SYSTEM PROGRAMMING
IN LINUX

SYSTEM PROGRAMMING IN LINUX

A Hands-On Introduction

by Stewart N. Weiss

no starch press®

San Francisco

Printed in China

First printing

29 28 27 26 25   1 2 3 4 5

ISBN-13: 978-1-7185-0356-4 (print)
ISBN-13: 978-1-7185-0357-1 (ebook)

 ® Published by No Starch Press®, Inc.
245 8th Street, San Francisco, CA 94103
phone: +1.415.863.9900
www.nostarch.com; info@nostarch.com

Publisher: William Pollock
Managing Editor: Jill Franklin
Production Manager: Sabrina Plomitallo-González
Production Editor: Miles Bond
Developmental Editor: Jill Franklin
Cover Illustrator: Octopod Studios
Interior Design: Octopod Studios
Technical Reviewer: Mitch Frazier
Proofreader: Lisa McCoy
Indexer: BIM Creatives, LLC

Sunflower photograph by Gilberto da Silva Moraes used under license from Shutterstock.com.

Library of Congress Control Number: 2025017198

For customer service inquiries, please contact info@nostarch.com. For information on distribution, bulk sales, corporate sales, or translations: sales@nostarch.com. For permission to translate this work: rights@nostarch.com. To report counterfeit copies or piracy: counterfeit@nostarch.com. The authorized representative in the EU for product safety and compliance is EU Compliance Partner, Pärnu mnt. 139b-14, 11317 Tallinn, Estonia, hello@eucompliancepartner.com, +3375690241.

[DC]

To

Joanna, my hero, love, and soulmate;

Shayna, light of my life;

and

my parents, who taught me what it means to be honorable.

About the Author

Stewart N. Weiss was a professor in the Department of Computer Science at Hunter College for 38 years and served on the faculty of the Graduate Center of the City University of New York as well. He has taught a broad range of courses, several of which he developed, including Unix system programming, parallel computing, software testing, and open source software development. He authored or co-authored nearly two dozen publications on aspects of software engineering, including software testing and reliability and open source software development. He was a principal investigator on several grants from the National Science Foundation.

Stewart holds a PhD in computer science from the Courant Institute of Mathematical Sciences at New York University. He started working with Unix and C in 1983 while he was a graduate student there and has been a Unix enthusiast ever since. He has always loved teaching and is very passionate about sharing his appreciation and knowledge of Unix and Linux.

About the Technical Reviewer

Mitch Frazier is a programmer who works for Emerson Electric doing mostly embedded systems programming in C. He also occasionally writes code in Golang, Python, Tcl, JavaScript, and bash. He previously worked for *Linux Journal*, both as a technical editor and as a system administrator.

BRIEF CONTENTS

CONTENTS IN DETAIL

2
FUNDAMENTALS OF SYSTEM PROGRAMMING   49

3
TIME, DATES, AND LOCALES 93

4
BASIC CONCEPTS OF FILE I/O 149

5
FILE I/O AND LOGIN ACCOUNTING   187

6
OVERVIEW OF FILESYSTEMS AND FILES 247

7
THE DIRECTORY HIERARCHY 311

8
INTRODUCTION TO SIGNALS 383

9
TIMERS AND SLEEP FUNCTIONS   435

10
PROCESS FUNDAMENTALS   491

11
PROCESS CREATION AND TERMINATION   539

12
INTRODUCTION TO INTERPROCESS COMMUNICATION   597

13
PIPES AND FIFOS   645

14
CLIENT-SERVER APPLICATIONS AND DAEMONS   679

15
INTRODUCTION TO THREADS   709

16
THREAD SYNCHRONIZATION   739

ACKNOWLEDGMENTS

I thank many people for their help, support, and guidance in the creation of this book. Foremost is my wife, Joanna Klukowska, who had been encouraging me to write this book for a long time and who gave me constant support throughout the entire process. She was always ready and eager to step through my code and find the bugs that seemed to escape my eyes, and she was far more steadfast and successful at it than I. In what little spare time she had, she also proofread many of the chapters.

I am sincerely grateful to Jill Franklin, the managing editor at No Starch Press, who read my manuscript meticulously, made many improvements in my writing, and offered many suggestions about making the big picture clearer. The book would not be what it is without her help and guidance. I'm also indebted to Mitch Frazier, the technical reviewer, for catching several mistakes and inaccuracies in the manuscript, for finding bugs in the code, and for detecting inconsistencies between the code that appears in the book and its counterpart in the repository. It was reassuring when a chapter passed his muster. I also thank everyone at No Starch Press who helped in the production of the book.

This book's origins date back to when I started teaching a course in Unix system programming at Hunter College at the City University of New York. That course was inspired by one taught by Matthew Smosna at New York University, who was a friend and fellow graduate student there. He passed away many years ago, but his legacy lives in this book. Many of the students who took my course made comments and suggestions that ultimately altered my lecture notes and found their way into this book. Thanks go to all of them. I give particular thanks to Zhi Peng Lin and Syeda Rahman, who took the course while I was writing the manuscript and made several suggestions for the first Early Access edition that improved the book. My brother-in-law, Jay Militscher, an IT professional, made several useful comments that led to rewrites of the introductory material.

Lastly, I am grateful to the many authors who've written excellent books about the Unix and Linux operating systems. Those resources were invaluable during the writing of this book.

PREFACE

The story of this book can trace its origins to 1983. In that year, I was a graduate student in the Courant Institute of Mathematical Sciences at New York University. The Courant, as it was called, had acquired Sun Microsystems workstations, which were running Berkeley Software Distribution 4.1, an early version of Unix. After I learned the rudiments of Unix, it didn't take long for me to become a Unix convert.

When I was hired to teach in a full-time position at Hunter College in 1987, I set up a small Unix network with my research computers. I couldn't imagine working efficiently without a Unix system to help me.

Some time later, I decided that my students should also have the opportunity to learn how to work in a Unix environment. If it was a good thing for me, I reasoned, then it could be a good thing for them too. I didn't give much thought to it back then, but I had become what these days people would call a Unix evangelist. In 1996, my dear friend Matthew Smosna was teaching an elementary course in the use of Unix tools and scripting at NYU and was kind enough to share his lecture notes and slides with me. Using his notes as a starting point, I created a similar course at Hunter College in

1997. Matthew passed away unexpectedly that year, but my gratitude to him has endured.

The course began as a tutorial on a rather large collection of Unix tools, ranging from text filtering tools such as sed, awk, and grep, to shell scripting and a smattering of Perl, to an overview of the Unix operating system and its structure. Many of the students whom I taught returned to me after graduation, thanking me for giving them the chance to learn Unix, as they had landed their first jobs because of it. Many students wanted to learn it in more depth, and so, in 2001, I converted the course to an introduction to system programming in Unix.

My goal was to teach a course in Unix system programming that was accessible to any computer science student who had taken a year of programming (in C++ at the time) and who had taken a class in operating systems. I started putting all of my lecture notes on my website and began to receive thank-you notes from people around the world for making them available. It was nice to get this kind of feedback, but at the same time, it made me realize that because the notes were highly visible, I needed to perfect them.

Eventually, the focus on Unix became more of a focus on Linux, the free and open source variant of it, because more and more students were making it their first choice of operating system. The material then became a blend of Unix concepts and Linux-specific programming interfaces. As the course became more popular among mid-level students, I redesigned it so that a course in operating systems was no longer a prerequisite. This change allowed students with good programming skills and a sincere desire to learn to master the material.

Throughout my years of teaching, I've learned that most, if not all, students learn programming only if they get a chance to write lots of programs and see many examples of each concept or interface as we cover it. A lot of research on how people learn supports this principle. Therefore, I've always created and shared many programs, which I call *demo programs*, with the students and told them that they should copy them and make lots of modifications to see how their changes affect its behavior. To facilitate this, I put a license on the software, the GNU General Public License, that granted them the right to make changes and redistribute the programs. There is nothing like hands-on work to drive ideas home. This book is modeled on this principle. It is also modeled on my belief that a good teacher teaches students how to learn.

INTRODUCTION

I designed this book to help you learn how to write system and utility programs on Linux. Much of it applies to other Unix systems as well. Whether you're a Unix/Linux user or computer science student who wants to dive deeper into the Unix/Linux programming interface, or you've been told by someone else that you'd benefit from learning more about it, or you're just plain curious and ready to explore a new path, this book will guide you to that end. No matter how you arrived here, I'm glad to have your ear, and I hope that I keep your interest through the journey.

What Will You Learn from This Book?

Unlike many other books on this subject, this one doesn't require you to have any prior programming experience with Unix or Linux in particular, and it doesn't require you to be an expert programmer already. It assumes that you know little to nothing about the Linux programming interface, and it builds your knowledge and ability to learn more, one small step at a time. If you flip through the book now and see material in later chapters that seems too advanced to understand, don't fret. By the time we get there, you should understand all of it easily. For the details about exactly what you need to know to benefit from this book, see "What Should You Know to Understand This Book?" on page xxxii.

I had several different goals when I designed and wrote this book that reflect the various ways that we interact with Unix/Linux:

- To teach you how to write programs on and for the Unix operating system, and Linux in particular

- To improve your ability to work efficiently within a Unix/Linux environment

- To teach you how the Unix operating system is designed and structured so that you have a deeper understanding of what happens "under the hood," so to speak

- To give you an appreciation of the marvel and magic of Unix so that you'll want to learn more

These are pretty hefty objectives, and they may seem to be too much to attain in a single book. To do so, the book is neither thorough nor comprehensive. It isn't a reference book on everything Unix. It doesn't cover every aspect of programming in the Unix environment, and it doesn't go deeply into each topic that it does cover.

Instead, it's a hands-on tutorial, and it covers what I believe is enough to give you a solid background and show you how you can learn more about each topic on your own. It's also conceptual, showing you not just *what* various features do and how to use them but also *how* they work so that you understand *why* you need to do what you do and why something is not working the way you expected it to when things go wrong.

How Will This Book Teach You?

I've written this book as if I, like you, know very little about the Unix programming interfaces, and we are going to learn about them together. I don't just tell you how this or that works. Instead, I share my thought processes as if I'm exploring new topics with you, and we both have to find the resources that explain these new topics. I follow this same approach when developing programs in the book, sharing my thinking about a program's design and details in the course of taking it from initial concept to executable code. I decided to take this approach because, as a teacher, I believe that my first goal is to teach you a method of learning.

In this sense, my approach tries to adhere to the principles embodied in the well-known proverb often attributed to the Chinese philosopher Lao Tzu, paraphrased as follows:

> Give a person a fish and they will eat for a day. Teach a person to fish and they will eat for a lifetime.

I strongly believe in this teaching philosophy.

I make one exception to this strategy when, in the course of covering a particular programming concept or interface, I decide that you ought to know more about the underlying operating system structures or workings, and then I put on a different hat, becoming the knowledgeable teacher and sharing what I know. At these times, I don't pretend that I know nothing.

Using Open Source Software

The fact that Unix has been an open source operating system is fundamental to the teaching method on which this book is based. Each time I introduce a new topic, my strategy is to explain the underlying concepts, perhaps look at the design and structure of the relevant interfaces, and then pick a command to implement. We'll go through a few iterations together to get it right, fixing problems and learning about what did and didn't work until we're satisfied with the solution. Then, after it's all tidied up, we may sometimes look at fragments of actual Linux or GNU library implementations. None of this would be possible with proprietary code.

Presenting Different Perspectives

When I present material about a particular subject, I often do so from three different perspectives, reflecting the roles that you might play at different times:

- That of a nonprogramming user, because it presents the command-level view of Unix. As a programmer, you need to understand how a nonprogramming user will work with the code you develop.

- That of a system programmer, in that it presents the information needed to write system programs in a Unix/Linux system. When developing new code, you need to become comfortable choosing the best interfaces for your project.

- That of a computer scientist, because it examines the internal structure of the GNU/Linux operating system. Very often, understanding the concrete representations and abstractions employed by the operating system enables you to write more efficient code.

I'll usually begin by looking at a topic through the eyes of an ordinary user and then switch to the eyes of a programmer. Sometimes, before changing to the programmer's view, I'll explore the structures and operating system concepts to appeal to the computer scientist in you. Seeing the material from all of these perspectives can make you a better system programmer.

Using Example Programs

This book is predicated on a learning model in which you and I investigate new components of the Unix/Linux programming interface and then develop code based on them. To this end, I've written about 200 example programs to accompany the book. You can download all of these programs in order to read and experiment with them. However, I strongly believe that the best way to learn how to program is to write code. I encourage you to start by modifying those programs and then writing programs like them from scratch. The more you do this, the better and more efficient you'll be at developing software on Linux systems. See "Online Materials" on page xxxvii for details about how to obtain copies of the programs.

What Should You Know to Understand This Book?

I've tried to make the prerequisite background for the book minimal, but this is a technically challenging subject. You should have the following background to get the most out of this book:

- You must be able to write programs in either C or C++ with ease. Your level of experience should correspond to a year of programming at the college level. For example, you should be familiar with standard data structures such as stacks, lists, queues, and trees. If you're a Java programmer or a Python programmer, you'll be at a disadvantage because the interfaces in Unix are written in C, and you'll have to transition to C.

- You should be comfortable enough working in the command line in Unix to be able to perform routine tasks such as navigating directories, listing their contents, and viewing and editing files.

- You should know how to compile and build programs from the command line.

The Role of C in This Book

C is the native language of the programming interfaces in Unix systems. You could write C++ programs that use these interfaces, but all of the programming examples I use are written in C. This implies that you should be able to read and understand simple C programs. If you can write in C++, you're sufficiently prepared to write in C, although many C++ programmers don't realize this.

Many people who know C++ often think that they don't know C and they get discouraged needlessly. The C++ language is more or less a superset of C. If you know C++, you know a great deal of C. There are a few minor differences in syntax here and there. The bigger problem is that most C++ programmers don't know how to use the C libraries. Most use C++ stream I/O and don't know how to use the functions from C's Standard I/O Library, which they see as archaic. These functions are usually much more useful and efficient than those found in C++. Where I taught for more than 40 years, the basic programming classes used C++, but most students who took my classes in Unix system programming quickly adapted to C, and some preferred it.

Utility Programs

At the very least, you need to know how to compile and build programs on Linux or other Unix systems. I don't cover how to use any program development tools in this book other than showing you how to build the programs using the GNU gcc compiler collection. However, you'll be a more efficient programmer if you know how to use a few software development system utilities. The most important of these tools are:

make   For maintaining program collections

gdb   An indispensable command line debugging tool

valgrind   To help find memory leaks and bad pointers in code

git   A command line tool for version control

If you're used to using an integrated development environment (IDE) such as Eclipse or NetBeans, try to toss its training wheels away and learn how to use these tools instead.

System Requirements

The book assumes that you have access to a Linux system on which you can develop programs. It doesn't matter which flavor of Linux you use. I've been using Ubuntu for several years; many other distributions are available. You don't need to install it on your machine if you have remote access to a Linux system, although working remotely is generally slower. You can also install a Linux virtual machine on your host computer as your work environment for this book.

If you don't have superuser privilege for your system, you'll either need to get sudo privilege or ask the person who maintains the machine to make sure the system has the needed packages, which include:

- The GNU compiler collection (gcc)

- All man pages, including manpages-dev, man-db, manpages-posix, and manpages-posix-dev

- The man-db package, which lets you search through man pages, but you'll have to run the command mandb as a superuser to initialize the database for searching

- The make utility, gdb, git, and valgrind

You'll have to check which package manager your variant of Linux uses for installing packages if you need to install any of these.

About UNIX, Unix, Linux, and More

Unix has a history dating back to 1969, and since that time many different variants have been developed, of which Linux is one. In 1969, and for many years after that, Unix was always written as *UNIX* because its name was a pun based on an earlier system named *MULTICS* on which its original developers worked. In fact, for a very short period of time, it was called UNICS. In 1993, *UNIX* became a registered trademark of The Open Group, a consortium of companies. The term *Unix* is not trademarked and doesn't refer to any one operating system. In general, it refers to any operating system that is what people often call *Unix-like*. In the interest of clarity, when the term *UNIX* appears in the text, it refers very narrowly to any operating system that has been certified by The Open Group as conforming to its branding of the term or to those versions of Unix predating the trademark whose name was written as UNIX at the time. I mostly use the word *Unix*, which in some contexts has a precise meaning and in others does not.

One important consequence of the fact that there are so many different varieties of Unix is that a program that works on one Unix system may not work on another. This problem led over time to the standardization of Unix. Chapter 1 contains a brief history of the various applicable standards. The general problem of writing programs that work across a variety of operating systems is called *portability*. Chapter 1 also describes steps that you can take to make your code portable to Unix systems other than the one on which you wrote it, provided that they conform to one standard or another.

The term *Linux* poses a slightly different problem. Technically speaking, Linux is not an entire operating system with all of its utilities and programs that come bundled together in an installation package. It's just what's commonly called the *kernel*, a term defined in Chapter 1. The rest of the operating system is mostly programs and libraries developed by GNU as part of the GNU Project (*https://www.gnu.org/gnu/gnu.html*). (GNU is a recursively defined acronym for GNU's Not Unix.) For this reason, many people believe it should be called *GNU/Linux*. I am one of those who believe that its name should reflect the major contribution to it by the GNU Project; therefore, when I want to refer specifically to the entire operating system, I'll sometimes call it GNU/Linux as a reminder, but when I refer specifically to its kernel, I'll call it Linux.

Scope, Content, and Organization

This book covers most of the basic programming interfaces in Linux, but not all of them. In particular, it covers locales and internationalization, files and filesystems, various methods of I/O from basic to advanced, signals, timers, processes, threads, many interprocess communication facilities, client-server programming, terminals and terminal I/O, the *ncurses* library, login accounting, and other system databases. It does not cover access control lists, capabilities, sockets, or pseudoterminals.

Chapter Organization

The book has 19 chapters that build upon one another. I wrote this book as if I were teaching in a classroom and you're there with me, and we've embarked on a journey in which we learn this material together. I don't expect a reader who starts in Chapter 7 to understand it any more than I would expect a student who missed the first six classes of a course to understand much in the seventh class.

Chapter 1: Core Concepts   Explains what system programming is and how it differs from other kinds of programming. It introduces the fundamental concepts and components of the Unix operating system, such as users and groups, files and directories, processes, and so on, and it explains the man pages and how we'll use them. It also covers some of the history of Unix and the key standards.

Chapter 2: Fundamentals of System Programming   Introduces concepts related to programming in a Unix environment and working with the kernel application programming interface (API). It covers object libraries and the difference between static and shared libraries, system calls, error handling, portability and feature test macros, system limits, and internationalization of programs. It also covers how programs can access the environment strings and their command line arguments, and process command line options.

Chapter 3: Time, Dates, and Locales   Presents the methodology for learning system programming that the rest of the book follows and explains how the source code repository that contains all example programs is organized. It applies this methodology to the development of programs that work with dates and times in Unix and introduces basic methods of internationalizing programs.

Chapter 4: Basic Concepts of File I/O   Introduces core concepts of files and file I/O in Unix, including universal I/O, open file connections, file descriptors, and the parts of the kernel API relevant to I/O. It also covers file permissions, the types of user IDs, and the setuid facility. It develops a simplified copy command and explores issues related to performance and buffering.

Chapter 5: File I/O and Login Accounting   Introduces the file pointer, seeking operations, and a few more advanced methods of I/O. It introduces system data files related to users and logins, and it develops simplified versions of the lastlog and last commands.

Chapter 6: Overview of Filesystems and Files   Dives into the structure of disks, disk partitions, disk filesystems, and their internals. It introduces parts of the kernel API for accessing filesystem attributes, file attributes, and more, and it also introduces the Linux virtual filesystem and how it works. It then develops simple versions of the stat and statfs commands.

Chapter 7: The Directory Hierarchy   Explains the structure of directories and the directory hierarchy. It explores the parts of the kernel API and the standard libraries for processing directories and the directory hierarchy, including methods of traversing the hierarchy. Here, we develop simple ls, pwd, and du commands.

Chapter 8: Introduction to Signals   Covers the core concepts of signals and how they're used in Unix systems. It introduces the parts of the kernel API related to sending signals, signal handling, signal registration, and signal blocking. It also discusses the design of signal handlers and the concept of asynchronous signal safety.

Chapter 9: Timers and Sleep Functions   Introduces timing elements for programs and explains fundamental concepts related to timing, such as clocks, hardware interval timers, and more. It introduces several different sleep functions and software interval timers, and it also develops a couple of programs that act like system monitors.

Chapter 10: Process Fundamentals   Introduces the fundamentals of processes: what they are, how they're organized, and how they're managed and represented internally by the kernel. It introduces the Executable and Linking Format (ELF) file format and how it is used to create process images, and it also introduces the *proc* pseudofilesystem. Here we develop a simplified ps command.

Chapter 11: Process Creation and Termination   Introduces the parts of the kernel API related to the creation, termination, and management of processes, including calls for the synchronization of parent and child processes. It develops a simplified shell program.

Chapter 12: Introduction to Interprocess Communication   The first of two chapters dedicated to interprocess communication (IPC). It covers POSIX shared memory, semaphores, and POSIX message queues. It develops a few programs that demonstrate the application of these IPC facilities.

Chapter 13: Pipes and FIFOs   Introduces unnamed pipes and named pipes, also called FIFOs, and goes into details of the semantics of opening, reading, writing, and closing pipes and FIFOs. It develops a simple FIFO-based server.

Chapter 14: Client-Server Applications and Daemons   Covers concepts related to the development of client-server applications, including system logging facilities and conversion of processes into daemons. It develops both an iterative server similar to the calc command and a concurrent server.

Chapter 15: Introduction to Threads   The first of two chapters on multithreaded programs. It covers thread basics, explores much of the *Pthreads* library related to thread creation and management, and develops a multithreaded server.

Chapter 16: Thread Synchronization   Covers the parts of the *Pthreads* API related to the synchronization of threads, including mutexes, condition variables, barriers, and read-write locks.

Chapter 17: Alternative Methods of I/O   Explores I/O models beyond the standard blocking I/O model. In particular, it covers nonblocking I/O and polling, signal-driven I/O, POSIX asynchronous I/O, and multiplexed I/O using the `select()` system call.

Chapter 18: Terminals and Terminal I/O   Covers terminals and terminal I/O, beginning with the special needs of interactive programs. It examines the structure of terminal driver software and support for terminal configuration in the kernel, after which it explores methods of configuring the terminal such as the `termios` and `ioctl` interfaces. It develops a simplified `stty` command.

Chapter 19: Interactive Programming and the ncurses Library   Covers configuring the terminal for interactive programs, including noncanonical mode programming. It introduces the *ncurses* library's API and develops a few programs based on it, ending with a simple version of the `top` command.

Appendix A: Creating Libraries   Shows how to create and manage static and shared libraries.

Appendix B: Unicode and UTF-8   Offers a short tutorial on Unicode and the variable-length representation of Unicode known as UTF-8.

Appendix C: Date and Time Format Specifiers   Presents a table of the date and time specifiers, with examples, used in the formatting of dates and times by various functions and system utilities.

Online Materials

To keep the book from becoming too long, programs are generally not presented in their entirety. Instead, they're available online along with other materials. You can access them on the book's web page at *https://nostarch .com/introduction-system-programming-linux*.

Source Code

All of the source code that appears in this book, as well as other example programs, is available for download at *https://github.com/stewartweiss/intro -linux-sys-prog* and as a ZIP file from *https://nostarch.com/introduction-system -programming-linux*. The programs are organized by chapter. Each chapter directory contains a makefile for building and maintaining the programs in that directory, and I include a master makefile that can build and maintain all of the programs in this repository. The top-level directory has a *README* file that explains the licensing and has instructions for maintaining the programs. I have tried to write thorough inline documentation for all programs.

There are also three directories named *common*, *include*, and *lib*. The first contains source code and header files for functions that are used in multiple chapters. The makefile there can build a library file that is copied into *lib* and copy the headers into *include*.

All complete programs in the repository are covered by the GNU General Public License (Version 3), a copy of which is in the repository. The source code for all library functions in the *common* directory is covered by the GNU Lesser General Public License (Version 3), a copy of which is also in the repository.

Command Line Online Chapter

The book also includes in its online resources a short summary of the basics of using the command line, titled "Working in the Command Interface." This covers the set of basic commands needed to perform essential tasks.

make Tutorial

I've written a make tutorial for those who want to know how to use this utility program in elementary ways. The book's web page has a link to a GitHub repository that contains the tutorial and instructions for how to use it.

Solutions to Exercises

Solutions to selected exercises from the ends of each chapter are available online in a single ZIP file that you can download from the website.

Conventions and Format

I've tried to follow fixed conventions and style throughout the book to make it easier to read. These include the book's typography, the format of command input and output, names of things, dates and times, and more.

Typographical Conventions

I use a monospaced font for all code, input and output of programs, file contents, and the names of all commands and executable programs. For example, I would write "bash is a popular shell in Linux." I use *italic* text for the names of all files and directories, as in "The executable program file for the bash shell is */bin/bash*."

Notation

In the description of a command or function I use square brackets ([ ]) to enclose optional elements. The brackets are not part of the command. Italic text denotes placeholders, not actual text that you type. An ellipsis (...) means more than one copy of the preceding token. For example, in the description

```
ls [option] ... [directory_name] ...
```

the words *option* and *directory_name* are placeholders. The square brackets indicate that both the option specifiers and the argument to the ls command are optional but that all option specifiers must precede any directory names and that option specifiers and directory names can occur multiple times, as in:

```
ls -l -t chapter01 chapter02
```

Here, -l and -t are two options and chapter01 and chapter02 are two arguments.

I use a vertical bar (|) to indicate exactly one choice among multiple alternatives. For example, the description

```
bash [option] ... [command_string | file]
```

indicates that after all options, you can supply either a command string or the name of a file but not both.

Throughout the book, I'll use the $ character as the prompt string displayed inside a terminal window. Any text that you would enter is shown in **boldface**. For example, the echo command just prints whatever text you enter after it on the command line. I would demonstrate how you use it as follows:

```
$ echo 'Is this really how echo works?'
Is this really how echo works?
$
```

Notice that the prompt character is displayed again. This is how I indicate that you're seeing *all* of the command's output and that the command terminated. When showing all output would require too many lines, I'll snip some of the lines by putting the word *--snip--* in place of the removed output, as in:

```
$ ls /var
backups/
cache/
--snip--
$
```

I'll also use an ellipsis on a single line when I've deleted some of the text on that line. In the Unix system that you use for following along with this book, the prompt character that you see might be something other than $. Many systems might have a default prompt that includes more information, such as your login name or the name of the computer. In fact, you are usually able to customize your prompt.

In code listings, I'll sometimes omit parts of the code to save space. I'll indicate this either with a *--snip--* in place of multiple lines of code, as in

```
int main()
    --snip--
    return 0;
}
```

or, when I want to specify what's missing, I'll use this notation:

```
if ( argc < 2 )
    // OMITTED: Handle missing argument
else
```

I'll also write all pseudocode that appears in code listings in //-style comment blocks, reserving /*...*/-style blocks for actual comments.

Example Program Naming Conventions

I try to adhere to a program naming convention for the example programs that I've written for the book. Using a convention helps you (and me) guess what a program does from its name. The chapters in general contain three types of example programs:

- Programs that implement a simplified version of an existing Unix command. In this case, the program name is formed by prefixing the actual command name by spl_. For instance, spl_ls is the book's version of ls, and the source file is named *spl_ls.c*.

- Programs that do nothing except demonstrate basic use of a function introduced in a chapter. These have names that end in the suffix *_demo.c*, such as *getenv_demo.c*.

- Programs that don't implement an existing command but do more than just demonstrate how to call and use a function. I try to give these names that describe what they do. The program *showallusers.c* in Chapter 5 is an example of one.

If a chapter has multiple versions of a program, a sequence number is appended to the basename of the function, as in *spl_date1.c* and *spl_date2.c*.

Dates and Identities

It's common practice in the computer book industry to change any dates and timestamps in program and command output to either a point very far in the past or to some future time well beyond the book's release date so that the book isn't dated. I do this whenever possible, but sometimes when date and time themselves are the subject of a chapter and altering true output would make an explanation more difficult, I don't.

None of the usernames that appear in the output of programs are those of real people, except for mine. Any similarity to a real person's name is coincidental. I alter the output of commands that display actual usernames so that they aren't those of real people.

Suggestions and Corrections

I've tried my best to find bugs and mistakes in the example programs and the text of the book, but I can't imagine that I found and corrected them all. Along the same lines, I sometimes rewrote an explanation many times over, trying to make sure it is easy and enjoyable to read and accurate, but again, I am not perfect, and you may find places in the book that you think could be written better.

If you'd like to make suggestions or corrections to the text of the book, please email me at *stewart.weiss@acm.org* or email *errata@nostarch.com*. Include either a page number or a piece of identifying text that is long enough to be unique. If you find bugs or more serious flaws in the code (I hope not), if you're familiar with Git, please open an issue on *https://github.com/stewartweiss/intro-linux-sys-prog*.

I hope that you learn a lot from this book. Even more important, I hope that it shows you how you can learn what it doesn't cover on your own. Finally, I hope it's enjoyable to read and that you gain an appreciation for the marvel and magic of Unix.

1

CORE CONCEPTS

This first chapter presents the big picture of system programming and basic background information on Unix. We begin with an exploration of what system programs are and how they are different from other kinds of programs. Next, I'll introduce many of the fundamental concepts that underlie the Unix family of operating systems, and we'll conclude with a brief discussion of the history and standardization of Unix and the C programming language.

When we examine the various concepts that make Unix what it is, we start with the kernel because it is essentially the core of a Unix system. From there, we move on to Unix shells, which are the programmable, interchangeable user interfaces in Unix systems, separate and distinct from the Unix kernel. After that, we'll cover the concepts of users and groups. I then explain how the distinction between privileged and unprivileged instructions in Unix enables the kernel to manage resources securely and efficiently. Next, I'll introduce the concept of a user *process*, a representation of a running user program managed by the kernel, and *threads*, which are particular types of processes in Unix. I'll also explain the idea of an *environment list*, which is a set of variables and values passed to new processes, and I'll describe the Unix directory hierarchy and present an overview of files, directories, and permissions.

One important part of any Unix system is its online documentation, which plays a critical role in how you'll learn system programming in this book. We'll cover its organization and use in this chapter as well.

What Is System Programming?

The first programs people learn to write are simple ones, but despite their simplicity, we can use them to explain what system programming is. The simplest possible program that actually does something has no input and just prints a message onto the screen. One such program is the ubiquitous "Hello, world" program that you most likely wrote at the beginning of your development as a programmer. The first C version of this program appeared in Kernighan and Ritchie's *The C Programming Language* (Prentice Hall, 1978) and has since become the de facto first program that students learn to write when they are learning a new programming language. Listing 1-1 shows the original version of that program.

hello_world.c
```
#include <stdio.h>
void main()
{
    printf("hello, world\n");
}
```

Listing 1-1: Kernighan and Ritchie's original "Hello, world" program

The first line is an *include directive*, which starts with the keyword #include and is followed by the specification of a file. It tells the C preprocessor to read the contents of the file, in this case, the C header *stdio.h*, at that point in the program. We need that action to take place because the main program makes a call to the C printf() function, whose declaration is in *stdio.h*. Without it, the compiler could not tell whether printf() was being called properly. The C preprocessor has to find the header file before it can read it, and header files can be in many possible places. The angle brackets (<>) around the name of the file tell the preprocessor that it's in one of the standard places that it searches.

The Magic of Input and Output

The printf() function is one way in C to print information on the screen. I'm using the word *screen* as a synonym for the more technical term, *terminal window*. In this simple example, printf() has a single string, "hello, world.\n", as its argument. The \n is the *newline* character, which causes the next character following it to appear at the beginning of the next line on the screen.

Let's assume that this code is stored in a file named *hello_world.c* and that we've already compiled it into an executable program named *hello_world*. Because we don't want to be sidetracked by the details of how to compile code on a Unix system, we omit that compilation procedure here.

Running this program in a terminal window causes the string "hello, world" to be displayed, and then the prompt reappears. To run the program, we enter its name, preceded by ./, and press ENTER:

```
$ ./hello_world
hello, world
$
```

For someone who has never written a program before, this seems like magic. All you have to do is include the *stdio.h* header file in the code and give the printf() function the string that you want to print, and voilá: When you run the program, the string appears.

It clearly isn't magic though, and a lot must be going on behind the scenes to make the characters appear on the screen. C has given us a very powerful tool, printf(), so that we can write programs that print to the screen without needing to learn a lot about terminals and other technology.

Let's take this one step further. The preceding program outputs text but has no input. Listing 1-2 performs both input and output.

hello.c
```
#include <stdio.h>
void main() {
❶  char username[256];
    printf("Enter your name: ");
❷  scanf("%255s", username);
    printf("hello, %s\n", username);
}
```

Listing 1-2: A program that performs both input and output

This program begins with a declaration of a char array named username of length 256 ❶. This array can store up to 255 characters plus a terminating NULL byte. A *NULL byte* is the nonprinting character whose code is zero. As a character, it's written as \0. In many programming languages, a NULL byte is required at the end of a string. The program then prints a prompt message to the screen asking the user to enter their name. Then the C scanf() function ❷ reads characters from the keyboard until either 255 characters are entered or it finds a whitespace character (blank, tab, or newline), and it stores this data into the username array. The program prints hello followed by the contents of that array.

THE SCANF() FUNCTION

The scanf() function is the C library's formatted input function. It reads input, by default from the keyboard, following a format that you give it. In general, its first parameter is a string enclosed in double quotes followed by one or more

(continued)

---

pointers. The double-quoted string is called the *format specification*. In this example, it is "%255s", which specifies that the input data should be stored as a string (s for string) with a maximum width of 255 characters. The argument following the format specification must be a pointer to the start of a character array large enough to hold 255 characters plus the NULL byte. Since array names can be used in C wherever a constant pointer is expected, the array username is a valid argument.

Let's think about how this input and output actually take place. The program makes calls to the scanf() and printf() functions, but where is their code and how is it executed? Many beginning programmers mistakenly believe that the header files included by their programs contain the function implementations because all they have to do is put appropriate #include directives into their programs for them to work. However, those implementations are not in the header files.

The Role of the C Library in I/O

In general, when functions are not defined in the same file as the code calling them, they need to be linked into that code. When a compiler is processing a file and finds a function call not defined in the same file, it marks the call as an *unresolved symbol* because it can't assign an address for that function. The same is true if it finds unknown type names, variable names, and so on. Linking is the act of assigning addresses to these unresolved symbols. The compiler does not link. The *linker* is the component of the compiler collection that resolves undefined symbols. A *compiler collection* is a set of programs that build programs from source code.

The C language provides no built-in facilities for performing operations such as input/output, memory management, and string manipulation. Instead, they're defined in a standard library, which you link into your program. In the case of scanf() and printf(), their definitions are part of the C Standard Library. The linker automatically searches through this library without your needing to do anything special, thereby finding the function definitions. In "Object Libraries" on page 50, I explain exactly what a library is and how you can see what it contains.

Inside that library, the scanf() function makes calls to a lower-level function named read(). The code that implements read() is not part of the library; it's part of the Unix operating system itself. You'll get a better picture of this in the following section, "System Resources," and a more detailed explanation in Chapter 2. The read() code performs the actual transfer of bytes from the input device to the program's memory. Similarly, the printf() function makes calls to a lower-level function named write(), which is also implemented within the operating system. The write() code handles all of the details of writing to the output device. In short, the operating system performs all transfers of data to and from the output device, which is often the terminal. Figure 1-1 illustrates how this happens.

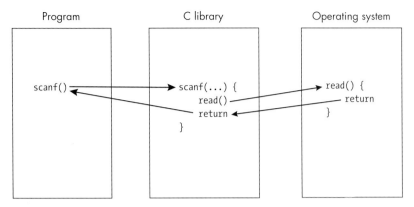

Figure 1-1: The execution flow of input operation

When we run a program like *hello.c* in Listing 1-2, we have the illusion that the program is connected directly to the keyboard and the display device via C library functions. If you run the program on your own personal computing device, this illusion may not be far from reality. However, we can also run it on a multiuser system in a terminal window, and the results will be exactly the same. This fact complicates the picture even further. In a Unix system, and in almost all modern operating systems, many people can work on the system at the same time, and programs belonging to different people can run at the same time, each receiving input from a different keyboard and sending output to a different display. Each person will see the same output as if they had run the program on a single-user machine. The operating system is what makes this possible. It has to ensure that each user's programs do not interfere with each other.

System Resources

We can frame this problem in terms of resources. *Resources* are objects that software uses and/or modifies. For example, a program's input and output data are resources, as are the values that it stores in its internal data structures. A program has the privilege to access or modify any of its own resources.

In Unix systems, some resources are protected from access by ordinary programs and are accessible only by the operating system. These protected resources are called *system resources*. System resources include hardware, such as the CPU, physical memory, screen displays, storage devices, and network connections. They also include objects that aren't hardware, such as system data structures and files. These are sometimes called *soft resources*. Figure 1-2 illustrates the way an operating system is layered in order to control access to system resources.

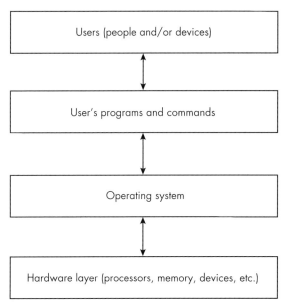

Figure 1-2: An operating system has layers to protect resources.

A modern operating system such as Unix provides an interface that programs can use for requesting access to system resources. This interface is called its *application programming interface (API)*. In computer science jargon, the term *application* is often used to refer to programs intended to be run by ordinary users. An API typically consists of a collection of function, type, and constant definitions and sometimes variable definitions as well. The API that an operating system provides in effect defines the means by which an application can request services from it. The functions in the API are called *system calls*.

NOTE   *If you're familiar with object-oriented programming, you may notice a resemblance between the operating system's API and a class interface. Both provide a set of methods for accessing protected data only through a well-defined set of access points.*

System Programs Explained

We've now set the stage to make a distinction between ordinary programs and system programs. A program that's not a system program is designed as if it has exclusive access to all of the resources it uses. It doesn't deal with the complexity of connecting to monitors and keyboards and isn't cognizant of the fact that the operating system must manage these resources.

In contrast, a program that makes direct requests for the services exposed in an operating system's API is called a *system program*, and when we write this kind of program we are *system programming*. System programs make requests for resources and services directly from the operating system. Sometimes people write them to extend the functionality of the operating system itself or provide functions that higher-level applications can use. For example, we could write a program that gets the current time from the operating system's internal clock and displays it in various formats for any user. This would be a system program.

The term *system program* also applies to any program that can run independently of the operating system and extend its functionality, even if it doesn't make any direct calls to the API. Tools such as compilers, assemblers, linkers, terminal emulators, and so on are considered to be system programs, and they play a fundamental role in a computer system. As Richard Stallman wrote, "The kernel is an essential part of an operating system, but useless by itself; it can function only in the context of a complete operating system" [40]. In this view, system programs are like an extension to the operating system, even though their definition is a bit fuzzy. The primary purpose of this book is to show you how you can write programs of this nature, namely those that interact directly with the operating system and, in effect, act like a part of that system.

Fundamental Concepts of Unix

This section introduces the core concepts that underlie the design of the Unix operating system. From its beginning, Unix was designed around a small set of clever ideas, as its authors, Dennis Ritchie and Ken Thompson, put it: "The success of UNIX lies not so much in new inventions but rather in the full exploitation of a carefully selected set of fertile ideas, and especially in showing that they can be keys to the implementation of a small yet powerful operating system" [33]. Those "fertile ideas" included, in the order in which we discuss them, the concepts of a programmable shell, users and groups, privileged and unprivileged instructions, environments, files and the directory hierarchy, device-independent input and output, and most important, processes. I describe these concepts in this section, not in great detail, preceded by a brief overview of that "small yet powerful operating system" itself, now known as the Unix *kernel*. Along the way, I introduce some Unix commands to demonstrate the concepts.

Before we dive into all of this material, we need to address one sticky point having to do with standards. Unix has many different varieties, which many people call *flavors*. This is a consequence of its history, and in "Unix History and Standards" on page 41, I'll summarize this problem and how it's been resolved, in particular by making reference to the most important family of standards: POSIX, an acronym for Portable Operating System Interface. Between here and that section, I'll sometimes make reference to the fact that something does or does not conform with POSIX.1-2024, which is the most recent version as of this writing. We cannot overstate the importance of conformance; commands and functions that are either not specified by or not conforming to the POSIX.1 standard are not portable and not guaranteed to work on all Unix systems that conform to the standard. I'll point this out when it is relevant.

The Unix Kernel

It is perhaps unfortunate that the term *operating system* has no single, universally agreed upon definition. If you look at almost any textbook on operating systems [37, 41], you'll find two different views of what constitutes an operating system:

- The operating system is the collection of all software that provides services to applications and users and manages and protects all hardware resources. In this view, tools like user interfaces and browsers are part of the operating system.

- The operating system is only the program that is loaded into memory on startup and remains in memory, controlling all computer resources, until the computer is powered off.

Regardless of which definition you decide to adopt, the term *kernel* is unambiguously used as another name for the second definition. It's an appropriate name, since it's the core of the Unix system. In the seminal book on the design of the 4.4BSD operating system, *The Design and Implementation of the 4.4BSD Operating System*, McKusick and co-authors define a kernel as "a small nucleus of software that provides only the minimal facilities necessary for implementing additional operating system services" [26]. In this book, I use the narrow definition of an *operating system*, namely that it is the kernel and nothing more.

The *kernel* is a program, or a collection of interacting programs, depending on the particular implementation of Unix, with many entry points. An *entry point* is an instruction in a program at which execution can begin. Each of these entry points provides a service that the kernel performs. If you are used to thinking of programs as always starting at their first line, this may be disconcerting.

Most likely, in the programs that you have written so far, there has been a single entry point, namely the main() function. However, it's possible to create code that can have several entry points. Software libraries are code modules with multiple entry points. You can think of entry points as functions that can be called by other programs. They perform services such as opening, reading, and writing files, creating new processes, allocating memory, and so on. Each of these functions expects a certain number of arguments of certain types and produces well-defined results. The collection of kernel entry points makes up a large part of its API. In fact, you can think of the kernel as containing a collection of separate functions, bundled together into a large package, and its API as the collection of signatures or prototypes of these functions.

Kernel Roles and Responsibilities

What are the kernel's responsibilities, and what does it do? The goal for now is to paint a picture of *what* the kernel does and not to describe *how* it does this.

When a Unix system boots, a combination of firmware and software loads the kernel into the portion of memory called *system space* or *kernel space*, where it stays until the machine is shut down. User programs are not allowed to access system space. If they try, the kernel terminates them.

The kernel has full access to all of the hardware attached to the computer. The kernel maintains various system resources in order to perform services for user programs. These system resources include many different data structures that keep track of input/output (I/O), memory, and device usage, for example.

The Unix kernel manages and protects all of these resources and provides an operating environment that allows all users to work efficiently, safely, and happily. It prevents users and the programs that they run from accessing any hardware resources directly. In other words, if a user's running program wants to read from or write to a disk, it must ask the kernel to do that on its behalf, rather than doing it on its own. The kernel will perform the task and transfer any data to or from a portion of memory that the user's program can access.

To understand why this is necessary, consider what would happen if users' programs could access the hard disk directly. A user could run a program that could try to acquire all disk space, or even worse, try to erase the disk, subverting the kernel's ability to protect its resources.

The Unix kernel also protects users from each other and protects itself from users, while simultaneously giving users the impression that they each have the computer entirely to themselves. This is precisely the illusion described in the section "What Is System Programming?" on page 2. Somehow, everyone is able to run programs that seem as if they have the computer all to themselves, as if no one else were using the machine. Users have their own disk space, their own private portion of memory, their fair share of time on the CPU, and so on.

In order to achieve these objectives, the inventors of Unix incorporated several key principles into its design:

- The system designates two levels of privilege (user privilege and kernel privilege) such that certain instructions can be executed only with kernel privilege.

- Each user has a unique identity. A privileged user can create groups of users, and those groups have unique identities as well. These user and group identifiers are assigned privileges and protections for all user resources such as disk storage, running programs, and so on.

- The system of files supports creation, modification, retrieval, and removal of persisted data and programs, as well as privacy, protection, and the ability to share software and data.

- Physical memory is divided into two regions: *user space*, where ordinary user programs are loaded, and *system space*, which is where the operating system itself is stored.

- The kernel has exclusive control of the use of the processor, and it decides at any given time what runs next.

- The kernel has the exclusive ability to load programs into memory, run them, and terminate them. A running program cannot even terminate itself; the best it can do is to ask the kernel to terminate it!

- The kernel has complete and exclusive control of all computer hardware.

We'll describe each of these principles in more depth in the remaining sections of this chapter.

Kernel Services

I've mentioned reading and writing files and terminal I/O as some of the types of services that the kernel provides, but to give you an even better sense of the scope of its services, the following list shows the types of services it performs:

- Process scheduling and management

- I/O handling

- Physical and virtual memory management

- Device management

- Filesystem management

- Signaling and interprocess communication

- Multithreading

- Protection and security

- Networking services

Figure 1-3 depicts how users and their programs access system resources and services through the kernel's application programming interface.

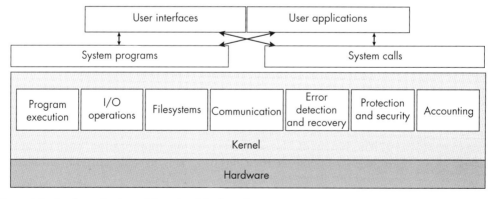

Figure 1-3: A schematic view of the role of the kernel

Each of the boxes inside the kernel region represents a different service category. The box labeled "System calls" represents the part of the API that programs use to request and obtain these services, whereas the box labeled

"System programs" is the set of stand-alone programs that users can run to obtain these services.

Shells and Commands

The kernel provides services to running programs, but not directly to users; instead, users interact with Unix by entering commands through a command line interpreter running in a terminal window or by interacting with a graphical user interface (GUI), which I do not discuss in this book. A *command line interpreter* is a program that reads commands and carries them out.

Commands

A *command* is an instruction that you enter by inputting text, usually (but not always) using a keyboard. Commands may have options and arguments following the command name. *Options* modify the behavior of the command, whereas *arguments* are the command's inputs. For example:

```
$ gcc -g -o myprog myprog.c
```

The following list explains each part of that command line:

gcc   The command name (the GNU Compiler Collection).

-g   An option to gcc that tells it to include debugging information in the generated executable.

-o myprog   An option with an option argument, myprog. The -o option tells gcc to put the output into the file named immediately after it, in this case, *myprog*, which is its argument.

myprog.c   The command's only argument, which is the name of its input file.

The command line is everything that you type up to but not including the newline character produced when you press ENTER. In this example, the command is the entire command line, but sometimes a single line can have multiple commands separated by command-separator characters such as the semicolon, as in:

```
$ gcc -g -o myprog myprog.c ; gcc -g -o hello hello.c
```

Technically, a *simple command* is a single command, not a sequence of commands. When we use the term *command*, we usually mean a simple command.

In GNU/Linux and some other Unix systems, some commands have two kinds of command options, *short* and *long*:

- Short options begin with a single dash (-) and are a single character, as in -a and -H.

- Long options start with a double dash (--) and can be words, such as --date and --file-type.

POSIX.1-2024 does not require conforming systems to provide long options, but GNU/Linux has them.

Both types of options can have option arguments. For example, in

```
$ gcc -g -o myprog myprog.c
```

the -o option has the myprog argument.

In Unix systems that conform to the POSIX.1-2024 standard, if an option has an argument, the argument is required; you cannot omit it. On the other hand, GNU/Linux permits a command to have options with nonrequired arguments. For example, you can enter the Firefox web browser's name to start it from the command line in GNU/Linux:

```
$ firefox
```

If you give it the -P myprofile option, it starts up with the user profile named myprofile. If you enter just

```
$ firefox -P
```

it displays a dialog asking you to pick a profile from a list. The profile name is a nonrequired argument to -P.

The rules for giving option arguments are:

- The argument to a short option follows it immediately, possibly with intervening space or TAB characters, as in -ohello or -o hello. The one exception is that nonrequired arguments can't have space before them.

- The argument to a long option follows the = operator *without intervening space*, as in --date='Jan 01,1970'.

The typical command consists of the command name followed by options and then arguments, but some commands allow the options and arguments to be intermixed. For example:

```
$ gcc -g myprog.c
$ gcc myprog.c -g
```

These command lines are equivalent.

Shells

The word *shell* is the Unix term for a particular type of command line interpreter. Command line interpreters have been provided with operating systems since their inception. Early mainframes and personal computer operating systems required people to interact with them exclusively through a command line interpreter. DOS, for example, provided a command line interpreter, which became the basis for the Microsoft Command window, which was simply a DOS emulator.

A command line interpreter presents a prompt of some kind, indicating that it's waiting for you to enter a command. At the prompt, you type a command and press ENTER, causing the command to be executed, after which the prompt reappears:

```
$ hostname
harpo
$
```

If you enter the `hostname` command, it shows the name of the computer on which you're working. Here it printed `harpo`, the name of my computer, and redisplayed the prompt. The shell continues to run until you give it a command to terminate itself, such as `exit`.

In Unix, a shell is not just a command line interpreter; it's also a programming language interpreter. You can use it to define variables, evaluate expressions, perform I/O, use conditional control-of-flow statements such as loops and branching statements, define and call functions, and much more. In short, it has most of the features of a high-level programming language such as C. You can save a sequence of shell commands into a file to be executed at another time. Such a file is called a *shell script*. You can arrange for the shell to execute these shell scripts in a few different ways.

Most shells also implement various frequently used commands as functions inside the shell itself, which are called *shell builtins* or just *builtins*. Building a command directly into the shell speeds up its execution because calling a function takes much less time than starting a separate program, which requires kernel intervention.

In a typical Unix system, you can choose which shell you'd like to use from among several different shells, depending on your preferences.

The oldest of the most commonly distributed shells, which was part of Seventh Edition UNIX (released in 1979 by Bell Labs), is known as the *Bourne shell*, so named because it was written by Stephen Bourne [3]. The name of the shell program was `sh`, which is what you had to enter to run it. It was the first extension to the original UNIX shell, written by Ken Thompson. The Bourne shell is important because it is always part of any Unix distribution and many administrative scripts are written in it, requiring that it's installed. Some commands will fail if it isn't found on the system.

Other common shells that have been around a long time include the C shell (`csh`) and the Korn shell (`ksh`).

However, the most commonly used shell in GNU/Linux systems is the Bourne Again SHell, whose program name is `bash`, and that is the shell we'll use in this book. The GNU Project created `bash` by extending the Bourne shell with features from the Korn shell and the C shell (*https://www.gnu.org/software/bash/*).

Users and Groups

Historically, *users* in Unix were people who were given access to the system and could run programs and own files. Part of the security of Unix rests on the principle that every user of the system must be authenticated. *Authentication* is a form of security clearance, like showing an ID card before entering a building or passing through a scanner at an airport.

The traditional method of authentication in Unix gives every user a unique username and an associated unique, nonnegative integer user ID, or UID for short. The username is the name a person enters to log in to the system. Each user also has an associated password. Unix uses the username/password pair to authenticate a user attempting to log in. If the username does not exist or the password doesn't match it, the system rejects the user. System files store passwords in an encrypted form.

LOGGING IN

To *log in* to a system is to *log* into it. One of the dictionary meanings of the verb *to log* that existed long before computers did is to record something in a log-book, as a sea captain or airplane pilot does. The term *login* conveys the idea that the action is being recorded in a logbook. In Unix, logins are recorded in a file that acts like a logbook. The system maintains a list of names of users who are allowed to log in. We take this term for granted. We use the noun *login* as a single word only because it has become a single word on millions of login screens around the world. To log in, as a verb, really means to log *into* something; it requires an indirect object.

To be precise, in modern Unix systems, a user is any entity that can run programs and own files. This entity need not be an actual person. For various reasons, the definition of a user was generalized to allow abstract entities as well as programs to be users as well. For example, root, syslog, and lp are each nonperson users.

A *group* is a set of users. Just as each user has a username and user ID, each group has a unique group name and an associated unique, nonnegative integer group ID, or GID for short. Unix uses groups to provide a means of resource sharing. For example, a file can be associated with a group, and all users in that group would have the same access rights to that file. Since a program is just an executable file, the same is true of programs; an executable program can be associated with a group so that all members of that group will have the same right to run that program.

Every user belongs to at least one group, called the user's *primary group*. You can use the id command to print your username and user ID and the group name and group ID of all groups to which you belong:

```
$ id
uid=500(stewart) gid=500(stewart)
groups=500(stewart),4(adm),24(cdrom),27(sudo)
```

In fact, you can supply id with any username, and it will list their information:

```
$ id syslog
uid=102(syslog) gid=106(syslog) groups=106(syslog),4(adm),5(tty)
```

Alternatively, you can use the groups command to print a list of groups to which you (or another user) belongs:

```
$ groups
stewart adm cdrom sudo
$ groups syslog
syslog : syslog adm tty
```

In Unix, the *superuser* is a distinguished user whose username is (usually) root and whose UID is 0. The superuser can perform actions that ordinary users cannot, such as changing a person's username or modifying the operating system's configuration. Anyone who can log in as root in Unix has absolute power over that system. For this reason, most Unix systems record every attempt to log in as root, so that a system administrator can monitor and catch break-in attempts.

Privileged and Nonprivileged Instructions

In order to prevent ordinary users and their programs from accessing hardware and performing other operations that may corrupt the state of the computer system, Unix requires that the processor support two modes of operation, known as *privileged* and *unprivileged* mode. These modes are also known as *supervisor mode* and *user mode*, respectively. *Privileged instructions* are instructions that can alter system resources, directly or indirectly. Examples of privileged instructions include:

- Acquiring more memory
- Changing the system time
- Raising the priority of the running process
- Reading from or writing to the disk
- Entering privileged mode

Only the kernel is allowed to execute privileged instructions. Programs run by ordinary users can execute only unprivileged instructions. The security, reliability, and integrity of the operating system depend upon this separation of powers.

Environments

When a program is run in Unix, one of the steps that the kernel takes prior to running the program is to make available to it an array of name-value pairs called the *environment list*, or simply the *environment*. Each name-value pair in this list is a string of the form *name=value*, where *value* is a NULL-terminated C string and there are no spaces around the = character. The *name* is called an *environment variable* and *name=value* is called an *environment string*. For example

```
LOGNAME=stewart
```

is an environment string that specifies that the variable named LOGNAME has the value stewart. Variable names are not allowed to contain the = character, but otherwise they have no restrictions. However, for portability of any programs that use these variables, and by convention, they should contain only uppercase letters, digits, and underscores and should not begin with a digit (see *The Open Group Base Specifications*, Issue 7, 2018, Chapter 8 [14]).

In this example

```
COLUMNS=80
```

COLUMNS is an environment variable whose value is 80. Even though 80 is a number, it is stored as a string inside the environment list. If this environment variable exists, it stores the number of columns in the currently open terminal window, and as you resize the window, its value changes accordingly.

Environment variables can influence the behavior of many programs, including the shell itself. When you log in to a Unix system, the operating system creates the environment for you, using configuration information from various files in the system. From that point forward, whenever you run a program, it inherits a copy of the current values of the environment. That program can use the environment variables to customize its behavior, and it can also modify its own copy of the environment. In the online chapter "Working in the Command Interface," available in the online resources for the book at *https://nostarch.com/introduction-system-programming-linux*, I explain how the environment is passed to a program, how it affects the behavior of the shell, and how you can customize it. In Chapter 10, I explain in detail how the environment is represented and where it is stored in memory when a program is running.

You can see the values of environment variables from the command line in various ways. The printenv command displays the values of all environment variables, as does the env command. Both may produce more lines than one screen can display. Soon you'll see how to *page* output one screenful at a time. If you want to see the values of selected environment variables, give their names as arguments to the printenv command:

```
$ printenv LINES COLUMNS SHELL
23
80
/bin/bash
```

A program can call the getenv() function to retrieve a particular environment string. To demonstrate, the following small program, named *getenv_demo.c*, prints out the name of the user's shell:

getenv_demo.c
```c
#include <stdio.h>
#include <stdlib.h>

void main()
{
    char *shell = getenv("SHELL");
    printf("The current shell is %s.\n", shell);
}
```

The program needs to include the *stdio.h* header file because it calls the printf() function and the *stdlib.h* header file because it calls getenv(), which is declared in that header. We compile it and run it as follows:

```
$ gcc getenv_demo.c -o getenv_demo
$ ./getenv_demo
The current shell is /bin/bash.
```

This is a sneak preview of how we compile code using the GNU gcc compiler. We give gcc the name of the source code file, *getenv_demo.c*, and the option -o getenv_demo to store the output of the compiler in the executable file named *getenv_demo*. Without that option, it would store the executable in a file named *a.out*. In the next chapter we'll explain thoroughly the process of building executable code.

Files, Directories, and the Single Directory Hierarchy

In their seminal article, "The UNIX Time-Sharing System," Ritchie and Thompson stated that the single most important role of the operating system is to provide a filesystem [33]. Kernighan and Pike, in their now-famous book on programming in the Unix environment, *The UNIX Programming Environment*, point out that the very first aspect of Unix that Ritchie and Thompson discussed while designing the system was the structure of its system of files because that determined how everything else was going to work; they went so far as to state that "everything in the UNIX system is a file" [19].

Files

For most people who use computers, files are simply objects that store information. These objects usually reside on *nonvolatile storage* devices, which are storage devices that retain data even when power is not applied to them, such as magnetic tapes and magnetic, optical, and electronic disks. (In contrast, *volatile storage*, such as main memory, does not retain data when it is powered off.) These nonvolatile storage devices are called *secondary storage* devices or *external storage* devices, even though they might appear to you to be "inside" the computer. The nomenclature is a historical artifact.

In many non-Unix systems, the operating system recognizes different types of files, each having its own specific structure, such as word processor documents, image files, or spreadsheets. In fact, in those systems, files often have names or extensions that can be used to infer their structure or even cause a specific program to load them.

In Unix, however, the story is very different. From the kernel's viewpoint, an ordinary file is just an object that contains a linear sequence of bytes. It does not impose any structure on the contents of this kind of file; any structure that it might have is given to it by the user or program that creates it. These files are called *regular* or *plain* files. Some of these files are what we commonly call *text files* because when we open them we see plaintext. These files contain sequences of characters with lines demarcated by newline characters; programs that are designed to display them use the embedded newline characters to create the line structure on the screen. *Binary files*, in contrast, are files that contain byte sequences that are not necessarily text characters, such as a program's executable code.

File Types

The Unix kernel does define a small set of file types other than these regular files:

- Directories
- Device files
- Pipes
- Sockets
- Symbolic links

Directories are described in "Directories" on page 19. Device files, pipes, and sockets are collectively called *special files*. Special files are an unusual feature of the Unix system of files. They were invented to provide a method of programming I/O in a device-independent way. Chapters 6 and 13 cover device files, pipes, and device-independent I/O. *Sockets* are a type of device file that allows processes to communicate with each other, and they're primarily used in network communication. Because they are a complex topic that can fill a book by themselves, I don't cover them in this book. I define and discuss symbolic links in "Symbolic Links" on page 24.

File Attributes, Permissions, and Contents

All files, regardless of their type, have *attributes*. Attributes include all of the important information about the file, such as the time the file was last modified, the time it was last accessed, the user ID of its owner, its size expressed as a number of bytes, who is allowed various types of access to the file, and so on. The attributes that describe restrictions on access to the file are called the *file mode* or the file's *permissions*. Permissions play an important role in the security of a Unix system. We'll explore them in detail in Chapter 4.

The attributes of a file are collectively called the *file status*. The word *status* may sound misleading, but it's the word that was used by Ritchie and Thompson in the original UNIX system. Another word often used to describe a file's attributes or status is *metadata*. Unix systems make a clear distinction between the contents of a file and its status. *Contents* are a file's data; most, but not all, files have contents. Some files, such as device files and certain other special files, do not have contents; they do not store data. They are interfaces that the kernel uses to implement device-independent input and output.

The contents of a file don't contain any status information. They have no end-of-file characters to denote the end of the file, for example, or any other means of representing its length. The contents and status aren't even stored together. The status is stored in a data structure called an *inode*, whereas the contents may be spread out in multiple blocks on the same storage device as the inode.

An important fact about files is that *filenames are not part of the status of the file.* In fact, a nondirectory file can have multiple names, and those names aren't an inherent property of the file itself, but of the directories that contain them.

Directories

A *directory*, often called a *folder* in other operating systems, is a type of file that, from the user's perspective, appears to contain other files. We tend to visualize them as shown in Figure 1-4.

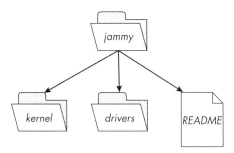

Figure 1-4: A directory with three children

This is only an illusion; directories don't contain files any more than the table of contents contains the chapters of the book. What then is a directory?

To be precise, a directory is a file that contains a table of *directory entries*, which are properly called links. A *link* is an object that associates a filename to an actual file. It has two components: the filename and a reference to a file's inode. The links may reference any type of file, including directories, implying that directories can be members of directories. However, a link isn't allowed to refer to a file that's on a different device from the directory itself.

Directories are never empty because every directory contains two links, named . (dot) and .. (dot-dot). These entries have a predefined meaning: . is a link to the directory itself, and .. is a link to the directory containing this directory, which is called the *parent* directory. Figure 1-5 shows what the actual directory table for the directory named *jammy* in Figure 1-4 looks like.

jammy directory

Reference to file	Name
53	.
2	..
12	kernel
185	drivers
282	README

Figure 1-5: A table for the jammy *directory*

The numbers in the left-hand column are just illustrative and are supposed to represent references to the inodes for the given files. For example, drivers is the name in this directory for the file whose inode has number 185.

When you work in a shell, it maintains a unique directory for you called the current working directory. The *current working directory* is the one in which you're working. The idea of being "in a directory" deserves clarification.

We often say when speaking out loud about a computing session that we're "in a directory." Give a moment's thought to this statement. What does it actually mean? It's more intuitive when you work in a GUI and the file browser displays a window whose contents are the files inside a single directory. In this case, the directory whose files are in that window is the directory in which you're currently working. The same thing is true in a command line interface; you have a unique working directory.

Two directory-related commands will demonstrate these ideas. The ls command can display the contents of directories. Entering ls without arguments displays the contents of the current working directory:

```
$ ls
chapters/    fonts/    images/    main.tex    main.bib
```

Alternatively, we can give ls one or more directory names as its arguments to see their contents:

```
$ ls chapters images
chapters:
appendix_a.tex    chapter_02.tex    chapter_05.tex        preface.tex
back_matter.tex   chapter_03.tex    front_matter.tex
chapter_01.tex    chapter_04.tex    intro.tex

images:
chapter_01/   chapter_2/   chapter_3/   chapter_4/   chapter_5/
```

Notice that each directory's name appears first, followed by the files that are in that directory. The number of columns that ls uses is based on how many names the directory has and their lengths.

We can change the current working directory with the cd command:

```
$ cd chapters
$ ls
appendix_a.tex    chapter_02.tex    chapter_05.tex        preface.tex
back_matter.tex   chapter_03.tex    front_matter.tex
chapter_01.tex    chapter_04.tex    intro.tex
```

Notice that now the ls command displays the contents of the new working directory, which is *chapters*. We can return to the previous directory via the .. link:

```
$ cd ..
$ ls
chapters/    fonts/    images/    main.tex    main.bib
```

The output of ls shows that the working directory is once again the parent of *chapters*, since the list of filenames is the same as it was before we changed directory to *chapters*.

Filenames

Files and filenames, as noted earlier, are different things. A *filename* is a string that names a file. It is part of the link contained inside a directory. A single nondirectory file may have names in different directories (on the same logical device) and can therefore appear to be a member of many directories. However, files exist independently of the directories in which they appear. If the same file has names in different directories, the references associated to those names in the links all point to the exact same inode, namely the unique inode for that file. It's like a person traveling with several passports. The passports might have different names for the person and be used in different countries, but they each represent the same person. Figure 1-6 illustrates this idea.

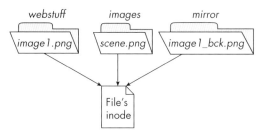

Figure 1-6: A file with three names

In this figure, one file is known by three different names, each being a link to a different directory.

Filenames are allowed to be quite long. The maximum number of characters in a filename is defined by a system-dependent constant NAME_MAX, which is usually 255 characters. They can contain almost any character except a forward slash (/) and the NULL character (\0), but you shouldn't use certain characters in filenames even if they're allowed. For example, a filename can have spaces and newlines, but if it does, you'll usually need to put quotes around the name to use it as an argument to commands. Certain characters, such as *$*, *&*, ***, and others, have a distinct meaning to various programs and must be *escaped* by preceding them with a backslash if they're used in those contexts, so it's best to avoid them. The convention is to use only alphanumeric characters, the underscore, and the hyphen in filenames. Unix is case-sensitive, such that *source* and *Source* would be treated as two different filenames.

Unlike most other operating systems, Unix doesn't use filename extensions for any purpose, although user-level software such as compilers and word processors might use them as guides. Desktop environments such as GNOME and KDE can create associations based on filename extensions in much the same way that Windows and macOS do, but Unix itself doesn't have a notion of file type based on content, and it provides the same set of operations for all files, regardless of their type. In Unix, we use the word *suffix* for the part of a filename after a period, such as the *c* in *myprog.c*.

The Directory Hierarchy

Unix organizes files into a tree-like hierarchy that most people erroneously call the filesystem. It's more accurately called the *directory hierarchy* because the term *filesystem* refers to a set of data structures written onto an unstructured disk device to enable the creation and management of files and directories.

Each node in this tree-like hierarchy is either a nondirectory file or a directory. Each edge is a *directed edge* from a nonempty directory to each file that is contained in that directory, including files that are directories, and we call the contained files the *children* or *child nodes* of that directory. The directory is called the *parent* of those child nodes. This hierarchy's base is a single *root* directory whose name is the / character. Even though the base is named /, when people refer to this directory, they usually call it the root directory, since saying "forward slash" is not very descriptive and is also a mouthful.

Because a single file can have names in different directories, a file may have more than one parent node, as shown in Figure 1-6. This is why the hierarchy is tree-like but not a tree, since in a tree, every node has a unique parent.

In a typical, modern Unix system, the directory hierarchy is a *directed acyclic graph*, which is a directed graph that contains no cycles. It has no cycles because a directory, unlike a nondirectory file, can't have more than one name, which implies that it's an entry in exactly one parent directory. This implies that no edge can be pointing to it from any descendant node, and hence the graph has no cycles. Some Unix implementations do allow the superuser to give directories more than one name, in which case, it is possible for the hierarchy to have cycles.

This idea of a single directory hierarchy is a defining characteristic of Unix. Other operating systems, such as Microsoft Windows, have separate directory hierarchies for each distinct device. In Unix, even though the files in this single tree might be on different devices, the directory hierarchy on any device can be attached to the single tree by a procedure called *mounting*. After that hierarchy is mounted on the tree, its files can be accessed in the same way as all other files.

The typical Unix directory hierarchy, a portion of which is illustrated in Figure 1-7, has several directories just under the root. These directories are called the *top-level directories*.

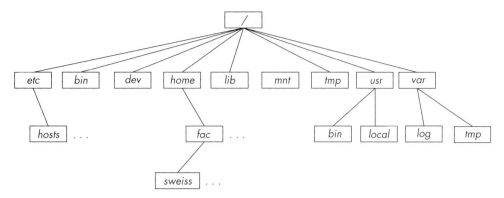

Figure 1-7: A portion of the top of a typical UNIX directory hierarchy

The following list describes the top-level directories present in most Unix systems. The only directories actually required by POSIX.1-2024 are */dev* and */tmp*.

bin   All essential binary executables, including those shell commands that must be available when the computer is running in single-user mode (something like safe mode in Windows).

boot   Static files of the bootloader.

dev   Essential device files (covered in Chapters 6 and 18).

etc   Almost all host configuration files, roughly like the registry file of Windows.

home   If present, all users' home directories.

lib   Essential shared libraries and kernel modules.

media   Mount point for removable media.

mnt   Mount point for mounting a filesystem temporarily.

opt   Add-on application software packages.

sbin   Essential system binaries.

srv   Data for services provided by this system.

tmp   Temporary files created by applications.

usr   Originally, this was the top of the hierarchy of user data files, but now it's the top of a hierarchy containing nonessential binaries, libraries, and sources. Typical subdirectories are */usr/bin* and */usr/sbin*, which contain binaries; */usr/lib*, containing library files; and */usr/local*, the top of a third level of local programs and data.

var   *Variable* files, meaning files whose contents can change.

All files, including directories, can be characterized by two independent binary properties: their shareability and their variability. *Shareable* files can be stored on one host and used on others. *Unshareable* files aren't shareable. For example, the files in user home directories are shareable because they don't depend on where they are stored, whereas bootloader files are specific to a given machine and aren't shareable.

Variable files are files whose contents can change, whereas *static* files are those whose contents cannot. They include, for example, executable binaries, libraries, documentation files, and other files that don't normally change in the day-to-day operation of the computer. In modern Unix systems, the shareability and variability of files are factors in deciding which ones are in which parts of the hierarchy. Files that differ in either of these attributes are placed into different directories, which makes it easy to store files with different usage characteristics on different filesystems and also makes backing up easier. For example, the */etc* directory is unshareable—it contains files specific to the particular computer—and it's static because its contents are configuration files that are modified only when we apply updates, install new software, or the superuser decides to change configurations. The */var* directory is so named because it is variable. It contains many different types of logfiles that the kernel and applications update on a regular basis. Some of its subdirectories, such as */var/mail*, may be shareable, whereas others such as */var/log* may be unshareable. The */usr* directory is shareable and static. It contains application binaries, libraries, and static data.

Symbolic Links

An ordinary link is a directory entry that points to the inode for a file, but a *symbolic link* is a file whose contents are just the name of another file. The file to which the link points is called the *target* of the link. The inode for a symbolic link identifies that file as a symbolic link. It's similar to a *shortcut* in the Windows operating system. Symbolic links are often called *soft links* in contrast to ordinary links, which are called *hard links*.

Usually, commands, programs, and the kernel itself, when they are given a symbolic link when a filename is expected, will operate on the target of the link, not the link itself. They can easily see that the file is a symbolic link because the inode indicates it. We say that a link is *dereferenced* or is *followed* when the link is opened to access its target.

Symbolic links pose hazards for the operating system and applications because of the possibility of circular references and infinite loops. The danger is that a symbolic link can point to a directory, which means that if a program follows symbolic links, it might return to a directory that it already visited and end up in a cycle. Chapters 6 and 7 address issues related to symbolic links in more detail.

Pathnames

A *pathname* is a character string that identifies a file. There are two types of pathnames: absolute and relative. An *absolute* pathname starts at the root of the directory hierarchy and starts with a leading forward slash, */*. Zero or more filenames separated by slashes follow that leading slash, such as */data/jammy/kernel/sched/sched.h*. All filenames except the last must be directory names or symbolic links whose targets are directory names. Each of the names in the example pathname except *sched.h* is a directory. The last name in the path may be any type of file. Other examples of absolute pathnames are */usr/bin/*, */usr/local/share/man*, and */home/stewart/unixbook/figures/figure01.png*.

Terminating a pathname with a slash is acceptable if the last filename in it is a directory, as in the pathname */usr/bin/*.

If you accidentally insert more than one slash between the names in the path, it will be ignored. The two absolute pathnames */usr/local/share/man* and */usr/local///share/man* are the same.

If a pathname doesn't start with a leading slash, it's called a *relative pathname*. A relative pathname starts in the current working directory, which we can now accurately define. The *current working directory* (also called the *present working directory*) is the directory that any running program uses to resolve pathnames that do not begin with a */*. For example, if the current working directory is */home/stewart/unix_book*, the pathname *chapters/chapter_01* refers to a file whose absolute pathname is */home/stewart/unix_book/chapters/chapter_01*.

The environment variable PWD contains the absolute pathname of the current working directory. The pwd command prints the value of PWD:

```
$ pwd
/home/stewart/unix_book
$ printenv PWD
/home/stewart/unix_book
```

Pathnames can become very long if they contain symbolic links, and Unix systems limit their length, expressed in bytes. POSIX.1-2024 specifies that the constant PATH_MAX is the maximum number of bytes allowed in a pathname, including the terminating NULL byte. On many Linux systems, it is 4096 bytes.

Processes

People (and sometimes programs) write programs. Programs are sequences of instructions to the computer, written in a programming language. The language might be a high-level one, such as C or C++, or it might be a low-level one, such as an assembly language. In general, programs can't be executed in the form in which they're written; they must be translated into an executable form. The exceptions to this are programs written in scripting languages, such as JavaScript, PHP, and BASIC. These aren't translated into an executable; an interpreter program reads the source code directly and executes their instructions one after another.

We call the first form of a program the *source code* and the second form the *executable code* or, simply, the *executable*. For example, the source file *hello_world.c* from Listing 1-1 is a human-readable text file. You can use the GNU C compiler to build an executable from it named *hello_world* with the following command:

```
$ gcc hello_world.c -o hello_world
```

The file *hello_world* will be an executable file residing, by default, in the same directory as *hello_world.c*. You can't use ordinary text editors to see or modify the contents of this file because it's not plaintext; it's a binary file.

Perhaps surprisingly, even running a program is a complex procedure (we'll cover the details in Chapter 11). The executable form of most programs isn't something we can actually run. We can't just load it into memory and tell the machine to start running that file from its first byte. That file is usually a conglomeration of executable code, various tables, and instructions to a linker/loader. When you enter the command

```
$ ./hello_world
```

a sequence of actions takes place that causes a linker/loader to use the information in that *hello_world* executable to load the file, as well as any shared objects that it needs, into memory, prepare the program for execution, and run that program.

Many users can run a single program at the same time on a given machine, or a single user can run one multiple times in different terminal windows. Either way, it means that one executable can have many running instances, which is what leads us to distinguish between programs and processes. A *process* is an instance of a running program. Each separate instance is a different process, although each and every one of them is executing the exact same executable file.

This formal definition of a process doesn't really tell you what a process is in concrete terms, even though it's the one you'll likely see in an operating systems textbook. It's like defining a baseball game as an instance of the implementation of the set of rules created by Alexander Cartwright in 1845 by which two teams compete against each other on a playing field. Neither definition gives you a mental picture of what's being defined. Let's make it more concrete.

When a program is run on a computer, it uses resources such as primary memory and secondary storage space; kernel memory (kernel space) for mappings and tables of various kinds, such as a table of which parts of primary memory it uses; privileges, such as the right to read or write certain files or devices; and much, much more. As a result, at any moment of time, a process is associated with the collection of all resources allocated to that instance of the running program, as well as any other properties and settings that characterize that instance, such as the values of the processor's registers. Thus, although the idea of a process sounds like an abstract idea, it is, in fact, a very concrete thing, and an operating system must manage it.

Unix systems assign to each process a unique nonnegative integer called its *process identifier*, or *PID* for short. We can learn a bit about processes using the ps command, which can display a list of running processes, as well as selected information about each of them. It has various options to control which processes it displays and what information it outputs. In its simplest form, with no options, we can use it to see the PIDs of our own running processes:

```
$ ps
    PID TTY          TIME CMD
  10278 pts/0    00:00:00 bash
  11087 pts/0    00:00:00 ps
```

This lists two processes: one running bash and the other running the ps command itself. They use so little time that it shows up as zeros, and their respective PIDs are 10278 and 11087. They're both running in a terminal whose device name is pts/0.

At the programming language level, we can call the getpid() function to obtain the PID of the process that invokes it. We demonstrate this in the *getpid_demo.c* program:

```
getpid_demo.c  #include <stdio.h>
            ❶ #include <unistd.h>
               void main()
               {
               ❷ printf("I am the process with process-id %d\n", getpid());
               }
```

All this program does is print its own PID, but it illustrates how to use getpid(). The program includes the header file <unistd.h> ❶ because the getpid() function, called inside the argument list of printf() ❷, is a system call, and almost all system call declarations are in <unistd.h>. This is our first program to make a system call.

The return value of getpid() is the PID of the process that calls it. Because PIDs are integers in the format string of printf(), we use the %d format specification to print the return value as a fixed decimal numeral. Assuming that *getpid_demo.c* is in our working directory, we can compile and run it with these commands:

```
$ gcc getpid_demo.c -o getpid_demo
$ ./getpid_demo
I am the process with process-id 18805
```

If we were to run this same program again, it would print a different PID, proving a new process is created whenever it is run.

Threads

The programs that we've described so far in this chapter are assumed to have a single thread of control. A *thread of control* is a single sequence of instructions that's executed one instruction at a time, one after the other, during the execution of a program. Originally, all programs had a single thread of control. As the cost of computer processors became smaller and smaller, hardware vendors started building computers containing multiple processors, and computer scientists sought ways to take advantage of this new technology. They designed and created programming languages and libraries that would allow a program to contain more than one thread of control, each of which could run on the separate processors simultaneously. These threads of control were named *threads* for simplicity.

POSIX.1-2024 formally defines a *thread* as a single flow of control through a process together with the required system resources to support a flow of control [14].

The traditional Unix process is a single thread, but in modern operating systems, processes in general can have multiple threads. When a process has multiple threads, it's called a *multithreaded process*. A multithreaded process has two types of resources: those that are shared among all of its threads, which are generally called *global* or *shared*, and those that are unique to each thread, commonly called either *thread local*, *private*, or *per-thread*. In Chapter 15, we detail exactly which process resources are shared and which are thread local.

Unix systems in general support multithreading, and Linux in particular supports several different types of threads. Linux handles threads in an interesting way; it treats all threads as standard processes. It doesn't provide any special scheduling or data structures for threads. To the Linux kernel, processes and threads are both called *tasks* and are both represented internally by the same data structure, called a task_struct [4]. In Linux, a *task* is an entity that's assigned system resources and can be scheduled on a processor. The difference between threads and ordinary processes in Linux is that threads can share resources, such as their address space, whereas processes don't share any resources.

In many Unix implementations, a thread has a *thread identifier (TID)* that is unique in the operating system, but POSIX.1-2024 doesn't require this. It requires only that within a single process, each thread's TID is unique. Linux handles TIDs with a two-pronged approach: In a single-threaded process, the TID is equal to the process ID, whereas in a multithreaded process, all threads have the same PID, but each one has a unique TID. In Linux, a thread can call the gettid() function to obtain its thread ID. The *gettid_demo.c* program demonstrates this idea:

gettid_demo.c
```
#define _GNU_SOURCE
#include <stdio.h>
#include <unistd.h>
#include <sys/types.h>

void main()
{
    printf("I am a thread with thread ID %d\n", gettid());
}
```

The program uses the C preprocessor #define directive to define the symbol _GNU_SOURCE. Unless this symbol is defined, the compiler won't see the various declarations in the header files that are needed for the program to call gettid(). This is an example of a *feature test macro*, which is explained in

"Portability" in Chapter 2. The #define directive must appear before all include directives. We can compile and run it as shown in the following sample session:

```
$ gcc gettid_demo.c -o gettid_demo
$ gettid_demo
I am a thread with thread ID 1810
```

If we run this program again, it too will display a different TID each time for the same reasons as before: A new process runs, and its TID is the same as its PID when it has one thread.

Online Documentation

Unix systems provide several different types of online documentation. In this context, *online* means on the computer that you are using, not on the World Wide Web.

The Man Pages

In 1971, shortly after the release of First Edition UNIX, Dennis Ritchie and Ken Thompson, with help from Joseph Ossanna and Robert Morris, wrote the first *UNIX Programmer's Manual*, which is still available online (*https://www.nokia.com/bell-labs/about/dennis-m-ritchie/1stEdman.html*). This manual was initially a single volume, but in short order it grew into a set of seven volumes, organized by topic. It was available in both printed form and as formatted files suitable for display on an ordinary character display device. Over time it grew in size. Every Unix distribution now comes with this set of manual pages, called *man pages* for short. The manual usually has eight numbered sections in a typical Unix system as of this writing, as shown in Table 1-1. Some Unix systems have additional sections.

Table 1-1: Manual Sections

Number	Common name	Description
1	User commands	Executable programs and shell commands
2	System calls	Functions provided by the kernel
3	Library calls	Functions within program libraries
4	Special files	Files usually found in /dev
5	File formats and conventions	Formats of system files
6	Games	Various games and humorous programs
7	Miscellaneous	Macro packages and conventions
8	System administration commands	Usually only for root

The man pages are an important part of Unix documentation. They act as an online reference when you want to learn about any part of the Unix system, such as a command, a function from one of the libraries, a system call, a device interface, a system file, various file formats, and much more. Although the documentation is very thorough and detailed, it's usually not tutorial in nature. It can be overwhelming sometimes, but many pages have code examples that you can compile, modify, and run.

Over the years in which I taught Unix system programming, students would sometimes say that they didn't need to learn how to use the man pages because all that information is on the web and they just had to google it. It's true that you can find copies of the man pages on many websites and read posts on discussion boards, but the reasons for reading the man pages on your own Unix installation go beyond this:

- The versions of the man pages on your system were installed at the time that the software they document was installed, and they are updated whenever you update the software itself and the software has updates to apply to them.

- Man pages are written by the people who wrote and maintain the software and are trustworthy and accurate.

- The man pages on your system are self-contained in the sense that any cross references they make are also on your system.

- You can read them even if your internet connection isn't available.

To view the man page for a given topic, enter `man` followed by the topic in which you're interested, meaning the command name, function name, and so on. For example, enter `man man` to read the man page for the `man` command itself:

```
$ man man
MAN(1)                          Manual pager utils                         MAN(1)


NAME
        man - an interface to the system reference manuals
--snip--
```

The output is just the first few lines of that page. The first line shows that the `man` command is in Section 1 of the man pages because the title contains `MAN(1)`. The text `Manual pager utils` is not the name of Section 1; we'll call it the *man page header* or the *header* when the meaning is clear. Different man pages in Section 1 may have different headers. After the word `NAME` is the name of the command followed by a very brief description of what the command does. This is the very first man page you should read, and we'll revisit it shortly.

All POSIX-conforming Unix systems are required to contain man pages for all of the header files that might be included by a function in the kernel's API. To put it more precisely, each function in the System Interfaces volume of POSIX.1-2024 specifies the headers that an application must include to use that function, and a POSIX-conforming system must have a man page for each of those headers. They may not be installed on the system you're using, but they're available. They're installed only if the system administrator installed the application development files.

The man page for the scanf() function starts with the following lines:

```
SCANF(3)                    Linux Programmer's Manual                    SCANF(3)
NAME
       scanf, fscanf, sscanf, vscanf, vsscanf, vfscanf
       - input format conversion

SYNOPSIS
       #include <stdio.h>
--snip--
```

It tells us that we need the header file *stdio.h* to use scanf(). We can enter **man stdio.h** to read about that header file, which outputs the following:

```
stdio.h(7POSIX)             POSIX Programmer's Manual             stdio.h(7POSIX)

PROLOG
       This manual page is part of the POSIX Programmer's Manual. The Linux
       implementation of this interface may differ (consult the corresponding
       Linux manual page for details of Linux behavior), or the interface may
       not be implemented on Linux.

NAME
       stdio.h - standard buffered input/output
--snip--
```

Notice that this man page is in a section whose number is 7posix. On your system, this page might be in a different section, such as Section 0.

One challenge with using the man pages is that you need to know the name of the command or function in which you're interested for them to be of help. The man pages do have a relatively simple search mechanism, but they are really intended as a reference manual for people who already have a sense of what it is they need to look up, so if you know what you want to do but don't know the command name, the challenge is how to find it.

The man pages play a key role in helping you solve problems on your own. My method of teaching how to write system programs is based on using the man pages to guide the learning process. They're inextricably linked to learning system programming in this book, so I've included a separate section, "Using the Manual Pages" on page 34, that explains their structure and how to use them in greater depth, including the syntax they use for specifying options and arguments.

The Info Documentation System

Because of some deficiencies in the man pages, the GNU project developed an alternative documentation system named *Info*, which it based on the *Texinfo* documentation system. Texinfo (pronounced "Tekinfo") is a documentation system that uses a single source file to produce both online and printed output. It's based on a help system that Richard M. Stallman created for the Emacs text editor in 1975 and 1976 (*https://www.gnu.org/software/texinfo/manual/texinfo/html_node/History.html*).

The Info pages for various commands and utility programs sometimes contain much more information than their man page counterparts. In some cases, the man page for a command refers the reader to the Info page. To read an Info page, enter the `info` command (lowercase). For example, to learn about the `ls` command, enter **info ls**:

```
$ info ls
Next: dir invocation,  Up: Directory listing

10.1 'ls': List directory contents
==================================

The 'ls' program lists information about files (of any type, including
directories). Options and file arguments can be intermixed arbitrarily,
as usual.
--snip--
```

When there isn't a page for a particular topic in the Info system, the Info reader opens up the man page for that topic instead.

The Info pages use a method of navigation similar to the one in Emacs, which people often find hard to use. There's a method of reading an Info document and bypassing the navigation in it by piping its output into a pager program such as `more` or `less`, as shown here:

```
$ info ls | more
File: coreutils.info, Node: ls invocation, Next: dir invocation, Up: Directory
listing

10.1 'ls': List directory contents
==================================

The 'ls' program lists information about files (of any type, including
directories). Options and file arguments can be intermixed arbitrarily,
as usual.
--snip--
```

The same information is displayed, but it also mentions the file in which it's contained: *coreutils.info*. We'll explain how this works and what pagers are in "The Pager" on page 34.

Application-Provided Documentation

Sometimes you can also find information about a particular application or program in one of the directories in */usr/share/doc*. Many applications and higher-level program installers place their documentation there. This documentation sometimes includes extensive usage examples, development notes, and hints on where to find further information.

Some commands have a means of displaying their own help, usually by providing an option such as `--help`:

```
$ ls --help
Usage: ls [OPTION]... [FILE]...
List information about the FILEs (the current directory by default).
Sort entries alphabetically if none of -cftuvSUX nor --sort is specified.
--snip--
```

The rest of the output is primarily a description of the various options of ls and their arguments.

Shell Help

Certain shells have a help feature for commands that are built into the shell. In particular, bash has a help command, which when entered without arguments prints a two-column list of all bash builtins with options and arguments listed:

```
$ help
GNU bash, version 5.1.16(1)-release (x86_64-pc-linux-gnu)
These shell commands are defined internally. Type `help' to see this list.
Type `help name' to find out more about the function `name'.
Use `info bash' to find out more about the shell in general.
Use `man -k' or `info' to find out more about commands not in this list.

A star (*) next to a name means that the command is disabled.

 job_spec [&]                            history [-c] [-d offset] [n] or hist>
 (( expression ))                        if COMMANDS; then COMMANDS; [ elif C>
 . filename [arguments]                  jobs [-lnprs] [jobspec ...] or jobs >
 :                                       kill [-s sigspec | -n signum | -sigs>
 [ arg... ]                              let arg [arg ...]
 [[ expression ]]                        local [option] name[=value] ...
 alias [-p] [name[=value] ... ]         logout [n]
 bg [job_spec ...]                       mapfile [-d delim] [-n count] [-O or>
 bind [-lpsvPSVX] [-m keymap] [-f file>  popd [-n] [+N | -N]
 break [n]                               printf [-v var] format [arguments]
 builtin [shell-builtin [arg ...]]      pushd [-n] [+N | -N | dir]
--snip--
```

When given the name of a particular bash builtin, it prints a short summary of how to use that command:

```
$ help pwd
pwd: pwd [-LP]
    Print the name of the current working directory.

    Options:
      -L print the value of $PWD if it names the current working directory
      -P print the physical directory, without any symbolic links

    By default, `pwd' behaves as if `-L' were specified.
```

```
Exit Status:
Returns 0 unless an invalid option is given or the current directory
cannot be read.
$
```

The help command uses the same syntax as the man pages.

Other Sources of Documentation

You can download many manuals from the organizations that wrote and maintain the code. The single most important manual to have on hand is the GNU C Library Reference Manual, available at *https://www.gnu.org/software/libc/manual/*.

Using the Manual Pages

To make the most of the man pages, you need to learn how to use the pager that displays the pages and to read the man page for the man command itself, so that you can understand man page structure and what options the man command has.

The Pager

A *pager* is a program that displays its input one screen at a time. The man pages are stored in a compressed format in the directory hierarchy. The man command decompresses and formats them and then displays them with its pager. The default pager is actually named pager, but it's usually a symbolic link to the less command. Therefore, when you view a page, you'll most likely be using less. The : at the bottom of the screen is followed by your cursor because the : is the less command's prompt for you to type something on the keyboard. You can change the pager that man uses by changing the value of the PAGER environment variable. The following list describes some of the basic navigation controls when you use the default pager:

- To see the next screen, press SPACEBAR or enter **f** (for forward).

- To go back one screen, enter **b** (for backward).

- To stop reading, enter **q** for quit.

- To go to line *N*, enter *N***G**. If you just enter **G**, you'll go to the bottom of the page.

- To search forward for *keyword*, enter */keyword*. Enter **n** to find the next occurrence downward, or enter **N** to search upward.

- To search backward for *keyword*, enter **?<keyword>**. Enter **n** to find the next occurrence upward, or enter **N** to search downward.

To see the list of all possible navigation operators, read the man page for the pager. Both of the search operators accept patterns with wildcards, which you can read about in the man page for the pager command.

The Structure of Man Pages

Entering `man` followed by the name of any command or topic that has a man page displays that man page. We saw earlier that the `man` command has a page for itself as well. We're about to study that page, but before we do, let's take a look at a couple of other, simpler pages.

Since we've already seen the `echo` command in the Introduction, let's start with that. If you want to learn more about how to use `echo`, you'd enter `man echo` and you'd see several screens of output, beginning with:

```
echo(1)                        User Commands                        echo(1)


NAME
       echo - display a line of text

SYNOPSIS
       echo [SHORT-OPTION]... [STRING]...
       echo LONG-OPTION

DESCRIPTION
       Echo the STRING(s) to standard output.

       -n     do not output the trailing newline
       -e     enable interpretation of backslash escapes
       -E     disable interpretation of backslash escapes (default)
--snip--
```

The top of the page often has everything you need to know, such as what options are available and whether there are multiple forms of the command.

Sometimes the name of the man page `man` displays is different from the name of the command that you entered as an argument. For example, entering `man view` produces the following output:

```
VIM(1)                      General Commands Manual                      VIM(1)


NAME
       vim - Vi IMproved, a programmer's text editor
       SYNOPSIS
       vim [options] [file ..]
       vim [options] -
       --snip--
       ex
       view
       gvim gview evim eview
       rvim rview rgvim rgview
--snip--
```

This is the page for `vim`, but the `view` command is listed on that page. Sometimes a single man page provides information about related commands.

Notice too that instead of the title `User Commands`, this page's title is `General Commands Manual`. People who write man pages follow a standard, but that standard allows some variation, such as in the title of the page.

The sections of a man page are somewhat standardized. A few sections are required, but most sections are optional. The following list shows some common section names and describes their contents:

`NAME`   The name of this manual page

`SYNOPSIS`   A brief summary of the command's or function's interface

`DESCRIPTION`   An explanation of what the program, function, or format does

`OPTIONS`   For commands only; a description of the command line options accepted by a program and how they change its behavior

`USAGE`   For commands; a more thorough description of the use of the command

`ENVIRONMENT VARIABLES`   A list of all environment variables that affect the command or function and how they affect it

`EXIT STATUS`   For commands; a list of exit values returned by the command

`RETURN VALUE`   For functions; a list of the values the function will return to the caller and the conditions that cause these values to be returned

`ERRORS`   For functions; a list of the values that may be placed in the static variable errno in the event of an error, along with information about the cause of the errors

`FILES`   A list of the files used by the command or function, and files that might be modified

`ATTRIBUTES`   Architectures on which it runs, availability, code independence, and so on

`VERSIONS`   A brief summary of the kernel or library versions where a function appeared or changed significantly in its operation

`CONFORMING TO`   The standards to which the implementation conforms

`BUGS`   A list of limitations, known defects or inconveniences, and other questionable activities

`EXAMPLES`   If present, examples of how to use the command or function

`AUTHORS`   A list of authors of the documentation or program

`SEE ALSO`   A list of commands related to this command

`NOTES`   General comments that do not fit elsewhere

NOTE   *It's unfortunate nomenclature that the word* section *is used in two different ways. Do not confuse the sections of a man page with the sections of the manual.*

The most important sections to study when reading a man page for the first time are `NAME`, `SYNOPSIS`, `DESCRIPTION`, and `SEE ALSO`, and if you're reading about a command, check the `OPTIONS` section also. The `SYNOPSIS` section contains a brief summary of the command or function's interface. If there's an `EXAMPLES` section, I often look at it at right after reading the `SYNOPSIS`, which is usually my first stop on the page. The examples typically include programs you can copy and run or commands that you can try out.

The `SYNOPSIS` section for commands shows the command's syntax, including all arguments and options. Square brackets ([ ]) surround optional elements, a vertical bar (|) (sometimes called an *alternation* operator) separates choices among elements, angle brackets (< >) surround placeholders, and an ellipsis (...) represents elements that can be repeated. When multiple option letters are enclosed in square brackets, such as in [-aHvW], all of them can be given together. If it were written as [-a | -H | -v | -W], only one of the choices would be allowed. To illustrate, the git command, which is a version control program, has the following complex synopsis:

```
git [--version] [--help] [-C <path>] [❶ -c <name>=<value>]
    [--exec-path[=<path>]] [--html-path] [--man-path] [--info-path]
 ❷ [-p|--paginate|-P|--no-pager] [--no-replace-objects] [--bare]
    [--git-dir=<path>] [--work-tree=<path>] [--namespace=<name>]
 ❸ [--super-prefix=<path>] [--config-env=<name>=<envvar>]
 ❹ <command> [<args>]
```

From this synopsis we can conclude several rules:

- The placeholder `<command>` ❹ is the only required element after the command name.

- The element [`-c <name>=<value>`] ❶ is an option to git, but if the `-c` is present, it must be followed by the name-value assignment.

- The vertical bar | ❷ is used to indicate that at most one of `-p`, `--paginate`, `-P`, or `--no-pager` can be used.

- `--super-prefix` ❸ is a long option that has a required argument.

For functions, the `SYNOPSIS` shows any required data declarations or `#include` directives, followed by the function declaration. If there are *feature test macro* requirements, which we cover in "Feature Test Macros" on page 67, these are described as well. When you read about a function, you must read the `ERRORS` and `RETURN VALUE` sections; they tell you what possible errors the function reports, what values it can return, and how you need to handle them.

For learning how to use commands and functions, the man page by itself is usually sufficient. To understand how a command interacts with the operating system or how it might be implemented, we'll need to do more research. In Chapter 3, we'll go through an exercise that shows how to use the man pages in more detail.

Searching Through the Man Pages

The man command has a number of options for performing searches. Let's look at the beginning of the man page for man:

```
MAN(1)                        Manual pager utils                        MAN(1)


NAME
       man - an interface to the system reference manuals

SYNOPSIS
       man [man options] [[section] page ...] ...
       man -k [apropos options] regexp ...
       man -K [man options] [section] term ...
       man -f [whatis options] page ...
       man -l [man options] file ...
       man -w|-W [man options] page ...

DESCRIPTION
       man is the system's manual pager. Each page argument given to man is
       normally the name of a program, utility or function. The manual page
       associated with each of these arguments is then found and displayed. A
       section, if provided, will direct man to look only in that section of
       the manual. The default action is to search in all of the available
       sections following a pre-defined order (see DEFAULTS), and to show only
       the first page found, even if page exists in several sections.
--snip--
```

You may not see all of the options that appear here. The POSIX.1-2024 standard (*https://pubs.opengroup.org/onlinepubs/9699919799/utilities/man.html*) requires only the -k option, but most implementations provide more. The output shown in this example is from the most recent version of the man page from the the Linux man-pages Project (*https://www.kernel.org/doc/man-pages/*), which provides and standardizes man pages separately from the POSIX.1-2024 standard. A number of Linux distributions, including Debian, Fedora, Gentoo, openSUSE, and Ubuntu, as well as macOS and a few proprietary Unix systems, conform to this latter standard. (See *https://man-db.gitlab.io/man-db/* for an alternative set of man pages that can be installed on other systems.)

The most important options for us are -k and -K, which allow us to search through the man pages for keywords. If you read further in the man page, you'll see the following example:

```
man -k printf
    Search the short descriptions and manual page names for the
    keyword printf as regular expression. Print out any matches.
    Equivalent to apropos printf.
```

Further down the page, you'll see a description of what this and the -K do:

```
     -k, --apropos
           Equivalent to apropos. Search the short manual page descriptions
           for keywords and display any matches. See apropos(1) for details.
     -K, --global-apropos
           Search for text in all manual pages. This is a brute-force
           search, and is likely to take some time; if you can, you should
           specify a section to reduce the number of pages that need to be
           searched. Search terms may be simple strings (the default), or
           regular expressions if the --regex option is used.
```

The -k option allows us to search through all man pages to find those short
descriptions that match the word we give it. The *short description* is the NAME
section and its one-line description. The -K option searches the entire page,
not just the short description, for a match. We are warned that this is slow,
but we may occasionally find use for it.

   The page also suggests that we should read about the apropos command.
If we look at its man page, we find exactly what we need:

```
$ man apropos
APROPOS(1)                    Manual pager utils                    APROPOS(1)


NAME
       apropos - search the manual page names and descriptions

SYNOPSIS
       apropos  [-dalv?V] [-e|-w|-r] [-s list] [-m system[,...]] [-M path] [-L
       locale] [-C file] keyword ...


DESCRIPTION
       Each manual page has a short description available within it. apropos
       searches the descriptions for instances of keyword.

       keyword is usually a regular expression, as if (-r) was used, or may
       contain wildcards (-w), or match the exact keyword (-e). Using these
       options, it may be necessary to quote the keyword or escape (\) the
       special characters to stop the shell from interpreting them.
--snip--
```

We can use apropos for searching. If we give it the -r option, we can supply a
regular expression, which is a particular type of pattern, or we can give it -w
and use a different kind of pattern called *wildcards*, which are patterns used
for matching filenames. If we give it the -e option, it will match the keyword
exactly.

   If we read more in this page, we'll see that by default, matching is case-
insensitive. Also by default, apropos searches through all sections (volumes)
of the manual, but we can limit searches to specific sections with the -s option. The -a option forces the match to return only those pages that match

all of the search terms rather than any of the search terms. A few examples will demonstrate:

```
$ apropos case
$ apropos Case
```

Both of these match any line containing the word *case*, case insensitively.

Matches can include lines that contain words that have *case* as a substring, such as *lowercase*, *case-insensitive*, and so on, and the search will check all sections. Here are two examples that clarify this:

```
$ apropos -s2,3 file
$ apropos -e file
```

The first command limits the search to Sections 2 and 3 and matches descriptions with any words containing *file*, such as *filename*, *FileProducer*, and so on. The second matches only lines that have the exact word *file*, so it excludes *filename*, *FileProducer*, and so on.

NOTE *The apropos command may be implemented differently on your system than what I describe here. The options may have slightly different usage. For example, in Ubuntu Linux, the option -s3 searches through Sections 3, 3posix, 3perl, and so on. On your system, you may have to specify all sections explicitly. You should base your use of it on what your system's apropos man page states.*

Consider this example:

```
$ apropos -a convert case
```

This command matches all pages whose short descriptions contain the two words *convert* and *case*, not necessarily next to each other, such as *convert lowercase*.

The following command matches just those lines containing a word starting with *case* or a word in which *case* is part of a hyphenated word such as *case-sensitive*:

```
$ apropos ' case' 'case-'
alsaucm (1)          - ALSA Use Case Manager
strcasecmp (3)       - compare two strings ignoring case
strcasecmp (3posix)  - case-insensitive string comparisons
strncasecmp (3)      - compare two strings ignoring case
strncasecmp (3posix) - case-insensitive string comparisons
wcscasecmp (3)       - compare two wide-character strings, ignoring case
wcscasecmp (3posix)  - case-insensitive wide-character string comparison
wcsncasecmp (3)      - compare two fixed-size wide-character strings, ignor...
wcsncasecmp (3posix) - case-insensitive wide-character string comparison
```

In summary, apropos is a valuable tool for searching for help. We'll be using it extensively in the rest of the book when we need to do background research to implement various system programs.

Unix History and Standards

Finally, the number of UNIX installations has grown to 10,
with more expected.

—Ken Thompson and Dennis Ritchie, *UNIX Programmer's Manual,*
2nd edition, 1972

Why should you learn anything about the history of Unix if all that you care about is how to write system programs? The most compelling answer is that Unix's complex, haphazard history is the cause of its lack of a single standard and the consequent need to read documentation very carefully to decide whether your code will be portable or even be able to run on your own system. By knowing something about its history you'll see that certain features originated in different Unix distributions and are sometimes incompatible and that some are fusions of ideas from different branches of the Unix family tree.

Unix has a colorful history filled with many stories [36]. Many articles, websites, and books describe that history in great detail, and at the end of this section I include references to several of them. Here, I describe the major milestones on the path from its birth as an experimental platform for Ken Thompson's "Space Travel" game through the present.

The Birth of UNIX

Ken Thompson wrote the first version of UNIX in assembly language in 1969 while he was working for AT&T Bell Labs. He also revised an old programming language named B so that the system would have a compiler to build programs to run on this new system. By 1970, Dennis Ritchie began working with Thompson on his system. From 1971 through 1973, he worked on a new language, C (based on B), to facilitate the development of Unix, and in 1973, almost all of the UNIX kernel was rewritten in C. This made it possible to port UNIX to any machine with a C compiler. This was the first time an operating system was made portable, and it's also why so much of modern Unix is based on C. In 1974, they presented their ideas in a seminal paper at the ACM Symposium on Operating Systems at IBM Yorktown Heights, the result of which was that awareness of this new operating system grew rapidly.

Meanwhile, work on UNIX continued in Bell Labs, and its popularity within the Labs spread as well. In those early years, the UNIX systems were called *research systems* by Bell Labs, and each new release was called an *edition*, with their numbers corresponding to the numbers of the *UNIX Programmer's Manual* released at the same time. These editions were given the names V1, V2, and so on. In 1974, AT&T began licensing UNIX to universities. Because of government restrictions, it wasn't allowed to sell it.

Early Branches

The University of California at Berkeley (UCB) was one of the universities that obtained a copy of V4 from AT&T, and it embarked on a mission to add more features to the operating system, thereby starting a new fork in its development. When Ken Thompson spent 1975 and 1976 visiting UCB, he and the students there added even more features to their copy of Unix. These features weren't present in the AT&T system from which it derived.

From 1974 to 1979, UCB and AT&T worked on independent copies of Unix. By 1978, the various versions of Unix had most of the features found in it today, but not all in one system. In the late 1970s, legal actions began under US antitrust legislation to break up AT&T, the result of which was that by 1982, when the breakup was complete, it was allowed to sell its own brand of UNIX. AT&T then staked proprietary rights to this UNIX and sold it commercially. AT&T's first major commercial Unix was called System V, released in 1983.

The versions of Unix developed at UCB were named Berkeley Software Distributions (BSDs) and had names such as 1BSD, 2BSD, and so on. BSD systems were released under a much more generous license than AT&T's and didn't require a license fee or a requirement to be distributed with source code. The result was that much BSD source code was incorporated into various commercial Unix variants. By the time that 4.3BSD was written, almost none of the original AT&T source code was left in it. FreeBSD, NetBSD, and OpenBSD were all forks of 4.3BSD, having none of the original AT&T source code and no right to the UNIX trademark, but much of their code found its way into commercial Unix operating systems as well. In short, two major versions of UNIX had emerged: those based on the BSD family and those based on the AT&T version.

The Free Software Foundation and GNU

In 1983, another event changed the face of computing. Richard Stallman, who had worked in the Artificial Intelligence Lab at the Massachusetts Institute of Technology (MIT), published *The GNU Manifesto*. His idea, radical at the time, was that software should be free: not free of cost, but free as in *freedom*. He founded the Free Software Foundation (FSF) in order to campaign and advocate for software whose source code would always be open and free, and for other freedoms associated with its use. He also started the GNU Project under the auspices of the FSF. (GNU is a recursive acronym for GNU's Not Unix.)

The objective of the GNU Project was to build a free alternative Unix system, starting from scratch. The project also developed a vast collection of free software tools and libraries, including compilers, text editors, debuggers, and so on. Although the kernel of the operating system, known as Hurd, did not receive widespread use, the collection of tools and libraries that GNU created has been adopted in Unix systems worldwide.

The Rise of Linux

In 1991, the picture was further complicated by the creation of a new kernel named Linux. The Linux kernel was developed from scratch, unlike the BSD systems, which made Linux a lot less like AT&T UNIX than BSD was. Because Linux was just a kernel, without any tools or libraries, it was bundled together with the GNU Project software to turn it into a full-fledged operating system.

Linux was started by Linus Torvalds, who at the time was a student at the University of Helsinki. Many of his ideas were based on the Minix operating system written by Andrew Tanenbaum, who was a professor in Vrije Universiteit in Amsterdam. Tanenbaum made the sources for Minix available with copies of his book on operating systems [41]. Minix ran on Intel 386 processors but wasn't efficient. Torvalds wanted to build a Unix kernel to run more efficiently on the Intel 386.

Many Unixes

In 1993, AT&T divested itself of UNIX, selling it to Novell, which one year later sold the trademark to an industry consortium known as X/Open. There are now dozens of different Unix distributions, each with its own behavior. There are systems such as Solaris and UnixWare that are based on SVR4, the AT&T version released in 1989, and FreeBSD and OpenBSD based on the UCB distributions. Systems such as Linux are hybrids, as are AIX, IRIX, and HP-UX.

It is natural to ask what makes a system Unix. The answer is that over the course of the past 30 years or so, standards have been developed in order to define Unix. Operating systems can be branded as conforming to one standard or another. In the next section, we'll explore the various Unix standards.

You can read more about the history of various aspects of Unix in resources such as Dennis Ritchie's telling of its history [31]; Salus and Reed's *The Daemon, the Gnu, and the Penguin* [36]; Salus's comprehensive telling in *A Quarter Century of UNIX* [35]; Brian Kernighan's memoir, *Unix: A History and a Memoir* [17]; *UNIX Internals* [28]; and *The Design and Implementation of the 4.4BSD Operating System* [26]. You can read transcripts of interviews with many UNIX developers in the *Oral History of UNIX* [23] and read the history of the GNU project at *https://www.gnu.org/gnu/gnu.html*. Torvalds and Diamond published an account of Linux development [46], and Appendix A of *Open Sources: Voices from the Open Source Revolution* [7] has an interesting exchange of ideas between Torvalds and Tanenbaum germane to the design of the Linux kernel. The bibliography also has additional references on Unix history [20] [32] [35] [38].

Unix and Related Standards

One widely accepted Unix standard is the POSIX standard, an acronym for Portable Operating System Interface. Technically, POSIX doesn't define

Unix in particular; it's more general than that. POSIX is a family of standards known formally as IEEE 1003. It was also published by the International Standards Organization (ISO) with the name ISO/IEC 9945:2003; these were one and the same document.

NOTE   *The most recent version of POSIX as of this writing is IEEE Std 1003.1-2024, also known as POSIX.1-2024. It is simultaneously known as the Open Group Base Specifications Issue 8. The POSIX.1-2024 standard consolidates the major standards preceding it, including POSIX.1, and the Single UNIX Specification, Version 4 (SuSV4).*

The spirit of POSIX is to define a Unix system, as is stated in the introduction to the specification (*http://pubs.opengroup.org/onlinepubs/9799919799/*):

> POSIX.1-2024 defines a standard operating system interface and environment, including a command interpreter (or "shell"), and common utility programs to support applications portability at the source code level. It is intended to be used by both application developers and system implementors.

The Single UNIX Specification was derived from an earlier standard written in 1994 known as the X/Open System Interface, which itself was developed around a Unix portability guide called the *Spec 1170 Initiative*, which contained a description of exactly 1,170 distinct system calls, headers, commands, and utilities covered in the spec.

The Single UNIX Specification was revised many times starting in 1997 by The Open Group, which was formed in 1996 as a merger of X/Open and the Open Software Foundation (OSF), both industry consortia. The Open Group owns the UNIX trademark. It uses the Single UNIX Specification to define the interfaces an implementation must support to call itself a UNIX system. The most recent edition, revised in 2018, contains 1,833 distinct interfaces.

The specification standardizes the collection of all system calls, libraries, and those utility programs such as grep, awk, and sed that make Unix feel like Unix. The collection of system calls is what defines the Unix kernel. The system calls and libraries together constitute the Unix application programming interface, whereas the utility programs constitute the Unix user interface.

There are four major parts to the standard:

Base definitions   General terms, concepts, and interfaces common to all volumes of the standard, including utility conventions and C language header definitions

System interfaces   Definitions for system service functions and subroutines; language-specific system services for the C programming language; function issues, including portability, error handling, and error recovery

Shell and utilities   Definitions for a standard source code−level interface to command interpreters and common utility programs for application programs

Rationale An informative section, which contains historical information concerning the contents of POSIX.1-2024 and why features were included or discarded by the standard developers

POSIX.1-2024 also defines areas as being outside of its scope:

- Graphics interfaces

- Database management system interfaces

- Record I/O considerations

- Object or binary code portability

- System configuration and resource availability

All interfaces defined by POSIX are written in C because much of Unix was originally developed in C. Therefore, POSIX depends upon a standard definition of C; in particular, POSIX.1-2024 is based on C17, whose official standard is ISO/IEC 9899:2018. I'll discuss more about C standards in the next section.

The Single UNIX Specification, Version 4, from 2018 is essentially the same as POSIX.1-2024, except that it includes a standard for the *ncurses* library, which is a terminal control library that can be used to create interactive programs that run in terminal windows, such as text editors and games.

The fact that there are standards doesn't imply that all Unix implementations adhere to them. Although there are systems such as AIX, Solaris, and macOS that are fully POSIX conformant, most are partly compliant. Systems such as FreeBSD and various versions of Linux fall into this category.

Any single Unix system may have features and interfaces that do not comply with a standard. The challenge in system programming is being able to write programs that will run on a broad range of systems in spite of this.

A Unix man page generally shows to which standards the topic of the man page conforms. The `standards` man page, in Section 7, lists all of the names used for the standards referenced in the man pages. If you enter the command `man standards`, you will see the full list. In Chapter 2, we'll go over how feature test macros are used to provide a means to compile a single program on a variety of different Unix systems.

C Standards

The C programming language has undergone several revisions since it was first invented by Dennis Ritchie, each adding new features and sometimes fixing defects. The most recent version as of this writing is C23. You can download the latest free draft of the C23 standard as well as drafts of older versions from various websites, such as *https://iso-9899.info/wiki/The_Standard*. It's a good idea to keep a local copy of the current standard for those times when you encounter an unfamiliar construct in a program.

Because POSIX specifies not just what Unix must do but what the various parts of the C Standard Library must do, in effect, it specifies an extension to the C language. Therefore, a Unix system that is POSIX conformant contains all of the library functions of the C language, such as the C Standard I/O Library and the C Math Library, all part of what's commonly called the C Standard Library.

The C Standard Library provided for Linux as well as several other Unix distributions is the GNU C Library, called GNU `libc`, or `glibc`. GNU often extends the C library, and not everything in it conforms to the ISO standard, nor to POSIX. What all of this amounts to is that the version of the C library on one system is not necessarily the same as that found on another system.

This is one reason why it's important to know the standard and know what it does and doesn't define. In general, the C standard describes what's required, what's prohibited, and what's allowed within certain limits. Specifically, it describes the following:

- The representation of C programs

- The syntax and constraints of the C language

- The semantic rules for interpreting C programs

- The representation of input data to be processed by C programs

- The representation of output data produced by C programs

- The restrictions and limits imposed by a conforming implementation of C

Not all compilers and C runtime libraries comply with the standard, and this complicates programming in C.

The GNU compiler has command line options that let you compile according to various standards. For example, if we wanted our *hello.c* program to be compiled against the ANSI standard, we would enter:

```
$ gcc -ansi hello.c -o hello
```

Since C90 is the same standard as ANSI, we could also enter:

```
$ gcc -std=c90 hello.c -o hello
```

As another example, to compile *hello.c* against the ISO C11 standard, we could enter:

```
$ gcc -std=c11 hello.c -o hello
```

Even though there are later ISO C standards, if we use the previous command, it will apply the most recent C standard anyway.

Understanding how to write programs for Unix requires knowing which features are part of C and which are there because they are part of Unix. In other words, you'll need to understand what the C libraries do and what the underlying Unix system defines. Having a good grasp of the C standard will make this easier.

Summary

System programs are fundamentally different from the kinds of programs that most beginning students learn how to write because they access protected resources inside the computer system. What actually happens when a program makes a relatively simple call to print onto the terminal window involves much more than what meets the eye. The sequence of steps includes the use of system calls, which are function calls into the kernel code. The kernel is the core of the operating system, the part that is memory resident as long as the computer is powered on, and is responsible for protecting, managing, and making available the wide range of resources in the computer system.

Unix introduced many novel ideas in the design of operating systems. Some of the most innovative ideas that made it so successful are the following:

- A programmable, interchangeable command line interpreter, called a shell, that runs in userspace rather than as a part of the kernel

- The concept of processes and the method of process creation

- The use of two levels of privilege to provide protection of the kernel and its resources

- Device-independent I/O operations

- The representation of files as sequences of bytes without structure

- I/O redirection and pipes in particular

- The concepts of users and groups and file permissions

- The single directory hierarchy

- The environment concept

The growth and spread of Unix led to many different Unix varieties and distributions and a need for standardization. This in turn led to the creation of a consortium that created the POSIX standards for its interfaces and behavior.

Exercises

1. Who are the authors of the bash shell? (Hint: Use the man pages to find out.)

2. What is the return type of the read() system call?

3. Using the man pages, find the names of all of the header files that you would need to include to use the following functions in a program. There might be more than one needed for some of these.
   (a) _exit()
   (b) setuid()
   (c) fstat()

4. If your current working directory is */usr/share/gcc/python*, what is the shortest relative pathname of the file */usr/lib32/libc.so.6*?

5. What command can be used to print the creation date of a file? (Hint: This information is part of a file's status.)

2

FUNDAMENTALS OF SYSTEM PROGRAMMING

The first chapter explained how system programs differ from the typical programs that you write in an introductory software development course. In this chapter, we turn our attention to the core concepts that you need to understand, not just for writing programs in general but for writing system programs. I'll cover several basic principles of programming in a Unix environment as well as those specifically related to system programming. In addition, I'll explain how to solve certain problems that are common to all projects, such as handling errors, parsing and checking the command line, and obtaining environment strings.

We'll start with the topics related to general programming and then move on to the fundamentals of system programming, including system calls, the relationship between system calls and libraries, handling system call and library function errors, and making your programs portable.

Whereas ordinary programs typically interact only with a user and the user's files, system programs usually interact with many different types of system resources. Writing them requires a deeper understanding of the system interfaces to these resources as well as their structure and purpose.

For example, if your program has to acquire data from a shared resource, such as a file that another process may have already opened, you'll be better equipped to write it if you know what happens when files are opened, how Linux manages open files, and how processes interact with them. If your program has to control a different type of shared resource, such as a terminal window, you'll need to understand how terminals work.

A completely different problem is how to design a program that might get a delivery of data not when it asked for it, but at some later, unpredictable time. This is an example of asynchronous I/O, which we explore in Chapter 17. Similarly, a process may need to pause its execution until some other process has performed some other task, such as when a program plays a game of chess against another program. Neither program is allowed to make a move until the other has finished its turn. Writing these types of programs requires familiarity with the system resources for process synchronization.

Object Libraries

Most likely, almost every program you've written has made calls to functions you didn't write but that are part of some library installed on your system. The functions that you call to read from or print to the screen are contained in a library, most likely a standard library, such as the C Standard Library (for example, `printf()`) or the C++ Input/Output Library based on `iostreams` (for example, the insertion operator of the `ostream cout` object). You may not have thought much about libraries before, but they play a key role in programming.

When you've been writing programs for a while, you might realize that you keep writing certain functions over and over again for different projects. To avoid rewriting them each time, perhaps you copy them from one directory to another, possibly tweaking them a bit depending on how you plan to reuse them.

Suppose you discover while working on your latest project that one of the functions you're reusing in this way has a bug. You can fix it in the current copy, but then you'll have to find all of the other projects that use that function and fix the bug in them as well. It's not a very efficient organizing principle.

Wouldn't it be better if you could create a repository of those frequently used functions in such a way that each new project could just link to it? Although such a repository could be a collection of source code files, it would be even better if it were a bundle of *object modules*, code that's already compiled and ready to link into a program.

One advantage of an object code bundle instead of a source code bundle is that you don't have to compile it every time. Also, if you plan on sharing your work with others, you could distribute the object code and not worry that it might be modified, unintentionally or otherwise, or possibly broken. Those issues are possible if you distribute just the source code. If you did distribute the object code, you'd most likely need to distribute a header file that contained all declarations of the functions and other symbols contained in the object code.

In Unix systems, doing so isn't just possible, it's also relatively easy. Unix has tools that let you create your own libraries and tools that can view and modify libraries. Appendix A contains detailed instructions on how to create libraries in Unix.

An *object library*, also called a *software library*, is a file that bundles together, in a structured way, the compiled object code from multiple functions so that programs can call them easily. Libraries aren't stand-alone executables; they don't have a main() function, and you can't run them. They contain function implementations and sometimes type definitions and constants needed by those functions or by code that calls them. Figure 2-1 depicts a hypothetical library named *libsnw.a*.

libsnw.a

Figure 2-1: A small object library with three modules and an index that serves as a table of contents

The index in Figure 2-1 is essentially a look-up table that contains the addresses relative to the start of the file of all symbols defined in the library, which makes those symbols easy to find.

System Libraries

System calls are usually very low-level primitives. They do very simple tasks because the Unix operating system was designed to keep the kernel as small as possible. For the same reason, the kernel typically doesn't provide many routines that do similar things. For example, the kernel has a single function to perform almost all read operations, and when it reads from storage devices such as disks, it reads large blocks of data from a specified device to specified system buffers. It doesn't have a different system call to read a character at a time, nor one that reads formatted input, both of which are useful functions to have. In short, just a single kernel function performs almost all input operations!

To compensate for the kernel's simplicity, Unix's designers augmented the programming interface with an extensive set of higher-level routines that are kept in libraries. These routines provide a much richer set of primitives for programming in Unix. Many library functions ultimately make system calls to the kernel, but some don't because they don't need any kernel services. We say that these functions operate entirely *in user space*, meaning that they never need kernel services.

Unix systems also contain libraries for various specialized tasks, such as asynchronous input and output, sharing memory, terminal control, login and logout management, and so on. Using any of these libraries requires that the library's header file be included in the code with the appropriate `#include` directive (for example, `#include <termios.h>`) and, sometimes, that the library be linked explicitly because it isn't in a standard place. Volume 3 of the Unix Manual Pages contains man pages for all functions that are part of libraries.

Static and Shared Libraries

Unix systems support two kinds of libraries: static and shared. A *static library*, short for "statically linked library," is a library whose code can be linked to the program statically, after the program is compiled, to create the program executable file. In other words, the linker copies the library functions referenced by the program out of the library and inserts them into the program executable, after which it resolves all unresolved symbols to enable jumps into and out of those functions. Static libraries in Unix have filenames that end in *.a*, such as *libm.a* and *libc.a*. The *.a* suffix is a reminder that these libraries used to be called *archives*.

In contrast, a *shared library* is a library whose object code is not copied into the executable, but is instead linked to the program at runtime. *Runtime* is the interval of time during which the program is actually running. Because the code in these libraries is linked at runtime, they're also called *dynamic libraries* or *dynamically linked libraries*.

NOTE *The fact that a shared library is also called a dynamically linked library doesn't imply that they're the same as what Microsoft calls a* DLL. *While DLL is short for "dynamically linked library" also, DLLs are different from Unix shared libraries. I'll use the term* shared library *so as not to cause any confusion.*

With shared libraries, calls to functions or references to other symbols in the library are linked only when the program actually executes the calls or accesses the symbols for the first time. Shared libraries have names ending in *.so*, possibly followed by a numeric suffix of the form *.<number>*, such as *libc.so.6*, where the number refers to a specific version. The *.so* suffix is short for "shared object."

Static linking, which was the original form of linking used in most operating systems, including Unix, resolves references to externally defined symbols such as functions by copying the library code directly into the executable file when the executable file is built. The *linkage editor*, also called the *link editor* or simply the *linker*, performs static linking. The term *linker* is a bit ambiguous, so I avoid using it. The `ld` program is the static linker in Linux.

The primary reason to use static linking, perhaps now the only reason, is that statically linked executables are self-contained and can run reliably on multiple platforms. For example, a program might use a particular version of a graphical toolkit such as GTK that may not be present on all systems. If the toolkit's libraries are statically linked into the executable, the executable can run on other systems with the same machine architecture without requiring that the users on those systems install the specific library files.

When a library is dynamically linked to a program, the linkage editor inserts records into the program for symbols from the library to indicate that these symbols will be resolved when they are first reached during the program's execution. When the program is loaded into memory, the dynamic linker checks whether that library is already in memory and, if not, finds a place in memory for it and loads it. As the program executes, each time a new symbol is reached, the dynamic linker links it to the library. Programs can experience slightly longer running times with dynamic linking, because whenever an unresolved symbol is found and must be resolved, there's a bit of overhead in locating the library and linking to it.

Linux systems have two dynamic linkers: `ld.so` and `ld-linux.so`. The former links and loads the old-style executable format known as *a.out* binaries, and the latter links and loads executables in the modern Executable and Linking Format (ELF). ELF is a standard format for executable files, object files, and libraries. It replaces the older *a.out* format and the Common Object File Format (COFF), which was created to replace *a.out*. ELF was developed by UNIX System Laboratories and has been adopted by almost all Unix vendors.

The Advantages of Shared Libraries

Shared libraries have several advantages over static ones. One is that because the executable program file doesn't contain the code of the libraries that must be linked to it, the executable file is smaller. Its reduced size means that loading into memory is faster and it uses less space on disk as well. Shared libraries also result in more efficient use of memory. Instead of multiple copies of a library being physically incorporated into multiple programs, a single memory-resident copy of the library is linked to each program, reducing the amount of memory in use. Shared libraries are designed so that when processes execute their code, it isn't modified.

Another advantage of linking to shared libraries is that when a library is updated, the programs that link to it don't need to be modified or recompiled, provided that the library interfaces aren't changed by the update. For example, if bugs are discovered and fixed in these libraries, all that's necessary is to obtain the modified libraries and install them. In contrast, if libraries are statically linked, all programs that use them would need to be recompiled.

Still other advantages are related to security issues. Hackers often try to attack applications through knowledge of specific addresses in the executable code. Methods of deterring such types of attacks involve randomizing the locations of various relocatable segments in the code. With statically linked executables, only the stack and heap address can be randomized; all instructions always have a fixed address when the executable is run. With dynamically linked executables, the kernel has the ability to load the libraries at arbitrary addresses, independent of each other, so that library code can have different addresses in each run, which makes such attacks much harder.

Commands to Query a Library's Contents

We have a choice of commands for seeing what a library file contains. For static libraries, we can use the ar command, which can print a wide range of information. In the simplest case, we can print out a table of contents with its t option. We don't need a hyphen before the t because technically it's not an option but an *operation code*. For example, to see the objects in the C++ standard library, you can enter:

```
$ ar t /lib/gcc/x86_64-linux-gnu/11/libstdc++.a
compatibility.o
--snip--
array_type_info.o
atexit_arm.o
atexit_thread.o
atomicity.o
bad_alloc.o
--snip--
```

The path to *libstdc++.a* may be different on your system. You can also use the objdump command to view executable program files and shared libraries. The -a option prints the index with information about the original object files:

```
$ objdump -a libsnw.a
In archive libsnw.a:

sort.o:     file format elf32-i386
rw-r--r-- 1220/400   2032 Apr 23 21:56 2007 sort.o

cardinal.o:     file format elf32-i386
rw-r--r-- 1220/400   1580 Apr 23 21:56 2007 cardinal.o

bsearch.o:     file format elf32-i386
rw-r--r-- 1220/400   1784 Apr 23 23:13 2007 bsearch.o
```

The -t option limits output to static symbols:

```
$ objdump -t libsnw.a
In archive libsnw.a:

sort.o:     file format elf32-i386

SYMBOL TABLE:
00000000 l    df *ABS* 00000000 sort.cpp
00000000 l    d  .text 00000000 .text
00000000 l    d  .data 00000000 .data
00000000 l    d  .bss 00000000 .bss
00000000 l    d  .gcc_except_table 00000000 .gcc_except_table
00000000 l    d  .gnu.linkonce.t._ZStgtIcSt11char_traitsIcESaIcEEbRKSbIT...
00000000 l    d  .eh_frame 00000000 .eh_frame
00000000 l    d  .note.GNU-stack 00000000 .note.GNU-stack
--snip--
```

The man page for objdump explains how to read its output.

For shared libraries, you can use the nm command with the -D or --dynamic option. The following shows how to use it to view the dynamically linkable symbols in the C standard library:

```
$ nm -j -D /lib/x86_64-linux-gnu/libc.so.6
--snip--
_IO_do_write@@GLIBC_2.2.5
_IO_doallocbuf@@GLIBC_2.2.5
_IO_enable_locks@@GLIBC_PRIVATE
_IO_fclose@@GLIBC_2.2.5
_IO_fdopen@@GLIBC_2.2.5
_IO_feof@@GLIBC_2.2.5
_IO_ferror@@GLIBC_2.2.5
_IO_fflush@@GLIBC_2.2.5
--snip--
```

The -j forces nm to print just the symbols and suppress other information.

Another tool you can use is readelf, which can display the contents of any ELF file, including object files. The readelf command is an example of a *binary utility*, a command designed to work with binary files such as ELF files. On some systems such as Solaris, you need to use elfdump because readelf isn't available.

To understand the output of readelf, you need to understand the structure of ELF files and the notation used by readelf. But if all you want to do is check what functions or other symbols are in an executable, you can enter **readelf -s *elf-file* | more**, and you'll see a large amount of output, a screenful at a time.

For example, I can run readelf on a program, say *myprogram*, that was linked to a *libutils.so* shared library and see all symbols, as shown here:

```
$ readelf -s myprogram
Symbol table '.dynsym' contains 17 entries:
```

```
Num:    Value Size  Type    Bind    Vis       Ndx Name
  0: 00000000    0 NOTYPE  LOCAL   DEFAULT   UND
  1: 00000000    0 FUNC    GLOBAL  DEFAULT   UND show_time
  2: 00000000    0 NOTYPE  WEAK    DEFAULT   UND __gmon_start__
  --snip--
```

The fact that show_time has a value of 0 means that it is not yet bound to an address. This is to be expected, because the actual binding will not take place until runtime.

To learn more, first read the man page for ELF and then read the page for readelf. You can also download the specification of ELF from various websites such as the Linux Foundation (*https://refspecs.linuxfoundation.org/ LSB_4.1.0/LSB-Core-generic/LSB-Core-generic/elf-generic.html*). Chapter 10 explains the structure of ELF files in detail.

Two other tools, hexdump and od, short for "octal dump," are sometimes useful. Each can display a file's raw, uninterpreted bytes starting from byte 0, with byte addresses, in various output formats such as character when possible, hexadecimal, octal, and decimal.

Commands to Show the Libraries Linked to a Program

Another useful tool for determining which shared libraries are linked into your program is ldd. You can give it the names of one or more executables or object modules, and it will print those dependencies. The following listing shows how to run it on our hello executable, built from the *hello.c* program from Listing 1-2:

```
$ ldd hello
    linux-vdso.so.1 (0x00007ffdbe564000)
    libc.so.6 => /lib/x86_64-linux-gnu/libc.so.6 (0x00007fc2e26a4000)
    /lib64/ld-linux-x86-64.so.2 (0x00007fc2e28f6000)
```

This shows that hello is linked only to the dynamic linker *ld-linux-x86-64.so.2* and the GNU C Library, *libc.so.6*, as well as a library named *linux-vdso.so.1*. We don't need to know much about this library; it's used by the C Standard Library at runtime to solve some performance issues. Section 7 of the man page for vdso explains its purpose in more detail.

Let's look at what dynamic libraries the ls program uses:

```
$ ldd /bin/ls
    linux-vdso.so.1 (0x00007ffd591a7000)
    libselinux.so.1 => /lib/x86_64-linux-gnu/libselinux.so.1 (0x00007efc6271...
    libc.so.6 => /lib/x86_64-linux-gnu/libc.so.6 (0x00007efc624f6000)
    libpcre2-8.so.0 => /lib/x86_64-linux-gnu/libpcre2-8.so.0 (0x00007efc6245...
    /lib64/ld-linux-x86-64.so.2 (0x00007efc62793000)
```

This output shows that ls is linked to two libraries besides the linking loader and the C standard library. The *libpcre2* library has functions for working with Perl regular expressions, and *libselinux* is the SELinux runtime library.

SELinux is a security system for Linux that defines access controls for the applications, processes, and files.

We can also use the `ltrace` and `strace` tools for seeing which functions are actually called when a program runs. You can learn how to use them from their man pages.

The C Standard Library

You'll find several different C library implementations across Unix systems, but the one you'll most likely encounter on a GNU/Linux system is the GNU C Library, GNU's implementation of the C Standard Library. People refer to it as *glibc*. The name of the C Standard Library is expected to be *libc.so* on Unix systems, whether it is the GNU implementation or another.

You can run the `ldd` command mentioned previously against any C program to see the absolute pathname to *libc.so.<n>*, where *<n>* is the latest version number. In the previous example, *libc.so.6* is the file */lib/x86_64-linux-gnu/libc.so.6*.

On most Linux systems, this file's execute bit is set, so that just by running the file, you'll see version information, as shown here:

```
$ /lib/x86_64-linux-gnu/libc.so.6
GNU C Library (Ubuntu GLIBC 2.39-0ubuntu3.1) stable release version 2.39.
Copyright (C) 2024 Free Software Foundation, Inc.
This is free software; see the source for copying conditions.
There is NO warranty; not even for MERCHANTABILITY or FITNESS FOR A
PARTICULAR PURPOSE.
Compiled by GNU CC version 11.4.0.
libc ABIs: UNIQUE IFUNC ABSOLUTE
For bug reporting instructions, please see:
<https://bugs.launchpad.net/ubuntu/+source/glibc/+bugs>.
```

Because some functions behave differently in different versions of the library, you might need to design a program so that its execution flow depends upon which library version is installed. GNU/Linux systems provide a way to do this with the `gnu_get_libc_version()` function, which returns a pointer to a string containing the version number. Your program can use this number in conditional instructions, so that at runtime, it can alter its behavior depending on the version. Its synopsis is as follows:

```
#include <gnu/libc-version.h>
const char *gnu_get_libc_version(void);
```

The following program demonstrates its use; it just prints out the version number:

get_glibc
_version.c
```
#include <gnu/libc-version.h>
#include <stdio.h>
int main()
{
```

```
        printf("The version of glibc is: %s\n",gnu_get_libc_version());
        return 0;
}
```

We can compile it and run it as follows:

```
$ gcc get_glibc_version.c -o get_glibc_version
$ ./get_glibc_version
The version of glibc is: 2.35
```

This tells us that we have 2.35 installed on this system.

System Calls

An ordinary function call is a jump into and return from a routine that is part of the code linked into the program making the call, regardless of whether the routine is statically or dynamically linked to the code. A system call is like a conventional function call in that it causes a jump to a routine followed by a return to the caller. But it's significantly different because it's a call to a function that is a part of the Unix kernel.

It's easy to tell whether a function is a system call or a library function. System call man pages are usually in Section 2, whereas library functions are usually in Section 3. If when you read the man page for a function, its SYNOPSIS shows you that you need to include *unistd.h*, then it's most likely a system call. If the function is in Section 3, *unistd.h* is not required.

The code that's executed during a system call is actually kernel code. Since the kernel code accesses hardware and contains privileged instructions, it must be run in privileged mode. Since only the kernel runs in privileged mode, this mode is also commonly called *kernel mode* or *privileged mode*. Therefore, during a system call, the process that made the call runs in kernel mode.

Unlike an ordinary function call, a system call causes a change in the execution mode of the processor; systems usually implement this with a *trap instruction*.

NOTE *A trap is a machine instruction that changes the processor mode and jumps to a specific location in memory. In older systems, the trap is implemented with the int 0x80 instruction. Linux kernels from 2.6 and later use the sysenter instruction, and the GNU C Library glibc 2.3.2 and later use sysenter.*

The kernel supports a fixed number of system calls on any given system. The syscalls man page lists the names of all calls supported on the system. Each call is associated with a number that's used as an index into a table of addresses to which control is transferred inside the kernel. These numbers are system dependent, but each has a symbolic name defined by a macro. For example, the symbolic name for the getpid() system call number is __NR_getpid (as well as SYS_getpid for backward compatibility). As of this writing, the latest Linux kernel has about 450 different system calls. The trap instruction is typically invoked with a parameter that references this number to specify which system call to run.

The number of parameters in system calls varies, and the method by which they're transferred to the kernel depends on how many there are. Linux systems use a combination of two different methods:

Register method   Parameters are placed into known registers in a specific order. When the number of parameters exceeds the number of available registers, the block method is used instead.

Block method   The parameters are stored in a block of consecutive bytes in memory, and the address of the block is passed in a register.

The latest version of Linux does not allow more than six parameters to a system call.

Wrapper Functions

Processes don't usually invoke system calls directly. Instead they call wrapper functions. A *wrapper function* for a function named foo() does very little other than repackage the parameters of the call to foo(), call foo(), collect its return value, and possibly supply it in a different form to the caller. The GNU C Library *glibc* has wrapper functions for almost all system calls.

Wrapper functions for system calls usually have the same name as the call itself. They also have to execute the trap instruction to trap to kernel mode.

A wrapper is said to be *thin* if it does almost nothing but pass the arguments in and receive the return values. The GNU C Library wrapper functions are often very thin, doing little more than copying arguments to the right registers before invoking the system call and then setting the value of a global error variable.

Sometimes a wrapper is not so thin, as when the library function has to decide which of several alternative functions to invoke, depending upon what is available in the kernel. The truncate() system call is a good example. It can truncate a file to a specified length, discarding the data beyond that length.

The original truncate() function could handle only lengths that could fit into a 32-bit integer. When filesystems were able to support very large files, a newer version named truncate64() was added. The newer function can process lengths representable in 64 bits. The wrapper for truncate() decides which one is provided by the kernel and calls it.

System Call Execution

The following list summarizes the steps that take place during a system call:

1. The user program makes a normal function call to the wrapper function in the library.

2. The wrapper function copies the arguments of the call off of the stack and puts them into the registers where the kernel expects them.

3. The wrapper executes the trap, passing the number of the system call as its argument. This causes the mode switch to supervisor mode and the jump to the kernel's system call handler.

4. The kernel's system call handler uses the number passed to it to access the system call vector at that offset. The vector contains the address in system space of the actual kernel code for that call.

5. The actual call code is executed, and it passes the return value back to the system call handler.

6. The handler passes the return value to the wrapper; the return instruction executed by the handler causes the switch back to user mode. If an error occurred, the wrapper function makes the error code available to the program.

Figure 2-2 illustrates these steps schematically from the moment the system call is executed in a user program until it returns from the call.

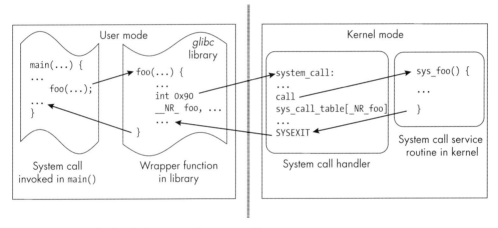

Figure 2-2: A sample detailed system call execution flow

Some system calls don't have wrappers in the library, and for those, the programmer has no other choice but to invoke the system call with the syscall() function, passing the system call's number and arguments. Generally speaking, for a system call named foo, its number is defined by a symbolic constant named either __NR_foo or SYS_foo. These macro definitions are exposed by the header file *sys/syscall.h*, which you'd need to include in the code. They may not be in that file itself, but in an included file, such as *asm/unistd_32.h* or *asm/unistd_64.h*. The man page for syscall() lists the headers to include.

An example of a system call that may not have a wrapper is gettid(), which returns the caller's thread ID. (A wrapper was added to *glibc* starting in version 2.30.) In Chapter 1, we saw a slightly different program that called this function. It's the same as getpid() for a process with a single thread. The *gettid_demo.c* program in Listing 2-1 uses syscall() to call gettid() and prints the returned ID on the screen.

```
gettid_demo.c   #include <unistd.h>
                #include <sys/syscall.h>
                #include <sys/types.h>
                #include <stdio.h>

                int main(int argc, char *argv[])
                {
                    printf("Thread id %ld\n", syscall(SYS_gettid));
                    /* Could also pass __NR_gettid */
                    return 0;
                }
```

Listing 2-1: A program that uses the `syscall()` function to make a system call

Because gettid() has no arguments, it isn't necessary to pass anything other than the system call number to syscall(). If it did have arguments, they would be passed as parameters after the call's number.

Multiple Paths to Kernel Services

In summary, some of the services that a program needs are satisfied by the following:

- Calling a library function that doesn't need to make a system call

- Calling a library function that does make a system call

- Making a system call through a wrapper function

- In rare cases, using syscall() to make a system call

Figure 2-3 illustrates these various paths to the kernel.

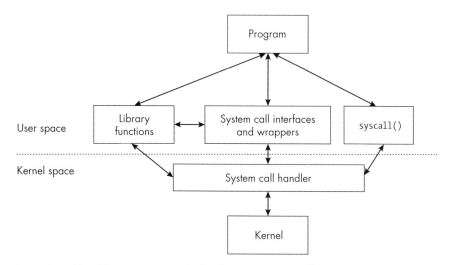

Figure 2-3: The different control paths for obtaining services, showing the relationship between library function calls and system calls

The figure shows, for example, that if a program calls a library function that needs to make a system call, the path to the kernel is through library functions, system call interfaces or wrappers, and then the system call handler.

Handling Errors from System Calls and Library Functions

A good program should be robust enough to terminate normally even when system calls and library functions return errors, which means you need to understand how these errors are returned and know the tools at your disposal for handling them. System calls and library functions use two different methods for indicating that an error occurred.

System Call Errors

Almost all system calls return a negative number when an error occurs in their execution. The absolute value of that number is meaningful; it indicates the type of error. The fact that it is negative is what indicates that it failed. A handful of system calls don't behave this way, but their man pages indicate when that's the case. When the system call returns to the C library wrapper function, if the return value is negative, the wrapper stores the absolute value of the return value into a static variable named errno, defined in the *errno.h* header file. It also returns -1 to the calling program. By including *errno.h* in your program, you can read the value stored in errno.

A robust program should check the return value of system calls and handle every possible error. Read the man page to find the list of error values that the particular system call can return. In the ERRORS section on that page, you'll see the list of error codes that can be returned, expressed as symbolic constants. You don't need to know the actual numbers, just their symbolic names.

> **USING THE ERRNO VARIABLE**
>
> Your program must not declare the errno variable. Because errno is declared in *errno.h*, including the header also includes its declaration. If you put another declaration of it in your program, it would hide the real errno variable and the one your program uses wouldn't contain the error values. Also, the program must inspect errno immediately after the system call because, if your program calls any other function or makes another system call before it inspects that variable, the error value may be overwritten by the error value resulting from the later call.

You can also enter the `errno -1` command to see the list of all possible error codes from all system calls. This command is part of the moreutils package, which may not be installed on your system. If you see an error message after entering that command, you need to install the package. A normal run looks like:

```
$ errno -l
EPERM 1 Operation not permitted
ENOENT 2 No such file or directory
```

```
ESRCH 3 No such process
EINTR 4 Interrupted system call
EIO 5 Input/output error
ENXIO 6 No such device or address
E2BIG 7 Argument list too long
ENOEXEC 8 Exec format error
--snip--
```

Let's work through an example to demonstrate how to put this together. We'll use a small program that makes a relatively simple system call to gethostname(), which stores the hostname of the computer in its first parameter or returns -1 if it fails. Because gethostname() can return just a few possible error values, it's a good choice for showing how to handle errors. The first step is to read the gethostname() man page to understand how to call it and respond to the errors. The man page, which also documents sethostname(), shows us its prototype:

```
#include <unistd.h>
int gethostname(char *name, size_t len);
```

The type of the second parameter, size_t, is an unsigned integer type that is defined by the POSIX.1 standard. Unix systems that conform to the standard employ this type for all symbols that are supposed to store the size of any kind of object. It's our first example of a Unix system type.

The man page explains the behavior of gethostname():

> gethostname() returns the NULL-terminated hostname in the character array name, which has a length of len bytes. If the NULL-terminated hostname is too large to fit, then the name is truncated, and no error is returned. POSIX.1-2024 states that if such truncation occurs, then it is unspecified whether the returned buffer includes a terminating NULL byte.

Based on this explanation, our program must check the value returned and handle the error, because if the name array was truncated and is missing the terminating NULL byte, the program will generate some type of fault, most likely a segmentation fault, when we try to print the name.

The ERRORS section on the man page for gethostname() lists three possible errors:

EFAULT   When name is an invalid address

EINVAL   When len is negative

ENAMETOOLONG   When len is smaller than the actual size

This list implies that we should have code to handle each case. Because there are only three, a sequence of if statements can handle them.

Listing 2-2 contains a complete program, *gethostname_demo.c*, that demonstrates one way to handle the errors from the call to gethostname().

gethostname _demo.c
```
#include <unistd.h>
#include <stdio.h>
```

```
❶ #include <errno.h>

void main()
{
    char   name[4]; /* Declare string to hold returned value.   */
    size_t len = 3; /* Purposely too small so error is revealed */
    int    returnvalue;

    returnvalue = gethostname(name, len);    /* Make the call. */
❷ if ( -1 == returnvalue ) {
        switch ( errno ) {
        case EFAULT:
            printf("A bad address was passed for the string name\n"); break;
        case EINVAL:
            printf("The length argument was negative.\n"); break;
        case ENAMETOOLONG:
            printf("The hostname is too long for the allocated array.\n");
        }
    }
    else
        printf("%s\n", name);
}
```

Listing 2-2: A program that demonstrates how to handle system call errors by inspecting the errno variable

The program needs to include *unistd.h* on the first line because gethost name() is a system call. It includes *errno.h* ❶ in order to use the errno variable. If the if condition ❷ is true, an error occurred and the switch statement selects a custom error message to print, after which the program terminates. If not, the program prints the name returned in the else clause. I purposely made the array too small for most machine names so that when this program is run we get to see the error message. By changing the array size to a large enough number, we prevent the error from occurring.

The following run of the program shows what it outputs, assuming the hostname is *harpo* and the executable is named *gethostname_demo*:

```
$ ./gethostname_demo
The hostname is too long for the allocated array.
```

An alternative to writing your own messages based on the value in errno is to use either the perror() library function declared in *stdio.h* or the strerror() library function declared in *string.h*. Both of these functions are *locale aware*, which means that if the program in which they're called is being run by a user who uses a language other than English, the message will be translated into that language, provided that the system supports it. Locales are described briefly in "Internationalization" on page 71 and covered in more depth in Chapter 3.

The perror() function writes a message onto the standard error stream describing the last error encountered during a call to a system or library function. Its synopsis is:

```
#include <stdio.h>
void perror(const char *s);
```

This function prints the string argument followed by a predefined message. Usually you pass it the name of the function as the string, as shown in *perror _demo.c*, displayed in Listing 2-3. This program doesn't need a switch statement because the selection logic is in perror(). It just calls perror() instead.

perror_demo.c
```
#include <unistd.h>
#include <stdio.h>

void main()
{
    char   name[4]; /* Declare string to hold returned value.        */
    size_t len = 3; /* Purposely declared too small so error is revealed */
    int    returnvalue;

    returnvalue = gethostname(name, len);            /* Make the call. */
    if ( -1 == returnvalue )
        perror("gethostname");
    else
        printf("%s\n", name);
}
```

Listing 2-3: A program that uses perror() to handle system call errors

Running this program, assumed to be compiled to *perror_demo*, shows what perror() prints:

```
$ ./perror_demo
gethostname: File name too long
```

The major drawback to relying on perror() is that by removing the switch, we've eliminated the chance to take different actions depending on the type of error. We can't, for example, terminate the program for some errors and not others. A lesser drawback is that we can't customize the error message. Like using errno, your program must call perror() immediately after the call, because otherwise it won't have the message for the error from the call.

The strerror() function's synopsis is:

```
#include <string.h>
char *strerror(int errnum);
```

It returns a pointer to a string containing the error message for the error number passed to it. Therefore, strerror(errno) is the error message associated with errno.

We can modify the preceding example by replacing the call to perror() with a call to strerror(errno). Here's the changed portion of the program, which I've named *strerror_demo.c*:

strerror_demo.c
```
#include <unistd.h>
#include <string.h>
#include <stdio.h>
#include <errno.h>
--snip--

    returnvalue = gethostname(name, len); /* Make the call. */
    if ( -1 == returnvalue )
        printf("gethostname failed: %s\n", strerror(errno));
    else
        printf("%s\n", name);
}
```

This function is not safe to use in a multithreaded program. Two different thread-safe versions of the program are available in GNU/Linux systems, both of which are described on the strerror man page.

Errors from Library Functions

Library functions don't necessarily respond to errors in the same way as system calls. In general, they fall into four different categories with respect to error handling:

- Functions that behave exactly the same way as system calls, returning -1 and setting the value of errno

- Functions that don't return -1 on error but do write the value of the error into errno, such as the C malloc() function, which returns a NULL pointer on error and sets the value of errno to the only possible error it can have, ENOMEM (out of memory)

- Functions that don't use errno for reporting the type of error, such as the character I/O functions fgetc() and getc(), which return EOF (the end-of-file return value, defined in *stdio.h*) on error and don't set errno

- Functions from the *Pthreads* library, which we discuss in Chapter 15, that return 0 on success and a positive number as an error value on failure

The only way to know how to handle the errors for the specific function your program is using is to read its man page.

Portability

Portability refers to the degree to which your program can run on other computers with little or no modification of the code itself. If, for example, your code uses features available only in GNU/Linux and you try to run it on another Unix system without that support, it won't behave the same way, and you may not even be able to build it unless you modify the source code.

Unix's haphazard growth is partly the cause of this problem, because over time, three major variants of Unix evolved: BSD, GNU/Linux, and System V (see Chapter 1). These variants had different features and capabilities, and people created standards to specify how those various systems were supposed to behave. One Unix system can have functions with the same names as another but whose semantics are different because they evolved in different variants. We need to know which version of a function our program uses when we compile it on the development machine and whether it will be the same when we compile the program on a different machine.

If you're distributing source code to be built on other computers, ideally you would design it so that it will compile into an executable whose behavior is what you expect even on other computers.

Portability is tied to the concept of standards because, for example, if your program is intended to adhere to the POSIX.1-2024 standard but must be built on a system conforming to a different, perhaps older, POSIX standard, you need to know how to design the code so that it uses features available on the other computer when the ones you hoped to use aren't available. The macro preprocessor's ability to compile code conditionally based on the values of macro objects is the key to solving this problem.

Feature Test Macros

A *feature test macro* is a macro designed to expose features such as constant and function prototypes in a header file when a program is compiled. For example, the following code is found in the *stdio.h* header:

```
#ifdef __USE_GNU
    /* Close all streams... */
    extern int fcloseall (void);
#endif
```

In this example, the declaration of the closeall() function will be exposed, meaning included in the program when you use the #include <stdio.h> directive, only if the symbol __USE_GNU is defined when the preprocessor reaches that directive in the program's code.

The header files and other source code files in the libraries and system call interfaces contain these conditional compilation directives in order to enable or disable the inclusion of various features. These feature test macros are designed to allow the libraries and interfaces to conform to multiple standards.

Feature test macros cannot be used to ensure that your program conforms to a limited standard, because they won't prevent you from including header files that haven't been written to conform to their use. They're primarily intended to control which standards to follow in the code.

Let's consider how to use them to control which features you want to enable or disable in your program. Suppose you're about to embark on a new project and want to use some functions you've never used before. Suppose one of them is the C getline() function, which has many versions. When you look at its man page, you'll probably see something like the following description:

```
NAME
       getline, getdelim - delimited string input

SYNOPSIS
       #include <stdio.h>
       ssize_t getline(char **lineptr, size_t *n, FILE *stream);
       ssize_t getdelim(char **lineptr, size_t *n, int delim, FILE *stream);

   Feature Test Macro Requirements for glibc (see feature_test_macros(7)):

       getline(), getdelim():
           Since glibc 2.10:
               _POSIX_C_SOURCE >= 200809L
           Before glibc 2.10:
               _GNU_SOURCE
--snip--
```

The page explicitly mentions Feature Test Macro Requirements. What are they, and how are you supposed to use this information?

If the SYNOPSIS section of a function's man page lists feature test macro requirements, it means that the given prototype or constant declaration will be read by the preprocessor only if the macro is defined *before* including *any* header files, not just the one in which it is declared, but all of them, as in:

```
#define _GNU_SOURCE
#include <unistd.h>
#include <stdlib.h>
#include <string.h>
--snip--
```

If you understand how the header files use these definitions, the code will make much more sense to you. I'll use a simplified version of the *stdio.h* header file to illustrate, because the actual header file is much more complex. The declaration of the prototype for getline() in this file looks roughly like this:

```
#ifdef __GNU_SOURCE
    ssize_t getline (char **__lineptr, size_t *__n, FILE *__stream);
#endif
```

Unless the symbol __GNU_SOURCE is defined when the preprocessor reads the #ifdef __GNU_SOURCE line, the getline() function will be skipped over. Therefore, in order for your program to use this version of the function, you need to define that symbol before any header file is included, like so:

```
#define __GNU_SOURCE
#include <stdio.h>
--snip--
```

Doing this causes the lines that #ifdef __GNU_SOURCE ... #endif protects to be read.

The man page in essence tells us that if we want to use either of the two functions getline() or getdelim(), if our version of *glibc* is 2.10 or later, we need to include the definition:

```
#define _POSIX_C_SOURCE 200809L /* Or any number >= 200809 */
#include <stdio.h>
```

If our version of *glibc* is older than 2.10, we need to use this macro:

```
#define _GNU_SOURCE
#include <stdio.h>
```

If you don't remember how to find which version of *glibc* you have, see the "The C Standard Library" on page 57.

As an alternative to defining the macro in the program source code, we can enable the definition when we compile the code on the command line using the -D option to gcc, as in

```
$ gcc -D__GNU_SOURCE myprog.c -o myprog
```

or

```
$ gcc -D_POSIX_C_SOURCE=200809L myprog.c -o myprog
```

Some feature test macros are intended to make your program more portable by preventing nonstandard definitions from being exposed. Other macros serve the opposite purpose, exposing nonstandard definitions that aren't exposed by default. The syntax of the feature test macros on the man page uses the logical-OR and logical-AND operators: || and &&. The example shown in the feature_test_macros man page is for the acct() function. It's not important what this function does:

```
SYNOPSIS
    #include <unistd.h>
    int acct(const char *filename);
```

```
Feature Test Macro Requirements for glibc (see feature_test_macros(7)):

   acct():
       Since glibc 2.21:
           _DEFAULT_SOURCE
       In glibc 2.19 and 2.20:
           _DEFAULT_SOURCE || (_XOPEN_SOURCE && _XOPEN_SOURCE < 500)
       Up to and including glibc 2.19:
           _BSD_SOURCE || (_XOPEN_SOURCE && _XOPEN_SOURCE < 500)
--snip--
```

The interpretation of the logical-OR operator || is that in order to obtain the declaration of acct() from <unistd.h>, either of two options can be applied. One is to include the macro definition #define _BSD_SOURCE before including any header files. The other option contains a logical-AND. You can include the macro #define _XOPEN_SOURCE but only if it has a numeric argument after it whose value is less than 500.

The following list describes a few common macros we'll encounter when reading code and man pages:

_POSIX_SOURCE   Exposes the functionality from the POSIX.1 standard as well as all of the ISO C features

_POSIX_C_SOURCE   Controls which POSIX functionality is made available, determined by its assigned value

_XOPEN_SOURCE   Exposes features from POSIX.1, POSIX.2, and X/Open standards

_GNU_SOURCE   Applies only to the *glibc* library and exposes everything in ISO C89, ISO C99, POSIX.1, POSIX.2, BSD, SVID, X/Open, LFS, and all GNU extensions (if POSIX.1 conflicts with BSD, POSIX takes precedence)

_BSD_SOURCE   Exposes functionality derived from 4.3 BSD Unix, ISO C, POSIX.1, and POSIX.2

_SVID_SOURCE   Exposes functionality derived from SVID (System V Interface Definitions), ISO C, POSIX.1, POSIX.2, and X/Open

Read the feature_test_macros man page to get a good understanding of why these macros are needed and how you can use them in general. We'll revisit them in later chapters as the need arises.

Other Portability Issues

As we start to develop system programs, we'll see that other factors affect how portable they are, including the following:

- The sizes of various data types
- The values of configuration parameters

- The sizes and ordering of data members in structures

- The set of macros actually available in header files

We'll address these issues as they arise.

System Limits

All Unix systems set limits on system resources and properties, such as the maximum length of a filename or a pathname and the maximum length of a username. Various standards specify minimum values for these maximums. For example, POSIX.1-2024 specifies that `_POSIX_NAME_MAX` is the least value that any conforming system can use as the maximum length of a filename. These specified values are called *system limits*.

A portable application needs to know what these limits are on each system on which it runs, and it should be able to adjust its use of resources accordingly. There are a few different means for getting these limits, depending on their category. POSIX.1-2024 divides system limits into three such categories:

Runtime invariant Those whose values are constant for any particular Unix system

Pathname variable Filesystem-related limits whose values can vary on a single system, depending on which filesystem they limit

Runtime increasable Those whose values can be increased at runtime

For example, most runtime invariant limits are defined in the header file *limits.h*. A program can call the functions `pathconf()` and `sysconf()` to get the values of various limits at runtime. Several programs in later chapters of the book provide examples of how to do this.

Internationalization

In the early days of computing, almost all software was developed for English speakers. Now, computer systems are used throughout the world, and we need to design software so that it accommodates local languages and cultural conventions. Sometimes differences in cultural conventions can lead to ambiguities with serious consequences. Two simple examples illustrate this issue:

- In the United States, people express dates in the format *MM/DD/YYYY*, where *MM* is a two-digit month, *DD* is a two-digit day of the month, and *YYYY* is a four-digit year, such as 07/11/2033. In Europe, the convention is *DD/MM/YYYY*. If a program is transported from one side of the Atlantic to another and dates are input or output, it would be hard to know which date is meant by 07/11/2033. Is it November 7 or July 11, 2033?

- In the United States, people use commas to separate the three-digit decimal groups of large numbers, and they use the period as the *radix character*, commonly called the decimal point, when numbers are written in base 10, such as 1,048,576.00. In Europe, people use periods to separate the three-digit decimal groups of large numbers, and they use a comma as the *radix character*, as in 1.048.576,00. Programs designed to parse only one representation will fail unless they know in which environment they're running.

Several other cultural conventions differ from one region to another, such as written languages, paper sizes, monetary units, time units, and measurement units.

The concept of a locale is intended to consolidate the cultural differences that affect the computational environment. POSIX.1.2024 and SuSv4 [14] simultaneously define a *locale* as "the definition of the subset of a user's environment that depends on language and cultural conventions." When a program is designed so that it works correctly no matter where it's used and performs input and output consistent with the location in which it's run, we say the program has been *internationalized*. *Internationalization* is the process of writing programs that accommodate variations in locales across the globe. Unix systems are required to provide certain basic support for internationalizing programs. Chapter 3 contains an introduction to this complex topic.

Processing the Command Line and Environment

In a Unix environment, commands such as

```
$ gcc -o main main.c utils.c fileio.c  # Build executable main from sources.
```

and

```
$ rm -r f1 f2 f3 dir  # Recursively remove f1, f2, and f3 from dir.
```

are examples of *simple commands*. In a simple command, a whitespace-separated list of words may follow the name of a program. In most shells, the *whitespace* characters that separate words are either a space or a tab. Newline characters terminate commands and do not separate their words.

A *word* is usually defined to be any sequence of non-whitespace characters not containing shell reserved characters unless they are escaped with a backslash or enclosed in single quotes. The first word of a simple command is typically the name of a program to be executed, which might be an executable file or a shell builtin. In the preceding two examples, the programs are gcc and rm, respectively.

In shells that conform to POSIX.1-2024, the command can begin with one or more variable assignments as well; we'll see examples of this in Chapter 3. In the rest of this section, when I use the term *command*, I mean a simple command.

When you type a command and press ENTER, the shell makes the words following the command name available to the program executing that command. The program needs to distinguish between the words that are non-option arguments to the command, such as `main.c`, `utils.c`, and `fileio.c` from the previous example, and those that are command options, such as `-o main` and `-r`. In this section, I'll explain how you can design your programs to extract words from the command line, separate them into options and arguments, and obtain the values of any environment variables that may influence the behavior of the program.

Extracting Command Line Arguments

To start, we'll assume that all of the words following the command name are non-option arguments. In "Extracting Command Line Options" on page 81, we'll remove this assumption and revisit how to process a command line that contains options.

In Unix and other POSIX-conforming operating systems, the operating system, in conjunction with the shell, arranges for the list of words from the command line, which includes both the program name and the command line arguments, to be made available to the program itself as a NULL-terminated array of strings passed into the second parameter of the `main()` function. The shell takes care of parsing the line, finding the arguments, finding the redirection operators, and possibly evaluating variables and other expressions. For example, in the command

```
$ ls dir1 dir2 > listing dir3
```

the arguments the shell finds are `dir1`, `dir2`, and `dir3`. The phrase `> listing` is a redirection; you're allowed to put redirections between those arguments, even though it's a confusing thing that you should never do.

A program's `main()` function is allowed to have no parameters, as in

```
int main() { /* Program here ... */ }
```

but in this case, it's unable to access its command line arguments.

The C standard requires compliant implementations of C (C compilers) to accept a `main()` function with two parameters, as follows:

```
int main (int argc, char *argv[]) { /* Program here ... */ }
```

The first parameter is an integer that specifies the number of words on the command line, which includes the name of the program, implying that $argc \geq 1$. The second parameter is a NULL-terminated array of C strings that stores all of the words from the command line, including the name of the program, which is always in `argv[0]`. The command line arguments, if they exist, are stored in `argv[1]`, . . . , up to `argv[argc-1]`.

Although many programs use argc and argv as the names of these parameters, there's nothing special about them; they can be any valid identifiers you choose. It's a convention to use the names argc and argv, but you'll often find programs that use ac and av instead. You could name them foo and bar, for instance, but that would be pretty bad programming style. Figure 2-4 illustrates how the arguments are made available to the program.

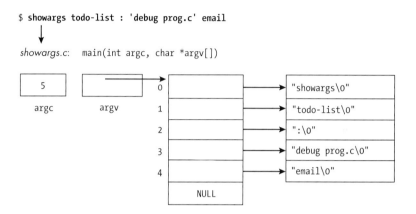

Figure 2-4: How command line arguments are passed to a program

Notice that a sequence of words enclosed in single quotes with embedded whitespace is a single word in the argument list. Also observe that the last element in the argument array is a NULL pointer.

Listing 2-4 is a simple program, *printargs1.c*, that shows one way for a program to access its command line arguments in a program.

printargs1.c
```
#include <stdio.h>

int main(int argc, char *argv[])
{
    printf("%s arguments:\n", argv[0]);
    for ( int i = 1; i < argc; i++ )
        printf("%d: %s\n", i, argv[i]);
    return 0;
}
```

Listing 2-4: A program that prints its command line arguments

It displays the command name that the user enters to execute the program, followed by the command line arguments that it receives from the shell, numbered to show their positions, one per line.

Notice that the last argument is in argv[argc-1], not argv[argc]. Because the array's last element is a NULL byte, we can also iterate through the arguments until the condition argv[i] == NULL is true, as shown in Listing 2-5.

printargs2.c
```
#include <stdio.h>

int main(int argc, char *argv[])
```

```
{
    int i = 1;
    printf("%s arguments:\n", argv[0]);
    while ( argv[i] != NULL )
        printf("%d: %s\n", i, argv[i++]);
    return 0;
}
```

Listing 2-5: A program that prints its command line arguments until it finds the NULL byte in the argv[ ] array

Using pointer arithmetic, we could dispense completely with the index variable i. (This is left as an exercise for the reader.)

Accessing the Environment

Within a program, you can also access any of the environment variables that the program inherited. I'll show three different ways to do this. Some are more efficient than the others, depending on the program's specific needs.

Using the getenv() Function

You can use getenv() to retrieve the value of any environment variable in the environment passed to the program. We saw its use in "Environments" on page 15. Its synopsis is as follows:

```
#include <stdlib.h>
char *getenv(const char *name);
```

Given name, it searches the environment list for a variable matching name, and if it finds one, it returns a pointer to its value; otherwise, it returns NULL. For example, the program in Listing 2-6 prints the value of the HOME environment variable, unless it's not in the environment, in which case it prints an error message.

getenv_demo.c
```
#include <stdlib.h>
#include <stdio.h>
int main()
{
❶  char *path_to_home;
   path_to_home = getenv("HOME");
   if ( NULL == path_to_home )
       printf("The HOME variable is not in the environment.\n");
   else
       printf("HOME=%s\n", path_to_home);
   return 0;
}
```

Listing 2-6: A program that uses getenv() to access the environment

The getenv() function returns a pointer to the string inside the actual environment list, not to a copy of that string, which means that if you modify it in your program, you're modifying the environment. It also means that in your program, the variable that you declare to receive the return value should be a char*, not a local array. For example, path_to_home ❶ would be declared incorrectly by making it an array of characters, such as

```
char path_to_home[256];
```

since this allocates storage for it and makes path_to_home a constant char pointer. The function wouldn't be able to assign a value to it, and the compiler will flag it as an error.

POSIX.1-2024 allows an implementation of this function to store the string whose address is returned in a statically allocated storage location, which means it will be overwritten by a subsequent call. If you intend to call it again, copy the return value to a local variable. For example, the following code may not work on some systems, because by the time that the value of home is evaluated, the storage has been overwritten by the return value of getenv() in user = getenv("USER"):

```
--snip--
    char *home, *user;
    home = getenv("HOME");
    if ( NULL != home ) {
        user = getenv("USER");
        if ( NULL != user )
            printf("USER=%s and HOME=%s\n", user, home);
    }
--snip--
```

Instead, you could use a string copying function such as strncpy() to copy the return value into home, as in:

```
char home[256];
strncpy(home, getenv("HOME"), sizeof(home));
```

If you do this, make sure to include the *string.h* header file, since the declarations of the string copying functions are there.

Using the environ Variable

When a program starts, it's given access to an externally defined global variable named environ of type char**, which is initialized to point to the start of the environment list inherited by the program, as illustrated in Figure 2-5.

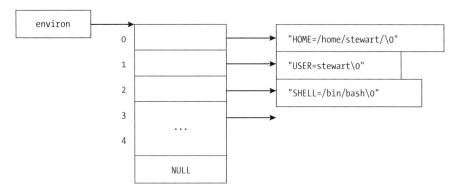

Figure 2-5: The environ pointer

In Figure 2-5, instead of enclosing the environment strings in quotes, they're shown as sequences of characters terminated by a NULL byte (\0). The environ array is terminated by a NULL byte as well.

You can use this variable to access any of the environment strings by a sequential search through the list. The program in Listing 2-7 demonstrates how to use environ to print the values of all environment variables inherited by the program.

environ_demo.c
```
#include <stdlib.h>
#include <stdio.h>

extern char **environ;      /* environ is declared extern because it */
                            /* is defined outside of the program.    */
int main()
{
    char **envp = environ; /* Set pointer to start of list.          */
    while ( NULL != *envp ) {
        printf("%s\n", *envp);
        envp++;
    }
    return 0;
}
```

Listing 2-7: Using char **environ to search the environment sequentially and print its environment strings

In effect, *environ_demo.c* does exactly what the printenv command does.

If all you need are the values of a few environment variables, using environ is not the best way to obtain them, because you'd need to search the environment linearly, and in the worst case, since the list is unordered, you'd need to compare every environment variable to the one(s) you're trying to find. Since each string comparison can look at every character of every variable name in the worst case, this search can take time proportional to the total number of characters in all environment variables. The getenv() function does this searching efficiently, so it's a better choice.

Using a Third Parameter to main()

The third method for accessing the environment list is to declare the main() function of any program with a prototype that has a third parameter:

```
int main(int argc, char *argv[], char *envp[])
```

This envp parameter points to the start of the environment list inherited by the program in the same way that the environ variable does.

You could then access the environment list with a loop such as:

```
int n = 0;
while ( NULL != envp[n] ) {
    /* Do something with envp[n]. */
    printf("%s\n", envp[n++]);
}
```

If you need only a few variables' values, it's better to use getenv(). Even though many systems support this feature, POSIX.1-2024 doesn't support it, which implies that on some systems, your code won't work if you use it, so I advise you not to use it.

Reporting Usage Errors

A program that expects one or more command line arguments must check whether it was provided what it expected. Otherwise, it will attempt to access locations in the array of arguments that don't exist, resulting in a fatal error.

For example, suppose you write a program that expects the names of two files on the command line, the first being the name of a file to open for reading and the second being the name of a file to open for writing. Let's say the program executable is named myprog. The correct usage of myprog would be of the form:

```
$ ./myprog inputfile outputfile
```

The command line must have at least three words for this program to run properly. If there are more than three, it can ignore the extras. The program should be allowed to run only if the first parameter to main(), which is int argc, is at least 3. The program in Listing 2-8 demonstrates how to check for correct usage properly.

usagecheck
_demo.c
```
#include <stdio.h>
#include <stdlib.h>

int main(int argc, char *argv[])
{
    if ( argc < 3 ) { /* Too few arguments  */
        /* Handle the incorrect usage here. */
❶      fprintf(stderr, "usage: %s file1 file2\n", argv[0]);
        exit(1);
```

```
    }
    printf("About to copy from %s to %s\n", argv[1], argv[2]);
    /* But no code for copying just yet */
    return 0;
}
```

Listing 2-8: A program that checks for correct usage, printing a message if it is used incorrectly

If the user doesn't supply two or more arguments, the program exits after displaying a message by calling the C fprintf() function ❶, whose first parameter is the C Library file stream to which to print, in this case, the standard error stream (stderr). Otherwise, it prints a message saying that it will copy from the first named file to the second. We'll see how to copy files in Chapter 4. For now, we just say we're doing so.

Extracting the Program Name

Suppose that we compile *usagecheck_demo.c*, putting the executable into a different directory from our working directory. This command puts it into the *bin* subdirectory of our home directory:

```
$ gcc -o ~/bin/usagecheck_demo usagecheck_demo.c
```

The ~ character is a shell special character that expands to the pathname of a user's home directory.

We'll now run usagecheck_demo from the current working directory without giving it the name of the output file:

```
$ ~/bin/usagecheck_demo infile
usage: /home/stewart/bin/usagecheck_demo file1 file2
```

When the program runs, the tilde ~ is expanded to the path */home/stewart* and argv[0] contains the entire pathname, */home/stewart/bin/usagecheck_demo*.

If you don't want to display the entire pathname of the program but prefer that it displays only the more concise message

```
usage: usagecheck_demo file1 file2
```

regardless of where the executable is, then before you print it, strip off the leading part of the argv[0] string so that the only thing left is what comes after the final / character. There are two relatively portable ways to do this, one more general than the other.

One way is to use the strrchr() function declared in *string.h*, whose prototype is:

```
char *strrchr(const char *source, int ch);
```

This function returns a pointer to the rightmost occurrence in source of the ch character. (In C, we can declare characters as int.) If ch isn't found in source, it returns a NULL pointer.

An algorithm for displaying the characters of the program name after the final / can search for the rightmost slash in the pathname and, if found, display the string that follows it. If it isn't found, no leading directories exist in the path, so it can print the entire path. If it is found and is the rightmost character, it's a usage error, since it means the pathname ends in a slash. Trying to run a command whose name ends in a slash causes most shells to report an error. Listing 2-9 demonstrates this method.

progname `#include <stdio.h>`
_demo.c `#include <string.h>`

```
int main(int argc, char *argv[])
{
    char *forwardslashptr;
    char *suffixptr = NULL;

    forwardslashptr = strrchr(argv[0], '/');
    if ( forwardslashptr != NULL )
     ❶ suffixptr = forwardslashptr + 1;
    else
        suffixptr = argv[0];
    if ( *suffixptr == '\0' )
        fprintf(stderr, "Program name ends in a / character\n");
    else
        printf("Program name is %s\n", suffixptr);
    return 0;
}
```

Listing 2-9: A program that strips the program name of any leading directories using strrchr()

For those unfamiliar with C, or if your C is a bit rusty, the instruction suffixptr = forwardslashptr + 1; ❶ performs *pointer arithmetic* to make suffixptr point to the first character after the forward slash.

When pointer arithmetic appears in code, the compiler translates addition of an integer n to a pointer of type basetype* into the addition of sizeof (basetype) * n bytes to the pointer's value. For example, if dblptr is a pointer of type double* that contains the address 1024, and a double uses 8 bytes, then dblptr + 6 is the address $1024 + (6 \times 8) = 1072$. It's worth remembering the strrchr() function because it's a useful function for other purposes as well. For example, we can use it to get the suffix of a filename or to get the portion of the filename before the suffix.

An easier, but less general, method of stripping the directories from the pathname in argv[0] is to use the basename() library function, of which there are both POSIX and GNU versions. Their prototypes are the same

```
char *basename(char *path);
```

but the POSIX function is declared in *libgen.h*, whereas the GNU version is declared in *string.h*. The POSIX function modifies argv, but the GNU version doesn't. Furthermore, the man page for basename() states that the

POSIX version implemented in *glibc* has bugs. For these reasons, we'll use the GNU version to demonstrate.

To use the GNU version, we need to define the `_GNU_SOURCE` macro before including any header files. Listing 2-10 shows the program.

basename `#define _GNU_SOURCE`
_demo.c

```
#define _GNU_SOURCE
#include <stdio.h>
#include <string.h>

int main(int argc, char *argv[])
{
    char *progname;
    progname = basename(argv[0]);
    printf("Program name is %s\n", progname);
    return 0;
}
```

Listing 2-10: A program using basename() to strip the program pathname of its leading directories

We'll compile this into an executable in the *~/bin* directory as we did with *usagecheck_demo.c* and run it in the same way:

```
$ gcc -o ~/bin/basename_demo basename_demo.c
$ ~/bin/basename_demo
Program name is basename_demo
```

Only the program name is printed, not the full pathname.

Extracting Command Line Options

Almost all commands have options, which might be short or long or both. Some commands allow the order of options and arguments to vary. For example, the following two command lines are equivalent:

```
$ gcc myprog.c -o myprog -Wall -I includedir
$ gcc -Wall -o myprog -I includedir myprog.c
```

POSIX.1-2024 requires that all options should precede all of the arguments, but some commands don't conform to this requirement. If a command has several short options, none of which have arguments, we can write them in various combinations, such as the following:

```
$ ssh -acCfGgKkMN
$ ssh -a -c -CfGg -Kk -M -N
$ ssh -CfGg -Kk -M -a -c -N
```

If options do have arguments, their arguments must follow them immediately, with whitespace allowed between the option letter and its argument.

The Utility Syntax Guidelines of the POSIX.1.2024 standard (Section 12.2) contain rules about options that programs should follow to conform to the standard. In particular, a program that conforms to these requirements should support the following option syntax:

- One or more short options that have no option arguments, followed by at most one option that has an option argument, can be grouped behind one hyphen (-) delimiter.

- The order of different options relative to one another should not affect program behavior, with one exception. Repeated options that have required arguments must be interpreted in the order that they appear. The make utility is an example of a command that allows this. It can have multiple -f options, and their order does matter.

GNU allows long options, but POSIX.1-2024 doesn't require them. Also, GNU allows options to have optional arguments, which POSIX.1-2024 forbids. Finally, GNU allows arguments to precede options, which POSIX.1-2024 forbids.

Writing a program that allows the user to enter options in various forms and in any order, consistent with these requirements, makes parsing the command line to find all of the options and their arguments a complex task.

Fortunately, Unix systems usually have two library functions named getopt() and getopt_long() that can do this work for you. The latter is a GNU function that can parse command lines with long options, for which you need to define _GNU_SOURCE before the header file inclusions. Their combined man page is as follows:

GETOPT(3)   Linux Programmer's Manual   GETOPT(3)

NAME
       getopt, getopt_long, getopt_long_only, optarg, optind, opterr, optopt -
       Parse command-line options

SYNOPSIS
       #include <unistd.h>

       int getopt(int argc, char * const argv[],
               const char *optstring);

       extern char *optarg;
       extern int optind, opterr, optopt;

       #include <getopt.h>

       int getopt_long(int argc, char * const argv[],
               const char *optstring,
               const struct option *longopts, int *longindex);
       int getopt_long_only(int argc, char * const argv[],
               const char *optstring,
               const struct option *longopts, int *longindex);

```
Feature Test Macro Requirements for glibc (see feature_test_macros(7)):
    getopt(): _POSIX_C_SOURCE >= 2 || _XOPEN_SOURCE
    getopt_long(), getopt_long_only(): _GNU_SOURCE
--snip--
```

Even though these are library functions, to use them you must include *unistd.h*. The variables optarg, optind, opterr, and optopt are externally defined, and you must not declare them in your program.

The man page explains everything we need to know to use these functions. If our program expects all arguments to follow all options before the header files are included, it should define _POSIX_C_SOURCE with a value greater than or equal to 2 or define _XOPEN_SOURCE. If we want to allow a user to intermingle options and arguments, it doesn't need to define either of these macros.

As mentioned previously, we must define _GNU_SOURCE to use getopt_long().

The getopt() function parses the command line arguments. Its first two arguments, argc and argv, are the argument count and array passed to the main() function. The third argument, optstring, is a string that identifies the options and their arguments. The string is interpreted according to the following rules:

- A letter by itself is an option without arguments. For example, b represents -b.

- A letter with a single colon (:) after it has a *required* argument, and getopt() will place a pointer to the argument in optarg if it exists, and if it's missing, it will return ?. (See the final rule regarding how a leading : in optstring is used.)

- A letter with a double colon (::) after it has an *optional* argument, and getopt() will place a pointer to it in optarg or will set optarg to 0 if it's missing.

- If getopt() finds an undefined option, it will put the character in optopt, print an error message on stderr, and return ?. You can set opterr to 0 to suppress the message. It will also perform these actions if a required option argument is missing.

- If the leading character is a :, then if getopt() finds a missing required option argument, instead of returning a ?, it returns a :, which makes it possible to distinguish the type of error. A : implies a missing option argument, and a ? implies an invalid option character.

Let's look at a small program that uses getopt(). The option string ":hb::c:1" specifies that -h and -1 are options without arguments, -b is an option with an optional argument, and -c is an option with a required argument.

The getopt() function initializes the external variable optind to 1. When getopt() is called repeatedly, it returns each of the option characters from each of the option elements on the command line. When it can't find any more options, it sets optind to be the index in the argv array of the next element to be processed, and it returns -1. Thus, when it returns -1, optind is the index in argv of the first argv element that isn't an option. (By default, the GNU version of getopt() rearranges the contents of argv as it scans, so that eventually all the nonoptions are at the end.)

A program that uses getopt() to parse the command line should consist of two parts:

- A loop that calls getopt() repeatedly to find and record all options, option arguments, and any errors in usage, after which it stores the command arguments in the argv array into suitable variables

- Conditional code that uses the presence or absence of options and arguments found earlier to control the program's execution

Listing 2-11 demonstrates this idea. It uses the same set of options as in the example we just described. This program doesn't do anything other than print list of the options that it finds as well as its arguments, but it shows how to collect the options found into a set of variables to be used later by the program.

getopt_demo.c
```c
#include <stdio.h>    /* For printf() */
#include <stdlib.h>   /* For exit()   */
#include <unistd.h>   /* For getopt() */
#include <string.h>

#define TRUE   1
#define FALSE  0

int main(int argc, char *argv[])
{
    int  ch;
    char options[] = ":hb::c:1";
    int  opt_h = 0;
    int  opt_1 = 0;
    int  opt_b = 0;
    int  opt_c = 0;
    char b_arg[32] = "";
    char c_arg[32] = "";

    opterr = 0;        /* Turn off error messages by getopt().      */
    while ( TRUE ) {
        /* Call getopt, passing argc and argv and the options string. */
        ch = getopt(argc, argv, options);
        /* It returns -1 when it finds no more options. */
        if ( -1 == ch )
            break;
        switch ( ch ) {
        case 'h':                          /* h is a switch (no arg).    */
            opt_h = TRUE; break;
        case 'b':                          /* b has an optional argument. */
            opt_b = TRUE;
```

```
        if ( 0 != optarg )
            strcpy(b_arg, optarg); break;
    case 'c':                       /* c has a required argument.  */
        opt_c = TRUE;
        strcpy(c_arg, optarg); break;
    case '1':                       /* 1 is a switch (no arg).      */
        opt_1 = TRUE; break;
    case '?':
        printf("Found invalid option %c\n", optopt); break;
    case ':':
        printf("Missing required argument\n"); break;
    default:
        printf("?? getopt returned character code 0%o ??\n", ch);
    }
}
/* Finished processing the command line                            */
/* Process the options - in this case, just print what was found. */
printf("Options found:\n");
if ( opt_h ) printf("-h \n");
if ( opt_1 ) printf("-1 \n");
if ( opt_b ) {
    printf("-b ");
    if ( strlen(b_arg) > 0 )
        printf("with argument %s\n", b_arg);
    else
        printf("with no argument \n");
}
if ( opt_c )
    printf("-c with argument %s\n", c_arg);

/* optind is the index of the 1st non-option word in the argv[] array. */
/* If optind < argc, there is at least one word that is not an option. */

if ( optind < argc ) {
    printf("non-option ARGV-elements:\n");
    while ( optind < argc )
        printf("%s ", argv[optind++]);
    printf("\n");
}
return 0;
}
```

Listing 2-11: A program that parses the command line for options and arguments

Listing 2-11 models the usual way to process the options, using a loop and an embedded switch statement in which the fact of finding an option is recorded in a variable associated with that option. This variable is checked later in the program.

For example, if the -h option is a flag to indicate whether to print a help message, the switch code fragment would look like this:

```
switch ( ch ) {
--snip--
case 'h':
    print_help = TRUE;
    break;
```

Then somewhere in the main program's body, we'd put code such as:

```
if ( print_help )
    print_help_message();          /* Print the help information. */
```

If the program allows the same option to be present multiple times on the command line with different arguments, the switch case for that option needs to store the successive arguments in a suitable data structure.

Extracting Numbers from Strings

Command line arguments and environment values are stored as strings, even if they represent numbers. When a program receives strings that are actually numeric, it needs to parse those strings to obtain the numbers they represent. Fortunately, various library functions can do this, although some are preferable to others.

Two different classes of functions convert strings to numbers: atoi() and its cousins atof() and so on, as well as strtol() and its cousins. Table 2-1 summarizes the functions available in a typical Linux system.

Table 2-1: String to Number Conversion Functions

Function	Result type	Remarks
atoi(const char *nptr)	int	No error checking
atol(const char *nptr)	long int	No error checking
atoll(const char *nptr)	long long int	No error checking
atof(const char *nptr)	double	No error checking
strtol(const char *nptr, char **endptr, int base)	long int	Sets errno on error
strtoll(const char *nptr, char **endptr, int base)	long long int	Sets errno on error
strtof(const char *nptr, char **endptr)	float	Sets errno on error
strtod(const char *nptr, char **endptr)	double	Sets errno on error
strtold(const char *nptr, char **endptr)	long double	Sets errno on error
strtoul(const char *nptr, char **endptr, int base)	unsigned long int	Sets errno on error
strtoull(const char *nptr, char **endptr, int base)	unsigned long long int	Sets errno on error

The functions whose names are of the form ato* have some disadvantages. One is that they don't set the errno variable if errors occur, returning 0 instead, which makes it hard to distinguish between a numeric 0 and an error. Second, they don't do much error checking. Finally, they can be used only for base 10 numerals, which is not a major limitation, since that's the base we use most often. If you look at their man pages, you'll see that their use is discouraged. In spite of this, I'll occasionally code with atoi() when I'm writing software for my own use that will be used only a few times and I don't need to error-check—what people commonly call *throw-away code*.

It's a better idea to learn how to use strtol() and the related functions because they're more general and provide robust error-checking. I'll describe how to use strtol(); learning how to use the related functions that return numbers of types unsigned long, long long, unsigned long long, and so on is similar.

The synopsis of the strtol() function is as follows:

```
#include <stdlib.h>
long strtol(const char *nptr, char **endptr, int base);
```

The first parameter (nptr) is a pointer to the string to be converted. If the second parameter (endptr) isn't NULL, then after the call, strtol() will store the address of the first invalid character it finds into *endptr. The last parameter (base) is the base of the numeral, which can be any base from 2 to 36. If you expect base-10 numerals, set the base to 0. Listing 2-12 shows a simple program, *strtol_demo.c*, that converts base-10 numerals.

strtol_demo.c
```
#include <stdlib.h>
#include <stdio.h>
#include <errno.h>

int main(int argc, char *argv[])
{
    char *endptr;
    long  val;

    if ( argc < 2 ) {
        fprintf(stderr, "Usage: %s str \n", argv[0]);
        exit(EXIT_FAILURE);
    }
❶  errno = 0;          /* To distinguish success/failure after call */
    val = strtol(argv[1], ❷ &endptr, 0);

    /* Check for various possible errors. */
❸  if ( errno != 0 ) {
        perror("strtol");
        exit(EXIT_FAILURE);
    }
    /* errno == 0 */
```

```
❹ if ( endptr == argv[1] ) {
      /* The first invalid char is the first char of the string. */
      fprintf(stderr, "No digits were found\n");
      exit(EXIT_FAILURE);
  }
❺ if ( *endptr != '\0' )
      /* There are non-number characters following the number,
          which we can call an error or not, depending. */
      printf("Characters following the number: \"%s\"\n", endptr);

  /* If we reached here, strtol() successfully parsed a number. */
  printf("strtol() returned %ld\n", val);
  exit(EXIT_SUCCESS);
}
```

Listing 2-12: A program that calls strtol() *to convert its first argument to a number*

Let's study some of the details in Listing 2-12. We set errno to 0 ❶ so that after the call, if it's nonzero we'll know that an error occurred. We need to do this because the actual number might be 0, implying that we can't interpret a return value of 0 as an error.

We pass the address of endptr, not endptr itself ❷, to strtol(). After the call, endptr contains the address of the first invalid character. We also check whether errno is 0 ❸ when strtol() returns. If it isn't 0, a conversion error occurred, and in this case we exit the program because the number might be out of range and we don't want to attempt to store it.

If errno is 0 ❹, there was no error, but it's possible that the string was not a number. If endptr points to the start of the string, it wasn't a number.

Finally, we check for a different possibility ❺. It's possible that the string is something like 1234abc, which has valid digits followed by nondigits. If endptr doesn't point to the end of the string, the string must have nondigits. It's best in this case to let the calling program know this.

If we run this program with several different types of input, we'll see how it behaves. Assume the executable is named strtol_demo:

```
$ ./strtol_demo 100000000000000
strtol() returned 100000000000000
$ ./strtol_demo -817238172
strtol() returned -817238172
$ ./strtol_demo +871237abns
Characters following the number: "abns"
strtol() returned 871237
$ ./strtol_demo kjasdksd
No digits were found
$ ./strtol_demo 712381723812736872368817236
strtol: Numerical result out of range
$ ./strtol_demo 032
strtol() returned 26
```

The very last run is revealing. The leading 0 is interpreted by strtol() as an indicator that the number is octal.

Because we'll need to convert strings to numbers frequently, in Chapter 3 we'll develop a few functions based on the strto* functions that we'll use in subsequent chapters of the book.

Before leaving this topic, however, let's consider another very simple way to extract the numeric value of a string using the sscanf() function. It's essentially the same as scanf() except it reads from a C string passed to it in its first parameter instead of from the standard input stream. Its synopsis is:

```
#include <stdio.h>
int sscanf(const char *str, const char *format, ...);
```

Like scanf(), its return value is the number of items successfully read and converted to the format specified. By giving it the %d format specifier and passing the address of an integer as the second argument, we can obtain the integer value of the string.

Listing 2-13 shows how to do this.

str2int.c
```
#include <stdio.h>
#include <stdlib.h>
#include <string.h>

int main(int argc, char *argv[])
{
    int x;

    if ( argc < 2 ) {
        fprintf(stderr,"usage: %s <number>\n", argv[0]);
        exit(1);
    }
    sscanf(argv[1], " %d", &x);
    printf("The number is %d\n", x);
    return 0;
}
```

Listing 2-13: A program that uses sscanf() to convert strings to numbers

This program calls sscanf() just once. I wouldn't recommend using scanf() when your program needs to convert thousands of strings to numbers, because it is slower than the other methods I described. Also, like atoi(), it doesn't handle errors as robustly as strtol().

Summary

System programs make requests to the kernel for services that require kernel-level privileges through the use of system calls. System calls are calls to functions implemented within the kernel.

A library is a file that bundles together the compiled object code from multiple functions so that they can be called from other programs. Some libraries are static and are linked to a program as the last stage of compilation, and others are dynamic (or shared) and are linked during program execution. Using dynamic libraries makes executable files smaller and makes them load faster. It also saves memory and makes recompiling programs unnecessary if the libraries are updated without changes to their interfaces. Several command line tools can inspect libraries and executable files.

The C Standard Library contains a wide range of functions. Some of its functions make system calls, and others work only in user space. Both library functions and system calls have very specific ways of returning error information. Any program that you write must handle errors from these functions.

Because different Unix systems follow standards to varying degrees, making programs portable can be challenging. Using feature test macros is a well-supported method to improve the portability of your programs.

Internationalization is an aspect of programming that is not covered in a typical programming curriculum, but it's important because programs might run in a variety of different cultural environments. Modern programs should be designed to respond to its user's locale settings. In the next chapter, we'll see how to do this.

This chapter showed how to process the command line, extracting the arguments and options to commands; how to access environment variables; and how to parse strings to extract their numeric value when they represent numbers. It's laid the foundation for the rest of the book. Starting in the next chapter, we'll apply much of what we've just covered.

Exercises

1. This exercise is open ended. Navigate to the */usr/bin* directory on the host you're using. There, run the 1dd command on every executable, and examine the sets of dynamic libraries to which each executable is linked. Which libraries are used the most? Which commands link to the most libraries?

2. The *printargs2.c* program in Listing 2-5 used an integer to iterate through the argv[] array. Write a version of it that does not print the argument numbers and does not use any local variables.

3. Write a program that prints out the words it receives on the command line in reverse order, one per line.

4. Write a program that prints out the words it receives on the command line sorted by their lengths, from shortest to longest, one per line. Words of the same length can be in any order.

5. The program *perror_demo.c* in Listing 2-3 purposely used an array of characters too small for the hostname. Read the man page that describes the *limits.h* header file, find the system constant that specifies the maximum hostname length, and rewrite the program so that this error cannot occur.

6. The seq command prints out sequences of numbers. In the simplest case, seq *num1 num2* prints every number from *num1* through *num2*. Write a program that implements this simple form of the command. If any arguments are missing, if they are not two integers such that the first is less than or equal to the second, it should print an error message.

3

TIME, DATES, AND LOCALES

In this chapter, I introduce the paradigm we'll employ to design and implement system programs in the rest of this book. I'll present the common code used by the projects that we'll develop and explain its organization. We'll also explore how Unix represents dates, times, and other information that depends on regional and cultural norms, such as character sets, monetary units, and numbers. Finally, I'll explain the concept and implementation of locales and describe the steps needed to internationalize programs so that their interfaces conform to the settings users choose for their locales.

Learning System Programming

Trying to learn all of the intricacies and details of the kernel API by reading through reference manuals and other documentation is not just a painstaking task but an ineffective means for learning how to write system programs.

There are too many system calls and library functions to remember. My experience teaching computer science for roughly 40 years is that people often learn well by following examples and then solving programming problems related to the examples, using them as starting points for their code, and this is the paradigm I use here.

Rather than concentrating exclusively on the manuals and knowledge bases, you'll learn the API little by little by writing programs that use it and exploring the documentation as needed to understand how to use the relevant parts of the API. We'll start with simple programs and over time increase the complexity of the projects.

This method wouldn't be possible if we were using a different operating system. Linux, like several other Unix distributions, is an open source operating system. Not only can we see its source code, but because of its licensing, we also can share it, redistribute it, and even modify it. For us, this means we're not infringing on any copyright when we share those sources here or elsewhere.

This strategy is not my own invention. In his book *Understanding Unix/Linux Programming* [27], Bruce Molay uses a similar strategy for teaching system programming. Here, we'll use the following procedure:

1. Choose an existing command or program that interacts with the kernel, such as a shell utility.

2. Read the man page for that command to make sure we understand what the command does and what system resources it uses.

3. Using the man pages and other online information, investigate the system calls and kernel data structures that we discovered it uses.

4. Write a similar version of that command, not one that is identical, but one that adds, modifies, or removes features and that uses those same system resources.

5. After finishing the given exercise, evaluate how well we did, identifying areas in which we could improve the program.

By repeating this procedure, we'll gradually familiarize ourselves with the relevant portions of the API as well as the resources needed to learn about it. Finding information in the man pages will become easier the more we do this, and with enough practice, we'll be more comfortable in tackling a more difficult and complex command. When we first try to read the actual sources, we won't understand much, but over time it will get easier and easier.

The content of the man pages may not be identical from one system to another, since it depends on factors such as which version of Unix you're using, which updates have been applied, and what third-party software is installed. The man pages I present in this book are the latest versions at the time of this writing. Pages in Sections 2 through 7 are from the Linux man-pages Project, *https://www.kernel.org/doc/man-pages/*. Pages in Sections 1 and 8 of the man pages are mostly from the GNU Project, *https://www.gnu.org*. When following along, compare the pages to which you have access to these, and make sure the programs you write are based on the man pages for your specific system.

Organization of Common Code

As we develop the programs in this book, we'll discover that certain functions are common to multiple projects. For example, in many projects, we'll need functions to extract the numeric values of command line arguments, as well as functions to handle errors of various kinds. Rather than implementing these functions in every project independently, we'll put their implementations into a single common directory and put their prototypes into header files in another common directory. We'll also create a static library containing all of the object modules for these shared functions and link that library to every program that needs them.

The same holds true for definitions of various types and macro constants that we might need. We'll place macros that define the maximum sizes of strings and other programming elements into a header file named *common_hdrs.h*.

For the programs that we'll create in this book, header files fall into one of two separate categories:

System-wide headers   Those provided by the operating system distribution

Local headers   Those containing declarations specific to the book's projects

The source code repository that accompanies the book, at *https://github .com/stewartweiss/intro-linux-sys-prog*, has two top-level directories, named *include* and *lib*. The *include* directory contains header files, and *lib* contains libraries and object modules created for the book. All system-wide header files that may be needed in more than one project are included in the file *include/sys_hdrs.h*. The file *include/common_hdrs.h* includes *sys_hdrs.h* as well as local headers, and therefore, by including *common_hdrs.h* in a project, we include the system header files as well as the ones we've created ourselves.

A fragment of *sys_hdrs.h* follows (the source distribution for the book contains the complete listing):

```
#include <sys/types.h>    /* Type definitions used by many programs   */
#include <stdlib.h>       /* Prototypes of many C functions and macros */
#include <stdio.h>        /* C standard I/O library                    */
#include <string.h>       /* String functions                         */
#include <limits.h>       /* System limit constants                   */
#include <unistd.h>       /* Prototypes of most system calls          */
#include <errno.h>        /* errno and error constants and functions  */
```

Listing 3-1 contains the complete *common_hdrs.h* header.

```
common     #ifndef COMMON_HDRS_H
_hdrs.h    #define COMMON_HDRS_H

           #include "sys_hdrs.h"
           /* Non-system headers */
           #include "get_nums.h"     /* String to number conversions    */
```

```
#include "error_exits.h"  /* Error-handling and exit functions */

/* Define various constants and types used throughout the examples. */
#define STRING_MAX 1024
#define MAXLEN STRING_MAX /* Maximum size of message string */
/* Create a BOOL type. */
#ifdef FALSE
    #undef FALSE
#endif
#ifdef TRUE
    #undef TRUE
#endif
#ifdef BOOL
    #undef BOOL
#endif
typedef enum{FALSE, TRUE} BOOL;

/* Definitions used by locale-related programs */
#define FORMAT "%c"                /* Default format string              */
#define BAD_FORMAT_ERROR    -1     /* Error in format string             */
#define TIME_ADJUST_ERROR   -2     /* Error to return if parsing problem */
#define LOCALE_ERROR        -3     /* Non-specific error from setlocale() */

/* General errors */
#define READ_ERROR          -4     /* Incomplete read of a file          */
#define MEM_ERROR           -5     /* Insufficient memory                */
#endif /* COMMON_HDRS_H */
```

Listing 3-1: The common_hdrs.h *include file*

The following lines are called a *header guard*:

```
#ifndef COMMON_HDRS_H
#define COMMON_HDRS_H
--snip--
#endif /* COMMON_HDRS_H */
```

See the "Header Guards" box if these are unfamiliar to you. Every header file should have a header guard to prevent multiple-definition errors.

HEADER GUARDS

Suppose that a file named *func.c* contains the directive #include "common.h". When the macro preprocessor cpp sees this directive, it copies the named file *common.h* into a copy of *func.c* at the point at which the #include directive was found. Every included file is copied into this temporary copy of the file that cpp is processing.

Suppose that a second header file, *mylist.h*, which contains the prototypes for functions in *mylist.c*, uses some functions declared in *common.h* (as well as other functions), and it therefore includes *common.h*. Finally, suppose that the main program, *main.c*, uses functions declared in both *common.h* and *mylist.h*. Then *main.c* will contain these directives:

```
#include "common.h"
#include "mylist.h"
```

When you run the compiler to build the executable for *main.c*, cpp sees the #include directive to copy *common.h* and will copy it into its temporary copy of *main.c*. It then sees the #include "mylist.h" directive and copies the file *mylist.h* after it. But this file also includes *common.h*, so any definitions in *common.h* will now appear twice in the copy of *main.c* that cpp passes to the compiler, which will cause the compiler to report definition errors.

A *header guard*, also called an *include guard*, is a conditional macro-based construction designed to prevent this.

By enclosing a header file, say one named *file.h*, in a conditional macro of the following form, we prevent the file from being included twice:

```
#ifndef FILE_H
#define FILE_H
--snip--
#endif
```

This is because the first line #ifndef FILE_H has the meaning, "If the macro symbol FILE_H is not defined, continue reading and processing code until the matching occurrence of #endif." In this case, the line immediately after this conditional test, #define FILE_H, causes cpp to store the definition of FILE_H.

On the other hand, if when #ifndef FILE_H is executed, the symbol FILE_H is defined, then cpp skips reading code until immediately after the matching #endif. This implies that any code enclosed in the header guard will be included only once, and the multiple definitions cannot occur.

Notice that the *common_hdrs.h* file in Listing 3-1 includes a header named *get_nums.h* as well as *error_exits.h*. In the following section, we discuss the first of these, and in "Common Error-Handling Functions" on page 102, we discuss the second.

Functions for Extracting Numbers

The *get_nums.h* header declares prototypes and constants for functions that extract the numeric values of string data. (In Chapter 2, we saw how to use strtol() for this purpose.) The header contains prototypes for two functions based on the use of strtol() as well as associated constants that those functions use.

We create these functions because the error handling that should be done after calling the library functions can be lengthy. Rather than putting that error-handling code into every program that calls the function, we can integrate it into separate functions, like wrapper functions, making the calling programs smaller.

We name the two functions in that header get_long() and get_int(). Listing 3-2 shows the part of the header file containing the get_long() prototype and the defined constants.

```
#ifndef GET_NUMS_H
#define GET_NUMS_H

#include "sys_hdrs.h"

❶ /* Flags to pass to functions */
#define NO_TRAILING           1    /* Forbid trailing characters.        */
#define NON_NEG_ONLY          2    /* Forbid negative numbers.           */
#define ONLY_DIGITS           4    /* Forbid strings with no digits.     */
#define POS_ONLY              8    /* Forbid zero and negative numbers.  */
#define PURE NO_TRAILING | ONLY_DIGITS

❷ /* Return codes */
#define VALID_NUMBER          0    /* Successful processing              */
#define FATAL_ERROR          -1    /* ERANGE or EINVAL returned by strtol() */
#define TRAILING_CHARS_FOUND -2    /* Characters found after number      */
#define OUT_OF_RANGE         -3    /* int requested but out of int range */
#define NO_DIGITS_FOUND      -4    /* No digits in string                */
#define NEG_NUM_FOUND        -5    /* Negative number found but not allowed */

/** get_long()
    On successful processing, it returns VALID_NUMBER and stores the resulting
    number in *value; otherwise, it returns one of the nonzero error codes
    and puts a suitable message into *msg. flags is used to decide whether
    trailing characters, negative values, and zeros for strings without any
    digits are allowed or should be errors.
 *  @param  char*    arg    [IN]  String to parse
 *  @param  int      flags  [IN]  Flag specifying how to handle anomalies
 *  @param  long*    value  [OUT] Returned long int
 *  @param  char*    msg    [OUT] If not empty, error message
 *  @return int             VALID_NUMBER or a negative error code indicating the
                            type of error
 */
int get_long(char *arg, int flags, long *value, char *msg);
--snip--
#endif
```

Listing 3-2: Portions of the get_nums.h *header file*

The get_long() function is designed to allow the caller to specify whether to accept certain types of strings, such as those with trailing nonnumeric characters, or to accept a zero when the string has no digit at all, or to report negative values. Its return value, if negative, indicates some type of anomaly or error ❷. If there are no errors or anomalies, it returns `VALID_NUMBER`, which is defined as zero. Callers can easily ignore the specific error codes or take different actions depending on which they are.

The prototype has four parameters. The first is the string to be parsed. The second argument is an integer interpreted by the function as a set of flags. The following list includes the four possible flags ❶ and their meanings:

NO_TRAILING   Returns a `TRAILING_CHARS_FOUND` value for any string containing trailing nonnumeric characters, including those that have no digits at all, returning the value of the digits it found

NON_NEG_ONLY   Returns `NEG_NUM_FOUND` if the numeric value is negative

POS_ONLY   Returns `NEG_NUM_FOUND` if the numeric value is not positive

ONLY_DIGITS   Return `NO_DIGITS_FOUND` if the string has no digits and set *value to zero

Because they're independent, they can be bitwise-ORed into a flag to pass to the function, as in:

```
int flag = 0;
flag = flag | NO_TRAILING | ONLY_DIGITS;
```

The third parameter is a pointer to a location that can store the `long int` on successful return.

The fourth argument is the location in which to store an error message if things go wrong. Thus, if get_long() returns `VALID_NUMBER`, the number is in *value. If it returns anything else, the error message that it constructs is in msg.

Because the definition of get_long() is lengthy, to conserve space, I omit parts of it as well as comments in Listing 3-3 (the book's source code repository provides the complete listing).

get_long()
```
int get_long(char *arg, int flags, long *value, char *msg)
{
    char *endptr;
    long  val;
    errno = 0;
    val = strtol(arg, &endptr, 0);

    if ( errno == ERANGE ) {
        if ( msg != NULL )
            sprintf(msg, "%s\n", strerror(errno));
        return FATAL_ERROR;

    } else if ( errno == EINVAL && val != 0 ) {
        /* Bad base; shouldn't happen */
        if ( msg != NULL )
            sprintf(msg, "%s\n", strerror(errno));
        return FATAL_ERROR;
    }
```

```
        if ( endptr == arg ) {
    ❶ if ( flags & (ONLY_DIGITS | NO_TRAILING) ) {
            if ( msg != NULL )
                sprintf(msg, "No digits in the string\n");
            return NO_DIGITS_FOUND;
        }
        else {                    /* Accept a zero result.              */
            *value = 0;
            return VALID_NUMBER;
        }
    }
    if ( *endptr != '\0' ) { /* Non-number characters follow the number. */
    ❷ if ( flags & NO_TRAILING ) {
            if ( msg != NULL )
                sprintf(msg, "Trailing characters follow the number: 
                    \"%s\"\n", endptr);
            return TRAILING_CHARS_FOUND;
        }
    }
    --snip--
    *value = val;
    return VALID_NUMBER;
}
```

Listing 3-3: A partial listing of the get_long() function

The function uses sprintf() to construct the message string. We use it
the way we would use printf(), except we give it a string parameter preceding the format string. Instead of printing to standard output, it prints to the
string. In the various places where we might call sprintf(), we first check that
this pointer is not NULL before attempting to pass it to sprintf().

After calling strtol(), it checks for the two possible error values that it
might return. The ERANGE code implies a nonrecoverable error (number out
of the range of long int), and EINVAL implies either that there were no digits or that the base was bad. Since we set base to 0, implying actual base-10
numbers, we shouldn't get an EINVAL code unless there were no digits, but
to be safe, we check for this possibility. For either of these errors, the caller
receives the FATAL_ERROR code.

If strtol() succeeded, we start the process of looking at the flags that
the caller sent and deciding whether the returned value violates any of them.
Checking the flags uses the bitwise-AND and bitwise-OR operators ❶. For
example, the expression flags & (ONLY_DIGITS | NO_TRAILING) bitwise-ANDs
the bits of flags with the bitwise-OR of ONLY_DIGITS and NO_TRAILING. The expression is true if and only if flags has one or both of these bits set. If
NO_TRAILING is set but endptr is not at the end of the string ❷, it implies that
there are trailing characters and that the caller wants to be informed about it,
so the function returns TRAILING_CHARS_FOUND. It returns VALID_NUMBER if the flag
is not set because it implies that the calling code doesn't care whether there

are trailing characters. Similar logic applies to the remaining flags, but that code is not shown.

The get_int() function, displayed in Listing 3-4, is much shorter, because it just calls get_long() and checks whether the number is within range for an integer using the system constants INT_MAX and INT_MIN.

get_int()
```
int get_int(char *arg, int flags, int *value, char *msg)
{
    long val;
    int  res = get_long(arg, flags, &val, msg);

    if ( VALID_NUMBER == res ) {
        if ( val > INT_MAX || val < INT_MIN ) {
            sprintf(msg, "%ld is out of range\n", val);
            return OUT_OF_RANGE;
        }
        else {
            *value = val;
            return VALID_NUMBER;
        }
    }
    else { /* get_long failed in one way or another. */
        return res;
    }
}
```

Listing 3-4: A function to get the integer value of a string

Observe that get_int() doesn't have to check for any errors other than the numbers being out of range. It just passes the other error codes from get_long() to its caller. What may not be obvious is that the message that get_long() constructs will also be passed to the caller if get_int() doesn't overwrite it for a number that is out of range.

I wrote a couple of programs to call these functions (available in the source code), passing various flags to illustrate some of their error handling. The following shows some of their runs:

```
$ ./test_get_long 32kjk    # With NO_TRAILING passed
return:  TRAILING_CHARS_FOUND.
message: Trailing characters follow the number: "kjk"
$ ./test_get_long 32kjk    # Without NO_TRAILING passed
return:  VALID_NUMBER
$ ./test_get_long sdfskjk # With ONLY_DIGITS passed
return:  NO_DIGITS_FOUND
message: No digits in the string
$ ./test_get_int -287348987987987987988879879
return:  FATAL_ERROR
message: Numerical result out of range
```

In the first run, I passed the NO_TRAILING flag, and it reported seeing nondigit characters attached to the number. In the second run, I gave it the same input but without that flag, and it silently accepted the number without error. In the third run, I gave it a string with no digits and passed the ONLY_DIGITS flag, and it rejected the input, identifying the error. The last run was to show that it would successfully handle inputs that are too large and out of range.

Common Error-Handling Functions

All of the projects in this book share a few error handling functions, whose declarations are consolidated into a header file named *error_exits.h* in the *include* top-level directory. Having a few common error-handling functions simplifies the programs and reduces redundant code. Listing 3-5 shows the header file.

error_exits.h
```
#ifndef ERROR_EXITS_H
#define ERROR_EXITS_H
#include "sys_hdrs.h"

/** error_message()
    This prints an error message associated with errnum on standard error
    if errnum > 0. If errnum <= 0, it prints the msg passed to it.
    It does not terminate the calling program.
    This is used when there is a way to recover from the error.          */
void error_mssge(int errornum, const char *msg);

/** fatal_error()
    This prints an error message associated with errnum on standard error
    before terminating the calling program, if errnum > 0.
    If errnum <= 0, it prints the msg passed to it.
    fatal_error() should be called for a nonrecoverable error.           */
void fatal_error(int errornum, const char *msg);

/** usage_error()
    This prints a usage error message on standard error, advising the
    user of the correct way to call the program.                         */
void usage_error(const char *msg);

#endif /* ERROR_EXITS_H */
```

Listing 3-5: The header file with declarations of common error-handling functions

The error_message() function expects a number and a string. If the number is positive, it is an errno value and it uses strerror() to format a string describing that error and prints that string to standard error. If the number is not positive, it prints the string passed into it instead.

The fatal_error() function is the same as error_message() except that it terminates the program after printing the message, calling exit() with the system-defined `EXIT_FAILURE` number as its argument. The `usage_error()` function prints a usage message on standard error and terminates the program. Listing 3-6 provides their implementations.

error_exits.c

```
void error_mssge(int errornum, const char *msg)
{
    if ( errornum > 0 ) /* An errno value                       */
        fprintf(stderr, "%s\n", strerror(errornum));
    else /* Project-defined error number - ignore and just print msg */
        fprintf(stderr, "%s\n", msg);
}

void fatal_error(int errornum, const char *msg)
{
    error_mssge(errornum, msg);
    exit(EXIT_FAILURE);
}

void usage_error(const char *msg)
{
    fprintf(stderr,"usage: %s\n", msg);
    exit(EXIT_FAILURE);
}
```

Listing 3-6: Three error handling functions

Although the `fatal_error()` and `usage()` functions look similar, it's convenient to have a separate function for displaying a message specifically when the user ran the program incorrectly.

File Organization

The numeric parsing and error-handling functions just described are used by almost all programs in this book. To facilitate using them, I place their source code into a single top-level directory named *common* at the same level as the *include* and *lib* directories. Each chapter has a directory at this same level, containing the sources for all programs referenced in the chapter. The *lib* directory contains a static library named *libspl.a* that contains all common object files from the *common* directory. This directory structure is depicted in Figure 3-1.

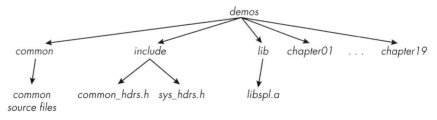

Figure 3-1: The structure of the demo program directories with common code

To create the *libspl.a* library, I use the GNU ar command. Appendix A contains an explanation of this command and detailed instructions for how to create static and shared libraries in general.

Planning Our First System Program

The first program we'll write is a warm-up exercise, one that won't require much background knowledge. Its purpose is to show how we'll go through the steps described previously. We'll write a command that displays the current date and/or time in various formats. We know the operating system maintains this information somewhere, because lots of applications display the date and time.

This exercise also has a few side benefits. You'll learn how Unix represents and processes dates and times. You'll learn the various components of the API related to time and date, and when we're finished, we'll have a few utility functions that'll be useful in later projects.

The first step is to check whether a command like this already exists and try to mimic its behavior. We can search the man pages to find such a command using apropos. The most obvious keywords to try first would be *date* and *time*. Since we're searching for commands, we limit the search to Section 1, first trying to match the keyword *date*, as follows:

```
$ apropos -s1 date
aa-features-abi (1)   - Extract, validate and manipulate AppArmor feature abis
apport-bug (1)        - file a bug report using Apport, or update an existin...
apport-collect (1)    - file a bug report using Apport, or update an existin...
autoreconf (1)        - Update generated configuration files
autoupdate (1)        - Update a configure.ac to a newer Autoconf
--snip--
```

On my system, 64 lines of output were displayed, but I'm showing only the first five lines. Several of these lines are descriptions of commands that have nothing to do with dates or times. Why is this? Remember that keyword searches in their simplest form display any short descriptions that contain the keyword, even as a substring.

We need to request an exact match instead:

```
$ apropos -s1 -e date
cal (1)             - displays a calendar and the date of Easter
date (1)            - print or set the system date and time
date (1posix)       - write the date and time
hp-timedate (1)     - Time/Date Utility
idevicedate (1)     - Display the current date or set it on a device.
mate-time-admin (1) - set date and time
ncal (1)            - displays a calendar and the date of Easter
timedatectl (1)     - Control the system time and date
```

From this short list, we can see that there are two man pages for a command named date, one in Section 1 and the other in Section 1posix.

Here's part of the man page for date in Section 1posix:

```
DATE(1POSIX)                POSIX Programmer's Manual              DATE(1POSIX)

PROLOG
       This manual page is part of the POSIX Programmer's Manual. The Linux
       implementation of this interface may differ (consult the corresponding
       Linux manual page for details of Linux behavior), or the interface may
       not be implemented on Linux.
NAME
       date - write the date and time
SYNOPSIS
       date [-u] [+format]
       date [-u] mmddhhmm[[cc]yy]
--snip--
```

This page describes what a POSIX-conforming version of the date command should do; it's a specification. It warns us that it isn't necessarily a description of the command that actually runs on our Linux system.

Let's look at the page in Section 1. That page begins as follows:

```
DATE(1)                         User Commands                         DATE(1)

NAME
       date - print or set the system date and time
SYNOPSIS
       date [OPTION]... [+FORMAT]
       date [-u|--utc|--universal] [MMDDhhmm[[CC]YY][.ss]]
--snip--
```

This version has more options. If we were running a version conforming to POSIX, several options wouldn't be available.

To start, we'll just run the command without options to see its output:

```
$ date
Wed Mar 26 02:54:17 PM EDT 2025
```

This output raises a few questions:

- It displays not just the current date, but the time of day and the day of the week. How does it know what day of the week it is?

- It outputs the string EST, which is short for "Eastern Standard Time." This implies that the system stores time zone information and that there's some way to determine in which time zone we're running. How can we find that information?

- How does it retrieve the current time? Is this a system call?

- How does date choose the format of date/time to print?

The rest of the Section 1 man page shows that the command has several useful options that aren't available in POSIX. If we try a few, we'll see that we're running the Linux version of the command:

```
$ date -d  'next Thu' # Note that we can put space between -d and its argument
Thu Mar 27 12:00:00 AM EDT 2025
$ date -d'next month'
Sat Apr 26 02:55:05 PM EDT 2025
$ date -d"2038-01-19 03:14:07 UTC" # Time of end of Unix Epoch
Mon Jan 18 10:14:07 PM EST 2038
$ date -d'5 years ago'
Thu Mar 26 02:56:13 PM EDT 2020
```

The -d option lets us request that date print dates other than the current one, which is a useful feature, and it even allows expressions such as *five years ago* and *next Thursday*. This option is not detailed much in the man page. Instead, its author wrote the following note there: "The date string format is more complex than is easily documented here but is fully described in the info documentation."

More important for us right now is that it has options for controlling the format of the output date/time string. We can change the format by supplying an option of the form +"*FORMAT*", where *FORMAT* is a string that contains ordinary character sequences as well as character sequences called *format specifications*, each of which is introduced by a % character and followed by a second character called a *format specifier character*. Each format specification defines one or more pieces of date or time information formatted in a particular way. For example, %m is replaced on output by a two-digit month number, such as 04.

The ordinary character sequences in *FORMAT* (called *literals*) are output exactly as they're written in the string. For example, the format "The month is %m" is output as "The month is 04" if the current month is April.

Some common format specifiers are %a, which is replaced by the three-letter weekday name, such as Sun for Sunday; %b, which is replaced by the three-letter month name, such as Dec for December; and %D, which is replaced by a date in the form *mm/dd/yyyy*, such as 01/01/1972. Appendix C contains a comprehensive list of specifiers with examples.

Here are a few examples of output when the date is the end of the Unix Epoch, January 19, 2038, at 03:14:07 UTC:

```
$ date +"%A, %D"          # Full day name, literal comma, and American date
Monday, 01/18/38
$ date                    # Default format
Mon Jan 18 10:14:07 PM EST 2038
$ date +"%c"              # Locale's date and time
Mon 18 Jan 2038 10:14:07 PM EST
$ date +"It is %A at %R." # Full day name, 24-hour time
It is Monday at 22:14.
```

Notice that the format string contains a mix of format specifiers and literals. The literals are displayed uninterpreted, where they appear relative to the format specifiers. The %c format specifier is called the *locale's date and time* in the documentation.

Several of the format specifiers refer to the user's locale in their descriptions. For example, the %a and %A are the locale's abbreviated and full weekday names, respectively. In the United States, these are names such as Sun and Sunday, respectively, but we have yet to see what they would be if we could choose a different locale. We'll see how to do this in "Working with Locales" on page 128.

The man page for date doesn't specify what its default format is. We can see what it looks like, and we know that it's the locale's format, but we don't know why it's in that form. However, the SEE ALSO section tells us that the full documentation is available in two places: the Info documentation and on the GNU website (*https://www.gnu.org/software/coreutils/date*). Both sources state that "invoking date with no *format* argument is equivalent to invoking it with a default format that depends on the LC_TIME locale category." In the default C locale, this format is +"\%a \%b \%e \%H:\%M:\%S \%Z \%Y", so the output looks like Thu Mar 3 13:47:51 PST 2005. Clearly, we need to know more about locales to understand this explanation, but for now we'll focus on writing some simple programs that behave like date, and we'll explore locales later in this chapter.

Our first goal is to write a much simpler version of the date command without any of its command line options to reproduce its default behavior. Once we do that, we'll add the ability to customize the output format using format specifiers, and after that we'll see how to make a version of it that's sensitive to locale settings. We'll name the first version of the command spl_date1 and name the program's source code file *spl_date1.c*.

Designing the First Version of spl_date

For spl_date1, we'll follow this program logic:

1. Get the current time.

2. Format the time in the default form of the date command, storing it into a string.

3. Print the string on standard output.

The first two steps imply that we need to understand how time is represented in Unix and find ways to change its representation to different kinds of human-readable forms.

Whenever you embark on a new project, it's a good idea to search for help in Section 7 of the man pages. Section 7 contains overviews of various topics. It might have an overview on the topic of interest, in this case, time. If so, it will contain background concepts and possibly references to functions that you might need.

To check whether Section 7 has a page that might help, enter the command **apropos -s7 -e time**. It returns, among others, the following pages:

```
RESET (7)            - restore the value of a run-time parameter to the def...
SET (7)              - change a run-time parameter
```

```
bootparam (7)          - introduction to boot time parameters of the Linux ke...
SHOW (7)               - show the value of a run-time parameter
sys_time.h (7posix)    - time types
systemd.time (7)       - Time and date specifications
time (7)               - overview of time and timers
time.h (7posix)        - time types
time_namespaces (7)    - overview of Linux time namespaces
```

Of these, the time (7) man page looks like the best starting point. It summarizes what we need to understand about time in Unix and Linux.

About Calendar Time in Unix

The man page explains that Unix has two types of time: process time and real time. *Process time* is the time a process spends in the CPU (Chapter 4 covers how to obtain process time). *Real time* is elapsed time measured from some reference point. When that reference point is not fixed, real time is called *elapsed time*. *Timers* are objects in Unix that can be set and used to keep track of elapsed time. They're important, and we'll revisit them in later chapters, but they're not what we want right now.

Calendar time is real time with respect to a particular fixed time point called the Epoch. The *Epoch* is defined as January 1, 1970, at 00:00:00 UTC. It's approximately when the first Unix system was released. UTC is short for "Coordinated Universal Time," which used to be called Greenwich Mean Time. The initialism is correct; the order of the letters was a compromise by the international advisory group that created it. See the NIST.gov website for an explanation (*https://www.nist.gov/pml/time-and-frequency-division/how-utcnist-related-coordinated-universal-time-utc-international*). Since its inception, in Unix, calendar time has been measured as the number of seconds elapsed since the Epoch.

Broken-Down Time

The time (7) man page also mentions a type of time representation called *broken-down time*, which is a time representation that's broken down into various commonly used components. As Robert Grudin put it in *Time and the Art of Living* [11]:

> Our units of temporal measurement, from seconds on up to months, are so complicated, asymmetrical and disjunctive so as to make coherent mental reckoning in time all but impossible. . . . It is as though architects had to measure length in feet, width in meters and height in ells; as though basic instruction manuals demanded a knowledge of five different languages.

We measure time in years, months, weeks, days, hours, minutes, and seconds, but we also use days of the week, days of the month, months of the year, and so on. These units have little consistency, other than the number of seconds in a minute and minutes in an hour being the same.

A broken-down time structure consolidates all of this information into a single data structure, called a struct tm, which is used by several functions that convert time and date formats from one form to another. The man page mentions some of them and suggests looking at the ctime() man page. If we look at that page, we see that asctime(), ctime(), gmtime(), localtime(), mktime(), strftime(), and strptime(), as well as various thread-safe versions of these, are all time-conversion functions.

We'll examine these functions in "Time Conversion Functions" on page 112 to decide which we should use, but first we'll examine the struct tm data structure, which is defined in the *time.h* header file as follows:

```
struct tm {
    int tm_sec;     /* Seconds (0-60)                    */
    int tm_min;     /* Minutes (0-59)                    */
    int tm_hour;    /* Hours (0-23)                      */
    int tm_mday;    /* Day of the month (1-31)           */
    int tm_mon;     /* Month (0-11)                      */
    int tm_year;    /* Year - 1900                       */
    int tm_wday;    /* Day of the week (0-6, Sunday = 0) */
    int tm_yday;    /* Day in the year (0-365, 1 Jan = 0) */
    int tm_isdst;   /* Daylight saving time              */
};
```

The fields have their expected meanings, but there are two details to note:

- The tm_sec field stores the number of seconds after the minute, which is normally in the range 0 to 59, but it can be up to 60 to allow for leap seconds.

- The tm_isdst field is a flag that indicates whether daylight saving time is in effect at the time described. The value is positive if daylight saving time is in effect, zero if it is not, and negative if the information is not available.

Now that we know that functions exist to convert formats and that they use this broken-down time structure, we can turn to the question of how to get the current time.

Calendar Time System Calls

The time (7) man page suggests two different system calls for obtaining the calendar time: clock_gettime() and time(). From the man page for clock_gettime(), we learn the following.

- The general-purpose clock_gettime() function provides the time of a specified clock. Its synopsis is:

```
#include <time.h>
int clock_gettime(clockid_t clockid, struct timespec *tp);
```

The function is given the ID of a clock and a pointer to a `timespec` struct, in which, on return, it stores the time on that clock, measured in nanoseconds.

- The predefined constant `CLOCK_REALTIME` of type `clockid_t` is the ID of the clock that keeps track of calendar time. The `timespec` struct is defined in *time.h* as:

```
struct timespec {
    time_t tv_sec;  /* Seconds     */
    long   tv_nsec; /* Nanoseconds */
};
```

The `time_t` type is a signed integer type whose size is implementation dependent but is at least 32 bits.

- To make sure the function is exposed in the header files, there is a feature test macro requirement:

```
_POSIX_C_SOURCE >= 199309L
```

This implies that we need to set `_POSIX_C_SOURCE` to that value or higher before including any header files.

- The man page also states that on POSIX systems on which this function is available, the symbol `_POSIX_TIMERS` is defined in *unistd.h* to a positive value. If we want to design a program to choose a different method of getting calendar time in case this function is not available, we would insert conditional code of the following form:

```
#if _POSIX_TIMERS > 0
    /* Use clock_gettime() to get time. */
#else
    /* Use some other function such as time(). */
#endif
```

- In the SEE ALSO section, it suggests a few pages that we should read: gettimeofday() and time(), both in Section 2. We should also read the man page for *time.h*.

The time() system call is much simpler to use and understand. Its man page tells us the following:

- time() returns the number of seconds since the Epoch.

- Its synopsis is:

```
#include <time.h>
time_t time(time_t *tloc);
```

The argument is a pointer to an integer of type time_t, but it's allowed to be NULL because its return value is also the current time.

• When tloc is NULL the function cannot fail, obviating the need for error handling.

Before we decide which of these two functions to use, we look at the man page for the gettimeofday() function suggested in the SEE ALSO section. Its synopsis is

```
#include <sys/time.h>
int gettimeofday(struct timeval *tv, struct timezone *tz);
```

where the tv argument is a pointer to timeval struct defined in *<sys/time.h>* as follows:

```
struct timeval {
    time_t      tv_sec;  /* Seconds      */
    suseconds_t tv_usec; /* Microseconds */
};
```

On return, this stores the number of seconds and microseconds since the Epoch. The timezone struct pointer tz should always be set to NULL because it has been *deprecated*.

WARNING *Whenever you see a feature marked as deprecated in documentation, avoid using it. If the organization that supports the software has deprecated it, that means it will no longer support it and it will become obsolete.*

In fact, the CONFORMING TO section notes that the function itself has been marked as obsolete since POSIX.1-2008, and it recommends using clock_gettime() instead.

The choice is thus reduced to clock_gettime() and time(). The difference is in how the returned time is represented and its granularity. Since the tv_sec field of the struct timespec returned by clock_gettime() is the number of seconds since the Epoch, it should be the same as the value returned by time(). For our program, we don't need subsecond granularity, so there's little benefit to using clock_gettime(). On the other hand, it's a more adaptable function.

Another factor to consider is performance. To check whether there is a price to pay for obtaining the finer resolution of the timespec structure, I wrote two programs that called each function 10 million times and measured their elapsed times when run on my x86-64 system running Linux 5.15.0. The program that called time() required 0.032 seconds, whereas the one running clock_gettime() required 0.171 seconds. Repeated runs had similar results. Taking everything into consideration, we'll choose time() for getting the current time in this first version of our program.

Time Conversion Functions

The functions asctime(), ctime(), gmtime(), localtime(), and mktime() are all described on the same man page. Entering **man ctime** will display it. Here's the relevant portion of that page, with some lines removed:

```
#include <time.h>

char *asctime(const struct tm *tm);
char *ctime(const time_t *timep);

struct tm *gmtime(const time_t *timep);
struct tm *localtime(const time_t *timep);

time_t mktime(struct tm *tm);
```

We observe that:

- asctime() is given a broken-down time struct and returns a string.

- ctime() is given a time_t value and returns a string.

- gmtime() and localtime() are each given a time_t value and return a pointer to a broken-down time struct.

- mktime() is given a broken-down time struct and returns a time_t value.

- None of these functions require time resolution smaller than seconds, reinforcing our decision to use time() instead of clock_gettime() to get the current time.

This shows that we need to use either asctime() or ctime() to create a formatted time string, but if we use asctime() we need to convert from calendar time to the broken-down time first. Reading the DESCRIPTION section reveals that the difference between gmtime() and localtime() is that gmtime() converts its time_t argument to broken-down time expressed in UTC, whereas localtime() converts its time_t argument to broken-down time expressed relative to the user's specified time zone. We'll have more to say about time zones in "About Time Zones" on page 131.

The CONFORMING TO section of that page, however, states that both asctime() and ctime() are marked as obsolete and that strftime() should be used in their place, ruling them out. Reading the man page for strftime(), we learn that it's a much more powerful function than either of them:

```
$ man strftime
--snip--
SYNOPSIS
    #include <time.h>
    size_t strftime(char *s, size_t max, const char *format,
                    const struct tm *tm);
```

DESCRIPTION
       The strftime() function formats the broken-down time tm according to
       the format specification format and places the result in the character
       array s of size max.
--*snip*--

The rest of its description tells us that strftime() lets us customize the
output date and time string by using a *format specification*, which is its third
parameter. In fact, the set of format specifiers is almost identical to those
used by the date command, making our job fairly easy.

As a start, to approximate the default format of date, we can use %c.
(Although the man page states that there's a format specification %+ that
produces a string in the exact same format as the date command, it isn't
supported in *glibc* version 2.) Thus, to obtain a string in roughly the same
format as date such as

Fri 09 May 2025 12:34:10 PM EDT

we'll pass the format specification %c to strftime().

We can put together the *spl_date1.c* program based on what we've learned.
Figure 3-2 displays the program logic.

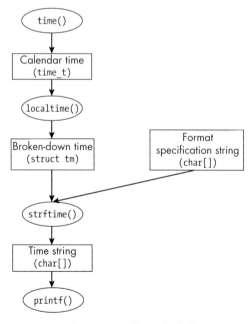

Figure 3-2: The program flow of spl_date1.c

We use time() to get the current time in calendar time units and pass
that return value to localtime(), which constructs a broken-down time object.
We pass that in turn to strftime() in addition to the format specification %c,
stored in a variable. Finally, we print out the string produced by strftime().

The resulting program, *spl_date1.c*, is displayed in Listing 3-7 with some comments omitted to save space.

```
#define _GNU_SOURCE
#include "common_hdrs.h"

int main(int argc, char *argv[])
{
    char    formatted_date[200];
    time_t current_time;
    struct tm *broken_down_time;
    char    format_str[MAXLEN];

    strcpy(format_str, "%c");
    current_time = time(NULL); /* Get the current time. */

    /* Convert current time into broken-down time. */
    if ( (broken_down_time = localtime(&current_time)) == NULL )
        fatal_error(EOVERFLOW, "localtime");

    /* Create a string from the broken down time using the %c format. */
    if ( 0 == strftime(formatted_date, sizeof(formatted_date),
                  ❶ format_str, broken_down_time) ) {
        fatal_error(EXIT_FAILURE, "Conversion to a date-time string"
                  " failed or produced an empty string\n");
    }
    printf("%s\n", formatted_date);
    return 0;
}
```

Listing 3-7: The first version of the spl_date program

Rather than hardcoding the %c format specifier ❶ directly into the call to strftime(), we store it in a string variable named format_str of length MAXLEN (defined in *common_hdrs.h*) that we pass to the function. This makes it easier to change the program in the next version.

Designing a Second Version of spl_date

We'll now improve *spl_date1.c* by allowing the user to enter different date formats on the command line. For example, it would be useful if we could enter commands such as the following:

```
$ ./spl_date +"Today is %A. Current time: %R"
Today is Sunday. Current time: 13:45
```

In this way, different users could see the time in their format of choice.

To accomplish this, we have to make only a small change to the program. Specifically, we need to check whether the command has an argument, and if so, whether it starts with a + and is small enough to fit into format_str. If so, we can pass the string following the + to strftime(). If that string isn't a valid format string, strftime() will return an error that we can report. Otherwise, we print the string that it produces. If there's no argument to the program, we just print the current time in the default format.

We can incorporate this logic into a function named getformat(), which is passed a pointer to the command line and extracts the format string from it:

getformat()
```
void getformat(int nargs, char *argvec[], char *format_str)
{
    char err_msg[MAXLEN];              /* For error messages    */
    if ( argvec[nargs-1][0] == '+' ) /* Argument starts with + */
        if ( strlen(argvec[nargs-1] + 1 ) < MAXLEN )
            strncpy(format_str, argvec[nargs-1] + 1, MAXLEN - 1);
        else {
            sprintf(err_msg, "Format string length is too long\n");
            fatal_error(BAD_FORMAT_ERROR, err_msg);
        }
    else {
        sprintf(err_msg,"%s: Format should be +\"format-string\"\n",
                basename(argvec[0]));
        fatal_error(BAD_FORMAT_ERROR, err_msg);
    }
}
```

The function expects its first parameter nargs to be passed argc; this way, argvec[nargs-1] is the last word on the command line.

We add this function to the program, which we'll name *spl_date2.c*. We'll call it immediately before the call to time() (see Listing 3-8). No other changes are needed. The complete program is in the source code distribution for the book.

```
--snip--
int main(int argc, char *argv[])
{
    char    formatted_date[MAXLEN];
    time_t current_time;
    struct tm *broken_down_time;
    char    format_string[MAXLEN];

    if ( argc < 2 )
        strcpy(format_string, "%c");
    else
        getformat(argc, argv, format_string);
    current_time = time(NULL); /* Get the current time. */
    --snip--
    if ( 0 == strftime(formatted_date, sizeof(formatted_date),
                    format_string, broken_down_time) ) {
        fatal_error(BAD_FORMAT_ERROR, "Conversion to a date-time string"
                " failed or produced an empty string\n");
```

```
    }
    printf("%s\n", formatted_date);
    return 0;
}
```

Listing 3-8: A partial listing of the second version of spl_date, allowing an optional user-supplied format string argument

Following are a few runs of this program that show how it handles some possible errors and produces the expected output:

```
$ ./spl_date2
Wed Mar 26 15:07:25 2025
$ ./spl_date2 today
spl_date2: format should be +"format-string"
$ ./spl_date2 +"Today is day %e of %B. It is now %r"
Today is day 26 of March. It is now 03:08:49 PM
$ ./spl_date2 +"a very long string, longer than 1024 characters..."
spl_date2: format string length is too long
```

The last run is given a format string whose length exceeds the size of the buffer that the program uses to show how it handles this error. You can see that it detects it and exits without crashing.

Designing a Third Version of spl_date

The preceding program wasn't too hard to develop, but it prepared us to go one step further and add the ability to display dates in the past and future by allowing the user to specify lengths of time to add to or subtract from the current time. This program will be a bit more challenging to write.

The User Interface

First, we need to decide how the user should call the program. Then we'll write a precise specification against which we can test our implementation. Since the ability to add an amount of time is optional, the program should have a command line option with a required argument that specifies the amount of time to add or subtract to the current time. We'll call the amount of time that we want to add or subtract the *time-adjustment*, and we'll use the option character -d (for *difference*).

We should also get into the habit of providing a help feature for every nontrivial program we write. The Unix convention is to give commands an -h option that displays their usage information. If that option is present, the convention is to ignore all other words on the command line.

To summarize, our program's synopsis should be of the form

```
$ spl_date3 [-h] | [-d "time-adjustment"] [+"format-specification"]
```

where the *time-adjustment* argument to -d is a string that we need to define, and the *format-specification* is the same as it was in spl_date2.

Time Adjustment Specifications

When we write amounts of time in noncomputer contexts, we understand that the expressions "1 month, 8 days," "one month and eight days," and "one month, eight days" are equivalent amounts of time. If we allowed users to enter amounts of time with that degree of flexibility, we'd be making the task of parsing the input much harder than if we limited the form of the input to something simpler. It amounts to a trade-off between what's easy for the user and what's easy for the programmer. Since we're not trying to write production software yet, we need a compromise that provides a convenient interface for the user and a relatively easy syntax to parse.

My compromise is to allow the user to enter time differences in the customary units we use, specifically, years, months, weeks, days, hours, minutes, and seconds, but not to enter phrases such as "next Monday" or "last month," which would add more parsing to the program.

To make the parsing easier, we'll require the user to enter numerals rather than words for the amounts. For example, the program should accept a phrase such as "2 years 3 weeks" but not "two years three weeks" or "two years, three weeks."

Also, we'll give users the ability to enter times in the past by allowing negative numbers for the time quantities, so we'll accept a phrase such as "-4 hours 5 minutes," which could also be entered as "-3 hours -55 minutes." Note that a negative number applies only to the time unit next to it—"-4 hours 5 minutes" is not "-(4 hours 5 minutes)."

To simplify the program, we'll forbid fractional amounts, such as "3.5 days," but we'll allow users to enter the same unit multiple times. For example, they could enter a time adjustment such as:

```
1 year 4 months -2 days -3 weeks +1 day
```

The way that I've formulated this, commas between the units are not allowed.

I'll write a specification of the time adjustment using the following grammar, which uses the same syntax as the man page synopsis:

```
time-adjustment = <num> <time-unit> [<num> <time-unit> ... ]
num             = [+|-]<integer>
time-unit       = year[s] month[s] week[s] day[s] hour[s] minute[s] second[s]
integer         = [1-9][0-9]...
```

Notice that the time units can have an optional s on the end, numbers can start with an optional + or -, and they cannot start with leading zeros. If they use a leading zero, the number will be interpreted as an octal number.

Here are some examples:

```
$ ./spl_date3 -d "1 year 2 months"
$ ./spl_date3 -d " +1 year 2 months" +"%D %r"
$ ./spl_date3 -d " 3 weeks 5 days 4 hours 30 minutes" +"%D %r"
$ ./spl_date3 -d" -5 months -3 days" +"%D"
```

The first shows the date one year and two months from today in the default format. The next shows the same date but in a different format of the form "*mm/dd/yyyy hh:mm:ss AM|PM.*" The third shows the date that is three weeks, five days, four hours, and 30 minutes from the current time using the same format as the preceding example. The last shows a date five months and three days earlier, using the default format.

Fuzzy Time

The last consideration before we start to map out the program logic concerns the fuzziness of months and years as units of time. The number of days in a month depends on the month, and the number of days in a year changes for leap years. If we subtract one month from July 31 what is the date? Since there is no June 31, is it June 30?

If you read the Info page for the date command, you'll see that its implementation uses the rule that adding (or subtracting) a month increments (or decrements) the month number, and if the date doesn't exist in that month, it's adjusted to the nearest date that's valid.

We can test how the real date adjusts these dates using its --date= option:

```
$ date --date='Dec 29, 2024 +2 months'
Sat Mar  1 12:00:00 AM EST 2025
# Because Feb 29 does not exist, date makes it one day after Feb 28,
# which is Mar 1.
$ date --date='Dec 30, 2024 +2 months'
Thu Mar  2 12:00:00 AM EST 2025
# Because Feb 30 does not exist, date makes it two days after Feb 28,
# which is Mar 2.
$ date --date='Mar 30, 2025 -1 month'
Sun Mar  2 12:00:00 AM EST 2025
# date uses the same idea as before. It does not matter whether it got the
# day by adding or subtracting.
$ date --date='Dec 30, 2023 +2 months'
Fri Mar 1 12:00:00 AM EST 2024
# date knows that 2024 is a leap year, so it makes it one day past Feb 29.
```

For consistency, our program should use this same date calculation logic, but that raises the question: Is there a library function that does this calculation, or do we have to implement it ourselves?

If we return to the man page for ctime(), we'll see that it has relevant information about the mktime() function:

> The mktime() function modifies the fields of the tm structure as follows: tm_wday and tm_yday are set to values determined from the contents of the other fields; if structure members are outside their valid interval, they will be normalized (so that, for example, 40 October is changed into 9 November); tm_isdst is set (regardless of its initial value) to a positive value or to 0, respectively, to indicate whether DST is or is not in effect at the specified time.

In short, `mktime()` encapsulates the corrections for invalid dates and times used in the `date` command, saving us from having to implement this logic ourselves. Therefore, we can add time adjustments to a broken-down time structure `bd_time` and call `mktime(bd_time)` to have `mktime()` normalize the time for us.

Program Logic

How this version of `spl_date` differs from the preceding one will guide the changes in the program logic. The first step is to list the changes:

- We have to add option parsing.

- We have to parse the time adjustment, if it's present, into the numbers of seconds, minutes, hours, and so on, that need to be added (or subtracted) from the current time.

- We need to add the time adjustment to the current time and display the resulting time.

We can incorporate these differences into the program's control flow, ignoring error handling for the moment, in the following sequence of steps:

1. Parse the command line, checking whether the `-d` or `-h` option is present.

2. If `-h` is present, ignore all other arguments and options, print out help information, and exit.

3. Otherwise, if `-d` is present, allocate memory to store its argument and copy the argument into that memory.

4. If there is a format specification, copy it into a string of sufficient size.

5. Obtain and store the current time into a `time_t` variable using `time()`.

6. Convert the current time into a broken-down time representation using `localtime()`.

7. If `-d` is present, parse the argument, creating a temporary broken-down time structure that stores the time to add to the current time in terms of years, months, days, and so on, and add the value of the temporary structure to the broken-down current time.

8. Use the `strftime()` function to format the output string representation of the broken-down time.

9. Print the formatted string using `printf()`.

Figure 3-3 shows the control flow with the new logic in bold.

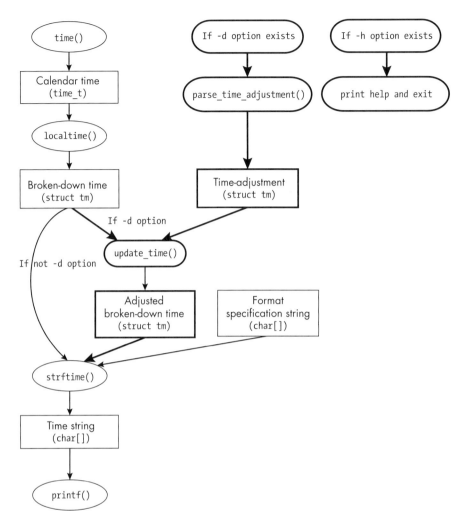

Figure 3-3: The control flow of spl_date3.c

We can now prototype and design the function that parses the time-adjustment string. Since the function should receive a time-adjustment string as its input and create a broken-down time representation of that string as its output, a reasonable prototype for it is the following:

```
int parse_time_adjustment( /* IN  */ char *datestring,
                           /* OUT */ struct tm *datetm );
```

Following convention, the return value is an indication of success or failure, and the broken-down time structure is a result parameter.

Given the string time_adjust_string passed to the program following the -d option and the address of a broken-down time structure, parse_time _adjustment() parses the string and sets the individual members of the structure accordingly. For example, if the time_adjust_string is

```
2 years   4 months   12 days   -6 hours   -2 days
```

it should set the structure's members as follows:

```
datetm->tm_year = 2
datetm->tm_mon = 4
datetm->tm_mday = 10
datetm->tm_hour = -6
--snip--
/* All other members set to zero */
```

In principle, we can design this code from scratch and parse the string without any need to call a library function, reading each character from left to right, processing them as needed. For example, we could skip whitespace, build numbers when we see a plus or minus sign or a digit, and build time-unit strings when the characters are alphabetic. Processing this way makes one pass over the string and is the fastest possible approach. However, we need to process only the command line, not thousands of large strings, implying that the amount of time we'll save with this approach is imperceptible. It would be far better to take advantage of existing library functions that have been well tested, even if we end up making two passes across the string.

PERFORMANCE AND DESIGN CONSIDERATIONS

There's usually a trade-off between code that's easy to read and code that performs well. In designing a system program, we should certainly aim for good performance, but we also want to write code that's easy to understand and maintain. What principles can guide the algorithms we choose?

- Code that isn't executed much doesn't need to be fast because even if it's a few orders of magnitude slower than it could be, it won't add any noticeable amount to the total running time. In contrast, code that's executed frequently should be fast.

- It's safer to use code that has been already written and tested thoroughly than to write new code to solve the exact same problem.

- Code that will be in service a long time should be easier to maintain than code that you know will be obsolete sooner.

I usually ask myself these questions when I design algorithms and need to decide how to make the trade-offs.

What functions can we use? Again, the first step is to consult the man pages. If we try using **apropos -s3 string** or **apropos -s3 -e string** to see which man pages in Section 3 are related to strings, we'll get a very long list that we can search by hand. Or, we could see if there's a man page named string. If we do that, we'll discover a new resource:

```
$ man string
STRING(3)               Linux Programmer's Manual               STRING(3)

NAME
       stpcpy, strcasecmp, strcat, strchr, strcmp, strcoll, strcpy, strcspn,
```

```
        strdup, strfry, strlen, strncat, strncmp, strncpy, strncasecmp,
        strpbrk, strrchr, strsep, strspn, strstr, strtok, strxfrm, index,
        rindex - string operations

SYNOPSIS
        #include <strings.h>

        int strcasecmp(const char *s1, const char *s2);
                Compare the strings s1 and s2 ignoring case.

        int strncasecmp(const char *s1, const char *s2, size_t n);
                Compare the first n bytes of the strings s1 and s2 ignoring case.
--snip--
```

We could also read the *string.h* man page, but this one is better because
the *string.h* man page is a POSIX page saying what should be present in
a POSIX-compliant system, whereas this one is what actually is on our system. On GNU/Linux, all of the functions listed in the *string.h* man page are
available, possibly with different behavior than POSIX.1-2024 requires. No
matter which you choose, it will be informative and will provide guidance
and clues for picking the right tool for the job.

The list of functions in the *string.h* man page includes one named strtok()
with this prototype:

```
#include <string.h>
char *strtok(char *s, const char *delim);
```

The description states that it extracts *tokens* from the string s that are delim-
ited by one of the bytes in delim. *Tokens* are pieces of a string to be parsed.

The strtok() library function is a great tool for breaking up a line into
tokens separated by any types of delimiters. For example, if you're given a
comma-separated values (CSV) file and need to extract its fields, you could
use this function passing a comma as a delimiter.

The delim string is the set of characters that act as delimiters. If the string
is :,;, then each of those characters will be treated as a character separating
two tokens. For our purpose, we set delim = " \t" because the tokens in the
time-adjustment string are separated by whitespace characters, including tab
characters.

The first time we call strtok(), we pass the string to be parsed in the first
argument. Its return value will be a pointer to the first token it finds. All
returned tokens are terminated with a NULL byte (\0) so that string-processing
functions can be used safely with them.

In subsequent calls, we pass the NULL pointer in the first parameter. If
there are no more tokens, it returns NULL, so the standard way to use it is essentially as follows:

```
char *delim = " \t"; /* Space and tab */
char *token;
token = strtok(mystring, delim);
while ( token != NULL ) {
```

```
    /* Process the token just found. */
    token = strtok(NULL, delim);
}
```

The strtok() function actually makes a copy of the string that you pass to it, and as it finds each token, it replaces the delimiter at the end of it with a terminating NULL byte (\0).

Since our program expects the time-adjustment string to be a sequence of pairs of the form *<number> <whitespace> <time-unit>*, each iteration of the loop should call strtok() twice: the first time to get a number and the second to get a time unit. We'll declare the following variables:

```
char *delim   = " \t";       /* Space and tab              */
char *token;                  /* Returned token             */
int   number;                 /* To store number token      */
char  err_msg[STRING_MAX];    /* For error messages         */
int   flags = ONLY_DIGITS | NO_TRAILING;
int   res;                    /* Return value of get_int() */
```

By setting flags to ONLY_DIGITS | NO_TRAILING, we reject numbers that have any nondigits following them and strings that have no digits at all where numbers are expected.

The pseudocode structure of the loop is:

```
token = strtok(time_adjust_string, delim);
while ( token != NULL ) {
    res = get_int(token, flags, &number, err_msg); /* Get number.        */
    /* If error, handle it. */
    token = strtok(NULL, delim); /* Get time unit, such as year, month. */
    /* If error, handle it. */
    /* Add number of time units to appropriate member of datetm. */
    token = strtok(NULL, delim); /* Try to get the next number.        */
}
```

The function tries to get the first token before entering the loop. If successful, it enters the loop and calls get_int() to extract the number from the returned token, exits for any possible errors from a failed call to get_int(), and calls strtok() to get the associated time unit. It exits if the time unit is missing; otherwise, it adds the amount of time to the datetm structure before calling strtok() again. Listing 3-9 contains the complete function implementation, with some comments omitted to save space.

```
parse_time     int parse_time_adjustment(char *time_adjust_string, struct tm *datetm)
_adjustment()  {
                   char *delim = " \t";        /* Space and tab              */
                   char *token;                 /* Returned token             */
                   int   number;                /* To store number token      */
                   char  err_msg[STRING_MAX];   /* For error messages         */
                   int   flags = ONLY_DIGITS | NO_TRAILING;
                   int   res;                   /* Return value of get_int() */
```

```
token = strtok(time_adjust_string, delim);
while ( token != NULL ) {
    res = get_int(token, flags, &number, err_msg); /* Get an integer. */
    if ( VALID_NUMBER != res )
        fatal_error(res, err_msg);
    /* number is the quantity of time-adjustment units to be read next. */
    /* Get the next token in time adjustment; should be a time unit.   */
    token = strtok(NULL, delim);
    if ( NULL == token )
        /* End of string encountered without the time unit */
        fatal_error(TIME_ADJUST_ERROR, "missing a time unit\n");

    if ( NULL != strstr(token, "year") ) datetm->tm_year += number;
    else if ( NULL != strstr(token, "month") ) datetm->tm_mon += number;
    else if ( NULL != strstr(token, "week") ) datetm->tm_mday += 7*number;
    else if ( NULL != strstr(token, "day") ) datetm->tm_mday += number;
    else if ( NULL != strstr(token, "hour") ) datetm->tm_hour += number;
    else if ( NULL != strstr(token, "minute") ) datetm->tm_min += number;
    else if ( NULL != strstr(token, "second") ) datetm->tm_sec += number;
    else
        fatal_error(TIME_ADJUST_ERROR,
            "Found invalid time time_unit in amount to adjust the time\n");
    token = strtok(NULL, delim);
}
return 0;
}
```

Listing 3-9: The parse_time_adjustment() function

To add the time adjustment to the datetm structure, I use the strstr()
function, also described in that time man page. This is essentially a substring
searching function. Its man page shows the prototype:

```
#include <string.h>
char *strstr(const char *haystack, const char *needle);
```

As the parameter names suggest, it searches for the first occurrence of substring needle in string haystack, returning a pointer to that occurrence or NULL
if it's not there. As it's presented here, this function will parse a string such
as "4 megadays" as "4 days." It can be modified so that it is successful only
if the time units are exact words such as "day" or "days." I leave this as an
exercise.

NOTE   *You might wonder why I use a sequence of cascading if statements in parse_time
_adjustment() instead of a switch statement. In C, the switch statement requires an
integer type, but I need to compare strings, which are not an integer type. There are
more efficient ways to do this, but since this code is executed only relatively few times,
and since it's clear and simple, it's suitable.*

The last function we'll use is one that adds the values from one broken-down time structure into another, which I name adjust_time(). It's displayed in Listing 3-10.

```
int adjust_time(struct tm *datetm, struct tm *time_to_add)
{
    datetm->tm_year += time_to_add->tm_year;
    datetm->tm_mon  += time_to_add->tm_mon;
    datetm->tm_mday += time_to_add->tm_mday;
    datetm->tm_hour += time_to_add->tm_hour;
    datetm->tm_min  += time_to_add->tm_min;
    datetm->tm_sec  += time_to_add->tm_sec;

    errno = 0;
    mktime(datetm);
    if ( errno != 0 )
        fatal_error(errno, NULL);
    return 0;
}
```

Listing 3-10: A function that adds time amounts to a broken-down time structure and normalizes the fields

The only point to emphasize about adjust_time() is that it's possible for mktime() to fail, and because of this, the function checks for an error after the call and terminates the program if something went wrong.

Listing 3-11 shows fragments of the *spl_date3.c* program with the preceding functions omitted to save space.

```
#define _GNU_SOURCE                    /* Needed for get_long()            */
#include "common_hdrs.h"

#define FORMAT "%c"                     /* Default format string           */
#define MAXLEN STRING_MAX               /* Maximum size of message string  */
#define BAD_FORMAT_ERROR      -1        /* In case user supplied bad format */
#define TIME_ADJUST_ERROR     -2        /* Error to return if parsing problem */

--snip-- // OMITTED: Definition of parse_time_adjustment()

int main(int argc, char *argv[])
{
    char       formatted_date[MAXLEN]; /* String storing formatted date   */
    time_t     current_time;           /* Timeval in seconds since Epoch  */
    struct tm *bdtime;                 /* Broken-down time                */
    struct tm  time_adjustment= {0};   /* Broken-down time for adjustment */
    char       format_string[MAXLEN];  /* String storing  format spec     */
    char       usage_msg[512];         /* Usage message                   */
    char       ch;                     /* For option handling             */
    char       options[] = ":d:h";     /* Getopt string                   */
    BOOL       d_option = FALSE;        /* Flag to indicate -d found       */
```

```
char      *d_arg;                    /* Dynamic string for -d argument  */
int        d_arg_length;             /* Length of -d argument string    */

opterr = 0;  /* Turn off error messages by getopt(). */
while ( TRUE ) {
    ch = getopt(argc, argv, options);
    if ( -1 == ch )
        break;
    switch ( ch ) {
    case 'd':                        /* Has required argument           */
        d_option = TRUE;
        d_arg_length = strlen(optarg);
        d_arg = ❶ malloc(d_arg_length * sizeof(char));
        if ( NULL == d_arg )
            fatal_error(EXIT_FAILURE,
                        "calloc could not allocate memory\n");
        strcpy(d_arg, optarg);
        break;
    case 'h':
        sprintf(usage_msg, "%s [-d <time adjustment>]"
                " [+\"format specification\"]", basename(argv[0]));
        usage_error(usage_msg);
    case '?':
        fprintf(stderr,"Found invalid option %c\n", optopt);
        sprintf(usage_msg, "%s [-d <time adjustment>]"
                " [+\"format specification\"]", basename(argv[1]));
        usage_error(usage_msg);
    case ':':
        fprintf(stderr,"Missing required argument to -d\n");
        sprintf(usage_msg, "%s [-d <time adjustment>]"
                " [+\"format specification\"]", basename(argv[0]));
        usage_error(usage_msg);
    }
}
/* optind-1 is the number of valid options found, so argc-(optind-1) is
   the number of non-option words on the command line, implying that if
   argc-optind == 0 or optind == argc, there is no format string. */
if ( 0 == argc - optind )
    strcpy(format_string, "%c");
else
    getformat(argc, argv, format_string);

current_time = time(NULL);
bdtime = localtime(&current_time);
if ( bdtime == NULL )
    fatal_error(EOVERFLOW, "localtime");
if ( d_option ) {
```

```
        parse_time_adjustment(d_arg, &time_adjustment);
        update_time(bdtime, &time_adjustment);
   ❷ free(d_arg); /* Allocated in option handling above */
    }
    if ( 0 == strftime(formatted_date, sizeof(formatted_date),
                    format_string, bdtime) )
        fatal_error(BAD_FORMAT_ERROR, "Conversion to a date-time string "
                "failed or produced an empty string\n");
    printf("%s\n", formatted_date);
    return 0;
}
```

Listing 3-11: The main program of spl_date3

This listing introduces the C malloc() function ❶, which is part of a family of memory allocation functions including calloc() and realloc().

The malloc() function allocates memory from the heap and returns a pointer to the start of the newly allocated memory. Its prototype is:

```
#include <stdlib.h>
void *malloc(size_t size);
```

Because it returns a void* result, we can assign that address to any C pointer, such as a utlist* or a char*. Although unlikely, it can fail because there's no memory left to allocate and will return NULL and set errno to ENOMEM in this case.

The listing also introduces free() ❷, which is used to free the memory space pointed to by ptr, which must have been returned by a previous call to malloc(), calloc(), or realloc(). Its synopsis is:

```
#include <stdlib.h>
void free(void *ptr);
```

If the memory ptr pointed to has been freed already, the consequences are unpredictable. We'll discuss allocating and deallocating memory more in Chapter 10. Note that the absence of a break after each call to usage_error() in the switch statement is justified because the function terminates the program.

A few runs demonstrate the program's behavior:

```
$ ./spl_date3 -h
usage: spl_date3 [-d "<time adjustment>"] [+"format specification"]
$ ./spl_date3 +"%a %b %d, %Y, at %R"
Wed Mar 26, 2025, at 15:24
$ ./spl_date3 -d "1 year" +"%a %b %d, %Y, at %R"
Thu Mar 26, 2026, at 15:30
$ ./spl_date3 -d "1 week 2 hours" +"%a %b %d, %Y, at %R"
Wed Apr 02, 2025, at 17:33
$ ./spl_date3 -d "-2 months +4 months" +"%a %b %d, %Y, at %R"
Mon May 26, 2025, at 15:38
$ ./spl_date3 -d '+120 minutes -2 hours' +"%a %b %d, %Y, at %R"
Wed Mar 26, 2025, at 15:39
```

Notice that subtracting two months and adding four months results in a net of two months later than the current time and that adding 120 minutes and subtracting two hours leaves the time unchanged.

Working with Locales

Imagine now that the user of our spl_date3 program is someone from another region of the world who doesn't speak English and doesn't use our representation of dates and times. As it's written so far, its output won't be in a form that they can understand. How can we change it so that it is?

This question leads into a deeper study of the internationalization of software and the concept of a locale. The POSIX.1-2024 definition of a locale given in Chapter 2 is "the definition of the subset of a user's environment that depends on language and cultural conventions," which is very abstract. We need to know how to program with locales and what they are in more concrete terms.

In particular, we need to know the following:

- What exactly is a locale?

- What conventions does a locale influence?

- What kinds of information does a locale encapsulate?

- How many different locales are there, and where are they stored?

- Is there some standard, default locale?

- At the user level, what commands can we use to view and change our locale?

- How is the information associated with a locale structured?

- At the programming level, what library functions get and set locale contents so that programs can be internationalized?

The first step is to search the man pages for answers. Searching for the keyword *locale* using apropos locale results in a long list of man pages, many of which are in Section 3, Library Functions. Section 7 and 5 man pages often have overviews and are a good starting point. The POSIX *locale.h* header file page might be useful too. User-level commands that display information about locales would be in Section 1. We start with the general description page in Section 7:

```
$ man 7 locale
LOCALE(7)                    Linux Programmer's Manual                    LOCALE(7)

NAME
       locale - description of multilanguage support
```

```
SYNOPSIS
       #include <locale.h>

DESCRIPTION
       A locale is a set of language and cultural rules. These cover aspects
       such as language for messages, different character sets, lexicographic
       conventions, and so on. A program needs to be able to determine its
       locale and act accordingly to be portable to different cultures.

       The header <locale.h> declares data types, functions and  macros which
       are useful in this task.

       The functions it declares are setlocale(3) to set the current locale,
       and localeconv(3) to get information about number formatting.
--snip--
```

This page refers us to the *locale.h* header file for details about the data types, functions, and macros. It also mentions two functions, setlocale() and localeconv(), that we may need in our modified program. The rest of the man page describes important fundamental concepts, summarized next.

Locale Categories

A locale consists of a collection of categories. *Categories* are parts of the locale that control related aspects of a user's cultural and language settings. For example, the LC_CTYPE category consists of data that specifies character classification, case conversion, and other character attributes, such as which characters are letters, which are digits, which are punctuation, and so on.

The names that identify categories all begin with LC_ (short for "locale category"). These names are integer-valued macros declared in *locale.h* for use by programs. The names can also be placed into the environment, in which case they're also environment variables. Thus, LC_CTYPE is the macro name of a category and can also be the name of an environment variable.

POSIX.1-2024 defines six categories, all of which should be in the environment of most Unix systems that you might use. Some systems do not add them to the environment by default. The GNU C library, starting with version *glibc* 2.2, extends the set with six more categories.

Table 3-1 contains all of the categories present in the latest GNU/Linux distribution as of this writing, with an indication of whether it is part of POSIX or a GNU extension and a brief synopsis of what it controls.

Table 3-1: Locale Categories and Their Meanings

Category	Availability	Meaning
LC_COLLATE	POSIX.1-2024	Collation order (how characters are sorted)
LC_CTYPE	POSIX.1-2024	Character classification and case conversion, such as which characters are in the character set and what their classes are
LC_MESSAGES	POSIX.1-2024	Formats of informative and diagnostic messages and interactive responses
LC_MONETARY	POSIX.1-2024	Monetary formatting, such as currency symbols and conventions
LC_NUMERIC	POSIX.1-2024	Numeric, nonmonetary formatting
LC_TIME	POSIX.1-2024	Date and time formats
LC_ADDRESS	GLIBC-2.2	Formats of locations and geography-related items, such as names of places
LC_IDENTIFICATION	GLIBC-2.2	Metadata for the locale
LC_MEASUREMENT	GLIBC-2.2	Measurement systems (for example, metric vs. US customary units)
LC_NAME	GLIBC-2.2	Words used to address people (for example, "Frau," "Mme")
LC_PAPER	GLIBC-2.2	Dimensions of standard paper sizes (for example, US letter vs. A4)
LC_TELEPHONE	GLIBC-2.2	Formats used with telephone services

These 12 categories cover a broad spectrum of information. A few other environment variables, shown in Table 3-2, control the locale in addition to the categories listed in Table 3-1.

Table 3-2: Environment Variables That Affect the Locale Settings

Variable	Availability	Meaning
LC_ALL	POSIX.1-2024	Represents the set of all locale categories and has special meaning and precedence
LANG	POSIX.1-2024	Determines the locale category for native language, local customs, and coded character set in the absence of the LC_ALL and other LC_* variables
LANGUAGE	GLIBC-2.2	Used by the glibc function gettext in language translation
TZ	POSIX.1-2024	Time zone information
NLSPATH	POSIX.1-2024	A path variable (same format as PATH) used for finding message catalogs for translation to other languages
LOCPATH	POSIX.1-2024	A path variable for finding locale data files

The variables in Table 3-2 are not locale categories, but with the exception of TZ, they're used for managing locale information. For example, LC_ALL acts like a global locale setting, overriding the values of all locale variables; setting it to a specific locale assigns that locale to all of the categories, whether or not they were set to a specific locale.

The Section 7 man page also describes how to pass locale data to the setlocale() function and shows the declaration of the lconv struct that localeconv() returns. Although we'll eventually need to learn about these two functions, we'll visit them later in this chapter in "The Programming Interface to Locales" on page 138.

Before we explore how to manage locales at the user level, we need to understand a bit about time zones.

About Time Zones

The TZ environment variable listed in Table 3-1 stores the time zone associated with the current user, which is not necessarily the same as the system time zone. For example, a large institution such as a university or a corporation might have a Linux server that people can log in to from around the world. The server lives in its own time zone. Individual users can be in different time zones, and they can set their TZ variable to their own time zones, usually in their shell configuration files, such as ~/.bashrc. This way the programs that they run will use their time, not the time of the server.

We assign a string representation of the time zone to the TZ variable. For example, ":America/New York" is my time zone. To understand what values you can assign to it, you need to know how time zones are managed in Unix.

Time zone information is stored in a standardized binary format, defined by the Internet RFC 8536 standard. This format also includes information about daylight saving time.

The individual time zone files that contain this data are in the */usr/share/zoneinfo* directory. Most of the files there are directories, but some are plain files, and some are symbolic links. For example, it contains a directory named *America* and a directory named *Europe*, as well as a symbolic link named *Greenwich*. Each directory has ordinary files with the names of cities or regions. Each of these can be specified as a time zone, using the pathname starting in */usr/share/zoneinfo*. For example, under *Europe*, there's a file named *Paris* and another named *Dublin*. All of the following are valid assignments:

```
TZ=":Europe/Paris"
TZ=":Europe/Dublin"
TZ=":Greenwich"
```

There is a more complex way to assign time zone information to the TZ variable, but I don't describe it here. See the POSIX.1-2024 standard for more details.

We won't delve into the form of the system time zone files either. Fortunately for us, the C Library does all of the work to take time zone information into account. Those functions that return times and dates, other than those that specifically ignore time zones, such as gmtime(), all behave correctly without our needing to do anything special.

The Command-Level Interface to Locales

The search for man pages with which we started, apropos locale, returned references to two pages describing the locale command. One is in Section 1, and the other is in Section 1posix:

```
locale (1)          - get locale-specific information
locale (1posix)     - get locale-specific information
```

The POSIX page is a specification of what the command should do. The other page describes the command implemented on the system you're using. Both are useful, but let's see what the first page tells us:

```
$ man 1 locale
LOCALE(1)                       Linux User Manual                       LOCALE(1)


NAME
       locale - get locale-specific information

SYNOPSIS
       locale [option]
       locale [option] -a
       locale [option] -m
       locale [option] name...

DESCRIPTION
       The locale command displays information about the current locale, or
       all locales, on standard output.

       When invoked without arguments, locale displays the current locale
       settings for each locale category (see locale(5)), based on the
       settings of the environment variables that control the locale
       (see locale(7)). Values for variables set in the environment are
       printed without double quotes, implied values are printed with
       double quotes.
--snip--
```

Let's run it without arguments to see what it outputs (you'll likely see something different):

```
$ locale
LANG=en_US.UTF-8
LANGUAGE=en_US
LC_CTYPE=en_US.UTF-8
LC_NUMERIC=en_US.UTF-8
LC_TIME=en_US.UTF-8
LC_COLLATE=C.UTF-8
LC_MONETARY=en_US.UTF-8
LC_MESSAGES="en_US.UTF-8"
LC_PAPER=en_US.UTF-8
LC_NAME=en_US.UTF-8
```

```
LC_ADDRESS=en_US.UTF-8
LC_TELEPHONE=en_US.UTF-8
LC_MEASUREMENT=en_US.UTF-8
LC_IDENTIFICATION=en_US.UTF-8
LC_ALL=
```

On my system the locale is set to be en_US.UTF-8 for all but one category, LC_COLLATE, which is set to C.UTF-8. The LANG is en_US.UTF-8 as well. The LANGUAGE variable has the same value, but the name is the short form of it. The LC_ALL variable is assigned an empty string because if it were assigned a nonempty string, it would override the values for all other categories, which would prevent me, for example, from changing one category to a different value from the others.

Locale names are typically of the form

```
language[territory][.codeset][@modifier]
```

where *language* is an ISO 639 language code, *territory* is an ISO 3166 country code, *codeset* is a character set or encoding identifier such as ISO-8859-1 or UTF-8, and *modifier* is any string used to further refine the name.

In the locale name en_US.UTF-8, en is the English language, US is the United States, and UTF-8 is the codeset. It has no modifier.

A *codeset* is a mapping from graphical characters to numeric values. The numeric values are called *code points*, and codesets are also sometimes called *character maps* or *character sets*. For example, ASCII is an early codeset that maps the set of characters commonly found on old keyboards, as well as certain other nonprinting characters, to 7-bit unsigned integers. It does not map characters with diacritical marks or non-Latin characters.

The UTF-8 codeset is a variable-length codeset that is capable of representing all Unicode code points in anywhere from 1 to 4 bytes per point.

Unicode is a numeric representation of the alphabets of almost all known ancient and modern languages, including Japanese, Chinese, Greek, Cyrillic, Canadian Aboriginal, and Arabic. Appendix B contains a brief history and description of Unicode with detailed examples.

The locale command with the -a option outputs a list of the available locales on your system. This is a fragment of the output on my system, for example:

```
$ locale -a
C
C.utf8
POSIX
en_AG.utf8
en_AU.utf8
--snip--
fr_BE.utf8
fr_FR.utf8
pl_PL.utf8
--snip--
```

Except for the first three lines, these are the names of locales I've *generated* for my use, either temporarily to run some program under them or permanently as a locale in which I want to work. You can ignore the fact that the utf8 suffix is lowercase and doesn't have the hyphen. Codeset names are case-insensitive, and the hyphen is optional. The first three, C, C.utf8, and POSIX, are predefined locales. POSIX.1-2024 requires systems to have a POSIX locale and for it to be the default locale for all C programs. The C locale is the same as the POSIX locale if a system conforms to POSIX.1-2024, but if not, the latter is usually more extensively defined.

From the names of the locales listed in the previous example, you might be able to infer what they are, but if you add the -v option, you'll get much more detail. The following shows two examples of the details that you'd see:

```
$ locale -av
--snip--

locale: en_IE.utf8      archive: /usr/lib/locale/locale-archive
-------------------------------------------------------------------------------
     title | English locale for Ireland
    source | RAP
   address | Sankt Jørgens Alle 8, DK-1615 København V, Danmark
     email | bug-glibc-locales@gnu.org
  language | English
 territory | Ireland
  revision | 1.0
      date | 2000-06-29
   codeset | UTF-8


  --snip--

 locale: pl_PL.utf8      archive: /usr/lib/locale/locale-archive
-------------------------------------------------------------------------------
     title | Polish locale for Poland
    source | RAP
   address | Sankt Jørgens Alle 8, DK-1615 København V, Danmark
     email | bug-glibc-locales@gnu.org
  language | Polish
 territory | Poland
  revision | 1.0
      date | 2000-06-29
   codeset | UTF-8
```

You can change your locale to any of the ones this command lists by assigning the environment variables their full names. For example, if I change the LC_ALL variable to pl_PL.utf8, all of those functions and commands that are sensitive to the locale will use the Polish settings for my locale.

The locales locale -a lists are a small subset of those that you can generate. In some versions of Linux, the file */etc/locale.gen* contains a list of locales that you can generate by uncommenting them and rerunning the `locale-gen` command, provided that you have superuser privilege. After you do that, the locale's name will be in the list that `locale -a` displays.

The */etc/locale.gen* file typically contains several hundred locale names, mostly commented out. Linux maintains a list of all supported locales in the */usr/share/i18n/SUPPORTED* file. The exact path might vary depending on the particular Linux distribution that you're using.

The directory name *i18n* in this path is the abbreviation that people use for "internationalization" (that word has 18 letters starting with *i* and ending with *n*). That file usually has about as many entries as *etc/locale.gen*.

TEMPORARILY CHANGING THE ENVIRONMENT

In bash, you can precede a command with one or more variable assignments. If these variables are environment variables, the change in their value will be in effect only for the execution of that individual command, because a temporary environment is created with those changes and passed to a subshell in which the command is run.

To demonstrate, I'll run `date +"%c"` first and then set the time zone variable TZ to be the current time in Spain and override all other category settings using the territorial locale for Spain, `es_ES.utf-8`. Then I'll run `date +"%c"` again, so you can see the difference:

```
$ date +"%c"
Mon 06 Mar 2023 01:11:45 PM EST
$ TZ=Spain LC_ALL=es_ES.utf-8 date +"%c"
lun 06 mar 2023 18:11:47
```

The day `lun` is short for *Lunes*, the Spanish word for *Monday*, and `mar` is short for *marzo*, the word for *March*.

The Structure of Locales

The information associated with each given locale category is represented in a precise, structured format, specified by POSIX.1-2024. This makes it possible to write functions that use locale data and to create new locales for different regions. Since Section 5 of the man pages generally documents file formats and data structures in system and library interfaces, it's a good place to look for information about the format of locale data.

The locale man page in Section 5 describes the form and data of a *locale definition file*. Locale definitions are written in a markup language that resembles XML (Extensible Markup Language). They are given as input to the `localedef` command, which generates a compressed binary file with the same data. Programs that use locales read the binary data, not the locale definition files.

Different locale categories have different data, but their definition files all have the same form. Each is defined by its own set of *keywords* and associated values. The value for a keyword depends upon the keyword. To illustrate, I've included part of the actual definition file for the LC_NUMERIC category used by the en_US.utf8 locale. It's the smallest locale category:

```
LC_NUMERIC

decimal_point      "<period>"
thousands_sep      "<comma>"
grouping           "3;0"
--snip--
END LC_NUMERIC
```

Every file begins with the name of the category and ends with END *category name*. This category has three keywords: decimal_point, thousands_sep, and grouping. The first two values are self-explanatory. The value for grouping indicates that groups of three digits are separated by commas for all groups to the left of the decimal point. The first digit (3) is the size of the first group to the left of the decimal point. The second, 0, means that all groups to the left have 3 as well.

The LC_CTYPE category has much more extensive data. So that you can see how their definitions can vary, Listing 3-12 provides a fragment of a typical definition file for the en_US.utf8 locale.

```
escape_char    /
LC_CTYPE

upper   <A>;<B>;<C>;<D>;<E>;<F>;<G>;<H>;<I>;<J>;<K>;<L>;<M>;/
        <N>;<O>;<P>;<Q>;<R>;<S>;<T>;<U>;<V>;<W>;<X>;<Y>;<Z>
lower   <a>;<b>;<c>;<d>;<e>;<f>;<g>;<h>;<i>;<j>;<k>;<l>;<m>;/
        <n>;<o>;<p>;<q>;<r>;<s>;<t>;<u>;<v>;<w>;<x>;<y>;<z>
space   <tab>;<newline>;<vertical-tab>;<form-feed>;/
        <carriage-return>;<space>
cntrl   <alert>;<backspace>;<tab>;<newline>;<vertical-tab>;/
        <form-feed>;<carriage-return>;<NUL>;<SOH>;<STX>;/
        <ETX>;<SEL>;<RNL>;<DEL>;<GE>;<SPS>;<RPT>;<SI>;<SO>;<DLE>;<DC1>;/
        <DC2>;<DC3>;<RES>;<POC>;<CAN>;<EM>;<UBS>;<CU1>;<IFS>;/
        <IGS>;<IRS>;<ITB>;<DS>;<SOS>;<fs>;<WUS>;<BYP>;<LF>;/
        <ETB>;<ESC>;<SA>;<SM>;<CSP>;<MFA>;<ENQ>;<ACK>;/
        <SYN>;<IR>;<PP>;<TRN>;<NBS>;<EOT>;<SBS>;<IT>;<RFF>;/
        <CU3>;<DC4>;<NAK>;<SUB>
punct   <exclamation-mark>;<quotation-mark>;<number-sign>;<dollar-sign>;/
        <percent-sign>;<ampersand>;<apostrophe>;<left-parenthesis>;/
        <right-parenthesis>;<asterisk>;<plus-sign>;<comma>;/
        <hyphen-minus>;<period>;<slash>;<colon>;<semicolon>;/
        <less-than-sign>;<equals-sign>;<greater-than-sign>;/
        <question-mark>;<commercial-at>;<left-square-bracket>;/
```

```
        <backslash>;<right-square-bracket>;<circumflex>;/
        <underscore>;<grave-accent>;<left-curly-bracket>;/
        <vertical-line>;<right-curly-bracket>;<tilde>
digit   <zero>;<one>;<two>;<three>;<four>;/
        <five>;<six>;<seven>;<eight>;<nine>
--snip--
tolower (<A>,<a>);(<B>,<b>);(<C>,<c>);(<D>,<d>);(<E>,<e>);/
        (<F>,<f>);(<G>,<g>);(<H>,<h>);(<I>,<i>);(<J>,<j>);/
        (<K>,<k>);(<L>,<l>);(<M>,<m>);(<N>,<n>);(<O>,<o>);/
        (<P>,<p>);(<Q>,<q>);(<R>,<r>);(<S>,<s>);(<T>,<t>);/
        (<U>,<u>);(<V>,<v>);(<W>,<w>);(<X>,<x>);(<Y>,<y>);(<Z>,<z>)
--snip--
END LC_CTYPE
```

Listing 3-12: A locale definition file for the English language in the United States

Notice the syntax that's used for defining the keyword values in this category. The `tolower` keyword provides the data that functions would need to convert uppercase to lowercase, so it's a semicolon-separated sequence of pairs that essentially defines a function that maps characters to characters. In contrast, the `digit` keyword's value is just a list of the names of the decimal digits that we use in the United States.

If you want to know what the keywords and values are for a locale category, you could read the documentation, but fortunately, the `locale -k` command will list them. Give it the name of the category, and it outputs a list:

```
$ locale -k LC_TIME
abday="Sun;Mon;Tue;Wed;Thu;Fri;Sat"
day="Sunday;Monday;Tuesday;Wednesday;Thursday;Friday;Saturday"
abmon="Jan;Feb;Mar;Apr;May;Jun;Jul;Aug;Sep;Oct;Nov;Dec"
mon="January;February;March;April;May;June;July;August;September;October;
     November;December"
am_pm="AM;PM"
d_t_fmt="%a %d %b %Y %r %Z"
d_fmt="%m/%d/%Y"
t_fmt="%r"
t_fmt_ampm="%I:%M:%S %p"
--snip--
```

You can also give it a keyword. To see the format used by `date`, enter the following:

```
$ locale -ck date_fmt
LC_TIME
date_fmt="%a %b %e %r %Z %Y"
```

The -c option prints the locale category, in this case LC_TIME, on a separate line. With the -k *keyword* option, locale prints the supplied keyword and its value, in this case date_fmt and its value, %a %b %e %r %Z %Y. Consulting Table C-1 in

Appendix C, we can verify that this is what date prints, but we can also enter that command to double-check:

```
$ date +"%a %b %e %r %Z %Y"
Wed Mar 26 03:43:21 PM EDT 2025
$ date
Wed Mar 26 03:43:30 PM EDT 2025
```

You can see that date with no format outputs exactly the same fields as the format string "%a %b %e %r %Z %Y".

The Programming Interface to Locales

We started this exploration of locales partly so that we could internationalize the spl_date program. When we read the locale(7) man page, it mentioned the setlocale() function. Let's see what its man page says about it:

```
$ man setlocale
SETLOCALE(3)                  Linux Programmer's Manual                  SETLOCALE(3)

NAME
       setlocale - set the current locale

SYNOPSIS
       #include <locale.h>
       char *setlocale(int category, const char *locale);

DESCRIPTION
       The setlocale() function is used to set or query the program's current
       locale.
--snip--
```

This is a library function for setting a program's locale, as well as finding out what locale is in effect for it. Its first parameter is the category name. If the second parameter is NULL, it doesn't change the locale, but returns the name of the locale currently assigned to the passed-in category. If the second parameter is the full name of the locale, such as "en_US.UTF-8", it will set the category's value to that locale; otherwise, it returns NULL. If the second parameter is an empty string (""), setlocale() will set the category's value to the locale setting it finds in the current environment.

The rule it uses depends on the version of Unix that you're running. In GNU/Linux, the steps for deciding which locale to assign to the category in the first parameter when the second is an empty string are as follows:

1. If there is a non-NULL environment variable LC_ALL, the value of LC_ALL is used.

2. If an environment variable with the same name as the category exists and is non-NULL, its value is used.

3. If there is a non-NULL environment variable LANG, the value of LANG is used.

A program must call `setlocale()` in order for it to be internationalized. In the absence of a call to this function, the program will use the "C" locale. If it calls `setlocale(LC_ALL, "")`, it will assign to all categories the value of the locale it determined from the steps listed previously. If the program uses library functions whose behavior is dependent on the locale, they will use the values that `setlocale()` determined. Therefore, calling `setlocale()` is the first step in internationalizing your programs. For spl_date, it's the only step we need to take.

An Internationalized Version of the spl_date Program

The program *spl_date4.c* is an internationalized version of *spl_date3.c*. The only change needed is to insert a call to `setlocale()` into main() before calls to any other library functions, right before the option-handling code.

The man page for `strftime()` states that the only environment variables that it uses are TZ and LC_TIME. In other words, it uses the time zone setting in TZ, and it uses the values of the keywords in the LC_TIME category to format the time, based on the format specification that we pass to it.

We don't need to do anything for the program to report the correct time for the user's time zone, because we assume that when the user set up their account, they supplied their time zone, which was stored in the TZ environment variable. If not, the time zone defaults to the system's time zone, which is usually stored in */etc/timezone* or in a file to which */etc/timezone* is a soft link.

Therefore, we'll call `setlocale()`, passing LC_TIME as its first argument rather than LC_ALL. We could pass it LC_ALL if we thought it might influence the behavior of other functions in our program, but in this case it isn't necessary:

```
if ( setlocale(LC_TIME, "") == NULL )
    fatal_error(LOCALE_ERROR,
                "setlocale() could not set the given locale");
```

The program doesn't save the return value, but it checks whether it's NULL, which is returned if the locale couldn't be set. If we want to save the name of the locale for later use, we copy it into a local string variable.

Because the program is nearly identical to *spl_date3.c*, Listing 3-13 contains only the part of it containing the updated code. The complete program is in the source code distribution for the book.

spl_date4.c
```
#define _GNU_SOURCE
#include <locale.h>
#include "common_hdrs.h"
--snip-- // OMITTED: Definitions of other macros, parse_time_adjustment(),
       //           and adjust_time()

int main(int argc, char *argv[])
{
    --snip-- // OMITTED: Variable declarations
```

```
    char *mylocale;
    if ( (mylocale = setlocale(LC_TIME, "")) == NULL )
        fatal_error(LOCALE_ERROR,
                    "setlocale() could not set the given locale");
    while ( TRUE ) {
    --snip-- // OMITTED: Rest of main program
}
```

Listing 3-13: The internationalized spl_date *program, with most code omitted*

Let's see how this program behaves. We'll run it under several different locales, leaving the time zone unchanged, and with both the default format and a custom format:

```
$ LC_TIME=da_DK.utf8 ./spl_date4
ons 26 mar 2025 15:50:40 EDT
$ LC_TIME=da_DK.utf8 ./spl_date4 "+%A, %d %B %Y"
onsdag, 26 marts 2025
$ LC_TIME=de_DE.utf8 ./spl_date4 "+%A, %d %B %Y"
Mittwoch, 26 März 2025
$ LC_TIME=es_ES.utf8 ./spl_date4 "+%A, %d %B %Y"
miércoles, 26 marzo 2025
$ LC_TIME=fi_FI.utf8 ./spl_date4
ke 26. maaliskuuta 2025 15.56.07
$ LC_TIME=fi_FI.utf8 ./spl_date4 "+%A, %d %B %Y"
keskiviikko, 26 maaliskuu 202
$ LC_TIME=fr_FR.utf8 ./spl_date4
mer. 26 mars 2025 15:57:15
$ LC_TIME=ja_JP.utf8 ./spl_date4
2025年03月26日 15時57分40秒
$ LC_TIME=ja_JP.utf8 ./spl_date4 "+%A, %d %B %Y"
水曜日, 26 3月 2025
```

This final version of spl_date is able to display dates and times following the conventions of a wide range of geographic locales. In the end, enabling this feature required only a small modification to the previous program, but understanding why and how it works was the real goal. Now, we'll turn our attention to other aspects of internationalization.

Other Ways to Internationalize Programs

The System Interfaces section of the POSIX.1-2024 standard specifies which functions in the C library should take locale information into account and which parts of the locale they should use. In general, a library implementation in a Unix system may or may not conform to these requirements. For the most part, the GNU C Library in Linux meets the standard's requirements and goes beyond them by providing some features not specified in POSIX.1-2024. Here we limit discussion to the GNU C Library's internationalization features.

The underlying philosophy of the GNU C Library is that the programmer should be freed as much as possible from the burden of handling internationalization. If a program sets its locale using `setlocale()` or one of a few other similar functions I haven't mentioned yet, before calling any library functions, all of the functions that are designed to use locale data will modify their behavior according to the locale's rules.

This reduces our problem to knowing which functions use locale information and which locale categories they use. Unfortunately, the documentation doesn't contain a complete list of precisely those library functions that use locale information, so I'll provide some guidance that overcomes this deficiency. Following is a list of functions that do use locale data:

fprintf()	islower()	iswcntrl()	iswupper()	strcoll()	toupper()
fscanf()	isprint()	iswctype()	iswxdigit()	strerror()	towlower()
isalnum()	ispunct()	iswdigit()	isxdigit()	strfmon()	towupper()
isalpha()	isspace()	iswgraph()	mblen()	strftime()	wcscoll()
isblank()	isupper()	iswlower()	mbstowcs()	strsignal()	wcstod()
iscntrl()	iswalnum()	iswprint()	mbtowc()	strtod()	wcstombs()
isdigit()	iswalpha()	iswpunct()	perror()	strxfrm()	wcsxfrm()

Most of these use data from either the `LC_CTYPE` or `LC_COLLATE` category, but some also use `LC_NUMERIC`, `LC_TIME`, or `LC_MONETARY`. Their man pages specify which of these categories the function uses, either by naming which locale-specific environment variables it uses or by stating that the function uses the locale in a specific way. You can search for the keyword *locale* or the pattern `LC_` in the page using the pager's search operator `/` followed by the keyword, as in **/LC_** to jump to the part of the page that references these terms.

If this list isn't accessible and you can't remember which functions use the locale, refer to the `SEE ALSO` section of the Info page for `setlocale()` or visit the POSIX.1-2024 website page for it at *https://pubs.opengroup.org/onlinepubs/9699919799/functions/setlocale.html*, where many of the functions are listed.

The `strcoll()` function is worth singling out. Here's its prototype:

```
int strcoll(const char *s1, const char *s2);
```

It compares two strings, s1 and s2, and returns a negative integer if s1 < s2, zero if s1 == s2, and a positive integer if s1 > s2.

Most people use `strcmp()` for comparing two strings in C. Its prototype is the same, but `strcmp()` doesn't use locale data in its comparisons, which means that sorting algorithms based on `strcmp()` won't sort according to the true ordering of characters in the user's locale.

In contrast, `strcoll()` does use the locale's `LC_COLLATE` data. The following program demonstrates its use:

strcoll_demo.c
```
#define _GNU_SOURCE
#include "common_hdrs.h" /* Includes <locale.h> */

int main(int argc, char *argv[])
```

```
{
    char *smallest;
    char  usage_msg[256];
    int   i = 1, j;

    if ( argc < 3 ) {
        sprintf(usage_msg, "%s string string ...\n", basename(argv[0]));
        usage_error(usage_msg);
    }
    if ( NULL == setlocale(LC_COLLATE, "") )
        fatal_error(LOCALE_ERROR,
                    "setlocale() could not set the given locale");
    smallest = argv[i];
    for ( j = i + 1; j < argc; j++ )
        if ( strcoll(smallest, argv[j]) > 0 )
            smallest = argv[j];
    printf("%s\n", smallest);
    return 0;
}
```

If we compile and run this program, setting a different temporary locale for
each run, we see how it behaves:

```
$ LC_COLLATE=C ./strcoll_demo Zebra lion camel ape
Zebra
$ LC_COLLATE=en_US.utf8 ./strcoll_demo Zebra lion camel ape
ape
```

The C locale uses the ASCII ordering of characters, with all uppercase preceding all lowercase. In contrast, the en_US.utf8 locale sorting order is case-
insensitive. If, in *strcoll_demo.c*, we replaced strcoll() with strcmp() and ran
this program, in both locales the output would be Zebra, showing that strcmp()
doesn't use locale data.

Sometimes no library function can handle the problem you're trying to
solve in a locale-sensitive way. In that case, you need to access locale data directly. The library has ways to do this. When we first searched for functions
to internationalize our spl_date program by entering apropos locale, the output listed a few library functions that we overlooked. We'll search again but
limit the search to Section 3:

```
$ apropos -s3 locale
--snip--
localeconv (3)        - get numeric formatting information
localeconv (3posix)   - return locale-specific information
--snip--
nl_langinfo (3)       - query language and locale information
nl_langinfo_l (3)     - query language and locale information
--snip--
```

I removed lines that aren't relevant.

The `localeconv()` and `nl_langinfo()` functions can each be used for obtaining information about the values of keywords in the current locale of the calling program. If you read their man pages, you'll learn that the difference between them is that `localeconv()` returns all of the information available in the locale in one very large data structure, `struct iconv`, whereas `nl_langinfo()` is given a keyword from a locale category and returns the value of that particular keyword. The GNU C Library Reference Manual calls `nl_langinfo()` *pinpoint access* to the locale.

The `localeconv()` function is more portable than `nl_langinfo()`, but it's slow because it has to gather all of the locale data, it isn't extensible, and it's not general enough, since it gives access to only `LC_MONETARY` and `LC_NUMERIC` data. In contrast, `nl_langinfo()` also provides extensive access to information from the `LC_TIME` category and limited access to `LC_MESSAGES`.

Here's a simple example that uses `nl_langinfo()` to print the days of the week in the language of the current locale:

nl_langinfo *_demo1.c*

```
#define _GNU_SOURCE
#include <langinfo.h>
#include "common_hdrs.h"

int main(int argc, char *argv[])
{
    char *mylocale;
    if ( (mylocale = setlocale(LC_TIME, "")) == NULL )
        fatal_error(LOCALE_ERROR,
                    "setlocale() could not set the given locale");
    printf("The current locale is %s\n", mylocale);

    /* DAY_1 is a keyword defined in langinfo.h. When passed to nl_langinfo,
       the function returns the name of the first day of the week in the
       current locale. The second day is DAY_2, and so on. Because they are
       consecutive integers, we can increment to advance through them. */
    for ( int dayofweek = DAY_1; dayofweek < DAY_1+7; dayofweek++ )
        printf("%s\n", nl_langinfo(dayofweek));
    return 0;
}
```

This program uses the knowledge that the keywords `DAY_1`, `DAY_2`, and so on are integers with consecutive values of an enumeration type, defined in the header file *langinfo.h*, so that we could loop through the keywords.

We compile and run the program, changing the locale to see its effect:

```
$ LC_ALL=es_ES.utf8 ./nl_langinfo_demo1
The current locale is es_ES.utf8  # Spanish in Spain
domingo
lunes
martes
miércoles
jueves
```

```
viernes
sábado
$ LC_ALL=da_DK.utf8 ./nl_langinfo_demo1
The current locale is da_DK.utf8  # Danish in Denmark
søndag
mandag
tirsdag
onsdag
torsdag
fredag
lørdag
```

The nl_langinfo() function can access many other keywords, which makes it possible to write your own functions that are locale-sensitive, provided that they depend only on the categories of data that they are able to retrieve.

Locale Objects

Although it's an advanced topic, I'll briefly describe the manipulation of locales. You might at some point decide that you want to create your own custom locales. A *locale object* is an object of type locale_t. Locale objects can be created by two functions: newlocale() and duplocale(). These functions were added to the locale interface as multithreading became more common in software. Individual threads in a process can call them to create locale objects independently, so that each can have its own locale. However, even a single-threaded process can call them to create create multiple locales between which it can switch.

The synopsis for newlocale() is as follows:

```
#include <locale.h>
locale_t newlocale(int category_mask, const char *locale, locale_t base);
```

The first parameter, category_mask, is a set of the locale categories you want to modify, such as LC_TIME. To modify more than one, you give it a bitwise-OR of category names, such as LC_TIME | LC_NUMERIC. The second parameter, locale, is the string name for the locale that you want to apply to this category, such as es_ES.utf8. The last parameter, base, is the locale object that you want to modify. If base is the value (locale_t) 0, meaning the value zero typecast to type locale_t, then a new locale object is created; otherwise, the locale object in base is modified.

This function allows you to process different categories of locale data in one locale and then process other data in a different locale during a computation. The program in Listing 3-14, based on the example from the newlocale() man page, demonstrates how to use it. It expects two locale names on the command line. It combines the LC_NUMERIC settings of the first one and the LC_TIME settings of the second one in a new locale object. It also uses the uselocale() function, whose prototype is:

```
#include <locale.h>
locale_t uselocale(locale_t newloc);
```

The uselocale() function is given a locale object and makes it the locale for the calling thread, in this case the entire process, and returns the locale object in use before the call. Comments in the program are mostly omitted to save space. The fully documented program is in the book's source code distribution.

newlocale
_demo.c

```c
#define _XOPEN_SOURCE 700
#include "common_hdrs.h"
#define TESTNUM 123456789.12        /* Number to test locale       */
#define BASE0 ((locale_t) 0)

int main(int argc, char *argv[])
{
    time_t    t;                    /* To store current time       */
    struct tm *tm;                  /* To store broken-down time   */
    char      buf[100];             /* To store formatted time string */
    char      err_msg[STRING_MAX];  /* For error messages          */
    locale_t  loc, newloc;          /* Temporary locale objects    */

    if ( argc < 2 ) {
        sprintf(err_msg, "Usage: %s locale1 [locale2]\n", argv[0]);
        usage_error(err_msg);
    }
    if ( (loc = newlocale(LC_NUMERIC_MASK, argv[1], BASE0)) == BASE0 )
        fatal_error(EXIT_FAILURE, "newlocale");

    if ( argc > 2 ) {
        if ( (newloc = newlocale(LC_TIME_MASK, argv[2], loc)) == BASE0 )
            fatal_error(EXIT_FAILURE, "newlocale");
        loc = newloc;
    }
    uselocale(loc);
    printf("With numeric settings of %s, number is: %'8.2f\n", argv[1],
            TESTNUM);
    t = time(NULL);
    if ( (tm = localtime(&t)) == NULL )
        fatal_error(EXIT_FAILURE, "localtime");
    if ( 0 == strftime(buf, sizeof(buf), "%c", tm) )
        fatal_error(EXIT_FAILURE, "strftime");
    printf("With time settings of %s, date/time is: %s\n", argv[2], buf);

    uselocale(LC_GLOBAL_LOCALE);    /* loc is no longer in use. */
    freelocale(loc);                /* Release storage for loc. */
    return 0;
}
```

Listing 3-14: A program that uses newlocale() to create a custom locale object

Notice that the last step this program takes is to change the process's locale to `LC_GLOBAL_LOCALE` and then free the locale object that it created. The locale object was allocated memory by `newlocale()`. We need to free that memory. The `NOTES` section of the `newlocale()` man page indicates that our programs must free that memory using `freelocale()`, but we can't free it if it's in use, so we change locale to `LC_GLOBAL_LOCALE`, which is not a real locale object; it's a special value that can't be used as a locale.

To illustrate how this program works, here's a run with the numeric settings from Spain and the date and time settings from Japan:

```
$ ./newlocale_demo es_ES.utf8 ja_JP.utf8
With numeric settings of es_ES.utf8, number is: 123.456.789,12
With time settings of ja_JP.utf8, date/time is: 2023年09月25日 09時55分36秒
```

The GNU C Library includes functions that explicitly use locale objects as parameters. They're easily recognized because their names end in `_l` and they're documented on the same man pages as their non-`_l` counterparts. For example, `isalpha()` and `isalpha_l()` share a man page. Whereas the `isalpha()` function implicitly uses the locale set by a call to `setlocale()` or `uselocale()`, `isalpha_l()` is passed a locale object explicitly in its last parameter. This allows different threads of a process to use different locale objects. These functions were added to the POSIX standard in 2008, but not all systems support them. To use them, you need to provide a feature test macro in your programs. The man pages contain the specific macros that you need, depending on which function you want to use.

Summary

The hands-on approach we use for learning how to write system programs is to try to write programs that are similar to existing commands, researching those commands to understand which resources they use and how they use them. Because all of the projects that we develop share a core of common code, in this chapter we showed what that code is, how it's organized, and how we'll incorporate it into our projects. We chose to start by implementing a simplified version of the `date` command because that command doesn't use system resources other than access to the system clock. Through a search of the man pages, we learned that we needed the `time()` system call and the `localtime()` and `strftime()` library functions to implement `date`. We went through a few incremental revisions of the program to demonstrate how to add optional formats, how to add the user option to display dates other than the current one, and finally, how to internationalize the program.

Learning how to internationalize the `date` program allowed us to explore the more general subject of internationalization. We explored the concept of a locale, studying the kinds of data that it encapsulates, the commands available for viewing and manipulating them, and the programming interface to them as specified by the POSIX standards and as implemented in

GNU/Linux. In particular, the GNU/Linux C Library has many functions that are locale-aware and several functions for extracting information from locale objects.

Exercises

1. Write a program that expects one or more hexadecimal numbers on the command line and, for each number, prints its value as a decimal integer, one per line. If any argument is not a valid hexadecimal number or has trailing characters that aren't hexadecimal digits, it should display `not a valid number` for that word. It should allow a leading `0x` or `0X` but not require it. For example, if the executable is named `hex2int`, it should work like this:

```
$ ./hex2int 0xa b 0xf00 foo abe
a = 10
b = 11
f00 = 3840
foo: not a valid number
abe = 2750
```

2. Write a program that sorts the words entered on the command line and prints them on the standard output, one per line. It should sort according to the collating sequence of the user's locale. A word is any sequence of characters other than whitespace. (Hint: You'll need to store the words in an array.)

3. Read the man page for `strtod()`, the function that parses floating-point decimals and returns their values. Based on that page, write a function named `get_longdbl()` with the prototype

```
int get_longdbl(char *arg, int flags, long double *value, char *msg);
```

that stores into `value` the numeric value of its first argument. Based on the possible error value, design a set of flags to pass to this function to control what should constitute an error versus just a warning, such as whether it has trailing characters or is negative or too large.

4. Write a program named `yearday2date` that, when given an integer argument, returns the date in the current year that it represents in the format *<Monthname> <dayofmonth>, <current year>*. January 1 is always day one of a year. For example, if you entered `yearday2date 100` in the year 1970, a non-leap year, it would print `March 10, 1970`. If the number is zero, it should report an error. If the number is greater than the number of days in the current year, it should calculate the date in the future, and if it is negative, it should calculate the date in the past. For example, if you ran it in 1970, `yearday2date -1` should print `December 31, 1969` and `yearday2date -365` should print `January 1, 1969`. (Hint: Read the man page for `mktime()`.)

5. The `locale` command without any arguments or options prints out the values of the categories in the current locale. Write a program that does this. This program will be very easy if you examine the source code in the file */usr/include/langinfo.h*. You'll see that a macro is defined there to make this easy.

6. Modify the `parse_time_adjustment()` function from the chapter so that it rejects tokens that contain valid time units as strict substrings. For example, it should reject *megaday* and *saturday* as day time units and only allow *day* and *days*.

4

BASIC CONCEPTS OF FILE I/O

One of the most fundamental operations that system programs perform is the transfer of data to and from files. The transfer of data from a file to the memory space of a process is called *file input*, and the transfer in the opposite direction is called *file output*. Together, they're called *file I/O*. Because most system programs perform file I/O and because even the simplest of problems will require our programs to perform it as well, we study it next.

Our primary objectives in this chapter are to explain the issues and concepts related to accessing files in Unix and to demonstrate how to use the file-handling part of the kernel API. In addition, we'll explore file-handling issues that impact the performance and portability of the programs we write.

We start with an overview of the Unix I/O model and then cover some key background concepts related to file permissions and processes in order to understand how Unix decides whether a process is allowed to access a file in a particular way. Following this, we examine in detail the elementary parts of the Unix kernel API related to file I/O. We'll implement a simplified version of the `cp` command, and we'll consider how various design decisions affect its overall performance.

High-Level vs. Low-Level File I/O

High-level language libraries usually provide many different functions to perform I/O conveniently. In previous chapters, we saw examples of these, such as `scanf()` and `printf()` for input and output of textual data. Functions like these are often sufficient to solve some problems, but for other problems they aren't suitable, either because they don't give us enough control over how a read or write operation should be performed or because our program needs to work with data that isn't plaintext. In addition, the cost of their convenience is usually longer running time compared to what's possible using system calls directly. If a program is not going to read or write large amounts of data, it may not matter how fast it transfers data, but it does make a big difference in performance when we want our programs to handle large datasets. Therefore, it's important to know how to use the lower-level functions for file I/O provided by the kernel.

Universal I/O

From its inception, Unix employed a *universal* model of I/O. As Ritchie and Thompson wrote in 1974, "the system calls to do I/O are designed to eliminate the differences between the various devices and styles of access" [33]. In other words, the same system calls that are used to perform I/O on disk files are also used on all other types of files, including device files. A program that can read from or write to disk files can also read from or write to devices such as terminals, network interfaces, and peripheral devices. From a program's perspective, there's no distinction between random access devices, such as disks, and sequential access devices, such as tapes.

Unix frees you as a programmer from needing to know the details of devices such as disks, tapes, network interfaces, and terminals, allowing you to write programs that transfer data to or from any of them. This is why Unix is said to provide device-independent I/O. You don't need to understand how the kernel performs this magic in order to write a system program, but we'll explain a bit about how it does so in Chapter 6.

File Permissions Revisited

The online chapter "Working in the Command Line Interface" introduces the concept of file permissions in Unix. Now we introduce one more key concept that comes into play in the context of file creation, namely the file creation mask.

Every process has a *file creation mask*, which is a set of 9 bits that restricts which permissions are enabled when the process creates a file. The file creation mask is commonly called a *umask*. Because this name is shorter, we'll call it a umask henceforth.

When a process calls a function that creates a file, that file is given an initial set of permissions, such as who can read it, who can write to it, and so on. Functions that create files usually have a mode argument that lets the process set those initial permissions, but the umask is applied to the mode that the process tries to put on the file, possibly removing some permissions specified by that mode. The resulting initial permissions set on the file are what the process attempted to set on it, minus those that the umask removed.

Applying the Umask

The umask is essentially an inverted mask: a 1-bit in the umask disables the corresponding permission in the created file, but a 0-bit in the umask does not disable the corresponding permission in the file if the process tries to enable it. We can view a umask's 9 bits as three groups of 3 bits each, corresponding to the permission bits in the file mode. For example, the umask

```
000010010
```

can be viewed as

```
000 010 010
```

The first group controls user permissions, the second controls group permissions, and the third controls others permissions:

```
0 0 0    0 1 0    0 1 0
r w x    r w x    r w x
user     group    others
```

Because an octal digit is equivalent to three binary digits, octal numbers are used to represent umask values. The previous umask value is octal 022, for example.

When a process calls a function to create a file with a mode of *mode*, the system applies the umask to it using the bitwise C operation (*mode* & ~*umask*). In other words, the umask is inverted and bitwise-ANDed to the mode. For example, suppose that *mode* is 110110010 and *umask* is octal 022, or binary 000010010. The complement of *umask* in binary is 111101101. The operation is thus

```
  110 110 010
& 111 101 101
= 110 100 000
```

Interpreting this as a permission string, it gives the user read and write permission, the group only read permission, and no permissions on the file to anyone else. The umask value 022 is a common value because it disables writing to a file by anyone other than its owner, but it doesn't limit reading. If we wanted an even more secure value that prevented reading by others for every created file, we'd set the process's umask to octal 066, or binary

000110110. The complement of 066 is 111001001, and applying it to the previous mode

```
   110 110 010
&  111 001 001
=  110 000 000
```

disables read and write by anyone except the user. Some people find it easier to apply a umask using a modified form of subtraction in which 0 − 1 = 0. The original, noninverted umask is subtracted from the mode as in:

```
   110 110 010
-  000 110 110
=  110 000 000
```

When we treat its application as a form of subtraction, it's easier to remember that the umask acts like a filter that removes permissions.

Setting and Getting Umasks

When you log in to a Unix system, the shell started up for you is assigned an initial default value for the umask, often octal 022. This default value depends on the operating system and the shell. You can view your umask with the umask command. To see the octal value of the umask, enter:

```
$ umask
0022
```

This shows that the umask value is octal 022. The first 0 means the following digits are octal.

If you want to see the permissions that are *not masked* by the umask in symbolic form, use the -S option:

```
$ umask -S
u=rwx,g=rx,o=rx
```

This shows that the umask doesn't mask out any permissions for the user because u=rwx, and it doesn't mask out read and execute permissions for anyone else (g=rx,o=rx).

You can use the umask command to change the umask by giving it a umask value argument:

```
$ umask
0022
$ umask 033
$ umask
0033
```

You can put a umask command into one of your shell configuration files if you want the shell's umask to be something other than the default value.

For example, in bash, you could add the following lines into your *.bashrc* file if you want every interactive shell to use that umask:

```
# Set my umask to turn off group writes; others: no read, no write
umask 026
```

All shells that start up when you open a terminal window are interactive and read that file. If you put them into your *.bash_profile* file, then only the login shell will use that umask.

Propagating Umasks

Whenever you run a process from the command line, its umask is inherited from the shell, so unless that process changes its umask, its value will be the one your shell had when you ran that command. Any processes created by that process will also have that umask, so the umask propagates downward to every process running on your behalf, unless one of these processes changes it.

A process can change its umask with the umask() system call. In Chapter 11, we'll go over examples of programs in which processes change their umasks.

A Process's User IDs

File permissions exist to control which users can access files and how they can access them. The only way that a user can actually access a file is by running a command or a program, which is to say, running a process. Therefore, file permissions must determine which user processes can access files and how they can access them.

The essential idea that underlies how permissions are used is that every process is associated with at least one user ID. To be precise, on Linux, every process has four user IDs:

- A real user ID
- An effective user ID
- A saved set-user-ID
- A filesystem user ID, which is Linux specific

On most Unix systems, the kernel uses the effective user ID when it needs to determine whether to grant a process permission to access a resource, such as memory, or to access files. On Linux, it uses the filesystem user ID to determine access to files, but the filesystem user ID is always equal to the effective user ID, the result being that it too uses the effective user ID.

Normally, when you run a program, the process that's created is assigned an effective user ID and a real user ID that are both equal to your user ID and thus the same. Sometimes, however, a process can have different effective and real user IDs. Usually, when they're different, the effective user ID gives the program greater privileges than the real user ID. A program can be run in such a way that the effective user ID of the running process is not that of the user who runs it, but is instead the user ID of the owner of the program file. In the next section, we explain what makes this possible.

The setuid Bit

The file mode contains 12 bits, of which the highest-order bit is a bit named the *setuid* bit. In Chapter 6, I'll explain more about all of the mode bits. If this bit is set, or enabled, for a file containing an executable program, then when a user who doesn't own the file runs that program, the process will have an effective user ID that is different from its real user ID. Specifically, whenever the program is run, the created process has an effective user ID equal to the user ID of the owner of the program file and a real user ID equal to the user ID of the user that ran the program. You can see whether the setuid bit is enabled with the ls -l command. When it's set for a file, the permission string that ls -l displays will have an s instead of an x for the user's execute permission letter.

Programs with the setuid bit enabled often have a need to temporarily change their effective user ID to the real user ID and then restore the effective user ID to what it was. The purpose of the saved set-user-ID is to store the effective user ID in such programs for later retrieval. Programs that modify their effective user IDs are called *setuid programs*.

A good example to illustrate these concepts is the passwd command. The passwd command is usually contained in the */usr/bin/passwd* file. If we view the permissions on that file using ls -l /usr/bin/passwd, we see:

```
-rwsr-xr-x 1 root    root        59976 Nov 24 07:05 passwd
```

The s in the permission string indicates that the setuid bit is on. The file is owned by root, whose user ID is 0. When we run the passwd command, its effective user ID will be 0, but its real user ID will be our own user ID.

Try this experiment: Open two terminal windows, and in one, run the passwd command without entering anything. In the second terminal, look at the passwd process's status by entering ps -o euid,ruid,pid,args -C passwd. This command displays the effective and real user IDs, the process ID, and the command name for every running instance of passwd. You'll see that the real and effective user IDs are different:

```
$ ps -o euid, ruid, pid, args -C passwd
 EUID  RUID    PID COMMAND
    0   500  14561 passwd
```

The column labeled EUID is the effective user ID, and the RUID column is the real user ID. The RUID column will contain your actual user ID. When you're finished, press CTRL-D twice in the terminal with the passwd program waiting for input. It will terminate without making any changes to your password.

The role of a process's credentials in file input and output should now be clear. A process can access only files for which it has permission to do so.

This is determined by the file's permissions and the effective user ID of the running process.

Input/Output Mechanics

Before a process can access a file, it needs to establish a connection to that file in order to communicate with it. A *connection* is an object that manages and controls a process's access to the file. It contains data such as the *file offset*, also called the *file pointer*, which is the offset in the file at which the next operation takes place, various flags and mode bits that control the manner in which operations are performed, information to locate the file, and pointers to kernel functions that the process can invoke. To create this object, a process must *open* the file. In fact, the POSIX specifications call the connection object an *open file description (OFD)*, which is the term we'll use here.

In Unix, a process can open a file to access it in one of three modes:

Read mode   Exclusively to read from it

Write mode   Exclusively to write to it

Read/write mode   To both read and write

These are called the *access modes* of the opened file. The access mode is one of the items stored in the OFD.

The operation that opens a file returns an identifier that serves as a reference to the newly created OFD. This identifier is called a *file descriptor*. A file descriptor is a typically small, nonnegative integer. Once you've opened a file and have a file descriptor for the connection, you must pass that descriptor to all subsequent operations on that file.

Traditionally, Unix systems did not prevent multiple processes from opening the same file, and POSIX codified that behavior. POSIX-conforming systems allow multiple processes to access the same file at the same time, which is an important feature of Unix. It's why it is possible for multiple users to run the same command or change their passwords at the same time. In fact, a single process can open the same file multiple times as well. Unix systems do provide locking mechanisms so that a process can prevent other processes from opening a file while it's accessing it.

Each open operation on the file creates a distinct open file description for that file and returns to its caller a unique file descriptor for that description. A process may also have multiple file descriptors that refer to a single OFD because Unix provides a means by which a process can duplicate the descriptor that refers to an OFD, so that the new descriptor and the original both point to the same OFD. We'll study the duplication of file descriptors in Chapter 13, and we'll examine the various data structures that the kernel uses for terminal I/O in Chapter 18.

Figure 4-1 depicts a portion of the tables and data structures created to manage I/O operations on files.

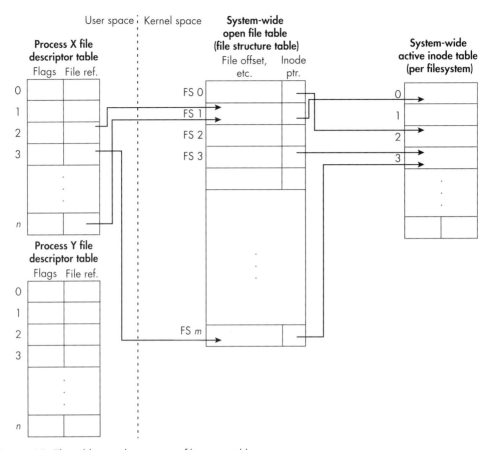

Figure 4-1: The tables used to manage files opened by processes

Figure 4-1 shows the kernel's in-memory *open file table*, also known as the *file structure table*. Open file descriptors point to entries in this table. The entries in this table have many members, among which is a pointer to the inode that represents the actual file. In Figure 4-1, Process X has two open files with OFDs at locations 1 and *m*. It duplicated a descriptor (2) so that descriptors 2 and *n* point to the same OFD at index 1 in the file structure table. Process Y and Process X each opened the file with inode 3, so they have two different OFDs at locations *m* and 3, respectively, pointing to it.

When a program has finished all reading and writing and no longer needs access to the file, it needs to *close* it. Closing the file breaks the connection between the program and the file. It frees the file descriptor, so that it no longer refers to the OFD. If there are no other descriptors pointing to the OFD, the resources used for the OFD are freed and the OFD is removed. (One field in the OFD is a reference count that keeps track of how many descriptors point to it.) Even more importantly, if your program doesn't close a file to which it was writing, some of the data may be lost. This can happen because usually writing to a file is not direct—the data is first written to kernel buffers that the kernel eventually writes to the underlying hardware. In "Buffering and Running Time" on page 182, I explain more about this concept.

Closing the descriptor is necessary to *flush* these buffers to the device, but even closing it may not be sufficient. See the close(2) man page for an explanation.

In summary, a process performs file I/O in three steps:

1. Open a connection to the file to read or write.

2. Perform the reads and/or writes through that connection.

3. Close the connection to the file.

Standard File Descriptors

When a process is started from a shell, it inherits three open file descriptors, numbered 0, 1, and 2. These descriptors refer to connections that have already been opened by the time the process starts execution:

- File descriptor 0, called the *standard input*, refers to the connection from which it receives input.

- File descriptor 1, called the *standard output*, refers to the connection to which it sends output.

- File descriptor 2, called the *standard error*, refers to the connection to which it sends error messages.

For clarity, programs can use the symbolic constants STDIN_FILENO, STDOUT_FILENO, and STDERR_FILENO, defined in *unistd.h*, for the numbers 0, 1, and 2, respectively.

If the shell that creates the process is an interactive shell, meaning a shell that you're using to enter commands, the three descriptors are usually connected to the terminal device in which the shell is running. The input comes from the keyboard, and the output and error are written to the terminal screen. However, if any shell redirection operators were applied to the command that the process is executing, those descriptors may be pointing elsewhere. We'll explain how that works in Chapter 18.

When the process terminates, these descriptors are closed automatically, which is why you never have to explicitly open and close them in your programs.

The Kernel I/O Interface

The cp command is the Unix command for copying files. The simplest form of that command

---

cp *file1 file2*

---

copies the contents of *file1* to *file2*. If the latter file already exists, cp will silently overwrite its contents; otherwise, it creates a new file with that name.

Writing our own version of this command without using any library functions is a good way to learn how to use the kernel's I/O interface. We'll first research the kernel's system calls for opening, reading, writing, and closing files. We'll follow the same approach that we used when writing the spl_date programs in Chapter 3, namely, we'll search the man pages to find the system calls we need, starting with one that opens files.

Opening Files

Since we're looking for system calls related to opening files, we restrict the apropos search to Section 2 and give it the keyword open:

```
$ apropos -s2 open
creat (2)               - open and possibly create a file
epoll_create (2)        - open an epoll file descriptor
epoll_create1 (2)       - open an epoll file descriptor
flock (2)               - apply or remove an advisory lock on an open file
mq_open (2)             - open a message queue
name_to_handle_at (2) - obtain handle for a pathname and open file via a ha...
open (2)                - open and possibly create a file
open_by_handle_at (2) - obtain handle for a pathname and open file via a ha...
openat (2)              - open and possibly create a file
openat2 (2)             - open and possibly create a file (extended)
perf_event_open (2)     - set up performance monitoring
pidfd_open (2)          - obtain a file descriptor that refers to a process
```

The four contenders from the returned list that warrant further inspection are creat(), open(), openat(), and openat2().

It turns out that creat(), open(), and openat() share a single man page. The man page for openat2() states that this system call extends the functionality of openat(), that it's a system call without a *glibc* wrapper and therefore has to be called using the syscall() function, and that it's a Linux-specific call, meaning that it isn't required by POSIX.1-2024. If we use it, our program would be limited to Linux systems only. For these reasons, we'll focus on the other functions and examine their man pages. The SYNOPSIS section there is:

```
#include <sys/types.h>
#include <sys/stat.h>
#include <fcntl.h>

int open(const char *pathname, int flags);
int open(const char *pathname, int flags, mode_t mode);
int creat(const char *pathname, mode_t mode);
int openat(int dirfd, const char *pathname, int flags);
int openat(int dirfd, const char *pathname, int flags, mode_t mode);
```

First we see that even though these are system calls, they're not declared in *unistd.h*. Certain system calls are declared in other headers, in this case, in *fcntl.h*. The *sys/stat.h* and *sys/types.h* headers contain type and constant declarations needed by these calls. On some Linux systems, you may not need to include the *sys/types.h* header file. Check your local documentation to be sure.

Doing a quick scan of the page without reading all of the details, we discover first that `creat()` is essentially a special case of `open()` and that `openat()` is also an extension of `open()` that gives us the ability to name the file to be opened relative to a given directory. We can safely conclude that `open()` is the function we need to research.

The open() System Call

There are two prototypes for `open()`, their only difference being the presence of a third argument. Some man pages present these instead as a single prototype:

```
int open(const char *pathname, int flags, ... /* mode_t mode */);
```

The declarations are equivalent because the third argument is optional.

The first argument, named `pathname`, is a character string containing the pathname of the file to be opened. The second argument, named `flags`, is a bit mask. A *bit mask* is an integer whose individual bits represent distinct Boolean values that can be inspected or modified. This argument specifies the access mode for the file: reading only, writing only, or reading and writing, but other flags can be bitwise-ORed into it to control how the file is opened or created and how file operations are performed. We'll get to those shortly.

The optional third argument is also a bit mask, but it's used only when `open()` is being called to create a new file, in which case it specifies the permissions on that file.

If successful, the call to `open()` creates a new open file description and returns an integer file descriptor that refers to it and can be used in subsequent operations on the file. This descriptor is the lowest-numbered file descriptor not already in use by the process. We'll see in Chapter 18 why this fact is important. If the call isn't successful, it returns -1, and the error code is set in `errno`. Note that a process can open the same file multiple times; each call to `open()` creates a new open file descriptor.

The `flags` bit mask must include one of the following access modes, defined in *fcntl.h*, and zero or more *file creation flags* and *file status flags* bitwise-ORed into the mask:

O_RDONLY Open the file for reading only.

O_WRONLY Open the file for writing only.

O_RDWR Open the file for reading and writing.

For example, to open an existing file named *infile* in the working directory for reading, we'd write:

```
int fd;
fd = open("infile", O_RDONLY);
if ( -1 == fd )
    // Handle error.
```

If we try to open a file for reading that doesn't exist, open() will return -1 and store the EACCES error code in errno.

Similarly, to open an existing file named *outfile* for writing, we'd write:

```
int fd;
fd = open("outfile", O_WRONLY);
if ( -1 == fd )
    // Handle error.
```

This second example raises a few additional questions:

- If the file to which we want to write doesn't exist, will open() return an error or will it create a new file?

- If the file to which we want to write exists but isn't empty, will open() return an error or silently overwrite it?

- If that file exists and isn't empty and open() doesn't return an error, will writes to the file start at its beginning, replacing its contents, or will they be appended to the end of the current contents?

The answers to these questions depend on the values that we bitwise-OR into the flags argument. These flags fall into two categories: file creation flags and file status flags. *File creation flags* influence the behavior of the open() call itself, whereas *file status flags* modify the actual file operations.

The man page has a complete list of all flags, but to understand many of them, we need to know more about advanced methods of I/O, which we'll cover in Chapter 18. For now, I'll explain the file creation flags that are relevant to the preceding questions:

O_CREAT   Creates the file specified by pathname if it does not already exist

O_EXCL   Used with O_CREAT; forces open() to fail if pathname already exists

O_TRUNC   If pathname exists and is a regular file, truncates it to zero length before writing to it

To answer the first question, if we try to open a file for writing, using either O_WRONLY or O_RDWR with no other flags and the file doesn't exist, open() will fail. If we bitwise-OR the O_CREAT flag to O_WRONLY, as in

```
int fd = open("outfile", O_WRONLY | O_CREAT);
if ( -1 == fd )
    // Handle error.
```

it will instead create a new file with the given name. In short, trying to open a new file for writing fails unless the O_CREAT flag is bitwise-ORed into the second argument.

If we pass O_CREAT and no other flags to the call but the file exists, open() will not fail, but the file's contents will be written starting at the beginning of the file. If we write N bytes to the file, the first N bytes of the original file will be replaced but the rest of the file will remain.

If we want the entire file to be replaced, we need to bitwise-OR the O_TRUNC flag as well. This sets the file to zero length before the first write to it:

```
int fd = open("outfile", O_WRONLY | O_CREAT | O_TRUNC);
if ( -1 == fd )
    // Handle error.
```

This is a typical way of opening a file for writing, but it's not the only way.

You also can bitwise-OR the O_EXCL flag to O_CREAT to produce a different behavior, as in

```
fd = open("outfile", O_WRONLY | O_CREAT | O_EXCL);
```

which returns an error if *outfile* exists and, if it doesn't, creates it. In short, if you want to replace the file if it exists or create it if it doesn't, use O_WRONLY | O_CREAT | O_TRUNC as the second argument. If you want to prevent the file from being overwritten if it exists and create it if it doesn't, pass O_WRONLY | O_CREAT | O_EXCL instead.

Most of the other possible combinations of these file creation flags, used with read, write, or read/write access, will have either undefined or undesirable behavior. For example, if you try to open a file for read/write access and pass the following flags, the call will truncate the file when it's opened, leaving nothing to read initially:

```
fd = open(argv[1], O_RDWR | O_CREAT | O_TRUNC);
```

Make sure that's really what you want to do.

None of the flags just introduced will allow your program to open an existing file for writing and start writing to it at the end of the file, so that successive opens of the file for writing enlarge the file. You might want to do that if a program needs to maintain a logfile and append to it when it's running. In Chapter 11, we'll see an example of how to do this.

Attributes of Created Files

Let's consider the last parameter of the open() call, which is needed only when the call creates a file, meaning that it's called in either read/write or write mode, with the O_CREAT flag in the second argument. It has no effect otherwise.

When open() creates a file, we need to know the following:

- Which user is the owner of the file?

- What group is associated with the file?

- What are the permissions on the file?

The man page tells us that the owner is set to the effective user ID of the calling process, not the real user ID.

The answer to the group ownership question depends on the particular Unix system, but there is no simple answer. Just as a process has real and effective user IDs, it also has real and effective group IDs, with analogous meanings. In Linux, the file's group ownership is either the effective group ID of the calling process or the real group ID of the directory in which the file is created. It depends on several factors. Most of the time, it's going to be the effective group ID of the calling process, which is most likely the same as the real group ID. Check your local documentation to know for sure.

Finally, we focus on what permissions the file is given when it's created. If you don't supply a third parameter but you've passed O_CREAT in flags, the permission is unpredictable. You must provide that parameter. If you do, the permissions are the mode that you pass to it, modified by the process's umask. You can specify the mode either by supplying a literal number, such as the octal value 0600, or by a bitwise-OR of one or more of the symbolic constants defined in the *sys/stat.h* system header file and shown in Table 4-1.

Table 4-1: Symbolic Constants for File Mode

Constant	Numeric value	Permission
S_IRWXU	00700	User has read, write, and execute permission.
S_IRUSR	00400	User has read permission.
S_IWUSR	00200	User has write permission.
S_IXUSR	00100	User has execute permission.
S_IRWXG	00070	Group has read, write, and execute permission.
S_IRGRP	00040	Group has read permission.
S_IWGRP	00020	Group has write permission.
S_IXGRP	00010	Group has execute permission.
S_IRWXO	00007	Others have read, write, and execute permission.
S_IROTH	00004	Others have read permission.
S_IWOTH	00002	Others have write permission.
S_IXOTH	00001	Others have execute permission.

For example, you can specify the rw-r--r-- permission on the file by passing the bitwise-OR S_IRUSR | S_IWUSR | S_IRGRP | S_IROTH in the third parameter.

Errors When Opening Files

The open() call can fail for various reasons, and the man page describes all of the associated error values. A good program would try to inform its user why it failed so they can correct the error. Some of the causes of failure follow:

- The specified file doesn't exist.

- The user doesn't have permission to open the file.

- One or more flags passed to the open call are invalid.

- The open call tried to create a file and couldn't, either because it didn't have permission in the specified directory or the file exists and O_CREAT and O_EXCL were passed.

Because a failure to open a file will most likely prevent any useful computation from continuing, the easiest way to handle the errors is to display an error message and terminate. The fatal_error() function presented in Chapter 2 does this, so a pseudocode fragment for opening a file should be of the form:

```
int fd;  /* File descriptor to receive */
fd = open(pathname, file_opening_flags, mode);
if ( -1 == fd )
    fatal_error(errno, "name of function");
```

The program might also have to release any resources that it acquired, such as other files it might have opened successfully and modified but has not yet closed.

Closing Files

It's best to learn the proper way to close files before we consider how to read from or write to them for a few reasons:

- Closing a file shouldn't be an afterthought, because the close operation performs important tasks, as we noted previously in this section.

- We won't be able to write any programs to demonstrate how to read from or write to files unless we know how to open and close them.

- Opening and closing are somewhat symmetric operations that act like bookends surrounding actual I/O operations, respectively acquiring file descriptors and relinquishing them, so it's natural to learn about the closing operation right after opening.

The System Call to Close a File

We need to find the system call that closes a file. A search in Section 2 of the man pages for the keyword close produces a single page:

```
$ apropos -s2 close
close (2)            - close a file descriptor
```

Notice that this man page's one-line description states that this call closes a *file descriptor*, not a *file*. Although we think of the open operation as opening a file, we think of the close operation as closing a file descriptor. The man page for close() starts with:

```
SYNOPSIS
        #include <unistd.h>
        int close(int fd);

DESCRIPTION
        close() closes a file descriptor, so that it no longer refers to any
        file and may be reused...
```

> If fd is the last file descriptor referring to the underlying open file
> description (see open(2)), the resources associated with the open file
> description are freed; if the file descriptor was the last reference to
> a file which has been removed using unlink(2), the file is deleted.

RETURN VALUE
> close() returns zero on success. On error, -1 is returned, and errno
> is set appropriately.

Observe that the header file needed for close() is not the same as the one
for open(). It's declared in *unistd.h*, whereas open() is declared in *fcntl.h*.

This function has a single argument, which is the file descriptor of the
connection to be closed. The call closes that file descriptor. If a file has been
opened by a process via multiple calls to open(), the close() call doesn't close
the other connections; it closes only the one corresponding to fd.

The second paragraph of the man page DESCRIPTION implies that there
can be multiple file descriptors referring to the *same* OFD. When we introduced the open() call, we pointed out that each call to it creates a new OFD
and returns a descriptor that refers to it, so how is that possible? The answer lies in the fact that file descriptors can be duplicated using the dup() or
dup2() system call. These calls create copies of file descriptors that point to
the same OFDs.

Errors When Closing Files

If close() is successful, its return value is 0, but if not, it returns -1. You might
wonder what could possibly go wrong when closing a file and why close()
can fail.

One reason might be that we passed it a bad file descriptor when we
called close(), in which case it returns -1 and sets errno to EBADF. Another
reason could be that the kernel, in the middle of executing code within the
close() system call, may be given an urgent task to complete, one so urgent
that it has to drop the close() call immediately to handle that task. In this
case, the call returns -1 and sets errno to EINTR. Further still, the file may not
have been on the local machine or local drive. It might be a file on a remote
system that we're accessing across a network. The network connection might
have gone down, in which case the close operation cannot complete its actions, and again, we'd get a -1 return value, and most systems will set errno
to EIO.

Finally, if this file had been opened for writing, many other problems
could cause close() to fail. For example, the kernel may discover in the
close() call that it cannot complete a transfer of data to a disk file, because,
for example, we've run out of disk space. On some systems, this error isn't
reported until we close the file, when errno would be set to ENOSPC, meaning
no more disk space, or EDQUOT, meaning this write exceeded our quota.

The NOTES section of the man page provides guidance on how to handle
the various errors if close() fails. If close() returns -1, we should not retry
calling it, because doing so might cause other problems, particularly for programs with multiple threads. The failure value is supposed to be used only

for diagnostic or remedial purposes, which means it's best to try rewriting the data to the file or writing to a new file if possible. In fact, the most recent version of the man page as of this writing states, "A careful programmer who wants to know about I/O errors may precede close() with a call to fsync(2)." The fsync() function forces any remaining writes to a file to be flushed to the underlying device, so that a failure in closing isn't related to the attempted writes to it. By calling fsync() before calling close(), we'd see any I/O errors related to writing first and could handle them before closing the descriptor, but the fsync() man page points out that it can only be called when the file descriptor is that of a disk file. It will return EINVAL otherwise.

Handling the EINTR error in a comprehensive and portable way in POSIX-conforming systems is difficult because different implementations handle this error differently. POSIX.1-2024 doesn't specify what an implementation is supposed to do if the kernel is interrupted while executing code in the close() function. Therefore, some implementations guarantee that the file descriptor has been closed despite the error. Others don't close the file descriptor and require that close() be called again, which, as noted previously, can cause other problems. To handle closing errors in a portable way, a program would have to respond to this error in a different way depending on which implementation it's running. This in turn requires checking at runtime which kernel is running and which libraries it's using.

At this point, I present a simpler way to handle closing errors in which we call fsync() before close(). If fsync() returns EINVAL, we'll ignore the error. If close() sets errno to EINTR, the program exits:

```
errno = 0;              /* Need to include <errno.h>. */
/* On some Unix systems, we need to check whether fd has been used
   for writing. On Linux, we don't need to do this. */
return_val = fsync(fd);    /* Flush data to device. */
if ( -1 == return_val ) {
    /* Error trying to flush data to device. Depending on application, we
       might need other actions here. */
    if ( EINVAL != errno ) fatal_error(errno, "fsync() to pathname");

/* fsync() was successful. */
errno = 0;
if ( -1 == close(fd) )
    fatal_error(errno, "closing pathname");
```

The preceding code is safe to use in Linux because it isn't an error in Linux to call fsync(fd) when fd was opened for reading only.

Reading from Files

We need to find the system call that can read the contents of a file, not just text files but arbitrary files. In Chapter 1, we saw that in Unix, from the kernel's perspective, a nondirectory file is simply a sequence of bytes without structure; we need a function to read such a file. We'll resort to our usual method for finding the right call, namely a man page search. We try the obvious search, using the exact (option -e) keyword read, limiting the search to Section 2:

```
$ apropos -s2 -e read
--snip--
pread (2)          - read from or write to a file descriptor at a given offset
pread64 (2)        - read from or write to a file descriptor at a given offset
preadv (2)         - read or write data into multiple buffers
preadv2 (2)        - read or write data into multiple buffers
pwrite (2)         - read from or write to a file descriptor at a given offset
pwrite64 (2)       - read from or write to a file descriptor at a given offset
pwritev (2)        - read or write data into multiple buffers
pwritev2 (2)       - read or write data into multiple buffers
read (2)           - read from a file descriptor
readdir (2)        - read directory entry
--snip--
```

On my Linux system, the search returned more than 20 hits. This list is a fragment of those results; however, it does contain two functions that warrant further research:

```
pread (2)       - read from or write to a file descriptor at a given offset
read (2)        - read from file descriptor
```

The first, pread(), may not be suitable. When we read its man page, we see that it's more general than we need it to be and is really intended for multi-threaded programs.

We want to read the man page of the second, read(). If we enter

```
$ man read
READ(1POSIX)                    POSIX Programmer's Manual                    READ(1POSIX)
--snip--
NAME
       read - read from standard input into shell variables
--snip--
```

we get the page for a read command, not the one for the read() system call. We need to specify the section number in the man command:

```
$ man 2 read
--snip--
NAME
       read - read from a file descriptor

SYNOPSIS
       #include <unistd.h>
       ssize_t read(int fd, void *buf, size_t nbytes);
```

```
        read() attempts to read up to nbytes bytes from file descriptor fd into
        the buffer starting at buf.
--snip--
```

Note that to use read(), we need to include the *unistd.h* header file. The function has three parameters: an integer file descriptor fd, a void pointer named buf, and one of type size_t, named nbytes. The man page states that it reads up to nbytes many bytes from the file descriptor fd into the buffer whose starting address is buf.

The bytes that are read are stored into memory locations starting at buf, which is declared as type void* so that any address can be passed to it. It's worth pointing out that this parameter is named buf to emphasize that it's memory in the calling process that temporarily holds data to be transferred from the file. A program calling read repeatedly with the same buffer argument needs to copy the data out of the buffer after each call. The third parameter, nbytes, is the number of bytes to read.

The return value is of type ssize_t. This is a system type similar to size_t except that it's a *signed integer* type, so that it can store negative numbers. The return value is either the number of bytes actually read, which can never be larger but might be smaller than nbytes, or -1 if something went wrong, in which case errno contains the error value.

Figure 4-2 represents the actions resulting from a call to read(3,buf,len).

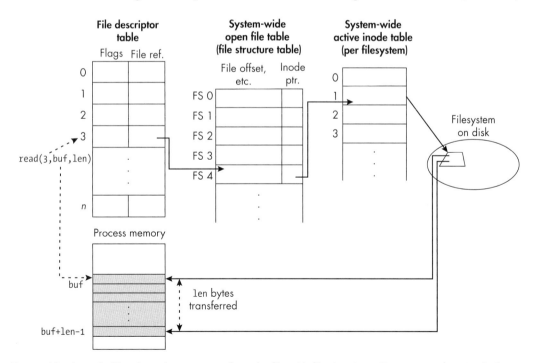

Figure 4-2: A read of len bytes by a process from the file with file descriptor 3 to memory location buf

The kernel uses file descriptor 3 to locate the OFD in the file structure table. It uses that OFD to locate the inode for the file, which stores the address on disk of the file's data. When we first discussed OFDs in "Input/Output Mechanics" on page 155, we noted that one of the members of an OFD is a file offset, which always points to the place in the file to perform the next operation. The reading of data starts at the file offset and in this case attempts to read len bytes. The data is copied into the memory locations in the process's address space starting at buf. The read operation advances the file offset by len bytes.

Let's take a look at a code fragment that puts some of these ideas together. Suppose that fd is a valid file descriptor that we've opened for reading, buffer is a char array of size 100, and return_val is a variable of type ssize_t. The following code fragment shows how to repeatedly read 100 bytes of data at a time from the file associated with fd until there's no more data to read:

```
BOOL done = FALSE;   /* Flag to indicate no more data  */
while ( !done ) {
    return_val = read(fd, buffer, 100);
    if ( 0 > return_val )
        /* An error code was returned during reading.  */
    ❶ fatal_error(errno, "error reading file...");
    else if ( 0 == return_val )
        /* The end of file was reached - stop reading. */
        done = TRUE;
    else
    ❷ /* buffer[0...return_val-1] contains the bytes just read. */
        // OMITTED: Transfer this data to its final destination before
        //          it is overwritten by the next call to read().
}
```

This is the structure of a typical read loop. The loop repeatedly calls read() until it returns either zero or a negative value. A negative value indicates an error during reading, in which case we handle the error by calling the fatal_error() function ❶ (which we presented in Chapter 2) to print a message and exit the program. A zero return value just means we've read all there is to read, so we set the flag done to TRUE to break the loop. Any other value means that read() was successful. That case is handled in the else clause ❷, which in this fragment is just a comment indicating that buffer contains the data just read. That comment tells us we need to transfer the data before it's overwritten, which might mean writing it to a file or copying it into some data structure, for example.

There's no guarantee that the read() call will actually read 100 bytes; it might have read fewer bytes, which is why the comment states that buffer [0...return_val-1] is the data just read. If, for example, only 256 bytes remained in the file at the current position of the file offset, then the next two calls to read() would read 100 bytes each, and the third just 56 bytes, as depicted in Figure 4-3.

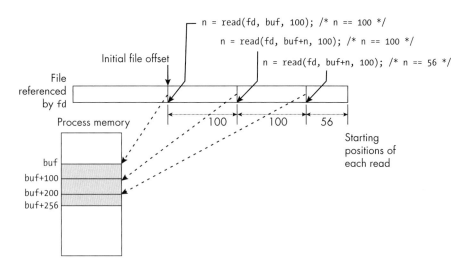

Figure 4-3: Three successive reads with the third returning fewer bytes than requested

You can't assume that the number of bytes requested is the same as the number received, and it's not an error when it isn't.

Remember that each successive call to read(fd, buf, nbytes) starts reading in the file referenced by fd at the byte immediately following the last byte read by the previous call, because the file offset is advanced by the read. This is why successive calls will eventually read the entire file without missing or duplicating bytes. The ability to read the entire file correctly hinges on read()'s advancing that file offset.

The next step is to find the system call that we can use for writing to files. Once we know that, we'll be ready to create a program to copy files.

Writing to Files

To find the system call that can write to files, an obvious choice of a search in the man pages would be

```
$ apropos -s2 write
```

This search on my system returns about 20 different man pages. Depending on which distribution you're running, it might be more or less than that.

We can refine the search to produce a smaller set of pages with the -a option to apropos, which lets us search for pages that match *all* of the supplied keywords, and give it both write and file, since we want to write to files in particular:

```
$ apropos -s2 -a write file
_llseek (2)          - reposition read/write file offset
llseek (2)           - reposition read/write file offset
lseek (2)            - reposition read/write file offset
pread (2)            - read from or write to a file descriptor at a given offset
pread64 (2)          - read from or write to a file descriptor at a given offset
pwrite (2)           - read from or write to a file descriptor at a given offset
```

```
pwrite64 (2)       - read from or write to a file descriptor at a given offset
write (2)          - write to a file descriptor
```

The very last hit is the one we want: the function that writes to a file descriptor. Its man page begins with:

```
SYNOPSIS
       #include <unistd.h>

       ssize_t write(int fd, const void *buf, size_t nbytes);

DESCRIPTION
       write() writes up to nbytes bytes from the buffer starting at buf to
       the file referred to by the file descriptor fd.
--snip--
RETURN VALUE
       On success, the number of bytes written is returned. On error, -1 is
       returned, and errno is set to indicate the cause of the error.
--snip--
```

The write() system call is a symmetric counterpart to the read() call. It writes nbytes bytes starting at the address given by buf to the file associated with the fd file descriptor. The return value when it's successful is the number of bytes actually written. It'll never be greater than nbytes. If there's an error, it returns -1, and errno contains the error code. Like the buffer parameter of the read() call, this buffer parameter is declared as a void pointer, so that it can be used to transfer any type of data.

The man page provides the details for using write(). A call such as

```
write(fd, buffer, num_bytes)
```

attempts to transfer num_bytes bytes from the memory location pointed to by buffer to the current position of the file offset in the file opened for writing via the fd file descriptor. The initial position of the file offset depends on how the file was opened. For example, if you opened the file for writing, passing the O_WRONLY | O_CREAT | O_TRUNC flags, the file offset will be at the start of the file. After each call to write(), it's incremented by the number of bytes actually written, so that the next call will write its data immediately after the data just written. Thus, no *holes* are created in the file under normal usage.

A program calling write() should check whether it returns -1, which indicates a write error, and handle the error appropriately. If write() doesn't return -1, there was no error in writing, but it's possible that the number of bytes actually written is less than the number of bytes that were supposed to be written. This *partial write* to an ordinary disk file can be caused by a variety of reasons: The file might have reached a predefined maximum size, the disk might be full, or the user's disk quota might be reached. After a partial write, your program can either just display a suitable error message and exit or try to write the remaining data again. If it calls write() again after the partial write, it'll either transfer the remaining bytes or return an error, which it can then handle.

A simple way to call `write()` that doesn't try to rewrite after a partial write is of the form:

```
errno = 0;
result = write(fd, buffer, num_bytes);
if ( result == -1 )
    // Error in writing - use errno value to print a message to use,
    // exiting if appropriate.
else if ( result < num_bytes )
    // Some but not all data was written; display message and exit.
else
    // write() was successful and all data was written.
```

It is always a good idea to check whether a partial write occurred and, at the very least, inform the user that it did.

NOTE *A successful call to `write()` to a disk file doesn't necessarily transfer the data to the disk. In fact, on most modern Unix systems, writing to a file doesn't cause any immediate disk I/O. Instead, the data is transferred to kernel buffers, which are written to the disk at a later time. This practice generally reduces disk I/O, saves time in the kernel, and speeds up the writes. Chapter 18 covers this concept of kernel buffering.*

We're now ready to write a simple version of the Unix `cp` command, which we name `spl_cp1` (because we'll write a second version later).

Writing a copy Command

The simplest form of `cp` makes a copy of one file to a file with a different name, using the syntax:

```
cp source_file target_file
```

The two arguments to `cp` can be any pathnames, including those with symbolic links.

To illustrate, suppose our current working directory has a symbolic link named *backups*:

```
$ ls -F
file1  backups@
```

The `-F` option to `ls` classifies the directory entries with an *append indicator*, which is one of *, /, =, >, @, or |. The @ symbol indicates that an entry is a symbolic link, showing in this example that *backups* is a symbolic link.

We can see what the target of the *backups* symbolic link is with the `readlink` command:

```
$ readlink backups
/data/backups/
```

The `readlink` command displays the full pathname to which a symbolic link refers, showing in this case that *backups* is a link to a directory, since it's displayed with a trailing slash. You can use the `realpath` command also; for this simple case they behave exactly the same.

If we issue the command

```
$ cp file1 backups/current/file1_bkup
```

cp makes a copy of *file1* in the directory */data/backups/current/* with the name *file1_bkup*.

Although the command seems simple enough, several questions about its behavior come to mind immediately:

- If *target_file* already exists, will cp replace it, or will it refuse to replace it and issue a warning instead?

- After a successful copy, what permissions will *target_file* have, and which user and group will own it?

- Can *source_file* and *target_file* refer to the same file? In other words, can cp replace a file by itself, or is that an error? Remember that the two files can be different links to the same file in Unix systems.

- If *source_file* is a symbolic link to another file, does cp copy the file referenced by the link or the link itself?

- Can cp make copies of special files and directories?

The POSIX specification of cp [14] answers all of these questions for systems that conform to POSIX requirements:

- If *target_file* exists, cp truncates the file and replaces its contents with the contents of *source_file*, an action known as *clobbering*. This is dangerous, as you cannot recover a file once you've clobbered it, so many people use the interactive option -i to cp, which prompts the user before overwriting the file:

```
$ cp -i README README.md
cp: overwrite 'README.md'? n
$
```

Any answer that begins with y or Y is interpreted as *yes*, and anything else is taken as a negative answer.

- The permissions and ownership given to *target_file* depend on whether it existed before the copy operation. If it existed before, they will remain the same as they were. If it is newly created, its mode will be the mode of *source_file* modified by the user's umask, and its user and group IDs will be those resulting from a call to open() with the O_CREAT flag. (You can refer back to "The open() System Call" on page 159 for how the group ID is chosen by open() in this case.)

- POSIX doesn't require an implementation of cp to detect whether the source and target pathnames refer to the same file, but most implementations do. Suppose, for example, that *linux_cheatsheet*

and *commands* are links to the same file, which we can verify with the
`ls -i` command, which prints the inode numbers of the files:

```
$ ls -i
6690145 commands  6690145 linux_cheatsheet
```

Then if we enter

```
$ cp linux_cheatsheet commands
cp: 'linux_cheatsheet' and 'commands' are the same file
```

we see that cp looks not at the names but at the files to which they refer.

- If *source_file* is a symbolic link to another file, then cp copies the
  target of that link, not the link itself.

- Without options, cp does not copy directories, but it can copy special files that a user has the privilege to read.

Copying a file does not preserve any attributes other than the mode and
ownership. To preserve the timestamps and other attributes when copying,
we can use the -p (short for "preserve") option.

A final point to remember is we cannot create a file in a directory unless
we have write permission on that directory. Therefore, if cp needs to create
the target file, we must have write permission on the target directory.

Design of the copy Program

With all of the preceding considerations in mind, we can now outline the
structure of our `spl_cp1` program:

1. Check that the command line has two arguments and exit with a
   usage error if it doesn't.

2. Open the first argument file for reading, which we'll call the *source*
   file. If it cannot be opened for reading, report the error and exit.
   This should take care of detecting whether it's a directory or a file
   that we don't have permission to read.

3. Open the second argument file for writing, passing the bitwise-OR
   of the `O_CREAT` and `O_TRUNC` flags to allow it to be created if it doesn't
   exist and overwritten if it does.

4. Enter a loop that performs the following sequence of instructions
   until either an error occurs or it has read the entire source file:
   (a) Read a chunk of data from the source file into a buffer
       and store the number of bytes read into a variable named
       `num_bytes_read`. If there is no data left or a read error oc-
       curred, break out of this loop.
   (b) Write `num_bytes_read` many bytes of data from the buffer to
       the target file. If a write error occurred or the amount of
       data written is less than `num_bytes_read`, report the error and
       break out of the loop.

5. Close the source file.

6. Close the target file.

7. Return a value indicating whether or not the program copied the file successfully.

We've already covered everything we need to know to implement that logic, so writing the program will be relatively straightforward. We just have a few decisions to make about the variables our program will need.

Implementation of the copy Program

The read() and write() system calls both require a buffer. We need to decide how large that buffer should be, and that decision will affect the program's performance. For now, we'll choose its size somewhat arbitrarily, and after creating the initial version of the program, we'll consider how the buffer size affects its performance. Listing 4-1 shows the complete program.

```
spl_cp1.c   #define _GNU_SOURCE
            #include "common_hdrs.h"
        ❶ #ifndef BUFFER_SIZE
            #define BUFFER_SIZE   4096
            #endif
            #define MESSAGE_SIZE 512
            #define PERMISSIONS   S_IRUSR|S_IWUSR|S_IRGRP|S_IWGRP|S_IROTH /* rw-rw-r-- */

            int main(int argc, char *argv[])
            {
                int     source_fd;              /* Source file descriptor   */
                int     target_fd;              /* Target file descriptor   */
                int     num_bytes_read;         /* Return value of read()   */
                int     num_bytes_written;      /* Return value of write()  */
                mode_t  permissions = PERMISSIONS; /* Permissions to assign */
                char    buffer[BUFFER_SIZE];    /* Buffer for transfers     */
                char    message[MESSAGE_SIZE];  /* Error message string     */

                /* Check for correct usage. */
                if ( argc != 3 ) {
                    sprintf(message, "%s source destination", basename(argv[0]));
                    usage_error(message);
                }
                /* Open source file for reading. */
                errno = 0;
                if ( (source_fd = open(argv[1], O_RDONLY)) == -1 ) {
                    sprintf(message, "unable to open %s for reading", argv[1]);
                    fatal_error(errno, message);
                }
                /* Open target file for writing. */
                if ( (target_fd = open(argv[2], O_WRONLY | O_CREAT | O_TRUNC,
                                    permissions)) == -1 ) {
```

```
            sprintf(message, "unable to open %s for writing", argv[2]);
            fatal_error(errno, message);
        }
        /* Repeatedly transfer BUFFER_SIZE bytes at a time from source_fd to
           target_fd. */
        errno = 0;
❷ while ( (num_bytes_read = read(source_fd, buffer, BUFFER_SIZE)) > 0 ) {
            errno = 0;
            num_bytes_written = write(target_fd, buffer, num_bytes_read);
        ❸ if ( errno != 0 )
                fatal_error(errno, "copy");
            else
                if ( num_bytes_written != num_bytes_read ) {
                ❹ sprintf(message,"write error to %s\n", argv[2]);
                    fatal_error(-1, message);
                }
        }
        if ( num_bytes_read == -1 )
            fatal_error(errno, "error reading");

        /* Close files. */
        if ( close(source_fd) == -1 ) {
            sprintf(message, "error closing source file %s", argv[1]);
            fatal_error(errno, message);
        }
        errno = 0;
        if ( -1 == fsync(target_fd) )  /* Flush data to device. */
            fatal_error(errno, "fsync");
        /* fsync() was successful. */
        if ( close(target_fd) == -1 ) {
            sprintf(message, "error closing target file %s", argv[2]);
            fatal_error(errno, "error closing target file");
        }
        return 0;
}
```

Listing 4-1: A complete implementation of a simple file copy program

The conditional macro ❶ that defines the buffer size allows us to change the buffer size without having to change the program itself. For example, by entering the command

```
gcc -DBUFFER_SIZE=4096 spl_cp1.c -I ../include -L ../lib -lspl -o spl_cp1
```

to compile and build the executable spl_cp1, the value 4096 assigned to the symbol BUFFER_SIZE on the command line will override the value it's given in the source code. Recall from Chapter 2 that various functions needed by all of our programs were placed into our own static library, named *libspl.a*, in the directory *demos/lib*, whose relative pathname from this chapter's demo

directory is *../lib*. That's why the compilation command needs the options
`-L../lib -lspl`.

The `while` loop ❷ condition uses a common C paradigm:

```
while ( (returnvalue = func(...) ) conditional_operator expression)
```

To evaluate the condition, the function is called, and its return value is assigned to *returnvalue*, which is then compared to *expression* using the given *conditional_operator*. If the comparison is true, the loop is entered; otherwise, it is not.

The `while` loop does the main work. The loop is entered each time that the `read()` call transferred one or more bytes to the `buffer`. The loop body attempts to write those bytes to the target file descriptor. The return value of `write()` is checked to see whether the number of bytes transferred equals the number requested by the call. If not, something went wrong and the program exits ❹. The program also checks whether `write()` set errno to a nonzero value ❸ and exits if it does.

It's time to run the program and see how it works.

Testing of the copy Program

Let's run the `spl_cp1` command to make a copy of its own source code:

```
$ ./spl_cp1 spl_cp1.c spl_cp1_backup.c
```

We can check whether *spl_cp* and *spl_cp_backup.c* are identical with the `diff -s` command, which compares two files:

```
$ diff -s spl_cp1.c spl_cp1_backup.c
Files spl_cp1.c and spl_cp1_backup.c are identical
```

In this case it copied the file correctly, but more generally, how do we know whether the program is correct? *Correctness* in this context means:

1. It should make identical copies of the source files every time it's called, regardless of their size.

2. It should report incorrect usage and report errors whenever errors occur.

We can't verify the first condition because that would require running the program on every possible file. However, we can convince ourselves with high probability that the program is correct by running it on as many files as is reasonably possible, with varying sizes, from empty files to extremely large files that might possibly exhaust system resources.

How can we compare two arbitrary files to see if they're identical? We can't use the `diff` command, because it can compare only text files, but the `cmp` command can compare any two files, text or otherwise. For example, we can run `spl_cp1` to make a copy of itself and then check whether the copy is identical to the original:

```
$ ./spl_cp1 spl_cp1 spl_cp1.bkup
$ cmp spl_cp1 spl_cp1.bkup
$
```

It will display the first position at which they differ if they're not the same or nothing if they're identical. You can use `cmp -l` to see all differences in the two files.

Thus, to convince ourselves of its correctness, we can run our `spl_cp1` program on files of size zero, files of moderate size, and extremely large files, checking with `cmp` to see whether the copies are the same as the originals or whether writing fails because there's not enough disk space to make the copies.

To start, here's a run on an empty file:

```
$ du -b /temp/emptyfile      # Show actual size of /temp/emptyfile.
0 /temp/emptyfile
$ spl_cp1 emptyfile emptyfile.bkup
$ du -b /temp/empty*
0 /temp/emptyfile
0 /temp/emptyfile.bkup
```

There's no need to compare them since they're both empty.

A run on a file of medium size looks like this:

```
$ du -b /temp/mediumfile
57569256 /temp/mediumfile
$ ./spl_cp1 /temp/mediumfile /temp/mediumfile.bkup
$ cmp mediumfile*
$
```

Try running this program on extremely large files, and you'll see that it copies them correctly. To test for write errors, I ran it to make a copy of a very large file, a guest virtual machine image file for Ushahidi Ubuntu, which was 13,129,809,920 bytes, on a disk whose capacity was only about 8GB, as follows:

```
$ ./spl_cp1 /data/Ushahidi-Ubuntu.vmdk /temp/largefile
write error to /temp/largefile
```

Referring to Listing 4-1, you can see that this error message is the one that's written when errno == 0 after the call to `write()` and `write()` wrote fewer than the number of bytes it was supposed to. If we modify the program so that it calls `write()` one more time after this, errno would be set to `ENOSPC` and we'd see the message `copy: No space left on device`.

The Universality of the copy Program

At the beginning of this chapter, I pointed out that the Unix model of I/O is universal. Now that we've written the `spl_cp1` program, we can demonstrate concretely how it works. Open a terminal window, and in bash, navigate to the directory containing the spl_cp1 executable. Create a small text file in that directory named *testfile*. It doesn't matter how large or small it is or what it contains. The file I'll work with has the following lines:

```
####        ####
        ^
    ---
```

First, copy *testfile* to the terminal:

```
$ ./spl_cp1 testfile /dev/tty
####        ####
        ^
    ---
$
```

The contents of *testfile* appeared on the terminal screen because the system calls work on *all* files, and */dev/tty* is a device file that represents the terminal window in which you're working. This shows that the spl_cp1 program copied the file to the terminal.

Now try it the other way around. Enter any text followed by CTRL-D after the command line and then look at the contents of *newfile* with the cat command:

```
$ ./spl_cp1 /dev/tty newfile
####        ####
        ^
    ---
CTRL-D
$ cat newfile
####        ####
        ^
    ---
```

This time, spl_cp1 read the terminal device file and wrote what it contained to a new file named *newfile*. The read() system call returns 0 only when it receives a CTRL-D, the keyboard character sequence that sends an end-of-file signal to it; that's why we need to enter that CTRL-D.

You can also use spl_cp1 to send what you enter in one terminal window to another. Open a second terminal window and enter **tty** in it. The tty command prints the pathname of the terminal's device file. You'll see a string such as /dev/pts/2, which is the device file for that terminal window. Enter the following command, substituting the pathname that tty printed in your window, and then enter whatever text you like after it, followed by CTRL-D:

```
$ ./spl_cp1 /dev/tty /dev/pts/2
Hello there.
I'm trying to reach you.
```

```
I'm on terminal /dev/pts/1.
Bye.
CTRL-D
```

You should see whatever you typed in one window in the other. In your second window, press ENTER to get the prompt again. It's not magic; it's Unix.

Timing Programs

The correctness of a program is the most important aspect of its quality, but not the only one. Other measures of program quality relate to how well it performs. Running time is usually the most important performance metric. For example, we'd like to know how fast our spl_cp1 program is at copying files, on average, and how long will it take to copy very large files. This raises the question of how can we measure the amount of execution time that programs take in Unix.

When we researched the man pages in Chapter 3 to investigate time in Unix (in particular, in "About Calendar Time in Unix"), we learned about real time and process times. In that chapter, we weren't interested in process times, so we didn't dwell on them, but now we need to know more about them. The Section 7 man page for time mentioned that the time command could be used to determine the amount of CPU time consumed during the execution of a program.

The time command's man page explains that it can be used to provide data on various system resources used by a program. By default, it displays information about resources besides running time, such as memory usage and I/O activity. To restrict its output to just running times, enter

```
$ time -p command
```

where *command* is the command whose running time you want to measure. The -p option tells time to display the traditional POSIX output, which consists of three values, each measured in seconds up to two decimal places:

- Elapsed clock time, listed in the output as real time

- User time, listed as user time

- System time, listed as sys time

Reported *real* time is the number of seconds that elapse from when the command was invoked until it completed. Reported *user time* is the total amount of time that the process, and any child processes or their descendants executing on its behalf, spent running in user mode. Reported *sys time* is the total amount of time spent on the process's behalf running within the kernel—that is, in privileged mode, including such time spent by its children as well.

Note that time writes its output to the standard error stream rather than the standard output stream. You can supply different options to control the format of the output as well as the kinds of resources about which you'd like time to report. The man page contains a detailed list of all of the resource usage that it reports. Also, shells such as bash typically define their own version of the time command, so you should always type the full pathname of the time program when using it if you want the non-bash version. Since time is usually installed in */usr/bin/*, you would enter:

```
$ /usr/bin/time -p command
```

For example, I'll run our spl_cp1 program on a relatively large file, a disk image of Chimera Linux, a non-GNU Linux, approximately 116MB:

```
$ /usr/bin/time -p ./spl_cp1 chimera-1.9-linux_x86_64.bin /temp/chimera
real 0.73
user 0.02
sys 0.14
```

This output shows that 0.73 seconds elapsed between when the program started and when it finished, and that it spent about 0.02 seconds running in user mode and about 0.14 seconds running in kernel mode.

Notice that the sum of user and system times is much less than the real time. The real time can never be less than their sum, but it's usually much larger. Processes often spend time waiting for I/O operations to complete. This waiting time is not part of user or system times. When a process issues a request for I/O, it's removed from the CPU until the I/O is complete. We say that the process is *blocked* when it isn't allowed to use the CPU because it doesn't have a required resource to run, which in this case is a completed I/O operation. In addition, when many processes are running, they share the CPU(s) with each other. Each ends up waiting in a queue until it acquires a CPU. This waiting time isn't part of user or system times either. These waiting times account for the difference between elapsed (real) time and the sum of user and system times. Our ls_cp program spent 0.73 − 0.16 = 0.57 seconds not on the CPU, either waiting for I/O or the CPU.

Although the amount of time that a process spends waiting depends heavily on what else the system is doing, the more calls it makes, the longer it will take, on average.

When we try to copy larger and larger files, we should expect the process times to become larger. To test this hypothesis, we'll need a set of large files. Also, we'll change the options to the time command so that it puts the output on a single line rather than three lines and sends it to a file instead. The -f *format-string* option controls both output content and format. We'll use the format string "\t%e \t%U \t%S", which reports real, user, and system times on a single tab-separated line. We'll send the output to a file with the -o *output-file* option and ask it to append output to the file instead of overwriting it with the -a option.

I created a set of four files, *f1, f2, f3*, and *f4*, such that *f1* is 60MB and the others double in size successively, and I ran the following bash for loop:

```
$ for i in 1 2 3 4 ; do
    let size=$((60*(2**(i-1))))
    echo -n $size >> results
```

```
    /usr/bin/time -f "\t%e \t%U \t%S" -o results -a ./spl_cp1 f${i} f${i}.bk
done
```

The loop uses bash arithmetic operations to calculate the value of size to
print and prints that value to the *results* output file, without a trailing newline character. It then copies each of the files into a new file, recording the
times in the same *results* file. Table 4-2 shows the results of this experiment.

Table 4-2: Process Times in Seconds of the spl_cp
Program on Four Successively Larger Files

File size (MB)	Real time	User time	System time
60	0.32	0.00	0.08
120	0.75	0.01	0.13
240	1.47	0.03	0.26
480	3.07	0.06	0.50

Notice in Table 4-2 that the real and system times increase approximately
in proportion to the size of the file over this small dataset, but the user times
do not. This isn't a coincidence; the system time is related to the number of
system calls that the program makes, and the user time is independent of
how many calls it makes. Most of the work is being done in the kernel, not in
the program code.

THE OVERHEAD OF SYSTEM CALLS

System calls in general take much more time than calls to library functions. In
"System Calls" in Chapter 2, we summarized the sequence of actions that take
place when a program makes a system call. Steps such as copying the arguments of the call to a place that the kernel can access them, trapping to kernel
mode, and locating the code to be executed inside the kernel and jumping to
it all take time.

We can get an estimate of how much overhead a system call requires by timing a small program that does nothing other than make a large number of system calls. The uname() system call is a relatively small system call that retrieves
information about the kernel from data stored internally. It makes few function
calls itself inside the kernel and runs pretty quickly. I wrote a small program,
spl_syscalloverhead.c (available in the book's source code distribution), that
calls uname() 100,000,000 times. The time command reported that it ran for
about 42.25 seconds. As a means of comparison, I replaced the system call
in that same program by a call to the GNU C Library function rand(), which
returns a random integer. The rand() function is a wrapper for a hidden
__random() function, which performs some integer arithmetic using a very
efficient algorithm for random number generation based on saved state information. It finished in about 1.47 seconds. Both programs were run on a
host with a Linux 5.15 kernel. That program (*spl_libcalloverhead.c*) is available in the book's source code distribution as well. The difference in time is
primarily due to the overhead required to execute a system call.

Buffering and Running Time

In our *spl_cp1.c* program, we chose a buffer size of 4096 bytes. If we increase the buffer size, the program will make fewer system calls to copy a fixed size file. For example, if our file is 4,096,000 bytes, with a buffer of size 4096 bytes, it makes 1,000 read() and write() calls, but if we double the buffer size, it makes 500 calls to each. Decreasing the buffer size increases the number of calls to each. Given that these system calls have overhead, it stands to reason that our programs will run faster with larger buffer sizes. We test this hypothesis by modifying our *spl_cp1.c* program so that the buffer size is a command line argument. We named the modified version of the program *spl_cp2.c* (it's available in the book's source code distribution). We can then conduct an experiment in which we run the program with varying size buffers and measure how much time it takes for each buffer size. For each buffer size, we need to run it multiple times and take the average time of the runs. This by itself won't give us a good picture of the effect of buffer size, because the kernel itself performs *buffering* when transferring data to and from disk devices to improve the performance of I/O.

When a user process calls read() for data from a disk file, the kernel doesn't transfer the data directly from the disk to the address space of the user process. Instead, it transfers the data from the disk to a storage area in kernel memory, and when all of the data has been transferred, it copies it into the user process's address space.

Symmetrically, when a user process calls write() to transfer data to a disk file, the data it sends is copied to a storage area in kernel memory, and at some future time the kernel transfers it to the disk file. This buffering scheme is depicted in Figure 4-4. The kernel's storage area for these disk I/O operations is called its *buffer cache*, and the kernel's use of it is called *system buffering*.

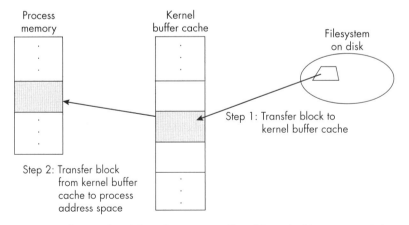

Figure 4-4: The transfer of data during a read() call from the filesystem on disk to the kernel's buffer cache and then to the process's address space

The kernel is designed to use this buffer cache to improve overall performance. For one, the read() and write() calls don't have to wait for the slow disk operations to complete. They return as soon as data is transferred in memory.

Second, on a read request by a process, the kernel searches its buffer cache to see whether the disk data being requested is there. If a buffer is found with that data, it doesn't have to access the disk. Instead, the data is read directly from memory without any physical I/O. Write requests are slightly more complex but similar. In both cases, the average effect is that the kernel spends less time involved in actual physical I/O. In Chapter 17, we'll explore system buffering in greater depth.

The reason that this system buffering of disk data is relevant is that if our program repeatedly copies the same file to the disk, the Linux kernel will not do the same work each time. Once it reads the input file, it won't have to access the disk each time because it will have all of its data in its buffer cache, provided the machine has enough memory, and as soon as it writes the file once, it won't have to write it again. To prevent this behavior, we'll *unmount* and *remount* the filesystem on which the file resides between runs, which has the effect of emptying the cache data. Filesystem mounting is covered in Chapter 7.

The following bash script was used to test the effect of buffer size on the performance of the *spl_cp2.c* program:

```
#!/bin/bash
umount /temp
printf "%s\t%s\t%s\t%s\n" Size Elapsed User System >> $1
for i in 1 2 4 8 16 32 64 128 256 512 1024 2048 4096 8192 16384 32768 65536
do
    for j in 1 2 3 4 5 ; do
        mount /temp
        echo -n "$i"  >> resultfile
        /usr/bin/time -f "\t%e \t%U \t%S" -o resultfile -a \
                        ./spl_cp2  /temp/src  /temp/cpy  $i
        umount /temp
    done
done
mount /temp
```

The file and the copy were stored on a filesystem that had no other activity and could be mounted and unmounted easily. The script creates a file in tabular form, which can be imported into a spreadsheet program for further analysis. Table 4-3 displays the results of the experiment.

Table 4-3: Effect of Buffer Size on Running Time of the *copy.c* Program

Buffer size (B)	Real time	User time	System time
1	214.242	58.556	155.608
2	107.516	29.388	78.020
4	53.874	14.784	38.870
8	27.254	7.298	19.556
16	14.002	3.700	9.772
32	7.328	1.792	4.992
64	3.986	0.920	2.562
128	2.272	0.428	1.338
256	1.470	0.216	0.718
512	1.010	0.110	0.396
1,024	0.816	0.046	0.252
2,048	0.686	0.030	0.166
4,096	0.640	0.012	0.134
8,192	0.636	0.006	0.112
16,384	0.642	0	0.108
32,768	0.586	0	0.106
65,536	0.608	0	0.108

Notice that for the small buffer sizes, doubling the buffer size roughly halves the system time, but as the buffer size gets larger and larger, the decrease in system time diminishes, and eventually, for the last few sizes, it shows no change. Consider the fact that no matter how many calls to read() the program makes, by the time the program finishes, the entire file has to be transferred from the kernel's buffer cache to the program's memory area. The buffer size affects how many transfers are needed, but it doesn't change the total number of bytes to be transferred. In short, the time to transfer the data cannot be diminished by making fewer system calls. The total overhead of the calls becomes smaller as the buffer size grows, but not the total transfer time. The same principle applies to the write operations. It's a law of diminishing returns; the gain in performance obtained with larger buffer sizes is limited by the time it takes to do the transfer operations.

The experiment's results suggest that, for this particular filesystem and host computer, the total time used by the program doesn't change much for buffer sizes larger than 4096. It's certainly clear that buffers smaller than 512 bytes aren't good choices if we're trying to make our program run quickly. In general, the larger the buffer size, the less system call overhead our spl_cp program has. On the other hand, if we make the buffer so large that it's larger than the file to be copied, our program will incur needless overhead in the kernel when it tries to allocate unnecessary memory in its buffer cache.

The `cp` command in GNU/Linux is implemented in the GNU *Coreutils* library. In the most recent stable release (9.6) of that library as of this writing, for ordinary files, the choice of buffer size is determined at runtime by the `io_blksize()` function, which chooses an appropriate block size for I/O transfers. It defaults to 128KB (2^{17} bytes), much larger than our choice of 4096 bytes!

Finally, although our experiment tells us something about system call overhead, it doesn't measure the effect of the buffer size on actual disk I/O transfer times. We'll explore file I/O again in Chapter 17.

Summary

Unix employs a simple model of I/O that rests on four pillars: the `open()`, `close()`, `read()`, and `write()` system calls. To transfer data to or from a file, a program opens it, performs the transfer using either `read()` or `write()`, and closes it. This model is universal, in that these same four system calls can be applied to all nondirectory files, including device files. A program does not need to call specialized functions to perform I/O on devices.

Every process inherits a file creation mask, also called a umask, that partly determines the permissions assigned to any files that it creates. Users can define the umask given to all of their processes in their `bash` startup files.

In Unix, a process has four user IDs: a real user ID, an effective user ID, a saved user ID, and, specifically in Linux, a filesystem user ID that serve as its credentials. When a process tries to access a resource such as a file, the kernel makes sure that it has the proper credentials for the type of access it is attempting. Linux kernels use the filesystem user ID to do so, and other Unix kernels use the effective user ID. The kernel only grants permission for a resource if the type of access requested is allowed for its user ID. This is how the file permission is used.

When a process opens a file, the kernel creates a data structure called an open file description that represents its connection to that file, and it gives that process an integer file descriptor associated with that description. Files may be opened by multiple processes, and even by the same process multiple times, and each open operation results in a new open file description. All operations on an open file, such as reading and writing, must be given its file descriptor. Every process started in an interactive shell is given three file descriptors, numbered 0, 1, and 2, that refer to the standard input, the standard output, and the standard error. Standard input is connected to the terminal device keyboard and the other two to its screen.

Processes can open files for reading, writing, or both. The `open()` call allows a process to control other aspects of its connection to the file, such as what to do if a file to be written already exists and what permissions to assign to newly created files. The `read()` and `write()` system calls each have three parameters: the file descriptor, the memory address of a buffer, and a number of bytes to transfer to or from that buffer, called the buffer size. The choice of buffer size is up to the programmer. In this chapter, we demonstrated how to use the file I/O system calls by implementing an elementary file-copying program that can make a copy of a file specified on the command line with a new or existing filename.

Unix provides commands that we can use for measuring the amount of time that our program takes, so that we have a way to improve its performance. The time command is one of them. It can report on three different times associated with a process: the system time, which is time spent in kernel mode; user time, which is time spent in user mode; and real or elapsed time, which is the time elapsed from when the process began to run and when it terminated.

The running time of a process that performs file I/O is greatly influenced by the size of the buffer used for the transfers. In general, larger buffer sizes result in shorter running times, up to a limit, but when we really want to find optimal values, we need to take into consideration other factors, such as the size of the file and the size of the blocks used by the filesystem and kernel for transfers.

Exercises

1. For each umask, write the permissions given to the file after the specified command.
    (a) The umask is 024 and the new file is created by the touch command.
    (b) The umask is 023 and the file is created by gcc when you compile a program successfully.
    (c) The umask is 066. A file named *foo* has permissions rwxrwxrwx. A new file is created with the command cp foo foo.copy.

2. Rewrite the *spl_cp1.c* program so that the buffer size is a command line option of the form -B *bufsize* and it uses a default value of 4096 if the option is not present.

3. Implement a command named transcript so that when a user enters transcript myfile, all of its standard input will be copied to both its standard output and to the file named *myfile*. Name the program file *transcript.c*. (Hint: The *spl_cp1.c* program can be modified to do this. This command can also be used in a pipeline, as in ls | transcript mydir.)

4. The cat command can be used to concatenate files. For example, cat f1 f2 f3 concatenates files *f1*, *f2*, and *f3* and displays their concatenation on standard output. Implement this command. Assume that the total number of files allowed on the command line is 10. Remember that the program does not need to open or close standard output.

5

FILE I/O AND LOGIN ACCOUNTING

In the preceding chapter, we learned the fundamental concepts of file I/O as well as how to use the basic system calls related to it. Here, we'll add a few more advanced tools to our repertoire so we can create more sophisticated programs. First, we'll consider ways to control the position of the file offset, which is the component of an open file description that stores the position of the next byte to read or write in a file. Being able to control the file offset will give us the means to solve problems we currently can't solve that require reading from nonconsecutive parts of files. We'll apply this new knowledge to develop a few programs for displaying various types of information about login records.

All Unix systems record and maintain information about who has logged in, when they did so, and more, in order to answer questions such as who is currently logged in, who has logged in within some past length of time, and when was the last time that one or more users logged in. We'll examine the files and data structures that store this information as well as the programming interfaces to them.

When we do the background research to write these programs, we'll discover that there are parts of the kernel API that simplify access to particular system databases, and we'll explore what they do and how we can use them. We'll then create a few programs that manipulate some of that data. Finally, we'll discuss a few performance issues and design choices in the programs we developed.

Controlling the Position of I/O Operations

In Chapter 4, the read operation that we use in the spl_cp1 program is oblivious to the structure of the files it copies; it doesn't matter whether the transfers are aligned with any structural elements in the file. Figure 5-1 illustrates this idea.

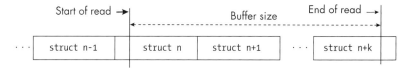

Figure 5-1: The positions at the start and end of a read operation with respect to structures in a file

The diagram depicts a portion of a file that consists of a sequence of C structs of uniform size. The buffer size in the system call read(fd, buf, bufsize) of that program is not chosen to align with any internal structure that the file might have. If neither buf nor bufsize is an exact multiple of the size of these structures, the beginning and ending positions of read operations can fall in the middle of these C structs. For the spl_cp1 program, this doesn't matter—it ultimately copies all the bytes from one file to another, preserving their sequence—but other programs might need to align the starting points of read operations to the starts of these structures.

Programs that need to align their reads and writes with particular offsets in a file need the ability to move the file offset to the position at which they need to perform their next I/O operation.

The lseek() System Call

When a file is first opened, the file offset is set to the start of the file, unless the O_APPEND flag was passed to the open() call. We haven't yet discussed the significance of the O_APPEND flag, but we'll do so in Chapters 11 and 17. If read() is called to read *N* bytes from the file, and it succeeds, the file offset is automatically advanced *N* bytes. Similarly, if a write operation writes *N* bytes, the file offset is advanced *N* bytes. We don't control this.

When a program explicitly moves the file offset, it's called *seeking*. Unix kernels provide a system call named lseek(), which changes the current file offset's position. Its man page begins with:

```
#include <sys/types.h>
#include <unistd.h>
off_t lseek(int fd, off_t offset, int whence);
```

DESCRIPTION

lseek() repositions the file offset of the open file description associated with the file descriptor fd to the argument offset according to the directive whence as follows:

SEEK_SET

The file offset is set to offset bytes.

--snip--

The lseek() system call has three parameters: a file descriptor (fd), a distance in bytes (offset), and an integer flag (whence), which can take on one of the following macro constants: SEEK_SET, SEEK_CUR, or SEEK_END. The offset value, which can be given any integer value including negative numbers, is the number of bytes to move the file offset. A positive value moves it forward, and a negative value moves it backward. The value of whence determines the starting position from which it is to be moved. It has three possible values:

SEEK_SET   The file offset moves offset bytes relative to the file's start.

SEEK_CUR   The file offset moves offset bytes relative to the current value of the file offset.

SEEK_END   The file offset moves offset bytes relative to the file's end.

Figure 5-2 illustrates how the file offset is adjusted based on the different parameter values.

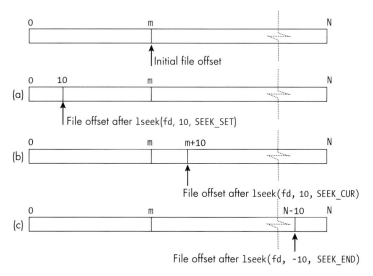

Figure 5-2: The effect of the whence parameter on the movement of the file offset. In (a) it's moved using whence = SEEK_SET, in (b) using whence = SEEK_CUR, and in (c) using whence = SEEK_END.

If the resulting value of the file offset would be negative, it's an error, and it isn't moved. Instead, lseek() returns -1 and sets errno to EINVAL. There are several other ways it can fail, and in all cases it returns -1 and sets errno to an error value. The man page lists all of the possible errors.

If lseek() is successful, its return value is the resulting position of the offset as measured in bytes from the beginning of the file. This return value is useful for two purposes. One is that we can get the current position of the offset with the call:

```
off_t current_pos = lseek(fd, 0, SEEK_CUR);
```

This call doesn't move the file offset, and current_pos is its current position.

We can also use lseek() to get the size of a file by seeking to the end and getting the return value:

```
off_t size = lseek(fd, 0, SEEK_END);
```

Since the file offset is now at the end of the file, the return value is the size of the file in bytes, which we store in size.

Other examples of using lseek() are:

```
lseek(fd, 20, SEEK_SET)    /* Byte 20 of the file               */
lseek(fd, -1, SEEK_END)    /* The last byte of the file         */
lseek(fd, -1, SEEK_CUR)    /* The byte before the current offset */
lseek(fd,  0, SEEK_SET)    /* The first byte in the file        */
```

In all of the preceding examples, we didn't try to move the file offset past the end of the file. Let's look at what happens when we do.

File Holes

Although we can't move the file offset to a position preceding the start of the file, we can move it to a position *after* the end of the file! For example, when the value of offset is positive and whence is SEEK_END, the file offset is moved beyond the end of the file. Data can be written to this position, and this in effect creates a gap in the file between the original end of the file and the start of the data just written. This gap is called a *file hole*. If we then call lseek(fd, 0, SEEK_END), the file offset is advanced to the new end of the file.

The read() system call doesn't return an error when the file offset is inside a file hole. Instead, it treats the hole as a sequence of NULL bytes (bytes whose value is zero). To be precise, if the file offset is inside a file hole, the call read(fd, buffer, count) fills buffer with a NULL byte for every byte in the hole that it reads. Thus, if all count bytes are within the hole and the buffer is at least count bytes long, buffer[0...count-1] will be filled with zeros. If count is large enough that the file offset plus count contains data after the hole, then that data will be stored into buffer following the zeros. Figure 5-3 illustrates a file hole.

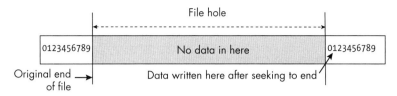

Figure 5-3: A file hole created by seeking past the end of a file and writing data there

Figure 5-3 depicts a situation in which a process opened a file consisting of the 10 consecutive characters 0123456789, after which it performed a seek that moved the file offset 1,000,000 bytes past the end and then wrote the same sequence of characters (0123456789) at the new file offset. The file size then became 10 + 1,000,000 + 10 = 1,000,020 bytes, even though the file has a hole of 1,000,000 bytes within it. Listing 5-1 is a program that creates such a file.

makefilehole.c
```
#define MESSAGE_SIZE    512
#define BUFFER_SIZE      10

int main(int argc, char *argv[])
{
    int  fd;
    char buffer[BUFFER_SIZE];
    char message[MESSAGE_SIZE];

    if ( 2 > argc ) {
        sprintf(message, " %s <file-to-create>\n", basename(argv[0]));
        usage_error(message);
    }
    /* Create a new file named file_with_hole in the pwd. */
    if ( (fd = open(argv[1], O_WRONLY | O_CREAT | O_EXCL, 0644)) < 0 )
        fatal_error(errno, "open");

    /* Fill buffer with a string. */
    strncpy(buffer, "0123456789", BUFFER_SIZE);

    /* Write the string at the beginning of the file. */
    if ( write(fd, buffer, BUFFER_SIZE) != BUFFER_SIZE )
        fatal_error(errno, "write");
    /* Seek 1,000,000 bytes past the end of the file. */
    if ( lseek(fd, 1000000, SEEK_END) == -1 )
        fatal_error(errno, "lseek");
    /* Write the small string at the new file offset. */
    if ( write(fd, buffer, BUFFER_SIZE) != BUFFER_SIZE )
        fatal_error(errno, "write");
    if ( close(fd) == -1 )
        fatal_error(errno, "close");
    exit(EXIT_SUCCESS);
}
```

Listing 5-1: A program that creates a file with a hole

We run it to create a file named *file_with_hole* and inspect its size with the command ls -l file_with_hole:

```
$ ./makefilehole file_with_hole
$ ls -l file_with_hole
-rw-r--r-- 1 stewart stewart 1000020 Jun  3 11:57 file_with_hole
```

However, the file doesn't actually contain 1,000,020 bytes.

We can see its actual disk allocation with a few different commands. One way is to use ls -s --block-size=1. The -s option of ls shows the number of blocks allocated to the file, and the --block-size=1 option specifies that the -s option should use units of 1 byte. The command

```
$ ls -s --block-size=1 file_with_hole
8192 file_with_hole
```

shows that this file actually has 8192 bytes. Since disk blocks on the device where the file resides are 4096 bytes (4KB) each, the file is allocated two 4096-byte blocks. We'll explain why it has these two blocks shortly.

A second method of seeing its actual disk allocation is to use the du command, which displays disk usage for the files specified as its arguments. It also accepts a --block-size=1 option to show block size units of 1 byte:

```
$ du --block-size=1 file_with_hole
8192 file_with_hole
```

Even though the file appears to have a size of 1,000,020 bytes when we use ls -l, it's allocated only two disk blocks of 4KB each. Files are allocated storage in fixed-size blocks. A write of $N \leq 4096$ bytes at the start of the file requires one 4KB block. Any remaining bytes of that block are filled with NULLs. Since we wrote the second string 1,000,010 bytes from the start of the file, the filesystem allocated a second block for the file. The start of that block must be a multiple of 4096 bytes from the start of the file. The largest multiple of 4096 less than 1,000,010 is $\lfloor 1{,}000{,}010 / 4096 \rfloor \times 4096$, which is 999,424. Thus the second block starts at byte offset 999,424 in the file. Since 1,000,010 − 999,424 = 586, the start of that second string in the second block is 586 bytes after the start of that block. All bytes preceding that string in that block are filled with zeros, and all bytes after it are filled with zeros. There are no other blocks. Figure 5-4 illustrates where the string starts in the file and its relationship to the start of the block.

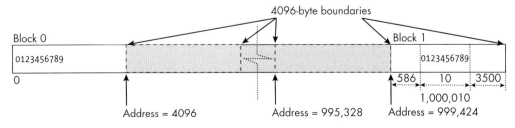

Figure 5-4: A not-to-scale diagram of the disk blocks allocated to the file with holes that is depicted in Figure 5-3

The od command can show us the actual file contents. We can give it two options: -a displays any bytes containing characters as the characters themselves rather than their numeric codes, and -Ad displays addresses in decimal instead of the default radix, which is octal:

```
$ od -a -Ad file_with_hole
0000000   0   1   2   3   4   5   6   7   8   9 nul nul nul nul nul nul
0000016 nul nul nul nul nul nul nul nul nul nul nul nul nul nul nul nul
*
1000000 nul nul nul nul nul nul nul nul nul nul   0   1   2   3   4   5
1000016   6   7   8   9
1000020
```

The * notation in the third row of output indicates that the missing lines are identical to the preceding line of 16 NULL bytes. In all other rows, the first column is the decimal address of the first byte in that row. The remaining fields in a row are the values of the bytes at the 16 successive addresses starting at that address. The nul string means that the byte is zero filled. If the low-order 7 bits of a byte represent a character, the character is displayed. That's why we see the actual characters in the output. Even though they look like numbers, they are just characters.

The next time the output of ls -l suggests that a file is of a large size, remember that the actual amount of disk space used by the file might be less. In general, files that appear to be of a large size but really use only a small fraction of that size are called *sparse files*.

Displaying Last Login Information

One problem for which we need to control the position of the file offset is the retrieval and update of login records. Unix systems, like most operating systems, keep track of logins and logouts. They record the times that a user logs in and logs out, as well as other information associated with those events. Ordinary users have permission to read this data; we don't need to be a system administrator or have superuser privilege to see it. The data is structured, usually stored as C structures in binary form in disk files. In order to read, update, or write new records located in particular positions in a file, a program needs to move the file offset to those positions.

We're going to implement a command that reads data from this type of file so that we can get experience in managing the file offset. In particular, we'd like to know which commands print data associated with previous logins on our system, such as the last time that a user logged in or out. We expect that the man page descriptions of such commands will include words such as *login*, *logout*, or *logged*, as well as the word *last*. Although most commands are in Section 1 (Commands) of the man pages, commands used for system administration may also be found in Section 8 (System Management Commands).

We'll use apropos with the -a option to search for all pages containing both *log* and *last* in these two sections:

```
$ apropos -s1,8 -a log last
last (1)              - show a listing of last logged in users
lastb (1)             - show a listing of last logged in users
lastlog (8)           - reports the most recent login of all users or of
                        a given user
pam_lastlog (8)       - PAM module to display date of last login
                        and perform inactive account lock out
```

The output lists three commands of interest: last, lastb, and lastlog. The first two have the same description, and their man pages are worth examining. In fact, they have a shared man page, which states that the last command searches back through a file whose typical pathname is */var/log/wtmp* and displays a list of users who have logged in and possibly logged out since the date the file was created. The lastb command is similar, but it reports only on bad login attempts. We'll revisit the last command later in this chapter.

THE PATHS.H FILE

Although the man page tells us that the *wtmp* file is in */var/log/*, it may not be in that location on all systems. The locations of common system files and directories vary from one Unix distribution to another. To allow applications to be written in a portable way, when a Unix system is installed, the system header file */usr/include/paths.h* is populated with macros for the actual pathnames of common system files. For example, it defines _PATH_WTMP as a macro name for the pathname of the *wtmp* file

```
#define _PATH_WTMP "/var/log/wtmp"
```

and _PATH_MAN as the pathname to the directory storing the compressed man pages:

```
#define _PATH_MAN "/usr/share/man"
```

Whenever possible, instead of hardcoding actual pathnames in a program, it's better to use the macros. This way, if the program is compiled and run on a machine in which the system file is in a different location than the one on which we developed the code, it will still locate the file.

If you'd like to use the macros from */usr/include/paths.h*, you can modify the header file *sys_hdrs.h* introduced in Chapter 2 to include that header as well, or include *paths.h* in each program needing those macros.

The lastlog Command

The lastlog command displays a list of the most recent logins of all users who have ever logged in or, if a username is given to it, the most recent login of that user. Sample output of the command looks like this:

```
$ lastlog
--snip--
sam            pts/2      192.168.1.112    Wed Feb 19 22:01:56 -0400 2025
lightdm                                       **Never logged in**
nm-openvpn                                    **Never logged in**
brit           pts/1      192.168.1.165    Mon Jan 20 11:20:50 -0400 2025
sshd                                          **Never logged in**
--snip--
```

This command displays the username for every user of the system who has ever logged in, the terminal line on which the login occurred, the host IP address or hostname, whether it was a remote login, and the time and the date of the login. The time is given in the locale's time format, because if I run it changing the locale's LC_TIME category to the Spanish language

```
$ LC_TIME=es_ES.utf8 lastlog
--snip--
sam            pts/2      192.168.1.112    mié abr 19 22:01:56 -0400 2023
--snip--
```

it displays the date and time in Spanish.

We're going to try to implement the lastlog command. Its man page starts with:

```
LASTLOG(8)                   System Management Commands                   LASTLOG(8)


NAME
       lastlog - reports the most recent login of all users or of a given user

SYNOPSIS
       lastlog [options]

DESCRIPTION
       lastlog formats and prints the contents of the last login log
       /var/log/lastlog file. The login-name, port, and last login time will
       be printed. The default (no flags) causes lastlog entries to be
       printed, sorted by their order in /etc/passwd.
--snip--
```

After the OPTIONS section, there's more detailed information about the command and its database file, which the page states is *var/log/lastlog*. The *paths.h* header file has a macro for this file's pathname

```
#define _PATH_LASTLOG "/var/log/lastlog"
```

which we'll use when we implement it.

The lastlog File

The *lastlog file* is a database that contains information about each user's last login. The `lastlog` command accesses records from this file. The page tells us that the database file is sparse, which implies that the file holes in it account for most of its size. We can infer something about the organization of the file from the following remark in the CAVEATS section of the page:

CAVEATS

Large gaps in UID numbers will cause the lastlog program to run longer with no output to the screen (i.e. if in lastlog database there is no entries for users with UID between 170 and 800 lastlog will appear to hang as it processes entries with UIDs 171-799).

We now know the following:

- There are no entries for users who have never logged in.

- The `lastlog` command produces no output and appears to hang when it reaches a sequence of user IDs of users who have no entries.

- The file can be sparse.

- The file appears to be large if there are users with high user IDs.

Since the file's size increases as user IDs get higher, and since the command takes time even though it produces no output when there's no record for a user, and since it's sparse, we can infer that the file is like a large array of records for all possible users such that the location in the file of a user's record is proportional to the user's user ID, as shown in Figure 5-5.

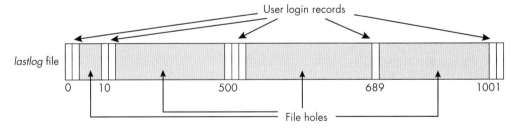

Figure 5-5: The structure of the lastlog file

Figure 5-5 shows five clusters of user login records, and the rest of the file has no data. In other words, it has file holes. The `lastlog` command spends time in these holes only to discover that the associated users have never logged in.

The lastlog Structure

The man page doesn't show us each record's structure; for that, we need to do more research. To learn about the form and content of this structure, we check whether there's a man page for the file itself, perhaps in the FILES section of the man pages, but there isn't. We then check whether there's a header file that defines the structures. That file would most likely be named *lastlog.h* and be located in */usr/include*. Sure enough, that file exists and has just four lines:

```
$ more /usr/include/lastlog.h
/* This header file is used in 4.3BSD to define `struct lastlog',
   which we define in <bits/utmp.h>. */

#include <utmp.h>
```

The comment states that the definition of struct lastlog is in *bits/utmp.h*. If you try to find a directory named *bits* on your system, you'll discover many of them, and they may not even contain an entry for the *lastlog.h* file.

This leads to a more general question. When we write an #include directive in a program, such as

```
#include <utmp.h>
```

and there are multiple files named *utmp.h* in the filesystem, which of them does the compiler use?

The compiler searches through a sequence of directories for included files in a well-defined order. Technically, it's not the compiler, but the compiler's preprocessor, cpp on GNU/Linux, that defines and uses this sequence. To display the preprocessor's search sequence on a GNU/Linux system, we can run the following command:

```
$ cpp -v /dev/null -o /dev/null
```

The -v is a gcc option that tells cpp to produce *verbose* output. The first argument is the program to preprocess, in this case /dev/null, which is an empty file. The -o /dev/null tells it to throw away the processed code, which in this case is nonexistent. The command runs the preprocessor on an empty program in verbose mode, outputting its diagnostic report on the standard error stream (the screen) and throwing away the standard output.

You'll see many output lines of messages, but there'll be a line starting with #include <...> search starts here:. The lines following that line show the search path for included header files. On my system, I see the following:

```
--snip--
#include <...> search starts here:
 /usr/lib/gcc/x86_64-linux-gnu/11/include
 /usr/local/include
 /usr/include/x86_64-linux-gnu
 /usr/include
End of search list.
```

To find the correct *bits/utmp.h* file, we look in each directory in turn, starting with the first. On my system, the first (and only) occurrence of the *bits/utmp.h* file is */usr/include/x86_64-linux-gnu/bits/utmp.h*.

Let's look at that file:

```
--snip--
#ifndef _UTMP_H
#error "Never include <bits/utmp.h> directly; use <utmp.h> instead."
#endif

#include <paths.h>
#include <sys/time.h>
#include <sys/types.h>
#include <bits/wordsize.h>

#define UT_LINESIZE   32
#define UT_NAMESIZE   32
#define UT_HOSTSIZE 256

/* The structure describing an entry in the database of previous logins */
struct lastlog {
❶ #if __WORDSIZE_TIME64_COMPAT32
    int32_t ll_time;
#else
    __time_t ll_time;
#endif
    char ll_line[UT_LINESIZE];
    char ll_host[UT_HOSTSIZE];
};
--snip--
```

The warning at the top is that a program should never include *bits/utmp.h* directly. Instead it should include *utmp.h*, because that file includes *bits/utmp.h*.

The lastlog structure has three members. The first is named ll_time and is either of type __time_t or int32_t. The value of the __WORDSIZE_TIME64_COMPAT32 ❶ macro determines whether the ll_time member of the lastlog structure is declared as __time_t or int32_t.

How and where is this macro defined? The included file <bits/wordsize.h> is most likely where it's defined. Its full path would be */usr/include/x86_64 -linux-gnu/bits/wordsize.h*. There, we see yet another conditional macro:

```
#ifdef __x86_64__
#define __WORDSIZE_TIME64_COMPAT32 1
/* Both x86-64 and x32 use the 64-bit system call interface. */
#define __SYSCALL_WORDSIZE 64
#else
#define __WORDSIZE_TIME64_COMPAT32 0
#endif
```

The macro __x86_64__ is set to true when the compiler is installed on a 64-bit architecture that is running in *32-bit compatibility mode*. This means that the machine can run applications that consist of instructions for a 32-bit architecture even though it's a 64-bit machine. On such machines,__WORDSIZE_TIME64 _COMPAT32 is set to true (1); otherwise, it's set to false (0).

The comment preceding the conditional macro explains the need for it. It ensures that if the machine is a 64-bit machine that allows 32-bit applications to run, such as an x86-64 or a ppc64, all applications will see int32_t as the type of ll_time, which is 4 bytes, and otherwise, they'll all see its type as __time_t, which is 8 bytes on a 64-bit machine and 4 bytes on a 32-bit machine. This implies that when we use the sizeof() function in C to obtain the number of bytes in the struct lastlog on our system, as in sizeof(struct lastlog), our program will have the correct size, independent of the architecture, implying that we can read the structure safely with a call of the form read(fd, ll_buffer, sizeof(struct lastlog)).

READING STRUCTURES FROM A FILE

You can read an arbitrary C struct such as struct lastlog from a file with file descriptor fd into a local variable, say, ll_record of type struct lastlog, using the following code:

```
size_t lastlog_struct_size = sizeof(struct lastlog);
size_t num_bytes_read = read(fd, &ll_record, lastlog_struct_size);
if ( num_bytes_read < 0 )
    // read() error - handle it.
else if ( num_bytes_read == lastlog_struct_size ) {
    // Success - can access members with code such as
    // printf("%s\n", ll_record.ll_line)
else
    // It was an incomplete read.
```

You would typically set errno to 0 before the call in order to determine after the call what, if any, error occurred.

The other two members, ll_line and ll_host, are character arrays. In the header file just shown, these are of size 32 and 256, respectively. There is no member that stores a user ID because the records are indexed by the user ID, and therefore, the address of a record in the file implicitly gives us the user ID. In other words, letting N = sizeof(struct lastlog) be the size of the lastlog structure in bytes, if a structure starts at byte address $m \times N$, then it represents the last login of the user whose user ID is m.

The lastlog structure doesn't have a username member either, so we need to find out how to obtain the username of a user whose user ID is given.

Usernames, User IDs, and the passwd File

If we enter **apropos -s2,3 user** to find either a system call or library function that returns the username associated with a given user ID, we'll get over

100 man pages that match the word *user*. We can inspect the output line by line for a candidate that might work, or we can reduce its size by piping it through the grep filter command. A *filter command* reads its input from the standard input, unless it's given a filename argument, in which case it reads from the file and outputs a modification of its input on the standard output. The grep filter expects a string argument. The string can be a pattern, which is best enclosed in single quotes. If it's not a pattern, grep searches for that string exactly in every line of its standard input. By default, it outputs only those lines that have a match, so grep `name` will output only those lines containing the word `name`. It acts like a sieve, throwing away lines that don't match. Here's the result:

```
$ apropos -s2,3 user | grep name    # Find all entries containing "name"
attr_list (3)        - list the names of the user attributes of a filesyste...
attr_listf (3)       - list the names of the user attributes of a filesyste...
cuserid (3)          - get username
getlogin (3)         - get username
getlogin_r (3)       - get username
getpwnam (3posix)    - search user database for a name
getseuserbyname (3)  - get SELinux username and level for a given Linux use...
User::grent (3perl)  - by-name interface to Perl's built-in getgr*() functions
User::pwent (3perl)  - by-name interface to Perl's built-in getpw*() functions
```

(If your output does not look like this, try explicitly including Section 3posix, as in `apropos -s2,3,3posix`.)

The one result that stands out is getpwnam in Section 3posix of the man pages, since it searches a user database for a name. The three functions whose description is get `username` return only the username of the calling process, which isn't what we want.

The POSIX man page for getpwnam is a specification of what the function should do. The relevant fragments of it are:

```
GETPWNAM(3POSIX)           POSIX Programmer's Manual           GETPWNAM(3POSIX)

PROLOG
       This manual page is part of the POSIX Programmer's Manual. The Linux
       implementation of this interface may differ (consult the corresponding
       Linux manual page for details of Linux behavior), or the interface may
       not be implemented on Linux.

NAME
       getpwnam, getpwnam_r - search user database for a name

SYNOPSIS
       #include <pwd.h>

       struct passwd *getpwnam(const char *name);
       int getpwnam_r(const char *name, struct passwd *pwd, char *buffer,
                 size_t bufsize, struct passwd **result);
```

The getpwnam() function shall search the user database for an entry with a matching name.

--snip--

This seems to be the opposite of what we want. It takes a name argument and searches for a matching user record in a database. We want a function that searches that database when it's given a user ID.

However, the page gives us a clue: The function returns a pointer to a struct passwd. We should investigate this structure. Also, we should scroll down to the SEE ALSO section of the page to see whether it mentions other functions that might be more like what we're after. There, it mentions the function getpwuid(). Let's look at its man page:

GETPWNAM(3)   Linux Programmer's Manual   GETPWNAM(3)

NAME

        getpwnam, getpwnam_r, getpwuid, getpwuid_r - get password file entry

SYNOPSIS

        #include <sys/types.h>
        #include <pwd.h>

        struct passwd *getpwnam(const char *name);
        struct passwd *getpwuid(uid_t uid);
        int getpwnam_r(const char *name, struct passwd *pwd,
                    char *buf, size_t buflen, struct passwd **result);
        int getpwuid_r(uid_t uid, struct passwd *pwd,
                    char *buf, size_t buflen, struct passwd **result);
        --snip--
        The getpwuid() function returns a pointer to a structure containing the
        broken-out fields of the record in the password database that matches
        the user ID uid.

        The passwd structure is defined in <pwd.h> as follows:
            struct passwd {
                char   *pw_name;   /* Username   */
                char   *pw_passwd;   /* User password   */
                uid_t   pw_uid;   /* User ID   */
                gid_t   pw_gid;   /* Group ID   */
                char   *pw_gecos;   /* User information */
                char   *pw_dir;   /* Home directory   */
                char   *pw_shell;   /* Shell program   */
            };

        See passwd(5) for more information about these fields.
--snip--

We've found the function we need. The getpwuid() function is given a user ID and returns a pointer to a passwd structure for the user with that user ID. The passwd structure is summarized on this man page, which also refers us to the *pwd.h* header file for its declaration. Furthermore, it tells us that there's a man page in Section 5 named passwd. Since Section 5 contains file formats, this is a description of the password file, named *passwd* in Unix (missing the *or* in *password*).

This man page provides enough information for us to use the getpwuid() function, but it's a better idea to learn more about the passwd structure and the *passwd* file before continuing.

The Password Database

In Unix systems, all users have an entry in the password database, whose pathname is always */etc/passwd*. That file is a plaintext file, unlike the *lastlog* file, and it's usually world readable, so you can view its contents with any of the commands for viewing files, such as less /etc/passwd. Each line in the file represents a single user account, and in Linux it contains seven fields separated by colons. POSIX.1-2024 requires an implementation to have only five of these fields; the actual password and user information fields are optional. This is what a typical entry looks like:

```
linus:x:501:600:Linus Torvalds:/home/linus:/bin/bash
```

The first field is the username (linus). The second is the actual encrypted password, unless it is marked with an x to indicate that the actual password is stored elsewhere. The third field is the user ID (501), and the fourth is the group ID (600). The fifth is traditionally called the *gecos* or *comment* field, and it can contain anything that the system administrator chooses to put there, but it's often used for the user's actual name. The next two fields are the absolute pathname of the user's home directory and their startup shell.

The passwd structure and all functions that work with it are declared in */usr/include/pwd.h*. The man page for *pwd.h* lists all of the relevant functions, as shown in Listing 5-2.

```
void          endpwent(void);
struct passwd *getpwent(void);
struct passwd *getpwnam(const char *);
int           getpwnam_r(const char *, struct passwd *, char *,
                         size_t, struct passwd **);
struct passwd *getpwuid(uid_t);
int           getpwuid_r(uid_t, struct passwd *, char *,
                         size_t, struct passwd **);
void          setpwent(void);
```

Listing 5-2: Functions that set and get password database information

We're going to explore several of these functions shortly, but first let's see how we can use the getpwuid() function.

The argument of getpwuid() is of type uid_t, which is an integer type. The return value is a pointer to a passwd structure. The function may allocate that structure in static memory, which means it can be overwritten by a subsequent call to any of the functions that return a pointer to a passwd structure. Therefore, if we want to access the structure's members at a later time, we have to copy the structure to a local variable in the program. If not, we just declare a local pointer variable.

Listing 5-3 illustrates how we can use getpwuid() to print the user ID and username of the user running the program.

getpwuid
_demo.c
```
#include "common_hdrs.h"
#include <pwd.h>
int main(int argc, char *argv[])
{
    uid_t userid;
    struct passwd *psswd_struct; /* To save pointer returned by getpwuid() */

    /* Get the real user ID associated with the process, which
       is the same as that of the user who runs this command. */
    userid = getuid();

    /* To get the user name, we retrieve the password structure
       from the real user ID using the following function. */
    psswd_struct = getpwuid(userid);

    /* Print out the user ID with the name, in the same format as the
       id command. */
    printf("uid=%d(%s)\n", userid, psswd_struct->pw_name);
    return 0;
}
```

Listing 5-3: A program that displays the user's username and user ID

We compile and build this program using gcc and run it as follows:

```
$ gcc -I../include getpwuid_demo.c -o getpwuid_demo
$ ./getpwuid_demo
uid=500(stewart)
```

If you do the same on your machine, you'll see your username and user ID.

Accessing All User Entries

The functions listed in Listing 5-2 have two separate man pages: getpwnam(), getpwnam_r(), getpwuid(), and getpwuid_r() are explained in one page, and setpwent(), getpwent(), and endpwent() are explained in the second. These last three functions can be used to iterate through all user entries in the *passwd* file. Their man page explains how this works:

- The getpwent() function returns a pointer to a record from the password database. The first time it's called, it returns the first entry; thereafter, it returns successive entries. It returns NULL when there are no more entries or if there's an error.

- The setpwent() rewinds the password database so that the next call to getpwent() returns the first entry.

- The endpwent() function closes the password database.

The man page notes that all three have feature test macro requirements. To use any of them we need to expose their declarations with the appropriate #define macros prior to including the header files. We can either define _XOPEN_SOURCE with a value of at least 500 or, on systems with version later than *glibc* 2.19, define _DEFAULT_SOURCE; on systems with older versions of *glibc*, we can instead define _BSD_SOURCE or _SVID_SOURCE.

It also notes that neither setpwent() nor endpwent() returns a value and that both always succeed, so we don't need to check for errors after calling them; however, because getpwent() can fail, we do have to check for errors after that call.

From their descriptions, it follows that we can first initialize the iterator with a call to setpwent() and then call getpwent() in a while loop, terminating the loop when its return value is NULL. The program in Listing 5-4 demonstrates this logic.

showallusers.c
```
#define _GNU_SOURCE
#define _XOPEN_SOURCE 500
#include "common_hdrs.h"
#include <pwd.h>

int main(int argc, char *argv[])
{
    struct passwd *psswd_struct;        /* Stores returned record */

    if ( NULL == setlocale(LC_TIME, "") )  /* Set the locale.     */
        fatal_error(LOCALE_ERROR,
                    "setlocale() could not set the given locale");
    setpwent();                          /* Initialize the iterator. */
    errno = 0; /* Set errno to 0 to detect error from getpwent(). */
    /* Repeatedly call getpwent() until it returns NULL. */
    while ( (psswd_struct = getpwent()) != NULL ) {
        /* Print the pw_name member of the struct. */
        printf("%s\n", psswd_struct->pw_name);
    ❶ errno = 0;
    }
    if ( errno != 0 ) {
    ❷ fatal_error(errno, "getpwent");
```

```
    endpwent();                        /* Close the passwd database. */
    return 0;
}
```

Listing 5-4: A program that displays all usernames in the password database

First note that the program calls `setlocale()` to print usernames in a locale-sensitive way, just in case it's run on a host computer where some usernames use character sets other than US English. (We discussed locales in Chapter 3.) Also, the program defines _XOPEN_SOURCE with a value of 500 to enable the features described in the man page. Finally, note that we repeatedly reset errno to 0 ❶ in order to check its value ❷ after calling `getpwent()`.

We build the executable with:

```
$ gcc -Wall -g showallusers.c -I../include -L ../lib -lspl -o showallusers
```

The following shows a portion of its output, with most lines deleted for brevity:

```
$ ./showallusers
root
daemon
bin
--snip--
stewart
--snip--
ssd
getpwent: No such file or directory
```

The error message at the very end of the output comes from the program's call to `fatal_error()` ❶.

In "System Call Errors" in Chapter 2, we mentioned that the `errno -l` command lists all error messages with their symbolic names, numeric values, and associated message strings. We can run that command, or we can use the `-s` option to search specifically for this message:

```
$ errno -s "No such file or directory"
ENOENT 2 No such file or directory
```

The man page for `getpwent()` did not explicitly list this as a return value, which is why we didn't check for it. It occurs only at the end of the file. If we want to suppress it, we can modify the preceding `if` conditional to be (errno != 0 && errno != ENOENT). Aside from this, it seems that the program's logic can serve as the basis for our implementation of a `lastlog` command.

Developing a lastlog Program

We'll design and implement a simple version of the `lastlog` command. Initially, it won't accept any command line options. It will print the last login times of all users of the system.

Design Considerations

In the section "Displaying Last Login Information" on page 193, we saw that the *lastlog* file is sparse with large gaps between user records. Figure 5-5 illustrated a hypothetical *lastlog* file with just a few user records. Because user IDs assigned to users aren't necessarily consecutive numbers, we just can't write a loop such as

```
for ( u = lowest_userid; u < highest_userid; u++ )
    // OMITTED: Process lastlog structure for user u.
```

because a user may not exist for a particular value of the index variable u, and if we try to process a nonexistent record, we'll be in a file hole. In short, this loop processes every valid record in the file, but it also tries to access nonexistent ones, so it isn't correct.

We can, however, use the logic from the *showallusers.c* program in Listing 5-4 to iterate over all users and get their user IDs. Specifically, we could use a loop of the following form:

```
setpwent();
while ( (psswd_struct = getpwent()) != NULL ) {
    u = psswd_struct->pw_uid;
    // OMITTED: Process lastlog structure for user u.
}
endpwent();
```

With this loop, the only records we would access would be those of actual users, but it also tries to access login records that may not exist. Some users may never have logged in and therefore would not have a record in the *lastlog* file. Our algorithm must detect this case. In addition, some user accounts could have been deleted even though there are valid login records for them in the file, and this loop would not find them.

Another, lesser problem with this approach is that if the *passwd* file has not been managed properly, the entries in the file may not be in numerically increasing order of user ID. In this case, the successive reads would bounce back and forth in the *lastlog* file unless we saved the user IDs into an array and sorted them before reading the file. To demonstrate, the following is a very small fragment of the sequence of user IDs in the *passwd* file of a system I log into frequently:

```
...14609,5463,13933,14978,15535,14100,15230,14203,14921,15434,15050,
14567,15414,14431,15508,6187,14903,14010...
```

This list is very unordered, and using these user IDs in the order getpwent() returns them would cause a lot of long movements of the file offset in the *lastlog* file. Figure 5-6 illustrates the sequence of reads in a hypothetical machine whose password database is very out of order.

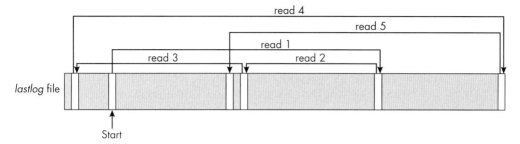

Figure 5-6: The order of reads in the lastlog file using the passwd structures returned by successive calls to getpwent() on a hypothetical host

If the *lastlog* file spans many disk blocks, the out-of-order reads would be slower than if they were closer together. The problem with out-of-order reads is a performance issue. The question is whether the time required to store all of the user IDs and sort them before reading any records from the file is greater than the time spent seeking because the records delivered by getpwent() are not in order. For this program, we won't sort the records. For a production version, we'd need to study this question further.

We have one other problem. Suppose the highest user ID of all users who have logged in is 1000. This implies that the *lastlog* file's highest entry starts at address 1000 × sizeof(struct lastlog). Suppose too that a user in the password database whose user ID is 1200 has never logged in. When the preceding loop tries to read the record for that user, which should be at location 1200 × sizeof(struct lastlog) in the file, the program will fail with some type of read error, since that address is beyond the end of the file. We need a way to determine whether the record we'd like to process is for a user whose user ID is higher than the highest one in the file.

We can solve this problem if we can obtain the size of the *lastlog* file before we start reading. If the file is of size *M* and isn't corrupted, meaning that it contains only complete lastlog structures, the highest user ID is (*M* / sizeof(struct lastlog)) − 1.

We can use lseek() to get the size of a file by seeking to the end and saving the returned value of the file offset in a variable:

```
off_t size = lseek(ll_fd, 0, SEEK_END);
```

We could also use the stat() system call to get the size of the file, but for this program, we'll use lseek().

Finally, we need to consider the matter of how time is represented. The lastlog structure's time representation is platform dependent, as we discovered in "The lastlog Structure" on page 196. The ll_time member might be one of two different data types, dependent on the macro condition:

```
#if __WORDSIZE_TIME64_COMPAT32
    int32_t ll_time;
#else
    __time_t ll_time;
#endif
```

The `localtime()` function, which we'll call to convert time to broken-down time, expects a value of type `time_t*`. We can't safely typecast `int32_t*` as an argument to `localtime()`. For example, if `ll_entry` is a lastlog struct, writing `localtime((time_t*)&(ll_entry.ll_time))` will fail, because all we'd be doing is casting the pointer type, but the underlying types might be different.

Instead, we'd have to assign the entry's time value to a variable of type `time_t`, as in

```
time_t ll_time = ll_entry.ll_time;
```

and pass that variable's address to `localtime()`. Since we need to do this only if `__WORDSIZE_TIME64_COMPAT32` is defined, the code will need to be conditionally compiled based on the value of that macro.

Program Logic

Let's sketch out the program's logic:

1. Open the *lastlog* file for reading and handle errors.
2. Get the size of the *lastlog* file.
3. Use the size to determine the largest user ID in the *lastlog* file.
4. Enable localization with a call to `setlocale()` so that dates and times are locale-sensitive.
5. Print a header row for the output.
6. For each entry in the password database:
   - (a) Get the user ID of this entry.
   - (b) Store the username associated with this user ID from the `psswd_struct->pw_name` member.
   - (c) Check whether the user ID is no greater than the highest user ID in the file. If it's greater, treat this as the case of a user who never logged in by printing a message that the user never logged in.
   - (d) If the user ID is within the bounds, seek to the start of the record in the *lastlog* file for that user ID.
   - (e) Read the lastlog structure into a temporary variable, `ll_entry`.
   - (f) If `ll_entry.ll_time` is 0, the user never logged in. Print a message that the user never logged in and skip to the next record.
   - (g) Either convert the login time stored in `ll_entry.ll_time` to a `time_t` type to pass to `localtime()`, or if it is already of type `time_t`, pass it directly.
   - (h) Use the broken-down time returned by `localtime()` in a call to `strftime()` to get a date/time string `lastlog_time` with the default format.
   - (i) Print a line on standard output with the user's name, the `ll_entry.ll_line`, the `ll_entry.ll_host`, and the login time, `lastlog_time`.

Implementing most of the preceding steps is straightforward, so our next task is to refine them, after which we can write the program. We'll start with the first step and continue in sequence.

Writing the Program

We know how to open the *lastlog* file and handle the potential error: We'll use the _PATH_LASTLOG macro defined in *paths.h* as the pathname of the file and let ll_fd store the file descriptor returned by the call to open the file:

```
errno = 0;
if ( (ll_fd = open(_PATH_LASTLOG, O_RDONLY)) == -1 )
    fatal_error(errno, "while opening " _PATH_LASTLOG);
```

We'll next get the size of a file with the method we described:

```
off_t ll_file_size = lseek(ll_fd,0, SEEK_END);
```

Then we'll get the largest user ID in the file as follows:

```
size_t ll_struct_size = sizeof(struct lastlog);
int highest_uid = ll_file_size/ll_struct_size - 1;
```

Given a user ID (uid), to seek to the start of the lastlog structure for that user ID, we simply multiply the user ID by the size of the structure:

```
offset = lseek(ll_fd, ll_struct_size*uid, SEEK_SET);
```

All of the pieces are now in place, and we can write the complete program, which appears in Listing 5-5. To save space, the listing does not contain thorough documentation. A fully documented version is available in the book's source code distribution.

spl_lastlog.c
```
#define _GNU_SOURCE
#include "common_hdrs.h"
#include <lastlog.h>            /* For lastlog structure definition   */
#include <paths.h>              /* For definition of _PATH_LASTLOG    */
#include <pwd.h>                /* For password file iterators        */

#define MESSAGE_SIZE   512
#define FORMAT         "%c"     /* Default format string              */

/* Prints a line for a username who has never logged in */
void print_never_logged_in(char *uname)
{
    printf("%-16s %-8.8s %-16s **Never logged in**\n", uname, " ", " ");
}

int main(int argc, char *argv[])
{
```

```
struct lastlog ll_entry;       /* To store lastlog record read from file */
struct passwd *psswd_struct;  /* passwd structure from password file    */
int           ll_fd;          /* File descriptor of lastlog file        */
off_t         ll_file_size;   /* Size of lastlog file, in bytes         */
size_t        ll_struct_size; /* Size in bytes of lastlog structure     */
size_t        num_bytes;      /* Number of bytes read in read()         */
uid_t         uid;            /* User ID of current search              */
char          *username;      /* Username of current search             */
int           highest_uid;    /* Highest user ID in lastlog file        */
char          lastlog_time[64]; /* Localized date/time string           */
time_t        ll_time;        /* Lastlog time converted to time_t       */
struct tm     *bdtime;        /* Broken-down time                       */

errno = 0;
if ( (ll_fd = open(_PATH_LASTLOG, O_RDONLY)) == -1 )
    fatal_error(errno, "while opening " _PATH_LASTLOG);


ll_file_size = lseek(ll_fd,0, SEEK_END); /* Get size of lastlog file.   */
ll_struct_size = sizeof(struct lastlog); /* Get size of lastlog struct. */

highest_uid = ll_file_size/ll_struct_size - 1;
if ( setlocale(LC_ALL, "")  == NULL )
    fatal_error(LOCALE_ERROR, "setlocale() could not set
               the given locale");


setpwent();  /* Initialize the passwd file iterator. */
printf("Username        Port     From          Last Login\n");

while ( (psswd_struct  = getpwent()) != NULL ) {
    uid = psswd_struct->pw_uid;
    username = psswd_struct->pw_name;
    if ( uid > highest_uid )
        print_never_logged_in(username);
    else {
        if ( lseek(ll_fd, uid * ll_struct_size, SEEK_SET) == -1 )
            fatal_error(errno, "lseek");
        errno = 0;
        if ( (num_bytes = read(ll_fd, &ll_entry, ll_struct_size)) <= 0 ) {
            if ( 0 != errno ) /* A read error occurred.              */
                fatal_error(errno, "read");
            else { /* Not a read error - shouldn't happen but continue */
                error_mssge(-1, "could not read the entry, skipping");
                continue;
            }
        }
        else if ( num_bytes != ll_struct_size )
            fatal_error(READ_ERROR, "incomplete read of lastlog struct");
```

```
            if ( 0 == ll_entry.ll_time )   /* No entry for this user */
                print_never_logged_in(username);
        else {
            /* Convert the lastlog time into broken-down time. */
#if __WORDSIZE_TIME64_COMPAT32
                ll_time = ll_entry.ll_time;
                bdtime = localtime(&ll_time);
#else
                bdtime = localtime(&(ll_entry.ll_time));
#endif
                /* The only possible error is EOVERFLOW. */
                if ( bdtime == NULL )
                    fatal_error(EOVERFLOW, "localtime");

                if ( 0 == strftime(lastlog_time, sizeof(lastlog_time),
                    FORMAT, bdtime) )
                    fatal_error(-1, "Conversion to a date-time string failed "
                            " or produced an empty string\n");
                printf("%-16s %-8.8s %-16s %s\n", username,ll_entry.ll_line,
                    ll_entry.ll_host, lastlog_time);
            }
        }
    }
    close(ll_fd);
    exit(EXIT_SUCCESS);
}
```

Listing 5-5: A complete program that prints the last login times for all users with entries in the password database

We'll build the executable and run it to see whether its output matches that of the actual lastlog command shown on page 195. I'll display the same portions of its output as we displayed there:

```
$ ./spl_lastlog
--snip--
sam             pts/2     192.168.1.105    Wed 19 Feb 2025 10:01:56 PM EDT
lightdm                                    **Never logged in**
nm-openvpn                                 **Never logged in**
brit            pts/2     192.168.1.105    Mon 20 Jan 2025 11:20:50 AM EDT
sshd                                       **Never logged in**
--snip--
```

We can manually compare the output of the actual command and our version of it to see how it differs, running them in separate terminal windows side by side, or we can pipe lastlog's output to the diff command, which will output the differences for us:

```
$ lastlog | diff - <(./spl_lastlog)
41c41
```

```
< sam              pts/2      192.168.1.105      Wed Feb 19 22:01:56 -0400 2025
---
> sam              pts/2      192.168.1.105      Wed 19 Feb 2025 10:01:56 PM EDT
45c45
< brit             pts/2      192.168.1.105      Mon Jan 20 11:20:50 -0400 2025
---
> brit             pts/2      192.168.1.105      Mon 20 Jan 2025 11:20:50 AM EDT
```

Here, `diff` is comparing its standard input stream, coming from `lastlog`, to the `<(./spl_lastlog)` pseudofile created by running the `spl_lastlog` command. The `bash` notation `<(command list)` treats the output of *command - list* as a filename. The hyphen tells `diff` that its first file argument is the standard input stream.

The only differences we find are in the date/time format. We passed the `%c` format to `strftime()`, whereas the Linux implementation passes the format string `"%a %b %e %H:%M:%S %z %Y"`. We can verify this by reading the source code file *lastlog.c*, found in the *shadow-utils* package (*https://github.com/shadow -maint/shadow*). Other implementations use still other formats. The differences aren't very important.

With our implementation, we can also change the locale and see that `showlastlog` displays the login time in the locale's format:

```
$ LC_TIME=es_ES.utf8 ./spl_lastlog
--snip--
sam              pts/2      192.168.1.105      mié 19 ene 2025 22:01:56
lightdm                                        **Never logged in**
nm-openvpn                                     **Never logged in**
brit             pts/2      192.168.1.105      lun 20 feb 2025 11:20:50
sshd                                           **Never logged in**
--snip--
```

We don't need to do much testing of this program to see that its output is correct. We also don't need to be concerned too much about its performance unless it's used on systems with a really large number of users. I leave it as an exercise to determine whether presorting the user IDs will improve performance.

Wrapping up, we chose to implement the `lastlog` command as a way to learn more about how to read from arbitrary positions in a file by seeking to and performing reads at those locations. In the process, we discovered that Unix provides an API for accessing entries in the *passwd* file. That API in effect provides us with an iterator, `getpwent()`, that returns successive password records.

These represent two different paradigms for file access. To obtain data from one file, *lastlog*, we have to explicitly move the file offset with `lseek()` and call `read()` to retrieve the file's data. We call this *explicit seeking and reading*. For the other file, *passwd*, we didn't need to move the file offset or read explicitly, but instead used functions from a small API associated with that file to retrieve data. We call this method *API-based reading*. The differences between them are:

- With explicit seeking and reading, we can control more precisely how and when the transfers are made than we can by using API-based reading.

- With explicit seeking and reading, the burden is on us to make sure that we haven't made mistakes in accessing the file, and if we don't design the code well, it may perform poorly.

- By using API-based reading, we simplify our programming task considerably because we use code implemented by the library's programmers.

- If the API changes, we might have to make changes to our program, which would not be the case if we were to explicitly read from the file.

Our implementation of `spl_lastlog` was a hybrid approach.

In the remainder of this chapter, we'll explore other system databases stored in world-readable files that have APIs for accessing their records.

Developing a last Command

In our search for commands that could display last login times (see "Displaying Last Login Information" beginning on page 193), we came across a command named `last`. There we learned that it extracts information from a file named *wtmp*. We're now going to develop an implementation of that command, along the way learning about the *wtmp* file, the structure of its data, and the various issues related to login records in general. Let's start by reading the man page for `last`, which begins with:

```
LAST(1)                        User Commands                        LAST(1)


NAME
       last, lastb - show a listing of last logged in users

SYNOPSIS
       last [options] [username...] [tty...]
       lastb [options] [username...] [tty...]

DESCRIPTION
       last searches back through the /var/log/wtmp file (or the file
       designated by the -f option) and displays a list of all users logged in
       (and out) since that file was created.
--snip--
```

The page also describes a `lastb` command, but when we read further, we discover that `lastb` only displays what it calls *bad login attempts*, meaning those that failed, and only users with superuser privilege can run it.

It's important to observe that last searches *backward* in the *wtmp* file, not forward. The most recent entries are listed first. If we run last without any options on a computer that has multiple active user accounts, we'll see output such as:

```
--snip--
l.fishburne pts/1       69.114.124.124  Fri Feb 28 19:19    still logged in
v.gallo     pts/21      104.162.60.115  Fri Feb 28 18:57 - 21:26  (02:29)
s.okonedo   pts/16      173.52.89.136   Fri Feb 28 18:53    gone - no logout
❶ m.sheen   pts/14      172.58.231.252  Fri Feb 28 18:29 - 02:53  (08:24)
csguest     tty3        tty3            Fri Feb 28 18:27 - 19:53  (01:36)
s.buscemi   pts/14      146.95.73.100   Fri Feb 28 18:26 - 18:27  (00:01)
❷ m.farrow  pts/9       151.202.41.80   Fri Feb 28 18:11 - 19:40  (1+01:29)
reboot      system boot 5.15.0-57-generi Thu Feb 27 13:56   still running
--snip--
wtmp begins Wed Jan 1 08:11:55 2025
```

The final line of output is the date of the first entry recorded in the database used by last.

If we run last -x, we get more system-related events, such as

```
runlevel   (to lvl 5)  5.15.0-71-generi Sat May 13 13:06 - 13:16  (00:10)
reboot     system boot 5.15.0-71-generi Sat May 13 13:06 - 13:16  (00:10)
shutdown   system down 5.15.0-71-generi Sat May 13 10:52 - 13:06  (02:13)
```

Neither the man page nor the Info page describes the individual fields of output, so let's go through what those fields contain. The default output is a sequence of lines, each containing information about either a user login or some type of system activity.

The first (leftmost) field is either a username or a description of a system event, such as reboot. For user logins, the next field is an indication of how the user was connected to the system. This can be through a pseudoterminal (for example, pts/21) or through a virtual console or the desktop environment (for example, tty3). For user logins, this field is also called the *line* (which is what we called it when we developed the spl_lastlog program). For system events, this field is a description of the event, such as system boot. A runlevel event is a change in the runlevel of the system. *Runlevels* essentially define the services available to ordinary users. The lowest user runlevel gives the user a terminal interface and no desktop, for example.

The next field indicates from where the user logged in, either the remote host's internet address or sometimes its fully qualified internet name or, for system events, the name of the kernel.

The next fields are, for user logins, the times at which the user logged in and then logged out followed by the total time of that session in the format (*hours*:*minutes*). The width of a line would be too long if last displayed both the start time and end time of a login session in the full date/time format, such as:

```
... Fri Feb 28 18:29:22 2025 - Sat Mar 01 15:53:31 2025 ...
```

Instead, it omits the seconds in both times and displays only the hour and minute of the ending time:

```
... Fri Feb 28 18:29 2025 - 15:53 ...
```

The nuance is that a login session can end on a day after the one in which it began at a time possibly earlier in the day than the login time, so that the end time is a smaller time value than the start time, such as Fri Feb 28 18:29 - 02:53 ❶. That second number by itself doesn't tell us that the time was the following day. It could be two, three, or more days later. The session length tells us this information. It can include a count of days and will look like (1+01:29) ❷, meaning one day, one hour, and 29 minutes. We need to look at the session length to know on which day the end time occurred.

If the session is still active, instead of a time value, the field contains the text still logged in. On rare occasions, and the previous output is such an occasion, instead of the still logged in message, the last command reports gone - no logout. This is the result of last's detecting corrupted information about a user, such as a change during a session in the user's username or user ID, or a user who was not logged out automatically when the system was rebooted or shut down. For system events, this field might contain status information such as still running or crash.

It is from this field that you can see that the more recent entries precede the older ones in the output.

Unix has a few other, similar commands for listing information about logins. One is the who command. Its man page states that it displays information about users who are currently logged in. It's useful on systems in which most people log in remotely and you're interested in knowing whether certain users are logged in. If we run who, we see output such as:

```
c.deneuve     pts/2    2025-02-01 00:14 (151.202.41.80)
s.aghdashloo  pts/1    2025-02-01 00:20 (73.48.77.155)
k.russell     pts/1    2025-02-01 09:39 (165.155.132.86)
c.rains       pts/2    2025-02-01 10:10 (146.111.116.2)
```

Here, each line represents a currently active login session. The first column is the username; the second is the device special file of the user's terminal; the third is the time at which that user logged in on that terminal; and the last is the source of the login, either the hostname if it's known or its internet address. For example, k.russell was logged in on terminal line pts/1, the session started at 9:39 on February 1, 2025, and the login was initiated from a device with internet address 165.155.132.86. Unlike last, who does not show anything about past logins.

Login Records

To learn more about login records, we first look at the NOTES, FILES, and SEE ALSO sections of last's man page. For last, NOTES are mostly for system administrators, and we can ignore them. The FILES section mentions two files: */var/log/wtmp* and */var/log/wtmpb*. The SEE ALSO section suggests reading the wtmp(5) man page. We'll read that page to learn about the files and data structures related to the command, hoping that they'll contain what we need to write the program. The wtmp(5) man page begins with:

```
UTMP(5)                    Linux Programmer's Manual                    UTMP(5)


NAME
       utmp, wtmp - login records
SYNOPSIS
       #include <utmp.h>
DESCRIPTION
       The utmp file allows one to discover information about who is currently
       using the system. There may be more users currently using the system,
       because not all programs use utmp logging.


       Warning: utmp must not be writable by the user class "other", because
       many system programs (foolishly) depend on its integrity...
--snip--
       The file is a sequence of utmp structures, declared as follows in
       <utmp.h> (note that this is only one of several definitions around;
       details depend on the version of libc):
--snip--
```

We observe first that utmp and wtmp share a man page and that both *wtmp* and *utmp* are files containing sequences of structures. The warning on the page is directed at system administrators—they should not set the *utmp* file's permissions too weakly because it makes the system vulnerable to attack. The page then describes the content and format of the *utmp* file, which stores information about logins in a sequence of utmp structures. The *wtmp* file is also a sequence of utmp structures, but they're processed in a slightly different way, which we'll cover shortly.

The utmp structure is declared in the *utmp.h* header file. The parenthetical note at the end is important; it tells us that this man page describes just one possible definition of the utmp structure, which may be different from that used by other Unix systems. If we design a program based on this definition, it may not run on other Unix systems. Whenever we see this type of warning, we should read the CONFORMING TO section of the man page. There, we learn that POSIX.1 doesn't specify a utmp structure, instead defining a utmpx structure, whose declaration is exposed by including the *utmpx.h* header file. We need to read about the differences and make a decision. If our program is designed to use the utmpx structure, it will be portable to POSIX-compliant systems, but if it is based on the utmp structure, it may not be.

We'll start by exploring the utmp structure, because that was the first one historically and also because the utmpx structure was derived from it. The remainder of this discussion is specific to Linux.

The utmp Structure

The man page description of the utmp structure begins with the following macros:

```
#define EMPTY          0    /* Record does not contain valid info
                                  (formerly known as UT_UNKNOWN on Linux) */
#define RUN_LVL        1    /* Change in system run-level          */
#define BOOT_TIME      2    /* Time of system boot                 */
#define NEW_TIME       3    /* Time after system clock changed     */
#define OLD_TIME       4    /* Time before system clock changed    */
#define INIT_PROCESS   5    /* Process spawned by init(1)          */
#define LOGIN_PROCESS  6    /* Session leader of user login        */
#define USER_PROCESS   7    /* Normal process                      */
#define DEAD_PROCESS   8    /* Terminated process                  */
#define ACCOUNTING     9    /* Not implemented                     */

#define UT_LINESIZE    32
#define UT_NAMESIZE    32
#define UT_HOSTSIZE    256
```

The first 10 are the possible values of the ut_type member of the structure, which defines the type of entry it represents, because Unix systems typically record events besides logins in the file. (We'll explain this shortly in "Logins, Logouts, and the utmp and wtmp Files" on page 220.) The next three are macros for the sizes, in bytes, of three members of the structure that are strings. After these, we see the type of the ut_exit member of the structure:

```
struct exit_status {        /* Type for ut_exit, below    */
    short int e_termination;    /* Process termination status */
    short int e_exit;           /* Process exit status        */
};
```

Finally, we see the declaration of the utmp struct itself:

```
struct utmp {
    short ut_type;             /* Type of record                     */
    pid_t ut_pid;              /* PID of login process               */
    char  ut_line[UT_LINESIZE]; /* Device name of tty - "/dev/"       */
    char  ut_id[4];            /* Terminal name suffix               */
    char  ut_user[UT_NAMESIZE]; /* Username                           */
    char  ut_host[UT_HOSTSIZE]; /* Hostname for remote login, or kernel
                                  version for run-level messages      */
    struct exit_status ut_exit; /* Exit status of a process marked as
                                  DEAD_PROCESS                        */

/* The ut_session and ut_tv fields must be the same size when
   compiled 32- and 64-bit. This allows data files and shared
   memory to be shared between 32- and 64-bit applications.    */
❶ #if __WORDSIZE == 64 && defined __WORDSIZE_COMPAT32
    int32_t ut_session;        /* Session ID (getsid(2)),
                                  used for windowing                  */
    struct {
        int32_t tv_sec;        /* Seconds                            */
        int32_t tv_usec;       /* Microseconds                       */
    } ut_tv;                   /* Time entry was made                */
#else
    long  ut_session;          /* Session ID                         */
    struct timeval ut_tv;      /* Time entry was made                */
#endif
    int32_t ut_addr_v6[4];     /* Internet address of remote
                                  host; IPv4 address uses
                                  just ut_addr_v6[0]                  */
    char __unused[20];         /* Reserved for future use            */
};
```

Before digging into the details of this data structure, let's get a sense of the content and purpose of its important members:

ut_type Indicates the type of the entry—whether it's a login entry, a boot entry, a shutdown entry, and so on

ut_pid Stores the process ID of the process that created the entry, which for login entries is the user's login process

ut_line   Stores the name of the terminal device of the login, such as *pts/1*, which is called the *line*

ut_id   A string that's unique to each entry, serving as an identifier for that entry

ut_tv   Records the time that the record was created (see "Logins, Logouts, and the utmp and wtmp Files" on page 220 for more details)

ut_user   For logins, contains the username, and for other types of entries, stores other identifying information

ut_host   Stores the name of the remote host from which the connection was made

Some of the details warrant more explanation. The conditional macro ❶ preceding the declaration of the ut_tv member has the same meaning as the one we saw in "The lastlog Structure" on page 196 in the definition of the struct lastlog. The preceding comment explains why it's there, and a comment in the NOTES section explains further. It ensures that if the machine is a 64-bit machine that allows 32-bit applications to run, ut_session is 4 bytes (int32_t) and ut_tv is 8 bytes (two int32_t members) for all applications. If it's a 32-bit machine, all applications see these same sizes for these members. If it's a 64-bit host not allowing 32-bit applications to run, these members are larger, since the struct timeval will be 16 bytes, and a long is 8 bytes. We'll have to use a feature test macro, as we did in Listing 5-5, in order to access the ut_session and ut_tv members in our final program.

The man page then describes how the entries in the utmp file are created and updated by various processes when you log in and log out, which we'll discuss soon. It also reiterates the following warning:

The file format is machine dependent, so it is recommended that it be processed only on the machine architecture where it was created.

The fact that this warning appears twice on the page is not to be overlooked. It implies that we should expect our program to run correctly only on the architecture on which we compile it.

The man page doesn't list any functions specifically tied to the utmp structure definition, but in the SEE ALSO section, it does reference various library functions such as getutent() and getutmp() from Section 3 of the man pages. The page for getutent() has a warning that this function, as well as all others sharing its page, are obsolete in non-Linux systems and that POSIX.1 instead defines a corresponding set of functions with an x in their names, such as getutxent() instead of getutent(). These functions are just aliases for their counterparts without the x, so we're not going to look at the functions in the Linux utmp API. Instead, we'll study and use the Linux utmpx API in order to make our programs more portable.

The utmpx API

Let's find the POSIX.1 specification of the `utmpx` API with this man page search:

```
$ apropos utmpx
getutmp (3)          - copy utmp structure to utmpx, and vice versa
getutmpx (3)         - copy utmp structure to utmpx, and vice versa
sessreg (1)          - manage utmpx/wtmpx entries for non-init clients
utmpx (5)            - login records
utmpx.h (7posix)     - user accounting database definitions
utmpxname (3)        - access utmp file entries
```

The `utmpx.h` man page is a POSIX specification of the API. It shows that the POSIX.1 `utmpx` structure has only six members:

```
char           ut_user[]  /* User login name                              */
char           ut_id[]    /* Unspecified initialization process identifier */
char           ut_line[]  /* Device name                                  */
pid_t          ut_pid     /* Process ID                                   */
short          ut_type    /* Type of entry                                */
struct timeval ut_tv      /* Time entry was made                          */
```

Even though POSIX.1 requires fewer members, the Linux `utmp` man page tells us that "Linux defines the `utmpx` structure to be the same as the `utmp` structure." In Linux, both structures contain the 10 members defined in the man page. If our programs reference the non-POSIX members, they may not run correctly on non-Linux systems.

The functions shown in the POSIX.1 `utmpx.h` man page are the following:

```
void          endutxent(void);
struct utmpx *getutxent(void);
struct utmpx *getutxid(const struct utmpx *);
struct utmpx *getutxline(const struct utmpx *);
struct utmpx *pututxline(const struct utmpx *);
void          setutxent(void);
```

They're declared in the *utmpx.h* header file, which our programs will need to include.

Logins, Logouts, and the utmp and wtmp Files

Both the *utmp* and *wtmp* files are updated when a user logs in and logs out, but they serve different purposes and are processed in different ways. In order to write any program that uses their data, we need to understand how both files are processed.

The *utmp* file stores information about who is currently logged in, but it's also used to record events such as boots, reboots, and changes in the operating system's runlevel. In contrast, the *wtmp* file is an audit file that records not just current logins but also logouts, as well as boots, reboots, and the same other events as *utmp* does.

When a user logs in, a record for that login is created in both the *utmp* and *wtmp* files. The contents of that record depend on how the user logged in: directly from the machine's GUI desktop, such as the GNOME Desktop Manager (GDM) on a Linux machine, remotely via a network protocol such as SSH, through an XTERM window, and so on. Following is a superficial description of the sequence of actions that take place when a user logs in:

- When a Unix system is booted, after the kernel performs all initializations, enables interrupts, and all other startup actions, it creates the first user-level process, whose process ID is 1. This process was traditionally named init, but in Linux it's now named systemd. We'll call it init here since it is still referred to in the documentation by this name. This init process is the ancestor of all processes in a UNIX system: All processes ever created are directly or indirectly created by it. It monitors the activities of all processes and also manages what takes place when the computer is shut down.

- The init process uses information about available terminal devices on the system, such as consoles, modems, network ports, and so on, to create, for each device, a process that will listen for activity on that device. These devices are called *lines*. Some of the listening processes have names like getty, mingetty, and so on. The name *getty* is short for "get tty."

> ### TTYS
>
> The term *tty* is short for "teletype." A *teletype* is the precursor to the modern computer terminal. Teletype machines came into existence as early as 1906, but it wasn't until around 1930 that their design stabilized. Teletype machines were essentially typewriters that converted the typed characters into electronic codes that could be transmitted across electrical wires. Modern computer terminals inherit many of their characteristics from teletype machines.

- Each getty process configures the terminal device, displays a prompt such as login:, and waits for the user to enter a username and password. Simplifying the rest of what takes place, once the login is authenticated, an entry is created in the *utmp* and *wtmp* files for that login.

Some systems use other means of authenticating logins, such as pluggable authentication modules (PAM), for this purpose. PAM is a library of dynamically configurable authentication routines that can be selected at runtime to do various authentication tasks, not just logins. When a system uses PAM, different software creates the login entries.

Similarly, the handling of network logins is different. These are usually derived from the BSD network login mechanism. Network logins don't use physical terminals, so there's no way to know in advance how many terminals must be initialized. In addition, the connection between the terminal and the computer is a network service, such as SSH or SFTP.

With network logins, `init` creates a process that will listen for the incoming network requests for logins. For example, if the system supports logging in through SSH, then `init` creates a process named `sshd`, the SSH daemon, which in turn creates a new process for each remote login. These new processes will in turn create a pseudoterminal driver, which then spawns the `login` process that does everything described previously, including creating the *utmp* and *wtmp* entries, but again with slightly different content.

To summarize, there are different paths to the creation of these login records in the two files, and these paths as well as the contents of the record depend on the login method. Regardless of how the login takes place, for each login, the `ut_type` of the record is set to `USER_PROCESS` in both the *utmp* and the *wtmp* files, and the `ut_user` member is set to the user's username.

When a user logs out, changes are made to both the *utmp* and *wtmp* files, and those changes depend on which processes handled the login entries. The changes made to the *utmp* file are different from the changes made to the *wtmp* file. In the *utmp* file, the login record of the user who is logging out is essentially erased. However, in the *wtmp* file, the process that updates the file appends a new record to it and doesn't modify the user's login record. The content of that record also depends upon on which form of login took place initially, whether through the console, over a network, and so on.

It would be a lot easier to understand if we could display the contents of these binary files. If we had a program that could display their raw contents converted to human-readable form, we'd also be able to debug our implementation of `last` when we start testing it. In addition, it's a good warm-up exercise for us to write this program. Since both files are sequences of `utmpx` structures, we'll design the program, which we'll name `spl_utmpdump`, so that by default it displays the *utmp* file but with the optional command line argument `wtmp`, displays the *wtmp* file, as in

```
$ ./spl_utmpdump          # Display the utmp file.
```

or:

```
$ ./spl_utmpdump wtmp     # Display the wtmp file.
```

The second form will always display the current *wtmp* file. This approach won't allow us to display older *wtmp* files such as */var/log/wtmp.1*. Printing the raw contents of a file in a human-readable format is commonly called *dumping* the file.

A Program to Show the utmp and wtmp Files

To start, since we'll be writing a few programs that require the *utmpx* header file, we'll append the line

```
#include <utmpx.h>
```

to the *sys_hdrs.h* header file that we defined in Chapter 3. We'll develop the program from the bottom up, starting with the functions that print various pieces of information.

First, we'll write a function, print_ut_type(), partially shown in Listing 5-6, for converting the integer ut_type field to a string such as "USER PROCESS" for the symbolic constant that the integer represents.

print_ut_type()
```
void print_ut_type(int t)
{
    switch ( t ) {
    case RUN_LVL:      printf("RUN_LVL       "); break;
    case BOOT_TIME:    printf("BOOT_TIME     "); break;
    --snip--
    case DEAD_PROCESS: printf("DEAD_PROCESS  "); break;
    case ACCOUNTING:   printf("ACCOUNTING    "); break;
    }
}
```

Listing 5-6: A function that prints the string associated with each ut_type value

We make the width of the field large enough to display the longest strings and pad the shorter ones with spaces on the right.

Next, we write a relatively simple function, print_one_rec(), that will display the fields of a single utmpx structure. The only challenges are in formatting field widths and using the feature test macro that ensures that it compiles correctly for 32-bit and 64-bit architectures, with and without 32-bit application support. We'll pick a field width of nine characters for the username. Many systems allow much longer usernames, so we may want to change this. Listing 5-7 contains the complete function.

print_one_rec()
```
void print_one_rec(struct utmpx *utbufp)
{
    struct tm *bdtime;
    char      timestring[64];

    print_rec_type(utbufp->ut_type);
    printf("%-6d ",  utbufp->ut_pid);        /* Process id */
    printf("%-8.8s ", utbufp->ut_user);      /* User name  */
    printf("%-8.8s ", utbufp->ut_id);        /* utmp id    */
    printf("%-8.8s ", utbufp->ut_line);      /* Line       */
❶ #ifdef SHOW_EXIT
    printf("%-3d ",   utbufp->ut_exit.e_exit);
    printf("%-3d ",   utbufp->ut_exit.e_termination);
#endif
    if ( utbufp->ut_host[0] != '\0' )
        printf(" %-18s", utbufp->ut_host);   /* Host       */
    else
        printf(" %-18s", " ");
```

```
❷ #if __WORDSIZE_TIME64_COMPAT32
       time_t utmp_time = utbufp->ut_tv.tv_sec;
       bdtime = localtime(&utmp_time);
   #else
       bdtime = localtime(&(utbufp->ut_tv.tv_sec));
   #endif
       if ( bdtime == NULL )
           fatal_error(EOVERFLOW, "localtime");

       if ( 0 == strftime(timestring, sizeof(timestring),"%c", bdtime) )
           fatal_error(-1, "Conversion to a date-time string failed "
                           " or produced an empty string\n");
       printf("%s\n", timestring);
   }
```

Listing 5-7: A function to print a single utmpx record

The code uses the printf() format specifier %-8.8s for the username field. In %-8.8s, the - means left justify, and the 8.8s means use exactly eight characters. If a string is smaller, it's padded on the left; if larger, it's truncated on the right. We also conditionally compile ❶ the code that displays the ut_exit status to reduce the width of the output when it's too long to display.

If we compile this program using

```
$ gcc -DSHOW_EXIT spl_utmpdump.c ...
```

the exit status fields will be part of the output.

If instead we compile with

```
$ gcc spl_utmpdump.c ...
```

they'll be omitted.

The feature test macro ❷ is just like the one we used in the spl_lastlog program. If the program is compiled on a 64-bit machine that can run 32-bit applications, it converts the time to a time_t value through assignment to a variable of type time_t and then passes this variable's address to localtime(). Otherwise, it passes the address of the struct timeval's tv_sec member directly. Also, notice that we continue to use the strftime() function for converting broken-down time to a string representation in a locale-sensitive way.

Next is a little function that prints the header row for the output, which is also conditionally compiled to include or exclude the exit status heading:

```
print    /* print_header_row prints a heading for the output. */
_header_row()  void print_header_row()
         {
             printf("%-14s%-7s%-9s%-9s%-9s", "TYPE", "PID", "USER", "ID", "LINE");
         #ifdef SHOW_EXIT
             printf("%-9s", "STATUS");
         #else
             printf(" ");
```

```
#endif
    printf("%-19s%-16s\n", "HOST", "TIME");
}
```

Field widths are hardcoded into it. If they need to be tweaked later, it would be better to pass them into the function as parameters, using the `printf()` feature that allows field widths to be passed as arguments, as in:

```
printf("%-*s", size, str) /* str will be printed left-justified
                             in a field of width size. */
```

We're ready to design the main program, which will use the utmpx API for reading the utmpx records rather than the kernel's read() system call. Its outline is:

1. Check whether the user passed wtmp as an argument.

2. If so, call utmpxname(WTMPX_FILE) to open the *wtmp* file.

3. Otherwise, call utmpxname(UTMPX_FILE) to open the *utmp* file.

4. Print a header row using print_header_row().

5. Initialize reading from the file with setutxent(), and set errno to 0.

6. While utmpx_entry = getutxent() is successful, call print_one_rec(utmpx _entry).

7. Check whether the loop exited because the end of the file was reached or because errno was set, and handle the error in this case.

8. Call endutxent() to close the file.

Listing 5-8 contains the complete program with the previously defined helper functions omitted to save space.

spl_utmpdump.c
```
#define _GNU_SOURCE
#include "common_hdrs.h"

void print_header_row()
{
    // OMITTED: Body of function
}

void print_rec_type(int t)
{
    // OMITTED: Body of function
}

void print_one_rec(struct utmpx *utbufp)
{
    // OMITTED: Body of function
}
```

```
int main(int argc, char *argv[])
{
    struct utmpx *utmp_entry;   /* For returned pointer from getutxent */

    if ( (argc > 1) && (strcmp(argv[1], "wtmp") == 0) ) {
        if ( -1 == utmpxname(WTMPX_FILE) )
            fatal_error(errno, "utmpname()");
    }
    else if ( -1 == utmpxname(UTMPX_FILE) )
            fatal_error(errno, "utmpname()");
    print_header_row();
    setutxent();
    errno = 0;
    while( (utmp_entry = getutxent()) != NULL )
        print_one_rec(utmp_entry);
    if ( 0 != errno )
        fatal_error(errno, "getutxent()");
    endutxent();
    return 0;
}
```

Listing 5-8: A program that dumps the utmp/wtmp *file in a human-readable format*

We'll build the showutmp executable defining SHOW_EXIT

```
$ gcc -DSHOW_EXIT spl_utmpdump.c -I../include -L ../lib -lspl -o spl_utmpdump
```

and run it on our *wtmp* file to see what we can observe from the output.

In the first run, we discover that both fields of the exit status of all records are zeros. To reduce the width of this output, we rebuild showutmp without defining SHOW_EXIT and run it again, which results in the following output:

```
$ ./spl_utmpdump wtmp
TYPE          PID   USER      ID        LINE   HOST             TIME
RUN_LVL       53    runlevel  ~~        ~      5.15.0-71-generic Tue Feb 25 08:11:55 2025
INIT_PROCESS  1993            tty1      tty1                    Tue Feb 25 08:11:55 2025
LOGIN_PROCESS 1993  LOGIN     tty1LOGI  tty1                    Tue Feb 25 08:11:55 2025
USER_PROCESS  2297  stewart   :0        tty7   :0               Tue Feb 25 08:13:03 2025
USER_PROCESS  6988  stewart   ts/0stew  pts/0  :0               Tue Feb 25 08:33:37 2025
DEAD_PROCESS  6965  stewart   ts/0stew  pts/0                   Tue Feb 25 10:50:08 2025
DEAD_PROCESS  0     stewart   :0        tty7   :0               Tue Feb 25 10:52:10 2025
RUN_LVL       0     shutdown  ~~        ~      5.15.0-71-generic Tue Feb 25 10:52:21 2025
BOOT_TIME     0     reboot    ~~        ~      5.15.0-71-generic Tue Feb 25 13:06:09 2025
RUN_LVL       53    runlevel  ~~        ~      5.15.0-71-generic Tue Feb 25 13:06:32 2025
INIT_PROCESS  1967            tty1      tty1                    Tue Feb 25 13:06:32 2025
LOGIN_PROCESS 1967  LOGIN     tty1LOGI  tty1                    Tue Feb 25 13:06:32 2025
USER_PROCESS  2327  stewart   :0        tty7   :0               Tue Feb 25 13:08:27 2025
DEAD_PROCESS  0     stewart   :0        tty7   :0               Tue Feb 25 13:16:30 2025
USER_PROCESS  7210  jl.trint  ts/1mero  pts/1  24.46.119.86     Sat Mar  1 09:16:43 2025
```

```
USER_PROCESS  7342    r.griffi ts/2njia pts/2    146.95.38.217    Sat Mar  1 10:13:57 2025
USER_PROCESS  7348    b.pepper ts/4meli pts/4    24.90.66.208     Sat Mar  1 10:16:08 2025
USER_PROCESS  7367    m.grace  ts/5harm pts/5    148.74.161.63    Sat Mar  1 10:16:21 2025
USER_PROCESS  7389    m.richar ts/6weig pts/6    67.245.64.80     Sat Mar  1 10:16:42 2025
DEAD_PROCESS  0                         pts/5                     Sat Mar  1 10:22:28 2025
DEAD_PROCESS  0                         pts/6                     Sat Mar  1 10:46:29 2025
--snip--
```

Notice that the program prints all of the fields correctly in suitable column widths. Also, observe that the file stores records other than user login and logout events. Our focus here isn't on those records, but on the USER_PROCESS and DEAD_PROCESS records.

In the very first USER_PROCESS record, the line is tty7 and the ID is :0. This corresponds to a login on the computer's desktop. GDM assigns lines of the form ttyx, where x is a number, to these logins. The ID is assigned the value :0, which refers to the computer's actual screen display. When I logged out on that day, a logout entry for that same line was written to the file:

```
DEAD_PROCESS  0     stewart  :0      tty7    :0          Tue Feb 25 10:52:10 2025
```

The username field was not erased. The same is true for the login on pts/0: when I logged out, as shown in that logout record:

```
USER_PROCESS  6988   stewart  ts/0stew pts/0   :0         Tue Feb 25 08:33:37 2025
DEAD_PROCESS  6965   stewart  ts/0stew pts/0              Tue Feb 25 10:50:08 2025
```

On the other hand, the logout records for all of the other logins on lines whose names are of the form pts/x have had their usernames erased. This difference is exactly what we discussed in "Logins, Logouts, and the utmp and wtmp Files." The man page for utmp and wtmp states only that "the wtmp file records all logins and logouts. Its format is exactly like utmp except that a NULL username indicates a logout on the associated terminal." The converse is not true. The entry for a logout on a terminal does not necessarily have a NULL username.

Analysis of the wtmp File

Our next goal is to use our observations about the *wtmp* file to develop an algorithm for the last command. To start, let's ignore the effect of system events on what it displays, concentrating exclusively on user logins and logouts. The command has to find, for each user login record, the matching user logout record.

We'll consider an abstract version of the file, in which we remove all information not relevant to this problem, including the PID, ID, HOST, TIME, and the exit status fields of each record. We'll also remove the records that are not either user logins or logouts. We're left with a file such as:

```
USER_PROCESS  stewart          tty7
USER_PROCESS  stewart          pts/0
```

DEAD_PROCESS	stewart	pts/0
DEAD_PROCESS	stewart	tty7
USER_PROCESS	stewart	tty7
DEAD_PROCESS	stewart	tty7
USER_PROCESS	jl.trint	pts/1
USER_PROCESS	r.griffi	pts/2
USER_PROCESS	b.pepper	pts/4
USER_PROCESS	m.grace	pts/5
USER_PROCESS	m.richar	pts/6
DEAD_PROCESS		pts/5
DEAD_PROCESS		pts/6
DEAD_PROCESS		pts/4
DEAD_PROCESS		pts/1
DEAD_PROCESS		pts/2

For every USER_PROCESS entry, if that user has logged out, there's a unique DEAD_PROCESS entry with the same terminal line. Terminal lines are unique—no two users can be logged in at the same time on the same line—and this implies that if we know the line on which a user logged in, we can find the logout record by searching for a DEAD_PROCESS record with the same line that occurs most recently in time after that login.

We can think of this problem in an even more abstract way. Suppose we represent a user login on a line with a unique left bracket. Since the keyboard doesn't have an unlimited supply of different types of left brackets, I'll use a notation consisting of a left square bracket symbol subscripted with a unique integer, such as $[_1$ or $[_2$, to represent a unique left bracket type. The matching logout record will be a right square bracket indexed with the same number, $]_1$ or $]_2$, respectively. A sequence of logins and logouts can then be viewed as a string of these brackets with the following constraints:

- For every right bracket $]_x$, there is a matching left bracket $[_x$ to the left of it in the string.

- There are no two occurrences of a left bracket $[_x$ without an intervening occurrence of its matching right bracket $]_x$.

- There are no two occurrences of a right bracket $]_x$ without an intervening occurrence of its matching left bracket $[_x$.

- For every left bracket $[_x$, the leftmost matching right bracket $]_x$ that occurs to the right of that left bracket is the matching right bracket for that left bracket. If no such right bracket exists, it implies that the user whose login is represented by that left bracket has not yet logged out.

If we use the number following the pts/ as the subscript of the bracket and a for the subscript of the tty7 line, then our data would be represented by the string:

$$[_a \quad [_0 \quad]_0 \quad]_a \quad [_a \quad]_a \quad [_1 \quad [_2 \quad [_4 \quad [_5 \quad [_6 \quad]_5 \quad]_6 \quad]_4 \quad]_1 \quad]_2$$

This abstraction of the *wtmp* data can help us to solve the problem of finding logouts that match logins. It's like searching a string of brackets.

The complication is that the `last` command searches backward through the file, printing the most recent login sessions first. In essence, it travels back in time as it processes the *wtmp* file, because at any given step, the record it has just read has a timestamp that is older than all of the ones it's read before it. By reading the entries in reverse order, it sees newer entries before older ones. Our algorithm needs to do the same, making it a bit harder to understand.

As we process this string in right-to-left order, in effect, we're going back in time. When we see a right square bracket, for example, we know that it should be the matching bracket for some left square bracket that we've yet to see, representing event that took place earlier in time. We don't know when we'll see it, meaning how far to the left it'll be. Therefore, we have to squirrel this bracket away in a safe place, such as in a linked list, and move on.

We'll solve this problem by creating an initially empty, doubly linked list, which makes deletions easier. For the sake of precision, let's name it `saved_ut_recs`. The idea will be to search the string in right-to-left order, starting from the rightmost entry, marching backward in time toward the beginning. When we find a right bracket, we push it onto the front of `saved_ut_recs`. When we find a left bracket, we search the `saved_ut_recs` list starting at its first node for the first occurrence of its matching right bracket. If we find it, we record the login and logout times that it represents and delete the right bracket from the list. If we don't find it, the user whose logout it represents is still logged in.

Notice that we can't use a stack to solve this problem because the brackets can be interleaved, as our sample data showed. We'd have to pop items off of the stack until we found the correct one and then push back the ones that we removed.

We haven't yet taken into consideration the effect of the records related to runlevel changes, boots, reboots, and shutdowns. When the machine is shut down or rebooted, under normal circumstances, any logged-in users are logged out automatically. The result is that `struct utmpx` entries of type `DEAD_PROCESS` are appended to the file for all of these logouts. Therefore, we need to identify shutdown and reboot records.

Shutdown records are those that satisfy the following equalities:

```
ut_type == RUN_LVL
ut_user == "shutdown"
ut_line == "~"
```

Boots and reboots are those that satisfy these equalities:

```
ut_type == BOOT_TIME
ut_user == "reboot"
ut_line == "~"
```

Although there are other types of runlevel change records, we'll ignore them because they don't have an effect on user logins or logouts.

If, as we're reading records backward in the file, we come across a record that represents either a boot, reboot, or shutdown, and if there are any remaining `DEAD_PROCESS` records in the `saved_ut_recs` list, they cannot be matching logouts for logins that we have yet to find; this is because any logins that we haven't found yet must have occurred prior to this boot/reboot/shutdown, which means those users would have been logged out prior to that event, not after it. Therefore, when we find such a record, we'll erase all entries from the `saved_ut_recs` list. That's their only effect on the behavior of our version of `last`, which we'll name `spl_last`.

Designing the spl_last Program

We begin by outlining the design of our program, which will accept a single option, -x. If this option is given on the command line, our program's output will include the system shutdown events and runlevel changes. Otherwise, it will display only user logins, logouts, and reboots, just like the actual `last` command. Our initial version won't attempt to be efficient; it will read only one `utmpx` record at a time, even though this takes more time. After we've written this version, we'll consider some changes that would make it more efficient.

These are the initializations that the program will need to perform:

1. Set up option handling by checking whether the -x option was supplied. If so, set a flag `show_sys_events` to `TRUE`, and if not, set it to `FALSE`.

2. Open the *wtmp* file. If this fails, exit with a suitable error message; otherwise, store the returned file descriptor into `fd_wtmp`.

3. Set the locale by calling `setlocale(LC_TIME, "")`. If it fails, display an error message and exit.

4. Read the first entry from the file and save the time in that entry's `ut_tv.tv_sec` field into `time_t start_time` to display as the final line of output. If the read fails, display an error message and exit. The code snippet should be:

    ```
    errno = 0;
    if ( read(fd_utmp, &utmp_entry, utsize) != utsize )
        fatal_error(errno, "read");
    start_time = utmp_entry.ut_tv.tv_sec;
    ```

5. Create an initially empty list of saved `utmpx` records, `saved_ut_recs`.

6. Initialize a `time_t` variable named `last_shutdown_time` to 0. This variable will be updated whenever a shutdown event is found in the file. The value 0 indicates that no shutdown record has been found yet.

After the initializations, the program will enter its main processing loop in which, for every `utmpx` record in the file, starting with the last (most recent) record, it will process that record. Let's assume for now that we've written a function with the prototype

```
int get_prev_utrec(int fd, struct utmpx *ut, int *finished);
```

which, when called the first time, retrieves the last utmpx record in the open file with descriptor fd and stores it into *ut, not modifying the *finished parameter, and when called all subsequent times, gets the record preceding the last one read, unless it has already read the first record in the file, in which case it sets *finished to TRUE.

The main loop is then of the form:

```
int done = FALSE;
while ( !done ) {
    if ( get_prev_utrec(fd_utmp, &utmp_entry, &done) ) {
        // OMITTED: Process the utmp_entry.
    else /* get_prev_utrec() did not read successfully. */
        if ( !done )
            fatal_error(2, " read failed");
}
```

When get_prev_utrec() reads the first entry in the file, it returns TRUE, but when it tries to read again, it returns FALSE and sets done to TRUE.

Let's outline the steps for processing each successfully read utmp_entry. Remember that we're travelling back in time with each iteration of the while loop.

The first step is to determine the type of utmp_entry. For most records, we can determine the type from the ut_type field, but as we noted previously, shutdowns are those records for which ut_type == RUN_LVL, ut_user == "shutdown", and ut_line== "~". If these conditions are true, the program must set the utmp_entry.ut_type field to SHUTDOWN_TIME, the utmp_entry.ut_line to "system down", and the utmp_entry.ut_user to "shutdown" before continuing.

The remaining processing is contingent on the value of utmp_entry.ut_type. The following list describes what the program should do for each of its possible values:

DEAD_PROCESS   If utmp_entry.ut_line is not NULL, insert utmp_entry onto the front of the saved_ut_recs list; otherwise, don't insert it, since it doesn't correspond to any user session.

USER_PROCESS   Search the saved_ut_recs list for a record whose ut_line is the same as that in utmp_entry. If it's found, print a line of output for this login record in which the start time is utmp_entry.ut_tv.tv_sec and the end time is the ut_tv.tv_sec member of the record found in the list. Also compute the total login time and print it. Finally, delete the saved record from the saved_ut_recs list. If no matching record is found, this user login does not have a matching logout. If last_shutdown_time > 0, print a line of output with the end time "gone - no logout". If last_shutdown_time == 0, the user is still logged in, so print a line of output with end time "still logged in". In either case, the printed start time is utmp_entry.ut_tv.tv_sec.

BOOT_TIME   Store the boot time into a variable last_boot_time and erase the saved_ut_recs list. Print a line of output whose ut_line field is "system boot" and whose start time is utmp_entry.ut_tv.tv_sec. If last_shutdown_time == 0, the system has not been shut down since this boot entry was recorded in the file, so the printed end time of this output line should be "still running". Otherwise, the end time should be the current value of last_shutdown_time, and the total time should be the time difference last_shutdown_time - utmp_entry.ut_tv.tv_sec.

SHUTDOWN_TIME   Save the ut_tv.tv_sec in this record into the last_shutdown _time variable, because for this shutdown, we don't yet know when the most recent preceding reboot took place, and we'll need it when we find that reboot entry, so that when we print the line for that reboot entry, we'll have its end time. We also need to print the end time for this shutdown. The end time of a shutdown event is the time after the shutdown when the system is next rebooted. In other words, the duration of a shutdown event is the time during which the machine is not running. The start time in the output line for a shutdown is when it was shut down, and its end time is when it was rebooted afterward. That reboot has already been read, and its reboot time was stored into the variable last_boot_time. Therefore, we print a line of output whose start time is utmp_entry.t_tv.tv_sec and whose end time is last_boot_time, print the total time, and erase the saved_ut_recs list, since any saved records in that list cannot match any logins that took place earlier in time than this shutdown event.

When the main loop ends, the program has to clean up a bit and print a final line of output. Cleanup involves freeing dynamically allocated memory in the saved_ut_recs linked list and closing the fd_utmp file descriptor. The final output line that our program should print should be the same as what the real last command prints, which is of the form

```
wtmp begins Thu 01 Jan 1970 12:00:00 AM
```

or something similar based on the user's locale settings. (In Chapter 3, we learned how to do this.) The following code fragment will work:

```
struct tm bd_start_time;
char    wtmp_start_str[128];
start_time = localtime(&start_time);
if ( 0 == strftime(wtmp_start_str, sizeof(wtmp_start_str),
                "%a %b %d %H:%M:%S %Y", bd_start_time) )
    fatal_error(BAD_FORMAT_ERROR,
              "Conversion to a date-time string failed or produced "
              " an empty string\n");
printf("\nwtmp begins %s\n", wtmp_start_str);
```

An extra newline character precedes the output string so that a blank line appears before the message, just like the real last command's output.

Support Functions

We still have to implement a few more functions for our program. One of these is the function that reads the file in backward order, whose prototype we defined earlier:

```
int get_prev_utrec(int fd, struct utmpx *ut, int *finished);
```

We also need a function that can compute the total time of a single ses-sion, whether it's a login, reboot, or shutdown; convert that time to a num-ber of seconds, minutes, hours, and so on; and format it as a string like the one printed by last.

Its prototype will be:

```
void format_time_diff(time_t start_time, time_t end_time, char *time_diff_str);
```

It will compute the total number of seconds in end_time - start_time and store its formatted string representation in time_diff_str.

We need a printing function as well. When processing utmpx records, the program needs to print a line of output for that record with a specific start and end time. We'll consolidate this printing into a function with the prototype

```
void print_one_line(struct utmpx *ut, time_t end_time);
```

which will print a line of output representing the utmpx record ut for a session that starts at time ut.ut_tv.tv_sec and ends at time end_time.

Finally, the program needs some doubly linked list processing support. The doubly linked list definition will be:

```
typedef struct {
    struct utmpx     ut;
    struct utmplist *next;
    struct utmplist *prev;
} utmplist;

utmplist *saved_ut_recs = NULL;  /* An initially empty list */
```

We'll use three functions for list-related actions: a function to save a utmpx record into the list, one that deletes one from the list, and one that erases the entire list. Their prototypes are:

```
void save_ut_to_list(struct utmpx *ut, utlist **list);
void delete_utnode(utlist *utptr, utlist **list);
void erase_utlist(utlist **list);
```

We'll start with get_prev_utrec(). We can't use the utmpx API for read-ing records from the list because it retrieves them in a forward direction, whereas our function has to get them in the opposite direction.

The first time the function is called, it has to position the file offset at the last record in the file. For all other times, the file offset has to point to the record preceding the record it previously read. Since it needs to do something different in the first call from what it does in subsequent calls, it needs to *remember* which call it's in. For this purpose, we'll use a static local Boolean variable is_first, initially TRUE, to indicate whether it's in the first call.

Our function also has to be aware of when it's being called to read the first record in the file, at offset zero, so that it doesn't seek to a negative file offset, which causes lseek() to fail. It could do this by getting the position of the file offset before it reads, with the call:

```
current_offset = lseek(fd,0, SEEK_CUR);
```

If current_offset == 0, this is the first record, so it should set finished to TRUE to indicate that it should not be called again. The disadvantage of this solution is that it makes an extra call to lseek() every time it's called. We can avoid this by maintaining a second static local variable, saved_offset, which would save the current value of the file offset prior to the read. It would decrease it in each call by the size of the utmpx structure.

The last problem is how to reposition the file offset to read the previous record each time. Figure 5-7 illustrates this.

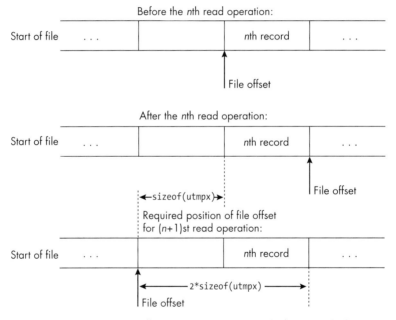

Figure 5-7: Where the file offset has to be repositioned after a read when reading backward in the file

After the read() system call reads the nth record of the file, the file offset is pointing to the first byte in the file after that record. This position is 2*sizeof(struct utmpx) bytes past where it has to be in order to read the preceding record. If we've saved the file offset into saved_offset before reading, then we just have to decrease saved_offset by sizeof(struct utmpx) bytes for it to be ready for the next read. All of this logic is incorporated into the function, presented in Listing 5-9.

get_prev_utrec()
```
int get_prev_utrec(int fd, struct utmpx *ut, BOOL *finished)
{
    static off_t saved_offset;      /* Where this call is about to read  */
    static BOOL  is_first = TRUE;   /* Whether this is first time called */
```

```
size_t      utsize = sizeof(struct utmpx);  /* Size of utmpx struct */
ssize_t     nbytes_read;                     /* Number of bytes read */

/* Check if this is the first time it is called. If so, move the file
   offset to the last record in the file and save it in saved_offset. */
if ( is_first ) {
    errno = 0;
    /* Move to utsize bytes before end of file. */
    saved_offset = lseek(fd, -utsize, SEEK_END);
    if ( -1 == saved_offset )  {
        error_mssge(errno,
                    "error trying to move offset to last rec of file");
        return FALSE;
    }
    is_first = FALSE; /* Turn off flag. */
}

*finished = FALSE; /* Assume we're not done yet. */
if ( saved_offset < 0 ) {
    *finished = TRUE;/* saved_offset < 0 implies we've read entire file.*/
    return FALSE;    /* Return 0 to indicate no read took place.        */
}
/* File offset is at the correct place to read. */
errno = 0;
nbytes_read = read(fd, ut, utsize);
if ( -1 == nbytes_read ) {
    /* read() error occurred; do not exit - let main() do that. */
    error_mssge(errno, "read");
    return FALSE;
}
else if ( nbytes_read < utsize ) {
    /* Full utmpx struct not read; do not exit - let main() do that. */
    error_mssge(READ_ERROR, "less than full record read");
    return FALSE;
}
else { /* Successful read of utmpx record */
    saved_offset = saved_offset - utsize; /* Reposition saved_offset. */
    if ( saved_offset >= 0 ) {
        /* Seek to preceding record to set up next read. */
        errno = 0;
        if ( -1 == lseek(fd, - (2*utsize), SEEK_CUR) )
            fatal_error(errno, "lseek()");
    }
    return TRUE;
}
}
```

Listing 5-9: The get_prev_utrec() function, which reads through the wtmp file backward

The beginning of the function checks whether it's the first time it's called and positions the file offset to the last record in the file. After that, it checks whether the saved offset is negative and, if so, it sets finished = TRUE and returns to end processing. If it makes it past this point, it reads the record and performs error handling if need be. If all goes well, it decrements saved _offset by the size of the record, and if not negative, it moves the file offset to the new position, setting up the next read.

Let's turn to the next function, format_time_diff(). Given the starting and ending times in seconds, it computes their difference and creates a formatted string representing that difference. It is shown in Listing 5-10.

```
format       void format_time_diff(time_t start_time, time_t end_time, char *time_diff_str)
_time_diff()  {
                  time_t secs = end_time - start_time;
                  int minutes = (secs / 60) % 60;
                  int hours   = (secs / 3600) % 24;
                  int days    = secs / 86400;

                  if ( days > 0 )
                      sprintf(time_diff_str, "(%d+%02d:%02d)", days, hours, minutes);
                  else
                      sprintf(time_diff_str, "(%02d:%02d)", hours, minutes);
              }
```

Listing 5-10: The format_time_diff() function

From the time difference, which is in seconds, it does a bit of arithmetic to calculate the equivalent time quantity in seconds, minutes, hours, and days. If the number of days is zero, it formats it one way, and if greater than zero, another, to be consistent with how the actual last command behaves.

The third support function is print_one_line(), shown in Listing 5-11.

```
print        void print_one_line(struct utmpx *ut, time_t end_time)
_one_line()   {
                  time_t      utrec_time;
                  struct tm *bd_end_time;
                  struct tm *bd_ut_time;
                  char       formatted_login[MAXLEN];  /* Formatted login date  */
                  char       formatted_logout[MAXLEN]; /* Formatted logout date */
                  char       duration[MAXLEN];         /* Session length        */
                  char      *start_date_fmt = "%a %b %d %H:%M";
                  char      *end_date_fmt   = "%H:%M";

                  utrec_time = (ut->ut_tv).tv_sec; /* Get login time in seconds. */

                  /* If the end time is 0 or -1, print the appropriate string
                     instead of a time. */
                  if ( ut->ut_type == BOOT_TIME && end_time == 0 )
                      sprintf(duration, "still running");
```

```
        else if ( ut->ut_type == USER_PROCESS && end_time == 0 )
            sprintf(duration, "still logged in");
        else if ( ut->ut_type == USER_PROCESS && end_time == -1 )
            sprintf(duration, "gone - no logout");
        else /* Calculate and format duration of the session. */
            format_time_diff(utrec_time, end_time, duration);

        /* Convert login time to broken-down time. */
        bd_ut_time = localtime(&utrec_time);
        if ( bd_ut_time == NULL )
            fatal_error(errno, "localtime");

        if ( 0 == strftime(formatted_login, sizeof(formatted_login),
                        start_date_fmt, bd_ut_time) )
            fatal_error(BAD_FORMAT_ERROR,
                        "Conversion to a date-time string failed or produced "
                        " an empty string\n");
        /* Convert end time to broken-down time. */
        bd_end_time = localtime(&end_time);
        if ( bd_end_time == NULL )
            fatal_error(errno, "localtime");

        if ( 0 == strftime(formatted_logout, sizeof(formatted_logout),
                        end_date_fmt, bd_end_time) )
            fatal_error(BAD_FORMAT_ERROR,
                        "Conversion to a date-time string failed or produced "
                        " an empty string\n");
        /* Add terminating NULL to host name, otherwise it will be too long. */
        ut->ut_host[sizeof(ut->ut_host)-1] = '\0';

        /* Print the whole line. */
        printf("%-8.8s %-12.12s %-18s %s - %s %s\n", ut->ut_user, ut->ut_line,
                ut->ut_host, formatted_login, formatted_logout, duration);
}
```

Listing 5-11: The print_one_line() function

The function prints a single line to standard output in the same format as the actual last command. The inline comments explain its steps.

The next three listings contain the linked list functions. The first of these adds the given utmpx record to the given list:

```
save_ut    void save_ut_to_list(struct utmpx *ut, utlist **list)
_to_list() {
                utlist* utmp_node_ptr;

                /* Allocate a new list node. */
                errno = 0;
```

```
    if ( NULL == (utmp_node_ptr = (utlist*) malloc(sizeof(utlist))) )
        fatal_error(errno, "malloc");

    /* Copy the utmpx record into the new node. */
    memcpy(&(utmp_node_ptr->ut), ut, sizeof(struct utmpx));

    /* Attach the node to the front of the list. */
    utmp_node_ptr->next = *list;
    utmp_node_ptr->prev = NULL;
    if ( NULL != *list )
        (*list)->prev = utmp_node_ptr;
    (*list) = utmp_node_ptr;
}
```

The next function removes the node pointed to by p from the given list
and frees the memory allocated for that node:

delete_utnode()
```
void delete_utnode(utlist *p, utlist **list)
{
    if ( NULL != p->next )
        p->next->prev = p->prev;

    if ( NULL != p->prev )
        p->prev->next = p->next;
    else
        *list = p->next;
    free(p);
}
```

The third function is used to delete the entire list, freeing all of the
memory allocated to its nodes:

erase_utlist()
```
void erase_utlist(utlist **list)
{
    utlist *ptr = *list;
    utlist *next;

    while ( NULL != ptr ) {
        next = ptr->next;
        free(ptr);
        ptr = next;
    }
    *list = NULL;
}
```

Notice that the parameter is a doubly indirect pointer. We need this because
the list head itself, saved_ut_recs, is modified by the call. If it weren't doubly
indirect, the call erase_utlist(saved_ut_list) would remove its nodes but on

return, saved_ut_recs would not be NULL, and the program would then have a dangerous dangling pointer.

We're ready to assemble the program. To save space here, since we've already seen the support functions, they're omitted from Listing 5-12. I also omit option processing and lengthy comments. The complete program is in the book's source code distribution.

spl_last.c
```c
#define _GNU_SOURCE
#include "common_hdrs.h"

#ifndef SHUTDOWN_TIME /*If SHUTDOWN_TIME record type not defined, define it.*/
#define SHUTDOWN_TIME 32 /* Give it a value larger than all other types.   */
#endif

typedef struct utmp_list { /* Type of the linked list of utmpx records      */
    struct utmpx ut;
    struct utmp_list *next;
    struct utmp_list *prev;
} utlist;

int get_prev_utrec(int fd, struct utmpx *ut, BOOL *finished);
void format_time_diff(time_t start_time, time_t end_time, char *time_diff_str);
void print_one_line(struct utmpx *ut, time_t end_time);
void save_ut_to_list(struct utmpx *ut, utlist **list);
void delete_utnode(utlist *p, utlist **list);
void erase_utlist(utlist **list);

int main(int argc, char *argv[])
{
    struct utmpx  utmp_entry;            /* Read info into here.            */
    size_t        utsize = sizeof(struct utmpx); /* Size of utmpx record    */
    int           fd_utmp;               /* Read from this descriptor.      */
    time_t        last_boot_time;        /* Time of last boot or reboot     */
    time_t        last_shutdown_time = 0; /* Time of last shutdown          */
    time_t        start_time;            /* When wtmp processing started    */
    struct tm     *bd_start_time;        /* Broken-down time representation*/
    char          wtmp_start_str[MAXLEN]; /* String to store start time     */
    utlist        *saved_ut_recs = NULL; /* An initially empty list         */
    char          options[] = ":x";      /* getopt string                   */
    int           show_sys_events = FALSE; /* Flag to indicate -x found     */
    char          usage_msg[MAXLEN];     /* For error messages              */
    BOOL          done = FALSE;          /* Flag to stop utmp loop          */
    BOOL          found = FALSE;         /* Flag to indicate match found    */
    char          ch;
    utlist        *p, *next;

    if ( (fd_utmp = open(WTMPX_FILE, O_RDONLY)) == -1 )
        fatal_error(errno, "while opening " WTMPX_FILE);
```

```
// OMITTED: Option parsing
if ( NULL == setlocale(LC_TIME, "") ) /* Set the locale. */
    fatal_error(LOCALE_ERROR, "Could not set the given locale");

/* Read the first struct in the file to get the time of first entry. */
errno = 0;
if ( read(fd_utmp, &utmp_entry, utsize) != utsize )
    fatal_error(errno, "read");
start_time = utmp_entry.ut_tv.tv_sec;
while ( !done ) {
    errno = 0;
    if ( get_prev_utrec(fd_utmp, &utmp_entry, &done) ) {
        if ( (strncmp(utmp_entry.ut_line, "~", 1) == 0) &&
             (strncmp(utmp_entry.ut_user, "shutdown", 8) == 0) ) {
            utmp_entry.ut_type = SHUTDOWN_TIME;
            sprintf(utmp_entry.ut_line, "system down");
        }
        switch ( utmp_entry.ut_type ) {
        case BOOT_TIME:
            strcpy(utmp_entry.ut_line, "system boot");
            print_one_line(&utmp_entry, last_shutdown_time);
            last_boot_time = utmp_entry.ut_tv.tv_sec;
            if ( saved_ut_recs != NULL )
                erase_utlist(&saved_ut_recs);
            break;
        case RUN_LVL: /* Not handled */
            break;
        case SHUTDOWN_TIME:
            last_shutdown_time = utmp_entry.ut_tv.tv_sec;
            if ( show_sys_events )
                print_one_line(&utmp_entry, last_boot_time);
            if ( saved_ut_recs != NULL )
                erase_utlist(&saved_ut_recs);
            break;
        case USER_PROCESS:
            found = 0;
            p = saved_ut_recs; /* Start at beginning. */
            while ( NULL != p ) {
                next = p->next;
                if ( 0 == (strncmp(p->ut.ut_line, utmp_entry.ut_line,
                           sizeof(utmp_entry.ut_line))) ) {
                    print_one_line(&utmp_entry, p->ut.ut_tv.tv_sec);
                    found = 1;
                    delete_utnode(p, &saved_ut_recs);
                }
                p = next;
            }
```

```
                if ( !found ) {
                    if ( last_shutdown_time > 0 )
                        print_one_line(&utmp_entry, (time_t) -1);
                    else
                        print_one_line(&utmp_entry, (time_t) 0);
                }
                break;
            case DEAD_PROCESS:
                if ( utmp_entry.ut_line[0] == 0 )
                    continue; /* There is no line in the entry, so skip it. */
                else
                    save_ut_to_list(&utmp_entry, &saved_ut_recs);
                break;
            case OLD_TIME:     /* Not handled */
            case NEW_TIME:     /* Not handled */
            case INIT_PROCESS: /* Not handled */
            case LOGIN_PROCESS: /* Not handled */
                break;
            } /* End of switch */
        }
        else /* get_prev_utrec() did not read correctly. */
            if ( !done )
                fatal_error(2, " read failed");
    }
    erase_utlist(&saved_ut_recs);
    close(fd_utmp);
    bd_start_time = localtime(&start_time); /* Convert to broken-down time. */
    if ( 0 == strftime(wtmp_start_str, sizeof(wtmp_start_str),
                    "%a %b %d %H:%M:%S %Y", bd_start_time) )
        fatal_error(BAD_FORMAT_ERROR, "Conversion to a date-time "
                    "string failed or produced an empty string\n");
    printf("\nwtmp begins %s\n", wtmp_start_str);
    return 0;
}
```

Listing 5-12: An implementation of the last *command, with stubs for the previously defined support functions*

The main() function consolidates the logic we discussed previously. When it sees DEAD_PROCESS records, it inserts them into the list, provided that their ut_line field is nonempty. When it sees USER_PROCESS records, it searches the list from the beginning for a record whose ut_line matches, deletes it from the list, and prints a line on output. If it doesn't find a matching record, either the user is still logged in or was never logged out properly. It checks which occurred (last_shutdown_time > 0) and prints accordingly. When it sees a SHUTDOWN_TIME or a BOOT_TIME record, it erases the list of saved records after printing a line of output.

Here's a sample of the program run without options:

```
$ ./spl_last
--snip--
o.isaac  pts/3        100.2.79.16       Thu Jul 03 22:35 - 22:49 (00:13)
w.housto pts/0        104.162.60.115    Thu Jul 03 10:45 - 23:24 (12:38)
szhang44 pts/1        104.162.60.115    Wed Jul 02 18:47 - 15:53 (5+21:05)
d.moore  pts/3        71.249.97.95      Wed Jul 02 12:15 - 12:41 (00:26)
d.moore  pts/0        104.162.60.115    Wed Jul 02 11:16 - 00:38 (13:22)
s.morton pts/0        49.43.217.131     Wed Jul 02 02:07 - 04:59 (02:52)
s.morton pts/3        49.43.217.131     Tue Jul 01 22:44 - 00:57 (02:12)
o.isaac  pts/1        104.162.60.115    Tue Jul 01 17:05 - 18:47 (1+01:42)
d.hopper pts/0        104.162.60.115    Tue Jul 01 10:40 - 00:14 (13:33)

wtmp begins Sat Jul 01 00:27:35 2023
```

This machine is almost never rebooted since it serves as a gateway for an internal network, so there are no reboot entries, but once a month its *wtmp* file is cleared, which is why the file begins on the first of the month.

Here's a run on a different host with the -x option:

```
sweiss   pts/1        146.95.214.131    Wed Jul 16 12:50 - 13:02 (00:12)
sweiss   pts/1        146.95.214.131    Wed Jul 16 12:44 - 12:45 (00:01)
--snip--
n.rapace pts/0        146.95.214.131    Sat Feb 01 00:47 - 00:49 (00:02)
a.george pts/0        146.95.214.131    Fri Jan 31 14:46 - 17:07 (02:21)
p.liant  pts/0        146.95.214.131    Sat Jan 25 20:15 - 20:19 (00:04)
w.beatty pts/0        146.95.214.131    Mon Jan 20 09:39 - 09:40 (00:00)
root     pts/0        146.95.78.229     Sun Jan 19 12:49 - 12:50 (00:00)
root     pts/0        146.95.78.229     Sat Jan 18 16:11 - 16:11 (00:00)
csguest  tty2         tty2              Fri Jan 10 13:42 - 13:42 (00:00)
csguest  tty2         tty2              Fri Jan 10 13:30 - 13:42 (00:11)
reboot   system boot  5.15.0-57-generic Fri Jan 10 13:30 - 19:00 still run...
shutdown system down  5.15.0-57-generic Fri Jan 10 13:30 - 13:30 (00:00)
reboot   system boot  5.15.0-57-generic Fri Jan 10 13:27 - 13:30 (00:02)
shutdown system down  5.15.0-43-generic Fri Jan 10 13:27 - 13:27 (00:00)
csguest  tty3         tty3              Fri Jan 10 13:22 - 13:22 (00:00)

wtmp begins Fri Jan 10 13:15:47 2023
```

This output shows that the host had a lot of system activity on a single day. It also shows that someone logged into it on a console as a guest on that same day, perhaps in order to reboot the machine.

User Space Buffering of Input

Our implementation reads one utmpx record at a time, which is not efficient, as we explained in Chapter 4. The implementation of the actual last command reads much larger chunks of the file at a time, but as a result its logic is more complex. Because our primary objective in this chapter was to learn how to manipulate file offsets without making the problems overly complex, we didn't attempt to add user buffering to the programs.

Before we leave this chapter though, we should explore user space buffering of input. The kernel buffers its reads and writes, as we discussed earlier, but our programs can also explicitly buffer input. Suppose that, instead of reading one record at a time, our program reads many records at a time. If a record is N bytes and the kernel reads 4096 bytes at a time from the disk, we can reduce the number of system calls our program makes by reading the largest number of records that fit into a 4096-byte block, or $M = \lfloor 4096 / N \rfloor$ records each time. The program's performance would improve, but we'd have to solve a few new problems.

The records would have to be stored into an array in our program's local memory, and we would need functions to get and remove the next record of the array and reload the array when it was empty. Since we're reading backward in the file, we'd have to read the records in backward order from the array. In other words, if we read M records at a time from the file into an array declared as struct utmpx utrecs[M], we'd have to retrieve them from the array in the order utrecs[M-1], utrecs[M-2], utrecs[M-3], . . . , utrecs[0]. The logic for processing records does not change, and the logic for reading backward is similar to that of the get_prev_utrec() function, except that instead of moving the file offset with lseek(), we'd use an integer variable that points to the next index in the array from which to retrieve a record. When that variable reaches 0, the program would have to reload the array from the file.

Let's formalize an interface that we could use for user-buffered input from the *wtmp* file. It needs just a few functions:

```
#define NRECS  16
#define UTSIZE (sizeof(struct utmpx))

/* Open the wtmp file specified by filename, obtaining a file descriptor,
   and if successful, allocate storage for a buffer *utbuf of size
   NRECS*UTSIZE (large enough to store NRECS utmpx structures).
   Return the file descriptor if successful, -1 on failure. */
int init_wtmp(char *filename, struct utmpx **utbuf);

/* Return a pointer to the next utmpx structure to process from
   the utbuf buffer at index next_ut, decrementing next_ut. */
struct utmpx *get_next_utrec(struct utmpx *utbuf, int *next_ut);

/* Try to read the next NRECS utmpx structures from fd_utmp into
   the buffer utbuf starting at the beginnning of the buffer.
   Return the number actually read, or -1 if reading failed. */
int load_buf(int fd_utmp, struct utmpx *utbuf);

/* Free all memory used by the buffer utbuf and close the file descriptor
   fd_wtmp. */
void wtmp_finalize(int fd_wtmp, struct utmpx **utbuf);
```

The program would call `init_wtmp()` to open the file and allocate an array that can hold `NRECS` utmpx structures. If this is successful, it would call `load _buf()` to read up to `NRECS` records from the file, starting `NRECS*UTSIZE` bytes before the end of the file, into the buffer. Subsequent calls to `load_buf()` would read that many bytes from the position `NRECS*UTSIZE` bytes before the previous call.

When the program reaches the beginning of the file, reloading may load fewer than `NRECS` records. It needs to check the return value of this call so that it knows where in the buffer to get the next utmpx record. Of course, if the return value is 0, it means there's nothing left to read.

Each time the program is ready to process the next utmpx record, it calls `get_next_utrec()`. It starts at the highest index in the array containing a valid record, which would be the return value of `load_buf()` minus one, and works downward. The function decrements this index. When it becomes -1, the program needs to reload the buffer. When loading returns 0, the file's contents have been read completely and the program should call `wtmp_finalize()`. Implementing the complete program is left as an exercise.

Summary

Reading and updating files in Unix may sometimes require moving the file offset around in the file. The `lseek()` system call allows us to reposition this offset so that read and write operations start at specific offsets in the file. Being able to move this offset well beyond the end of a file and write data at that position gives us the ability to create *file holes*, gaps in the file containing no data. The possibility that files may contain file holes implies that the actual disk usage of a file may be different from the size reported by commands such as `ls`.

Unix systems maintain records of user logins and logouts, as well as various system events such as boots, reboots, changes in runlevel, and shutdowns. The standard set of utilities in Unix typically contains commands that allow us to query these types of records. These include `who`, `lastlog`, `last`, and others. The files that store these records are generally world readable, so that any user can look up who's logged in currently, the last time that a particular user logged in, and so on. Most of these records are in binary format and must be read using system calls such as `read()` or library functions that can read binary data. They reside in files such as *lastlog*, *utmp*, and *wtmp*. We can access data from the *utmp* and *wtmp* files by using a POSIX API that does not require making system calls to read directly.

Most data associated with users contains the user ID of the user, not the username. The *passwd* file contains an entry for every user that associates the username to a user ID, and Unix provides functions for retrieving entries from this file either by supplying a user ID, `getpwuid()`, or by supplying a username, `getpwnam()`.

In the chapter, we developed a few programs to learn how to work with system files and move the file offsets around. In particular, we implemented simple versions of the `lastlog` and `last` commands, as well as a command that dumps the contents of any file based on `utmp` records, which we named `showutmp`.

Exercises

1. Rewrite the *spl_lastlog.c* program so that it accepts a `-u user1 user2 ...` option such that, instead of printing the last login information for all users, it prints the information for the listed users. You can limit the number of arguments to 16 for simplicity.

2. Rewrite the *spl_lastlog.c* program so that it accepts a `-t` option (t for "terse") that suppresses output for users who never logged in and just displays actual logins.

3. Rewrite the *spl_utmpdump.c* program to use the kernel's `read()` system call for reading the `utmp` records.

4. Write an implementation of the `spl_last` program with options that limit the range of dates for which it will output data. Specifically, give it two options, `-s start_time` and `-e end_time`, so that it only shows events that take place *after* start time and *before* end time.

5. Write an implementation of the `last` program that uses user-buffering of input, as described in "User Space Buffering of Input" on page 242. Experiment with different sizes of buffers. To do this, make the buffer size a command option `-b nrecs`, where *nrecs* is the number of records to read each time.

6. The implementation of `spl_lastlog` might be improved by storing all user IDs returned by `getpwent()`, sorting them, and then accessing the *lastlog* file. Write a version of this program based on this strategy. Then, time both versions on the same input files multiple times to compare their running times. If you have access to some Linux systems with many users, run the two versions on them to see which is faster.

6

OVERVIEW OF FILESYSTEMS AND FILES

In Chapter 1, we introduced the basic concepts of files, directories, and filesystems. The online chapter, "Working in the Command Line Interface," describes the user-level interface to the filesystem, namely the basic commands for working with files and directories. Here, we dig a little deeper into the hardware and software layers on which this interface is built.

We begin by examining the physical layer that underlies a typical disk-based filesystem. After that, we discuss the different types of filesystems supported by Linux, as well as the Linux virtual file system (VFS). We then describe the various data structures used to implement a traditional, generic Linux filesystem, which will make it easier to develop programs that interact with the filesystem with cognizance of portability considerations in the design of these programs. This leads us to an exploration of the programming interface to the filesystem, where we examine some of the functions of the Unix API for retrieving both file and filesystem attributes. Finally, we put this knowledge to use in the design and implementation of a few programs that print these attributes.

Disks and Disk Partitions

Files play a fundamental role in all Unix systems. Ordinary files can contain data and programs, directory files organize sets of files, and various types of special files allow us to interact with devices in the same way that we access regular files.

Filesystems are the framework for storing files. They organize the entire collection of files, providing both the infrastructure and an interface for accessing them. Most filesystems are *disk based*, meaning that they reside on some type of disk storage device, such as a magnetic disk. They can also reside on other types of physical storage devices such as magnetic or optical tapes, internal memory, and solid-state devices such as flash drives. Some are memory based. Because the most common filesystems are disk based, we begin this chapter with a brief overview of the structure of disks and the software that manages them.

Disk Geometry

Even though the term *hard disk* is in the singular, a hard disk typically consists of multiple disks, which we call platters. A *platter* is a circular, rigid disk that has two *surfaces*, each of which can store data magnetically. They're usually made from glass, aluminum, or ceramic. The platters rotate together at a constant fixed rotational speed around a spindle, which is connected to a motor. The rate of rotation is measured in rotations per minute (RPM).

Data is encoded on each surface in concentric circles. Each concentric circle is called a *track*. The set of all tracks on all surfaces that are at the same radius from the center of the disk is called a *cylinder*. The tracks in a cylinder are therefore aligned vertically. Tracks are divided into equal length segments called *sectors*, though sometimes different tracks can have a different number of sectors. *Physical blocks* consist of one or more sectors. Physical blocks are most often 512, 1024, or 4096 bytes in size, but they can be other sizes, usually, but not necessarily, multiples of 512 bytes. A block is the smallest unit of data that can be transferred to or from a disk. Sometimes groups of adjacent blocks are called *clusters*. Figure 6-1 is a schematic representation of a single surface.

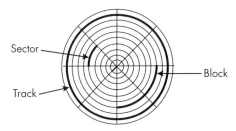

Figure 6-1: The structure of a typical disk surface, showing sectors, blocks, and tracks

In the figure, the thickened arcs represent sectors, blocks, and tracks. A block is shown having two adjacent sectors, and each track has eight sectors.

Figure 6-2 depicts schematically a cylinder for a five-platter disk drive, which would have 10 tracks in every cylinder.

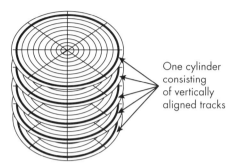

One cylinder consisting of vertically aligned tracks

Figure 6-2: A schematic representation of a cylinder for a five-platter disk

Each surface on a disk has a disk head, which moves like the tone-arm on a phonograph. The tracks of a single cylinder can all be read with the disk head in the same position.

Figure 6-3 shows a set of disk heads for a three-platter disk drive.

Figure 6-3: An opened hard disk drive, showing the disk heads. Photo courtesy of Geni via Wikimedia Commons, reproduced under CC BY-SA 4.0 (https://creativecommons .org/licenses/by-sa/4.0/).

The disk head can both read and write data on the disk, but it needs to be moved into position to do so.

To read data, for example, the disk head must be moved to the track containing the data. This is called *seeking*. The time it takes to move the head to the correct track is the *seek time*. Once the head is on the correct track, the disk must be rotated until the block to be read is under the head. The time that it takes to rotate the disk to this position is called the *rotational delay*. Once the head is over the needed sector, the data is transferred. The seek time and rotational delay are startup costs of an I/O operation, part of its overhead, with seek time dominating this overhead.

In comparison to the amount of time needed to read or write information in main memory, data transfers to or from a disk are slow because of seek time and rotational delay. The time it takes to transfer data is a function of the amount of data, but generally, it is orders of magnitude greater than the time to read memory.

Disk Device Drivers

The kernel interacts with disks through device drivers. A *device driver* is a collection of kernel functions that make a device respond to the various system calls such as read(), write(), lseek(), and so on, by communicating with the device. A *disk device driver*, or a *disk driver* for short, is a particular kind of device driver that interacts with disk drives. In essence it operates a disk device's controller, causing actions such as moving the disk head and activating reading and writing on the disk.

Each different disk has a different controller, and therefore, the disk drivers are specific to particular disk devices. On the other hand, no matter which type of disk the driver controls, its interface to the kernel is the same. In short, the kernel has a set of interface specifications with which each disk driver must conform. Figure 6-4 illustrates schematically the relationship between disks, disk drivers, the kernel, and the filesystem.

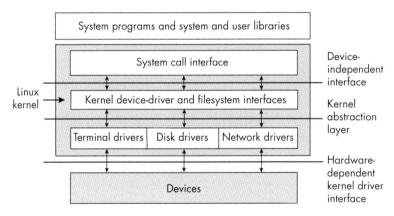

Figure 6-4: The layering of interfaces from the hardware up to user space applications

The hardware is the lowest level of the computer system, the device drivers interact directly with it, and the kernel interacts with them. This organization is part of the concept of device independence that is characteristic of Unix systems—processes and higher-level parts of the kernel are freed from having to be aware of the differences in devices.

Disk Partitioning

In the early days of Unix, a hard disk was formatted as a continuous sequence of blocks intended to contain a single filesystem. Over time, disk capacities increased and it became possible to divide a single disk into multiple non-overlapping logical entities, each containing a distinct filesystem. These separate portions of a hard disk were called *disk partitions*, or *partitions* for short. Disk partitions are also called *logical disks*. The act of dividing the disk into partitions is called *partitioning* the disk. Figure 6-5 shows the layout of a disk that has been partitioned. The first sector of the disk contains a record of how the disk has been subdivided. This record is often called a *master boot record* (*MBR*), but modern systems also call it the *globally unique identifier partition table* (*GPT*). In the figure it is named the *disk (master) record*.

Figure 6-5: The layout of a disk with five partitions

Partitions can be used for purposes other than filesystems. Unix systems define a type of partition called a *swap partition*, or *swap area*, for managing memory. When the kernel needs to make room in memory for a new process, it writes the memory images of selected memory-resident processes into this swap partition. Another use of partitions is for database systems. Database management systems often use the disk in *raw mode*, meaning without a filesystem.

Some of the key benefits of partitioning a disk include the following:

More control of file security   The files of different user groups can be placed into different partitions, each with its own mounting options, such as whether or not it is writeable or read-only, thereby allowing different degrees of security for different user groups.

More efficient use of the disk   Different partitions can employ different block sizes and file size limits so that filesystems that tend to have much larger files will have different parameters than those that have smaller ones.

More efficient operation   When a disk is partitioned, the distances that the disk head needs to travel to perform reads and writes tend to be shorter than if it is one large disk, thereby reducing the disk access times.

Selective backup procedures   Backups can be performed on individual partitions, rather than entire disks, thereby making it possible to back up different filesystems at different intervals.

Improved failure recovery   When disk media has failures, the damage can be restricted to a single partition rather than the entire disk, so that a smaller set of files needs to be repaired or restored.

Reliability   Partitioning can be used to create redundant copies of files, reducing the risk of data loss when one part of the disk is corrupted because of physical problems or malware attacks.

The biggest disadvantage of partitioning a disk is that partitions cannot be increased in size. If a partition is created with too small a size, it can reach capacity quickly and cannot be made larger. In this case the entire disk needs to be repartitioned.

Many, Many Filesystems

Neither the design nor the implementation of the Unix filesystem is part of any Unix standard. Over the years, various flavors of Unix developed their own filesystems, each of which had its own unique interface and implementation. For example, Tanenbaum [42] created the *Minix File System* when he wrote the Minix operating system in 1987, and McKusick et al. [26] later developed the *Berkeley Fast File System* (*FFS*) for BSD2. Several Unix distributions adopted and modified the Berkeley FFS. A filesystem derived from FFS is often called a *Unix File System*, or *UFS*. The developers of Solaris, for example, created *Solaris UFS* [24], based on FFS. As of this writing, there are dozens of UFS filesystems as well as many others supported by Unix distributions in general. The Wikipedia page, *https://en.wikipedia.org/wiki/Comparison_of_file_systems*, contains a long list of them. Here, we'll explore those that are supported by Linux kernels.

Filesystems Supported by Linux

Modern Unix systems such as Linux often support a wide range of different filesystems. We can learn which filesystems are supported on the machine we're using with a man page search. Entering `apropos filesystem` will output a long list of man pages related to filesystems, which we have to filter manually, but entering `apropos filesystems` results in a shorter list, among which we see the following:

```
$ apropos filesystems
--snip--
filesystems (5)     - Linux filesystem types: ext, ext2, ext3, ext4, hpfs, ...
--snip--
```

The `filesystems` man page shows that the current version of Linux as of this writing supports several filesystems, including:

Ext2 The high-performance disk filesystem used by Linux for fixed disks as well as removable media

Ext3 A journaling version of the Ext2 filesystem

Ext4 A performance upgrade of the Ext3 filesystem

Minix The original filesystem of the Minix operating system, which was the first to run under Linux

ISO9660 A CD-ROM filesystem type conforming to the ISO 9660 standard

NFS Sun's Network File System, which also supports other network filesystems

tmpfs   A filesystem whose contents reside in memory

proc   A pseudofilesystem which is used as an interface to kernel data structures

The first five are disk based, but the last three filesystems in this list are not. NFS is a network filesystem that supports access to files on different computers across a network. A tmpfs filesystem resides entirely in memory, and the */proc* filesystem is not a true filesystem; it looks like one, but in fact, it is just a file-like interface to a set of data structures managed by the kernel.

The Ext Filesystems

When Linus Torvalds wrote the first version of Linux, he incorporated the Minix operating system into it, mostly because it was already written and bug free [5]. Shortly after, he and others in the Linux development community implemented a new filesystem named the *extended filesystem* (*Ext*), which added many new features [4]. Subsequently, the Ext2 filesystem was written by Rémy Card, Theodore Ts'o, and Stephen Tweedie specifically for Linux in 1992 and released in 1994 [5]. It was widely used and was designed with provisions for future enhancements.

The next Linux filesystem was Ext3, which was developed by Stephen Tweedie and which differs from Ext2 only in that it contains journaling. *Journaling* is a way to maintain filesystem consistency in the event of hardware failures. A *journal file* records all of the actions that are supposed to be taken on the filesystem, such as creating and deleting files, changing their contents or attributes, and so on. In a journaling filesystem, this record can be used to recover the state of the filesystem without the lengthy task of examining every block on the disk. Ext2 and Ext3 are interchangeable in that one can be converted to the other while the filesystem is mounted because the difference is only in the journaling.

The fourth extended filesystem, Ext4, was released in 2008, mostly to improve performance. While Linux supports many types of filesystems, the Ext2, Ext3, and Ext4 filesystems are native to it and found on almost all Linux systems. Although there are now several different Linux filesystems, many are derived from Ext2. Since it's easier to understand filesystem concepts with a specific filesystem, the structure of the filesystem described in this chapter is mostly based on the Ext2/3/4 systems. For most discussions, it doesn't matter which it is, but for others, it will matter, and in those cases I'll be specific about which I mean.

Filesystem Structure

A filesystem is not just a collection of data structures written onto a disk; it is akin to a C++ object, consisting of data structures and *methods that act upon them*. In general, while the methods of a software system are important to understand, it is often sufficient to know just its data structures to understand how that system works. Linus Torvalds advocated this principle when he was discussing his design of the git version control system in 2006, writing, "I'm a huge proponent of designing your code around the data, rather than the other way around" (*https://lwn.net/Articles/193245/*) to emphasize the importance of good data structures. By examining the main data structures of the filesystem, we'll get a good sense of what takes place when our programs issue requests for the kernel to read or write data. Therefore, in this section, we'll focus first and foremost on the organization and the data structures of the Ext2/3/4 filesystems and touch only a bit on some of their methods.

Partition Layout

In a modern Linux filesystem, the very first block in the disk partition is the *boot block*. After the boot block, the rest of the space is subdivided into a sequence of equal-size chunks called *block groups*. This is depicted in Figure 6-6, which shows the organization of the partition as well as what is contained in each block group. The figure also shows how many physical blocks are used by each part of a block group.

Earlier Unix systems grouped blocks into *cylinder groups*, which were blocks contained in one or more adjacent disk cylinders. A cylinder group is a physical concept, tied to the geometry of the disk, but a block group is a logical concept, independent of the disk geometry, because modern hard disk drives hide the geometry from the operating system. If in your readings you encounter references to cylinder groups, think of them as block groups.

The boot block contains information needed by the operating system to boot the computer. Although there's a boot block in every filesystem on a disk, the operating system only uses the very first boot block on the disk for booting under normal circumstances.

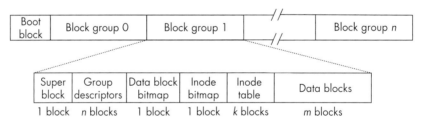

Figure 6-6: Layout of an Ext2 partition with n block groups and an exploded view of one block group

Unix systems other than Linux use a similar decomposition of a partition into equal-size groups; the Berkeley FFS called them cylinder groups. Shortly we'll see why it's more efficient to subdivide a partition into equal-size groups, but first let's see what components each block group contains, and then we'll go over what information these components store and how it's used.

Block Group Layout

In the Ext2/3/4 filesystems, every block group contains the following data:

- A copy of the filesystem's superblock

- A copy of the block group's set of group descriptors

- A data block bitmap

- An inode bitmap

- An inode table for the files in that block group

- The data blocks of all files in that block group

Now let's explore each of these components.

The Superblock

A copy of the superblock is the first block in each block group. The superblock is a large data structure with more than 100 members, containing parametric information about the filesystem such as how many inodes it has, the total number of blocks, the block size, the numbers of reserved and unused blocks, timestamps of various kinds, various flags indicating whether it is read-only or locked, information about the system's mount status, and much more. The term often used to describe this type of information is *metadata*—data about data. The kernel uses the superblock in block group 0 alone. Copies are kept in the other block groups in case of a filesystem failure.

Group Descriptors

Every block group has its own set of group descriptors. The group descriptors store information about the group such as the address of the starting block of each other component of the block group, how many blocks in the group are in use, how many are free, and so on. For example, the data structure in Ext4 that stores group descriptors is of type ext4_group_desc and has a couple dozen members. Each group contains the set of group descriptors of all groups in the partition for reliability in case of filesystem corruption.

Data Block Bitmap

The data block bitmap is a bitmap with 1 bit for every data block in that group. If the block is in use, the bit is 1, and if free, the bit is 0. The data block bitmap is allocated one block on the disk. If that block is 4096 bytes (4KB) in size, it has $8 \times 4096 = 2^{15}$ bits. In this case, the block group can have at most 2^{15} blocks, each of size 4096 (2^{12}) bytes, for a total of 2^{27} bytes (128MB) per block group.

Inode Bitmap

The inode bitmap serves a similar purpose for inodes as the data block bitmap does for data blocks. It contains a bit for each inode in the inode table, which indicates whether it is in use or free. Since this bitmap is also allocated exactly one 4096-byte block, the inode bitmap can keep track of 2^{15} inodes.

Inode Table

Inodes used to be stored in two separate lists: the free-list and the used-list. In modern systems, the inodes are usually in a table, and this is the case for Linux's Ext2/3/4 filesystems. The inode table stores all inodes for files whose data is in the block group. We introduced inodes in Chapter 1, noting that an inode stores a file's status, the original term for its attributes. The term *file metadata* is often used to describe the contents of the inode, especially in the context of filesystems.

The structure that represents an inode is of type struct ext4_inode in Ext4 and similarly named for the other filesystems. It has more then 20 members. In Ext2 and Ext3, the inode is a fixed size of 128 bytes. Doing a bit of arithmetic for Ext2 and Ext3, with a 4096-byte block size, each block can store 4096 / 128 = 32 inodes. The superblock determines how many inodes can be in each block group. If, for example, a block group can have 256 inodes, then storage for the inode table would require 256 / 32 = 8 blocks.

In Ext4, the inode can be larger. Ext4 added more fields to the inode than were present in the earlier systems. For example, the i_crtime member, which stores the file creation time, was not in the earlier inodes, but was added to the struct ext4_inode. The inode itself has a member named i_extra_isize that indicates how much larger than 128 bytes it is.

In Chapter 1, we saw that a defining characteristic of Unix file management is that file data is not stored with the file's metadata and that all of a file's metadata is stored in the inode. This includes timestamps such as when the file was created, last modified, and last accessed. It also includes its mode, its size in bytes, how many blocks it uses, and how many links refer to it. Most importantly, it's where the pointers to all of the file's data blocks are stored. This implies that the inode must be accessed many times in order to access the file's data.

The method of storing files in Unix is flexible and efficient. Its design was visionary because it allowed for huge files, even when there was no way to store huge files. The inode in a Unix system contains an array of (typically) 15 block pointers. A block pointer is usually 4 bytes long. In systems with 15 block pointers, they're used as follows:

- For regular files, the first 12 block pointers in this array are the addresses of the first 12 blocks of the file. If the block size is 4096 bytes (4KB), then a file of size at most 12 × 4096 bytes, or 48KB, can be accessed by one level of indirection through these pointers.

- If a regular file is larger than 48KB, then the 13th pointer contains the address of a *single-indirect block*, which is a 4096-byte block used to store block addresses. Since a block address is 4 bytes, there are 4096 / 4 = 1024 block addresses in this block. Since each of these 1024 blocks is 4096 bytes, the 13th pointer allows for addressing an additional 1024 × 4096 bytes (4MB). Therefore, using the first

12 pointers and the 13th allows for accessing files whose size is up to 48KB + 4MB.

- For still larger files, the 14th pointer is the address of a *double-indirect block* that similarly contains 1024 addresses of single-indirect blocks, each of which contains 1024 block addresses. This accommodates files with sizes up to 48KB + 4MB + $(1024 \times 1024 \times 4)$KB, which is 48KB + 4MB + 4GB.

- The 15th address is that of a *triple-indirect block*, which, needless to say, points to 1024 double-indirect blocks. Since each double-indirect block points to 1024×1024 data blocks, using this pointer, we can access $1024 \times 1024 \times 1024$ blocks, each of size 4KB, in addition to the blocks pointed to by the other pointers. This lets us address files whose total size is in excess of $1024 \times 1024 \times 1024 \times 4$KB, which is 4TB.

Figure 6-7 depicts the use of these direct and indirect blocks in the inode.

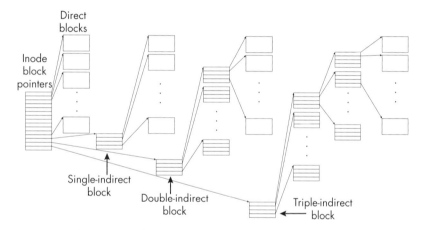

Figure 6-7: The structure of a inode, showing pointers to direct and indirect blocks

For clarity, only four addresses are shown in the indirect blocks. The number of addresses in a 4KB block would be 1024.

Data Block Area

The last part of a block group is the set of blocks reserved for file data. Every effort is made to store all of the blocks of a file in the same block group as its inode. For large files, this is not always possible, and their data blocks may be allocated in other block groups.

Performance Considerations

Modern filesystems do not try to store all of a file's data as a single sequence of consecutive blocks. Although accessing the data of a file would be faster if they did, the disk space would be utilized poorly because there would be many empty gaps that would be too small for entire files. In addition, finding space to write a new file would take more time, since the filesystem would have to find free space large enough for the file. Instead, filesystems divide the file's data into blocks and store the blocks in noncontiguous locations. This results in very high disk utilization, but it introduces other problems.

For one, it takes more time to find a file's data blocks. For another, because the blocks may not be close to each other, it causes more disk seeking between accesses, increasing file access *latency*, the time needed to set up the access before the transfer of data.

If a partition were not subdivided into block groups and there were a single inode table at the beginning of the partition, then every file access would require even more disk seeking for moderately large files, because the inode needs to be accessed each time a new data block must be accessed, implying that the disk head would have to travel back and forth between the inode table and the data blocks frequently. In addition, the blocks of a file could be very far away from each other, causing more seeking.

The use of block groups mitigates these problems while still allowing the blocks of a file to be stored on disk noncontiguously. It decreases overall seek time because the inodes and bitmaps that are used to locate data blocks are either in the same cylinder as the blocks or close to that cylinder. Also, the allocation method used by the inodes in Unix allows the kernel to calculate the starting address of a block with simple arithmetic. However, the use of double-indirect and triple-indirect pointers increases the CPU time needed to access data blocks, because several pointer dereferences are needed for each block. This increase in time is offset by the use of the kernel I/O buffering described earlier in Chapter 4.

Another issue regarding performance is the size of the block. Files are always allocated whole blocks, never pieces of a block. It's extremely rare for the size of a file to be an exact multiple of the block size. Because of this, the final block of storage is only partially filled. The unused, or wasted, space inside a block is called *internal fragmentation*. On average, the fraction of the last block that is unused is 50 percent. This implies that the larger the block size, the more space is wasted in that last block.

When most files are small, larger block sizes result in more wasted disk space, because small files have fewer blocks, so proportionately, the wasted space in the last block is a larger fraction of the file size. As an example, suppose that block size is 4KB. If files are 100KB in size on average, they use an average of 25 4KB blocks, of which 2KB in each last block is wasted space. Therefore, the unused space per file is 2KB/100KB or 2 percent of its allocation. On the other hand, if files are much smaller, about 16KB in size, they need just four 4KB blocks each, so their wasted space is 2KB/16KB per file, or 12.5 percent. Wasted space also translates to wasted time, since there's more disk activity and more disk waits on average.

Larger block sizes improve performance for filesystems expecting large files. Often a system administrator will choose smaller block sizes for the root filesystem, which tends to have smaller files, and larger ones for user data. How large are files on average? In 1993, one study that surveyed the sizes of files found on the internet, by collecting data on over 12 million files across

1,000 filesystems, found that the median file size was just under 2048 bytes, with the average size being 22KB [15].

The Kernel's Filesystem Interface

A filesystem has to provide methods that the kernel can call so that it can provide its services to user programs. Such methods include functions to create files, to read and write data, to retrieve file properties, to move the file offset, and so on. It also has to provide functions for retrieving information about disk usage and other filesystem properties. To get a better sense of the kernel's interaction with the filesystem, we'll work through an explicit example, namely creating a new file and writing data into it.

Creating a New File

Suppose that the current working directory is */home/snw/testing* and that we enter the command:

```
$ gcc -o myprog myprog.c
```

Assuming that the program is compiled and linked and that we have write and execute permission for the directory */home/snw/testing*, gcc will create a file named *myprog* in this directory. To create this file, gcc must either call open() with the O_CREAT flag or call creat(), requesting the kernel to create it. The kernel in turn must perform a sequence of actions, which it does by making calls to lower-level filesystem methods. In the following discussion, when I say that the kernel does this or that, I really mean that the kernel calls various filesystem methods that actually perform that action.

To create a file, the kernel takes the following steps, which leave out several details, such as handling errors:

1. It checks whether the filename is valid and whether the filename doesn't exist already in the given directory.

2. It checks whether the process has permission to create a file in this directory.

3. It acquires a new inode for the file.

4. It fills in the inode with the file status.

5. It creates a directory entry in the *testing* directory with the inode number and filename *myprog*.

Let's look at each of these steps in more detail.

Checking Whether the Filename Exists

The kernel checks whether the filename is too long or has invalid characters and so on. It then checks whether the filename does not already exist in the given directory, */home/snw/testing*. If any checks fail, it stops here, with a suitable message. If not, it continues to the next step.

Checking Permissions

The kernel checks whether the file can be created in the given directory before it continues. If all goes well, it continues.

Creating the Inode

The kernel tries to create an inode. It must get a free inode in the inode table. The inode bitmap is used for this purpose. If there are no free inodes, the kernel must report the error and stop here. In this case, we'll get a message that the filesystem is full. In this step, a copy of the inode table in memory is used; the disk version of it isn't accessed.

Updating the Inode

Assume that the kernel obtained an inode, say, one with index 47 in the inode table. The kernel fills the inode with the owner, permissions, time of last modification, and so on. It then saves the inode number, 47, of this inode, for later use. The updates to this inode are in the memory copy of the table, not the disk-resident copy. The disk copy is updated periodically by the kernel.

Recording the Filename in the Directory

If all of the preceding steps were successful, then the kernel creates a new entry in the current working directory consisting of the pair (47, *myprog*), because 47 is the inode number and *myprog* is the name.

Writing Data to a File

Our example command, `gcc -o myprog myprog.c`, also writes the executable code to the file, which means that the running process issues the `write()` system call to write that data to the file. Two major steps that must be performed by `write()` are:

1. Allocating data blocks for the file and storing the file data into these blocks

2. Recording the addresses of the data blocks in the inode

To write the data to the file, the kernel must acquire the right number of free blocks. While `gcc` is running, it is generating the data to write to the file, creating it in smaller pieces at a time. Each chunk is given to the kernel through the `write()` system call. Because the kernel does output buffering, the file is being stored in kernel buffers, which are not written to disk until the buffers are flushed. If the amount of data is small, all of it will fit in memory buffers and the kernel will know exactly how many disk blocks are needed for it. If the file is very large, the kernel may start allocating blocks before it knows the file's actual size. Assuming that there are enough free blocks, it will first allocate direct blocks. If the file is larger than the number of bytes that can fill all of the direct blocks, the kernel allocates single-indirect blocks as needed. If it is larger than the amount of storage they can provide, it starts allocating double-indirect blocks. It continues this procedure, using triple-indirect blocks if not even all of the double-indirect blocks will suffice.

Note that the data block bitmaps are used in this step to find free blocks and that the bitmaps are modified to mark blocks as being in use as they're allocated. Note too that the locations of the data blocks are implicitly recorded in the inode by these steps because the data block pointers point to them.

The Virtual Filesystem

The filesystem design just described is the basis for many Unix filesystems, but in general, filesystem implementations differ from each other. Furthermore, Unix systems almost always support the ability to mount different types of filesystems onto the directory hierarchy, which implies that different parts of the hierarchy can be on devices with different filesystems. This leads to a problem that we now introduce by example.

Many Unix systems allow users to mount Microsoft's FAT, FAT32, and NTFS filesystems. FAT stands for file allocation table and is the filesystem found on many Microsoft operating systems as well as on external storage devices such as USB flash memory drives. NTFS is Microsoft's New Technology File System, introduced in 1993 with Windows NT 3.1. In Chapter 1, we saw that a directory in Unix is a file that consists of a list of directory entries, each of which contains the name of a file and a reference to that file. In FAT and FAT32 systems, directories don't have this structure. In order to mount these systems and access the files in them, the kernel must make their directories look like the traditional Unix directories. This is just one problem.

The more general problem is that, when many different filesystems are mounted onto the directory hierarchy, the kernel can't have single implementations of the various file-related system calls such as `read()`, `write()`, and `lseek()` because the code in those functions depends on how the filesystem is implemented.

Consider our simple implementation of the `cp` command from Chapter 4, which we named `spl_cp1`. It makes calls to `open()`, `close()`, `read()`, and `write()`. Suppose that we insert a USB flash drive that has a FAT filesystem on it into a USB port on our machine. Suppose too that the drive's name is *MyDrive*. Modern machines automatically mount these flash drives by attaching them to the directory hierarchy either under */media* or under */mnt*. Assuming that it's mounted under */media* and we want to copy a file named *mywork* from that drive into our home directory, we'd enter the command

```
$ ./spl_cp1 /media/MyDrive/mywork ~/mywork
```

and it would successfully copy the file from a FAT filesystem to the native filesystem, say, Ext4. We explore why this works.

The locations and sizes of a file's data blocks vary from one system to another, making it almost impossible to have a single function that finds them without knowing the underlying filesystem implementation. As a result, the actual machine code that's executed when the file-related system calls are invoked is not bound to the system call names when the kernel is compiled.

Let's try to understand this problem in terms of a different problem with which we're more familiar, namely how pointers and virtual functions work in a programming language. When we don't know at compile time how much storage a variable will need for a running program because it depends on how much data is input, we don't declare that variable statically. Instead we declare a pointer and allocate memory to the structure at runtime. This is called *runtime* or *delayed binding* because the binding of the name of the variable to its storage location is delayed until runtime. In C++, when a class contains a virtual function, the code that's executed when that function is called is not bound to the function's name until runtime, which is another form of delayed binding. In the case of virtual functions, the solution is opaque to the programmer because the C++ runtime library handles the binding internally with a special table called a *virtual dispatch table*.

In Linux, as well as in several other Unix systems, this same idea underlies the kernel's interface to the filesystem. The designers of Ext2 created a layer of abstraction within the kernel on top of all mounted filesystem operations. This layer is called the *virtual filesystem (VFS)*. The VFS defines an abstract filesystem interface and hides its implementation. At runtime, it binds the implementations of filesystem-related calls to functions that are hardcoded in each mounted filesystem, which is, in essence, a form of delayed binding. The original Linux VFS was written by Chris Provenzano and later rewritten by Linus Torvalds.

The VFS defines a set of functions that every filesystem is required to implement. This interface is made up of a set of operations associated with three kinds of objects: filesystems, inodes, and open files.

When a process issues a file-oriented system call, the kernel calls a function contained in the VFS. This function handles the structure-independent operations and then redirects the call to a function contained in the physical filesystem code, which is responsible for handling the structure-dependent operations.

For example, let's consider the read() system call. When a program opens a file, it gets a file descriptor for the open file. That file descriptor is a reference to a data structure that represents the file, which we learned earlier is called the open file description. One field of this structure, in Linux named f_op, is a pointer to a table of function addresses. The actual function that's called when read() is invoked is f_op->read(...). If the file were on an MS-DOS filesystem, one function would be called, and if it were on an Ext4 filesystem, a different function would be called.

How is the table pointed to by f_op initialized with the addresses of the functions? The VFS stores information about filesystem types supported by the kernel in a table that's created during the kernel configuration. When a filesystem is mounted, the kernel uses this table to populate a mounted filesystem descriptor with the data needed by the VFS. A *mounted filesystem descriptor* contains several types of data, including data common to all filesystem types, pointers to the functions provided by the actual filesystem, and private data maintained by the actual filesystem code.

The VFS supports many different types of underlying physical filesystems. In fact, in Sun's variants of Unix, from SunOS through Solaris, and in BSD and FreeBSD, the concepts of inode and inumber (inode number) have been replaced with those of *vnode* and *vnumber*, with the *v* standing for "virtual." Linux continues to use the term *inode*. A schematic representation of these levels within the Ext2 filesystem, based on [5], is depicted in Figure 6-8.

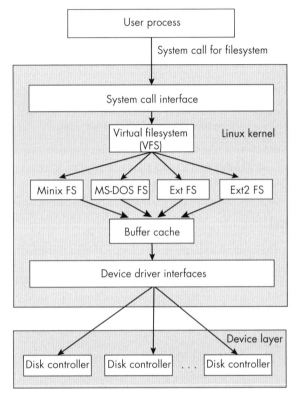

Figure 6-8: A schematic representation of the Linux VFS incorporating the Ext2 filesystem

Exploring the Filesystem API

Our next goal is to apply what we've learned about file and filesystem attributes to write a few programs that interact with the filesystem-related parts of the kernel API. Candidate programs could be ones that display the metadata of a given filesystem, or those that display a file's metadata. If we know how to retrieve a file's metadata, we could write many different useful commands, such as one that determines whether two filenames are links to the same actual file, or whether they're owned by the same user, or which of two files was created or modified more recently.

Our ultimate goal is to write a program that accesses filesystem metadata. If we can find a command that can display this metadata, we could model our program after it. We'll discover that, because the API related to filesystems is not a part of POSIX, navigating through it is a bit murky. Nonetheless, this will be a valuable exercise in system programming.

We'll begin by searching the man pages for a command that displays filesystem metadata, in the hope that its man page will lead to other resources. It isn't enough to search only for the one-word term *filesystem* because in the man pages it is sometimes one word and sometimes two, since different man pages are authored by different people.

In the following query, we limit the search to Section 1 and snip out matches that aren't relevant.

```
$ apropos -s1 "filesystem" "file system"
--snip--
lsattr (1)          - list file attributes on a Linux second extended file s...
--snip--
stat (1)            - display file or file system status
```

The first command, lsattr, isn't what we want, since it just displays a list of files and their attributes in an Ext2 filesystem. The second of the two, stat, is one we introduced briefly in Chapter 1.

The stat Command

Let's look at the stat man page in Section 1 to see if it leads us in the right direction:

```
$ man s1 stat
STAT(1)                        User Commands                        STAT(1)


NAME
        stat - display file or file system status
SYNOPSIS
        stat [OPTION]... FILE...
DESCRIPTION
        Display file or file system status.
        Mandatory arguments to long options are mandatory for short
        options too.

        -L, --dereference
                follow links

        -f, --file-system
                display file system status instead of file status
--snip--
```

When we used the stat command in Chapter 1, it was to view a file's status. Notice though that it can also be used to display attributes of filesystems by giving it the -f or --file-system option. In this case, it shows the status of the filesystem on which the given file resides. The difference in output with and without -f is illustrated here:

```
$ stat /etc/bash.bashrc  # status of file /etc/bash.bashrc
  File: /etc/bash.bashrc
  Size: 2319       Blocks: 8          IO Block: 4096    regular file
Device: 10302h/66306d Inode: 10486298     Links: 1
Access: (0644/-rw-r--r--) Uid: (    0/    root)  Gid: (    0/    root)
Access: 2018-06-05 14:03:30.199540534 -0400
Modify: 2018-04-04 14:30:26.000000000 -0400
Change: 2018-06-05 14:03:30.199540534 -0400
 Birth: 2018-06-05 14:03:30.199540534 -0400
$ stat -f /etc/bash.bashrc  # Status of filesystem containing /etc/bash.bashrc
  File: "/etc/bash.bashrc"
    ID: b07bc00fdedb9bf9 Namelen: 255     Type: ext2/ext3
Block size: 4096      Fundamental block size: 4096
Blocks: Total: 58651894   Free: 28744967   Available: 25747399
Inodes: Total: 14974976   Free: 13698698
```

Without the -f, stat displays some of the file's attributes whereas with it, it displays attributes of the filesystem containing that file.

The man page further states that stat has a -c *FORMAT* option to control which attributes it displays as well as their formats, where *FORMAT* is a string similar to that used in the date command (see Chapter 3). The format specifiers consist of a percent sign followed by a letter, such as %a, %b, and so on. The meanings of the various format specifiers depend on whether or not the -f option is present. Without it, they specify formats for file status, and with it, for filesystem status. For example, for files, %b is the number of blocks allocated to the file, whereas for filesystems, it is the total number of blocks in the filesystem. To demonstrate, we enter the two commands:

```
$ stat -c"Blocks allocated: %b" /etc
Blocks allocated: 24
$ stat -f -c"Total blocks in filesystem: %b" /etc
Total blocks in filesystem: 58651894
```

Some of the other format specifiers for filesystem status are as follows:

%b   Total data blocks in filesystem

%c   Total file nodes in filesystem

%d   Free file nodes in filesystem

%f   Free blocks in filesystem

%i   Filesystem ID in hex

%s   Fundamental block size (for block counts)

%T   Filesystem type in human-readable form

We'd like to write a limited version of this command that displays just filesystem metadata, as an exercise in using the Linux filesystem API. First, we check whether the man page has enough information in it to get started.

In the SEE ALL section of the page it mentions three system calls: stat(), statfs(), and statx(). The man pages for stat() and statx() tell us that they display the statuses of files, not filesystems. The third, statfs(), gets filesystem statistics and might be what we want, but out of curiosity, we'll look at the stat() man page in Section 2 because learning about stat() might give us some insights into writing our program, which we'll return to later.

The stat() System Call

Because there's both a command and a system call named stat, to view the stat() system call's man page, we need to specify Section 2 when issuing the man command:

```
$ man -s2 stat
STAT(2)                      Linux Programmer's Manual                      STAT(2)

NAME
       stat, fstat, lstat, fstatat - get file status
SYNOPSIS
       #include <sys/types.h>
       #include <sys/stat.h>
       #include <unistd.h>

       int stat(const char *pathname, struct stat *statbuf);
       int fstat(int fd, struct stat *statbuf);
       int lstat(const char *pathname, struct stat *statbuf);

       #include <fcntl.h>            /* Definition of AT_* constants */
       #include <sys/stat.h>
       int fstatat(int dirfd, const char *pathname, struct stat *statbuf,
                   int flags);
--snip--
DESCRIPTION
       These functions return information about a file, in the buffer pointed
       to by statbuf. No permissions are required on the file itself, but in
       the case of stat(), fstatat(), and lstat() execute (search) permission
       is required on all of the directories in pathname that lead to the file.
--snip--
```

The page describes several related functions, the first three of which return information about a given file in their second argument, which is the address of a stat structure. The differences among the first three are only in how the file is specified:

- The stat() function expects a pathname for the file, and if the file we name is a symbolic link, it gives us information about that link's target. For example, if *mylink* is a soft link to *target*, stat() returns information about *target*.

- The `lstat()` function also expects a pathname for the file, but if it's given a symbolic link, it returns information about the link itself, not its target. Using the same example, it would return information about *mylink*.

- The `fstat()` call is given a file descriptor instead of a pathname.

The fourth system call listed there, `fstatat()`, is a more general function, designed so that it can behave like any of the other three. We won't investigate it here.

It might be confusing that there's a command named stat, *a system call named* stat, *and a data structure named* stat! *We'll be very clear about which we mean. This type of overloading of names also occurs in other parts of the API.*

None of these functions can be used to access attributes of a filesystem per se, but studying them will help us to understand how to write programs that access this type of data because, as we'll see shortly, metadata is often stored in a form that requires some type of parsing or unpacking, and these will require similar preprocessing.

The `DESCRIPTION` section of the man page tells us that we need execute permission on the path to the file if we call `stat()` but not if we call `fstat()`. If we call `fstat()`, we need a file descriptor for the file, which we can get by opening the file, whereas we don't need to open a file to call `stat()`. We'll decide later which to use, but first let's read about the stat structure.

The stat Structure

The man page has the definition of the stat structure:

```
struct stat {
    dev_t     st_dev;     /* ID of device containing file   */
    ino_t     st_ino;     /* Inode number                   */
    mode_t    st_mode;    /* File type and mode             */
    nlink_t   st_nlink;   /* Number of hard links           */
    uid_t     st_uid;     /* User ID of owner               */
    gid_t     st_gid;     /* Group ID of owner              */
    dev_t     st_rdev;    /* Device ID (if special file)    */
    off_t     st_size;    /* Total size, in bytes           */
    blksize_t st_blksize; /* Block size for filesystem I/O  */
    blkcnt_t  st_blocks;  /* Number of 512B blocks allocated */

    /* Since Linux 2.6, the kernel supports nanosecond precision for the
       following timestamp fields. For details before Linux 2.6, see NOTES. */

    struct timespec st_atim; /* Time of last access          */
    struct timespec st_mtim; /* Time of last modification    */
    struct timespec st_ctim; /* Time of last status change   */
```

```
#define st_atime st_atim.tv_sec   /* Backward compatibility */
#define st_mtime st_mtim.tv_sec
#define st_ctime st_ctim.tv_sec
};
```

This structure has fields to store the most consequential members of a file's inode such as the ID of the device on which it resides, its inode number, the file mode and type, various data related to its size and allocation, time-stamps, and so on. The macros st_atime, st_mtime, and st_ctime are defined for older programs that were written before the kernel started supporting nanosecond time resolution.

The data types of all of these fields are not native C types, meaning that they're not part of the C programming language. They are *system data types*, which means that they're defined in header files in the system. The advantage of defining data structures with system data types is portability. The number of bytes in an integer type in C varies from one operating system to another. A long int might be 4 bytes on one machine and 8 on another. If a program declares a variable to be of type long int and it needs to store a value of type uid_t, it may not have enough bytes on some machines. In contrast, the system data types are defined internally as typedefs of native C types, so that if a value is of type uid_t and a program declares a variable of type uid_t to receive that value, it is guaranteed to have the required number of bytes.

To write a program to extract and print the data from the fields of the stat structure, we have to know more about these types. Because this is most likely going to be true for our planned spl_statfs program, we need to learn what these types are and how we can work with them. This man page has a lot of information, especially in the DESCRIPTION and NOTES sections; almost everything we need to know is there.

For the st_dev field, the page suggests reading about the major() and minor() functions

```
st_dev  This field describes the device on which this file resides.
        (The major(3) and minor(3) macros may be useful to decompose the
        device ID in this field.)
```

and for the st_mode field, it suggests reading the man page inode(7):

```
st_mode  This field contains the file type and mode. See inode(7) for
         further information.
```

For all remaining fields, it refers us to the inode(7) man page. Section 7 pages are always very informative:

```
$ man -s7 inode
INODE(7)                    Linux Programmer's Manual                    INODE(7)

NAME
     inode - file inode information
```

DESCRIPTION
    Each file has an inode containing metadata about the file. An application
    can retrieve this metadata using stat(2) (or related calls), which
    returns a stat structure, or statx(2), which returns a statx structure.
--snip--

Following this brief description is a list of the inode members available for
access through these system calls, with detailed descriptions of each. Some
members of an inode are for internal use and not exposed in the kernel API,
so they aren't mentioned in this page. The page also shows us how we can
extract the file type and permission bits in the st_mode member, which we'll
return to shortly, and describes feature test macros and conformance to
standards.

    How can we learn more about the other system data types appearing
in the structure? In previous chapters, we encountered types such as off_t,
size_t, and time_t, which are also system data types. If we want to learn more
about them, we could see if there's a man page that describes or explains
more about them. A reasonable search would be apropos "system data type":

```
$ apropos "system data type"
FILE (3)                - overview of system data types
aiocb (3)               - overview of system data types
clock_t (3)             - overview of system data types
clockid_t (3)           - overview of system data types
dev_t (3)               - overview of system data types
div_t (3)               - overview of system data types
--snip--
system_data_types (7) - overview of system data types
--snip--
```

    We get a very long list of matches, but they're all for the same page in
Section 7. That page has a long list of almost all system types, with entries
such as the following:

```
dev_t
        Include: <sys/types.h>. Alternatively, <sys/stat.h>.

        Used for device IDs. According to POSIX, it shall be an integer
        type. For further details of this type, see makedev(3).

        Conforming to: POSIX.1-2001 and later.
        See also: mknod(2), stat(2)
--snip--
```

For each listed type, it tells us which header file has its declaration; what
it's used for; what kind of type it is, such as whether it's an integer type or
a structure of some kind; what the various standards say about its size; and
which interface functions use it. In general, when we want to learn what a
specific type is, this page is our starting point.

The File Mode

The file mode is stored in the st_mode member of the stat structure. POSIX.1 -2024 specifies the purpose of each of its 16 bits. The highest-order 4 bits are called the *file type* bits. The low-order 12 bits are called the *file mode bits*. Among these 12 bits, the low-order 9 bits are the *permission bits*. The 3 bits above them are the *special bits*. Figure 6-9 illustrates the meanings of the bits.

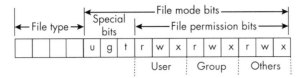

Figure 6-9: The file mode bits in the st_mode member

The file type bits define which of the seven possible file types the file is, such as whether it's a regular file, a directory, a symbolic link, or one of the special files. The special bits alter permissions in a few different ways. The highest order special bit is the setuid bit, which we introduced in Chapter 4. The next two bits are the setgid bit and the sticky bit; we'll explain their significance and use in "The setgid Bit" and "The sticky Bit" sections next. The next 9 bits are the permission bits, grouped into three sets of 3 bits each. Each set has a read, write, and execute bit. The three sets of bits are respectively the permissions associated with the user, the group, and others. A 1-bit means the permission or property is on, and a 0-bit that it is off.

POSIX.1-2024 standardizes various macros that facilitate extracting the values of these bits. Some of the macros are masks and others are macro functions for querying the values. The <sys/stat.h> header file contains all of the macro definitions, and the inode man page describes them. The single-bit masks for the file mode component of the st_mode are:

```
S_ISUID    0004000    /* setuid bit                        */
S_ISGID    0002000    /* setgid bit (see below)            */
S_ISVTX    0001000    /* Sticky bit (see below)            */
S_IRWXU    00700      /* Mask for file owner permissions   */
S_IRUSR    00400      /* Owner has read permission.        */
S_IWUSR    00200      /* Owner has write permission.       */
S_IXUSR    00100      /* Owner has execute permission.     */
S_IRWXG    00070      /* Mask for group permissions        */
S_IRGRP    00040      /* Group has read permission.        */
S_IWGRP    00020      /* Group has write permission.       */
S_IXGRP    00010      /* Group has execute permission.     */
S_IRWXO    00007      /* Mask for permissions for others   */
S_IROTH    00004      /* Others have read permission.      */
S_IWOTH    00002      /* Others have write permission.     */
S_IXOTH    00001      /* Others have execute permission.   */
```

The following code snippet is an example of how they can be used, but without checking whether stat() returned an error:

```
stat("myfile", &statbuffer);
if ( statbuffer.st_mode & S_IROTH )
    printf("myfile is readable by others.\n");
```

The masks for retrieving file type are:

```
S_IFMT      0170000   /* Mask for file type bits */
S_IFLNK     0120000   /* Symbolic link          */
S_IFREG     0100000   /* Regular                */
S_IFBLK     0060000   /* Block device           */
S_IFDIR     0040000   /* Directory              */
S_IFCHR     0020000   /* Character device       */
S_IFIFO     0010000   /* FIFO                   */
```

For example, to retrieve the file type and test whether the file is a directory, we'd write the following code, again without checking for errors from stat():

```
stat("myfile", &statbuffer);
if ( S_IFMT & statbuffer.st_mode == S_IFDIR )
    printf("myfile is a directory.\n");
else
    printf("myfile is not a directory.\n");
```

Because retrieval of the file type is such a frequently performed action, POSIX.1-2024 defines macro functions for testing the file type, which are easier to use than the masks. In the following macros, the m argument is the 16-bit value of the st_mode member:

```
S_ISREG(m)     /* Is it a regular file? */
S_ISDIR(m)     /* Directory?            */
S_ISCHR(m)     /* Character device?     */
S_ISBLK(m)     /* Block device?         */
S_ISFIFO(m)    /* FIFO (named pipe)?    */
S_ISLNK(m)     /* Symbolic link?        */
S_ISSOCK(m)    /* Socket?               */
```

Using the macros, the previous example could be written as:

```
stat("myfile",&statbuffer);
if ( S_ISDIR(statbuffer.st_mode) )
    printf("myfile is a directory.\n");
else
    printf("myfile is not a directory.\n");
```

These macros make it easy to write code to determine whether a given file has specific permissions as well as to determine its type. Before we demonstrate with a few examples, let's explore the special bits mentioned previously.

The setgid Bit

In Chapter 4, we introduced the user IDs associated with a process. Processes have an analogous set of group IDs, namely a real group ID, an effective group ID, and a saved set-group ID. Their meanings are analogous as well.

The *setgid* bit is similar to the setuid bit except that, when a file has that bit set and it contains an executable program, when that program is run, the effective group ID of the process becomes the group ID of the group of the file. If the group of a file containing an executable program is *G*, for example, and the file's setgid bit is enabled, then when the program is run, it runs with its effective group ID equal to that of group *G* rather than the group ID of the user running the program, except in a few unusual circumstances.

The setgid bit has a different meaning when the file is a directory. In this case, all files created in that directory inherit their group IDs from the directory rather than from the process that creates them. This feature makes sharing files easier, since a directory with an enabled setgid bit will allow users of the same group to add files that all members of the group can use in the same way.

The setgid bit has a few interesting applications, one of which is the `write` command. The `write` command (/usr/bin/write, not the `write()` system call), is a command that lets users write to a terminal other than their own. The syntax is:

```
write username [ ttyname ]
```

If a user has multiple terminals open, the optional second argument lets us specify to which terminal to write. After we enter this command, everything we type will be displayed on the user's terminal, until we enter an end-of-input signal (CTRL-D). To try it, type who to see who's logged on and which terminals they're using.

Suppose I am logged in on terminal /dev/pts/2. You could type

```
$ write sweiss /dev/pts/2
Can I bother you?
CTRL-D
```

and wait for my response. Your typing will appear on my terminal window. How is it possible that one person can write on another person's terminal?

The `write` command needs write permission on the terminal on which it wants to write. First take a look at the list of pseudoterminal devices in /dev/pts. The list will look something like:

```
$ ls -l /dev/pts
crw-------  1 ariel   tty 136, 1 Mar  5 17:50 1
crw--w----  1 jake    tty 136, 3 Mar  3 16:22 3
crw--w----  1 lindy   tty 136, 5 Mar  3 15:40 5
crw--w----  1 sweiss  tty 136, 7 Mar  5 18:00 7
```

Some of these have the group-write bit set and others do not. All of these belong to the tty group, which means that any process that runs with the effective group ID equal to the group ID of tty can write to those terminals whose write bit is set.

Now take a look at the write command's mode bits:

```
$ ls -l /usr/bin/write
-rwxr-sr-x 1 root tty 10124 Jan 27 2025 /usr/bin/write
```

When the setgid bit is enabled, the x representing the execute-bit in the group sector of the mode is replaced by an s. You can see that the write executable is in the tty group and its setgid bit is enabled. When we run write, the process that executes it runs with the effective group ID of the write program, which is the tty group. This implies that the write command will be able to write to any terminal whose group-write bit is set.

Since it can be annoying to receive messages on your terminal while you're working, Unix provides a simple command to query, enable, or disable this bit:

```
$ mesg [ y/n ]
```

If you enter mesg alone, it will display y or n, depending on whether the bit is set. Entering mesg y enables writing and mesg n turns it off.

The sticky Bit

The *sticky* bit, also called the *save-text-image bit*, serves two different purposes when it is applied to files and directories. Originally, Unix was a pure swapping operating system—processes were swapped in and out of memory to maintain the multiprogramming level. The swapping store was a separate disk or a separate partition of a disk that was used exclusively for storing process images when they were swapped out. The executable code and other data were kept in contiguous bytes on the swapping store, making reads and writes faster.

A program that was used by many people might go through many memory loads and unloads each day. Putting it in the swapping store made loads and unloads easier, because the file was in one piece. Setting the sticky bit on a program file prevented it from being removed from the swapping store.

If a directory has the sticky bit enabled, then a file that someone creates in the directory will be protected from being deleted or renamed by anyone except that person, the directory's owner, and a process with superuser privileges. Setting the sticky bit on a directory lets all processes put files into it in such a way that only processes with the same effective user ID as the process that created the file can remove those files. For example, some Unix systems set the sticky bit on the directory */var/tmp/* so that it can be used as a place for processes to write temporary files. You can tell when the sticky bit is set on a directory because the letter x in the *others* part of the mode string displayed by commands such as ls -ld is replaced by a t, as in:

```
$ ls -ld /var/tmp
drwxrwxrwt 14 root root 4096 Nov 17 10:09 /var/tmp/
```

If you have that directory on your computer, try this experiment:

```
$ touch /var/tmp/emptyfile  # Create or update a file in /var/tmp.
$ ls /var/tmp/  # Prove that it's there.
emptyfile
--snip--
```

If you have a second user on your host, ask them to delete that file to see if they can. They won't be able to, but you can.

An Example lstat Program

Let's turn our attention to the stat() system call. The stat (2) man page has an EXAMPLES section containing a complete program that calls lstat() to print out a file's metadata. Since the stat() and lstat() calls differ only in how they treat symbolic links, we can use this program to see how we can print the members of the stat structure returned by the stat() system call also.

SAMPLE CODE IN MAN PAGES

Some man pages have an EXAMPLES section containing one or more example programs to help us understand how to use the function they describe. These example programs are often very helpful and can be used as a good starting point for writing a program, since they will compile and build successfully and are usually documented well enough so that we can understand how to use the functions from that man page.

The program, which I've copied into a file named *lstat_manpage_example.c*, is reproduced in the following listing. I've added a few comments.

lstat_manpage _example.c
```
#include <sys/types.h>
#include <sys/stat.h>
#include <stdint.h>
#include <time.h>
#include <stdio.h>
#include <stdlib.h>
#include <sys/sysmacros.h> /* Needed for major() and minor() */

int main(int argc, char *argv[])
{
    struct stat sb;

    if ( argc != 2 ) {
        fprintf(stderr, "Usage: %s <relative_pathname>\n", argv[0]);
        exit(EXIT_FAILURE);
    }
    if ( lstat(argv[1], &sb) == -1 ) {
        perror("lstat");
```

```
        exit(EXIT_FAILURE);
    }
❶ printf("ID of containing device: [%jx,%jx]\n",
        (uintmax_t) major(sb.st_dev),
        (uintmax_t) minor(sb.st_dev));
    printf("File type:                ");
❷ switch ( sb.st_mode & S_IFMT ) {
        case S_IFBLK:  printf("block device\n");     break;
        case S_IFCHR:  printf("character device\n"); break;
        case S_IFDIR:  printf("directory\n");        break;
        case S_IFIFO:  printf("FIFO/pipe\n");         break;
        case S_IFLNK:  printf("symlink\n");           break;
        case S_IFREG:  printf("regular file\n");      break;
        case S_IFSOCK: printf("socket\n");            break;
        default:       printf("unknown?\n");          break;
    }

    printf("I-node number:           %ju\n",  sb.st_ino);
    printf("Mode:                    %o (octal)\n", sb.st_mode);
    printf("Link count:              %ju\n", (uintmax_t) sb.st_nlink);
    printf("Ownership:               UID=%ju   GID=%ju\n",
        ❸ (uintmax_t) sb.st_uid, (uintmax_t) sb.st_gid);
    printf("Preferred I/O block size: %jd bytes\n", (intmax_t) sb.st_blksize);
    printf("File size:               %jd bytes\n", (intmax_t) sb.st_size);
    printf("Blocks allocated:        %jd\n", (intmax_t) sb.st_blocks);

    /* These next instructions use the older timestamp names. For example,
    rather then accessing &sb.st_ctim.tv_sec, it accesses &sb.st_ctime. */
    printf("Last status change:      %s", ctime(&sb.st_ctime));
    printf("Last file access:        %s", ctime(&sb.st_atime));
    printf("Last file modification:  %s", ctime(&sb.st_mtime));
    exit(EXIT_SUCCESS);
}
```

We can make several observations about the code:

- The major() and minor() functions extract the major and minor device IDs from the st_dev member of the structure, which are both cast to (uintmax_t). The printf() function ❶ is given the format specification %jx to print each value. The man page for printf(3) explains that j is a *length modifier* that we use when the integer conversion (in this case, a hexadecimal conversion x) following it corresponds to an intmax_t or uintmax_t argument. If we look up these two functions, we see that they return an unsigned int, which is cast to uintmax_t.

- The switch statement ❷ expression uses the macro bit masks explained in the preceding section. The expression switch (sb.st_mode & S_IFMT) is compared against each of the file type masks described there.

- Most of the other values are cast to either `uintmax_t` or `intmax_t` in this program ❸. If they were not cast, we would replace the `j` length modifier by the `l` (for `long`) modifier.

- The program converts timestamp values to strings using `ctime()`. Our programs thus far have used a combination of `localtime()` and `strftime()` so that they are locale-aware.

- This program does not convert the permission bits to their string representation, but leaves them in octal notation. With what we know now, we can make the permission output more human friendly.

If we build the executable, named `lstat_manpage_example`, we can run it and see what its output is:

```
$ ./lstat_manpage_example /var/log/lastlog
ID of containing device:  [8,33]
File type:                regular file
I-node number:            917611
Mode:                     100664 (octal)
Link count:               1
Ownership:                UID=0   GID=43
Preferred I/O block size: 4096 bytes
File size:                292292 bytes
Blocks allocated:         576
Last status change:       Mon Feb 24 14:21:21 2025
Last file access:         Fri Mar 28 07:58:12 2025
Last file modification:   Mon Feb 24 14:21:21 2025
```

Although the program doesn't attempt to mimic the output of the stat command, it extracts the data from all available members of the stat structure and displays it in a human-readable form. It doesn't convert the octal permissions in the mode to string form; soon we'll consider how to do that.

Since this program uses `lstat()` instead of `stat()`, let's see how it treats symbolic links. First, let's create a symbolic link to */var/log/lastlog* in our working directory and run the program with the link as its argument:

```
$ ln -s /var/log/lastlog ./ll  # ll is a soft link to lastlog.
$ ./lstat_manpage_example ll
ID of containing device:  [8,13]
File type:                symlink
I-node number:            6690311
Mode:                     120777 (octal)
Link count:               1
Ownership:                UID=500   GID=500
Preferred I/O block size: 4096 bytes
File size:                16 bytes
Blocks allocated:         0
Last status change:       Sat Mar 29 11:05:54 2025
Last file access:         Sat Mar 29 11:05:54 2025
Last file modification:   Sat Mar 29 11:05:54 2025
```

Comparing this output to the preceding listing, we see that lstat() prints information about the link itself, not the link's target. Notice that the link has its own inode number, that it has no data blocks, and that its timestamps are different from its target, /var/log/lastlog. Also notice that the permission bits that it displays for a symbolic link are 0777. Recall that POSIX.1-2024 does not require the permission bits in the returned st_mode of a symbolic link to have any meaning.

How does the stat command treat symbolic links? The man page showed that the stat command has a -L option. Without this option, when the command is given a symbolic link as its argument, it displays information about the link itself, not the link's target:

```
$ stat ll
  File: ll -> /var/log/lastlog
  Size: 16         Blocks: 0          IO Block: 4096    symbolic link
Device: 813h/2067d Inode: 6690311     Links: 1
Access: (0777/lrwxrwxrwx)  Uid: (  500/ stewart)   Gid: (  500/ stewart)
Access: 2025-03-29 11:05:54.227552506 -0400
Modify: 2025-03-29 11:05:54.227552506 -0400
Change: 2025-03-29 11:05:54.227552506 -0400
 Birth: 2025-03-29 11:05:54.227552506 -0400
```

The filename part of the output shows that *ll* is a symbolic link to */var/log/lastlog*, that it's just 16 bytes in size, and that it has no data blocks.

With the -L option, stat displays information about the target:

```
$ stat -L ll
  File: ll
  Size: 292292     Blocks: 576        IO Block: 4096    regular file
Device: 833h/2099d Inode: 917611      Links: 1
Access: (0664/-rw-rw-r--)  Uid: (    0/    root)   Gid: (   43/    utmp)
Access: 2025-03-28 07:58:12.831632025 -0400
Modify: 2025-02-24 14:21:21.610229965 -0500
Change: 2025-02-24 14:21:21.610229965 -0500
 Birth: 2023-03-10 08:09:20.962419140 -0500
```

The filename listed is *ll*, but the metadata is that of its target, */var/log/lastlog*. For files that are not symbolic links, the output is identical.

We could use the example code from the man page as a starting point to design a program that behaves like the stat command. However, looking back at its output, we don't see the file creation time. That's because the stat structure returned by the stat() family of system calls doesn't contain a timestamp for it. On the other hand, the stat command displays the file's creation time, called the *birth time* in its output. The fact that the stat command can display file creation time but that it isn't in the stat structure returned by the stat() or the lstat() system calls merits further investigation, since it must be getting this timestamp in another way.

At the bottom of the stat() page, the SEE ALL section references statx(), another system call. The inode (7) man page also mentions it. We also know that the inode contains the file creation time in Ext4, but that it wasn't part of the inode in Ext2 and many other filesystems. If we want to write a program that can display file creation time, we can't use stat(), but perhaps we can use statx(). Let's see what its man page has to say.

The statx() System Call

The statx() man page informs us that it's an extended version of stat(), returning information in a statx structure rather than a stat structure. The VERSIONS and CONFORMING TO sections of the page note that both the call and the data structure are later additions to Linux, appearing first in kernel version 4.11 (in 2017) and that they are Linux specific. Therefore, it isn't necessarily available in other Unix systems and hence programs calling statx() may not be portable.

Let's examine the statx() prototype shown in the SYNOPSIS on the man page:

```
SYNOPSIS
       #include <sys/types.h>
       #include <sys/stat.h>
       #include <unistd.h>
       #include <fcntl.h>   /* Definition of AT_* constants */

       int statx(int dirfd, const char *pathname, int flags,
               unsigned int mask, struct statx *statxbuf);
```

The statx() function has five parameters, unlike stat(), which has two, and calling it is a bit more complex. Also, the synopsis lists four header files that must be included to call this function, but if you're using a Linux system with a version of *glibc* older than 2.28, your program will need to include different header files. In particular, it will require the kernel header files *linux/stat.h* and *linux/fcntl.h*. In Chapter 2, we saw a few different methods for checking the version of *glibc*.

The statx Data Structure

We start by examining the statx structure returned by the function, which is its last parameter. The definition from the man page follows:

```
struct statx {
    __u32 stx_mask;        /* Mask of bits indicating filled fields */
    __u32 stx_blksize;     /* Block size for filesystem I/O         */
    __u64 stx_attributes;  /* Extra file attribute indicators       */
    __u32 stx_nlink;       /* Number of hard links                  */
    __u32 stx_uid;         /* User ID of owner                      */
    __u32 stx_gid;         /* Group ID of owner                     */
    __u16 stx_mode;        /* File type and mode                    */
    __u64 stx_ino;         /* Inode number                          */
    __u64 stx_size;        /* Total size in bytes                   */
```

```
    __u64 stx_blocks;        /* Number of 512B blocks allocated      */
    __u64 stx_attributes_mask; /* Mask to show what's supported
                              in stx_attributes                 */

    /* The following fields are file timestamps: */
    struct statx_timestamp stx_atime;  /* Last access       */
    struct statx_timestamp stx_btime;  /* Creation          */
    struct statx_timestamp stx_ctime;  /* Last status change */
    struct statx_timestamp stx_mtime;  /* Last modification */

    /* If this file represents a device, then the next two
       fields contain the ID of the device. */
    __u32 stx_rdev_major;  /* Major ID */
    __u32 stx_rdev_minor;  /* Minor ID */

    /* The next two fields contain the ID of the device
       containing the filesystem where the file resides. */
    __u32 stx_dev_major;    /* Major ID */
    __u32 stx_dev_minor;    /* Minor ID */
};

/* The file timestamps are structures of the following type: */
struct statx_timestamp {
    __s64 tv_sec;    /* Seconds since the Epoch (UNIX time) */
    __u32 tv_nsec;   /* Nanoseconds since tv_sec           */
};
```

This structure differs from the stat structure in that it has extra members, and the member types are different. We'll discuss these types shortly. The additional members in the statx structure are:

stx_mask   Has bits to indicate which other fields of the structure have been filled in by the kernel

stx_attributes   Contains the bitwise-OR of various flags that indicate additional attributes of the file, such as whether it's compressed or encrypted

stx_attributes_mask   Indicates which bits in the stx_attributes mask are actually used

stx_btime   Referred to as the birth time in the documentation, but is also called the *file creation time*

Since this structure does contain the birth time of the file, we can use the statx() function to implement our version of the stat command, but we need to read more of the man page to understand how to call the function and how to use the returned data.

Let's start with the data types of the structure's members. First, the timestamp members such as stx_mtime have type struct statx_timestamp, unlike the corresponding members of the stat structure, whose types are each struct timespec. The members of these structures have the same names, but the underlying integer types of the members differ.

The remaining members of the statx structure are either __u16, __u32, or __u64. It doesn't declare any members using system data types such as uid_t. Although we can take an educated guess that __u32 is an unsigned 32-bit integer and __u64 is an unsigned 64-bit integer, we don't really know that for sure. Finding confirmation of this guess is not so easy though. They're not mentioned in the system_data_types man page, nor are they native types in the C language. We can attempt various man page searches but none will turn up a page that describes these types. We might be tempted to search on the web for guidance, but before resorting to what might yield an unreliable answer online, we can try a more extensive search on our Linux host.

We can confirm that these are not native C types by reading the most recent C standard, *C23* [6]. Therefore, they must be defined in Linux. Since all type and function definitions exposed to user space programs are in a header file somewhere, we can do a recursive grep search for the pattern __u64, starting in */usr/include*, which is the root of all included header files in user space, piping the output through a pager:

```
$ grep -R '__u64' /usr/include | more  # -R for recursive search
asm-generic/int-ll64.h:31:__extension__ typedef unsigned long long __u64;
asm-generic/int-ll64.h:34:typedef unsigned long long __u64;
asm-generic/statfs.h:49: __u64 f_blocks;
--snip--
asm-generic/statfs.h:76: __u64 f_ffree;
asm-generic/int-l64.h:30:typedef unsigned long __u64;
--snip--
```

Fortunately, the very first file, */usr/include/asm-generic/int-ll64.h*, has a typedef for this type, as does the similarly named file, */usr/include/asm -generic/int-l64.h*. The initial comments in both files explain. In the first we see

```
/*
 * asm-generic/int-ll64.h
 *
 * Integer declarations for architectures which use "long long"
 * for 64-bit types.
 */
```

and in the second:

```
/*
 * asm-generic/int-l64.h
 *
 * Integer declarations for architectures which use "long"
 * for 64-bit types.
 */
```

Our compiler will pull in the appropriate header file for our own machine based on definitions it found when it was installed. We now know that this is an unsigned 64-bit integer, regardless of how the C types long and long long are represented. The definition of __u32 is also in these header files.

INTEGER TYPES IN THE KERNEL

Within the Linux kernel, the code has to have a guarantee that the integer type it uses has a specified number of bits, such as 32 or 64, and has the correct signedness. The kernel code cannot rely on C types for this purpose because the standard C integer types are not the same size on all architectures. Therefore, the kernel uses integer types such as s32, u32, s64, and u64 that are defined in such a way that they're guaranteed to have the correct number of bits.

Because some kernel data structures are exposed to user space, some user space header files contain declarations of types that correspond to those kernel types but whose names are preceded by double underscores, such as __s32, __u32, __s64, and __u64.

Although we could use the j conversion modifier in the printf() conversions, since we know that these types are a fixed number of bits, we can design the code that prints their values using C types. We just need to cast them to a corresponding C type and call printf() with the correct format conversions. Specifically, if smallnum and bignum are of types __u32 and __u64 respectively, then we would print them as follows

```
printf("%lu", (unsigned long) smallnum);
printf("%llu", (unsigned long long) bignum);
```

assuming we don't need to specify a minimum field width for formatting purposes.

Calling statx()

Let's see how we use the other parameters of the statx() system call. We begin with how to specify the file whose metadata we want. The statx() function lets us specify that file by one of four different methods:

An absolute pathname   If the second argument, pathname, starts with a slash, such as /var/log/lastlog, it is an absolute pathname that specifies the target file and the first argument is ignored, as in:

```
statx(0, "/var/log/lastlog", 0, STATX_ALL, &statxbuf);
```

A relative pathname   If pathname does not start with a slash and the first argument, dirfd, is the macro constant AT_FDCWD, then the target file is the one specified by the given pathname relative to the current working directory. If the current working directory is */var/run*, then the file */var/log/lastlog* would be specified using the call:

```
statx(AT_FDCWD, "../log/lastlog", 0, STATX_ALL, &statxbuf);
```

A directory-relative pathname   If `pathname` does not start with a slash and `dirfd` is an actual file descriptor that refers to a directory, then the target file is the one specified by the given pathname relative to the directory referred to by `dirfd`. If `varlog_fd` is a valid file descriptor for the directory */var/log*, then

```
statx(varlog_fd, "lastlog", 0, STATX_ALL, &statxbuf);
```

refers to the file */var/log/lastlog* regardless of what the current working directory is at the time of the call.

A file descriptor   If `pathname` is an empty string and the macro constant `AT_EMPTY_PATH` is bitwise-ORed into the third argument, `flags`, then the target file is the one referred to by the file descriptor in its first argument, which in this case does not have to refer to a directory. For example, if `fd` is a valid file descriptor for the file */var/loglastlog*, then

```
statx(fd, "", AT_EMPTY_PATH, STATX_ALL, &statxbuf);
```

refers to the file */var/log/lastlog*.

The second method, using a relative pathname, is easiest, and if we set the first parameter to `AT_FDCWD` but the pathname is absolute, then that parameter is ignored anyway, which means that the pathname may be either relative or absolute. We'll use this method in our program.

Let's turn to the third parameter of the function, which is an integer, a bitwise-OR of a set of flags. Their purpose is to modify how the target file is identified. For example, we already saw the use of the `AT_EMPTY_PATH` flag. Another flag of interest is `AT_SYMLINK_NOFOLLOW`. When this flag is bitwise-ORed into the parameter, if the pathname is a symbolic link, the function returns information about the link itself, rather than its target.

The fourth parameter, `mask`, is an unsigned integer that serves as a bitmask. It is how we can tell the kernel which metadata we want it to return in the structure, such as whether or not we want the timestamps or the file mode, and so on. The man page lists the constants that can be bitwise-ORed into mask:

STATX_TYPE	Want stx_mode & S_IFMT
STATX_MODE	Want stx_mode & ~S_IFMT
STATX_NLINK	Want stx_nlink
STATX_UID	Want stx_uid
STATX_GID	Want stx_gid
STATX_ATIME	Want stx_atime
STATX_MTIME	Want stx_mtime
STATX_CTIME	Want stx_ctime

STATX_INO	Want stx_ino
STATX_SIZE	Want stx_size
STATX_BLOCKS	Want stx_blocks
STATX_BASIC_STATS	[All of the above]
STATX_BTIME	Want stx_btime
STATX_ALL	[All currently available fields]

There is no constant to select the stx_blksize field.

From its man page we know that the stat command lets us specify which data we want to display by using the -c option. These constant bitmasks could be used to implement that option, given that the program has parsed the command line and recorded which fields need to be printed. It would just set the bits of this mask to indicate the fields that it wants to display. However, there's a catch. The man page warns us that

> It should be noted that the kernel may return fields that weren't requested and may fail to return fields that were requested, depending on what the backing filesystem supports. (Fields that are given values despite being unrequested can just be ignored.) In either case, stx_mask will not be equal to mask.

The kernel may choose to ignore the mask, and when statx() returns, the stx_mask bits indicate which fields have been assigned values by the kernel. The following snippet determines whether or not the stx_size field has been given a value and, if so, prints it, assuming that all variables in the statx() call have been declared and initialized:

```
if ( statx(AT_FDCWD, pathtofile, flags, mask, &statxbuf) == -1 )
    // OMITTED: Handle error.
else {
    --snip--
    if ( statxbuf.stx_mask & STATX_SIZE )
        // OMITTED: Print statxbuf.stx_size.
}
```

A program would need an if statement like this one for each different field of the statx structure.

If we wanted to design the program with the ability to print only selected fields, we'd need to introduce new Boolean variables with names like wants_size_field and wants_uid_field and modify this code. After a call to statx(), when our program needs to print the data in the structure, it would check the values of these variables and only print them if the corresponding wants_..._field variable is set. For example, to print the file size only if the user requested it, our code would be something like this:

```
// OMITTED: Set wants_size_field_ = TRUE if user requested it, FALSE if not.
--snip--
if ( statx(AT_FDCWD, pathtofile, flags, mask, &statxbuf) == -1 )
    // OMITTED: Handle error.
else {
    --snip--
```

```
    if ( wants_size_field && (statxbuf.stx_mask & STATX_SIZE) )
        // OMITTED: Print statxbuf.stx_size.
}
```

The last issue we need to address before designing the main function is how to determine whether the given file argument is a symbolic link, and if it is, how to find the name of its target. The first problem is solved once the program has called statx() because we can use the stx_mode member to get the file type and check whether it's a soft link with the macro S_ISLNK():

```
if ( statx(AT_FDCWD, pathname, flags, mask, &statx_buffer) < 0 )
    // OMITTED: Handle error.
else
    if ( S_ISLNK(statx_buffer.stx_mode) )
        // OMITTED: It's a sym link - process the link.
--snip--
```

A man page search solves how to find the name of the link's target:

```
$ apropos -s2 -a symbolic link
readlink (2)        - read value of a symbolic link
readlinkat (2)      - read value of a symbolic link
```

The readlink() system call has the prototype:

```
ssize_t readlink(const char *pathname, char *buf, size_t bufsiz);
```

We give it the name of the link in its first argument, and the address of a character string and its length in the second and third arguments. It fills in the character string with the pathname contained in the link itself, and returns the length of the string, or -1 on an error. The man page tells us that it doesn't add the terminating null byte, so our program has to append it to the returned string—for example:

```
if ( -1 == (nbytes = readlink(pathname, target, sizeof(target))) )
    error_mssge(errno, "readlink");
else
    target[nbytes] = '\0';   /* Add the null byte. */
    printf(" File: %s -> %s\n", pathname, target);
    --snip--
```

We're now ready to design and implement a first version of the stat command, which we'll call spl_stat. This initial version will allow a single option, -L. If a file argument is a symbolic link, then if that option is supplied, it will report on the link's target, and if the option is not supplied, it will report on the link itself, like the stat command.

Writing an spl_stat Command

We'll develop this program following a top-down strategy. We'll start with the main program and design the required utility functions afterward, using stubs in their place.

Designing the main() Function

The main() function logic is relatively simple:

1. Initialize variables such as the mask and flags. For the default behavior, the mask should be STATX_BASIC_STATS | STATX_BTIME.

2. Initialize a flag variable named report_on_link to contain the flag AT_SYMLINK_NOFOLLOW.

3. Localize the program by calling setlocale().

4. Parse the command line for options and arguments. If the -L option is found, set report_link_data to 0 so that the program reports on link targets instead of links.

5. If the command line is incorrect, exit with a usage message.

6. For each *pathname* found on the command line:
    - Call statx(AT_FDCWD, *pathname*, report_on_link, mask, &statx_buffer).
    - If the call was not successful, print an error message and skip to the next file.
    - If the call was successful, determine if *pathname* is a symbolic link. If it is, and report_link_data is 0, print the name of the link. If it is, but report_link_data is not 0, print the link and target in the form *pathname* -> *link-target*. If *pathname* is not a symbolic link, just print its name. In all cases, print the fields of statx_buffer afterward.

Let print_statx() be the name of the function that prints the fields of the returned statx structure. It will have two parameters, the address of a statx structure, and an array of integers:

```
void print_statx(struct statx *stx_buf, int what2print[]);
```

The array parameter will have a value for each field of the structure. If that value is 0, the function will not print it. If it's a 1, it will, provided that the field has been given a value in the structure. In this first version of the program, all elements of the array will be set to 1. In the second version, we'll add logic to main() to allow the user to select the fields to display.

Listing 6-1 shows the main program, with most comments omitted to save space. The complete program is in the book's source code distribution.

spl_stat.c
main()
```
#define _GNU_SOURCE    /* Needed to expose statx() function in glibc */
#include <sys/stat.h>  /* Required for statx()                       */
#include "common_hdrs.h"
```

```
#define NUM_FIELDS  13 /* Number of fields in statx structure        */
void print_statx(struct statx *stx, int what2print[]);

int main(int argc, char **argv)
{
    struct statx statx_buffer;     /* statx structure filled by statx()    */
    char         usage_mssge[128]; /* String to store usage message        */
    unsigned int mask;             /* Mask to pass to statx()              */
    char         options[] = "L";  /* String for getopt() processing       */
    int          report_link_data; /* Flag for whether to report on link   */
    ssize_t      nbytes;           /* Return value of readlink()           */
    char         target[256];      /* Pathname of link target              */
    int          to_print[NUM_FIELDS]; /* Flags for which fields to print  */
    int          i;
    char         ch;

    mask = STATX_BASIC_STATS | STATX_BTIME;
    for ( i = 0; i < NUM_FIELDS; i++ ) to_print[i] = 1;

    /* Default behavior is to report on symbolic links, not their targets. */
    report_link_data = AT_SYMLINK_NOFOLLOW; /* See the man page. */

    if ( setlocale(LC_TIME, "") == NULL )
        fatal_error(LOCALE_ERROR, "setlocale() could not set the
                                   given locale");

    // OMITTED: Option parsing

    /* If no file arguments, print a usage message. */
    if ( optind >= argc ) {
        sprintf(usage_mssge, "usage: %s [-L] files ...\n", basename(argv[0]));
        usage_error(usage_mssge);
    }
    /* For each file argument, call statx() and print its metadata. */
    for ( i = optind; i < argc; i++ ) {
        if ( statx(AT_FDCWD, argv[i], report_link_data, mask,
             &statx_buffer) < 0 )
            printf("Could not stat file %s\n", argv[i]);
        else {
            if ( S_ISLNK(statx_buffer.stx_mode) ) {  /* File's a soft link. */
                if ( report_link_data == AT_SYMLINK_NOFOLLOW ) {
                    /* Report is of the link itself, not its target, so
                       write the filename in the form 'link -> target'. */
                    errno = 0;
                    if ( -1 == (nbytes = readlink(argv[1], target,
                                sizeof(target))) )
                        error_mssge(errno, "readlink");
                    else {
```

```
                            target[nbytes] = '\0';
                            printf("  File: %s -> %s\n", argv[i], target);
                        }
                    }
                    else /* Report is of the target. */
                        printf("  File: %s\n", argv[i]);
                }
                else
                    printf("  File: %s\n", argv[i]);

                print_statx(&statx_buffer, to_print);
            }
            /* If there's another file, print a dashed separator line. */
            if ( i < argc - 1 )
                printf("-----------------------------------"
                       "----------------------------------------\n");
        }
        return 0;
    }
```

Listing 6-1: The main() function of our implementation of the stat command

Basically, the program performs its initializations, sets the locale, and gets
command line options, and then, for each file on the command line, it invokes statx() and prints out the data in the returned statx structure. It prints
a dashed line between each file's output, unlike the actual command.

Designing the print_statx() Function

Writing the function that prints the metadata is mostly an exercise in formatting information properly. Though it might seem tedious, it's a worth-
while endeavor to learn how to use printf(). One aspect of this is ensuring
we use the correct flags, length modifiers, field widths, and conversion specifiers in the printf() format specification strings. The other aspect is trying
to make our output conform to the way the actual command's output looks.
This is less important, but it's also a good exercise in using printf(). The
format of the output of stat may vary from one file to another and column
positions may move slightly, so we use its output just as an approximation
for how to format our program's output.

To facilitate planning the output, we redisplay the stat command's output here, together with a guide to help identify positions of the printed
fields. This time we give it a device file so that we can see how it displays the
device type:

```
$ stat /dev/pts/0
  File: /dev/pts/1
  Size: 0               Blocks: 0          IO Block: 1024   character special file
Device: 18h/24d Inode: 4            Links: 1      Device type: 88,1
Access: (0620/crw--w----)  Uid: (  500/ stewart)  Gid: (    5/     tty)
Access: 2023-09-10 10:34:16.146591494 -0400
```

```
Modify: 2023-09-10 10:34:16.146591494 -0400
Change: 2023-09-10 09:26:47.146591494 -0400
 Birth: -
```

```
123456789 123456789 123456789 123456789 123456789 123456789 123456789
         10        20        30        40        50        60
```

We'll shift the starting position of the text Inode:... to align with the Blocks:... above it, as in

```
$ stat /dev/pts/0
  File: /dev/pts/1
  Size: 0             Blocks: 0          IO Block: 1024    character special file
Device: 18h/24d       Inode: 4           Links: 1      Device type: 88,1
Access: (0620/crw--w----)  Uid: (  500/ stewart)  Gid: (    5/     tty)
--snip--
123456789 123456789 123456789 123456789 123456789 123456789 123456789
         10        20        30        40        50        60
```

The sequence of fields to be printed, with formatting information, is shown in Table 6-1. Some of the information about the data formatting comes from the field type in the stat structure described in the man page. For example, stx_size is of type __u64. All values are supposed to be left-justified except the user ID and the group ID, which are right-justified. Therefore, the table omits information about justification. The timestamp fields all have the same format, indicated by the term *timestamp format*, which is a localized date/time, followed by a nine-digit number of nanoseconds and a time zone shift.

Table 6-1: Fields of the statx Structure to Print, with Formatting Information

Data member	Label	Starting column	Formatting information
Pathname	File:	1	char* printed by main()
stx_size:	Size:	3	long unsigned int
stx_blocks	Blocks:	25	long unsigned int
stx_blksize	IO Block:	44	unsigned int
File type bits in stx_mode	None	61	char*
stx_dev_major, stx_dev_minor	Device:	1	Single long unsigned int in the format *hex/dec*
stx_ino	Inode:	25	long unsigned int
stx_nlinks	Links:	44	unsigned int
stx_rdev_major, stx_rdev_minor	Device type:	57	Two 32-bit unsigned integers in the format *d,d*
stx_mode	Access:	1	Octal numeral of file mode/ permission string
stx_uid	Uid:	28	unsigned int/username

Data member	Label	Starting column	Formatting information
stx_gid	Gid:	52	unsigned int/group name
stx_atime	Access:	1	Timestamp format
stx_mtime	Modify:	1	Timestamp format
stx_ctime	Change:	1	Timestamp format
stx_btime	Birth:	1	Timestamp format

Table 6-1 allows us to sketch out the print_statx() function, designing the printf() format specifications to match the corresponding data types and layout. Some of the members of the statx structure need no processing before they're printed, whereas others do. For those not requiring preprocessing, we can use a bit of arithmetic to determine the field widths and format conversion specifiers for the calls to printf().

For example, to determine the field width for the stx_blksize value, we reason as follows. Because the label "IO Block: " starts in column 44 and is 10 characters long including the space character, and because the next print field is the file type, starting in column 61, the field width for stx_blksize should be 61 – 10 – 44 = 7. Since stx_blksize is a 32-bit type that we cast upward to unsigned long (to be safe), the format specifier should be "%-7lu".

For those members that can be printed without any preprocessing, Table 6-2 shows the printf() format specifications based on these calculations. We'll visit how to print members that do require preprocessing shortly.

Table 6-2: Selected Fields of the statx Structure, with printf() Format Specifications for Printing Them

Data	Member name	printf() format specification
File size	stx_size	"Size: %-16llu"
Number of blocks	stx_blocks	"Blocks: %-10llu"
I/O block size	stx_blksize	"IO Block: %-7lu"
Inode number	stx_ino	"Inode: %-11llu"
Number of links	stx_nlinks	"Links: %-5u"
Device type	stx_rdev_major, stx_rdev_minor	"Device type: %lu,%lu"
File mode	stx_mode	"Access: (%04o / %s)"
User ID	stx_uid	"Uid: (%5ld / %s)"
Group ID	stx_gid	"Gid: (%5ld / %s)"

Let's turn our attention to the data that requires some preprocessing before printing. The particular problems that we need to solve are as follows:

- Although we can print the file mode as an octal number without any preprocessing, to print it as a permission string we need a function that, given a 16-bit file mode, returns a permission string representing that mode. Its prototype will be char *mode2str(int mode).

- Because the command displays both user ID and username, but we only have the user ID, we need a function that, given a user ID, returns the corresponding username as a string. If there is no username, it should return an empty string. This will have prototype `char *uid2name(uid_t uid)`.

- Similarly, we need a function to return the group name given a group ID. If there is no group name, it should return the group number. This will have prototype `char *gid2name(gid_t gid)`.

- We need to create the numeric representation of the device IDs. The device IDs are two separate 32-bit integers, but when they're printed by the stat command, they are encoded into a single number that is displayed in both hexadecimal and decimal, such as 813h/2067d. Because the `makedev()` function mentioned in the `system data_types(7)` man page encodes the two values into a single integer, we can employ it here.

- We need to print the file type as a string, such as `"regular file"`, based on the bits in the `stx_mode` member. We can use the method we described in "The File Mode" on page 270.

- The times displayed by the stat command contain nanosecond accuracy, as in `2010-09-07 10:31:41.823620843`, and the timestamp members of the statx structure also store time accurate to the nanosecond, but the `strftime()` function that prints localized time is given a time argument accurate only to the second (`struct tm`). In order to format time to the nanosecond, we need to print the nanoseconds as a decimal integer after the string printed by `strftime()`. We'll create a single function that prints the label followed by the localized time, formatted to include the nanoseconds and time zone after it. Its prototype is:

```
void print_time(const char *label, struct statx_timestamp *time_field)
```

Before implementing the functions we just described, let's look at the code for the print_statx() function, which makes calls to them.

print_statx()
```
void print_statx(struct statx *stx, int what2print[])
{
    char idstring[64];

    if ( stx->stx_mask & STATX_SIZE )
        printf(" Size: %-16llu", (unsigned long long)stx->stx_size);
    if ( stx->stx_mask & STATX_BLOCKS )
        printf("Blocks: %-10llu", (unsigned long long)stx->stx_blocks);
    /* stx_blksize is always returned - there is no mask for it. */
    printf(" IO Block: %-7lu", (unsigned long)stx->stx_blksize);

    /* Extract the file type from the stx_mode field with the S_IFMT mask. */
    if ( stx->stx_mask & STATX_TYPE )
```

```
        switch ( stx->stx_mode & S_IFMT ) {
            case S_IFIFO:  printf("  FIFO\n");                    break;
            case S_IFCHR:  printf("  character special file\n");  break;
            case S_IFDIR:  printf("  directory\n");               break;
            case S_IFBLK:  printf("  block special file\n");      break;
            case S_IFREG:  printf("  regular file\n");            break;
            case S_IFLNK:  printf("  symbolic link\n");           break;
            case S_IFSOCK: printf("  socket\n");                  break;
            default:
                printf("  unknown type (%o)\n", stx->stx_mode & S_IFMT);
                break;
        }
    else /* This should not happen, but just in case... */
        printf("  no known type\n");


    /* Print out the combined major and minor device ids in both
       hexadecimal and decimal. */
    ids2hexdecstr(stx->stx_dev_major, stx->stx_dev_minor, idstring);
    printf("Device: %-16s", idstring);


    if ( stx->stx_mask & STATX_INO )
        printf("Inode: %-11llu", (unsigned long long) stx->stx_ino);
    if ( stx->stx_mask & STATX_NLINK )
        printf(" Links: %-5lu", (unsigned long) stx->stx_nlink);
    /* If the file is a device file, such as a terminal, disk, and so on, the
       statx structure will have the device's major and minor device ids in
       stx_rdev_major and stx_rdev_minor respectively. These are __u32 values.
       We cast upward in case the machine doesn't have 32-bit integers. */


    if ( stx->stx_mask & STATX_TYPE )
        switch ( stx->stx_mode & S_IFMT ) {
        case S_IFBLK:
        case S_IFCHR:
            printf(" Device type: %lu,%lu",
                    (unsigned long) stx->stx_rdev_major,
                    (unsigned long) stx->stx_rdev_minor);
            break;
        }
    printf("\n");


    /* Print the mode in the form (octal/permissionstr), such as
       (0644/-rw-r--r--).
       To get the first part, bitwise-and with 0777 to zero out the file type
       upper 4 bits and print a 4-char wide field in octal. The second part
       is the call to mode2str(). */
    if ( stx->stx_mask & STATX_MODE )
        printf("Access: (%04o / %s)", stx->stx_mode & 07777,
                        mode2str((int) stx->stx_mode));
```

```
    if ( stx->stx_mask & STATX_UID )
        printf("  Uid: (%5ld / %s)  ", (long) stx->stx_uid,
                            uid2name(stx->stx_uid));
    if ( stx->stx_mask & STATX_GID )
        printf("  Gid: (%5ld / %s)\n", (long) stx->stx_gid,
                            gid2name(stx->stx_gid));
    if ( stx->stx_mask & STATX_ATIME )
        print_time("Access: ", &stx->stx_atime);
    if ( stx->stx_mask & STATX_MTIME )
        print_time("Modify: ", &stx->stx_mtime);
    if ( stx->stx_mask & STATX_CTIME )
        print_time("Change: ", &stx->stx_ctime);
    if ( stx->stx_mask & STATX_BTIME )
        print_time(" Birth: ", &stx->stx_btime);
}
```

The field widths in the `printf()` specifiers are based on the starting columns we identified in Table 6-1. For fields that are left justified, their specifiers start with a leading hyphen, as in `"%-12lu"`, which specifies a left-justified field of width 12 for an `unsigned long int`.

For all fields except `stx_blksize`, printing their values is preceded by testing that the corresponding bit in the `stx_mask` has been set. The inline comments provide further explanation.

Next, we'll turn our attention to the auxiliary functions called by `print _statx()`, namely `char *mode2str()`, `uid2name()`, `gid2name()`, `ids2hexdecstr()`, and `print_time()`.

Writing the Auxiliary Functions

Let's start with the `char *mode2str(int mode)` function. Its single argument is the file's mode, and its return value is a string pointer. Because it returns a pointer to a string, we declare a static string local to the function and return a pointer to it. Because it's static, it isn't on the stack and will stay in memory while the program is running.

```
mode2str()    char *mode2str(int mode)
              {
                  static char str[11];                         /* Initial string    */

                  strcpy(str, "----------");
                  if      ( S_ISDIR(mode) )  str[0] = 'd';  /* Directory           */
                  else if ( S_ISCHR(mode) )  str[0] = 'c';  /* Char devices        */
                  else if ( S_ISBLK(mode) )  str[0] = 'b';  /* Block device        */
                  else if ( S_ISLNK(mode) )  str[0] = 'l';  /* Symbolic link       */
                  else if ( S_ISFIFO(mode) ) str[0] = 'p';  /* Named pipe (FIFO) */
                  else if ( S_ISSOCK(mode) ) str[0] = 's';  /* Socket              */

                  if ( mode & S_IRUSR ) str[1] = 'r';
                  if ( mode & S_IWUSR ) str[2] = 'w';
```

```
    if ( mode & S_IXUSR ) str[3] = 'x';

    if ( mode & S_IRGRP ) str[4] = 'r';
    if ( mode & S_IWGRP ) str[5] = 'w';
    if ( mode & S_IXGRP ) str[6] = 'x';

    if ( mode & S_IROTH ) str[7] = 'r';
    if ( mode & S_IWOTH ) str[8] = 'w';
    if ( mode & S_IXOTH ) str[9] = 'x';

    /* Now check the setuid, setgid, and sticky bits. */
    if ( mode & S_ISUID ) str[3] = 's';
    if ( mode & S_ISGID ) str[6] = 's';
    if ( mode & S_ISVTX ) str[9] = 't';
    return str;
}
```

The function is relatively simple. It checks each bit of the mode argument. If it's set, it replaces the - in str by the corresponding letter, based on the bitmask constant bitwise-ANDed to it. After it checks the permission bits, it checks the special bits and, for each bit that's enabled, it replaces the corresponding execute bit in the string by either an s or a t.

The next two functions are uid2name() and gid2name(). They are nearly the same. In Chapter 5, we learned about the getpwuid() function, which returns a pointer to the passwd structure, given a user ID. We use that function to get the structure and return the username member of it:

uid2name()
```
#include <pwd.h>
char *uid2name(uid_t uid)
{
    struct passwd *pw_ptr;
    if ( (pw_ptr = getpwuid(uid)) == NULL )
        return "";
    else
        return pw_ptr->pw_name;
}
```

The required header file is shown in the listing as a reminder that we need to include it. If for some reason there is no entry in the password database, it returns an empty string.

We haven't yet needed to work with group information, but a good guess would be that there's a corresponding set of functions for groups. The corresponding function for getting the group name, given the group ID, might be getgrgid(). A man page search will confirm this—entering apropos -a 'gid' 'get' lists several functions, but the ones that mention a file's group are the ones we need:

```
getgrgid (3)        - get group file entry
```

This function returns a pointer to a group structure, which has a member named gr_name. Our function can use this in the same way that uid2name() used getpwuid():

gid2name()

```
#include <grp.h>
char *gid2name(gid_t gid)
{
    struct group *grp_ptr;
    if ( (grp_ptr = getgrgid(gid)) == NULL )
        return "";
    else
        return grp_ptr->gr_name;
}
```

The next task is to print the device IDs in the required format. We encapsulate that logic in a function named ids2hexdecstr(). That function needs to construct a string in which the first part is the hexadecimal code for the stx_dev_major and stx_dev_minor fields. The format specifier, "%02x%02xh", converts the next two integer values to hexadecimal with leading zeros without intervening space, each with a minimum field width of two characters, followed by the letter h. For example

```
printf("%02x%02xh", 255, 32);
```

prints ff20h.

The second part of the string is the decimal equivalent of the combined major and minor device IDs.

According to its man page, the makedev() function, given two 32-bit device IDs, constructs and returns a single dev_t (which is a long unsigned int) device ID:

```
#include <sys/sysmacros.h>
dev_t makedev(unsigned int maj, unsigned int min);
```

This function is not required by POSIX.1-2024, implying that this code may not be portable.

We could avoid using it if we want by converting the hexadecimal string we just constructed to a decimal using strtol() with a base of 16. We'll opt to use the less portable approach by calling makedev(), casting the dev_t return value to an unsigned long for printing:

```
#include <sys/sysmacros.h>
void ids2hexdecstr(unsigned int major, unsigned int minor, char *buffer)
{
    sprintf(buffer, "%02x%02xh/%lud", major, minor, makedev(major, minor));
}
```

The last part of this program is the `print_time()` function. In Chapter 3, we learned how to format date/time strings. Examining the output of the stat command, we see that the dates and times are in the format

---

yyyy-mm-dd hh:mm:ss.ddddddddd -hh:mm

---

where the *ddddddddd* is a number of nanoseconds in the range [0,999999999]. Table C-1 in Appendix C lists the date and time format specifiers that we can give to `stftime()`. They're also in its man page. If we look at that list, we can see that "%F %T" is the format that would give us the date and time as *yyyy-mm-dd hh:mm:ss*.

To print the nanoseconds in a left-justified field of nine characters with leading zeros, we can use "%09u". The resulting function follows:

print_time()
```c
void print_time(const char *label, struct statx_timestamp *time_field)
{
    struct tm *bdtime;              /* Broken-down time          */
    char       formatted_time[100]; /* String storing formatted time */
    char       timezone[32];        /* To store time offset      */
    time_t     time_val;            /* For converted tv_sec field */

    time_val = time_field->tv_sec;  /* Convert to time_t.        */
    bdtime = localtime(&time_val);  /* Convert to broken-down time. */
    if ( bdtime == NULL )           /* Check for error.          */
        fatal_error(EOVERFLOW, "localtime");

    if ( strftime(time_string, sizeof(time_string), "%F %T", bdtime) == 0 )
        fatal_error(BAD_FORMAT_ERROR,"strftime failed\n");

    printf("%s%s.%09u", label, time_string, time_field->tv_nsec);
    if ( 0 == strftime(timezone, 32, " %z", bdtime) )
        fatal_error(BAD_FORMAT_ERROR, "Error printing time zone\n");
    printf("%s\n", timezone);
}
```

We've completed the program. To save space here, the complete listing is omitted, but is in the source code distribution for the book.

We compile and build the program with the command

```
$ gcc -Wall -g -I ../include spl_stat.c -L../lib -lspl -o spl_stat
```

---

and run it on a few different files, comparing the output to that of the actual stat command, as shown here:

```
$ ./spl_stat  spl_stat.c
  File  spl_stat.c
  Size: 10777        Blocks: 24        IO Block: 4096     regular file
Device: 0813h/2067d  Inode: 6690318    Links: 1
Access: (0664/-rw-rw-r--) Uid: (  500 / stewart)   Gid: (  500 / stewart)
Access: 2023-09-10 15:31:57.754777183 -0400
```

```
  Modify: 2023-09-10 15:31:52.954929789 -0400
  Change: 2023-09-10 15:31:52.994928519 -0400
   Birth: 2023-09-10 15:31:52.950929916 -0400
$ stat spl_stat.c
   File: spl_stat.c
   Size: 10777         Blocks: 24          IO Block: 4096    regular file
  Device: 813h/2067d    Inode: 6690318     Links: 1
  Access: (0664/-rw-rw-r--)  Uid: (  500/ stewart)  Gid: (  500/ stewart)
  Access: 2023-09-10 15:31:57.754777183 -0400
  Modify: 2023-09-10 15:31:52.954929789 -0400
  Change: 2023-09-10 15:31:52.994928519 -0400
   Birth: 2023-09-10 15:31:52.950929916 -0400
```

This first run shows that our program's output is almost identical to that of the command.

Let's see how it compares when given a device file argument, which will require the device type to be printed:

```
$ ./spl_stat /dev/tty
  File: /dev/tty
  Size: 0              Blocks: 0          IO Block: 4096    character special file
Device: 0005h/5d      Inode: 12          Links: 1    Device type: 5,0
Access: (0666/crw-rw-rw-)  Uid: (    0/ root)    Gid: (    5/ tty)
Access: 2023-09-21 16:07:46.650574320 -0400
Modify: 2023-09-21 16:07:46.650574320 -0400
Change: 2023-09-21 16:07:46.650574320 -0400
 Birth: 2023-09-21 16:07:42.320000000 -0400
$ stat /dev/tty
  File: /dev/tty
  Size: 0              Blocks: 0          IO Block: 4096    character special file
Device: 5h/5d Inode: 12          Links: 1    Device type: 5,0
Access: (0666/crw-rw-rw-)  Uid: (    0/    root)    Gid: (    5/      tty)
Access: 2023-09-21 16:07:46.650574320 -0400
Modify: 2023-09-21 16:07:46.650574320 -0400
Change: 2023-09-21 16:07:46.650574320 -0400
 Birth: 2023-09-21 16:07:42.320000000 -0400
```

Our program prints leading zeros in the device ID, whereas the stat command does not; otherwise, the output is the same.

Finally, let's see how it behaves when the file is a symbolic link. We'll use the same *ll* link as before:

```
$ ./spl_stat -L ll
 File: ll
 Size: 292292         Blocks: 576        IO Block: 4096    regular file
 Device: 0833h/2099d   Inode: 917611     Links: 1
 Access: (0664/-rw-rw-r--)  Uid: (   0 / root)    Gid: (   43 / utmp)
 Access: 2023-09-11 21:21:13.592747728 -0400
 Modify: 2023-08-25 10:23:49.742860606 -0400
```

```
Change: 2023-08-25 10:23:49.742860606 -0400
 Birth: 2023-03-10 08:09:20.962419140 -0500
```

```
$ ./spl_stat ll
 File: ll -> /var/log/lastlog
 Size: 16            Blocks: 0          IO Block: 4096    symbolic link
Device: 0813h/2067d    Inode: 6690311    Links: 1
Access: (0777/lrwxrwxrwx) Uid: ( 500 / stewart)   Gid: ( 500 / stewart)
Access: 2023-09-11 20:22:36.919872028 -0400
Modify: 2023-09-02 09:19:55.041155595 -0400
Change: 2023-09-02 09:19:55.041155595 -0400
 Birth: 2023-09-02 09:19:55.041155595 -0400
```

You can see that the program implements the -L option, because with it, it reports on the target, and without it, it reports on the link itself.

Designing an Enhanced spl_stat Command

If we want to create a second version of the program that allows the user to suppress printing of selected fields, the only changes are in the option-handling code in the main program and in the print_statx() function. I outline the changes here and leave development of the actual program as an exercise.

First, we declare an enumerated type:

```
enum field2print {
    typef, modef, nlinkf, uidf, gidf, atimef, mtimef, ctimef,
    inof, sizef, blocksf, blksizef, btimef, NUM_FIELDS
};
```

We'll use this type as a set of index values into an array of flags named to_print, declared in the main() function. If to_print[nlinkf] is FALSE, for example, then the program should not print the stx_nlinks data, and if to_print[nlinkf] is TRUE, then it should. Initially, all fields are suppressed:

```
BOOL to_print[NUM_FIELDS];
for ( i = typef; i < NUM_FIELDS; i++ )
    to_print[i] = FALSE;
```

Next, in main(), we need to parse the option string. This is the most work. We don't have to use the same syntax as the stat command. We could simplify it and use options of the form

```
-a  # Show atime.
-b  # Show btime.
-c  # Show ctime.
-t  # Show type.
-p  # Show mode.
--snip--
```

choosing unique, mnemonic letters for each field when possible. If we want to be faithful to the syntax of the actual stat command, then we'd need to write a separate function that parsed an option of the form "%a %w ...", matching the syntax of that command. We'll choose the simpler method here. In the option-handling loop, when an option is found, the corresponding flag in the array would be set:

```
int main(int argc, char **argv)
{
    char   options[] = "abctpL...";
    BOOL   to_print[NUM_FIELDS];
    char   ch;
    --snip--

    /* Parse the command line for options. */
    while ( TRUE ) {
        /* Call getopt, passing argc and argv and the options string. */
        ch = getopt(argc, argv, options);
        if ( -1 == ch ) /* No more options */
            break;
        switch ( ch ) {
        case 'a': to_print[atimef] = TRUE; break;
        case 'b': to_print[btimef] = TRUE; break;
        case 'c': to_print[ctimef] = TRUE; break;
        case 'n': to_print[nlinkf] = TRUE; break;
        --snip--
        }
    }
}
```

The last changes would be in the print_statx() function. We would need to replace every if statement such as

```
if ( stx->stx_mask & STATX_ATIME )
```

with:

```
if ( to_print[atimef] && stx->stx_mask & STATX_ATIME )
```

If we make these changes throughout the function, then only those fields requested by the user will be printed. However, the formatting will not be the same as it is in the original program. The actual stat command does not attempt to preserve that formatting. We could, if we wanted, replace the missing fields by blank strings of the same length.

Writing an spl_statfs Command

Let's return to the original problem we wanted to solve, namely, developing a program that can display the metadata of a filesystem. What we learned while developing a stat command is good preparation for this task.

The statfs() System Call

Earlier, we discovered a system call named statfs() that prints a filesystem's metadata. We begin by looking at its man page:

```
$ man -s2 statfs
STATFS(2)                    Linux Programmer's Manual                    STATFS(2)


NAME
       statfs, fstatfs - get filesystem statistics
SYNOPSIS
       #include <sys/vfs.h>     /* Or <sys/statfs.h> */


       int statfs(const char *path, struct statfs *buf);
       int fstatfs(int fd, struct statfs *buf);
DESCRIPTION
       The statfs() system call returns information about a mounted filesystem.
       path is the pathname of any file within the mounted filesystem. buf is
       a pointer to a statfs structure defined approximately as follows:


           struct statfs {
               __fsword_t f_type;     /* Type of filesystem (see below)  */
               __fsword_t f_bsize;    /* Optimal transfer block size     */
               fsblkcnt_t f_blocks;   /* Total data blocks in filesystem */
               fsblkcnt_t f_bfree;    /* Free blocks in filesystem       */
               fsblkcnt_t f_bavail;   /* Free blocks available to
                                         unprivileged user               */
               fsfilcnt_t f_files;    /* Total inodes in filesystem      */
               fsfilcnt_t f_ffree;    /* Free inodes in filesystem       */
               fsid_t     f_fsid;     /* Filesystem ID                   */
               __fsword_t f_namelen;  /* Maximum length of filenames     */
               __fsword_t f_frsize;   /* Fragment size (since Linux 2.6) */
               __fsword_t f_flags;    /* Mount flags of filesystem
                                         (since Linux 2.6.36)            */
               __fsword_t f_spare[xxx]; /* Padding bytes reserved for
                                           future use                    */
           };
```

This is probably the function we need. This system call returns various pieces of information about the filesystem containing the file specified in its first parameter. That information is returned in the statfs structure, whose address is the second parameter.

Before we study the statfs data structure in detail, let's read more of the man page, particularly the relevant remarks and warnings.

- In the CONFORMING TO section, it states that this call is only available in Linux, implying that our code won't be portable unless we find alternative methods that are more portable and include macros to check on which system the program is compiled.

- In the NOTES section, it mentions that the __fsword_t type is an internal type in *glibc* that may not be recognized by our compiler. The recommended solution is to cast variables of this type to unsigned int, with the warning that it may not work.

- The page also warns us that "nobody knows what f_fsid is supposed to contain (but see below)." The following explanation elaborates— the f_fsid field is supposed to contain the filesystem's unique ID. Different Unix distributions return that ID in different ways. In Linux, the f_fsid field is of type fsid_t which is defined in *sys/vfs.h* as:

```
struct {int val[2];}
```

- The *Linux Standard Base* (*LSB*), another standard developed under the auspices of the Linux Foundation (see *https://wiki.linuxfoundation .org/lsb/lsb-introduction*) has deprecated the library call statfs() and advises us to use statvfs() instead. In fact, if we look through the POSIX list of system calls and library functions, we don't find statfs(2), but we do find statvfs().

In short, the man page has enough discouraging warnings that we should consider the alternatives before making any decisions about how to design our program.

The statvfs() Library Function

We begin by reading the statvfs() man page, in the hope that we'll be able to use this function instead:

```
STATVFS(3)              Linux Programmer's Manual              STATVFS(3)

NAME
       statvfs, fstatvfs - get filesystem statistics
SYNOPSIS
       #include <sys/statvfs.h>

       int statvfs(const char *path, struct statvfs *buf);
       int fstatvfs(int fd, struct statvfs *buf);
DESCRIPTION
       The function statvfs() returns information about a mounted filesystem.
       path is the pathname of any file within the mounted filesystem. buf is
       a pointer to a statvfs structure defined approximately as follows:
```

```
            struct statvfs {
                unsigned long  f_bsize;    /* Filesystem block size      */
                unsigned long  f_frsize;   /* Fragment size              */
                fsblkcnt_t     f_blocks;   /* Size of fs in f_frsize units */
                fsblkcnt_t     f_bfree;    /* Number of free blocks      */
                fsblkcnt_t     f_bavail;   /* Number of free blocks for
                                              unprivileged users         */
                fsfilcnt_t     f_files;    /* Number of inodes           */
                fsfilcnt_t     f_ffree;    /* Number of free inodes      */
                fsfilcnt_t     f_favail;   /* Number of free inodes for
                                              unprivileged users         */
                unsigned long  f_fsid;     /* Filesystem ID              */
                unsigned long  f_flag;     /* Mount flags                */
                unsigned long  f_namemax;  /* Maximum filename length    */
            };
```

Here the types fsblkcnt_t and fsfilcnt_t are defined in <sys/types.h>.
Both used to be unsigned long.

--*snip*--

This is a library function, not a system call. The rest of the man page explains that it is supported by calls to statfs() in Linux. The statement that the structure is "defined approximately" is not explained further, other than that some members will not have meaningful values on some filesystems.

On the positive side, the filesystem ID in this structure is a simple integer and there are no members whose types are internal *glibc* types. On the negative side, it doesn't have the f_type field, so we can't use this function to get the filesystem type. Lastly, the man page explains that, to get all mounting flags bitwise-ORed into f_flags, we need to define _GNU_SOURCE.

If we use this function, we need a different method of getting the filesystem type. If we use statfs(), our code will only work on Linux systems. This problem is unlike the problems we tackled in the previous chapters of the book, which all fell under the parts of the API standardized by POSIX.1-2024, because the lack of a single standard means that we either have to write a very complex program to make it portable, or write a simpler one that we know will only work on Linux.

It would be useful to see the filesystem type in our output. Getting the filesystem type without calling statfs() is much harder because we'd need to learn about how filesystems are mounted and where their types are stored in the kernel's data structures for maintaining information about mounts.

A Hybrid Solution

Given the preceding arguments, we'll follow a hybrid approach; we'll use statvfs() to get most of the metadata that we want to display, and call statfs() to get the filesystem type and nothing more.

As we did when we designed the spl_stat program, we'll use the output of stat -f as a guide to format the output of our program. Let's display that output again to see its format, putting column numbers underneath to help plan our output:

```
$ stat -f /var/log
  File: "/var/log"
    ID: 7e58ac747798a2a5 Namelen: 255      Type: ext2/ext3
Block size: 4096        Fundamental block size: 4096
Blocks: Total: 11936443   Free: 10290961   Available: 9676510
Inodes: Total: 3055616    Free: 3020523


123456789 123456789 123456789 123456789 123456789 123456789
0         10        20        30        40        50
```

If we run stat -f on several different files, we'll discover that the filesystem ID varies in length but that the Namelen: label always starts one space after the end of it and so has a variable starting position.

We need to map the displayed data items to the members of the statvfs structure. For most of the labeled data shown, reading the statvsf(3) and stat(1) man pages is enough determine to which members of the structure they correspond. The one member that does not seem obvious is f_frsize, but by process of elimination, we can conclude it must be the data appearing after the label Fundamental block size. The correspondence is therefore as follows:

ID   f_fsid

Namelen   f_namemax

Type   f_type, not part of struct statvfs

Block size   f_bsize

Fundamental block size   f_frsize

Blocks: Total   f_blocks

Blocks: Free   f_bfree

Blocks: Available   f_bavail

Inodes: Total   f_files

Inodes: Free   f_ffree

The filesystem type, is not part of that structure; we'll get it by calling statfs(). Table 6-3 shows the formatting information that the preceding output implies.

Table 6-3: Fields Output by `stat -f` with Formatting Information and Either `struct statvfs` Member Names or Other Source of Data

Data member	Label	Starting column	Type
Command argument	File:	3	char*, printed by main function
f_fsid	ID:	5	Hexadecimal un-signed long integer
f_namemax	Namelen:	❶	Unsigned long integer
External	Type:	43	char*
f_bsize	Block size:	1	Unsigned long integer
f_frsize	Fundamental block size:	24	Unsigned long integer
f_blocks	Blocks: Total:	1	Unsigned long integer
f_bfree	Free:	27	Unsigned long integer
f_bavail	Available:	44	Unsigned long integer
f_files	Inodes: Total:	1	Unsigned long integer
f_ffree	Free:	27	Unsigned long integer

The starting position ❶ of `Namelen:` is one space past the end of the filesystem ID. We can use the same method of calculating field widths as we used for the `spl_stat` program. For example, the printing field for `f_bfree` member starts in column 27, including its label, `"Free: "`, which is 6 characters long. The next printing field starts in column 44. Therefore, the width of the format specifier for `f_bfree` should be 44 – 6 – 27, or 11. The format specifier, since its type is `unsigned long`, should be `"%-11lu"`.

The last nontrivial part of the program is printing a string representation of the filesystem type, since the `statfs` structure's filesystem type field is an integer encoding that has to be decoded. Here's where Unix filtering tools and the `vi` editor come in handy. The `statfs()` man page has a list of filesystem types that can be values of the `f_ftype` member:

```
ADFS_SUPER_MAGIC      0xadf5
AFFS_SUPER_MAGIC      0xadff
AFS_SUPER_MAGIC       0x5346414f
ANON_INODE_FS_MAGIC   0x09041934 /* Anonymous inode FS (for
                                    pseudofiles that have no name;
                                    e.g., epoll, signalfd, bpf) */
--snip--
```

We can copy that list to a file and open it in the `vi` editor. In the editor, with just a few global substitutions, including deleting all comments, deleting all occurrences of `_SUPER_MAGIC`, deleting all occurrences of `_MAGIC`, and replacing the remaining underscores with hyphens, the file will look like:

```
ADFS      0xadf5
AFFS      0xadff
AFS       0x5346414f
```

```
ANON-INODE-FS    0x09041934
--snip--
```

We can then convert all uppercase to lowercase using the vi command
1,$s/./\L&/g

```
adfs        0xadf5
affs        0xadff
afs         0x5346414f
anon-inode-fs   0x09041934
--snip--
```

and rearrange each line using the command

```
:1,$s/^\([^ ]*\)  *\([0-9a-z]*\)[ ]*$/case \2: return "\1";/
```

so that they look like:

```
case 0xadf5: return "adfs";
case 0xadff: return "affs";
case 0x5346414f: return "afs";
case 0x09041934: return "anon-inode-fs";
--snip--
```

These lines become the cases of a switch statement inside a function
with the prototype char *fstype2name(struct statfs statfs_buf) that returns
the string associated with the number from the f_ftype member of the structure argument:

```
char *fstype2name(struct statfs statfs_buf)
{
    switch ( statfs_buf.f_type ) {
        case 0xadf5: return "adfs";
        case 0xadff: return "affs";
        case 0x5346414f: return "afs";
        case 0x09041934: return "anon-inode-fs";
        --snip--
        default: return "unknown type";
    return
}
```

To save space here, the complete function is only displayed in the book's
source code distribution.

The final step before compiling and building the program is to make sure
that our program will print the filesystem ID correctly. The man page for
statfs raised a red flag about this when, in the NOTES section, it mentioned
that in Linux and some other Unix systems, the type fsid_t of the f_fsid
member of the statfs structure is defined as struct { int val[2]; }—in other
words, as a pair of integers rather than a long integer. To check this, we write a
small program that does nothing except printing the filesystem ID contained

in the f_fsid member of the statvfs structure and comparing its output to that of the stat -f command. The program, named *fsidtest.c*, follows:

```
#define _GNU_SOURCE
#include <sys/types.h>
#include <sys/stat.h>
#include <unistd.h>
#include <stdio.h>
#include <sys/statvfs.h>

int main(int argc, char **argv)
{
    struct statvfs statvfs_buffer;
    if ( statvfs(argv[1], &statvfs_buffer) == 0 )
        printf("%lx\n", statvfs_buffer.f_fsid);
    return 0;
}
```

Sure enough, when we build and run the executable, the filesystem ID that it outputs is different from the one output by the stat -f command:

```
$ ./fsidtest /var/log
7798a2a57e58ac74
$ stat -c"%i" -f /var/log
7e58ac747798a2a5
```

The order of the upper 4 bytes and lower 4 bytes is the reverse of what stat -f displays. The f_fsid member is in fact a sequence of two 32-bit numbers, but the high-order 4 bytes should be printed after the low-order 4 bytes. This is easily handled in the print_statvfs() function by masking out the upper bytes first to get the low-order 4 bytes, storing them into a variable, right-shifting the upper 4 bytes into a second variable, and then printing them in reverse order, as follows:

```
unsigned int low = statvfs_buf.f_fsid & 0xFFFFFFFF;
unsigned int high = (statvfs_buf.f_fsid >> 32) & 0xFFFFFFFF;
printf("    ID: %08x%08x", low, high);
```

The complete program, with the preceding changes made in print_statvfs(), and the body of the fstype2name() function omitted, appears in Listing 6-2.

```
#define _GNU_SOURCE
#include <sys/stat.h>
#include <errno.h>
#include <sys/vfs.h>
#include <sys/statvfs.h>
#include "common_hdrs.h"

/* Given a statfs structure, this returns the human-readable filename stored
   in its f_ftype member. */
```

```c
char *fstype2name(struct statfs statfs_buf)
{
    switch ( statfs_buf.f_ftype ) {
    --snip--
    }
}

void print_stat(struct statvfs statvfs_buf, char *fstype)
{
    unsigned int low = statvfs_buf.f_fsid & 0xFFFFFFFF;
    unsigned int high = (statvfs_buf.f_fsid >> 32) & 0xFFFFFFFF;
    printf("    ID: %08x%08x", low, high);
    printf(" Namelen: %-8lu", statvfs_buf.f_namemax);
    printf("Type: %s\n", fstype);
    printf("Block size: %-11lu", (unsigned long) statvfs_buf.f_bsize);
    printf("Fundamental block size: %lu\n", statvfs_buf.f_frsize);
    printf("Blocks: Total: %-10lu", statvfs_buf.f_blocks);
    printf("Free: %-11lu", statvfs_buf.f_bfree);
    printf(" Available: %lu\n", statvfs_buf.f_bavail);
    printf("Inodes: Total: %-10lu", statvfs_buf.f_files);
    printf("Free: %lu\n", statvfs_buf.f_ffree);
}

int main(int argc, char **argv)
{
    struct statvfs statvfs_buffer; /* statvfs structure filled by statvfs()*/
    struct statfs  statfs_buffer;  /* statfs structure filled by statfs()  */
    char           mssge[128];     /* String to store error messages       */

    /* If no file arguments, print a usage message. */
    if ( argc < 2 ) {
        sprintf(mssge, "usage: %s file \n", basename(argv[0]));
        usage_error(mssge);
    }
    printf("  File: \"%s\"\n", argv[1]);
    errno = 0;
    if ( statvfs(argv[1], &statvfs_buffer) < 0 ) {
        sprintf(mssge, "Could not statvfs file %s\n", argv[1]);
        fatal_error(errno, mssge);
    }
    if ( statfs(argv[1],  &statfs_buffer) < 0 ) {
        sprintf(mssge, "Could not statfs file %s\n", argv[1]);
        fatal_error(errno, mssge);
    }
    print_stat(statvfs_buffer, fstype2name(statfs_buffer));
    return 0;
}
```

Listing 6-2: A program to output a filesystem's metadata, given any file contained in it

The `main()` function checks that there is a file argument and prints its name if it finds one. It then calls statvfs() to get the statvfs structure and calls statfs() to get the statfs structure. Its last step is to call print_stat(), passing the statvfs structure and the filesystem type string returned by the call to fstype2name(statfs_buffer).

Testing spl_statfs

We're ready to test the program and compare its output to that of the stat -f command. First, we'll run them both on the *dev* directory:

```
$ stat -f  /dev
  File: "/dev"
    ID: 986fcbcacd116e7e Namelen: 255     Type: tmpfs
Block size: 4096      Fundamental block size: 4096
Blocks: Total: 2016429   Free: 2016429    Available: 2016429
Inodes: Total: 2016429   Free: 2015803
$ ./spl_statfs /dev
  File: "/dev"
    ID: 986fcbcacd116e7e Namelen: 255     Type: tmpfs
Block size: 4096      Fundamental block size: 4096
Blocks: Total: 2016429  Free: 2016429    Available: 2016429
Inodes: Total: 2016429  Free: 2015803
```

The outputs are identical. They both identify the filesystem as a tempfs type, and all numeric values match. Next, we'll try them on the filesystem of a USB drive inserted into a USB port:

```
$ stat -f /media/guest/USB_stick/
  File: "/media/guest/USB_stick/"
    ID: 84000000000 Namelen: 1530     Type: msdos
Block size: 4096      Fundamental block size: 4096
Blocks: Total: 471778   Free: 347737    Available: 347737
Inodes: Total: 0        Free: 0
$ ./spl_statfs /media/guest/USB_stick/
  File: "/media/guest/USB_stick/"
    ID: 840      0        Namelen: 1530   Type: msdos
Block size: 4096      Fundamental block size: 4096
Blocks: Total: 471778   Free: 347737    Available: 347737
Inodes: Total: 0        Free: 0
```

Again the output is identical and our program correctly identified the filesystem type and the filesystem ID. Last, we show the output that both programs produce when the filesystem is on a CD-ROM disk:

```
$ stat -f /media/guest/music-files/
  File: "/media/stewart/music-files/"
    ID: b0000000000 Namelen: 255     Type: isofs
Block size: 2048      Fundamental block size: 2048
```

```
Blocks: Total: 2048681     Free: 0          Available: 0
Inodes: Total: 0           Free: 0
$ ./spl_statfs /media/stewart/music-files/
  File: "/media/guest/music-files/"
    ID: b0000000000 Namelen: 255     Type: isofs
Block size: 2048         Fundamental block size: 2048
Blocks: Total: 2048681     Free: 0          Available: 0
Inodes: Total: 0           Free: 0
```

These few sample runs do not constitute thorough testing of the program. Before we can make this code available for use, we should test it on a larger set of filesystems.

Completing this exercise has enabled us to solve a few other relatively easy problems. For example, we can design functions to display how many free blocks are available to users, or approximately what fraction of the blocks are in use. The df command does this, so we're now able to write our own version of df as well.

Summary

In a very real sense, files are the core of a Unix operating system. Ordinary files can contain data and programs, directory files organize sets of files, and device special files enable programs to interact with devices in the same way as they do with regular files. Files have metadata as well, which are the statistics and properties associated with them, such as their size, permissions, type, and so on. Filesystems are an integrated collection of data structures written onto a storage device, together with the software that maintains those data structures, designed to organize files and provide a programming interface for accessing them. A typical disk-based filesystem is decomposed into block groups, each of which contains a superblock, an inode table, and bitmaps for locating the inodes and data blocks.

Because Unix systems enable multiple distinct filesystems to be integrated into a single, tree-like directory hierarchy through a procedure called mounting, at any given time, more than one type of filesystem can be a part of this hierarchy. These different filesystems are implemented in different ways and have different interfaces for their services. Many Unix kernels, and in particular, Linux kernels, contain an abstraction layer named the virtual file system (VFS). The VFS creates a common interface for system calls needing access to files and the filesystem, regardless of their underlying types.

The Linux kernel provides a few system calls for obtaining the metadata associated to files, including stat(), lstat(), and statx(). It also provides a separate set of calls for accessing filesystem metadata, including statfs(), and the C library provides the POSIX-conforming statvfs(). This chapter shows how these calls can be employed to implement a few commands for users to enter to obtain information about files and mounted filesystems on their host machine.

Exercises

1. If the blocks in the filesystem are each 4096 bytes, and disk addresses are four bytes each, how many indirect blocks are needed to access the blocks of:

    (a) A file of size 5120KB?

    (b) A file of size 2048GB?

    Do not count the data blocks to which the indirect blocks point.

2. If a file is of size 1TB, how many disk addresses would be accessed to get the starting address of the very last block of the file once the inode has been read into memory, assuming the block size is 4KB?

3. If the blocks in a block group are each 2^B bytes, and the data block bitmap must fit into a single block, what is the maximum number of bytes of storage possible in this block group?

4. Write a function named newer() with the prototype

    ```
    int newer(const char *pathname1, const char *pathname2);
    ```

    that returns 1 if the file pathname1 was last modified no earlier than the file pathname2 and otherwise returns 0. If their last modifications happened at the exact same nanosecond of time, it returns 1. If it encounters errors that prevent it from returning, such as pathnames that do not exist, it returns -1. If either argument is a symbolic link, report on the link itself, not its target.

    (a) Write a main program with two expected command line arguments that calls this function and outputs the name of the newer file, or exits with an error message.

    (b) Modify this program to accept command line options -a, -b, -c, and -m that constrain the program to use access time, birth time, status change time, and modification time, respectively, instead of the default modification time.

5. Write a function named samefile() with the prototype

    ```
    int samefile(const char *pathname1, const char *pathname2);
    ```

    that returns 1 if pathname1 and pathname2 are links to the same file, and 0 if they are not. If it encounters errors that prevent it from returning, such as pathnames that do not exist, it returns -1. Write a main program with two expected command line arguments that calls this function and outputs a 1 or a 0 or exits with an error message. If either argument is a symbolic link, report on the link itself, not its target.

6. Write a function named sameowner() with the prototype

    ```
    int sameowner(const char *pathname1, const char *pathname2);
    ```

    that returns 1 if pathname1 and pathname2 are owned by the same user, and 0 if they are not. If it encounters errors that prevent it from returning, such as pathnames that do not exist, it returns -1. Write a main program with two expected command line arguments that calls this function and outputs a 1 or a 0 or exits with an error message. If either argument is a symbolic link, report on the link itself, not its target.

7. Write the complete program for version 2 of the `spl_stat` program, outlined in "Designing an Enhanced `spl_stat` Command" on page 297.

8. Read the man page for `df` and run it to see what it displays without any options. Design a version of this command that displays the same data for a filesystem when given its device file pathname as an argument, for example, `df /dev/sda1`.

7

THE DIRECTORY HIERARCHY

So far, we've concentrated on the programming interface related to regular files. We learned how to perform basic and more advanced I/O in Chapters 4 and 5 and how to retrieve file and filesystem attributes in Chapter 6. We've yet to explore the programming interface for working with directories and the directory hierarchy. For example, how can a program list all of the entries in a given directory, retrieve a single directory entry, change its current working directory, or get the absolute pathname of the current working directory? Still further, how can a program traverse selected parts of the directory hierarchy, such as by a depth-first or breadth-first search?

In this chapter, we explore the API related to directories and the directory hierarchy with the goal of being able to write programs to perform these types of tasks. I'll also provide an overview of filesystem mounting because, as you'll see, how filesystems are mounted plays a part in how programs can perform various tasks related to directories.

Directory Structure

Before we explore the API for interacting with directories, let's review what we know about them so far. First, as far as the kernel is concerned, directories are like regular files except that they have a more restrictive form:

- They have a precisely defined structure. A directory consists of a set of (*inode number, filename*) pairs called *links*. The inode number is an index into the inode table in the filesystem in which the directory resides, and the filename is the name in that directory for the referenced file. We often use the term *link* interchangeably with *filename*.

- They are never empty, because every directory has two unique entries: . (called *dot*) and .. (called *dot-dot*), which refer, respectively, to the directory itself and to the parent directory. The exception to this rule is that in the root directory, whose name is /, the directories . and .. refer to the same inode; or, put another way, / and /.. are the same directory.

- Directories can be created and modified only by specific system calls, unlike regular files, which can be created by open() and creat().

Some commands that read from files can also read from directories, but the results are usually unpredictable. Some commands that do this on one system may not do this on another. For example, on some systems, the cat and od commands may display the contents of a directory as a stream of bytes, but because a directory is not a text file, the output of cat will look garbled. The output of od may look normal. However, other implementations of these commands will output an error message if their argument is a directory, such as:

```
$ cat mydir
cat: mydir: Is a directory
```

The open() system call will open a directory, provided that it is opened in read-only mode, and the close() call will close it. Although we can open a directory with open(), on most systems, the read() system call will fail to read it. The reason that open() is allowed to open a directory is to access the metadata in its inode, not to read its contents. We'll see later that being able to open a directory and create an open file description for it is useful in a few situations, such as when we want to save our current working directory and return to it later.

On some Unix implementations, the read() system call may succeed when given a directory argument. You can run the following program to check whether read() succeeds in reading a directory on your system:

testdircalls.c
```c
#include "common_hdrs.h"

int main(int argc, char *argv[])
{
    int  fd;
    char buf[2];
```

```
    if ( argc < 2 )
        printf("usage: %s <directory-path>\n", argv[0]);
    else {
        errno = 0;
        fd = open(argv[1], O_RDONLY);
        if ( -1 == fd )
            fatal_error(errno, "open");
        if ( -1 == read(fd, buf, 1) )
            perror("read() was not successful");
        else
            printf("read() was successful.\n");
        errno = 0;
        if ( -1 == close(fd) )
            fatal_error(errno, "close");
    }
    return 0;
}
```

If we compile and build it with the command

```
$ gcc -I../include -L../lib -o testdircalls testdircalls.c -lspl
```

and run it with a directory argument, we'll see whether reading failed:

```
$ ./testdircalls .
read() was not successful: Is a directory
```

The calls to open() and close() succeeded, but not the call to read(). Our next goal is to find those system calls and library functions that are intended to work with directories.

Processing Directories

Some of the simplest commands that we routinely use involve directories. The most obvious example is the ls command, which lists the files in each directory entered on its command line. In fact, the arguments to ls can also be nondirectory files, such as regular files and special files, but without any options, all ls does is print out their names:

```
$ ls myfile yourfile
myfile  yourfile
```

Its more interesting usage is when the argument is a directory. In that case, it displays the links contained in that directory, and with various command options, it will display selected metadata as well.

Because ls outputs different information depending on whether it's given a directory or a nondirectory file, its main program must check the file type before it does much work. We already know how to do this, namely by calling stat() or statx() and checking the file type in the file type bits of the st_mode member of the returned structure, as in

```
if ( -1 != stat(argv[1], &statbuffer) ) {
    if ( S_ISDIR(statbuffer.st_mode) ) /* Display links in argv[1]. */
        list_dir_contents(argv[1]);
    else
        printf("%s", argv[1]);
}
```

where list_dir_contents() is some function that would list the directory's contents. We'd like to discover how, at the programming level, we can retrieve the contents of a directory. Following our usual procedure, we'll start with a man page search to find system calls or library functions that might help us. It's reasonable to search for the two terms *read* and *directory* exactly and occurring simultaneously:

```
$ apropos -s2,3 -e -a read directory
readdir (2)          - read directory entry
readdir (3)          - read a directory
readdir (3posix)     - read a directory
readdir_r (3)        - read a directory
```

The first match, readdir() in Section 2, must be a system call. We'll take a look at that man page first, after which we'll read the man page for what is likely to be a library function, readdir(), in Section 3:

```
$ man 2 readdir
READDIR(2)                 Linux Programmer's Manual                 READDIR(2)

NAME
       readdir - read directory entry
SYNOPSIS
       int readdir(unsigned int fd, struct old_linux_dirent *dirp,
                   unsigned int count);

       Note: There is no glibc wrapper for this system call; see NOTES.
DESCRIPTION
       This is not the function you are interested in. Look at readdir(3) for
       the POSIX conforming C library interface. This page documents the bare
       kernel system call interface, which is superseded by getdents(2).
--snip--
```

The DESCRIPTION tells us that we shouldn't be using this function but should instead look at the library function in Section 3. It does, however, mention a system call that has replaced this one, the getdents() call. If we read its man page

```
$ man getdents
GETDENTS(2)                Linux Programmer's Manual                GETDENTS(2)
```

we see the same warning. At this point, it's pretty clear that this is like posted
property and we should stay off it. For this project, we're going to work with
the POSIX-conforming library functions instead of system calls. One clear
advantage will be that our code will be portable.

The readdir() Library Function

We'll begin by reading the Section 3 man page for readdir(), which is the
Linux page for it, after which we'll take a look at the POSIX man page for
it in Section 3posix, since it might contain information not present in the
Linux page:

READDIR(3)   Linux Programmer's Manual   READDIR(3)

NAME
        readdir - read a directory
SYNOPSIS
        #include <dirent.h>

        struct dirent *readdir(DIR *dirp);
DESCRIPTION
        The readdir() function returns a pointer to a dirent structure
        representing the next directory entry in the directory stream
        pointed to by dirp. It returns NULL on reaching the end of the
        directory stream or if an error occurred.

        In the glibc implementation, the dirent structure is defined as
        follows:

            struct dirent {
                ino_t   d_ino;   /* Inode number   */
                off_t   d_off;   /* Not an offset; see below */
                unsigned short d_reclen;   /* Length of this record   */
                unsigned char d_type;   /* Type of file; not supported
                                               by all filesystem types */
                char   d_name[256]; /* Null-terminated filename */
            };

The only fields in the dirent structure that are mandated by POSIX.1 are d_name and d_ino. The other fields are unstandardized, and not present on all systems; see NOTES below for some further details.

--snip--

Given a pointer, `dirp`, to a *directory stream* this function returns a structure representing a directory entry. We don't know exactly what a directory stream is yet, nor how we get one, but based on the man page, we know that the DIR* type is a pointer to one. We'll address these issues later. The man page states a few important facts about calling the function:

- Successive calls to readdir() with the same directory stream pointer return successive entries in that directory stream, and when all entries have been accessed, it returns a NULL pointer.

- If an error occurs in a call, it returns a NULL pointer. To distinguish between an error and the end of the directory, we need to set errno to 0 before the call and check it after.

- The entry returned by readdir() may be overwritten by subsequent calls to readdir() for the same directory stream because it might be a statically allocated variable in the library. Therefore, before calling it again, if we want to save the returned data, we have to copy it into a local variable.

Now let's read about the dirent structure returned by the call to make sure we understand how to use it.

The dirent Structure

Despite this data structure having several fields, only the d_ino and d_name fields are guaranteed by POSIX to be part of it. The first field contains the inode number, and the second stores the NULL-terminated filename.

Filenames and the dirent Structure

The NOTES mention that POSIX.1 doesn't specify a length for this filename even though the Linux man page declares it as having 256 characters including the NULL byte. Programs should not depend on its having any particular length. POSIX only ensures that its length is at most NAME_MAX characters. Therefore, for the program to be portable, any variables that store the filename should be declared to be at least NAME_MAX+1 bytes. For example, if a local variable named filename has to store a name from the d_name member, it should be declared as

```
char filename[NAME_MAX+1];
```

to allow for the terminating NULL byte. The d_name member of the structure is the one member we're most interested in, but we'll also examine the d_type member.

It's natural to wonder whether a program calling readdir() will need to include some other header file to use this NAME_MAX value or whether including *dirent.h* is sufficient. In general, man pages usually list every header file needed to use the functions they describe. In this case, the *dirent.h* header file does expose the definition of NAME_MAX, albeit through several levels of nested #include directives. We can verify this by compiling the following one-line program:

```
#include <dirent.h>
void main()
{ int n = NAME_MAX; }
```

If the symbol weren't made available by including *dirent.h*, we'd get an error message from the compiler, but it compiles without errors. If we put a printf() instruction in this program, we'd most likely see that its value is 255, but this is implementation dependent. POSIX.1-2024 only requires it to be at least 14 bytes.

File Types and the dirent Structure

The dirent structure also has a d_type field, which contains the type of the entry, such as whether it's a regular file, a directory, a symbolic link, and so on. Because this field isn't required by POSIX.1-2024, it may not be a member of the structure on some systems. This implies that a program that uses this field will not be completely portable. On systems with *glibc*, such as Linux, a program can determine whether or not the field is actually in the structure with the macro _DIRENT_HAVE_D_TYPE; it's defined only if the structure has the d_type member. The code referring to d_type should then be protected by a conditional macro test:

```
#ifdef _DIRENT_HAVE_D_TYPE
    // OMITTED: We have d_type member so we can get type information with it.
```

```
#else
    // OMITTED: We don't have d_type; we need to call stat() to get type.
#endif
```

Even if d_type is a member of the structure, it may not have type information because not all filesystems provide it; the Ext2/3/4 and BSD filesystems do provide it. The reason it's present on some systems is that, if a program needs to know the type of the directory entry, it's faster to get it by using this field than by making a call to stat() or lstat(), which are more time consuming.

The *glibc* library exposes a set of macro constants with names such as DT_LNK, DT_DIR, DT_REG, and so on, for the value in d_type. To make them available on *glibc* 2.20 or later, the feature test macro _DEFAULT_SOURCE should be defined before any #include directives; on earlier versions of *glibc*, the macro _BSD_SOURCE must be defined. A program can define both macros safely. The readdir(3) man page has the complete list of these macro constants. If our programs don't need the type of the directory entry, we don't need to bother with the added complexity of using the d_type member in a portable way.

Directory Streams

Nowhere in the readdir(3) man page is there any information about what a DIR is, but the NOTES section tells us how to get one and provides a clue: "A directory stream is opened using opendir(3)." From this, we understand that a DIR object is a directory stream, and we learned how to obtain one. This opendir() function is also listed in the SEE ALSO section, along with several other functions that are likely to be part of the directory API.

Based on our experience in Chapter 5 with the passwd database API, it's likely that opendir() may serve a purpose similar to that of setpwent(), but with respect to directories, by initializing an iterator that retrieves successive directory entries until all have been accessed. This is a good time to look at the readdir(3posix) POSIX man page because it might explain more about directory streams. In fact, it has the following description:

> The type DIR, which is defined in the <dirent.h> header, represents a directory stream, which is an ordered sequence of all the directory entries in a particular directory. Directory entries represent files; files may be removed from a directory or added to a directory asynchronously to the operation of readdir().
>
> The readdir() function shall return a pointer to a structure representing the directory entry at the current position in the directory stream specified by the argument dirp, and position the directory stream at the next entry. It shall return a NULL pointer upon reaching the end of the directory stream.

Although we don't need to know the structure of a DIR to use readdir(), out of curiosity, we might like to see it. In fact, DIR is defined by a typedef in *dirent.h*

```
typedef struct __dirstream DIR;
```

but there is no definition of struct __dirstream in any user space header files in the system. This is because POSIX allows __dirstream to be an incomplete type. An *incomplete type* is a type that describes an object but lacks the information needed to determine its size. Each implementation of Unix must define it and is free to define it as it chooses, but it need not expose that implementation in any user space header files. The *dirent.h* header file declares struct __dirstream and makes DIR equivalent to it, but does not define its members. This gives programmers the ability to declare objects of type DIR*, but not the ability to access the members of a DIR object.

If you write a program that references a __dirstream object, the compiler will report an error that its size is unknown. If you instead declare a struct __dirstream variable, the program will compile, because the pointer's size is known. You will not be able to dereference this pointer and use what it points to because your program does not have access to its implementation, but it's implemented in the libraries that use it. This is a form of information hiding in C.*

If you download the source code for a recent version of *glibc*, such as 2.37 or later, you'll find the definition of this structure in the file *sysdeps/unix/sysv/linux/dirstream.h*.

It's time to look at the opendir() function, whose purpose is to return a directory stream.

The opendir() Library Function

The man page for opendir() begins as follows:

```
OPENDIR(3)                 Linux Programmer's Manual            OPENDIR(3)

NAME
       opendir, fdopendir - open a directory
SYNOPSIS
       #include <sys/types.h>
       #include <dirent.h>
       DIR *opendir(const char *name);
       DIR *fdopendir(int fd);

   Feature Test Macro Requirements for glibc (see feature_test_macros(7)):
       fdopendir():
           Since glibc 2.10:
               _POSIX_C_SOURCE >= 200809L
           Before glibc 2.10:
               _GNU_SOURCE
DESCRIPTION
       The opendir() function opens a directory stream corresponding to the
       directory name, and returns a pointer to the directory stream. The
       stream is positioned at the first entry in the directory.

--snip--
```

This function is much simpler than readdir(). We give it the pathname of a directory, and it returns a pointer to the beginning of a directory stream so that the first call to readdir() on that stream returns the first entry in the directory. Our program will need to declare a variable of type DIR* to receive the returned address. If the function fails, it returns a NULL pointer. Note that this function requires the *sys/types.h* header file. There's nothing significant in the NOTES section for us to be concerned about at this point. A code snippet illustrating how to call the function follows:

```
DIR          *dirp;
struct dirent *dir_entry;

dirp = opendir("/home/stewart");
if ( NULL != dirp )
    /* Call readdir(). */
    dir_entry = readdir(dirp);
--snip--
```

Whenever we open something, we ought to close it. That's the general rule in programming. If there's an opendir() function, there's likely to be a closedir() function that our programs should call to close a directory stream and free up its resources.

The closedir() Library Function

A man page search shows that there is a closedir() function. The closedir() function closes the given open directory stream. The relevant part of its man page is:

```
SYNOPSIS
        #include <sys/types.h>
        #include <dirent.h>
        int closedir(DIR *dirp);
DESCRIPTION
        The closedir() function closes the directory stream associated with
        dirp. A successful call to closedir() also closes the underlying
        file descriptor associated with dirp. The directory stream descriptor
        dirp is not available after this call.
RETURN VALUE
        The closedir() function returns 0 on success. On error, -1 is returned,
        and errno is set appropriately.
```

Notice that this function also needs the *sys/types.h* header file and that it returns -1 and sets errno on failure, like a system call. The only possible error is passing it an invalid directory stream pointer, such as one that's already been closed.

A Simple ls Program

To demonstrate the use of the few functions we've just discovered, we'll implement a simplified version of the ls command, which, for arguments that are directories, lists the filenames in them, and for arguments that are nondirectory files, just lists their names. We'll make it act like the real ls in that, when it isn't given any arguments, it lists the files in the working directory. This program won't accept any command line options.

We'll put the logic of listing all files in a single directory into a function named listdir(), which is given a directory stream pointer, dirp, and an integer, flags, that encodes a set of flags. The listdir() function repeatedly calls readdir(dirp) to get the next entry from the dirp stream and print its filename member until readdir(dirp) returns NULL. If readdir() reports an error when trying to read an entry, listdir() prints a message and skips the file. The flags parameter isn't used in this version of listdir(); it's there to make the function extensible.

EXTENSIBLE DESIGN

Extensibility is a measure of the ease with which the functionality of a software design or artifact can be extended. Designing with extensibility in mind allows for unanticipated future improvements and enhancements.

The main() function's job is to process the command line. For every pathname argument on the command line, main() will attempt to get a directory stream for it by calling opendir(). If the call fails and sets errno to ENOTDIR, it means that the argument is not a directory and therefore, instead of calling listdir(), it will print the argument. If opendir() fails for any other reason, it skips the argument without exiting. The complete program is shown in Listing 7-1. I've named the source file *spl_ls1.c* anticipating enhanced versions to follow.

spl_ls1.c
```
#include "common_hdrs.h"
#include <dirent.h>

/* listdir(dirp, flag) prints the filenames in the directory stream dirp,
   one per line, including . and .., in the order the stream delivers them. */
void listdir(DIR *dirp, int flags)
{
    struct dirent *direntp;       /* Pointer to directory entry structure  */
    BOOL           done = FALSE;  /* Flag to control loop execution        */

    while ( !done ) {
        errno = 0;
        direntp = readdir(dirp);                        /* Get next entry. */
        if ( direntp == NULL && errno != 0 ) /* Not the end of the stream   */
            perror("readdir");               /* but an error from readdir() */
```

```
        else if ( direntp == NULL ) /* errno == 0, nothing left in stream  */
            done = TRUE;
        else
            printf("    %s\n", direntp->d_name);        /* Print it.      */
    }
    printf("\n");
}

int main(int argc, char *argv[])
{
    DIR *dirp;
    int  ls_flags = 0;

    if ( 1 == argc ) {      /* No arguments; use current working directory. */
        errno = 0;
        if ( (dirp = opendir(".")) == NULL )
            fatal_error(errno, "opendir");            /* Could not open cwd */
        listdir(dirp, ls_flags);
    }
    else {          /* For each command-line argument, call opendir() on it. */
        for ( int i = 1; i < argc; i++ ) {
            errno = 0;
            if ( (dirp = opendir(argv[i])) == NULL ) {
                if ( errno == ENOTDIR )            /* It's not a directory. */
                    printf("%s\n", argv[i]);
                else                               /* It's an error.       */
                    error_mssge(errno, argv[i]);
            }
            else {                          /* A successful open of a directory */
                printf("%s:\n", argv[i]);
                listdir(dirp, ls_flags);
                closedir(dirp);
            }
        }
    }
    return 0;
}
```

Listing 7-1: A program that prints the contents of all directories in its argument list

To demonstrate the program's behavior, I created a directory named *testing* containing a few files and directories and removed read permission from one of the directories to see whether the program would handle this error well. The directory is depicted in Figure 7-1.

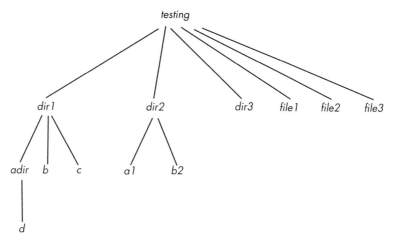

Figure 7-1: The testing directory

The following listing shows that *dir3* has no read permission:

```
$ ls -gG testing/dir3   # The -gG supresses owner and group information.
total 12
drwxr-xr-x 3 4096 Sep 27 10:26 dir1/
drwxr-xr-x 2 4096 Sep 27 10:27 dir2/
d-wx--x--x 2 4096 Sep 27 10:36 dir3/
--snip--
```

I compiled and built this program using:

```
$ gcc -Wall -g spl_ls1.c -L../lib -lspl -o spl_ls1
```

Two runs of it follow: one on *testing* and the other on some directories and files within it:

```
$ ./spl_ls1 testing
testing:
    dir1
    file3
    file1
    dir3
    file2
    dir2
    .
    ..
$ cd testing; spl_ls1 dir1 file1 dir3 file2
dir1:
    b
    c
    .
```

```
adir
..

file1
dir3: Permission denied
file2
```

Notice that it correctly listed the contents for the directories for which it had permission, but not for *dir3*, for which it correctly reported the permission error. The order in which it prints a directory's contents appears to be random. It isn't sorted in any obvious way. Also, unlike the real ls command, our program lists the dot (.) and dot-dot (..) entries.

This program is a good start. It was relatively easy to design and write, owing to the fact that the directory API provides functions that allow us to iterate over all directory entries. In addition, we didn't need to use any of the non-POSIX members of the dirent structure for this version of ls, which made the program simpler.

We could improve the program in a few different ways. First, we can easily suppress printing of the dot and dot-dot entries, as well as all entries that are supposed to be hidden because their names start with dot. Another relatively easy improvement would be to list more than one filename per line, which would require mostly just a bit of arithmetic and some output format planning. Other enhancements are more challenging. One would be to print the filenames according to some specified ordering, such as by their names or times of last modification, and so on. Another would be to filter the output so that we list only files that meet a supplied condition, such as those that are directories or those whose names match a pattern. These last two enhancements can't be implemented easily with just the set of functions we've seen so far. We need to do a bit of research to see what other tools are available in the directory API. Trying to implement some of these enhancements is a good exercise for learning more about this API.

Other Functions in the Directory API

The SEE ALSO section of the readdir(3) man page lists several library functions that work with directories in one way or another. The ones whose names end in dir include rewinddir(), seekdir(), telldir(), and scandir(). The others whose names don't match that pattern are ftw(), dirfd(), and offsetof().

The last two functions, dirfd() and offsetof(), are not as relevant to our immediate objectives as the others. The dirfd() function returns a file descriptor for the directory opened by a call to opendir(), and the offsetof() function is not specific to directories; it allows a program to obtain the offset within a C struct of one of its members, measured in bytes. It is needed occasionally because the sizes of some members of a structure can vary at runtime, such as the d_name member of the dirent structure. We'll examine the other functions listed there, starting with the ones whose names end in dir.

The first, rewinddir(), simply resets the directory stream so that reading begins at its first entry again. Its name is suggestive of this. Its prototype is:

```
#include <sys/types.h>
#include <dirent.h>
void rewinddir(DIR *dirp);
```

We need the `rewinddir()` function for those occasions when a program has to make another pass across all of the entries in a directory stream. One reason for a second pass is that, in the first pass, it didn't find the information it needed without calling `stat()` on the entries. In a second pass, it could call `stat()` on all of the files. Another use case is when a first pass is needed to count the number of files satisfying some condition, and if the count is above a threshold value, a second pass is made to process those files satisfying the condition.

The telldir() and seekdir() Library Functions

The two functions `seekdir()` and `telldir()` are interrelated, in that neither is useful in a program without the other. Their prototypes are:

```
#include <dirent.h>
long telldir(DIR *dirp);
void seekdir(DIR *dirp, long loc);
```

The first, `telldir()`, returns a `long` integer that can be used to return to the entry that would be read by the next call to `readdir()` in its directory stream argument, `dirp`. In essence, it's saving the current position of the stream iterator. The second, `seekdir()`, given the directory stream `dirp` and a `long` integer returned by `telldir()`, positions the stream's internal iterator so that the next call to `readdir()` reads the entry at that position in the stream. Combined, these two functions provide a way to save a position in the stream and return to it later.

NOTE   *The `telldir()` man page warns us not to assume that the long integer returned by `telldir()` is simply an offset relative to the start of the directory. Modern filesystems can represent directories using hash tables or search trees to improve performance. For these filesystems, the value returned by `telldir()` and used internally by `readdir()` is what the page calls a* cookie, *meaning an integer value from which the actual address of the entry can be derived.*

One application of these functions is to process the entries in a given directory that satisfy a given condition before those that don't. For example, we could use them to print all entries that are directories preceding all nondirectory entries. Because this is a good exercise in using the directory API, we'll write a second version of an `ls` command, named `spl_ls2`, that does exactly this.

Let's sketch out its algorithm. Each time the program reads an entry in the given directory stream, it checks whether or not it's a directory. If it's not a directory, it saves it in a list to print later, and if it is a directory, it prints it immediately. Since this requires knowing an entry's type, this exercise will also demonstrate how we can use the _DIRENT_HAVE_D_TYPE feature test macro to conditionally compile a program on systems that may or may not have the d_type member in the dirent structure. Therefore, our first task is to write a Boolean-valued function that determines whether or not an entry is a directory, which we'll name isdir().

Listing 7-2 contains the isdir() implementation. The function checks whether or not its struct dirent* argument is a directory entry. If our host system's dirent structure contains a d_type member, it uses it; otherwise, it calls stat() to get the type. Since this is a compile-time decision, the function uses the feature test macro to choose which code to include. Because we'll probably use this function in several other programs, we'll add it to our libspl library and create a header file named *dir_utils.h* that includes its prototype so that we don't need to include its code in every program that uses it.

isdir()
```
/* Returns TRUE if *direntp represents a directory, and FALSE otherwise */
BOOL isdir(const struct dirent *direntp)
{
#ifdef _DIRENT_HAVE_D_TYPE        /* We have the d_type member.     */
    return (direntp->d_type  == DT_DIR);
#else                             /* We don't have it - call stat(). */
    struct stat statbuf;
    stat(direntp->d_name, &statbuf);
    return (S_ISDIR(statbuf.st_mode));
#endif
}
```

Listing 7-2: A function that checks whether a dirent structure is a directory entry

This isdir() function makes the revised listdir() function simpler. Following is a rough outline of how this revised listdir() can process a single directory.

1. Given a directory stream argument dirp, which was opened successfully by the main program, it repeatedly performs the following steps:
    (a) Calls telldir() to save the current position, say, in a variable named pos
    (b) Reads the next entry: direntp = readdir(dirp)
    (c) Calls isdir(direntp) to check whether this entry is a directory
    (d) If it's a directory, processes it, meaning it prints its name; if it isn't, saves the position pos in a list of locations to process later
2. When all entries have been read, it exits the loop and, for each saved position pos in the list, seeks to that position using seekdir() and processes it (meaning, in this case, prints it).

Notice that the program must call telldir() before it calls reaaddir() because telldir() returns the position it is about to read, not the one just read.

We need to decide whether to use a linked list or an array to store the saved positions. A linked list has more overhead because of the possibly frequent calls to `malloc()` for each nondirectory entry and the extra code for linked list management. An array is faster but will need to be resized if it reaches capacity. Despite the linked list's greater overhead, it leads to a simpler design.

We'll modify the previously written `listdir()` function so that if its `flags` argument contains a flag to turn on directories-first processing, it will print directories before nondirectories, and if not, it will print the entries in the order presented to it by the calls to `readdir()`.

The revised function will need the support of a few linked list functions, namely, one to append a node to the end, one to print the list, and one to erase it. To save space, only their prototypes are included here; their implementations are included in the book's source code distribution. The list definition and the function prototypes are shown in Listing 7-3.

```
/* Linked list node that stores an offset returned by telldir() */
typedef struct listnode {
    long            pos;         /* The offset                     */
    struct listnode *next;       /* Pointer to nextnode in list    */
} poslist;                       /* Pointer to a list              */


/* save(p, &pos_listptr) saves position p onto the end of the list
   pointed to by pos_listptr. Because the list head might be
   changed, its address is passed, not its value. */
void save(long pos, poslist **list);


/* printlist(dirp, pos_list) prints the filenames whose offsets were
   saved into pos_list. */
void printlist(DIR* dirp, poslist *list)


/* eraselist(&list) erases the list pointed to by list. */
void eraselist(poslist **list)
```

Listing 7-3: Linked list utility functions for the revised `listdir()` function

The preceding functions are called by the revised `listdir()`, which is displayed in Listing 7-4. The parts of the function that have been modified are in bold.

```
listdir()   void listdir(DIR *dirp, int flags)
            {
                struct dirent *entry;
                long int      pos;
                poslist       *saved_positions = NULL;

                while ( 1 ) {
                    pos = telldir(dirp);          /* Save current position.  */
                    errno = 0;                    /* Try to read entry.      */
```

```
        if ( NULL == (entry = readdir(dirp)) && errno != 0 )
            perror("readdir");        /* Error reading entry      */
        else if ( entry == NULL )
            break;
        else {
            if ( (flags & LIST_DIRS_FIRST) && !isdir(entry) ) {
                save(pos, &saved_positions);
                continue;
            }
            printf("%s/\n", entry->d_name);
        }
    }
    if ( flags & LIST_DIRS_FIRST )
        printlist(dirp, saved_positions);
    eraselist(&saved_positions);
}
```

Listing 7-4: A revised listdir() *function that can list a directory's entries with all directory names preceding all nondirectory names*

The major changes to the revised function's code include the call to telldir() at the top of the loop, the inserted directory test, and the postprocessing at the end of the loop to print the saved entries. I also modified the output by appending a / character to the ends of directory names so that they can be identified.

The only changes to the main program are the declaration of the macro constant, LIST_DIRS_FIRST = 1, and the initialization of ls_flags to LIST_DIRS _FIRST instead of 0, so that the call listdir(dirp, ls_flags) turns on the new feature. I'll name this program *spl_ls2.c*. For brevity, I don't list the complete program here, but it's provided in the book's source code distribution. We can build the executable, naming it spl_ls2, and run it on the same directory on which we ran spl_ls1:

```
$ ./spl_ls2 testing
testing:
dir1/
dir3/
dir2/
./
../
file3
file1
file2
```

All directory names precede all nondirectory names. This output includes the dot (.) and dot-dot (..) entries, which are directories. You should run this program on other directories to convince yourself that it works correctly.

The scandir() Library Function

The name scandir() suggests that this function can scan a directory, possibly to look for something. We'll begin by looking at the synopsis on its man page:

```
#include <dirent.h>
int scandir(const char *dirp, struct dirent* **namelist,
        int (*filter)(const struct dirent *),
        int (*compar)(const struct dirent **, const struct dirent **));

int alphasort(const struct dirent **a, const struct dirent **b);
int versionsort(const struct dirent **a, const struct dirent **b);
```

Because this function's prototype is more complex than any we've seen so far, we'll begin by going through the mechanics of calling it. After that we'll consider what it does and how we can use it.

How We Call scandir()

Unlike other functions we've seen so far, scandir() has parameters that are functions. More accurately, filter and compar are both *pointers* to functions. A parameter that is a pointer to a function is called a *function pointer parameter*. The third parameter of scandir() is declared as:

```
int (*filter)(const struct dirent *)
```

This declares filter to be a pointer to a function whose single argument is a pointer to a constant dirent structure and whose return type is int. A function such as the following matches it:

```
int skipdot(const struct dirent *direntp)
{
    if ( strcmp(direntp->d_name, ".") == 0
      || strcmp(direntp->d_name, "..") == 0 )
        return 0;
    else
        return 1;
}
```

Similarly, the fourth parameter is declared as

```
int (*compar)(const struct dirent **, const struct dirent **)
```

which states that compar is a pointer to a function expecting two arguments, each of type const struct dirent**, that returns an int. The alphasort() and versionsort() functions shown in the man page have the exact same prototype as the fourth parameter (compar) and could be passed as the fourth argument to scandir().

The scandir() function also has a triply indirect parameter, namelist. This parameter is the address of a dynamic array of pointers to dirent structures. These structures are referred to by three levels of indirection—the address is the first, the array name is the second, and the array entries themselves are pointers, hence the third. If a program declares dp_array to store the address of a pointer to a dirent structure as follows

```
struct dirent* *dp_array; /* Not struct dirent* dp_array[] */
```

then it would pass dp_array's address, &dp_array, as the second argument to scandir(). Putting this all together, we could call scandir() as follows:

```
int returnval = scandir("/home/snw/", &dp_array, skipdot, alphasort);
```

Although we now know how to call scandir(), we still don't know what it does. That comes next.

FUNCTION POINTER PARAMETERS

In C, when a function has a function pointer parameter, a calling program can pass to it a pointer to a function whose prototype matches that of the parameter. Let's consider an example. Suppose that we declare the function f() as follows:

```
double f(int (*funcp)(int, int), int*);
```

Then the first parameter of f() is funcp, a pointer to a function whose prototype is

```
int function_name(int, int);
```

where *function_name* is any valid function name. A calling program can pass the address of any function whose prototype is of this form as the first parameter of f(). Suppose that g() is defined to be the following function:

```
int g(int x, int y) { return x * y; }
```

The prototype of g() matches that of *funcp. Therefore, we can pass g() in a call to f() as follows:

```
double res = f(g, 12);
```

Since the compiler replaces the name of a function by its address, it isn't necessary to call it like this, although it is also correct:

```
double res = f(&g, 12);
```

In contrast, if the function h() has the prototype

```
int h(int*, int*);
```

then it is an error to pass it to f(), because its prototype doesn't match the parameter's exactly. See the function *functionptr_demo.c* in the book's source code distribution for a more thorough example that also uses a typedef to declare a function pointer type.

What scandir() Does

Let's assume that the scandir() function's first argument is the pathname of a directory, dirp. It opens that directory and makes a pass across every entry in the directory's stream. For each entry, it calls the (*filter) function on that entry. The (*filter) function returns an integer. For each entry for which that return value is nonzero, scandir() stores a pointer to its dirent structure in namelist, sorted using the comparison function (*compar) on the pairs of entries. If the call passes NULL to the filter function parameter (*filter), all entries are stored in the array, and if it passes NULL to the comparison function parameter, no sorting takes place.

The comparison function is not limited to comparing the entries by their filenames—it can compare the two entries by examining any data in the entry, even if that involves calling lstat() on them. A comparison function must have two parameters that are constant pointers to dirent structures, and it must return an integer. The traditional return values of comparison functions are -1, 0, and 1, but it needs to return an integer less than, equal to, or greater than zero only if the first argument is considered to be, respectively, less than, equal to, or greater than the second. For example, the following function could be used to compare two entries by the sizes of the files:

```
int cmpbysize(const struct dirent **a, const struct dirent **b)
{
    struct stat a_sb, b_sb;
    stat((*a)->d_name, &a_sb);
    stat((*b)->d_name, &b_sb);
    return (a_sb.st_size - b_sb.st_size);
}
```

This example returns numbers that are not necessarily -1, 0, or 1. Also, it has no error handling, which is omitted to save space. If we just want to sort the entries alphabetically in accordance with the locale's LC_COLLATE value, we can pass the alphasort() function to scandir(), because alphasort() calls strcoll() internally, which is locale-aware.

When scandir() has returned, the namelist array contains all entries that met the filter's conditions, sorted by the sorting criteria embodied in the comparison function, and the return value of the function is the number of entries in that array. The scandir() function allocates its own memory for the namelist array. A program calling scandir() must not declare its own storage for it, but it must free the memory allocated to the array when it no longer needs it.

The man page has a simple example that illustrates how to call the function and free the memory. We include it here, modified slightly to reduce space:

scandir_manpage
_example.c
```
#define _DEFAULT_SOURCE
#include <dirent.h>
#include <stdio.h>
#include <stdlib.h>
```

```
int main(void)
{
    struct dirent **namelist;
    int            n;

    if ( (n = scandir(".", &namelist, NULL, alphasort)) == -1 )
        exit(EXIT_FAILURE);
    while ( n-- ) {
        printf("%s\n", namelist[n]->d_name);
        free(namelist[n]);
    }
    free(namelist);
    exit(EXIT_SUCCESS);
}
```

This program prints the entries in the current working directory. The first name printed is the last one in the array because it prints the directory entries in the reverse of the collating order.

We can use the scandir() function to write an improved version of *spl_ls2.c*, our program that lists directory contents with directories first. Not only will it print the directories first, but it will sort the entries alphabetically in the ordering of the current locale. It won't need to open the directory and read it using the opendir() and readdir() functions because scandir() bypasses that work. The first step is to write the comparison function, which is shown in Listing 7-5.

dirsfirstsort()
```
int dirsfirstsort(const struct dirent **a, const struct dirent **b)
{
    if ( isdir(*a) )
        if ( !isdir(*b) ) /* a is a directory but b is not.        */
            return -1;
        else /* Both a and b are directories; sort alpabetically.  */
            return(alphasort(a, b));
    else
        if ( isdir(*b) )  /* b is a directory but a is not.        */
            return 1;
        else /* Neither a nor b is a directory; sort alpabetically. */
            return(alphasort(a, b));
}
```

Listing 7-5: A comparison function that sorts directories before nondirectories and alphabetically if the two entries are both directories or both nondirectories

This function orders the entries by sorting directories ahead of nondirectories and breaks ties alphabetically. It calls the isdir() function presented in Listing 7-2 to determine whether an entry is a directory or not.

The next step is to write a function, which I've named scan_one_dir(), that prints a single directory's entries using scandir():

```
scan_one_dir()    int scan_one_dir(const char *dirname, void (*process)(const struct dirent*))
                  {
                      struct dirent **namelist;  /* An array of pointers to dirent structs  */
                      int            i, n;

                      errno = 0;
                      if ( (n = scandir(dirname, &namelist, NULL, dirsfirstsort)) < 0 )
                          fatal_error(errno, "scandir");

                      for ( i = 0; i < n; i++ ) { /* Process every entry saved into namelist.*/
                          process(namelist[i]);  /* Process this dirent structure.         */
                          free(namelist[i]);     /* Free the dirent structure.             */
                      }
                      free(namelist);            /* Free the namelist array that was
                                                     allocated by scandir().               */
                      return(EXIT_SUCCESS);
                  }
```

The function passes dirsfirstsort() to scandir() as its comparison function
and uses no filter, so that no entries are excluded from the namelist array.

Now that we've seen how to use function pointer parameters, I take advantage of them here. Rather than designing this function narrowly so that
it can only print the filenames in the entries, I make it more general. Specifically, its second parameter is a pointer to a function that will process the
dirent structures saved in namelist. The function pointer parameter is named
process() in the listing and has a dirent structure argument and a void return
value. We can pass any void function to it that has a single dirent structure
argument. Since our program just prints file and directory names, the function passed to this parameter is one that just prints the entry's name. Another program could pass a different function to it, for example, one that
calls stat() on the filename to retrieve its metadata and process that metadata in some particular way.

We're ready to assemble the program. To save space, Listing 7-6 does
not show those functions already displayed in previous listings; the complete
program is in the book's source code distribution.

```
spl_ls3.c   #define _DEFAULT_SOURCE     /* For glibc > 2.10                  */
            #define _BSD_SOURCE          /* For versions of glibc <  2.19    */
            #include "common_hdrs.h"
            #include <dirent.h>
            #include "dir_utils.h"       /* For isdir() and dirsfirstsort() */

            /* print(dp) prints the filename of entry *dp. If it's a directory, it
               appends a trailing '/' to its name. */
            void print(const struct dirent *direntp)
            {
                printf("%s", direntp->d_name);
```

```
    if ( isdir(direntp) )
        printf("/");
    printf("\n");
}

int main(int argc, char *argv[])
{
    if ( setlocale(LC_TIME, "") == NULL )
        fatal_error(LOCALE_ERROR,
                    "setlocale() could not set the given locale");
    if ( 1 == argc )            /* If no arguments, list the CWD.     */
        scan_one_dir(".", print);
    else {                      /* Otherwise, for each argument, scan it.  */
        for ( int i = 1; i < argc; i++ ) {
            printf("\n%s:\n", argv[i]);     /* Print the argument.       */
            scan_one_dir(argv[i], print);   /* Pass the print() function. */
            if ( i < argc-1 ) printf("\n"); /* Put a newline before next. */
        }
    }
    exit(EXIT_SUCCESS);
}
```

Listing 7-6: A program using scandir() to list all contents of all arguments, sorted in collating order, with directories preceding nondirectories

After setting up the current locale, the main program calls scan_one_dir(), passing it the print() function for each command line argument. We build it and run it on our test directory:

```
$ ./spl_ls3 testing
testing:
./
../
dir1/
dir2/
dir3/
file1
file2
file3
```

Because of space limitations, this output is intentionally small. You can run this program on much larger directories to see that it sorts the entries in the correct order.

The various library functions that we've examined in the directory API are all designed to work within a single directory as a flat structure. They don't descend into subdirectories. We need to know how to design programs that can descend into subdirectories and process entire directory hierarchies because many problems require this, as we'll see in the next section. We're about to explore various ways to accomplish this, including a few different APIs designed to recursively descend directories.

Processing the Directory Hierarchy

In Chapter 1, I pointed out that the directory hierarchy is tree-like, but is not a tree. Let's review why this is true. The first reason is that symbolic links can create cycles because a symbolic link can point back to an ancestor in the tree, as depicted in Figure 7-2. In the figure, directories are in bold, and the symbolic link is a dashed line.

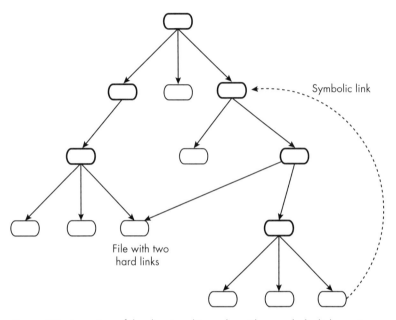

Figure 7-2: A portion of the directory hierarchy with a symbolic link creating a cycle

If none of the symbolic links created cycles, the hierarchy still wouldn't be a pure tree because hard links allow files to have multiple names in different directories, as Figure 7-2 illustrates. Files that are contained in more than one directory are nodes with more than one parent, but in a tree, each node other than the root has a single parent.

In Linux and most Unix systems, the hierarchy has no cycles if it has no symbolic links. This is because in these systems, a directory node can never be the target of a hard link, which implies that no node can have an edge leading back to an ancestor. For brevity, even though it isn't technically a true tree, we'll refer to a directory hierarchy as a *directory tree*, or just a *tree* when the meaning is clear.

The fact that the hierarchy is tree-like suggests that many of the algorithms that we use to process trees can be applied to process the hierarchy. Some of these algorithms are important enough for us to explore now, because the paradigms that they embody are the basis for many practical and useful Unix tools.

Some of the most useful tools in Unix allow us to traverse the entire directory tree rooted at a given node, performing some type of processing in each node. This is what the `find` command does, for example. It lets us search the tree rooted at a given directory, searching for files that satisfy specified conditions and performing actions on the files that satisfy those conditions. In the simplest case, we can use `find` to search for files whose names match a pattern and print out the relative pathnames of those that do.

Other commands such as `ls`, `rm`, `cp`, and `grep` have a recursive option, usually either `-R` or `-r`, that makes those commands act on every file in the directory trees rooted in their directory arguments. All of the preceding commands work top-down, usually in a depth-first manner, processing an entire subtree before processing any sibling subtrees.

Some tools, such as `tree` and `du`, short for "disk usage," also work on entire directory trees. The `tree` command displays the entire directory tree rooted at a given directory, visually indenting files at deeper levels of the tree. The `du` command summarizes the amount of disk space used by files in a given directory hierarchy. Its man page states that it acts recursively on directories. In other words, when we enter `du` *dirname*, `du` recursively descends *dirname*, collecting and reporting the total disk usage of every directory in its tree, after which it prints the grand total of all directories. For example, here is a run of it on the *testing* directory:

```
$ du testing
4 testing/dir3
4 testing/dir1/adir
8 testing/dir1
4 testing/dir2
32 testing
```

This output suggests that `du` processes all child nodes before it processes their parent, which is an example of a *postorder traversal*. The numbers in the output are counts of the number of 1024-byte blocks used by all files in each directory; we'll explore the command in more detail later in this chapter.

All of the preceding examples traversed the tree by *descending* it: visiting all nodes or selected nodes in the subtree rooted at a given node. Algorithms that traverse the tree in this manner are called *tree walks*. In contrast to tree walks, some commands *ascend* the tree. The `pwd` command is a good example of this; it travels up the tree starting in the current working directory until it reaches the root directory in order to construct the absolute pathname of the current working directory. Traveling up the tree presents interesting challenges that are very different from those that we'll encounter in trying to traverse the tree downward and recursively.

Among the various commands that walk the tree, the `du` command is a good one to implement; we'll learn a lot in the process. Since we already know how to use the `stat()` family of system calls to obtain disk usage metadata for a file, collecting disk usage metadata won't be difficult. The challenge is how to walk the tree recursively and, in particular, to process its nodes in a postorder manner. Therefore, our approach to solving this problem is first to develop a couple of programs that just walk the tree, not trying to collect disk usage information. When we've worked out the algorithm for performing the tree walk, we'll augment it with the ability to report disk usage.

We'll also learn a lot by tackling a problem that has to ascend the tree. Implementing a version of the pwd command is a good exercise in ascending the tree. We'll discover that it isn't as simple as it might seem.

Before we start researching solutions to these problems, we need to learn a bit more about the concept of filesystem mounting, which is what we cover next. After that, we'll explore potential ways to perform tree walks as preparation for implementing the du command. Once we decide on a good method, we'll implement a simplified version of that command.

Mounting File Systems

In Chapter 1, I introduced the concept of filesystem mounting, which I'll explain in more detail now because it's relevant to the problems we're about to solve. It's easiest to understand with a concrete example. The superuser can issue the mount command to mount a filesystem onto the directory hierarchy at a specific point; the command

```
$ mount device directory
```

attaches the filesystem on the given device into the directory hierarchy at the specified directory. That directory is then called the filesystem's *mount point*. In general, you need superuser privilege to mount a filesystem, and you typically need to provide the command more information than in this example, such as the filesystem type and its unique identifier.

When a filesystem is mounted onto the directory hierarchy, the root directory of that filesystem replaces the directory on which it's mounted, and that directory's previous contents are hidden by the mount. When the filesystem is *unmounted*, using the umount command (not unmount), the directory's contents are restored.

An Example of Filesystem Mounting

To illustrate, Figure 7-3 depicts a portion of the top of the directory hierarchy of a hypothetical Unix system.

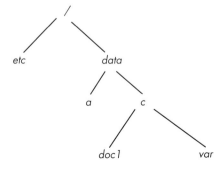

Figure 7-3: The initial file hierarchy without any mounts

The root of this hierarchy has a subdirectory named *data* with two subdirectories named *a* and *c*. The *c* directory is not empty. Suppose that there's another device, */dev/hdb*, that has a filesystem on it, depicted in Figure 7-4.

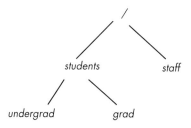

Figure 7-4: The filesystem /dev/hdb

The root of this filesystem has two subdirectories named *staff* and *students*, and *students* has the subdirectories *grad* and *undergrad*. Now suppose we mount this second filesystem on the directory */data/c* by entering (as superuser):

```
$ mount /dev/hdb /data/c
```

If the mount is successful, then */data/c* becomes the mount point for the filesystem */dev/hdb*, and we say that */dev/hdb* is mounted on the directory *c*. The files *doc1* and *var* are hidden until the filesystem is unmounted, at which point they'll reappear. The directory hierarchy after the mount is depicted in Figure 7-5.

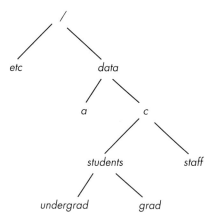

Figure 7-5: The directory hierarchy after the mount of /dev/hdb onto /data/c

The absolute pathnames of all files in the mounted filesystem start with */data/c* now, such as */data/c/students/grad*.

When a directory becomes a mount point, the kernel restructures the directory hierarchy. Although the directory contents are masked by the root directory of the mounted filesystem, the kernel stores the hidden contents and a record of the mount. Different versions of Unix implement mounting in different ways; implementation is not part of any standard. However, it's pretty much universally true that a process can recognize when a directory *dir* is a mount point because the device ID of the directory's parent, say, *parent*, is different from that of *dir*. This is because *dir* is the root of the mounted filesystem and *parent* is a node on the filesystem to which it's attached.

Commands for Finding Mount Points

There are a few ways to tell where the mount points are in the directory hierarchy. One is the df command, which is intended to show the amount of disk space available on the mounted filesystems that contain the filenames it's given on the command line. By default, the POSIX-conforming version of it outputs several fields on each line, but the GNU version, found on Linux, allows us to limit its output to just the name of the device and its mount point by giving it the --output=source,target option. Without any filenames it shows all mounted filesystems:

```
$ df --output=source,target
--snip--
/dev/sdc2     /
/dev/sdd3     /var
/dev/sdb3     /home
/dev/sdc1     /boot
/dev/sdd4     /data/research_resources/physics/articles/more_articles
```

If we want to know the filesystem and mount point for our current working directory, then entering **df --output=source,target .** shows us:

```
$ pwd  # To see what our working directory is
/home/stewart/unixbook/demos
$ df --output=source,target .
Filesystem     Mounted on
/dev/sdb3      /home
```

We can also use the mount command. Without any options, it displays all mounted filesystems with information about each. By giving it the -t *type* option, it limits the output to mounts of the requested type. For example, to see the Ext4 filesystems, I can enter:

```
$ mount -t ext4
--snip--
/dev/sdc2 on / type ext4 (rw,relatime,errors=remount-ro)
/dev/sdd3 on /var type ext4 (rw,relatime)
```

```
/dev/sdb3 on /home type ext4 (rw,relatime)
/dev/sdc1 on /boot type ext4 (rw,relatime,stripe=4)
/dev/sdd4 on /data/research_resources/physics/articles/more_articles...
```

This command also displays the mount options, which I haven't discussed here. You can read about mount options on the mount man page.

A third method is the findmnt command, which also displays mounted filesystems. By default, its output is presented in a tree-like format, and the fields are similar to df's output. We can limit the output to just the filesystem and mount point with the -o SOURCE,TARGET option and limit the types with -t type:

```
$ findmnt -t ext4 -o SOURCE,TARGET
SOURCE     TARGET
--snip--
/dev/sdc2  /
/dev/sdb4  /data
/dev/sdd4  /data/research_resources/physics/articles/more_articles
/dev/sdd3  /var
/dev/sdb3  /home
/dev/sdc1  /boot
```

This is just a brief summary of these commands. The mount command is also used for mounting filesystems, but you need superuser privileges on the computer for that purpose.

Duplicate Inode Numbers

The advantage of mounting is that it simplifies the user's conceptualization and navigation of the file hierarchy. One problem it introduces is that there may be files with the same inode number in the directory hierarchy, since inode numbers are unique only within a single filesystem.

In fact, in most Unix systems, and in Linux in particular, the root directory of every filesystem is inode number 2. Inode number 1 is used to record bad blocks in the filesystem, and index 0 is unused in the inode table. A typical Unix system may have several filesystems all mounted directly under /. Viewing the inode numbers in the top-level directory, you're likely to see several subdirectories, all of which have inode number 2, because they're all mount points for attached filesystems.

Given that multiple files can have the same inode numbers when filesystems are mounted on the directory hierarchy, the only way to uniquely identify a file is with a pair consisting of the inode number and the device ID of the filesystem on which it resides. That number is always stored in the inode. Without the device ID, the inode number is ambiguous. This is also why the kernel doesn't allow us to create a hard link for a file on a different filesystem.

To see this, suppose in the preceding example that the file *data/a/doc1* has inode number 52. Suppose that the file */students/undergrad/hwk1* on */dev/hdb* also has inode number 52. If we could create a hard link across filesystems, then the command

```
$ ln /data/a/doc1 /data/c/students/grad/doc1
```

would result in two links in the */dev/hdb* filesystem, each having the same inode number, but these two inode numbers would refer to two different inodes. This would break the filesystem, unless directories were able to store device numbers as well as inode numbers with filenames, which would require rewriting a lot of the kernel. All hard links to a file must be in a single filesystem.

The subject of mounting and mount points will play a role in our solutions to the remaining problems of this chapter.

Tree Walks

Let's turn to the problem of walking through a directory tree. One way to walk a directory's tree is to implement a recursive function using only the first set of library functions from the preceding section, namely opendir(), readdir(), and closedir(). With these, we need to modify our *spl_ls1.c* program only slightly.

A Recursive Tree Walk Using readdir()

To modify the *spl_ls1.c* program so that it can visit the entire tree rooted at a given directory, we need to change the main program slightly and revise listdir(). The main program will still open the root directory of the tree walk as it did before, by calling opendir(). However, since listdir() will also need to open any directory it finds as it's reading the directory stream, it will need the name of the directory it's processing. Let's redisplay the main loop of listdir() to make this clear:

```
while ( !done ) {
    errno = 0;
    direntp = readdir(dirp);
    if ( direntp == NULL && errno != 0 )
        perror("readdir");
    else if ( direntp == NULL )
        done = TRUE;
    else
    ❶ printf("    %s\n", direntp->d_name);
}
```

In this code, we need to replace the call to printf() ❶ by programming logic such as the following, which excludes the requisite error handling:

```
printf("%s\n", direntp->d_name);
if ( isdir(direntp) ) {
    subdirp = opendir(direntp->d_name);
    listdir(subdirp, flags);
    closedir(subdirp);
}
```

In other words, listdir() prints the entry's filename and then checks if it's a directory. If it is, it recursively calls listdir(). Unfortunately, this doesn't work, for two reasons.

The first is best explained with an example. Consider the fragment of a directory tree shown in Figure 7-6.

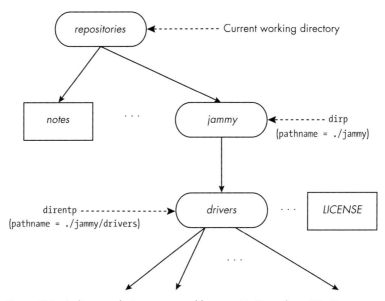

Figure 7-6: A directory being processed by opendir() and readdir()

The figure shows that the main program's working directory at the time it's called is *repositories*. Suppose that it was invoked with the command:

```
$ ./spl_ls1 jammy
```

The main() function in turn calls opendir("jammy"). Since *jammy* is a pathname relative to the current working directory *repositories*, the call is successful; the *jammy* directory is opened and the dirp directory stream pointer is returned, which main() passes in its call listdir(dirp). Inside listdir(), while processing the *jammy* directory, readdir() is called and returns a direntp pointer to the subdirectory named *drivers*. The isdir(direntp) function detects that it is a directory and calls opendir(direntp->d_name). This is the problem. At that point, direntp->d_name is the name "drivers", but the pathname *drivers* is relative only to *jammy*, not to the process's current working directory, *repositories*. Therefore opendir() will fail with the ENOENT error "No such file or directory." The pathname that should be passed to opendir() is *jammy/drivers*, not *drivers*.

More generally, the pathname passed to opendir() must be relative to the current working directory. In the current implementation of listdir(), the relative pathname of the directory being processed isn't available in the listdir() function's parameter list. Therefore, we need to modify its prototype to include it and also modify the calls to it in main(). The listdir() function needs to declare a variable to store the longest possible pathname that might be needed for this purpose. We'll therefore declare a variable, pathname, in it, with size PATH_MAX, defined in *limits.h*.

The second problem is related to the dot and dot-dot entries. They're both directories. When readdir() reads the entry for dot, isdir() returns true. The recursive call to listdir() will start right back in the beginning, and an infinite loop will ensue because the program will keep returning to process the same directory over and over again!

The solution to this problem is to check whether the current entry is . or .. and skip it if it is. We can now assemble a correct version of the recursive solution. The revised code for listdir() and the main program are shown in Listing 7-7. We'll name this recursive version of our program *spl_ls_rec1.c*. For brevity, the #include directives and some comments are omitted.

spl_ls_rec1.c
```
void listdir(DIR *dirp, char *dirname, int flags)
{
    struct dirent *direntp;      /* Pointer to directory entry structure */
    BOOL          done = FALSE;  /* Flag to control loop execution       */
    char          pathname[PATH_MAX]; /* Pathname of file to open        */
    DIR           *subdirp;      /* Dir stream for subdirectory          */
    char          *name;         /* Directory entry name copy            */

    while ( !done ) {
        errno = 0;
        direntp = readdir(dirp);
        if ( direntp == NULL && errno != 0 )
            perror("readdir");
        else if ( direntp == NULL ) /* Implies end of stream */
            done = TRUE;
        else {
            name = direntp->d_name;
            if ( (strcmp(name, ".") != 0) && (strcmp(name, "..") != 0) ) {
                sprintf(pathname, "%s/%s", dirname, name);
                printf("%s\n", pathname);
                if ( isdir(direntp) ) {
                    errno = 0;
                    if ( (subdirp = opendir(pathname)) == NULL )
                        error_mssge(errno, name);
                    else {
```

```
                        listdir(subdirp, pathname, flags);
                        closedir(subdirp);
                    }
                }
            }
        }
    }
    printf("\n");
}

int main(int argc, char *argv[])
{
    DIR   *dirp;
    int   ls_flags = 0;

    if ( 1 == argc ) {
        errno = 0;
        if ( (dirp = opendir(".")) == NULL )
            fatal_error(errno, "opendir");    /* Could not open cwd */
        else
            listdir(dirp, ".", ls_flags);
    }
    else { /* For each command line argument, call opendir() on it. */
        for ( int i = 1; i < argc; i++ ) {
            errno = 0;
            if ( (dirp = opendir(argv[i])) == NULL ) {
                if ( errno == ENOTDIR )    /* It's not a directory. */
                    printf("%s\n", argv[i] );
                else                            /* It's an error. */
                    error_mssge(errno, argv[i]);
            }
            else {           /* Directory was opened successfully. */
                printf("\n%s:\n", argv[i] );
                listdir(dirp, argv[i], ls_flags);
                closedir(dirp);
            }
        }
    }
    return 0;
}
```

Listing 7-7: A program to demonstrate recursive listing of a directory hierarchy

We'll build and run this program on the *testing* directory depicted in Figure 7-1:

```
$ ./spl_ls_rec1 testing
testing:
testing/dir1
```

```
testing/dir1/b
testing/dir1/adir
testing/dir1/adir/d
testing/dir1/c
testing/file3
testing/file1
testing/dir3
testing/file2
testing/dir2
testing/dir2/b2
testing/dir2/a1
```

You can see that it recursively displays the files and directories, but there's no apparent ordering of the files. This is a consequence of using readdir() to read the entries, since it doesn't return them in sorted order.

A Recursive Tree Walk Using scandir()

One way to overcome the lack of sorting is to base a recursive tree walk on *spl_ls3.c* instead. That program used the scandir() function, which sorted the filenames using alphasort(). To reduce the code size, we'll remove the directory-first processing that we coded into *spl_ls3.c* and concentrate on adding recursion to the program. We'll also remove the function pointer parameter to scan_one_dir() and the print() function. The scan_one_dir() function from that program, modified to include the recursive call, is shown in the following listing, with the changes highlighted in bold:

scan_one_dir()
(revised)
```
int scan_one_dir(const char *dirname)
{
    struct dirent **namelist;
    int             i, n;
    char            pathname[PATH_MAX];

    errno = 0;
    if ( (n = scandir(dirname, &namelist, NULL, alphasort)) < 0 )
        fatal_error(errno, "scandir");

    for ( i = 0; i < n; i++ ) {
        if ( strcmp(namelist[i]->d_name, ".") != 0
          && strcmp(namelist[i]->d_name, "..") != 0 ) {
            printf("%s/%s\n",dirname,namelist[i]->d_name);
            if ( isdir(namelist[i]) ) {
                sprintf(pathname, "%s/%s", dirname, namelist[i]->d_name);
                scan_one_dir(pathname);
            }
        }
        free(namelist[i]);
    }
}
```

```
    free(namelist);
    return(EXIT_SUCCESS);
}
```

Because the only change to the main program is the removal of the function argument to the two calls to scan_one_dir(), to save space, we won't redisplay it here. The revised program is named *spl_ls_rec2.c* in the book's source code distribution. We build and run this new version on the same *testing* directory:

```
$ ./spl_ls_rec2 testing
testing:
testing/dir1
testing/dir1/adir
testing/dir1/adir/d
testing/dir1/b
testing/dir1/c
testing/dir2
testing/dir2/a1
testing/dir2/b2
testing/dir3
testing/file1
testing/file2
testing/file3
```

You can see that the pathnames are all correct and that they're sorted by filename. It might be possible to base our implementation of du on this program, but before we make that decision, let's review what du does.

The du command traverses each directory tree it's given. It accumulates the disk usage of every file in a directory and then prints the disk usage of that directory. It does this recursively, so that if a file is a directory, it first descends into that directory to accumulate the usage and recursively descends into its subdirectories. This implies that it does, in fact, perform a postorder traversal of each directory tree.

The default block size that it uses for reporting is 1024 bytes, but it depends on the environment variables of the user running it, as well as some system settings. Also by default, du doesn't print the disk usage of ordinary files, even though they're added into the directory totals. With the -a option, it prints the block counts for all files, not just directories. Consider this run of it:

```
$ du -a testing
0 testing/dir1/b
0 testing/dir1/adir/d
4 testing/dir1/adir
0 testing/dir1/c
8 testing/dir1
4 testing/file3
4 testing/file1
4 testing/dir3
4 testing/file2
```

```
0 testing/dir2/b2
0 testing/dir2/a1
4 testing/dir2
32 testing
```

Studying its output, we can see that it descends into directories in a depth-first manner, reaches their leaf nodes, returns, and prints the total counts for the parent directories. It prints the counts for the directories only *after* it visits all of their children. Figure 7-7 illustrates the portion of the path taken by du on the *dir1* subdirectory.

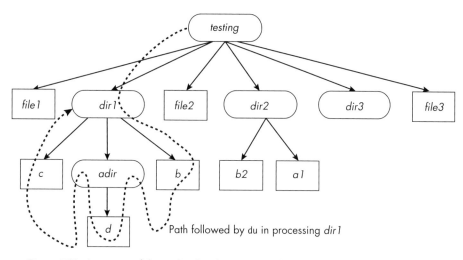

Figure 7-7: A portion of the path taken by du -a on the testing *directory*

It descended into *testing/dir1*, then *testing/dir1/b*, and since that was a leaf node, it then descended into *testing/dir1/adir* and then into *testing/dir1/adir/d* before backing out and visiting *testing/dir1/c*. Our goal is to write a program that can process the tree in the same way.

The nftw() Tree Walk Function

Before deciding how to write our program, let's consider the other potentially useful function mentioned in the readdir() man page, namely nftw(). Its man page is:

```
NAME
       ftw, nftw - file tree walk

SYNOPSIS
       #include <ftw.h>
       int nftw(const char *dirpath,
              int (*fn) (const char *fpath, const struct stat *sb,
                       int typeflag, struct FTW *ftwbuf),
              int nopenfd, int flags);
```

```
#include <ftw.h>
int ftw(const char *dirpath,
        int (*fn) (const char *fpath, const struct stat *sb,
                   int typeflag),
        int nopenfd);
```

Feature Test Macro Requirements for glibc (see feature_test_macros(7)):
   nftw(): _XOPEN_SOURCE >= 500

DESCRIPTION

nftw() walks through the directory tree that is located under the
directory dirpath, and calls fn() once for each entry in the tree. By
default, directories are handled before the files and subdirectories
they contain (preorder traversal).

--snip--

The nftw() function is designed to walk a directory tree. It has a function
pointer parameter that can be applied at each node of the tree. Its description states that directories are processed before their files and subdirectories, which implies that it's a preorder traversal, but further down in the man
page, it indicates that by supplying an appropriate flag, it can be made to
perform postorder processing.

The man page also has information about a second, related function,
ftw(), but it notes that this is an older function and that nftw() was designed
to replace it. The older ftw() function is now deprecated.

The nftw() function is given four arguments. The first is the pathname
of a directory, the second is a function that will be called on each entry that
it visits, the third is an integer that specifies the maximum number of file
descriptors it's allowed to use, and the last is a set of flags that influence its
behavior. Let's go through each of these arguments and how they're used.

The first argument is the root of the tree that it will process. Given the
pathname to a directory, dirpath, the nftw() function recursively descends
the directory hierarchy rooted in dirpath. For each entry that it finds, it calls
the function pointed to by its second argument, fn(), passing it the following
arguments:

fpath The pathname of the entry. If dirpath is a relative pathname,
then fpath is a pathname relative to the process's current working directory at the time nftw() was called. If dirpath is an absolute pathname,
then fpath is also an absolute pathname.

sb A pointer to a stat structure containing information about the object, filled in as if stat(fpath, sb) or lstat(fpath, sb) was called to retrieve the metadata.

typeflag An integer flag that encodes more information about the en-
try. Its value is exactly one of the following predefined constants:
   FTW_F The entry fpath is a regular file.
   FTW_D The entry fpath is a directory.

FTW_DNR   The entry fpath is a directory that cannot be read by the process. In this case, the fn() function won't be called for any of its descendants.

FTW_DP   The entry fpath is a directory and all of its files and subdirectories have been visited already because the FTW_DEPTH flag was set in the flags argument of nftw().

FTW_NS   The stat() function failed on the entry, most likely because the process did not have execute permission on the parent directory. In this case, the stat buffer passed to (*fn) is undefined.

FTW_SL   The entry fpath is a symbolic link, and the FTW_PHYS flag was set in the flags passwd to nftw().

FTW_SLN   The entry fpath is a broken, or *dangling*, symbolic link, one that doesn't point to an existing file, and the FTW_PHYS flag was not set in flags. In this case the stat buffer was filled with information about the link itself instead of its target.

ftwbuf   This is a pointer to an FTW structure, which is defined as follows:

```
struct FTW {
    int base;
    int level;
};
```

The FTW structure provides information about the filename in the fpath pathname passed to (*fn). Specifically, base is the character offset of the entry's filename in the fpath pathname. For example, if fpath is *testing/dir1/adir* and the entry being processed is the file *adir*, then base contains the length of the string *testing/dir1/*.

The level member of the structure indicates the depth of the entry relative to the root of the walk, which is the directory passed to the call to nftw(). The root directory is level 0. If a parent node has level n, then all of its children are at level $n + 1$. In this example, level would contain 2, since *adir* is two levels below *testing*.

Any programmer-defined function can be passed to the fn function pointer parameter, provided that its prototype matches that of the parameter. If so, nftw() calls this function for every entry that it visits. The function will have access to the stat structure returned by a call to stat() on that entry as well as the information encoded in its typeflag argument. A significant drawback of the (*fn) parameter's declaration is that it has no *hooks* that we can use to pass other data to it. In other words, there are no parameters in the function prototype that a program can use to pass other data items to the function. One consequence of this design is that, in order for this function to access any program variables that can retain data across calls, those variables must either be declared with static linkage or have file scope.

For example, to compute the total number of blocks used by all entries in the subtree rooted at a given directory, we would either have to make the total block count a static variable within the function that we define or declare the variable with global scope. This will be clear when we look at an example, which we'll do shortly.

The third parameter to the nftw() function, nopenfd, is the maximum number of file descriptors that nftw() should use while traversing the file tree. Each time that nftw() visits a directory, it opens it and obtains its file descriptor. After it descends that directory's subtree and returns to its parent, it closes that descriptor. Therefore, one open file descriptor is needed for each level of the tree from the root of the search to the current level. If nopenfd is smaller than the depth of the tree, then to reach the deeper entries, nftw() will be forced to close descriptors of ancestors in the tree in order to continue descending the tree. This degrades its performance. If a process makes nopenfd large enough, this problem is avoided, but the number of open file descriptors a process can have is limited by the kernel.

PROCESS RESOURCE LIMITS

The maximum number of open files that a process is allowed is an example of a *process resource limit*. A process requires many different types of resources, such as memory for its stack, time on the CPU, and storage for open file descriptions. The kernel sets limits on the amount of resources of each type that a process can use. With the appropriate system calls, a process can get the values of these limits and modify them.

At the command level, prlimit can be used to query and modify these resource limits. For example, prlimit -n lists the resource limit on open files:

```
$ prlimit -n
RESOURCE DESCRIPTION                SOFT    HARD UNITS
NOFILE   max number of open files 1024 1048576 files
```

The prlimit(2) man page explains the difference between soft and hard limits and contains a discussion of how a process can access and modify resource limits.

The fourth parameter of nftw() is an integer that can be used to pass in a bitwise-OR of zero or more of the following constants, which control aspects of its behavior, such as how ntfw() handles mount points and soft links, what it uses as its current working directory, and whether it follows a preorder or postorder traversal of the tree.

FTW_CHDIR If set, nftw() changes its current working directory to each directory as it processes the files in that directory. If it isn't set, nftw() doesn't change the current working directory.

FTW_DEPTH If set, nftw() processes all files in a directory before processing the directory itself; in other words, it performs a postorder traversal. If it isn't set, nftw() processes directories before any of their files, which we call *preorder traversal*.

FTW_MOUNT If set, nftw() does not cross mount points, meaning that it only processes files in the same filesystem as fpath.

FTW_PHYS   If set, nftw() performs a physical walk and does not follow symbolic links. If it visits a file that is a symbolic link, it processes the link itself, not its target. If it isn't set, it follows symbolic links but does not visit any file twice. If FTW_PHYS is not set and FTW_DEPTH is set, nftw() follows soft links but does not process any directory that would be a descendant of itself.

FTW_ACTIONRETVAL   This flag is available only under *glibc* 2.3.3 or later, with _GNU_SOURCE defined to expose it. If it's set, the next node that nftw() visits is determined by the return value of (*fn). The return values that it responds to are FTW_CONTINUE, FTW_SKIP_SIBLINGS, FTW_SKIP_SUBTREE, and FTW_STOP. For example, if (*fn) returns FTW_CONTINUE, then nftw() continues normal processing, whereas if (*fn) returns FTW_SKIP_SIBLINGS, then nftw() will skip visiting any remaining siblings of the current entry and instead return to the parent. The FTW_SKIP_SUBTREE flag will cause it to skip processing any subtrees of the entry if it's a directory, and FTW_STOP stops all processing and causes nftw() to return immediately.

The nftw() function visits the entries in the tree rooted at dirpath until one of the following conditions occurs:

- An invocation of (*fn) returns a nonzero value and FTW_ACTIONRETVAL is not set, in which case nftw() stops and returns that value.

- The FTW_ACTIONRETVAL flag is set and (*fn) returns FTW_STOP, in which case it stops and returns that value.

- It detects an error, in which case it returns -1 and sets errno to indicate the error.

- It has visited all nodes of the tree, in which case it returns 0.

Let's look at an example. Although the man page for nftw() has an example program, I created a slightly different one whose behavior is similar to that of the tree command. This program displays the name of every file in the tree rooted at its argument directory, indented on the line by an amount of space proportional to its depth in the tree, as a way to visualize the directory hierarchy. The program accepts three user-supplied options with the following meanings:

-m   The program does not cross mount points.

-d   The program does a postorder traversal instead of a preorder traversal.

-p   The program does not follow symbolic links. Without it, it does.

When we write a program that uses nftw(), all of the logic is essentially in the function that it calls at every node. In this first example, that function is named display_info(). Let's take a look at its code:

display_info()
```
#define _XOPEN_SOURCE 700
#include "common_hdrs.h"
#include <ftw.h>
```

```
#define  MAXOPENFD   20       /* Maximum number of file descriptors to open */

int display_info(const char *fpath, const struct stat *sb,
                 int tflag, struct FTW *ftwbuf)
{
    char        indent[PATH_MAX];                  /* A blank string       */
❶ const char *basename = fpath + ftwbuf->base; /* Filename of entry    */
❷ int         width    = 4*ftwbuf->level;       /* Length of leading path */

    /* Fill indent[] with a string of 4*level spaces and NULL-terminate it. */
    memset(indent, ' ', width);
    indent[width] = '\0';

    /* Print out indent followed by filename (not full path). */
    printf("%s%-30s", indent, basename);

    /* Check flags and print a message if need be. */
    if ( tflag == FTW_DNR )      printf(" (unreadable directory)");
    else if ( tflag == FTW_SL )  printf(" (symbolic link)");
    else if ( tflag == FTW_SLN ) printf(" (broken symbolic link)");
    else if ( tflag == FTW_NS )  printf(" (stat failed) ");

    printf("\n");
    return 0;       /* Tell nftw() to continue. */
}
```

This function is relatively simple; it doesn't use the stat structure argument, and it doesn't alter its behavior in response to its tflag argument other than by printing a message based on its value. It uses the level and base members of the FTW structure to indent and format the output. It prints the last component of the pathname by setting basename to point to the first character in the pathname after the first ftwbuf->base ❶ many characters. The indentation is 4*ftwbuf->level spaces ❷. The memset() function fills the memory pointed to by its first argument with a fixed number of identical bytes. It's a convenient and efficient way to create a string with a fixed number of spaces. The main program is also fairly simple:

```
int main(int argc, char *argv[])
{
    int  flags = 0;
    int  ch;
    char options[] = ":dpm"; /* Three possible options */
    opterr = 0;

    while ( TRUE ) {
        if ( -1 == (ch = getopt(argc, argv, options)) )
            break;
```

```
            switch ( ch ) {
            case 'd': flags |= FTW_DEPTH; break;
            case 'p': flags |= FTW_PHYS;  break;
            case 'm': flags |= FTW_MOUNT; break;
            default: fprintf (stderr, "Bad option found.\n");
                return 1;
            }
        }
        errno = 0;
        if ( optind < argc )
            while ( optind < argc ) {
                if ( -1 == nftw(argv[optind], display_info, MAXOPENFD, flags) )
                    fatal_error(errno, "nftw");
                optind++;
            }
        else if ( -1 == nftw(".", display_info, MAXOPENFD, flags) )
            fatal_error(errno, "nftw");
        else
            exit(EXIT_SUCCESS);
}
```

The main program checks the command line for options and arguments and
then calls nftw() for each command line argument, passing it the argument,
the function to call, the maximum number of open file descriptors it should
use, and optional flags. Without any arguments, it processes the current
working directory.

The complete program, named *nftw_demo.c*, is in the source code distribution for the book. To demonstrate its behavior, I created a test directory
named *testdir*, whose contents are displayed in a tree-like format here:

```
testdir
    linktosubdir1 -> subdir1
    subdir1
        subsubdir1
            link2tosubdir1 -> ../../subdir1
            subsubsubdir1
                testfile1
                testfile2
        subsubdir2
    subdir2
```

This directory has several levels of nested subdirectories, one of which has a
symbolic link, *link2tosubdir1*, that creates a cycle.

Here's a run of this program on this directory with the -p option passed
to it so that it does not follow symbolic links but instead displays them:

```
$ ./nftw_demo -p testdir
testdir
    linktosubdir1                    (symbolic link)
```

```
    subdir2
    subdir1
        subsubdir2
        subsubdir1
            link2tosubdir1                  (symbolic link)
            subsubsubdir1
                testfile1
                testfile2
```

Here's a run without the -p option:

```
$ ./nftw_demo testdir
testdir
    linktosubdir1
        subsubdir2
        subsubdir1
            subsubsubdir1
                testfile1
                testfile2
    subdir2
```

In the first run, it indicates which files are soft links and doesn't follow them. In the second run, it follows the links. It begins by following the *linktosubdir1* link and displays the tree rooted at *subdir1*. When it returns to *testdir*, it doesn't reenter *subdir1* because, as the man page tells us, nftw() does not report on any file twice by following symbolic links.

Now that we see what is possible with the nftw() function as well as the scandir() function, we need to decide which we should use to implement our initial version of the du command. If we use nftw(), the (*fn) function will need block-scoped (local) variables that have static duration or access to file-scoped variables. The alternative is a recursive solution based on scandir(). To avoid the recursion, which might be slow, we'll opt to write it based on nftw() and see how well we do.

Writing a du Command

The du command has several options, but we'll write a simple version of it that accepts no options. Because we'd like to see the disk usage of all files, we'll implement the equivalent of du -a and name it spl_du1.

The spl_du1 command won't follow symbolic links; otherwise, it might overcount file usage or count files that are not within the directory argument. For the first version, it won't cross mount points, so it reports disk usage only within a single filesystem. It's easy enough to add an option later to let it cross mount points.

Because the program has to do a postorder traversal of the tree, we'll pass the FTW_DEPTH flag to the nftw() function. We'll use Figure 7-8 to demonstrate its behavior. Since the way we draw the tree has nothing to do with the order of the files in the directories, for convenience we can assume that nftw() visits the children of a single node, from left to right. Therefore, in the tree in Figure 7-8, the files are visited in the order *srcs, cpy, bin, pics, stuff, data, work, ideas, projects, file2, garbage, play*, and finally, *snw*.

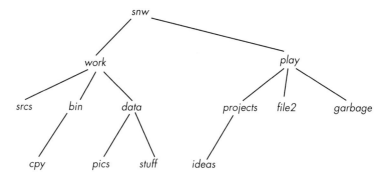

Figure 7-8: A sample tree hierarchy

The key problem is how the program can recursively accumulate the sizes of the files that it visits. It has to be able to print out the size of each file that it visits and, when it reaches a directory, to print out that directory's total usage. For example, in Figure 7-8, when it returns to the *data* entry after visiting its children, it has to print the total usage of *pics* and *stuff* and the size of the *data* directory itself. In addition, it has to add to this sum the sizes of *srcs* and the current accumulation in *bin* and add this amount to a running total to pass up to the *work* entry when it returns to it. This suggests that if the program keeps a set of running disk usage totals indexed by the level in the tree, it should be able to record the total disk usage at every directory in the tree, including the directory at the tree's root.

Let's call the function that we pass to nftw() file_usage(). Since file_usage() has no parameter that can be used to pass any program state information to it, the only way for separate invocations of it and the main program to share data is by putting state information in file scope. Therefore, to record the number of disk blocks used in each level of the tree, the program will need to declare an array

```
#define MAXDEPTH  50  /* Some large number to be determined */
static  uintmax_t total_usage[MAXDEPTH];
```

in file scope. It has to be in file scope because the main program needs to initialize each element of the array to 0 each time it begins a new tree walk for a directory passed to it, and the file_usage() function needs to update it.

The reason to declare the element type uintmax_t is that it's the largest unsigned integer type available. This type is declared in *stdint.h*, so we'll need to include that header in the main program. The system_data_types man page describes the type and notes that to print values of that type, the program needs to use the %ju format specifier in the printf() format specification list.

The choice of constant for MAXDEPTH is easily changed. If we want, the program could make a system call to obtain the maximum number of open files allowed for the process and dynamically allocate an array of that size, but for now, we'll assume that the depth of the tree is never greater than 50, so we'll define MAXDEPTH to be 50.

The prototype for file_usage() is:

```
int file_usage(const char *fpath, const struct stat *sb,
               int tflag, struct FTW *ftwbuf)
```

At any instant of time, file_usage() is visiting a specific file in the tree. Let's call this file the *current file* and call its level the *current level*, and let's use the variable cur_level to represent that level. We'll call the level of the file processed immediately before the current file the *previous level*, and we'll use the variable prev_level to store that level. We'll initialize prev_level to -1 to indicate that the directory tree has not yet been processed. Since the main program can be invoked with multiple directory arguments, it will set prev_level to -1 before calling nftw() on that argument. Since both main() and file_usage() modify prev_level, it will be file-scoped.

Both prev_level and cur_level take on values up to MAXDEPTH and no larger. The current file has a total usage that we can store in the variable named cur_usage. This is the usage of the actual file, not the sum of the disk usage of any children it may have. Directories are usually allocated a single block, with a default size of 4096 bytes on most systems. The file_usage() function can get the disk usage of the current file from the stat structure passed into the function; it's in the st_blocks member of the stat structure. This value is the number of 512-byte blocks; in order to print the number of 1024-byte blocks, we'll divide it by 2.

Let's think about what file_usage() has to do for each visited entry. Its actions depend entirely on the values of both cur_level and prev_level. To make the discussion precise, we define a *left sibling* of a tree node as a sibling that is to the left of that node in the tree's depiction and a *right sibling* analogously. The file_usage() function must ensure that the following *invariant* assertion is true immediately after it has finished processing a file:

> total_usage[cur_level] is the sum of the sizes of all trees whose roots are at level cur_level and are left siblings of the current file, plus the size of the subtree rooted at the current node.

Suppose first that prev_level < cur_level. This implies that either prev _level is -1 or we just descended from a node closer to the root of the tree. The latter case can happen only during a postorder traversal when we reach a leaf node that is the leftmost in its tree. For any other node, the previous node will be either at the same level or below it. If prev_level == -1, it implies that the tree is a single node and is therefore also a leftmost leaf node. Therefore, in either case, we've just reached a bottom level of the tree and we need to set total_usage[cur_level] to the current file's usage and copy this into total_usage[cur_level]:

```
cur_usage = sb->st_blocks/2;
total_usage[cur_level] = cur_usage;
```

Observe that total_usage[cur_level] satisfies the invariant assertion in this case.

Let's consider the next case, in which prev_level == cur_level. In this case, we're visiting a file that is a right sibling of the one previously visited, and it cannot be a nonempty directory because if it were, we'd be returning to it from a node at a greater level. This implies that we have visited all left siblings of the current file and that the current file has no children. Therefore, we need to update total_usage[cur_level] by adding the current file's disk usage to it:

```
cur_usage = sb->st_blocks/2;
total_usage[cur_level] += cur_usage;
```

Assuming that the invariant was true prior to this call to file_usage(), it remains true as a result of adding cur_usage to it, since cur_usage is the disk usage of the subtree rooted at this file and total_usage[cur_level] is now the total usage of the trees rooted at the left siblings of this node plus this node's total usage.

The last case to consider is when prev_level > cur_level. In a postorder traversal, this can occur only when the previous node is a child of the current node and the program has just returned to a directory whose children have all been visited. For example, in Figure 7-8, if the current node is *play*, the previous node must be *garbage*, since we visit them in a left-to-right order. Therefore, the total disk usage accumulated in the previous node's level must be added to the disk usage of this parent directory, and this sum must be printed as the total usage of this directory.

We now take advantage of the invariant assertion with respect to total _usage[prev_level]. The algorithm only returns to a parent directory immediately after visiting its rightmost child. Since the last node processed was the rightmost child and its level is prev_level, total_usage[prev_level] must be the sum of the usages of all subtrees of this directory. Therefore, the disk usage to display for this directory is the number of blocks used by the directory plus total_usage[prev_level]:

```
cur_usage = total_usage[prev_level] + sb->st_blocks/2;
```

To preserve the invariant assertion, we also need to add the new value of cur_usage to total_usage[cur_level]. You should convince yourself that, by doing so, the invariant is true for total_usage[cur_level]. The next step is the less obvious one—we must reset total_usage[prev_level] to 0 so that the combined actions are:

```
cur_usage = total_usage[prev_level] + sb->st_blocks;
total_usage[cur_level] += cur_usage;
total_usage[prev_level] = 0;
```

To see why we have to zero total_usage[prev_level], consider what would happen when file_usage() returns and is then called for the next file. Using the file tree in Figure 7-8, suppose the current file is the directory work, and file_usage() just processed the directory named *data*. Then cur_level = 1 and prev_level = 2. The next file that file_usage() will process is *ideas* and then *projects*. After it visits *ideas* and returns to *projects*, total_usage[1] must have the value 0; otherwise, the size of projects will include the sizes of *srcs*, *bin*, and *data*. In other words, every time that we finish a level of siblings in a subtree, having reached the rightmost sibling, and return to their parent, we must zero out the entry in the total_usage[] array for the children's level. The only chance to do this is when we've added its value into the total usage of the parent and are finished with that node. Doing this preserves the invariant, since no nodes are currently being visited in that level anymore.

We're ready to assemble the initial version of the spl_du1 command. Our command will print a message next to a filename if that file had a problem such as being a broken link or an unreadable directory. The real du command prints a message to the standard error stream instead. To reduce the size of Listing 7-8, I omitted comments. The complete listing is in the source code distribution.

spl_du1.c
```
#define _XOPEN_SOURCE 700
#include "common_hdrs.h"
#include <ftw.h>
#include <stdint.h>
#include <limits.h>

#define MAXDEPTH 100
static uintmax_t total_usage[MAXDEPTH];
static int      prev_level;

int file_usage(const char *fpath, const struct stat *sb,
               int tflag, struct FTW *ftwbuf)
{
    int       cur_level;
    uintmax_t cur_usage;

    cur_level = ftwbuf->level;
    if ( cur_level >= MAXDEPTH ) {
        fprintf(stderr, "Exceeded maximum depth.\n");
        return -1;
    }
    if ( prev_level == cur_level ) {
        cur_usage = sb->st_blocks/2;
        total_usage[cur_level] += cur_usage;
    }
    else if ( prev_level > cur_level ) {
        cur_usage = total_usage[prev_level] + sb->st_blocks/2;
        total_usage[cur_level] += cur_usage;
        total_usage[prev_level] = 0;
    }
    else {
        cur_usage = sb->st_blocks/2;
        total_usage[cur_level] = cur_usage;
```

```
        }
        printf("%ju\t%s", cur_usage, fpath);
        prev_level = cur_level;

        if ( tflag == FTW_DNR )       printf(" (unreadable directory)\n");
        else if ( tflag == FTW_SL )  printf(" (symbolic link)\n");
        else if ( tflag == FTW_SLN ) printf(" (broken symbolic link)\n");
        else if ( tflag == FTW_NS )  printf("stat() failed\n");
        printf("\n");
        return 0;    /* To tell nftw() to continue */
}


int main(int argc, char *argv[])
{
    int flags = FTW_DEPTH | FTW_PHYS | FTW_MOUNT;
    int status;
    int i = 1;

    if ( argc < 2 )  {
        memset( total_usage, 0, MAXDEPTH*sizeof(uintmax_t));
        prev_level = -1;
        if ( 0 != (status = nftw(".", file_usage, 20, flags)) )
            fatal_error(status, "nftw");
    }
    else
        while ( i < argc ) {
            memset(total_usage, 0, MAXDEPTH*sizeof(uintmax_t));
            prev_level = -1;
            if ( 0 != (status = nftw(argv[i], file_usage, MAXDEPTH, flags)) )
                fatal_error(status, "nftw");
            i++;
        }
    exit(EXIT_SUCCESS);
}
```

Listing 7-8: An implementation of a simplified version of the du command

Running spl_du1 and du -a on a test directory produces the same block counts and list of files:

```
$ du -a testdir
4 testdir/subdir2
0 testdir/subdir1/subsubdir1/subsubsubdir1/testfile2
0 testdir/subdir1/subsubdir1/subsubsubdir1/testfile1
4 testdir/subdir1/subsubdir1/subsubsubdir1
0 testdir/subdir1/subsubdir1/link2tosubdir1
8 testdir/subdir1/subsubdir1
4 testdir/subdir1/subsubdir2
16 testdir/subdir1
0 testdir/linktosubdir1
```

```
24 testdir
$ ./spl_du1 testdir
4 testdir/subdir2
0 testdir/subdir1/subsubdir1/subsubsubdir1/testfile2
0 testdir/subdir1/subsubdir1/subsubsubdir1/testfile1
4 testdir/subdir1/subsubdir1/subsubsubdir1
0 testdir/subdir1/subsubdir1/link2tosubdir1 (symbolic link)
0 testdir/subdir1/subsubdir1/testfile1.lnk
8 testdir/subdir1/subsubdir1
4 testdir/subdir1/subsubdir2
16 testdir/subdir1
0 testdir/linktosubdir1 (symbolic link)
24 testdir
```

However, this doesn't mean it's correct. If we test it on a few more directories, we'll discover a problem. I constructed another test directory, named *testdir2*, containing a file named *d1* with 560 1K blocks:

```
$ ls -s testdir2/d1
560
```

I then created a few hard links to *d1*

```
$ cd testdir2; ln d1 d2 ; ln d1 d3
$ cd ..
```

and ran du -a on *testdir*:

```
$ du -a testdir2
560 testdir2/d1
564 testdir2
```

Not only do we not see *d2* and *d3* in the output, but the total usage doesn't include them, as it shouldn't, because they're just different names for the single file *d1*. Running our version of the command produces different output:

```
$ ./spl_du1 testdir2
560 testdir2/d1
560 testdir2/d3
560 testdir2/d2
1684 testdir2
```

This program, as it stands, counts files with multiple links as many times as they have links. If a file has two names in two different subdirectories of our root directory, each will be counted. Since the purpose of this command is to report the amount of disk space a directory tree uses, it isn't useful in its current state; we need to modify it.

How can we fix it? Since every directory entry has the number of the inode for the file, we could just check each time whether we've already added the disk usage for the actual file by saving the inode number each time we process a file. The stat structure contains the inode number, st_ino, of the file and the link count, st_nlink. If the link count is only 1, we know there are no other links, but if it's greater than 1, there might be. Unfortunately, this idea won't work; I'll explain why.

On any single filesystem, every file is uniquely identified by its st_ino value. If we allow the program to cross mount points, then the inode number does not uniquely identify files, because there can be files with the same inode number in two different filesystems. The program might think it's already added disk usage for the current file when it hasn't, because the inode number refers to a file on a different device. We need to know the device as well. The stat structure contains the device ID, st_dev, of the filesystem in which the file is located, and we need to make it part of a file's unique identification.

Suppose that we create a set named visited that stores the (st_ino, st_dev) pairs of all nondirectory files that the tree walk has visited that have two or more links. Initially, visited would be empty. Each time that the tree walk visits a new entry, it would check whether it's a nondirectory file with a link count greater than 1. If so, it would check whether the entry is already in visited. If it is, it would skip the entry, and if not, it would process it and add the entry to the set. This modification would prevent double-counting files with more than one name. The only reason for checking whether the link count is greater than 1 is to save space in the set and save time because there's no benefit to storing entries in the set if they have only one name.

There are several ways to implement the visited set, but the two most efficient would be either a hash table or a search tree. The hash table can have close to $O(1)$ performance for each search and/or insertion if it has a good hash function and enough storage capacity. A balanced search tree would require $O(n \log n)$ steps to search a set of size n. I decided to use a hash table. Let's name a second version of the program with these corrections as *spl_du2.c*.

I don't include the implementation of the hash table here; the file *hash.c* is available in the source code distribution for the book. The header file *hash.h* exposes the following functions from *hash.c* that the program will call:

```
typedef unsigned long long hash_val;
BOOL insert_hash (hash_table* h, hash_val val);
BOOL is_in_hash  (hash_table  h, hash_val val);
void init_hash   (hash_table* h, int initial_size);
void free_hash   (hash_table* h);
```

Although the definition of the hash_table is also in *hash.h*, we don't need to see it to use these functions. However, for the same reason that total_usage[] needs to be in file scope, the hash table representing the visited set must also be in file scope in our program:

```
static uintmax_t  total_usage[MAXDEPTH];  /* Total disk usage for level n  */
static hash_table visited;                /* Set of inodes already visited */
```

The program needs to hash (st_ino, st_dev) pairs, but the functions is_in _hash() and insert_hash() expect a single number. Therefore, if the file _usage() function were to call is_in_hash() and insert_hash() directly, those functions would have to be modified so that they accepted both an inode number and a device ID as arguments.

Rather then designing them to accept two numbers, I took the approach of designing a more general hash table that could be used by other programs. Our program can encode the inode number and the device ID into a single unsigned long long int before calling these functions. We don't need a so-phisticated encoding algorithm to encode the inode number and the device ID. There are typically only a very small number of separate filesystems on a single computer, so multiplying the inode number by the device ID should be sufficient. We can always fine-tune the encoding at a later time. The fol-lowing two functions are essentially wrappers for the calls to the hash table functions:

```
/* was_visited(i, d) returns TRUE if the pair was already visited. */
BOOL was_visited(ino_t inode, dev_t dev)
{
    hash_val val = inode * dev;
    return is_in_hash(visited, val);
}


/* mark_visited(i, d) inserts (i, d) into the visited set and returns
   TRUE if successful and FALSE on an error. */
BOOL mark_visited(ino_t inode, dev_t dev)
{
    hash_val val = inode * dev;
    return insert_hash(&visited, val);
}
```

The revised file_usage() function follows, with the changed portions highlighted in bold:

file_usage() (revised)

```
int file_usage(const char *fpath, const struct stat *sb,
               int tflag, struct FTW *ftwbuf)
{
    static int prev_level = -1;
    int       cur_level;
    BOOL      already_visited = FALSE;
    uintmax_t cur_usage;

    cur_level = ftwbuf->level;
    if ( cur_level >= MAXDEPTH ) {
        fprintf(stderr, "Exceeded maximum depth.\n");
        return -1;
    }
```

```
❶ if ( prev_level == cur_level ) {
      if ( sb->st_nlink == 1 ) {
          cur_usage = sb->st_blocks/2;
          total_usage[cur_level] += cur_usage;
      }
      else {
          already_visited = was_visited(sb->st_ino, sb->st_dev);
          if ( !already_visited ) {
              cur_usage = sb->st_blocks/2;
              total_usage[cur_level] += cur_usage;
              if ( !mark_visited(sb->st_ino, sb->st_dev) )
                  fatal_error(-1, "Could not insert inode into hash table");
          }
      }
  }
❷ else if ( prev_level > cur_level ) {
      cur_usage = total_usage[prev_level] + sb->st_blocks/2;
      total_usage[cur_level] += cur_usage;
      total_usage[prev_level] = 0;
  }
❸ else {
      if ( sb->st_nlink == 1 || S_ISDIR(sb->st_mode) ) {
          cur_usage = sb->st_blocks/2;
          total_usage[cur_level] = cur_usage;
      }
      else {
          already_visited = was_visited(sb->st_ino, sb->st_dev);
          if ( !already_visited ) {
              cur_usage = sb->st_blocks/2;
              total_usage[cur_level] = cur_usage;
              if ( !mark_visited(sb->st_ino, sb->st_dev) )
                  fatal_error(-1, "Could not insert inode into hash table");
          }
      }
  }
  if ( !already_visited ) {
      printf("%ju\t%s", cur_usage, fpath);
      if ( tflag == FTW_DNR )      printf(" (unreadable directory)\n");
      else if ( tflag == FTW_SL ) printf(" (symbolic link)\n");
      else if ( tflag == FTW_SLN ) printf(" (broken symbolic link)\n");
      else if ( tflag == FTW_NS ) printf("stat() failed\n");
      printf("\n");
  }
  prev_level = cur_level;
  return 0;
}
```

Notice that we don't check for whether the entry is a directory when prev_level == current_level ❶. Because of the nature of the postorder traversal by nftw(), it cannot be a directory in this case, and therefore, we just check how many links it has. When prev_level > current_level ❷, it must be a directory and we don't need to check the link count. When prev_level < current_level ❸, it might be a directory with no children or an ordinary file. In this case, we check the link count only if it isn't a directory.

The only changes to the main program are the initialization of the hash table and the freeing of the memory it uses. The entire main() function is displayed in the following listing, with the changes highlighted in bold. The #include directives and the feature test macro (#define _XOPEN_SOURCE 700) are omitted:

spl_du2.c
main()

```
int main(int argc, char *argv[])
{
    int flags = FTW_DEPTH | FTW_PHYS /*| FTW_MOUNT */;
    int status;
    int i = 1;

    if ( argc < 2 ) {
        init_hash(&visited, INITIAL_HASH_SIZE);
        memset(total_usage, 0, MAXDEPTH*sizeof(uintmax_t));
        if ( 0 != (status = nftw(".", file_usage, 20, flags)) )
            fatal_error(status, "nftw");
        free_hash(&visited);
    }
    else
        while ( i < argc ) {
            init_hash(&visited, INITIAL_HASH_SIZE);
            memset(total_usage, 0, MAXDEPTH*sizeof(uintmax_t));
            if ( 0 != (status = nftw(argv[i], file_usage, MAXDEPTH, flags)) )
                fatal_error(status, "nftw");
            else {
                i++;
                free_hash(&visited);
            }
        }
    exit(EXIT_SUCCESS);
}
```

The INITIAL_HASH_SIZE is a macro value. The hash table insertion function is designed to resize the hash table if it gets more than half full, so the choice of initial size is not that important because it will grow as needed. I made it 1024 for this version of the program.

Also, in this version, the FTW_MOUNT flag is commented out. If we want to see whether the program correctly displays disk usage of files with the same inode number but on different filesystems, we have to allow the program to cross mount points. If you uncomment this flag and build the executable, it will cross mount points, allowing you to see what happens when files have the same inode but are on different devices.

We can build the executable and run it on a few directories that contain files with multiple links. For example, we can run it on the *testdir2* directory that started this discussion:

```
$ ./spl_du2 testdir2
560 testdir2/d2
564 testdir2
```

Only one of the files is counted. If you experiment with this revised version of the program, you'll see that it does not overcount any files with multiple names.

We could add enhancements to this program, such as options to limit the depth of the traversal, turn on and off crossing mount points, or change the display units, but these are not critical. We've achieved the goal of this exercise: to explore how to use the nftw() function and to implement a useful command. These enhancements are left as exercises.

The fts Tree Traversal Functions

The SEE ALSO section of nftw()'s man page mentions the fts functions. Before we leave the topic of tree traversals, let's take a brief look at them.

Unlike nftw(), fts is not a single function but an integrated set of related functions, in much the same way that opendir(), readdir(), rewinddir(), and closedir() are interrelated functions. The fts functions have their origin in the BSD distributions, starting with 4.4BSD, and they aren't POSIX functions. They are available in most Linux distributions though. The fts set of functions includes:

```
FTS     *fts_open(char * const *path_argv, int options,
                  int (*compar)(const FTSENT **, const FTSENT **));
FTSENT *fts_read(FTS *ftsp);
FTSENT *fts_children(FTS *ftsp, int instr);
int     fts_set(FTS *ftsp, FTSENT *f, int instr);
int     fts_close(FTS *ftsp);
```

Just as opendir() creates a directory stream object and returns a pointer to it, fts_open() creates a *handle* that is used by the other functions. A *handle* is a pointer to an FTS structure. Unlike nftw(), which does not allow the application to control the order in which files are searched other than whether it is preorder or postorder, fts allows the calling program to specify this order.

The fact that these functions are not part of the POSIX standard implies that any application that uses them may not be portable. On the other hand, we can do much more with the fts functions than we could with nftw() because these functions are much more flexible and have hooks for program data so that we don't need file-scoped or static variables to store the program's larger state information.

I'll explain the basics of these functions and give a small example to illustrate how they're used. This can be a powerful tool when the program you're writing does not need to be portable. We'll start with a summary of the fts functions:

- We call fts_open() first. We pass it an array of strings representing the roots of trees that we want to traverse, an integer that encodes various options, and a comparison function to be used for determining the order in which files are visited. It returns a handle for an FTS structure.

- The fts_read() function visits a file each time it's called. The handle returned by fts_open() is passed to fts_read(). Each file in the tree is visited just once, except for directories, which are visited before and after their children. fts_read() returns a pointer to an FTSENT structure for each file that it visits. The FTSENT structures have a member that allows them to be linked together.

- If the currently visited file is a directory, then a call to the fts_children() function returns a pointer to a linked list of FTSENT structures representing all of the children in this directory.

- The fts_set() function allows a file to be reprocessed after it has been returned by a call to fts_read().

- The fts_close() function is the cleanup function. After processing the entire directory tree passed to fts_open(), we call fts_close() to close the stream and clean up resources.

To use these functions, we need to know the contents of the FTSENT structure, because that's what characterizes each visited file. That structure is defined in the header file */usr/include/fts.h*:

```
typedef struct _ftsent {
    unsigned short fts_info;      /* Flags for FTSENT structure */
    char           *fts_accpath;  /* Access path               */
    char           *fts_path;     /* Root path                 */
    short          fts_pathlen;   /* strlen(fts_path)          */
    char           *fts_name;     /* Filename                  */
    short          fts_namelen;   /* strlen(fts_name)          */
    short          fts_level;     /* Depth (-1 to N)           */
    int            fts_errno;     /* File errno                */
    long           fts_number;    /* Local numeric value       */
    void           *fts_pointer;  /* Local address value       */
    struct ftsent *fts_parent;    /* Parent directory          */
    struct ftsent *fts_link;      /* Next file structure       */
    struct ftsent *fts_cycle;     /* Cycle structure           */
    struct stat    *fts_statp;    /* stat(2) information        */
} FTSENT;
```

Although this structure has many members, for relatively simple applications, we won't use many of them. The most important members are as follows:

fts_info An integer that encodes information about the type of object represented by this structure.

fts_accpath A path for accessing the file from the current directory.

fts_path The path for the file relative to the root of the traversal. This path contains the path specified to fts_open() as a prefix.

fts_name The filename.

fts_errno Upon return of an FTSENT structure from the fts_children() or fts_read() functions, with its fts_info field set to FTS_DNR, FTS_ERR or FTS_NS, the fts_errno field contains the value of the external variable errno specifying the cause of the error. Otherwise, the contents of the fts_errno field are undefined.

fts_number Provided for the use of the application program and not modified by the fts functions. It is initialized to 0.

fts_pointer Provided for the use of the application program and not modified by the fts functions. It is initialized to NULL.

fts_parent A pointer to the FTSENT structure referencing the file in the hierarchy immediately above the current file, that is, the directory of which this file is a member. A parent structure for the initial entry point is provided as well; however, only the fts_level, fts_number, and fts_pointer fields are guaranteed to be initialized.

fts_link Upon return from the fts_children() function, the fts_link field points to the next structure in the NULL-terminated linked list of directory members. Otherwise, the contents of the fts_link field are undefined.

fts_statp A pointer to a stat structure for the file.

The fts_info field provides information about the visited file encoded into an integer value. It contains exactly one of the following values:

FTS_D A directory being visited in preorder.

FTS_DC A directory that causes a cycle in the tree. The fts_cycle field of the FTSENT structure will be filled in as well.

FTS_DEFAULT Any FTSENT structure that represents a file type not explicitly described by one of the other fts_info values.

FTS_DNR A directory that cannot be read. This is an error return, and the fts_errno field will be set to indicate what caused the error.

FTS_DOT A dot file that wasn't specified as a filename to fts_open().

FTS_DP A directory being visited in postorder.

FTS_ERR This is an error return, and the fts_errno field is set to indicate what caused the error.

FTS_F A regular file.

FTS_NS A file for which no stat information was available. The contents of the fts_statp field are undefined. The fts_errno field will be set to indicate what caused this error.

FTS_NSOK A file for which no stat information was requested. The contents of the fts_statp field are undefined.

FTS_SL A symbolic link.

FTS_SLNONE A symbolic link with a nonexistent target. The contents of the fts_statp field reference the file characteristic information for the symbolic link itself.

Let's compare this family of functions to the nftw() function:

- The fts_info member has information similar to that found in the tflag argument to the (*fn) function by nftw(). It characterizes the visited file.

- Unlike the nftw() function, the structure representing the current file, FTSENT, has hooks for the application to use. Specifically, fts_number and fts_pointer can be used for application-specific data, making it possible to change state and data across different invocations of the fts_read() function.

- The fts_parent field provides a means to access the parent node, which ntfw() does not do.

- The FTSENT structure has stat information for the returned file through its fts_statp member, provided no error occurred.

- The name of the file is in the fts_name member. The fts_path member has the pathname of the file relative to the root of the tree walk.

Let's look at a small example that illustrates how we can use the fts_read() function in a tree walk. The program, which we'll name *fts_demo.c*, displays the sizes, in bytes, of all files in the directory's tree, and after processing all files, it prints out the name and size of the largest file that it found. The comparison function that it passes to the fts_open() function compares two entries by name using the current locale's collating sequence:

```
#include "common_hdrs.h"
#include <fts.h>

int namecmp(const FTSENT **s1, const FTSENT **s2)
{
    return (strcoll((*s1)->fts_name, (*s2)->fts_name));
}
```

The strcoll() function was introduced in Chapter 3. It compares two strings based on the current locale.

The main program processes the directory whose pathname is given as the program's first argument. In addition to printing a file's size, it indents each visited file's pathname by a number of spaces proportional to its level in the tree to make it easy to see the nested directory structure (see Listing 7-9).

fts_demo.c
main()

```
int main(int argc, char *argv[])
{
    FTS    *tree;
    FTSENT *file;
    char    errmssge[128];
    char    largest_file[PATH_MAX];
    size_t  max = 0, size;

    if ( argc < 2 ) {
        sprintf(errmssge, "%s directory\n", argv[0]);
        usage_error(errmssge);
    }
❶  char *dir[] = { argv[1], NULL };
    if ( NULL == (tree = fts_open(dir, FTS_PHYSICAL , namecmp)) )
        fatal_error(errno, "fts_open");

    errno = 0;
    while ( (file = fts_read(tree)) ) {
❷      switch ( file->fts_info ) {
        case FTS_DNR:  /* Cannot read directory */
            fprintf(stderr, "Could not read %s\n", file->fts_path);
            continue;
        case FTS_ERR:  /* Miscellaneous error   */
            fprintf(stderr, "Error on %s\n", file->fts_path);
            continue;
        case FTS_NS:  /* stat() error: Continue to next files. */
            fprintf(stderr, "Could not stat %s\n", file->fts_path);
            continue;
        case FTS_DP:  /* Ignore postorder visit to directory.  */
            continue;
        }
        /* Check if this is largest file so far. */
❸      size = file->fts_statp->st_size;
        if ( max < size ) {
            max = size;
            strncpy(largest_file, file->fts_path, 1+file->fts_pathlen);
        }
❹      printf("%12ld\t%*s%s\n", size,
                4*(file->fts_level), " ", file->fts_path);
        errno = 0; /* Set errno to 0 again before next fts_read(). */
    }
    if ( errno != 0 )
        fatal_error(errno, "fts_read");
```

```
        printf("Largest file is %s with size %lu\n", largest_file, max);
        if ( fts_close(tree) < 0 )
            fatal_error(errno, "fts_close");
        return(EXIT_SUCCESS);
}
```

Listing 7-9: A program that shows how to use the fts functions

The program starts by passing a NULL-terminated array of directory pathnames ❶ and the comparison function to the fts_open() function. In this
program the array has just a single pathname, argv[1], but in general, it can
have more. If the open succeeds, the program repeatedly calls fts_read().
The order in which files are visited is determined by the comparison function. For each file, it uses the fts_info field ❷ to determine if there were errors processing the file, and if not, it gets its size from the fts_statp pointer
to the file's stat structure ❸. If the file is larger than the current largest file,
it updates the variables that record this information. Since the fts_level
field is the level of the file relative to the root of the tree, it indents the filename by 4*fts_level spaces to emphasize its depth in the tree.

The printf() ❹ function's format string, "%12ld\t%*s%s\n", has something
new. The specifier %*s expects a number followed by a string. The number is
the minimum width of the field in which to print the string. Therefore

```
printf("%*s%s\n", 4*(file->fts_level), " ", file->fts_path);
```

prints a space in a field of width 4*(file->fts_level) followed by the string
stored in file->fts_path.

I built the executable (fts_demo) and ran it on the test directory to see
how it behaves:

```
$ ./fts_demo testdir
      4096  testdir
         7      testdir/linktosubdir1
     18893      testdir/newfile
      4096      testdir/subdir1
      4096          testdir/subdir1/subsubdir1
        13              testdir/subdir1/subsubdir1/link2tosubdir1
      4096              testdir/subdir1/subsubdir1/subsubsubdir1
         0                  testdir/subdir1/subsubdir1/subsubsubdir1/testf...
         0              testdir/subdir1/subsubdir1/testfile1.lnk
      4096          testdir/subdir1/subsubdir2
      4096      testdir/subdir2
Largest file: testdir/newfile; Size=18893
```

Although the program is a simple one, you can see the potential that these fts
functions have for implementing a variety of applications that need to walk
a directory tree. For example, we could implement du with it, or a recursive
ls, or even the more complex find command. In fact, the GNU versions of
commands such as grep, chmod, chown, rm, cp, and chgrp are implemented with
the fts functions to perform their recursive tree traversals. On BSD systems,
the find command is based on the fts functions.

The pwd Command

The `pwd` command prints the absolute pathname of the current working directory. Implementing it will expand our understanding of the structure of directories, but will also present a different set of challenges than we've encountered so far. To see this, we'll work through a small exercise.

An Exercise in Constructing a Directory Tree

We'll try to reconstruct a portion of a file hierarchy from the inode numbers in a set of directories. Let's suppose that we're given a directory named *scratch* that contains subdirectories and ordinary files and that the subdirectories also have subdirectories, and so on. Each of these subdirectories may have regular files as well. Let's assume for this example that all files are in the same filesystem, so that inode numbers uniquely identify files. The command

```
$ ls -1iaR scratch
```

can be used to recursively display the inode numbers and filenames of all files in the directory tree rooted at *scratch*, including the entries for dot and dot-dot in each directory. These dot and dot-dot entries play a critical role in navigating the directories. Suppose that entering `ls -1iaR scratch` produces the following output, in which the actual directory names have been omitted:

```
725 .
449 ..
753 README
727 work
728 misc

731 .
728 ..
733 TODOLIST
732 tests

727 .
725 ..
729 prog1
730 info
733 TODO

728 .
725 ..
729 docs
731 testing
748 prog2
```

The contents of these directories have enough information to reconstruct the file tree rooted at *scratch*. First, we'll draw a tree whose nodes are just inode numbers, after which we can use the directory listing to assign file-names to those numbers. For example, from the last five lines of output, we see that node 728 has three children, 731, 748, and 729, and that its parent is 725, so our first subtree looks like this:

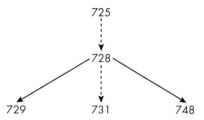

Similarly, the preceding five lines show that node 727 has children with inode numbers 729, 739, and 733, and that its parent is 725, which we can use to construct the combined subtree so far:

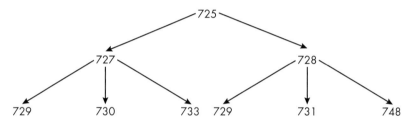

The lines above the last group show that the inode with number 731 has two child nodes with numbers 732 and 733 and that its parent is 728. This is a subtree of the first tree we constructed. We'll attach this subtree to our growing tree, and simultaneously, since inode 725 has children with numbers 728, 729, and 753, we'll create the new node, 753, and attach it as a child of node 725:

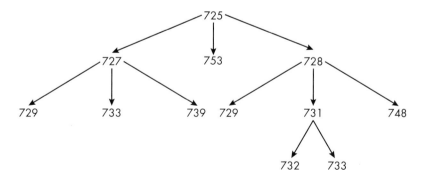

Looking at the resulting tree, we see that two of the inodes, 729 and 733, have links in two different directories; as we replace inode numbers with filenames, we'll use the filenames for those inodes that are contained in the respective directories:

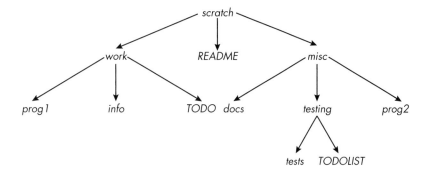

This exercise demonstrates that the parent entries in a given directory are the only means to obtain that directory's name and that the only way to do this when all files are in the same filesystem is to:

1. Save the inode number of the current directory, which is the one associated with the dot entry.

2. Find the inode number for the parent entry in the current directory, meaning the dot-dot entry.

3. Get the list of child inodes of the parent directory.

4. Find the inode number in this list that matches the inode number for dot in the current directory.

5. For the matching inode number, get the filename associated with it. This is the name of the current working directory.

In short, the parent directory entries in a directory play a vital role in the hierarchy, because they're essentially *backlinks*—they're the only practical way to know the name of the current directory and the only way to ascend the tree.

This strategy will not work in all cases because it doesn't account for the effect of mount points on this problem. When a part of this directory tree is in a different filesystem because one of the directories is a mount point, it isn't enough to use inode numbers alone. We need to use (*inode number, device ID*) pairs to represent files. In the preceding sequence of steps, each reference to an inode number must be replaced by an (*inode number, device ID*) pair. To make this convenient, we'll define a structure that represents such a pair:

```
typedef struct device_inode_pair {
    dev_t dev;
    ino_t ino;
} dev_ino;
```

All preceding references to inode numbers should now be thought of as references to elements of type dev_ino.

A Strategy for Implementing the pwd Command

Suppose our current working directory is *chap_dir_hierarchy*, which is located in the directory *demos*, which is in *lsp_book*, which is in *teaching*, which is in *snw*, which is in *home*, which is in the root directory, /. Then entering **pwd** will print the absolute pathname:

```
$ pwd
/home/snw/teaching/lsp_book/demos/chap_dir_hierarchy
```

Initially, pwd doesn't know where the working directory is with respect to the potentially very large directory tree; it doesn't have the path to it. From the preceding exercise it should be clear that to construct this path, it has to work upward, using the parent entries of each new directory as it ascends the tree.

In fact, there's a system call as well as a library function, both named getcwd(), that return the absolute pathname of the current working directory. If we wanted to, we could call either of them to solve this problem and we'd be finished; however, since the objective of this exercise is to learn how to climb the tree, that is not an option. Instead, we will try to write those functions from scratch.

The exercise we did gives us part of the strategy for implementing the pwd command. We find the name of the current directory using the steps we described on page 373, substituting dev_ino pairs for the inode numbers. We then step up to the parent directory and repeat these steps. We do this repeatedly until we've reached the root of the directory hierarchy. This strategy raises several questions:

- How can a program change its working directory to that of its parent?

- How can a program get the list of children of its parent directory?

- How can a program determine which directory entry in the parent matches the child representing the current directory?

- How can we tell when we've reached the root of the tree?

- How do we construct the string that stores the absolute pathname to the directory from right to left, since that's the order in which we'll discover the ancestor directories?

- Do we need to be concerned about the maximum length of a pathname? If so, what would we do if the pathname exceeded it?

To answer the first question, let's see what a man page search will give us:

```
$ apropos -s2,3 -a change directory
chdir (2)             - change working directory
chdir (3posix)        - change working directory
chroot (2)            - change root directory
fchdir (2)            - change working directory
fchdir (3posix)       - change working directory
--snip--
```

The chdir(2) and fchdir(2) functions share the same man page. The corresponding POSIX pages describe the POSIX requirements for these functions. The synopsis for them is:

```
#include <unistd.h>

int chdir(const char *path);
int fchdir(int fd);
```

The first function changes to the directory specified by the string path, whereas the second, fchdir(), changes to the directory specified by the file descriptor, fd. The second function requires opening the directory and obtaining its descriptor, whereas the first doesn't require this. As a system call, the second is faster, but for this program, speed is not an important factor. Both can fail for a variety of reasons, such as not having permission on the directory or encountering an I/O error. Although unlikely to fail in this case, we still need to error-check the return value. Therefore, changing the working directory to the parent is accomplished with:

```
errno = 0;
if ( -1 == chdir("..") )
    fatal_error(errno, "chdir");
```

To answer the second question, we can use any of the methods from earlier in this chapter to open a directory and retrieve its child entries. One choice is to use opendir() to open it and then repeatedly call readdir() to get its entries until we find the matching inode number. Another choice is to call scandir(), passing a filter function designed to select only the single entry whose (*inode number, device ID*) matches that of the current directory. Performance-wise, it's a toss-up: Repeated calls to readdir() may be faster in the case that we quickly find the match, but each call adds time, whereas the single call to scandir() may be a slower call, and we can't control which order it searches the directory. I'll choose to use repeated calls to readdir().

To determine which directory entry in the parent matches the child, before stepping up to the parent directory, the program can call stat() to get the inode number and device ID of ".", which is the entry for the current working directory, and store it into a dev_ino structure named dir_dev_ino. When it's changed the working directory to the parent directory using chdir("..") and it's searching through all of its entries, for each entry returned by readdir(), it would call lstat() on the d_name member of the dirent structure to retrieve the inode number and device ID of the entry, storing the pair into a dev_ino structure, say named this_dev_ino. If this_dev_ino and dir_dev_ino match, then the d_name in the dirent structure is the name of the directory. It's important that we use lstat() rather than stat(); the latter reports on the targets of symbolic links and not the links themselves and will lead to errors.

To make the code more readable, I'll define a Boolean-valued function that compares dev_ino structures:

```
BOOL are_samefile(dev_ino f1, dev_ino f2)
{
    return (f1.ino == f2.ino && f1.dev == f2.dev);
}
```

I'll also define a function, which I've named get_dev_ino(), that, given a file-name relative to the current directory, gets its inode number and device ID and stores them in a dev_ino structure:

```
void get_dev_ino(const char *fname, dev_ino *dev_inode)
{
    struct stat sb;
    errno = 0;
    if ( -1 == lstat( fname , &sb ) )
        fatal_error(errno, "Cannot stat ");
    dev_inode->dev = sb.st_dev;
    dev_inode->ino = sb.st_ino;
}
```

Assume that dir_dev_ino is the dev_ino pair for the directory whose name we're trying to find and that the program has changed directory into the parent directory. The code, missing its error checking, would then be roughly:

```
dir_ptr = opendir("."); /* Open parent directory. */
while ( (direntp = readdir(dir_ptr)) != NULL ) {
    get_dev_ino(direntp->d_name, &this_entry);
    if ( are_samefile(this_entry, dir_dev_ino) ) {
        // OMITTED: Found the matching entry
    else
        // OMITTED: Keep searching.
}
```

The next question is how we'll know when we've reached the root. There are two ways. One is to call stat("/", &sb) at the start of the program to get a stat structure for the root, extract its inode number and device ID, and store them. Each time we're about to change directory to the parent, we'd compare the inode and device against that of the root. If they match, we know we're at the root. A second method is to use the fact that in the root directory, and only in the root directory, the dot and dot-dot entries point to the same inode. Each time we're about to change directory to the parent, we'd check whether the parent and the current directory have the same dev_ino pair. If so, we'd stop; otherwise, we'd continue. I'll use the first method because it's simpler.

The last question is how to build the pathname. Because we're ascending the tree rather than descending it, we're discovering the names of the directories in the pathname in a right-to-left order. We can't just append the most recently discovered directory name to the pathname because the path would be backward if we did. Instead we have to *prepend* it to the existing partially constructed pathname. Figure 7-9 visualizes the steps to prepend the first directory name to an initially empty buffer of size PATH_MAX bytes storing the pathname. We've used the PATH_MAX macro before; it's the largest allowable size of a pathname on the system, typically 4096 bytes.

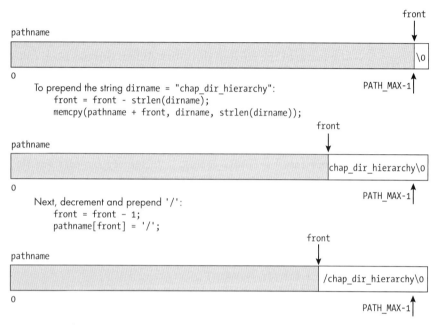

Figure 7-9: The steps to build the pathname in a right-to-left direction by prepending each new parent directory

The first step is to write a NULL byte to the rightmost position in the buffer in pathname[PATH_MAX-1]. At all times, front will be the index of the leftmost character of the partially built pathname. Initially, front = PATH_MAX-1. For each name that we want to prepend, we get the string length of the name

```
len = strlen{dirname};
```

and subtract it from front so that front points to where this name will start in the buffer. We then copy the directory name to this position. The C memcpy() function can copy it efficiently. It won't add a NULL byte to the end, but we already put it there. Lastly, we prepend a / to the string, decrementing front. This process is then repeated until the entire pathname has been constructed.

The only problem that this last algorithm does not consider is what will happen if the pathname is larger than the buffer. This can happen if directory names are very long and the working directory is very deep in the directory tree.

The easiest acceptable solution is to write a message that the full path was not constructed and replace the initial part of the pathname by a sequence of ellipsis characters. If we name the executable spl_pwd, with our previous example, the output would be something like:

```
$ ./spl_pwd
Error: File name too long
..../teaching/lsp_book/demos/chap_dir_hierarchy
```

It's not that hard to detect when this error would occur. In the listings that follow, which we're ready to assemble, we'll call out the code that handles it.

The first function is the one that searches in the parent directory to find the name of the current directory. When this has been called, the working directory is already the parent:

get_filename()
```c
char *get_filename(dev_ino child_entry)
{
    DIR            *dir_ptr;       /* The directory to be opened        */
    struct dirent  *direntp;      /* The dirent for each entry         */
    dev_ino        this_entry;    /* The dev_ino pair for the entry    */
    char           errmssge[256]; /* To store error messages           */
    int            len;           /* Length of a string                */
    char           *fname;        /* malloc-ed name to return to caller */

    errno = 0;
    dir_ptr = opendir(".");
    if ( dir_ptr == NULL )
        fatal_error(errno, "opendir");
    /* Search through the current working directory for a file whose
       inode number and device ID are that of entry. */
    while ( (direntp = readdir dir_ptr)) != NULL ) {
        errno = 0;
        get_dev_ino(direntp->d_name, &this_entry);
        /* If this entry matches, we found the file. */
        if ( are_samefile(this_entry, child_entry) ) {
            /* Copy the entry's d_name into a malloc-ed fname. */
            len = strlen(direntp->d_name);
            errno = 0;
            if ( NULL == (fname = malloc(len+1)) )
                fatal_error(errno, "malloc");
            strncpy(fname, direntp->d_name, len);
            closedir(dir_ptr);
            return fname;
        }
    }
    /* If we reach here, there is no matching entry in this directory. */
    sprintf(errmssge, "i-number %lu not found.\n", child_entry.ino);
    error_mssge(-1, errmssge);
    return NULL;
}
```

A call to get_filename(dir_dev_ino) in the parent directory of the current working directory returns the name of the current working directory by searching through the entries in the parent using the algorithm we described. If, for some reason, no entry is found that matches, an error is reported and a NULL pointer is returned instead.

Because the function is returning a pointer to the directory name, that name can't be on the stack. Instead, the function allocates memory for the name on the heap using malloc(). It has to be freed by the caller when it is no longer needed.

Listing 7-10 is of the main program. To save space, prototypes for the preceding functions replace their code. The complete program is in the book's source code distribution.

---

spl_pwd.c
```
#include "common_hdrs.h"
#include <sys/stat.h>
#include <dirent.h>

/* The following two functions are in preceding listings: */
void get_dev_ino(const char *fname, dev_ino *dev_inode);
char *get_filename(dev_ino child_entry);

int main(int argc, char *argv[])
{
    dev_ino     current;
    dev_ino     root;
    char        pathname[PATH_MAX];
    char        *dirname;
    ssize_t     front = PATH_MAX-1;
    ssize_t     namelength;

    get_dev_ino("/", &root);
    get_dev_ino(".", &current);
    if ( are_samefile(current, root) ) {
        printf("/\n");
        return 0;
    }
    pathname[PATH_MAX-1] = '\0';
    while ( !are_samefile(current, root) ) {
        /* Go up to parent directory. */
        chdir("..");
        /* Search in the parent directory for the fileame of this_inode. */
        if ( NULL == (dirname = get_filename(current)) )
            fatal_error(-1,
                        "Could not find entry in .. for current directory.");
        /* If successful, write this name to the left of the current path. */
        namelength = strlen(dirname);

        /* Check if the new path is too long. If so, fill with dots instead
           and report the error. */
```

```
❶ if ( front - namelength <= 0 ) {
      memset(&(pathname[0]), '.', front);
      front = 0;
      error_mssge(ENAMETOOLONG, "Error");
      break;
    }
    else {
      front = front - namelength;
      memcpy(pathname+front, dirname, namelength);
    }
    /* Free the memory allocated by get_filename() for this string. */
    free(dirname);
    front--;
    pathname[front] = '/';
    get_dev_ino(".", &current); /* To start next level */
  }
  printf("%s\n", &(pathname[front]));
  return 0;
}
```

Listing 7-10: A program that displays the absolute pathname of the current working directory

Just before prepending the next component of the pathname, the program checks ❶ whether the buffer would overflow if it did. If so, instead of prepending the component, it puts a string of dots there instead to indicate that something's missing. It also prints an error message.

We'll build the executable, naming it spl_pwd, and run it and pwd in the same directory. I'll pick one whose path crosses two mount points:

```
$ ./spl_pwd
/data/research_resources/physics/articles/more_articles/quantumstuff
$ pwd
/data/research_resources/physics/articles/more_articles/quantumstuff
```

The *more_articles* directory is the mount point for */dev/sdd4*, and *data* is the mount point for */dev/sdb4*

```
$ df --output=source,target . /data
Filesystem    Mounted on
/dev/sdd4     /data/research_resources/physics/articles/more_articles
/dev/sdb4     /data
```

which implies that the program crossed both mount points on its way up the tree.

The actual pwd command is usually implemented in a more complex way than the one we developed here. The implementations vary from one distribution to another. We could have used the getcwd() function to do most of the work. The GNU/Linux implementation avoids calling getcwd() because that function fails for pathnames that exceed PATH_MAX bytes, and their version is designed to be more robust. Their version handles pathnames of unlimited length. Our version fails if it doesn't have permission to open a directory, whereas the GNU version displays a more useful diagnostic. Finally, the GNU version will fall back to reading the PWD environment variable if things go awry, and we didn't consider that option.

Summary

The structure of a directory file in Unix is quite simple. A directory is just a sequence of entries, called links, of the form (*inode number, filename*), among which are two entries present even in empty directories: ".", called *dot*, and "..", called *dot-dot*, which refer, respectively, to the directory itself and to the parent directory. These two entries provide the means to connect the directories and files into a tree-like structure called the directory hierarchy.

There are a few different methods of processing the contents of directories. One approach uses an API that requires opening a directory using opendir(); getting a directory stream as a result; using successive calls to readdir() to read the entries in the directory, which are delivered in sequence; and closing the stream with closedir(). This API also contains a few other useful functions for saving a position in the directory stream (telldir()), returning to a saved position (seekdir()), and starting all over from the beginning (rewinddir()).

Another method is to use the scandir() function, which does not require the directory to be opened and which collects all of its entries into an array that can be accessed after the call returns. This option gives us the ability to filter the entries and also to order them by passing it a filtering function and/or a comparison function. We developed a few different programs for listing directory contents in the chapter to demonstrate how both of these methods could be used.

The directory hierarchy is a single tree-like structure whose nodes are directories and files. Even though it isn't technically a tree, it's convenient to call it one. Distinct filesystems can be attached to this single tree by a process called mounting. In mounting, the root of the filesystem to be mounted is attached to an existing directory in the tree, called its mount point. Mounting allows different types of filesystems to be a part of a single hierarchy.

There are many different ways to *walk* through a directory tree, such as a depth-first traversal and a breadth-first traversal. One can do preorder or postorder processing while walking the tree. The nftw() function allows us to walk a tree in various ways, as does the fts set of functions. The former is a POSIX standardized tree walk function whereas the latter is a BSD-derived set of functions that may not be present on all systems. These functions can be used to implement a wide range of directory tree tools, such as the find command and many others.

In this chapter, we showed how to walk a directory tree using recursive algorithms based on the readdir() and the scandir() functions. We also implemented a simple version of the du command based on the nftw() function and demonstrated with smaller programs how to use some of the fts functions. Lastly, we solved a different problem, that of walking up the tree, to implement the pwd command.

Exercises

1. Modify the *spl_ls1.c* program so that it does not display the . and .. entries and sorts the entries in the collating order of the current locale. You'll need an array to solve this problem.

2. Modify the *spl_ls1.c* program so that it omits the . and .. entries and sorts the entries by their times of last modification, with the more recent files preceding the less recent ones.

3. In "A Simple ls Program" on page 321, we purposely gave the `listdir()` function a `flags` parameter that it didn't need so that it was extensible. With that in mind, write a version of `ls` that accepts one or more of the following options:

   ```
   -l  # Display a listing for each file similar to the real ls.
   -F  # Add one of the characters */=>@| to the end of the file
        to indicate its type.
   -g  # Display each entry's group.
   ```

4. The filter function passed as the third argument to `scandir()` is used to select which entries are copied into the returned array of directory entries. Can it be used to limit those entries to the ones whose filenames match a pattern, such as a fileglob? Read the man page for `fnmatch()`.

   Try to use this strategy to implement a command `findmatches` that can recursively find all files in a directory tree whose names match the fileglob specified on the command line as follows:

   ```
   $ ./findmatches fileglob directory_name
   ```

   Remember that the filter function has no hooks, so you'll need to use globally scoped variables that it can access. An alternative solution would not pass a filter to `scandir()`. You could try that also. In either case, implement only the standard fileglobs, not any extensions.

5. Exercise 4 asks you to use `scandir()`. Solve this same problem using the `fts` set of functions instead.

6. Write a version of `spl_du` based on a recursive algorithm using `scandir()`.

7. Write a version of `spl_du` with an option `-dmaxlevel` that will not process any files whose level in the tree is greater than *maxlevel*.

8. The `find` command is a very powerful command. Its man page shows how many different ways it can be used. Write a limited version of `find` named `findlinks` that when run as

   ```
   $ ./findlinks dirpath pathname
   ```

   searches in the directory tree rooted at *dirpath* for all filenames that are links to the same file as *pathname* and prints out their pathnames relative to *dirpath*.

8

INTRODUCTION TO SIGNALS

In the past few chapters, we wrote programs to implement various commands as a way to learn different parts of the Unix/Linux API. Those were relatively short-running programs that had no interaction with users or other programs. Many programs don't behave that way. For example, some must run until a particular event takes place, and others run for a long time and need to respond to events that can happen any time while they're running. Programs such as text editors, games, and servers of various kinds fall into this category. In these types of programs, segments of code are executed only as a result of some external event, such as a user's keypress. Such programs must be designed to deal with signals, and since they're now on our programming horizon, this is a good time to cover them.

This chapter differs from the previous few because, rather than developing programs to implement existing commands, it primarily presents and explores a core concept in much the same way that Chapter 2 did. In particular, it introduces and discusses signals in Unix, including what they are and how, when, and why they're created and sent to processes. It explains how a process can control when signals are delivered to it and how it can respond when it does receive signals. In the course of presenting these ideas, it introduces the basic system calls and commands related to signals. To make all of this more concrete, we'll work through the development of a few simple programs that demonstrate how we can use these system calls in our programs. There is much more to signals than we discuss in this chapter, which covers just the basics.

The Role of Signals

Signals serve the same purpose in Unix as they do in the outside world; they're a form of notification about some event or condition of importance that's sent to a recipient. In the outside world, signals can be visual, such as the change in color of a traffic light at an intersection; they can be audible, such as the sounding of an alarm clock or smoke alarm; and they can even be mechanical, such as the vibration of a mobile phone. In Unix systems, signals are essentially software interrupts; they're empty messages delivered to a process that interrupt its normal instruction cycle. They're usually sent to a process to report exceptional situations, such as references to invalid memory addresses or a terminal being disconnected.

Many signals are like hardware interrupts in that they can occur at any time, independent of what a process is doing when they arrive. The kernel is almost always the source of the signal. Sometimes, under certain conditions, one process can send a signal to another, and it's even possible for a process to send a signal to itself, in which case it's delivered to that process immediately.

Examples of events that cause signals to be sent to a process include a user entering CTRL-C in the terminal of the process or resizing the terminal window in which the process is running. These can happen at any time with respect to the process's execution, and therefore we call them *asynchronous* signals. In contrast, when a process performs an arithmetic instruction that results in a divide-by-zero error, it will also be sent a signal, but this signal will always arrive whenever the process executes that same sequence of instructions. Because the delivery of the signal to the process always happens at the same time in its instruction sequence, we call this type of signal a *synchronous* signal.

Let's make this a bit more concrete. Every signal in Unix has a unique integer value that has a (unique) symbolic name. These symbolic names are of the form SIG followed by short strings that are descriptive of the purpose of the signal. For example, SIGINT, commonly called the interrupt signal, is the signal usually sent to a process because the user entered the interrupt character on the keyboard while the process was running, and SIGWINCH is the signal sent to it when the window in which the process is running was re-sized. On most architectures, the numeric value of SIGINT is 2, but because the numeric value of a signal is not standardized, it may vary from one archi-tecture to another. Therefore, programs use only their symbolic names. You can see a list of their names in the signal man page in Section 7. Later in this chapter I'll present a list of them as well, with more details about them.

A signal has no other information associated with it besides its name. It's like an email message with a subject and no body, the subject being the numeric value of the signal. The value of a signal by itself provides its infor-mation; if a process receives a SIGWINCH signal, for example, it knows that the terminal window was resized. For this reason, the value of a signal is called the *signal type*.

A Signal Delivery Example

Let's start with an example that describes the complete sequence of steps that results in a signal being delivered to a process. Entering CTRL-C in a terminal while a process is running usually terminates the process. Let's see how that happens and how signals are involved in it. Figure 8-1 illustrates the sequence we now describe.

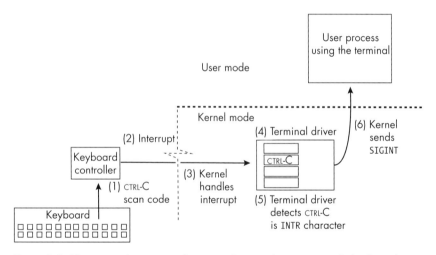

Figure 8-1: The steps taken to transform CTRL-C entered on a terminal's keyboard to a SIGINT delivered to processes using that terminal

1. In general, as you type on a keyboard, *scan codes*, which represent the entered key combinations, are generated by the circuits in the keyboard. When you enter CTRL-C, the scan code for that key com-bination is sent by the keyboard through the port to which it's con-nected to the keyboard controller.

2. When the controller receives the scan code, it causes a hardware interrupt. Every keystroke results in a hardware interrupt as you're typing, so that each individual character can be processed.

3. The interrupt causes the kernel to run briefly. The kernel determines with which terminal the keyboard is associated and transfers control to that terminal's terminal driver.

4. Inside the terminal driver, there's an array of character codes representing the terminal's special characters. The *special characters* are characters that cause actions other than simply being displayed, such as backspace and end-of-file. The terminal driver determines that the entered code matches the code in the entry in this array (at index VINTR) whose special meaning is *send the interrupt signal* (SIGINT).

5. The terminal driver checks whether a particular flag (isig) is set in the terminal's configuration settings. If isig is set, it calls the signal subsystem of the kernel to tell it to send the SIGINT signal to all processes whose control terminal is the one that received the CTRL-C.

6. The kernel sends the SIGINT signal to all of those processes.

7. Your process receives the signal. In general, unless a process has specified explicitly what it does when it receives this signal, which I'll explain later, it will terminate upon receiving it, because by default, processes are killed by SIGINT. Most programs do not take such explicit steps to handle SIGINT, and so they terminate abruptly. In this case, your program terminates.

All of these steps take place so fast that it's hard to believe that they all happen in that short amount of time, but they do!

Sources of Signals

The *source* of a signal is the component of the computer system in which the event or condition occurs, whether it is hardware or software. Regardless of the source of the event, it is only the kernel that sends signals to processes. The kernel is like a central signal processing station inside the machine. It sends a signal to one or more processes if it detects a condition requiring it or if a process issued a system call requesting that a signal be sent. Here is a summary of the different types of sources:

User   A user can type a key combination that causes the terminal driver to ask the kernel to send a signal. This is an asynchronous signal since it can arrive at a process at any time, independent of what the process might be doing. Examples include CTRL-C, CTRL-Z, and CTRL-S. The user can also issue the kill command, which can send a signal to one or more processes.

Kernel   Events such as the completion of an I/O operation, the loss of power, a network becoming disconnected, or a timer expiring are sources of signals that the kernel directly detects. The kernel sends the appropriate signal to the affected processes when these types of events occur. These are asynchronous signals because they are unpredictable and can arrive at any time with respect to a process's execution.

Hardware exceptions   A running process can cause an exception, an error condition, that is trapped by the hardware. These include floating-point exceptions, illegal instructions, addressing exceptions (such as attempts to access addresses outside of the process's address space), and other events generally caused by the process itself. The kernel runs as a result of these traps and sends a signal to the offending process. These are synchronous signals because if the process is run again, they will occur at the same point in the process's execution.

Other processes   Processes themselves can request the kernel to send signals to other processes to which it has permission to send signals. For ordinary user processes, these are any processes with the same real and effective user ID. A process can even issue a system call to have a signal sent to itself.

Signals, as a mechanism, were originally designed as a means for a process to be notified of errors and exceptional conditions [26]. They made their first appearance in the early Unix versions. The BSD distributions extended the use of signals so that processes could send signals to each other. However, the most common source of signals is still either the hardware or the kernel.

Signal Concepts

This section introduces the terminology and concepts associated with signals in the context of the sequence of events described in the example in the preceding section.

The Lifetime of a Signal

A signal has a lifetime that starts with some event or condition arising either in hardware or software and ends when it's delivered to the destination process. Some sources state that this causal event *generates* the signal. For example, the POSIX.1-2024 specification states that "a signal is said to be *generated* for (or sent to) a process or thread when the event that causes the signal first occurs."

From the kernel's point of view, a signal isn't generated until the kernel performs an action to create it. It isn't the occurrence of the event itself that generates the signal, but the action taken by the kernel. In Linux, when the kernel detects an event for which a signal should be sent to one or more processes or is requested by a process to send a signal to one or more processes, it updates a few data structures associated with each destination process to indicate that a new signal has been sent to that process. Among these data structures is a queue of signals that have been generated for, but not yet delivered to, that process. In Chapter 10, we'll examine these and other data structures associated with a process.

A process that's been sent a signal may not be executing at the time the signal was sent. For example, it might be waiting for an I/O operation to complete, or it may be ready to run but not currently running on a processor. Until it resumes execution and the signal is actually delivered to it, we say that the signal is *pending* for that process.

At any given time, there's at most one pending signal of a given type for each process. In other words, the kernel does not generate a signal of that same type for the process if one is already pending; if an event occurs for which it should send that same signal again while it's pending, it just discards it. It's easiest to remember this if you picture the set of pending signals as a set of bits, with one bit for each signal type.

Processes also have the ability to temporarily block certain types of signals by defining a signal mask. We'll cover this aspect of signals in "Blocking Signals" on page 405. If a process has blocked a signal that's been sent to it, the signal remains pending until the process unblocks it.

A signal is *delivered* to a process when it responds to the signal in one of the following ways:

- The process explicitly ignores the signal. (Some signals can't be ignored though.) Even if a process chooses to ignore the signal, it is still considered to be delivered to it.

- The process executes a signal handler. A *signal handler* is a function that the process executes when the signal is delivered. When the process's response is to execute a signal handler, we say that the signal has been *caught*. Signal handling is a large and complex topic that we'll explore in "Basic Signal Handling" on page 393 and "The sigaction() System Call" on page 416.

- The process accepts the default action associated with the signal. The default action can be one of the following:

    Terminate   The process is terminated.
    Ignore   The process ignores the signal and continues to execute.
    Stop   The process's execution is suspended; it can resume execution at a later time.
    Core dump   The kernel writes the contents of a process's logical memory and its context into a file called a *core dump file* and then terminates the process. The core dump can be opened by a debugger such as gdb to be inspected.
    Continue   If the process was stopped, the process can resume execution when it receives certain signals.

A signal handler is a function of a specific form. A program makes a system call to tell the kernel that this function is to be run when the specific signal is sent to the program. This is called *registering* or *installing* the handler. If a program has not registered a signal handler for a particular signal and doesn't have the explicit instructions that tell the kernel it wants to ignore that signal, its fate is determined by the default action of that signal. Most signals cause a process to terminate by default.

A process's *disposition* of a signal is the action that it takes when the signal is delivered. When you design a program, if you create and register a signal handler for a specific signal, you've set its disposition. By not registering a signal handler, you've also set its disposition to accept the default action.

Signal Types

Signals first appeared in Fourth Edition Unix in 1973 [38]. Initially there were nine different signal types, but over the years, the number of signal types increased. The way that signals were sent and delivered also changed over time, since the early methods were unreliable. The BSD systems developed one solution, and System V developed another. The first POSIX standard, adopted in 1990, defined a single reliable model of signals with 19 different signals. POSIX.1-2001 added nine more signals, and some Unix distributions added others that aren't standardized. As a consequence, the exact set of signal types varies from one system to another, but those standardized by POSIX are universally found in all Unix systems. There are typically about 30 to 35 different signal types in any Unix system.

The two most important resources for learning how to program with signals are the `signal(7)` man page and the `signal.h(7posix)` man page. The `signal.h(7posix)` man page contains the POSIX requirements for everything related to signals, including the definitions of all data types, macro constants, functions that work with them, and the signal types themselves. The `signal(7)` man page describes the different types of signals, how a process can send a signal, how signal handlers can be set up, when and how signals are delivered to processes, how processes can temporarily delay their delivery, and much more. Together, these two pages provide almost everything we need to know.

The `signal(7)` man page contains two tables of signals. The first lists the different types of signals and, for each one, which standard introduced it, what the default action is for it, and a brief summary of what causes it. The second table contains the numeric values of the symbolic constants. Because these aren't standardized, for some signals, it lists several values, depending on the processor architecture. Table 8-1 is a nearly complete list of all of the signals listed in the man page, with a few nonstandard signals omitted, sorted by their standard numeric value. In the table, the default action *Term* is short for "terminate" and *Core* is short for "core dump and exit." A *Yes* in the POSIX column means that it's a POSIX-standard signal; a *No* means it isn't a standard signal.

Table 8-1: Signal Names and Default Actions

Name	Number	POSIX	Default action	Comment
SIGHUP	1	Yes	Term	Hangup detected on controlling terminal or death of controlling process
SIGINT	2	Yes	Term	Interrupt from keyboard
SIGQUIT	3	Yes	Core	Quit from keyboard
SIGILL	4	Yes	Core	Illegal instruction
SIGTRAP	5	Yes	Core	Trace/breakpoint trap
SIGABRT	6	Yes	Core	Abort signal from abort(3)
SIGBUS	7	Yes	Core	Bus error (bad memory access)
SIGFPE	8	Yes	Core	Floating-point exception
SIGKILL	9	Yes	Term	Kill signal
SIGUSR1	10	Yes	Term	User-defined signal 1
SIGSEGV	11	Yes	Core	Invalid memory reference
SIGUSR2	12	Yes	Term	User-defined signal 2
SIGPIPE	13	Yes	Term	Broken pipe; write to pipe with no readers
SIGALRM	14	Yes	Term	Timer signal from alarm(2)
SIGTERM	15	Yes	Term	Termination signal
SIGCHLD	17	Yes	Ignore	Child stopped or terminated
SIGCONT	18	Yes	Cont	Continue if stopped
SIGSTOP	19	Yes	Stop	Stop process
SIGTSTP	20	Yes	Stop	Stop typed at terminal
SIGTTIN	21	Yes	Stop	Terminal input for background process
SIGTTOU	22	Yes	Stop	Terminal output for background process
SIGURG	23	Yes	Ignore	Urgent condition on socket (4.2BSD)
SIGXCPU	24	Yes	Core	CPU time limit exceeded (4.2BSD)
SIGXFSZ	25	Yes	Core	File size limit exceeded (4.2BSD)
SIGVTALRM	26	Yes	Term	Virtual alarm clock (4.2BSD)
SIGPROF	27	Yes	Term	Profiling timer expired
SIGWINCH	28	No	Ignore	Window resize signal (4.3BSD, Sun)
SIGIO	29	No	Term	I/O now possible (4.2BSD)
SIGPOLL	29	Yes	Term	Pollable event (System V); synonym for SIGIO
SIGPWR	30	No	Term	Power failure (System V)
SIGSYS	31	Yes	Core	Bad system call (SVR4)

You can list all signals with their numeric values on your host computer from the command line by entering `kill -1`. In bash, you can enter the built-in command `trap -1`, which displays the same output.

Note that the spelling of the symbolic signal names is correct; many correspond to English words but have missing letters. We can categorize these signals based on their source. We'll describe many, but not all, of the signals listed in Table 8-1 in the following summaries. Because there are circumstances in which we need to know the total number of signals, the *signal.h* header file defines a symbolic constant, NSIG, which is the total number of signals defined on the given system. Since signal numbers are assigned consecutively, NSIG equals the largest defined signal number plus one.

Signals from Program Errors

When a program receives any of the following errors, it should usually terminate. These signals are sent when the program has made a serious enough error that it can't feasibly continue. The purpose of the signal is to give the program a chance to clean up before exiting. For example, it might have changed the state of the terminal window and needs to restore it. After it cleans up, it can safely terminate.

SIGABRT A process can call abort() to have this signal sent to itself. Since this signal causes a core dump by default, this is how a process can terminate with a core dump.

SIGSEGV Sent when your program causes a segmentation fault with an attempt to access a part of memory for which it doesn't have permission. It indicates an invalid access to valid memory. This can happen when the program dereferences an uninitialized pointer or when it uses a pointer to step through an array but doesn't check for the end of the array.

SIGBUS Like a SIGSEGV except that it is generated when the program tries to access an invalid memory address. This causes a bus error.

SIGFPE Reports a fatal arithmetic error of any kind, not just floating-point errors, but errors such as division by zero and overflow.

SIGILL The ILL is short for "illegal instruction." This is usually sent when the program tries to execute data (typically because of a bad pointer dereference) or tries to execute a privileged instruction.

SIGEMT Short for "emulator trap." This is the signal sent when an instruction doesn't exist in hardware and must be emulated by software.

SIGSYS Sent when the program makes a bad system call, such as by passing the wrong number to the syscall() function (see Chapter 2).

SIGTRAP Used to implement debuggers and tracing programs such as strace and ptrace.

The next class of signals are those that are intended to terminate the program for one reason or another.

Termination Signals

These signals are sent, in general, to tell the process to terminate. The intention is to give it a chance to clean up, such as closing open files, saving its state information, restoring the state of the terminal, and so on.

SIGINT, SIGQUIT   Sent as a result of keyboard input. By default, SIGINT is sent when a user enters CTRL-C. It's a common way to abruptly terminate a process. If a process has a signal handler for it, it can perform cleanup before exiting, or even ignore it. By default, SIGQUIT is sent when the user enters CTRL-\. Unlike SIGINT, this produces a core dump and terminates the process.

SIGKILL   Will terminate a process without exception. It cannot be ignored, deferred, or caught by a signal handler.

SIGTERM   Also terminates a process by default, but unlike SIGKILL, can be caught by a handler. When you enter the kill command to kill a process, this is the signal that's sent to it.

SIGHUP   Sent to a process when its controlling terminal is closed or a remote connection is broken. By default, it terminates a process. Installing a signal handler for it is a way to do cleanup before the process exits.

Timer Expiration Signals

These signals are sent when a timer of some type expires. There are two different types of timers: those that measure real or clock time and those that measure processor time. We discuss timers in Chapter 9 and make use of them when we cover alternative methods of I/O in Chapter 17.

SIGALRM   Sent to a process by the kernel when a timer set by either the alarm() or setitimer() system call expires. These timers measure real time.

SIGVTALRM   Sent to a process by the kernel when a timer that measures the CPU time the process has used, called *virtual time*, expires.

We won't see much use for the SIGVTALRM signal, but we'll find the SIGALRM signal to play an important role in game programs.

Asynchronous I/O Signals

These signals are related to asynchronous I/O, which we'll cover in Chapter 18.

SIGIO   Sent to a process that has arranged in advance to be notified when data is available from a read operation from a terminal device (or a socket, which we don't cover in this book). In Chapter 17, where we learn about alternative methods of I/O, we'll make use of this signal.

SIGURG   Related to network programming. It is sent when out-of-band data is received on a socket.

Process and Job Control Signals

This category of signals includes those that are sent to a process for job control–related activities, such as the termination of a child process (covered in Chapter 11) or a request to temporarily stop the process.

SIGCHLD   Sent to a process that has created one or more children when one of those child processes terminates. (We'll learn about how a process can create new processes, called *child processes*, in Chapter 11.)

SIGSTOP   Will suspend, or stop, a process. Like SIGKILL, this signal cannot be ignored, deferred, or caught by a signal handler.

SIGTSTP   Short for *terminal stop* and typically sent when the user enters CTRL-Z. It suspends the process, which can be resumed at a later time with the fg command.

SIGCONT   Sent to resume a process that was previously stopped. If a running process receives it, it ignores it by default. It's useful because a signal handler for it can take specific actions when the process resumes.

While a process is suspended, it can't receive any signals until it is continued, except for the SIGKILL and SIGCONT signals.

Miscellaneous Signals

These signals are lumped together but are caused by very different events.

SIGPWR   An asynchronous signal sent when a power loss is detected.

SIGWINCH   Sent when the window in which the process is running is resized.

SIGUSR1, SIGUSR2   Have no predefined meaning. These two signals are intended to be used by ordinary user-level programs for synchronization or other notifications. We'll make use of these signals in Chapters 9, 11, and 17.

There are a few signals that we didn't describe. It's unlikely you'll ever need to handle them.

Signal Definitions

If you're curious to see the definitions of these symbolic names in the header file on your own machine, you'll need to rummage around a bit. The *signal.h* header file includes the definitions of all symbolic signal types indirectly, but does not usually contain them. Typically, *signal.h* is just a thin wrapper that includes other header files, including the one that contains the actual signal definitions. In Linux, the included files `<bits/signum-generic.h>` and `<bits/signum-arch.h>` together define the signal names. User-level programs should never include these; they should include just *signal.h*.

Now that we know what the various signals are and what types of events cause them to be sent, we'll consider how we can control what our program does when it receives a given signal. This is called *setting the signal disposition*.

Basic Signal Handling

As noted earlier, a program doesn't have to accept the default action caused by a signal. It can be designed to respond in its own way to any signal except

SIGKILL and SIGSTOP, which cannot be caught. In short, we can change the disposition of our programs with respect to every possible signal except those two. This involves two steps:

1. Defining a function, called a *signal handler*, to be executed on receipt of a specific signal. A simple signal handler has the prototype

   ```
   void sighandler(int signum);
   ```

   in which the integer argument is the number of the signal it has caught. By default, this signal handler is executed, like any other function, on the process's runtime stack, but it's possible to have it run on an alternate stack. There are many limitations on what kind of code can be put into a signal handler; we'll address this in "Guidance on Designing Signal Handlers" on page 431.

2. Informing the kernel that this function is to be executed when the specific signal is delivered to the process. This is called *registering* or *installing* the signal handler.

Figure 8-2 depicts how the handler is run. When a handler has been registered for a signal and that signal is delivered to a process, the kernel runs briefly, arranges for the signal handler to be run, and returns control to the user process starting inside the handler code.

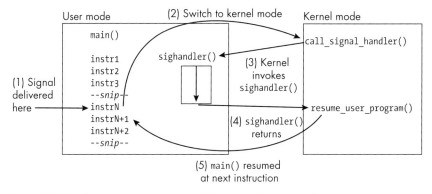

Figure 8-2: A schematic representation of the steps that occur when a process receives a signal for which it has registered a signal handler named sighandler()

When the signal handler finishes executing, the kernel runs briefly again, this time to ensure that the main program is resumed in the instruction right after the one that was executed just before the signal was delivered. Registering a handler requires making a system call. The original system call designed for this purpose was signal(). Although it isn't the preferred way to do this, it is simple to use and easy to understand, and is therefore worth the effort to learn. We'll examine it first.

The signal() System Call

The signal() function was first designed only as a way to notify processes of exceptional events; signals weren't intended as a general-purpose notification system [26]. When a signal was delivered to a process and its signal handler ran, its disposition was reset to the default action, which meant that if a second signal of the same type arrived, rather than its handler running again, the default action would be taken. If the default action was process termination, the process would die. Programmers worked around this problem by calling signal() within the handler to catch the second signal, as in

```
void sig_handler(int sig)
{
    signal(sig, sig_handler);
    // OMITTED: Take actions in response to signal.
}
```

but this wasn't a real solution. The second signal could arrive before the handler was set up again, thereby terminating the process, or after, in which case the handler might be reentered a second time, like a recursive function call. Because of its unpredictable nature, the signal() call and the consequent signal handling were deemed unreliable.

Later versions of the signal() function in 4.4BSD and in System V corrected this problem in different ways, the consequence being that its semantics depended on which Unix system was being run. POSIX adopted the 4.4BSD model, incorporating a slightly modified specification of it in its first standard, whereas System V continued to use the original semantics. Although current versions of Linux and BSD combine the semantics of each, POSIX and most documentation recommend not using this function anymore. It has been replaced by a reliable method of signal handling based on the sigaction() system call, which we'll examine in the section "The sigaction() System Call" on page 416.

The signal() function's man page is in Section 2. Its prototype, from the SYNOPSIS, is:

```
#include <signal.h>

typedef void(*sighandler_t)(int);
sighandler_t signal(int signum, sighandler_t handler);
```

Programs must include *signal.h* to use this function. The synopsis contains a declaration of the sighandler_t type, which is a pointer to a function whose prototype is void *sighandler*(int signum). This is both the return type of signal() and the type of its second argument.

On success, the return value of signal() is the old disposition of the signal passed to it in its first argument, which is the number of the signal to be handled. For this argument, it's best to use its symbolic name, such as SIGINT or SIGQUIT, rather than an actual number. The second argument is the disposition we want this signal to have. It need not be the address of a signal handler function; it can also be either of the two constants SIG_DFL and SIG_IGN. Both of these are defined indirectly in *signal.h* as *fake signal functions*, along with the return value SIG_ERR, which indicates an error:

```
/* Fake signal functions */
#define SIG_ERR ((__sighandler_t) -1) /* Error return   */
#define SIG_DFL ((__sighandler_t)  0) /* Default action */
#define SIG_IGN ((__sighandler_t)  1) /* Ignore signal  */
```

If SIG_DFL is supplied, the default action will be taken, and if SIG_IGN, the signal will be ignored. If instead it's the name of a signal handler, then that handler will be invoked.

Let's take a look at a simple example that uses signal(). Listing 8-1 shows how a program can install signal handlers to catch the SIGINT and SIGQUIT signals generated when the user enters CTRL-C and CTRL-\, respectively. When compiling on Linux, using the typical default compiler options, signal() will have the BSD-style semantics in which the disposition is not reset to the default action when the signal is delivered. It's as if _BSD_SOURCE were defined when compiling.

signal_demo1.c
```
#include "common_hdrs.h"
#include <signal.h>

void catch_sigint(int signum)
{
    printf("I'm not terminated by CTRL-C!\n");
}

void catch_sigquit(int signum)
{
    printf("I'm not terminated by CTRL-\\!\n");
}

int main()
{
    if ( SIG_ERR == signal(SIGINT, catch_sigint) )
        fatal_error(errno, "signal()");
    if ( SIG_ERR == signal(SIGQUIT, catch_sigquit) )
        fatal_error(errno, "signal()");
    for ( int i = 20; i > 0; i-- ) {
        printf("Try to terminate me with ^C or ^\\.\n");
        sleep(1);
    }
    return 0;
}
```

Listing 8-1: A simple program that catches SIGINT and SIGQUIT

The two functions, catch_sigint() and catch_sigquit(), are signal handlers for SIGINT and SIGQUIT, respectively. Observe that their prototypes match the definition of sighandler_t. In the main() function, the two calls to signal() install catch_sigint() as the signal handler for SIGINT and catch_sigquit() as the signal handler for SIGQUIT. Until signal() is executed, the program is subject to the default action for each. Like previous programs we've written, this one checks for an error from the system call and exits if it's detected. First let's compile the program with the command:

```
$ gcc -o signal_demo1 -I../include signal_demo1.c -L../lib -lspl
```

When we run signal_demo1 and enter CTRL-C in the same terminal, the SIGINT signal is sent to the process executing signal_demo1; as a result, catch_sigint() runs, and when it returns, the program resumes execution. In *signal_demo1.c*, the only action taken by either handler is to print a message on the screen, simply to show that the function was executed.

NOTE *Normally, we shouldn't call printf() in a signal handler because it isn't an async-signal-safe function. Some functions are not safe to call in signal handlers; those that can be called safely are* async-signal-safe*. Because the point of many of the small programs presented here is to show when handlers are called, I put calls to printf() in them; otherwise, I'll avoid it. Henceforth, I'll often remind you of this by writing* UNSAFE *in a comment where they occur. I discuss async-signal-safety in more detail in* "Guidance on Designing Signal Handlers" *on page 431 and describe how a handler can safely print messages.*

You can enter CTRL-C many times, and each time the program will just print a message; the disposition is not reset. This is the BSD-style semantics.

The System V signal() Semantics

On some systems, if you enter CTRL-C a second time, the program will terminate because signaling is based on the System V Interface Definition (SVID) model, in which the disposition is reset to the default action when the signal is delivered. As I mentioned before, with the default compiler options in Linux, this won't happen, because the version of signal() that's called doesn't reset the disposition after the handler runs. However, we can change the behavior of signal_demo1 by defining the macro _XOPEN_SOURCE when we compile it. Doing so exposes a different version of the signal() function with the semantics defined in the SVID. If we compile with the command

```
$ gcc -D_XOPEN_SOURCE -o signal_demo1 -I../include signal_demo1.c \
  -L../lib -lspl
```

and rerun the program, we'll see different behavior, as the following run shows. The ^C is what appears on the terminal when we enter CTRL-C:

```
$ ./signal_demo1
Try to terminate me with ^C or ^\.
^CI'm not terminated by CTRL-C!
```

```
Try to terminate me with ^C or ^\.
^C
$
```

The first CTRL-C is caught, but the second terminates the program. Linux provides an explicit way to obtain the SVID behavior with the sysv_signal() system call. We use it in the exact same way as signal(), but we need to define _GNU_SOURCE to employ it, since it's a GNU extension (see Listing 8-2).

sysv_signal *_demo.c*
```c
#define _GNU_SOURCE
#include "common_hdrs.h"
#include <signal.h>

void catch_sigint(int signum)
{
    printf("I'm not terminated by the first CTRL-C!\n");   /* UNSAFE */
}

void catch_sigquit(int signum)
{
    printf("I'm not terminated by the first CTRL-\\!\n"); /* UNSAFE */
}

int main()
{
    if ( SIG_ERR == sysv_signal(SIGINT, catch_sigint) )
        fatal_error(errno, "sysv_signal()");
    if ( SIG_ERR == sysv_signal(SIGQUIT, catch_sigquit) )
        fatal_error(errno, "sysv_signal()");
    for ( int i = 20; i > 0; i-- ) {
        printf("Try to terminate me with ^C or ^\\.\n");
        sleep(1);
    }
    return (0);
}
```

Listing 8-2: A program that catches SIGINT and SIGQUIT using unreliable signaling

When you compile and run this program and enter CTRL-C or CTRL-\more than once, the program terminates. The purpose of these examples is to show how this unreliable signaling mechanism behaves. Unless I state otherwise, the executables of all remaining programs that use the signal() system call for setting the disposition are assumed to be built using the default, BSD-style semantics.

The next program, shown in Listing 8-3, is the same as *signal_demo1.c* with one exception: The dispositions of SIGINT and SIGQUIT are set to be ignored by calling signal() with SIG_IGN as the second argument.

signal _demo2.c
```
#include "common_hdrs.h"
#include <signal.h>

int main()
{
    if ( SIG_ERR == signal(SIGINT, SIG_IGN) )  /* Ignore Ctrl-C. */
        fatal_error(errno, "signal()");
    if ( SIG_ERR == signal(SIGQUIT, SIG_IGN) ) /* Ignore Ctrl-\. */
        fatal_error(errno, "signal()");
    for ( int i = 10; i > 0; i-- ) {
        printf("Try to kill me with ^C or ^\\. "
                "Seconds remaining: %2d\n", i);
        sleep(1);
    }
    return 0;
}
```

Listing 8-3: A simple program that sets the dispositions of SIGINT and SIGQUIT to be ignored

When you run this program and enter CTRL-C and CTRL-\ repeatedly, nothing happens. The program runs as if you didn't enter any keyboard input. The program calls sleep(), a system call that suspends the calling process for the given number of seconds. Because the process spends almost all of its time suspended in the call to sleep(), the signals are most likely being sent to the process while it's suspended in that call. When a signal is sent to a process that's not running, the kernel records that signal's arrival and marks it as pending, if it wasn't already marked as pending. The process is then scheduled to run. As soon as it runs, its signal handler is executed. When it returns, the interrupted function, in this case the sleep() call, may or may not be restarted, depending on the particular Unix distribution on which it's run.

In Linux, the call isn't restarted; it's one of many functions that aren't restarted when they're interrupted by a signal handler. This implies that, in our example program, at most one signal can be sent to the process during its sleep() call. The signal(7) man page has a comprehensive discussion detailing the responses of all system calls to interruptions by signal handlers.

Before we explore some of the more advanced topics, including the use of sigaction() for setting the signal disposition, let's find some user-level commands for sending signals to processes and some system calls and library functions that programs can call to do the same, so that we have a way to test out some of the signal handling programs that we write.

Sending Signals

We'll search the man pages for commands that we can use to send signals:

```
$ apropos -s1 -a send signal
kill (1)              - send a signal to a process
skill (1)             - send a signal or report process status
snice (1)             - send a signal or report process status
```

Among these is the `kill` command. We've used the `kill` command before to list signal types; `kill -l` displays the list of all signals. In spite of its name, the `kill` command sends signals. If we enter

```
$ kill pid
```

where `pid` is the process ID of a process, it will send the `SIGTERM` signal to that process. For example, `kill 1234` sends the signal to the process whose PID is 1234. If we replace the PID with −1, as in

```
$ kill -1
```

then the `SIGTERM` signal will be sent to every process that we're allowed to kill, which, since we are nonprivileged users, are (roughly speaking) all of our currently running processes, but not those of other users. By default, `kill` sends the `SIGTERM` signal, but it can send any other signal as well.

The more general form of the command is

```
$ kill -s signal-val pid [pid] ...
```

where *signal-val* can be one of the following:

- The full signal macro name, such as `SIGKILL`

- The part of the signal macro name after `SIG`, such as `KILL`

- The numeric value of the signal, such as, for `SIGKILL`, `9`

The `kill` command requires that you know the PID of the process you want to signal. You can always get it using `ps`, but there's a faster method mentioned in the `SEE ALSO` section of `kill`'s man page, namely the `pkill` command, which doesn't need the PID. The `pkill` command's syntax is essentially the same as `kill`'s, but you can give it a pattern to match the command that you'd like to signal rather than its PID, and it will send the signal to all commands that match the pattern. For example

```
$ pkill signal_demo
```

will send the `SIGTERM` signal to any process that was run by entering `signal _demo...`, such as `signal_demo1` or `signal_demo2`.

Let's turn to the programming interface. We'll search the man pages in Sections 2 and 3 for system calls or library functions for sending signals:

```
$ apropos -s2,3 -a send signal
kill (2)              - send signal to a process
kill (3posix)         - send a signal to a process or a group of processes
killpg (3)            - send signal to a process group
killpg (3posix)       - send a signal to a process group
--snip--
raise (3)             - send a signal to the caller
raise (3posix)        - send a signal to the executing process
tgkill (2)            - send a signal to a thread
tkill (2)             - send a signal to a thread
```

This list includes functions that send signals to threads, which I omitted from its output. We see that there are a few functions for sending signals to either a single process or to a process group. Process groups are covered in Chapter 10.

Let's look at the man page for the kill() system call. This call allows a process to send a signal to one or more processes or even itself. Its synopsis is:

```
#include <sys/types.h>
#include <signal.h>

int kill(pid_t pid, int sig);
```

The first parameter can be used to specify the PID of the process to receive the signal. The second parameter is the type of signal to send. In the simplest case, a call such as

```
kill(942, SIGTERM);
```

sends the SIGTERM signal to the process whose PID is 942. One process cannot send a signal to another target process if the sender's real or effective user ID doesn't equal either the real or saved set-user-ID of the target and the sender is not root. If a process doesn't have permission to send a signal to the specified process, kill() returns -1.

The first argument can also be 0, -1, or another negative number, and it means something different in each case:

0   The signal will be sent to all processes in the same process group.

-1   If the sender is not the superuser, it's sent to all processes for which it has permission to send signals, which are all those processes whose real or saved set-user-ID is the same as the real or effective user ID of the sending process.

n < -1   It's sent to all processes in the process group whose process group ID is the absolute value of n. When we run a command such as

```
$ last | grep pts/0 | sort | uniq
```

a process is created for each separate program in the command, and all of those are placed into a single process group. Being able to send a signal to all of the processes involved in the command with a single call is convenient.

One application of the kill() system call is to enable related processes that have created new processes to coordinate and synchronize their behavior with these child processes. We'll explore how to write programs that can create new processes in Chapter 11. Here we'll use an artificial example to show how kill() works. We begin by writing a small program that sends two consecutive signals to the process whose PID is passed to the program on the command line. That program is displayed in Listing 8-4.

kill_demo.c

```c
#include "common_hdrs.h"
#include <signal.h>

int main(int argc, char *argv[])
{
    int   res, pid;
    char message[128];
    if ( argc < 2 )
        usage_error("kill_demo <PID of a process to signal>");

    if ( VALID_NUMBER != (res = get_int(argv[1], NO_TRAILING, &pid, message)))
        fatal_error(res, message);

    printf("Sending SIGINT to  process %d.\n", pid);
    if ( -1 == kill(pid, SIGINT) )
        fatal_error(errno, "kill() sending SIGINT");
    sleep(1); /* Give a chance for signal to be sent. */
    printf("Now sending SIGTERM to  process %d.\n", pid);
    if ( -1 == kill(pid, SIGTERM) )
        fatal_error(errno, "kill() sending SIGTERM");
    return 0;
}
```

Listing 8-4: A program that sends a SIGINT and then a SIGTERM to the process whose PID is given on its command line

The program sends a SIGINT followed by a SIGTERM, the idea being that the target process is designed to catch the SIGINT but not the SIGTERM, and will terminate after receiving it.

We'll need a second program for the target process to execute, which I'll name *signal_demo3.c*. The program has a handler only for SIGINT. It prints its PID when it starts up, produces no input prompts, and runs until it receives any other terminating signal such as SIGTERM. This gives us a chance to send it signals from a different terminal. Printing the PID allows us to record the PID and pass it to kill_demo. Listing 8-5 shows that program.

signal_demo3.c

```c
#include "common_hdrs.h"
#include <signal.h>
```

```
static char *progname;

void catch_sigint(int signum)
{
    printf("%s caught CTRL-C!\n", progname);  /* UNSAFE */
}

int main(int argc, char *argv[])
{
    progname = argv[0];
    printf("PID=%d\n", getpid());
    if ( SIG_ERR == signal(SIGINT, catch_sigint) )
        fatal_error(errno, "signal()");
    while ( TRUE ) continue; /* Wait for a signal to be received. */
    return 0;
}
```

Listing 8-5: A small program that catches SIGINT and no other signal and runs idly until it is sent a terminating signal

We perform the following two steps to show how `kill()` works:

1. We run `signal_demo3` in the background and record the PID that it displays.

2. While `signal_demo3` is running, we run `kill_demo`, giving it the PID displayed by `signal_demo3`.

When we perform this small experiment, we'll see that `kill_demo` sent the two signals to `signal_demo3` because `signal_demo3` prints a message when it receives SIGINT and it terminates when it receives the SIGTERM:

```
$ ./signal_demo3 &
[1] 18268
PID=18268
$ ./kill_demo 18268
kill_demo sending SIGINT to  process 18268.
signal_demo3 caught CTRL-C!
kill_demo sending SIGTERM to terminate process 18268.
[1]+  Terminated              signal_demo3
```

If we try to pass the PID of a process that isn't our own to `kill_demo`, we'll see a message like

```
kill() sending SIGINT: Operation not permitted
```

as proof that a process can send signals only to those processes whose real or saved set-user-IDs are the same as either the real or the effective user ID of the process.

A process can send a signal to itself using the raise() library function

```
int raise(int signal);
```

which returns 0 on success and -1 on failure. Since the only possible error is passing a bad signal number, I don't check the return value in any of the programs in the listings. If the process has installed a handler for the signal that it sends to itself, the handler will run and, only after it terminates, will raise() return from the call. A process can also send a signal to itself by calling getpid() and using kill(), as in:

```
kill(getpid(), signal);
```

Why would a process ever need to send a signal to itself? Here's one common reason. Suppose that your program has modified the terminal settings, or created temporary files, or taken other actions that might require immediate cleanup if a user tries to stop or terminate it. Proper behavior would be to perform all cleanup and then terminate or stop, depending on the signal sent by the user. Therefore, in the handler for a job control signal, it can raise a signal to terminate the program after it performs the cleanup. Listing 8-6 contains a small program, based on an example in the GNU C Library manual, that shows how to do this:

raise_demo.c
```
#include "common_hdrs.h"

void sigtstp_handler(int signum)
{
    if ( SIG_ERR == signal(SIGTSTP, SIG_DFL) )
        fatal_error(errno, "signal()");
    printf("\ncleaning up in progress...\ndone\n");
    raise(SIGTSTP);
    printf("raise() called to stop process.\n");
}

void sigcont_handler(int signum)
{
    /* When the process is resumed, reset the sigtstp handler so that it
       cleans up again before stopping. */
    if ( SIG_ERR == signal(SIGTSTP, sigtstp_handler) )
        fatal_error(errno, "signal()");
}

int main(int argc, char *argv[])
{
    if ( SIG_ERR == signal(SIGTSTP, sigtstp_handler) )
        fatal_error(errno, "signal()");
    if ( SIG_ERR == signal(SIGCONT, sigcont_handler) )
        fatal_error(errno, "signal()");
    for ( int i = 20; i > 0; i-- ) {
```

```
        printf("Enter CTRL-Z to stop the process, or CTRL-C to end it.\n");
        sleep(2);
    }
    return 0;
}
```

Listing 8-6: A program that shows how to clean up when receiving a job control signal and then comply with the signal's default action

The main program installs handlers for SIGTSTP and SIGCONT. The signal handler for SIGTSTP first sets the disposition back to the default, which is to stop the process, then performs all cleanup, and then calls raise(SIGTSTP) to send itself the signal and force itself to stop.

NOTE *The SIGTSTP signal is not the same as SIGSTOP. While your programs can't ignore, defer, or catch SIGSTOP, they can do so for SIGTSTP.*

Once the program has stopped, if the user resumes it by entering fg on the command line, the sigcont_handler() will run, setting the disposition of SIGTSTP back to calling sigtstp_handler() so that it can clean up again if it's stopped another time. We'll compile and run this program and enter CTRL-Z, then resume it after it stops and enter CTRL-C:

```
$ ./raise_demo
Enter CTRL-Z to stop the process, or CTRL-C to end it.
^Z
cleaning up in progress...
done
raise() called to stop process.

[2]+  Stopped                 raise_demo1
$ fg
raise_demo
Enter CTRL-Z to stop the process, or CTRL-C to end it.
^C
$
```

You should try this a few times to convince yourself that it's doing what I've just described, each time entering CTRL-\ a few times before terminating it with CTRL-C.

Blocking Signals

Another way in which we have control over how our programs can respond to signals is by blocking them. *Blocking* a signal means informing the kernel to hold onto that signal for a short time until we're ready for it to be delivered. If the kernel generates a signal that a process has blocked, the kernel won't send it to the process until it unblocks it. Blocking a signal is best viewed as putting a short-term hold on its delivery while our program performs some actions that we don't want to be interrupted. If we wanted it to be blocked for a long time, it would be better to just set its disposition to SIG_IGN. There are various circumstances under which short-term blocking is useful:

- A program might be executing a short section of code that updates shared variables or data structures, which is called a *critical region* or *critical section*. In particular, if the signal handler for a given signal or the main program modifies some variable that they both modify, then we don't want the program to receive that signal while the main program is modifying that data; otherwise, the signal handler will run and possibly corrupt the data that the main program was updating. Therefore, we'd block it before and unblock it after the access.

- The program might need to execute some code before a particular signal has been delivered to it. It could block that signal until it executes the code and unblock it when it's done.

- When a program is in the midst of handling one signal, it may need to block the delivery of other signals until it finishes what it's doing.

The only two signals that cannot be blocked are SIGKILL and SIGSTOP. It isn't an error to try to block them; the attempt will just be ignored.

NOTE *Blocking a signal is not the same as ignoring it. An ignored signal is actually delivered to a process, which then ignores it, whereas a blocked signal is not delivered to the process, but might be later. When the signal is delivered, the process may then choose to ignore it.*

The kernel manages the blocking of signals by maintaining a *signal mask* for every process. When we study threads in Chapter 15, we'll see that a signal mask is also maintained for every thread of a multithreaded process. The signal mask is the set of signals that are currently blocked for that process (or thread). We can think of it as a bit mask with a bit for every signal type; a signal is blocked if and only if its corresponding bit in the mask is set, as depicted in Figure 8-3. The mask may not be implemented like this, but it's an easy way to conceptualize it.

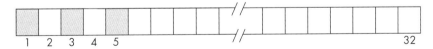

Figure 8-3: A conceptualization of the signal mask for a process in which shaded cells represent blocked signals

Let's search the man pages to try to find functions related to the blocking and unblocking of signals:

```
$ apropos -s2,3 -a signal block
--snip--
```

```
rt_sigprocmask (2)      - examine and change blocked signals
sigblock (3)            - BSD signal API
sigpause (3)            - atomically release blocked signals and wait for inte...
sigprocmask (2)         - examine and change blocked signals
sigprocmask (3posix) - examine and change blocked signals
```

Reading their man pages, we learn that the sigblock() function is obsolete and sigpause()'s man page tells us not to use it. The preferred function is sigprocmask(), which is a system call described in the same man page as rt_sigprocmask(). The sigprocmask() function can be used to block or unblock one or more signals anywhere in a program. It isn't the only means of blocking signals; when we examine the sigaction() system call, we'll see that we can use it to specify which signals are blocked during execution of an installed signal handler.

The synopsis for sigprocmask() is

```
#include <signal.h>

int sigprocmask(int how, const sigset_t *set, sigset_t *oldset);
```

where the first parameter (how) takes one of three symbolic integer values: SIG_BLOCK, SIG_UNBLOCK, or SIG_SETMASK. We'll explain them shortly. On success, this call returns 0, and on failure, -1. The remaining two parameters are of type sigset_t. The sigprocmask() man page suggests reading the Section 3 sigsetops man page for more information about it.

That page presents the general concept of signal sets as well as a collection of functions that act on them.

Signal Sets

A *signal set* is a data structure that specifies a set of signals. The system data type sigset_t represents a signal set. The sigsetops man page lists five functions for working with signal sets:

int sigemptyset(sigset_t *set)   Initializes the parameter (set) to be empty or, in other words, to exclude every defined signal type. It always returns 0.

int sigfillset(sigset_t *set)   Initializes the parameter (set) to be full or, in other words, to include every defined signal type. It always returns 0.

sigaddset(sigset_t *set, int signum)   Given a particular signal (signum), adds that signal type to the given signal set, set. It returns 0 on success and -1 on failure. The only possible failure occurs if signum isn't a valid signal number.

sigdelset(sigset_t *set, int signum)   Given a particular signal (signum), deletes that signal type from the given signal set, set. It returns 0 on success and -1 on failure. The only possible failure occurs if signum isn't a valid signal number.

int sigismember(const sigset_t *set, int signum)   Tests whether signum is a member of the signal set set. It returns 1 if the signal is in the set, 0 if not, and -1 on error, which only occurs if signum isn't a valid signal number.

The first two functions create empty and full signal sets, respectively. The next two add or delete individual signals from the specified sets. This gives us two ways to build a set of signals. We can either create an empty set and add signals to it or create a full set and delete from it. If we want a set with fewer than half of the possible signals in it, then it makes sense to do the former; otherwise, the latter.

Although the sigset_t data type may be implemented as a bit mask, we can't count on that, and we need to use these functions exclusively for defining sets of signals.

The sigsetops man page also lists three other support functions in *signal.h* that can be exposed by defining the _GNU_SOURCE feature test macro:

```
int sigisemptyset(const sigset_t *set);
int sigorset(sigset_t *dest, const sigset_t *left, const sigset_t *right);
int sigandset(sigset_t *dest, const sigset_t *left, const sigset_t *right);
```

The first is useful for determining whether a signal set is empty, returning 1 if the set has no signals and 0 if it does. The next two fill the signal set dest with the union of their last two arguments (sigorset()) or their intersection (sigandset()). These are not POSIX functions, implying that if we use them, our programs may not be portable.

The sigprocmask() Function

Now that we know how to create and modify signal sets, we can return to the sigprocmask() function. Its first parameter (how) should be one of the following three values:

SIG_BLOCK   With this value, the signal set passed as the second parameter (set) will be added to the set of currently blocked signals in the signal mask. In effect, the new mask is the union of the old mask and the supplied set. If a signal is already blocked and is part of the set, it has no effect.

SIG_UNBLOCK   With this value, the signal set passed as the second parameter (set) will be subtracted from the set of currently blocked signals in the signal mask. If a signal in set is not currently blocked, it has no effect.

SIG_SETMASK   With this value, the signal set passed as the second parameter (set) replaces the entire signal mask by the signals in set, effectively ignoring the old mask.

The last parameter is the old value of the mask. If we don't want to use it later in the program, we can just pass a NULL to it; otherwise, we'd pass the address of a signal set in which to save it. A common reason for saving it is being able to restore the previous mask after temporarily changing the mask of blocked signals.

Let's look at a code fragment that illustrates the general paradigm. The following code snippet blocks delivery of SIGINT during a section of code:

```
sigset_t blocked_signals, old_mask;
--snip--
sigemptyset(&blocked_signals);
sigaddset(&blocked_signals, SIGINT);

/* Add SIGINT to set of blocked signals in mask. */
if ( -1 == sigprocmask(SIG_BLOCK, &blocked_signals, &old_mask) )
    fatal_error(errno, "Error trying to change signal mask");

// OMITTED: Do critical work here, and then unblock the signal.

❶ if ( -1 == sigprocmask(SIG_SETMASK, &old_mask, NULL) )
    fatal_error(errno, "Error trying to restore old mask");
```

This prevents delivery of SIGINT while it's executing critical code. Other signals that aren't currently blocked can still be delivered, and this fragment doesn't show their dispositions. The unblocking method ❶ used in this code fragment does not necessarily unblock SIGINT. If SIGINT had been blocked before this code fragment ran, it would still be blocked afterward, because when we restore the old mask using SIG_SETMASK, we're replacing the entire current mask with the old one, and if it was blocked in the old mask, it will still be blocked. If the intent is to unblock SIGINT, it's better to explicitly do so, with the call

```
sigprocmask(SIG_UNBLOCK, &blocked_signals, NULL);
```

which removes it from the mask without blocking or unblocking any other signals.

This raises another question, which is how we can tell whether one or more signals are currently blocked. If a program calls sigprocmask() with NULL as its second argument, as in

```
if ( -1 != sigprocmask(SIG_BLOCK, NULL, &old_mask) )
    fatal_error(errno, "Error calling sigprocmask()");
```

then the mask is unaffected but its current state is saved in old_mask. To test whether a particular signal, say SIGINT, is in the returned mask, we can write:

```
if ( sigismember(&old_mask, SIGINT) )
    printf("SIGINT is currently blocked.");
```

We'll put some of these ideas together to write a small program named *sigprocmask_demo1.c* that blocks SIGINT while the program sleeps a bit, then unblocks it and sleeps intermittently again. Listing 8-7 introduces the use of a new system call, usleep(), which has finer granularity than sleep(). This call suspends the process for the given number of *microseconds* rather than seconds. Therefore, calling usleep(5000) suspends the process for 5,000 microseconds, which is 5 milliseconds, and usleep(500000) suspends it for 0.5 seconds.

sigprocmask _demo1.c

```c
#include "common_hdrs.h"

void catch_sigint(int signum)     /* Signal handler for SIGINT */
{
    printf("  Caught SIGINT\n");  /* UNSAFE                     */
}

int main(int argc, char *argv[])
{
    int     i;
    sigset_t blocked_set;

    if ( SIG_ERR == signal(SIGINT, catch_sigint) )
        fatal_error(errno, "signal()");
    /* Create a signal set with just SIGINT, and block with it. */
    sigemptyset(&blocked_set);
    sigaddset(&blocked_set, SIGINT);
    if ( -1 == sigprocmask(SIG_BLOCK, &blocked_set, NULL) )
        fatal_error(errno, "sigprocmask()");

    printf("SIGINT is blocked; sleeping for 5 seconds."
           " Try entering a few CTRL-Cs.\n");
    for ( i = 1; i <= 1000; i++ )
        usleep(5000);

    if ( -1 == sigprocmask(SIG_UNBLOCK, &blocked_set, NULL) )
        fatal_error(errno, "sigprocmask()");
    printf("SIGINT is no longer blocked. Enter a few CTRL-Cs.\n");
    for ( i = 1; i <= 5; i++ )
        usleep(800000);
    return 0;
}
```

Listing 8-7: A program that shows the effect of blocking and unblocking a signal

Listing 8-7 is designed to demonstrate a few different properties of signals and blocking. After you build this executable, run it, enter several CTRL-Cs immediately, and observe what happens. After you see the message SIGINT is no longer blocked. Enter a few CTRL-Cs, enter them again and observe the difference. For example, I ran this program following these instructions, and the session looked like this:

```
$ ./sigprocmask_demo1
SIGINT is blocked; sleeping for 5 seconds. Try entering a few CTRL-Cs.
```

```
^C^C^C^C^C^C  Caught SIGINT
SIGINT is no longer blocked. Enter a few CTRL-Cs.
^C  Caught SIGINT
^C  Caught SIGINT
^C  Caught SIGINT
^C  Caught SIGINT
^C  Caught SIGINT
```

The following rules explain its output and behavior:

- Blocked signals are not queued. While a signal is blocked, if it is generated multiple times, only one instance of it will be delivered when that signal is unblocked. If we enter CTRL-C 6 times while it is blocked, when it becomes unblocked, the handler will run just once, not 10 times. That's why you'll see just one message, Caught SIGINT.

- POSIX requires that when a signal is unblocked with a call to sigprocmask(), if it is pending, the signal should be delivered to the process immediately, before the sigprocmask() call returns. That's why the handler's message, Caught SIGINT, appears before the message printed by the following printf(), namely SIGINT is no longer blocked. Enter a few CTRL-Cs.

- The second for loop suspends the process five times, each time for 0.8 seconds. If you observe the output, the number of signals caught, no matter how many you enter, will be five. If a signal is delivered during a system call, it interrupts that call. Some system calls that are interrupted by signals automatically restart and others don't. Whether or not the call restarts after the handler runs depends on which call it is. The signal(7) man page has a detailed list describing how most system calls respond to the interruption. The usleep() system call is not restarted after the handler runs; it just terminates. This is why the number of messages printed by the handler is equal to the number of iterations of the for loop.

In the displayed session, you can see that only one CTRL-C was delivered when it was unblocked and that usleep() returned and did not resume whenever it was interrupted; otherwise, we'd be able to enter more than five CTRL-Cs during that for loop.

Listing 8-8 presents another very small program that shows how to block all signals that user programs are allowed to block while it executes a small fragment of code.

*sigprocmask
_demo2.c*
```
#include "common_hdrs.h"
#include <signal.h>

int main(int argc, char *argv[])
{
    sigset_t signals, prevsignals;
```

```
    printf("PID=%d\n", getpid());
    sigfillset(&signals);
    if ( -1 == sigprocmask(SIG_BLOCK, &signals, &prevsignals) )
        fatal_error(errno, "sigprocmask()");

    while ( TRUE ) {
        printf("Try sending signals to me. "
                "Use SIGKILL to terminate me, SIGSTOP to stop me.\n");
        sleep(5);
    }

    if ( -1 == sigprocmask(SIG_SETMASK, &prevsignals, NULL) )
        fatal_error(errno, "sigprocmask()");
    return 0;
}
```

Listing 8-8: A program that blocks all signals

Build and run this program in one terminal window, copy its PID, and in a second terminal window, send lots of signals to the program with the `kill` command, such as `kill -s SIGABRT` *pid*, where *pid* is the PID you copied. This is an easy way to temporarily prevent a portion of code from being interrupted by almost any signal.

Because a signal handler has just a single parameter, which is just the signal number, the only way that it can share data with the program is through file-scoped, or global, variables. At the start of the discussion about blocking signals on page 405, I mentioned that when a signal handler modifies variables that are shared with the rest of the program, in order to access them safely outside of the handler, the program should prevent the handler from running by blocking the signal while it accesses those variables. The next program, *sigprocmask_demo3.c*, will demonstrate how to do this. It will count how many times the signal handler was called and print the count. If we didn't block the signal from arriving while the `main()` function updated and printed the count, the program might fail to count some delivered signals. The program will declare a global variable, `sig_received`, as volatile `sig_atomic_t`, which is shared by the handler and `main()`.

THE SIG_ATOMIC_T TYPE

The signal.h(7POSIX) man page defines `sig_atomic_t` as a "possibly volatile-qualified integer type of an object that can be accessed as an atomic entity, even in the presence of asynchronous interrupts." Let's break this down.

Variables that are declared to be `sig_atomic_t` can be read or written with a single uninterruptible machine instruction. They are *atoms*, in the sense that they are moved around as single chunks in the machine. A data type consisting of larger pieces, such as a `struct`, is not an atom. Standard int types are usually atomic, but this is not guaranteed. A 64-bit integer might be moved as two

---

32-bit chunks on some architectures. The sig_atomic_t type is often declared as a typedef for int, though this is machine dependent.

When compilers optimize code, they sometimes put variables into registers temporarily. If a variable is in a register and another part of the program updates the in-memory copy, the value in the register is no longer valid. The volatile qualifier tells the compiler that it's not safe to do this, because the variable might be updated asynchronously by other parts of the same program. Therefore, it's common to see variables declared as volatile sig_atomic_t in code intended to access them atomically and possibly asynchronously.

In general, a sequence of code is called *atomic* if it is always executed without interruption, as if it were one indivisible instruction.

Listing 8-9 contains the *sigprocmask_demo3.c* program. It sets this sig _received variable and does nothing else. The main program tests this variable and, if it's set, increments a counter. The program has to block delivery of SIGINT while it tests the shared variable.

sigprocmask_demo3.c

```c
#include "common_hdrs.h"

static volatile sig_atomic_t sig_received = 0;

void catch_sigint(int signum)
{
    sig_received = 1;
}

int main (int argc, char *argv[])
{
    sigset_t blockedset;
    int     i;
    int     count = 0;

    /* Initialize the signal mask and install the handler. */
    sigemptyset(&blockedset);
    sigaddset(&blockedset, SIGINT);
    if ( SIG_ERR == signal(SIGINT, catch_sigint) )
        fatal_error(errno, "signal()");
    printf("PID=%d\n Enter CTRL-\\ to end this program.\n", getpid());
    while ( TRUE ) {
        /* Block the signal while we print the count. */
        if ( -1 == sigprocmask(SIG_BLOCK, &blockedset, NULL) )
            fatal_error(errno, "sigprocmask()");
        if ( sig_received ) {
            count++;
            sig_received = 0;
        }
        printf("\n%d SIGINTs received so far\n", count);
```

```
        /* Unblock the signal, allowing handler to run. */
❶   if ( -1 == sigprocmask(SIG_UNBLOCK, &blockedset, NULL) )
            fatal_error(errno, "sigprocmask()");
❷   pause();
    }
}
```

Listing 8-9: A program in which the signal handler updates an atomic variable accessed by the main() function

Listing 8-9 introduces a new system call, pause() ❷, which suspends the calling process until it receives a signal that either terminates the process or causes a signal handling function to run. If the program doesn't have a signal handler for the signal and the default action is to ignore it, pause() does not return. Using pause() here is intended to serve two purposes. The first is to give us as much time as we need to send a signal, either by entering the kill -s SIGINT command in another terminal window or by entering CTRL-C in the process's terminal. The second is to ensure that the program's count of received SIGINTs is correct, because they can only be delivered while the process is suspended in the pause(), which would cause the handler to run and the process to wake up, block signals again, and update and print the count. When you run this program, enter sequences of CTRL-C and check whether the number is counted correctly by the main program. You'll need to terminate it with a signal other than CTRL-C, such as CTRL-\. It might be correct for all of your tests of it, but unfortunately, it isn't correct.

Although it's hard to arrange it, we could send a SIGINT between the unblocking of signals ❶ but before the call to pause() and then again during the pause(). Both will cause the signal handler to run and set sig_received to 1, but the count will be updated only once for the two calls.

The problem is that this sequence of unblocking and immediately suspending the process to wait for a signal has a tiny window of time during which a signal can arrive; the pause() system call isn't sufficient for this purpose. We need to atomically unblock and suspend the process. One system call that can do this is sigsuspend():

```
#include <signal.h>
int sigsuspend(const sigset_t *mask);
```

This system call atomically replaces the signal mask of the calling process by mask and suspends the process. If a signal in the mask terminates the process, then sigsuspend() does not return. If it's caught by a handler, then sigsuspend() returns after the handler returns, and the signal mask is restored to what it was before the call to sigsuspend(). In effect, it's like executing

```
sigprocmask(SIG_SETMASK, &mask, &orig_mask);
pause();
sigprocmask(SIG_SETMASK, &orig_mask, NULL);
```

atomically. If we modify *sigprocmask_demo3.c* by replacing the lines

```
if ( -1 == sigprocmask(SIG_UNBLOCK, &blockedset, NULL) )
    fatal_error(errno, "sigprocmask()");
pause();
```

with

```
if ( (-1 == sigsuspend(&unblockedset)) && errno != EINTR )
    fatal_error(errno, "sigsuspend()");
```

where unblockedset is an empty set of signals, then the program will count
the signals correctly. A program that does this, *sigsuspend_demo.c*, is available
in the book's source code distribution.

The expected way to use sigsuspend() is in conjunction with sigprocmask()—
the program blocks signals, executes a critical section of code, and calls
sigsuspend() to unblock the signals and wait for delivery of a signal. This still
requires writing a signal handler for the signals. An alternative that's useful
in other situations and that frees us from having to write the signal handlers
is to use either sigwait() or sigwaitinfo(). A process can call either of these to
wait for the delivery of a specific set of signals. The difference between them
is that the latter can return information about a signal through a siginfo_t
parameter.

The sigwait() system call, whose prototype is

```
int sigwait(const sigset_t *set, int *sig);
```

suspends the calling process until one of the signals in set becomes pending. It accepts the signal, removing it from the pending list of signals, and
returns its number in sig. If signals in the set were already pending when
sigwait() is called, it returns immediately. If a signal in the set was previously
blocked and is sent to the process (and is therefore pending), sigwait() removes it from the pending list and returns. In other words, blocked signals
can be waited for by sigwait().

The sigwait() and sigwaitinfo() system calls are useful when we want to
write programs that respond to specific signals in a synchronous way, meaning without writing signal handlers that run whenever the signals are sent,
but instead responding to them within the program's ordinary functions.
The normal paradigm is to block all of the signals in which we're interested
and then enter a loop in which the program waits for one of those signals to
become pending. If multiple signals are pending, the one that is removed
is based on a set of rules specified in the signal(7) man page. The program
then performs an action based on which signal was removed. We don't write
signal handlers for these signals, though we do need them for any signals
not in the signal set. The program only responds to the signals when they're
accepted by sigwait() and removed from the pending list. The typical code
structure is:

```
sigprocmask(SIG_BLOCK, &mask, &oldmask);
if ( sigwait(&mask, &sig) != 0 )
    // OMITTED: Handle error.
```

```
switch ( sig ) {
case SIGINT:
    // OMITTED: Take some action for SIGINT.
    break;
case SIGUSR1:
    // OMITTED: Take some action for SIGUSR1.
    break;
--snip--
default:
    // OMITTED: Take some action for all other waited-for signals.
}
sigprocmask(SIG_SETMASK, &oldmask, NULL);
```

A sample program that follows this approach, *sigwait_demo1.c*, is available in
the book's source code distribution.

The sigaction() System Call

The sigaction() system call was introduced to replace the use of signal() for
installing signal handlers and controlling their behavior. It overcomes the
deficiencies of signal() that we described in "The signal() System Call" on
page 395, and it allows a programmer to specify how the handler will respond when multiple signals are sent to a program while it's executing a
signal handler. It also provides a way for a program to obtain detailed information about the source and cause of delivered signals. However, this
increased functionality comes with a cost, because it's harder to learn and
understand, and it raises new questions we've yet to consider.

We'll start by reading its man page. Its prototype is

```
#include <signal.h>

int sigaction(int signum, const struct sigaction *act,
              struct sigaction *oldaction;
```

where

- signum is the value of the signal to be handled

- act is a pointer to a sigaction structure that specifies the handler,
  masks, and flags for the signal

- oldact is a pointer to a structure to hold the currently active
  sigaction data

When called, it sets the disposition of signal (signum) based on the contents
of the sigaction structure act and saves its current disposition in oldact. If
successful, it returns 0; otherwise, it returns -1 and sets errno accordingly.
The man page tells us that we need to define the _POSIX_C_SOURCE feature test
macro to use this function. Notice that the function name is the same as the

name of the structure whose address is passed to it, like the stat() function and the stat structure.

Let's examine the sigaction structure first to learn what roles its various members play.

The sigaction Structure

The sigaction structure is declared in the *signal.h* header file. The man page states that it's "something like":

```
struct sigaction {
    void      (*sa_handler)(int);
    void      (*sa_sigaction)(int, siginfo_t *, void *);
    sigset_t  sa_mask;
    int        sa_flags;
    void      (*sa_restorer)(void);
};
```

The ambiguity is intentional, because the definition is more complicated than this. The page warns us that the two members sa_handler and sa_sigaction on some machines might be defined as a C union. A union is like a struct in which the members can have overlapping storage and therefore cannot have different values simultaneously. Figure 8-4 depicts a small union.

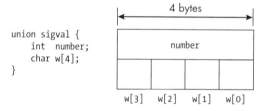

Figure 8-4: A C union with a 4-byte integer and a four-character string

In the sigaction structure, the two members are both pointers to functions. The fact that the functions have different prototypes is not a problem, since they're both pointers, which have a fixed number of bytes regardless of what they point to.

The sigaction structure allows us to install either the old-style signal handler that we've been using, whose prototype has a single integer parameter, or, if we include the appropriate flag in the sa_flags member, the newer POSIX-compliant type of signal handler whose prototype is:

```
void  (*sa_sigaction)(int signum, siginfo_t *info, void *ucontext);
```

But we must choose one or the other. Since we already know enough about the older method, we'll concentrate on the newer sa_sigaction type of signal handler. If the SA_SIGINFO flag is bitwise-ORed into the sa_flags member, then the sa_sigaction member of the structure will be installed as the signal handler, not the `sa_handler` member, and the pointer must point to a function whose prototype matches it.

The remaining members of the `sigaction` structure are as follows:

sa_mask   By default, the signal that caused the handler to run will be blocked during execution of the handler. This integer bitmask defines which other signals should also be blocked while the handler is running.

sa_restorer   This function pointer is not used by any application. It is strictly for the use of the C libraries, and we can safely ignore it.

sa_flags   This is an integer that encodes a set of flags that control how subsequent signals of the same type as the one that caused the handler to run are handled. For example, if a handler has caught a `SIGINT` signal and another `SIGINT` arrives while the handler is executing, then the flags in `sa_flags` will determine how to dispose of the second `SIGINT`, in effect overriding the default behavior of blocking it. The `sa_flags` member has no effect on arriving signals of other types. This `sa_flags` field is a bitwise-OR of several flags, the most important of which are:

> **SA_NODEFER**   If set, the kernel will not automatically block signals of the same type while it's being handled, which it does by default. This implies that an arriving signal of the same type will cause the handler to be interrupted and a second instance of it reentered with the second signal. A stack frame for the second instance is pushed on top of the stack frame for the first instance.
>
> **SA_RESETHAND**   When set, the signal action is reset to `SIG_DFL`. This means that as soon as the signal is delivered, the default action will take place. This flag implies the `SA_NODEFER` flag because signals are not blocked. The difference is that instead of a second handler instance running, the process takes the default action for the signal. The intention is to make the handler behave like the old-style, mouse trap–like `signal()` handler, since any signal of the same type arriving after the first will cause the default behavior.
>
> **SA_RESTART**   When set, certain system calls that would otherwise be terminated if a signal were delivered during their execution will be restarted automatically. The `signal(7)` man page lists and describes the system calls that would be restarted if this flag were set.
>
> **SA_SIGINFO**   When set, the newer-style `sa_sigaction` handler is installed, with three arguments passed to it. The first is the signal number. If the second argument is not `NULL`, it points to a `siginfo_t` structure containing the reason why the signal was generated; the third argument points to a `ucontext_t` structure containing the receiving process's context when the signal was delivered.

Two other flags that we'll make use of in Chapter 11 are `SA_NOCLDSTOP` and `SA_NOCLDWAIT`.

We'll explore how `sigaction()` works by way of some examples. We've got several different aspects of its behavior to study. In particular:

- What information can a signal handler obtain when the `SA_SIGINFO` flag is enabled in the call to `sigaction()`?

- When a synchronous signal such as a SIGFPE is delivered to a process and a handler for it runs, when the handler returns, is the instruction with the error executed from the point after the error, or will the error occur again?

- How do the various combinations of the SA_NODEFER, SA_RESETHAND, and SA_RESTART flags that can be bitwise-ORed into sa_flags affect how a program responds when signals of the same type as the one currently being handled are delivered to the process?

- When a signal handler is running and a signal of the same type is delivered because it's not blocked, the handler is interrupted and a second instance of it runs. How do we make the handler reentrant so that data is not corrupted when this happens?

Signal Information Passed to the Handler

When SA_SIGINFO is enabled in sa_flags, the signal handler that sigaction() installs is expected to have a prototype with three parameters, which are:

int signum The number of the signal causing the handler to run.

siginfo_t* info A pointer to a siginfo_t structure containing information about the signal such as what caused it, who the sender is, and so on.

void* ucontext A pointer to a ucontext_t structure, cast to void*. This structure contains information about the context of the program at the time the signal was delivered, such as what signals were blocked at the time and the location of the process stack. It is rarely used.

The first parameter is just the signal number, and the last is a structure that is rarely needed by the handler, so we'll concentrate on the second parameter, the siginfo_t structure.

The sigaction() man page on Linux contains a definition of this structure that shows all possible members it can have, as partially reproduced here:

```
siginfo_t {
    int          si_signo;  /* Signal number                              */
    int          si_errno;  /* An errno value                             */
    int          si_code;   /* Signal code                                */
    int          si_trapno; /* Trap num that caused hardware-generated sig */
    pid_t        si_pid;    /* Sending process ID                         */
    uid_t        si_uid;    /* Real user ID of sending process            */
    int          si_status; /* Exit value or signal                       */
❶  union sigval si_value;  /* Signal value                               */
    --snip--
    int          si_syscall; /* Number of attempted system call           */
    unsigned int si_arch;    /* Architecture of attempted system call     */
}
```

Although the definition makes it appear as though all of these members are present in this structure, they aren't. The narrative following the definition explains that the structure is essentially a union and that the set of members actually present when the handler runs depends on which signal the handler caught. Most of these members are filled in by only a few signals, but not others. In Linux, the only three members that are guaranteed to be part of the structure regardless of the signal type are si_signo, si_errno, and si_code. In contrast, POSIX.1-2024 specifies a different set of mandatory members, namely:

```
int          si_signo;    /* Signal number                        */
int          si_code;     /* Signal code                          */
pid_t        si_pid;      /* Sending process ID                   */
uid_t        si_uid;      /* Real user ID of sending process      */
int          si_status;   /* Exit value or signal                 */
union sigval si_value;    /* Signal value                         */
void         *si_addr;    /* Memory location which caused fault   */
```

The si_value field ❶ has type union sigval, which is defined in *siginfo.h*.

Which fields are filled in depends on the manner by which the signal is sent, the source of the signal, and the actual signal type. The idea is that when a particular signal is sent to a process and the handler catches it, some of this information is stored into selected fields that have meaning for that particular signal. For example, if a signal is sent by the kill() system call or the kill command, regardless of the signal type, then the si_pid and si_uid are filled in. In contrast, if a hardware-generated signal such as SIGILL or SIGSEGV is caught, then si_addr is filled with the address of the instruction causing the trap.

The simple program in Listing 8-10 is an example that demonstrates the first case.

sigact_demo1.c
```c
#include "common_hdrs.h"

void sig_handler(int signo, siginfo_t *info, void *context)
{
    printf("Signal number: %d\n", info->si_signo);    /* UNSAFE */
    printf("PID of sender: %d\n", info->si_pid);       /* UNSAFE */
    printf("UID of sender: %d\n\n", info->si_uid);     /* UNSAFE */
    /* Force the process to terminate by raising SIGTERM,
       for which we have no handler. */
    if ( signo == SIGINT )
        raise(SIGQUIT);
    else
        raise(SIGTERM);
}

int main(int argc, char *argv[])
{
```

```
    struct sigaction the_action;

    the_action.sa_flags     = SA_SIGINFO;
    the_action.sa_sigaction = sig_handler;

    if ( -1 == sigaction(SIGINT, &the_action, NULL) )
        fatal_error(errno, "sigaction()");
    if ( -1 == sigaction(SIGQUIT, &the_action, NULL) )
        fatal_error(errno, "sigaction()");
    printf("Open a second terminal window and send SIGINT "
           "by entering kill -s SIGINT %d\n", getpid());
    pause();
    return 0;
}
```

Listing 8-10: A program in which the signal handler displays information about the source of a signal

The main() function sets the handler for both SIGINT and SIGQUIT to be the sig_handler() function.

NOTE *Although I may occasionally use a single function to catch more than one signal, in general it's not a good idea to do so. It's better to install separate handlers for each signal type. I use a shared handler here only to save space.*

After installing the handlers, the program prints instructions to open a second terminal window and then pauses, so that we can take our time in setting up the terminal.

The handler begins by printing out the values of the three members of the siginfo_t structure that are guaranteed to have data. Then, if it received a SIGINT, it raises a SIGQUIT so that it will run a second time. When it runs the second time, it will have received a SIGQUIT and will raise SIGTERM, which is unhandled and will terminate the program. This design allows us to compare the information delivered when the kill() system call sent the signal (through the kill command) as opposed to when it was sent by the process itself through raise(). Since raise(signo) is equivalent to kill(getpid(), signo), the same fields are filled in by the two calls but the values will not be the same. A sample run of the program will look something like this:

```
$ ./sigact_demo1
Open a second terminal window and send SIGINT by entering kill -s SIGINT 12461
Signal number: 2
PID of sender: 4978
UID of sender: 500

Signal number: 3
PID of sender: 12461
UID of sender: 500

Terminated
```

Notice that the PID listed for the received SIGQUIT (signal number 3) is the same as the process's PID, whereas the one listed for the SIGINT is different because it's that of the kill command entered in a bash shell.

Let's look at another example in which the signal is caused by hardware. We can force a SIGFPE signal to be sent to a process by intentionally dividing by zero in our program and then examine the information in the signal handler. The only field filled in when a SIGFPE is received is the si_code field. The possible values for si_code and their meanings are described in the POSIX.1-2024 standard (*https://pubs.opengroup.org/onlinepubs/9699919799/ basedefs/signal.h.html*). The POSIX specification of the header file *signal.h*, which we can read by entering man signal.h, also contains the codes.

Because the compiler might optimize our intentional arithmetic errors out of the code, we'll turn off optimization when we compile this program, which appears in Listing 8-11. Running this program lets us see some of the codes generated by floating-point exceptions.

sigact_demo2.c

```
#define _GNU_SOURCE
#include "common_hdrs.h"
#include <signal.h>
#include <math.h>
❶ #include <fenv.h>

void fpe_handler(int signo, siginfo_t *info, void *context)
{   /* These calls to printf() are all UNSAFE. */
    printf("Signal: %s\n", strsignal(info->si_signo));
    switch ( info->si_code ) {
    case FPE_INTDIV:
        printf("Code: FPE_INTDIV (Integer divide by zero)\n"); break;
    case FPE_FLTDIV:
        printf("Code: FPE_FLTDIV (Floating-point divide by zero)\n"); break;
    case FPE_FLTOVF:
        printf("Code: FPE_FLTOVF (Floating-point overflow)\n"); break;
        --snip--
    }
❷ raise(SIGTERM);
}

int main(int argc, char *argv[])
{
    struct sigaction action;
    float            y = 2.0, z = 0.0;
    BOOL             float_divzero = FALSE;
    BOOL             float_overflow = FALSE;
    signed int       n = 1, m = 2;

    if ( 2 == argc )
        switch (argv[1][0]) {
        case 'f': float_divzero  = TRUE; break;
        case 'o': float_overflow = TRUE; break;
```

```
    case 'o': noreturn    = TRUE; break;
    }

action.sa_sigaction = fpe_handler;
action.sa_flags = SA_SIGINFO;
sigemptyset(&(action.sa_mask));
int excepts = FE_DIVBYZERO|FE_INEXACT|FE_INVALID|FE_OVERFLOW|FE_UNDERFLOW;
feenableexcept(excepts);
if ( sigaction(SIGFPE, &action, NULL) == -1 ) {
    fatal_error(errno, "sigaction");
    exit(1);
}

m = 2*n - m;   /* m == 0 but compiler doesn't detect it. */
if ( float_divzero )
    n = (int) y/z;
else if ( float_overflow )
    feraiseexcept(FE_OVERFLOW);
else
    n = n/m; /* Prevent compiler from warning about unused n. */

return n;
}
```

Listing 8-11: A program in which the signal handler displays information about a hardware-generated signal

Because the program uses functions from C's floating-point exception library, it must include the *fenv.h* ❶ header file and the math library must be linked into the code (with -lm). This program is designed to produce three different types of floating-point errors. If an f is given as the program argument, it will execute the statement, n = (int) y/z. Since z is really zero, this results in a floating-point divide-by-zero. If a o is given, it will raise a floating-point overflow artificially by calling feraiseexcept(FE_OVERFLOW). Otherwise, it will evaluate n/m, in which m is exactly 0, resulting in an integer-divide-by-zero. In order to force the floating-point traps to occur, the program enables them by calling feenableexcept(), passing a mask ❸ containing all allowable traps. The *fenv.h* ❶ header exposes the various floating-point exception-related functions and constants. To save space, only the relevant parts of the signal handler's switch statement are displayed.

The handler's call to raise(SIGTERM) ❷ forces the program to terminate. Without it, the program would enter an infinite loop. To experience this yourself, comment out this call and recompile and run the program. You'll see that it repeatedly outputs the following two lines:

```
Code: FPE_INTDIV (Integer divide by zero)
Signal: Floating point exception
```

This is because when a signal handler returns from execution, the program normally resumes execution in the instruction that was interrupted. In the case of hardware-detected errors such as floating-point exceptions, the very code that caused the trap will be reexecuted, causing an infinite cycle of traps. A signal handler must either terminate the program explicitly or raise an exception such as SIGTERM that causes it to terminate.

We compile and run this program, first without any arguments and then with f followed by o:

```
$ ./sigact_demo2
Signal: Floating point exception
Code: FPE_INTDIV (Integer divide by zero)
Terminated
$ ./sigact_demo2 f
Signal: Floating point exception
Code: FPE_FLTDIV (Floating-point divide by zero)
Terminated
$ ./sigact_demo2 o
Signal: Floating point exception
Code: FPE_FLTOVF (Floating-point overflow)
Terminated
```

This output confirms that the si_code member of the info parameter can be used to determine the exact type of error that was trapped when the program ran.

To obtain similar information about the causes of other signals, we need to consult the sigaction man page, which has the remaining details about exactly which signals populate the various members of the siginfo_t structure. As an alternative, the POSIX.1-2024 specification has tables that show the possible values assigned to si_code, as well as the remaining fields, for each signal type. We can refer to them as needed when writing code that needs this type of information.

Effect of sa_flags on Signal Handler Execution

Let's turn our attention to studying the effects of the different possible sa_flags on a program's signal handling. The three flags we consider are SA_RESETHAND, SA_NODEFER, and SA_RESTART. The best way to understand what these flags do is to write a program that lets us see these effects, both in isolation and in combination with each other. We'll develop a small program that does exactly this.

First, let's review the difference between how a handler behaves with and without the SA_NODEFER flag being enabled. Suppose that a signal handler is running because it received a signal of some hypothetical type SIGX. If SA_NODEFER was not enabled when the handler was installed, signals of type SIGX will be blocked by default. In this case, if a second SIGX is sent, it will not be delivered to the process until the signal handler terminates. If more than one SIGX arrives while it's blocked, only a single instance is delivered. On the other hand, if the SA_NODEFER flag is enabled, a signal of type SIGX will be delivered while the handler is running, interrupting the handler. A second instance of the handler will run. If another SIGX arrives, it will interrupt the second instance of the handler, and so on. It behaves like a recursive function.

With this in mind, we can design a handler. So that we can tell whether a second call of the handler interrupted a first, as opposed to the second call starting after the first finished executing, we'll have the handler generate a unique number based on the time it was called, accurate to the millisecond, and print a message containing that number as soon as it starts running and just before it exits. The printed messages will show us the ordering of the calls. Therefore, our handler's logic, step by step, should be as follows:

1. On entry, the handler gets the current time with at least millisecond accuracy and uses that time to generate a unique number, which we'll name call_id.

2. It prints a short message that the handler was entered, along with its call_id and the type of signal it received.

3. To allow enough time for multiple signals to be delivered while the handler is running, it then spins in a loop that does nothing, just to prolong its running time.

4. When it is about to exit, it prints a second message that it is exiting, along with its call_id and signal type.

Suppose the entry and exit messages are of the form:

```
Entered handler for signal SIGINT, ID=1234567
Leaving handler for signal SIGINT, ID=1234567
```

Then, with this design, if signals aren't blocked, meaning SA_NODEFER is set, and they're sent quickly enough that the handler is running when they're sent, the sequence of printed messages should look like matching bookends:

```
Entered handler for signal SIGINT, ID=521400
Entered handler for signal SIGINT, ID=521500
Entered handler for signal SIGINT, ID=521600
--snip--
Leaving handler for signal SIGINT, ID=521600
Leaving handler for signal SIGINT, ID=521500
Leaving handler for signal SIGINT, ID=521400
```

On the other hand, if they're blocked (SA_NODEFER not set), the sequence will instead be a sequence of interleaved entrance and exit messages, such as this:

```
Entered handler for signal SIGINT, ID=521400
Leaving handler for signal SIGINT, ID=521400
Entered handler for signal SIGINT, ID=521500
Leaving handler for signal SIGINT, ID=521500
Entered handler for signal SIGINT, ID=521600
Leaving handler for signal SIGINT, ID=521600
--snip--
```

When we researched functions for working with time in Chapter 3, we came across one named clock_gettime(). We decided we didn't need it for implementing the date command because it was accurate to the nanosecond, but we'll use it now. Its prototype is:

```
#include <time.h>
int clock_gettime(clockid_t clockid, struct timespec *tp);
```

The clockid is a constant indicating which clock to use. In our case, we'll use the one named CLOCK_REALTIME, which is like a wall clock's time. The struct timespec is defined by:

```
struct timespec {
    time_t   tv_sec;      /* Seconds     */
    long     tv_nsec;     /* Nanoseconds */
};
```

The handler will call clock_gettime() to get the current time, accurate to the nanosecond, storing it into a timespec structure (t). To generate the call_id, it will multiply the number of seconds (tv_sec) by 1,000 and add the number of nanoseconds (tv_nsec) divided by 1,000,000 to get a number of milliseconds. To make call_id shorter, we'll drop the high-order digits in the number of seconds. The instruction is therefore:

```
call_id = 1000*(t.tv_sec & 0xFFF) + (t.tv_nsec / 1000000);
```

We're ready to assemble the handler function, which is in Listing 8-12.

sig_handler()
```
void sig_handler(int signo, siginfo_t *info, void *context)
{
    int             call_id; /* Num to uniquely identify sig handler run */
    int             i, j = 0;
    struct timespec t;       /* Time handler starts                      */

    /* Get current time in nanoseconds. */
    if ( -1 == clock_gettime(CLOCK_REALTIME, &t) )
        raise(SIGTERM);
    /* Create an ID to uniquely identify this call to handler. */
    call_id = (t.tv_sec & 0xFFF)*1000 + (t.tv_nsec / 1000000);
    printf("Entered handler for SIG%s ID=%d\n",
            sigabbrev_np(info->si_signo), call_id);
    /* Artificially delay handler to allow time for signals to arrive. */
    for ( i = 0; i < 200000000; i++ ) { j++; }
    printf("Leaving handler for SIG%s ID=%d\n",
            sigabbrev_np(info->si_signo), call_id);
}
```

Listing 8-12: The signal handler for sigact_demo3.c

Let's turn to the main program now. Because we're also interested in the effect of the SA_RESTART flag, which determines whether or not system calls are restarted if a signal arrives while they're executing, the program needs to make a system call, not just any call, but one that blocks waiting for the user to do something. The ideal candidate is the read() call. The signal(7) man page listed this call as one that can be restarted if it's waiting for a slow device. Reading from the terminal is considered slow; therefore, our main program will have a while loop that repeatedly calls read() to read a small number of characters from the terminal.

The program will prompt the user to enter a few characters and provide a way for them to terminate the program by entering quit. It'll check the return value of read() each time. If it's -1, we'll see if the errno value is EINTR, which indicates it was interrupted by a signal. If so, we'll print a message; otherwise, we'll print whatever the user entered.

There are a few complications. First, we've never used read() to read from a terminal. Unlike a read from a file, a read from a terminal does not return until the user presses ENTER. When we study terminals, we'll see how to prevent that, but for now, we have to work with this limitation. Also, it's inadvisable to mix calls to the I/O library functions such as printf() with system calls such as read() in the same program; the library functions can interfere with the reads. Therefore, we'll use write() to write our messages to the terminal.

The last problem is what happens if the user enters too many characters. For example, suppose the program asks the user to enter 12 characters but they enter 20. Where are those characters stored? Are they discarded? Are they saved for the next read()? These questions all pertain to the subject of terminals, which we'll study in Chapter 18. A simplified answer, for now, is that there's a hidden queue that contains the characters that the user enters and that if a call to read() requested N characters, as soon as N characters are in the queue, read() returns, leaving any other entered characters in the queue for the next call to read() (see Figure 8-5).

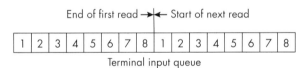

Figure 8-5: A read of eight characters from the terminal, showing where the next read operation will start

If we don't want those extra characters in the queue, we can discard them by calling tcflush(), which is a function in the TERMIOS library. We give this function the file descriptor for the terminal and an operation code:

```
tcflush(STDIN_FILENO, TCIFLUSH); /* Flush all input from terminal. */
```

We empty the input buffer before each read operation in case characters might be remaining from a preceding read.

The pseudocode loop body is therefore as follows:

1. Zero the buffer into which read() will store the user's text, using memset(buffer, 0, buffer_size).

2. Flush the terminal queue in case there's anything there with tcflush(STDIN_FILENO, TCIFLUSH).

3. Display a prompt string with write(STDOUT_FILENO, prompt, strlen(prompt)).

4. Read from the terminal with chars_entered = read(STDIN_FILENO, &buffer, buffer_size).

5. If the read was interrupted, display a message to that effect; otherwise, display what the user entered.

We put all of this together into the program shown in Listing 8-13, omitting the handler code. The complete program is available in the source code distribution for the book.

sigact_demo3.c
```c
#include "common_hdrs.h"
#include <signal.h>
#include <termios.h> /* Needed for tcflush */

/* Prototype for handler, shown in previous listing */
void sig_handler(int signo, siginfo_t *info, void *context);

int main(int argc, char *argv[])
{
    const int    maxsize = INPUTLEN; /* Maximum input size               */
    const char   intr_message[] = "    read() was interrupted.\n";
    const char   out_label[]    = "Entered text:";
    char         buffer[maxsize+2];  /* INPUTLEN plus newline and null byte */
    struct sigaction action;
    sigset_t     blocked;               /* Set of blocked sigs           */
    int          flags = 0;
    int          n, i = 1;
    char         prompt[128];
    int          reply_len = strlen(out_label);
    int          intr_message_len = strlen(intr_message);
    int          prompt_len;

    sprintf(prompt, "Type at most %d characters, then <ENTER>"
                    "(or 'quit' to quit):", maxsize);
    prompt_len = strlen(prompt);

    /* Get command line arguments and check which ones user entered. */
    while ( i < argc ) {
        if ( 0 == strncmp("reset", argv[i], strlen(argv[i])) )
            flags |= SA_RESETHAND;
```

```
        else if ( 0 == strncmp("nodefer", argv[i], strlen(argv[i])) )
            flags |= SA_NODEFER;
        else if ( 0 == strncmp("restart", argv[i], strlen(argv[i])) )
            flags |= SA_RESTART;
        i++;
    }

    /* Set up sigaction. */
    action.sa_sigaction = sig_handler;      /* SIGINT handler          */
    action.sa_flags = SA_SIGINFO | flags;   /* Add the entered flags.   */
    sigemptyset(&blocked);                  /* Clear all bits of mask.  */
    action.sa_mask = blocked;               /* Set blocked mask.        */

    /* Install sig_handler as the SIGINT handler. */
    if ( sigaction(SIGINT, &action, NULL) == -1 )
        fatal_error(errno, "sigaction");

    while ( TRUE ) {
        memset((void*)buffer, 0, maxsize+2);    /* Zero input buffer.      */
        tcflush(STDIN_FILENO,TCIFLUSH);         /* Remove bytes never sent. */
        write(STDOUT_FILENO, prompt, prompt_len); /* Write prompt string.   */
        n = read(STDIN_FILENO, &buffer, maxsize+1); /* Read user input.     */
        if ( -1 == n  &&  EINTR == errno )      /* If interrupted by signal */
            write(STDOUT_FILENO, intr_message, intr_message_len);
        else {
            if ( strncmp("quit", buffer, 4) == 0 )  /* User wants to quit.  */
                break;
            else {              /* Write the entered characters to terminal. */
                write(STDOUT_FILENO, &out_label, reply_len);
                if ( buffer[n-1] != '\n' ) /* If so, terminate with newline */
                    buffer[n-1] = '\n';
                write(STDOUT_FILENO, &buffer, n);
            }
        }
    }
    return 0;
}
```

Listing 8-13: A program that can be used to test the effects of several different sa_flags

We can run this program without any arguments or with any combination of the words reset, nodefer, and restart. First, run it with just reset and don't even enter any characters. Just enter two CTRL-Cs slowly:

```
$ ./sigact_demo3 reset
Type at most 12 characters, then <ENTER>(or 'quit' to quit):^CEntered handler
for SIGINT ID=53264325
Leaving handler for SIGINT ID=53264325
    read() was interrupted.
```

```
Type at most 12 characters, then <ENTER>(or 'quit' to quit):^C
$
```

The flag puts the handler into mouse trap mode so that the second CTRL-C terminates the program. It never reaches the second call to read(). If you run it again but enter the CTRL-Cs faster, you won't even see the first message that the read was interrupted.

Now try running it with the restart argument and nothing else. This time, enter a few CTRL-Cs rapidly:

```
$ ./sigact_demo3 restart
Type at most 12 characters, then <ENTER>(or 'quit' to quit):^CEntered handler
for SIGINT ID=53551971
^C^CLeaving handler for SIGINT ID=53551971
Entered handler for SIGINT ID=53552390
^CLeaving handler for SIGINT ID=53552390
Entered handler for SIGINT ID=53552785
Leaving handler for SIGINT ID=53552785
```

The display does not show the prompt character because the program is still in the read() system call, waiting for input, evidence that the read() was restarted. You can enter quit or terminate it with CTRL-\, or you can continue by pressing ENTER, in which case you'll get the prompt back. Notice that the signals are not blocked; all of them were delivered to the handler, but they were queued, so that the handler got them one after another. Try this again, but enter some text to see that it outputs the text.

The next test is to run it with the nodefer argument. It's best to try it by itself first, without entering text:

```
$ ./sigact_demo3 nodefer
Type at most 12 characters, then <ENTER>(or 'quit' to quit):^CEntered handler
for SIGINT ID=53972397
^CEntered handler for SIGINT ID=53972556
^CEntered handler for SIGINT ID=53972732
^CEntered handler for SIGINT ID=53972868
Leaving handler for SIGINT ID=53972868
Leaving handler for SIGINT ID=53972732
Leaving handler for SIGINT ID=53972556
Leaving handler for SIGINT ID=53972397
    read() was interrupted.
Type at most 12 characters, then <ENTER>(or 'quit' to quit):quit
$
```

The signals were all delivered, and each interrupted the previous one.

If you run this program and enter more than 12 characters at the prompt, the excess will be discarded. But you should try the following experiment: Comment out the call to flush the input queue, recompile the program, and enter dozens of characters at the prompt. What do you see?

The preceding program showed how to detect when a read() from the terminal was interrupted by a signal. If we want to design a handler for a signal such as SIGINT, enabling restarting of interrupted system calls, the handler should print a suitable message to the terminal when it runs, telling the user to reenter the text. The following simple, old-style handler demonstrates this idea:

```
/* File-scoped variables */
volatile sig_atomic_t got_interrupt = 0;
char alert[] = "\nSignal caught; re-enter input.\n>";
int  alertlen; /* In main(), assign with alertlen = strlen(alert). */

void on_interrupt(int signo)
{
    // OMITTED: Other signal handling code
    got_interrupt = 1;
    write(1, alert, alertlen);
}
```

Notice that in this example, we call write() instead of printf() because it's signal safe. If this handler is installed in a program to catch SIGINT and that signal is delivered, the user will see a message such as

```
Signal caught; re-enter input.
>
```

with the prompt (>) indicating that it is waiting for more input.

Guidance on Designing Signal Handlers

This section provides a short list of dos and don'ts in the design of signal handlers. We've already mentioned a few of these.

- Most of the time, it's best to do as little as possible inside a signal handler. If receiving a particular signal requires that a significant amount of work needs to be done, the handler should set a sig_atomic_t flag that the main program can monitor periodically. The main program should then do the work. The exception to this rule is when the main program does essentially nothing and all of the work is performed by signal handlers. When we explore the design of interactive programs, we'll see how this works.

- Many functions are considered to be unsafe when called from inside a signal handler. The complete list of them, as well as an explanation and guidance on signal safety, is in the signal-safety(7) man page. Your programs should not call any of these functions from within a signal handler. Since printf() isn't safe, to print messages from within a handler, we can try to use the write() system call. If the message requires the kind of formatting available only with printf(), then if it's possible, we can create a formatted string and pass it to write(). Sometimes it's possible to just set a flag in the handler and write outside of it. The following code snippet suggests how to do this:

```
static volatile sig_atomic_t flag = 0;

void catch_sigint(int signum)
{
    flag = 1;
}

int main(int argc, char *argv[])
{
    --snip--
    sigprocmask(SIG_BLOCK, &blockedset, NULL);
    if ( flag ) {
        printf("SIGINT received\n");
        flag = 0;
    }
    else
        printf("SIGINT not received\n");
    sigprocmask(SIG_UNBLOCK, &blockedset, NULL);
}
```

- Signal handlers are usually meant to be the last code executed when a signal is delivered to a process. Usually, the program should exit after the handler runs, but sometimes it needs to perform a few short tasks first. There are advanced techniques for jumping to a different part of a program's code in this case, but we don't discuss them here. You can read about sigsetjmp() and siglongjmp() in their man pages.

- It isn't a good idea to use the same handler for more than one signal type; it makes it all the harder to design the handler to be reentrant.

You can find more extensive guidance on the design of signal handlers in the GNU C Library Reference Manual (*https://www.gnu.org/software/libc/manual/*).

In short, signal handlers are usually called asynchronously, at unpredictable times, to do as little as possible. The call can happen between the beginning and the end of a C operator that requires multiple instructions. Even copying one integer variable into another can take two instructions on most machines. If a handler uses global or static variables that are not sig_atomic_t, results can be unpredictable. If it spends too much time, there's a chance another signal might arrive. Keep them short and simple whenever possible.

Summary

Signals are essentially empty messages that are sent to processes to notify them of events requiring their attention. They were originally designed for exceptional events such as arithmetic errors or attempts by users to terminate a process, but now they're used more extensively, and they also serve as a simple means of interprocess communication. There are many different types of signals, with each distinct type represented by a unique number that has a symbolic name beginning with `SIG`, such as `SIGINT` or `SIGTERM`.

Signals can be sent to a process by the kernel, by users with the `kill` command, and by other processes with the `kill()` system call. Users and processes require appropriate permission to send signals to a process. A process can also send a signal to itself with the `raise()` system call. Technically, the kernel does all of this sending; users and processes only make requests to the kernel to send signals. Despite this, we usually say that users and processes send the signals.

When a request is made to send a signal to a process or an event occurs that requires that a signal be sent to that process, the kernel generates the signal by updating some data structures representing the state of that process. The signal is considered to be delivered to a process when the process receives and responds to it. Until it's delivered, it's called a pending signal.

Processes can temporarily block the delivery of most types of signals by creating signal masks. Blocked signals are delivered when the process unblocks them. If multiple signals of the same type are delivered to a process that has blocked them, all but one of them will be discarded.

Signal delivery is usually asynchronous with respect to process execution, which means that the time at which the process receives it is independent of where the process is in its computation. Signals sent by users, other processes, and the kernel are typically asynchronous. In contrast, a signal that's due to a hardware exception caused by the process itself is delivered synchronously—each time the process runs, the signal is delivered at the exact same time in the process's execution.

A process's disposition of a signal is what it does in response to it. There are three possible responses. One is to accept the default action associated with the signal's type, which is typically termination of the process. Another is to ignore the signal explicitly. The third is to execute a function that the process previously designated to be invoked whenever a signal of that type is delivered to it. This type of function is called a signal handler, and when it's run, we say the signal's been caught by it. Designating a signal handler function to be invoked on receipt of a signal is called registering or installing it.

The `signal()` system call was the original method of installing signal handlers in early UNIX systems, and it's still available in most systems, but because it isn't standardized, it should not be used. Modern applications should use the POSIX-conforming `sigaction()` system call. This latter call provides much finer and greater control over how signals are handled. For example, it lets us control what a signal handler does when signals arrive during its execution and what types of information are available for the handler to access.

Exercises

1. Write a function with the prototype

   ```
   int printsigset(sigset_t set);
   ```

   that prints, on a single line of standard output, a list of the numbers of all standard signals in the set set or prints empty set if it has none. It should return -1 on error and 0 on success. Use functions from *glibc* as needed and the appropriate feature test macro.

2. One function that we didn't explore is sigpending(). Read its man page and then write a function that prints on a single line of standard output a list of the numbers of all pending signals or prints no pending signals if there are none. It should return -1 on error and 0 on success.

3. The abort() library function terminates the calling process by sending it a SIGABRT signal. However, because the caller might have a signal handler for SIGABRT, it has to do more than simply raise this signal. Read its man page and then write an implementation of it.

4. In this chapter, we didn't explore methods of waiting for signals other than the pause() system call. That call suspends a process until a signal arrives and its signal handler runs or it is unhandled and terminates the process. Why would a process want to suspend itself until a signal arrives? Can you think of applications for which this is useful? List a few of them.

5. The sigwait() function suspends the calling process until a signal of a specified type arrives. Read its man page and write a program that
   - Prints its process ID and then blocks all signals
   - Sleeps for 30 seconds
   - Suspends itself waiting for signals to become pending
   - Prints a list of all signals that are pending

   It should be designed so that a SIGINT will terminate it after the pending signals are printed. You can open a second terminal to send signals to this process.

9

TIMERS AND SLEEP FUNCTIONS

In Chapter 8, in learning how to design programs that respond to signals, we took another step toward being able to write interactive and event-driven programs, but we still have a few more concepts to understand. These types of programs, whether they're system programs or other types of applications, often treat time and time intervals as part of their input data.

For example, a program that pops up a message such as "Are you still there?" when it hasn't detected any user activity for a while uses the length of a time interval to decide when it needs to display a message to its user. Some programs display flashing cursors, which blink at regular time intervals. A large class of system programs that monitor resource usage are capable of producing some type of animated or dynamic output, such as a graph that updates regularly as time progresses or a terminal display that refreshes itself at regular intervals. Commands that fall into this category include:

`top`   Displays extensive information about all processes in the system

`pidstat`   Displays information about selected processes

vmstat   Displays information about memory usage

iostat   Displays information about input/output activity

By default, the top command refreshes its information every few seconds. The others do so when the user enters a refresh interval as an option. For example, entering vmstat 3 tells the vmstat command to append new data to its report every 3 seconds. These types of programs have a way of controlling the precise times at which they execute specific functions.

In this chapter, we'll learn how to design and develop programs that can time their behavior in the same way. To do so, we'll need to learn a bit about time and time measurement in Unix systems. This journey will take us through an exploration of clocks and hardware timers as well, since they underlie the management of time in any computer system. We'll explore the concept of software timers and examine the relationship between timers, sleeping, and clocks. Although our primary focus is the part of the kernel's API related to timing and timers, we'll also examine two sleep functions we haven't yet seen. We'll put all of these ideas to use in the design and development of a few programs that work with time.

Keeping Track of Time

Programs that are capable of doing specific tasks at regular intervals must have a way to keep track of time and perform tasks at scheduled times. Let's think about some real-world analogues to this problem. In the real world, when we need to perform tasks at precise intervals of time, we often use a timer. For example, when we need to adjust the temperature of an oven in 30 minutes, to remember to do this, we set a timer to notify us when that time elapses. If we're conducting some experiment that requires collecting data every 10 minutes, we use a more advanced type of timer that can repeatedly signal us every 10 minutes. In general, we use timers to inform us when a specified amount of time has elapsed. When that amount of time has elapsed, we call it a *timeout*. We set a timer by giving it a length of time. Usually, setting a timer also arms the timer. To *arm* a timer means to start it, whereas *setting* it specifies the length of the interval. When the interval expires, it notifies us, usually with some type of audible or visual indication.

Alarm Clocks and Timers

A timer is not the same as an alarm clock. Normally, we wouldn't use an alarm clock in the preceding situations. When our goal is to be notified when a fixed amount of time has passed, using an alarm clock is inconvenient. We use alarm clocks to notify us when a specific wall clock time has been reached, not when a timeout has occurred. We set an alarm clock with a specific wall clock time, and at that time, it notifies us. A timer's input, on the other hand, is the length of a time interval. It doesn't need the time of day in order to work, but it does need some type of internal timekeeping device to keep track of the elapsed time. Although alarm clocks do serve a purpose in a computer system, such as scheduling jobs that have to take place at a certain time of day, they're not a solution to the types of problems we just considered.

Sleep Functions and Timers

Up until now, our programs relied entirely on sleep functions such as `sleep()` and `usleep()` to insert some form of time-dependent delay into their executions. When a process calls a sleep function, it specifies an interval of time as the argument to the call, and it's immediately suspended. When that time has elapsed, it wakes up and resumes execution at the instruction following the call, unless an unhandled signal interrupted its sleep, in which case it was most likely terminated. For example, if we wanted a program to check whether some file will have been modified within the next 30 seconds, with what we know now, we'd make it sleep for 30 seconds and then check the file when it wakes up. The problem with this solution is that the program can't do anything while it's waiting, which is neither useful nor efficient.

Let's consider how we could program a progress bar if all we had at our disposal were sleep functions. Suppose that our process performs some very lengthy task, such as copying a large number of files from one filesystem to another, and that we'd like it to display a dynamic indicator of how much it's accomplished and update it at regular intervals. This is what a progress bar does. Suppose that at any instant of time, the program can compute what fraction of the task has been completed. If the only way to schedule an update of the progress bar at some future time is by sleeping for that amount of time, we couldn't do the work whose progress we're trying to measure! Clearly sleep functions are useless for solving this problem.

Suppose instead that we could use some type of software timer analogous to a real-world timer. If a program needed to do some particular task at a future time, like checking a file, it could set a timer, just like a real-world timer, to interrupt it when that amount of time elapsed. In this way, it could continue to do its work in the meantime. When the timer expired, it would temporarily stop what it was doing, perform the scheduled task (such as checking the file), and return to the interrupted work. Let's consider how we could program a progress bar if we had timers at our disposal. Suppose that a program could set a timer to expire repeatedly at regular intervals. Each time that it received a notice of a timeout, the program could compute the amount of work completed and update the indicator. Assuming that the calculation and update are fast, this is an efficient way to keep the user informed of its progress.

With this in mind, let's see what we can learn from the online documentation about timers and related functions. Our objective is to learn what services the kernel provides for user programs so that they can use timers. There are questions though, such as how fine a granularity we can expect from a timer and how accurate they are. We also need to know how they notify our programs when timeouts occur. We need the answers to these questions.

Time, Clocks, and Timing

We'll begin our exploration as we've done in previous chapters: by trying to find a man page that contains an overview, guidance, and possibly references to other resources. Whenever they exist, the man pages in Section 7 are always a good place to start. Therefore, we'll search Section 7 for a page about timers or something similar, trying the keywords time and timers:

```
$ apropos -s7 time timer
--snip--
sys_time.h (7posix)  - time types
sys_times.h (7posix) - file access and modification times structure
systemd.time (7)     - Time and date specifications
time (7)             - overview of time and timers
time.h (7posix)      - time types
time_namespaces (7)  - overview of Linux time namespaces
utime.h (7posix)     - access and modification times structure
❶ timer: nothing appropriate.
```

Among the matches is the time (7) man page that we first discovered in Chapter 3. Back then we were interested in dates and times, not timers, but this page has information about timers as well. We'll start by reviewing it, but notice before we continue that there isn't a man page about timers specifically ❶, suggesting that this is the right place to start.

Overview

The time (7) man page is divided into brief sections with background information about general topics. It starts with information about distinctions between real and process time, distinctions between hardware and software clocks, concepts of time measurement and time representation, and finally, a brief discussion of timers, with references to specific system calls related to timers. We do need to understand something about clocks and time measurement to use timers properly, but let's first see what kinds of timers are available.

The set of available timers is listed in the section entitled "Sleeping and Setting Timers" on the man page. There it mentions several timer system calls, including alarm(), getitimer(), timerfd_create(), and timer_create(). It also mentions two system calls for sleeping that we haven't examined yet: nanosleep() and clock_nanosleep(). We'll read about them shortly. Before we do, we'll explore the basic concepts underlying clocks and time measurement.

Hardware Clocks and Hardware Timers

Most computers have a designated hardware clock called the *real-time clock* (*RTC*) that keeps wall clock time, which we called *calendar time* in Chapter 3. Some computers have more than one hardware clock, and they're also called RTCs. Among all of the RTCs, there's one that is backed up by a battery while the computer is turned off or in a low-power state so that it keeps its time. To avoid confusion, we'll call this battery-backed hardware clock the RTC and ignore the fact that there might be other real-time clocks in the computer.

The principal purpose of the RTC is to record the wall clock time. Linux systems use it only to initialize various software structures that store time and date for functions such as time() and gettimeofday(), which return the correct date and time. The RTC does have other capabilities though, one of which is that it can be programmed to generate periodic interrupts on a dedicated interrupt line at selected frequencies ranging between 2 Hz and 8,192 Hz. It can also generate an interrupt for every clock tick, which is usually once per second. Lastly, it can be programmed so that when it reaches a prespecified number of recorded ticks, it generates an interrupt so that it can function like an alarm clock. Exactly how it works is architecture dependent.

Many computers also have a hardware device called a *programmable interval timer* (*PIT*). The PIT issues an interrupt, called a *timer interrupt*, whenever it times out. The PIT is essentially a hardware timer, like a kitchen timer, except that it continues to generate interrupts at the same rate as long as the machine is powered. Linux kernels typically program the PIT to issue interrupts about once every millisecond, a frequency of 1,000 Hz. The interval between adjacent interrupts is called a *tick*. The PIT's ticks are like a metronome inside the computer; they are used by the kernel to control all aspects of its timing. Multimedia playback and media streaming depend upon these ticks for smooth playing. The kernel constant HZ is the frequency at which these ticks are generated, and the term *jiffy* refers to the length of each tick of this timer.

A third type of timekeeping device is called the *Time Stamp Counter*. Linux systems sometimes use this hardware counter for higher-precision timing; the oscillator in this device can have much higher frequencies than the PIT, as high as 1 GHz, making it useful for finer-resolution timing.

Lastly, many modern computers have high-resolution timers, called *High Precision Event Timers* (*HPETs*). These timers are supported in Linux kernels from version 2.6 onward. They contain internal counters that they update at least once every 10 microseconds, meaning a frequency of at least 100 KHz. They have internal circuitry so that they can be programmed to generate interrupts at periodic intervals or only once, when a counter reaches a specific value. They're used by the kernel to support the high-resolution timers that we'll learn about later in this chapter.

The System Clock

The system clock is a *software clock*, which means that time is recorded and updated entirely by software. Whenever the computer is rebooted, the kernel initializes the system clock, either by reading the time from the RTC or, if it has a network connection, by getting it from a network time service such as an *NTP (Network Time Protocol)* server. Until it's initialized, the time on a system clock is just the time that elapsed since the machine was rebooted. Once it's initialized, the system clock stores the calendar time, meaning the number of seconds since the Epoch.

The system clock is updated every time it receives an interrupt from the PIT. In other words, the system clock is initialized from a hardware clock when the computer boots, but after that, it keeps time by recording ticks from a hardware timer. As just mentioned in "Hardware Clocks and Hardware Timers," the length of these clock ticks is a jiffy. If the PIT generates ticks at a rate of 100 Hz, each jiffy is 0.01 seconds. If the rate is 250 Hz, then a jiffy is 0.004 seconds. There is no single value for a jiffy; it is machine dependent. On some systems it might be 0.01, on others 0.004, and so on.

This discussion about clocks and clock ticks is both relevant and important because on older Linux kernels, the resolution of software timers depends on the value of a jiffy; a timer can't be more accurate than the length of a jiffy. The man page tells us as much. On newer kernels, some timer system calls aren't based on jiffies but are based on the high-resolution timers (HRTs) such as the HPETs.

High-Resolution Sleep Functions

We've used the `sleep()` system call extensively so far. One problem with `sleep()` is that its resolution is 1 second, which is too coarse for many applications. We also used `usleep()`, which has a resolution of 1 microsecond. The u in `usleep()` is the Roman character set's approximation of the Greek letter μ, the symbol for *micro*. Even though its unit is a microsecond, a call such as `usleep(usecs)` doesn't guarantee that the length of the interval during which the process sleeps will be exactly usecs microseconds—only that it's at least this much. According to the man page, it can be longer either because the underlying timers are not fine enough or because of "system activity."

Sleep functions such as `sleep()` and `usleep()` are implemented with hidden software timers. One problem with both of them is that they share a single software timer given to the process, which implies that multiple overlapping calls to `usleep()` or `sleep()` can interfere with each other, causing unexpected results. They also share the same timer as the `alarm()` system call, with similar consequences. Furthermore, they may interfere with signal generation and delivery because their implementations rely on signals. The man page for `usleep()` suggests that to avoid this signal problem, programs should use `nanosleep()` instead.

The nanosleep() System Call

POSIX requires implementations of Unix to provide a nanosleep() system call, which is guaranteed not to interact with signals and has, as its name suggests, nanosecond resolution. The SYNOPSIS on its man page is:

```
#include <time.h>
int nanosleep(const struct timespec *req, struct timespec *rem);

Feature Test Macro Requirements for glibc (see feature_test_macros(7)):
    nanosleep(): _POSIX_C_SOURCE >= 199309L
```

A calling program must define _POSIX_C_SOURCE with a value of at least 199,309 before including any header files. The call's two parameters are pointers to timespec structures. We first encountered the timespec structure in Chapter 3, in the man page for clock_gettime(), which we opted not to use because time() was a simpler function. I redisplay its definition for convenience:

```
struct timespec {
    time_t tv_sec;  /* Seconds     */
    long   tv_nsec; /* Nanoseconds */
};
```

The value in tv_nsec must be an integer in the range 0 to 999,999,999, so that it doesn't exceed 1 second, but it can represent any fraction of a second accurate to the nanosecond. This implies that, unlike sleep() and usleep(), the nanosleep() function lets us specify time intervals with nanosecond resolution.

The nanosleep() function's first argument is required; it's the length of the time interval during which the process should sleep. The second argument may be NULL. If it isn't NULL, then it should point to a timespec structure that will be filled with the remaining time if the call to nanosleep() is interrupted by a signal, in which case nanosleep() returns -1 and sets errno to EINTR. The following code snippet shows how we can detect when nanosleep() was interrupted in order to continue the sleep, assuming that requested_delay and remaining_time are timespec structures:

```
if ( -1 == nanosleep(&requested_delay, &remaining_time) )
    if ( errno == EINTR )
        /* remaining_time contains the time left in the interval. */
```

Since timespec structures will play a part in several programs from this point on, I've written a few utility functions to make it easier to use them. Their declarations, which follow, are in the file *include/time_utils.h* of the source code repository:

time_utils.h
```
/** dbl_to_timespec(t, *ts) converts the number of seconds represented by the
    double-precision float t into a timespec structure, storing it in *ts. */
int dbl_to_timespec(double t, struct timespec *ts);
```

```
/** timespec_to_dbl(ts, *t) converts the time represented by the timespec
      ts to a double-precision float and stores it in *t. */
void timespec_to_dbl(struct timespec ts, double *t);

/** add_dbl_to_timespec(t, &ts, &newtime) adds the number of seconds
      represented by double t to timespec ts, storing the sum into timespec
      newtime. */
void add_dbl_to_timespec(double t, struct timespec *ts,
                                struct timespec *newtime);

/** timespec_diff(ts1, ts2, *diff) computes the difference ts1 - ts2,
      storing it in *diff. */
void timespec_diff (struct timespec ts1, struct timespec ts2,
                        struct timespec *diff);

/** timespec_add(ts1, ts2, &sum) stores the sum of timespecs ts1 and ts2
      into &sum. */
void timespec_add(struct timespec ts1, struct timespec ts2,
                        struct timespec *sum);
```

The implementations are in the file *common/time_utils.c* in the book's source code distribution. The only implementation displayed here is for timespec_diff(), which requires a tiny bit of finesse:

timespec_diff()
```
void timespec_diff(struct timespec ts1, struct timespec ts2,
                        struct timespec *diff)
{
    long temp;
    diff->tv_sec = ts1.tv_sec - ts2.tv_sec;
    temp = ts1.tv_nsec - ts2.tv_nsec;
❶  if ( temp < 0 ) {
        /* Because temp < 0, we need to borrow 1 sec from tv_sec and
           add it to tv_nsec as 1000000000 nanoseconds. */
        diff->tv_sec--;
        diff->tv_nsec = 1000000000 + temp;
    }
    else
        diff->tv_nsec = temp;
}
```

It's easy to overlook the need to adjust the structure when temp is negative ❶ in this function. A similar problem occurs in timespec_add().

Let's look at a small program that demonstrates how to use nanosleep(). The program appears in Listing 9-1.

nanosleep
_demo1.c
```
#include "common_hdrs.h"
#include "time_utils.h"
```

```
void sigint_handler(int signum)
{
    return; /* Just catch the signal and return to main(). */
}

int main(int argc, char *argv[])
{
    struct timespec  initial_sleep, remainder;
    char             errmssge[100];
    int              retval;
    double           delay = 5;  /* Default delay if no command argument  */
    struct sigaction act;

    if ( argc >= 2 ) {           /* User supplied a delay on command line. */
        retval = get_dbl(argv[1], NON_NEG_ONLY | PURE, &delay, errmssge);
        if ( retval < 0 )        /* Not a valid number                    */
            fatal_error(retval, errmssge);
        else if ( delay <= 0 )   /* Valid number but negative             */
            fatal_error(retval, "get_dbl requires a positive number"
                                " without trailing characters.\n");
    }
    /* Convert delay in seconds to a timespec. */
    dbl_to_timespec(delay, &initial_sleep);
    /* Set up and install SIGINT handler. */
    act.sa_flags = 0;
    sigemptyset(&act.sa_mask);
    act.sa_handler = sigint_handler;
    if ( -1 == sigaction(SIGINT, &act, NULL) )
        fatal_error(errno, "sigaction");

    printf("About to sleep for %10.10f seconds...\n", delay);
    if ( (-1 == nanosleep(&initial_sleep, &remainder)) && (errno == EINTR) ) {
        /* Sleep was interrupted by a handled signal (SIGINT). */
        timespec_to_dbl(remainder, &delay);     /* Convert remaining time.  */
        printf("nanosleep() had %10.10f seconds left when it was "
                "interrupted.\n", delay);
    }
    return 0;
}
```

Listing 9-1: A program showing how to use nanosleep()

Most of the pieces of the program are self-explanatory. It installs a signal handler to catch a CTRL-C, but it doesn't do anything except return. Why? We want the call to nanosleep() to be interrupted by a signal so that we can test the code that extracts how much time is left. Therefore, we need to catch the signal so that the program is not terminated, and we want execution to resume in main() after the handler is called. That's why the handler does nothing except call return.

When we build and run this program, we want to give it a delay long enough that we can enter CTRL-C and witness its output, as well as show that it accepts real-valued delays:

```
$ ./nanosleep_demo1 5.67891234
About to sleep for 5.6789123400 seconds...
^Cnanosleep() had 3.9501537770 seconds left when it was interrupted.
```

From the output, you can see that I entered CTRL-C about 1.73 seconds into the sleep. This program is designed to catch only SIGINT; it will be killed by any other signal. It's left as an exercise to write a similar program that reports the remaining time regardless of which signal was delivered other than SIGKILL and SIGSTOP.

Let's consider the more interesting problem of ensuring that the program sleeps for the entire duration that the user requested no matter how many signals are delivered to it. For simplicity, let's limit the set of handled signals to SIGINT. To get nanosleep() to run again for the remaining time after an interruption, we'd need to execute instructions such as the following pseudocode:

```
if ( nanosleep(&initial_sleep, &remainder) was interrupted ) {
    // Set initial_sleep to value of remainder.
    /* Call function again. */
    nanosleep(&initial_sleep, &remainder);
}
```

This works if it gets one more signal. However, what if a third or a fourth signal is delivered and interrupts the call? In this case, we would need to call nanosleep() over and over until it completes the sleep without being interrupted, implying that the remainder is at last zero. We need to replace the if statement with a loop, something like this:

```
while ( nanosleep(&initial_sleep, &remainder) is interrupted ) {
    initial_sleep = remainder;  /* Sleep for remainder. */
}
```

If nanosleep() is not interrupted by a signal, the loop will terminate. If it is, it will run again with the remaining time as its initial_sleep. Since the remaining time is strictly smaller than the initial time, eventually the call completes because the sleep time requested is strictly smaller in each iteration.

The following C do-while loop is the proper way to do this:

```
do {
    retval = nanosleep(&initial_sleep, &remainder);
    if ( retval == -1 ) {       /* An error or an interruption occured.  */
        if ( errno == EINTR ) /* Received SIGINT                         */
            initial_sleep = remainder;
```

```
        else                      /* Some other non-recoverable error occurred. */
            fatal_error(errno, "nanosleep");
    }
} while ( retval < 0 );
```

The loop exits when retval >= 0, which can be true only if nanosleep() wasn't interrupted and had no other errors.

The next question is whether the total amount of time that the process sleeps equals the original requested time. The man page tells us that the duration of the sleep is at least the time specified in the request, not equal to it. It also warns in its NOTES that the interval is rounded up in case it isn't an exact multiple of the granularity of the underlying clock. Yet another source of possible increase is the scheduling activity of the kernel—the process will always experience some small delay before it runs again after a sleep. Inside a loop, these tiny increases in the sleep time build up into what people call *timer drift*, a slowly increasing change in the accuracy of the timer. We'll have more to say about this shortly.

To test whether the preceding loop ensures that a program sleeps for at least the full duration requested, we can get the time just before the loop and immediately after it and compute the difference. There's a hitch though; the only function that we've used so far for getting the current time is time(), and this has 1-second resolution. The deprecated gettimeofday() that we discovered in Chapter 3 has microsecond resolution—still not fine enough— but we did read about clock_gettime() there, and its man page synopsis is:

```
#include <time.h>
int clock_gettime(clockid_t clockid, struct timespec *tp);
--snip--

Feature Test Macro Requirements for glibc (see feature_test_macros(7)):
clock_gettime()
    _POSIX_C_SOURCE >= 199309L
```

We chose not to use it to implement spl_date because of performance considerations, but we need it now since it's the only function with the same resolution as nanosleep(). Its man page suggests that for the first parameter we use either the real-time clock ID, CLOCK_REALTIME, or the monotonic clock ID, CLOCK_MONOTONIC. The former is actual wall clock time but can sometimes have small discontinuous jumps, sometimes decreasing, whereas the latter is smooth but measures time differently. I'll use the monotonic clock since all we need is the time difference, not the actual wall clock time. The main program, with only the relevant code displayed, is in Listing 9-2.

nanosleep
_demo2.c
```
#include "common_hdrs.h"
#include "time_utils.h"

void handler(int signum)
{
    const char mssge[] = "Signal received.\n";
```

```
        write(STDOUT_FILENO, mssge, strlen(mssge)); /* SAFE */
}

int main(int argc, char *argv[])
{
    struct timespec initial_sleep, remainder, starttime, endtime, difftime;
    --snip--
    if ( -1 == clock_gettime(CLOCK_MONOTONIC, &starttime) ) /*Get starttime.*/
        fatal_error(errno, "clock_gettime");
    do {
        retval = nanosleep(&initial_sleep, &remainder);
        if ( retval == -1 ) {
            if ( errno == EINTR )        /* Received SIGINT */
                initial_sleep = remainder;
            else          /* Some other nonrecoverable error */
                fatal_error(errno, "nanosleep");
        }
    } while ( retval < 0 ); /* Repeat until retval is zero. */
    if ( -1 == clock_gettime(CLOCK_MONOTONIC, &endtime) ) /* Get endtime.   */
        fatal_error(errno, "clock_gettime");

    /* Compute the time difference (endtime - starttime) as timespecs. */
    timespec_diff(endtime, starttime, &difftime);

    timespec_to_dbl(difftime, &total); /* Convert to double and then print. */
    printf("Sleep lasted %10.10f seconds, "
           "%10.10f seconds longer than requested.\n", total, total - delay);
    return 0;
}
```

Listing 9-2: Excerpts of a program that sleeps for the entire duration of the original requested sleep time, calling nanosleep() repeatedly and measuring the total elapsed time of the sleep

The complete program, named *nanosleep_demo2.c*, is in the book's source code distribution. The signal handler, handler(), prints a message when it's run so that we can see how many signals were delivered. The program uses a few of the utility functions for working with timespec structures that were described earlier. Their declarations are in *time_utils.h*. I built the program, naming it nanosleep_demo2, and ran it, entering several CTRL-Cs:

```
$ ./nanosleep_demo2 6.789123456
Delaying for 6.7891234560 seconds...
^CSignal received.
^CSignal received.
^CSignal received.
^CSignal received.
Sleep lasted 6.7895459130 seconds, 0.0004224570 seconds longer than requested.
```

This output shows that the total elapsed time (6.7895459130 seconds) is less than a half-millisecond greater than the requested sleep time (6.789123456 seconds). Repeated runs with the same number of delivered signals have similar timer drifts, but as the number of signals increases, the drift increases. For example, when I send 14 signals without changing the requested delay interval, the drift is 0.0011846140 seconds: still relatively small. When I send 32 signals, the drift is 0.0035780350 seconds.

The nanosleep() man page NOTES contains a brief discussion about timer drifts caused by repeated restarts of nanosleep(). It recommends calling a different function, clock_nanosleep(), specifying an absolute time value to avoid this.

The clock_nanosleep() System Call

Why do we need a sleep function that avoids timer drifts when it's interrupted frequently? Consider designing a video game or some other program with animated output that requires very high-frequency updates to its output display. In these types of programs, signals are generated frequently because of user input and, with a sleep function like nanosleep(), timer drifts will increase and the animation can start to appear nonuniform.

The synopsis from the clock_nanosleep() man page shows that this system call has two parameters not needed for nanosleep():

```
#include <time.h>
int clock_nanosleep(clockid_t clockid, int flags,
                    const struct timespec *request,
                    struct timespec *remain);
Link with -lrt (only for glibc versions before 2.17).

Feature Test Macro Requirements for glibc (see feature_test_macros(7)):
clock_nanosleep():
    _POSIX_C_SOURCE >= 200112L
```

The first (clockid) is a clock ID, like the ones used by the clock_gettime() function, and the second (flags) is a flag set. This function accepts fewer choices of clock ID than clock_gettime(). For our purposes, CLOCK_REALTIME and CLOCK_MONOTONIC are the ones we'll consider. The man page has information about the other clock IDs that can be passed to it. The flags parameter can either be 0 or the symbolic constant TIMER_ABSTIME.

When flags is 0, the requested time (*request) is interpreted as a time interval, as it would be with nanosleep(). In this case we say clock_nanosleep() is called to do a *relative* sleep, and the function behaves like nanosleep()—if it's interrupted by a signal, the remaining time is stored in *remain so that it can be called again to complete the relative sleep. We'd call it, passing it either the real time or monotonic clock ID, as follows:

```
clock_nanosleep(CLOCK_REALTIME, 0, &requestedtime, &remainingtime);
```

Unlike nanosleep(), it lets us choose the clock source.

Its more interesting use is to make a program do an absolute sleep by passing it the TIMER_ABSTIME flag. When we pass this flag to the function, the requested time (*request) is interpreted as an absolute time as measured by the clock with ID (clockid). It's like setting an alarm clock—we give it a future clock time, the process is immediately suspended, and when the clock reaches that time, the process wakes up. If *request isn't later than the current time on the clock, then clock_nanosleep() returns immediately without suspending the process; that would be like setting an alarm clock to a past time! With absolute sleeps, the last parameter is ignored and can be set to NULL because the requested time is absolute—if the process is not interrupted, it's guaranteed to sleep until the clock reaches the time specified in *request, and if it is interrupted, it can be called again with the same time in *request to continue the sleep until that time. Figure 9-1 illustrates the difference between absolute and relative sleep requests.

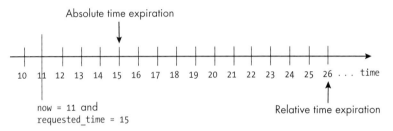

Figure 9-1: The difference between an absolute time specification and a relative one when the current time is 11 and the request is 15

To be clear, suppose that the time at which it's called is *t1* seconds since the epoch, and the requested time is *t2* seconds since the epoch, where *t1* < *t2*. If no signal is delivered to the process, the sleep caused by calling

```
clock_nanosleep(CLOCK_REALTIME, TIMER_ABSTIME, t2, NULL);
```

will end at time *t2*, not *t1* + *t2*. The time isn't treated as an interval; it's taken as a point of time in the future. Therefore, in order to use clock_nanosleep() to delay for an interval of time (a relative sleep), such as sleep_interval, a program must call clock_gettime() with the same clock ID, such as CLOCK_REALTIME, add sleep_interval to the returned time, and call clock_nanosleep() with that later time as its third parameter, as in the following semi-pseudocode:

```
clock_gettime(CLOCK_REALTIME, &current_time);
stop_time = current_time + sleep_interval;
clock_nanosleep(CLOCK_REALTIME, TIMER_ABSTIME, &stop_time, NULL);
```

The last issue regarding clock_nanosleep() is its relationship to signals and signal handlers. Like nanosleep(), clock_nanosleep() doesn't interfere with signal disposition. Also like nanosleep(), if clock_nanosleep() is interrupted by a signal that the process catches, it isn't restarted, even if the SA_RESTART flag is set in the sigaction structure when the handler is installed. Lastly, as noted before, if it's interrupted by a signal, the time interval is relative, and remaining is not NULL, then the unfinished time is stored in *remaining. The similarities end there, because these two functions are different in a subtle way that has dire consequences if it's overlooked, namely in their return values. The library wrappers for most system calls return -1 when they fail, but this one does not.

A SUBTLE AND SIGNIFICANT DISTINCTION

When nanosleep() is interrupted by a signal handler's execution, it returns -1 and sets errno to the value EINTR. When clock_nanosleep() is interrupted by a signal handler, it returns the error code EINTR, not -1. Error codes are *positive* numbers. Therefore, checking whether it was interrupted requires a different test, such as:

```
retval = clock_nanosleep(CLOCK_REALTIME, TIMER_ABSTIME, &timetoresume, NULL);
if ( retval == EINTR )
    /* Call was interrupted by a signal. */
else if ( retval > 0 )
    /* Some other error occured. */
else
    /* Call was successful and returned at time timetoresume. */
```

To compare the behaviors of clock_nanosleep() and nanosleep(), I modified *nanosleep_demo2.c* slightly so that it calls clock_nanosleep() instead. To make it sleep for the specified interval (a relative sleep), I used the strategy described in the preceding pseudocode. The relevant portions of this revised program, named *clock_nanosleep_demo.c*, are in Listing 9-3. The complete program is in the book's source code distribution.

---

clock_nanosleep _demo.c
```
#include "common_hdrs.h"
#include "time_utils.h"
--snip--

int main(int argc, char *argv[])
{
    --snip--
    printf("Delaying for %10.10f seconds...\n", delay);
    if ( -1 == clock_gettime(CLOCK_MONOTONIC, &starttime) )
        fatal_error(errno, "clock_gettime");

    /* Add delay time to clock time. */
    add_dbl_to_timespec(delay, &starttime, &endsleep);

    /* Repeatedly call clock_nanosleep() until it returns 0. */
    do {
        retval = clock_nanosleep(CLOCK_MONOTONIC, TIMER_ABSTIME,
                                &endsleep, NULL);
        if ( retval != EINTR && retval > 0 ) /* An error, not an interrupt */
```

```
        fatal_error(errno, "nanosleep");
    } while ( retval != 0 );              /* Repeat until retval is zero. */
    if ( -1 == clock_gettime(CLOCK_MONOTONIC, &endtime) ) /* Get time now. */
        fatal_error(errno, "clock_gettime");
    timespec_diff(endtime, starttime, &difftime);
    --snip--
}
```

Listing 9-3: Parts of a program using clock_nanosleep() to sleep for a relative time interval

I built the executable and ran it with the same delay as I used for *nanosleep _demo2.c*, entering four CTRL-Cs as well:

```
$ ./clock_nanosleep_demo 6.78912345
Delaying for 6.7891234500 seconds...
^CSignal received.
^CSignal received.
^CSignal received.
^CSignal received.
Sleep lasted 6.7892145100 seconds, 0.0000910600 seconds longer than requested.
```

The *nanosleep_demo2.c* run had a timer drift of 0.0004225 seconds, whereas this is only 0.0000911 seconds. I ran it several more times, forcing 14 interrupts, and each time the timer drift was about 0.00012 seconds. A final set of runs with 30 interrupts each time resulted in an average drift of about 0.00012 seconds. This shows that even with repeated interrupts, the drift stays at the same magnitude. It is mostly the result of system activity such as scheduling delays.

Software Timers

We'll begin our study of software timers with the lower-resolution ones based on traditional software clocks, because they're easier to use and understand. We'll start with the alarm() system call, after which we'll take a look at the higher-resolution timers commonly known as POSIX timers.

The alarm() System Call

The very first timer to appear in Unix was the alarm() system call, making its appearance in Seventh Edition Unix in 1979. It's the easiest timer to use and understand. The alarm() system call has limited functionality; let's see what its man page tells us:

```
ALARM(2)               Linux Programmer's Manual               ALARM(2)

NAME
       alarm - set an alarm clock for delivery of a signal
```

```
#include <unistd.h>
unsigned int alarm(unsigned int seconds);
```

DESCRIPTION

alarm() arranges for a SIGALRM signal to be delivered to the calling process in seconds seconds. If seconds is zero, any pending alarm is canceled. In any event any previously set alarm() is canceled.

RETURN VALUE

alarm() returns the number of seconds remaining until any previously scheduled alarm was due to be delivered, or zero if there was no previously scheduled alarm.

--snip--

This is very straightforward. Summarizing alarm()'s features:

- Its resolution is 1 second.

- It notifies the calling process of its timeout by sending it a SIGALRM signal.

- A program cancels a previously set alarm by calling it again with an argument of 0, as in alarm(0).

- If it's called while a previously set alarm is active, the previous one is canceled, and alarm() returns the number of seconds remaining on the previous alarm.

Let's clarify this last point. Suppose that at some point in time, a process calls alarm() to have a SIGALRM sent to itself in 10 seconds

```
alarm(10);
```

and that exactly 4 seconds later, the same process calls alarm() again, this time setting it for 20 seconds:

```
seconds_left = alarm(20);
```

The return value of alarm() is 10 − 4 = 6 seconds, and it's stored into seconds _left. The alarm is reset to 20 seconds, and the next SIGALRM will be delivered to the process 20 seconds after this second call.

The alarm() system call has a few different applications. For one, a process can set an alarm prior to starting a long task that it might not complete if the input dataset is unexpectedly large. When it receives the SIGALRM, it can stop the task. This way, the alarm prevents the process from spending too much time on a potentially endless task. A process can also set an alarm to perform a task at some future time, perhaps dependent upon the state of its data.

The first program we'll write is a trivial one that just calls alarm() and then calls pause() to put itself to sleep until it receives a signal. In effect, this program will act like the sleep command. It expects the user to enter the number of seconds to sleep. We'll name it *alarm_demo1.c*, shown in Listing 9-4.

alarm_demo1.c
```
int main(int argc, char *argv[])
{
    int k, resultcode;

    if ( 2 > argc )
        usage_error("alarm_demo1 <alarm-interval>");

    resultcode = get_int(argv[1], NON_NEG_ONLY | PURE, &k, NULL);
    if ( resultcode < 0 || k < 1 )
        fatal_error(resultcode, "get_int expects a positive integer");
    printf("Sleeping for %d seconds...\n", k);
    alarm(k);   /* Set the alarm for k seconds.                   */
    pause();    /* Suspend itself indefinitely (until a signal arrives) */
    return 0;
}
```

Listing 9-4: A program like the sleep command that suspends itself for a given amount of time using alarm() and pause()

Because this program doesn't have a signal handler, when it receives the SIGALRM signal, the default action is taken, meaning the program terminates. I built the executable, naming it alarm_demo1, and ran it to demonstrate its behavior:

```
$ ./alarm_demo1 10
Sleeping for 10 seconds...
Alarm clock  # 10 seconds later
```

The string "Alarm clock" is written to the terminal when a process receives a SIGALRM and doesn't handle it. The next example is a modification of the preceding program. It differs in two ways:

- Instead of calling pause(), it enters a loop in which it prints the elapsed time every second by calling nanosleep() for a 1-second sleep and printing when it times out.

- This program catches the SIGALRM with a signal handler that prints a message to the terminal.

The program, *alarm_demo2.c*, is displayed in Listing 9-5.

alarm_demo2.c
```
#include "common_hdrs.h"
#include <signal.h>
#define DEFAULT_DELAY   5
char MESSAGE[] = "Received a wake-up signal!\n";

void catchalarm(int signum)  /* The signal handler for SIGALRM */
{
```

```
    write(STDOUT_FILENO, MESSAGE, sizeof(MESSAGE));
    exit(EXIT_SUCCESS);       /* Exit the program.              */
}

int main(int argc, char *argv[])
{
    int retval = 0, k = 0, delay = DEFAULT_DELAY;
    struct timespec  sleeptime = {1, 0}; /* 1 second, 0 nanoseconds */
    struct sigaction act;

    if ( argc >= 2 ) {
        retval = get_int(argv[1], NON_NEG_ONLY | PURE, &delay, NULL);
        if ( retval < 0 || delay < 1 )
            fatal_error(retval, "get_int expects a positive integer");
    }
    act.sa_handler = catchalarm;
    sigemptyset(&(act.sa_mask));
    sigaction(SIGALRM, &act, NULL);
    printf("About to sleep for %d seconds\n", delay);
    alarm(delay);     /* Turn on alarm.                          */
    while ( TRUE ) { /* Print seconds elapsed until SIGALRM is received. */
        nanosleep(&sleeptime, NULL);
        printf("  %d second(s) elapsed\n", ++k);
    }
    return 0;
}
```

Listing 9-5: A program like the sleep command that suspends itself for a given amount of time using alarm() and a loop based on nanosleep()

Notice that the signal handler for SIGALRM is safe since it doesn't call any functions that aren't async-signal-safe. It's an old-style handler with a single argument, installed with sigaction(). If the user doesn't supply an argument to this program, it defaults to a 5-second timeout; otherwise, it uses the timeout specified by the user on the command line. A run of it looks like this:

```
$ ./alarm_demo2 4
About to sleep for 4 seconds
  1 second(s) elapsed
  2 second(s) elapsed
  3 second(s) elapsed
Received a wake-up signal!
```

The alarm() system call is a *one-shot* timer—it isn't intended to be used to create a sequence of timeouts. Nonetheless, by calling it again from within the SIGALRM handler, we can approximate the same effect as a timer that repeatedly expires. Our next program will demonstrate how to do this.

A Progress Bar Based on Alarms

The alarm() system call might be simple, but we can still use it to implement a terminal-based progress bar, partly because progress bars don't need to update more frequently than once per second and partly because it doesn't matter if the intervals between updates are perfectly even.

Suppose that a program starts some very lengthy operation that might take a long time to complete. User-friendly programs often display some indication of their progress. Sometimes it's not possible because there's no way to measure the progress, but sometimes there is. If it's possible to measure progress, then a program can display a progress bar. The idea is that, at fixed intervals of time, the program can compute the fraction of the work completed and update a progress bar in the terminal to show the user how far along the operation has progressed.

To do this though, we need to reset the alarm each time it expires. Therefore, the signal handler itself will call alarm() after it updates the progress bar and will have the form

```
void refresh_progressbar(int signum)
{
    // Refresh the progress bar.
    alarm(refresh_interval);
}
```

where *refresh_interval* is the number of seconds in the next interval of the timer. The main program logic should be something like the following:

1. Initialize a file-scoped (global) variable named fraction_completed to 0. It has to be global because both the main program and the signal handler need access to it, and it can't be passed as a parameter to a handler.

2. Draw the frame for a progress bar that indicates zero progress.

3. Install a signal handler for SIGALRM. We'll name it refresh_progressbar() to make its purpose explicit.

4. Set the first alarm to expire in 1 second. That should be a reasonable update interval. Because both the main program and the signal handler call alarm() with this value, we make it a macro constant named REFRESH_INTERVAL. It is important that this step comes *after* the preceding one—we don't want to start sending signals until a signal handler has been installed.

5. Start the lengthy task. To simulate a lengthy task, the program will enter a while loop of the form

```
while ( the fraction of the task completed < 1.0 )
    // Simulate the task's completing more work.
```

Rather than simulating a long task, we could make the program perform some very long computation, such as calculating tens of thousands of digits of π, but there's no need to do that to demonstrate the principles underlying the use of the timer. Instead, the program will simulate the progress of a lengthy task by repeatedly sleeping a tiny amount of time and increasing a variable representing the fraction of work it completed. To make the simulation a bit more natural, we make the increases in the fraction of work completed random by basing them on the values returned by a random number generator. We can also control approximately how long the simulation runs with a macro constant, MIN_SIMULATION_SECS, set to 16. To control how quickly the simulated task runs, we'll introduce another variable, progress_rate, that stores the maximum increase in the fraction of work completed in each iteration of the simulating loop.

We'll consolidate this behavior in a function named lengthy_task(). Its logic, partly in pseudocode, is essentially:

```
// Let dt be a tiny amount of time in seconds.
❶ // Let progress_rate = dt / MIN_SIMULATION_SECS.
while ( fraction_completed < 1.0 ) {
    // Sleep for dt seconds.
    // Let randfraction be a random number generated in the interval [0,1.0].
    fraction_completed = fraction_completed + (progress_rate * randfraction);
    if ( fraction_completed > 1.0 )
        fraction_completed = 1.0;
}
```

Since the generated random number, randfraction, is in the range [0,1], the expression progress_rate * randfraction is in the range [0, progress_rate]. This limits the maximum increase of fraction_completed in any single loop iteration to progress_rate. Since 1/progress_rate is the fewest number of iterations of the loop and each takes dt many seconds, the least amount of time that the task runs is

$$MIN\_SIMULATION\_SECS = dt \times (1/progress\_rate)$$

and on average, it should take about double this much time, because the average of a large number of uniformly generated random numbers in the interval [0,1] is 0.5. This explains why, in the code, progress_rate is assigned dt / MIN _SIMULATION_SECS ❶ so that the simulation runs for at least that much time.

We'll use nanosleep() to do the sleeping in this code because it doesn't interact with any signals, including SIGALRM. We'll also make the number of nanoseconds in the timespec passed to nanosleep() a macro, SLEEPNSECS, defined as 480,000,000, so that the sleep is about a half-second.

As it stands, there's a race condition on the update to fraction_completed, because if a SIGALRM is delivered to the program in the middle of an update, the refresh_progressbar() handler will run.

A race condition *occurs when two or more processes or threads access some shared resource and the outcome of their sharing it is that the correctness of the computation depends on the order in which they do so. If all processes just read the resource without modifying it, there is no possibility of a race condition. But if one or more can modify it, then a race condition might exist.*

Although the handler doesn't modify `fraction_completed`, the value it sees when it runs may be stale. To prevent the race condition, we'll use `sigprocmask()` (see Chapter 8) to block the signal during the update in `lengthy_task()`, calling it before and after the update to block and unblock it, respectively. Therefore, we'll declare

```
sigset_t blocked_signals;
```

make it empty, and add `SIGALRM` to it:

```
sigemptyset(&blocked_signals);
sigaddset(&blocked_signals, SIGALRM);
```

The update would then be nested in between calls to `sigprocmask()`:

```
sigprocmask(SIG_BLOCK, &blocked_signals, NULL);
fraction_completed += progress_rate * randfraction; /* Need to generate */
if ( fraction_completed > 1.0 )
    fraction_completed = 1.0;
sigprocmask(SIG_UNBLOCK, &blocked_signals, NULL);
```

The last issue is how to generate a random number between 0 and 1.0. We search the man pages for a random number generator by entering `apropos -s2,3 random`. The search returns many possibilities, but most share a single man page. All but one of these return integers. It would be easier if it returned a fraction. The one that does is `drand48()`, which returns double-precision floats in the range 0 to 1.0. Its synopsis is:

```
#include <stdlib.h>
double drand48(void);
```

It requires no argument and doesn't need to be seeded. For example, `x = drand48()` assigns some random number between 0 and 1.0 to x.

Putting all of these ideas together, the `lengthy_task()` is as follows:

`lengthy_task()`
```
void lengthy_task()
{
    double      sleep_secs    = (double) (1.0*SLEEPNSECS) / 1000000000;
    double      progress_rate = sleep_secs / MIN_SIMULATION_SECS;
    struct timespec dt        = {0, SLEEPNSECS}, rem;
    sigset_t    blocked_signals;

    sigemptyset(&blocked_signals);
    sigaddset(&blocked_signals, SIGALRM);
```

```
    while ( fraction_completed < 1.0 ) {
        if ( -1 == nanosleep(&dt, &rem) )
            nanosleep(&rem, NULL);
        sigprocmask(SIG_BLOCK, &blocked_signals, NULL);
        fraction_completed += progress_rate * drand48();
        if ( fraction_completed > 1.0 )
            fraction_completed = 1.0;
        sigprocmask(SIG_UNBLOCK, &blocked_signals, NULL);
    }
}
```

The next step is to develop the signal handler code that updates and displays the progress bar. For the sake of simplicity, the progress bar will be a fixed length and will contain two types of characters. An initial prefix of hash mark (#) characters will represent the completed segment. The remainder of the bar, meaning the portion representing the unfinished work, will be represented by hyphens (-). The entire bar will be enclosed in square brackets, and the percent completed as an actual percentage will be written to the right of the bar. For example, a few snapshots of the bar would look like the following:

```
[#####--------------------------------------------------] %8
Time passes.
[###########--------------------------------------------] %21
More time passes.
[##################-------------------------------------] %32
```

Let's develop the code to animate this bar. The program will be easier to modify if we declare a few macro constants:

```
#define MIN_SIMULATION_SECS   16      /* Minimum simulation time (seconds)   */
#define REFRESH_INTERVAL       1      /* Number of seconds between refreshes */
#define BAR_LENGTH            64      /* Length of progress bar between [ ]   */
#define DONE_CHAR            '#'      /* Character for completed part        */
#define NOT_DONE_CHAR       '-'       /* Character for incomplete part        */
#define SLEEPNSECS     480000000      /* Nanoseconds in simulated dt          */
```

The signal handler will need two variables:

```
char bar[BAR_LENGTH+1];    /* The string representing the progress bar     */
int  finished_work;        /* The number of chars in the completed segment */
```

The extra character in the bar is for a NULL byte.

The instruction to calculate the length of the completed segment is therefore:

```
finished_work = (int) (fraction_completed * BAR_LENGTH);
```

The cast to int does not round; it removes the fractional part of the number.

The next question is whether there's a way to fill a string with multiple copies of the same character without looping. A man page search for a suitable library function or system call with apropos -s2,3 fill outputs:

```
$ apropos -s2,3 fill
getentropy (3)      - fill a buffer with random bytes
memset (3)          - fill memory with a constant byte
--snip--
wmemset (3)          - fill an array of wide-characters with a constant wid...
```

The memset() library function is exactly what we need; we used it in Chapter 7 in the implementation of spl_pwd to pad the pathname with leading periods. We give it the starting address of the string to fill, the character to fill it with, and the number of characters to write. It doesn't add a terminating NULL byte and cannot detect if we write too many characters at that address. The function returns a pointer to the memory area, which we don't need to use. We can create a bar representing fraction_completed work with the following instructions:

```
finished_work = (int) (fraction_completed * BAR_LENGTH);
bar[BAR_LENGTH] = '\0';
memset(bar, NOT_DONE_CHAR, BAR_LENGTH);
memset(bar, DONE_CHAR, finished_work);
```

This first memset() call writes all of the hyphens, and the second replaces the leftmost finished_work many hyphens by number signs.

In order to make the bar appear as if hyphens are being replaced by hash marks in each update, we need to redraw the entire line. If we try using the instruction

```
printf("[%s]", bar);
```

the bar will not overwrite itself; we'll get multiple bars one after the other, as in:

```
[-----------...------][##---------...-------][###--------...-------]
```

The solution requires some knowledge about the characters that control how lines are displayed in a terminal, inherited from those ancient machines called typewriters. The *line feed* character (\n), also called *newline*, is the character that causes the cursor to go to one line below its current position in the same column, like rotating the knob on an old typewriter. The *return character* is the character that moves the cursor back to the start of the current line. By writing a return character before writing the bar

```
printf("\r[%s]", bar);
```

in effect, we make each new print instruction overwrite the previous one. We need to include the percentage after the bar as well. To write a percent sign, we need to use double percent signs:

```
printf("\r[%s] %%%d", bar, (int)(100 * fraction_completed));
```

The signal handler is almost complete. As it stands, it won't work the way we expect. That's because of the way the C Library buffers its output. Unless you put a newline in a printf(), the output won't appear immediately. This is because the C Library uses line buffering for all I/O to or from terminal devices.

LINE BUFFERING IN THE C I/O LIBRARY

The C I/O Library uses a method of buffering called *line buffering* for terminal devices. When a process uses C library functions for output, that output is put into buffers. The contents of these buffers are not sent immediately to the terminal. They are sent only when one of the following actions takes place:

- The process tries to do output and the output buffer is full.
- The stream is closed or the process terminates.
- A newline is written to the stream.
- An input operation on the terminal stream (the standard input stream) takes place.
- fflush(stdout) is called to force the output to the terminal.

When output is not terminated with a newline and it needs to appear immediately, calling fflush(stdout) *flushes* it to the terminal.

To make the progress bar appear to be refreshed incrementally, the signal handler needs to call fflush(stdout) after calling printf(). The entire signal handler follows:

refresh
_progressbar()

```
void refresh_progressbar(int signum)
{
    char bar[BAR_LENGTH + 1];
    int  finished_work = (int) (fraction_completed * BAR_LENGTH);

    bar[BAR_LENGTH] = '\0';
    memset(bar, NOT_DONE_CHAR, BAR_LENGTH);
    memset(bar, DONE_CHAR, finished_work);
    printf("\r[%s] %%%d", bar, (int)(100 * fraction_completed));
    fflush(stdout);
    alarm(REFRESH_INTERVAL);
}
```

Before coding the main() function, there are a few other issues to address. The first is that a progress bar ought to appear on the screen immediately, without the user feeling a pause or delay in the program's reaction time. A function to draw this initial progress bar follows:

draw_initial_bar()

```
void draw_initial_bar()
{
    char initial_bar[BAR_LENGTH + 1];
```

```
    memset(initial_bar, NOT_DONE_CHAR, BAR_LENGTH);
    initial_bar[BAR_LENGTH] = '\0';
    printf("\r[%s]", initial_bar);
    fflush(stdout);
}
```

It draws the square brackets with BAR_LENGTH-many NOT_DONE_CHARs.

Another issue is whether the bar should remain in the terminal window when the program finishes, and yet another is what the program should do if a terminating keyboard signal such as SIGINT or SIGQUIT is sent to it. Usually, progress bars disappear when the monitored task completes. Ours should too. The program will replace the bar and the percentage indicator with a blank line. The following function does this and returns the cursor to the leftmost position in the same line so that it looks like it just disappeared:

erase
_progress_bar()
```
void erase_progress_bar()
{
    char blanks[BAR_LENGTH + 10];      /* Allows for percentage after bar */

    memset(blanks, ' ', BAR_LENGTH + 9); /* Fill blanks with space chars. */
    blanks[BAR_LENGTH + 9] = '\0';       /* NULL-terminate it.            */
    printf("\r%s\r", blanks);            /* Return to left, write spaces. */
    fflush(stdout);                      /* Force output.                 */
}
```

To address the second issue, we'll catch the two signals with a single handler, which will erase the progress bar and then force the program to terminate by raising SIGTERM:

sig_handler()
```
void sig_handler(int signum)
{
    erase_progress_bar();  /* Erase the bar.     */
    raise(SIGTERM);        /* Force termination. */
}
```

The main program is displayed, without the macro definitions and functions already presented, in Listing 9-6. The program is named *progress_bar1.c*; when we get to interval timers, we're going to write another version based on them.

progress_bar1.c
```
#include "common_hdrs.h"
#include <signal.h>
// OMITTED: Macros and functions
double fraction_completed = 0;    /* Fraction of operation completed    */

int main(int argc, char *argv[])
{
    struct sigaction    act;
    const struct timespec slight_pause = {2, 0}; /* 2-second interval  */
    struct timespec     remaining_sleep;
```

```
    draw_initial_bar();
    sigemptyset(&(act.sa_mask));
    act.sa_flags = 0;
    act.sa_handler = sig_handler;
    if ( sigaction(SIGINT, &act, NULL) == -1 )
        fatal_error(errno, "sigaction");
    if ( sigaction(SIGQUIT, &act, NULL) == -1 )
        fatal_error(errno, "sigaction");

    act.sa_handler = refresh_progressbar;
    if ( sigaction(SIGALRM, &act, NULL) == -1 )
        fatal_error(errno, "sigaction");
    alarm(REFRESH_INTERVAL);  /* Set first alarm.      */
    lengthy_task();           /* Run the simulated task. */
    if ( -1 == nanosleep(&slight_pause, &remaining_sleep) )
        nanosleep(&remaining_sleep, NULL);
❶ alarm(0);                  /* Turn off the alarm.   */
    erase_progress_bar();     /* Erase the progress bar. */
    printf("Done\n");         /* Print 'Done' at end.  */
    return 0;
}
```

Listing 9-6: A program that displays a simulated progress bar, using alarm() *as its timer*

The program turns off the last alarm in case it's outstanding by calling
alarm(0) ❶ so that the bar is not redrawn after it's erased.

There's no way to show how this program runs on paper, of course. You
can build it and run it to see how the bar progresses. By changing the various macro parameters, you can adjust the rate of progress.

Interval Timers

The 1-second time granularity, or resolution, of alarm() is too coarse to be
useful for many applications. Furthermore, although we used alarm() to generate signals at regular intervals for our progress bar program, it isn't designed to do this, and we have to call it within the signal handler to achieve
this effect. The resulting SIGALRM signals are then subject to cumulative delays
contributed to partly by the time that elapses in the handler before it calls
alarm() to arm the timer again and partly by scheduling and other system activities that delay the start of the handler. This solution will not work when
the measurements require more accuracy and finer resolution.

Overview

Interval timers were developed to overcome this deficiency. Their first appearance was in 4.2BSD as well as in SVR4 (1988), and they were standardized
in POSIX.1-1994, also known as the Single UNIX Specification, Issue 4. The
original interval timer interface defined two system calls, setitimer() and

getitimer(). The CONFORMING TO section in their shared man page states that POSIX marked them as obsolete in 2008 and recommends the use of the POSIX timer API, specifically timer_gettime() and timer_settime(), instead.

Regardless of whether we use the older interval timers or the newer ones, the principles are the same, so before we take a look at the man pages, let's begin with an overview of how they work.

An interval timer has two components: an initial value and a repeat interval, which is often just called the *timer interval*. The *initial value* is the amount of time that elapses until the first timer expiration. The *repeat interval* is the amount of time between successive timer expirations after the first one. For example, if the initial value is 5 milliseconds (msecs) and the timer interval is 2 msecs, then the sequence of timer expirations will occur 5, 7, 9, 11 msecs (and so on) from the time that the timer was set. More generally, if an interval timer is started at time t_0, with initial value α and repeat interval β, then it will expire at times $t_0 + \alpha$, $t_0 + \alpha + \beta$, $t_0 + \alpha + 2\beta$, $t_0 + \alpha + 3\beta$, and so on until the process terminates or turns off the timer.

When a timer expires, a timer notification is sent to the process (or thread) that started the timer. With the older interval timer interface using setitimer() to set a timer, the notification is always a signal, one of SIGALRM, SIGVTALRM, or SIGPROF, depending on the type of interval timer it set up. The newer POSIX timers, as we'll see, are more general and give the process a choice of how it should be notified. In addition, a process can have more than one POSIX timer of the same type, unlike the older interval timers.

POSIX Timers

The setitimer() man page suggests using timer_settime() instead of setitimer() in new code, referring us to the timer_create() system call in its SEE ALSO section. We'll begin our exploration of POSIX timers by learning how to create and delete them, after which we'll examine how to arm and disarm them and retrieve their settings. We'll put them to use in a few different programs, the first of which will be a second version of the progress bar program we implemented using the alarm() system call. Lastly, we'll discuss the concept of timer overruns.

Creating and Deleting Timers

The timer_create() system call creates an interval timer for the calling process. Its SYNOPSIS is:

```
#include <signal.h>
#include <time.h>
int timer_create(clockid_t clockid, struct sigevent *sevp,
                 timer_t *timerid);
Link with -lrt.
```

The note about linking tells us that programs calling timer_create() need to link to the *real-time* library, *librt*, with the linker option -lrt. The timer_create() call creates a new interval timer for the calling process, initially unarmed, and returns its ID in the buffer pointed to by its third argument (timerid). The man page refers to this timer as a per-process timer because it's accessible only to the calling process.

The first argument, clockid, is the ID of the clock that the timer will use for measuring time. I introduced clock IDs when we worked with clock_nanosleep(). There are several other types of clocks that can be used with these interval timers, but for now we'll use only CLOCK_REALTIME and CLOCK_MONOTONIC clocks.

One of the major differences between the older timers and POSIX timers is that POSIX timers provide more choices for how a process is notified when they expire. The second argument to timer_create() (sevp*) serves this purpose; it points to a sigevent structure, which has its own man page. This structure specifies the details about event notifications. Its declaration is

```
struct sigevent {
    int        sigev_notify;        /* Notification method        */
    int        sigev_signo;         /* Notification signal        */
    union sigval sigev_value;       /* Data passed with notification */
    void (*sigev_notify_function) (union sigval);
    /* Function used for thread notification (SIGEV_THREAD) */
    void  *sigev_notify_attributes;
    /* Attributes for notification thread (SIGEV_THREAD) */
    pid_t  sigev_notify_thread_id; /* ID of thread to signal; Linux-specific */
};
```

The sigev_notify member specifies the method of notification, which can be one of the following symbolic values:

SIGEV_NONE   The process is not notified.

SIGEV_SIGNAL   The process is sent the signal specified by sigev_signo. If the process used sigaction() to install a handler for this signal, then the si_code field of the siginfo_t structure passed to the handler will have the value SI_TIMER and the si_signo field will have the signal number.

SIGEV_THREAD   The function specified by sigev_notify_function is run in a new thread for the process. This function is given sigev_value as its only argument.

SIGEV_THREAD_ID   This is like SIGEV_SIGNAL except that the signal is sent to the thread of the process whose thread ID is stored in sigev_notify _thread_id.

If we're willing to accept the default notification method, we can just set sevp* to NULL. This has the same effect as if it pointed to a sigevent structure in which sigev_notify were set to SIGEV_SIGNAL and sigev_signo were set to SIGALRM. In this case, the timer ID of the expiring timer is made available to a handler with a siginfo_t argument in that structure's si_value member.

The following code snippet demonstrates how to create a timer that uses a CLOCK_MONOTONIC clock that delivers a SIGUSR1 signal when it expires, making the timer ID available to the handler. The code declares a variable named timerid, of type timer_t, and a struct sigevent variable named sig_event:

```
timer_t        timerid;        /* To store returned timerid     */
struct sigevent sig_event;     /* sigevent to pass to timer_create() */
--snip--
/* Set up sigevent structure. */
sig_event.sigev_notify = SIGEV_SIGNAL;    /* Notify by signal.    */
sig_event.sigev_signo = SIGUSR1;          /* Send SIGUSR1.        */
sig_event.sigev_value.sival_ptr = &timerid;  /* Make timer ID available. */

if ( timer_create(CLOCK_MONOTONIC, &sig_event, &timerid) == -1 )
    // OMITTED: Failed - handle the error.
```

This code fragment sets the timer to send a SIGUSR1 signal. Recall from Chapter 8 that SIGUSR1 and SIGUSR2 are the two signals that programs can use for whatever purpose they choose because they have no predefined meaning. Soon I'll introduce the class of real-time signals, which we can use instead.

Whenever a program dynamically creates a resource, it should delete it; it's a good housekeeping principle. Creating a timer obliges us to delete it when we no longer need it. Timers use system resources; by deleting them right away, we make our programs more efficient and allow other processes to access them. The SEE ALSO section of timer_create()'s man page mentions the system call for deleting timers, timer_delete(). It's a relatively simple function, whose synopsis is:

```
#include <time.h>
int timer_delete(timer_t timerid);
Link with -lrt.
```

It deletes the timer whose ID is passed to it. If the timer is armed at the time of the call, it is first disarmed. The man page notes that POSIX doesn't specify what an implementation is supposed to do if there are any pending signals from this timer. Linux systems let pending signals stay pending. Other Unix implementations may handle them differently.

Arming and Disarming Timers

The timer_settime() system call arms the timer whose timer ID is passed to it. The SYNOPSIS on its man page is:

```
#include <time.h>
int timer_settime(timer_t timerid, int flags,
                const struct itimerspec *new_value,
                struct itimerspec *old_value);
--snip--
Link with -lrt.
```

The function simultaneously sets and arms the timer specified in its first argument (timerid). The clock that it uses for measuring time is the one that was specified when that timer was created. The third and fourth arguments (new_value and old_value) each point to an itimerspec structure. This structure specifies an initial value and a timer interval based on the nanosecond resolution timespec structure, the same structure passed to both nanosleep() and clock_nanosleep(). The *new_value structure contains the value with which to set the timer, and *old_value will be used to save the previous setting and remaining time, which I'll explain shortly. We can pass a NULL to it if we don't need the old setting. The function can fail for a few reasons, and if it does, it returns -1 and sets errno to the reason code.

The itimerspec structure, as given on the man page, is

```
struct itimerspec {
    struct timespec it_interval;  /* Timer interval     */
    struct timespec it_value;     /* Initial expiration */
};
```

The it_value member specifies the initial value, and it_interval specifies the timer interval, also called its *period* in the documentation.

If the initial value (it_value) is 0 and the timer was already armed, it's disarmed; that's how we can turn off a timer. If it isn't 0, meaning that either it_value.tv_sec or it_value.tv_nsec is not 0, then the timer is armed and it will expire for the first time after the interval specified by it_value, provided flags is 0. The timer starts at the time of the call. If the initial value is nonzero and the timer was previously armed, the old settings are overwritten and the new value is used.

The it_interval field specifies the repeat interval of the timer. If this value is 0, it doesn't repeat; it's a one-shot timer. Otherwise, each time that the timer expires, it's reloaded from the value in this field and is armed again. This implies that from the time of the first call to timer_settime(), the timer will send endless notifications to the process at this regular interval. It's up to the process to stop them, either by calling timer_settime() with new_value->it_value set to 0 or by calling timer_delete().

If old_value isn't NULL, then the it_interval from the previous call is copied into old_value->it_interval and the amount of time until the timer would have expired next is copied into old_value->it_value.

The flags parameter can be used to change the interpretation of the initial value (new_value->it_value) from a relative time to an absolute time. The discussion in "The clock_nanosleep() System Call" on page 447 explained absolute time. If flags = TIMER_ABSTIME then the initial value is interpreted as the absolute time at which to send the notification, based on the underlying clock of the timer. If that time has passed already, the timer expires immediately.

Counting Timer Overruns

Sometimes a timer sends more signals to a process than it can handle. This can happen for a couple of reasons. One is that, because of kernel scheduling or other system activities, there can be a long delay between when a signal is generated by a timer and when it's delivered. In the interim, additional timer expirations can occur, generating more signals. The other situation is when a process has temporarily blocked the signal, because the timer notifications can't be delivered until the signal is unblocked.

The kernel queues at most one signal per timer for a process. The consequence is that some timer notifications are never delivered. Event notifications that are generated but never delivered or accepted are called *timer overruns*. The timer *overrun count* is the number of these overruns. A process can call timer_getoverrun() to get this count. Its synopsis is:

```
#include <time.h>
int timer_getoverrun(timer_t timerid);
```

The single argument is of type timer_t; the calling program passes the timerid that was returned by a call to timer_create(). For example:

```
if ( -1 == timer_create(CLOCK_MONOTONIC, &sev, &timerid) )
    fatal_error(errno, "timer_create");
--snip--
if ( -1 == timer_settime(timerid, 0, &interval, NULL) )
     fatal_error(errno, "timer_settime");
--snip--
printf("Timer overruns: %d\n", timer_getoverrun(timerid));
```

This function can also be called within the handler that catches the signal sent by the timer. As long as the timer is still active, timer_getoverrun() can be called; once it's disarmed, the returned count will be 0 regardless of whether there were overruns or not. The program *timer_overrun_demo.c* in the book's source code distribution shows how to use this function. It counts the number of timer overruns in a given interval. The man page for timer_create() also has a sample program that counts these overruns, which is also available as *posix_timer_manpage_example.c* in the source code distribution.

Timer overrun counting is significant because it's a way to keep track of exactly how many timer notifications were generated, even if the process never saw them. If, for example, each notification is supposed to result in some value being incremented, the count could be used to apply the missing increments. Missed notifications may make a computation invalid.

We're ready to create some programs that put the preceding concepts and tools to use. We'll begin by rewriting the progress bar program that we implemented with the low-resolution, one-shot alarm() timer. After that, we'll develop two other programs: one that simulates a system resource monitor similar to the iostat command we mentioned earlier, and one that shows how to employ real-time signals and multiple timers.

A POSIX Timer-Based Progress Bar

The opening remarks about interval timers mentioned the two deficiencies of using the alarm() system call as an interval timer: its low resolution and the timer drift that occurs because of repeated small delays introduced in the signal handler. We eliminate both of these problems by using a POSIX timer instead. Therefore, our first application of a POSIX timer will be an enhanced version of the progress bar program, named *progress_bar2.c*.

This version gives the user the option to enter the timer interval so that the refresh rate of the progress bar can be chosen at runtime. If the user doesn't provide it, the program will use a default value. We'll also set the sigevent notification method to deliver a SIGUSR1 signal instead of a SIGALRM to eliminate any possibility of interference with other functions that might use SIGALRM.

Allowing the user to specify the refresh interval introduces a few new problems. First, consider the part of the lengthy_task() function shown here:

```
while ( fraction_completed < 1.0 ) {
    if ( -1 == nanosleep(&dt, &rem) )
        nanosleep(&rem, NULL);
    sigprocmask(SIG_BLOCK, &blocked_signals, NULL);
    fraction_completed += progress_rate * drand48();
    --snip--
}
```

In lengthy_task(), the delay time (dt), which is the requested sleep time, is currently 0.48 seconds, which means that if the period of the timer is smaller than that, it is likely that the sleep will be interrupted. The code handles this by calling nanosleep(&rem, NULL) to complete the sleep. However, if the period is small enough, say 0.2 seconds or less, then that call will also be interrupted. The effect on the simulation is that the length of the simulated task can be shortened considerably because each small delay that nanosleep() was intended to impart is much smaller because the repeated sleeps are much shorter. This prevents us from seeing the effect of very small timer intervals on the progress bar's behavior.

One solution is to temporarily block the SIGUSR1 signals for the duration of nanosleep(). This will prevent the interruptions and consequent speeding up of the simulation. We'd only need to make the following small change, highlighted in bold, in the simulated task:

```
while ( fraction_completed < 1.0 ) {
    sigprocmask(SIG_BLOCK, &blocked_signals, NULL);
    if ( -1 == nanosleep(&dt, &rem) )
        nanosleep(&rem, NULL);
❶   sigprocmask(SIG_UNBLOCK, &blocked_signals, NULL);
    sigprocmask(SIG_BLOCK, &blocked_signals, NULL);
    fraction_completed += progress_rate * drand48();
    --snip--
}
```

If we did this, there'd be just a tiny window of time ❶ between when the signal was unblocked and when it was blocked again, during which a signal could be delivered. Since only one signal per timer is queued when they're blocked, many signals might be discarded and the program would have timer overruns, signals that were never delivered.

The alternative solution is to replace the call to `nanosleep()` by a call to `clock_nanosleep()`, passing the `TIMER_ABSTIME` flag to it, using the paradigm described in "Arming and Disarming Timers" on page 464. That function, when in absolute time mode, doesn't lose any time when it's restarted after an interrupt. Although it's a bit more complex to code up, there won't be any timer overruns, because each signal will be delivered, barring scheduling activity in the kernel and provided that the period of the timer is not extremely small. It's worth the extra trouble to take this approach.

The revised function uses the same logic as was used in the *clock_nanosleep _demo.c* program (Listing 9-3). It's partially displayed in Listing 9-7 with these changes highlighted in bold.

`lengthy_task()` *(revised)*

```
void lengthy_task()
{
    --snip--
    struct timespec endts, startts;
    int     ret;

    sigemptyset(&blocked_signals);
    sigaddset(&blocked_signals, SIGUSR1);
    while ( fraction_completed < 1.0 ) {
        if ( -1 == clock_gettime(CLOCK_MONOTONIC, &startts) )
            fatal_error(errno, "clock_gettime");
        timespec_add(dt, startts, &endts);
        do {
            ret = clock_nanosleep(CLOCK_MONOTONIC, TIMER_ABSTIME, &endts,
                                  NULL);
            if ( ret != EINTR && ret > 0 )
                fatal_error(errno, "clock_nanosleep");
        } while ( ret != 0 );
        sigprocmask(SIG_BLOCK, &blocked_signals, NULL);
        fraction_completed += progress_rate * drand48();
        if ( fraction_completed > 1.0 )
            fraction_completed = 1.0;
        sigprocmask(SIG_UNBLOCK, &blocked_signals, NULL);
    }
}
```

Listing 9-7: The long running task simulation, using `clock_nanosleep()` *instead of* `nanosleep()`

Allowing the user to choose the refresh interval introduces another problem. If the refresh interval is too large, when the task has finished, the last refresh to the progress bar (the one that shows that it has reached 100 percent), won't appear on the terminal unless the program delays long enough before erasing it and cleaning up. It will be discarded. On the other hand, if the refresh interval is short and the program waits a long time, the shell prompt will take more time to return than it should. Clearly, the amount of time between when the simulated task ends and when the program should start its cleanup depends on the refresh interval.

The revised main program accounts for this by making the sleep time passed to nanosleep() near the end of main() a function of the refresh interval, but this introduces a different problem if the refresh interval is very small. In this case, the progress bar will disappear before the user ever gets a chance to see that it reached 100 percent because it could be just a few milliseconds before it disappears—too short a time to see it. Therefore, the program needs a lower bound on the length of time before it erases the progress bar.

The following function incorporates all of these ideas. The second parameter (refresh_timespec) is the refresh interval entered by the user converted to a timespec value. For example, if the user enters 2.75, then refresh_timespec .tv_sec will be 2 and refresh_timespec.tv_nsec will be 750,000,000.

short_pause()
```
void short_pause(double refresh_secs, struct timespec refresh_timespec)
{
    struct timespec slight_pause;
    struct timespec remaining_sleep;

    if ( refresh_secs > 3.0 )
        slight_pause = refresh_timespec;
    else {
        slight_pause.tv_sec  = 3;
        slight_pause.tv_nsec = 0;
    }
    if ( -1 == nanosleep(&slight_pause, &remaining_sleep) )
        nanosleep(&remaining_sleep, NULL);
}
```

Using POSIX timers instead of alarm() requires more setting up; the main() function needs the following new variables as a result:

```
double            refresh_secs = 0.5;    /* Default refresh interval       */
double            max_interval;          /* Max allowed refresh interval   */
timer_t           timerid;               /* Timer ID from timer_create()   */
struct timespec   zero_interval = {0,0}; /* For zeroing a timer value      */
struct timespec   refresh_timespec;      /* timespec for refresh interval  */
struct itimerspec refresh_interval;      /* The timer value and repeat     */
struct sigevent   sev;                   /* Notification structure         */
```

The program also has a few more steps than the first version had, which are:

1. Checking whether the command line has a refresh interval argument, and if so, checking that it's within limits

2. Setting up the interval timer's sigevent structure and the timer values in the itimerspec argument

3. Disarming the timer and changing the signal disposition after the simulated task finishes

The last step is included in a small function that consolidates all of the program's cleanup activities:

```
void clean_up()
{
    struct sigaction act;
    act.sa_handler = SIG_IGN;
    if ( sigaction(SIGUSR1, &act, NULL) == -1 )
        fatal_error(errno, "sigaction");
    erase_progress_bar();
    printf("Done\n");
}
```

The main() function of the revised program, named *progress_bar2.c*, is displayed in Listing 9-8. The variable declarations and some code that wasn't changed are omitted to save space. The complete program is available in the book's source code distribution.

progress_bar2.c
    main()

```
int main(int argc, char *argv[])
{
    --snip--
    max_interval = (double) MIN_SIMULATION_SECS / 2.0;

    /* Check if command line has a refresh interval. */
    if ( argc >= 2 ) {
        retval = get_dbl(argv[1], NON_NEG_ONLY, &refresh_secs, errmssge);
        if ( retval < 0 )
            fatal_error(retval, errmssge);
        else if ( refresh_secs <= 0 )
            fatal_error(retval, "get_dbl requires a positive number.\n");
    }
    /* Check that refresh interval is a suitable size. */
    if ( refresh_secs > max_interval || refresh_secs < 0.001 ) {
        sprintf(errmssge, "Argument must be between  0.001 and %4.1f",
                max_interval);
        usage_error(errmssge);
    }

    draw_initial_bar(); /* Draw empty bar. */
    OMITTED: Set up signal handling.

    /* Set sigevent struct to send SIGUSR1 signal when timer expires. */
    sev.sigev_notify = SIGEV_SIGNAL;
    sev.sigev_signo  = SIGUSR1;
    sev.sigev_value  = (union sigval) 0; /* Zero this field. */

    /* Create the timer with this sigevent structure. */
    if ( -1 == timer_create(CLOCK_MONOTONIC, &sev, &timerid) )
        fatal_error(errno, "timer_create");
```

```
    /* Convert refresh_secs to a timespec. */
    dbl_to_timespec(refresh_secs, &refresh_timespec);

    /* Set the timer initial value and timer interval to refresh_timespec. */
    refresh_interval.it_value    = refresh_timespec;
    refresh_interval.it_interval = refresh_timespec;

    /* Arm the timer with the itimerspec interval. */
    if ( -1 == timer_settime(timerid, 0, &refresh_interval, NULL) )
        fatal_error(errno, "timer_settime");

    lengthy_task();  /* Simulate the task. */
    short_pause(refresh_secs, refresh_timespec);

    /* Zero the timer to disarm it. */
    refresh_interval.it_value = zero_interval;
    if ( -1 == timer_settime(timerid, 0, &refresh_interval, NULL) )
        fatal_error(errno, "timer_settime");
    clean_up();
    return 0;
}
```

Listing 9-8: A revised progress bar simulation that uses POSIX timers instead of alarm() to generate signals for updating the progress bar

Because the program's output changes over time, the only way to see its behavior is by building it and running it with different values for the command line argument. If you do this, you'll see that you can control the refresh rate of the progress bar at runtime.

Resource Monitors

In the beginning of the chapter, I mentioned a few commands that dynamically monitor real-time resource usage over a period of time, including top, pidstat, vmstat, and iostat. Each of these displays a report in the terminal window with statistics about a particular type of resource, such as process-related events, memory, or I/O activity. Most are user configurable, letting us customize their behavior, and most also have some limited interaction with the user while they're running. For example, the user can force refreshes, suspend them, or terminate them by entering various key combinations.

With what we know about timers now, we could, with effort, implement one of these commands. It would be sufficiently challenging, we'd have written a useful and fairly large program as a result, and it would be a good application of POSIX timers. However, there are a few reasons not to try this yet. One is that we haven't covered processes yet and wouldn't really understand much about the data that these programs collect and display. Another reason is that, in order to format and update their output dynamically, most of them use features of terminal I/O that we've yet to explore.

In fact, several of them depend on the *ncurses* library, which is a library of terminal-independent functions that programs can use for updating character screens dynamically. We'll cover these topics in later chapters: processes in Chapters 10 and 11, terminal I/O in Chapter 18, and the *ncurses* library in Chapter 19.

Instead, we'll implement a dynamic resource monitor that's similar to those commands and equally useful but only builds on what we've covered in the preceding chapters, namely a dynamic file I/O monitor.

Sometimes, a program that writes a large amount of data to a file takes a long time to finish, either because of the amount of data or the amount of time it takes to generate the data. Often when this happens, we can't do more work until all of the data is written to the file. For example, when I copy a very large file from a remote server and I want to work on the copy, I have to wait for the file transfer to finish. File transfers over a network can take a long time, making the operation take longer than expected. I know I've often wanted to monitor the file in a separate terminal window that I can watch while I do other work so that as soon as the transfer is complete, I can work on that file. Sometimes the program that drives the transfer notifies us when it's complete, but not all do.

The program, which I'll name `watchfiles`, will accept a list of file pathnames on the command line. It will display, for each valid file, its name and size, updating the size at regular intervals, until the size of the file stops changing. It will also give us the option to terminate the program by entering q (for "quit") at any time. For now, we'll have to limit the number of files to watch because if that number isn't smaller than the number of rows in the screen, we won't be able to see them all. We don't yet know how to get the current number of rows in a terminal and therefore can't check whether the number of files exceeds that actual number of rows. In Chapters 18 and 19, we'll see how to handle this type of problem.

As an example of the program's behavior, if we run it as

```
$ ./watchfiles /tmp/zoom_amd64.deb /tmp/linux-6.1.37.tar.gz bigfile
```

then once it starts, it would clear the screen and display the files and their current sizes in two labeled columns, one for filenames and one for their sizes, updating the sizes periodically. For example, for the preceding run of `watchfiles`, the initial display might look like Listing 9-9.

```
File                      Size
/tmp/zoom_amd64.deb       16789823
/tmp/linux-6.1.37.tar.gz  872838217
bigfile                   0923331

Enter 'q<RETURN>' to quit:
```

Listing 9-9: A snapshot of watchfiles at an arbitrary time t

Then, after some short time interval, in the very next screen refresh, the screen might look like Listing 9-10.

```
File                       Size
/tmp/zoom_amd64.deb      23781637
/tmp/linux-6.1.37.tar.gz  879145201
bigfile                  12008657

Enter 'q<RETURN>' to quit:
```

Listing 9-10: Snapshot of watchfiles at time t + 1

The only differences in the displayed data are the sizes of the files.

To make the program a bit more versatile and challenging to develop, we'll add a few of the features that commands such as top have. One is a command line option that specifies how often the data will be refreshed. Another is a command line option that specifies how many screen refreshes without a change in any file's size are needed to decide that the file sizes have stabilized and that the program can terminate. The program's synopsis is therefore:

```
watchfiles [ options ] file [file ...]
where options can be one or more of
   -i <seconds>    The length of the update interval [default = 1]
   -l <count>      The number of updates in which no files changed
                   size to force the program to terminate [default = 10]
```

Developing this program will pose many of the same challenges that top would. Summarizing its behavior:

1. On startup, it checks the command line, gets the options and pathname arguments, and checks each pathname to make sure it has the permission to access its metadata. It removes any file it can't access from the list of files it will watch. It checks whether the number of files is less than the maximum allowed number of files (20) and exits with a usage message if it isn't.

2. It clears the screen completely.

3. It sets up the signal handlers and creates, sets, and arms the timer whose expirations drive the updates to the file sizes.

4. Each time the timer expires, a signal handler runs to check every file. If any disappeared, it replaces its size with the word disappeared. (This can happen if someone deleted the file after the program started.) For each file, the handler gets its current size. If the current size is different from the previous size, it records this. It then updates the display with the new file sizes or messages.

    If none of the files being watched changed size, the handler increments a count of the number of consecutive intervals without a change in any file's size. If one or more files changed, it resets this count to zero. If the count exceeds the threshold value, it notifies the program to terminate by setting a global flag that the main program can check.

5. The main program also checks whether the user entered a q and, if so, it terminates.

Let's explore how to implement these steps in the order they're listed.

Setting Up the File List

The first step is pretty routine at this point: parsing the command line and getting the options and arguments. For each file, the program needs to get its size. We can use stat(), lstat(), or statx() to get the size of a file as long as the program has execute permission on every directory in its pathname (see Chapter 6). It doesn't have to open the file. If the program can't stat the file, it should display a message and delete it from its list of files to display.

This implies that the program needs to create a list of files to display from the argv[] array passed to it. There's no need to duplicate the filenames in the argv[] array in order to do this. We can create an array, say filelist[], whose entries are pointers to the filenames in the argv[] array that we can watch. Figure 9-2 shows how this second array would simply point to the elements of argv[] that can be watched. The shaded pathnames and argv[] entries are the ones that can't be watched for one reason or another.

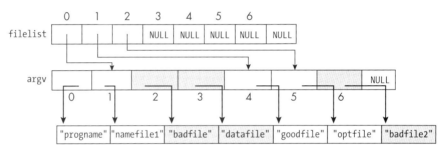

Figure 9-2: The filelist[] array that points to only those pathnames in argv[] that can be stat-ed and watched

However, there's another problem. The terminal window has a fixed width. What if the user enters a pathname so long that it's impossible to display a single line for the file in the terminal? We could just accept it and wrap it across multiple lines, but it would be nicer to truncate the pathname so that it fits on the line, replacing the leading directory names in the pathname by an ellipsis, the way we did in the implementation of the spl_pwd command in Chapter 7. We can define a constant, MAX_LENGTH, equal to the maximum length of a displayed pathname. Ideally it should depend on the number of columns in the terminal, but for this version of the program we'll just set it to 50. Thus, if one of the supplied pathnames is

```
/data/ubuntu-22.04.2-src-1/pool/main/a/alsa-topology-conf   # length = 57
```

the program would truncate it on the left and replace the deleted part with an ellipsis, as follows:

```
...u-22.04.2-src-1/pool/main/a/alsa-topology-conf           # length = 50
```

This in turn implies that for each file that the program will watch, it needs to store a separate display name as well as its actual pathname. The simplest solution is to check the length of every pathname and, for each, if this length is small enough, copy the actual pathname into the display name, and if not, copy a truncated version of it into the display name. Therefore, we'll need an array of display names, one for each watched file. The main program can allocate this array once it knows how many files it's watching.

We'll left-align the displayed names and right-align the file sizes on the screen. We'll make the width of the first column a fixed size equal to a declared constant, MAX_LENGTH. This makes it possible to construct the output string using only async-signal-safe functions from the string library such as strcat() and strncpy(), without needing the formatted output functions from *glibc*. The main program will right-pad all display names that are shorter than MAX_LENGTH with blanks. Listing 9-11 shows the code fragment in main() to create the display names padded with blanks as needed (without error handling).

```
for ( i = 0; i < numfiles; i++ ) {
    len = strlen(filelist[i]);
    displayname[i] = calloc(MAX_LENGTH + 1, sizeof(char));
    if ( len > MAX_LENGTH ) {
        sprintf(displayname[i], "...%*s",
                MAX_LENGTH - 3, filelist[i] + len - MAX_LENGTH + 3);
    }
    else {
        memset(displayname[i], ' ', MAX_LENGTH);
        displayname[i][MAX_LENGTH] = '\0';
        strncpy(displayname[i], filelist[i], len);
    }
}
```

Listing 9-11: A code fragment that truncates or right-pads all filenames with space characters as needed

Files whose names exceed MAX_LENGTH aren't padded. To pad the shorter names, the displayname string is first filled with blanks, after which the leftmost part of the string is overwritten by strncpy() when it copies the filename into it.

Refreshing the Screen

Before we explore how a program can clear the screen, it's best if we clarify what this means and get a basic understanding of terminals.

There's a difference between the terms *screen*, *console*, and *terminal*. We use the term *screen* to refer to the visible area in what we've been calling a *terminal window* so far. For example, to *clear the screen* means to make that area completely blank. Similarly, if we refer to the *top of the screen*, we mean the highest line in the terminal window. The term *console* usually refers to the physical display device and keyboard attached to the computer through which we interact with it. In Linux, a *virtual console* is a software representation of

a keyboard and display device. The device files whose names are of the form
/dev/tty* are virtual consoles in Linux.

The word *terminal* has a few meanings. Some people use it to refer to a
piece of hardware through which we interact with the computer. This is rare
these days. Some use it to mean the software emulated terminal that appears
in a window on the display device, which, on a bit-mapped display, is technically called a *terminal emulator*. Some people use the term more generally to
refer to the interface that both hardware and software terminals present to
the user. In this sense, hardware terminals, terminal emulators, and virtual
consoles all present a terminal to a user. In Unix, a terminal is represented
by a device special file. Here, I use the word *terminal* in this last sense, as the
interface, whether hardware or software emulated, that allows the kernel
and processes to send text output to a user and allows the user to enter text
input. In this section, we'll explore just enough about terminals to solve the
current programming problem. Terminals and terminal I/O are covered in
more depth in Chapter 18.

Terminals normally perform two functions: to accept input and to display output. When character codes are delivered to the terminal driver,
they undergo some preliminary processing. Some codes are actual characters to be displayed, called *printable* characters, such as letters, numbers, and
punctuation. Their graphical representations on the screen are called *glyphs*.
Other codes are control characters. You're familiar with some of them, such
as CTRL-C and CTRL-\, but there are several others. Some sequences are consecutive bytes that tell the driver where to position the cursor, or what colors
to use to display text, whether to wrap text, clear the screen, and so on.

In the early years of computing, there were different types of terminals
sold by various manufacturers. Each different type had its own set of control sequences. This made it hard to write portable programs. In 1976, the
set of control sequences was standardized by the European Computer Manufacturers Association (ECMA). The standard was updated several times
and ultimately adopted by the International Organization for Standardization (ISO) and the International Electrotechnical Commission (IEC) and was
named ISO/IEC 6429. It was also adopted by the American National Standards Institute (ANSI) and known as ANSI X3.64. These sequences are now
commonly called the ANSI escape sequences, even though ANSI withdrew
the standard in 1997.

An ANSI escape sequence is a sequence of ASCII characters, the first
two of which are the ASCII *escape* character, whose decimal code is 27, followed by the left-bracket character [. The escape character is often written as
the octal code \033 or the hexadecimal code \x1b. The string \033[is known
as the *Control Sequence Introducer (CSI)*. The character or characters following
the CSI are an alphanumeric code that specifies a particular keyboard or display function. For example, the ANSI escape sequence "\033[2J" is the CSI
"\033[" followed by the control code 2J. The code "2J" erases the entire video
display. Therefore, if we want to clear the screen, we can send the sequence
"\033[2J" to the terminal by printing it as a string to standard output:

```
printf("\033[2J");
```

Almost all terminal emulators running on Unix systems interpret these ANSI escape sequences in the same way, which means that, in principle, a program that uses these sequences should behave the same regardless of which terminal is being emulated; however, this is not guaranteed. This is why the *curses* library (now called *ncurses*) was developed. This library provides a consistent, standardized interface to the terminal. We'll cover the *ncurses* library in Chapter 19.

It's surprisingly easy to find the escape sequences that are available:

```
$ apropos -a escape sequence
console_codes (4)    - Linux console escape and control sequences
--snip--
```

The console codes man page describes the different types of control codes and escape sequences that are supported by Linux consoles, including software-emulated terminals. It also includes a summary of the steps that take place when character codes are sent to the terminal driver, but we'll explain how that works in Chapter 18.

The subsection entitled "Linux Console Controls" has tables of the different types of control codes and escape sequences, not just the ANSI ones, but others as well. The notation might be a bit confusing at first; it requires a careful reading. It explains that command letters such as H and J in the tables are the final characters in the sequence and that they're preceded by one or more parameters separated by semicolons. The whitespace is not part of the syntax. Table 9-1 shows some examples to clarify this.

Table 9-1: Examples of Terminal Escape Sequences

Man page notation	Example	Action
ESC [1 J	\033[1J	Erase from top of display to cursor
ESC [2 J	\033[2J	Erase entire display
ESC [H	\033[10;20H	Move cursor to row 10, column 20 (origin at 1,1)
ESC [E	\033[5E	Move cursor to column 1, 5 lines down

These are the only escape sequences we'll need. We can use them to clear the screen in a couple of different ways and to move the cursor to any position on the screen. The book's source code distribution has two programs that demonstrate how to use several different escape sequences. One, *escapeseq_demo1.c*, writes a sequence of symbols on the terminal periodically, and the other, *escapeseq_demo2.c*, displays a screen menu and lets you enter different commands that alter the screen.

Continuing along, a few macros will make our program easier to read:

```
#define   REFRESH       write(STDOUT_FILENO, "\033[1J", 4)
#define   CLEARDISPLAY  write(STDOUT_FILENO, "\033[2J", 4)
#define   MOVETOHOME    write(STDOUT_FILENO, "\033[1;1H", 6)
#define   MOVETO(row)   write(STDOUT_FILENO, "\033[",2); \
```

```
                              write(STDOUT_FILENO, row, strlen(row)); \
                              write(STDOUT_FILENO, ";1H", 3)
```

The MOVETO(row) macro moves the cursor to position (*row*,1). For example, MOVETO(22) moves it to (22,1). We already know how to do the third step, setting up the signal handlers and timer, so we'll move on to the issue of updating the file sizes.

Updating the File Sizes

The set of files is updated with every timer expiration, implying that the code to determine and print the changes should be in the signal handler, which we'll name update_files(). The handler's code is essentially a loop that calls stat() on each file in the list of files.

Most of the major variables accessed by the handler have to be either global (file-scoped) or static locals. For example, in order for the handler to keep track of whether a file's size has changed from one update to the next, file sizes have to be preserved across calls to the handler. Since the number of files isn't known until runtime, the array of file sizes has to be allocated dynamically. It's better if main() allocates the storage as soon as it has parsed the command line and counted the files that can be stat-ed successfully. Hence the array must be global. Similar reasoning applies to the array of display names.

There are two ways to replace the displayed file size at each update. One is, for each file, to move the cursor to the start of its size in the display area, erase the current size, and write the new size. The other is to erase the screen from the top line down to the line containing the last file, construct a single string in memory with all of the new sizes, and print that entire string to the screen all at once at cursor position (1,1). The second method is a lot cleaner and easier than the first. Figure 9-3 illustrates this idea.

Figure 9-3: A depiction of the terminal window showing the region above the static prompt that needs to be refreshed by the signal handler every time the timer expires

To avoid calling the output functions declared in *stdio.h*, none of which are async-signal-safe, the handler will construct the strings to print using strcpy() and strcat(), after which it can use write() to print the entire string to the terminal.

The preceding discussion suggests the following sequence of steps that the signal handler should perform.

1. Erase the screen from line 1 down to the last line of filenames.

2. Move the cursor to the upper-left screen corner (1,1).

3. Create a string with a heading of the form "*File ... Size*".

4. For each file *i*, do the following:
   (a) Call lstat() on file *i*, filling a stat buffer.
   (b) If not successful because the file doesn't exist, create an output line with the filename and the word disappeared where the size was before. If it isn't successful for any other reason, create an output line with an error message that stat() failed.
   (c) Otherwise, get the new size from the stat buffer, create an output line for the file with the new size, compare the old and new sizes, and if different, set changed to TRUE.
   (d) Append the output line just constructed to the string to be printed using strcat().

5. Call write() to write the string constructed in the preceding loop to the terminal.

6. If changed is FALSE, no file's size changed in this update, so increment the count of unchanged updates: stable_cnt++. Otherwise, at least one file's size changed, so reset stable_cnt to 0.

7. If stable_cnt has reached the stopping criterion limit nochange_limit, set a flag named stopflag so that the main program can terminate.

8. Move the cursor 2 lines below the last file's line and display a prompt of the form Enter 'q<ENTER>' to quit:.

We're ready to assemble the pieces of the program.

Assembling the Program

Based on the preceding discussion, several of the variables must be declared with file scope. They are:

```
char      **filelist;        /* Files for processing                     */
char      **displayname;     /* Name to display in case path too long    */
int         numfiles = 0;    /* Number of files to be processed          */
char        linecnt_str[3];  /* String storing count of lines to refresh */
long long *prevsize;         /* Array of file sizes in previous update    */
int         stable_cnt = 0;  /* Count of consecutive unchanged updates   */
int         nochange_limit;  /* When stable_cnt reaches it, time to stop  */
const int  MAX_LENGTH = 50;  /* Width of filename field in output         */
```

```
const int  MAX_FILES  = 20;     /* Maximum number of files allowed to track   */
char       heading[66];         /* Heading with column labels to be displayed */
char       rownum[3];           /* Row number of line containing the prompt    */
volatile sig_atomic_t stopflag = 0; /* Flag that handler sets to stop main    */
```

The signal handler code follows. It makes no calls to unsafe functions; the file size is converted to a string by a function lltostr() whose source is in the file *common/llongtostr.c* in the source code repository. The inline comments explain the steps:

```
void update_stats(int signum)
{
    const char  prompt[] = "Enter \'q\' to quit:";
    struct stat statbuf;         /* stat structure filled by statx()    */
    char        outbuffer[4096]; /* String to display w/ every update   */
    char        one_line[256];   /* Buffer to store one file's line     */
    long long   newfilesize;     /* New size of file                    */
    char        size_str[20];    /* Size of filename stored as a string */
    static BOOL changed = FALSE; /* Flag to indicate if a file changed  */
    int         i = 0;

    MOVETO(rownum);          /* Move cursor to prompt line.            */
    REFRESH;                 /* Clear the screen from top to this line. */
    MOVETOHOME;              /* Move cursor to upper left.             */
    strcpy(outbuffer, heading); /* Copy heading to buffer.             */
    for ( i = 0; i < numfiles; i++ ) {
        if ( lstat(filelist[i], &statbuf) < 0 )
            if ( errno == ENOENT ) {
                strcpy(one_line, displayname[i]);
                strcat(one_line, " disappeared\n");
            }
            else {
                strcpy(one_line, displayname[i]);
                strcat(one_line, " stat failed\n");
            }
        else {  /* Valid stat of file */
            newfilesize = statbuf.st_size;      /* Get new size.       */
            if ( prevsize[i] != newfilesize ) { /* Size changed        */
                changed = TRUE;                 /* Make a note of it.  */
                prevsize[i] = newfilesize;      /* Save new size.      */
            }
            lltostr(newfilesize, size_str, 15);
            strcpy(one_line, displayname[i]);
            strcat(one_line, size_str);
            strcat(one_line, "\n");
        }
        strncat(outbuffer, one_line, strlen(outbuffer));
    }
    /* Write the outbuffer to the terminal display. */
```

```
    if ( -1 == write(STDOUT_FILENO, outbuffer, strlen(outbuffer)) )
        fatal_error(errno, "write");
    if ( !changed )
        stable_cnt++;    /* No file changed in this update increment count. */
    else
        stable_cnt = 0;  /* A file changed - reset count to start again.    */
    if ( stable_cnt >= nochange_limit )
        stopflag = 1;
    MOVETO(rownum);         /* Move cursor to line where prompt is written. */
    write(STDOUT_FILENO, prompt, strlen(prompt));        /* Display prompt. */
}
```

The last task is to write up the main() function. It's primary work is to perform all initializations and setup, in the following order:

- Get the command line options and arguments.

- Check that all argument files exist and that the program has the appropriate permissions to get their sizes using lstat(). The logic for accomplishing this is:

```
for ( k = 0, i = optind; i < argc; i++ ) {
    if ( lstat(argv[i], &statbuf) < 0 ) {
        fprintf(stderr, "Could not stat %s, skipping it. \n",
                argv[i]);
        numfiles--;  /* Reduce file count. */
    }
    else
        filelist[k++] = argv[i];
}
```

When this loop finishes, the entries in the filelist[] array will point to only those elements of argv[] that can be accessed, as we discussed in "Setting Up the File List" on page 474.

- Create the display names for each file, truncating or padding them as needed. This code was presented in Listing 9-11.

- Initialize all global variables shared by the signal handler.

- Install a signal handler for SIGUSR1 and a handler that catches SIGINT and SIGQUIT and cleans up before terminating the process.

- Set up and arm the timer.

- Wait for the user to enter q to terminate the program.

Listing 9-12 has fragments of the main() function. The complete program is available in the source code repository. The missing parts are described in the comments.

watchfiles.c
    main()
```
int main(int argc, char **argv)
{
```

```
    // OMITTED: Declarations of local variables in main(), initializations of
    //          the usage_message, the heading to be displayed, option parsing
    //          code, checks that each file in the argument list can be
    //          stat-ed, checks for number of files, allocating storage for,
    //          truncating, and padding the display names

    act.sa_handler = sig_handler;
    act.sa_flags   = 0;
    sigemptyset(&(act.sa_mask));
    if ( sigaction(SIGINT, &act, NULL) == -1 )
        fatal_error(errno, "sigaction");
    if ( sigaction(SIGQUIT, &act, NULL) == -1 )
        fatal_error(errno, "sigaction");

    CLEARDISPLAY;   /* Completely erase the terminal window. */

    /* Install update_stats() SIGUSR1 handler. */
    act.sa_handler = update_stats;
    if ( sigaction(SIGUSR1, &act, NULL) == -1 )
        fatal_error(errno, "sigaction");

    /* Set up sigevent structure for timer and create the timer. */
    sev.sigev_notify = SIGEV_SIGNAL;
    sev.sigev_signo  = SIGUSR1;
    sev.sigev_value  = (union sigval) 0;
    if ( -1 == timer_create(CLOCK_MONOTONIC, &sev, &timerid) )
        fatal_error(errno, "timer_create");
    // OMITTED: Setting and arming the timer
    while ( !stopflag ) {
        n = read(STDIN_FILENO, &c, 1);
        if ( -1 == n && errno == EINTR )
            continue;
        else if ( c == 'q' )
            break;
    }
    tcflush(STDIN_FILENO, TCIFLUSH); /* Remove last newline character. */
    refresh_interval.it_value = ZERO_TS;            /* Disarm timer. */
    if ( -1 == timer_settime(timerid, 0, &refresh_interval, NULL) )
        fatal_error(errno, "timer_settime");
    if ( stopflag ) /* Loop exited because no file size changed. */
        printf("\nNo changes were detected in the last %2.1f"
                " seconds in any file.\n", nochange_limit*refresh_secs);
    cleanup();      /* A function that frees all calloc-ed memory */
    exit(EXIT_SUCCESS);
}
```

Listing 9-12: A partial listing of the main() function of watchfiles

The purpose of the call to tcflush() on the standard input stream is to remove the newline character from the terminal's input queue. We haven't yet covered how to read characters from the terminal without requiring the user to enter a newline. If we leave it in the queue, bash will receive an empty command when the program terminates and display an extra prompt line.

Running the Program

Because the program uses a POSIX timer, it has to be built with the extra linker flag, -lrt:

```
$ gcc -D_XOPEN_SOURCE=700 -D_DEFAULT_SOURCE I../include -L ../lib \
  watchfiles.c -lspl -lm -lrt -o watchfiles
```

I'll display a few snapshots of the running program to show its behavior. In the first run, I set the interval to 0.75 seconds and the limit to 10 intervals with no change, giving it two files for which it has permission to access the file metadata, one with a name that's too long to display:

```
$ ./watchfiles -l10 -i0.75 /var/log/syslog \
~/.local/share/recently-used.xbel.EPDEU1 \
/home/stewart/.mozilla/firefox/hjas8j.profile/webappsstore.sqlite
```

It clears the screen and displays the files and their sizes. Following is a snapshot during a run:

File	Size
.../stewart/.local/share/recently-used.xbel.EPDEU1	5351
/var/log/syslog	3943250
...fox/xdjb3t0l.latest_profile/webappsstore.sqlite	29360128
Enter 'q' to quit:	

If I let it run until there are no changes, I see the output:

File	Size
.../stewart/.local/share/recently-used.xbel.EPDEU1	7864
/var/log/syslog	3943250
...fox/xdjb3t0l.latest_profile/webappsstore.sqlite	29360128
Enter 'q' to quit:	
No changes were detected in the last 7.5 seconds in any file.	

This time, I'll give it a few more files, a few of which are either nonexistent or can't be stat-ed because I don't have execute permission on some directory in the pathname. I'll redirect standard errors to a file to save the errors that the program reported:

```
$ ./watchfiles -l5 -i0.75 ../testdata/foo nosuchfile /var/spool/cron/atjobs/anotherbadfile \
~/.cache/mozilla/firefox/xdjb3t0l.latest_profile/cache2/entries/ \
1247B9C6A8F1003F00AE7A3789C91F3487255EF9  2> errors
```

I let it run until it detects no changes:

File	Size
../testdata/foo	400
/var/spool/cron/atjobs	4096

```
Enter 'q' to quit:
No changes were detected in the last 3.8 seconds in any file.
```

Notice that several files are missing. The *errors* file contents are:

```
Could not stat nosuchfile, skipping it.
Could not stat anotherbadfile, skipping it.
Could not stat .cache/mozilla/firefox/xdjb3t0l.latest_profile/cache2/entries/
1247B9C6A8F1003F00AE7A3789C91F3487255EF9, skipping it.
```

The error messages do not distinguish between nonexistent files and those without appropriate permissions.

Developing this small resource monitor gave us the chance to employ a timer in a useful program. The principles involved are the same regardless of what resource is being monitored. In addition, we discovered how to control the terminal just enough to clear the screen and move the cursor to those positions on the screen where we wanted to display output. Soon we'll see other, easier, and yet more powerful functions for terminal control when we explore the *ncurses* library.

Real-Time Signals and Multiple Timers

The programs we've developed so far have used a single timer, but in many cases, a program needs more than one. For example, system programs that control or monitor the activities of many resources need multiple timers. Animations in which multiple sprites move independently in a screen require a timer for each sprite.

If a program is limited to just the two unassigned standard signals, SIGUSR1 and SIGUSR2, the only way it could use more than two timers would be to design the signal handler to extract the timer ID from the siginfo_t parameter to determine which timer expired and base its action on that ID. The handler code would be larger and the handler would take longer to execute. Since version 2.2, Linux has supported an extended set of signals that incorporates real-time signals, and POSIX.1-2001 made these signals part of the standard. Real-time signals have no preassigned meaning. A program can use them for its own purposes.

Unlike standard signals, multiple real-time signals of the same type are queued if delivery is temporarily blocked. Furthermore, they're queued in the order they were sent. Their range of values is defined by two macros: SIGRTMIN, the lower bound, and SIGRTMAX, the upper bound. POSIX requires that any conforming system have at least eight real-time signals.

A program should not use actual numbers to refer to any of these signals. Instead, it should use an expression such as SIGRTMIN+n, where n is a small enough nonnegative integer. A program can safely use signals SIGRTMIN,

SIGRTMIN+1, and SIGRTMIN+2, up to SIGRTMIN+7 in Linux, but the correct way to use them is to make sure that SIGRTMIN+*n* is never more than SIGRTMAX. Also, signals with smaller numeric values have higher priority in the sense that if two or more are sent at the same time, the lower-valued signal will be delivered before the higher-valued one.

To illustrate the use of multiple timers and real-time signals, I wrote a short program that creates several timers, each using a unique real-time signal number. A single handler catches all of these signals. When it runs, it prints a number that's unique to the timer that expired, based on the timer ID associated with the timer that sent the signal. Recall from the discussion about timer creation in "Creating and Deleting Timers" on page 462 that a three-parameter sigaction handler can access the timer ID used if, when the timer was created, the sigevent structure's sigev_value.sival_ptr contained the address of that timer ID—the siginfo_t parameter's si_value.sival_ptr will contain that timer ID when the handler runs.

The program, named *posix_timer_demo1.c*, creates eight timers, fewer if the system does not support at least eight real-time signals. Each timer's interval is unique: Timer *n*'s interval is a constant multiple of the *n*th prime number, which reduces the frequency with which two timers expire at the exact same time. When a timer expires, the signal handler writes the prime number length of the timer's interval on the screen. It calls write() for this purpose so that writing is async-signal-safe. Although the sequence of numbers displayed on the screen appears somewhat random, it isn't. Each number is printed at a frequency inversely proportional to its value, so that 2 appears most frequently and 19 the least. Because all timer signals are caught by the same handler, which blocks all signals while it's running, some get queued, and their associated numbers may not be printed in the order in which they were generated:

---

posix_timer _demo1.c

```c
#include "common_hdrs.h"
#include <stdint.h>
#include "time_utils.h"

#define CLOCKID CLOCK_MONOTONIC
#define NUMTIMERS 8
char *idstr[] =
    {" 2", " 3", " 5", " 7", " 11", " 13", " 17 ", " 19 "};

void sighandler(int sig, siginfo_t *si, void *uc)
{
    long timerid = *(long*) (si->si_value.sival_ptr);
    write(STDOUT_FILENO, idstr[timerid], strlen(idstr[timerid]));
    fflush(stdout);
}

int main(int argc, char *argv[])
{
    timer_t         timerid[NUMTIMERS];
```

```
struct sigevent    sev;
struct itimerspec timer_setting[NUMTIMERS];
struct sigaction  sa;
char               c;
int                i, nbytes;
int                numtimers = NUMTIMERS;
const double       BASE_UNIT = 0.4; /* Seconds */
int                interval[NUMTIMERS] = {2, 3, 5, 7, 11, 13, 17, 19};

if ( SIGRTMIN+NUMTIMERS > SIGRTMAX )
    numtimers = SIGRTMAX - SIGRTMIN;

/* Install signal handlers. */
sa.sa_flags = SA_SIGINFO | SA_RESTART;
for ( i = 0; i < numtimers; i++ ) {
    sa.sa_sigaction = sighandler;
    sigfillset(&sa.sa_mask); /* Block all other signals. */
    if ( -1 == sigaction(SIGRTMIN+1+i, &sa, NULL) )
        fatal_error(errno, "sigaction");
}
/* Create the timers. */
sev.sigev_notify = SIGEV_SIGNAL;
for ( i = 0; i < numtimers; i++ ) {
    sev.sigev_signo = SIGRTMIN + 1 + i;
    sev.sigev_value.sival_ptr = &(timerid[i]);
    if ( timer_create(CLOCKID, &sev, &(timerid[i])) == -1 )
        fatal_error(errno, "timer_create");
}
for ( i = 0; i < numtimers; i++ ) {
    /* Set the intervals for the timers. */
    dbl_to_timespec(interval[i]*BASE_UNIT, &(timer_setting[i].it_value));
    timer_setting[i].it_interval = timer_setting[i].it_value;
}
for ( i = 0; i < numtimers; i++ )
    if ( timer_settime(timerid[i], 0, &(timer_setting[i]), NULL) == -1 )
        fatal_error(errno, "timer_settime");

printf("Enter 'q' to terminate this program.\n");
while ( TRUE ) {
    if ( -1 == (nbytes = read(STDIN_FILENO, &c, 1)) )
        fatal_error(errno, "read");
    else if ( c == 'q' )
        break;
}
exit(EXIT_SUCCESS);
}
```

A run of the executable produces the following output. Due to space limitations, only a small portion of it is shown:

```
$ ./posix_timer_demo1
Enter 'q' to terminate this program.
 2 3 2 5 2 3 7 2 3 2 5 11 2 3 13 2 7 3 5 2 17  2 3 19  2 5 3 7 2 11 2 3
5 2 13 3 2 7 2 3 5 2 3 11  ^C
```

The pattern is not regular because signals are blocked while the handler is running, and when they're delivered, because lower-numbered real-time signals have higher priority than higher ones, their IDs will be printed ahead of the others. More importantly, this program demonstrates the way in which a program can use multiple timers, each with its own unique signal.

Summary

Timers and sleep functions provide a means for processes to control the points in time at which they perform specific actions. The older sleep functions such as sleep(), usleep(), and nanosleep() suspend the process for a program-supplied interval of time. The first two have the weakness that they interact with signals, whereas nanosleep() does not. The newer clock_nanosleep() function also allows the program to specify a wall clock time at which to wake up, rather than after an interval of time has elapsed, and it lets the program choose which hardware clock it should use for measuring time.

Modern computers contain several different types of time measurement devices. Most have a designated hardware clock called the real-time clock (RTC) that keeps wall clock time, also called calendar time, backed up by a battery while the computer is turned off or in a low-power state. Some computers have several RTCs. An RTC on x86 hardware, for example, can be programmed to generate periodic interrupts at selected frequencies ranging between 2 Hz and 8,192 Hz, or at every clock tick.

Many computers also have a programmable interval timer (PIT). The PIT issues a timer interrupt whenever it times out. Linux kernels typically program the PIT to issue interrupts about once every millisecond. Linux systems sometimes use the Time Stamp Counter for higher-precision timing, as high as 1 GHz, for finer resolution. Lastly, many modern computers have high-resolution timers called High Precision Event Timers (HPETs), which can be programmed to generate interrupts at regular intervals or only once, when a counter reaches a specific value. These timers are used to provide high-resolution timers for user programs.

Software interval timers are based on these different hardware clocks and timers. A program can set an interval timer to expire after an elapsed time. When the timer expires, it sends the process a notification, which is usually a signal but need not be. Unlike a sleep function, a timer does not suspend the process. Timers allow a process to schedule the execution of code at regular intervals, making it possible to implement commands and applications such as resource monitors, progress bars, and animations.

Unix systems provide a few different types of interval timers. The simplest of these is alarm(), which generates a SIGALRM signal when the timer expires and whose interval is expressed in units of 1 second. The setitimer() function is a higher-resolution timer than alarm(), but it is marked as obsolete by POSIX.1-2008. POSIX recommends the use of a newer type of timer called a POSIX timer that has nanosecond granularity. POSIX timers are created by timer_create() and armed with timer_settime().

This chapter showed how to use several different sleep functions and timers. We developed a progress bar program based on both the simple alarm() timer and a POSIX timer. We also developed a simple resource monitor based on a POSIX timer.

Exercises

1. Write a program like *nanosleep_demo1.c* that catches all terminating signals that can be caught instead of just SIGINT and reports the remaining time when it receives them, just like *nanosleep_demo1.c*. Exclude signals caused by hardware errors or I/O, such as SIGBUS, SIGSEGV, and SIGIO.

2. Implement a command named snooze that behaves like the sleep command except that:
   - It allows the user to enter a fractional number of seconds, such as 5.25, defaulting to 1 second if no argument is supplied.
   - While the shell is suspended, it displays the message

   ```
   Delaying for n seconds...
   ```

   and on the line below this message, it prints a forward slash alternating with a backslash every 0.1 seconds.
   - When it is finished, it erases the alternating slashes and writes the word Done.
   If the program receives a terminating signal, it should terminate.

3. Implement a command line countdown timer named countdown that is given a number of minutes as its first argument and an optional refresh interval in minutes as its second argument:

   ```
   $ ./countdown duration [refresh_interval]
   ```

   It clears the screen completely, and at the top of the cleared screen it displays Number of minutes remaining: followed by the number of minutes remaining until the duration expires. If the refresh interval is not supplied, it updates the remaining time every minute; otherwise, it refreshes it after every *refresh_interval* minutes. When it reaches zero, it clears the message from the screen completely and returns control to the shell. If either argument is anything other than a positive integer, it displays a suitable usage message and exits.

4. Modify the preceding program so that it accepts a command line option -s that, when present, means that the values entered by the user should be taken as seconds instead of minutes. If the program receives a terminating signal, it should terminate.

5. Write a program named `wallclock` that clears the screen and displays the current wall clock time, using the user's LC_TIME locale setting, on the top line of the screen, updating it every second. It should replace the previous time with the new time each second. There are a few different ways to implement this command. Consider whether to use the `time()` system call or `clock_gettime()`. Will it sleep or use a timer?

6. The `timer_overrun_demo` program in the chapter counts the number of timer overruns in a given time period. It's run as

```
$ ./timer_overrun_demo duration timer_interval
```

in which *duration* is the number of seconds during which the program sends itself SIGRTMIN signals and *timer_interval* is the number of nanoseconds between successive timer expirations that generate this signal. For example, if the duration is 2 seconds and the timer interval is 10,000 nanoseconds, then the program will generate and attempt to deliver 2,000,000,000 / 10,000 = 200,000 signals. When the timer intervals are very small, the counting is inaccurate. Experiment with successively smaller intervals to see when it starts to miscount. Run it with the same arguments repeatedly. What are some possible explanations for why the overrun count changes and why it becomes less accurate as the timer interval gets smaller and smaller?

7. The `watchfiles` program in the chapter is unable to detect how many rows are in the terminal screen. Because of this, it will crash if the user enters more file arguments than they should. Read the man page for `ioctl()` and look at the header file *sys/ioctl.h*. Using `ioctl()`, write a function named `winsize()` that gets the size of the screen. (The macro TIOCGWINSZ will be its second argument.) Use your function to prevent `watchfiles` from crashing if the user enters more file arguments than can fit in the window.

10

PROCESS FUNDAMENTALS

In this chapter, we examine the structure and representation of a process in Linux. If we think of a process as something that performs a task for an ordinary nonprivileged user such as you or me but that is managed by the kernel, it leads to two very different views of a process. One is the way that nonprivileged users see it, and the other is the way that the kernel represents it. We begin by exploring the user-visible manifestation of a process. After that, we'll look at it from the kernel's perspective.

More specifically, we start by examining the kinds of relationships that can exist among sets of processes. Since processes execute programs, we'll then delve into what executable programs actually are and their relationship to processes. After that, we'll examine the structure of the *memory image* of a process, which is the contents of the memory assigned to the process while it's running.

Turning to how a process is manifested within the kernel, we'll study how the kernel represents a process, what types of attributes are associated with it, what kinds of resources a process can have, and what kinds of resources and internal structures are needed by the kernel to manage the process. We'll look at the ways in which user programs can view some of the kernel's representation of a process. Along the way, we'll implement a few programs that use or access various process attributes, such as a simplified version of the `ps` command.

Processes Revisited

In the first chapter of the book, I defined a process as an instance of a running program. This is the traditional definition of a process. Another way to conceptualize a process is that it's an entity that executes a program. As long as it's alive, it's executing some program, and it may not be the same program as the one it began to execute when it came into existence. The POSIX definition formalizes this viewpoint; POSIX.1-2024 defines a process as "an address space with one or more threads executing within that address space, and the required system resources for those threads" (Base Definitions: 3.210). If we think of a process as an address space with something executing within it, then it's not hard to accept the idea that whatever it's executing can be changed and that a process is not tied to a particular program. It's like a person and their job—when a person changes their job, they remain the same person, even though they're *executing* a new job.

To execute a program, a process requires physical memory for the program's instructions and data, as well as other system resources such as disk space and access to the CPU. All resources are finite, and it's the kernel's responsibility to allocate them among the processes. To make decisions about which processes should be given which resources, the kernel has to have a clear picture of what every process is doing at a given time. For example, it needs to know a process's privileges and scheduling priority, its runtime status, the state of any pending timers or signals, tables of open file descriptions, tables for managing signals, memory maps, and so on. Therefore, the kernel must have a representation of a process that includes all of the information it needs to manage that process as well as all other processes and their resources. For each process, this information, called the *process metadata*, is aggregated into a kernel data structure that's associated with the process by means of the unique process ID (PID) that the kernel assigned to it when it was created. In "The Kernel's Process Representation" on page 517, we'll explore the various resources and attributes associated with the process under the kernel's control and how programs can access them.

Users such as you and I need the PID to access process metadata. Commands such as `ps` and `top` print the PIDs with the rest of their output so that we can identify which lines of output correspond to which processes. With the PID, we can also access more process metadata by examining the files in the */proc* pseudofilesystem. The */proc* pseudofilesystem is not a filesystem in the usual sense; it's an interface to the kernel's data structures. Ordinary commands and functions that access files can access process metadata, so that we can easily "see" the kernel's internal data, like reading an X-ray of the kernel. We'll explore the */proc* pseudofilesystem in "The */proc* Pseudofilesystem" on page 521.

The kernel maintains other IDs for each process. For example, every process has a few user IDs, such as an effective UID and a real UID (see Chapter 4). It also has a parent process ID, a process group ID, and a session ID. Soon you'll see the role that the various IDs play in process management.

The Process Tree

On a typical Unix system, at any moment in time you'll probably find a few hundred active processes. An *active*, or *live*, process is one that's been created and has not terminated. Enter `ps -e` to see information about the complete set of them, or just pipe its output to `wc -l` to count them, as in:

```
$ ps -e | tail -n +2 | wc -l   # Throw away heading line of ps.
266
```

With the exception of the init (systemd) process, whose PID is 1, all of these processes came into existence because some other process created them. The init process is created at system startup by the kernel and then goes on to create other processes, which in turn create other processes, which create others, and so on. This implies that every process other than init was either created directly or indirectly by the init process, in essence forming a process tree whose root is init. In fact, the pstree command displays this tree, in whole or in part, depending on the options and arguments you give it.

The terminology associated with processes is very anthropomorphic; we call the creating process the *parent process*, the created one the *child process*, and all processes created by the same process *siblings*. Terms such as *ancestor* and *descendant* have the expected analogous meanings. Thus, we say that init is the ancestor of every other process and that all other processes are descendants of init.

Process Groups

Modern Unix systems introduced the concept of a *process group* as an abstraction of a job [4]. The motivation for this feature was to simplify the way in which a pipeline could be terminated with a signal [13]. When we enter a shell pipeline such as

```
$ last | cut -d' ' -f1 | sort -u
```

separate processes are created to execute each subcommand, but they're all placed into a single process group created by the shell. When a user enters a termination or job control signal such as CTRL-C from the keyboard, the signal is delivered to all processes in the group, making it possible to terminate every process in the pipeline easily.

POSIX.1-2024 defines a *process group* as "a collection of processes that permits the signaling of related processes" (Base Definitions: 3.296). Each process group has a unique positive-integer *process group ID*, which I'll refer to as its PGID. Every process belongs to exactly one process group at any time. The process's process group ID, which I'll refer to as its PGRP, is set to the PGID of the process group to which it belongs. To be clear, a PGID is the ID of a process group, whereas a PGRP is the group ID of a process.

When a process is created, it's given the PGRP of its parent and therefore begins execution as part of its parent's group. When a user enters a pipeline in a shell that supports job control such as bash, the shell creates a new process group as well as a process for each executable program in the pipeline and places all of these child processes into that group. The assignment of a PGID for that group is fairly simple—the very first process that the shell creates becomes the group's *process group leader*, and its PID is used as the PGID for the new group. Each other process's PGRP is then set to this PGID.

To see this, open two terminal windows. In the first, enter the pipeline:

```
$ cat | sort | uniq | wc
```

Since cat is waiting for user input, all of these commands will remain active until you enter CTRL-D in this terminal, which delivers an EOF to cat. In a second terminal, enter a ps command that displays the PGRP of each process. You can view the PGRP of a process in the output of ps with the -o option, specifying the format to include pgrp. To see the PID, the parent process ID (PPID), the PGRP, and the executed command, I'll enter the command:

```
$ ps -opid,ppid,pgrp,cmd
   PID   PPID   PGRP CMD
--snip--
  8294   4685   8294 bash
 16779   4716  16779 cat
 16780   4716  16779 sort
 16781   4716  16779 uniq
 16782   4716  16779 wc
 16783   8294  16783 ps -u stewart -opid,ppid,pgrp,cmd
```

(You might need to add a -a option to ps for this to work on other Linux distributions.) I removed the unrelated processes from this output. Notice that cat's PID is the same as its PGRP. This tells us that cat is the group leader. The remaining processes in the pipeline are all in this group because they have the same PGRP as cat.

Because process groups were introduced primarily for job control, if I had entered CTRL-C while the pipeline was active, every process would have received a SIGINT and would terminate. What if, instead, I tried to terminate the set of processes using the kill command? The man pages for kill, both the Linux page and the POSIX page, state that we can send a signal to an entire group by sending it to the negated GPID of the group. In the preceding example, I could have entered kill -SIGINT -16779 to terminate the entire group.

The preceding discussion leads to a few questions:

- How can bash change the PGID of its child processes after it creates them?

- Are there system calls that let a process change its own PGRP or change the PGRP of another process, and if so, what limitations are imposed?

- Are there calls that allow one process to get the PGRP of another process if it has its PID?

I'll search the man pages to seek answers using apropos:

```
$ apropos -s2 'process group'
getpgid (2)         - set/get process group
getpgrp (2)         - set/get process group
setpgid (2)         - set/get process group
setpgrp (2)         - set/get process group
setsid (2)          - creates a session and sets the process group ID
```

The first four system calls share one page, whose SYNOPSIS is:

```
#include <sys/types.h>
#include <unistd.h>

int setpgid(pid_t pid, pid_t pgid);
pid_t getpgid(pid_t pid);

pid_t getpgrp(void);              /* POSIX.1 version */
pid_t getpgrp(pid_t pid);         /* BSD version     */

int setpgrp(void);                /* System V version */
int setpgrp(pid_t pid, pid_t pgid); /* BSD version     */
--snip--
```

These calls have feature test macro requirements, but we don't need them if we're not using the BSD or System V functions shown here. The page tells us that the preferred way for a process to get the PGID of the process group to which it belongs is by calling getpgrp() and otherwise by calling getpgid(0). It can get the PGID of another process with PID p by calling getpgid(p). We're discouraged from using the BSD versions of these calls, and in fact they aren't exposed in *unistd.h* unless we use the appropriate feature test macro.

The setpgid() system call allows a process to change the PGRP of processes in a few different ways:

```
  setpgid(0, pgid)    /* Set the PGRP of the calling process to pgid.   */
  setpgid(pid, 0)     /* Set the PGRP of process pid to pid.            */
  setpgid(0, 0)       /* Set the PGRP of the calling process to its PID. */
❶ setpgid(pid, pgid)  /* Set the PGRP of process pid to pgid.           */
```

The last use of it ❶ is intended only to allow one process to move another from one group to another, provided that both groups are part of the same session (a concept we'll discuss shortly) and that the calling process has the same owner.

Sessions

Modern Unix systems also introduced the concept of a login session, usually just called a session, to facilitate job control. You can think of a session as the collection of all processes created directly or indirectly when you log in. Formally, a *session* is a collection of process groups, and every process group belongs to exactly one session. This implies that every process belongs to one session since each process is a member of some process group. It also implies that all processes in a process group belong to the same session, and that we can think of process groups and sessions as a two-level hierarchy. Each process has a unique *session ID (SID)* that identifies the session to which it belongs.

The primary purpose of a session is to organize processes around their controlling terminals. The controlling terminal for a process, discussed in Chapter 8, is the terminal that delivers signals to the process when the user enters certain key combinations or sequences, such as CTRL-C, in that terminal. When a user logs in, the kernel creates a session, places all processes and process groups of that user into the session, and links the session to the terminal as its controlling terminal. In each session, one process is the *session leader*, which is the only process whose SID equals its PID.

Any process that isn't a group leader may detach itself from its session by calling setsid(). The setsid() system call creates a new session whose session ID is the PID of the calling process. It also creates a new process group in that new session and makes the calling process the session leader of the session and the group leader of the group. Initially, this new session has no controlling terminal, which implies that the process is immune to keyboard interrupts. This is exactly how a daemon process is created—it detaches itself from the session of which it's a member and goes off on its own. A *daemon* is a process that has no controlling terminal and usually runs until the computer is powered off. In Chapter 14, we'll explore how to create daemon processes. If the process is not intended to be a daemon and needs a controlling terminal, it can acquire one by opening a terminal with the open() system call, passing the device file associated with the terminal.

A process can get its session ID with the getsid() system call: getsid(0) returns the SID of the calling process, and getsid(p) returns the SID of process whose PID is p. Some versions of Unix require that the caller and p belong to the same session; otherwise, the call returns -1.

We can add a session ID column to the ps command's output to see the SIDs of the printed processes by adding sid to the list of output format specifiers, as in

```
$ ps -opid,ppid,pgrp,sid,tty,cmd
   PID   PPID   PGRP    SID TT       CMD
```

```
  4716    4685    4716    4716 pts/0    bash
 23010    4716   23010    4716 pts/0    ps -opid,ppid,pgrp,sid,tty,cmd
```

which also added in the controlling terminal to the output. Notice that bash is the session leader because its SID is equal to its PID.

Foreground and Background Processes and Process Groups

There are two types of process groups, called *foreground* groups and *background* groups. If a process is in a foreground process group, it's called a *foreground process*, and if it's in a background process group, it's called a *background process*. The idea, informally, is that foreground processes are connected to the terminal, whereas background processes aren't. When people say they're running something in the foreground (or the background), they mean that the process is a foreground (or background) process. Every session can have multiple process groups, but at most one of them can be a foreground group; the others must be in the background. There's no limit to the number of background processes.

When we enter a command from the shell, terminating it with a newline, as in

```
$ ps -u stewart -opid,pgid,cmd | tail +2 | sort -k3 | awk '{print $2, $3}'
```

all of the processes created to execute the command are in the foreground. In contrast, when we append an ampersand (&) to the command line, as in

```
$ rsync -avH $HOME /backups/backup_$(date +"%m-%d-%y") &
$
```

all of the created processes are placed into a background group. When the command is placed into the background, the prompt returns immediately. The background job runs while we continue to work in the foreground.

One difference between foreground and background processes is that foreground processes can read from their controlling terminal, whereas background processes cannot. If a background process tries to read from the controlling terminal, the kernel will send it a SIGTTIN signal, which will stop, but not terminate, the process. If it tries to write to the terminal, the kernel will send a SIGTTOU signal to it. The default action of a SIGTTOU signal is to stop the process, but many shells override the default action to allow background processes to write to the terminal.

Another difference is that when you enter a key combination that generates a signal in the terminal, the signal is sent only to the foreground process group. Entering CTRL-C, for example, will not cause a SIGINT to be sent to background processes. You can still send a SIGINT to a background process group with the kill command.

The SIGHUP signal will be sent to all processes in the session, whether they're foreground or background. The SIGHUP signal is usually generated when a terminal connection is broken for one reason or another. When this happens, by default, all processes are killed. When you log out from a session, SIGHUP is sent to all background processes. If you want to run a background job and have it continue even after you log out, you can use the nohup command to run it. This will allow it to run, ignoring SIGHUP signals. For example, if you want to run a backup program named do_backup in the background and close your terminal connection, you can enter:

```
$ nohup do_backup &
$ logout
```

Of course, the do_backup program must not read from or write to the terminal; it's a good idea to redirect standard error when you run nohup.

Program Files

A program starts out as a source code file, from which we create an executable file by compiling and linking it. When we issue a command to run the executable file, between the time at which we issue that command and the time it begins to run, a process is created with all of the resources it needs to execute the program's code. This implies that the executable program file contains enough information to create this process, but it raises two questions:

- What information is in the executable file that enables the kernel to create the process image in memory?

- What steps take place to create this process?

In this section we'll examine the form and content of an executable program file. In the next chapter, we'll concentrate on process creation and related topics.

The Contents of an Executable File

An executable program file must contain enough information to create a process image. This includes, at a minimum, the following types of information:

- The executable machine instructions, which are called its *text*.

- The address of the machine instruction at which to start execution, called the *entry point*. A program file may contain several functions in addition to the main() function; the entry point identifies which instruction in the code is the start of main().

- *Relocation tables*, which are tables used for connecting unresolved symbols, meaning those without addresses, to actual addresses when the program is loaded into memory and run.

- A *symbol table*, which is a table that the compiler creates to map symbolic names to logical addresses and store the attributes of these symbols. If a program is built with debugging symbols enabled, the symbol table is loaded into memory with the program at runtime.

- *String tables*, which are tables containing various strings used in the program, such as the names of variables, string literals, and functions, as well as strings needed for dynamic linking of the program.

- All of the initialized data used by the program, such as string and numeric literals.

- Information about which dynamic libraries need to be loaded when the program runs, including the pathname of the dynamic linker to link those libraries to the program at runtime.

All of this information must be structured in a precise way so that loaders, linkers, and other utility programs can find and interpret it correctly. For example, when we run the `file` utility command to print information about an executable file

```
$ file /bin/bash
/bin/bash: ELF 64-bit LSB pie executable, x86-64, version 1 (SYSV),
dynamically linked, interpreter /lib64/ld-linux-x86-64.so.2, BuildID[sha1]=
33a5554034feb2af38e8c75872058883b2988bc5, for GNU/Linux 3.2.0, stripped
```

it's able to extract this metadata about the `bash` executable from its file only because its format is standardized. Right now, it doesn't matter whether you know what all of this output means; the point is that `file` is able to parse the executable file to extract it.

The Executable and Linking Format

If you've ever run the gcc compiler and didn't specifically name the executable file with the `-o` *output-file* option, as in

```
$ gcc myprog.c
```

the linker named the resulting executable file *a.out*. If you've ever wondered why it's called *a.out*, it's because *a.out* is short for "assembler output"; it wasn't just the name of the output file but was also name of the format of all binary executable files on Unix systems for many years. It isn't anymore. In 1993, a more portable and extensible format now known as *Executable and Linking Format* (*ELF*) was published by UNIX System Laboratories as part of the *Application Binary Interface* (*ABI*) specification. It was revised in 1995 by the Tool Interface Standards (TIS) Committee, an industry consortium that included most major companies, including Intel, IBM, Microsoft, Novell, Santa Cruz Operation, and several others. While compilers continue to create files named *a.out*, on most modern machines, they are actually ELF files.

Version 1.2 of the ELF specification [45] defines the format and content of four different file types:

Relocatable file　Stores code and data suitable for linking with other object files in order to create an executable or a shared object file.

Executable file　Contains a program suitable for execution. The file specifies how to construct the *memory image* that a process will execute.

Shared object file   Stores code and data for linking under two different circumstances. In one case, the link editor processes it with other relocatable and shared object files to create yet another shared object file. In the second case, the dynamic linker combines it with an executable file and other shared objects to create the memory image that a process will execute.

Core file   Produced by a core dump. A *core dump* is a snapshot of a process's memory image written to a file. Certain signals, when unhandled, cause core dumps if they're enabled by the system configuration. Core dump files are large and often disabled by default.

In short, the content and structure of the file depend on which type of file it is. Here, we're interested in the form of the ELF executable type file; a good grasp of the form and content of an ELF file gives us a better understanding of how programs are executed and what their memory images look like. Most of what I describe in the remainder of this section is based on version 1.2 of the ELF specification, which can be downloaded from *https://refspecs.linuxbase.org*.

ELF File Structure

Regardless of the file type, an ELF file always starts with a structure called the *ELF header*. The ELF header acts like a road map to the rest of the file, detailing its organization. It identifies and provides the addresses and sizes of the tables needed to access all other components of the file. Because it's designed to be used for both linking and execution of a program, it embeds two different parallel, overlapping views called the *linking view* and the *execution view*. Figure 10-1 depicts the two different views of an ELF file.

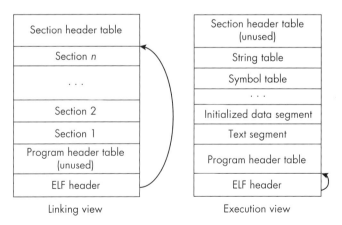

Figure 10-1: The linking and execution views of an ELF file with low addresses at the bottom

The difference between them is summarized as follows:

- The linking view is the view of the file needed by the link editor in order to link and relocate components in the file. In this view, the file is organized into sections. *Sections* contain most of the information needed for linking, such as the instructions, data, symbol table, relocation information, and so on. Every section is described by a *section header*, which contains information such as the type of information the section contains, its offset in the file, its size, and more. The section headers are organized into a *section header table*.

- The execution view is the view used to load and execute the program. In this view, the information is organized into segments. *Segments* are the parts of the file that are loaded into memory to form the process's memory image; they consist of one or more consecutive sections in the file. Each segment is described by a *program header*, which contains information such as the segment's location in the file, size, virtual address at which it should be loaded, and so on. The program headers are organized into a *program header table*.

Segments and sections are two different ways to look at the exact same data in the file. The difference between them isn't what data they contain, but how they reference and use that data. To quote the ELF specification:

> A program header table, if present, tells the system how to create a process image. Files used to build a process image (execute a program) must have a program header table; relocatable files do not need one. A section header table contains information describing the file's sections. Every section has an entry in the table; each entry gives information such as the section name, the section size, and so on. Files used during linking must have a section header table; other object files may or may not have one.

In other words, segments correspond to the different regions of a process's memory image, such as its executable code, called the text segment in the figure; its initialized data; its uninitialized data; and so on.

When an executable is loaded into memory, the segments are mapped not to physical addresses, but to logical addresses, which are also called virtual addresses.

VIRTUAL AND PHYSICAL MEMORY ADDRESSES

The addresses generated by the CPU during a program's execution are called *logical* or *virtual* addresses. *Physical* addresses are actual addresses in physical memory. For example, a process might generate a set of logical addresses between 0x08048000 and 0xc0000000, but that does not mean that it actually accesses physical memory locations from 0x08048000 and 0xc0000000. Modern operating systems use a method of memory management called *virtual memory management*, in which the addresses generated by the CPU are mapped to actual physical memory addresses by a *memory management unit*. The most common virtual memory scheme is *paging*, in which physical memory is partitioned into uniform-size *page frames*, each process's address space is partitioned into *pages* of the same size as the page frames, and these logical pages are mapped to physical pages by the kernel and the hardware.

Both the section header table and the program header table can be viewed as an array of structures. The section header table is like a table of contents for the sections in the file. It is located at the end of the file. The program header table functions as a table of contents for the segments. It is located immediately following the ELF header. Neither the sections nor the segments in the file have to be in particular locations because the header tables store their positions. Figure 10-2 illustrates this idea, with the start of the file at the bottom of the image.

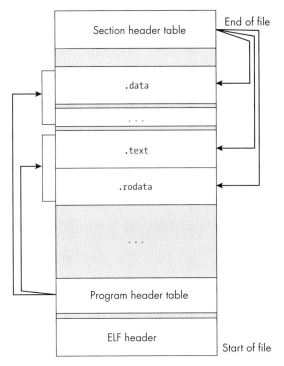

Figure 10-2: The overlapping views of the ELF file, showing that multiple sections may be part of a single segment

The figure also shows that segments may consist of multiple sections. For example, the .text section and .rodata section are part of a single loadable segment indexed by the program header table, but each is an individual section indexed in the section header table.

ELF File Contents

The purpose of this section is to present an overview of the organization and structure of an ELF file, with enough detail so that you could design programs to access its data. We have several resources for learning more about its contents, including:

- The ELF man page. A search of the man pages using `apropos -e elf` reveals that there's a Section 5 man page for ELF, which contains a description of its structure and contents, including C structure declarations, with enough detail to write simple programs that can access its data.

- The */usr/include/elf.h* header file, which contains declarations and definitions of all constants and C structures.

- The ELF specification.

In addition to these resources, on GNU/Linux systems, we also have at our disposal the `readelf` command. This command has options that control which subset of the information in an ELF file to display. Here are a few of the basic options:

`-a`   Show almost everything.

`-a --use-dynamic`   Show everything.

`-e`   Show all headers.

`-h`   Show the ELF file header.

`-l`   Show all program headers (segments).

`-S`   Show all section headers.

`-t`   Show section details.

`-s`   Show all symbols.

GNU provides several other utilities for working with ELF files, such as `scanelf` and `dumpelf`, which are part of the *pax-utils* package. This is in most systems' repositories, and the sources can be downloaded from the git repository at *https://github.com/gentoo/pax-utils*.

To make this more concrete, I compiled the original *hello_world.c* program from Chapter 1 into the executable file *hello_world* so that we can explore its ELF file. This is about the smallest nontrivial program we can examine.

An ELF file begins with the ELF header. The header contains the most basic information about the file. To see the header of the *hello_world* executable, you can use `readelf -h`:

```
$ readelf -h hello_world
ELF Header:
 Magic:   7f 45 4c 46 02 01 01 00 00 00 00 00 00 00 00 00
 Class:                             ELF64
 Data:                              2's complement, little endian
 Version:                           1 (current)
 OS/ABI:                            UNIX - System V
 ABI Version:                       0
 Type:                              DYN (Position-Independent Executable file)
 Machine:                           AdvancedMicro Devices X86-64
 Version:                           0x1
```

```
Entry point address:                0x1060
Start of program headers:           64 (bytesinto file)
Start of section headers:           13984 (bytesinto file)
Flags:                              0x0
Size of this header:                64 (bytes)
Size of program headers:            56 (bytes)
Number of program headers:          13
Size of section headers:            64 (bytes)
Number of section headers:          31
Section header string table index: 30
```

The first 4 bytes of the file are 0x7f followed by the string *ELF*. The next 3 bytes encode the class of the file (32 versus 64 bit), whether it's little-endian or big-endian, the version of ELF (1 meaning current), and the operating system and ABI. These are all part of the output labeled `Magic`. The class of the file determines whether certain members, such as the entry point address and the start of the section headers, are 32 bits or 64 bits. This implies that before the entire header is read, the first few bytes need to be read to determine how much memory to allocate for the header.

The rest of the header provides metadata such as the machine type, file type, and location and size information for the program headers and section headers, from which the locations of the program header and section header tables can be calculated. This information allows us to read all of the program headers and section headers into memory so that we can access the segments and sections that they describe. In "A Program to Print the ELF Program Header Table" on page 506, we'll demonstrate how to access this data by developing a program that can display the program header file of an ELF file.

The ELF header for *hello_world* indicates that it has 13 program headers and 31 section headers. To see a list of the program headers in the file, we can enter `readelf -lW hello_world`, part of whose output follows in Listing 10-1.

```
There are 13 program headers, starting at offset 64


Program Headers:
  Type          Offset   VirtAddr           PhysAddr           FileSiz  MemSiz   Flg Align
  PHDR          0x000040 0x0000000000000040 0x0000000000000040 0x0002d8 0x0002d8 R   0x8
  INTERP        0x000318 0x0000000000000318 0x0000000000000318 0x00001c 0x00001c R   0x1
      [Requesting program interpreter: /lib64/ld-linux-x86-64.so.2]
  LOAD          0x000000 0x0000000000000000 0x0000000000000000 0x000628 0x000628 R   0x1000
  LOAD          0x001000 0x0000000000001000 0x0000000000001000 0x000171 0x000171 R E 0x1000
  LOAD          0x002000 0x0000000000002000 0x0000000000002000 0x0000fc 0x0000fc R   0x1000
  LOAD        ❶ 0x002db8 0x0000000000003db8 0x0000000000003db8 0x000258 0x000260 RW  0x1000
--snip--
  GNU_RELRO   ❷ 0x002db8 0x0000000000003db8 0x0000000000003db8 0x000248 0x000248 R   0x1

 Section to Segment mapping:
  Segment Sections...
```

```
00
01      .interp
02      .interp .note.gnu.property .note.gnu.build-id .note.ABI-tag  ...
03      .init .plt .plt.got .plt.sec .text .fini
04      .rodata .eh_frame_hdr .eh_frame
05      .init_array .fini_array .dynamic .got .data .bss
--snip--
12      .init_array .fini_array .dynamic .got
```

Listing 10-1: Sample output of readelf

This output lists the program (segment) headers, followed by a mapping that shows which sections are part of each segment. The header whose type is INTERP contains the pathname to the dynamic linker, which loads the executable, resolves links, and ultimately passes control to hello_world when it is finished. The segments of type LOAD are loadable segments—they become part of the memory image. Offsets are the number of bytes from the start of the ELF file at which the segment starts. The virtual address is the offset in the memory image at which the segment loads. The physical address is ignored.

The column labeled FileSiz is the size of the segment in the file. The flags indicate access mode (R for read, W for write, E for execute), and the last column is the byte alignment in virtual memory. For example, LOAD-type segments must align on 4096 (0x1000) byte boundaries.

The section to segment mapping shows that the dynamic linker (.interp) is the only section in segment 1 and that the text section (.text) is part of segment 3, along with a few other sections. The read-only data section (.rodata) is in segment 4, and the initialized data section (.data) and the uninitialized data section (.bss) are part of segment 5.

When a segment consists of more than one section, the sections must be adjacent to each other in the file, and their section headers are adjacent in the section header table. For example, the output shows that segment 3 contains the following sections:

```
03      .init .plt .plt.got .plt.sec .text .fini
```

If we were to look at the sections in this file using readelf -S hello_world, we'd see the following:

```
[Nr] Name        Type      Address          Off    Size   ES Flg Lk Inf Al
--snip--
[12] .init       PROGBITS  0000000000001000 001000 00001b 00  AX  0   0  4
[13] .plt        PROGBITS  0000000000001020 001020 000020 10  AX  0   0 16
[14] .plt.got    PROGBITS  0000000000001040 001040 000010 10  AX  0   0 16
[15] .plt.sec    PROGBITS  0000000000001050 001050 000010 10  AX  0   0 16
[16] .text       PROGBITS  0000000000001060 001060 000117 00  AX  0   0 16
[17] .fini       PROGBITS  0000000000001178 001178 00000d 00  AX  0   0  4
```

Notice that the offsets (Off column) are increasing and that the offset of each successive section is obtained by adding the previous size to the previous offset and, if it does not fall on the byte boundary specified by the align (Al) column, bumped up so that it falls on a multiple of that alignment.

Also observe that some sections are part of more than one segment. For example, look at Listing 10-1 again. Segment 12, the last segment ❷, of type GNU_RELRO, is a subset of segment 5 ❶, a loadable segment. Their virtual addresses are the same, but segment 12 is smaller in size. Section 12 is not loadable; it's used by the dynamic linker to mark those sections as read-only when they're relocated into the memory image. Figure 10-3 illustrates this idea.

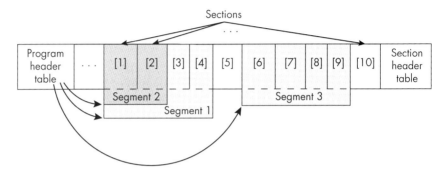

Figure 10-3: Illustration of how sections are part of segments and may be in more than one segment

The preceding observations focused on the segments and sections, but we can also examine all of the symbols, both the statically linked and the dynamically linked ones, using the command readelf -s hello_world. A tiny snippet of the output shows the kind of information stored for each symbol:

```
$ readelf -s hello_world
--snip--
Symbol table '.symtab' contains 36 entries:
   Num:    Value          Size Type    Bind   Vis      Ndx Name
--snip--
    23: 0000000000000000     0 FUNC    GLOBAL DEFAULT  UND printf@GLIBC_2.2.5
--snip--
    30: 0000000000004010     0 NOTYPE  GLOBAL DEFAULT   26 __bss_start
    31: 0000000000001149    46 FUNC    GLOBAL DEFAULT   16 main
--snip--
```

Notice that the printf symbol is part of *glibc* and has no value. The value of a symbol is its address, and it has no address until runtime. In contrast, main() has a value because it's the address of the main program.

A Program to Print the ELF Program Header Table

We can use what we discovered in the preceding sections about the structure and content of ELF files to write a small program that accesses a small piece of that file. Specifically, we'll write a program that displays all of the program headers in a given file, trying to mimic the output of the readelf -l command, without the section to segment mapping. The goal of this exercise is to show you how to use the various road maps in the file to locate and read any part of the file. We're using the program headers simply to illustrate the general method.

The current ELF specification supports both 32-bit and 64-bit architectures, and the complication is that the sizes of the members of various structures depend on the architecture. To simplify this small project, we'll design the program to work with the 64-bit versions of all structures. It is a minor extension to add the logic for the 32-bit versions as well.

The *elf.h* header file defines types used by the file based on whether it's 32-bit or 64-bit. For example, here's a small part of it:

```
/* Type for a 16-bit quantity */
typedef uint16_t Elf32_Half;
typedef uint16_t Elf64_Half;
--snip--
/* Type of addresses */
typedef uint32_t Elf32_Addr;
typedef uint64_t Elf64_Addr;

/* Type of file offsets */
typedef uint32_t Elf32_Off;
typedef uint64_t Elf64_Off;
```

With this in mind, here's how the 64-bit ELF header structure is defined:

```
typedef struct {
    unsigned char   e_ident[EI_NIDENT]; /* Magic number and other info     */
    Elf64_Half      e_type;             /* Object file type                */
    Elf64_Half      e_machine;          /* Architecture                    */
    Elf64_Word      e_version;          /* Object file version             */
    Elf64_Addr      e_entry;            /* Entry point virtual address     */
    Elf64_Off       e_phoff;            /* Program header table file offset */
    Elf64_Off       e_shoff;            /* Section header table file offset */
    Elf64_Word      e_flags;            /* Processor-specific flags        */
    Elf64_Half      e_ehsize;           /* ELF header size in bytes        */
    Elf64_Half      e_phentsize;        /* Program header table entry size */
    Elf64_Half      e_phnum;            /* Program header table entry count */
    Elf64_Half      e_shentsize;        /* Section header table entry size */
    Elf64_Half      e_shnum;            /* Section header table entry count */
    Elf64_Half      e_shstrndx;         /* Section header string table index */
} Elf64_Ehdr;
```

The very first member, e_ident, is a 16-byte array (EI_NIDENT = 16). The first 4 bytes read \0x7fELF. The fifth byte indicates whether the rest of the file is a 32-bit ELF or a 64-bit ELF. We need to begin by reading this byte and making sure we have a 64-bit ELF header. Assuming we do, we can read the entire header from the file and examine its members. We'll need to allocate storage for it before reading, of course.

The offset in the file to the program header table is stored in the e_phoff member, each header has size e_phentsize, and there are e_phnum many headers. This implies that the entire program header table is e_phnum × e_phentsize bytes in size. Therefore, after reading the ELF header, our program should allocate storage for the program header table of size e_phnum × e_phentsize and read that many bytes from the file offset e_phoff.

The program header table is not an actual table; it's just a sequence of structures whose definition is:

```
typedef struct
{
    Elf64_Word    p_type;    /* Segment type           */
    Elf64_Word    p_flags;   /* Segment flags          */
    Elf64_Off     p_offset;  /* Segment file offset    */
    Elf64_Addr    p_vaddr;   /* Segment virtual address   */
    Elf64_Addr    p_paddr;   /* Segment physical address */
    Elf64_Xword   p_filesz;  /* Segment size in file    */
    Elf64_Xword   p_memsz;   /* Segment size in memory  */
    Elf64_Xword   p_align;   /* Segment alignment       */
} Elf64_Phdr;
```

If prog_header_table is a pointer to the first of these, then we can access all of them using array subscripting of the form prog_header_table[0], prog_header_table[1], and so on.

Our program has to read the data in each structure and format it in the same way as the readelf command.

There's one catch. The INTERP segment is treated differently from the others. In the output from readelf it is displayed as:

```
INTERP    0x000318 0x0000000000000318 0x0000000000000318 0x00001c ...
    [Requesting program interpreter: /lib64/ld-linux-x86-64.so.2]
```

According to the man page, the pathname of the interpreter is the actual content of the INTERP segment. That string is in the ELF file at offset p_offset and is of size p_filesz. Therefore, as our program reads each program header, it needs to check whether it has found this header, and if so, it needs to read the string from the file at that offset in order to print it.

We're ready to outline the steps in a mix of prose and actual code. The following steps omit all of the required error handling:

1. Open the ELF file for reading, and let fd be the returned file descriptor.

2. Read the first 16 (EI_NIDENT) bytes from fd into a buffer.

3. Read the fifth byte of the buffer to determine the file class. It's either ELFCLASS32 or ELFCLASS64. For simplicity, the remaining steps are based on its being the 64-bit class.

4. Allocate storage for the header:

```
Elf64_Ehdr *elf_header64 = calloc(1, sizeof(Elf64_Ehdr));
```

5. Seek to the start of the file and read `sizeof(Elf64_Ehdr)` bytes into the header just allocated:

```
lseek(fd, 0, SEEK_SET);
read(fd, elf_header64, sizeof(Elf64_Ehdr));
```

6. From this ELF header, `*elf_header64`, get the offset (`elf_header64->e_phoff`) and size (`elf_header64->e_phentsize`) of the first program header, as well as the total number of program headers (`elf_header64->e_phnum`).

7. Allocate memory to store all of the program headers. This requires (`elf_header64->e_phentsize`) × (`elf_header64->e_phnum`) bytes.

8. Let `Elf64_Phdr*` phtable be the starting address of this memory. Equivalently, phtable may be treated as an array of `elf_header64->e_phnum` program headers, since they are stored consecutively in the file.

9. Seek `elf_header64->e_phoff` bytes from the start of the ELF file.

10. Read the entire set of program headers into the memory allocated at phtable that location:

```
read(fd, phtable, elf_header64->e_phnum * sizeof(Elf64_Phdr));
```

11. Print a line of output stating how many program headers are in the file and where the first header begins. Then print a line with column labels.

12. Print out each program header one after the other, using a loop such as

```
for ( i = 0; i < elf_header64->e_phnum; i++ ) {
    print_progheader64(fd, &(phdr64[i]));
}
```

in which the `print_progheader()` function prints out one line for the header passed as its argument. The function needs the file descriptor argument so that it can read the pathname of the program interpreter when it finds the segment that contains it.

When the program interpreter segment is found, it needs to seek to position `progheader->p_offset` and read `progheader->p_filesz` bytes into an allocated string, after which it can print the path to the interpreter.

The entire program based on this logic is called *print_elfphdr.c* and is included in the source code distribution for the book. The main program is shown here, with limited error handling to save space:

print_elfphdr.c
main()
```
int main(int argc, char *argv[])
{
    int         fd;
    ssize_t     nbytes;
```

```
                    unsigned char ident[EI_NIDENT];
                    int          class, i;
                    Elf64_Ehdr   *elf_header64 = NULL;
                    Elf64_Phdr   *phdr64 = NULL;

                    if ( argc < 2 )
                        usage_error("expecting executable file");
                    if ( (fd = open(argv[1], O_RDONLY)) == -1 )
                        fatal_error(errno, "open");
                    if ( (nbytes = read(fd, ident, EI_NIDENT)) != EI_NIDENT )
                        fatal_error(errno, "read");

                    lseek(fd, 0, SEEK_SET);
                    class = ident[EI_CLASS];
                    if ( class != ELFCLASS64 )
                        fatal_error(-1, "Expecting  64-bit ELF file");

                    elf_header64 = calloc(1, sizeof(Elf64_Ehdr));
                    if ( read(fd, elf_header64, sizeof(Elf64_Ehdr)) == -1 )
                        fatal_error(errno, "read");
                    printf("There are %d program headers, starting at offset %lu.\n\n",
                            elf_header64->e_phnum, elf_header64->e_phoff);
                    printf("Program Headers:\n");
                    printf("  Type           Offset    VirtAddr          PhysAddr"
                           "          FileSiz  MemSiz   Flg Align\n");
                    phdr64 = read_ph64table(fd, elf_header64->e_phoff, elf_header64->e_phnum);
                    for ( i = 0; i < elf_header64->e_phnum; i++ )
                        print_progheader64(fd, &(phdr64[i]));
                    return 0;
                }
```

A sample run on an executable such as *hello_world* produces output like the readelf command:

```
There are 13 program headers, starting at offset 64.

Program Headers:
  Type           Offset    VirtAddr          PhysAddr          FileSiz  MemSiz   Flg Align
  PHDR           0x000040  0x0000000000000040 0x0000000000000040 0x0002d8 0x0002d8 R   0x8
  INTERP         0x000318  0x0000000000000318 0x0000000000000318 0x00001c 0x00001c R   0x1
      [Requesting program interpreter:/lib64/ld-linux-x86-64.so.2]
  LOAD           00000000  00000000000000000 000000000000000000 0x02e188 0x02e188 R   0x1000
  LOAD           0x02f000  0x000000000002f000 0x000000000002f000 0x0def6d 0x0def6d R E 0x1000
  LOAD           0x10e000  0x000000000010e000 0x000000000010e000 0x039b08 0x039b08 R   0x1000
--snip--
  GNU_STACK      00000000  00000000000000000 000000000000000000 00000000 00000000 RW  0x10
  GNU_RELRO      0x148a90  0x0000000000149a90 0x0000000000149a90 0x003570 0x003570 R   0x1
```

The same method can be used to print the contents of section headers and symbol tables. I've included another program named *printelf.c* in the source code distribution that prints just the ELF header to show how to handle the individual members of that structure.

The Virtual Memory Layout of a Process

Let's turn to the memory image of a process. The goal is to construct a mental picture of what a process looks like in its *virtual address space*—meaning what pieces go where, not in physical memory, but in virtual memory. The virtual memory layout is architecture dependent; I'll describe the typical layout in a Linux system running on an x86-64 processor. Although it's derived from the traditional layout used in early Unix systems, it has diverged in a few important respects, which I'll discuss.

There are five different regions of the user-space part of a process, of which four are called *segments*, a term derived from early Unix systems that implemented these memory regions using the memory management scheme known as *segmentation* [4]. From the lowest location to the highest, they are:

- The text segment
- The initialized data segment
- The uninitialized data segment
- The stack segment
- The heap

The C library defines three variables, etext, edata, and end, whose addresses are the first address after the text segment, the initialized data segment, and the uninitialized data segment, respectively. These are not part of any standard, but most Unix systems provide them. A program uses them by declaring them as extern. In Listing 10-2 I show how to use them.

Figure 10-4 shows how these segments as well as other parts of a process's address space are organized in logical memory and their relationship to the segments of the ELF file. The figure is drawn with low-order addresses at the bottom. The shaded portion of the figure represents logical addresses that are currently allocated and addressable by the process. The area below the text segment is where the dynamic linker is mapped into the process's virtual memory. The process can't access that portion of its address space. When we run a program, the dynamic linker runs first. The dynamic linker sets up its internal data structures so that it can create the links needed by the process, and only after it has loaded and mapped libraries into the process's address space does it transfer control to the first instruction in the program.

The area between the stack and the heap is unused. If the process were to generate an address in this region, it would cause an exception. The bottom of the user stack contains the pointers to the command line arguments and the environment strings. The arguments and the strings are above the stack, which grows downward.

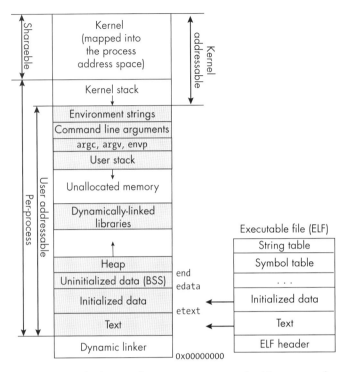

Figure 10-4: The layout of a process in its virtual address space for a typical Linux system, showing the correspondence between the ELF file's segments and the process's segments

The region above the environment strings is where the kernel is mapped into the process's address space. When a process is executing in unprivileged (user) mode, it can't access any of this memory. When it makes a system call and its privilege changes, it can access that part of its virtual memory. Mapping the kernel into the address space of each process simplifies the way in which system calls are implemented. Notice in the figure that a part of the kernel-addressable portion of the process's virtual memory is labeled *per-process*; this is where the metadata associated with the process is located. I'll explain more about this metadata later in the chapter.

The starting locations of each of these regions were, at one time, in fixed positions. For example, the text segment always started at logical address 0x08048000. However, because of the ever-increasing number of attempts to exploit memory vulnerabilities when the addresses of libraries and executables were at known locations, a technique known as *address space layout randomization (ASLR)* was introduced into the Linux kernel.

With ASLR, the relative positions of the memory regions is preserved, but the actual locations of the different regions are shifted by random numbers of bytes. To support ASLR, compilers generate position-independent code. In Figure 10-4, the relative positions of the various regions are shown, but their distances from each other do not reflect actual distances. Following are brief descriptions of each of the memory regions.

The Text Segment

The text segment contains the process's executable code, including all functions that are statically linked into it. It is a fixed size and is almost always a read-only segment, shared by all other processes executing the same program. The fact that it is read-only and shareable implies that:

- A process cannot inadvertently modify it.

- Only one copy is needed in physical memory.

- The overhead of swapping is reduced because if the process is swapped out of memory, it doesn't have to be copied to secondary storage since it hasn't changed, and if it already resides in memory, there's no need to copy it back from secondary storage when a process is swapped back into memory.

The segment is made shareable by mapping its memory pages into the page table of every process that executes this code.

The Initialized Data Segment

The initialized data segment is memory allocated for all file-scoped (global) and static variables that are explicitly initialized in the program's source code. The size of this segment is fixed when the program is loaded, based on the information in the ELF file.

The Uninitialized Data Segment

The uninitialized data segment contains global and static variables that haven't been given initial values. It's also called the *BSS* segment. BSS is an initialism for *Block Started by Symbol*, an old FORTRAN assembly instruction. Because uninitialized data has no starting value, the loader only needs to reserve the space for them and typically fills their memory with zero bytes. The latest C standard requires it to be zero-filled. Unlike the initialized data segment, uninitialized data takes up no space in the ELF file, which just needs to record its locations and sizes. When the process is loaded, the size of this segment is fixed.

The Heap

The heap is technically not a segment; it's an extension of the uninitialized data segment. The heap is the region of memory above the BSS used to satisfy a process's requests for dynamically allocated memory. The top of the heap is called the *program break*. It used to be true that the initial position of the program break was the first address after the BSS segment, but this is not true in current systems. The following program, available in the book's source code distribution, shows that the program break is not at the same address as end when you run it:

showbreak.c
```
#include <unistd.h>
#include <unistd.h>
#include <stdio.h>

extern char etext, edata, end;

int main(int argc, char *argv[])
{
    void *break_location = sbrk(0);
    printf("Location of end           = %10p\n"
           "Location of program break = %10p\n", &end, break_location);
    printf("Difference in decimal     = %ld\n",
           (long) (break_location - (void*) &end));
    return 0;
}
```

The program calls sbrk(0) to get the current position of its program break. The brk() and sbrk() system calls move the program break. Their man page SYNOPSIS is:

```
#include <unistd.h>

int brk(void *addr);
void *sbrk(intptr_t increment);
```

The call sbrk(*n*) moves the break by *n* bytes and returns the new position. Passing 0 to it leaves the position unchanged and returns the current position. Moving the break upward allocates memory, and moving it downward deallocates memory. These functions should not be called by user programs, which should instead call the C Library functions malloc() or calloc() to allocate more memory and free() to deallocate it. I'm using sbrk() just to get the break's position.

The Stack Segment

The stack segment contains the program stack for calls made by the process to functions that are executed in user space. Each call causes a stack frame to be pushed onto this stack. The stack frame provides storage for the automatic (local) variables and return values and addresses.

The starting address of the stack is near the top of the user-addressable portion of the process's address space.

The stack grows upside-down relative to the address space in most Unix systems, meaning that a push onto the top makes the stack top a lower memory address, and a pop makes it point to a higher address. This implies that the stack grows toward the heap, and vice versa. If the stack ever meets the top of the heap, it causes an exception.

A Program That Displays Virtual Memory Locations

The preceding sections described the various places in virtual memory where the different categories of program symbols are located. To make this more concrete, the book's source code repository contains a program, *displayvm.c*, that displays the virtual addresses of some of its symbols as well as the locations of etext, edata, end, and the program break (returned by sbrk(0)) in order to show within which segments each symbol is placed. The program, with some parts omitted to save space, is presented in Listing 10-2. It prints the virtual addresses of the following symbols:

Global initialized variable   title

Global uninitialized variable   string

Local variable in main program   i

Parameters to main program   argc, argv, and envp

Static uninitialized local in main program   diff

Main function   main()

Non-main function   sort()

Library function   strcpy()

System call wrapper   write()

Address returned by a call to malloc()   *inheap

To make it easier to identify the memory regions, high-order addressed elements are printed first and programmatic elements are indented so that the segment boundaries are more visible:

displayvm.c
```
#include "common_hdrs.h"
typedef unsigned long long ull;
extern int etext, edata, end;
char *title = "Layout of virtual memory\n";  /* Initialized data      */
char string[256];                            /* Uninitialized data (BSS) */

typedef struct { /* Type definitions are not in memory image! */
    ull  loc;
    char name[16];
} symbol;

void sort(symbol addresses[], int count)        /* Text segment          */
{
    // OMITTED: Function that sorts symbols by addresses
}

int main(int argc, char *argv[], char *envp[])  /* Text segment          */
{
    int        i;                               /* Stack variable        */
    static long diff;                           /* Global in BSS         */
```

```
char        *inheap = (char *) malloc(4096); /* In heap */
int          num_symbols;
void        *progbreak = sbrk(0);

symbol addresses[] = {
    {(ull) &main, "  main"},      {(ull) &sort, "  sort"},
    {(ull) &strcpy, "  strcpy"}, {(ull) &write, "  write"},
    {(ull) &etext, "etext"},      {(ull) &title, "  title"},
    {(ull) inheap, "  *inheap"}, {(ull) &string, "  string"},
    {(ull) &diff, "  diff"},      {(ull) &edata, "edata"},
    {(ull) &end,  "end"},         {(ull) &argc, "  argc"},
    {(ull) &(argv[0]), "  argv"}, {(ull) &(envp[0]), "  envp"},
    {(ull) progbreak, "progbreak"},{(ull) &i, "  i"}
};

num_symbols = sizeof(addresses) / sizeof(addresses[0]);
strcpy(string, title);
write(1, string, strlen(string) + 1);
sort(addresses, num_symbols);
printf("ID                        HEX_ADDR        DECIMAL_ADDR\n");
for ( i = 0; i < num_symbols; i++ )
    printf("%-10s   is at addr:%16llX%20llu\n", addresses[i].name,
           addresses[i].loc, addresses[i].loc);
return 0;
}
```

Listing 10-2: A program that displays the addresses of etext, edata, and end as well as the virtual addresses of its symbols

I compiled and built the program with the default compiler setting that generates a position-independent executable on a kernel with ASLR enabled. This implies that the displayed addresses will differ from one run to the next and that they will not be the virtual addresses in the ELF file for the program. A run of it produced the following output:

```
$ ./displayvm
Layout of virtual memory
ID                      HEX_ADDR        DECIMAL_ADDR
  envp      is at addr:  7FFE101EA268    140729168863848
  argv      is at addr:  7FFE101EA258    140729168863832
  i         is at addr:  7FFE101E9F88    140729168863112
  argc      is at addr:  7FFE101E9F7C    140729168863100
  strcpy    is at addr:  7FD86DD36CB0    140567532235952
  write     is at addr:  7FD86DCAC870    140567531669616
progbreak   is at addr:  561D306D8000     94683366522880
  *inheap   is at addr:  561D306B72A0     94683366388384
end         is at addr:  561D2EB40148     94683337589064
  diff      is at addr:  561D2EB40140     94683337589056
  string    is at addr:  561D2EB40040     94683337588800
```

```
edata      is at addr:    561D2EB40018      94683337588760
  title    is at addr:    561D2EB40010      94683337588752
etext      is at addr:    561D2EB3D7D9      94683337578457
  main     is at addr:    561D2EB3D39B      94683337577371
  sort     is at addr:    561D2EB3D1F9      94683337576953
```

By examining the locations of etext, edata, end, and program break relative to the program symbols, you can verify that the symbols are mapped into the text, data, BSS, heap, and stack regions described earlier in accordance with their scope and storage qualifications. Also notice that the library functions, including the call to the write() wrapper function, are above the program break and below the lowest stack location; they're loaded into virtual memory dynamically, as depicted in Figure 10-4, which implies that they're not in the heap.

The program displays both hexadecimal and decimal addresses because sometimes it's easier to calculate the number of bytes between adjacent entries in hexadecimal and sometimes it's easier in decimal. For example, the starting address of string is exactly 0x100 bytes below that of diff. This is 256 bytes, the size of string.

You might wonder why the lowest virtual address, 0x561D2EB3D1F9, is so large. Why put a program so high in its logical address space? Despite the fact that the lowest virtual address is 0x561D2EB3D1F9, the highest is 0x7FFE101EA268. The difference between them is more than 46TB ($> 2^{45}$ bytes)! On a 64-bit machine, the size of the virtual address space depends on whether the virtual memory management system uses four- or five-level page tables, but in either case, it's typically 128TB or even more. The address space for this executable was chosen to be smaller by the kernel based on the information in the ELF file. If the process ends up requiring more memory, the memory image will be resized. The actual amount of physical memory used by a process can be much smaller than the size of the virtual address space, since the actual allocated physical memory is based on the sizes of the segments that are used at runtime.

The Kernel's Process Representation

We turn now to the kernel's view of processes. Understanding how processes are represented within the kernel and what types of kernel-managed data are accessible to user space programs is necessary for writing programs that manipulate and manage processes. Many of the functions that act on processes have an effect on their attributes, and unless we know what those attributes are, we won't understand how to use those functions correctly.

Process Metadata

The kernel is involved in all aspects of a process's execution and management. It creates them, it decides when they run and when they don't, it decides which resources to give them and when they get them, and it manages all manner of resources that they use, such as memory, signals, timers, open files, masks, and interprocess communication mechanisms. It also handles what happens when processes terminate, the release of their resources, and the notifications sent to other processes that might need to know about their demise. If all of this isn't enough, it also performs a multitude of different types of accounting tasks and records historical information about each process's execution.

To accomplish this, it needs to maintain a significant amount of information for each distinct process. In all operating systems, this metadata is aggregated into a large data structure known by a variety of names, such as a *process control block*, *process structure*, *task structure*, or *process descriptor*, which is what it's called in Linux. In Linux, the process descriptor has pointers to several smaller substructures rather than being a large, bulky object, and it's implemented by a data structure of type struct task_struct.

In early Unix systems, prior to 4.4BSD, the process descriptor was divided into two types of data to improve the kernel's handling of multithreaded programs. The *user structure* contained the subset of data that was thread-specific and did not need to be in memory when that thread was swapped to secondary storage. The *process structure* contained information needed by all threads of the process and which had to be in memory as long as the process was active. This division has since been replaced in many Unix implementations, but remnants of its design remain. Here, we'll look at how more recent Linux systems organize the process metadata contained in the process descriptor.

Overview of the Process Descriptor

The Linux task_struct is large and complex, with many attached substructures, many of which also have substructures. As of version 6.13, it contains about 300 members. Some of the parts of this structure are process attributes, some are descriptions of resources assigned to the process, and some are data used by the kernel for managing the process, such as lists of pending signals and timers, hardware context information, scheduling information, and so on.

Some of the substructures contain the following types of information:

- Thread information

- Memory maps for the process

- Open file descriptions

- Accounting information

- Signal handling structures (queues of pending signals, actions, flags)

- Timers and timer management data

In addition, there are members related to the management of the kernel mode process stack, called the *kernel stack* for short. This stack is used when a process issues a system call. During a system call, the process has switched to privileged mode. The kernel needs a separate stack to execute the call and any other functions within the kernel that are called while in privileged mode. Unlike user programs, the kernel's maximum stack size is predictable, which is why, in Figure 10-4, the kernel stack is bounded above and below by fixed boundaries.

Figure 10-5 depicts the Linux process descriptor schematically, showing how some parts of it are in separate substructures and some are embedded in the task_struct itself.

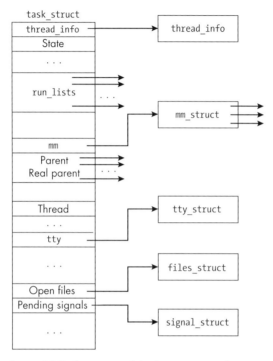

Figure 10-5: Fragments of the Linux process descriptor of type task_struct

Much of the data in the process descriptor is tied to the program that the process is executing, such as the memory maps, stack descriptions, per-process timers, and locale information. When it changes the program it's executing, that information is cleared. Other information is preserved because it is inherently part of the process itself. For example, the process descriptor contains various IDs, including:

- Process ID (PID)
- Parent process ID (PPID)
- Process group ID (PGID)
- Session ID (SID)
- Real user ID
- Real group ID
- Supplemental group IDs

These IDs are attributes of the process, independent of the code that it's executing. If the process changes the program it's executing, it retains these attributes. Other preserved metadata include:

- Current working directory

- Root directory

- File mode creation mask (umask)

- Signal mask

- All pending signals

- Time remaining on alarm clocks

- List of ignored signals

- All signals for which the process accepts the default disposition

- Interval timers (not those created by timer_settime())

- Controlling terminal

- Most resource limits, such as the maximum file size

The process descriptor has been carefully designed so that attributes that are not part of the process but tied to the executed program are easily replaced when it changes the program it executes. It's also been designed to make multithreading efficient. Chapter 15 will revisit this topic.

The set of process descriptors for all processes is maintained in a doubly linked list called the *process list* in Linux. In fact, a process descriptor is usually a part of many linked lists, including lists of children, siblings, and threads, to name just a few. The kernel uses a clever method of achieving this; it defines a doubly linked list node type named struct list_head with no content other than a pair of links to nodes of that type:

```
struct list_head {
    struct list_head *next, *prev;
};
```

The list_head structure points to the previous node and next node in a doubly linked list. Embedding various members of the task_struct as struct list_head makes the task structure a part of multiple doubly linked lists.

For example, the lists for children, siblings, and threads are declared this way:

```
struct list_head children;
struct list_head sibling;
struct list_head thread_group;
```

A single task structure is thus a node in a list of children, a list of siblings, and a list of the threads in a thread group. The kernel has a means to obtain a pointer to the task structure of which a given list_head structure is a member.

The kernel doesn't expose any of these internal structures to user space programs in a direct way. Some system calls, such as getpid() and getppid(), return IDs, but most of the information in the process descriptor is not accessible through the system call interface. For example, there aren't system calls that return information about child processes or memory maps of our process. On the other hand, we do know a couple of commands that print information about one or more processes, such as top and ps. If we knew how they obtained their data, we might be able to access selected metadata in our programs. Consulting the man page for ps offers a clue, as does the page for the related command, pstree; they refer us to the proc(5) man page. The proc(5) man page is the key that unlocks a door to another realm of data.

The proc Pseudofilesystem

The */proc* filesystem was introduced in Eighth Edition UNIX in 1984 [21]. A modified version of it was later added to 4.4BSD [26]. Enter the command **ls /proc** and you'll see a large collection of directories, the majority of whose names are integers, as well as some whose names are alphabetic, such as *irq* and *drivers*. You'll also see regular files with alphabetic names such as *cmdline*, *cpuinfo*, and *uptime*. Sprinkled among them is a handful of symbolic links such as *mounts*, *net*, and *self*. Most of the regular files in */proc* are world readable and can be viewed with any command that can read text files, such as cat and more. For example:

```
$ cat /proc/uptime
2677.36 20616.89
$ cat /proc/version
Linux version 6.6.10-76060610-generic (buildd@lcy02-amd64-037) ...
```

The named regular files expose system-wide information, some of which is not necessarily related to processes (despite the name */proc*), such as statistics and status information about memory allocation, interrupts, and scheduling. A few of these can only be read with superuser privileges.

Numbered Directories

The numbered directories contain files and subdirectories that expose information about the process whose PID is that number. There is one for every running process on the system. They all have the same set of subdirectories and files, and these files and subdirectories expose information specifically about that process. Entering ls /proc/1 will display the files for the init process, whose PID is 1. There are more than 50 files in each directory, but we'll take a look at a few of the smaller and more easily understood ones. You may not be able to do this on your system because some administrators configure the */proc* directory with tight security, preventing you from snooping at files that aren't in your own process directories:

```
$ cat /proc/1/cmdline
/sbin/initsplash$
```

This output is misleading because many files use NULL bytes to separate the words instead of spaces and may not have a newline at the end of the text. We can fix that by converting the NULLs to spaces and then replacing the ending space with a newline:

```
$ cat /proc/1/cmdline | tr '\0' ' ' | sed 's/ $/\n/'
/sbin/init splash
$
```

The *cmdline* file in any numbered directory contains the complete command line that invoked the process, including its arguments. In contrast, *comm* contains the filename of the actual executable program, which can be different and can also be changed by the process itself:

```
$ cat /proc/1/comm
systemd
```

Now let's look at the *status* file for the running bash shell. Its PID is in the shell variable $$. I'll truncate the output because it's lengthy:

```
$ cat /proc/$$/status
Name: bash
Umask: 0022
State: S (sleeping)
Tgid: 5521
Ngid: 0
Pid: 5521
PPid: 3486
TracerPid: 0
Uid: 500 500 500 500
Gid: 500 500 500 500
FDSize: 256
Groups: 4 24 27 30 46 116 126 500
--snip--
```

The proc(5) man page explains what each of these values means, but most are self-explanatory. If this output looks a lot like the information displayed by commands such as ps and top, it's because those commands read these files for their data; they do not have direct access to any internal kernel data structures. We'll explore the other files in the numbered directories shortly.

The Magic of /proc

The */proc* directory appears to contain many files and a lot of very useful information for uncovering properties of the system and the processes that are currently running. However, none of what looks like a file is actually a file with storage on disk; everything that appears in this directory is actually just stored in kernel memory and becomes visible only when you list */proc* using a command such as ls.

The *proc* directory is actually a *pseudofilesystem*, not a real one. Everything that you see when you list what's in it is just an interface constructed for you, on the fly, to the kernel's internal data structures. This is true when you read one of its files as well. It is something like the opposite of the principle underlying Schrödinger's cat in the box thought experiment—by trying to observe something that is ordinarily not there, it becomes visible to us. In fact though, Linux implements this seemingly magical filesystem in effect by replacing the standard calls to open(), read(), and so on with calls to functions that act on internal hidden data structures. To give you just a hint of how this works, it defines a function type

```
ssize_t (*proc_read)(struct file *, char __user *, size_t, loff_t *);
```

that looks like the read() system call (and even more like pread(), which is covered in Chapter 11) but which reads from an object of type struct file. When a program calls read() on a file in this filesystem, it invokes a function that matches this prototype instead.

As if all of this magic weren't enough, the */proc* filesystem also contains an even more magical *self* symbolic link. This link always points to the numbered directory of the process that accesses it. To illustrate:

```
$ cat /proc/self/comm
cat
$ cat /proc/self/status | grep '^PPid:'
PPid: 12812
```

Because the *self* directory was read when cat made a call to read one of its files, the directory to which *self* linked at the time of the call was that of the process created to execute cat.

Useful Per-Process Files

Some of the most useful files in the numbered directories are as follows:

cmdline   The complete command line for the process.

comm   The executable file that the process is executing.

cwd   A symbolic link to the process's current working directory.

environ   The initial environment that was set when the program being executed was started. It might have been changed by the program subsequently. The strings are NULL separated.

exe   A symbolic link containing the pathname to the executed command.

fd   A subdirectory containing links to each open file descriptor.

io   Input/output statistics for the process.

maps   The currently mapped memory regions and their access permissions. This shows information such as where the heap and stack and linked libraries are loaded. The program *memlayout.c* in the book's source code respository uses this file to display the virtual addresses of dynamic libraries, the heap, and so on.

stat   Status information about the process. This file is not as easily readable as *status* but is used by ps.

statm   Memory usage, measured in pages.

status   Similar status information to that in *stat*, but easier to read.

To demonstrate how we can use the information in these files, we'll create some short but useful programs.

An ancestors Command

Earlier in the chapter, we explored the process tree. Every process descends from process 1. There isn't a command that let's us see the PIDs of all ancestor processes of a given process. Let's write one named ancestors. We can't use getppid() because that returns the PPID of the caller, not an arbitrary process. However, the *status* file has a line of the form

```
PPid: 3486
```

in each process's directory. This leads to a solution, provided we have permission to view all of the files. We just have to repeatedly read the *status* file of each ancestor process, find the line containing the PPID, and open that directory's file until the PPID is 1. We'll use the C Library's getline() function instead of the read() system call.

We'll consolidate this logic into a function named getparentid() that we can call repeatedly until the PID is 1. That function will read the file line by line, using sscanf() on each line to search for the string "PPid:". The complete function is in Listing 10-3.

getparentid()
```
pid_t getparentid(pid_t p)
{
    pid_t   parentpid = 0;  /* The parent PID found by the function  */
    char    *buf = NULL;    /* The line read by getline()            */
    char    pathname[32];   /* Pathname to file to open              */
    size_t  len = 512;      /* Length of line getline() returned     */
    ssize_t nbytes= 0;      /* Bytes read by getline()               */
    FILE    *fp;            /* File stream to read                   */

    memset(pathname, '\0', 32);
    sprintf(pathname, "/proc/%d/status", p);
    if ( NULL == (fp = fopen(pathname, "r")) )
        fatal_error(errno, "fopen");

    if ( NULL == (buf = malloc(len)) )
        fatal_error(errno, "malloc");
    while ( TRUE ) {
        if ( -1 == (nbytes = getline(&buf, &len, fp)) )
```

```
            fatal_error(errno, "getline()");
        else if ( 1 == sscanf(buf, "PPid: %d", &parentpid) )
            break;
        if ( 0 == nbytes )
            break;
    }
    free(buf);
    return parentpid;
}
```

Listing 10-3: The getparentid() function

Most of its code is for error handling. The real work is done by sscanf(),
which parses the line. If the line contains the string "PPid:", it reads the
word after that string, converts it to an integer, and stores that number into
parentpid.

The main program follows:

ancestors.c
main()
```
int main(int argc, char *argv[])
{
    pid_t pid, parentpid;
    char  errmessage[128];
    if ( argc > 1 ) {
        if ( VALID_NUMBER != get_int(argv[1], 0, &pid, errmessage) )
            usage_error("bad number");
    }
    else
        pid = getpid();
    while ( (parentpid = getparentid(pid)) > 0 ) {
        printf("%d\n", parentpid);
        pid = parentpid;
    }
    return 0;
}
```

If there are no command line arguments, it prints the ancestors of the caller;
otherwise, it prints those of the given PID. It's essentially a while loop that
calls getparentid() until it returns 0. Since process 1's PPID is 0, that is when
it reached the init process and it stops. Because getparentid() returns a 0 on
error, it will also stop in that case.

Some sample runs follow:

```
$ ./ancestors
5521
3486
2953
2619
2229
2003
```

```
1
$ ./ancestors $(pidof -s mate-terminal)
2953
2619
2229
2003
1
```

The second run uses the pidof command, which searches the */proc* directory for the subdirectory whose executable's name is the given command. It can sometimes return more than one value because several processes are running programs with the same name, but with -s it returns one. It's better to give it the absolute pathname of the program when you know it.

A Simple ps Command

Our next exercise is to implement a simplified version of ps. Doing so will give us practice in the basic techniques for working with */proc* filesystem data; there's really no easy way to implement ps without the */proc* files. In fact, the GNU implementation of ps gets its data from */proc*.

From the proc man page we learn that, for each running process with PID *p*, there is a directory named */proc/p*, and within that directory there's a file named *stat* that contains all of the data that ps prints, but not necessarily in a human-readable form. The man page provides information about how to decode each item in the *stat* file and what that item describes.

The implementation of the ps command is complex for two reasons. One is that, historically, its behavior across different Unix systems varied greatly. The modern ps command is able to emulate most of the different behaviors when given specific command line options. The other reason is that it has many options. In particular, the user gets to pick exactly which process metadata to display as well as which processes' information should be displayed. We'll implement a much simpler version of it, since our objective is to learn how to work with */proc* files, not to implement a more complete version of ps. Specifically, we'll hardcode which types of information our command will display, and we'll choose a few fields that require some transformations to human-readable form to demonstrate how to do this.

Fortunately, the proc man page has, for each field, the field's name, a scanf() format specifier that one can use to read that field from the file, and a brief description of the field. The page lists them in the order in which they're contained in the file, which is critical, because we have to read them from the file in that order and assign them to the appropriate variables. In particular, data in the file that we are going to ignore still has to be read, but our program will not display it. Table 10-1 shows the fields that our program will display, their positions in the file, their format specifiers, and brief descriptions. The very first field in the output will be the username associated with the process, but this isn't part of the file; we'll have to get it by calling stat() on the file.

Table 10-1: Fields of the */proc/[pid]/stat* File and Their Descriptions

Position	Name	Format	Description
1	pid	%d	Process ID
2	comm	%s	Filename of the executable
3	state	%c	State (R: running; S: sleeping; D: sleeping in an uninterruptible wait; Z: zombie; T: traced or stopped)
4	ppid	%d	Process ID of the parent process
5	pgrp	%d	Group ID of the process
6	sid	%d	Session ID
7	tty_nr	%d	The tty the process uses
14	utime	%lu	User mode clock ticks
15	stime	%lu	Kernel mode clock ticks
18	priority	%ld	Priority level
19	nice	%ld	Nice level
22	start_time	%llu	Time the process started after system boot (seconds)
23	vsize	%lu	Virtual memory size (bytes)

Our program will add up the user time and system time (items 14 and 15) and display their sum as a single number representing the total time that the process has used so far. All of the data in a */proc/[pid]/stat* file is on a single newline-terminated line, which can be read with the C getline() function and stored into a string to be parsed by scanf() using the format specifiers from Table 10-1. We'll define a data structure, struct procstat, that contains a member for each field that we want to print, as well as the user ID:

```
typedef struct
{
    int         uid;        /* User ID of process                 */
    int         pid;        /* Process PID                        */
    char        *comm;      /* Command that process executes      */
    char        state;      /* State of the process               */
    int         ppid;       /* PID of parent process              */
    int         pgrp;       /* Process group ID                   */
    int         session;    /* Session ID of process              */
    int         tty_nr;     /* Integer encoding of control terminal */
    unsigned long utime;    /* Time spent in user mode            */
    unsigned long stime;    /* Time spent in kernel (system) mode */
    long        priority;   /* Process priority                   */
    long        nice;       /* Nice value                         */
    unsigned long long start_time; /* Time after boot that process started */
    unsigned long vsize;    /* Amount of virtual memory in use    */
} procstat;
```

Provided that the /proc filesystem has been mounted with relaxed enough security that ordinary users can read every process's *stat* file, we can open the /proc directory and read each *stat* file, extracting the required fields, transforming them into human-readable form, and printing them, one line per file, with suitable tabular alignments.

A rough outline of the program's logic follows.

1. Print a column heading for each output column.

2. Open the /proc directory, getting a DIR* pointer, say dirp.

3. Read each directory entry (using readdir()). For each directory entry, do the following:
    (a) If the entry name does not consist of only numerals, skip it. Otherwise, it must be a directory containing a *stat* file. Open its *stat* file for reading. Because we're using getline(), we'll open with fopen(), getting a FILE* pointer (fp).
    (b) Call fstat() on the file to get a stat buffer and extract the user ID from the stat buffer, storing it into the struct procstat.
    (c) Call getline() on the file, storing the line into a buffer (buf).
    (d) Parse buf, storing all of the fields that the program will print into the members of the struct procstat.
    (e) Print this process's data on a single line, converting those fields requiring conversion into appropriate form.

The following function parses the line from the file returned by getline():

```
parse_buf()   int parse_buf(char *buf, procstat *ps)
              {
                  int retval = 0;
                  retval = sscanf(buf, " %d %ms %c %d %d "/* pid, comm, state, ppid, pgrp */
                                  " %d %d "        /* session, tty_nr              */
                              ❶ " %*d %*u %*u " /* Skipping tty_pgrp, flags, min_flt   */
                                  " %*u %*u %*u " /* Skipping cmin_flt, maj_flt, cmaj_flt */
                                  " %lu %lu "      /* utime, stime                 */
                                  " %*d %*d "      /* Skipping cutime, cstime       */
                                  " %ld %ld "      /* priority, nice                */
                                  " %*d %*d "      /* Skipping num_threads, alarm   */
                                  " %llu %lu ",    /* start_time, vsize             */
                                                   /* Skipping everything after vsize */
                                  &ps->pid, &ps->comm, &ps->state, &ps->ppid, &ps->pgrp,
                                  &ps->session, &ps->tty_nr, &ps->utime, &ps->stime,
                                  &ps->priority, &ps->nice, &ps->start_time, &ps->vsize );
                  return retval;
              }
```

The parse_buf() function takes advantage of scanf()'s assignment-suppression character (*) ❶, which tells scanf() to read the input but to discard it. This is how the single call to scanf() can read everything we need, skipping over the data we're going to ignore.

After calling parse_buf() to store the data in the procstat structure, the program has to process some of the data items before it prints them. The items requiring some type of preprocessing follow:

comm   The name of the executed command in the file has enclosing parentheses that should be removed.

tty_nr   The controlling terminal for the process is stored as a single number encoding the major and minor device IDs of the terminal, but it should be displayed as a string such as "pts/2". We can use the major() and minor() functions for extracting these numbers (see Chapter 7). Getting the actual string names, such as "tty1" or "pts/1", will require more work, to be explained shortly.

utime, stime   The units for these fields are clock ticks. We need to add them, divide by ticks per second, and then create a string representation in the format HH:MM:SS.

start_time   This one is a little tricky. This stores the number of clock ticks since the system was booted. We need to convert the time to seconds, get the boot time (somehow), add the seconds to it, and format it either in the form HH:MM or, if the start time is not today but still in the same calendar year, in the form Month Day (Mar 05), or if its start time was in an earlier year, with just the year number (2025).

We'll go through the various conversion functions first, after which we'll develop the code that drives the program.

The following function strips the parentheses from the command name.

strip_cmmd
_parens()
```
char *strip_cmmd_parens(char *comm)
{
    int i = 0;

    if ( NULL == comm )
        return comm;
    if ( comm[0] != '(' )
        return comm;
    else {
        while ( comm[i] != '\0' && comm[i] != ')' ) i++;
        comm[i] = '\0';
        return comm + 1;
    }
}
```

It replaces the right parenthesis with a NULL byte and returns a pointer to its second character.

Getting the terminal string associated with a major and minor device number requires a bit of research. The proc man page mentions the file */proc/tty/drivers*. This file contains a list of the tty drivers currently available, showing, in order, the name of the driver, the default node name, the driver's major number, the range of minor numbers used by the driver, and the driver type. A fragment of it, augmented with column headings, is here:

Driver Name	Driver Node	Major Number	Minor Range	Driver Type
/dev/tty	/dev/tty	5	0	system:/dev/tty
/dev/console	/dev/console	5	1	system:console
--snip--				
serial	/dev/ttyS	4	64-111	serial
pty_slave	/dev/pts	136	0-1048575	pty:slave
pty_master	/dev/ptm	128	0-1048575	pty:master
unknown	/dev/tty	4	1-63	console

The second column is the device filename, which is what we want to print, without the leading /dev/. For example, the (*major*,*minor*) pair (136,8) would be pts/8, the (*major*,*minor*) pair (4,11) would be tty11, and the pair (5,1) would be console. A function to construct a device name string from the major and minor device numbers is essentially a large switch statement. Its prototype is

```
int tty_name(char *buf, unsigned maj, unsigned min);
```

and a small fragment of its switch is:

```
switch ( maj ) {
case 4:
    if ( min < 64 ) {
        sprintf(buf, "tty%d", min); break;
    }
    sprintf(buf, "ttyS%d", min-64); break;
--snip--
case 136 ... 143:    /* ... is a GNU extension to C. */
    sprintf(buf, "pts/%d", min + (maj - 136) * 256); break;
--snip--
```

The function is available in the book's source code distribution.

Creating the time string for the total time used by the process and creating the starting time string both require division by the number of clock ticks per second. That number is a system parameter that is usually either stored in a system macro named HZ or is obtained by another macro _SC_CLK_TCK(), which is defined in *sys/sysmacros.h*. A function based on these assumptions is:

```
get_hertz()   long get_hertz()
              {
                  long freq;
              #ifdef _SC_CLK_TCK        /* If this is defined, prefer it. */
                  if ( (freq = sysconf(_SC_CLK_TCK)) > 0 )
                      return (hz = freq);
              #endif
              #ifdef HZ                 /* If this is defined, use it.    */
                  return (hz = HZ);
```

```
#endif
    return (hz = 100);      /* Hopefully we never need this.  */
}
```

The variable `hz` in which the `get_hertz()` function stores this value is declared as a global so that the other functions have access to it.

The function to convert the `utime` and `stime` values to a time string is:

`make_cpu_time()`
```
void make_cpu_time_str(procstat ps, char *cputimestr)
{
    long cputime = (ps.stime + ps.utime) / hz;
    int minutes  = cputime / 60;
    int hours    = minutes / 60;
    int seconds  = cputime % 60;
    sprintf(cputimestr, "%02d:%02d:%02d", hours, minutes, seconds);
}
```

The last utility function is the one that creates a time string representing the starting time of the process. It requires the boot time. The files in */proc* that are not in numbered directories are system-wide data. In particular, */proc/stat* contains system statistics. One of its entries, according to the proc man page, is `btime`, which is the system boot time in seconds since the epoch. Our program can read and store this value.

A function to do this follows:

`get_boot_time()`
```
void get_boot_time(unsigned long long *btime)
{
    char    *buf;                 /* Storage for call to getline()          */
    char    *bootline = NULL; /* Pointer to line in file with btime entry  */
    size_t  len = MAX_LINE;   /* Set to zero so getline() allocates buf.   */
    FILE    *fp;

    *btime = 0;   /* In case we fail to get it */
    if ( NULL == (fp = fopen("/proc/stat", "r")) )
        return;
    if ( NULL == (buf = malloc(MAX_LINE)) )
        fatal_error(errno, "malloc");
    do {
        if ( -1 == getline(&buf, &len, fp) )
            break;
        if ( (bootline = strstr(buf, "btime ")) )
            sscanf(bootline, "btime %llu", btime);
    } while ( bootline == NULL );
    free(buf);
}
```

This function opens the */proc/stat* file and reads lines until it finds the line of the form `btime` *number*. When it finds this line, it uses `sscanf()` to read the string after the word `btime` and convert it to an `unsigned long long`. Setting `buf` to NULL and len to 0 before the call tells getline() to allocate memory for each line that it reads. The user program has to free it.

The function that creates the starting time string for the process is next. To save space, the error checking and handling code are removed:

```
void make_start_time_str(procstat ps, char *start_time)
{
    unsigned long long start;
    struct tm          *bdtime;
    struct tm          *current_time;
    struct tm           saved_start_time;
    const char         *fmt = START_FORMAT;
    unsigned long long boot_time;
    static unsigned long long seconds_since_epoch;

    get_boot_time(&boot_time);
    if ( 0 == boot_time )
        fatal_error(-1, "Could not get boot time");
    start = boot_time + ps.start_time / hz;
    bdtime = localtime((time_t*) (&start));
    saved_start_time = *bdtime;
    current_time = localtime((time_t*) (&seconds_since_epoch));
    if ( saved_start_time.tm_yday != current_time->tm_yday ) fmt = "%b%d";
    if ( saved_start_time.tm_year != current_time->tm_year ) fmt = "%Y";
    strftime(start_time, 8, fmt, &saved_start_time);
}
```

The function gets the boot time, converts the time in ps.start_time to seconds, and adds the boot time to it to get the calendar time in seconds at which the process started. It also gets the current time, because the format that ps uses to display the starting time depends on whether it started on the same day, on a previous day in the same calendar year, or in a previous calendar year. It uses localtime() to make these decisions by getting the broken-down time for both the current time and the starting time.

The function print_one_ps() prints the metadata for a single process:

```
void print_one_ps(procstat ps, char *buf)
{
    char    start_time[10];
    char    ttyname[10];
    char    cputimestr[16];
    char    *cmd;
    make_start_time_str(ps, start_time); /* Create the start time string. */

    /* Use tty_nr field to create a name for the tty. If it returns 0,
       set the name to "?". */
    if ( ! tty_name(ttyname, major(ps.tty_nr), minor(ps.tty_nr)) )
        strcpy(ttyname, "?");
```

```
/* Create a time string for the total cpu time (user + sys time). */
make_cpu_time_str(ps, cputimestr);

cmd = strip_cmmd_parens(ps.comm);

sprintf(buf, "%-11s%5d%8d%3c %4ld  %4ld   %s  %-6s%10s%10ld    %s \n",
  ❶ uid2name(ps.uid), ps.pid, ps.ppid, ps.state, ps.priority,
    ps.nice, start_time, ttyname, cputimestr,
  ❷ ps.vsize/1024, cmd);
free(ps.comm);
}
```

The uid2name() function ❶ was defined in Chapter 6. We divide the virtual memory size from the file by 1024 ❷ because the output units are KB.

Printing the metadata for all running processes amounts to iterating over all subdirectories in */proc* whose names are numeric and opening and reading their *stat* files. The function that does this, printallprocs(), is shown next, without any error checking or handling:

printallprocs()
```
void printallprocs(DIR *dirp)
{
    struct dirent *direntp;      /* Pointer to directory entry structure  */
    char   *accepts="0123456789"; /* For matching directory names         */
    char    pathname[PATH_MAX];  /* Pathname to file to open              */
    char    heading[MAX_LINE];   /* String containing heading             */
    char    psline[MAX_LINE];    /* String containing one proc's data     */
    size_t len = MAX_LINE;       /* Length of line getline() returned      */
    FILE*  fp;                   /* File stream to read                   */
    char   *buf;
    procstat ps_fields;
    struct stat statbuffer;

    memset(heading, 0, MAX_LINE);
    printheadings(heading);
    printf("%s", heading);
    if ( NULL == (buf = malloc(MAX_LINE)) ) /*Allocate buffer for getline().*/
        fatal_error(errno, "malloc");

    while ( TRUE ) {
        errno = 0;
        direntp = readdir(dirp);                     /* Get next entry. */
        if ( direntp == NULL && errno != 0 )
            perror("readdir"); /* Not end of stream, but a readdir() error  */
        else if ( direntp == NULL )   /* The end of the stream was reached. */
            break;
        else if ( strspn(direntp->d_name, accepts) == strlen(direntp->d_name))
        {   /* Directory name is a number. */
```

```
            memset(pathname, '\0', PATH_MAX);
            sprintf(pathname, "/proc/%s/", direntp->d_name);
            if ( -1 == stat(pathname, &statbuffer) ) /* Stat directory */
                continue;
            /* The /proc/[pid]/stat file doesn't store real uid. */
            ps_fields.uid = statbuffer.st_uid;

            sprintf(pathname + strlen(pathname), "stat");
            if ( NULL == (fp = fopen(pathname, "r")) )
                continue;

            if ( -1 == getline(&buf, &len, fp) )
                fatal_error(errno, "getline()");
            parse_buf(buf, &ps_fields);
            print_one_ps(ps_fields, psline);
            printf("%s", psline);
            fclose(fp);
        }
    }
    free(buf);
    printf("\n");
}
```

The main program is omitted; the complete program is available in the book's source distribution.

All of the support functions described in this section, except for printall procs(), are in a file named *ps_utils.c* in the *common* directory. The main program file includes the header file *ps_utils.h* in the *include* directory. A fragment of a sample run of the program, which is named spl_ps, follows:

UID	PID	PPID	S	PRI	NI	STIME	TTY	TIME	SIZE	CMD
root	1	0	S	20	0	06:54	?	00:00:02	168720	systemd
root	2	0	S	20	0	06:54	?	00:00:00	0	kthreadd
root	3	2	I	0	-20	06:54	?	00:00:00	0	rcu_gp
--snip--										
stewart	9714	3220	S	20	0	08:59	pts/4	00:00:00	29112	bash
stewart	9807	3255	R	20	0	09:01	pts/0	00:00:00	5852	spl_ps

The program as it stands does not format the command name in the same way that ps does. The ps command puts square brackets around the command name when the arguments to the command are not available. This is true of kernel threads and daemon processes, among others. Adding them is left as an exercise.

Summary

A process is not just an abstraction; it's a precisely defined object. A typical Unix system can have hundreds of processes running at any instant of time.

Because processes come into existence only because some other process creates them, a natural parent/child relationship ensues, and the set of running processes can be viewed as a tree of ancestral/descendant relationships, like a genealogical tree. Unix systems also support the creation of process groups, which are sets of processes created to execute multiple programs as part of a larger job. There are two types of process groups: foreground and background groups. Roughly speaking, foreground processes are connected to the terminal, whereas background processes aren't. Modern Unix systems define the concept of a (login) session. A session is the collection of all process groups created directly or indirectly when you log in. All process groups belong to exactly one session.

A running process has a memory image, which is the set of all virtual addresses that it's allocated. That memory image has a very structured form, consisting of regions called segments. At the low end of its memory, it has the text segment, containing all of its executable code. Directly above that lie two different regions for statically allocated data, and above that is what we usually call the heap, the region from which dynamically allocated memory is assigned. At the opposite end are the environment strings, the argument strings, and the process stack.

A process is created to execute a program, which exists as a file on a secondary storage device. The executable program file is a structured file that adheres to a format known as the Executable and Linking Format (ELF). The ELF specification describes exactly what information must be in the file and its relative location within it. In addition to describing the structure of executable programs, it also defines the structure of shared object modules, relocatable object modules, and core files. In this chapter, we examined the detailed information contained in an ELF file for executable programs and developed a program to display some of that information.

The kernel representation of a process is known by many names. In Linux, it's called a process descriptor and is represented by a structure of type task_struct. The process descriptor has hundreds of individual members that describe the resources allocated to the process, the attributes of the process, and lists of child processes, siblings, and much more. The kernel doesn't expose this structure in a direct way, but in most Unix systems, it provides most of it in the */proc* pseudofilesystem.

The */proc* filesystem has a directory for every active process, and with each directory, it has text files containing the information that the kernel stores in the file descriptor for the process. This filesystem is not a real one; it has no disk storage and is constructed on the fly when we view its contents with commands such as ls and cat. In the final section of the chapter, I showed how to use the information in this filesystem to implement a simplified version of the ps command.

Exercises

1. Enhance the `ancestors` command so that it also outputs the name of the command of each ancestor process. Depending on the security level of the system, you may not be able to see command names other than those of your own processes.

2. Write a command named `nca`, short for "nearest common ancestor," which, when given two process IDs on the command line—say, `p1` and `p2`—outputs the PID and the name of the command executed by the process `q` such that `q` is an ancestor of `p1` and `p2`, and `q` has no descendants that are ancestors of both `p1` and `p2`. For this program, assume a process is its own ancestor, so that `nca p1 1` is `1` and `nca p p` is `p`. Depending on the security level of the system, you may not be able to see command names other than those of your own processes.

3. Write a command named `pgroup` that when run as

   ```
   $ ./pgroup pid
   ```

   prints the PIDs of all processes in the same group as *pid*.

4. Write a command named `psiblings` that when run as

   ```
   $ ./psiblings pid
   ```

   prints the PIDs of all processes that are siblings of *pid*.

5. The `pstree` command displays the tree of processes descending from init or, if it's given the PID on the command line, it displays the tree descended from the process with that PID. It indents the child processes by a few spaces and also draws lines to connect the parent to its children. By default, `pstree` compacts its output using a few optimizations. The `-c` option turns off compaction. Read its man page and run it to see how it works.

   Write a simplified version of `pstree -c` that when given an argument, `pid`, prints the tree of all processes that descend from `pid`, one per line. Like `pstree`, it should print the commands executed by each process. All children of a process should be indented by four spaces recursively so that the output is like the output of `pstree`. (Hint: Look at the directory */proc/[pid]/task/[pid]*. If it has a nonempty file named *children*, then that file lists the PIDs of its children.)

6. Compile the *displayvm.c* program with PIE disabled, using the command:

   ```
   $ gcc -no-pie -fno-pie -O0 -o displayvm_no_pie -I../include \
     displayvm.c
   ```

   Run the executable a few times. What do you observe?

7. The *print_elfphdr.c* program printed the program headers in an ELF file but did not handle the possibility that the file might be a 32-bit ELF file. Fix that problem by adding the code to handle that case.

8. The *print_elfphdr.c* program prints the program headers in an ELF file. Write a similar program named *print_elfsect_info.c* that prints the names and sizes of every section in a given ELF file. For example

```
$ ./print_elfsect_info myobjfile
```

would print the names and sizes of every section in `myobjfile`, one per line. (Hint: The ELF man page explains which section stores section names, and the ELF header file stores the index of this section.)

9. Write a program based on the previous exercise that prints the size of an executable's text segment.

10. Modify *spl_ps.c* so that the user can limit the type of information it lists, using the syntax:

```
$ ./spl_ps -o "%pid,%ppid,%start..."
```

The format specifiers can be of your own choosing, but if you look at the man page for ps, you'll see that there is a list of specifiers in this form that you can emulate.

11

PROCESS CREATION AND TERMINATION

In the previous chapter, we examined the content and structure of various objects associated with a process, such as the executable program file that it runs, the process descriptor by which the kernel represents it, and its memory image, which is the set of all virtual addresses that it can reference. These objects are static in the sense that they're snapshots taken at a moment in the lifetime of the process, like the frames of a movie. But a process is dynamic, changing over time, and we've yet to explore the transformations that a process undergoes.

In this chapter, we look at this aspect of a process. Specifically, we explore how one process can create another process, how it can interact with the processes that it creates, how it can change the program that it executes, and how it can terminate itself.

The Lifetime of a Process

Before we explore the details of process creation and other operations that act on a process as a whole, let's get a big picture of the ways in which a process can change itself or cause other processes to change during its lifetime. We'll concentrate on the most important system calls related to these changes.

A process comes into existence as a result of another process's creating it. The fork() system call is the most common means of creating a new process, and it will be the first call that we examine. When a process is created by a call to fork(), it executes the same program as its parent. This by itself is of limited use, because much of the time we want the new process to execute some other program. A process can change the program that it executes, along with its complete memory image, by calling execve() or any of a small set of library functions that wrap execve() to make it easier to use in one way or another. These are sometimes called the *exec() family of functions*. We'll examine how to use these functions in "Executing Programs" on page 560.

A process can terminate its execution at any time by calling either the C Library's exit() function or the lower level _exit() system call. When a process terminates itself this way, it's said to have terminated *normally*. When a process detects an unrecoverable error condition, it can terminate itself by calling the abort() library function; this is called *abnormal termination*. When a process is killed by a signal that it didn't catch, this is also called abnormal termination. In "Terminating Processes" on page 557, we'll explore the effects of the different methods of process termination and the steps that the kernel takes when a process is terminated by any means.

Both exit() functions have an integer argument, the least significant byte of which stores its exit status. When a process calls exit(e_status), the value stored in e_status is transmitted back to its parent process, which can access it by calling wait() or one of its variants. The wait() system call allows a parent to monitor when and how its children terminate. After a process creates one or more children, it can call wait() to wait for their termination. It's then suspended until some child terminates. The combination of exit() and wait() are a simple means by which a parent can receive information about how its children terminate. We'll study the wait() system call and its use in "Waiting for Children" on page 569.

The fork(), execve(), _exit(), and wait() system calls and related library functions are the four pillars of dynamic process control. They are the means by which we can create processes, change what they execute, synchronize their actions to a limited degree, and terminate them. Knowing how to use these four primitives is the key to writing programs that can multitask.

Creating Processes

Many types of programs benefit from being able to create new processes as they're running. For example, many servers are designed so that incoming service requests can be handled independently by separate processes. When a new request arrives, they create a new process to service it. Programs such as shells create new processes to execute the commands that users enter, and desktop managers such as GNOME and MATE create new processes to run various applets such as panels, file system browsers, and power managers. Creating a new process is a fundamental operation in Unix.

We can search the man pages for system calls that create new processes by entering `apropos -s2 -a create process`. On Linux, we'll discover three options:

- `fork()`
- `clone()` and variants of it
- `vfork()`

Of these, `fork()` is the most important call to understand—the `clone()` function and its variants are Linux specific and not specified by any version of POSIX, and `vfork()` was removed in POSIX.1-2008. The portable way, and the original way, of creating new processes is `fork()`.

The Basics of fork()

The `fork()` system call's synopsis is:

```
#include <sys/types.h>
#include <unistd.h>


pid_t fork(void);
```

It has no arguments and returns a process ID, returning -1 if it fails. The man page states that "fork() creates a new process by duplicating the calling process." The syntax seems simple enough, as does this description, but in fact exactly what it does is far from simple; it's both remarkable and initially perplexing. What's remarkable is that the new process is an almost exact copy of the calling process (I'll make this statement more precise shortly). What's perplexing is what happens after the call returns; we've not yet seen a function quite like `fork()`. Let me explain by way of an example.

When a process *p* executes the system call

```
pid_t returnval = fork();
```

assuming it was successful, the kernel runs on its behalf and creates a new process *c* that is an almost identical copy of the calling process *p*. When the system call finishes, the very next instruction to be executed in both the new process *c* and the calling process *p* is the one immediately after the call in the program! In this example, the instruction is the assignment of the call's return value to the variable `returnval`. Both processes execute this assignment, but the difference is that the value returned to the parent is the PID of the newly created process (its child, *c*), and the value returned to the child is 0, so that they each have a different value stored in `returnval`.

In short, before the system call is executed, there's a single process executing this program, but by the time the call has returned, there are two. There has been a *fork* in the stream of executed instructions, just like a fork in a road. It is almost like process mitosis. Figure 11-1 illustrates the instruction flow.

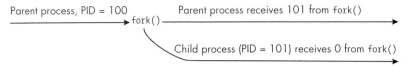

Figure 11-1: A conceptualization of the fork() system call

The fact that the parent and child receive different return values from fork() is the key to writing programs that call it. Because the value returned to the parent is the PID of the newly created child process, which is never 0, but the value returned to the child is 0, immediately after the call, the program can test whether the return value is 0 or not. If it's 0, it's the child executing the code, and if not, it's the parent. The typical coding paradigm is therefore:

```
pid_t returnval = fork();
if ( -1 == returnval )
    // OMITTED: Handle the error.
else if ( 0 == returnval )
    // OMITTED: Code for the child to execute
else
    // OMITTED: Code for the parent to execute
```

Some people use a switch statement instead.

I'll demonstrate with a very simple example, named *fork_demo1.c*, shown in Listing 11-1.

fork_demo1.c
```
#include "common_hdrs.h"

int main(int argc, char *argv[])
{
    pid_t returnval;

    if ( -1 == (returnval = fork()) )
        fatal_error(errno, "fork");
    else if ( 0 == returnval )   /* Child executes this branch. */
        printf("I am the child process. My PID is %d\n", getpid());
    else                         /* Parent executes this branch. */
        printf("I am the parent process. My PID is %d\n", getpid());
    return 0;
}
```

Listing 11-1: A program that creates a single child process, with the parent and child each printing to the terminal

When we build and run this executable, we'll see something like the following output:

```
$ ./fork_demo1
I am the parent process. My PID is 9386
I am the child process. My PID is 9387
```

The two lines might appear in a different order from one run to another because of system scheduling activity. The order in which parent and child execute is not standardized and, on some systems, the parent might be scheduled first, while on others, the child will be.

The fact that the parent and child print different PIDs is proof that a new process was created by fork(). The output is also proof that the child executes the same program as the parent. The fork() man page tells us that the child process and the parent process run in separate memory spaces and that "at the time of fork() both memory spaces have the same content." In other words, when the child process is created, the kernel makes an exact copy of the memory space of the parent and gives that copy to the child. The parent and child have different return values from the call to fork(), but these values are in the kernel stack of each process. When fork() returns, they're copied into the user-addressable memory space of each process.

The Child's Memory Image

The statement that, initially, the child has an exact copy of the memory image of the parent means that all parts of the memory image are copied, including the stack, the heap, the data segments, and so on. They are not shared! To make this point clear, I've written a small program that demonstrates it.

NOTE *In modern Linux systems, the physical pages of the parent's memory image aren't actually copied until the child process attempts to modify them. Until then, the child's and parent's logical pages are mapped to the same physical pages. This is called copy-on-write.*

The program in Listing 11-2 declares a few variables whose storage is in different parts of the address space. It has a file-scoped globalvar, which will be in the initialized data segment; a local localvar in the runtime stack; and a local variable that will point to dynamically allocated memory in the heap, named heapvar. Before the child is created, the parent prints the values of these variables. When the child is created, it also prints their values and subsequently modifies each of them. When it has finished, both processes print the values of these variables again. Their final values in the child and parent will be witnesses to fork()'s behavior.

fork_demo2.c
```
#include "common_hdrs.h"

const char str[] = "On the heap.";
int   globalvar = 10;    /* In the initialized data segment */

int main(int argc, char* argv[])
{
    int     localvar = 0;  /* A stack variable                        */
    char   *heapvar;       /* A pointer that will point into the heap */
    pid_t  result, mypid; /* For storing return value of fork() and PID */
```

```
        if ( NULL == (heapvar = calloc(sizeof(str) + 1, 1)) )
            fatal_error(errno, "calloc");
    memcpy(heapvar, str, strlen(str));
    heapvar[strlen(str)] = '\0';        /* Heap variable now has a string. */
    printf("This is printed by the parent process before the call"
            " to fork():\npid = %d, localvar = %d, globalvar = %d, "
            " heapvar = \"%s\" \n\n", getpid(), localvar, globalvar, heapvar);

    if ( -1 == (result = fork()) )
        fatal_error(errno, "fork");

    else if ( 0 == result ) { /* Child executes this branch.   */
        mypid = getpid();
        printf("This is printed by the child process:\n");
        printf("Child PID = %d, localvar = %d, globalvar = %d, "
                "heapvar = \"%s\"\n", mypid, localvar, globalvar, heapvar);
        localvar = 1;               /* Make changes to these variables. */
        globalvar = mypid;
        memset(heapvar, 'x', strlen(heapvar)); /* heapvar = "xxx...x" */
        printf("Child process will now assign new values to
                these variables.\n\n");
    }
    else {                          /* Parent executes this branch. */
        mypid = getpid();
        sleep(2); /* Sleep long enough for child's output to appear first. */
    }
    /* Both processes continue here. */
    if ( 0 == result )
        printf("Child printing:");
    else
        printf("Parent printing:");

    printf("\nMy pid is %d. The variables "
            "have the following values in my address space:\n "
            "localvar = %d, globalvar = %d, heapvar = \"%s\" \n\n",
            mypid, localvar, globalvar, heapvar);
    return 0;
}
```

Listing 11-2: A program that shows that the child and parent do not share their data

When we build and run this program, we see the following output, of course with different PIDs each time:

```
$ ./fork_demo2
This is printed by the parent process before the call to fork():
pid = 3686, localvar = 0, globalvar = 10,  heapvar = "On the heap."

This is printed by the  child process:
```

```
Child PID = 3687, localvar = 0, globalvar = 10, heapvar = "On the heap."
 Child process will now assign new values to these variables.

Child printing:
My pid is 3687. The variables have the following values in my address space:
 localvar = 1, globalvar = 3687, heapvar = "xxxxxxxxxxx"

Parent printing:
My pid is 3686. The variables have the following values in my address space:
 localvar = 0, globalvar = 10, heapvar = "On the heap."
```

I make the parent sleep for 2 seconds so that the child's changes and output will appear first. The values of the three variables being tracked by the program did not change in the parent after the child modified them. This is proof that the child and parent have separate copies of the stack, the data segments, and the heap. They do not share them.

The Child's Process Descriptor

The documentation for fork() states that the new process is created by duplicating the old one. Recall from Chapter 10 that the kernel represents each process by a process descriptor. To *duplicate* a process means to make a new copy of that descriptor and to create the memory image for the new process.

The man page also tells us that the child process is an exact copy of the parent, except in a few specific ways. We need to understand what's the same and what's different to avoid some common programming pitfalls. As mentioned earlier, the entire virtual address space of the parent is duplicated in the child. This includes all of the environment strings, stack contents, text and data segments, and data in shared libraries that are mapped into this address space. This also includes items such as buffers for open file and directory streams that are allocated in the parent process's heap.

Almost all of the parent's process descriptor is duplicated in the child, including items such as the working and root directories, masks, controlling terminal, and so on. But some parts of the descriptor are modified in the child. The list of differences between the parent and child is documented in the man page. I'll point out a few of the differences that are relevant to what we've covered so far:

- The child has its own unique PID, which is also different from any active PGID.

- The child's PPID is its parent's process PID.

- The child's set of pending signals is initially empty.

- The child does not inherit any timers, including per-process timers, from its parent.

The other significant ways in which the parent and child differ are related to areas such as multithreading, synchronization operations of various kinds, memory mapping, and message queues.

Sharing of Open Files

Among the items that are copied into the child are all of the open file descriptors from the parent. Recall that each process has a table of open file descriptors and that these descriptors are pointers into the kernel's table of open file descriptions (the file structure tables). In Chapter 4, Figure 4-1 depicts the relationship between the open file descriptors that are part of a process and the open file descriptions maintained by the kernel. Figure 11-2 shows the effect of fork() on the open file descriptors.

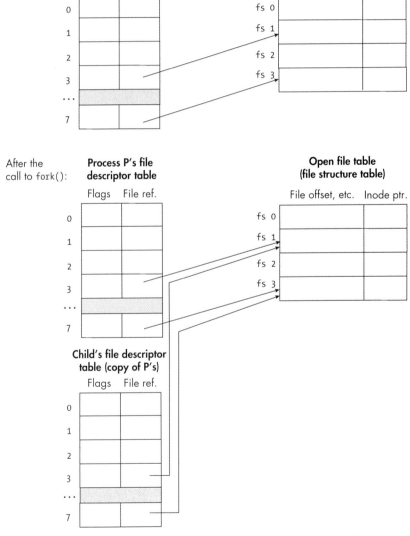

Figure 11-2: The before and after of the duplication of a process's open file descriptor table in the new child process

The file offset, in particular, is part of the open file description. Because the child has copies of the open file descriptors, it has pointers to the same open file descriptions as the parent does in the kernel's file structure table. This means that parent and child share the file offset in every file previously opened by the parent. When either process moves that file offset, either by a read or write operation or by explicitly moving it with lseek(), the file offset seen by the other process is moved. It also means that the parent and child can read data written into the file by the other. In short, parent and child can access the same file, but if they don't do so in a coordinated (synchronized) way, unexpected outcomes can ensue. To demonstrate this sharing of a file, consider the following program:

fork_demo3.c
```
#include "common_hdrs.h"

int main(int argc, char *argv[])
{
    int    fd, i;
    pid_t retval;

    if ( -1 == (fd = open("newfile", O_CREAT | O_WRONLY | O_TRUNC, 0644)) )
        fatal_error(errno, "open");
    if ( -1 == (retval = fork()) )
        fatal_error(errno, "fork");
    else if ( 0 == retval )   /* Child executes this branch.  */
        for ( i = 0; i < 10; i++) {
            if ( 0 >= write(fd,"c", 1) )
                fatal_error(errno, "write");
            usleep(300000);
        }
    else                        /* Parent executes this branch. */
        for ( i = 0; i < 10; i++ ) {
            if ( 0 >= write(fd, "p", 1) )
                fatal_error(errno, "write");
            usleep(200000);
        }
    write(fd, "\0", 1);
    close(fd);
    if ( retval != 0 )
        printf("File \"newfile\" is ready for viewing.\n");
    return 0;
}
```

The parent process opens a file named *newfile* for writing in its current working directory. It then calls fork(). The child inherits a copy of the open file descriptor for the file and can therefore write to it, because the file access mode is part of the descriptor. Both the child and the parent write characters into the file, one at a time. The child writes *c*'s and the parent *p*'s. The calls to usleep() decrease the chance that one process will perform all of its output before the other. Both processes close the file when they finish writing.

If you look at the file that is created, it will have interspersed characters from the parent and child:

```
$ ./fork_demo3
File "newfile" is ready for viewing.
$ cat newfile
pcpcpcppcpcppcpcpcccc
```

This shows that parent and child processes share the file offset. If they had their own private copies of it, the output of one could overwrite the other's output. The fact that the child process has access to the same open files as the parent is going to play an important role in interprocess communication (Chapter 13).

Listing 11-3 shows another small program with a not-so-obvious flaw. This program models the situation in which an application creates many child processes to perform subtasks, roughly the way a desktop manager might.

fork_demo4.c
```
#include "common_hdrs.h"

int main(int argc, char *argv[])
{
    pid_t newpid;
    int   num_children = 4;

    printf("About to create many processes...\n");
    while ( num_children-- > 0 ) {
        newpid = fork();   /* Create a child process.                 */
    ❶ if ( newpid == 0 ) /* If this is a new process, don't create others.*/
            break;
    }
    /* Each process calls getpid() and prints it process ID. */
    printf("Process ID = %d\n", getpid());
    return 0;
}
```

Listing 11-3: A program that creates a fixed number of child processes, with a subtle error

Notice that in the while loop, if the return value from fork() is 0, the process exits the loop ❶. I leave it as an exercise to predict the output when this code is removed. When you build and run this program, you'll see output like the following:

```
$ ./fork_demo4
About to create many processes...
Process ID = 36690
Process ID = 36691
Process ID = 36692
Process ID = 36689
```

Now run it again, this time piping the output to the cat command:

```
$ ./fork_demo4 | cat
About to create many processes...
Process ID = 36747
About to create many processes...
Process ID = 36748
About to create many processes...
Process ID = 36745
About to create many processes...
Process ID = 36749
```

What explains why the output is different? Here are some relevant facts about I/O in the C Library as well as what's shared by parent and child.

- When a child process is created, its standard output descriptor points to the same open file description as the parent's and they share the file offset. Therefore, all children and their parent share the file offset.

- The `printf()` function is part of the C I/O Library and acts on objects of type `FILE`, which are called *file streams*. The C Library uses stream buffering for all operations that act on `FILE` streams. It uses three different kinds of stream buffering methods:

    Unbuffered streams Characters written to or read from an unbuffered stream are transmitted individually to or from the file as soon as possible.

    Line-buffered streams Characters written to a line-buffered stream are transmitted to the file in blocks when a newline character is found or if certain other conditions hold. The other conditions are described in detail in Chapter 9.

    Fully buffered streams Characters written to or read from a fully buffered stream are transmitted to or from the file in blocks of an arbitrary size, but not less than 256 bytes.

- By default, streams are fully buffered. The exception is when a stream is connected to a terminal device, in which case it is line buffered.

- The buffer used by the C Library is part of the process's address space because the dynamically linked libraries are mapped into that address space. We saw that demonstrated in Chapter 10.

- When `fork()` is called, the child gets a copy of the parent's buffer. Unless that buffer was flushed, it retains any characters that the parent wrote into it since the last time it was flushed.

- No C Library function is atomic. It is entirely possible that output can be intermingled or even lost if the timing of calls by separate processes sharing a file offset leads to this.

Now let's put these facts together. The fork_demo4 program begins with the instruction:

```
printf("About to create many processes...\n");
```

If output has not been redirected, then stdout points to a terminal device and is therefore line buffered. Because the string "About to create many processes...\n" is newline terminated, it is written to the terminal immediately and removed from the buffer. When the process forks the children, they get empty buffers and write their individual messages to the terminal. There's a small chance that one process can overwrite the data sent by another to the terminal, but it isn't likely when the number of processes is small, as is the case in this example. Therefore, we see the single string written by the parent, followed by the messages written by the children.

When standard output is redirected to a file or to a pipe, it no longer points to a terminal device. In this case, the library will use full buffering on the stream. The block size used for full buffering is much larger than the total size of the string written by the parent process, and therefore, when fork() is called the buffer has not been emptied. The consequence is that the string "About to create many processes...\n" will remain in the buffers of all child processes when they are forked, and when they each call

```
printf("Process id = %d\n", getpid());
```

each will output lines of the form

```
About to create many processes...
Process id = 36754
```

and roughly twice as many lines will be written to the stream as there were without redirection.

A program that creates child processes and that also has been performing I/O using the C Library's stream buffering has to flush the buffers before calling fork() if the output is to be the same, regardless of whether it is redirected. The fflush() library function will flush a buffer; a program can call it before calling fork(), but there's no need to call it if the output is not redirected. Fortunately, there's a function, isatty(), that tests whether a file descriptor refers to a terminal device:

```
#include <unistd.h>
int isatty(int fd);
```

We can get the file descriptor for stdout, the C Library's output file stream, with the fileno() function. Putting this together, we can insert the lines

```
if ( !isatty(fileno(stdout)) );
    fflush(stdout);
```

just after the first printf():

```
printf("About to create many processes...\n");
if ( !isatty(fileno(stdout)) )
    fflush(stdout);
```

We'll add this correction to the program in a revised version, *fork_demo5.c*, but we also need to address the issue of possible intermingled or lost output.

Potential Race Conditions

The preceding program raised the prospect of potential race conditions. A *race condition* exists in a fragment of code when the outcome of its execution depends on the order in which two or more independent processes or threads access and/or modify data that is referenced within that code. In the preceding example, multiple child processes all try to write to the same stream without any attempt to synchronize their writes to it. The C printf() function does not write atomically, and in principle, the output from different processes can become intermingled on the screen. As the number of processes increases and the amount of time spent in output increases, the probability of race conditions increases.

We can model this mathematically. Suppose that N identical processes try to print to the screen using printf(). If the fraction of its time that each process spends in that printf() is p, then we can think of this as a *success* event in a binomial probability distribution. The probability that at least 2 processes out of N are executing the printf() at the exact same time is 1 minus the probability that no process is executing it, minus the probability that exactly 1 is. This is defined by the expression:

$$1 - ((1 - p)^N + N \cdot p(1 - p)^{N-1})$$

Calculating the value of this expression for $p = 0.05$ and $N = 16$, for example, the probability of a race (and hence lost output) is about 0.19. For $N = 32$, it is 0.48, and for $N = 64$, it is about 0.84. In short, as the number of processes increases, it becomes almost inevitable that lines will be lost, regardless of whether they are written to the terminal or to a file, because the race condition is independent of how the output stream is buffered.

One solution that prevents these race conditions is two-fold. First, we use system calls instead of the library functions. Writes with write() are not buffered in user space, and, starting with the Linux 3.14 kernel, they are guaranteed to be atomic; in older kernels, updates to the file offset were not atomic. Second, we take advantage of the O_APPEND file status flag, which is described in the open() man page, which we first examined in Chapter 4. We didn't explore this flag in that chapter because it's needed only when multiple processes or threads try to write to the same file. When we bitwise-OR it into the flags when opening a file, every write operation is preceded immediately and atomically by a seek to the end of the file. This guarantees that each write occurs at the end of the file, regardless of how many other processes are trying to do the same thing simultaneously.

The question is how we can set that flag on our standard output stream, because our programs don't explicitly open the standard streams—they're opened automatically when our process starts execution. The only method of setting that we know of is in the call to open(). We need another way to set the flag. Luckily, the SEE ALSO section of the open() man page references the fcntl() system call, whose synopsis is

```
#include <unistd.h>
#include <fcntl.h>

int fcntl(int fd, int cmd, ... /* arg */);
```

This call can be used for modifying a file descriptor after it's been opened. It returns -1 on failure. The third argument (arg) is needed for only certain values of cmd.

Using fcntl() to modify the set of flags on a file descriptor is a three-step procedure:

1. Retrieve the existing flags into an integer variable:

```
flags = fcntl(fd, F_GETFL);
```

2. Bitwise-OR the new flag into the integer:

```
flags = flags | O_APPEND;
```

3. Copy the modified integer back to the descriptor:

```
fcntl(fd, F_SETFL, flags);    /* F_SETFL requires a third argument. */
```

Therefore, we can put standard output into atomic auto-append mode in our program with the following code snippet:

```
int flags;
/* Put standard output into atomic append mode. */
flags = fcntl(stdout, F_GETFL);
flags |= (O_APPEND);
if ( -1 == fcntl(STDOUT_FILENO, F_SETFL, flags) )
    exit(EXIT_FAILURE);
```

This is the easiest method of preventing race conditions involving output to terminals and files. It isn't the best, though; the rest of the man page for fcntl() contains a discussion of advisory record locks, which can be used by a process to lock all or part of a file while it is accessing it. We won't explore record locks in this book, but we do explore other methods of preventing race conditions in Chapters 12 and 16 and the use of fcntl() more thoroughly in Chapter 17. The program *fork_demo5.c*, with all of the preceding changes, is not shown in the book, but is available in the book's source code distribution online.

Process Synchronization with Signals

Using auto-append mode on a file descriptor eliminates the race condition when multiple processes write to the end of a file concurrently, but it isn't a general solution to preventing races related to the shared file offset when some processes read as well.

One situation in which this occurs is when the child and parent processes are in a producer-consumer relationship. A *producer-consumer* paradigm is one in which there are two kinds of processes: producers and consumers. Producer processes write data into a buffer that is read exclusively by consumer processes. Producers don't read from the buffer, and consumers don't write into it. In general, there can be multiple producers and multiple consumers, but suppose for now that the child is the only producer and that the parent is the only consumer. The child generates data of some kind and writes it to the shared file, which was opened in read/write mode by the parent before creating the child process. Suppose further that the child writes data as soon as it generates it, appending to the end of the previously written data, whereas the parent, which is the consumer, reads data starting at the beginning of the file, in fixed-size chunks. Each process needs to move the file offset for its own purpose. Figure 11-3 depicts this situation.

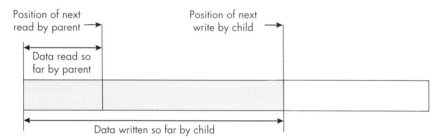

Figure 11-3: The two different positions that the shared file offset must have for parent and child processes

The file is essentially a shared buffer between the child and the parent. The child has to write its data without its being lost or duplicated, and the parent has to read the data in the order it was written without loss or duplication. Since they share the file offset, they cannot access the file at the same time. We can solve this problem with signals. It isn't an efficient solution or the best in general, but it demonstrates how signals can solve relatively simple synchronization problems. In "The `waitpid()` System Call" on page 574, we'll explore a different approach that doesn't require signals.

This solution uses the `SIGUSR1` and `SIGUSR2` signals. The child's structure in pseudocode is:

```
Repeat
    Generate and write some data.
    Signal parent using SIGUSR1 that it's okay to read.
    Pause and wait for signal from parent that it's okay to write again.
Until all data has been written.
Signal parent using SIGUSR2 that all data's been written, and exit.
```

The parent's structure is symmetrical:

```
Repeat
    Wait for a signal from the child that it's okay to read.
    Read the data and write to the terminal until no data is left.
    Signal the child that  it's okay to write again, using SIGUSR1.
Until the child has sent a SIGUSR2 signal.
On receipt of the SIGUSR2, read what's left in the file and exit.
```

Listing 11-4 contains fragments of the program mixed with pseudocode. Some error handling is omitted as well. The complete listing is available in the book's source code distribution.

sync_io_demo.c
```
volatile sig_atomic_t
done = FALSE;

void usr_handler(int sig)
{
    if ( sig == SIGUSR2 )
        done = TRUE;
}

void produce_data(int fd)   /* Child process      */
{
    char data[] = "abcdefghijklmnoprst:";
    int  pos   = 0;
    int  count = 0;

    // OMITTED: Set up signal handlers.
    pid_t ppid = getppid(); /* Get parent's PID. */

    while ( !done ) {
      ❶ usleep(random() % 400000);   /* Delay a random bit to slow program. */
        lseek(fd, pos, SEEK_SET);    /* Move to saved last position in case
                                        parent moved file offset.           */
        if ( -1 == write(fd, data, strlen(data)) ) /* Write more data.      */
            fatal_error(errno, "write");
        pos = lseek(fd, 0, SEEK_END); /* Save file offset.                  */
        if ( ++count < 20 ) {        /* Continue writing.                   */
            kill(ppid, SIGUSR1);     /* Notify parent to keep reading.      */
            pause();                 /* Wait for signal from parent.        */
        } else {
            kill(ppid, SIGUSR2);     /* Notify parent that writing is done.*/
            done = TRUE;             /* Exit loop.                          */
        }
    }
    exit(EXIT_SUCCESS);
}
```

```
int main(int argc, char *argv[])
{
    const int CHUNKSIZE = 8;
    char      buffer[CHUNKSIZE+1];
    int       pos = 0;

    // OMITTED: Check usage and exit if incorrect.
    int    fd = open(argv[1], O_CREAT | O_RDWR |  O_TRUNC, 0644 );
    pid_t pid = fork();
    if ( -1 == pid )
        fatal_error(errno, "fork");
    else if ( 0 == pid )
        produce_data(fd);    /* Child produces data and writes to file. */
    else {
        // OMITTED: Install SIGUSR1 and SIGUSR2 handlers.
        while ( TRUE ) {
            pause();
            int unread_bytes = lseek(fd, 0, SEEK_END) - pos;
            lseek(fd, pos, SEEK_SET);       /* Move offset to saved position. */
            while ( unread_bytes >= CHUNKSIZE ) {
                if ( -1 == (bytes_read = read(fd, buffer, CHUNKSIZE)) )
                    fatal_error(errno, "read");
                if ( bytes_read != CHUNKSIZE )
                    fatal_error(-1, "read");
                unread_bytes -= CHUNKSIZE;
                buffer[CHUNKSIZE] = '\0';
                printf("%s\n", buffer);
            }
❷     if ( done ) {  /* Child exited, so read last bytes of the file. */
                if ( -1 == read(fd, buffer, unread_bytes) )
                    // OMITTED: Handle error.
                buffer[unread_bytes] = '\0';    /* Null-terminate to print. */
                printf("%s\n", buffer);         /* Print to terminal.    */
                close(fd);                      /* Close descriptor.     */
                exit(EXIT_SUCCESS);             /* Exit.                 */
            }
            else {
                pos = lseek(fd, 0, SEEK_CUR); /* Save position of last read.*/
                kill(pid, SIGUSR1);         /* Signal child to produce data. */
            }
        }
    }
}
```

Listing 11-4: A program that synchronizes parent and child access to a shared file using signals

Both processes register the same signal handler, usr_handler(), which does nothing when it catches SIGUSR1 since there's nothing for it to do, but when it catches SIGUSR2, it implies that the child sent the signal to the parent, and it sets the global atomic variable done to TRUE. When the parent reaches the test of done ❷, if the child has terminated, the parent executes the code that drains the last data in the file, prints it, and exits.

The child has an artificial delay to slow the program down ❶, and it iterates a fixed number of times to print a small amount of data to the file. Both processes save the offset as they work because the other process moves it to do its work. When you run this program, you'll see the output from the parent process, eight characters per line:

```
$ ./sync_io_demo /tmp/newfile
abcdefgh
ijklmnop
rst:abcd
efghijkl
--snip--
```

You can verify from the output that no data is lost or duplicated. You can also look at the file, folded into eight-character lines, to compare:

```
$ fold -w8 /tmp/newfile
abcdefgh
ijklmnop
rst:abcd
efghijkl
--snip--
```

This example is a prelude to the topic of interprocess communication, which we cover in depth in Chapters 12, 13, and 14.

Other Functions That Create Processes

The original implementation of fork() was time consuming and wasteful of memory because it duplicated the parent's entire memory image. Very often, after a fork(), the child process replaced the program it was executing immediately, making all of that copying needless. Because of this, 3.0BSD Unix introduced an alternative method of process creation which was named vfork(). This call was more efficient. Rather than making a complete copy of the address space of the old process, the vfork() call created a new process without copying the data and stack segments of the parent and instead allowed the child process to share these.

This saved time and memory but also raised the possibility that the child would inadvertently corrupt the state of the parent process. It wasn't intended to be used to allow the child and parent to share data; on the contrary, its purpose was to avoid the extensive memory copying in the case that the child would replace its program anyway with a call to execve(), which we'll discuss soon. The vfork() system call disappeared for a while and was reincarnated in a different form in NetBSD and then incorporated into Linux. The call has significant problems. The Linux man page states

> Some consider the semantics of vfork() to be an architectural blemish, and the 4.2BSD man page stated: "This system call will be eliminated when proper system sharing mechanisms are implemented."

There is also a clone() system call in Linux systems. The clone() function, which is technically a library routine wrapping a system call, allows the child to share the address space with its parent, and also lets the programmer pass a function and arguments for the child to execute.

Terminating Processes

Most beginning C programmers use the return statement to terminate their programs. Sometimes this is sufficient. In fact, executing the C return statement in the main() function is equivalent to calling the exit() function if the return type is integer. If it isn't an integer type, the value returned to the host environment (for example, bash) is undefined.

We've used the exit() function many times in various demonstration programs. We did this as a way to terminate the calling process no matter where it was in the program code in order to bail out and return an integer value when some error condition arose. But the exit() function does much more than this. Its synopsis is:

```
#include <stdlib.h>
void exit(int status);
```

Three actions take place when exit() is called:

1. The process's registered exit functions run.
2. The system gets a chance to clean up after the process.
3. The process gets a chance to have a status value delivered to its parent.

An *exit function* is a function that has been registered to run when the exit() library function is called. The atexit() function is used for registering exit functions. I'll explain how to register exit functions shortly.

There are several reasons why we might want a function to run when exit() is called. Imagine that when your program terminates, it has to update a log file. Suppose the function that does this is named update_log(). Suppose also that the program is very large, that there are multiple points at which exit() is called, and that more than one programmer is maintaining this program. If the exit() function didn't provide a means of invoking user-defined exit routines, then each time that anyone modified the program to insert a new call to exit(), they'd have to remember to call update_log() first. However, by registering update_log() to run whenever exit() is called, it makes the programmer's job easier, since they don't have to worry about forgetting to include the call when the program is modified.

To be precise, when exit() is called, the following actions take place in the given order:

1. All functions registered to run with atexit() are run in the reverse order in which they were registered.

2. All of the file streams opened through the Standard I/O Library are flushed and closed.

3. The kernel's _exit() function is called, passing the status argument of exit() to it.

We can register an exit function by calling atexit(). There is a non-portable *glibc* function like it named on_exit() as well, but we're discouraged from using it. The atexit(3) man page explains how to register exit functions. Its synopsis is:

```
#include <stdlib.h>
int atexit(void (*function)(void));
```

It's given the name of a function with a void return type and no arguments and returns 0 on success. For example:

```
void paythebill()
{
    printf("I'll pay the bill before I leave.\n");
}
if ( 0 != atexit(paythebill) )
    // OMITTED: Handle not being able to register paythebill().
```

Child processes inherit the exit functions registered by the parent when fork() created them.

If more than one function is registered, they're run in the reverse of the order in which they were registered (in other words, in last-in-first-out order). After the registered functions run, the exit() function flushes the streams and closes the files. The exit() function then calls _exit(), passing it whatever argument it received from the calling process. The kernel's _exit() function does the following:

1. Closes any open file descriptors, not just those opened through Standard I/O Library functions

2. Releases all memory belonging to the process

3. Makes init the parent of all children of the exiting process

4. Makes the low-order 8 bits of the integer argument to exit(), called its *exit status*, available to the parent process (I'll discuss how the parent can retrieve this exit status in "Waiting for Children" on page 569)

5. Under normal circumstances, which I'll explain in "Waiting for Children," generates a SIGCHLD signal to be sent to the parent process

Let's look at a simple example that shows how to use exit functions. The program in Listing 11-5 registers four functions prior to exiting by executing its return statement.

atexit_demo.c
```
void lockingup(void)
{
    printf("Locking up. Goodbye.\n");
}

void mopper(void)
{
    printf("Mopping the floors.\n");
}

void sweeper(void)
{
    printf("Sweeping the floor and wiping down counters.\n");
}

void supervisor(void)
{
    printf("Time to clean up.\n");
}

int main(void)
{
    long max_exit_functions = sysconf(_SC_ATEXIT_MAX);

    printf("The maximum number of exit functions is %ld\n",
            max_exit_functions);
    if ( (atexit(lockingup)) != 0 )
        fatal_error(errno, "cannot set exit function\n");
    if ( (atexit(mopper)) != 0 )
        fatal_error(errno, "cannot set exit function\n");
    if ( (atexit(sweeper)) != 0 )
        fatal_error(errno, "cannot set exit function\n");
    if ( (atexit(supervisor)) != 0 )
```

```
        fatal_error(errno, "cannot set exit function\n");
    return EXIT_SUCCESS; /* return invokes exit(). */
}
```

Listing 11-5: A program that registers a few exit functions and then returns

When we build the executable and run it, we'll see that the order of execution of the functions is opposite to the order in which they were registered:

```
$ ./atexit_demo
The maximum number of exit functions is 2147483647
Time to clean up.
Sweeping the floor and wiping down counters.
Mopping the floors.
Locking up. Goodbye.
```

Process termination plays an important role in programming when we start to write programs that create other processes. When a process that we've created terminates, we need to make sure we've cleaned up after it so that we don't hold onto unneeded resources. We'll also see that when we do it the right way, it's a chance for the parent process to be notified of the reason that its child terminated. That's the subject of "Waiting for Children" on page 569.

Executing Programs

Typically, when a process calls fork(), it's so that the new process can execute a different program. If there were no way for the new process to do that, then every process in the system would be executing the same program! In "The Lifetime of a Process" on page 540, I mentioned that execve() is the system call that a process calls to change the program that it executes. We could also discover this via a man page search:

```
$ apropos -s2 -a execute program
execve (2)            - execute program
execveat (2)          - execute program relative to a directory file descriptor
```

The execve() system call, as well as each of a set of library functions collectively known as the exec() functions, provides the means for a process to change the program that it's executing as well as its entire memory image. Although there are several different library functions in this exec() family, they have one thing in common—they change the program that the calling process executes to a program identified in their argument list. They differ in the way that the program and its arguments are passed to them. We'll first look at the system call and then at the various library functions built on top of it.

The execve() System Call

The man page synopsis for execve() is:

```
#include <unistd.h>
int execve(const char *pathname, char *const argv[], char *const envp[]);
```

The execve() system call replaces the program being executed by the calling process with the program whose pathname is its first argument. The filename must be a binary executable or a script whose first line is:

```
#! interpreter [optional-arg]
```

The filename must be the absolute or relative pathname of the program, since execve() does not use the PATH environment variable to search for the directory containing that filename. The second and third arguments are NULL-terminated arrays of arguments and environment strings, respectively. In other words, each is an array of strings followed by a NULL pointer, such as was depicted in Figure 2-4 in Chapter 2. For convenience, the argv[] parameter is shown in Figure 11-4.

argv[0]	argv[1]	. . .	argv[n-1]	NULL
0	1		n-1	

Figure 11-4: The argv array passed to execve()

The environment strings are expected to be in the proper format, meaning each is of the form *key=value*.

The execve() system call is so-named because arrays are also called *vectors*; the *ve* part of the name is a reminder that execve expects vectors for its second and third arguments. (The original implementation referred to argv[0], argv[1], ..., 0 as a vector.) The execve() function passes these vectors to the program to be executed, which will be able to access them in its own argument list:

```
int main(int argc, char *argv[], char **envp)
```

Since all programs expect the program name in argv[0] and their first argument in argv[1], it's important that our programs arrange the argument list to satisfy this condition before they call execve(). The examples that follow shortly will demonstrate.

Remember that the process itself is not being replaced, just what it executes. In particular, the call to execve() causes the program currently run by the process to be replaced by the given program. That program is in a new text segment, with a new stack, heap, initialized data segment, and uninitialized data segment. Since the same process continues to execute the new program, almost all of its attributes remain the same. For example, all of its identifiers, such as its PID, PPID, and so on, are preserved. Particularly important is that the process's control terminal stays the same; open file descriptors remain open after the call, with a few exceptions; and the working directory is preserved. We'll see why this is important in Chapter 13.

The execve() man page has a complete list of what is and is not preserved in the process descriptor, and Chapter 10 contains a summary as well. Some key points to remember are:

- Signal dispositions are reset to their defaults if they had handlers.

- Pending signals are preserved.

- Masks such as the umask and signal mask are preserved.

- Open directory streams are closed.

- Time remaining on alarm clocks is preserved.

- Interval timers are preserved but POSIX timers (those created by timer_create()) are not.

- Exit functions are not preserved.

- The locale is set to the default C locale.

A successful call to execve() does not return. If it does return, something went wrong; the program that was supposed to be executed never ran, and execve() returns -1. For example, given this code

```
execve("myprog", argv, envp);
printf("If you're seeing this, myprog did not run.\n");
```

printf() can be executed only if execve() returned. There's no need to check its return value since it must be -1, but the error code in errno will indicate what went wrong.

We'll begin our exploration with a trivial example named *execve_demo1.c* that shows the mechanics of calling execve(). After that, we'll look at a program designed to provide some insight into more general ways to invoke it. After these two programs, we'll look at how to use the different library wrappers for execve().

The following program hardcodes the name of the executable to run, */bin/date*, into the call to execve() so that it always runs the date command and passes its command line arguments to date:

execve_demo1.c
```
#include "common_hdrs.h"

int main(int argc, char *argv[], char *envp[])
{
    if ( argc < 2 )
        usage_error("execve_demo1 <words to display>\n");
    argv[0] = "date";
    execve("/bin/date", argv, envp);
    fatal_error(errno, "execve");  /* If we reach here, it's bad news! */
}
```

The program replaces the contents of argv[0] with date because the */bin/date* program should be given its own name, not the name *execve_demo1*. If the date program finds an error in its usage, it will use the name in its argv[0] string in its usage message. When we run it

```
$ ./execve_demo1 -d tomorrow +"Tomorrow is %A."
Tomorrow is Tuesday.
```

we see that the program just runs the date command with the arguments that it's given. Try changing argv[0] to some other string and running the program with invalid options; you'll see how argv[0] is used.

The second program, *execve_demo2.c*, is in Listing 11-6. It runs the program specified as its first command line argument, passing it the remaining command line arguments. The program is designed to demonstrate a few ideas about the use of execve().

execve_demo2.c
```
#define _GNU_SOURCE          /* For basename() */
#include "common_hdrs.h"

int main(int argc, char *argv[])
{
    if ( argc < 2 )
        usage_error("execve_demo1: program-to-execute [arguments]");
    char *new_env[] = {"AUTHOR=stewart", "CHAPTER=Process Creation", NULL};
    char *path = strdup(argv[1]);
    argv[1] = basename(argv[1]);
    printf("Program being executed is %s.\n", argv[1]);
    execve(path, argv+1, new_env);
    fatal_error(errno, "execve() failed to run.\n");
}
```

Listing 11-6: A program that calls execve(), with its first argument as the program to execute

First, this demonstrates that the environment vector passed to execve() can be any NULL-terminated array of strings in the proper form, not just the process's current environment. In this program, it replaces it completely with an environment consisting of two environment strings.

Second, the argument vector passed to execve() in its second argument is the set of words after the program name from the command line, which is pointed to by argv+1. The first word to be passed, argv[1], is the pathname of the actual program file to be executed. Although execve() must be given the path to the executable file as its first argument, the entire pathname shouldn't be the first word in the argument vector passed to it; in fact, many commands expect it to be just the base name of the file. For this reason, argv[1] is first copied into a second variable, path, and then it's stripped of the leading directories by a call to basename(). The copy, path, is passed to execve() as the program to execute.

You can run this program by passing the pathname to any executable file and the arguments for that file, as in:

```
$ ./execve_demo2 /bin/echo Hello World
Program being executed is /bin/echo.
Hello World
```

That file does not have to be a binary. For example, we can pass it the name of a shell script. The file *simplescript.sh* has two lines

```
#!/bin/bash
/usr/bin/echo "Hello World"
```

and because it's an executable file, we can pass it to execve_demo1 to execute

```
$ ./execve_demo2 simplescript.sh
Program being executed is simplescript.sh.
Hello World
```

showing that as long as the first line is that of an interpreter that can execute the rest of the file, execve() can run it.

The program in Listing 11-7, will be useful for showing how the various exec functions behave. It displays its argument vector and environment strings and does nothing else.

print_args_env.c
```
#include <stdio.h>
extern char **environ;

int main(int argc, char *argv[])
{
    for ( int i = 0; argv[i] != NULL; i++ )
        printf("argv[%d] = %s\n", i, argv[i]);
    char **envp = environ;
    while ( NULL != *envp) {
        printf("%s\n", *envp );
        envp++;
    }
    return 0;
}
```

Listing 11-7: A program that prints its arguments and environment strings

Let's suppose that the executable is installed in the */opt* directory so that we have to pass /opt/print_args_env to execve() to execute it. When we pass this program's pathname and a few arguments to execve_demo1, the output verifies that the environment was replaced:

```
$ ./execve_demo2 /opt/print_args_env This too shall pass.
Program being executed is /opt/print_args_env.
argv[0] = print_args_env
argv[1] = This
```

```
argv[2] = too
argv[3] = shall
argv[4] = pass.
AUTHOR=stewart
CHAPTER=Process Creation
```

Notice that the externally defined environ variable is pointing to the environ-ment constructed in execve_demo1 prior to calling execve(). This variable is initialized by execve() so that the process has access to the new environment when it runs the specified program.

The exec() Library Functions

Shortly after the first version of Unix was released, the Unix library was ex-tended to include a family of six functions layered on top of execve(), mostly to give programmers alternative ways to obtain its functionality. This family of functions is collectively called the exec() family. The differences among the functions are:

- Whether a pathname must be supplied to the function or a filename without any slashes can be given to it, in which case it searches for the file in the directories given in the PATH environment variable

- Whether the arguments are supplied as a NULL-terminated vector of strings or as a NULL-terminated list of strings

- Whether the environment for the new process image is passed by the calling process in a third argument envp or is instead taken from the external environ variable from the caller

The functions share a single man page, whose SYNOPSIS follows:

```
#include <unistd.h>

extern char **environ;

int execl(const char *pathname, const char *arg, ...  /* (char *) NULL */);
int execlp(const char *file, const char *arg, ...     /* (char *) NULL */);
int execle(const char *pathname, const char *arg, ... /* (char *) NULL,
           char *const envp[] */);
int execv(const char *pathname, char *const argv[]);
int execvp(const char *file, char *const argv[]);
❶ int execvpe(const char *file, char *const argv[], char *const envp[]);
```

Each of these contains either an *l* or a *v* in its name. The versions that contain an *l*—execl(), execlp(), and execle()—expect a NULL-terminated *list* of NULL-terminated string arguments, whereas the versions that contain a *v*—execv(), execvp(), and execvpe()—expect an array of NULL-terminated string arguments. The execvpe() function ❶ is a GNU extension, not necessarily available in POSIX-conforming distributions, and you need to define _GNU_SOURCE to use it.

The functions are also distinguished by whether or not they contain a *p* in their names. The versions that don't contain a *p* in their names—execl(), execle(), and execv()—require that the first argument is either an absolute pathname or a relative pathname to the executable program file. The versions that do contain a *p*—execlp() and execvp()—don't require a pathname to the executable program file; if the filename contains no slashes, they use the PATH environment variable to search for the file. If the environment doesn't contain a PATH variable, they search a standard sequence of directories, which is system dependent. Table 11-1 summarizes the different functions based on these categories.

Table 11-1: The exec Family of Functions

Function name	Executable's specification	Argument specification	Environment
execl()	Pathname	List	Caller's environ variable
execlp()	Filename	List	Caller's environ variable
execle()	Pathname	List	envp argument
execv()	Pathname	Array	Caller's environ variable
execvp()	Filename	Array	Caller's environ variable
execvpe()	Filename	Array	envp argument

If our program calls one of the functions that expects an array for the second argument, it should arrange for argv[0] to be the name of the executable file. If it calls a function that expects a list after the executable's name, it should arrange for the first list element to be the name of the executable.

The advantage of the functions expecting a list is that the calling program doesn't need to construct a vector to pass as an argument, which takes extra steps. The major disadvantage of these list-expecting functions is that we can only use them if we know at compile time exactly how many arguments the executable needs. To make this clear, suppose that we'd like to call execl() to execute */bin/ls* on the directories that we pass on the command line. Suppose our program is named do_ls and we can call it with an unpredictable number of arguments, such as:

```
$ ./do_ls dir1 dir2 dir3 > /dev/null
$ ./do_ls dir1 dir2 dir3 dir4 dir5 > /dev/null
```

What should the call to execl() look like in *do_ls.c*? For the first call, it can be

```
execl("/bin/ls", "ls", argv[1], argv[2], argv[3], (char*) NULL);
```

but for the second, it needs to be:

```
execl("/bin/ls", "ls", argv[1], argv[2], argv[3], argv[4], (char*) NULL);
```

There's no easy way to use this function if we don't know how many arguments it needs at the time we write the program. The vector-expecting functions don't pose this problem, since we can pass an entire vector by its address. Therefore, in the example programs that follow, which are designed to show the differences between how you call the various functions, I've assumed a fixed number of arguments. In practice, we wouldn't code like this!

Each of the following programs demonstrates how to use one of these library functions to run a command given as its first command line argument, expecting at least three words after the command name. If the number of arguments is fewer than three, it exits. I give examples of each of execl(), execlp(), and execle(), but not of execv() or execvpe(), since the first is essentially like execve() without the last parameter, and the second is like a combination of execvp() and execve(). I'll start with an example of the use of execl(), in Listing 11-8.

execl_demo.c
```
#define _GNU_SOURCE
#include "common_hdrs.h"

int main(int argc, char *argv[])
{
    if ( argc < 5 )
        usage_error("execl_demo command arg1 arg2 arg3\n");
    char *path = strdup(argv[1]);
    char *filename = basename(path);
    execl(argv[1], filename, argv[2], argv[3], argv[4], (char *) NULL);
    fatal_error(errno, "execl");
}
```

Listing 11-8: A program using execl() to run a given command on its argument list, consisting of three words

Notice that the command line options have to be passed as separate words in the list. This program checks that there are at least five words on its command line; it ignores extras if there are any.

When we pass /opt/print_args_env a b c to this program, the output is:

```
$ ./execl_demo /opt/print_args_env a b c
argv[0] = print_args_env
argv[1] = a
argv[2] = b
argv[3] = c
SHELL=/bin/bash
COLORTERM=truecolor
LANGUAGE=en_US
```

The program in Listing 11-9 uses execlp() instead. The only difference is that it doesn't need a pathname; we can pass print_args_env on the command line and the program finds its location.

execlp_demo.c
```
#include "common_hdrs.h"

int main(int argc, char *argv[])
{
    char *p;
    if ( argc < 5 )
```

```
        usage_error("execl_demo command arg1 arg2 arg3\n");
    if ( NULL == (p = strrchr(argv[1], '/')) )  /* No '/' in name */
        execlp(argv[1], argv[1], argv[2], argv[3], argv[4], (char *) NULL);
    else                            /* Pass the string after the '/'. */
        execlp(argv[1], p+1, argv[2], argv[3], argv[4], (char *) NULL);
    fatal_error(errno, "execlp");
}
```

Listing 11-9: A program using execlp() to run a given command on its argument list, consisting of three words

If the user passes a pathname instead of a filename, the program needs to pass only the portion of that pathname after the last / character. It could call basename(), but calling strchr() avoids allocating memory for basename(), which can alter its argument. Running this instead of execlp_demo, we see:

```
$ ./execlp_demo print_args_env a b c
argv[0] = print_args_env
argv[1] = a
argv[2] = b
argv[3] = c
SHELL=/bin/bash
COLORTERM=truecolor
LANGUAGE=en_US
```

The execle() function is like execve() except that it expects a list instead of a vector. In Listing 11-10, we get a chance to pass it an environment in its last parameter.

execle_demo.c
```
#define _GNU_SOURCE
#include "common_hdrs.h"

int main (int argc, char *argv[])
{
    if ( argc < 5 )
        usage_error("execl_demo command arg1 arg2 arg3\n");
    char *new_env[] = {"AUTHOR=stewart", "CHAPTER=Process Creation", NULL};
    char *path = strdup(argv[1]);
    char *file = basename(path);
    execle(argv[1], file, argv[2], argv[3], argv[4], (char*) NULL, new_env);
    fatal_error(errno, "execve() failed to run.\n");
}
```

Listing 11-10: A program using execle() to run a given command on its argument list, consisting of three words

Running this program on the same arguments as the previous two, we see:

```
$ ./execle_demo /opt/print_args_env a b c
argv[0] = print_args_env
argv[1] = a
```

```
argv[2] = b
argv[3] = c
AUTHOR=stewart
CHAPTER=Process Creation
```

The last library function that I will include here is execvp(), shown in Listing 11-11. It is like execve() except that it uses the caller's environ variable and it does not need a pathname.

execvp_demo.c
```
#define _GNU_SOURCE
#include "common_hdrs.h"

int main(int argc, char *argv[])
{
    char *p;
    if ( argc < 5 )
        usage_error("execvp_demo command arg1 arg2 arg3\n");
    if ( NULL == (p = strrchr(argv[1], '/')) )
        execvp(argv[1], argv+1);
    else {
        argv[1]= p+1;
        execvp(argv[1], argv+1);
    }
    fatal_error(errno, "execvlp");
}
```

Listing 11-11: A program using execvp() to run a given command on its argument list, consisting of three words

If you run this program with the same command line as the previous exec programs, you'll see that the output is exactly the same as the output of execlp_demo.

Waiting for Children

When a parent process creates one or more child processes, it usually needs to know when they completed the tasks they were delegated and whether they exited normally or encountered errors or other abnormal conditions that prevented their completing them successfully. A parent process is also supposed to assist the kernel in releasing resources held by its child processes when they terminate. The wait() system call and its relatives serve this purpose; they complete the quartet of system calls related to process control—fork(), exec(), exit(), and now, wait(). Although in "The Lifetime of a Process" on page 540 I mentioned the wait() system call, if we didn't know about it, we'd discover it through a man page search such as:

```
$ apropos -s2,3 -a child process
--snip--
wait (3posix)        - wait for a child process to stop or terminate
--snip--
```

This page is the POSIX specification of the wait() system call, not the Linux page for it. There's a separate Section 2 man page for wait() as well.

Since Linux 2.6, the Linux version has conformed to the POSIX requirements; let's look at the Linux wait(2) man page first. That page's SYNOPSIS is:

```
#include <sys/types.h>
#include <sys/wait.h>

pid_t wait(int *status);
pid_t waitpid(pid_t pid, int *status, int options);
int   waitid(idtype_t idtype, id_t id, siginfo_t *infop, int options);
```

The status parameter in wait() and waitpid() is the address of an integer variable in which to store the terminated child's exit status. If the parent doesn't care about that status, it can pass NULL as an argument instead. These two calls suspend the calling process until a child terminates. Termination is a state change, but not the only one. When a process is stopped by a signal or resumed by one, these are also state changes. The third system call, waitid(), is more general than the others because it allows a parent to wait for any of these state changes in a child.

The wait() and waitpid() System Calls

The wait() and waitpid() system calls serve a few purposes:

- To allow a parent process to block itself until a child has terminated.

- To allow a parent process to collect, or *reap*, the status of a child that has terminated.

- To allow the kernel to release the resources associated with the child process. If a parent does not perform a wait of one kind or another, the kernel must retain certain information and resources for that child, and the terminated child remains in a *zombie* state.

ABOUT ZOMBIE PROCESSES AND WAITS

A child that has terminated but hasn't been waited for is called a *zombie* in Unix. The kernel can't release all of the resources held by this zombie process in case its parent performs a wait for it later. In particular, it preserves, at the very least, its slot in the kernel's process table, its PID, termination status, and resource usage information. As long as a zombie is not removed from the system by a wait operation, it occupies this slot. If the table fills, the kernel won't be able to create new processes. Processes such as continuously running servers that create child processes can quickly cause this problem if they don't reap their children. If a parent process terminates, its zombie children are adopted by init, which eventually performs a wait to remove the zombies. By calling one of the wait functions, parent processes tell the kernel that it can release these resources.

To facilitate the description of these system calls, the Unix and POSIX documentation define a child process that has terminated to be *waitable* if its parent has not yet waited for it.

The wait() System Call

I'll begin by discussing the simpler of these two calls: wait(). When a process calls wait(), if it has no waitable children, it's blocked until *any one* of its children terminates. If it has one or more waitable children, it isn't blocked and the call returns immediately. The return value of a successful wait() is the PID of some child that terminated, whether it's one of the waitable ones or one that terminated after the call. It doesn't matter which child terminated; the call returns if any child did. If a process calls wait() but has no unwaited-for children, this is an error; wait() returns -1 immediately and sets errno to ECHILD. Note that waitable children are unwaited-for children.

In the simple case of a process creating a single child and waiting for it, the typical way to use wait() is of the form:

```
int   child_status, exit_value;
pid_t child_pid, result;

if ( -1 == (result = fork()) )
    fatal_error(errno, "fork");
else if ( 0 == result ) {        /* Child does stuff here. */
    exit(exit_value);
}
else { /* Parent waits for child. */
    if ( (child_pid = wait(&child_status)) == -1 )
        if ( ECHILD != errno )
            fatal_error(errno, "wait");  /* Error in wait() */
    /* Parent does stuff using child's pid and exit status. */
}
```

When a process has created multiple children, it's a bit different. In order to wait for all of them, it needs to put the call to wait() in a loop. Since wait() sets errno to ECHILD when a process has no unwaited-for children, we can make that the stopping condition of the loop, as shown in Listing 11-12.

```
wait_demo1.c   #include "common_hdrs.h"
               #include <sys/wait.h>

               int main(int argc, char *argv[])
               {
                   pid_t pid;
                   int   i, num_children = 4;

                   for ( i = 0; i < num_children; i++ ) {
                       switch ( fork() ) {
                       case -1:
```

```
            fatal_error(errno, "fork");        /* Error in fork()  */
        case 0:
            sleep(2);                  /* Children sleep and then exit. */
            exit(i);
        default:
            break;                  /* Parent just waits for children. */
        }
    }
    while ( (pid = wait(NULL)) != -1 )     /* Ignore exit status. */
        printf("Child %d terminated.\n", pid);
    if ( ECHILD != errno )
        fatal_error(errno, "wait");
    exit(EXIT_SUCCESS); /* If we reach here, we waited for all children. */
}
```

Listing 11-12: A program that creates multiple child processes and waits for all of them

The parent process in *wait_demo1.c*, ignores the exit status of its terminating children by passing NULL to wait(). The loop iterates until wait() returns -1 and ECHILD == errno.

Let's focus on the status parameter of wait() and waitpid(). When a child calls any of the exit() family of functions, passing an integer exit status, or if it executes a return statement from its main() function and passes an integer to it, the kernel arranges for the least significant byte (LSB) of that value to be collectible by the parent process through a call to any of the wait() family of system calls. In a call such as wait(&status), the parameter (status) is the address of an int variable that receives information about how the child terminated. POSIX doesn't specify how this variable is structured, but the traditional layout, which is the one currently used by Linux, is visualized in Figure 11-5.

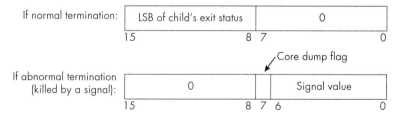

Figure 11-5: A traditional arrangement of bits of the status available from the call wait(&status)

If the child terminated normally by calling exit(), then the second byte (bits 8 through 15) of status contains the low-order byte of the value the child passed to the exit() call, and the low-order byte of status is 0. If the child terminated abnormally because of an unhandled signal, the low-order seven bits of status contain the signal value. If the child was terminated by a signal that caused a core dump, then bit 7 is set.

The fact that a core dump is supposed to occur does not mean that there will be a core file in your working directory. If the system administrator has disabled them for all users or if your shell limits them, then it won't exist.

Because the exact layout is system dependent, code based on this layout may not be portable. Instead, we're encouraged to use the macros specifically designed for this purpose, which are described in the wait(2) man page and specified in POSIX.1-2024. In these macros, status_val is the actual integer pointed to by the status parameter; it isn't its address.

WIFEXITED(status_val)   Evaluates to nonzero if the child exited normally

WEXITSTATUS(status_val)   If the value of WIFEXITED(status_val) is nonzero, evaluates to the low-order 8 bits of the argument that the child passed to exit() or _exit(), or the value that it returned from main()

WIFSIGNALED(status_val)   Evaluates to nonzero if the child was terminated by a signal

WTERMSIG(status_val)   The number of the signal that terminated the child, but only if WIFSIGNALED(status_val) is nonzero

WCOREDUMP(status_val)   If WIFSIGNALED(status_val) is nonzero, evaluates to nonzero if the signal caused a core dump

Note that systems that aren't POSIX compliant may not support these macros; if you want to make your program portable, you'll need feature-test macros in your code.

Let's take a look at an example program that puts all of these macros to use. The program *wait_demo2.c*, shown in Listing 11-13, creates a single child process and waits for its termination.

wait_demo2.c
```c
#include "common_hdrs.h"
#include <sys/wait.h>

int main(int argc, char *argv[])
{
    pid_t pid;
    int    status;

    switch ( fork() ) {
    case -1:
        fatal_error(errno, "fork");
    case 0:
        if ( argc == 1 ) {
            printf("Child PID = %d\n", getpid());
            pause();              /* Wait for signal.     */
        }
        exit(atoi(argv[1]));    /* No error-checking here! */
    default:
        if ( (pid = wait(&status)) != -1 ) {
            printf("Child %d terminated ", pid);
```

```
            if ( WIFEXITED(status) )
                printf("with exit status %d.\n", WEXITSTATUS(status));
            else if ( WIFSIGNALED(status) ) {
                printf("as a result of signal %d", WTERMSIG(status));
                if ( WCOREDUMP(status) )
                    printf(" and a core dump took place");
                printf(".\n");
            }
        }
        else if ( ECHILD != errno )
            fatal_error(errno, "wait");
        exit(EXIT_SUCCESS);
    }
}
```

Listing 11-13: A program that shows how to use the status-checking macros

If the program is run with an integer command line argument, that argument is used as the argument to exit() in the child. If you run it without a command line argument, the child process prints its PID so that you can send it a signal. It will remain suspended in this case until it receives a terminating signal. The parent waits for the child and uses the macros to check the child's termination status. Here are a few runs of the program:

```
$ ./wait_demo2 32
Child 17176 terminated with exit status 32.
$ ./wait_demo2 356
Child 17193 terminated with exit status 100.
$ ./wait_demo2
Child PID = 17238    # From a second terminal, issue "kill -1 17238
Child 17238 terminated as a result of signal 1.
$ ./wait_demo2
Child PID = 18175
Child 18175 terminated as a result of signal 3 and a core dump took place.
```

The first run causes the parent to display the child's normal termination exit status, the number entered as the command line argument. The second run shows that only the low-order byte is taken as its exit status, since 356 = 256 + 100. The next two runs show that the parent detects that the child was killed by a signal, one causing a core dump and the other not.

The waitpid() System Call

One problem with wait() is that if a process has multiple children, wait() can't be used to wait for a specific child. Another problem is that if no children have terminated when the parent calls it, the parent blocks until some child terminates. Sometimes it would be better if the parent could call it and return immediately if no child exited yet. A third problem is that wait() can't be used to detect when a child process has been stopped by a signal, such as SIGSTOP.

The `waitpid()` call addresses all of these deficiencies. It has three parameters:

```
pid_t waitpid(pid_t pid, int *wstatus, int options);
```

The first parameter specifies the set of child processes for which the calling process should wait:

pid > 0 Wait for the child with PID = `pid`.

pid = 0 Wait for only those children in the same process group as the parent.

pid = -1 Wait for any child, like `wait()`.

pid < -1 Wait for any child whose process group ID is equal to the absolute value of `pid`.

In this sense it is a generalization of `wait()`, since the call

```
pid_t child_pid = wait(&child_status);
```

is equivalent to:

```
pid_t child_pid = waitpid(-1, &child_status, 0);
```

The second parameter in `waitpid()` serves the exact same purpose as it does in `wait()`. The third (`options`) is a bitwise-OR of zero or more of the following flags:

WNOHANG When set, the process returns immediately if no child has exited yet.

WUNTRACED When set, in addition to returning if a child terminates, the process also returns when a child has stopped.

WCONTINUED When set, since Linux 2.6.10, the call also returns if a child is resumed by receiving a `SIGCONT` signal.

These enhancements make it possible to track children in a more precise way. Being able to wait for a specific child allows the parent to take different actions depending on which child finished. This feature is needed when different functions within a process must wait for different children to terminate. Being able to return immediately if no children have terminated makes it possible for the parent to periodically check for termination of children inside a loop and continue to perform other work. The ability to detect whether a child has been stopped or restarted is mostly useful for job control, as when a user suspends and resumes processes from the keyboard. In this case, a parent process, such as a shell that has spawned multiple children, can detect when any of these have changed state.

The next program demonstrates some of the functionality of `waitpid()` that `wait()` lacks. It models the producer-consumer problem that I described earlier in "Process Synchronization with Signals" on page 553. In the *sync_io _demo.c* program in that section, the child and parent processes played the role of the producer and consumer, respectively. Here, the program will create two children that will act as the producer and the consumer, and the parent process will monitor their behavior. The producer will write text to a shared file, and the consumer will read text from that file and convert it to uppercase before printing it.

The structure of this program is similar to the way in which a shell sets up the execution of a two-step pipelined command such as:

```
sort myfile | cut -d, -f1
```

A shell such as bash creates two child processes: one to run the left-hand side command (sort) and the other to run the right-hand side (cut). The shell itself is their parent, and it's able to monitor the two child processes in the same way that this program will. Figure 11-6 depicts this program structure.

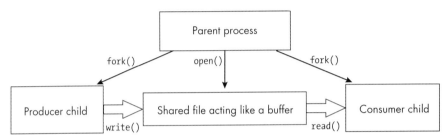

Figure 11-6: The structure of the producer-consumer program in which the main program forks two children that act as producer and consumer

The significance of this exercise is not in the actions of the child processes, but in how the parent process utilizes waitpid() to detect state changes in the children as they're running. Additionally, it presents another way for two processes that share an open file descriptor to read and write that open file without a race condition.

To simplify its design and to show why being able to wait for a specific process is useful, the program is designed to detect whether the producer process stopped or terminated before it checks on the consumer child. If it detects any state change in the producer, it prints a message to the terminal, but if the producer terminated, it stops monitoring the producer and starts to monitor the consumer. It could be modified so that if the producer stopped, the parent would send a signal to the consumer to stop as well and to resume only when the producer continues. We could also modify it so that when the producer terminates, the parent would automatically terminate the consumer. This version, for the sake of simplicity, does neither.

The basic logic of the main program in pseudocode is as follows:

```
Open a temporary file for reading and writing.
Create the producer (PID = pid[0]) and consumer (PID = pid[1]) processes.
Repeat the following instructions until the producer terminates: {
    Call waitpid(pid[0], ..., WNOHANG) to check on state changes in the
        producer without blocking;
    If the producer's state changed,
        Print a message to the terminal indicating the state change, and
```

If it terminated,
Break out of this loop.
Simulate doing other work by sleeping a bit.
}
Repeat the following instructions until the consumer terminates: {
Call waitpid(pid[1], ..., WNOHANG) to check on state changes in the
consumer without blocking;
If the consumer's state changed,
Print a message to the terminal indicating the state change, and
If it terminated,
Break out of this loop, close the file, and terminate.
Simulate doing other work by sleeping a bit.
}

The call to waitpid() becomes:

```
retval = waitpid(pid[i], &status, WUNTRACED | WCONTINUED | WNOHANG)
```

It will return a positive number only if the process has exited or was terminated or stopped by a signal or continued by a signal after it was stopped. If
it returns 0, there was no state change in the process.

The loops to reap the producer and consumer are easily merged into a
single loop in the main() function whose form, without error checking, is:

```
int i = 0;
do {
    if ( -1 == (retval = waitpid(pid[i],&status,WUNTRACED|WCONTINUED|WNOHANG)))
        // OMITTED: Handle the error from waitpid().
    else if ( 0 == retval )
        continue;  /* No state change detected.   */
    else {         /* A state change was detected. */
    ❶ // OMITTED: Call a function to print child state change.
        if ( WIFEXITED(status) || (WIFSIGNALED(status)) )
            if ( i++ == 0 )
                // OMITTED: Print a message that producer terminated.
    }
    sleep(1); /* Would do other work here */
} while ( i < 2 );
```

To handle the printing of the state change ❶, we'll create a utility function that
uses the predefined macros to print the detected status information. This is
called only after the program receives a successful return from waitpid():

print_status()
```
void print_status(pid_t pid, int status)
{
    if ( WIFEXITED(status) )
        printf("Process %d exited with status %d\n", pid, WEXITSTATUS(status));
    else if ( WIFSIGNALED(status) )
        printf("Process %d terminated by signal %d\n", pid, WTERMSIG(status));
```

```
    else if ( WIFSTOPPED(status) )
        printf("Process %d stopped by signal %d\n", pid, WSTOPSIG(status));
    else if ( WIFCONTINUED(status) )
        printf("Process %d continued\n", pid);
}
```

Because the rest of the main() function is straightforward, we'll turn to the design of the producer and the consumer processes. These will be encapsulated into two functions within this single program, rather than as separate programs to be exec-ed. The processes therefore share the open file descriptor that they inherit from the parent. As an abstraction of what a producer and consumer do, the producer will write a sequence of *p* characters to the file and the consumer will read them and print them to the terminal as proof that it received them.

In *sync_io_demo.c*, the child and parent prevented race conditions on the shared file offset by two measures:

- The file is opened with the O_APPEND file status flag so that writes by the producer are atomically appended to the end of the file.

- Access to the file by the child and parent was alternated by each sending a signal to the other when it was okay to access the file.

This is not ideal. To remove the race condition on the file offset in this program, we'll introduce a new system call. The race can occur, even with the O_APPEND flag set, because the consumer has to perform two actions to read its next character. It has to seek to the position in the file after the last character it read and then perform the read. If pos_to_read is the saved file offset after its last read, it needs to do

```
lseek(fd, pos_to_read, SEEK_SET);
read(fd, &nextchar, 1);
```

but the producer could slip in between these two steps, which are not a single atomic operation. We need a way to perform these two steps atomically.

Let's search the man pages for system calls related to reading and the file offset:

```
$ apropos -s2 -a read file offset
--snip--
pread (2)          - read from or write to a file descriptor at a given offset
pread64 (2)        - read from or write to a file descriptor at a given offset
pwrite (2)         - read from or write to a file descriptor at a given offset
pwrite64 (2)       - read from or write to a file descriptor at a given offset
```

The pread() and pread64() system calls do the same thing, but the latter is newer. According to the documentation, in recent versions of *glibc* (*glibc* version 2.12 or later), the wrapper function for pread() transparently chooses the best one for the given system. The synopsis for pread() is:

```
#include <unistd.h>
ssize_t pread(int fd, void *buf, size_t count, off_t offset);
```

This system call atomically reads from the open file descriptor fd at the specified offset relative to the beginning of the file. In other words, it moves the file offset, performs the indicated read, and restores the file offset afterward, without the possibility of interruption. The pwrite() call is analogous, and we could, if we wanted, use that instead of setting the O_APPEND flag on the file, but that would make the producer a bit more complex.

The producer code follows:

producer()
```
void producer(int fd)
{
    int   i;
    char mychar = 'p';
    printf("Producer is about to start producing data.\n");
    for ( i = 0; i < PRODUCE_TIME; i++ ) { /* PRODUCE_TIME is adjustable.  */
        usleep(500000);                    /* Delay a bit to slow program. */
        if ( -1 == write(fd, &mychar, 1) ) /* Atomically append to file.   */
            fatal_error(errno, "write");
    }
    printf("\nProducer (PID=%d) finished producing data; exiting\n", getpid());
    exit(PRODUCER_EXIT_VAL);               /* Some fixed exit value        */
}
```

The usleep() is inserted into the loop so that the producer doesn't finish before we get a chance to send it some signals and watch how the program reacts.

The consumer's code follows:

consumer()
```
void consumer(int fd, int flag)
{
    int    i;
    off_t pos_to_read = 0;
    int    nbytes;
    char   buffer, ch;

    if ( flag > 0 ) {
        printf("Send a signal to consumer (%d) to terminate it.\n", getpid());
        pause();  /* Wait for signals. */
    }
    printf("Data from producer, converted to uppercase:\n");
    for ( i = 0; i < CONSUME_TIME; i++ ) { /* CONSUME_TIME is adjustable. */
        sleep(1);                          /* Slow down the process.      */
❶      if ( -1 == (nbytes = pread(fd, &buffer, 1, pos_to_read)) )
            fatal_error(errno, "read");
        else if ( nbytes == 0 )
            break;                         /* End of data                 */
```

```
    else {
        pos_to_read++;                  /* Advance saved file offset.  */
        ch = toupper(buffer);           /* Convert to uppercase.       */
        write(STDOUT_FILENO, &ch, 1);   /* Print the character.        */
    }
}
exit(CONSUMER_EXIT_VAL);                 /* Some fixed exit value       */
}
```

The consumer is designed to allow the user to send signals to it without
having to rush. By passing it a positive flag value, we prevent it from printing
anything. Instead it suspends itself to wait for delivery of a signal. Since the
pause() system call returns only upon delivery of a terminating signal or one
for which a signal handler is installed, this design gives us a chance to send
SIGSTOP and SIGCONT signals to it repeatedly and watch how the parent responds
to them. Notice that the consumer calls pread() ❶ with the file offset that it
incremented in the previous loop iteration.

The last piece of the program is the main() function, most of which is
shown in Listing 11-14. The complete program, named *waitpid_demo.c*, is in
the book's source code distribution.

waitpid_demo.c
  main()
```
int main(int argc, char *argv[])
{
    pid_t pid[2];                       /* Store PIDs of two children.    */
    pid_t ret;                          /* Return value of waitpid()      */
    int   fd;                           /* File descriptor of opened file */
    int   status;                       /* Status of waited-on process    */
    --snip--
    if (-1 == (fd = open("/tmp/temp", O_CREAT|O_RDWR|O_TRUNC|O_APPEND, 0644)))
        fatal_error(errno, "open");
    switch ( pid[0] = fork() ) {
    case -1:
        fatal_error(errno, "fork");
    case 0:
        printf("Producer PID = %d\n", getpid());
        producer(fd);
    }
    switch ( pid[1] = fork() ) {
    case -1:
        fatal_error(errno, "fork");
    case 0:
        printf("Consumer PID = %d\n", getpid());
        consumer(fd, consumer_off);
    }
    int i = 0;
    do {
        if (-1 == (ret=waitpid(pid[i],&status,WUNTRACED|WCONTINUED|WNOHANG))){
            if ( errno != ECHILD ) fatal_error(errno, "waitpid()");
        }
```

```
        else if ( 0 == ret ) continue;
        else {
            print_status(ret, status);
            if ( WIFEXITED(status) || (WIFSIGNALED(status)) ) {
                if ( i++ == 0 ) printf("\nProducer finished; waiting for "
                                        "consumer to finish.\n");
            }
        }
        sleep(1);
    } while ( i < 2 );
    close(fd);
    exit(EXIT_SUCCESS);
}
```

Listing 11-14: A program that uses waitpid() *to monitor child processes*

The program can be run with a command line argument for the flag passed to the consumer. If no argument is supplied, its default behavior is for the consumer to print inside its loop. When you run this program, open a second terminal window and use the kill command to send SIGSTOP and SIGCONT signals to both the producer and consumer processes and watch the responses from the program.

While it's running, it will output a sequence of *p* characters until it terminates or is killed. You can send any signal to either child process. If you send a terminating signal to the producer, the consumer will run until it exits, unless you send it a signal as well:

```
$ ./waitpid_demo
Producer PID = 37837
Producer is about to start producing data.
Consumer PID = 37838
Data from producer, converted to uppercase:
PPPPP
Process 37837 stopped by signal 19   # Issued kill -19 37837 from 2nd terminal
PPPP
Process 37837 continued              # Issued kill -18 37837 from 2nd terminal
Producer finished; waiting for consumer to finish.
Process 37838 stopped by signal 19   # Issued kill -19 37838 from 2nd terminal
Process 37838 continued              # Issued kill -18 37838 from 2nd terminal
PPPPPPPPP
Process 37838 terminated by signal 8 # Issued kill -8 37838 from 2nd terminal
$
```

If, when you run the program, you send signals to the consumer before the producer, you won't see messages on the terminal until the producer has terminated. This is because the program does not monitor the consumer until the producer has terminated. If we replace the first argument to waitpid() with -1, then it will monitor state changes to both processes, but you'll also need to change some of the rest of the main() function to use the return value to decide which process was waited for.

The waitid() System Call

The third system call mentioned on the man page for wait() is waitid(). This call adds slightly different functionality to waitpid(). For one, the first argument can be used to identify the process to be monitored in a way not possible with waitpid(), namely by a PID file descriptor, which we haven't explored. It also returns more information about the monitored process in a siginfo_t structure. One interesting extra flag that we can bitwise-OR into its last argument is the WNOWAIT flag. If this is set, the waited-for process remains waitable even after the call, so that its status can be retrieved at a later time. I won't discuss this system call any further here, since it doesn't add that much more to our toolkit than what we now have. The program *waitid_demo.c* in the book's source code distribution is an example of how to use this system call.

The SIGCHLD Signal and Asynchronous Waiting

In general, a parent process cannot predict when any of its children will terminate. Children run independently, and their terminations are asynchronous with respect to the parent's execution—they don't terminate at the exact same point in time during the parent's execution each time the process runs. They might be terminated by an unexpected signal or may take longer to run at times because of scheduling activity. Consider what happens when you run a command in a shell such as bash in the background, as when you end it with an ampersand (&). It returns the prompt to you immediately and runs the command asynchronously in a background process. The shell doesn't know when that command will terminate.

The methods of waiting for a child process that we've seen so far are all synchronous with respect to the parent's execution—the parent calls wait() in its instruction stream at the exact same point in time relative to the parent's execution, but this call can happen at any time relative to the child's execution. When the parent calls wait(), it might be a long time after or a long time before the waited-for child terminates. Therefore, with this synchronous method of waiting, a process has just two choices for how it can wait:

- It can block itself until some child terminates or otherwise changes its state.

- It can periodically check, without blocking, whether a child terminated or changed state.

Neither of these is ideal. The first option implies that the parent does no work until a child terminates, however long in the future that might be. The second option is a form of polling, wasting CPU cycles each time it tries to reap its child's status without reward.

An entirely different approach is to utilize the SIGCHLD signal. Normally, when a process terminates by calling an exit function or is killed or stopped by a signal, the kernel generates a SIGCHLD signal and sends it to that process's parent, provided that it's still running. There are exceptions to this rule that I'll explain shortly, but for now let's assume that the SIGCHLD signal is always sent to the parent process in these circumstances. In this alternative method, we put the call to wait() or waitpid() inside the SIGCHLD handler.

Since the handler's running implies that some child terminated, the appropriate call to wait() returns immediately. The parent doesn't block and doesn't need to poll; it reaps the status of the terminated child only when it actually terminated. Since the call to wait() is within the handler, which can run at any time with respect to the parent's execution, this method of reaping a child's status is called *asynchronous waiting*. On the surface, asynchronous waiting is simple, but there are several issues that make it extremely complex to design a handler that's guaranteed to reap all of the children. Following are the major problems:

Standard signals are not queued.
If another child terminates while the handler is running, that signal is blocked and will be delivered when the handler returns, but if more than two children terminate in close proximity, all except the first of these signals may be lost because the kernel cannot deliver each of them immediately. When this happens, those children will remain zombies.

Reentrant handlers are hard to design.
Setting the SA_NODEFER flag on the handler when it's installed in the hope of preventing lost signals introduces the possibility that the handler will be interrupted by another signal and thus reentered. Making a reentrant handler that contains system calls is very hard to do because many calls themselves are non-reentrant. It also means that the handler cannot use C stream functions such as printf() for any I/O.

A handler should only call async-signal-safe functions.
In particular, all I/O should use the async-signal safe write() system call rather than the buffered C Standard Library functions.

A process has just one copy of the errno variable.
All of the wait()-like functions set errno on error, as do all other system calls that might be called from within the handler. Since the handler runs asynchronously with respect to the rest of the parent program and a process has just a single copy of the errno variable in its memory, the handler could overwrite that value, so that when it returns, the other parts of the program that needed to query it will see an incorrect value.

The documentation advises against waiting for *any* child in a handler.
Calls that wait for *any* child, such as waitpid(-1, &status, ...) or wait(&status), can sometimes interfere with other processes waiting to reap their children's status. Instead, within the handler, the wait should be for a specific child process. This implies that the handler needs access to the PID of the child that terminated.

The handler must be established before any child processes are created.
If child processes are created before the program establishes the SIGCHLD handler, there's a chance that they may terminate before the handler's installed, and if the parent can collect their status only from within the handler, they'll become zombies. Therefore, installation of the SIGCHLD handler should always precede creation of child processes.

Despite these problems, it's possible to design a SIGCHLD handler that reaps the terminated child that caused the signal to be sent to the parent. It won't be able to overcome the lost signal problem described in the first item, but the main program will compensate for it. First, we need to understand a bit more about the SIGCHLD signal, because it's not always the case that when a child terminates, the kernel generates a SIGCHLD signal for the parent. We need to understand when it doesn't.

The SIGCHLD Signal

The SIGCHLD signal is the means by which a parent is notified of its child's demise. A parent can opt out of receiving this signal by setting the disposition of SIGCHLD to SIG_IGN. In this case, when a child terminates, no SIGCHLD is sent, its status is discarded, and the child does not become a zombie. A process doesn't need to, and should not, wait for any children as long as the disposition of SIGCHLD is SIG_IGN.

Note that this is different from not establishing a handler for SIGCHLD, even though its default action is to be ignored. If a program does not establish a handler, the SIGCHLD signal will still be sent, but the process will ignore it, and if the process does not reap the child's status through a call to wait(), the child will become a zombie.

Another nuance associated with the SIGCHLD signal is its relationship to the SA_NOCLDWAIT sigaction flag. In Chapter 8, when I described the flags that could be set in the sa_flags member of the sigaction structure, I mentioned the SA_NOCLDWAIT flag, but didn't say much about it. Now it matters.

When a program establishes a SIGCHLD handler using sigaction, it can set the SA_NOCLDWAIT flag on the handler, as in:

```
void some_handler(int signum);

sigaction sigact;
sigemptyset(&sigact.sa_mask);
sigact.sa_flags = SA_NOCLDWAIT;
sigact.sa_handler = some_handler;
sigaction(SIGCHLD, &sigact, NULL);
```

It can set this flag even if the disposition of SIGCHLD is set to SIG_DFL:

```
sigaction sigact;
sigemptyset(&sigact.sa_mask);
sigact.sa_flags = SA_NOCLDWAIT;
sigact.sa_handler = SIG_DFL;
sigaction(SIGCHLD, &sigact, NULL);
```

The effect of SA_NOCLDWAIT is to prevent child processes from being turned into zombies when they terminate by discarding their status immediately, so that the parent doesn't have to wait for them to reap their status and prevent their becoming zombies.

What if a parent does make a call to one of the wait() functions after having set this flag? In this case POSIX specifies that a call to wait() or waitpid() will block until all children have terminated and will then fail, setting errno to ECHILD. Linux conforms to POSIX in this regard.

However, POSIX leaves the relationship between this flag and the delivery of the SIGCHLD signal up to the implementation: "If SA_NOCLDWAIT is set, it is implementation-defined whether a SIGCHLD signal is sent to the parent process." On Linux systems, a SIGCHLD signal is generated even if SA_NOCLDWAIT is set. The consequence of this is that if the parent waits inside the SIGCHLD handler, the handler will be called but the wait will fail, setting errno to ECHILD.

Summarizing, we shouldn't set the SA_NOCLDWAIT flag on a SIGCHLD handler within which we plan to reap children's status with a call to one of the wait() system calls. It is a bit contradictory—it's saying in effect, "I don't want to wait for my children, but I'm going to do it anyway."

A Reaping SIGCHLD Handler

Based on the preceding observations and conclusions, let's describe the design of a SIGCHLD handler that can reap the status of a terminated child.

- The second item from the preceding list suggests that we shouldn't set the SA_NODEFER flag on the handler, because making it reentrant will be difficult and complex. By a careful design we can avoid losing SIGCHLD signals almost all of the time. The handler will not be able to catch every signal if they happen to arrive too close in time.

- A working handler should not call printf() to comply with the third item. The print_status() function we saw earlier in the chapter shouldn't be used in a production handler. In this demo version, we'll use it just because it's simpler code. An async-signal-safe version of it is included in the book's source code distribution.

- The fourth item implies that the handler should begin by saving the value of errno on entry into a stack variable such as saved_errno and restore it before returning.

- The fifth item implies that, within the handler, we need to wait explicitly for the process that terminated (or changed state), and therefore, within the handler, we need the PID of the process that caused the SIGCHLD to be delivered. This implies that we need to use the type of handler with a siginfo_t parameter, because the siginfo_t structure has a member that contains the PID of the child process. The man page for waitpid() explains exactly which members of that structure are filled when the signal is sent. The ones we need are:

    si_code   This contains one of a set of symbolic constants describing the child process's reason for termination (or state change). It can be CLD_EXITED, CLD_KILLED, CLD_DUMPED, CLD_STOPPED, CLD_CONTINUED, or CLD_TRAPPED.
    si_pid   This contains the PID of the terminating process.

The following handler satisfies these constraints. The program that uses it, named *sighandler_wait_demo.c*, will be presented afterward. Some of the code in this function is there just to produce informative output while the program is running. To compensate for the possibility of lost SIGCHLD signals, the program will declare a volatile-qualified, file-scoped integer variable, sigchld_count, that the handler will increment each time it reaps a terminated child. It isn't a count of terminated children because some of their signals can be lost. The main program will compare this count to the number of children it created and, if needed, reap the ones that are still zombies before it exits.

handle
_sigchld()

```
void handle_sigchld(int signum, siginfo_t *siginfo, void *unused)
{
        int        status;        /* To store collected status              */
        sigset_t   blocked_set;   /* For blocking SIGCHILD to count signals */
        pid_t      waitedfor;     /* Return value of waitpid()              */
        static char errmssge[] = "waitpid in SIGCHLD handler found no"
                               " more reapable children.\n";

        int saved_errno = errno;  /* Save the errno on entry to the handler. */
        sigemptyset(&blocked_set);
        sigaddset(&blocked_set, SIGCHLD);  /* Set up signal mask.            */
        waitedfor = waitpid(siginfo->si_pid, &status, WUNTRACED | WCONTINUED);
        if ( waitedfor  < 0 )              /* No child to wait for           */
            write(2, errmssge, sizeof errmssge);
        else if ( siginfo->si_code == CLD_EXITED ||
                  siginfo->si_code == CLD_KILLED ||
                  siginfo->si_code == CLD_DUMPED  ) {

            /* The child terminated one way or another.
               Block SIGCHLD while incrementing a signal counter
               and printing the status because we use printf(). */

            if ( -1 == sigprocmask(SIG_BLOCK, &blocked_set, NULL) )
                error_mssge(errno, "sigprocmask()");
            sigchld_count++;
            printf("Handler reaping: ");
            print_status(siginfo->si_pid, status);

            /* Unblock SIGCHLD now. */
            if ( -1 == sigprocmask(SIG_UNBLOCK, &blocked_set, NULL) )
                error_mssge(errno, "sigprocmask()");
        }
        else { /* A stop or continue signal */
            if ( -1 == sigprocmask(SIG_BLOCK, &blocked_set, NULL) )
                error_mssge(errno, "sigprocmask()");
            print_status(siginfo->si_pid, status);
            if ( -1 == sigprocmask(SIG_UNBLOCK, &blocked_set, NULL) )
                error_mssge(errno, "sigprocmask()");
        }
        errno = saved_errno;
}
```

When the handler is run, it saves errno, creates a signal set containing just SIGCHLD, and calls waitpid(), passing the PID of the child that terminated (in siginfo->si_pid). If the return value is -1, the child was already reaped. I'll explain how that's possible shortly. Otherwise, it checks siginfo->si_code to see if it's one of the termination codes. If so, because of the remote possibility that the handler could be run without SIGCHLD being blocked, it blocks SIGCHLD so that it can safely increment the count and print the status, after which it unblocks it. If the handler ran because of a nonterminating state change, it prints the status, also after blocking the signal.

The child processes that we'll use to test the handler will each execute the following function:

```
child()   void child(int exit_val)
          {
              if ( exit_val == 0 )
                  pause();
              else
                  sleep(exit_val);
              exit(exit_val);
          }
```

If the exit_val passed into it is 0, it waits to be sent a signal. Otherwise, it sleeps for exit_val seconds and exits with that value as its exit value. This design gives us time to send a signal if we want or to let a child terminate normally, so that we see the effects of both signals and normal exits.

The main program that uses handle_sigchld() as its SIGCHLD handler, is shown in Listing 11-15.

```
main()    int main(int argc, char *argv[])
          {
              pid_t          pid[NUM_CHILDREN], w;
              int            exitval[NUM_CHILDREN] = {0,0,0,0}; /* Default values
              struct sigaction sigact;                                      for children */
              int            status, n;
              sigset_t       blocked_set;

              sigemptyset(&blocked_set);         /* Create the signal mask. */
              sigaddset(&blocked_set, SIGCHLD);
              /* Get child process exit codes from command line. */
              if ( argc > 1 ) {
                  for ( int i = 0; i < argc-1 && i < NUM_CHILDREN; i++ )  {
                      n = atoi(argv[i+1]);
                      exitval[i] = n > 0? n : 0;
                  }
              }
              /* Establish SIGCHLD handler. */
              sigemptyset(&sigact.sa_mask);
              sigact.sa_flags = SA_SIGINFO;
              sigact.sa_sigaction = handle_sigchld;
              sigaction(SIGCHLD, &sigact, NULL);
```

```
/* Create the child processes with their exit codes to run child(). */
for ( int i = 0; i < NUM_CHILDREN; i++ ) {
    switch ( pid[i] = fork() ) {
    case -1:
        fatal_error(errno, "fork");
    case 0:
        printf("Child %d PID = %d\n", i, getpid());
        child(exitval[i]);
    default:
        break;
    }
}
/* Delay to give time for sending signals and letting child processes
   run until they exit. The amount of time is easily adjusted. If the
   sigchld_count equals the number of child processes, they all are
   terminated and the loop breaks. Otherwise, it continues sleeping. */
for ( int i = 0; i < NUM_CHILDREN; i++ ) {
    if ( sigchld_count == NUM_CHILDREN )
        break;
    sleep(6);
}
/* Because it's possible that signals were lost, there may be zombies when
   the program is ready to exit. The following loop reaps the zombies and
   prints a message that main() did the reaping, not the handler.
   This code MUST block SIGCHLD because there is a possibility that some
   child did not yet terminate when we reach here. If so, a SIGCHLD will
   be sent and the handler will run. It is possible for the wait in the
   handler and the wait here to interrupt one another, and for the status
   to be corrupted. By blocking SIGCHLD, it forces the handler to run
   after the main program reaps the children. */
if ( -1 == sigprocmask(SIG_BLOCK, &blocked_set, NULL) )
    fatal_error(errno, "sigprocmask()");
do {
    w = waitpid(-1, &status, WNOHANG ); /* Nonblocking wait         */
    if ( -1 == w ) {      /* -1 means no more children need reaping. */
        printf("All child processes are reaped.\n");
    }
    else if ( 0 < w ) { /* It reaped a child.                        */
        printf("main() reaping:  ");
        print_status(w, status);
    }
} while ( w >= 0 );      /* Run until all have been reaped.          */
if ( -1 == sigprocmask(SIG_UNBLOCK, &blocked_set, NULL) )
    fatal_error(errno, "sigprocmask()");
exit(EXIT_SUCCESS);
}
```

Listing 11-15: The main program for sighandler_wait_demo.c

The program creates four child processes. When you run it without arguments, each child will need to be terminated by a signal. If instead you supply $0 < N < 4$ positive integers on the command line, the first N child processes will use those values as both the number of seconds to sleep before exiting and their exit value. It's easiest to open two terminal windows to run it, although you can background it and enter `kill` commands in the same terminal.

The program will indicate whether the handler reaped a child or whether it wasn't reaped until `main()` was ready to exit. If the child processes have very different sleep times, the handler will reap them all. If they're all the same, some signals can be lost and `main()` will reap them. The entire program is in the book's source code distribution. Here are a few runs that demonstrate this:

```
$ ./sighandler_wait_demo 1 2 3 4
Child 0 PID = 36957
Child 1 PID = 36958
Child 2 PID = 36959
Child 3 PID = 36960
Handler reaping: Process 36957 exited with status 1
Handler reaping: Process 36958 exited with status 2
Handler reaping: Process 36959 exited with status 3
Handler reaping: Process 36960 exited with status 4
All child processes are reaped.
```

In this case, the handler reaped them all:

```
$ ./sighandler_wait_demo 1 1 1 1
Child 0 PID = 36979
Child 1 PID = 36980
Child 2 PID = 36981
Child 3 PID = 36982
Handler reaping: Process 36979 exited with status 1
Handler reaping: Process 36980 exited with status 1
Handler reaping: Process 36982 exited with status 1
main() reaping:  Process 36981 exited with status 1
All child processes are reaped.
```

Because the children terminated at roughly the same time, process 36981's SIGCHLD signal was discarded and it wasn't reaped by the handler. Eventually the main program reaped it.

Lastly, here's a run in which some of the children are killed by signals. A second terminal window was used to send the signals.

```
$ ./sighandler_wait_demo 6 10   # First two will sleep, others need signal.
Child 0 PID = 37249
Child 1 PID = 37250
Child 2 PID = 37251             # Sent signal 3 (SIGQUIT) to this one
Child 3 PID = 37252             # Sent signal 2 (SIGINT) to this one
```

```
Handler reaping: Process 37251 terminated by signal 3 and a core dump took...
Handler reaping: Process 37249 exited with status 6
Handler reaping: Process 37252 terminated by signal 2.
Handler reaping: Process 37250 exited with status 10
All child processes are reaped.
```

In this run, I sent signals to two of the processes and let the others exit normally.

To summarize, there are several different ways to wait for a child process to finish. The first two methods were synchronous and either required the parent to block itself or required that it periodically check whether any child terminated. The last method is an asynchronous one in which the parent does not stop what it's doing until the child terminates, at which point the parent's SIGCHLD handler runs to reap the child's status. This last method may still require the parent to reap any zombies before it exits.

Putting It All Together: A Simple Shell

To illustrate how the family of system calls we've just explored in this chapter can be used together, we'll design a very simple shell with almost no features other than for running commands. A shell in its simplest form is just a command line interpreter—you enter a command followed by a newline character, and the shell executes that command and returns the prompt back when it's finished. We'll implement a shell that does little more than this, which we'll name spl_sh.

We'll give this shell two features other than the ability to run a command:

- Entering exit terminates it.

- Entering help displays a usage message.

Adding these features lets us model how a shell built-in command is implemented because the shell itself implements them, not a spawned process. Essentially, the program logic in pseudocode is:

```
do {
    Display a prompt.
    Read the user's input.
    Parse the user's input into a command of the form:
        commandname argument vector
    If the first word is "exit," exit the program.
    Otherwise, if the first word is "help," display a usage message.
    Otherwise:
        Fork a new process.
        In the child process,
            Execute the program named by the command with its arguments.
        In the parent process, wait for the child to finish.
} forever
```

We can put together a simple version of this program. We'll assume that command names are not required to be absolute pathnames and that the arguments to the command are whitespace-separated words. We'll also assume that whatever program is specified by the command eventually terminates. With this in mind, the next refinement, without any error checking, is:

```
do {
    printf("Command:");              /* Print a prompt.                */
    ret = getline(&line, &len, tty);  /* Read a line from the terminal. */
    if ( ret <= 1 ) break;
    token = strtok(line, " \t");      /* Parse the line using strtok(). */
    i = 0;
    while ( token != NULL ) {
        argvec[i++] = token;
        token = strtok(NULL, delim);
    }
    if ( 0 == strcmp(argvec[0], "exit") )
        exit(EXIT_SUCCESS);
    else if ( 0 == strcmp(argvec[0], "help") ) {
        display_help();
        continue;
    }
    if ( (pid = fork()) == 0 )         /* Create a new process.          */
        execvp(argvec[0], argvec);     /* Child executes command argvec[0]. */
    else
        waitpid(pid, &status, 0);      /* Parent waits for child.        */
} while ( TRUE )
```

The program uses execvp() for two reasons. First, this function uses the PATH environment variable to find the command so that the user doesn't need to enter the absolute pathname. Second, because the number of arguments is not fixed, a list-based exec() function can't be used.

The complete program, named *spl_sh.c*, easily follows from this pseudo-code. The main program is displayed in Listing 11-16.

spl_sh.c main()
```
int main(int argc, char *argv[])
{
    char    *line = NULL;    /* Buffer to store input from user        */
    size_t  len = 0;         /* Length of buffer                        */
    ssize_t nread;           /* Number of bytes read by getline()       */
    char    *argvec[128];    /* Array to store command line from user  */
    char    *token;          /* Used by strtok() to parse command       */
    pid_t   pid;             /* Return value from fork, child's PID     */

    do {
        printf("spl_sh$ ");              /* Print the prompt.              */
        if ( 0 >= (nread = getline(&line, &len, stdin )) )
            break;                        /* An input error                 */
        if ( 1 == nread )                 /* Just the newline, so continue  */
            continue;
```

```
        line[nread-1] = '\0';               /* Replace newline at end.       */
        token = strtok(line, " \t");        /* Parse the line using strtok(). */
        int i = 0;
        while ( token != NULL ) {
            argvec[i++] = token;
            token = strtok(NULL, " \t");
        }
        argvec[i] = NULL;                    /* NULL-terminate the vector.    */
        if ( 0 == strcmp(argvec[0], "exit") ) {
            free(line);                      /* Exit the program.             */
            exit(EXIT_SUCCESS);
        }
        else if ( 0 == strcmp(argvec[0], "help") ) { /* Display help.         */
            printf("command arg arg ...\n");
            continue;
        }
        if ( (pid = fork()) == 0 )       /* Create a new process.             */
            execvp(argvec[0], argvec); /* Child executes command argvec[0]. */
        else if ( -1 == pid )
            fatal_error(errno, "fork");
        else
            if ( -1 == waitpid(pid, NULL, 0) ) /* Parent waits for child.     */
                fatal_error(errno, "waitpid()");
        free(line);                          /* Free the line allocated by getline. */
        line = NULL;
        len = 0;
    } while ( TRUE );
    return 0;
}
```

Listing 11-16: A very simple shell program

Because the child process immediately replaces its program with a call to execvp(), we don't see its call to exit(), but if it terminates normally, the program that it executes does make the call. This program has only two built-in commands, so it's fine to check in the main loop which command the user entered. If there were more, we'd be better off replacing that code with a call to a function that did that work. A sample run shows how it works:

```
$ ./spl_sh
spl_sh$ help
command arg arg ...
spl_sh$ echo hello out there!
hello out there!
spl_sh$ date
Sat May 11 09:06:37 AM EDT 2024
spl_sh$ exit
$
```

Note that this simple shell has no I/O redirection. It can't handle any redirection operators! I'll leave it as an exercise to add backgrounding to spl_sh.

The system() Library Function

Sometimes, within a program, it's convenient to execute a shell command, or some other executable program, without changing the program currently executed, almost like executing that shell command as a function within the program. The system() library function is designed for this purpose; it makes it possible for a program to execute another program within a forked shell process, as in:

system_demo.c
```
#include "common_hdrs.h"
int main(int argc, char *argv[])
{
    if ( argc < 2 )
        usage_error("Usage: system_demo command ");
    int ret = system(argv[1]);
    if ( ret == -1 )
        fatal_error(errno, "system");
    exit(EXIT_SUCCESS);
}
```

You can run this as follows:

```
$ ./system_demo 'hostnamectl | grep Kernel'
        Kernel: Linux 5.15.0-107-generic
```

It's a pretty convenient function, and I sometimes see it being used by beginning programmers. However, there are two issues regarding the use of the system() function:

It isn't efficient. It forks a shell, which in turn forks processes as needed to execute the given command.

It is unsafe in several circumstances. If the call executes a command supplied by a user on the command line, as this example does, the entered text must be carefully checked. The command can try to manipulate environment variables to run unintended programs. It should never be used in setuid programs or in those running with superuser privilege. The man page has more details.

This function is not indispensable the way fork() is; we can get the same effect with a combination of fork(), execl(), and some complex signal handling. The only reason to know about it is that at times it's convenient, and it's a good program to try to implement.

Summary

This chapter examined various system calls and library functions related to the creation and termination of processes as well as those that processes can use to change the programs that they execute.

Except for the very first process, init, which is created by the kernel, all processes are created by some other process. The fork() system call is the most common means of creating a new process. When a process is created by a call to fork(), it executes the same program as its parent. Over the years, fork() has been revised to make it more efficient, and some Unix systems introduced alternative process creation functions such as vfork() and clone(). This chapter did not explore either of these system calls.

Usually, when a new process is created, the reason is to execute a different program. A process can change the program that it executes, along with its complete memory image, by calling execve() or any of a small set of library functions that wrap execve().

A process terminates its execution by calling either the C Library's exit() function or the lower-level _exit() system call. This is called *normal termination*. When a process detects an unrecoverable error condition, it can choose to terminate itself by calling abort(), which causes *abnormal termination*. When it's killed by a signal that it didn't catch, this is also abnormal termination.

The exit() function's integer argument is called its *exit status*. When a process calls exit(e_status), that status is transmitted back to its parent process, which can *reap* it by calling wait(), waitpid(), or waitid(). The wait() functions are the means by which a parent can receive some information about state changes in its children. When a parent returns from one of these system calls, the child's status has been collected and the child's resources are all released. Until a terminated child's status has been reaped by one of these calls, it is called a *zombie* process. The kernel keeps track of it and maintains some limited information about it.

The fork(), execve(), _exit(), and wait() system calls and related library functions are the four pillars of dynamic process control. They are the means by which a program can create processes, change what they execute, monitor their actions to a limited degree, and terminate them.

Exercises

1. Study the following program:

```
int main(int argc, char *argv[])
{
    int N = 8;
    printf("About to create many processes...\n");
    for ( int i = 0; i < N; i++ )
        if ( -1 == fork() )
            exit(1);
    printf("PID = %d\n", getpid());
    return 0;
}
```

   Without running the program, answer these questions:
   - (a) How many child processes are created by this program?
   - (b) As a function of *N*, how many are created?
   - (c) How many lines are printed to the terminal when this is run?
   - (d) If this program is named makechildren and it is run as

   ```
   $ ./makechildren | wc -l
   ```

   will the output be the same as your answer to the previous question? Why or why not?
   - (e) Define the *depth* of a process *p* as follows: If *p* was created directly by the process that bash created to execute makechildren, *depth(p)* = 1. Otherwise, if *p* was created by another process *q*, *depth(p)* = *depth(q)* + 1. What is the maximum depth of all child processes created by makechildren?

2. Add a backgrounding operator to spl_sh. Specifically, modify it so that when a user enters a command terminated by &, such as

   ```
   spl_sh$ ./myprog &
   ```

   the prompt returns immediately, the command is executed in a new process, and when the process terminates, spl_sh collects its status asynchronously inside the SIGCHLD handler.

3. Add a sequence operator (;) to spl_sh. Specifically, modify it so that when a user enters a command such as

   ```
   spl_sh$ echo hello ; date ; who
   ```

   each command is executed in a separate process that only starts after the preceding one terminated, either normally or abnormally.

4. Write a program named cascade that when run as

   ```
   $ ./cascade N
   ```

creates N child processes, p1, p2, . . . , pN. The program can assume that $N < 128$. Each process prints its PID and then suspends itself. After 10 seconds, the main() function sends a SIGTERM to p1. When p1 receives it, it prints the message Process *<pid1>* terminated where pid1 is p1's PID, after which each of the remaining processes terminate in the sequence, p2, p3, and so on, each printing the same message, after which the program terminates. Do not expect the child process output to be in the same order in which they terminate.

5. Test your understanding of SIGCHLD handlers and reaping of child processes:

   (a) If a program has a handler for SIGCHLD that does not reap any child processes and the program calls wait() after a child terminates and the handler has run, will the child's status be available for reaping after the handler runs?

   (b) What if, instead of registering a SIGCHLD handler, the program creates a mask named sigmask containing SIGCHLD and blocks the signals in sigmask, after which it calls sigwait(&sigmask, &sig)? To prevent a terminated child from becoming a zombie, what must the program do in the case that the value returned in sig is SIGCHLD?

12

INTRODUCTION TO INTERPROCESS COMMUNICATION

Some applications and system programs run as a collection of multiple processes that work together, rather than as a single process. Web servers, database servers, desktop managers, and web browsers often consist of many running processes. Some applications consist of multiple threads instead of multiple processes, and some are even more complex, running as several multithreaded processes. Processes that work together need to coordinate their actions by communicating with each other. Communication, in general, is the exchange of information, and *interprocess communication* (*IPC*) in particular refers to the exchange of information between processes.

Mechanisms by which two or more processes can communicate, or that facilitate the coordinated exchange of data, are called *IPC facilities*. This definition is broad—for example, one IPC facility covered earlier in the book is the Unix signal facility, which we introduced in Chapter 8. Because signals can be used as a simple method of process synchronization, they facilitate the safe exchange of data and are therefore considered to be an IPC facility. Now, we're mostly interested in learning about what facilities are available in Unix systems for the exchange of data, without creating race conditions. This chapter begins with the big picture, categorizing IPC facilities conceptually, and then examines some of the IPC facilities based on the use of shared memory in Unix. It also explores the use of semaphores for synchronization.

Why Do We Need IPC?

In Chapter 11, we created two different programs, *sync_io_demo.c* and *waitpid _demo.c*, to demonstrate how a parent and child process could communicate with each other. In both of these, the two processes exchanged data through a shared disk file, with one writing data to it and one reading data from it. Exchanging data through a disk file is slow, but unlike the threads within a single program, which can share data through the global variables in the program, processes don't share any memory—their address spaces are disjoint from each other. Because of this, the only way that we knew of at that point for related processes to exchange data was through a file.

Sharing data through a file requires preventing race conditions on writes to the file. In *sync_io_demo.c*, to prevent these race conditions, the processes synchronized their accesses to the file through the use of signals, and in *waitpid_demo.c*, they prevented them with a combination of the O_APPEND flag and the pread() system call. Both of these solutions worked, but they were an ad hoc approach that we used simply because we didn't know a better alternative. These programs also ignored the possibility that some third process could open and modify that file while the two processes created by the program were running. We didn't explore the possibility of advisory file locks for those two programs, but we should know something about them. Although sharing data through a file is possible, it isn't an efficient way for processes to communicate. Fortunately, Unix systems have several other types of IPC facilities that make data exchange easier and more robust. Our goal is to learn more about them.

An Overview of Interprocess Communication

Conceptually, data can be exchanged between processes either through a shared storage medium, such as memory or a file, or by transferring it through some channel that the operating system manages. I'll summarize the two approaches briefly.

Shared Memory Methods

With an IPC facility based on shared memory, multiple processes access a shared region of memory that is mutually accessible to all of them.

- Since processes don't have access to each others' address spaces, the region of memory that they share has to be created. Once it's been created, ordinary store and fetch operations on that memory are the means of sharing data. In other words, one process modifies a variable in memory and another fetches its value.

- With shared-memory IPC, preventing race conditions is the job of the programmer, and some form of synchronization has to be used.

- The memory region used for sharing is in the processes' address spaces. The kernel is not involved in the transfer of data to and from this memory, making it a fast means of data exchange.

- In principle, data can also be exchanged through shared open files, but this isn't practical, because reading from and writing to disk files is much slower. There are ways, however, to map a disk file into physical memory that is shared by two or more processes and to use ordinary fetches and stores in place of reads and writes. In effect, it's like using shared memory except that the memory is backed by a disk file.

Figure 12-1 visualizes the differences.

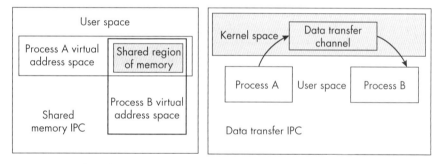

Figure 12-1: Shared memory–based IPC in comparison to data transfer–based IPC

Data Transfer Methods

With an IPC facility based on data transfer, processes pass data through some type of communication channel that's managed by the kernel.

- For some types of data transfer facilities, the data is transferred using the same read and write operations that are used in file I/O. Pipes and sockets fall into this category.

- For other types, specific send and receive system calls or library functions transfer the data. The most prevalent examples of this are message queues.

- Unlike shared memory IPC, data transfer IPC methods provide the mutual exclusion needed to prevent race conditions, freeing the programmer from having to prevent them explicitly.

- The communication channels that are used for data transfer are managed by the kernel and reside in kernel memory. This makes these methods slower than shared memory methods, since the kernel is involved in the exchange of data.

Two Different APIs

Unix systems provide several different IPC facilities based on both shared memory and data transfer. To decide which is best to use in a particular application, we should know what all of the choices are. If we search for man pages whose summaries contain the term *interprocess communication* by entering `apropos interprocess communication`, we'll find pages including the following:

perlipc (1)	- Perl interprocess communication (signals, fifos, pipes,...
pipe (3posix)	- create an interprocess channel
socket (3posix)	- create an endpoint for communication
svipc (7)	- System V interprocess communication mechanisms
sysvipc (7)	- System V interprocess communication mechanisms
unix (7)	- sockets for local interprocess communication

These man pages are a sufficient starting point. The `perlipc` reference is intriguing because it mentions specific facilities such as signals, FIFOs, and pipes, the last two of which are new terms for us. In particular, the `perlipc` man page begins by stating:

> The basic IPC facilities of Perl are built out of the good old Unix signals, named pipes, pipe opens, the Berkeley socket routines, and SysV IPC calls. Each is used in slightly different situations.

Also, the `pipe(3posix)`, `svipc(7)`, and `unix(7)` man pages deserve further examination. We'll explore many of these man pages to learn about the programming interfaces available, but before we dive into any details, we need to understand the difference between the POSIX and System V interfaces.

System V is the name given to AT&T's 1983 UNIX release, which incorporated many features previously not present in UNIX. System V integrated three different IPC mechanisms into UNIX: message queues, semaphores, and shared memory. Their interfaces have much in common, and having learned how to use any one of them, learning the others is much easier. The `svipc(7)` man page contains an overview of all of them, stating,

> System V IPC is the name given to three interprocess communication mechanisms that are widely available on UNIX systems: message queues, semaphores, and shared memory.

POSIX IPC refers to a different API that includes the same IPC facilities as System V—message queues, semaphores, and shared memory—but with a completely different interface to them. The POSIX API is consistent with the traditional Unix I/O model, unlike the System V API; it is also very self-consistent, in that the three different facilities are programmed in similar ways.

Summary of the Common IPC Facilities

Given that both POSIX and System V IPC consist primarily of message queues, semaphores, and shared memory, I'll continue by summarizing what the documentation says about each of them.

Message queues allow processes to exchange chunks of data called *messages* by putting them into, and removing them from, a queue. POSIX and System V use different APIs for working with message queues, and they provide similar, but not identical, functionality. Both provide the means for processes to send messages to or receive messages from a specified message queue. The sysvipc(7) man page refers us to the POSIX man page, mq_overview(7), for a comparison of the two APIs. Of the two, the POSIX API is newer and easier to use, and it provides more functionality.

Message queues are like mailboxes. A process can post, or write, a message into a message queue and can read a message from it. Unlike ordinary reads though, reads from a message queue are *destructive*—the message is removed from the queue by the act of reading, like removing mail from a mailbox. Unlike read operations on a file, a read operation reads a whole message, meaning the entire message that was placed into the message queue when it was written, like retrieving a single piece of mail. One way that a message queue is not like a mailbox is that a process cannot read more than one message at a time.

Although semaphores are included in both lists of IPC facilities, they're not exactly a method of exchanging data; they're primarily a *synchronization mechanism*, a means for processes to synchronize their accesses to a shared object or region of code to prevent race conditions. They're needed when a program uses shared memory IPC facilities. As with message queues, there are System V semaphores and POSIX semaphores.

A semaphore is essentially an integer variable on which two operations can be performed: increment and decrement. Its value is not allowed to fall below zero. These operations have gone by various names over the years; in POSIX, for example, to increment a semaphore, a program calls sem_post(), and to decrement it, it calls sem_wait(). Semaphores serve as a synchronization method for two reasons:

- The increment and decrement operations are *atomic*—if two or more processes try to call increment or decrement functions at the same time, the operations are serialized. No two processes can execute that code at the same time.

- If a process tries to decrement a semaphore whose value is 0, it is blocked by the kernel and remains blocked until the semaphore value becomes positive.

If two processes both try to decrement a semaphore whose value is currently 1, one will succeed, setting it to 0, and the other will be blocked. The one that succeeded can later increment the semaphore, unblocking the other process, after it has finished updating some shared resource. System V semaphores are harder to use than POSIX semaphores, but the biggest difference is that System V semaphore operations act on sets of semaphores rather than a single one.

Both System V and POSIX shared memory are IPC facilities that allow processes to share regions of memory. These memory regions go by different names; System V calls them *memory segments*, and POSIX calls them *memory objects*. The basic idea is that a process can request the kernel to create a shareable region of memory, and it gets some type of identifier that can be used for all subsequent operations in that memory region. Other processes that know this identifier and also have appropriate permission can access that memory as well. Once the memory region is established, a process can access that memory in the same way that it accesses the rest of its address space.

The System V API is the original shared memory model. The shm _overview(7) man page has this to say about it:

> System V shared memory (shmget(2), (shmop(2), etc.) is an older shared memory API. POSIX shared memory provides a simpler, and better designed interface; on the other hand POSIX shared memory is somewhat less widely available (especially on older systems) than System V shared memory.

The major advantage of the System V shared memory API used to be that it was more portable, but over time that advantage has diminished as more Unix distributions have incorporated the POSIX API.

The rest of this chapter will explore each of these IPC facilities, starting with shared memory, then looking at semaphores, and concluding with message queues. The next chapter will explore the other mechanisms that were mentioned at the start: pipes and FIFOs. There isn't room in this book to include a complete examination of both the System V IPC facilities and the POSIX ones. I've decided to explain the POSIX API because it is easier to learn and has a simple interface. I'll briefly describe System V semaphores, so that you can compare them to POSIX semaphores.

POSIX Shared Memory

Let's begin by searching for the relevant man pages:

```
$ apropos -a posix shared memory
shm_open (3)        - create/open or unlink POSIX shared memory objects
shm_overview (7)    - overview of POSIX shared memory
shm_unlink (3)      - create/open or unlink POSIX shared memory objects
```

The shm_overview(7) man page contains a summary and overview of the POSIX shared memory model and its API. We'll start there.

Overview

POSIX refers to shared memory objects in its documentation. A *shared memory object* is a data structure that represents a shareable memory region. It is analogous to an open file description. Recall from Chapter 4 that when a process opens or creates a file in Unix, the kernel creates an open file description and returns a small integer file descriptor that references that open file description. Similarly, when a process creates a shared memory region, the kernel creates a shared memory object and returns a small integer that is also called, somewhat confusingly, a file descriptor. A shared memory object encapsulates all of the metadata associated with the memory region created by the kernel. On Linux, it's created in an in-memory *tmpfs* filesystem and has a name visible in the */dev/shm* directory.

The shm_overview(7) man page lists the functions related to the creation and management of POSIX shared memory objects, with brief descriptions. The ones that are used for creating and using and removing the shared memory are as follows:

shm_open() Creates and opens a new shared memory object or opens an existing one.

ftruncate() Sets the size of the given shared memory object. Newly created shared memory objects have a length of 0.

mmap() Maps the shared memory object into the virtual address space of the calling process. A newly created object is not part of the virtual address space of a process until it is mapped into it.

munmap() Unmaps the shared memory object from the virtual address space of the calling process. Unmapping the memory object doesn't delete it; it marks the memory addresses assigned to it in the calling process as no longer part of the process's memory image.

shm_unlink() Removes a shared memory object name. It does not delete the actual memory object as long as one or more processes still have it mapped. Once all processes have unmapped the object, this deallocates and destroys the contents of the associated memory region.

close() Closes the file descriptor allocated by shm_open().

The preceding functions are listed in the order in which they're typically called. Before getting into the details, I'll summarize the steps involved in setting up a shared memory region:

1. The first step is for one of the processes to create the memory object with a call to shm_open(). One of the arguments to the call is the name for the memory object. That name has to be known by every other process that's going to share the memory. The call to shm_open() returns a file descriptor that refers to the memory object.

2. The created memory is 0 bytes long initially. The next step is to call the ftruncate() function to allocate memory to the object. Although

its name suggests that it is making the memory smaller, it can also increase the size of a memory object. The result of the call to ftruncate() is that physical memory has been allocated to the shared memory object, but this memory is not part of the calling process's virtual address space.

3.   The next step is to map the new physical memory into the address space of the calling process with a call to mmap(). This function assigns addresses inside the process for the physical memory created by ftruncate(). It's actually a more general-purpose function than this, since it is also used for creating memory-mapped files, which we haven't discussed. When a process maps memory with a call to mmap(), the kernel updates its page table to point to the shared physical pages. These pages are usually mapped above the shared libraries in the heap in the address space of the process, as shown in Figure 12-2.

4.   The memory is ready to be used. When this process is finished using it, it calls munmap() to unmap the virtual addresses assigned to it. The memory object as well as the physical memory continue to exist.

5.   The process that created the memory object with shm_open() should unlink, or remove, its name by calling shm_unlink(). The object's name is removed, and the object is deleted when all other processes unmap it.

Figure 12-2 depicts the mapping by mmap() of a part of physical memory into the address space of the calling process.

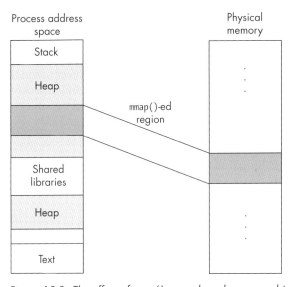

Figure 12-2: The effect of mmap() on a shared memory object

A process that wants to share an existing shared memory object performs fewer steps:

1. It calls shm_open(), passing the same name that its creator gave to the object, but with arguments that indicate it's not trying to create a new object.

2. It calls mmap() to map the object into its own address space. It *does not* call ftruncate()! The object already has associated memory and just needs to be mapped into the calling process.

3. It can now use the shared memory. When it's finished, it unmaps it. It doesn't have to unlink it.

Before looking at a few examples that show how to use shared memory, we need to study the prototypes and semantics of all of these functions in the API to understand exactly how to use them.

The Shared Memory API

Let's start with shm_open(). Its synopsis is:

```
#include <sys/mman.h>
#include <sys/stat.h>       /* For mode constants */
#include <fcntl.h>          /* For O_* constants  */


int shm_open(const char *name, int oflag, mode_t mode);
```

The man page notes that programs calling it must link to the real-time library with -lrt. This function is very much like open(): It's given a string containing a name, like a filename, a set of flags that controls the memory object's behavior, and a permission mode, and if it's successful, it returns a file descriptor that references the object.

The first argument is a string that will be used as the shared memory object name. This name must be of the form /*object-name*, where *object-name* can be up to NAME_MAX (255) characters. The leading slash is required by POSIX; without it, the code will not be portable. It's common for a program to put its own name somewhere in this string, as in /progmem1. Since the *tmpfs* filesystem is usually mounted on */dev/shm*, the shared memory object will look like an ordinary file there:

```
$ ls -1 /dev/shm
PostgreSQL.184558000
progmem1
```

The second argument is a bitwise-OR of flags that controls the opening mode. It must include one of O_RDONLY or O_RDWR. If one or more processes will modify the memory, the flag should be O_RDWR. The other flags are just like the flags we can pass when we open files, such as O_CREAT, O_EXCL, and O_TRUNC, with the same meanings.

The last argument is the file mode. The process that creates the memory object should set the mode to 0600 (S_IRUSR | S_IWUSR) so that only processes whose effective user ID is the same as that of the calling process can access that memory. For example

```
int shmfd = shm_open("/myprogmem", O_CREAT | O_EXCL | O_RDWR,
                                    S_IRUSR | S_IWUSR);
```

creates a new shared memory object that all of the user's processes can read and write. If the name exists already, it will fail. Another example is

```
int shmfd = shm_open("/myprogmem", O_RDWR, 0);
```

which will fail if */dev/shm/myprogmem* does not exist already. This is how a process would open the shared memory object already created by another process. It does not assign a mode to an existing object.

The ftruncate() system call is simpler to use. Its prototype is:

```
#include <unistd.h>
#include <sys/types.h>
int ftruncate(int fd, off_t length);
```

This function truncates or increases the size of the object referenced by the file descriptor fd. It does this to ordinary files as well as memory objects, so we can use it to lengthen or shorten any file. The second argument is the number of bytes to make the shared memory object (or file). Some examples of its use are:

```
ftruncate(fd, 100*sizeof(int));      /* Allocate for an array of 100 ints. */
ftruncate(fd, 128*sizeof(struct stat)); /* Allocate to hold an array of 128
                                            struct stat objects.          */
ftruncate(fd, MAX_INPUT);            /* Allocate bytes to store a string
                                            input by the user.            */
ftruncate(fd, 65536);                /* Allocate 65,536 bytes.           */
```

On success, it returns 0; otherwise, it returns -1 and sets errno accordingly.

The mmap() system call creates a new mapping in the virtual address space of the calling process. A mapping is essentially an assignment of a set of virtual addresses that corresponds to a set of physical addresses. In Chapter 10, we showed that shared libraries are mapped into a process's address space. That's an example of a mapping. The mmap() and munmap() prototypes follow:

```
#include <sys/mman.h>

void *mmap(void *addr, size_t length, int prot, int flags, int fd,
           off_t offset);
int munmap(void *addr, size_t length);
```

The first argument to mmap(), addr, is the virtual address at which the mapping should start, but this is just taken as a hint by the kernel, which decides where that mapping should start. Normally, we pass NULL in this argument to tell the kernel we don't care where it starts. The next argument, length, is the size, in bytes, of the mapping. If it isn't positive, the call fails. The next argument, prot, specifies access rights to the mapped region. It's either the symbolic constant PROT_NONE or a bitwise-OR of one or more of:

PROT_EXEC   Pages may be executed.

PROT_READ   Pages may be read.

PROT_WRITE   Pages may be written.

The fourth argument, flags, is a bitwise-OR of flags that control various aspects of the mapping. It must contain exactly one of the following constants, which define how updates to the region are applied:

MAP_SHARED   All processes see updates.

MAP_PRIVATE   When a process modifies the region, the kernel creates a separate copy of the region for that process and applies those modifications only to that copy. All future changes that the process makes are applied to that copy. Other processes continue to see only the original, unmodified region.

Several other flags can be bitwise-ORed into this argument, but I won't describe them here. The man page has a complete list of them.

The last argument, offset, is intended for when mmap() is called to set up a memory-mapped file. In this case, it is the offset in the file where the mapping starts. We can just set it to 0.

A Shared Memory Example Program

The first pair of programs that we'll create simply demonstrates the mechanics of setting up the shared memory. The first program, *shm_creator_demo1.c*, creates the shared memory object and fills it with a pair of strings at fixed offsets relative to the start of the mapping. The second program, *shm_user_demo1.c*, opens the same shared memory object, maps it into its own memory, and then prints the strings it finds at the given offsets. Both programs will include the same common header file, named *shm_demo1.h*, whose contents are:

shm_demo1.h
```
#include "common_hdrs.h"
#include <sys/mman.h>
#include <fcntl.h>
#include <sys/stat.h>


#define BUF_SIZE     8192
const   int offset1 = 0x64;
const   int offset2 = 0xC8;
```

The BUF_SIZE macro is the size of the memory region to be created.

The creator program is next:

```
#include "shm_demo1.h" /* For definitions of constants              */

int main(int argc, char *argv[])
{
    int    fd;          /* File descriptor referring to shared memory object */
    char *shmp;         /* Pointer to start of shared memory region          */
    char  usage[256];   /* For error message                                 */
    if ( argc != 2 ) {
        sprintf(usage, "Usage: %s /shm-path\n", argv[0]);
        usage_error(usage);
    }
    /* Create the named shared memory object for reading and writing. */
    if ( (fd = shm_open(argv[1], O_CREAT | O_EXCL | O_RDWR,
                        S_IRUSR | S_IWUSR)) == -1 )
        fatal_error(errno, "shm_open");

    if ( ftruncate(fd, BUF_SIZE) == -1 )  /* Make it a fixed size.    */
        fatal_error(errno, "ftruncate");

     /* Map the object into the process address space. */
    if ( (shmp = mmap(NULL, BUF_SIZE, PROT_READ | PROT_WRITE,
                      MAP_SHARED, fd, 0)) == MAP_FAILED )
        fatal_error(errno, "mmap");

    if ( -1 == close(fd) )          /* Close unneeded file descriptor. */
        fatal_error(errno, "close");

    /* Write two strings at fixed locations into this memory. */
❶ strcpy(shmp + offset1, "Hello");
    strcpy(shmp + offset2, "World");
    exit(EXIT_SUCCESS);
}
```

This particular program allocates a fixed number of bytes to the shared memory region, but it doesn't use very much of the region. Notice how it writes strings into the memory by adding an integer offset to the pointer shmp ❶.

Now let's look at the code for the program that reads the strings from this shared memory:

```
#include "shm_demo1.h" /* For definitions of constants              */

int main(int argc, char *argv[])
{
    int    fd;          /* File descriptor referring to shared memory object */
    char *shmp;         /* Pointer to start of shared memory region          */
    char  usage[256];   /* For error message                                 */
```

```
    if ( (argc != 2) || (argv[1][0] != '/') ) {
        sprintf(usage, "Usage: %s /shm-name\n", argv[0]);
        usage_error(usage);
    }
    /* Open the named shared memory object for reading and writing. */
❶ if ( (fd = shm_open(argv[1], O_RDWR, 0)) == -1 )
        fatal_error(errno, "shm_open");

    /* Map the object into the process's address space. */
    if ( (shmp = mmap(NULL, BUF_SIZE, PROT_READ | PROT_WRITE,
                    MAP_SHARED, fd, 0)) == MAP_FAILED )
        fatal_error(errno, "mmap");

    if ( -1 == close(fd) )  /* Close unneeded file descriptor.        */
        fatal_error(errno, "close");

    /* Print the two strings that are supposed to be in the locations
       offset1 and offset2 away from the region start. */
❷ printf("%s\n", shmp + offset1);
    printf("%s\n", shmp + offset2);

    shm_unlink(argv[1]);     /* Remove this reference to memory object. */
    exit(EXIT_SUCCESS);
}
```

This program looks very similar to the first. The significant differences are in how the shared memory object is opened ❶ and in the fact that this program doesn't call ftruncate(). Notice that this program prints by referencing the strings to be printed by adding integer constants to the start of the memory region ❷.

I built both programs, naming the executables shm_creator_demo1 and shm_user_demo1. I'll first run the creator program:

```
$ ./shm_creator_demo1 /shmdemo1
$ ls -l /dev/shm/shmdemo1
-rw------- 1 stewart stewart 8192 Jun  7 10:14 /dev/shm/shmdemo1
```

I ran ls -l after to show that the device file */dev/shm/shmdemo1* contains 8192 bytes, the size passed to ftruncate(). (You can also view its contents as if it were a regular file—for example, by entering cat /dev/shm/shmdemo1—but you'll see that it has no newlines.)

Now I'll run the user program:

```
$ ./shm_user_demo1 /shmdemo1
Hello
Goodbye
```

The user program successfully read the data written by the first program and printed it.

Pointer Pitfalls in Shared Memory

When a shared memory region is created and used by two or more processes, it is mapped into each process's virtual address space by the kernel. The starting address in each process is not necessarily the same. To make this clear, modify each of the two preceding programs by including the following instruction:

```
printf("Memory is mapped in process starting at address %p\n", shmp);
```

Recompile and build both programs and run them again, and you'll see something similar to this:

```
$ ./shm_creator_demo1 /test2
Memory is mapped in process starting at address 0x7f75cd792000
$ ./shm_user_demo1 /test2
Memory is mapped in process starting at address 0x7fa439bb9000
Hello
World
```

In fact, each time you run either program, the shared memory will be mapped to a different starting address. Let me make this concrete. In the preceding runs, the first process copied the string "Hello" to the location starting at address 0x7f75cd792000 + 0x64, whereas the second mapped it to address 0x7fa439bb9000 + 0x64. If the second program tried to read that string by using a pointer to its location, the program would likely fail because the address 0x7f75cd792000 + 0x64 in the second program is not necessarily a valid address, and it certainly doesn't contain the string "Hello". Figure 12-3 visualizes this particular shared memory mapping.

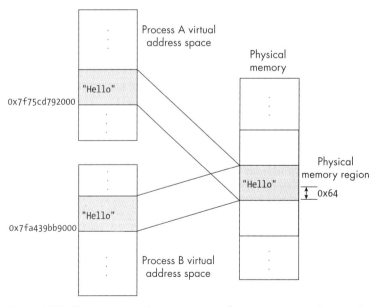

Figure 12-3: Two processes sharing a mapped memory region, showing that the starting address of the region is different in each process

Let's consider a second pair of programs. In this example, the header file that they share declares a structure containing an array and two char* pointer variables:

```
typedef struct _shared
{
    char *ptr1;
    char *ptr2;
    char  data[4096];
} shareddata;
```

I'll create a variation of the *shm_creator_demo1.c* program, named *shm _creator_demo2.c*, in which each pointer is assigned a particular value that will highlight a pitfall of shared memory programming. The rest of the program is essentially the same:

shm_creator _demo2.c
```
int main(int argc, char *argv[])
{
    int         fd;    /* File descriptor referring to shared memory object */
❶  shareddata *shmp;  /* Pointer to start of shared memory region          */
    char        usage[256];  /* For error message                          */

    if ( (argc != 2) || (argv[1][0] != '/') ) {
        sprintf(usage, "Usage: %s /shm-name\n", argv[0]);
        usage_error(usage);
    }
    if ( (fd = shm_open(argv[1],O_CREAT|O_EXCL|O_RDWR,S_IRUSR|S_IWUSR)) == -1)
        fatal_error(errno, "shm_open");
❷  if ( ftruncate(fd, sizeof(shareddata)) == -1 )
        fatal_error(errno, "ftruncate");
    if ( (shmp = (shareddata*) mmap(NULL, sizeof(shareddata),
            PROT_READ | PROT_WRITE, MAP_SHARED, fd, 0)) == MAP_FAILED )
        fatal_error(errno, "mmap");

    shmp->ptr1 = (char*)
❸  malloc(20);
    strcpy(shmp->ptr1, "Problem");
    strcpy(shmp->data, "Hello World");
❹  shmp->ptr2 = (char*) &(shmp->data);

    exit(EXIT_SUCCESS);
}
```

The variable shmp is a pointer to a shareddata structure ❶. The size of the memory object is made the size of that structure ❷. Now comes the interesting part. This program calls malloc() to allocate more memory ❸. This memory is not in the shared memory region; it's just in the heap of the calling process. It stores the address of this malloc-ed memory in the variable shmp->ptr1, which is part of the shared memory, and copies the string "Problem" into the malloc-ed memory. It then makes a copy of the string "Hello World" in the shareddata structure's array, starting at index 0. The last instruction stores the address of the start of this array, shmp->data, in the pointer shmp->ptr2 ❹. Figure 12-4 illustrates where the various objects reside in virtual memory.

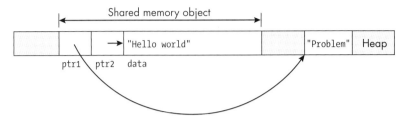

Figure 12-4: The arrangement of data in the shared memory created by shm_creator_demo2.c

The program that reads this shared memory, named *shm_user_demo2.c*, has a few small changes, shown next. The listing omits the code that hasn't changed:

shm_user
_demo2.c
```
int main(int argc, char *argv[])
{
    int       fd;    /* File descriptor referring to shared memory object */
    shareddata *shmp; /* Pointer to start of shared memory region        */
    char      usage[256];  /* For error message                          */
    --snip--
    if ( (shmp = (shareddata*) mmap(NULL, BUF_SIZE, PROT_READ | PROT_WRITE,
        MAP_SHARED, fd, 0)) == MAP_FAILED )
        fatal_error(errno, "mmap");
    --snip--
❶ printf("%s\n", shmp->ptr1);
❷ printf("%s\n", (char*) (shmp->ptr2));
    --snip--
}
```

When we compile and run both of these programs, first shm_creator_demo2 and then shm_user_demo2, the second will cause a segmentation fault. What is wrong?

The first problem is that shmp->ptr1 stores the address that malloc() returned to the other process, not to this one. It's an address in a different process's heap. It refers to junk here, or to an invalid address at best. Printing its contents ❶ causes a dereference that fails. If we comment out that first line, the program will also segfault, because when it tries to print the string starting at the address stored in shmp->ptr2 ❷, it has to dereference that pointer. But that dereference fails because that pointer stores an address in the other process's address space.

POINTERS, OFFSETS, AND SHARED MEMORY

When two or more processes establish a POSIX shared memory region, none of them should use the addresses in that region to access any part of it. Addresses will vary from one process to another, and dereferencing them will result in segmentation faults or other invalid memory access failures. In short, *do not use pointers inside shared memory!*

Instead, programs must use *offsets*, which are integer values that store the locations in the shared memory relative to the start of that memory. Pointer arithmetic can then be used with care to dereference the locations. For example, if startp is the start of the shared memory region, and int offset stores the number of bytes between the start and some data item, then (char*)(startp) + offset is the correct expression for the starting address of the data item. Of course, an offset must lie within the shared memory region; otherwise, if the program tries to dereference it, an invalid memory access occurs.

Lastly, a program cannot store the address returned by malloc() or any other function that creates memory outside of the shared memory region in any variable inside that region, because it references a meaningful memory address only in the address space of the process that created it.

Race Conditions

When several processes all read, but don't modify, some shared object, the order in which they read doesn't change their collective behavior; since reading doesn't modify the object, there's no race condition. However, when at least one process (or thread) modifies a shared object that is read by one or more other processes, the code is susceptible to race conditions.

To illustrate, suppose that counter is a variable in a shared memory region and that two or more processes execute the instruction

```
counter = counter + 1;
```

at some point in time. This instruction isn't atomic; it is typically compiled into three separate machine instructions of the form:

```
mov register1, @counter
add register1, 1
mov @counter, register1
```

If two different processes execute these three machine instructions and their computations are interleaved in time, either because one was interrupted by the second, which ran briefly, and then the first ran again, or because they're running on separate processors at the same time, then the result can be incorrect.

To make this concrete, suppose that counter is initially 5. If two processes each execute counter = counter + 1 and no race occurs, the value of counter should be 7 afterward. But it's possible for the instructions to be executed in such a way that the result is not 7. Consider the following sequence, where t0, t1, t2, and so on represent successive points in time, and P1 and P2 are two different processes incrementing counter:

```
t0: P1  executes mov register1, @counter      {register1 == 5 }
t1: P1  executes add register1, 1             {register1 == 6 }
t2: P2  executes mov register2, @counter      {register2 == 5 }
t3: P2  executes add register2, 1             {register2 == 6 }
t4: P1  executes mov @counter, register1      {counter   == 5 }
t5: P2  executes mov @counter, register2      {counter   == 6 }
```

The final value of counter is 6, not 7 as it should be. Programs using shared variables must take steps to prevent this behavior.

We need a way to guarantee that when one process executes an instruction such as counter = counter + 1, no other process can modify the value of counter until the first process completes the instruction and the value of counter is stored in memory. For many decades, computer scientists have investigated and proposed a variety of solutions to this problem, which are generally called *synchronization* methods. Some of them, such as semaphores and mutex locks, have found their way into Unix systems.

A *mutex lock* is an object on which two operations are defined: locking it and unlocking it. These operations are atomic in the sense that if two processes or threads try to acquire the lock at the same time, only one will succeed and the other will be blocked in the call to lock the mutex. We examine mutex locks in Chapter 15. In this chapter, we explore the use of semaphores.

Semaphores

Semaphores were invented by Edsger Dijkstra in 1963 while he was trying to solve synchronization problems in the design of the *THE* operating system [9]. Dijkstra originally defined two operations that acted on semaphores, which he named *P* and *V*, short for the two Dutch words that translate to English as *probe* and *increase*. People have used other names for these operations; the *P* operation is sometimes called *wait* or *down*, and the *V* operation *post*, *up*, or *signal*. I'll use *wait* and *post* here, since they're the names adopted in the POSIX.1-2024 specification.

Overview

A *semaphore* is an integer variable whose value is not allowed to become less than zero, and upon which two atomic operations are defined:

wait()   Decrements the semaphore if its value is positive. If its value is 0, the function blocks the process or thread that tried to decrement the semaphore and puts it on a list of waiting processes associated with the semaphore. For semaphore S, its operation is described by:

```
if ( S <= 0 )
    // Block calling process and put on S waitlist.
S--;
```

post()   Increments the semaphore, and if the semaphore's value becomes positive after incrementing it, the function wakes up a process or thread currently blocked in its wait list. For semaphore S, its operation is described by:

```
S++;
if ( S > 0 )
    // Resume a process currently on S waitlist in its call to wait().
```

There is no requirement that the waiting list of a semaphore be implemented as a first-in-first-out queue. It's up to an implementation to decide which process to wake up. Notice that, when a process wakes up, it continues to execute the code in wait(), which means that it immediately decrements S and returns from the call.

Both of these operations are atomic, or indivisible. They run from start to completion without being interrupted. When the post() operation wakes up a process, no other process can execute the code inside wait() or post() until the newly awakened process returns from the call to wait().

If the initial value of a semaphore is 1, then only one process can successfully decrement it. Any other processes that subsequently try to decrement it are then blocked. If a semaphore's value is initially 1 and post() operations are only applied to it when its value is 0, then its value is always either 0 or 1. Such a semaphore is called a *binary semaphore*. If post() operations could be applied to it when its value is 1, its value would exceed 1, and it would not be a binary semaphore.

If the initial value N of the semaphore is greater than 1, the number of processes that can successfully decrement it is equal to N. This type of semaphore is called a *counting semaphore*.

Binary semaphores can be used to ensure that only a single process executes a critical section of code. The idea is that, to protect a data structure from race conditions, we create a semaphore for it and we bracket all attempts to access that data structure by calls to wait() and post(), as follows:

```
wait(S);
    // Critical section code that modifies a shared data structure
post(S);
```

Because only one process can decrement S, only one process at a time can execute the critical code. We say that a process *acquires* or *locks* a binary semaphore when it has decremented it without being blocked. This is an abstraction. It doesn't describe, for example, how we create and how we initialize semaphores. It's time to search for an API for programming with them in Unix.

System V Semaphores

In order to compare the POSIX and System V APIs for the use of semaphores, I've included this brief description of the System V semaphore API. The System V semaphore API is described by the man pages:

semctl (2)	- System V semaphore control operations
semget (2)	- get a System V semaphore set identifier
semop (2)	- System V semaphore operations
semtimedop (2)	- System V semaphore operations

This API is older than the POSIX one. It was designed to be very general, and as a result, it's more complex to learn and use. There aren't explicit equivalents of the wait() and post() operations. Instead of operating on a single semaphore, the System V methods act on sets of semaphores. They also allow the semaphores in the set to be increased or decreased by amounts greater than 1. The creation of a semaphore in System V is a separate function from its initialization. This opens up the possibility of race conditions, which adds to the complexity of using them. The sequence of steps that we need to follow to create and use System V semaphores is roughly as follows:

1. Request a semaphore set using a System V IPC *key*. A key must be generated before this step.

2. Initialize the semaphore set by setting the value of each semaphore in the set.

3. Set up operations to be used with these semaphores.

4. Use the semaphore operations set up in the previous step.

5. Delete the semaphore set.

In short, we need to read about System V keys and how to generate them. We also need to learn how to invoke operations on semaphore sets with the functions semctl() and semop(). You'll see soon that POSIX semaphores are easier to program.

POSIX Semaphores

The sem_overview(7) man page presents an overview of POSIX semaphores. POSIX semaphores have a simple, well-designed interface. POSIX defines two types of semaphores, named and unnamed:

Named semaphore   Has a name of the form /*name*, in which *name* is a string of up to NAME_MAX-4 nonslash characters, similar to a shared memory region name. Two processes operate on the same named semaphore by passing that name to the sem_open() function.

Unnamed semaphore   Has no name. It must be created in an address space common to all processes or threads that operate on it. This means that, for processes, it must be in a shared memory object shared by the processes.

Early versions of Linux implemented only unnamed semaphores, but starting with version 2.6, Linux supports named ones as well. There are eight different functions related to the use of named and unnamed semaphores. Some are used only for named semaphores, some for unnamed semaphores, and some for both. Figure 12-5 shows which functions are used for which types of semaphores.

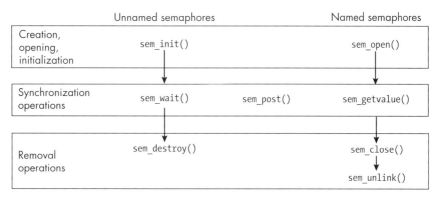

Figure 12-5: A comparison of the sequence of steps for using named and unnamed POSIX semaphores

The differences between named and unnamed semaphores are in how they are created and removed. The wait() and post() operations are the same for both. POSIX adds a sem_getvalue() function to the API, but it's unlikely you'll ever need to call it, and it isn't part of the conventional interface.

Unnamed Semaphores

Unnamed semaphores are memory based; for processes to access them, they must be placed in a shared memory region accessible to all processes. If they're used by threads, they must be either global in the program or in its heap. The functions used for unnamed semaphores are as follows:

sem_init()   Creates an unnamed semaphore

sem_wait()   Decrements and locks the given semaphore

sem_post()   Increments the given semaphore

sem_getvalue()   Gets the current value of the semaphore

sem_destroy()   Deallocates resources of the semaphore

Programs using any POSIX semaphore function must include the *semaphore.h* header file and link the program to the *pthread* library with the linker flag -lpthread. The semaphore type in POSIX is sem_t:

```
int sem_init(sem_t *sem, int pshared, unsigned int value);
```

The first argument is the address of a sem_t variable. The second argument (pshared) indicates whether the semaphore is shared by threads or by processes. If it's 0, the semaphore is shared by threads and should be placed in either the heap or declared globally. If its value is 1, it's process-shared and the semaphore must be in a shared memory region. The initial value of the semaphore is passed in its third parameter and must be a nonnegative integer.

The two synchronization operations are prototyped as:

```
int sem_wait(sem_t *sem);
int sem_post(sem_t *sem);
```

Each expects the address of a semaphore variable and returns 0 on success and -1 on failure. The function to release the semaphore resources is:

```
int sem_destroy(sem_t *sem);
```

This should be called only after all processes are no longer using the semaphore.

Listing 12-1 contains a simple program that uses an unnamed semaphore to prevent race conditions on updates to a shared counter variable. To save space, it has no error handling; the complete program is available in the book's source code distribution.

unnamedsem *_demo.c*
```
#include "common_hdrs.h"
#include <sys/mman.h>
#include <sys/wait.h>
#include <semaphore.h>
#define  ITERATIONS    1000000

typedef struct shmbuf {
    sem_t  sem;                    /* POSIX unnamed semaphore   */
    size_t count;                  /* A shared counter          */
} sharedmem;
char *shmpath = "/SHMDEMO";        /* Shared memory object name */
sharedmem *shmp;                   /* Pointer to shared memory  */

int main(int argc, char *argv[])
{
    int fd, i;

     /* Create shared memory object and set its size. */
    fd = shm_open(shmpath, O_CREAT | O_EXCL | O_RDWR, S_IRUSR | S_IWUSR);
    ftruncate(fd, sizeof(sharedmem));

    shmp = mmap(NULL,      /* Map mem object into process memory.          */
              sizeof(sharedmem), PROT_READ | PROT_WRITE, MAP_SHARED, fd, 0);
❶ sem_init(&shmp->sem,1,1);/* Initialize binary process-shared semaphore. */
    shmp->count = 0;       /* Set count to 0 before creating a child process. */
    switch( fork() ) {
    case -1:
        fatal_error(errno, "fork");
    case 0:                        /* Child process  */
        for ( i = 0; i < ITERATIONS; i++ ) {
            sem_wait(&shmp->sem);
```

```
            shmp->count++;
            sem_post(&shmp->sem);
        }
        exit(EXIT_SUCCESS);
    default:                    /* Parent process */
        for ( i = 0; i < ITERATIONS; i++ ) {
            sem_wait(&shmp->sem);
            shmp->count--;
            sem_post(&shmp->sem);
        }
        wait(NULL);             /* Wait for child to terminate. */
        printf("The final value of count, which should be 0, is %ld.\n",
                shmp->count);
        shm_unlink(shmpath); /* Remove shared memory object. */
        exit(EXIT_SUCCESS);
    }
}
```

Listing 12-1: A program that uses an unnamed POSIX semaphore to protect updates to a shared variable in a memory region shared by parent and child processes

If you build this program, naming it unnamedsem_demo, and run it, you should see the following output:

```
$ ./unnamedsem_demo
The final value of count, which should be 0, is 0.
```

You can run it any number of times and its output will be unchanged. Now change the semaphore's initial value ❶ to 2, recompile, and run the program a few times. You'll see that the count is wrong with each run:

```
$ ./unnamedsem_demo
The final value of count, which should be 0, is -169841.
$ ./unnamedsem_demo
The final value of count, which should be 0, is 17422.
```

When the semaphore is initialized to 2, neither process is blocked in its call to sem_wait() and the semaphore serves no purpose at all. The race condition still exists, and the parent and child corrupt the value of the counter.

Named Semaphores

Named semaphores are like unnamed semaphores in that we use the same wait() and post() operations for each. The difference is in how they're created and removed. Named semaphores are created with sem_open(), closed with sem_close(), and removed with sem_unlink().

The sem_open() synopsis is:

```
#include <semaphore.h>
sem_t *sem_open(const char *name, int oflag);
sem_t *sem_open(const char *name, int oflag, mode_t mode, unsigned int value);
```

A program calls the first form to open a semaphore that's already been created. It calls the second form to create a new semaphore. In both cases, the first argument (name) is a NULL-terminated string of the form "/*somename*", in which *somename* is, at most, NAME_MAX-4 characters and has no slash. The second argument should be one of the three values shown in Table 12-1. The table explains what the function does depending on the value of oflag and whether or not the name exists before the call.

Table 12-1: The Semantics of a Call to sem_open()

oflag	Name exists	Name doesn't exist
0	Opens existing semaphore successfully	Fails, setting errno to ENOENT
O_CREAT	Opens existing semaphore and ignores remaining arguments	Creates a new semaphore with the given name and properties
O_CREAT | O_EXCL	Fails, setting errno to EEXIST	Creates a new semaphore with the given name and properties

If the second argument includes the O_CREAT flag, the call must include the mode and initial value arguments. The mode can be specified with an octal numeric constant such as 0600 or, if the *fcntl.h* header file is included, then with symbolic definitions such as S_IRUSR and S_IWUSR. The process umask is applied to the requested mode. The initial value must be nonnegative. Some examples are:

```
sem_open("/MYSEM", 0);          /* Opens /MYSEM. Fails if it does not exist. */
sem_open("/MYSEM", O_CREAT, 0660, 1); /* Creates /MYSEM with initial value
                                1 and mode rw-rw----           */
sem_open("/MYSEM", O_CREAT | O_EXCL, 0660, 1); /* Like the preceding call but
                                        fails if /MYSEM exists  */
```

In all cases, if sem_open() is successful, it returns a pointer to the address of either the new semaphore or the existing one. If it fails, it returns SEM_FAILED and sets errno to indicate the error.

When a process no longer needs to use the semaphore, it should call sem_close(), passing the address of the semaphore. The semaphore will be closed when the process terminates if it doesn't close it explicitly. Closing it frees the resources associated with the process having it open; it does not remove the semaphore object itself, just the process's connection to it.

A process calls sem_unlink() to remove a semaphore's name and mark the semaphore object for deletion. The semaphore object is not removed until there are no more processes using it. It's safe to call sem_unlink() after all processes that want to use the semaphore have called sem_open(), since its name is no longer needed once all processes have opened it.

There aren't many situations in which we'd need a named semaphore, because in many cases, an unnamed semaphore is sufficient, as in the following two cases:

- Threads within a single program can use an unnamed semaphore on the heap or declared globally.

- Processes that set up a shared memory object can access an unnamed semaphore in that object. Since the object's declaration must be visible to the processes anyway, the semaphore itself is visible as well.

One use of named semaphores is when unrelated processes that don't share a memory region need to synchronize with each other. For example, they might need to synchronize accesses to a shared file. In this case, using a named semaphore is easier than setting up a shared memory region that contains an unnamed semaphore. But in the case of accessing a shared file, it's probably better to use file locks, a topic I don't cover in the book.

To demonstrate the use of a named semaphore, I created a program in which a process forks a child, after which both processes use the fprintf() library function to write very long, newline-terminated strings to the file inside for loops. The strings are long enough that they won't be written atomically by fprintf(), assuming the typical I/O block size of 4096 bytes. If there were no race conditions between parent and child, every line of the file would have been written by exactly one process, but if the outputs are intermingled, then the lines will have a mix of strings from each process. The program is displayed in part in Listing 12-2, without most error handling.

namedsem _demo.c

```
#define  ITERATIONS    1000
#define  SIZE          8192          /* 2 I/O blocks */
#define  SEMNAME       "/DEMOSEM"
#define  WAIT(S) if ( -1 == sem_wait(S) ) fatal_error(errno, "sem_wait")
#define  POST(S) if ( -1 == sem_post(S) ) fatal_error(errno, "sem_post")

int main(int argc, char *argv[])
{
    sem_t *sem;
    int    i;
    FILE  *fp;
    char   str1[SIZE], str2[SIZE];

    memset(str1, 'a', SIZE-1);
    memset(str2, 'b', SIZE-1);
    str1[SIZE-1] = '\0';        /* str1 = "aaaa...aaa" */
    str2[SIZE-1] = '\0';        /* str2 = "bbbb...bbb" */

    fp = fopen(argv[1], "w");
    if ( SEM_FAILED == (sem = sem_open(SEMNAME, O_CREAT | O_EXCL, 0660, 1)) )
        fatal_error(errno, "sem_open");
    switch ( fork() ) {
    case -1: fatal_error(errno, "fork");
    case 0:
        for ( i = 0; i < ITERATIONS; i++ ) {
```

```
            WAIT(sem);
            fprintf(fp, "%s\n", str1);
            fflush(fp);
            POST(sem);
        }
        exit(EXIT_SUCCESS);
    default:
        for ( i = 0; i < ITERATIONS; i++ ) {
            WAIT(sem);
            fprintf(fp, "%s\n", str2);
            fflush(fp);
            POST(sem);
        }
        wait(NULL);
        fclose(fp);
        sem_unlink(SEMNAME);
        exit(EXIT_SUCCESS);
    }
}
```

Listing 12-2: A program using a named semaphore to prevent race conditions when parent and child write to a file

Build and run this program, creating a new file. It won't produce output, but we can run a check using grep on the file:

```
$ ./namedsem_demo tempfile
$ wc tempfile
    2000     2000 16384000 tempfile   # As expected, it has 2000 lines.
$ grep -E -c 'ba|ab' tempfile
0                                      # No lines have ab or ba.
```

This output shows that the lines are not intermingled. Now change the initial value of the semaphore to 2 so that it no longer provides the locking effect, and repeat these instructions:

```
$ ./namedsem_demo tempfile
$ wc tempfile
    2000     2000 16384000 tempfile   # As expected, it has 2,000 lines.
$ grep -E -c 'ba|ab' tempfile
993                                    # Most lines have ab or ba.
```

The fact that some lines have both *a*'s and *b*'s implies that the calls to fprintf() were interrupted and that sometimes their string arguments were only partially written to the file.

A Shared Memory Producer Consumer Program

We're now ready to implement a solution to the producer-consumer problem by using POSIX shared memory. Earlier we had to use a shared file to implement it, and that solution had several deficiencies.

For this program, the producer writes integers into the shared buffer and the consumer reads those integers. Writing numbers simplifies the program and doesn't distract us with the messy details of writing string data into a shared memory object. This solution works when there are multiple producers and multiple consumers.

The common buffer, an array of ints, is created inside a shared memory object. Because the producer needs an index to the next place to write its data and the consumer needs the index of the next location from which it reads the data, the buffer and these variables should all be part of a single structure that will be created in a shared memory object, such as:

```
#define BUF_SIZE 512      /* Buffer capacity                    */
typedef struct _shmbuf {
    int front, rear;      /* Index of next read, write in buffer */
    int buf[BUF_SIZE];    /* Stores data being transferred       */
} sharedbuf;
```

The rear member is the next index to fill in the buffer, and the front member is the next index to read. They're both initialized to 0.

To add a new data item to the buffer, assuming the data structure is pointed to by sharedbuf, the producer would execute code of the form

```
sharedbuf->buf[sharedbuf->rear] = data;
sharedbuf->rear = (sharedbuf->rear + 1) % BUF_SIZE;
```

and the consumer would remove a data item similarly:

```
data = sharedbuf->buf[sharedbuf->rear];
sharedbuf->rear = (sharedbuf->rear + 1) % BUF_SIZE;
```

Because it's possible that rear and front may be the same location, these updates represent a race condition on the buf array itself. Therefore, we need to lock the buffer before this update and unlock it after. We can use a binary semaphore for this. We'll include it in the shared memory object:

```
typedef struct _shmbuf {
    sem_t mutex;           /* To prevent race condition on buffer */
    int   front, rear;     /* Index of next read, write in buffer */
    int   buf[BUF_SIZE];   /* Stores data being transferred       */
} sharedbuf;
```

Each process calls sem_wait() before the update and sem_post() after it.

The two processes need to keep track of how many items are in the shared buffer. More accurately, producers need to know whether there are available slots to fill in the buffer pool, and the consumer needs to know whether there are no items to consume. We could use a counter variable for this purpose and design the producer and consumer to update it accordingly, but then their main program loops would be busy waiting loops. For example, the consumer's loop, in pseudocode, would be

```
while ( TRUE ) {
    if ( sharedmem_counter > 0 )
        value = get_next_item(sharedmem_buffer)
        print value
}
```

and the producer's would be

```
while ( TRUE ) {
    if ( sharedmem_counter < BUF_SIZE )
        generate new value
        add_next_item(sharedmem_buffer, value)
}
```

The producers and consumers would execute millions of needless instructions, polling the value of the counter until it satisfied the `if` condition. This is where the idea of a counting semaphore comes into play. Instead of using a single counter variable, we can use two counting semaphores to keep track of the number of empty and filled buffer slots.

One semaphore, initialized to 0, would be the number of filled buffers. The producer would increment it with `sem_post()` each time it fills a buffer, and the consumer would decrement it with `sem_wait()` each time it emptied a buffer. A second semaphore, initialized to `BUF_SIZE`, would be the number of empty buffers. The producer would decrement it with `sem_wait()` each time it fills a buffer, and the consumer would increment it with `sem_post()` each time it emptied a buffer. Using semaphore operations in this way obviates the need for a counter variable and extra calls to lock and unlock a binary semaphore before and after the update to it.

Adding these semaphores to the shared memory object, its final form is:

```
#define BUF_SIZE 512       /* Buffer capacity                      */
typedef struct shmbuf {
    sem_t  filledbuf_count; /* To count filled buffers             */
    sem_t  emptybuf_count;  /* To count empty buffers              */
    sem_t  mutex;           /* To prevent race condition on buffer */
    int    front, rear;     /* Index of next read, write in buffer */
    int    buf[BUF_SIZE];   /* Stores data being transferred       */
} sharedbuf;
```

Before writing the producer and consumer programs, I'm going to define three macros to simplify the error handling and clarify the code:

```
#define WAIT(S)      if (-1 == sem_wait(S)) fatal_error(errno, "sem_wait")
#define POST(S)      if (-1 == sem_post(S)) fatal_error(errno, "sem_post")
#define INITSEM(S,N) if (-1 == sem_init(S,1,(N))) fatal_error(errno,"sem_init")
```

With these macros, which I put into the header file, the operations are easily discerned in the code.

The function that a producer calls to add an item to the buffer is now:

```
void add_next(sharedbuf *bufpool, int data)
{
    WAIT(&bufpool->emptybuf_count);
    WAIT(&bufpool->mutex);                  /* Lock buffer array.   */
    bufpool->buf[bufpool->rear] = data;
    bufpool->rear = (bufpool->rear + 1) % BUF_SIZE;
    POST(&bufpool->mutex);                  /* Unlock buffer array. */
    POST(&bufpool->filledbuf_count);
}
```

The consumer will call get_next() to remove an item:

```
int get_next(sharedbuf *bufpool)
{
    int val;
    WAIT(&bufpool->filledbuf_count);
    WAIT(&bufpool->mutex);                  /* Lock buffer array.   */
    val = bufpool->buf[bufpool->front];
    bufpool->front= (bufpool->front + 1) % BUF_SIZE;
    POST(&bufpool->mutex);                  /* Unlock buffer array. */
    POST(&bufpool->emptybuf_count);
    return val;
}
```

The producer will get its data from standard input. This way we can pipe numbers from a file into it or enter them interactively in the terminal. The consumer process will print the numbers it gets onto its standard output. This design implies that we shouldn't background the consumer process. Instead we'll run the two processes in the foreground in separate terminals.

We'll make the consumer process the one that creates the shared memory object and the semaphores. It will be responsible for removing the shared memory and for destroying the semaphore. It will run forever until we kill it with a signal. For this reason, it will need a cleanup function that should be run when it's sent a signal, and the shared memory object pointer will have to be file-scoped.

The consumer program is named *shm_consumer.c* and is presented in Listing 12-3, with some functions, signal handling setup, and error handling omitted. The complete program is in the book's source code distribution.

shm_consumer.c
```
#include "shm_prodcons.h"
char      *shmpath;
```

```
sharedbuf *shmp;

int get_next(sharedbuf* bufpool)
--snip--

void cleanup(int signo)
--snip--

int main(int argc, char *argv[])
{
    struct sigaction sigact;
    int         fd;
    int         val;

    if ( argc != 2 ) {     /* Get the shared memory name from command line. */
        fprintf(stderr, "Usage: %s /shm-path\n", argv[0]);
        exit(EXIT_FAILURE);
    }
    shmpath = argv[1];
     /* Create shared memory object and set its size to the size
        of our structure. */
    fd = shm_open(shmpath, O_CREAT | O_EXCL | O_RDWR, S_IRUSR | S_IWUSR);
    ftruncate(fd, sizeof(sharedbuf));

    shmp = mmap(NULL, sizeof(sharedbuf), /* Map object into address space. */
                PROT_READ | PROT_WRITE, MAP_SHARED, fd, 0);
    // OMITTED: Signal handler setup

    /* Initialize semaphores as process-shared. */
    INITSEM(&shmp->filledbuf_count, 0);
    INITSEM(&shmp->emptybuf_count, BUF_SIZE);
    INITSEM(&shmp->mutex, 1);

    shmp->front = 0;     /* Initialize counters. */
    shmp->rear = 0;

    while ( TRUE ) {
        val = get_next(shmp);
        printf("%d\n", val);
      ❶ // Add an artificial random delay here.
    }
    cleanup(1);
    exit(EXIT_SUCCESS);
}
```

Listing 12-3: The consumer program in the shared memory implementation of the producer-consumer problem

The while loop is no longer a busy waiting loop because the consumer will be blocked in the get_next() function when it tries to wait on the filledbuf_count semaphore and will be awakened when a producer adds more data. I'll explain the comment about adding a delay ❶ after we run this pair of programs.

The producer is simpler because it doesn't have to create anything. It's presented in Listing 12-4, with error handling omitted.

shm_producer.c
```
#include "shm_prodcons.h"
char *shmpath;

void add_next(sharedbuf *bufpool, int data)
--snip--

int main(int argc, char *argv[])
{
    int fd;
    int val;

    if ( argc != 2 ) {
        fprintf(stderr, "Usage: %s /shm-path\n", argv[0]);
        exit(EXIT_FAILURE);
    }

    shmpath = argv[1];
    fd = shm_open(shmpath, O_RDWR, 0);
    sharedbuf *shmp = mmap(NULL, sizeof(sharedbuf),
                           PROT_READ | PROT_WRITE, MAP_SHARED, fd, 0);
    while ( TRUE ) {
        if ( scanf("%d", &val) > 0 )
            add_next(shmp, val);
      ❷ // Add a print statement to show what we're sending.
        else
            break;
    }
    exit(EXIT_SUCCESS);
}
```

Listing 12-4: The producer program in the shared memory implementation of the producer-consumer problem

Both programs expect the name of the shared memory object on the command line. To set them up, you have to start up the consumer first, since it creates the semaphore. In one terminal, enter

```
$ ./shm_consumer /PRODCONS
```

and in the second, start up the producer:

```
$ ./shm_producer /PRODCONS
```

You can enter numbers interactively this way, and they'll appear in the other terminal. Alternatively, try

```
$ ./shm_consumer /PRODCONS > outputfile
```

and in the second, enter:

```
$ seq 1 10000 | shm_producer /PRODCONS
```

The numbers 1, 2, . . . , 10,000 will be sent to the consumer, which will send them to its standard output, redirected to *outputfile*. Kill the consumer with CTRL-C and browse the output file or run wc on it to verify that it has exactly 10,000 lines.

When the producer and consumer work at the same pace and do nothing else besides filling and emptying the buffers, they will run in lock-step, and the buffer will be empty most of the time. Each time the producer fills a buffer, it's emptied immediately. In practice, the producer and consumer process would be performing other actions, and the buffer might fill up while the consumer was busy or it might stay empty for a while when the producer was busy. If we make the buffer capacity small enough, the producer and consumer will spend more time waiting for the other. The consumer and producer code in the example has no artificial delay.

To see how a pair of programs might actually coordinate their updates, replace the commented line in the consumer program ❶ with a large randomized delay of several seconds, and in the producer program, replace the comment about printing ❷ with a print instruction that shows which number was written into the buffer, as well as another randomized delay. Make the buffer size small, say 20, and run the pair of programs. You'll see that the producer and consumer each wait for the other periodically. This simulates the way a pair of processes actually work together.

POSIX Message Queues

The mq_overview(7) man page contains a good summary of POSIX message queues and refers us to the man pages that describe how to use them. Message queues serve a different purpose than IPC facilities such as pipes and FIFOs, which we discuss in Chapter 13, for several reasons.

First, a message queue doesn't transfer data as a stream of bytes. If a process puts a message of size N bytes into a message queue, when the message is retrieved from the queue, it must be retrieved in its entirety. A process cannot, for example, request to read only $M < N$ bytes of a message. If it tries, the operation will fail.

Equally important, POSIX message queues are not first-in-first-out queues; the order in which messages are placed into a message queue is not necessarily the order in which they're retrieved, because each message is assigned a priority, and the queue itself is, in effect, a priority queue. When a message queue contains several messages, the next receive operation always removes the highest-priority message. Since messages can have the same priority, there can be multiple messages that have the highest priority. In this case, the oldest of them is retrieved. Priorities are integers from 0 up to MQ_PRIO_MAX − 1, which is a system-dependent constant. A program can get its value by calling sysconf(_SC_MQ_PRIO_MAX).

The POSIX message queue API is similar to the POSIX shared memory API. When a message queue is created, an *open message queue description* is also created, and a small integer like a file descriptor is returned to the process that created it. This descriptor is called a *message queue descriptor*. The relationship between message queue descriptors and open message queue descriptions is exactly the same as the one between file descriptors and open file descriptions. If you look back at Figure 4-1 in Chapter 4 and mentally replace the word *file* in that figure with *message queue*, you'll have a visualization of their relationship.

The functions for establishing a message queue, using it to exchange data, and closing and removing it when it's no longer needed have names that are similar to those in the POSIX shared memory API:

mq_open()   Creates and opens a new message queue or opens an existing one. Message queues are given names in the same form as shared memory objects and semaphores.

mq_send()   Puts a message into a message queue.

mq_receive()   Removes the oldest highest-priority message from a message queue if the queue is not empty. If the message queue is empty, by default the process is blocked until a message arrives.

mq_getattr(), mq_setattr()   Can be used to get or modify the attributes of a message queue, such as the maximum number of messages that it can hold or the maximum message size.

mq_notify()   Allows a process to request asynchronous notification of the arrival of messages in the queue. It uses the same event notification data structures as are used with POSIX timers, namely the struct sigevent. Setting up asynchronous notification frees a process from having to wait in a blocked state for messages to arrive in the queue or to poll it periodically in nonblocking mode. When a message is delivered to the queue, a notification, such as a signal, is sent to the process, which can then call mq_receive() inside the signal handler.

mq_close()   Closes a connection to a message queue.

mq_unlink()   Removes a message queue name and marks the message queue for removal. Once all processes have closed it, the message queue is deleted. Message queues have kernel persistence and will continue to exist until they're explicitly removed or the system is shut down.

The typical sequence of steps that a process takes to create a message queue and use it are as follows:

1. A process creates a new message queue, calling mq_open() and passing a name to it that other processes can use to open it. If a message queue has been created by another process and this process just wants to open it, it also calls mq_open(), but with different flags.

2. If a process wants to receive asynchronous notifications when messages are delivered, it then calls `mq_notify()`.

3. A process calls `mq_send()` to transfer messages into the message queue and calls `mq_receive()` to receive them.

4. When a process is finished using the message queue, it calls `mq_close()` to close its open message queue descriptor. This does not remove the description itself.

5. The process that created the message queue is the one that should remove it by calling `mq_unlink()`, which also removes the message queue name.

It's time to look at the prototypes of these functions, after which we'll create a few programs that demonstrate how to use message queues. We'll start with `mq_open()`:

```
#include <fcntl.h>          /* For O_* constants  */
#include <sys/stat.h>       /* For mode constants */
#include <mqueue.h>

mqd_t mq_open(const char *name, int oflag);
mqd_t mq_open(const char *name, int oflag, mode_t mode,
            struct mq_attr *attr);
```

This is similar to the `sem_open()` function. A program calls the first form to open a message queue that's already been created or calls the second form to create a new message queue. In either case, a successful call returns a message queue descriptor that we can use for the remaining operations. A message queue name is passed in the first argument and is of the form */mqname*. The same flags are used here as were used with the `shm_open()` and `sem_open()` functions.

The second argument is a bitwise-OR of flags that controls the opening mode. It must include one of `O_RDONLY`, `O_WRONLY`, or `O_RDWR`. These control the type of access that the calling process will have. If the caller will only receive messages, it opens it for read-only access, for example. We can optionally include `O_CREAT`, `O_EXCL`, and `O_TRUNC`, which have their usual effects, and we can also set `O_NONBLOCK` to set nonblocking mode on the descriptor. In this case, if `mq_receive()` or `mq_send()` would normally block, these functions would instead fail, setting errno to `EAGAIN`.

The attribute parameter can be set to `NULL` if we are satisfied with the default attributes. The members of a struct `mq_attr` are:

```
struct mq_attr {
    long mq_flags;      /* Flags (ignored for mq_open())   */
    long mq_maxmsg;     /* Max. # of messages on queue     */
    long mq_msgsize;    /* Max. message size (bytes)       */
    long mq_curmsgs;    /* # of messages currently in queue */
};
```

We're only allowed to modify the mq_maxmsg and mq_msgsize members when calling mq_open(); the values in the remaining fields are ignored.

The prototype for the send operation is:

```
#include <mqueue.h>
int mq_send(mqd_t mqdes, const char *msg_ptr,
            size_t msg_len, unsigned int msg_prio);
```

We give this function a message queue descriptor (mqdes) returned by the call to mq_open(), a pointer to data we want to send (msg_ptr), its length (msg_len), and a nonnegative integer priority (msg_prio). The message size cannot exceed the message size attribute of the queue, and it can be of size zero.

Messages are placed in the queue in decreasing order of priority, with newer messages of the same priority being placed after older messages with the same priority. If the queue is full, the process will be blocked until space is available, provided that the O_NONBLOCK flag was not set. If it is set, the call fails and errno is set to EAGAIN.

The prototype for the receive operation has almost the same prototype as the send operation. The only difference is that the last parameter is the address of a variable in which to store the received message's priority:

```
#include <mqueue.h>
int mq_receive(mqd_t mqdes, const char *msg_ptr,
               size_t msg_len, unsigned int *msg_prio);
```

This function places the oldest, highest-priority message into the buffer pointed to by msg_ptr. That buffer's size must be at least the mq_msgsize value of the queue's attribute structure. If the message queue is empty, the process is blocked, provided that the O_NONBLOCK flag was not set. If it is set, the call fails and errno is set to EAGAIN.

The mq_unlink() prototype looks the same as that of the other POSIX IPC facilities:

```
#include <mqueue.h>
int mq_unlink(const char *name);
```

It removes the name and destroys the open message queue description when all other processes have closed their connections to it. Let's look at a couple of example programs.

A Simple Message Queue Example

The first pair of demonstration programs exchange string data using a message queue. We'll design them so that running them confirms that higher-priority messages are received before lower-priority ones. One easy way to do this is to define the priority of a string to be its length. For example, the message "hello there" would have priority 11.

The receiving program creates the queue. It then enters a loop in which it retrieves messages from the queue and displays them on standard output.

It has a delay before it enters the loop so that the sending program has a chance to fill the queue with messages of varying priorities. If it doesn't delay, then each message would be displayed immediately and we wouldn't see the impact of its priority.

The receiving program is displayed in Listing 12-5.

mqrcv_demo.c
```c
#include <mqueue.h>
#include <sys/wait.h>

char *mqname;

int main(int argc, char *argv[])
{
    mqd_t    mqdes;               /* The message queue descriptor     */
    struct  mq_attr attr;         /* Message queue attribute structure */
    char    *msg_buffer;          /* Stores the received message      */
    ssize_t msg_size;             /* Size of buffer                   */
    unsigned int priority;        /* Priority of received message     */
    struct sigaction sigact;      /* To set up signal handler for SIGINT */
    if ( argc != 2 ) {
        fprintf(stderr, "Usage: %s <mq-name>\n", argv[0]);
        exit(EXIT_FAILURE);
    }
    mqname = argv[1];
    if ( (mqd_t) -1 == (mqdes = mq_open(mqname,O_CREAT|O_RDONLY,0660,NULL)) )
        fatal_error(errno, "mq_open");
    if ( -1 == mq_getattr(mqdes, &attr) )
        fatal_error(errno, "mq_getattr");
    if ( NULL == (msg_buffer = malloc(attr.mq_msgsize)) )
        fatal_error(errno, "malloc");

    // OMITTED: Set up signal handling.
❶  sleep(20);
    while ( TRUE ) {
        memset(msg_buffer, 0, attr.mq_msgsize);
        msg_size = mq_receive(mqdes, msg_buffer, attr.mq_msgsize, &priority);
        if ( msg_size != -1 ) {
❷          printf("Message (priority=%d):  %s\n", priority, msg_buffer);
        }
    }
    free(msg_buffer);                      /* Free the buffer.          */
    if ( -1 == mq_unlink(mqname) )         /* Mark queue for destruction. */
        fatal_error(errno, "mq_unlink");
    exit(EXIT_SUCCESS);
}
```

Listing 12-5: A program that receives messages from a message queue and prints them on its standard output

This receiver program is forced to sleep before retrieving messages ❶ to give a sending process a chance to fill the message queue with messages of varying priorities before the first mq_receive() operation. When it receives a message, the program prints it together with its priority ❷ so that we can verify that higher-priority messages are read before those with lower priority.

The sending program is displayed in Listing 12-6.

mqsend_demo.c
```
#include "common_hdrs.h"
#include <mqueue.h>

int main(int argc, char *argv[])
{
    mqd_t   mqdes;              /* The message queue descriptor      */
    struct  mq_attr attr;      /* Message queue attribute structure */
    char    *msg_buffer;       /* Stores the data read from stdin   */
    unsigned int priority;     /* Priority of sent message          */
    unsigned int length;       /* Length of sent message            */

    if ( argc != 2 ) {
        fprintf(stderr, "Usage: %s /<mq-name>\n", argv[0]);
        exit(EXIT_FAILURE);
    }
❶  if ( (mqd_t) -1 == (mqdes = mq_open(argv[1], O_WRONLY)) )
        fatal_error(errno, "mq_open");
❷  if ( -1 == mq_getattr(mqdes, &attr) )
        fatal_error(errno, "mq_getattr");
    if ( NULL == (msg_buffer = malloc(attr.mq_msgsize)) )
        fatal_error(errno, "malloc");

    while ( TRUE ) {
        if ( scanf("%ms", &msg_buffer) > 0 ) {
            length = strlen(msg_buffer);
            if ( length <= attr.mq_msgsize )
                mq_send(mqdes, msg_buffer, length, length);
            else
                fatal_error(-1, "String data too long");
        }
        free(msg_buffer);
    }
    mq_close(mqdes);
    exit(EXIT_SUCCESS);
}
```

Listing 12-6: A program that sends text from its standard input to a message queue

After opening the message queue for writing only ❶, the sender gets the queue's attributes ❷, because it needs to know the maximum message size that the queue allows. It uses scanf() to read the strings from standard input, with the %ms format specifier. The m requests scanf() to allocate a buffer of whatever size is large enough to store the data. This prevents a buffer overflow. If the size of the string exceeds the maximum message size, it doesn't send it. In fact, it exits. The program is required to free the buffer. Since the scanf() documentation does not say whether it will reuse a buffer from a previous call, it's safer to free it after each call. Also, as a reminder, with the %s conversion specifier, scanf() uses whitespace to delimit strings, not the end of the line.

This program can be run either interactively or by redirecting standard input into it. Let's see how they work. Create a file named *mqinput* with the single line:

```
a aa aaa aaaa aaaaa aaaaaa aaaaaaa aaaaaaaa
```

Name the executables mqrcv_demo and mqsend_demo and start up the receiving process in one terminal window

```
$ ./mqrcv_demo /MQ
```

and in a second terminal window, enter:

```
$ ./mqsend_demo /MQ < mqinput
```

After the 20-second delay, in the first terminal, you'll see:

```
Message (priority=8):    aaaaaaaa
Message (priority=7):    aaaaaaa
Message (priority=6):    aaaaaa
Message (priority=5):    aaaaa
Message (priority=4):    aaaa
Message (priority=3):    aaa
Message (priority=2):    aa
Message (priority=1):    a
```

Terminate both processes with a CTRL-C entered on the keyboard. You'll see the exact same output if you run the sender interactively:

```
$ ./mqsend_demo /MQ
a aa aaa aaaa aaaaa aaaaaa aaaaaaa aaaaaaaa
```

If you remove the delay from the receiving program, the output will be very different because the receiver will get the strings as soon as they're sent and print them immediately.

Message Queues and Asynchronous Notification

Consider a process that has a significant amount of computation to perform but which occasionally receives messages from another process. It can't call a blocking receive instruction on a message queue because a message may never even arrive. It could periodically poll the queue by issuing a nonblocking receive, but the two problems with this are:

- The sender may require immediate attention once it sends the message, and if the process is polling, it may not detect that it received the message in time.

- The program would have to use some type of timer to periodically stop what it was doing and check for messages, even if none were available, which wastes its time.

This is the situation in which to establish asynchronous notification when messages arrive in the message queue, using mq_notify(). Its prototype is:

```
int mq_notify(mqd_t mqdes, const struct sigevent *sevp);
```

The mq_notify() function allows a process to register or unregister for delivery of an asynchronous notification when a new message arrives in the message queue mqdes so that it doesn't have to repeatedly check in nonblocking mode or wait in a blocked state for them. However, the constraints on this notification system are:

- The notification is only sent when a new message arrives into an empty queue; if the queue is not empty at the time mq_notify() is called, then a notification will be sent only after the queue is emptied and a new message arrives.

- Only one process can register to receive notifications on the same message queue.

- Notification occurs once; after a notification is delivered, the notification registration is removed, and another process can register for message notification.

The mq_notify() function isn't really intended to let a process receive notifications for every arriving message. Rather, it's intended to alert a process that a first message has arrived in the message queue. It can be subverted though, so that a process can get most of its messages asynchronously.

The sigevent structure allows a process to either receive a signal or have a thread started up as a notification. We haven't covered threads yet, but the rough idea is that a new thread would run and could call mq_receive() to retrieve the new message. Instead, let's consider how to use signals. If we wanted our program to run a signal handler when a new message arrives in an empty queue, we'd need to take the following steps:

1. Configure a sigevent structure sigev as follows:

```
sev.sigev_notify = SIGEV_SIGNAL; /* Want a signal, not a thread */
sev.sigev_signo  = SIGRTMIN;     /* Use first real time signal. */
```

2. Create a three-parameter (siginfo-type) signal handler function to run when the signal is generated. Let's call it msg_handler(). Its prototype is:

```
void msg_handler(int signo, siginfo_t *info, void *context)
```

3. Register the signal handler to run when `SIGRTMIN` is received:

```
struct sigaction sa;
sigact.sa_sigaction = msg_handler;
sigact.sa_flags = SA_SIGINFO;
sigemptyset(&(sigact.sa_mask));
if ( sigaction(SIGRTMIN, &sigact, NULL) == -1 )
    // Handle the error.
```

4. Call `mq_notify()` to register this notification method:

```
if ( mq_notify(mqdes, &sigev) == -1 )
    // Handle the error.
```

The signal handler must take the following steps:

1. Prepare a buffer to receive a message and call `mq_receive()` to get it.
2. Call `mq_notify()` within the handler to reregister notifications.
3. Drain the message queue of any messages that might have arrived after the time the one for which the notification was sent, using a nonblocking call to `mq_receive()` in a loop.

It's important that the call to `mq_notify()` be made before emptying the queue. If you reverse the order, a message could arrive into the queue before the call to `mq_notify()` and then no signals will ever be sent because the queue is no longer empty.

A Program Receiving Asynchronous Notifications

There are many different types of programs that display information about some part of the computer system and update that display immediately when the state of the system changes. For example, network managers detect when a new network is available and add it to their list. Similarly, programs that display a list of currently logged-in users automatically add a new user to the list immediately after a new user logs into the system. File browsers update the display when a file is created, renamed, or deleted in some other window.

These types of programs receive an immediate notification about a change and respond to it. That notification is not necessarily a result of messages delivered through a message queue, but we can take this opportunity to write a program that gets such notifications from a message queue. In particular, let's suppose that the program receives messages from a message queue about logins to some particular service. Each message will contain:

- A name, not necessarily the system username, that the user chooses to be a display name

- A line on which the user logged in, such as `pts/2`

If the program uses mq_notify() to register immediate notifications, then the siginfo_t structure that is available to the signal handler will also provide the PID of the process that sent the message and the real user ID of that process. Our program can collect this information as soon as it receives the message from the message queue. It can then update its internal data structures and update the display device with the new login information.

A real program might be busy doing tasks other than updating a display, but since our objective isn't to create a real program, this program will just suspend itself until a message arrives. The program source file will be named *ulogger.c*. We'll also write a short program named *ulogger_client.c* that will send a login message to the ulogger process when a new login occurs. A shared header file, *ulogger.h*, will contain the definitions needed by both programs. Rather than providing the name of the message queue as a command line argument, its name will be defined in the shared header file. The content of the message sent by the client will be a structure containing the name and line as strings, which is also defined in the header file. Let's define that file now:

```
#define MAX_NAME  24
#define MAX_LINE  10
/* The structure of a login message sent to the logger process */
typedef struct _msgtype {
    char name[MAX_NAME];   /* Chosen user name  */
    char line[MAX_LINE];   /* Supplied TTY line */
} msgtype;

char mqname[] = "/MQ_logger"; /* Name of the message queue */
```

The client program is relatively short and very similar to *mqsend_demo.c*. It is different in two respects:

- It isn't interactive. It expects the name and line to be command line arguments.

- It packs the two strings into a structure and sends a structure into the message queue rather than two separate strings.

Let's take a look at its code in Listing 12-7.

ulogger_client.c
```
#include "ulogger.h"

int main(int argc, char *argv[])
{
    mqd_t   mqdes;          /* The message queue descriptor    */
    struct  mq_attr attr;   /* Message queue attribute structure */
    char    *msg_buffer;    /* Stores the data read from stdin */
    msgtype msg;            /* The message to be sent          */
    char    errstr[128];    /* For error messages              */

    if ( argc != 3 )
        usage_error("mqregister nickname line\n");
```

```
    /* Check that the entered strings are not too long. */
    if ( strlen(argv[1]) > MAX_NAME - 1 ) {
        sprintf(errstr, "Name must be less than %d characters\n", MAX_NAME);
        fatal_error(-1, errstr);
    }
    if ( strlen(argv[2]) > MAX_LINE - 1 ) {
        sprintf(errstr, "Line must be less than %d characters\n", MAX_LINE);
        fatal_error(-1, errstr);
    }
    strcpy(msg.name, argv[1]); /* Copy the arguments into the message. */
    strcpy(msg.line, argv[2]);

    /* Open the message queue for writing. */
    if ( (mqd_t) -1 == (mqdes = mq_open(mqname, O_WRONLY)) )
        fatal_error(errno, "mq_open");

    if ( -1 == mq_getattr(mqdes, &attr) )      /* Get max message size. */
        fatal_error(errno, "mq_getattr");

    if ( NULL == (msg_buffer = malloc(attr.mq_msgsize)) )
        fatal_error(errno, "malloc");

❶ mq_send(mqdes, (char*) &msg, sizeof msg, 0);
    mq_close(mqdes);
    exit(EXIT_SUCCESS);
}
```

Listing 12-7: A client program for the ulogger process

The program sends a structure into the message queue ❶ by casting its
address to char*. The receiving process has to cast it back to the structure
type when it gets it. Here are two examples of how we'd run this program:

```
$ ./logger_client stewart pts/4
$ ./logger_client gandalf pts/6
```

Let's turn to the design of the ulogger process.

Whenever a user logs in, it will store the supplied name, the line, the
time of the login, and the real user ID of the person. The following uinfo
structure encapsulates this data:

```
#define  MAX_TIMESTR  16
#define  MAX_USERS   256
typedef struct _user {
    uid_t uid;
    char  nickname[MAX_NAME];
    char  line[MAX_LINE];
    char  start_time[MAX_TIMESTR];
} uinfo;
```

The program uses two real-time signals, SIGRTMIN and SIGRTMIN+1. I created two macro names for them to make it easier to understand how they're used:

```
#define  SIGMSGAVAIL  SIGRTMIN    /* The notification when a message arrives */
#define  SIGUPDATE    SIGRTMIN+1 /* The signal sent to force screen updates */
```

Much of the work performed by the program is inside the signal handler that runs when a message is received. On the other hand, the main program needs access to some of the variables updated by the handler, so these will be declared globally in the program:

```
char          *msg_buffer;        /* The received message      */
ssize_t        msg_size;          /* Max allowed size of message */
mqd_t          mqdes;             /* Message queue descriptor  */
struct sigevent sev;              /* Notification setup        */
uinfo          users[MAX_USERS]; /* Array of logged in users  */
int            count = 0;         /* Number of current users   */
unsigned short int rows, cols;    /* Size of terminal window   */
```

The main program will perform all of the required setting up and then enter a loop. Inside that loop it will print the list of current users on the screen, updating it whenever a new user arrives. If the list is longer than the number of rows in the terminal, it will display only the most recently logged in rows-2 users. It will get the window dimensions with a call to ioctl():

```
void get_winsize(int fd, unsigned short *rows, unsigned short *cols)
{
    struct winsize size;
    if ( ioctl(fd, TIOCGWINSZ, &size) < 0 )
        fatal_error(errno, "TIOCGWINSZ error");
    *rows = size.ws_row;
    *cols = size.ws_col;
}
```

For each user, a line of output will contain the user's chosen name, the line, and the login time, such as:

```
Name                    Line      Time
gandalf                 pts/22    12:10:18
clarence                cloudnine 12:10:52
jessica                 tty7      12:11:19
--snip--
Arrived at 12:11:19:  Nickname = jessica (UID = 500)
```

The most interesting part of the program is the signal handler that's run when a message arrives; it does the following:

1. Gets the current time and formats it as a string

2. Retrieves the new message from the queue

3. Updates the array of users to include the new login

4. Writes the line that appears in the last row of the terminal

5. Reregisters notification by calling `mq_notify()`

6. Drains the message queue in case any new messages arrived

7. Signals the `main()` function that a new user arrived so that it can update its display

The handler raises a different real-time signal in the last step to wake up the `main()` function, which is blocked in a call to `sigwait()`. When it receives the signal, it updates the display.

Let's look at some of the pieces of the program, starting with the signal handler, named `msg_handler()`:

```
void msg_handler(int signo, siginfo_t *info, void *context)
{
    ssize_t    nbytes;
    time_t     arrival_time;
    struct tm *bdtime;
    char       timestr[MAX_TIMESTR];

    if ( info->si_code != SI_MESGQ )
        fatal_error(-1, "Signal handler invoked but not for arriving message");

    /* (1) Get current time and convert to string. */
    time(&arrival_time);
    bdtime = localtime(&arrival_time);
    strftime(timestr, MAX_TIMESTR, "%X", bdtime);

    /* (2) Retrieve the message. */
    memset(msg_buffer, 0, msg_size);
    nbytes = mq_receive(mqdes, msg_buffer, msg_size, NULL);
    if ( nbytes != -1 ) {
      ❶ newmsg = *((msgtype*) msg_buffer);
      ❷ print_status_line(timestr, newmsg.name, info->si_uid);
      ❸ update(&newmsg, info->si_uid, timestr);
    }
    if ( mq_notify(mqdes, &sev) == -1 ) /* (5) Reregister notification. */
        fatal_error(errno, "mq_notify");

    /* (6) Drain the queue. */
    while ( -1 != mq_receive(mqdes, msg_buffer, msg_size, NULL) )
        continue;
    if ( errno != EAGAIN )
        fatal_error(errno, "mq_receive");

    if ( nbytes != -1 )
        raise(SIGUPDATE);                 /* Signal main program.        */
}
```

The mq_receive() function's second parameter is of type char*, but the message content is a structure of type msgtype. The handler casts it ❶ to msgtype* so that it can dereference it. It then calls a function that prints the status line ❷, not shown, and calls another function that adds the new user to the array of users ❸, provided there's room for another user.

The main program is partially shown in Listing 12-8 (without any error handling). The auxiliary functions are omitted. The complete program is available in the book's source code distribution.

ulogger.c
```
int main(int argc, char *argv[])
{
    struct mq_attr   attr;
    struct sigaction sigact;
    sigset_t         mask;
    int              signo;

    /* Only run this without redirection. */
    if ( isatty(STDIN_FILENO) == 0 )
        fatal_error(-1, "Not a terminal\n");

    get_winsize(STDIN_FILENO, &rows, &cols);

    mqdes = mq_open(mqname, O_CREAT | O_RDONLY | O_NONBLOCK, 0660, NULL);
    mq_getattr(mqdes, &attr);
    msg_size = attr.mq_msgsize;
    msg_buffer = malloc(attr.mq_msgsize);

    sigact.sa_sigaction = msg_handler;
    sigact.sa_flags = SA_SIGINFO;
    sigemptyset(&(sigact.sa_mask));
    sigaction(SIGMSGAVAIL, &sigact, NULL);

    sigemptyset(&mask);
    sigaddset(&mask, SIGUPDATE);
    sigprocmask(SIG_BLOCK, &mask, NULL);

    sev.sigev_notify = SIGEV_SIGNAL;
    sev.sigev_signo = SIGMSGAVAIL;
    mq_notify(mqdes, &sev);

    setup_sighandlers(&sigact, 0);
    clearscreen();

    while ( TRUE ) {
        sigwait(&mask, &signo);    /* Wait for SIGUPDATE. */
        if ( signo == SIGUPDATE ) {
            print_column_headings();
            int first = count - rows + 2;
```

```
            first = first >= 0 ? first : 0;
            for ( int i = first; i < count; i++ ) {
                moveto(i - first + 2, 1);
                printf("%-*s %-*s %-*s\n", MAX_NAME, users[i].nickname,
                        MAX_LINE, users[i].line, MAX_TIMESTR,
                        users[i].start_time);
            }
        }
    }
    cleanup(1);
}
```

Listing 12-8: The main() *function of the* ulogger.c *process*

The main() function spends its time blocked in the call to sigwait(). When
a message arrives in the message queue, msg_handler() runs, and before it
returns, it raises SIGUPDATE to unblock the main program, which then updates
the terminal window to display the newly logged-in user.

Summary

Many real-world applications are actually multiple processes that work together to provide their services or manage their data. Processes that coordinate their actions need to communicate. This chapter introduced the fundamental concepts of interprocess communication (IPC). It categorized the
different methods of IPC as either shared memory or data transfer methods.

In shared memory IPC, a process can obtain a memory region from the
kernel that it can then share with other processes. Exchange of data is relatively easy except that it is up to the programmer to explicitly prevent race
conditions on the data that can be modified by multiple processes. When
processes exchange data in shared memory, the kernel is not involved in any
of the operations.

In contrast, methods of IPC based on data transfer, such as message
queues and pipes, are based on the transfer of data through some type of
communication channel that is created and managed by the kernel. The programmer does not need to prevent race conditions because the operations
for data exchange generally prevent these races.

A mechanism by which two or more processes can communicate, or
which facilitates the coordinated exchange of data, is called an *IPC facility*.
Signals are an IPC facility covered in earlier chapter. There are two different
APIs for IPC facilities: the POSIX API and the System V API. Both consist of
interfaces for shared memory, semaphores, and message queues. Programs
that communicate via shared memory have to be careful about the use of
pointers. In general, addresses within shared memory regions must be referenced by integer offsets relative to the start of the region. Programs also
need to prevent race conditions, and binary semaphores are one way to accomplish that. Binary semaphores can be used like a lock; a process enters a

portion of code only after it successfully acquires a semaphore, but only one process at a time can hold it.

Message queues are an IPC facility that let processes exchange data by send and receive operations on a queue. The queue itself is a priority queue—when a process retrieves a message from a nonempty message queue, it always gets the oldest, highest-priority message. Unlike shared memory, message queues are maintained by the kernel and all operations result in system calls.

In this chapter, we presented the POSIX API and described how it is different from the System V API. We developed examples that used shared memory IPC, as well as semaphores, both for preventing race conditions and also as counters. Lastly, we developed programs that communicated through message queues. The next chapter introduces pipes.

Exercises

1. Write a program that determines the maximum value that a POSIX semaphore can attain on your computer.

2. In Chapter 11, *sync_io_demo.c* used signals to coordinate access to a shared file. Rewrite that program so that it uses named semaphores to achieve the same synchronization effect.

3. Rewrite the shared memory–based producer and consumer programs so that they use a message queue instead. In this case, the consumer retrieves data from the queue and the producer puts data into it. Write it so that data items are integers. Assume all data items have the same priority.

4. The data items exchanged in the shared memory producer-consumer program in this chapter are numbers. Write a version of this program in which the items are strings whose maximum size is 64 characters each. An array of strings is ordinarily an array of char* pointers. In this program, the array elements are integer offsets to strings that are allocated elsewhere in the shared memory object. Since the strings are all of at most 64 bytes in size, the program can reserve memory inside the shared memory region for $64 \times$ BUF_SIZE bytes of string data.

5. Write a program that, given the name of any POSIX message queue, prints how many unread messages are in the queue at 1-second intervals until the message queue is removed. The program should terminate automatically when the queue no longer exists. You can modify this exercise by allowing an option that specifies an alternative time interval in seconds.

6. This is a challenging problem that you can tackle if you've had a course in operating systems and learned about memory management algorithms. Design a set of library functions to manage memory allocation in a shared memory segment. Specifically, design functions named shmalloc() and shfree(), with prototypes

```
int shmalloc(int shmd, int numbytes);
int shfree(int shmd, int location);
```

that allocate and free memory from a shared memory object with the shared memory descriptor shmd. As a start, don't try to compact the free space in the memory object—if shmalloc() cannot find enough memory for a request, let it fail. You can use ftruncate() to help with this problem.

13

PIPES AND FIFOS

This chapter concentrates exclusively on pipes and FIFOs. A *pipe* is an interprocess communication facility that acts the way its name suggests—a stream of bytes flows into it at one end and comes out in the same order at the other end. A *FIFO* is a particular kind of pipe that's also called a *named pipe*. FIFOs differ from ordinary pipes, which are called unnamed pipes, only in the way that they're created, opened, closed, and removed. A FIFO can be used by any pair of processes, whereas an unnamed pipe can only be used by processes with a common ancestor that created and passed it down to them.

An Overview of Pipes

We're familiar with the concept of a pipe at the command level. Most shells, bash included, have a pipe operator. A command such as

```
last | grep 'reboot'
```

connects the output of last to the input of grep. In this case, grep removes all lines from its input stream that don't contain the string *reboot*, so that it only outputs lines that are produced by last and also contain the word *reboot*. The | character is the bash pipe operator; its position between last and grep tells bash to start up two processes, one to run last and the other to run grep, and to arrange for the standard output of last to be redirected into the standard input of grep.

This pipe functionality has an interesting origin; it was introduced into Third Edition UNIX in 1973 [25]:

> The basic redirectability of input-output made it easy to put pipes
> in when Doug McIlroy finally persuaded Ken Thompson to do it.
> In one feverish night Ken wrote and installed the pipe system call,
> added pipes to the shell, and modified several utilities.

The shell pipe operator and a system call of the same name were invented simultaneously. Here we'll explore pipes, both named and unnamed, and the system calls and functions related to programming them.

Pipe Basics

In Chapter 12, the terms *pipe* and *FIFO* were mentioned in a few of the man pages we explored. We'll have to read a few more man pages to learn more about them, such as the pipe(3posix) man page. But before looking at that one, since I always like to check whether there's an overview about a new topic in Section 7, let's search that section:

```
$ apropos -s7 pipe
fifo (7)                - first-in-first-out special file, named pipe
pipe (7)                - overview of pipes and FIFOs
```

The first line of output answers one question—a FIFO is a first-in-first-out special file and is the same thing as a named pipe. In fact, the fifo(7) man page confirms this:

> A FIFO special file (a named pipe) is similar to a pipe, except
> that it is accessible through the filesystem—in other words, it has
> a *name*. It can be opened by multiple processes for reading or writ-
> ing. When processes are exchanging data via the FIFO, the kernel
> passes all data internally without writing it to the filesystem.

The man page uses the term *pipe* as a synonym for an unnamed pipe and prefers the term *FIFO* over *named pipe*, so I'll do the same here. Although FIFO is written in uppercase, the functions that work with them use the lowercase fifo within their names. The page basically tells us in the NOTES section that we should read the pipe(7) man page for further details.

The pipe(7) man page explains much more. Pipes and FIFOs provide a unidirectional interprocess communication channel. *Unidirectional* means that data can flow only in one direction through the pipe. The end of the pipe into which bytes are written is called the *write end* of the pipe, and the end from which bytes are read is the *read end*. All bytes that are written to the write end can be read from the read end. You can visualize it like a pipe through which water flows; water enters at the write end of the pipe and leaves through the read end of the pipe, but instead of water, it's a stream of bytes going in and out, as depicted in Figure 13-1.

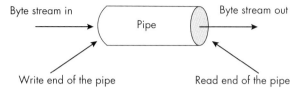

Figure 13-1: A unidirectional pipe through which a stream of bytes flows

The only difference between FIFOs and pipes is how they're created and how they're opened. Once they've been established, how they work is the same. The man page explains the important properties of both kinds of pipes, which I summarize here. In this context, I'm using the term *pipe* to refer to both kinds of pipes, since their semantics are the same.

Creating a pipe returns two file descriptors. One descriptor refers to the read end of the pipe, and the other refers to the write end. All communication takes the form of reads from and writes to these descriptors.

Pipes transmit byte streams. The bytes written into a pipe have no boundaries, the way that messages do. A reading process can attempt to read any number of bytes out of a pipe, independent of the number of bytes written by a writing process into it. For example, a writer might write 100 bytes into a pipe, and a reader might then read just 32 of those bytes.

Pipes preserve the order of the data written into them. Pipes are first-in-first-out channels; the bytes read from read end of the pipe are in the same order in which they were written into the pipe.

Reads from the pipe drain the pipe. In other words, when a process reads some number of bytes from the pipe, they're removed so that only one process can read those bytes. Reads like this are also called *destructive*.

Reads are blocking by default. A read operation on a pipe is *blocking* if it causes the process to wait if the pipe is empty. The O_NONBLOCK file status flag controls whether file operations are nonblocking or blocking. The pipe() system call leaves this flag clear on both ends of the pipe when it creates it. This means that, unless the process subsequently sets that flag, if a process tries to read from an empty pipe and the write end is open, then the process is blocked until either the write end is closed or data is written into it. If the write end is closed, a read operation returns 0 immediately as if it encountered the end of a file.

Pipes have limited capacity. If the pipe is full, a write will either block or fail, depending on whether the O_NONBLOCK flag was set on the write end of the pipe. When the pipe is created, it isn't set; writes to a full pipe will block the calling process until a process reads from the pipe to drain some bytes from it. The capacity of the pipe is system dependent. In the most recent Linux kernel, the capacity is 16 pages; if the page size is 4096 bytes, the capacity is 65,536 bytes.

Writes of at most `PIPE_BUF` bytes are atomic.   `PIPE_BUF` is a system-defined constant, defined by POSIX to be at least 512. On Linux it is 4096. A write of at most `PIPE_BUF` bytes is written to the pipe as a contiguous sequence. If two or more processes each attempt to write to the pipe at the same time, if the number of bytes they're each writing is at most `PIPE_BUF`, their writes will each be contiguous. On the other hand, if a process writes more than `PIPE_BUF` bytes, the kernel may interleave the data with data written by other processes.

There's a lot more to understand about pipes and FIFOs, such as how they're created, how we can read from and write to them, and so on. We'll start with pipes, after which we'll read about FIFOs. The pipe(3posix) man page is the POSIX specification of the pipe() system call. It has a brief description of the call and some example code. Since pipe() is a system call, there'll be a Linux man page for it in Section 2. It turns out that the Linux system call conforms to the POSIX requirements, so we'll read that page to learn about this call. Henceforth, I use the word *pipe* to mean an unnamed pipe.

Unnamed Pipes

An unnamed pipe is created with the pipe() system call. Its synopsis on most architectures is:

```
#include <unistd.h>
int pipe(int pipefd[2]);
```

On Alpha, IA-64, MIPS, SuperH, and SPARC/SPARC64 architectures, it has a different prototype, but the *glibc* wrapper for pipe() hides the difference, so that on systems with *glibc*, we can use this single prototype.

Assuming that pipefd is declared as

```
int pipefd[2];
```

the system call pipe(pipefd) creates a unidirectional channel called a *pipe* that can be used by two or more processes to communicate. The two file descriptors, pipefd[0] and pipefd[1], refer to the read end and write end of the pipe, respectively. If the call fails, it returns -1; otherwise, it returns 0.

Data written to the write end of the pipe is buffered by the kernel until it is read from the read end of the pipe. A process can read from the read end (pipefd[0]) using the read() system call and write to the write end (pipefd[1]) using the write() system call. The read and write ends are opened by the pipe() call—there's no separate call to open a pipe.

Let's look at a simple example. Listing 13-1 demonstrates the basic principles of how a process should use a pipe, with some error handling omitted. It illustrates the steps that most programs will need to take.

```
pipe_demo1.c   #include "common_hdrs.h"
               #include <sys/wait.h>
               #define  READ_FD  0    /* Make it easier to see the read end.    */
               #define  WRITE_FD 1    /* Make it easier to see the write end.   */

               int main(int argc, char *argv[])
               {
                   int  pipefd[2];    /* The array of file descriptors for pipe() */
                   char buffer;       /* A single char to receive and print       */

                   if ( argc < 2 )
                       usage_error("Usage: pipe_demo0 <arg> ");

               ❶ if ( pipe(pipefd) == -1 )
                       fatal_error(errno, "pipe");

                   switch ( fork() ) {
                   case -1:
                       fatal_error(errno, "fork()");

                   case 0: { /* Child code */
                       char label[] = "Child received: ";
                   ❷ close(pipefd[WRITE_FD]);     /* MUST DO THIS otherwise child will
                                                      never terminate!!               */
                       write(STDOUT_FILENO, &label, strlen(label));
                       /* Loop while not EOF and not a read error. */
                       while ( (read(pipefd[READ_FD], &buffer, 1)) > 0 )
                           write(STDOUT_FILENO, &buffer, 1);

                       write(STDOUT_FILENO, "\n", 1);
                       close(pipefd[READ_FD]);
                       exit(EXIT_SUCCESS);
                   }
                   default:                       /* Parent code                      */
                   ❸ close(pipefd[READ_FD]);    /* Parent is writing, so close read end. */
                   ❹ write(pipefd[WRITE_FD], argv[1], strlen(argv[1]));
                       close(pipefd[WRITE_FD]);  /* Reader will see EOF.              */
                       wait(NULL);               /* Wait for the child.              */
                       exit(EXIT_SUCCESS);
                   }
               }
```

Listing 13-1: A program in which a parent creates a pipe, forks a child, and sends data to the child through the pipe

The program creates a pipe after which it forks a single child process. The parent writes its single command line argument into the pipe, and the child reads and prints whatever it reads from the pipe to the terminal.

There are several important points to make about this program. The first is that the parent must create the pipe ❶ before it forks the child; otherwise, the child won't have a copy of the file descriptors. After the parent creates the pipe, but before it has forked the child, only the parent has file descriptors for it, as depicted in Figure 13-2.

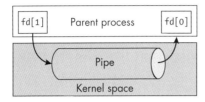

Figure 13-2: The pipe immediately after creation by the parent process

The figure illustrates another important fact: The pipe object does not reside in the process's address space; it's in kernel space and is managed by the kernel. In contrast, the process owns the file descriptors that point to the open file descriptions for the two ends of the pipe (see Figure 4-1 in Chapter 4). After the fork, the picture is different, as shown in Figure 13-3(a). The descriptors are duplicated, but the pipe itself is not.

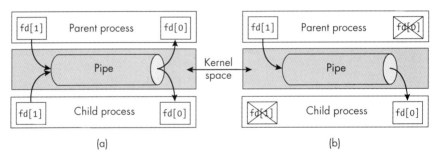

Figure 13-3: The pipe after the parent forks the child. (a) The state of the pipe before parent and child close their respective read and write descriptors. (b) Its state after.

The fact that a pipe is unidirectional has an important implication—*every process that has a copy of the pipe's open file descriptors must close the end of the pipe it is not going to use.* In this first program, the child must close the write end ❷ because it is reading, and the parent must close the read end ❸ because it is writing. The close() system call closes a pipe's file descriptor. Because of the way that read and write operations work, which I'll explain shortly, if the child reads from the pipe but has the write end open, it will block permanently when it tries to read and the pipe is empty. This is also why the parent has to close the write end ❹ when it finishes writing; otherwise, the child will block when it tries to read from the pipe.

It is a very common and hard-to-debug mistake to forget to close the unused file descriptor on a pipe. In particular, always make sure that a process intended to read from a pipe closes the write end of the pipe before anything else.

The last observation about this program is that no synchronization is needed when parent and child exchange data through the pipe. The kernel manages the pipe and ensures that all accesses are free of race conditions.

Here are two sample runs of `pipe_demo1`:

```
$ ./pipe_demo1 hello
Child received: hello
$ ./pipe_demo1 'Mr. Watson, come here. I want you.'
Child received: Mr. Watson, come here. I want you.
```

In the second run, the argument is enclosed in single quotes because this program expects a single command line argument.

PIPES AND LINUX PLUMBING

A pipe is not a file. When pipe() is called, the kernel creates two open file descriptions (file structures), one for the read end and one for the write end of the pipe. Even though these are file structures, they do not have any disk storage. The kernel also creates an inode for the pipe, but this inode is part of a special, hidden filesystem called a *pipefs*. This filesystem is not mounted in the system's directory hierarchy. The open file descriptions and the inode are used by the kernel to manage the pipe. They include internal storage buffers in kernel memory, queues of blocked processes, file offsets, and so forth.

The Behavior of Read Operations on Pipes

The semantics of reading from a pipe are much more complex than the semantics of reading from a file, primarily because the POSIX requirements for reads from a pipe are themselves complex. Whether or not a read blocks, succeeds, or fails depends on factors such as whether the O_NONBLOCK flag is set on the pipe, whether the pipe is open for writing, whether any writers are currently sleeping, whether the pipe buffer is empty or has enough bytes to satisfy the read, and so on. In the following discussion, I'll use the term *pipe* interchangeably with *pipe buffer*. Table 13-1 summarizes what happens when a process tries to read n bytes from a pipe that currently has p bytes in it.

Table 13-1: The Semantics of Reading *n* Bytes from a Pipe Containing *p* Bytes

| Pipe size (*p*) | At least one process has the pipe open for writing | | | No writing process |
| | Blocking read | | Nonblocking read | |
	At least one sleeping writer	No writer is sleeping		
p = 0	Repeatedly wait for sleeping writers to write data until *n* bytes have been written and copied, returning *n*.	Block until data is available, copy it, and return its size.	Return -EAGAIN.	Return 0.
0 < *p* < *n*		Copy *p* bytes and return *p*, leaving the pipe empty.		
n <= *p*	Copy *n* bytes and return *n*, leaving *p* − *n* bytes in the pipe buffer.			

The read semantics depend upon whether a writer has been put to sleep; if it tried to write into the pipe previously but the pipe buffer was full, it is made to sleep. On a blocking read request, if the number of bytes requested (*n*) is greater than what is currently in the pipe (*p*) and at least one writer was forced to sleep because the pipe was full when it tried to write, the read will obtain as many bytes as are currently available. It will then wait for the remaining bytes to be written by the writing processes that are woken up by the read that emptied the pipe. The read will continue to read until it obtains all *n* bytes. If no writer is sleeping and the pipe is empty, the read will block until some data becomes available.

The Behavior of Write Operations on Pipes

The writing semantics are also somewhat complex. Table 13-2 summarizes the POSIX requirements for a write() system call requesting to write *n* bytes into a pipe that has *f* free bytes in the pipe buffer. POSIX defines the requirements in terms of the constant PIPE_BUF defined earlier, currently equal to 4096 bytes. The amount of free space, *n*, is at most PIPE_BUF.

Table 13-2: The Semantics of Writing *n* Bytes into a Pipe with *f* Free Bytes

| Free space in buffer *f* | At least one reading process | | No reading process |
	Blocking write	Nonblocking write	
f < *n* <= PIPE_BUF	Block until *n* - *f* bytes are removed, copy *n* bytes, and return *n*.	Return -EAGAIN.	Send SIGPIPE signal and return -EPIPE.
PIPE_BUF < *n*	Copy *n* bytes, blocking as needed, and return *n*.	If *f* > 0, copy *f* bytes and return *f*; otherwise, return -EAGAIN.	
n <= *f*	Copy *n* bytes and return *n*.		

Let's start with the easy parts of this. First, if no process has the read end of the pipe open, the write fails, `write()` returns `-EPIPE`, and the kernel sends a `SIGPIPE` signal to the process. Let's assume now that at least one process is reading from the pipe. Then the response by `write()` depends on the amount of data to be written.

If the number of bytes to transfer (n) is at most the amount of free space (n <= f <= `PIPE_BUF`), all of the bytes are transferred and the call returns n. In this case, data is written atomically. Now let's also assume that writes are blocking. A write of at most `PIPE_BUF` bytes is performed atomically, whether the writing is blocking or not. If the space is not available, it blocks until it is. If n is greater than `PIPE_BUF`, the writes are broken up into smaller chunks and transferred nonatomically, and `write()` returns n when it completes the transfer. The last cases to consider are when the `O_NONBLOCK` flag is set. If not enough space is available in the pipe buffer but the amount to transfer is at most `PIPE_BUF`, `write()` returns `-EAGAIN` immediately. If `PIPE_BUF` < n, then if there is any free space (f > 0), f bytes are transferred, filling the pipe buffer, and `write()` returns f. Otherwise, it returns `-EAGAIN`.

This might seem pretty daunting to understand. Let's develop a few more programs that use these unnamed pipes to get more of a feel for them.

A Producer-Consumer Example

In Chapter 11, we developed the *waitpid_demo.c* program to demonstrate how to use the `waitpid()` system call, but we also used that program to present a race-free solution to the producer-consumer problem. That program created two child processes: One produced text and wrote it to a file, and the other read from that file. The program used a two-pronged approach consisting of the `pread()` system call and the `O_APPEND` flag set on the file's descriptor to prevent race conditions.

Equipped with our new knowledge, we can create a more efficient producer-consumer program in which the two child processes communicate through a pipe. To reduce the program size, we can exclude the code related to collecting the status of terminated child processes, as well as some of the error-handling code. An actual program should not do this!

The most important parts of this program are how it works with the pipe. The `main()` function does very little, but what it does is crucial:

1. The `main()` function creates the pipe and then forks the two child processes.

2. Since the parent is not involved in the communication between the two children, it immediately closes both ends of the pipe. Failure to do so can cause the consumer process to hang, because the write end of the pipe would be held open by the parent and it would block permanently in its call to `read()` even after the producer terminated.

3. The `main()` function then calls `wait()` so that the two child processes do not become zombies when they terminate.

The main program code follows:

pipe_demo2.c
main()

```c
#include "common_hdrs.h"
#include <sys/wait.h>
#include <ctype.h>
#define  READ_FD  0          /* Make it easier to see the read end.   */
#define  WRITE_FD 1          /* Make it easier to see the write end.  */

int main(int argc, char *argv[])
{
    int pipefd[2];            /* The array of file descriptors for pipe() */
    if ( pipe(pipefd) == -1 ) /* Create the pipe.                        */
        fatal_error(errno, "pipe");

    /* Create the producer process. */
    switch ( fork() ) {
        case -1:
            fatal_error(errno, "fork");
        case 0:
            producer(pipefd);
        default:
            break;
    }

    /* Create the consumer process. */
    switch ( fork() ) {
        case -1:
            fatal_error(errno, "fork");
        case 0:
            consumer(pipefd);
        default:
            break;
    }
    /* Close both ends of the pipe. */
    close(pipefd[READ_FD]);
    close(pipefd[WRITE_FD]);

    /* Wait for children to terminate. */
    for ( int i = 0; i < 2; i++ )
        if ( wait( NULL) == -1 )
            break;
    exit(EXIT_SUCCESS);
}
```

The producer process will execute slightly different code than it did in the *waitpid_demo.c* program. Instead of generating a few characters, it reads user input from the terminal and sends it to the consumer through the pipe.

We'll have to terminate the program by sending it a CTRL-D. The producer must close the read end of the pipe:

pipe_demo2.c
producer()

```
void producer(int fd[])
{
    char    *line = NULL;
    size_t   len = 0;
    ssize_t nread;

    close(fd[READ_FD]);  /* Cannot read and write.                     */
    while ( (nread = getline(&line, &len, stdin)) != -1 )
        write(fd[WRITE_FD], line, nread);

    free(line);          /* line was allocated by getline().           */
    close(fd[WRITE_FD]); /* Closing write end allows consumer to terminate. */
    exit(EXIT_SUCCESS);
}
```

The producer writes what we enter in the terminal window into the pipe. We'll be able to use this program to send arbitrarily large amounts of data into the pipe.

The consumer, in contrast, reads one byte at a time, intentionally, to emphasize that once the data is in the pipe, it's just a stream of bytes; it isn't efficient to read a byte at a time. The consumer converts all lowercase text to uppercase. In a production version of the program, we'd make sure to set the locale so that the rules for uppercase and lowercase are consistent with the user's locale settings:

pipe_demo2.c
consumer()

```
void consumer(int fd[])
{
    char buffer, ch;

❶   close(fd[WRITE_FD]);
    /* Loop while not EOF and not a read error. */
    while ( read(fd[READ_FD], &buffer, 1) > 0 ) {
        ch = toupper(buffer);
        write(STDOUT_FILENO, &ch, 1);
    }
    if ( close(fd[READ_FD]) == -1 )
        fatal_error(errno, "close");
    exit(EXIT_SUCCESS);
}
```

A run of the executable, named pipe_demo2, follows:

```
$ ./pipe_demo2
LET us go then, you and I,
LET US GO THEN, YOU AND I,
When the evening is spread out against the sky
```

```
WHEN THE EVENING IS SPREAD OUT AGAINST THE SKY
Like a patient etherised upon a table
LIKE A PATIENT ETHERISED UPON A TABLE
^D
```

Try commenting out the code in the consumer that closes the write end of the pipe ❶ and rebuilding and running the program. What happens? Do the same with the main program.

A Shell Pipe Simulation

When we enter a pipelined command such as

```
$ last | grep reboot
```

the shell creates a pipe like the one depicted in Figure 13-4.

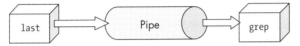

Figure 13-4: The state of the processes' open file descriptors after pipe creation

We can verify this by performing an experiment in which we look at a few files in the */proc* pseudofilesystem while running a pipelined command. Instead of last, we'll use cat as the first command, because cat won't terminate until we enter CTRL-D or kill it with a signal. For each process, say with PID <*p*>, the directory */proc/<p>/fdinfo/* contains a file for each open file descriptor, named *0, 1, 2,* and so on, and the directory */proc/<p>/fd/* contains symbolic links, *0, 1, 2,* and so on, to the actual open files. The files in *fdinfo* contain information about those descriptors, such as the position of its file offset, the flags passed when it was opened, and its inode number.

Open two terminals, and in the first, enter the command:

```
$ cat | grep reboot
```

In the second terminal, use pidof to get the PIDs of the processes running cat and grep. If pidof isn't available on your system, use ps -u instead:

```
$ pidof cat
13325
$ pidof grep
13326
$
```

Now look at the *fdinfo* files for descriptors 0 and 1 of the cat process:

```
$ cat /proc/13325/fdinfo/0
pos: 0
flags: 02000002
mnt_id: 27
```

```
ino: 5
$ cat /proc/13325/fdinfo/1
pos: 0
flags: 01
mnt_id: 14
ino: 94990
```

The ino field is the inode for the file. Notice the inode numbers for descriptors 0 and 1. The inode for 1 is a much larger number. Now look at the symbolic links for both of these file descriptors:

```
$ for i in 0 1; do echo -e -n "$i: "; readlink /proc/13325/fd/$i; done
0: /dev/pts/2
1: pipe:[94990]
```

The descriptor for standard input points to the device file */dev/pts/2*, but the descriptor that usually points to the terminal points to a pipe whose pipe inode number is 94990. This is proof that bash redirected standard output of this process to a pipe.

Let's repeat this for the process running grep:

```
$ cat /proc/13326/fdinfo/0
pos: 0
flags: 00
mnt_id: 14
ino: 94990
$ cat /proc/13326/fdinfo/1
ppos: 0
flags: 02000002
mnt_id: 27
ino: 5
```

The descriptor for standard input points to the same pipe inode as the descriptor for standard output of the cat command. Let's look at the symbolic links also:

```
$ for i in 0 1; do echo -e -n "$i: "; readlink /proc/13326/fd/$i; done
0: pipe:[94990]
1: /dev/pts/2
```

This proves that the shell performed the magic of connecting the two processes with a pipe. We just don't know how.

There are key differences between what bash has to do to arrange this pipe and what our pipe_demo2 program does.

For one, our program's child processes execute code that's part of our own program, whereas the child processes created by the shell execute code that isn't part of the shell program. In our program, the code that the two child processes executed explicitly closed the file descriptors. In contrast, the programs executed by the processes that the shell created, in this case cat and grep, are filters whose input and output are the standard input and standard output streams of the process. For example, the output of cat is written to the terminal unless it is redirected, and the input of grep is the standard input stream, unless it has a filename argument on its command line. Their code cannot be altered!

Instead, the shell itself has to arrange for the descriptor that normally points to the standard output stream of the process executing cat to be replaced by the descriptor for the write end of a pipe, and it similarly has to arrange for the descriptor that points to the standard input of the process executing grep to be replaced by the descriptor for the read end of the same pipe.

Figure 13-5 illustrates the state of the descriptors and the pipe after bash created the pipe and the two processes in our experiment. The read and write ends of the pipe are file descriptors 3 and 4 in each process, assuming that no files were opened before. In other words, if pipefd is the array filled by the call to pipe(), then pipefd[0] == 3 and pipefd[1] == 4.

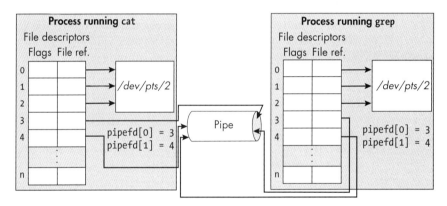

Figure 13-5: The state of the pipe and file descriptors immediately after bash created the pipe

Replacing what one descriptor, say firstfd, points to with what another descriptor, say secondfd, points to can be thought of as a two-step procedure:

1. Close the descriptor firstfd.

2. Duplicate the descriptor secondfd into firstfd.

We need a function that can duplicate a file descriptor, meaning that it creates a second pointer to the file structure pointed to by the original and copies it into another descriptor. If such a function existed, we could copy the pipe's write end descriptor into the descriptors for standard input and output.

We can search the man pages for functions that copy, or duplicate, descriptors with apropos -s2,3 -e descriptor | grep -E 'copy|duplicate' and discover the dup(), dup2(), and dup3() system calls, as well as the POSIX specification of dup(). The dup3() call is a Linux-specific extension. Let's examine the first two. Their synopsis is:

```
#include <unistd.h>
int dup(int oldfd);
int dup2(int oldfd, int newfd);
```

The dup() system call has one argument, whereas dup2() has two. The call dup(oldfd) creates a copy of the file descriptor oldfd, using the lowest-numbered unused file descriptor for the new descriptor.

LOWEST-NUMBERED UNUSED FILE DESCRIPTORS

The dup() system call is one of several system calls that, when they need to allocate a new descriptor, choose the lowest-numbered unused file descriptor. POSIX requires that any function that allocates a new file descriptor must always choose the lowest-numbered unused descriptor in that process. Others include open(), creat(), pipe(), and socket().

As an example, the following code redirects the standard output for the current process to a file, previously opened, named *f*, to which fd refers:

```
int fd;
--snip--
close(1);   /* Close descriptor 1, which is now the lowest unused descriptor.*/
dup(fd);    /* Now descriptor 1 points to the same file as fd.           */
close(fd);  /* Close the original descriptor.                            */
```

This code hinges on the fact that dup() always chooses the lowest-numbered unused file descriptor. Figure 13-6 illustrates the state of the descriptors before and after the code is executed.

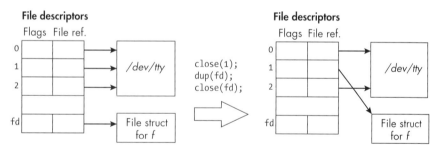

Figure 13-6: The redirection of standard output to a file f *referred to by descriptor fd, using dup()*

We could use this same strategy to redirect standard output to a pipe:

```
int pipefd[2];

if ( pipe(pipefd) == -1 )
    // Handle error and exit.
--snip--
close(1);         /* Close descriptor 1, making it lowest unused descriptor.*/
dup(pipefd[1]);   /* Now descriptor 1 points to the write end of the pipe.  */
close(pipefd[1]); /* Close the pipe's write end descriptor.                 */
```

Neither of these code snippets is guaranteed to work in all circumstances. The problem is that if a program has any signal handlers and a signal arrives after the closing of descriptor 1 but before the call to dup(), the signal handler might open a new file descriptor, using slot 1, and dup() will not duplicate the descriptor into standard output. This race condition is the reason why dup2() was created.

The dup2(fd, fdtoreplace) system call atomically performs the two steps of closing fdtoreplace and replacing it with fd. It eliminates the potential race condition I just described. In fact, dup() is now deprecated. To redirect standard output into the pipe, we can use the following, assuming the pipe was already created:

```
dup2(pipefd[1], 1); /* Now descriptor 1 points to the write end of the pipe.*/
close(pipefd[1]);   /* Close the pipe's write end descriptor.                */
```

A similar strategy works for redirecting standard input to a pipe's read end descriptor:

```
dup2(pipefd[0], 0); /* Now descriptor 0 points to the read end of the pipe. */
close(pipefd[0]);   /* Close the pipe's read end descriptor.                 */
```

Going back to our example, if the child process that executes cat performs the steps

```
dup2(pipefd[1], fileno(stdout)); /* Now stdout points to write end of pipe. */
close(pipefd[0]);                /* Close read end of pipe.                  */
close(pipefd[1]);                /* Close write end of pipe.                 */
```

and the child process that executes grep performs the steps

```
dup2(pipefd[0], fileno(stdin)); /* Now stdin points to pipefd[1].           */
close(pipefd[0]);               /* Close read end of pipe.                  */
close(pipefd[1]);               /* Close write end of pipe.                 */
```

the pipe will be set up properly, and the state of each process's open file descriptors will be as shown in Figure 13-7.

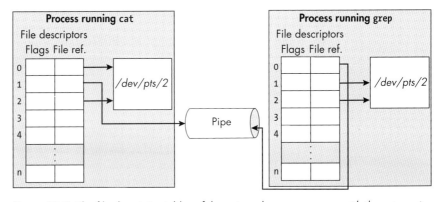

Figure 13-7: The file descriptor tables of the cat and grep processes with the set-up pipe

There's just one hitch. If, for some reason, either of the standard descriptors were closed prior to creating the pipe, one or both of the pipe's descriptors would be either 0 or 1, since pipe() will allocate the lowest-numbered unused descriptors. Suppose standard input had been closed. Then the preceding code would be equivalent to

```
dup2(0, 0));
close(0);
close(1);
```

and the process would crash when it tried to read from the pipe. Therefore, safe code should test that pipefd[0] != 0 and pipefd[1] != 1 before calling dup2().

The book's source code repository has a complete program named *shellpipe_demo.c* that shows how to simulate the shell's creation of a two-command pipeline. Its usage is:

```
shellpipe_demo <prog> [options] [args] '|' <prog> [options] [args]
```

The vertical bar must be enclosed in quotes to prevent the shell from treating it as its own pipe operator. Here is a sample run of this program:

```
$ ./shellpipe_demo ls -lt . '|' grep 'demo[12].c'
-rw-rw-r-- 1 stewart stewart  3168 May 25 17:03 pipe_demo2.c
-rw-rw-r-- 1 stewart stewart  2998 May 24 12:40 pipe_demo1.c
```

A version of the program follows, pared down and with some error handling omitted to save space. This version's usage is shellpipe_demo *prog1 prog2*, in which the two programs cannot have options or arguments:

shellpipe_demo.c
```
#include "common_hdrs.h"
#include <sys/wait.h>
#define  READ_FD  0        /* Make it easier to see the read end.      */
#define  WRITE_FD 1        /* Make it easier to see the write end.     */

int main(int argc, char *argv[])
{
    int fd[2];

    if ( argc < 3 )
        usage_error("Usage: shellpipe_demo command command");
    if ( -1 == pipe(fd) )
        fatal_error(errno, "pipe");

    switch ( fork() ) {
    case -1:
        fatal_error(errno, "fork");
    case 0:                                    /* Child 1              */
        dup2(fd[WRITE_FD], fileno(stdout));    /* Now stdout points to fd[1]. */
        close(fd[READ_FD]);                    /* Close read end of pipe.    */
```

```
        close(fd[WRITE_FD]);                    /* Close write end of pipe.    */
        execlp(argv[1], argv[1], (char*) NULL);  /* Run the first command.  */
        fatal_error(errno, "execlp");
    default:
        break;
    }
    switch ( fork() ) {
    case -1:
        fatal_error(errno, "fork");
    case 0:
        dup2(fd[READ_FD], fileno(stdin));    /* Now stdin points to fd[0].  */
        close(fd[READ_FD]);                  /* Close read end of pipe.     */
        close(fd[WRITE_FD]);                 /* Close write end of pipe.    */
        execlp(argv[2], argv[2], (char*) NULL);  /* Run the second command. */
        fatal_error(errno, "execlp");
    default:
        close(fd[READ_FD]);  /* Parent closes its ends of the pipe.        */
        close(fd[WRITE_FD]);
        for ( int i = 1; i <= 2; i++ )
            if ( wait(NULL) == -1 )
                fatal_error(errno, "wait");
        exit(EXIT_SUCCESS);
    }
}
```

Here's a run of this program:

```
$ ./shellpipe_demo ls wc
    79      79    1065
```

Best Practices Regarding Pipes

Quite a bit can go wrong when working with pipes, and there are some important facts to remember about using pipes with nonblocking reads and writes. Some of these have been mentioned already and some not. The following list consolidates them into a single place:

- If a write() is made to a pipe that is not open for reading by any process, a SIGPIPE signal will be sent to the writing process, which, if not caught, will terminate that process. If it is caught, after the SIGPIPE handler finishes, the write() will return with a -1, and errno will be set to the value EPIPE.

- If there are one or more processes writing to a pipe, if a reading process closes its read end of the pipe and no other processes have the pipe open for reading, each writer will be sent the SIGPIPE signal, and the preceding rules regarding handling of the signal apply to each process.

- As long as one writer has a pipe open for writing, a call to read() will remain blocked until there is data in the pipe. Therefore, if all writers finish writing to the pipe but a single writer fails to close the write end of the pipe, if a reader calls read(), the reader will remain permanently blocked. Once all writers close the write ends of the pipe, the read() will return 0.

- A write() to a full pipe will block the writer until there are PIPE_BUF free bytes in the pipe.

- Unlike reads from a file, read() requests to a pipe drain the pipe of the data that was read. Therefore, when multiple readers read from the same pipe, no two read the same data.

- Writes are atomic as long as the number of bytes is smaller than PIPE_BUF.

- Reads are atomic in the sense that, if there is any data in the pipe when the call is initiated, the read() will return with as much data as is available, up to the number of bytes requested, and it is guaranteed not to be interrupted.

- Processes cannot seek() on a pipe.

The popen() and pclose() Library Functions

The system() library function introduced at the end of Chapter 11 allows a program to execute an arbitrary shell command, but it doesn't enable the calling program to send data to the standard input of that command or to read the data from the standard output of that command. For this we can use popen(). The pipe(2) man page mentioned popen(3) in its SEE ALSO section.

Like system(), popen() can execute an arbitrary shell command line, but unlike system(), the shell command runs in parallel to the calling process. It has the same cost overhead as system() because it creates a process in which to run a shell and executes that shell, passing it a NULL-terminated string containing a shell command line to execute; this in turn causes that shell to create child processes to execute one or more commands from the command line string.

Unlike system(), before it forks any processes, popen() sets up a pipe between the calling process and the command to execute and establishes a C FILE* stream pointer that can be used to read from or write to the pipe, depending on the mode of operation.

The synopsis on its man page is:

```
#include <stdio.h>
FILE *popen(const char *command, const char *mode);

int pclose(FILE *stream);
```

The first argument is a string containing the command to execute. The second argument (`mode`) is a string that specifies its I/O mode. It must contain either `r` for reading or `w` for writing but not both. If successful, it returns a `FILE*` pointer to a stream that can be used to either read from or write to the pipe. On failure, it returns `NULL`.

NOTE *It's helpful to remember that the popen() function has the same syntax as the C Library function fopen(). In popen(), the first argument is a command to execute, whereas in fopen(), it's the pathname of a file. Both return a file stream pointer and, in each, the second argument indicates whether that stream is open in read-only or write-only mode.*

In effect, popen() creates a pipe, forks a new process, closes and duplicates file descriptors as needed, and within that child process runs the system-dependent default shell (`sh`) by exec-ing

```
execl(shell_path, "sh", "-c", command, (char *)0);
```

where *shell_path* is the absolute pathname of `sh`. The `-c` flag passed to the shell tells it to execute the *command* argument, and popen() ensures that any streams from previous calls to popen() that are still open in the calling process are closed in the new child process to prevent potential race conditions.

The mode argument defines whether the calling process can read from or write to the returned stream. The internal actions are as follows:

- If it contains `r`, the calling process is returned a `FILE*` pointing to the read end of the pipe and the child process's standard output is attached to the write end of the pipe so that the command that it executes puts its output into the pipe instead of the terminal.

- If it contains `w`, , the calling process is returned a `FILE*` pointing to the write end of the pipe, and the child process's standard input is attached to the read end of the pipe so that the command that it executes gets its input from the pipe instead of the standard input device.

- If it contains both, it results in an error.

In Linux, the mode may optionally contain `e`, which if present, enables the close-on-exec flag for the file descriptor underlying the returned file stream pointer.

THE CLOSE-ON-EXEC FLAG

In Chapter 11 we saw that open file descriptors remain open by default when a process calls execve(). Enabling the *close-on-exec* flag on an open file descriptor causes it to be closed instead. This is useful when a child process executes a new program that shouldn't access this descriptor.

Figure 13-8 depicts the two possible modes of communication.

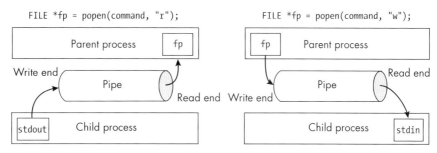

Figure 13-8: The two different methods of establishing communication with popen()

The pclose() function closes the stream opened by popen() and waits for the command to terminate. It returns the termination status of the child process created by popen(), unless that status is unavailable to pclose(), in which case it returns -1 and sets errno to ECHILD. This can happen if the parent process called any wait function while the child was running to wait for some other child process it forked.

WARNING *File streams created with popen() must be closed with pclose(), not fclose()!*

Let's look at a simple example program in which the parent process simulates a pipe between two commands given on the command line, without explicitly creating a pipe. Instead, it makes two calls to popen() and becomes the intermediary between the child processes executing the two commands. In effect, the parent replaces the pipe by transferring the output of one process to the input of the other:

popen_demo.c
```
#include "common_hdrs.h"
#include <sys/wait.h>

int main(int argc, char *argv[])
{
    int    nbytes;             /* Number of bytes read from pipe      */
    FILE   *fin;               /* Stream pointing to read end of pipe */
    FILE   *fout;              /* Stream pointing to write end of pipe */
    char   buffer[PIPE_BUF];   /* Buffer for transferring data        */
    int    status1, status2;   /* For collecting status of processes  */

    if ( argc < 3 )
        usage_error("Usage: popen_demo  command1 command2\n");
    if ( (fin = popen(argv[1], "r")) == NULL )
        fatal_error(errno, "popen");
    if ( (fout = popen(argv[2], "w")) == NULL )
        fatal_error(errno, "popen");
```

```
        /* Read the output of first command through the descriptor for fin
           and write that output into the descriptor for fout, the write end
           of the pipe that the second command reads as its input. */
        while ( (nbytes = read(fileno(fin), buffer, PIPE_BUF)) > 0 )
            if ( -1 == write(fileno(fout), buffer, nbytes) )
                fatal_error(errno, "write");
        if ( nbytes < 0 )
            fatal_error(errno, "read");

        status1 = pclose(fin);
        status2 = pclose(fout);
        if ( status1 == -1 || status2 == -1 )
            fatal_error(errno, "pclose");
        if ( WIFSIGNALED(status1) )
            printf("'%s' terminated by signal %d\n",argv[1], WTERMSIG(status1));
        if ( WIFSIGNALED(status2) )
            printf("'%s' terminated by signal %d\n",argv[2], WTERMSIG(status2));
        return 0;
}
```

Listing 13-2: A program that simulates a pipe using two calls to popen( )

You can run this program with multiword commands by enclosing the entire command in single quotes. For example, assuming the executable has been named popen_demo, the following pipes the man page search for *pipe* into grep:

```
$ ./popen_demo 'apropos -s2,3 pipe' 'grep posix'
pclose (3posix)      - close a pipe stream to or from a process
pipe (3posix)        - create an interprocess channel
popen (3posix)       - initiate pipe streams to or from a process
```

The same caveats apply to the use of popen( ) as to system( ) (see Chapter 11). We haven't explored other issues related to popen( ), including how the C Standard I/O Library's buffering of input and output affects reading and writing of the pipe through the C I/O stream and how various signals affect the execution of this function. For example, because popen( ) is using C file streams, which use block buffering for pipes and files, writes into the pipe are only written into the pipe when the buffer is full or the pipe is closed, and consequently the data isn't seen at its read immediately. To force the writes to appear immediately, you have to disable block buffering or flush frequently. The POSIX specification of popen( ) has a more detailed discussion of some of the nuances of using this function.

FIFOs

Unnamed pipes are an elegant mechanism, but their usefulness is somewhat limited. For one, they can only be shared by *related processes*, meaning those with a common ancestor that created a pipe which propagated down through calls to fork(), such as when a parent creates a pipe and then forks a child. Also, they cease to exist as soon as the processes that are using them terminate, which implies that they must be re-created every time they're needed. If we want to use them in a program with which any other process can communicate, the other processes will need to know the name of the pipe to use, but an unnamed pipe has no such name.

Named pipes, or FIFOs, make up for these limitations. A FIFO has the same reading and writing semantics as an unnamed pipe; all of the rules described in "Unnamed Pipes" on page 648 in terms of reading and writing apply to named pipes as well. The difference between named and unnamed pipes is only in how they're created and opened. Named pipes are unlike unnamed pipes in that:

- They exist as directory entries in the file system and therefore have associated permissions and ownership.

- They can be used by processes that are not related to each other.

- They can be created and deleted at the shell level or through the system API.

Although they have directory entries, they have no contents in the filesystem: They have no disk storage, even when they're being used, because they exist only in kernel memory. The directory entry for a FIFO serves only as a means for processes to access it using a name in the filesystem.

All of the preceding programs we developed were single stand-alone programs. FIFOs enable us to create client-server applications. A *client-server application* consists of two components: a server and a client. A *server* program is one that can provide services to other processes. The processes that request these services are called its *clients*. In Chapter 14 we'll study how to create true client-server applications. Here we'll concentrate on the use of FIFOs for creating programs that communicate but which are not necessarily true client-server applications. Specifically, one process will act like a server in the sense that it will be the only process reading from the FIFO, but it will not send any data back to processes that send data to it, and one process will act like a client in that it sends data to the server, but it will not be designed to receive any response from the server. I'll call these applications *client-server–like* applications.

Creating Named Pipes in the Shell

Before we explore how to create and use FIFOs in programs, let's look at how we can create them at the user level. Searching for commands related to

FIFOs with `apropos -s1 fifo` yields a Linux man page for the `mkfifo` command and a POSIX man page for it. POSIX also specifies another command, `mknod`, which is a general-purpose utility for creating device special files, including FIFOs, but POSIX recommends that FIFOs should be created with `mkfifo`, not `mknod`. Since the `mkfifo` command is also simpler to use, we'll work with that one.

We'll create a FIFO named *MYFIFO* in the */tmp* directory. The */tmp* directory exists on every Unix system; it's intended as a place for programs to create temporary files and is usually configured to allow all users to create files there. It usually has the sticky bit enabled, so that only the owner and the superuser can delete them:

```
$ ls -ld /tmp
drwxrwxrwt 20 root root 12288 May 29 09:47 /tmp/
```

To create *MYFIFO* there, enter:

```
$ mkfifo /tmp/MYFIFO
```

This creates the FIFO */tmp/MYFIFO*. It's fairly common to use uppercase names for FIFO names to make them easier to spot in directory listings.

The default mode on a FIFO is `rw-rw-rw-` prior to applying the `umask` value. Since my `umask` is 022, the new FIFO's permissions are `rw-r--r--`:

```
$ ls -l /tmp/MYFIFO
prw-r--r-- 1 stewart stewart 0 May 29 09:53 /tmp/MYFIFO
```

Notice that FIFOs are identified in the output of `ls -l` by the `p` file type. The `-m` option can be used to override the default mode. It's easiest to give it the mode in octal; if you use a symbolic mode string such as "go+w" or "go-w", the `+` and `−` operators are interpreted as adding or subtracting from `rw-rw-rw-`. Thus, the two commands

```
$ mkfifo -m644 /tmp/FIFO1
$ mkfifo -m"go-w" /tmp/FIFO2
```

create */tmp/FIFO1* and */tmp/FIFO2* with the same permission `rw-r--r--`.

NOTE   *In Linux, the mode supplied to the `mkfifo` command is not modified by the `umask`, but POSIX.1-2024 doesn't specify exactly how this mode must be used. It only requires that the actual mode created with the `-m` option should be at least as restrictive as the argument supplied to `-m`.*

Let's demonstrate the FIFO's operation with a small experiment. If the FIFO */tmp/MYFIFO* does not exist, create it with permission 666. Open a second terminal window. In the first terminal, enter the command:

```
$ cat < /tmp/MYFIFO
```

The shell prompt will not return because the cat command is now waiting for input from the FIFO, which is still empty. If you background it, the shell prompt will return. In the second terminal, enter:

```
$ echo "Today's lesson is about FIFOs. " > /tmp/MYFIFO
```

In the first terminal you'll now see

```
Today's lesson is about FIFOs.
```

which shows that the data put in the FIFO by echo was read by cat. Although this is interesting to observe, FIFOs are really intended as an IPC facility for programs, not user-level utilities, so let's now turn to programming with them.

Creating FIFOs

The first step is finding the function that can create a FIFO. A search limited to Sections 2 and 3 of the man pages turns up the mkfifo(3) man page, and possibly a reference to the mknod(2) page, but both POSIX and Linux advocate using mkfifo() instead, which is easier to use than mknod(). Therefore, we'll use mkfifo() to create all FIFOs. Its synopsis is:

```
#include <sys/types.h>
#include <sys/stat.h>

int mkfifo(const char *pathname, mode_t mode);
```

The call mkfifo(MYFIFO, 0666), when successful, creates a FIFO named MYFIFO with permission 0666 & ~ umask and returns 0. If it fails, it sets errno and returns -1. Notice that, unlike the mkfifo command, the umask is applied to the mode passed to the mkfifo() function.

One of our first decisions in designing client-server–like applications is where to put the FIFO. The server has to create it, which implies that it has to be in a directory that it has privilege to modify. Also, clients need to know where to find it. It's useful to distinguish between public and private FIFOs. A *public FIFO* is one that is known to all clients. There's no specific function that makes a FIFO public; rather, it's just that it's given a name that's easy to remember and its location is made known so that client programs can find it. Some authors call these *well-known FIFOs* because they are analogous to the well-known ports used for network sockets. A *private FIFO*, in contrast, has a name that's known only to the process that creates it and the processes to which it chooses to divulge it.

Common choices for the location of a public FIFO are:

- The */tmp* directory
- The */var/tmp* directory
- A subdirectory of */run* dedicated to the server, provided it has superuser privilege to create it

In most modern implementations of Unix, the */tmp* directory is cleaned on reboot. If the FIFO needs to survive reboots, this is not a good location for it; instead, it should be created in the */var/tmp* directory, since it doesn't get cleaned as often. If we're developing a system program that will be owned by root, then it's best to create the FIFO in */run/<servername>/*, since this will not be purged at all. The file-hierarchy(7) and hier(7) man pages contain more detailed information about the different choices, and a discussion of security issues regarding the location of the FIFO can be found at *https://systemd.io/TEMPORARY_DIRECTORIES/*.

Opening FIFOs

Whereas unnamed pipes are opened by the pipe() call, FIFOs are opened as if they were ordinary files, with the open() system call. The POSIX requirements for the opening semantics of FIFOs make opening them a bit more complicated than you might expect. These requirements are described in the fifo(7) man page. Because the intended use of FIFOs is for a writing process to send data to a reading process, the requirements are designed to synchronize the opening of each end of the FIFO by stipulating the following:

- A FIFO must be opened on both ends, meaning both reading and writing, before data can be written into it.

- If the O_NONBLOCK flag is clear, a process that opens one end of a FIFO will block until the other end is opened.

One way to satisfy these requirements is to open the FIFO for reading and writing with the O_RDWR flag, and Linux does support this, but POSIX does not and warns against it; programs using this approach may not work properly on other Unix systems. The POSIX requirements for the semantics of opening a FIFO for reading or writing and in both blocking and nonblocking mode are summarized in Table 13-3. If the other end of the FIFO is open, the call to open() always succeeds. The table describes what happens when the other end isn't open.

Table 13-3: The Semantics of Opening a FIFO When the Other End Is Not Open

Operation	Blocking mode	Nonblocking mode
Reading	Process blocks	Call returns 0 immediately
Writing	Process blocks	Call fails, setting errno to ENXIO

Now consider how a server works. Once it starts up, it remains running until it is terminated explicitly, say by an administrator. In the simplest case, it should block itself while no clients have sent it any data. In the next chapter, we'll consider more complex servers that perform other work and periodically check whether data is available.

Since the server needs to create a FIFO in order to receive messages from clients, it needs to open it for reading, but if it opens it for reading in blocking mode, Table 13-3 shows that it will immediately block unless a client already opened it for writing. This by itself may not be a problem, depending on what else the server has to do before clients start sending data to it. On a busy system, there may be a short delay between the time when the first client opens the FIFO for writing and the time that the server runs again.

A symmetric problem occurs when a client tries to open a FIFO for writing before the server has opened it for reading. In this case the client will be blocked. If instead the client were allowed to continue and then tried to write to a FIFO that had no reading process, its write would fail and the client would be sent a SIGPIPE signal.

The bigger problem is what happens after the server has opened the FIFO. Assume that the server's main loop is of the form

```
while ( read(thefifo, buffer, PIPE_BUF) > 0 )
    // Process data in buffer.
```

and that the server opened the FIFO only for reading in blocking mode. It blocks until a client opens it for writing.

Consider what happens once a client does open it for writing. When the client process finishes writing and closes the write end of the FIFO, the next time the server tries to read from the FIFO, there'll be no writer and the call will return 0 based on the semantics described in Table 13-1 on page 652. At this point, the main loop will break, the server will terminate, and no other clients will be able to send data to it. This violates the principle that the server must remain running.

The solution to this problem is to have the server open the FIFO for writing immediately after it opens it for reading:

```
if ( (publicfd = open(PUBLICFIFO, O_RDONLY)) == -1 )
    fatal_error(errno, "open");
if ( (dummyfd = open(PUBLICFIFO, O_WRONLY)) == -1 )
    fatal_error(errno, "open");
```

The only reason it opens it for writing is to keep itself from terminating; hence, the returned descriptor is called a dummy descriptor. Whereas a process should not open unnamed pipes for both reading and writing, it must do this for FIFOs. We'll base our first example on this server-like program design.

Putting It All Together: A Simple FIFO-Based Server-Like Program

Let's demonstrate the use of a FIFO by creating two programs that establish a one-way communication through it. One program will monitor a FIFO; it will first create a public FIFO and then listen to it for incoming messages. When it receives a message, it will update a counter and print the message on standard output, preceded by the counter value. It's like a server, except that it doesn't perform a service for the sending process, and it doesn't send anything back to it. With a few modifications, it could be turned into a server. In Chapter 14, you'll learn how to create true servers.

The other program is one that sends data to the monitor. That program is a little like a client program because its messages could be requests for service. Since a client needs to know the name of the FIFO to which it has to send its messages, we'll create a single header file that contains the FIFO's absolute pathname as well as any other shared data. The monitor, as well as any program that wants to send messages to it, will need to include this header file.

The monitor program is named *fifomonitor.c*, and the client program is *fifosender.c*. The common header file, shown next, is *fifodef.h*:

```
#include "common_hdrs.h"
#include <sys/stat.h>
#define  PUBLIC "/tmp/SIMPLE_FIFO"
```

This file doesn't need the included header files; they're included as a convenience so that when a program includes it, it doesn't need to explicitly include the common header files. Ideally, the FIFO's name should be chosen so that no other processes in the system would ever choose the same filename and no malicious software could guess it. For simplicity, I use a simple name that may not be unique. I put the FIFO into */tmp* because it does not need to persist across reboots.

The Monitor Program

In this first example, the monitor writes the messages it receives, together with a timestamp, to its standard input. Therefore, we won't run it in the background; otherwise, its output will appear after the prompt printed by the shell. Also, since it's intended to run forever, it doesn't terminate on its own, and we'll need to send it a terminating signal, either from the keyboard or from another terminal by entering pkill -3 fifomonitor. For this reason, it has a signal handler that does cleanup when it receives a terminating signal. The program is shown in Listing 13-3.

fifomonitor.c
```
#include "fifodef.h"
int public_fd;    /* File descriptor to read end of PUBLIC FIFO       */
int dummy_fd;     /* File descriptor to unused write end of PUBLIC FIFO */

void clean_up(int sig)
{
    close(public_fd); /* Close both FIFOs.                 */
    close(dummy_fd);
    unlink(PUBLIC);   /* Delete the filename for the FIFO. */
    exit(sig);
}

int main(int argc, char *argv[])
{
```

```
    int             nbytes;         /* Number of bytes read from client   */
    int             msg_count = 0;  /* Number of messages received        */
❶   static char     buffer[PIPE_BUF+1];  /* Buffer for received message   */
    struct sigaction handler;       /* sigaction for registering handlers */
    struct timespec tp;             /* timespec for message arrival time  */
    struct tm       *bdtime;        /* Broken-down time for tp            */
    char            timestr[64];    /* Arrival time as a string           */
    char            msgnum[16];     /* String for message number          */


    /* Register the signal handler to handle termination signals. */
    handler.sa_flags = 0;
    handler.sa_handler = clean_up;
    sigemptyset(&handler.sa_mask);
    if ( ((sigaction(SIGINT,  &handler, NULL)) == -1 ) ||
         ((sigaction(SIGHUP,  &handler, NULL)) == -1 ) ||
         ((sigaction(SIGQUIT, &handler, NULL)) == -1)  ||
         ((sigaction(SIGTERM, &handler, NULL)) == -1) )
        fatal_error(errno, "sigaction");

    if ( mkfifo(PUBLIC, 0666) == -1 )   /* Create the FIFO. */
        if ( errno != EEXIST )
            fatal_error(errno, "open");


    /* Open the FIFO for reading. */
    if ( (public_fd = open(PUBLIC, O_RDONLY)) == -1 )
        fatal_error(errno, "open");


    /* Open the FIFO for writing. */
    if ( (dummy_fd = open(PUBLIC, O_WRONLY)) == -1  )
        fatal_error(errno, "open");


    /* Repeatedly do a blocking read, waiting for a message from a client. */
    while ( TRUE ) {
        memset(buffer, 0, PIPE_BUF); /* Zero the buffer for the next read. */
        if ( (nbytes = read(public_fd, buffer, PIPE_BUF)) > 0 ) {
            buffer[nbytes] = '\0';   /* Add NULL byte to print it.        */
            /* Get the current time. */
            if ( -1 == clock_gettime(CLOCK_REALTIME, &tp) )
                fatal_error(errno, "clock_gettime()");

            /* Convert the current time into broken-down time. */
            bdtime = localtime(&tp.tv_sec);
            if ( bdtime == NULL )
                fatal_error(EOVERFLOW, "localtime");
            strftime(timestr, sizeof(timestr), "%X", bdtime);
            sprintf(msgnum, "[%d]", ++msg_count);
            printf("%-5s %s: %s", msgnum, timestr, buffer);
```

```
                    fflush(stdout);  /* In case there's no newline */
            }
            else
                printf("No bytes left in buffer\n");
                break;
        }
        exit(EXIT_SUCCESS);
}
```

Listing 13-3: A monitor program that prints the messages sent to it through a FIFO

The two file descriptors used by the main program are global because the
signal handler needs access to them. The buffer for storing messages from
the FIFO is declared to be of size PIPE_BUF+1 ❶ because the maximum number
of bytes from a single atomic write is PIPE_BUF, and in case it is that long, since
the program needs to append a NULL byte to it, the buffer has an extra byte.

   After installing the handler for the signals and opening the read and
write ends of the public FIFO, the program enters its loop. There, it erases
the read buffer and then calls read() on the FIFO. It appends the NULL byte
and prints it to standard output. Just in case the client sent a message without
a terminating newline character, it flushes the I/O buffer used by printf().

The FIFO Client Program

The client program shown in Listing 13-4 is smaller. It too needs a signal
handler, not for terminating signals, but for SIGPIPE, because if the monitor
disappears or the read end of its pipe is closed, when the client writes next,
it will be sent a SIGPIPE signal. To handle it gracefully, it prints a message and
exits.

fifosender.c
```
#include "fifodef.h"
#define  QUIT "quit"

void on_sigpipe(int signo)
{
    fprintf(stderr, "Monitor is not running; terminating.\n");
    exit(1);
}

int main(int argc, char *argv[])
{
    int     nbytes;           /* Number of bytes read from standard input   */
    int     public_fd;        /* File descriptor to write end of PUBLIC FIFO */
    char    text[PIPE_BUF];   /* Buffer to store user entered text          */
    struct sigaction sigact;  /* sigaction for registering handler          */

    /* Register the signal handler for SIGPIPE. */
    sigact.sa_handler = on_sigpipe;
    sigact.sa_flags = SA_RESTART;
```

```
    if ( (sigaction(SIGPIPE, &sigact, NULL)) == -1 )
        fatal_error(errno, "sigaction");

    /* Open the public FIFO for writing. */
    if ( (public_fd = open(PUBLIC, O_WRONLY)) == -1 )
        fatal_error(errno, "open");

    printf("Type 'quit' to quit.\n");
    while ( TRUE ) {
        memset(text, 0, PIPE_BUF);     /* Zero the buffer for the next read. */
        if ( (nbytes = read(STDIN_FILENO, text, PIPE_BUF)) == -1 )
            fatal_error(errno, "read");
        if ( !strncmp(QUIT, text, nbytes - 1)) /* If text is 'quit', exit. */
            break;
        if ( write(public_fd, text, nbytes) == -1 )
            break;                     /* Might get SIGPIPE here, so no need to exit. */
    }
    /* User quit, so close the write end of public FIFO. */
    close(public_fd);
    return 0;
}
```

Listing 13-4: A client program that sends the text entered by a user to the monitor through a FIFO

The client opens the FIFO for writing and then enters its loop, in which it repeatedly clears the buffer that stores the user's entered text, waits for the user to enter up to PIPE_BUF many bytes of text, checks whether it matches *quit* and, if not, writes it into the FIFO. If the user entered *quit*, then the client exits.

Client-Server Interaction

To see the behavior of this pair of programs, we have to start up the monitor first. Because it's really designed to run in the foreground, we can run the client in a second terminal window. The effect is more dramatic this way, because the text that we enter in the client appears in the terminal of the monitor. We start up the monitor first:

```
$ ./fifomonitor
```

The prompt will not return. In a second terminal, start up the client and enter a few lines:

```
$ ./fifosender
Type 'quit' to quit.
This is a test of our first FIFO application.
Does it work?
```

Look at the first terminal window. It now looks like this:

```
$ ./fifomonitor
[1]   09:57:24: This is a test of our first FIFO application.
[2]   09:58:06: Does it work?
```

Now instead of entering quit in the client, terminate the server with CTRL-C, enter **more text**, and then check whether the FIFO still exists:

```
$ ./fifosender
Type 'quit' to quit.
This is a test of our first FIFO application.
Does it work?
more text
Monitor is not running; terminating.
$ ls /tmp/SIMPLE_FIFO
ls: cannot access '/tmp/SIMPLE_FIFO': No such file or directory
```

This was a good warm-up exercise. It differs from a real client-server application in the following ways:

- The monitor doesn't do anything really. It doesn't provide a service to its clients, such as computing something in response to client requests and sending data back to the clients.

- It runs in the foreground and is connected to the terminal. Control signals sent from the terminal will kill it.

- If multiple clients send it messages at the same time, it can't distinguish among them—all of their messages are intermingled on the terminal.

The next step is to learn how to design a client-server applications in which the server actually serves multiple clients.

Summary

This chapter primarily explored pipes, both named and unnamed, as a means of IPC. Pipes were introduced into UNIX in 1973. A pipe is a unidirectional, finite-capacity byte stream, with first-in-first-out semantics. Every pipe has a read end and a write end; data written into the write end is read from the read end in the same order as it was written. It's a byte stream because successive writes are simply appended to the stream without any separating boundaries. The read and write ends of a pipe are represented by file descriptors, so that reading and writing use the same functions as are used with ordinary files.

Writing into a named or unnamed pipe is guaranteed by the kernel to be atomic as long as the amount of data written is at most PIPE_BUF bytes. On modern systems, this is typically the page size of the system: 4096 bytes. Reading from a pipe drains the pipe, so that no two processes can read the same data.

Unnamed pipes can be used only by related processes, such as parent and child, siblings, and so on. Named pipes, which are also called FIFOs, can be used by any processes that know their names. Unlike unnamed pipes, named pipes are visible in the filesystem, although they have no associated storage in it. Both named and unnamed pipes are implemented entirely within memory by the kernel. Although the semantics of reading from and writing to pipes is the same for both named and unnamed pipes, how they're created and how they're opened is different. In general, unexpected behavior can happen if we don't close unused descriptors or, in certain situations, fail to open descriptors even if we don't plan on using them.

The chapter also looked at a few topics related to pipes. For one, it introduced the popen() function, which is a convenient way to create a process to execute a command line without needing to call fork() or exec(). Second, it looked at the dup() and dup2() system calls for duplicating file descriptors. These calls play a fundamental role in setting up pipes to be shared by related processes and, within the shell, to implement I/O redirection.

Exercises

1. Modify *shellpipe_demo.c* to work with any number of commands, so that the command

    ```
    $ shellpipe_demo cmmd '|' cmmd '|' cmmd '|' ... '|' cmmd
    ```

    will act like:

    ```
    $ cmmd | cmmd | cmmd | ... | cmmd
    ```

2. This exercise explores possible implementations of the popen() and pclose() functions. To start, create an implementation file *mypopenclose.c* and a header file *mypopenclose.h* containing the prototypes of your versions of these functions, which I'll assume you've named mypopen() and mypclose().

    (a) Create a main program that you can use to call your versions of the functions. For this purpose, it's easiest to modify the *popen_demo.c* program from the chapter. Make it read the commands from the command line. I'll assume it's named *testpopen.c* in the rest of this description. Initially *testpopen.c* should call mypopen() instead of popen(), but should call pclose() until you implement mypclose().

    (b) Write your version of mypopen() in *mypopenclose.c*. You'll find it useful to use fdopen(). Read its man page for details. Build testpopen and run it, making sure that it works as expected.

    (c) Now write mypclose(). As you write it, you should realize that, from the file stream pointer fp it's given, it needs to determine which process is connected to fp in order to reap its status. Find an easy solution to this problem.

(d)   Will your two functions behave correctly when a process
calls mypopen() more than once before it calls `mypclose()`? If
you based *testpopen.c* on *popen_demo.c*, then it calls mypopen()
twice before calling `mypclose()`. What is the problem, and
how can it be solved? Try to write a version of these two
functions that works when a single program makes many
calls to mypopen().

(e)   The POSIX.1-2024 specification contains a possible implementation of these functions designed to be thread-safe.
Compare your solution to these implementations.

3.   Write a program that empirically determines the maximum capacity
of an unnamed pipe and empirically determines whether `PIPE_BUF` is
the least number of free bytes in an unnamed pipe so that a write to
it succeeds.

  •   To determine the maximum capacity, the program should
write one byte into it at a time until it is full. It should output the total number of bytes that it wrote.

  •   To determine whether `PIPE_BUF` is the least number of free
bytes necessary to write into it, remove bytes from this full
pipe in such a way that the program can determine exactly
how many bytes must be available for a successful write. Report the number on standard output.

4.   Modify *fifodef.h*, *fifomonitor.c*, and *fifosender.c* so that they can be used
for message logging. Specifically:

  •   Declare a fixed size structure in *fifodef.h* that contains a process ID and a message of at most 128 characters.

  •   Modify *fifomonitor.c* so that, when it reads from the FIFO
into its buffer, it extracts the process ID and the message
from the buffer and writes one line of the form `PID`: *message*
into a file named *logfile*. It should create this file when it
starts up if it does not already exist.

  •   Modify *fifosender.c* so that it expects a message as its only
command line argument, creates a structure containing its
process ID and that message, and writes that structure into
the FIFO whose name is in the *fifodef.h* file. If the message
on the command line is too long, decide how to handle it.

14

CLIENT-SERVER APPLICATIONS AND DAEMONS

In this chapter, we'll examine how to create client-server applications. To design a client-server application, we have to design both the client and the server and make sure that they work together.

A client-server application consists of two types of processes:

- A *server* process, which receives requests from other processes to provide some type of service. It performs the specific service and sends back a response to the other process.

- A *client* process, which issues service requests to a server by sending it a message and then receiving its response.

Clients typically interact with a user, whereas the server doesn't. In fact, the server is usually detached from any terminal. There can be multiple client processes, but there is almost always just a single server.

Servers can provide a wide variety of services, such as providing files, serving web pages, and controlling one or more hardware resources such as printers or other I/O devices. Not having an attached terminal, they record their error messages in a file or perhaps on a console, either directly or through a logging service provided by the kernel.

Although the client and server processes don't have to run on the same computer, in this chapter we limit our exploration to the design of client-server applications that run on the same host and communicate through one or more FIFOs. We'll begin by looking at the logging services provided by the kernel, after which we'll examine the steps that a process must take to turn itself into a daemon process. We'll then introduce the concepts of iterative and concurrent servers and develop one of each type.

Introduction to Client-Server Applications

There are many types of computing problems that benefit by breaking up the functionality of a potential solution into a client-server application. For example, when multiple users need to access a shared database, client programs can present the user interface and collect user inputs, send requests to a server, and present the returned results to the user. Similarly, suppose multiple processes need the services of a printer, and the system has multiple printers. Rather than having to collectively manage their privileges, authentication, priorities, and so on, these processes could send requests to a single print server that can manage the printers and handle distribution of the work. This decomposition has several benefits:

- By limiting access to a shared resource to a single server process, it is easier to detect breaches or failures because only that one process needs to be monitored. Other processes that need access to that resource become clients of this server process.

- It is more efficient for a single process to control a shared resource than for multiple processes to coordinate their accesses to it. For example, if multiple processes need to update some shared database, they can send their updates to a server, which can apply them in a controlled way, rather than competing with each other for access.

- Maintenance and debugging are easier when the clients encapsulate all local variations and customizations and the server presents a consistent, uniform interface to all clients.

Developing a client-server application requires that we separate out what the client does from what the server does and decide on the way in which they will communicate. The client and server code become tightly integrated in the sense that changes to the server will dictate changes to the client code. Therefore, when we develop a client-server application, we'll need to answer the following questions:

- What does the server do? What message or data does it expect from a client, and what does it return to the client?

- What does the client do? What form should its request to the server take, and in what form does it need its response?

- What IPC facilities will be used? Will there be a single public FIFO, for example? Will each client have a dedicated FIFO or perhaps more than one?

- How will errors and failure be handled? Will the server log its status and errors by some logging service?

In this chapter, we'll develop two different types of client-server applications to illustrate how these questions are addressed. First, though, we'll explore the logging services provided by the kernel. After that, we'll cover how a process can make itself a daemon.

System Logging Facilities

An application can write all of its error messages to an application-specific file, but when many applications do this, the set of logfiles grows, and managing them becomes difficult. The alternative is that all applications use a single logging facility, which writes to the logfiles that it maintains. If you've ever browsed through the */var* subdirectories, you might have discovered the file */var/log/syslog*. By default, this file can be read only by someone with superuser privilege or who is a member of the adm group. Let's see whether our programs can write their errors to that file.

A search of the man pages for system calls or functions that a process could use to log its errors and other events turns up a few relevant pages:

```
$ apropos -s2,3,7 logging
--snip--
openlog (3posix)    - open a connection to the logging facility
syslog.h (7posix)   - definitions for system error logging
```

The syslog.h(7posix) page briefly describes a facility called syslog() and refers us to the page for closelog(), which summarizes how to use this facility. The syslog() function writes messages to one of several possible system logfiles. By default, it will write to */var/log/syslog*. More accurately, syslog() is a function that a client process uses to send messages to the syslogd daemon, which decides where to write all messages. Some messages are written to */var/log/syslog*, some to a terminal, and some to other files. Usually, there's a configuration file such as *syslog.conf* that controls where messages are written. The openlog() function lets us configure how syslog() logging works. The syslog() function can be called by any process to record a message in the logfile.

It isn't necessary to call openlog() before calling syslog(). If we're willing to accept the default parameters and options, our program can just call syslog(), passing the appropriate arguments. The synopsis for this pair of functions is:

```
#include <syslog.h>
void openlog(const char *ident, int option, int facility);
void syslog(int priority, const char *format, ...);
```

The first parameter of openlog() is the name of the program to be recorded in the logfile; usually we pass it the program name. The second parameter is a bitmask that can be the bitwise-OR of several possible symbolic constants. These control different aspects of logging, such as whether to send messages to standard error as well as to the system logfile (LOG_PERROR), or whether to log the caller's PID (LOG_PID) with each message. The man page has the full list of available options.

The third parameter is named the facility. This is a value that helps to identify the calling process in subsequent calls of syslog(). For example, it could be LOG_CRON to indicate it's the cron daemon, LOG_KERN to indicate it's from the kernel, or LOG_USER to indicate the messages are from a user process. Another set of possible values our application can use are LOG_LOCAL0 through LOG_LOCAL7, which are reserved for application use.

Calling syslog() is relatively easy. We call it as if we were calling fprintf(), passing a priority level in the first argument and a format string with variables to be used within the string for conversions. Some of the priority-level constants are:

LOG_EMERG   Emergency or panic condition

LOG_CRIT   Critical condition, such as a disk error

LOG_ERR   General error condition

LOG_WARNING   Warning message

LOG_ALERT   Immediate attention needed

LOG_INFO   Informational message

When a process has finished calling syslog(), it can call closelog() to close the socket that the function uses to talk to the daemon.

It is important that the calling process does not pass a user-supplied string into the format parameter of the call. In other words, this type of call

```
scanf("%s", message);      /* Get string from standard input.   */
syslog(priority, message);  /* Pass string directly to syslog(). */
```

is a security risk. Instead, it should be called as follows:

```
scanf("%s", message);
syslog(priority, "%s", message);
```

The following program demonstrates sending messages to the file */var/log/syslog*:

syslog_demo.c
```
#include "common_hdrs.h"
#include <syslog.h>

int main(int argc, char *argv[])
{
    char msg[512];

    openlog(argv[0], LOG_PID | LOG_CONS, LOG_LOCAL0);
```

```
    strcpy(msg, "Starting logging demonstration.");
    while ( strcmp(msg, "quit") != 0 ) {
        syslog(LOG_INFO, "%s", msg);
        printf("Message to log: ");
        fflush(stdout);
        scanf("%s", msg);
    }
    exit(EXIT_SUCCESS);
}
```

The LOG_PID option causes each message to include the caller's PID. The last parameter was set to LOG_LOCAL0 to tell the logging facility that it will be a user program sending the messages. A line written to the logfile would look like this:

```
Jun 19 15:46:56 harpo syslog_demo[8259]: Message to log: user-entered-string
```

This is a short summary of system logging; you can read the man pages and the POSIX specification if you're interested in customizing the logging even more.

Daemons

A daemon is a process that runs in the background without a controlling terminal. In this section, we'll explore daemon processes and how to convert an ordinary process into a daemon.

Overview

Putting a process into the background does not make it a daemon. The important property of daemons is that they execute without an associated terminal or login shell, usually waiting for an event to occur. The event might be a request for a service such as printing or connecting to the internet, or a clock tick indicating that it is time to run. The word *daemon* is from Greek mythology and refers to a lesser god that did helpful tasks for the people it protected. Daemons are like these lesser gods; they are created at boot time and exist, hidden, ready to provide services when called upon.

Because daemons must not be connected to a terminal, one of their first tasks is to close all open file descriptors (in particular, standard input, standard output, and standard error). They usually make their working directory the root of the filesystem. They then take additional steps to break their association with any shell or terminal, among which are leaving their process group and registering their intent to ignore all incoming signals.

Daemon names often (but not always) end in d. This is one way to identify a daemon in the output of the ps -ef command: Run it and find the program names ending in d, such as httpd, sshd, syslogd, and telnetd. If their entry in the column labelled TTY is a ?, they have no associated terminal and are most likely a daemon.

Converting Processes into Daemons

Usually, daemons are started by system initialization scripts at boot time. If you've written a server and want to turn it into a full-fledged daemon, it isn't enough to put it into the background. This will only tell the shell not to wait for it; it will still have a control terminal and can still be killed by any signals from that terminal.

Some daemons are started by other programs. For example, sshd creates new daemons for new connections. Some are started by programs such as the cron daemon, which runs scheduled jobs (and has no d in its name). Some are invoked at the user terminal. For example, sometimes the printer daemon is stopped and restarted from the terminal by the superuser.

Because daemons don't have a controlling terminal, they don't write messages to standard output or to the standard error stream. This leaves them with just two choices for recording errors and logging their actions:

- Write to a logfile

- Use a system logging facility

In Linux, it's possible for a daemon to write to the standard error stream without turning its associated device into a control terminal. I'll explain more about that shortly. We'll address this issue after determining the steps that a process must take to turn itself into a daemon. These steps are:

Putting itself in the background It does this by forking a new process, exiting the parent process, and executing as the child. When the parent exits, the shell that started it collects its exit status and sees that the invoked process has terminated. The child, which is now executing the server code, is no longer in the foreground, but it is still controlled by the terminal.

Making itself a session leader We discussed sessions in Chapter 10. A process can detach itself from a terminal by becoming a session leader, but only processes that are neither session leaders nor process group leaders can do this. Since the current process is now a child of the original process, it is neither, so it can call setsid(), which makes it a session leader of a new session and a group leader of a new process group, neither of which has any other members.

Registering its intent to ignore SIGHUP Daemons should ignore this signal. The reason for ignoring it is that when a session leader terminates, all of its children are sent a SIGHUP, which would otherwise kill them. Since the process is currently a session leader and it will create child processes that should not be killed when this process terminates, its children should inherit the disposition to ignore SIGHUP.

Executing its code as a new child of the existing process The process again forks a child process, terminates itself, and lets the new child, which is the grandchild of the original process, continue to execute this code. This step is needed in some versions of Unix in which, when a session leader opens a terminal device, that terminal is automatically made the control terminal for the process. By running as the child of a session leader, the process is now protected against this possibility. In Linux, we can achieve this same effect by making the process set the O_NOCTTY flag on any call it makes to open() on a terminal device, obviating the need for this step; however, it's not as portable to do this.

Changing the current working directory to / If the current working directory of the daemon is on a filesystem other than /, that filesystem cannot be unmounted while the daemon is running. Since daemons usually run until the system is shut down, this step ensures that all filesystems can be unmounted while the system is running.

Clearing the umask A nonzero umask can change the permissions of files and directories created by the daemon. We don't want those permissions to be different than the ones specified when the daemon creates those files and directories.

Closing any open file descriptors The daemon might have inherited open file descriptors from its parent or grandparent. These are best closed, especially the standard descriptors 0, 1, and 2. In fact, to be safe, it's even better to make them point to */dev/null*.

A function that carries out the preceding steps, converting the calling process into a daemon, follows in Listing 14-1. I've named it make_me_a_daemon(). This opens a connection to the syslog facility as its last step.

make_me_a _daemon()
```
BOOL make_me_a_daemon(const char *pname)
{
    int    max_descriptors;
    pid_t pid;

    if ( (pid = fork()) == -1 )
        fatal_error(errno, "fork");
    else if ( pid != 0 )
        exit(EXIT_SUCCESS);  /* Parent terminates. */

    /* Child continues from here. */
    setsid();                /* Detach itself and become a session leader */
    signal(SIGHUP, SIG_IGN); /* Ignore SIGHUP.                            */

    if ( (pid = fork()) == -1 )
        fatal_error(errno, "fork");
    else if ( pid != 0 )
        exit(EXIT_SUCCESS);  /* First child terminates. */

    /* Grandchild continues from here. */
    chdir("/");              /* Change working directory.   */
    umask(0);                /* Clearfile mode creation mask */

    /* Get maximum number of allowed open descriptors. */
```

```
    if ( -1 == (max_descriptors = sysconf(_SC_OPEN_MAX)) )
        max_descriptors = MAXFD;
    else
        for ( int i = 0; i < max_descriptors; i++ )
            close(i);                       /* Close all open file descriptors. */
    openlog(pname, LOG_PID | LOG_CONS, LOG_LOCAL0); /* Start syslog logging.*/
    return TRUE;
}
```

Listing 14-1: A function that converts the calling process into a daemon

The pname parameter passed to the function is intended to be the program name, since it is written with each message. The function uses the
sysconf() function, which we've used in Chapters 10 and 11, to get the value
of a system parameter, in this case, the maximum allowed number of open
file descriptors. Many of the descriptors that it closes will not have been
opened, and close() will return -1, but we can ignore the return value in this
case. It returns TRUE to the caller to indicate that it is now a daemon.

An Iterative Server

An *iterative server* is a server that services the requests from its clients in an
iterative fashion, meaning one after another. In contrast, a *concurrent server*
is one that forks a separate process (or perhaps a thread) to handle each request. Here, we'll design and develop an iterative server.

Unlike our simple server from Chapter 13, an iterative server needs to
send replies back to clients. It cannot use a shared FIFO for this purpose;
every client has to have its own dedicated FIFO for receiving replies from
the server. Therefore, before a client establishes a connection to the server,
it needs to create its own, private FIFO. The clients' private FIFOs need to
have names that are unique, so that no two clients try to create a FIFO with
the same name. The program that we'll develop now will show one way to
solve this problem.

Overview of the Application

In this application, the server has two-way communication with each client,
processing incoming client requests one after the other. In order to achieve
this, the server creates a public FIFO that it uses for reading incoming messages from clients wishing to use its services. This raises the first issue. Since
a FIFO is a byte stream, if all clients send requests to a single queue, how will
the server know where one request ends and the next one starts in the pipe?
There are a few possible solutions:

Make messages fixed size   If all messages are the same size, the server
can just read the pipe in chunks of that size.

Put a separator byte at the end of each message   This allows variable
size messages. The server has to read until it finds the separator.

Start each message with a header   Every message can start with a header of fixed size (like the ELF file format) that contains the number of bytes in the message and possibly the offsets of other items in the message.

I decided, for this application, to go with the first choice, making each message the same size. Each incoming message is a structure with two members. The first is a string containing the name of the private FIFO that the client creates when it starts up and that is used by the server for sending a reply. The second is a string that contains the actual message data, for instance, a specific command or data it wants the server to process.

Figure 14-1 depicts the relationship between the clients and the server with respect to the shared pipes.

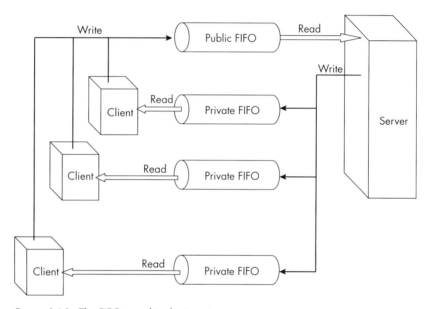

Figure 14-1: The FIFOs used in the iterative server

When the server receives a message, it looks at the FIFO name in it and tries to open it for writing. If successful, the server will use this FIFO for sending data to the client. After the client sends its message to the server, it opens its private FIFO for reading. It will block until the server opens the write end of this FIFO. When the server opens the write end, the client will read from it until it receives a return value of 0, indicating that the server has finished writing and closed its end of the pipe.

For the purpose of learning how to develop client-server applications, it doesn't matter much what service the server actually performs for the client, since it will have the same software architecture in most cases. Since I don't want what the server does to distract us from how it's designed, the service should be easy to implement and understand.

One simple service is lowercase-to-uppercase conversion for clients. In this case, the clients would send the server a piece of text and the server would send a copy of it back to the client in which every lowercase letter was converted to uppercase. The server could instead provide an arithmetic calculation service: The client would send an arithmetic expression to be evaluated, and the server would perform the calculation and send the result back to the client.

One benefit of developing the calculator server is that we'll get to see a good application of the popen() function. A benefit of developing the uppercase conversion server is that the issues regarding the handling of potentially large amounts of data can be demonstrated with it. Therefore, for the iterative server that we'll develop here, we'll implement the calculation service, and when we develop a concurrent server after this, we'll implement the uppercase conversion.

Since Linux already has a command named calc with similar functionality, the server executable will be named spl_calcd (for *calculator daemon*) and the client executable will be named spl_calc. For simplicity, I'll refer to the server as either the *calc server* or the *calc daemon*. Assuming that the calc server has been started up in the background by entering spl_calcd &, the client could be run as follows:

```
$ ./spl_calc '10 * 2 + 100/25'
24                              # Server's returned result
$ ./spl_calc 'sqrt(10.000)'
3.162                          # Server's returned result
$ ./spl_calc 'sqrt(10.00000)'
3.16227                        # Server's returned result
$ ./spl_calc 2.50^2
6.25                           # Server's returned result
```

The expression must be enclosed in quotes if it has any whitespace or shell special characters. This application is based on the bc arbitrary-precision arithmetic calculator language, which is specified in POSIX.1-2024. The POSIX specification (*https://pubs.opengroup.org/onlinepubs/9799919799/*) contains a complete grammar for the bc language. It's a pretty intuitive language and is essentially like ordinary C arithmetic expressions, but as shown earlier, it also has an exponential operator. It has most of the usual programming constructs, such as loops, branching, and functions. By default, the precision of the result is based on the maximum scale of any of its arguments, where *scale* is the number of digits to the right of the decimal point.

The bc command evaluates all compatible bc expressions and writes the result on standard output. But it expects these expressions in a file or in its standard input. We can give it a single expression from the shell in a few different ways, such as:

```
$ echo "6 + 4.00" | bc
10.00
$ bc <<< " 6 + 4.00"  # This puts the expression on bc's standard input.
10.00
```

We can also run it interactively.

Because bc can be run as a shell command, we can use popen() to execute it. When the user runs the calc client, the client will send its command line argument to the server, which stores it into a variable. For example, suppose that variable is named expression. The server stores the string 'echo "expression" | bc' into a string variable named command

```
sprintf(command, "echo \"%s\" | bc", expression);
```

and passes it to popen() for execution:

```
fp = popen(command, "r");
```

It will then use the returned file stream pointer fp to read bc's calculated result, which it places on its standard output, now connected to the write end of the pipe created by popen().

In effect, the server that we're about to create does little more than allow multiple independent clients to request calculations from bc. It doesn't have much utility in this sense because anyone can run a command in the shell to run bc. Its importance lies in the lessons we learn by developing it.

The spl_calc Common Header File

Because client and server need to share certain parameters, such as the pathname to the public FIFO and sizes of various variables, they will each include a common header file named *spl_calc.h*, displayed in Listing 14-2. The header file contains the absolute pathname to the FIFO and a declaration of a structure that clients will send to the server when they want a calculation performed.

spl_calc.h
```
#include "common_hdrs.h"
#include <sys/stat.h>

#define PUBLIC       "/tmp/CALCFIFO"
#define FIFOPATHLEN (PIPE_BUF/4)
#define TEXTLEN     (PIPE_BUF - FIFOPATHLEN)

struct message {
❶ char fifo_name[FIFOPATHLEN];
❷ char text[TEXTLEN];
};
```

Listing 14-2: The spl_calc shared header file

The message has to contain the name of the private FIFO that the client created when it started up, as well as the text string containing the expression to be evaluated. In principle, the FIFO name can contain as many as PATH_MAX characters, but the structure itself cannot be larger than PIPE_BUF bytes; otherwise, the structure will not be sent in a single atomic write operation. On most Unix systems, PATH_MAX is at least as large as PIPE_BUF. Using the getconf command, we can obtain the values of these configuration parameters. Running it on my current version of Linux

```
$ getconf PATH_MAX /usr/include/limits.h
4096
$ getconf PIPE_BUF /usr/include/limits.h
4096
```

we see they're equal. Allowing the FIFO name to be as large as it's allowed to be would complicate the design of both client and server, and it's very unlikely it will need to be so long. Therefore, I restrict the FIFO pathname ❶ to be one quarter of the size of PIPE_BUF (1024), leaving 3072 bytes for the text to be sent. This limits the size of the expression.

POSIX specifies that the maximum length of a shell command line (ARG_MAX) should be at least 4096 bytes, but on many systems, ARG_MAX is 2,097,152 bytes. Technically, this is the length of a string that can be passed to any of the exec() functions. To allow such large expressions complicates the client and server design. Therefore, for the sake of simplicity, I simply limit the expression to be at most 3*PIPE_BUF/4 bytes ❷.

The spl_calc Client Program

Since the client program is less complex than the server, let's look at it first. The client takes the following sequence of actions:

1. Checks if the command line argument is too long and, if so, exits.

2. Copies the command line argument into msg.text.

3. Constructs a name for and creates its private FIFO in *tmp* and sets its name into *msg*.fifo_name, where *msg* is of type struct message.

4. Registers its signal handlers.

5. Tries to open the public FIFO for writing in nonblocking mode. It uses nonblocking mode in case the server no longer has the FIFO open for reading, because the open will fail and the client can detect this and exit. (Refer back to Table 13-3 for a summary of FIFO opening semantics.)

6. Writes the message msg to the server. through the public FIFO.

7. Opens its private FIFO for reading.

8. Reads the server's reply from the private FIFO.

9. Copies the server's reply to its standard output.

10. Closes the read end of its private FIFO.

11. Closes the write end of the public FIFO and removes its private FIFO.

The client program, *spl_calc_client.c*, is shown in Listing 14-3. To save space, most comments are omitted. The complete program is available in the book's source code distribution.

```c
#define _GNU_SOURCE
#include "spl_calc.h"
const char startup_msg[] =
    "calcd server does not seem to be running. "
    "Please start the service by entering 'calcd &'\n";

volatile sig_atomic_t sig_received = 0;
struct message msg;
int             privatefd; /* File descriptor to read end of PRIVATE */
int             publicfd;  /* File descriptor to write end of PUBLIC */

void on_sigpipe(int signo)
{
    fprintf(stderr, "Server is not reading the pipe.\n");
    unlink(msg.fifo_name);
    exit(1);
}

void on_signal(int signo)
{
    close(privatefd);
    close(publicfd);
    unlink(msg.fifo_name);
}

int main(int argc, char *argv[])
{
    int             bytesRead;        /* Bytes received in read from server */
    static char     buf[PIPE_BUF];    /* Buffer to store returned data      */
    char            usage[NAME_MAX];  /* Usage message                      */
    struct sigaction handler;

    if ( argc < 2 ) {
        sprintf(usage, "%s <expression>", basename(argv[0]));
        usage_error(usage);
    }
    memset(msg.text, 0, TEXTLEN);
    if ( strlen(argv[1]) >= TEXTLEN )
        fatal_error(-1, "Expression too long");
    strcpy(msg.text, argv[1]);

    sprintf(msg.fifo_name, "/tmp/fifo%d", getpid()); /* Create FIFO name. */
    if ( mkfifo(msg.fifo_name, 0666) < 0 )           /* Create private FIFO. */
        fatal_error(errno, msg.fifo_name);

    handler.sa_handler = on_signal;
    if ( ((sigaction(SIGINT,  &handler, NULL)) == -1) ||
```

```
        ((sigaction(SIGHUP,  &handler, NULL)) == -1) ||
        ((sigaction(SIGQUIT, &handler, NULL)) == -1) ||
        ((sigaction(SIGTERM, &handler, NULL)) == -1) )
        fatal_error(errno, "sigaction");
    handler.sa_handler = on_sigpipe;
    if ( sigaction(SIGPIPE, &handler, NULL) == -1 )
        fatal_error(errno, "sigaction");

    if ( (publicfd = open(PUBLIC, O_WRONLY | O_NONBLOCK)) == -1 ) {
        if ( ENXIO == errno )
            fprintf(stderr, "%s", startup_msg);
        else
            error_mssge(errno, PUBLIC);
        exit(EXIT_FAILURE);
    }
    write(publicfd, (char*) &msg, sizeof(msg));           /* Send message.   */
    if ( (privatefd=open(msg.fifo_name,O_RDONLY)) == -1 ) /* FIFO for reply */
        fatal_error(errno, msg.fifo_name);

    while ( (bytesRead=read(privatefd,buf,PIPE_BUF)) > 0 ) /* Read reply.    */
        write(fileno(stdout), buf, bytesRead);

    close(privatefd);    /* Clean up. */
    close(publicfd);
    unlink(msg.fifo_name);
    exit(EXIT_SUCCESS);
}
```

Listing 14-3: The spl_calc client program

We could add a few enhancements to the design of this client. They're left as exercises at the end of the chapter.

The spl_calc Server Program

The server has more work to do than the client. It takes the following sequence of steps:

1. Sets up all signal handling.

2. Creates the public FIFO. If it finds it already exists, it displays a message and exits.

3. Opens the public FIFO for both reading and writing, even though it will only read from it. The write end is assigned to a *dummy* (unused) file descriptor.

4. It enters its main loop, where it repeatedly:
    (a) Performs a blocking read on the public FIFO.
    (b) On receiving a message from read(), tries to open the private FIFO of the client that sent it that message. It tries MAXTRIES (five) times, sleeping a bit between each try, in case

the client was delayed in opening its end of the FIFO for reading. After five attempts, it gives up on this client.

(c) If it was successful in opening the client's FIFO for writing, constructs a string containing the command line that it will pass to popen().

(d) Calls popen(), getting the fp file stream point that it needs to read to get the value computed by bc.

(e) Clears the memory for the return from popen(), reads the result, and writes it to the private FIFO of the client.

(f) Calls pclose() to collect the status of the subshell that ran bc, and closes the write end of the private FIFO.

In this design, the main loop never exits on its own. It loops forever because it never receives an end-of-file on the public FIFO, since it keeps the write end open itself. The server must be terminated by sending it a signal such as SIGTERM. The server program is displayed in part in Listing 14-4. Parts of it, such as signal handlers and their setup, as well as some error handling, are omitted to save space. The complete program is available in the book's source code distribution.

spl_calc_server.c
```c
#include "spl_calc.h"
#define  WARNING  "\nServer could not access client's private FIFO\n"
#define  MAXTRIES 5
int dummyfd;        /* File descriptor to write end of PUBLIC  */
int publicfd;       /* File descriptor to read end of PUBLIC   */
int privatefd;      /* File descriptor to write end of PRIVATE */

int main(int argc, char *argv[])
{
    int            tries;        /* Number of tries to open private FIFO */
    int            nbytes;       /* Number of bytes read from popen()    */
    int            done;         /* Flag to stop loop                    */
    struct message msg;          /* Private FIFO name and command        */
    char           result[PIPE_BUF+1];  /* Result to return to client    */
    char           command[TEXTLEN+32]; /* Command for popen() to execute */
    FILE           *fp;          /* FILE stream to read end of popen()   */

    // OMITTED: Register the signal handlers.

    /* Create public FIFO. */
    if ( mkfifo(PUBLIC, 0666) < 0 ) {
        if ( errno != EEXIST )
            fatal_error(errno, "mkfifo");
        else
            fprintf(stderr, "%s already exists. Delete it and restart.\n",
                    PUBLIC);
        exit(EXIT_FAILURE);
    }
```

```
        publicfd = open(PUBLIC, O_RDONLY);
        dummyfd = open(PUBLIC, O_WRONLY | O_NONBLOCK);

        while ( read(publicfd, (char*) &msg, sizeof(msg)) > 0 ) {
            tries = done = 0;
            privatefd   = -1;
            do {
                if ( (privatefd = open(msg.fifo_name, O_WRONLY|O_NONBLOCK)) < 0 )
                    sleep(1);          /* Sleep if failed to open.          */
                else {                 /* Create command to give to popen(). */
                    memset(command, 0, strlen(command)); /* Clear command. */
                    sprintf(command, "echo \"%s\" | bc  ", msg.text );
                    fp = popen(command, "r");
                    memset(result, 0, PIPE_BUF);
                    nbytes = read(fileno(fp), result, PIPE_BUF);
                    if ( -1 == nbytes )
                        error_mssge(errno, "Read from bc");
                    else if ( 0 == nbytes )
                        error_mssge(errno, "Null output from bc");
                    else {             /* Send result to client.   */
                        result[nbytes] = '\0'; /* Null-terminate. */
                        write(privatefd, result, nbytes + 1);
                    }
                    pclose(fp);        /* Wait for popen status.           */
                    close(privatefd); /* Close write end of private FIFO. */
                    done = 1;          /* Terminate loop.                  */
                }
            } while ( ++tries < MAXTRIES && !done );
            if ( !done )
                write(fileno(stderr), WARNING, sizeof(WARNING));
        }
        exit(EXIT_SUCCESS);
}
```

Listing 14-4: The spl_calc server program

The signal handling, which is not in the listing, is slightly different than it is
in the client. This server sets privatefd to -1 at the start of each loop, and if it
opens the private FIFO successfully, privatefd is no longer -1. It can use this
to determine, in the signal handler, whether it had a private FIFO open for
writing and needs to close it. If it gets a SIGPIPE because a client closed the
read end of its private FIFO immediately after sending a message but before
the server wrote back the converted string, it handles SIGPIPE by continuing
to listen for new messages and giving up on the write to that pipe.

    Here are a couple more runs of our client, assuming we built and ran
this server in the background:

```
$ ./spl_calc 2^10
1024
$ ./spl_calc 2^256
115792089237316195423570985008687907853269984665640560394575840\
07913129639936
```

We could have implemented this server without using popen() by writing our own functions to evaluate infix arithmetic expressions and letting the server call them directly. This would have made the server faster, because it would not need to fork a shell and a subshell to exec the bc command, but speed wasn't an important objective for this program. This design allowed us to quickly and easily create a useful server while learning the mechanics of opening, reading, writing, and closing FIFOs, with all the associated subtleties.

A Concurrent Server

One drawback of an iterative server is that it handles each client request sequentially. If some client requests are time consuming and others aren't, the server would be busy servicing one client to the exclusion of all others, and the others would experience delays. This can be avoided by designing the server to handle multiple client requests concurrently. Such a server is called a *concurrent server*. In this section, we'll develop a concurrent server and a client that communicates with it, but instead of implementing a concurrent version of the calc server, we'll develop one that performs lowercase-to-uppercase conversion of arbitrarily large amounts of text data using the user's current locale, which will present a few different problems to solve.

One way to create a concurrent server is to fork a child process for each client. The alternative is to multithread the server, creating a thread for each client instead. Our server will fork a process for each client. With this approach, the server's role is reduced to:

- Listening to the public pipe for incoming requests

- Forking a child process to handle a new request

- Waiting for the child process to finish

We don't want the server to block while waiting because it has to return immediately to the task of reading the public pipe. Therefore, it will call waitpid() only inside a SIGCHLD handler. We'll convert the process to a daemon by calling make_me_a_daemon().

The server program's main() function essentially takes this sequence of steps:

1. Registers its signal handlers.

2. Creates the public FIFO. If it finds it already exists, it displays a message and exits.

3. Opens the public FIFO for both reading and writing, although it will not write into that FIFO.

4. Enters its main loop, where it repeatedly:
    (a) Performs a blocking read() on the public FIFO.
    (b) Upon returning successfully from read(), forks a child process to handle the client request.

This server differs from the iterative calc server in another fundamental way. The client sends it raw text, which the server converts to uppercase and sends back. Because this is a two-way communication, the client and server need a pair of private FIFOs for this exchange. The client writes the raw text into one FIFO, and the server sends the converted text back to the client in a second FIFO. The client has to create these FIFOs and send their names to the server in its public FIFO when it requests this translation service. In addition, the client has to send the name of the locale to the server so that the server can set the locale before it performs the translation to uppercase. Therefore, the structure of the request message is different in this program than it was in the iterative server.

In this application, the only purpose of the request message that the client sends is to establish the means by which the client and the server can exchange data privately. The message structure has no data content. For this reason, I'll call it a *connection message*. A connection message contains the names of two FIFOs and the name of the locale. The *upcase.h* header file contains its definition:

---

upcase.h
```
#include "common_hdrs.h"
#define PUBLIC      "/tmp/UPCASE_FIFO"
#define LOCALELENGTH 128
#define NAMELENGTH  (PIPE_BUF - LOCALELENGTH)/2

typedef struct _message {
    char upcased_fifo [NAMELENGTH];
    char raw_text_fifo[NAMELENGTH];
    char locale[LOCALELENGTH];
} message;
```

The message structure is a total of PIPE_BUF bytes, divided equally between the two FIFO names after subtracting the maximum allowed length of a locale name, artificially set to 128 characters.

Each child process forked by the server begins by opening the read end of the client's raw_text FIFO. It then repeatedly reads from this raw_text _fifo, translates the text into uppercase, opens the write end of the client's converted_text_fifo, writes the converted text into it, and closes its write end until there's no more data in the raw_text_fifo.

The Concurrent Server Client

The client is structurally different from the iterative server's client. It takes the following major steps:

1. Determines whether it has a filename argument. If it does, it makes that the input source; otherwise, it uses standard input as its source.

2. Registers its signal handlers.

3. Calls `setlocale()` to enable all library functions to use the current locale settings.

4. Creates two private FIFOs in the */tmp* directory with unique names and writes their names and the name of the current locale into the connection message.

5. Opens the server's public FIFO for writing, handling errors as needed.

6. Sends the connection message to the server to establish the two-way communication.

7. Attempts to open its raw text FIFO in nonblocking, write-only mode. If it fails, it delays a second and retries. It retries a few times and then gives up and exits. If it fails, it means that the server has probably terminated.

8. Until it receives an end-of-file on its standard input, it repeatedly:
   (a) Reads a line from standard input.
   (b) Breaks the line into `PIPE_BUF`-sized chunks.
   (c) Sends each chunk successively to the server through its raw text FIFO.
   (d) Opens the `upcased` text FIFO for reading.
   (e) Reads the `upcased` text FIFO and writes its contents to its standard output.
   (f) Closes the read end of the `upcased` text FIFO.

9. Closes all of its FIFOs and removes the files.

Figure 14-2 shows how the client processes and the server parent and child processes use the various FIFOs. Compare this to Figure 14-1.

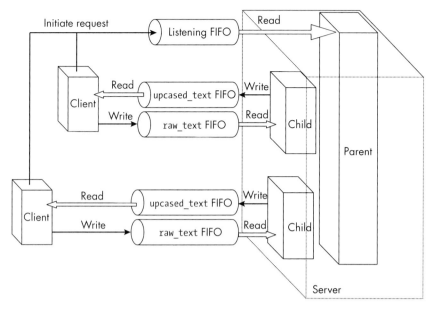

Read

Listening FIFO

Read

Initiate request

Read

upcased_text FIFO

Write

Client

Write

raw_text FIFO

Read

Child

Parent

Read

upcased_text FIFO

Write

Client

Write

raw_text FIFO

Read

Child

Server

Figure 14-2: Concurrent server and client communication

The code for the client is shown in Listings 14-5 and 14-6. Some code has been omitted to save space, such as setting up signal handlers and handling errors from system calls. The complete program, *upcase.c*, is available in the book's source code distribution.

```
upcase.c    #include "upcase.h"
globals     #define MAXTRIES 5
            const char server_no_read_msg[] = "The server is not reading the pipe.\n";
            const char noserver_msg[] = "The server does not appear to be running. "
                                        "Please start the service.\n";
            const char missing_pipe_msg[] =
                    "Cannot communicate with the server due to a missing pipe.\n"
                    "Check if the server is running and restart it if necessary.\n";
            int       upcased_fd;   /* File descriptor for READ PRIVATE FIFO   */
            int       rawtext_fd;   /* File descriptor for WRITE PRIVATE FIFO  */
            int       publicfd;     /* File descriptor for write end of PUBLIC */
            FILE      *inputfp;     /* File pointer to input stream            */
            message   msg;              /* Connection message                  */

            void clean_up()
            {
                if ( upcased_fd != -1 )
                    close(upcased_fd);
                if ( rawtext_fd != -1 )
                    close(rawtext_fd);
                unlink(msg.upcased_fifo);
                unlink(msg.raw_text_fifo);
            }
```

```
void on_sigpipe(int signo)
{
    fprintf(stderr, "%s Exiting...\n", server_no_read_msg); /* UNSAFE */
    unlink(msg.raw_text_fifo);
    unlink(msg.upcased_fifo);
    exit(EXIT_FAILURE);
}


void on_signal(int sig)
{
    if ( publicfd != -1 )
        close(publicfd);
    if ( upcased_fd != -1 )
        close(upcased_fd);
    if ( rawtext_fd != -1 )
        close(rawtext_fd);
    unlink(msg.upcased_fifo);
    unlink(msg.raw_text_fifo);
    exit(EXIT_SUCCESS);
}
```

Listing 14-5: The static and file-scoped functions and data for the upcase *client of the* upcase *server*

The signal handlers close open file descriptors and remove FIFOs from the filesystem as needed. The client's main program is in Listing 14-6, with some error handling omitted.

upcase.c
main()
```
int main(int argc, char *argv[])
{
    int           strLength;   /* Number of bytes in text to convert   */
    int           nChunk;      /* Index of text chunk to send to server */
    int           bytesRead;   /* Bytes received in read from server    */
    int           tries = 0;   /* Count of attempts to open FIFO        */
    static char   buffer[PIPE_BUF];
    static char   textbuf[BUFSIZ];
    struct sigaction sigact;

    if ( argc < 2 )
        inputfp = stdin;
    else if ( NULL == (inputfp = fopen(argv[1], "r")) )
        fatal_error(errno, argv[1]);

    publicfd   = -1;
    upcased_fd = -1;
    rawtext_fd = -1;

    // OMITTED: Register the signal handlers and set the locale.
```

```
/* Create unique names for private FIFOs using process ID. */
sprintf(msg.upcased_fifo, "/tmp/fifo_rd%d", getpid());
sprintf(msg.raw_text_fifo, "/tmp/fifo_wr%d", getpid());
sprintf(msg.locale, "%s", current_locale);

/* Create the private FIFOs. */
if ( mkfifo(msg.upcased_fifo, 0666) < 0  ||
     mkfifo(msg.raw_text_fifo, 0666) < 0 ) {
    clean_up();
    fatal_error(-1, "Error creating private FIFOs");
}

/* Open the public FIFO for writing. */
if ( (publicfd = open(PUBLIC, O_WRONLY | O_NONBLOCK)) == -1 ) {
    if ( ENXIO == errno )
        fprintf(stderr,"%s", noserver_msg);
    else if ( errno == ENOENT )
        fprintf(stderr,"%s %s", argv[0], missing_pipe_msg);
    else
        fprintf(stderr,"%d: ", errno);
    clean_up();
    exit(EXIT_FAILURE);
}
write(publicfd, (char*) &msg, sizeof(msg));

while ( ((rawtext_fd = open(msg.raw_text_fifo,
        O_WRONLY | O_NDELAY)) == -1) && (tries < MAXTRIES) )  {
    sleep(1);
    tries++;
}
if ( tries == MAXTRIES ) {
    /* Failed to open client private FIFO for writing */
    clean_up();
    fatal_error(-1, server_no_read_msg);
}
while ( TRUE ) {
    memset(textbuf, 0, BUFSIZ);
    if ( NULL == fgets(textbuf, BUFSIZ, inputfp) )
        break;
    strLength = strlen(textbuf);

    /* Break input lines into chunks and send them one at a
       time through the client's write FIFO. */
    for ( nChunk = 0; nChunk < strLength; nChunk += PIPE_BUF - 1 ) {
        memset(buffer, 0, PIPE_BUF);
        strncpy(buffer, textbuf + nChunk, PIPE_BUF - 1);
```

```
        buffer[PIPE_BUF-1] = '\0';
        write(rawtext_fd, buffer, strlen(buffer));

        /* Open the private FIFO for reading to get output of command
           from the server. */
        if ( (upcased_fd = open(msg.upcased_fifo, O_RDONLY)) == -1 ) {
            clean_up();
            fatal_error(errno, msg.upcased_fifo);
        }
        memset(buffer, 0, PIPE_BUF);
        while ( (bytesRead = read(upcased_fd, buffer, PIPE_BUF)) > 0 )
            write(fileno(stdout), buffer, bytesRead);
        close(upcased_fd);
        upcased_fd = -1;
    }
}
clean_up();
exit(EXIT_SUCCESS);
}
```

Listing 14-6: A client program that talks to the upcase server

After sending the names of the private FIFOs, the client tries to open
the write end of its raw text FIFO in nonblocking mode. If the server is delayed in opening the read end, this will fail. The server doesn't fail if it opens
the read end too soon. Assuming that the server isn't delayed, the client will
succeed in opening the raw text FIFO. We could insert a short sleep in case
the server is delayed.

If we were to open the raw text FIFO before sending the server the
connection message, we'd have a problem. We would need to open it in read-
write mode since the server is blocked on its read of the public FIFO and the
two processes would deadlock otherwise. But if we open the raw text FIFO in
read-write mode, then if the server terminates unexpectedly and never reads
the raw text FIFO again, the client wouldn't get a SIGPIPE signal because the
client itself has the read end open, preventing the kernel from generating the
signal. The client would never be notified that the server died! The order is
critical here.

The client then keeps the write end of its raw text FIFO open for the
duration of its main loop. Within the loop, the client first writes to its raw
text FIFO and then opens its upcased text FIFO, after which, if all goes well,
it reads and closes it again. Thus, it repeatedly opens and closes this FIFO
within the loop. We could just let it stay open for the duration of the loop,
but by closing it and reopening it, we give ourselves the chance to detect in
the open() call that the server closed its write end of the FIFO unexpectedly.

The error handling in the client is similar to what it was in the iterative
server's client. A clean_up() function simplifies the error handling, consoli-
dating the cleanup code.

The Concurrent Server

Let's turn to the design of the server. The main program uses several file-scoped variables and constants that it shares with signal handlers and a few utility functions. These are as follows:

```
#define  MAXFD    64
#define  WARNING  "\nNOTE: SERVER ** NEVER ** accessed private FIFO\n"
#define  MAXTRIES 5

int    dummyfd;         /* File descriptor for write end of PUBLIC  */
int    clientreadfd;    /* File descriptor for write end of PRIVATE */
int    clientwritefd;   /* File descriptor for write end of PRIVATE */
int    publicfd;        /* File descriptor for read end of PUBLIC   */
pid_t server_pid;       /* Stores parent PID                        */
BOOL   is_daemon = FALSE; /* Am I a daemon?                         */
```

It also declares the following locally scoped variables:

```
message          msg;       /* Connection message                   */
struct sigaction sigact;    /* sigaction for registering handlers   */
int              pid;       /* Return value from fork()             */
```

We're going to turn this server into a daemon process shortly after the program starts up by calling the function make_me_a_daemon(), shown in Listing 14-1 on page 685.

Since daemon processes should not write to the terminal, their error messages are logged in a file using syslog(). But if the server is unable to create its FIFO for any reason and cannot start up, it ought to write a message on the terminal. Therefore, before it turns itself into a daemon, it tries to create the public FIFO and prints an error message to standard error if it can't:

```
if ( mkfifo(PUBLIC, 0666) < 0 ) {
    if ( errno != EEXIST )
        fprintf(stderr, "mkfifo() could not create %s", PUBLIC);
    else
        fprintf(stderr, "%s already exists. Delete it and restart.\n",
                PUBLIC);
    exit(EXIT_FAILURE);
}
```

It then:

- Converts itself into a daemon

- Sets up signal handlers

- Opens its public FIFO for reading (and writing in nonblocking mode)

- Records its PID, which it will need later

Having done all of this, it's ready to enter its listening loop. In its listening loop, it's essentially blocked as it waits for incoming client connection messages. When it receives one, it forks a child process to do all of the work:

```
while ( read(publicfifo, (char*) &msg, sizeof(msg)) > 0 )
    if ( -1 == (pid = fork()) )
        syslog(LOG_ERR, "Could not create child process.");
    else if ( 0 == pid )
        /* Service the incoming client request based on the
           private FIFO names in msg. */
        process_client( &msg); /* Child process executes. */
```

The process_client() function is executed by the child process. Let's outline what it does:

1. Uses its pointer to the message read from the public FIFO to extract the names of the raw text FIFO and upcased text FIFO, as well as the locale.

2. Tries to open the client's raw text FIFO for reading. If it fails, the child exits.

3. Sets the locale to the one that the client passed to it.

4. Enters a loop in which it repeatedly:
   (a) Reads the raw text from the raw text FIFO.
   (b) Converts that text to uppercase.
   (c) Tries a fixed number of times to open the client's private upcased text FIFO. It may take a few tries because of scheduling delays or because the client terminated unexpectedly. If it fails, it exits.
   (d) Writes the converted text into the private upcased text FIFO, closes it, and clears the buffer for the next read from the raw text buffer.

The process_client() function, with some error handling and comments omitted, is in Listing 14-7.

process_client()
```
void process_client(message *msg)
{
    char buffer[PIPE_BUF]; /* Buffer for reads                      */
    int  tries;            /* Number of tries to open private FIFO */
    int  nbytes;           /* Number of bytes read from FIFO       */

    clientwritefd = -1;
    if ( (clientwritefd = open(msg->raw_text_fifo, O_RDONLY)) == -1 )
    ❶ log_and_exit("Client did not open pipe for writing");

    memset(buffer, 0, PIPE_BUF);  /* Clear the buffer. */
    if ( setlocale(LC_CTYPE, msg->locale) == NULL )
        syslog(LOG_ERR, "Could not set the locale to %s", msg->locale);
```

```
    while ( (nbytes = read(clientwritefd, buffer, PIPE_BUF)) > 0 ) {
        for ( int i = 0; i < nbytes; i++ )
            buffer[i] = toupper(buffer[i]);

        tries = 0;
        while ( ((clientreadfd = open(msg->upcased_fifo,
                    O_WRONLY | O_NONBLOCK)) == -1) && (tries < MAXTRIES) ) {
            sleep(1);
            tries++;
        }
        if ( tries == MAXTRIES )
            log_and_exit(WARNING);

        if ( (-1 == write(clientreadfd, buffer, nbytes)) && (EPIPE == errno) )
            log_and_exit("%m: Trying to write to client");
        close(clientreadfd);   /* Close write end of private FIFO. */
        clientreadfd = -1;
        memset(buffer, 0, PIPE_BUF);
    }
    exit(EXIT_SUCCESS);
}
```

Listing 14-7: The function executed by each forked child process in the concurrent server

The function parameter is a pointer to the message structure rather than a copy of it. There's no need to make a copy; since the code is executed by a new process, the copying takes place within fork(), which means that there's no danger that two different child processes try to read from the same private FIFOs in case the clients connect at almost the same time.

The log_and_exit() ❶ function records a message in a logfile and exits. We'll look at its code shortly.

Even if the child process successfully opens the FIFO, it still has to check whether a write() to it fails, since anything can happen in between, and if so, the child exits. Otherwise, it writes the data, closes its end of the FIFO, and waits to read more text from the client. When it receives the end-of-file, it exits.

Notice that the server repeatedly opens and closes the write end of the client's upcased text FIFO. This is the only way that the client will receive an EOF when it calls read(). If the client doesn't get the EOF, it will remain blocked in its read() of the upcased text FIFO and won't be able to send any more data to the server. This would put the client and this child process into deadlock, because this process would go back to the read() of the client's raw text FIFO and block waiting for data from the client, which would never arrive. Therefore, although it seems inefficient to open and close this FIFO each time, it is the simplest means of preventing deadlock.

The error handling is accomplished with the log_and_exit() function, whose code is:

```
void log_and_exit(char *errmssge)
{
    if ( is_daemon )
        syslog(LOG_ERR, "%s", errmssge);
    else
        error_mssge(-1, errmssge);
    exit(EXIT_FAILURE);
}
```

If the process has been turned into a daemon, it writes messages to the system logging facility, as discussed in "System Logging Facilities" on page 681; otherwise, it writes them to the standard error stream. The program has been designed so that we could, if we wanted, make conversion to a daemon optional with a command line option that controls it. It would amount to disabling the call to make_me_a_daemon().

The other utility functions for the server's main program are its signal handlers, which we look at now. The server process waits asynchronously for its spawned child processes to terminate by calling the wait function inside the SIGCHLD handler:

```
void on_sigchld(int signo)
{
    int status;
    while ( waitpid(-1, &status, WNOHANG) > 0 )
        continue;
    return;
}
```

It doesn't record the child's exit status in this version of the program, but it should really log it if the child terminated abnormally. The handler uses waitpid() to wait for all children, and it remains in its loop as long as there is a zombie to be reaped. The WNOHANG flag is used to prevent it from blocking in the waitpid() call.

If the server receives any terminating signal that it can handle, it cleans up after itself.

```
void on_signal(int sig)
{
    close(dummyfd);
    if ( clientreadfd != -1 )
        close(clientreadfd);
    if ( clientwritefd != -1 )
        close(clientwritefd);
    /* If this is the parent executing it, remove the public FIFO. */
    if ( getpid() == server_pid )
        unlink(PUBLIC);
    exit(EXIT_SUCCESS);
}
```

This signal handler checks whether the parent process is executing it. The child processes have copies of the signal handlers, and the handler might be executed by a child process. If the parent has been signaled, it should remove the public FIFO, but if it's a child, it shouldn't. We don't want child processes to remove this FIFO! A few sample runs demonstrate the client-server behavior. First we start the server:

```
$ ./upcased      # Start up the server; the prompt reappears.
$
```

Next let's run a client:

```
$ ./upcase
hello world
HELLO WORLD
^D
$ echo hello world | upcase
HELLO WORLD
$ ./upcase <  <(sed -n 2p upcase.c)
  TITLE          : UPCASE.C
$
```

When it's run interactively, you need to enter CTRL-D to send an EOF, or you can kill the process with a keyboard signal. When run with standard input redirected from a pipe or from a file or pseudofile, as shown here, the EOF is sent when the actual end-of-file is reached or the process on the write end of the bash pipe closed its write end, causing the next read operation to receive the EOF.

The complete server program, *upcased.c*, is available in the book's source code distribution. If you comment out the call to make_me_a_daemon() in the program and run the program as a background process, it will still provide its services, but will be susceptible to being killed by keyboard signals.

Summary

In this chapter, we explored concepts related to client-server software architectures. We began with an introduction to system logging services because most servers need to log their messages in a centralized location. We then turned to daemon processes. A daemon is a process that runs in the background without a controlling terminal. Most servers run as daemons so that they cannot be terminated by keyboard signals.

Servers can be iterative or concurrent. An iterative server handles requests from clients one after the other, in a single process, sharing its time among them. A concurrent server, in contrast, creates a child process to handle every distinct client. In this chapter, we developed two different iterative servers and a concurrent server.

Exercises

1. The `logger` command lets a user write a message to the system logfile from the command line. For example:

```
$ logger "This is a test message"
$ tail -1 /var/log/syslog
Jun 19 16:09:52 harpo stewart: test message
```

The command has several options. Read its man page and write an implementation of this command that accepts the `-i` option.

2. Modify *calc_client.c* so that if it has no command line argument, it reads the expression from standard input.

3. Modify *spl_calc.h*, *calc_client.c*, and *calc_server.c* so that if the user supplies a `-l` command line option to the client, the server will request `bc` to load its standard math library, as described on its man page.

4. Modify both *calc_client.c* and *calc_server.c* so that if the user supplies an `-s` *value* command line option, the number of digits to the right of the decimal point for all answers will be the supplied *value*.

5. Write a version of *calc_server.c* that still relies upon the `bc` command but does not call `popen()` to run it.

6. Add a `-d` option to *calc_server.c* that, when present, turns it into a daemon, and when not, requires the user to run it in the background.

15

INTRODUCTION TO THREADS

The first chapter of the book introduced the concept of threads and multithreaded programs without much detail. In subsequent chapters, we touched on threads, usually because they were mentioned in the documentation about something else we were studying, such as how a process could be notified of a timer expiration. At those points in the book, we ignored thread-related topics. In this chapter, we'll examine threads, and in particular, POSIX threads, in greater detail.

We'll start with an overview of threads in general, including

- How threads are different from processes

- How threads are represented by the kernel

- What resources are associated with threads

- How program design is different when programs have multiple threads

We'll then present an overview of the POSIX threads API, known as the *Pthreads* library, including the data types and broad categories of functions available for programming with threads. After that, we'll dive into the details of using the basic functions related to the management and operation of threads.

We'll also examine the complex relationship between signal handling and threads. When we first introduced signals, we didn't have to think about questions such as which threads of a process receive a signal sent to that process or whether a signal handler registered by one thread is run when another thread receives the signal it's supposed to catch.

Equipped with this new knowledge and the collection of tools from the *Pthreads* library, we'll write a multithreaded version of the concurrent server from Chapter 14. The POSIX threads API is very large, and we'll explore just a small part of it. This chapter's objective is primarily to show you the basics of POSIX threads and a path toward learning more about them.

Background

Processes require many kernel resources, such as a map of its entire memory image, a description of its hardware state, and various kinds of attributes and metadata. On the other hand, a process has just a single flow of control, a single execution path. In this sense, a process is an inefficient consumer of system resources because, though it requires a lot of resources, it can execute just one instruction at a time. It would be more efficient if those resources could support a program's ability to perform multiple tasks concurrently. Creating concurrency in a program by forking new processes that then work together doesn't really achieve this, because each process still uses its own resources, and this introduces two other problems:

- Processes must rely on interprocess communication facilities to communicate because they cannot share their address spaces with each other. Using any such facility is much slower than ordinary fetches and stores of shared variables and data within a single memory image.

- Creating processes with the fork() system call is time consuming. Recent versions of fork() in Linux use copy-on-write memory pages, making fork() faster, but it is still a slow operation.

In the 1980s, the idea of creating multiple threads of control within a single process took hold. The basic idea was to identify the smallest subset of a process's resources that would represent a single thread of control's execution state. Copies of this subset of resources would allow multiple threads of control to execute on their own within the process's address space. The copied resources included the hardware state and the stack. These threads existed within the process. The Unix community explored various ways to standardize this concept of threads. In 1995, The Open Group defined a standard interface for UNIX threads (IEEE POSIX 1003.1c) that they named *Pthreads* (*P* for *POSIX*). This standard was supported on multiple platforms, including Solaris, macOS, FreeBSD, OpenBSD, and Linux. In 1996, these requirements were incorporated into the POSIX standard. The threads described by POSIX were known as *POSIX threads*, and the API was dubbed the *Pthreads API*. In 2005, a new implementation of the interface was developed by Ulrich Drepper and Ingo Molnár of Red Hat, Inc., called the *Native POSIX Thread Library* (*NPTL*), which was much faster than the original library and has since replaced that library. The Open Group further revised the standard in 2008. Today, most Unix systems provide the *Pthreads* API.

Threads and Processes

Each thread of a process is a flow of control through the code of its parent program. In fact, we can think of every process as consisting of a memory image containing executable code together with one or more threads that execute a stream of instructions through that code. In this sense, an ordinary Unix process is the special case of a multithreaded process with just a single thread. In a process with multiple threads, the threads can execute different tasks concurrently, and in many Unix variants, including current versions of Linux, each thread is scheduled individually to run on a processor.

Support in the Kernel

Older versions of Unix and Linux had no support for multithreading; a program that was multithreaded using a threading library such as *Pthreads* was seen by the kernel as a single process. The individual threads within that process weren't visible to the kernel and were not scheduled individually. Books on operating system design refer to this as a *many-to-one (M:1)* threading model [37]. The major problem with this design was that if one thread made a blocking system call, the entire process was blocked. Modern Linux kernels recognize the individual threads of a process as distinct scheduling entities. This is usually known as a *one-to-one (1:1)* threading model.

In the Linux 2.6 kernel, and with versions of *glibc* since 2.3.2, threading support is provided by the kernel using the NPTL. Each user-level thread, meaning the threads that our programs create, is assigned to a kernel scheduling entity called a *lightweight process*.

Pros and Cons of Multithreading

Multithreaded programs have advantages over singly threaded programs. Some of the most significant advantages are the following:

- Code to handle each asynchronous event, such as a timer expiration or receipt of a message, can be executed by a separate thread. Each thread can handle its event using an ordinary synchronous programming model.

- Unlike cooperating processes, which have to use IPC facilities to share data, threads share the process's virtual address space, so they can share any data within it using ordinary fetch and store operations, which is faster than using IPC facilities in general.

- Even on a single processor machine, performance can be improved by putting calls to system functions with expected long waits in separate threads. This way, just the calling thread blocks and not the whole process.

- The response time of interactive programs can be improved by spawning threads to handle tasks that are inherently asynchronous, such as receiving and responding to various input devices.

Multithreaded programs have several disadvantages of which the following are the most significant:

- They have potential race conditions and synchronization problems that arise from the threads' accessing shared data.

- They are much harder to write, to test, and to debug. This stems in part from the difficulty of reasoning about concurrent activities, in part from the much larger number of possible states in which a program might be when it has multiple threads, and in part from the difficulty of using debugging and testing tools on multithreaded programs.

- Not all library functions are thread-safe. If two threads of the same process execute a non-thread-safe library function at the same time, the result of their combined execution is unpredictable because it causes a race condition inside the function. If a multithreaded program's threads have to call non-thread-safe library functions, the programmer needs to use synchronization methods to prevent their being in the call at the same time.

- Signal handling in a multithreaded program is much harder than it is in a singly threaded program, in part because signals were designed when multithreading did not exist and the interaction between signals and threads is complex.

For any particular programming problem, these pros and cons have to be weighed against each other.

Shared Resources and Attributes

Threads share some of the process resources and have private copies of the other resources. All threads share the memory image of the process. In particular, they share the text segment, its data segment, and heap memory. This implies that threads share the program's global variables, the command line arguments, the environment variables, and the data allocated in the heap, provided that they have pointers to that data.

Threads do not share the process stack. In order for each thread to run independently, each one needs its own runtime stack, and in order for the kernel to make scheduling decisions about them, much of the metadata maintained in the process descriptor must be replicated for each thread. POSIX.1 stipulates exactly which resources of a process should be shared by all of its threads and which resources must be private. In particular, the following parts of a process are not shared and must be unique to each thread:

- A thread ID
- A runtime stack and an alternate stack
- The stack pointer and registers
- The signal mask
- The errno value
- Scheduling attributes
- Thread-specific data

On the other hand, most of the metadata in the process descriptor is shared by all the threads. In addition to the text, data, and heap regions of the process, POSIX requires that the following metadata be shared by all threads:

- Environment variables
- Process ID
- Parent process ID
- Process group ID and session ID
- Controlling terminal
- User and group IDs
- Open file descriptors
- Record locks
- Signal dispositions
- File mode creation mask (the umask)
- Current working directory and root directory
- Interval and POSIX timers
- Nice value
- Resource limits
- Measurements of the consumption of CPU time and resources

In Linux, the process descriptor data structure, task_struct, is used to represent both threads and processes. Each thread has its own task_struct. This may sound inefficient, but it isn't. The Linux task_struct mostly contains pointers to other data structures. Instead of embedding resources in the task structure directly, it has pointers to these resources. This makes it easy to separate which resources are private to each thread and which are shared.

If two threads are part of the same process and share a particular resource, their pointers point to the same resource structure instance. If a particular resource is not shared, their pointers point to unique copies of it.

Figure 15-1 is a schematic representation of the task_struct showing some parts that are linked into it and parts that are embedded in it.

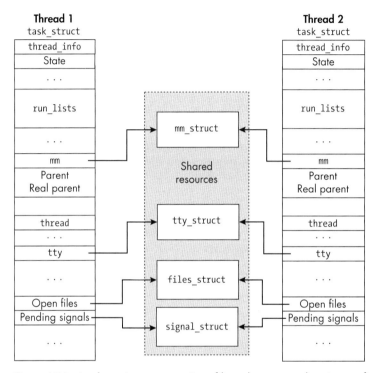

Figure 15-1: A schematic representation of how the process descriptors of two threads that are part of the same process facilitate sharing of memory, open files, and other shared data of the parent process

The substructures of the parent process descriptor, such as the mm_struct containing the memory maps and the files_struct that contains a pointer to all open files, are shared by the process's threads. In contrast, the thread member of the process descriptor, which stores the entire hardware state, including saved register values and stack pointers, needed when the thread is not running, is embedded in the process descriptor and distinct for each thread.

In Linux, thread stacks are allocated in the heap, often but not always above where the shared libraries are mapped into it. Figure 15-2 depicts the virtual memory of a process with three thread stacks allocated above the shared libraries.

0x0   Increasing virtual addresses ⟶

Figure 15-2: The location of the thread runtime stacks in process virtual memory

In Linux, the default stack size for each thread stack varies depending on the machine architecture. The `bash ulimit -s` command returns the default maximum stack size for a thread in KB. On Linux 6.9 on an x86-64 processor, for example, it is 8MB.

Program Design Considerations with Threads

Multithreading is suitable for certain types of concurrent programming. In general, in order for a program's performance to be improved by multithreading, it has to be organized into discrete, independent tasks that can execute concurrently. The first consideration is how to decompose the program into such discrete tasks. Other questions to be answered include the following:

- How can the load be balanced among the threads so that no one thread becomes a bottleneck?

- How will threads communicate and synchronize to avoid race conditions?

- What type of inherent data dependencies exist in the problem, and how will these affect thread design?

- What data will be shared and what data will be private to the threads?

- How will I/O be handled? Will each thread perform its own I/O, or will a single thread handle all I/O?

Each of these questions deserves some thought at the start of a project, and to some extent, each arises in most programming problems. Determining data dependencies, deciding which data should be shared and which should be private, and determining how to synchronize access to shared data are very critical aspects to the correctness of a multithreaded program. Load balancing and the handling of I/O usually affect performance but not correctness.

Knowing how to use a thread library is just the technical part of multithreaded programming. The harder part is designing the program so that it is free of race conditions and makes efficient use of resources. This chapter's main objective is to explore the threading API, *Pthreads*, with examples to show how it can be used. Here and there, we'll also explore design issues in multithreaded programs.

Overview of the Pthreads Library

The *Pthreads* library provides a very large number of primitives for the management and use of threads; over 100 different functions are defined in the 2024 POSIX standard. The functions in the *Pthreads* API fall into one of four groups:

Thread management   Functions that work directly on threads, such as creating, detaching, joining, and so on. This group also contains functions to set and query thread attributes and functions to set and query thread scheduling properties.

Mutexes   Functions for handling critical sections using mutual exclusion. Mutex functions provide support for creating, destroying, locking, and unlocking mutexes. These are supplemented by mutex attribute functions that set or modify attributes associated with mutexes.

Condition variables   Functions that address communications between threads that share a mutex based upon programmer-specified conditions. These include functions to create, destroy, wait, and signal, based upon specified variable values, as well as functions to set and query condition variable attributes.

Synchronization   Functions that manage read-write locks and barriers.

To get a feeling for how the API looks in general, we can look at the *Pthreads* analogues to the basic process control primitives that we've learned about. Table 15-1 shows a comparison of selected system calls to their analogous *Pthreads* primitives.

Table 15-1: The Correspondence Between *Pthreads* Functions and System Calls

Process primitive	Thread primitive	Description
fork()	pthread_create()	Creates a new flow of control (a thread) with a function to execute
exit()	pthread_exit()	Exits from the calling flow of control
waitpid()	pthread_join()	Waits for a specific flow of control to exit and collect its status
getpid()	pthread_self()	Gets the ID of the calling flow of control
kill()	pthread_cancel()	Potentially causes termination of another thread

All thread functions in the *Pthreads* API start with the prefix pthread_. Some have names that suggest what they do, such as pthread_create(), but not all, such as pthread_cancel(), which is a call to terminate another thread. To use any of the *Pthreads* library functions, a program must include the *pthread.h* header file and must be linked with the -pthread linker option (not -lpthread!).

The *Pthreads* API added new system data types needed by the functions in the API. The POSIX standard specifies that this set of functions must be exposed by including the *sys/types.h* header file. That file may not have their declarations directly. It might instead include them from another header. For example, on my Ubuntu Linux 6.9, *sys/types.h* file includes *bits/pthreadtypes.h*, which defines the added data types, some of which are described here:

pthread_attr_t   Used to identify a thread attribute object

pthread_barrier_t   Used to identify a barrier

pthread_barrierattr_t   Used to define a barrier attributes object

pthread_cond_t   Used for condition variables

pthread_condattr_t   Used to identify a condition attribute object

pthread_mutex_t   Used for mutexes

pthread_mutexattr_t   Used to identify a mutex attribute object

pthread_rwlock_t   Used for read-write locks

pthread_spinlock_t   Used to identify a spin lock

pthread_t   Used to identify a thread

Next, we'll explore the functions for managing threads.

Thread Management

We'll start with the fundamental thread operations: creating them, terminating them in various ways, and waiting for child threads. We'll review each of them and then put together a few small programs that demonstrate how to use them. We won't explore the more advanced features of thread management related to scheduling or concurrency control. If you're interested in learning about them, the relevant functions are pthread_setschedprio(), pthread_getschedparam(), pthread_setschedparam(), pthread_setconcurrency(), and pthread_getconcurrency().

Creating a Thread

The function that creates a new thread is easy to find in the man pages. (Using apropos -a create thread works.) The pthread_create() function's prototype is:

```
int pthread_create(pthread_t *thread, const pthread_attr_t *attr,
                    void *(*start_routine) (void *), void *arg);
```

It's very different from the fork() system call. It creates and starts execution of a new thread. The first parameter, thread, stores the address of a variable of type pthread_t. On successful creation of the new thread, *thread contains its thread ID. Unlike fork(), this call passes the address of a function, *start_routine(), that the new thread will execute. This function is called the *start function* of the thread. It has exactly one argument of type void*, and it returns a void*. The fourth argument, arg, is the address of the argument that is passed to start_routine() when the thread starts.

The second argument is a pointer to a pthread_attr_t structure, which can be used to define attributes of the new thread. These attributes include properties such as its stack size, scheduling policy, and *joinability*, which I'll explain shortly. If we pass a NULL in this parameter, the default values are used instead. We'll examine thread attributes in more detail later.

The pthread_create() man page's SEE ALSO section refers us to the remaining pages related to thread management. In particular, we'll look next at pthread_exit(3), pthread_join(3), and pthread_self(3).

Exiting a Thread

A thread can terminate itself in a few different ways. It can execute an ordinary return instruction, in which case the return value will be saved for later retrieval by another thread. It can also call pthread_exit(), whose prototype is:

```
void pthread_exit(void *retval);
```

This function terminates the calling thread. Like the _exit() system call, pthread_exit() never returns. The single parameter (retval) can be used to pass an exit status from the thread. Another thread in the same process can obtain that exit status by calling pthread_join(), which we'll examine shortly. The value pointed to by retval should not be located on the calling thread's stack, since the contents of that stack are undefined after the thread terminates. It can be a global variable, a static-qualified local variable of the start function, or a variable allocated on the heap.

When pthread_exit() is called, it causes cleanup handlers to run. This is similar to what the exit() library function does (see "Terminating Processes" in Chapter 11). A cleanup handler is the thread analogue to a function registered with atexit(). It is registered with pthread_cleanup_push(). They're executed in the reverse order in which they were pushed. This function also frees all other thread-specific resources, but not process-shared resources such as mutexes and file descriptors.

WARNING *Any thread can call exit(). However, in a multithreaded program, if any thread, including the master thread (the one executing main()) calls exit(), all currently running threads will be terminated. If the master thread executing main() executes a return instruction, all other threads will be terminated. If this isn't desirable, the main() function should terminate itself by calling pthread_exit(). In this way, threads that are still running will continue to run.*

After the last thread in a process terminates, the process terminates as if it called exit(0). At that point, process-shared resources are released and all functions registered with atexit() are run.

Joining a Thread

The pthread_join() function is similar to waitpid(), except that it cannot be used to wait for any thread to terminate the way that waitpid(-1, &wstatus, 0) does. Joining is a way for one thread to wait for another thread to terminate, in much the same way that the wait() system calls let a process wait for a child process. Joining a thread, like waiting for a process, is a way to synchronize the execution of threads. Its prototype is:

```
int pthread_join(pthread_t thread, void **retval);
```

The calling thread must specify the thread ID of the thread for which it wants to wait. Calling pthread_join() suspends execution of the calling thread until the target thread terminates, unless the target thread has already terminated, in which case it returns immediately.

The thread specified in the first parameter must be joinable. A thread is *joinable* if it can be joined. Some threads aren't joinable. By default, newly created threads are joinable. Threads that aren't joinable are called *detached* threads. A thread can be created in a detached state or it can be detached at a later time. We'll say more about this topic in "Detaching Threads" on page 722.

If retval is not NULL, then the value passed to pthread_exit() by the terminating thread will be available in the location referenced by retval, provided that pthread_join() succeeds. The double indirection is needed because the parameter of pthread_exit() has type void* and retval stores the address of the variable into which that value was copied.

We need to be careful when calling pthread_join() for the following reasons:

- Multiple simultaneous calls to pthread_join() by different threads specifying the same target thread have undefined results.

- The behavior is undefined if the thread argument to pthread_join() doesn't refer to a joinable thread.

- The behavior is undefined if the thread argument refers to the calling thread itself; a thread cannot wait for itself.

- If a thread that terminates is never joined, it becomes a *zombie* thread. A zombie thread consumes some system resources, and when the number of zombie threads is large enough, the system won't be able to create new threads or processes.

Let's look at an example that shows how the preceding three functions are used together. Listing 15-1 creates a single thread, after which the master thread joins it.

*pthread_create
_demo.c*
```
void *hello_world(void *world)
{
    long exit_value = 0; /* Exit value must be the same size as a pointer. */
    printf("Hello world from %s!\n", (char*) world);
    pthread_exit((void*) exit_value);
}

int main(int argc, char *argv[])
{
    pthread_t newthread;                    /* Stores thread ID        */
```

```
long    *status;   /* To store thread exit status, this must be long. */

if ( 0 != pthread_create(&newthread, NULL, hello_world, "Pluto") )
    fatal_error(errno, "pthread_create");

/* Now wait for the child thread. */
if ( 0 != pthread_join(newthread, (void**) (&status)) )
    fatal_error(errno, "pthread_join");
printf("Child exited with status %ld\n", (long) status);
return 0;
}
```

Listing 15-1: A program that creates a single thread and joins it when it terminates

Although it isn't shown in Listing 15-1, all programs include the *pthread.h* header file. Observe that we can pass the string "Pluto" in the last argument in the call to pthread_create(); it is converted to void*, and in the start function, we have to explicitly cast it back to a string type for printing. A run of this program follows:

```
$ ./pthread_create_demo
Hello world from Pluto!
Child exited with status 0
```

Passing Data to Threads

A thread's start_routine() has just a single void* parameter, which has implications for the design of a program. It's similar to the problem we had with signal handlers, which are even more constrained because they have just a single int argument. The void* parameter lets us overcome this.

When the threads in a program need access to more than a single data item, there are a few possible solutions:

- Declare variables needed by multiple threads to be global, in other words, file-scoped.

- Allocate shared variables on the heap through file-scoped pointers.

- Define a data structure containing all data to be shared, and pass a pointer to that structure to the thread start routine. This works because we can pass any address into a void* parameter.

The first two choices would look something like the following:

```
int   counter = 0;
int *on_heap = (int*) malloc(sizeof int);

void *start_function(void *arg)
{
    --snip--
```

```
    counter++;      /* Increment the global counter. */
    *on_heap = 1;   /* Assign 1 to *on_heap.          */
    --snip--
}
```

Using global, shared variables inside threads invites race conditions, and if there's a way to avoid doing so, we should. The third idea is to pack a data structure with everything each thread needs and pass a pointer to it as the start function's argument. For example, suppose that a large number of threads is created to process an even larger dataset. To make it concrete, suppose the data is in an array of integers that's been allocated on the heap. Suppose also that each thread processes a consecutive segment of this array and therefore needs the first and last indices of its segment in the array. Then we could define a structure such as

```
typedef struct _task_data {
    pthread_t tid;      /* Thread ID assigned to thread         */
    int       id;       /* Program's internal ID for the thread */
    int       first;    /* Index of first element for thread    */
    int       last;     /* Index of last element for task       */
    int       *array;   /* Pointer to start of array            */
    int       result;   /* Location where thread's result is stored */
} task_data;
```

to pass to each thread. Each thread will have its own values of first, last, and task_id. The tid member will contain the thread ID assigned to the thread when it is created; the task_id is a small integer that the program assigns to each thread so that it can be used to calculate which part of the array each thread is assigned. Figure 15-3 shows how the array is partitioned among the threads with this approach.

Figure 15-3: An array partitioned into N segments for N tasks, such that all segments except the last are the same size

The array pointer may or may not be needed in the data structure. If the pointer to it is in file scope, the threads will have access to it anyway, but if the pointer is a local variable in the main program, then a copy of the pointer should be in the structure. Suppose that the array is declared as a static local variable named array in the main program. Then a code fragment to initialize the thread data and create the threads would be as shown in Listing 15-2, assuming array_size is the number of array elements, nthreads is the number of threads to be created, and nthreads < array_size.

```
task_data thread_data[nthreads];

for ( t = 0; t < nthreads; t++ ) {
    thread_data[t].first   = (t * array_size) / nthreads;
    thread_data[t].last    = (((t + 1) * array_size) / nthreads) - 1;
    thread_data[t].task_id = t;
    thread_data[t].array   = array;
    if ( 0 != pthread_create(&(thread_data[t].tid), &attr, add_array,
                             (void *) &thread_data[t]) )
        fatal_error(errno, "pthread_create");
}
```

Listing 15-2: Initializing and starting threads to process a shared array

This would create and start nthreads-many threads, each executing add_array()
with its own structure containing the parameters of its execution. This
method of partitioning the array guarantees that the sizes of the array segments differ by at most 1. I leave proof of this as an exercise.

Identifying Threads

A thread can get its thread ID by calling pthread_self(), whose prototype is:

```
pthread_t pthread_self(void);
```

This is the analogue to getpid() for processes. This function is the only way
that the thread can get its ID, because the thread ID isn't provided to it by
the creation call, unless the program explicitly stores this thread ID for the
thread when it's created, as the preceding example code did. This function
never fails.

A thread can check whether two thread IDs are equal by calling pthread
_equal(), whose prototype is:

```
int pthread_equal(pthread_t t1, pthread_t t2);
```

This returns a nonzero value if the two thread IDs are equal and 0 if they are
not. This function never fails.

Detaching Threads

Because pthread_join() has to retrieve the status and thread ID of a terminated thread, this information must be stored someplace, and therefore uses
system resources. Until a terminated thread is joined by some other thread,
it is a zombie thread.

Sometimes threads are created that don't need to be joined. Consider
a process that spawns a thread for the sole purpose of writing output to a
file, which might take longer than the remaining execution time of the process. If the master thread is forced to call pthread_join() to reap this zombie

```
```

thread, it has to wait around until the thread terminates, which wastes more resources.

If a thread doesn't need to be joined, it can be created as a *detached thread*. When a detached thread terminates, no resources are saved; the system cleans up all resources related to the thread. A thread that wasn't initially detached can be detached later.

Being joinable or detached is a thread attribute. In order to set it, we need to modify the thread's attribute object, of type `pthread_attr_t`. This is a two-step procedure:

1. Initialize the thread attribute object with the default values by calling `pthread_attr_init()`.

2. Change the individual detachment state of the attribute object by calling `pthread_attr_setdetachstate()`.

The documentation for `pthread_attr_init()` warns us not to call this function more than once. Calling it after the object has been initialized results in undefined behavior. Its prototype is:

```
int pthread_attr_init(pthread_attr_t *attr);
```

The prototype for `pthread_attr_setdetachstate()` is:

```
int pthread_attr_setdetachstate(pthread_attr_t *attr, int detachstate);
```

The second parameter must be either `PTHREAD_CREATE_DETACHED` or `PTHREAD_CREATE_JOINABLE`.

Putting this together, the code for creating a detached thread is:

```
pthread_t      tid;                    /* Thread ID                   */
pthread_attr_t attr;                   /* Thread attribute            */
pthread_attr_init(&attr);              /* Initialize attribute object. */
pthread_attr_setdetachstate(&attr, PTHREAD_CREATE_DETACHED);
pthread_create(&tid, &attr, start_routine, arg);  /* Create the thread.  */
```

Converting a joinable thread to a detached thread is easier because *Pthreads* has a `pthread_detach()` function. Its prototype is:

```
int pthread_detach(pthread_t thread);
```

It can be called by any thread, including the thread itself. It marks the thread identified by `thread` as detached. Attempting to detach an already detached thread results in unspecified behavior. A thread can detach itself by calling:

```
pthread_detach(pthread_self());
```

Detaching a thread is irreversible—it cannot become joinable afterward. Listing 15-3 contains a program that creates a detached thread. The `main()` function creates the detached thread and terminates by calling `pthread_exit()` to allow its detached child to run after `main()` terminates. The call to `usleep()` in the thread loop slows the thread so that it continues after `main()` exits.

```
void *thread_routine(void *arg)
{
    printf("Child is running...\n");
    for ( int i = 0; i < strlen(arg); i++ ) {
        usleep(500000);
        write(1, arg + i, 1);
    }
    printf("\nChild is exiting.\n");
    return(NULL);
}

int main(int argc, char *argv[])
{
    char *buf = "abcdefghijklmnopqrstuvwxyz";
    pthread_t       thread;
    pthread_attr_t attr;
    pthread_attr_init(&attr);
    pthread_attr_setdetachstate(&attr, PTHREAD_CREATE_DETACHED);
    if ( pthread_create(&thread, NULL, thread_routine, (void *)(buf)) )
        fatal_error(errno, "error creating a new thread");
    printf("Main is now exiting.\n");
    pthread_exit(NULL);
}
```

Listing 15-3: A program that creates a detached thread and exits while the thread is running

Build this program and run it without arguments:

```
$ ./pthread_detach_demo
Main is now exiting.
Child is running...
abcdefghijklmnopqrstuvwxyz
Child is now exiting.
```

This output shows that the thread continued to run after the main program terminated.

Canceling a Thread

Threads can be canceled. *Cancellation* is essentially a request to terminate a thread. When a thread is canceled, its resources are cleaned up and it is terminated. A thread can request that another thread be canceled by calling pthread_cancel(), the prototype for which is:

```
int pthread_cancel(pthread_t thread);
```

Canceling is just a request; it isn't necessarily honored. When this function is called, a cancellation request is sent to the thread given as the argument.

Whether or not that thread is canceled depends upon the thread's cancelability state and type. The *cancelability* of a thread is the attribute that specifies whether or not a thread will allow itself to be terminated.

A thread can enable or disable cancelability, and it can also specify whether its cancelability type is asynchronous or deferred. If a thread's cancelability type is *asynchronous*, then it will be canceled immediately upon receiving a cancellation request, assuming it has enabled its cancelability. On the other hand, if its cancelability is *deferred*, then cancellation requests are deferred until the thread enters a cancellation point. Certain functions are *cancellation points*. To be precise, if a thread is cancelable, and its type is deferred, and a cancellation request is pending for it, then if it calls a function that is a cancellation point, it will be terminated immediately. The list of cancellation point functions required by POSIX can be found on the man page for *Pthreads* in Section 7.

A thread's cancelability state is enabled by default. It can be changed after it's created by calling pthread_setcancelstate(), whose prototype is:

```
int pthread_setcancelstate(int state, int *oldstate);
```

The two possible values for the first parameter (state) are PTHREAD_CANCEL_ENABLE and PTHREAD_CANCEL_DISABLE. The second parameter is the address of an integer to store the old state, or NULL if the program doesn't need it. If a thread disables cancellation, then a cancellation request remains queued until it enables cancellation. If a thread has enabled cancellation, then its cancelability type determines when cancellation occurs.

A thread's cancellation type is deferred by default. It can be set with pthread_setcanceltype():

```
int pthread_setcanceltype(int type, int *oldtype);
```

The possible values for the first parameter are PTHREAD_CANCEL_ASYNCHRONOUS and PTHREAD_CANCEL_DEFERRED.

Setting Thread Stack Size

The POSIX standard doesn't specify the size of a thread's stack, which can vary from one implementation to another. Furthermore, with even moderately demanding computational problems, exceeding the default stack limit is not that unusual. Thread stacks are usually no more than 8192 bytes, which is easily exceeded by many kinds of programs. If the stack limit is exceeded, the program will terminate, possibly with corrupted data.

Safe and portable programs don't depend upon the default stack limit but instead explicitly allocate enough stack space for each thread by calling the pthread_attr_setstacksize() function, whose prototype is:

```
int pthread_attr_setstacksize(pthread_attr_t *attr, size_t stacksize);
```

The first argument is the address of the thread's attribute object. The second is the new size for the stack. This function will fail if the attribute object doesn't exist or if the stack size is smaller than the allowed minimum (PTHREAD_STACK_MIN) or larger than the allowed maximum. The man page lists more caveats about its use.

To get the stack's current size, a thread can call:

```
int pthread_attr_getstacksize(pthread_attr_t *attr, size_t *stacksize);
```

This stores the current size of the stack in the variable whose address is passed in stacksize. It will fail if attr doesn't reference an existing attribute object.

To use this function, the thread has to have access to its current attribute object. There is no POSIX function that returns the attribute object of the calling thread, but there is a GNU extension, pthread_getattr_np(). However, this is a nonportable extension, not specified by POSIX. If we want our code to be portable, we can't rely on this function.

An alternative is to pass a reference to the attribute object to the thread in the start function so that it can change its attributes at a later time. The program *pthread_setstacksize.c* in the book's source code distribution shows how to do this. The following program fragment shows the key parts of the solution:

```
void thread_routine(void *arg)
{
    --snip--
    pthread_attr_t attr = (pthread_attr_t*) arg;
    pthread_attr_getstacksize(attr, &stack_size);
    --snip--
}
int main()
{
    pthread_t       thr;
    pthread_attr_t attr;
    --snip--
    pthread_attr_init(&attr);
    --snip--
    pthread_create(&thr, &attr, &thread_routine, &attr);
}
```

Regardless of whether your program increases the thread stack size, it's always a good idea to be mindful of how the thread uses memory. For example, if a thread needs local buffer storage for fairly large amounts of data, it should not declare an array on its stack. It should dynamically allocate storage on the heap instead (and free it when it no longer needs it).

Threads have several other attributes, but exploring them is an advanced topic that we won't cover here. The POSIX standard has a list of functions with names of the form `pthreads_attr_get*` that return specific attribute values. We know enough about threads at this point to create a nontrivial multithreaded program, but first we should explore the relationship between signals and threads.

Signals and Threads

The interaction between signals and threads is complex, but we need to understand it if any of our multithreaded programs have any signal handling capabilities. Some of the questions that we should answer include:

- If a signal is sent to a process, such as by `kill()`, is it sent to all of its threads or just one of them, and if just one, which one?

- Is there a distinction between signals sent to a process and signals directed at a specific thread?

- Can each thread register its own signal handlers, or do all threads share them?

- More generally, can different threads have different signal dispositions?

- Can each thread have its own signal mask, or are they all shared?

We can find answers to most of these questions in the signal(7) man page. First, let's distinguish between *thread-directed* and *process-directed* signals.

Thread-Directed Signals

These are signals directed at a specific thread. There are several ways to direct a signal to a specific thread:

- A signal can be directed at a specific thread if another thread in the same process sends it a signal using `pthread_kill()` or `pthread_sigqueue()`.

- A thread can send a signal to itself by calling `raise()`.

- If a thread executes an instruction that causes an exception of any kind resulting in generation of a signal, such as SIGSEGV, that signal will be sent just to that thread.

- If a thread tries to write to a pipe, named or unnamed, but no processes have it open for reading, the SIGPIPE signal is sent just to that thread.

These are essentially the only ways to send a signal to a specific thread. The `tgkill()` system call can do so, but it is meant for internal thread library use only.

Process-Directed Signals

These are signals targeted at the whole process and therefore pending for the whole process. Essentially, all signals sent by means other than the ones listed in the preceding section are process-directed. These are some explicit ways to send process-directed signals:

- A process or thread issues either a kill() or sigqueue() system call directed at the process of any of its threads.

- The kill command specifies the process of any of its threads.

- A user generates a signal from the keyboard, such as SIGINT.

- The kernel generates a signal as a result of some hardware exception unrelated to the process's execution, such as a SIGPWR.

- A signal is sent as a result of a timer expiration, possibly as a result of an I/O operation.

These are the most common ways for a process-directed signal to be generated.

Signal Masks and Dispositions

In a multithreaded program, every thread begins by inheriting its parent's signal mask, but it can also have its own signal mask. A thread calls pthread_sigmask() to create or modify its own mask. It has the same prototype as sigprocmask(). Every thread also has its own list of pending signals. A thread can retrieve the set of signals pending for it specifically as well as pending process-directed signals by calling sigpending().

In contrast, signal dispositions are process wide. In particular, signal handlers are process wide. This means that if a signal is delivered to any thread, whether that thread registered a handler for that signal or some other thread did, the handler will run, assuming the thread did not block the signal. It doesn't matter whether the signal is directed at a specific thread or is process directed. For example, if thread A registers a handler named sighandler() to catch SIGINT, and a signal is sent to thread B, which did not register this handler, sighandler() will run anyway. Similarly, if the disposition was set to SIG_IGN, then all threads that have not changed their signal masks will ignore SIGINT. There are complicating factors though.

NOTE   *If a process-directed signal is sent to a process, it's delivered to any one of the threads that do not have the signal blocked at the time of delivery. If more than one thread has the signal unblocked, the kernel chooses an arbitrary thread to which to deliver the signal.*

For example, if a program has three threads, A, B, and C, and only A has blocked SIGINT, then if a user enters CTRL-C on the keyboard, the signal will be delivered to either B or C but we cannot predict which one. If a signal handler for SIGINT is registered, then the handler will be run by the thread that receives the signal.

The program in Listing 15-4 is designed to experiment with threads and signals so that you can corroborate these behaviors. Some error handling has been removed to save space. The complete program is in the book's source code distribution.

pthread_signal
_demo.c

```c
#include "common_hdrs.h"
#include <pthread.h>

#ifndef SLEEP
#define SLEEP 10
#endif

sigset_t  mask;      /* Signal mask */
pthread_t thr[3];    /* Thread IDs  */

void sighandler(int sig)
{
    printf("Received %d; handler run by thread %ld\n", sig, pthread_self());
}

void *t1(void *arg)   /* Thread t1 start function */
{
#ifdef BLOCK1
    pthread_sigmask(SIG_BLOCK, &mask, NULL);
#endif
    sleep(SLEEP);
    pthread_exit((void*) arg);
}

void *t2(void *arg)   /* Thread t2 start function */
{
#ifdef SIGHANDLE
    struct sigaction sa;
    sigemptyset(&sa.sa_mask);
    sa.sa_flags = 0;
    sa.sa_handler = sighandler;
    sigaction(SIGINT, &sa, NULL);
#endif
    sleep(SLEEP);
    pthread_exit((void*) arg);
}

void *t3(void *arg)   /* Thread t3 start function */
{
    sleep(SLEEP);
    pthread_exit((void*) arg);
}
```

```
int main(int argc, char *argv[])
{
    long *status;
    sigemptyset(&mask);
    sigaddset(&mask, SIGINT);
    pthread_create(&thr[0], NULL, t1,(void*) 1);
    pthread_create(&thr[1], NULL, t2,(void*) 2);
    pthread_create(&thr[2], NULL, t3,(void*) 3);
    pthread_sigmask(SIG_BLOCK, &mask, NULL);
    sleep(1);
#ifdef MAINSIGNALS
    printf("Sending SIGINT to thread 1\n");
    pthread_kill(thr[0], SIGINT);
#endif
    for ( int i = 0; i < 3; i++ ) {  /* Wait for the child threads. */
        pthread_join(thr[i], (void**) (&status));
        printf("Child exited with status %ld\n", (long) status);
    }
    return 0;
}
```

*Listing 15-4: A program that can show different signal dispositions when multiple threads
are running*

By compiling the program and defining zero or more of the three symbols, MAINSIGNALS, BLOCK1, and SIGHANDLE, such as

```
$ gcc -I../include -L../lib pthread_signal_demo.c -o pthread_signal_demo\
  -lspl -lm -lrt -pthread -DBLOCK1  -DSIGHANDLE
```

you can run it to confirm the signaling semantics. The main() function creates three threads and then waits for them. If MAINSIGNALS is defined when
you compile it, main() will send a thread-directed SIGINT signal to thread 1.
If SIGHANDLE is defined, then a signal handler will be registered by thread 2.
If BLOCK1 is defined, then thread 1 blocks SIGINT. If you run it without any of
these symbols defined, the three threads will exit normally:

```
$ ./pthread_signal_demo
Child exited with status 1
Child exited with status 2
Child exited with status 3
```

If you allow the main program to send a signal to thread 1 without registering the signal handler, you see

```
$ gcc -I../include -L../lib pthread_signal_demo.c -o pthread_signal_demo\
  -lspl -lm -lrt -pthread -DMAINSIGNALS
$ ./pthread_signal_demo
Sending SIGINT to thread 1
$
```

showing that the main program never made it to the `pthread_join()` calls and all threads terminated.

Define `SIGHANDLE` and rerun it:

```
$ ./pthread_signal_demo
Sending SIGINT to thread 1
Received 2; handler run by thread 140223239542336
Child exited with status 1
Child exited with status 2
Child exited with status 3
```

Now increase the sleep time when you compile it and open a second terminal window before running it. Run the program, and in the second terminal, enter:

```
$ ps -L -eopid,ppid,tid,cmd | grep pthread_signal_demo
  23691    6442    23691 pthread_signal_demo
  23691    6442    23693 pthread_signal_demo
  23691    6442    23694 pthread_signal_demo
```

If you have enough time, send a `SIGINT` using `kill -2` to any of the threads and observe what happens. All threads are killed if the handler isn't registered, no matter which thread you signaled.

The implications for program design are significant. Because we can't predict which thread receives the signal if none of them block it, we can't predict whether the thread that runs the signal handler will have a race condition because of where it was interrupted. In general, handling signals asynchronously presents problems with multithreaded programs.

For this reason, it's better to handle signals synchronously in a dedicated thread. Kerrisk [20] suggests the following:

- Before creating any child threads, the main program's thread should block all asynchronous signals. The child threads will inherit this mask.

- Create a single thread that synchronously waits for these masked signals using `sigwait()`.

We'll put this idea to work in the next program.

A Multithreaded Concurrent Server

The concurrent server that we developed in Chapter 14 forked a new process for each client interaction. Here, we'll convert this server to a multithreaded concurrent server instead. Specifically, for each client request, it will create a new thread. Changing the server design won't require any changes to the client-side program, *upcase.c*, nor the shared header file, *upcase.h*, but it will require a change in how some data is organized and how it handles signals.

The process-based concurrent server's main loop is of the form:

```
while ( read(publicfd, (char*) &msg, sizeof(msg)) > 0 ) {
    if ( -1 == (pid = fork()) )
        syslog(LOG_ERR, "Could not create child process.");
    else if ( 0 == pid )
        // OMITTED: Fork a new process to service the incoming client
        //          request based on the private FIFO names in msg.
        process_client(&msg); /* Child process executes. */
        exit(EXIT_SUCCESS);   /* Should never get here!  */
}
```

The process_client() function is executed by a newly created process. We can instead make process_client() the start function of a new thread. Its prototype is almost the correct form:

```
void process_client(message *msg)
```

However, there are a few catches:

- When the process-based concurrent server forks a new process to execute this function, the entire address space is replicated and, in particular, msg is duplicated in the new process. Each child process has its own copy of msg. When we create a new thread with process _client() as the start function, nothing is replicated. If we pass the address of msg in the start function of a thread, then multiple threads will have pointers to the same message structure, a local variable in the main program. As the content of this structure changes in the master thread, the child threads can have corrupted data and incorrect results.

- The process_client() function from the process-based concurrent server accesses global variables such as clientwritefd and clientreadfd. The thread start function has to have its own copies of these and other variables that are globals.

- We need to change the signal handling, since as it is, it can lead to errors if a signal arrives when multiple threads are running.

- The threads should be created in a detached state so that the parent process does not have to call pthread_join() to collect their statuses when they terminate.

The solution to the first problem is to allocate memory on the heap every time a new client sends a request message, copy the request memory into that new memory, and pass a pointer to it to the start function of the new thread. Without any error handling, this is roughly:

```
message *client_data = (message*) malloc(sizeof(message));
memcpy(client_data, &msg, sizeof(msg));
pthread_create(&child_thread, &attr, process_client, (void*) client_data))
```

The second problem has an easy solution. All variables used in the start function other than its parameter should be local.

Regarding the signal issue, we can follow the approach we outlined in "Signals and Threads" (see page 731). The main program will block all potentially terminating asynchronous signals. It will then create a signal-handling thread whose only purpose is to synchronously handle any pending signals by calling `sigwait()`. The only signal handler needed by the threads is one for `SIGPIPE` because a thread can receive this signal if it tries to write to its private raw text FIFO but the server closed its read end of it.

The start function for this signal-handling thread is as follows:

sighandler()

```
void *sighandler( void *data)
{
    int      sig;
    sigset_t mask = *(sigset_t*) data;
    if ( sigwait(&mask, &sig) != 0 )
        fatal_error(errno, "sigwait");

    close(dummyfd);       /* Close global descriptors.  */
    close(publicfd);
    unlink(PUBLIC);       /* Remove FIFO name.          */
    exit(EXIT_SUCCESS);   /* Force all threads to exit. */
}
```

The `main()` function will pass it a pointer to a signal mask with each of the blocked signals set in it. This thread calls `sigwait()`, waiting for any of these signals to be sent. Since they're blocked, they become pending as soon as the process receives them, and the `sigwait()` call will return 0. Regardless of which signal it removed from the set of pending signals, it closes the open file descriptors, removes the public FIFO name from the filesystem, and calls `exit()`. Calling `exit()` causes all other threads to terminate as well.

Listing 15-5 contains the parts of the main program that are different in this multithreaded server from the previous one. The complete program is in the book's source code repository.

threaded _upcased.c main()

```
int main(int argc, char *argv[])
{
    message          msg;          /* Connection message                   */
    struct sigaction sigact;       /* sigaction for registering handlers   */
    sigset_t         mask;         /* Signal mask of blocked signals       */
    pthread_t        child_thread; /* Thread ID for created child          */
    pthread_t        sig_thread;   /* Thread ID for signal-handling thread */
    pthread_attr_t   attr;         /* Attribute structure for threads      */
    message          *client_data; /* message structure to send to thread  */
    --snip--

    /* Set the attribute structure to create detached threads. */
    pthread_attr_init(&attr);
```

```
        pthread_attr_setdetachstate(&attr, PTHREAD_CREATE_DETACHED);
        pthread_attr_setstacksize (&attr, 65536);

        /* Block likely asynchronous signals. */
        sigemptyset(&mask);
        sigaddset(&mask, SIGINT);
        sigaddset(&mask, SIGHUP);
        sigaddset(&mask, SIGTERM);
        sigaddset(&mask, SIGQUIT);
        sigaddset(&mask, SIGABRT);
        if ( -1 == sigprocmask(SIG_BLOCK, &mask, NULL) )
            log_and_exit("sigprocmask failed");

        /* Create signal-handling thread. */
        if ( 0 != pthread_create(&sig_thread, &attr, sighandler, (void*) &mask) )
            syslog(LOG_ERR, "Could not create child thread.");

        while ( read(publicfd, (char*) &msg, sizeof(msg)) > 0 ) {
            if ( NULL == (client_data = (message*) malloc(sizeof (message))) )
                log_and_exit("malloc");
            memcpy(client_data, &msg, sizeof(msg));
            if ( 0 != pthread_create(&child_thread, &attr, process_client,
                                     (void*) client_data) )
                syslog(LOG_ERR, "Could not create child thread.");
            memset(&msg, 0, PIPE_BUF);
        }
        close(dummyfd);
        close(publicfd);
        unlink(PUBLIC);
        exit(EXIT_SUCCESS);
    }
```

Listing 15-5: The main() function for the multithreaded concurrent server

If the parent needed to wait for the child threads, it would need to save the thread IDs of each one. Since the threads were created in a detached state, it doesn't have to wait and doesn't do anything with the thread IDs, so the main loop just reuses the same variable.

The thread start function is the remaining piece of this program. It is almost identical to the function executed by the child processes of the process-based concurrent server. I show only the changed parts in Listing 15-6.

```
process_client()   void *process_client(void *data)
                   {
                       int nbytes;
                       int tries;
                       int clientwritefd; /* This was global in the process-based server. */
                       int clientreadfd;  /* This was global in the process-based server. */
```

```
    /* This must be allocated on the heap for each thread. */
    char *buffer = (char*) malloc(PIPE_BUF);
    if ( NULL == buffer )
        log_and_exit("malloc");

    /* Cast argument to message pointer. */
    message *client_msg = (message*) data;

    --snip--

    free(buffer);
    free(client_msg);
    pthread_exit(EXIT_SUCCESS);
}
```

Listing 15-6: The thread start function for threads that process client requests

The function allocates its buffer on the heap. If the buffer is stored in the stack as a local variable, the thread stack might overflow unless I increase the stack size. Since heap memory is so much larger, it's easier just to store it in the heap and free it when the thread exits. The thread also has to free the memory of the message itself. This was allocated in the master thread, but the master thread can't free it because it has no idea when the child thread will be finished.

This program will produce the same output as the previous server. It should be able to handle many more clients and run faster for each. A good experiment is to set up a script that runs many clients nearly simultaneously, discarding their output, to see how many concurrent threads this server can handle. I leave this as an exercise.

Summary

A process requires many kernel resources but executes just a single sequence of instructions from its executable code. As a result, an ordinary process can't perform multiple tasks simultaneously. Multiple processes working together don't alter this inefficiency, since they don't share any resources. Threads are a solution to this problem. A multithreaded process consists of multiple threads of control through the executable code of a program. Each thread executes an independent path within the program's address space, and therefore, at any given time, multiple instructions are executed within the same program.

Threads share the program's data and heap segments, but each thread has its own private runtime stack. Each thread also has its own registers, signal mask, errno variable, and scheduling attributes. All other process attributes, such as the environment variables, controlling terminal, working directory, open file descriptors, and so on, are shared among all of the threads.

The fact that threads can share data easily is the primary reason that some problems have more efficient solutions in a multithreaded program than they would in a program with multiple processes that share data. However, the sharing of data among threads introduces the possibility of race conditions and data corruption in the code, because two or more threads can modify the same variable in an uncontrolled way. Solving this problem requires the use of primitive operations that can protect these critical sections of code from simultaneous access.

POSIX threads, commonly known as *Pthreads*, is an API consisting of data types and functions for writing multithreaded programs. It includes over 100 different functions for the management and control of threads with a program, falling into one of the following categories:

- Thread management

- Mutex management

- Condition variable management

- Synchronization primitives

The thread management group, for example, contains operations for creating, initializing, and destroying threads; modifying thread attributes; and controlling how threads can terminate themselves and each other.

Signals and the signal handling mechanisms were designed long before threading libraries were created. The interaction between signals and threads is complex because signals were designed to work with processes, not threads. Questions such as which threads get which signals and which threads execute signal handlers do not always have simple answers.

This chapter presented an overview of the *Pthreads* API and examined the various functions in the thread management category. It examined how signals work in multithreaded programs. Lastly, it developed a multithreaded version of the concurrent upcased server from Chapter 14. The next chapter explores parts of the *Pthreads* API related to mutexes, condition variables, and synchronization.

Exercises

1. Prove that the method of partitioning the elements of an array of size N among p threads shown in Listing 15-2 has the property that the number of elements assigned to each thread differs by at most 1 and the thread that has the last segment of the array always has $\lceil N/p \rceil$ elements.

2. Write a multithreaded version of *spl_ls2.c* (from Chapter 7) that creates a separate thread for each directory command line argument.

3. Write a program that creates as many threads as possible, using the default attributes for each thread, with a start function that prints `Hello World` and then exits. Design the program so that it reports the largest number of threads it was able to create before it exits. Run this program on several computers. Is the reported number always the same?

4. Write a script to determine the maximum number of simultaneous clients the multithreaded `upcased` server can serve at a time without failing. Each client should get its text interactively so that it stays running until it receives a signal or an EOF from the terminal. Design the script so that it creates new clients until the server fails and then kills the clients.

5. Write a multithreaded program named *search.c* that is given the pathname of a text file consisting of an unlimited number of unique integers, not in any order, followed by a single integer, n. The program outputs its 1-based position in the file if it's there and 0 otherwise. The program must create a number of threads equal to the number of processors in the computer. Each thread has to search its own set of numbers using the method of partitioning shown in Listing 15-2. If a thread finds the number, it should modify a global variable to cause the other threads to exit immediately. The main program should output the position. Read the man page for `get_nprocs(3)` and/or `sysconf()` to learn how to get the processor count.

6. Write a multithreaded version of *spl_du1.c* (from Chapter 7) that creates a separate thread for each directory command line argument. (The `nftw()` function is thread-safe provided that the `FTW_CHDIR` is not passed to it.)

16

THREAD SYNCHRONIZATION

Multithreaded programs can take advantage of the fact that the threads share global memory in the heap and data segments. It's easy to be lulled into thinking that they're relatively easy to design and write because it's so easy to share that data in memory. However, multithreaded programs require us to have a different mindset during their design and development than sequential programs do because this sharing of data comes at a cost. Specifically, we have to be ever mindful of the consequent race conditions and synchronization issues tied to this benefit. To solve these problems, we need tools for controlling access to shared objects. The *Pthreads* library contains an assortment of tools for this purpose, such as mutexes, condition variables, barriers, and read-write locks.

In this chapter, we explore the use of these tools for solving some synchronization problems. We begin with an overview of how to evaluate a multithreaded program. After that we'll look at specific tools from the *Pthreads* API, starting with mutexes, then condition variables, barriers, and read-write locks. Along the way, we'll write multithreaded versions of a few programs from previous chapters such as the producer-consumer program from Chapter 14. We'll also develop a few new programs. Although some of the algorithms we're studying are parallel, the intention in this chapter is not to explore theoretical concepts about concurrent programming; still, here and there I toss in a few concepts to clarify a more relevant point.

Correctness and Performance Considerations

One of the primary reasons for multithreading a program is to improve its performance. Before we dive into the details of the collection of synchronization tools provided by *Pthreads*, let's make sure we have a means of deciding whether a program performs well.

All programs have functional requirements, those that determine whether their output is correct. Most programs also have performance requirements, such as how long they run or how much memory they consume. Multithreaded programs have additional functional and performance requirements. A multithreaded program has to be functionally correct regardless of the timing of execution of its threads. If it fails sometimes due to how its threads are scheduled, it isn't correct. This is an example of a safety property, a concept defined by Leslie Lamport in 1977. A *safety* property is one that means, essentially, *bad things don't happen* [22].

A multithreaded program also has to have certain liveness properties, such as being free from deadlock, starvation of one or more threads, and livelock, which occurs when two or more threads continuously attempt an action that fails. (Think of two people trying to pass each other in a narrow corridor, with each telling the other to go first, but neither ever passing the other.) A *liveness* property, also defined by Lamport [22], is one that means *good things do happen*.

When we develop any multithreaded program, we need to be cognizant of these issues and convince ourselves that the program satisfies both functional and performance requirements.

Mutexes

A *mutex* is one of the tools of the *Pthreads* library that makes it possible to grant mutually exclusive access to critical sections. We discussed them briefly in Chapter 12 when we examined race conditions among processes. A mutex is like a software version of a lock—a thread locks it, uses the shared resource, and unlocks it. Its name is a portmanteau of "mutual exclusion." A mutex can be held, or *owned*, by only one thread at a time. Like a binary semaphore, the typical use of a mutex is to surround a critical section of code with calls to lock and then to unlock the mutex, as in the following code:

```
pthread_mutex_lock(&mutex);
// OMITTED: Critical section code
pthread_mutex_unlock(&mutex);
```

This is also depicted visually in Figure 16-1.

Figure 16-1: Calls to lock and unlock a mutex to ensure exclusive access to a critical section

We'll examine the functions to lock and unlock mutexes shortly.

Mutexes are a low-level form of critical section protection, providing the most rudimentary features. They were intended as the building blocks of higher-level synchronization methods. Nonetheless, they can be used in many cases to solve critical section problems. In the remainder of this section, we'll explore the fundamentals of working with them.

NOTE   *A mutex is different from a binary semaphore in one important respect—the only thread allowed to unlock a given mutex is the one that locked it, whereas a thread that didn't decrement a semaphore can increment it. They serve different purposes.*

Declaring and Initializing a Mutex

In *Pthreads*, a mutex is declared as an object of type pthread_mutex_t. It has to be initialized before it can be used. A man page search for how to initialize a mutex (apropos -a mutex initialize) yields a page for pthread_mutex_init(), but that page has little information and refers us instead to the page for pthread_mutex_destroy(). I'll summarize what that page states. There are two ways to initialize a mutex:

- Statically when it is declared, using the PTHREAD_MUTEX_INITIALIZER macro:

  ```
  pthread_mutex_t mutex = PTHREAD_MUTEX_INITIALIZER;
  ```

- Dynamically with the pthread_mutex_init() routine:

  ```
  int pthread_mutex_init(pthread_mutex_t *mutex,
                         pthread_mutexattr_t *attr);
  ```

The static initializer initializes a mutex with its default attributes, whereas the pthread_mutex_init() function is given a pointer to a mutex and to a mutex attribute object. It initializes the mutex to have the attributes of that object. Unlike the static initializer, this also performs error checking when invoked. Passing NULL in the second argument initializes the mutex with the default attributes and performs error checking in the process. The call to `pthread_mutex_init()` can fail for a few different reasons, such as a malformed attributes object or a lack of sufficient memory, resources, or privileges. It returns an error code if it fails and 0 on success.

Regardless of how it is initialized, a mutex is initially unlocked.

Locking and Unlocking a Mutex

There are two functions for locking a mutex, and one for unlocking it:

```
int pthread_mutex_lock(pthread_mutex_t *mutex);
int pthread_mutex_trylock(pthread_mutex_t *mutex);
int pthread_mutex_unlock(pthread_mutex_t *mutex);
```

Let's begin with `pthread_mutex_lock()`. The semantics of this function are a bit complex, in part because there are four different types of mutexes, called normal, recursive, error-check, and default. The default mutex type is usually the same as the normal mutex; in describing how the various mutex functions behave, I'll assume it's a normal mutex. The rules describing its semantics are:

- If the mutex is not locked, the calling thread succeeds in acquiring the referenced mutex and becomes its owner. The mutex is in a locked state as a result and the call returns 0.

- If the mutex is in a locked state when a thread tries to lock it, the calling thread is blocked until the mutex is unlocked.

- If a thread tries to lock a mutex that it has already locked, this results in deadlock.

- If a thread attempts to unlock a mutex that it hasn't locked or a mutex that is unlocked, undefined behavior results.

- If a signal is delivered to a thread that is blocked on a mutex, when the thread returns from the signal handler, it resumes waiting for the mutex as if it hadn't been interrupted.

In short, if several threads try to lock a mutex, only one thread succeeds in acquiring the lock. The other threads will be in a blocked state until the mutex is unlocked by its owner. Since only one thread returns successfully from the call to lock the mutex, in code like this

```
pthread_mutex_lock(&mutex);
// OMITTED: Critical section code
pthread_mutex_unlock(&mutex);
```

only one thread at a time can enter the critical section.

The `pthread_mutex_trylock()` function behaves similarly to `pthread_mutex_lock()` except that it never blocks the calling thread. Specifically, if the mutex is unlocked, the calling thread acquires it and the function returns 0, and if the mutex is already locked by any thread, the function returns the error value `EBUSY`. This means that on return from a call to `pthread_mutex_trylock()`, the code has to check the return value before entering a critical section. We won't explore this function further.

The `pthread_mutex_unlock()` function will unlock a mutex if it is called by the owning thread. If there are threads blocked on the mutex object referenced by `mutex` when `pthread_mutex_unlock()` is called, resulting in the mutex becoming available, the scheduling policy determines which thread next acquires the mutex. If the mutex is a normal mutex that used the default initialization, there is no specific thread scheduling policy associated with the mutex, and the kernel scheduler chooses which thread to unblock. The behavior of this function for non-normal mutexes is different.

Destroying a Mutex

When a mutex is no longer needed, it should be destroyed. The prototype for `pthread_mutex_destroy()` is:

```
int pthread_mutex_destroy(pthread_mutex_t *mutex);
```

The function destroys the unlocked mutex object referenced by `mutex`, and the mutex object becomes uninitialized. A locked mutex cannot be destroyed; if a thread attempts to do so, the effect is undefined. The result of referencing the mutex object after it has been destroyed is undefined. A destroyed mutex object can be reinitialized using `pthread_mutex_init()`.

A Program Using a Normal Mutex

We've developed a few programs in previous chapters that had critical sections, which we protected in a few different ways. For example, in Chapter 8, we wrote two different progress bar programs: *progress_bar1.c* and *progress _bar2.c*. In each, we employed a global variable named `fraction_completed` that kept track of the fraction of work completed by the program on an imaginary job. This variable was updated by a function named `long_running_task()` and used inside the signal handler that refreshed the progress bar. Because the signal handler could run asynchronously with respect to `long_running_task()`, the accesses to `fraction_completed` could be concurrent and subject to race conditions. We prevented them by blocking signals during the update to `fraction _completed` inside `long_running_task()`. Both programs were driven by signals generated at regular intervals. The first used the `alarm()` function, which was reset with each expiration in a signal handler. The second used a POSIX timer instead. The second was a bit more complex than the first because of the steps needed to set up and use the timer.

The *progress_bar1.c* program is a good candidate in which we can integrate the ideas about threads, mutexes, and signal handling that we've just explored, in part because it's simpler. We'll create a multithreaded version of that program, named *threaded_progbar.c*. Specifically, instead of a single thread executing the `long_running_task()`, we'll create multiple threads that do. This models the situation in which multiple threads work together to complete a common task. As a result, though, their mutual updates to fraction_completed are a critical section, which we'll protect with a single mutex. We'll also have to change how the SIGALRM signal is handled in this version. Specifically, we'll make the following changes:

- The main() function will create NUMTHREADS many (four) compute threads to execute the long_running_task(). We'll modify long_running _task() so that it's in the correct form to be a thread start function.

- The main() function will create a signal mask containing SIGALRM and the terminating asynchronous signals and call sigprocmask() to block all of these signals. The threads will inherit this mask. It will also create a single signal-handling thread like the one in *threaded_upcased.c* (see "A Multithreaded Concurrent Server" in Chapter 14) that uses sigwait() to synchronously handle all pending signals. (Figure 16-2 depicts the program structure, with four compute threads.)

- The simulated delay in the long_running_task() will be proportional to the amount that the thread adds to fraction_completed in its loop iteration, which is based on a random value. We'll change how we generate that value.

- We'll create a logfile into which each thread writes its ID every time it increases fraction_completed inside its critical section. The logfile will be a way to check how randomized the updates were.

- When it terminates, the program will print the total percentage of the simulated task that each thread completed.

The program is driven by the steady beat of the refresh_progressbar() function, which generates the sequence of SIGALRM signals as it refreshes the screen. However, no thread is responding directly to the beat except for sig_thread(), which calls refresh_progressbar() each time the SIGALRM is delivered, as shown in Figure 16-2.

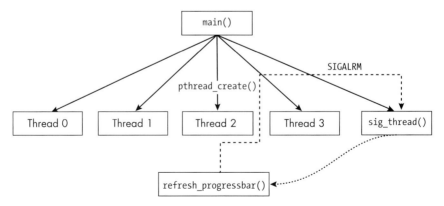

Figure 16-2: A schematic representation of threaded_progbar.c *showing four compute threads and one signal handling thread*

Let's look at the pieces of *threaded_progbar.c*. First, it needs a few global variables to simplify the code:

```
double fraction_completed = 0;        /* Fraction of operation completed   */
pthread_mutex_t frac_mutex = PTHREAD_MUTEX_INITIALIZER;  /* Shared mutex   */
double computedby[NUMTHREADS];        /* Fraction computed by each thread   */
pthread_t t[NUMTHREADS];              /* Thread IDs                         */

typedef struct _task_data {
    int fd;     /* File descriptor for logfile */
    long id;    /* Program's ID for thread      */
} thread_data;
```

The thread_data structure is the data type of the argument passed to the start function for a thread. Since the threads write to the logfile, they get a copy of the file descriptor to the open file description and share the file offset.

The revised long_running_task() is displayed in Listing 16-1.

long_running
_task()

```
void *long_running_task(void *arg)
{
    double progress_rate = 1.0 / (MIN_SIMULATION_SECS * NUMTHREADS);
    struct timespec differential, rem;

    thread_data td = *(thread_data*) arg;  /* Extract thread data from arg. */
    char str[5];
    sprintf(str, "%ld,", td.id);              /* Thread ID as a string        */

    while ( fraction_completed < 1.0 ) {
        pthread_mutex_lock(&frac_mutex);                 /* Lock mutex.        */
    ❶ double work = progress_rate * (1.0 * random()) / RAND_MAX;
        fraction_completed += work;                      /* Update is race free. */
    ❷ if ( fraction_completed > 1.0 ) {
            work -= (fraction_completed - 1.0);    /* Reduce work.       */
            fraction_completed = 1.0;
        }
        write(td.fd, str, strlen(str));    /* Record in logfile that I ran.  */
        pthread_mutex_unlock(&frac_mutex);          /* Unlock mutex.        */
        dbl_to_timespec(20 * NUMTHREADS * work, &differential);
        if ( -1 == nanosleep(&differential, &rem))/* Sleep proportionately. */
            nanosleep(&rem, NULL);
        computedby[td.id] += work;          /* Record fraction computed.    */
    }
    pthread_exit(EXIT_SUCCESS);
}
```

Listing 16-1: The thread start function for the compute threads

The program uses the mutex to protect all of the instructions in the critical section. The original program used the drand48() function, but it isn't thread-safe. Its man page notes this, stating that it records "global state information for the random number generator, so they are not thread-safe." Because it isn't thread-safe, we use random() ❶ instead, which is thread-safe.

When writing multithreaded programs, we need to check every library function's man page as we're working. All man pages have a section near their end named ATTRIBUTES *with a table indicating thread safety.*

The write() to the file is within the critical section not to protect the file offset, but to ensure that the order in which the thread IDs are written is the same as the order in which they acquired the mutex lock. If it came after the mutex was unlocked, two threads could write into the file in an arbitrary order. The file offset is protected from races because the file is opened with the O_APPEND flag in main() (see Chapter 11).

The if statement ❷ makes sure that the work variable is diminished if the last iteration causes the fraction of work completed to exceed 1.0. Lastly, the dbl_to_timespec() function is a utility function declared in the common header file *time_utils.h*, which the program includes.

The signal handling thread's start function, sighandler(), is similar in structure to that of the multithreaded concurrent server, *threaded_upcased.c*. It's shown next:

sighandler()
```
void *sighandler(void *data)
{
    int sig;
    sigset_t mask = *(sigset_t*) data;
    while ( TRUE ) {
        if ( sigwait(&mask, &sig) != 0 )
            fatal_error(errno, "sigwait");
        switch ( sig ) {
        case SIGALRM:
            refresh_progressbar(sig);
            break;
        default:
            erase_progress_bar();
            for ( int i = 0; i < NUMTHREADS; i++ )
                pthread_cancel(t[i]);   /* Terminate the other threads. */
            exit(EXIT_FAILURE);
        }
    }
    return data;
}
```

A pointer to the set of blocked signals for which sigwait() waits synchronously is passed into the function as its data. If it receives a SIGALRM, sigwait() returns and calls refresh_progressbar(). If it's any other pending signal, it's a terminating one, so it erases the progress bar and kills the compute threads explicitly. When it calls exit(), the main() function's thread exits and the file descriptor is automatically closed.

The last piece of the program that's different from the original is the main() function, partially shown in Listing 16-2. Most error handling is omitted; the complete program is available in the book's source code distribution.

```
#include "common_hdrs.h"
#include "time_utils.h"
#include <pthread.h>
--snip--
int main(int argc, char *argv[])
{
    const struct timespec slight_pause = {2,0};
    struct timespec     remaining_sleep;
    pthread_t           sig_thread;
    sigset_t            mask;
    int                 i, fd;
    thread_data         td[NUMTHREADS]; /* Thread data structures
                                           for each thread */

    fd = open("./taskorder", O_WRONLY | O_TRUNC | O_CREAT | O_APPEND, 0644);
    draw_initial_bar(); /* Draw the progress bar. */
    memset(computedby, 0, NUMTHREADS * sizeof (double));

    /* Block likely asynchronous signals and SIGALRM. */
    sigemptyset(&mask);
    sigaddset(&mask, SIGINT);
    // OMITTED: Add other signal to mask.
    sigaddset(&mask, SIGALRM);
    sigprocmask(SIG_BLOCK, &mask, NULL);

    pthread_create(&sig_thread, NULL, sighandler, (void*) &mask);
    alarm(REFRESH_INTERVAL);                    /* Arm the alarm.     */
    for ( long j = 0; j < NUMTHREADS; j++ ) {   /* Create the threads. */
        td[j].fd = fd;
        td[j].id = j;
        pthread_create(&t[j], NULL, long_running_task, (void*) &td[j]);
    }
    for ( i = 0; i < NUMTHREADS; i++ )
        pthread_join(t[i], NULL);
    close(fd);
    if ( -1 == nanosleep(&slight_pause, &remaining_sleep) )
        nanosleep(&remaining_sleep, NULL);
    alarm(0);                                   /* Disarm alarm.     */
    erase_progress_bar();
    printf("Thread#   Percent\n");
    for ( i = 0; i < NUMTHREADS; i++ )
        printf("%d         %f\n", i, 100 * computedby[i]);
    printf("The file ./taskorder has the sequence of thread accesses.\n");
    exit(EXIT_SUCCESS);
}
```

Listing 16-2: The main() function of threaded_progbar.c

I built the executable with

```
$ gcc -D_DEFAULT_SOURCE -DNUMTHREADS=4 -o threaded_progbar -L ../lib\
  -I../include threaded_progress_bar_mutex_synch.c -lspl -lm -lrt -pthread
```

and ran it. After displaying the progress bar growing, the output was:

```
$ ./threaded_progbar
Thread#    Percent
0          26.279767
1          24.309197
2          24.542369
3          24.868667
The file ./taskorder has the sequence of thread accesses.
```

Repeated runs show that the load is balanced fairly evenly among the threads. This is due mostly to the way that the random numbers are generated. The *taskorder* file for this run was:

```
0,1,2,0,3,1,2,1,2,0,3,1,3,0,2,0,2,0,0,1,0,3,1,2,3,0,2,0,1,1,3,0,\
0,2,1,1,3,1,3,0,2,1,1,3,3,0,1,2,1,3,2,1,3,0,1,0,2,0,1,3,1,2,0,0,\
3,2,1,2,2,3,1,0,1,2,3,0,1,2,3,1,3,0,0,3,
```

I wrote an awk script to parse this file to produce the following statistics for the number of times each thread acquired the mutex:

```
0 23
1 24
2 18
3 19
```

As the number of threads increases, contention for the critical section increases, and so does the system overhead. Creating the threads takes time, and each thread is locking and unlocking the mutex, which also takes time. If you increase the number of threads steadily and run the program under the time command, you'll see system time steadily increasing.

MUTEXES: KEEP THEM SHORT AND SWEET

Too much of a good thing is usually not good. A mutex is doing its job if there are usually threads blocked on it. After all, if no thread were ever blocked on a given mutex, then we ought to wonder whether we need it.

On the other hand, every thread blocked on the mutex is wasting its valuable time and not getting any work done. If there are many threads blocked on a mutex, it usually translates to longer running time since the mutex is, in effect, serializing the executable code. It forces each thread to execute that code in sequence.

In general, you should keep your critical sections as short as possible and use the fewest number of them possible. Locking and unlocking mutexes takes time too.

Other Types of Mutexes

The type of a mutex is determined by the mutex attribute structure used to initialize it. There are four possible mutex types:

PTHREAD_MUTEX_NORMAL   The type of mutex we've just examined

PTHREAD_MUTEX_ERRORCHECK   Used during development—instead of dead-locks when it's misused, it generates errors

PTHREAD_MUTEX_RECURSIVE   Can be used whenever a thread needs to lock a mutex more than once, such as locking it within a recursive function

PTHREAD_MUTEX_DEFAULT   Usually the same as PTHREAD_MUTEX_NORMAL

The default type is always PTHREAD_MUTEX_DEFAULT. To set the type of a mutex, use

```
int pthread_mutexattr_settype(pthread_mutexattr_t *attr, int type);
```

passing a pointer to a mutexattr_t structure and the type to which it should be set. Then you can use this mutexattr_t structure to initialize the mutex.

There is no function that, given a mutex, can determine the type of that mutex. The best one can do is to call

```
int pthread_mutexattr_gettype(const pthread_mutexattr_t *restrict attr,
                              int *restrict type);
```

which retrieves the mutex type from a mutexattr_t structure. But since there is no function that retrieves the mutexattr_t structure of a mutex, if a program needs to retrieve the type of a mutex, it needs to have the mutexattr_ structure that was used to initialize the mutex to know the mutex type. This means passing it to the thread's start function.

When a normal mutex is accessed incorrectly, either undefined behavior or deadlock results, depending on how the erroneous access took place. A thread will deadlock if it attempts to relock a mutex that it currently holds. If the mutex type is PTHREAD_MUTEX_ERRORCHECK, then error checking takes place instead of deadlock or undefined behavior. Specifically, if a thread attempts to relock a mutex that it has already locked, the EDEADLK error is returned, and if a thread attempts to unlock a mutex that it has not locked or a mutex that is unlocked, an error is also returned.

Recursive mutexes, meaning those of type PTHREAD_MUTEX_RECURSIVE, can be used when threads need to lock a mutex more than once, as in recursive functions. Basically, the mutex maintains a counter:

- When a thread first acquires the lock, the counter is set to 1.

- Unlike a normal mutex, when a recursive mutex is relocked, rather than deadlocking, the call succeeds and the counter is incremented. A thread can continue to relock the mutex up to some system-defined number of times.

- Each call to unlock the mutex by that same thread that locked it decrements the counter. When the counter reaches 0, the mutex is unlocked and can be acquired by another thread.

- Until the counter equals 0, all other threads attempting to acquire the lock will be blocked on calls to pthread_mutex_lock().

- A thread attempting to unlock a recursive mutex that another thread has locked is returned an error. A thread attempting to unlock an unlocked recursive mutex also receives an error.

Listing 16-3 contains an example of a program that creates two threads that use a recursive mutex to synchronize their accesses to a critical section of a recursive function. The program doesn't do much; it increments a counter and prints a message when the thread is inside its critical section.

recursive _mutex_demo.c
```
#define BOUND 4
pthread_mutex_t mutex;                          /* Lock for CS         */
struct timespec sleeptime = {0, 250000000};     /* 0.25 secs of delay */
int            count = 0;                        /* Shared by threads   */

void up(long int tid)
{
    pthread_mutex_lock(&mutex);
    printf("Thread %ld acquired lock in up();  count = %d\n", tid, count);
    nanosleep(&sleeptime, NULL);
    if ( ++count < BOUND )
        up(tid);
    else {
        count = 0;
        printf("Thread %ld returning from up();  count = %d\n", tid, count);
    }
    pthread_mutex_unlock(&mutex);
}

void *thread_routine(void *data)
{
    up((long) data);
    pthread_exit(NULL);
}

int main(int argc, char *argv[])
{
    pthread_t threads[2];
    pthread_mutexattr_t attr;

    pthread_mutexattr_settype(&attr, PTHREAD_MUTEX_RECURSIVE);
    pthread_mutex_init(&mutex, &attr);
    for ( int t = 0; t < 2; t++ )
```

```
            if ( 0 != pthread_create(&threads[t], NULL, thread_routine,
                                      (void *) t) )
                fatal_error(errno, "pthread_create");

    for ( int t = 0; t < 2; t++ ) {
        pthread_join(threads[t], (void**) NULL);
    }
    return 0;
}
```

Listing 16-3: A program that uses a recursive mutex

Before you run this program or read further, try to predict its output. The
output will show that when a recursive mutex is locked, it can be relocked by
the same thread without error but cannot be acquired by another thread.
Once a thread calls up(), it continues to call it recursively until count reaches
the upper bound. Then it returns from all nested calls. Only when the first
call returns does the other thread run. The output is not displayed here.

Condition Variables

A *condition variable* is a synchronization tool that serves a different purpose
from both mutexes and semaphores. It is an object that allows threads to
wait in a blocked state until some condition becomes true. Using a condition
variable requires associating it with two other entities:

- A Boolean condition, usually containing one or more shared
  variables

- A mutex that serializes the access to the code that tests the Boolean
  condition

There are no functions that connect the condition to the condition variable; it's the programmer's job to preserve this association throughout the
code. Although we don't need to know how a condition variable is implemented to use it, it's helpful to realize that it has two internal components:

- A queue of threads that are blocked on the condition

- A reference to a mutex that is bound to that condition variable

The condition variable can be associated with only a single mutex at any
time. I'll say more about this later. Figure 16-3 depicts the condition variable
object.

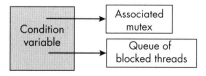

*Figure 16-3: A schematic representation
of a condition variable*

Condition variables are more complex to use than either mutexes or semaphores, mostly because they're more powerful. Before we dive into their details, let's consider the limitations of mutexes so that we understand why condition variables are an important tool to have on hand.

Why Do We Need Condition Variables?

A mutex is a low-level lock and unlock mechanism, intended to prevent simultaneous access to shared variables by more than one thread. It doesn't provide a way for one thread to notify another when some condition has changed its state. There are synchronization problems that can't be solved efficiently with only mutexes. Consider a problem in which there is some condition whose value depends on a shared variable. If that condition must be true for a thread to perform some action, the thread has to repeatedly test the value of the condition while it holds the mutex that protects that shared variable. This repeated testing loop wastes CPU cycles.

To make this concrete, let's reconsider the producer-consumer problem. In Chapter 12, we wrote a solution to this problem using POSIX shared memory and semaphores. It was designed to work with any positive number of producer and consumer processes. Let's try to use a mutex instead of semaphores to solve this problem.

Assume that the global shared variables are as follows:

```
pthread_mutex_t buf_mutex = PTHREAD_MUTEX_INITIALIZER;
size_t          count = 0;      /* Number of filled buffers           */
int             front = 0;      /* Index where consumer gets next item */
int             rear = 0;       /* Index where producer puts next item */
int             buf[BUF_SIZE]; /* Capacity of buffer                  */
```

The producer's main loop is of the form

```
while ( TRUE ) {
    pthread_mutex_lock(&buf_mutex);
    if ( count < BUF_SIZE ) {
        // Generate next data item and store in data.
        buf[rear] = data;
        rear = (rear + 1) % BUF_SIZE;
        count++;
    }
    pthread_mutex_unlock(&buf_mutex);
}
```

and the consumer's is of the form:

```
while ( TRUE ) {
    pthread_mutex_lock(&buf_mutex);
    if ( count > 0 ) {
```

```
        data = buf[front];
        front = (front + 1) % BUF_SIZE;
        count--;
        // Consume data.
    }
    pthread_mutex_unlock(&buf_mutex);
}
```

This code is correct in that it prevents race conditions on the buffer accesses and the updates to count; the problem is its performance. Suppose that the buffer is empty because the producer hasn't produced any data for a while. In each iteration of its loop, the consumer will lock the mutex, test whether there's anything in the buffer to consume (count > 0), and unlock the mutex. It will repeat this over and over, locking, testing, and unlocking until data is available. It would be more efficient if it could just block itself until data was available. This is where condition variables can be used.

The Typical Steps for Using Condition Variables

A condition variable allows a thread that has acquired a mutex but subsequently discovered that some condition is false to relinquish the mutex and block itself in the condition variable's internal queue, all in a single atomic step. The thread then remains blocked in that queue until some other thread, detecting that this condition became true, signals the condition variable, which wakes up one of the waiting threads. The programmer can associate the condition variable with any Boolean condition.

For example, suppose a condition variable named bufspace_available corresponds to there being at least one empty buffer in the buffer pool shared by producer and consumer threads. The condition might be associated with the Boolean expression count < BUF_SIZE, in this case. Then the producer's main loop would consist of the following sequence of actions:

1. Generate data to store into the buffer.

2. Try to acquire and lock a mutex, buf_mutex.

3. If the buffer is full (count == BUF_SIZE), *atomically* release the mutex and wait on bufspace_available's queue.

4. When bufspace_available is signaled because the buffer has space available (count < BUF_SIZE):
    (a) Reacquire the buf_mutex lock.
    (b) Insert the data into the buffer and increment the count.
    (c) Unlock buf_mutex.
    (d) Signal the consumer that there is data in the buffer.

The consumer would have symmetric code.

It's time to look at the *Pthreads* API related to condition variables.

Declaring and Initializing a Condition Variable

A condition variable is declared to be of type `pthread_cond_t`. Condition variable initialization is similar to mutex initialization. There are two ways to initialize a condition variable:

- Statically when it is declared, using the `PTHREAD_COND_INITIALIZER` macro, as in:

  ```
  pthread_cond_t condvar = PTHREAD_COND_INITIALIZER;
  ```

- Dynamically with the `pthread_cond_init()` function, whose prototype is:

  ```
  int pthread_cond_init(pthread_cond_t *restrict cond,
                        const pthread_condattr_t *restrict attr);
  ```

  This function is given the addresses of a condition variable and a condition attribute structure and initializes the condition variable to have the properties of that structure. If the `attr` argument is `NULL`, the condition is given the default attributes. Attempting to initialize an already initialized condition variable results in undefined behavior.

  The call

  ```
  pthread_cond_init(&condvar, NULL);
  ```

is equivalent to the static method except that error checking is performed. On success, `pthread_cond_init()` returns `0`; otherwise, it returns an error code.

Waiting on a Condition Variable

A thread can call one of two functions to wait on a condition variable: an untimed wait and a timed wait. Their prototypes are:

```
int pthread_cond_wait(pthread_cond_t *restrict cond,
                      pthread_mutex_t *restrict mutex);

int pthread_cond_timedwait(pthread_cond_t *restrict cond,
                           pthread_mutex_t *restrict mutex,
                           const struct timespec *restrict abstime);
```

Before a thread calls either of these functions, it must have locked the mutex referred to by the second argument; otherwise, the effect of the call is undefined. Calling either function causes the following two actions to take place atomically:

1. The `mutex` is released from the thread.
2. The thread is blocked on the condition variable `cond`.

The function is atomic in the sense that it guarantees that the calling thread will be blocked on the condition variable regardless of any actions by any other threads between the time it releases the mutex and is moved onto the condition variable's queue.

In the case of the untimed `pthread_cond_wait()`, the calling thread remains blocked in this call until some other thread signals `cond` using either of the two signaling functions about to be described in "Signaling a Condition Variable." If there are multiple threads in the condition variable's queue, it may not be the one to be awakened when the condition is next signaled.

When a thread returns from `pthread_cond_wait()`, the `mutex` is locked and owned by the now-unblocked thread.

In the case of `pthread_cond_timedwait()`, the calling thread remains blocked in this call until either some other thread signals `cond` or the absolute time specified by `abstime` is passed. If the time specified by `abstime` is passed before a thread signals the condition variable, the call returns with the error `ETIMEDOUT`; otherwise, it returns `0`.

ONE MUTEX PER CONDITION VARIABLE

If a condition variable is already associated with a mutex because one or more threads called one of the wait functions on it and are still in its queue, an attempt by any other thread to wait on this condition variable with a different mutex will fail. In other words, calling `pthread_cond_wait(&cond, &mutex)` creates a dynamic binding between cond and mutex that remains in effect as long as at least one thread is blocked on cond.

Signaling a Condition Variable

A thread can send a signal on a condition variable with one of two different functions, whose prototypes are:

```
int pthread_cond_broadcast(pthread_cond_t *cond);
int pthread_cond_signal(pthread_cond_t *cond);
```

Both of these functions unblock threads that are blocked on a condition variable. The difference is that `pthread_cond_signal()` unblocks one of the threads that are blocked on the condition variable, whereas `pthread_cond_broadcast()` unblocks all threads blocked on it. The man page notes that although any thread can call these functions, regardless of whether or not it currently owns the mutex associated with the condition variable, if predictable scheduling of the threads is required, the calling thread should own the mutex associated with the condition variable when it makes the call.

The `pthread_cond_signal()` is intended to unblock a single thread, but implementations of this function may unintentionally wake up more than one thread if more than one are waiting. These unintended wake-ups are called *spurious wake-ups*. They can happen because of the way that the calls are implemented. POSIX.1-2024 explicitly documents that spurious wake-ups may occur: "Correcting this problem would unnecessarily reduce the degree of concurrency in this basic building block for all higher-level synchronization operations."

Because of spurious wake-ups, the fact that a thread returns from a wait on a condition variable does not imply anything about the truth of the condition associated with this condition variable. Therefore, calls to wait on condition variables should be inside a loop, not in a simple if statement. For example, the producer code from earlier should be coded as:

```
// Generate data item to store into the buffer.
pthread_mutex_lock(&buffer_mutex);
while ( count == BUF_SIZE )
    pthread_cond_wait(&bufspace_available, &buf_mutex);
// Add data item to buffer.
pthread_mutex_unlock(&buf_mutex);
pthread_cond_signal(&data_available);
```

It is, in general, safer to code with a loop rather than an if statement, because if you made a logic error elsewhere in your code and it's possible that a thread can be signaled even though the associated condition isn't true, then having the wait occur inside a loop prevents the thread from being woken up erroneously, since it will reacquire the mutex, return from the call, retest the loop condition, and block again.

When multiple threads blocked on a condition variable are all unblocked by a broadcast, the order in which they are unblocked depends upon the scheduling policy. When they become unblocked, they reacquire the mutex associated with the condition variable. Therefore, the order in which they reacquire the mutex is dependent on the scheduling policy.

Condition variables have no record of how many signals have been received at any given time. Therefore, if a thread, say thread1, signals a condition cond before another thread, thread2, calls pthread_cond_wait() on cond, then thread2 will still wait on cond because the signal will have been lost—signals are not saved. Only a signal that arrives after a thread has called one of the wait functions can wake up that calling thread.

The man page clarifies the sense in which pthread_cond_wait() is atomic: When a thread, thread1, calls pthread_cond_wait(), the mutex is unlocked and thread1 is blocked on the condition variable. It is possible for another thread, say thread2, to acquire the mutex after thread1 has released it but *before* it is blocked. If thread2, or any other thread for that matter, signals this condition variable after this mutex has been acquired by another thread, then thread1 will respond to the signal as if it had taken place after it had been blocked. This means that it will be unblocked immediately and reacquire the mutex and the call will return.

Destroying a Condition Variable

When a condition variable is no longer needed, it should be removed with pthread_cond_destroy(), whose prototype is:

```
int pthread_cond_destroy(pthread_cond_t *cond);
```

This function destroys the given condition variable cond, after which it becomes, in effect, uninitialized. A thread can destroy an initialized condition variable only if no threads are currently blocked on it. Attempting to destroy a condition variable upon which other threads are currently blocked results in undefined behavior.

Condition Attributes

Condition variables have just two attributes: the process-shared attribute and the clock attribute. The former allows the condition variable to be accessed by a process other than the one in which it was created, provided that a memory mapping has made this possible. The clock attribute is used to select which clock should be used by the pthread_cond_timedwait() function. The condition variable attribute API consists of the following functions:

```
int pthread_condattr_init(pthread_condattr_t *attr);
int pthread_condattr_destroy(pthread_condattr_t *attr);
int pthread_condattr_getclock(const pthread_condattr_t *restrict attr,
                              clockid_t *restrict clock_id);
int pthread_condattr_setclock(pthread_condattr_t *attr, clockid_t clock_id);
int pthread_condattr_getpshared(const pthread_condattr_t *restrict attr,
                                int *restrict pshared);
int pthread_condattr_setpshared(pthread_condattr_t *attr, int pshared);
```

They're described by their respective man pages.

A Multithreaded Multiple Producer, Multiple Consumer Program

We'll use condition variables together with mutexes to create a multiple producer, multiple consumer program in which the producers and consumers are threads. We can base the design of the producer on the initial logic that I proposed in "The Typical Steps for Using Condition Variables" on page 753. The design of the consumer will be symmetric.

To simplify the program and reduce the amount of code, I've made the following design decisions:

- The data that producers "produce" will be integers.

- Each producer produces the same fixed number of items and then terminates.

- Each producer and consumer will have a program-given internal ID; the data produced by each producer will be derived from that ID and the fixed number of items in such a way that no two producers generate the same value.

- Consumers will run as long as there are active producers and exit when none are left.

The program will need the following file-scoped macros, constants, and variables:

```
#define MAX_ITEMS   20   /* Default for MaxItems (below) */
#define BUFFER_SIZE 16   /* Fixed buffer capacity        */

pthread_mutex_t buf_mutex       = PTHREAD_MUTEX_INITIALIZER;
pthread_mutex_t prodcount_mutex = PTHREAD_MUTEX_INITIALIZER;
pthread_mutex_t conscount_mutex = PTHREAD_MUTEX_INITIALIZER;
pthread_cond_t  space_available = PTHREAD_COND_INITIALIZER;
pthread_cond_t  data_available  = PTHREAD_COND_INITIALIZER;

int producer_count;        /* Number of current active producers      */
int consumer_count;        /* Number of current active consumers      */
int MaxItems = MAX_ITEMS;  /* Number of items each producer generates */
int front    = 0;          /* Index of next read from buffer          */
int rear     = 0;          /* Index of next write into buffer         */
int buffer[BUFFER_SIZE];   /* Buffer for storing data                 */
int buf_count;             /* Number of items currently in buffer     */
```

The condition variable space_available will be associated with the condition in which the buffer is not full, and data_available will be associated with the condition in which the buffer had data that hasn't been consumed. The buf_mutex will control access to the shared buffer and the index variables that producers and consumers update to access the elements of that buffer. I'll explain the need for the other two mutex variables, prodcount_mutex and conscount_mutex, shortly.

The producers will call add_buffer() to add a new item to the buffer queue, and consumers will call get_buffer() to retrieve the item in the front of the buffer queue. The two functions are shown next:

```
void add_buffer(long data)
{
    buffer[rear] = data;
    rear = (rear + 1) % BUFFER_SIZE;
    buf_count++;
}

int get_buffer()
{
    long v = buffer[front];
    front = (front + 1) % BUFFER_SIZE;
    buf_count--;
    return v;
}
```

These functions are called within critical sections protected by buf_mutex.

Producer Code

Based on the logic described in that earlier section, the producer thread's start function should look like Listing 16-4.

producer()
```
void *producer(void *data)
{
    int  i = 0;
    long tid = (long) data;
    while ( ++i <= MaxItems ) {
        pthread_mutex_lock(&buf_mutex);
        while ( BUFFER_SIZE == buf_count )
            pthread_cond_wait(&space_available, &buf_mutex);
        add_buffer(tid * (MaxItems) + i);
        pthread_cond_signal(&data_available);
        pthread_mutex_unlock(&buf_mutex);
    }
    --snip--
}
```

Listing 16-4: The producer thread start function

Each producer locks the mutex and then checks the buffer full condition. If it's full (BUFFER_SIZE == buf_count), it blocks itself on the space_available condition variable. The call to pthread_cond_wait() is in a while loop because of possible spurious wake-ups, discussed earlier. When space becomes available, a consumer thread will signal this condition variable, and some producer will wake up and proceed to the next instruction. The scheduling algorithm ensures that no producer will wait indefinitely in the condition variable queue.

In each iteration, the producer adds the number tid * MaxItems + i to the buffer. This implies that the producer with an ID tid adds the numbers tid * MaxItems + 1, tid * MaxItems + 2, . . . , tid * MaxItems + MaxItems, which equals (tid + 1) * MaxItems, guaranteeing that the numbers each generates are unique to it. For example, if MaxItems = 10, producer p generates $10p + 1$, $10p + 2$, $10p + 3$, . . . , $10(p + 1)$.

After adding the data to the buffer, a producer signals the data_available condition variable to wake up any consumers that were blocked waiting for some data to arrive in the buffer. It releases the mutex and repeats these steps until it has produced MaxItems data elements.

When the producer has exited its loop, it prints a message and decrements the count of active producers. Since all producers can modify this count, this code is protected by locking the prodcount_mutex. This is the code that was snipped from the start function shown in Listing 16-4:

```
printf("Producer %ld is exiting\n", tid);
pthread_mutex_lock(&prodcount_mutex);
producer_count--;
if ( producer_count == 0 )
    while ( consumer_count > 0 )
        pthread_cond_signal(&data_available);
```

```
pthread_mutex_unlock(&prodcount_mutex);
pthread_exit(NULL);
```

The very last producer to exit needs to make sure that no consumers are left waiting for more data. It checks whether consumer_count > 0. If so, it signals data_available for each consumer. There is no harm in sending too many signals, because consumers, like producers, wait inside a while loop.

Consumer Code

The consumer design is almost symmetric to that of the producer. It has to be different because a consumer thread cannot let itself be in a situation in which it's waiting for data but all of the producers have exited. Therefore, its main loop checks this possibility, as shown in Listing 16-5.

consumer()
```
void *consumer(void *data)
{
    long tid = (long) data;
    while ( TRUE ) {
        pthread_mutex_lock(&buf_mutex);
        while ( 0 == buf_count ) {
            if ( producer_count > 0 )   /* Any producers left? */
                pthread_cond_wait(&data_available,&buf_mutex);
            else { /* No producers left, so clean up and exit. */
                pthread_mutex_unlock(&buf_mutex);
                printf("Consumer %ld exiting because all producers left.\n",
                        tid);
                pthread_mutex_lock(&conscount_mutex);
                consumer_count--;
                pthread_mutex_unlock(&conscount_mutex);
                pthread_exit(NULL);
            }
        }
        long v = get_buffer();  /* If we reach here, data's available. */
        printf("Consumer %ld received %ld from buffer; buffer size = %d\n",
                tid, v, buf_count);
        pthread_cond_signal(&space_available);
        pthread_mutex_unlock(&buf_mutex);
    }
    pthread_exit(NULL);
}
```

Listing 16-5: The consumer thread start function

When a consumer finds that buf_count is 0, it blocks itself on the condition variable data_available. When it wakes up, it retrieves data from the buffer, prints a message, signals the space_available condition variable in case any producers are blocked in it, and unlocks the mutex.

The main program does very little. Since we might want to experiment with the numbers of producers and consumers, as well as the amount of data, it should have command line options to control for these. Therefore, the program's synopsis is

pthread_prod_cons [-p *num*] [-c *num*] [-m *num*]

in which the supplied numbers should be non-negative. The -p controls the number of producers (default = 1), the -c the number of consumers (default = 1), and the -m the total number of items generated by each producer (default = 20).

The main program is shown in Listing 16-6, with the option-parsing code and some error handling removed. The complete program, *pthread_prod_cons.c*, is available in the book's source code distribution.

pthread
_prodcons.c
main()
```
int main(int argc, char *argv[])
{
    long      i;               /* Thread data                        */
    int       numConsumers = 1; /* Defaults                          */
    int       numProducers = 1;
    pthread_t *producer_thread;  /* Dynamically allocated thread ID arrays */
    pthread_t *consumer_thread;
    // OMITTED: Option parsing

    producer_thread = (pthread_t*) calloc(numProducers, sizeof(pthread_t));
    consumer_thread = (pthread_t*) calloc(numConsumers, sizeof(pthread_t));
    producer_count = numProducers;
    consumer_count = numConsumers;
    if ( producer_thread == NULL || consumer_thread == NULL )
        fatal_error(errno, "calloc");
    buf_count = 0;

    /* Create consumers first so that signals from producers aren't lost. */
    for ( i = 0; i < numConsumers; i++ )
        pthread_create(&consumer_thread[i], NULL, consumer, (void*) i);
    for ( i = 0; i < numProducers; i++ )
        pthread_create(&producer_thread[i], NULL, producer, (void*) i);

    /* Wait for all child threads. */
    for ( i = 0; i < numProducers; i++ )
        pthread_join(producer_thread[i], NULL);
    for ( i = 0; i < numConsumers; i++ )
        pthread_join(consumer_thread[i], NULL);

    free(producer_thread);  /* Clean up. */
    free(consumer_thread);
    exit(EXIT_SUCCESS);
}
```

Listing 16-6: The main program for pthread_prodcons.c

We can run this with any numbers of producer and consumer threads. The output is designed so that we can check whether it's working as we expect. In particular, each time that a consumer thread retrieves an item, it writes a message to standard output. What must be true is that the number of messages equals the total number of producers times the maximum number of items per producer. For example:

```
$ ./pthread_prod_cons -m 100 -p8 -c4
Consumer 0 received 1 from buffer; buffer size = 9
Consumer 0 received 2 from buffer; buffer size = 8
--snip--
Consumer 1 received 700 from buffer; buffer size = 1
Producer 5 is exiting
Consumer 1 received 600 from buffer; buffer size = 0
Consumer 0 exiting because all producers left.
Consumer 1 exiting because all producers left.
Consumer 2 exiting because all producers left.
Consumer 3 exiting because all producers left.
```

The order in which consumers receive and print data is not controlled, but if the program is working correctly, the last lines of output will be those of exiting consumers.

Barrier Synchronization

In some applications, the individual threads need to periodically wait for all of the threads to reach a synchronization point before any of them proceed. This is common in multithreaded programs in which large numbers of threads have divided up a large dataset and each has computed some partial results, but all need the partial results of the other threads before they proceed. Programs that divide a computation into stages have to work this way. For example, the threads in a multithreaded version of the Floyd–Warshall algorithm for computing shortest paths in a finite graph need to synchronize this way. A more entertaining example is a multithreaded version of Conway's *Game of Life*.

The *Game of Life* simulates the growth of a colony of organisms over time. Imagine a finite, two-dimensional grid in which each cell represents an organism. Time advances in discrete time steps, t_0, t_1, t_2, ad infinitum. Whether or not an organism survives in cell (i, j) at time t_{k+1} depends on how many organisms are living in the adjacent surrounding cells at time t_k. Whether or not an organism is born into an empty cell (i, j) is also determined by the state of the adjacent cells at the given time. The exact rules aren't relevant.

A simple multithreaded simulation of the progression of states of the grid is to create a unique thread to simulate each individual cell and to create two grids, A and B, of the same dimensions. The initial state of the population is assigned to grid A. At each time step t_k, the thread responsible for cell (i, j) would perform the following tasks:

1. For cell A[i, j], examine the states of each of its eight neighboring cells A[m, n] and set the value of B[i, j] accordingly.

2. When all other cells have finished their step 1, copy B[i, j] to A[i, j], and repeat steps 1 and 2.

Notice that this solution requires that each cell wait for all other cells to reach the same point in the code. This could be achieved with a combination of mutexes and condition variables. Let's see how we could implement this.

The main program would initialize the value of a counter variable (count) to 0. Assuming there are N threads, each would execute a loop of the form:

```
loop forever {
    update_cell(i,j);
    pthread_mutex_lock(&update_mutex);
    count++;
    if ( count < N )
        pthread_cond_wait(&all_threads_ready, &update_mutex);
    /* count reached N, so all threads proceed. */
    pthread_cond_broadcast(&all_threads_ready);
    count--;
    pthread_mutex_unlock(&update_mutex);
    pthread_mutex_lock(&count_mutex);
    if ( count > 0 )
        pthread_cond_wait(&all_threads_at_start, &count_mutex);
    pthread_cond_broadcast(&all_threads_at_start);
    pthread_mutex_unlock(&count_mutex);
}
```

Essentially, after each thread updates its cell, it tries to acquire a mutex named update_mutex. The cell that acquires the mutex increments count and then waits on a condition variable, all_threads_ready, associated with the predicate count < N. As it releases update_mutex, the next thread does the same and so on until all but one thread has been blocked on the condition variable. Eventually, the last thread acquires the mutex, increments count and, finding count == N, issues a broadcast on the condition variable all_threads_ready, which unblocks all of the waiting threads, one by one.

One by one, each thread then decrements count inside the region of code locked by update_mutex. If each were allowed to cycle back to the top of the loop, this code would not work, because one thread could quickly speed around and increment count so that it equaled N again even though the others had not even started their updates. Instead, no thread is allowed to go back to the top of the loop until count reaches 0. This is achieved by using a second condition variable, all_threads_at_start. All threads will block on this condition except the one that sets the value of count to 0 when it decrements it. When that happens, every thread is unblocked and they all start this cycle all over again. This is visualized in Figure 16-4.

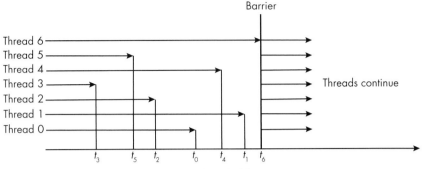

Figure 16-4: A conceptualization of a barrier synchronization point showing what time each thread reached it and that they all resume at the same time when the last thread arrives at it

This does work, roughly, but it adds so much serial code to the parallel algorithm that it defeats the purpose of using multiple threads in the first place! It ignores the possibility of spurious wake-ups and would be even more complex if these were taken into account. Fortunately, there is a simpler solution: The *Pthreads* library has a barrier synchronization primitive that solves this synchronization problem efficiently and elegantly.

A *barrier synchronization point* is an instruction in a program at which the executing thread must wait until all participating threads have reached that same point. If you've ever been in a group of people being taken on a guided tour of a facility or an institution of some kind, then you might have experienced this type of synchronization. The guide will wait for all members of the group to reach a certain point, and only then will they allow the group to move to the next set of locations.

Pthreads Barriers

The *Pthreads* implementation of a barrier lets the programmer initialize the barrier to the number of threads that must reach the barrier in order for it to be opened. There are only three functions in the *Pthreads* API specifically related to barriers: one to initialize a barrier, one to destroy one, and a third to wait on one.

A barrier is declared as a variable of type pthread_barrier_t. The function to initialize a barrier has the prototype:

```
int pthread_barrier_init(pthread_barrier_t *restrict barrier,
                         const pthread_barrierattr_t *restrict attr,
                         unsigned count);
```

It's given the address of a barrier; the address of a barrier attribute structure, which may be NULL to use the default attributes; and a positive value count. The count argument specifies the number of threads that must reach the barrier before any of them successfully return from the call. If the function succeeds, it returns 0. The function results are undefined if a thread attempts to initialize an existing barrier on which one or more threads are waiting.

A thread calls

```
int pthread_barrier_wait(pthread_barrier_t *barrier);
```

to wait at the barrier given by the argument. When the number of threads that have called `pthread_barrier_wait()` on a given barrier equals the count with which it was initialized, all threads waiting on the barrier return from the call. The constant `PTHREAD_BARRIER_SERIAL_THREAD` is returned to exactly one of these threads and 0 is returned to each of the remaining threads. There is no particular rule for which thread receives the special return value. At this point, the barrier is reset to the state it had as a result of the most recent call to `pthread_barrier_init()`.

Some programs may not need to take advantage of the fact that a single thread received the value `PTHREAD_BARRIER_SERIAL_THREAD`, but others may find it useful, particularly if exactly one thread has to perform a task when the barrier has been reached. A thread can check for errors when it returns from waiting at a barrier with

```
retval = pthread_barrier_wait(&barrier);
if ( PTHREAD_BARRIER_SERIAL_THREAD != retval && 0 != retval )
    pthread_exit((void*) retval);
```

which will force a thread to exit if it did not get one of the nonerror values. The return value can be retrieved by another thread that calls `pthread_join()` for this thread.

A barrier is destroyed using

```
int pthread_barrier_destroy(pthread_barrier_t *barrier);
```

which destroys the barrier and releases any resources used by it. The effect of any subsequent use of the barrier is undefined until the barrier is reinitialized by another call to `pthread_barrier_init()`. The results are undefined if `pthread_barrier_destroy()` is called when any thread is blocked on the barrier or if this function is called with an uninitialized barrier.

A Program Using Barrier Synchronization

Some accounting and system administrative commands need to compute the sums of various system statistics. For example, system monitors compute and display the amount of virtual memory currently used by all processes, as well as other sums, such as the total number of bytes received over a network interface, and commands such as `vmstat` and `iostat` report accumulated amounts of other resource consumption. When the amount of data is large enough, the computations performed by these types of programs can be sped up by multithreading them.

As exercise in multithreading with barrier synchronization, we'll develop a program, `vmem_usage` (short for "virtual memory usage"), that displays on standard output the total amount of virtual memory in KB used by all processes at the time that it's run. Writing this program will integrate the work we did in Chapter 10 in our implementation of a simplified ps command and the work in Chapter 7 in directory scanning with the ideas from this chapter about multithreading and synchronization barriers. In addition, we'll develop an algorithm for this program that will have much broader application than this one particular command. We can make the number of threads an argument to the program so that we can see the effect on performance easily, by running it with different numbers.

Design Strategies

The sequential algorithm for adding N numbers in a linear array of length N performs $N - 1$ additions. When N is very large, we can divide the work up among a number of threads. Let's consider the possible ways that the threads can cooperate in computing the total, the goal being to minimize running time. Assume in the following that p is the number of threads. The possible choices include:

- Declare a global variable named total. Every time that a thread needs to add one of its elements to total, it locks a mutex, adds the element to it, and unlocks the mutex. This is a poor idea because no two threads will be able to add their values at the same time, effectively serializing the summation, and the multithreaded program would take even longer than the sequential one because of all of the mutex operations!

- Assign each thread approximately N/p consecutive array elements. Each thread computes a partial sum of these elements and then adds its partial sum to total. Each thread would therefore perform about $N/p - 1$ additions to compute its partial sum, all concurrently with the other threads. Each thread would add its partial sum to total by locking a mutex, updating total, and unlocking the mutex. This serializes the updates to total and greatly improves the running time. In the worst case, it could require p additions, performed in sequence, to get the final value of total.

- Assign each thread approximately N/p consecutive array elements as just described, but when a thread finishes, it waits at a barrier until all threads have finished. When all threads reach the barrier, they can add their partial sums together with a divide-and-conquer strategy in such a way that the partial sums can be added together in about $\log_2 p$ steps.

The last choice is the best. Let's assume that the program creates an array named partial_sum of length p. Thread t stores its partial sum in partial _sum[t]. Somehow the threads need to add the elements in this array using a divide-and-conquer algorithm.

Parallel Reduction

When a mathematical expression such as $1 + 2 + 3 + 4$ is replaced by its value, 10, we say that it's been *reduced*. In mathematics, *reduction* is the rewriting of an expression into a simpler form. Binary arithmetic operators such as addition, multiplication, and maximum are associative, which means that

$$a + (b + c) = (a + b) + c$$

and:

$$\max(a, \max(b, c)) = \max(\max(a, b), c)$$

Operations with this property are amenable to parallelization because the operations can be applied in any order in parallel. An algorithm that performs a reduction such as this is called a *parallel reduction algorithm*.

We can add the elements of an array of size p in parallel with a divide-and-conquer algorithm as follows. Let's assume initially that p is a power of 2, say $p = 2^m$. We'll also assume that each thread has a unique ID in the interval $[0, p - 1]$.

1. The set of thread IDs is divided into a lower half and an upper half. Every thread t in the lower half has a *mate* in the upper half defined to be $t + p/2$. Correspondingly we'll say t is the mate of $t + p/2$. If $p = 16$, for example, then set of all mates is $(0,8), (1,9), \ldots, (7,15)$.

2. Each thread waits at a synchronization barrier until all threads have reached it.

3. Each thread in the lower half adds its mate's value to its own.

4. Since all values in the upper half have been added to corresponding values in the lower half, the upper half isn't needed any more, and the algorithm repeats but with the lower half treated as the entire array. In other words, the lower half is divided in a lower half of itself and an upper half of itself (by setting $p = p/2$). If p was originally 16, it is now 8 and the mates are $(0,4), (1,5), (2,6),$ and $(3,7)$. If the size of the set is greater than 1, go back to step 2.

5. When the set size is 1, the thread with ID 0 contains the total.

Figure 16-5 illustrates the flow of data for an array A of size 16. An arrow from element A[k] to element A[j] represents adding of A[k] to A[j].

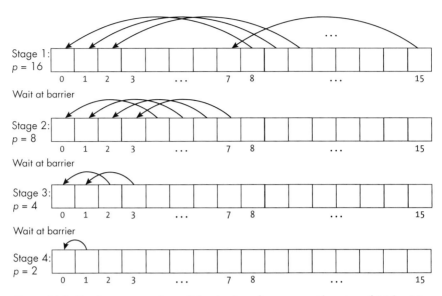

Figure 16-5: The four stages of parallel reduction of an array with a size of 16 by 16 threads

This algorithm takes $O(\log(p))$ steps when p is a power of 2. When p is not a power of 2, it has to do a bit more work, because there will be an unmated array element in the last position of the array. In this case, the thread with ID 0 just adds its value to its own in addition to adding its mate's value. The entire running time for the summation is on the order of $O((N/p) + \log(p))$.

The reduction algorithm executed in parallel by each thread is shown in Listing 16-7.

```
/* Executing thread's ID is tid. */
while ( p > 1 ) {
    pthread_barrier_wait(&barrier);/* Wait for all threads to reach barrier.*/
    if ( p % 2 == 1 && tid == 0 )       /* If thread[0] and p is odd number,
    ❶ partial_sum[0] += partial_sum[p-1]; add last element to 0th.        */
    p = p / 2;                     /* Iterate over lower half next time.    */
    if ( tid < p )                 /* If I'm in lower half, get mate's value. */
        partial_sum[tid] = partial_sum[tid] + partial_sum[tid+p];
}
```

Listing 16-7: The parallel sum reduction algorithm

The thread that owns element 0 of the array adds the last element of the array ❶ to element 0 if p is odd. Since this divides the array in half each time, after $\lceil log_2(p) \rceil$ iterations, it stops.

Program Design

The program consists of two separate stages. The first stage collects the data that will be summed, namely the total virtual memory size of each process. The second stage is the summation of that data. By separating out the two tasks, we can replace the first stage easily enough so that, instead of adding virtual memory sizes, it can add any other data, as long as it stores it in an array of the same type. The virtual memory size that the program will use is the value from the */proc[pid]/stat* file's 23rd field, which the documentation states is the process's virtual memory size. The same value is available in the */proc[pid]/status* file, measured in KB, on the line labeled VmSize:.

The program will declare the following data and types in file scope:

```
#define MAX_LINE   512          /* Size of buffers allocated for input */
long            *partial_sum; /* Array of partial sums of data       */
long            *vmsizes;     /* Dynamically allocated array of data */
pthread_barrier_t barrier;    /* Barrier for threads to synchronize  */


/* Data structure passed to each thread start function */
typedef struct _task_data
{
    int   first;        /* Index of first element for thread */
    int   last;         /* Index of last element for thread  */
    int   task_id;      /* Thread's program ID               */
    int   num_threads;  /* Total number of threads           */
    long *data;         /* Copy of pointer to array of data  */
} task_data;
```

The program will use the following functions:

```
/* Extract the 23rd field from the buffer and store into vsize. */
void extract_vmsize_from_buffer(char *buf, long int *vsize);


/* Gets the virtual memory size in /proc/[pid]/stat and stores in vmdata[i] */
void get_vmsize(const struct dirent *direntp, int i, long *vmdata);


/* Creates an array containing the virtual memory sizes of all processes,
   returning the size in *n. Program must free array. */
void get_all_vmsizes(long **array, long *n);


/* Thread start function. Adds the elements of thread_data->data. */
void *sum_reduce(void *thread_data);


/* Compute the sum of values[0]...values[size-1] with num_threads threads. */
long compute_sum(long *values, int size, int num_threads);
```

Let's look at the program in top-down order, starting with main(). To save space, the main program is displayed without most error handling in Listing 16-8.

```
vmem_usage.c  int main(int argc, char *argv[])
     main()  {
                long array_size;  /* Number of processes, and thus array size */
                long sum;         /* Total in kbytes                          */
                int  retval;      /* Return from call to get command line arg */
                int  num_threads; /* Number of threads this program will use  */
```

```
        if ( argc < 2 )    /* If no argument, use just one thread.    */
            num_threads = 1;

        retval = get_int(argv[1], NON_NEG_ONLY, &num_threads, NULL);
        if ( 0 >= num_threads )
            fatal_error(-1, "Negative number of threads");

        /* Get the virtual memory sizes of all processes; store in vmsizes. */
    ❶ get_all_vmsizes(&vmsizes, &array_size);

        /* Call a function that computes the sum, passing the
           array of data, its length, and the number of threads. */
        sum = compute_sum(vmsizes, array_size, num_threads);
        printf("%10ld KB\n", sum);
        free (vmsizes);
        return 0;
    }
```

Listing 16-8: The main program for vmem_usage.c

The function that gets the virtual memory sizes, get_all_vmsizes(), ❶ is based on the printallprocs() function used in the *spl_ps.c* program from Chapter 10. The difference between them is that, rather than calling readdir() repeatedly, this uses the scandir() function to populate an array of pointers to dirent structures, with a structure for each subdirectory within */proc* that represents a process. It is shown in Listing 16-9. We can easily modify this program so that it outputs the totals for a different set of process metrics.

```
get_all   void get_all_vmsizes(long **array, long *n)
_vmsizes()  {
                struct dirent **namelist;
                long           i = 0;

                errno = 0;
                if ( ((*n) = scandir("/proc", &namelist, numeric_dir_filter, NULL)) < 0 )
                    fatal_error(errno, "scandir");

                if ( NULL == (*array = (long*) calloc((*n), sizeof(long))) )
                    fatal_error(errno, "malloc");
                while ( i < (*n) - 1 ) {
                ❶ get_vmsize(namelist[i], i, *array);
                    free(namelist[i]);
                    i++;
                }
                free(namelist);
            }
```

Listing 16-9: The function that fills an array with the virtual memory sizes of all active processes

It uses a filtering function (numeric_dir_filter()) that limits namelist to contain only pointers to dirent structures of directories whose names are numeric. The filter function is not shown here. (See Chapter 7 to review filter functions or read the scandir(3) man page.) The call to get_vmsize() ❶ opens the *stat* file in the directory pointed to by namelist[i], parses the line in that file to get the virtual memory size of that process, and copies its value into array[i].

Its code, without any error handling, is displayed in Listing 16-10.

get_vmsize()
```
void get_vmsize(const struct dirent *direntp, int i, long *vmdata)
{
    char    pathname[PATH_MAX];      /* Pathname to file to open        */
    size_t  len = MAX_LINE;          /* Length of line getline() returned */
    FILE    *fp;                     /* File stream to read             */
    char    *buf;                    /* To store line from file         */
    long    vsize;                   /* Virtual memory size in bytes    */

    buf = calloc(MAX_LINE, 1);       /* Allocate buffer for getline(). */
    memset(pathname, '\0', PATH_MAX); /* Zero memory for path name.     */
    sprintf(pathname, "/proc/%s/stat", direntp->d_name);
    fp = fopen(pathname, "r");               /* Open file.             */
    getline(&buf, &len, fp );                /* Read the line.         */
    extract_vmsize_from_buffer(buf, &vsize); /* Parse line in buf.     */
    vmdata[i] = vsize/1024;                  /* Express in KB.         */
    free(buf);
}
```

Listing 16-10: The function that gets the virtual memory size of a single process whose directory pointer is passed to it

The extract_vmsize_from_buffer() function extracts the 23rd field in the *stat* file, which contains the virtual memory size in bytes. The program converts it to KB before storing it into the array. This function is not shown here. We could also get this same value from the *status* file in that directory, but the algorithm would have to read and parse more lines, similar to the *ancestors.c* program from Chapter 10. This solution is faster.

The remaining part of the program is the function that computes the array totals. The compute_sum() function encapsulates all of this logic, creating the threads and calling the thread start function, sum_reduce(), shown next in Listing 16-11. The compute_sum() function follows after that.

sum_reduce()
```
void *sum_reduce(void *thread_data)
{
    task_data *t_data; /* Thread data passed to each thread          */
    int       tid;     /* Thread internal ID                         */
    int       half;    /* Half the size of the partial_sums array    */
    int       retval;

    t_data = (task_data*) thread_data; /* Cast argument pointer. */
```

```
        tid    = t_data->task_id;          /* Get thread ID.         */

        /* Compute thread tid's partial sum sequentially: */
        partial_sum[tid] = 0;
        for ( int k = t_data->first; k <= t_data->last; k++ )
            partial_sum[tid] += t_data->data[k];

        /* Start the parallel reduction. Divide the array in half. */
        half = t_data->num_threads;
        while ( half > 1 ) { /* Repeat until sum is in partial_sum[0]. */
    ❶      retval = pthread_barrier_wait(&barrier);
            if ( PTHREAD_BARRIER_SERIAL_THREAD != retval && 0 != retval )
                pthread_exit((void*) 0);
            if ( half % 2 == 1 && tid == 0 )
                partial_sum[0] += partial_sum[half-1];
            half = half/2;      /* Reduce array size.                 */
            if ( tid < half )   /* If I am lower half mate, add mate to me. */
                partial_sum[tid] += partial_sum[tid+half];
        }
        pthread_exit((void*) 0);
    }
```

Listing 16-11: The thread start function, in which each thread computes a partial sum of its share of the array and then participates in a parallel reduction

This is where the barrier is used. No thread can advance past the barrier ❶ until all threads have reached this same place in the algorithm.

This thread start function is called by compute_sum(), which is displayed in part in Listing 16-12. Some error handling is removed.

compute_sum()
```
long compute_sum(long *values, int size, int num_threads)
{
    int        t;
    pthread_t *threads;
    task_data *thread_data;
    long       sum;

    pthread_attr_init(&attr);
    pthread_attr_setdetachstate(&attr, PTHREAD_CREATE_JOINABLE);

    /* Allocate the array of threads, task_data structures, data, and sums. */
    threads     = calloc(num_threads, sizeof(pthread_t));
    thread_data = calloc(num_threads, sizeof(task_data));
    partial_sum = calloc(num_threads, sizeof(double));
    // OMITTED: Check for errors.

    /* Initialize a barrier with a count equal to the number of threads. */
    pthread_barrier_init(&barrier, NULL, num_threads);
```

```
for ( t = 0; t < num_threads; t++ ) {
    thread_data[t].first       = (t * size)/num_threads;
    thread_data[t].last        = ((t + 1) * size)/num_threads - 1;
    thread_data[t].task_id     = t;
    thread_data[t].num_threads = num_threads;
    thread_data[t].data        = values;
    pthread_create(&threads[t], NULL, sum_reduce, (void*) &thread_data[t]);
}
for ( t = 0; t < num_threads; t++ )            /* Join all threads. */
    pthread_join(threads[t], (void**) NULL);
pthread_barrier_destroy(&barrier);
sum = partial_sum[0];
// OMITTED: Free all dynamically allocated memory.
return(sum);
}
```

Listing 16-12: The function that sets up all threads and thread data for execution and then creates the threads and joins them

The complete program, *vmem_usage.c*, is available in the book's source code distribution. A few runs of it with varying numbers of threads, run under the bash time command, show that there isn't a significant change in running time as the number of threads increases, but if that number is too large, the running time gets much worse because of the overhead of creating the threads. Here are a few runs to illustrate:

```
$ time ./vmem_usage 1
345082208  KB
real    0m0.011s
user    0m0.005s
sys     0m0.006s
$ time ./vmem_usage 4
345082208  KB
real    0m0.011s
user    0m0.006s
sys     0m0.004s
$ time ./vmem_usage 64
345082208  KB
real    0m0.015s
user    0m0.010s
sys     0m0.015s
```

This particular example doesn't show the benefits of multithreading in terms of runtime because the amount of data is small. I leave it as an exercise to replace the get_all_vmsizes() function with one that creates extremely large arrays of arbitrary data, just to see the effect on performance of increasing the number of threads.

Read-Write Locks

A mutex is a simple synchronization tool; it has just two states, locked and unlocked, and only one thread can lock it at a time. In some applications, a more sophisticated tool is needed. For instance, consider a multithreaded program that maintains a large dataset in which a single thread updates the dataset occasionally but multiple threads read it frequently. In this case:

- Reading threads should be allowed simultaneous access to the database.

- Writing threads must have exclusive access to the database when they write to it because during a write operation, the data might be in an unstable state.

This is a form of *categorical mutual exclusion*, which is a type of mutual exclusion based on the category of a process: A thread in the reader category being in a critical section does not exclude other threads in that same category, but the presence of a thread in the writer category in the critical section excludes threads from all categories.

It would be convenient if there were some mechanism that would allow this type of synchronization control. Searching for the keywords *reader* and *writer* in the man pages comes up empty, but the following search is successful:

```
$ apropos -s2,3 -a read write pthread
pthread_rwlock_destroy (3posix) - destroy and initialize a read-write lock...
pthread_rwlock_rdlock (3posix) - lock a read-write lock object for reading
--snip--
```

The POSIX threads API provides a tool called a *read-write lock*. Multiple readers can lock a read-write lock without blocking each other yet block writers from accessing it. If a single writer acquires the lock, it obtains exclusive access to it; any thread, whether a reader or a writer, will be blocked if it attempts to acquire the lock while the writer holds it.

This property of read-write locks allows for a higher degree of concurrency than a mutex. Unlike mutexes, they have three possible states:

- Locked in read mode

- Locked in write mode

- Unlocked

For simplicity, I may sometimes call a read-write lock that's currently locked for reading a *read lock* and one that's currently locked for writing a *write lock*. Multiple threads can hold a read-write lock in read mode, but only a single thread can hold a read-write lock in write mode. In effect, read locks can be shared, but write locks are exclusive; they're held by one thread at a time. This same effect could be achieved, although with significant overhead, with a combination of condition variables and mutexes; the *Pthreads* read-write lock API simplifies programming for us.

Read-Write Lock API Overview

Let's begin with a big picture of the read-write lock API. Because of their complexity, there are more functions for locking and unlocking read-write locks than for simple mutexes. The prototypes for the functions are listed by category here. A thread wishing to acquire a read-write lock for reading uses a different set of functions than one that wants to write. We'll examine their semantics afterward.

Initializing and Destroying Read-Write Locks

Like the other POSIX synchronization primitives, there are static and dynamic ways to initialize a read-write lock and a single function to destroy one:

```
int pthread_rwlock_init(pthread_rwlock_t *restrict rwlock,
                        const pthread_rwlockattr_t *restrict attr);
pthread_rwlock_t rwlock = PTHREAD_RWLOCK_INITIALIZER;
int pthread_rwlock_destroy(pthread_rwlock_t *rwlock);
```

The initializer macro PTHREAD_RWLOCK_INITIALIZER is equivalent to calling pthread _rwlock_init() with a NULL second argument.

Locking for Reading

Like locking a mutex, there are three ways to lock a read-write lock for reading:

```
int pthread_rwlock_rdlock(pthread_rwlock_t *rwlock);
int pthread_rwlock_tryrdlock(pthread_rwlock_t *rwlock);
int pthread_rwlock_timedrdlock(pthread_rwlock_t *restrict rwlock,
                               const struct timespec *restrict abstime);
```

The pthread_rwlock_tryrdlock and pthread_rwlock_timedrdlock versions are similar to the corresponding locking functions of a mutex.

Locking for Writing

There are also three different functions that will lock a read-write lock for writing, with analogous meanings:

```
int pthread_rwlock_wrlock(pthread_rwlock_t *rwlock);
int pthread_rwlock_trywrlock(pthread_rwlock_t *rwlock);
int pthread_rwlock_timedwrlock(pthread_rwlock_t *restrict rwlock,
                               const struct timespec *restrict abstime);
```

Notice the structure of these function names. The suffix of the function name, such as _wrlock, indicates the mode of the lock. The read versions have the suffix _rdlock.

Unlocking

There's but a single function to unlock a read-write lock:

```
int pthread_rwlock_unlock(pthread_rwlock_t *rwlock);
```

This unlocks the lock regardless of whether it was held for reading or writing.

Working with Attributes

Although these locks don't have many attributes that we're likely to set, the functions that do so follow:

```
int pthread_rwlockattr_init(pthread_rwlockattr_t *attr);
int pthread_rwlockattr_destroy(pthread_rwlockattr_t *attr);
int pthread_rwlockattr_getpshared(const pthread_rwlockattr_t
                              *restrict attr, int *restrict pshared);
int pthread_rwlockattr_setpshared(pthread_rwlockattr_t *attr, int pshared);
```

The process-shared attribute is not required to be implemented by a POSIX-compliant system, and there are no others that can be modified. Therefore, most of the time, we can accept the default attributes.

Use and Semantics of Read-Write Locks

I find it helpful to think about read-write locks as if they were keys to physical locks on the door of a room. The room is the code that the read-write lock protects. If the read-write lock is not currently held by any thread and a writing thread acquires it, it enters the room and locks the door so that no other thread can enter. On the other hand, if the read-write lock is not currently held by any thread and a reading thread acquires it, then it enters the room and leaves a guard at the door. If an arriving thread wants to write, the guard makes it wait in a line outside of the door until the reader leaves the room, or possibly later. All arriving writers will wait in this line while the reader is in the room. If an arriving thread wants to read, whether or not it's let into the room depends on the guard. The guard's decision depends on how *Pthreads* is configured.

Some systems support a *Pthreads* configuration option known as *Thread Execution Scheduling*, or *TES*. This option allows the programmer to control how threads are scheduled. If your system has functions to control thread scheduling, such as pthread_getschedparam(), then *TES* is enabled. If the system doesn't support this option and there's a reader in the room with writers standing in line waiting to enter, when a reader arrives at the door, it is up to the implementation to decide whether the reader can enter immediately or must wait outside along with the writers.

If *TES* is supported, then the decision is based on the scheduling policy that's in force. If either SCHED_FIFO, SCHED_RR (round-robin), or SCHED_SPORADIC scheduling is in force, then an arriving reader will stand in line behind higher or equal priority writers (and any readers whose priorities are higher than the arriving reader's). Figure 16-6 illustrates two possible scenarios when a reader arrives. If writers are queued up, the question is whether readers can enter or whether they wait. If readers can enter, writers can starve. If they wait, then a reader queue forms as well, and the next thread to acquire the lock is based on a scheduling decision.

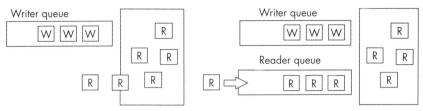

Figure 16-6: Two scenarios when writers are waiting for the read-write-lock while readers are "in the room" and readers arrive

These decisions about which threads must wait when threads are blocked on a lock can lead to unfair scheduling and even starvation. A discussion of this topic is outside of the scope of this book. Several of the operating systems books mentioned in the bibliography examine these issues [37] [42] [39]. At the very least, you should be aware that if the implementation gives arriving readers precedence over waiting writers when a reader has the lock, then a steady stream of readers could prevent a writer from ever writing. This isn't good.

Usually, a writer has something important to do, such as updating data, and it should be given priority over readers. This is why the *TES* option supports this type of scheduling and why some implementations always give waiting writers priority over waiting readers. However, it's also possible that a stream of writers will starve all of the readers, so if for some reason, there must be multiple writers, the code itself must ensure that they do not starve the readers by using mutexes and condition variables to prevent starvation.

To lock a read-write lock for reading, a thread calls `pthread_rwlock_rdlock()`. Whether or not it acquires the lock is based on the rules just described. If you don't want the thread to block in those cases where it might, the thread should call `pthread_rwlock_tryrdlock()` instead, which returns the error value `EBUSY` whenever it would block.

The `pthread_rwlock_timedrdlock()` function is like the `pthread_rwlock_rdlock()` function, except that if the lock cannot be acquired without blocking, the wait is terminated when the specified timeout expires. The timeout expires when the absolute time specified by the `abstime` parameter passes, as measured by the real time clock (`CLOCK_REALTIME`), or if the absolute time specified by `abstime` has already been passed at the time of the call. Notice that the time specification isn't an interval; it is absolute time (see Chapter 9). The function doesn't fail if the lock can be acquired immediately, and the validity of the `abstime` parameter isn't checked if the lock can be acquired immediately.

The differences between `pthread_rwlock_timedwrlock()`, `pthread_rwlock_tryrwlock()`, and `pthread_rwlock_wrlock()` are analogous.

As for unlocking, there is only one function to unlock. It doesn't matter whether the thread holds the lock for reading or writing; it calls `pthread_rwlock_unlock()` in either case.

Further Details About Pthreads Read-Write Locks

This section answers some more subtle, advanced questions about read-write locks in *Pthreads*.

- If the calling thread already holds a read lock on the read-write lock, another read lock can be successfully acquired by the calling thread. If more than one read lock is successfully acquired by a thread on a read-write lock, that thread is required to successfully call `pthread_rwlock_unlock()` a matching number of times. In this sense, it's similar to a recursive mutex.

- Some implementations of *Pthreads* will allow a thread that already holds a write lock on a read-write lock to acquire another write lock on that same lock. In these implementations, if more than one write lock is successfully acquired by a thread on a read-write lock, that thread is required to successfully call `pthread_rwlock_unlock()` a matching number of times. In other implementations, the attempt to acquire a second write lock on that same read-write lock will cause deadlock.

- If while either of `pthread_rwlock_wrlock()` or `pthread_rwlock_rdlock()` is waiting for the shared read lock, the read-write lock is destroyed, then the `EDESTROYED` error is returned.

- If a signal is delivered to the thread while it's waiting for the lock for either reading or writing, if a signal handler is registered for this signal, it runs, and the thread resumes waiting.

- If a thread terminates while holding a write lock, the attempt by another thread to acquire a shared read or exclusive write lock will not succeed. In this case, the attempt to acquire the lock does not return and will deadlock. If a thread terminates while holding a read lock, the system automatically releases the read lock.

- If a thread calls `pthread_rwlock_wrlock()` and currently owns the read-write lock for writing or reading, the call will either deadlock or fail, returning the error code `EDEADLK`.

- In an implementation in which a thread can hold multiple read and write locks on the same read-write lock, if a thread calls `pthread_rwlock_unlock()` while holding one or more shared read locks and one or more exclusive write locks, the exclusive write locks are unlocked first. If more than one outstanding exclusive write lock was held by the thread, a matching number of successful calls to `pthread_rwlock_unlock()` must be completed before all write locks are unlocked. At that time, subsequent calls to `pthread_rwlock_unlock()` will unlock the shared read locks.

As you can see, these locks have complex semantics that can have significant impact on the order in which threads access the shared data. Programming with them requires care. We'll develop an example program that demonstrates a basic application of them.

Read-Write Lock Example

Many system resources, such as the system time or the password database, are modified only occasionally but read from very frequently. When a thread has to modify the resource, it has to do so exclusively because the changes can involve several nonatomic operations. For instance, when the Linux kernel needs to add or remove a process from a linked list, there's a window of time during which the pointers have been changed but don't yet point to valid locations. A thread that tries to traverse this list during the update would dereference an invalid pointer. As another example, *glibc* supports message catalogs that allow applications to display messages in the language of a user's locale. A thread or process that needs to update a message in the catalog might have to change several lines of text. If another thread reads that message translation in the midst of an update, it will receive a corrupted translation or, even worse, an invalid memory address.

Because we can't, or shouldn't, modify actual system databases, our program simulates an update to a user dataset instead. The program creates a few kinds of threads: reader threads, writer threads, a signal-handling thread, and, if enabled, a monitor thread. The program requirements include the following:

- The dataset consists of an array of short strings of fixed maximum length, read from a file specified on the command line.

- To simplify the program, the only way to terminate all threads is by entering a terminating key combination such as CTRL-C or by sending a terminating signal such as SIGTERM.

- The number of reader threads is independent of the number of writer threads, but there should be more readers than writers.

- A writer thread changes one or more data strings in a single write operation.

- Each reader thread is assigned a range of lines in the data array that it reads.

- A writer thread doesn't write output on the terminal, but when it modifies the array, it will attach its unique, program-based ID and the time of modification to the modified lines as a form of audit.

- A reader thread reads its assigned entries from the array and writes them, along with their metadata, to its standard output.

- A writer thread will only write periodically, at fixed time intervals, sleeping in between write operations.

This last requirement will allow us to measure the performance of our program, because writers will wake up at fixed intervals and try to acquire the read-write lock immediately. If we use a high-precision timer to schedule their wake-ups, then we can compare the timestamp in the dataset to the time that the timer expired. The difference in time is the delay caused by being locked out. Our solution should keep this time as small as possible.

The challenge in using read-write locks is preventing starvation of both readers and writers. It would be a simple design if it didn't prevent starvation. Fortunately, *glibc* provides a nonportable extension to the *Pthreads* library, the `pthread_rwlockattr_setkind_np()` function, that lets a program modify the lock attributes to prevent writer starvation, provided that no reader acquires the lock recursively. However, if the number of writers is too large, readers can starve, so the key is to enable this feature only when the number of writers is not too large. The man page has all of the details.

To give all threads a fair chance at the lock, the program should be designed like a horse race—no thread can start until they're all in the figurative starting gate. Therefore, it will use a synchronization barrier at the start of each reader and writer start function to ensure that no thread enters its main loop until all threads have at least been created. Without the barrier, the threads that are created first in the main program will always get the lock first, and if these are writers, the readers might starve.

Writing this program has two purposes. One is to get some practice using the read-write lock. The other is to create a tool to explore the effects of the numbers of readers and writers and preferences on access to the critical section of code. To this end, it has a few ancillary features:

- It will have command line options to specify the number of readers (`-r` *nreaders*), the number of writers (`-w` *nwriters*), the number of nanoseconds that readers spend outside of their reading code section (`-s` *nanosecs*), and whether or not to give writers starvation prevention (`-R` turns it off).

- It creates a logfile named *rwlockdemo.log* in the current working directory. Every time any thread acquires or releases a lock, it writes to that file.

- When a writer writes its ID into the data array, it negates it. This way, writer entries are easy to recognize because their IDs on output are negative numbers.

- When a reader process reads an entry, it will write that entry to standard output, preceded by its program ID. Sample output could be:

```
Read by  7: -9     2670.176026554    [ 116] spruce
```

In this output, 7 is the reader's ID, 9 is the ID of the writer who last modified line 116 in the dataset, and the timestamp in seconds is 2670.176026554. The string spruce is the actual data.

- Setting the compile time symbol MONITOR will add code to the executable that writes additional information about the lock to the logfile.

We'll look at various fragments of the program, named *pthread_rwlock _demo.c*, which is available in the book's source code distribution in its entirety. To save space here, some code won't be displayed. Let's start with the global types, constants, and variable declarations:

```
#define NUM_READERS   8    /* Default number of readers */
#define NUM_WRITERS   2    /* Default number of writers */
#define LINESIZE      64   /* Maximum length of string  */
#define MAX_ARRAYSIZE 1024 /* Maximum array size         */


/* The data structure representing a single item in the shared array */
typedef struct _data {
    int            wrid;        /* Writer ID, negated         */
    struct timespec wrtime;     /* Time of last modification */
    char           text[LINESIZE];  /* Actual text data       */
} item;

typedef struct _task_data
{
    int   first;      /* Index of first element for thread */
    int   last;       /* Index of last element for thread  */
    int   task_id;    /* Thread's program ID               */
    int   num_threads; /* Total number of threads          */
    item *data;       /* Pointer to array of data          */
} reader_task_data;  /* Only readers need this structure. */

item            *shared_data;        /* Dynamically-allocated data array */
int             arraysize;           /* Actual size of the array         */
pthread_rwlock_t rwlock;             /* The reader/writer lock           */
pthread_barrier_t barrier;           /* Barrier to improve fairness      */
FILE            *logfp;              /* FILE stream for logfile          */
int             rdrsleep_ns = 200000; /* Nanosecs in reader delay time   */
#ifdef MONITOR
```

```
pthread_mutex_t    counter_mutex;       /* Used by the monitor code       */
int                num_threads_in_lock; /* For the monitor code           */
#endif
```

Although I included the conditionally compiled monitor variable declarations here, I won't show the monitor code in the next few listings.

The readers execute the start function shown in Listing 16-13.

```
reader()  void *reader(void *data)
          {
              int               retval;
              reader_task_data *t_data = (reader_task_data*) data;
              int               t = t_data->task_id;
              struct timespec   sleeptime = {0,rdrsleep_ns};
              struct timespec   rem = sleeptime;

              retval = pthread_barrier_wait(&barrier);   /* Wait for all threads. */
              if ( PTHREAD_BARRIER_SERIAL_THREAD != retval && 0 != retval )
                  fatal_error(retval, "pthread_barrier_wait");
              while ( TRUE ) {
          ❶  if ( 0 != (retval = pthread_rwlock_rdlock(&rwlock)) )
                      fatal_error( retval, "pthread_rwlock_rdlock");
                  // OMITTED: Lock print mutex (if you want all lines together).
                  for ( int k = t_data->first; k <= t_data->last; k++ )
                      printf("Read by %2d: %3d\t%6lu.%-12lu [%4d] %s", t,
                              t_data->data[k].wrid,
                              t_data->data[k].wrtime.tv_sec,
                              t_data->data[k].wrtime.tv_nsec,
                              k,
                              t_data->data[k].text);
                  fflush(stdout);
                  // OMITTED: Unlock print mutex (if it was locked before the loop).
                  fprintf(logfp, "Reader %d got the read lock\n", t);
                  fflush(logfp);

          ❷  if ( 0 != (retval = pthread_rwlock_unlock(&rwlock)) )
                      fatal_error( retval, "pthread_rwlock_unlock");
                  fprintf(logfp, "Reader %d released the read lock\n", t);
                  fflush(logfp);
                  nanosleep(&sleeptime, &rem);
              }
              pthread_exit(NULL);
          }
```

Listing 16-13: The start function executed by all reader threads

Most of the loop is enclosed in the calls to lock the read-write lock for reading ❶ and unlock it ❷.

If we wanted all of a reader's output to be printed together, we could enclose the print loop with mutex locking. The printf() function is thread-safe—it locks the output stream until it returns—so that the output lines will be preserved intact. As written, the output lines from different reader threads may be intermingled, but since each line shows which reader wrote it, it doesn't matter.

Let's look at the writer start function, which is shown in Listing 16-14.

writer()
```
void *writer(void *data)
{
    int             retval;         /* Return values from function calls */
    int             t = (int) (long) data; /* Thread's program ID      */
    struct timespec dt = {1,0};     /* Sleep time for clock_nanosleep   */
    struct timespec curtime;        /* Time of modification             */

    retval = pthread_barrier_wait(&barrier);    /* Wait for all threads. */
    if ( PTHREAD_BARRIER_SERIAL_THREAD != retval && 0 != retval )
        fatal_error(retval, "pthread_barrier_wait");
    while ( TRUE ) {
    ❶ if ( 0 != (retval = pthread_rwlock_wrlock(&rwlock)) )
            fatal_error(retval, "pthread_rwlock_wrlock");
    ❷ clock_gettime(CLOCK_MONOTONIC, &curtime);
        for ( int i = 0; i < arraysize; i++ ) {
        ❸ if ( random() > RAND_MAX/2 ) {
                shared_data[i].wrid = -t;
                shared_data[i].wrtime = curtime;
            }
        }
        fprintf(logfp, "Writer %d got the write lock\n", t);
        fflush(logfp);
        if ( 0 != (retval = pthread_rwlock_unlock(&rwlock)) )
            fatal_error(retval, "pthread_rwlock_unlock");
        fprintf(logfp, "Writer %d released the write lock\n", t);
        fflush(logfp);
        clock_nanosleep(CLOCK_MONOTONIC, 0, &dt, NULL);
    }
    pthread_exit(NULL);
}
```

Listing 16-14: The start function executed by all writer threads

The writer threads also wait at the barrier before entering their loop. Inside the loop, they immediately try to acquire a write lock on the read-write lock ❶. As soon as they acquire it, they get the current time ❷ and make a pass across the entire array, modifying a random number ❸ of entries. On average, each writer will modify half of the entries each time it writes.

Writers don't actually modify the text string. It isn't necessary for this program. Besides, not modifying it makes it easier to do a bit of post-mortem analysis in the output file. They add their negated ID to the entry and modify its timestamp.

After they release the lock, they sleep for 1 second. If they acquire the lock immediately after waking up, the next modifications will be close to one second after the preceding ones. If a writer is delayed, the timestamps will show how much it was delayed. By greping through the output, we can see the lines that each thread modified and the times it did so.

The main program calls an auxiliary function, load_data(), to load the lines from a text file into the array. That function, shown in Listing 16-15, ensures that lines are limited to the maximum allowed size, truncating them if necessary, and that the array length is not exceeded.

load_data()
```
int load_data(char *pathname, int maxsize, item *array)
{
    FILE   *fp;
    int    i = 0;
    char   *buffer = NULL;
    size_t len  = 0;

    if ( (fp = fopen(pathname, "r")) == NULL )
        fatal_error(errno, "fopen");
    while ( (i < maxsize) && (-1 != getline(&buffer, &len, fp)) ) {
        if ( len < LINESIZE )
            strncpy(array[i].text, buffer, len);
        else {
            strncpy(array[i].text, buffer, LINESIZE - 1);
            array[i].text[LINESIZE-1] = '\0';
        }
        array[i].wrid = 0;
        array[i].wrtime.tv_sec = 0;
        array[i].wrtime.tv_nsec = 0;
        i++;
    }
    free(buffer);
    return i;
}
```

Listing 16-15: The function that loads the data from a text file into the array shared by the readers and writers

The last piece is the main program. Excerpts of it are displayed in Listing 16-16. Some code has been removed, as indicated in the listing, and some error handling has been omitted as well.

pthread_rwlock
_demo.c
main()
```
int main(int argc, char *argv[])
{
    int            retval;
    int            nreaders = NUM_READERS;
    int            nwriters = NUM_WRITERS;
    long int       t;
```

```
unsigned int      num_threads;
pthread_t         *threads;
pthread_t         sig_thread; /* Thread ID for signal-handling thread */
sigset_t          mask;       /* Signal mask of blocked signals        */
pthread_attr_t    attr;       /* Attribute structure for threads       */
reader_task_data *thread_data;
BOOL              reader_preference = FALSE;
char              ch;

// OMITTED: Option-parsing, usage handling, blocking asynchronous signals

/* Set the attribute structure to create a detached thread. */
pthread_attr_init(&attr);
pthread_attr_setdetachstate(&attr, PTHREAD_CREATE_DETACHED);
pthread_attr_setstacksize (&attr, 65536);

/* Create one thread to handle asynchronous terminating signals. */
pthread_create(&sig_thread, &attr, sighandler, (void*) &mask);

pthread_rwlockattr_t rwlock_attributes;
pthread_rwlockattr_init(&rwlock_attributes);
/* The following nonportable function alters thread priorities when
   readers and writers are both waiting on a rwlock. */
❶ if ( nwriters > 1 ) {
    if ( reader_preference ) /* By default, this is FALSE. */
        pthread_rwlockattr_setkind_np(&rwlock_attributes,
                PTHREAD_RWLOCK_PREFER_READER_NP);
    else
        pthread_rwlockattr_setkind_np(&rwlock_attributes,
                PTHREAD_RWLOCK_PREFER_WRITER_NONRECURSIVE_NP);
}
pthread_rwlock_init(&rwlock, &rwlock_attributes);

num_threads = nreaders + nwriters;
arraysize = MAX_ARRAYSIZE;
/* Allocate memory for shared array and read data from file into it. */
if ( NULL == (shared_data = (item*) calloc(arraysize, sizeof(item))) )
    fatal_error(errno, "calloc");
arraysize = load_data(argv[optind], arraysize, shared_data);

logfp = fopen("rwlockdemo.log", "w");
thread_data = calloc(nreaders, sizeof(reader_task_data));
threads = calloc(num_threads, sizeof(pthread_t));

/* Initialize the barrier. */
if ( 0 != (retval = pthread_barrier_init(&barrier, NULL, num_threads)) )
    fatal_error(retval, "pthread_barrier_init");
```

```
    for ( t = 0; t < nreaders; t++ ) { /* Set up task data for readers. */
        thread_data[t].first     = (t * arraysize)/nreaders;
        thread_data[t].last      = ((t + 1) * arraysize)/nreaders - 1;
        thread_data[t].task_id    = t;
        thread_data[t].num_threads = nreaders;
        thread_data[t].data       = shared_data;
    }
    for ( t = 0; t < nreaders; t++ )            /* Create and run readers. */
        pthread_create(&threads[t], &attr, reader, &thread_data[t]);

    for ( t = nreaders ; t < num_threads; t++ ) /* Create and run writers. */
        pthread_create(&threads[t], NULL, writer, (void*) t);

    for ( t = 0; t < num_threads; t++ )         /* Join all threads.      */
        pthread_join(threads[t], NULL);

    exit(EXIT_SUCCESS);
}
```

Listing 16-16: The main program for pthread_rwlock_demo.c

The main() function basically sets everything up for its threads. The signal handling thread is run to wait for asynchronous terminating signals and clean up if any are delivered. If the user didn't provide the -R option for the run ❶, reader_preference is turned off and the attribute structure for the read-write lock will be given the PTHREAD_RWLOCK_PREFER_WRITER_NONRECURSIVE_NP attribute, which prevents writer starvation. The reader threads are created first. The writer threads are created in the second loop and given IDs with the integers starting with nreaders, up to num_threads - 1.

The program design lets us run it with changing numbers of reader and writer threads. The expected usage is:

```
./pthread_rwlock_demo [-r nreaders -w nwriters -s readersleep -R] datafile
```

It's best to redirect standard output into a file when we run the program. This way, we can analyze the file to see whether writers were able to perform their updates without much delay. The logfile will show the order in which each thread acquired and released the lock. I'll run the program with an input file consisting of the names of trees found in public places on the streets of New York City, which is part of an open dataset. It has 133 names:

```
$ ./pthread_rwlock_demo -r12 -w3 treenames > run1
^C
```

Looking at the contents of *run1*, we'll see lines like the following:

```
Read by  2:   0      0.0           [  32] cockspur hawthorn
Read by  1:   0      0.0           [  20] black pine
Read by  1:   0      0.0           [  21] black walnut
Read by  9: -14    3765.998855807  [  99] sawtooth oak
Read by  7: -13    3765.998929951  [  77] northern red oak
Read by  9: -13    3765.998929951  [ 100] scarlet oak
Read by  7: -14    3765.998855807  [  78] Norway maple
Read by 10: -14    3765.998855807  [ 110] silver maple
```

This shows that initially some readers read entries not yet modified (the metadata is zeros) but that different readers start to read modified entries. The -13 and -14 indicate that writers 13 and 14 modified these entries. If we search for all lines containing scarlet oak, as in

```
$ grep 'scarlet oak' run1
Read by  9: -13    3765.998929951  [ 100] scarlet oak
Read by  9: -13    3766.999128456  [ 100] scarlet oak
Read by  9: -13    3767.999340177  [ 100] scarlet oak
Read by  9: -12    3768.999343937  [ 100] scarlet oak
Read by  9: -12    3769.999540417  [ 100] scarlet oak
--snip--
```

we see that reader 9 always reads this entry and that two different writers modified it. The writes take place a little more than one second apart. The difference is on the order of 0.2 milliseconds, which is partly caused by the writers not acquiring the lock immediately.

The *rwlockdemo.log* file contains lines such as

```
Reader 4 got the read lock
Reader 4 released the read lock
Reader 3 got the read lock
Reader 3 released the read lock
Writer 13 got the write lock
Writer 13 released the write lock
Writer 12 got the write lock
Writer 12 released the write lock
Writer 14 got the write lock
Writer 14 released the write lock
Reader 8 got the read lock
--snip--
```

showing the order in which the threads accessed the file. This can be used to corroborate the output.

Summary

This chapter explored an assortment of programming tools provided by the *Pthreads* API for synchronizing threads and preventing race conditions.

A mutex is essentially a binary software lock. One thread at a time can lock it, and only that thread can unlock it. When multiple threads try to lock it at the same time, all but one is blocked until it is unlocked. A condition variable is a more complex object. The intended purpose of it is for a thread that has acquired a mutex but can't continue because some condition is false to atomically release the mutex and put itself on a queue of threads blocked on that variable. Another thread can signal the condition variable to indicate that the condition is true, and a single thread is then removed from its queue and can proceed.

A synchronization barrier is a function that programs can use to prevent any thread from advancing until all threads are at the barrier, like the gate at the start of a race. We looked at read-write locks as well. These can be held by multiple readers at a time, but if a writer wants to lock it, no other thread can lock it until the writer releases it. These locks are a challenge to use because it's not hard for some programs to cause all readers to starve or cause all writers to starve.

The chapter did not cover all possible *Pthreads* functions and synchronization tools. It omitted an exploration of spin-locks, real-time threads, and thread scheduling. It did not cover thread keys and thread-specific data. The man pages and the POSIX specification have more details about these topics.

Exercises

1. Modify *vmem_usage.c* so that it can report on the total of other process statistics besides virtual memory size. Specifically, it should accept the following command line options and associated meanings:

    -u Total user mode CPU time
    -k Total kernel mode time
    -r Total of resident set sizes as a number of pages

    Without options, it reports on virtual memory size. If more than one option is present, it reports on each, one metric per line, in any order, with a label indicating the metric, such as User mode CPU time:.

2. Modify the function get_all_vmsizes() in *vmem_usage.c* so that it creates multiple threads to construct the array of per-process virtual memory sizes. It should pick a number of threads no greater than the minimum of the number of processors and the number of active processes. Read the man page for get_nprocs(3) and/or sysconf() to learn how to get the processor count.

3. A *thread-shared semaphore* is one that can be used only by the threads of the same multithreaded program. Implement a thread-shared semaphore using nothing but *Pthreads* mutexes and condition variables. A program must make such a semaphore accessible to all threads by making it a global variable or putting it on the heap. Use the following structure definition:

```
typedef struct {
    pthread_mutex_t lock;
    pthread_cond_t  cond;
    int             value; /* Semaphore value (>= 0)                */
    BOOL            avail; /* True if initialized and not destroyed */
} _sem_t;
```

(a) Write implementations of the following semaphore operations that act on objects of type _sem_t:

```
/* sem_init() initializes *sem with initial value and makes it
   available. */
void sem_init(_sem_t *sem, int init_value);

/* sem_destroy() releases *sem resources, making *sem
   unavailable. */
void sem_destroy(_sem_t *sem);

/* sem_wait() implements a semaphore wait() on *sem.
   Returns 0 on success, else nonzero. */
int sem_wait(_sem_t *sem);

/* sem_post() implements a semaphore post() on *sem.
   Returns 0 on success, else nonzero. */
int sem_post(_sem_t *sem);
```

Your solution does not have to guarantee any particular scheduling of threads that are woken up by a post operation, and it does not have to handle the possibility of threads being cancelled during a semaphore operation.

(b) Modify *pthread_prodcons.c*, the multithreaded producer-consumer program from this chapter, so that it uses your semaphore operations instead of mutexes and condition variables.

4. Is there a set of command line options for the pthread_rwlock_demo program that will starve readers or starve writers? Try changing the numbers of readers and writers to see if you can cause either class to starve or perhaps "near starve," where the threads of that class almost never acquire the lock. Try changing the time that readers sleep (with the -s option). With a fixed number of readers and writers, is there a threshold value for the reader sleep time below which writers starve? You can analyze the logfile with tools such as grep and wc to determine with ease how often both readers and writers acquired the lock.

5. The Linux kernel has a reader-writer consistency mechanism of type seqcount_t with lockless readers (read-only retry loops) and no writer starvation. It's intended to protect updates to rarely updated data like the system clock. It is designed for a single writer and multiple readers. The idea is simple in principle: The sequence counter is either even or odd at any time. Initially it is 0. When the writer wants to write, it adds 1, writes, and subtracts 1. When a reader wants to read, it repeatedly loops, checking whether the counter is even or odd. It reads only when the counter is even. If the sequence count has changed between the start and the end of the read, the reader must retry. You can read more about it in the kernel documentation, in the repository file *Documentation/locking/seqlock.rst*.

Write a small program with a number of reader threads and a single writer that uses this method to allow the readers to read an integer variable that gets updated by the writer at random times.

17

ALTERNATIVE METHODS OF I/O

Most of the programs in previous chapters are based on a model of I/O in which read and write operations are blocking. These programs obtain their input from a single source, either the standard input stream or a disk file, and they send their output to a single source, either the standard output stream or a disk file. The exceptions are the programs in Chapters 12, 13, and 14, some of which open message queues and pipes in nonblocking mode, but only because this is needed to keep these facilities from closing prematurely or to prevent deadlock or some other unwanted behavior.

When a process issues a blocking read, it is suspended until the data from the input source is transferred to its address space. When it issues a blocking write, it's suspended until the data is transferred from its address space to a kernel buffer, which usually takes place so quickly that the delay is imperceptible.

For some types of applications, blocking I/O is unsatisfactory. Some examples are:

- Interactive programs, which need to respond immediately to infrequent user input in the terminal while they perform other tasks. If they have to block while waiting for the input, they can't make progress on the other tasks and waste time waiting for input that arrives at unpredictable times.

- Programs that have multiple input sources with intermittent data flow and that need to monitor all of them for possible input. Blocking while waiting for input from one source prevents their checking the other sources, which might have input waiting to be read, resulting in delays and inefficiencies.

In this chapter, we'll explore alternatives to this model of I/O. In particular, we'll consider:

- Nonblocking I/O achieved by enabling the O_NONBLOCK flag on the file descriptor

- Signal-driven I/O achieved by enabling the Linux and BSD-specific O_ASYNC flag on the file descriptor

- POSIX asynchronous I/O (AIO)

- Multiplexed I/O based on the select() system call

Signal-driven I/O is limited to terminals, pseudoterminals, sockets, pipes, and FIFOs. The other methods can be used with file descriptors for any device type, such as disk files, pipes, terminals, and so on.

Nonblocking I/O

Nonblocking input refers to any method of input in which the process returns immediately from a call to read() when no data is available for reading, and symmetrically, nonblocking output refers to any method of output in which the process returns immediately if it's unable to write to the file descriptor. This can happen with pipes, for example, when they're full, and it can even happen to terminals if the writing process sends data at a faster rate than the driver can process that data.

Enabling Nonblocking I/O

To enable nonblocking I/O on a file descriptor, we simply enable the O_NONBLOCK flag on it. If this flag is set, when a process calls read(), if no data's available, it doesn't wait; instead, read() returns -1 and puts an error code in errno. Similarly, if it calls write() and it's not possible to write to the target device, write() returns -1 and puts an error code in errno.

While it's useful to enable nonblocking reading on terminals, pipes, and sockets, for example, it makes little sense to do so with disk files. If a file isn't empty, a read operation will be satisfied, unless such a large number of bytes is requested that it takes a perceptible amount of time for the kernel to transfer the data to the process's address space, or the disk is so busy that the read operation is delayed. In either case, it's the kernel's decision to put the process into a noninterruptible sleep while the data is transferred. The open(2) man page states this clearly:

> Note that this flag has no effect for regular files and block devices; that is, I/O operations will (briefly) block when device activity is required, regardless of whether O_NONBLOCK is set.

Since we've already explored the use of nonblocking I/O on IPC facilities such as message queues and pipes, here I'll concentrate on how it can be used with interactive programs. The typical use of it in this case is of the form:

```
while ( TRUE ) {
    // Compute stuff.
    if ( read(0, &buf, numbytes) <= 0 )
        // Handle the case that no data is available.
    else
        // Process data read into buf.
}
```

In other words, the program's main loop calls read() in each iteration. If it returns -1, it just goes back to computing. If not, then it received data and can compute with it.

Chapter 11 introduced the fcntl() system call to enable the O_APPEND flag on a file descriptor to prevent race conditions. It's a three step-procedure. To enable O_NONBLOCK, we follow the same procedure:

```
int flagset = fcntl(fd, F_GETFL);       /* Get the existing flagset from fd. */
if ( flagset == -1 )                     /* Check if fcntl() failed.          */
    fatal_error(errno, "fcntl");         /* If so, handle it.                 */
flagset |= O_NONBLOCK;                    /* Bitwise-OR the flag.              */
if ( -1 == fcntl(fd, F_SETFL, flagset) ) /* Set the flagset into fd.          */
    fatal_error(errno, "fcntl");          /* If an error, handle it.          */
```

The call to fcntl() can fail for several reasons; a program should always check its return value.

A Program to Demonstrate Nonblocking Input

Listing 17-1 sets up nonblocking input on the standard input stream connected to the terminal. The program doesn't do much else; it repeatedly calls read() to read a single character entered by the user and prints a message on the terminal indicating either that read() failed or that it read the entered character. It terminates if the user enters q or after 500 iterations, whichever comes first.

`#include "common_hdrs.h"`
`#include <fcntl.h>`

```c
void set_non_block(int fd)
{
    int flagset = fcntl(fd, F_GETFL);
    if ( flagset == -1 )
        fatal_error(errno, "fcntl");
    flagset |= O_NONBLOCK;
    if ( -1 == fcntl(fd, F_SETFL, flagset) )
        fatal_error(errno, "fcntl");
}

int main(int argc, char *argv[])
{
    char ch;
    int   count = 0, failedcount = 0;
    char str[128];
    long delay = 500000;

    if ( argc > 1 )
        delay = strtol(argv[1], NULL, 0);

    set_non_block(STDIN_FILENO);    /* Turn off blocking mode.     */
    while ( count < 500 ) {
        count++;
        if ( -1 == usleep(delay) )   /* Delay a bit.               */
            fatal_error(errno, "usleep");
        if ( read(STDIN_FILENO, &ch, 1) > 0 ) {
            if ( ch == 'q' )
                break;
            else if ( ch != '\n' ) { /* Don't print entered newline. */
                sprintf(str, "\rUser entered %c\n", ch);
                write(1, str, strlen(str));
            }
        }
        else { /* read() returned -1, implying no data available.   */
            failedcount++;               /* Update counter.          */
            sprintf(str, "\rNo input; number of unsatisfied reads = %d\n",
                    failedcount);
            write(1, str, strlen(str));
        }
    }
    return 0;
}
```

Listing 17-1: A program using nonblocking input to read from the terminal

The default configuration of a terminal prevents a read operation from completing until a newline is entered. Therefore, when you run the program, you need to press ENTER to transmit anything you enter, even a single character. In the next chapter, we'll learn how to configure the terminal so that we don't have to enter those newlines.

The program is intentionally slowed down with a short sleep in each iteration of the loop so that we can see the changes in output as it runs and so that it doesn't produce output faster than we can read it on the screen. By default, it's 0.5 seconds, but it has a command line argument that can override the default. The program expects this argument to be the length of the delay in microseconds. For example

```
$ ./nonblock_demo1 250000
```

starts it with a delay of 0.25 seconds. On some systems, usleep() will fail if you supply it an argument larger than 999999.

When you run the program, you can type more than one character before the newline. In the following run, I entered the string abcd followed by a newline:

```
No input; number of unsatisfied reads = 1
No input; number of unsatisfied reads = 2
No input; number of unsatisfied reads = 3

User entered a
User entered b
User entered c
User entered d
No input; number of unsatisfied reads = 10
No input; number of unsatisfied reads = 11
No input; number of unsatisfied reads = 12
q
```

You can't see the input because the output strings overwrite it; the format string given to printf() starts with a carriage return character (\r), which causes the cursor to return to column 1 in the same line, overwriting whatever was on the line. If you enter successively longer strings before entering a newline, all of the characters are still read, implying that they're stored in a buffer before they're delivered to the process. How large is this buffer? We'll answer that question in Chapter 18.

A long delay in the program simulates the program's being busy doing other work and polling only infrequently. A short delay simulates much more frequent polling. The less frequently the program polls for input, the longer it will take to respond to it. This lack of responsiveness may be unacceptable in many applications. The more frequently it polls, the more system calls it makes, leading to more wasted CPU cycles.

As an experiment, run the program under the time command with successively smaller delay intervals and don't enter q, so that it always runs for

500 iterations. For example, two runs might produce output such as the following:

```
$ time ./nonblock_demo1 100000
--snip--
real    0m50.072s
user    0m0.005s
sys     0m0.012s
$ time ./nonblock_demo1 20000
--snip--
real    0m10.072s
user    0m0.005s
sys     0m0.010s
```

With longer delays, you're able to enter more input, and the number of unsatisfied reads decreases. With shorter delays, the fraction of failed reads increases. If the delay is so small that you can barely enter input and the user isn't some robot that can enter thousands of characters per second, the number of unsuccessful calls to read() is extremely large and the fraction of successful reads is extremely small. Each one of those reads is an expensive system call using kernel resources.

NOTE *When a program performs a nonblocking read inside a loop, we say that it's polling the input source, and we call this polling I/O. Polling I/O is wasteful of CPU resources. In short, the cost of improving the responsiveness of the program to user input by disabling blocking and polling frequently is wasted CPU cycles.*

A second version of this program, named *nonblock_demo2.c*, is available in the book's source code distribution. It is easier to use because the output is designed to take up just three lines of the terminal instead of scrolling off of the screen:

```
f
User entered f
No input; number of unsatisfied reads = 68
```

It uses ANSI escape sequences to move the cursor on the screen and hence is a little longer than the version shown here.

When you run it, observe that the reported system time is about the same, regardless of how many successful reads the program made. In other words, the kernel spends a lot of time in the read() system call, whether there's lots of input or not.

Signal-Driven I/O

We considered the use of polling (nonblocking) input because blocking input operations makes a process wait until all data is available, but we see that the big problem with polling is that it is wasteful of system resources. Blocking reads are a form of *synchronous* I/O, because the execution of the process is synchronized with the delivery of its input data.

Let's recall how system buffering works when reading from disk files. When a process issues a read() system call for some amount of data, the kernel attempts to satisfy the read from its buffer cache. If the buffer cache for the given file descriptor is empty, it initiates an input operation to transfer data from the device to a system buffer. When the data is in the buffer, it then transfers it to the process's address space. For block devices such as disks, this sequence of steps is depicted in Figure 4-4 in Chapter 4. For character devices such as terminals and serial ports, the kernel also buffers input, but in a different way, which I'll describe in Chapter 18. Regardless of the source, an input operation is considered complete only when the data has been transferred to the process's address space.

Before we explore how signal-driven I/O works, we need to understand the difference between edge-triggered and level-triggered notification methods.

EDGE-TRIGGERED AND LEVEL-TRIGGERED NOTIFICATION

I'll frame the explanation of these two different methods of notification in terms of processes waiting for notification about I/O activity on a file descriptor. They're more general than this, since they apply to electronic circuitry as well.

Consider an input source, such as a terminal or the read end of a pipe, represented by a file descriptor. When new data arrives, it's an event, a change of state in the monitored file descriptor. In an edge-triggered notification method, a notification is sent to a process only when the event takes place. It's sent once, at the time of the event. In a level-triggered notification method, a notification is sent when the monitored file descriptor is in a state in which input is available to read, not just when it first becomes available.

For example, if 100 bytes of data are written into a pipe whose read end is being monitored, in edge triggering, the process gets a signal when the pipe went from being empty to having data to read. If the process reads 50 bytes, leaving 50 in the pipe, if 100 more bytes arrive, the process won't get another signal, because the pipe didn't change state. If the process issues a wait for a signal that the pipe has data, it will block indefinitely. In level triggering, as long as any data is in the pipe, if the process issues a wait anytime after the data arrived, the wait will not block, because data is available to read.

Overview

In *signal-driven I/O*, a process informs the kernel in advance that it wants to be sent a signal whenever it's possible to read or write a given open file descriptor, and it establishes a signal handler to catch this signal. For a read operation, delivery of the signal implies that one or more bytes of data have been transferred to a kernel buffer and can be read by the process. Signal-driven I/O is an edge-triggered notification method.

Because it's edge triggered, if a process doesn't consume all of the available input at the time it receives the notification, it won't get another signal. For a write operation, receiving a notification that a descriptor is ready implies that it wasn't possible to write to it before but it is now, for example, because a buffer was full before but it now has space available. For terminal devices, signal-driven output is not available. We're primarily interested in signal-driven reading. Figure 17-1 visualizes when the signal is generated during the movement of data from the device to the process.

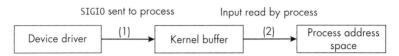

Figure 17-1: The sequence of data movement in a signal-driven input operation showing (1) when the signal is generated and (2) input being read by the process

Signal-driven I/O is available only in Linux and BSD; it isn't a portable method of I/O. It was originally part of an early POSIX standard, POSIX.1g, but it was subsequently removed [20].

Procedure for Enabling Signal-Driven I/O

Signal-driven I/O requires enabling the O_ASYNC flag on the file descriptor on which I/O will take place. The fact that this flag is named O_ASYNC leads many people to call this asynchronous I/O, but it isn't. In *asynchronous I/O*, a process initiates an I/O operation and then continues to execute. When the I/O operation has completed, the process is notified and the data is available in its own address space; the process doesn't need to call read() or any other function to get the data. In the next section, we'll examine the POSIX Asynchronous I/O (AIO) API, which is a true form of asynchronous I/O.

To set up signal-driven input, the program must take the following steps:

1. Establish a signal handler for the SIGIO signal. This is the signal that's generated by default when I/O is possible on a file descriptor. We know how to use sigaction() to do this. This should always be the first step.

2. Tell the kernel which process is to receive the signal. Usually it's the calling process. This requires a call to fcntl(). Its man page explains the steps. If fd is the descriptor, the program has to call:

```
fcntl(fd, SETOWN, getpid());          // OMITTED: Error handling
```

We haven't called fcntl() with the SETOWN command code in previous programs. This sets the owner of the signal to the process identified in the third argument. By making the return value of getpid() the third argument, we're telling the kernel that our process should receive the signal.

3. Enable the O_ASYNC flag on the file descriptor, and optionally enable the O_NONBLOCK flag on that descriptor. I'll explain why this is a good idea shortly:

```
int flagset = fcntl(fd, F_GETFL);      // OMITTED: Error handling
flagset |= O_ASYNC | O_NONBLOCK;
fcntl(fd, F_SETFL, flagset);           // OMITTED: Error handling
```

4. The program then executes the rest of its instructions.

5. When the SIGIO signal is delivered to the process, it implies that
    some input is available, but there's no indication of how many bytes
    are available. For terminal devices, the signal is also sent when end-
    of-file is detected. Because signal-driven I/O is edge triggered, the
    process receives this signal once when the descriptor receives data,
    having had none available before. Therefore, the process has to read
    as much data as is available; otherwise, it may not get future signals,
    even if more data is available.

Figure 17-2 shows the relative sequence of events in time.

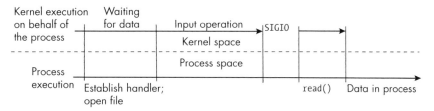

Figure 17-2: A timeline depicting the relative points in time at which events take place for signal-driven input

Receipt of the SIGIO signal implies only that some data is now available.
To ensure that it receives future notifications, the process should repeatedly call read() with a suitable number of bytes to read each time, depending on what type of data is expected. If the file descriptor does not have the
O_NONBLOCK flag set, then when data runs out, the read() will block, defeating
the purpose of signal-driven I/O. If O_NONBLOCK is enabled, then it will get a -1
return code instead, which it can query.

Events Causing Signal Generation

Listing 17-2, which we'll turn to soon, is designed to answer the question:
When is input possible on the file descriptor for a terminal device, and therefore, when is the signal sent? In addition, it models a safe design for a program that uses signal-driven I/O. This program and the one presented in "A
Program Using Signal-Driven I/O" on page 802 call the following function
to set up signal-driven I/O on the file descriptor:

setup_fd()
```
void setup_fd(int fd)
{
    int flagset = fcntl(fd, F_GETFL);
    if ( flagset == -1 )
        fatal_error(errno, "fcntl");
```

```
        if ( -1 == fcntl(fd, F_SETFL, flagset | O_ASYNC | O_NONBLOCK) )
            fatal_error(errno, "fcntl");
        fcntl(fd, F_SETOWN, getpid());
}
```

The setup_fd() function adjusts the status flags of the descriptor to enable
signal-driven I/O and nonblocking mode, and it also sets the owner of the
signal to the calling process.

The program in Listing 17-2 prints a count of the number of signals that
it receives due to input being ready on the standard input descriptor.

sigio_counter.c
```
#include "common_hdrs.h"
#include <fcntl.h>

volatile sig_atomic_t input_ready = 0;
volatile int          count = 0;

void setup_fd(int fd )
{
    // OMITTED: Body of function
}

void on_input(int signum)
{
    input_ready = 1;
    count++;
}

int main(int argc, char *argv[])
{
    struct sigaction sigact;
    sigset_t         blockedsigs;
    char             ch;
    BOOL             finished = FALSE;

    sigemptyset(&blockedsigs);          /* Create an empty signal mask. */
    sigaddset(&blockedsigs, SIGIO);   /* Add SIGIO to mask.            */
    sigact.sa_handler = on_input;     /* Establish the SIGIO handler. */
    sigact.sa_flags = SA_RESTART;
    sigemptyset(&sigact.sa_mask);
    if ( sigaction(SIGIO, &sigact, NULL) == -1 )
        fatal_error(errno, "sigaction");
    setup_fd(STDIN_FILENO);   /* Set up signal-driven I/O. */
    while( !finished ) {
        pause();
        if ( input_ready ) {  /* SIGIO delivered             */
            input_ready = 0;
            sigprocmask(SIG_BLOCK, &blockedsigs, NULL);   /* Block it.   */
```

```
    ➊ while ( read(STDIN_FILENO, &ch, 1)  > 0  && !finished ) {
          if ( ch == 'q' )
              finished = TRUE;
          printf("SIGIO count = %d; current char = %c\n", count, ch);
      }
          sigprocmask(SIG_UNBLOCK, &blockedsigs, NULL); /* Unblock it. */
      }
  }
  return 0;
}
```

Listing 17-2: A program that uses signal-driven I/O and shows when the signal is generated for the process

The signal handler for SIGIO sets a flag that indicates that it was called, implying input is available to be read. This program is counting signals, so it also increments a global counter (count). This is safe because no other part of the program modifies count and because, since SIGIO is blocked while the handler is running, it doesn't have to be reentrant—there's no race condition on the increment operation.

After main() has established the handler and called setup_fd(), it's ready to start reading input. Its main loop calls pause() to wait for any signal to arrive. When it wakes up, if the flag input_ready is set, it resets it to 0. Although it's unlikely, it's possible for a second SIGIO signal to arrive while main() is in the loop ➊ that reads the available input. If it did occur, it could interrupt the printf(). To be safe, the code section is protected by blocking the SIGIO signal with sigprocmask().

The loop repeatedly reads characters one at a time and prints the value of the counter and the character just read. A sample run looks like this:

```
$ ./sigio_counter
abc
SIGIO count = 1; current char = a
SIGIO count = 1; current char = b
SIGIO count = 1; current char = c
SIGIO count = 1; current char =

d
SIGIO count = 2; current char = d
SIGIO count = 2; current char =

# I entered a blank line here by pressing ENTER and nothing else.
SIGIO count = 3; current char =

q
SIGIO count = 4; current char = q
$
```

Each line of input was terminated by pressing ENTER. The newline character was read by the loop, and when it printed it, there was a blank line of output. Notice that the signal is generated exactly when a newline character is entered in the terminal. In Chapter 18, you'll see that this is an attribute of the terminal itself, which we can modify.

Real-Time Signals and Signal-Driven I/O

In modern Linux, we have the option to establish a real-time signal instead of SIGIO. POSIX doesn't specify this. SIGIO is a standard signal; this implies that it isn't queued. If multiple signals are sent to the process while it's in the handler, they'll all be lost. Real-time signals are queued. We saw examples of their use in Chapter 9. If a program expects to receive a high volume of input in small intervals of time, it's safer to establish a handler for a real-time signal instead. In addition, if we use the standard signal instead of a real-time signal and our program is receiving input from more than one file descriptor, it would have to check all descriptors to determine which descriptor had input.

A Program Using Signal-Driven I/O

The *sigio_counter.c* program presents the structure of a program that really doesn't do anything other than wait for input. Now we'll create a program that actually does something besides this. We'll name it *sigio_demo.c*. This is the first of several interactive programs that we'll create.

A common type of interactive program displays information on the screen that's updated at regular intervals and also allows the user to enter commands to change its display. Two different design patterns solve this problem. In one, the main program's loop checks for input in each iteration, reading and responding to it if it's available. Then the loop sleeps a fixed amount of time and then updates the display, as shown in the following pseudocode:

```
Set up signal-driven I/O.
while ( TRUE ) {
    if ( input is available )
        Process it.
    Sleep a fixed interval of time.
    Update display.
    Do a small amount of work.
}
```

This design would use signal-driven I/O to cause the loop to be interrupted. The handler would set a flag, and when the main program returns to test for input, it would process it. This design works when the main program doesn't need to do much else.

An alternative is:

```
Set up an interval timer.
Set up signal-driven I/O.
while ( TRUE ) {
    if ( input is available )
```

```
        Process it.
    if ( timer expired )
        Update display.
    Do a small amount of work.
}
```

This design shifts the burden of timing the updates to a signal handler for the timer expirations. That handler could do the updates itself rather than setting a flag. It depends on whether it can perform them using async-signal-safe functions. The program we'll develop here employs the second strategy, in part so that you can see how to write this kind of program and in part because it models the more common type of interactive program.

We'll begin by defining the program's required behavior, its inputs, and its outputs. This program will have a few shortcomings, which I'll describe shortly. Its limitations stem from our not knowing enough about controlling the behavior of a terminal window.

- The program is invoked without arguments. When it starts up, it clears the screen. The screen's coordinate system, for our purposes, has origin (1,1) in the upper-left corner. I'll call position (1,1) *home*. Moving the cursor to its home is called *homing the cursor*.

- A single character, 0, which I'll call the *sprite*, is printed in the top-most row. At fixed time intervals, it moves to the right one character position, which I'll call a *screen cell*. When it reaches the rightmost column of the terminal window, it moves to the row below into the leftmost cell.

- The bottom row of the terminal is forbidden ground—the sprite is never allowed to move into it. If the preceding rules would move it to the bottom row, instead it restarts in the cell (1,2).

- Moving the sprite means that it is erased from its previous position and printed in the new position.

- While the sprite is moving, the user can enter any characters followed by a newline. The program tries to keep the cursor in the home cell so that the characters entered by the user appear on the screen in that cell.

- The refresh rate must be fast enough to make the animation appear smooth and to prevent the user from entering too many commands, such as up and then down, in a single interval.

- Every time the user enters text followed by a newline, the program prints a message in the bottom row showing the last character entered before the newline.

- Three characters are supposed to cause changes in the program's state: q causes the program to quit, u moves the sprite up one row, and d moves the sprite down one row. No other characters cause any changes to the program's state.

The program will employ two signal handlers, one for the SIGIO signal and one for the timer expiration signal, which we'll set to be SIGUSR1. Both will be one-liners, setting a global flag to indicate that they were called. The program structure is therefore:

```
volatile sig_atomic_t input_ready   = 0;  /* Indicates SIGIO received   */
volatile sig_atomic_t timer_expired = 0;  /* Indicates timer expiration */

void on_input(int signum)
{
    input_ready = 1;
}

void on_timer(int signum)
{
    timer_expired = 1;
}

--snip--
int main(int argc, char *argv[])
{
--snip--
finished = FALSE;
while ( !finished ) {
    if ( input_ready ) {
        input_ready = 0;
        // Process all user input.
    }
    if ( timer_expired ) {
        timer_expired = 0;
        // Update the screen display based on program's state variables.
    }
    pause();
}
```

I won't explain any of the parts of the program related to creating and arming the timer. You can review Chapter 9 for a refresher. The program depends heavily on the moveto() function, which we've employed in programs in a few previous chapters. The call moveto(r,c) moves the screen's cursor to the cell (r,c) so that the next output appears there. It also calls get_window_size(), which we've used in other programs. To save space, I don't display either of these functions here, nor will I display the signal handling and timer setup.

The program defines the following two macros:

```
#define  FREQ_NS  100000000    /* Number of nanosecs in the timer interval */
#define  TOP_ROW  2            /* Highest row in which sprite can be       */
```

The main program's variables are as follows:

```
int main(int argc, char *argv[])
{
    struct  sigaction sigact;               /* For installing handlers      */
    struct  timespec refresh_timespec = {0, FREQ_NS}; /* Refresh rate       */
    struct  itimerspec refresh_interval; /* The timer value and repeat      */
    struct  sigevent sev;                   /* Notification structure       */
    timer_t timerid;                        /* Timer ID from timer_create() */
    char    ch;                             /* User input                   */
    BOOL    finished = FALSE;               /* Loop exit condition          */
    int     row = TOP_ROW, oldrow;          /* Drawing position row coordinate */
    int     col = 1, oldcol;                /* Drawing position col coordinate */
    char    sprite = 'O';                   /* The sprite to draw           */
    char    blank = ' ';                    /* For erasing                  */
    int     numrows;                        /* Window row dimension         */
    int     numcols;                        /* Window column dimension      */
    char    msg[32];                        /* To print in bottom row       */
    int     user_row_adjust = 0;            /* Net row change caused by user */
    const   char CLEAR_SCREEN[] = "\033[2J"; /* Escape seq to clear screen  */
    const   char CLEAR_ABOVE[]  = "\033[1J"; /* Clears all lines above      */
    int     clr_above_len = strlen(CLEAR_ABOVE); /* Length of CLEAR_ABOVE   */
```

The structure of the main program is presented in pseudocode here:

```
Set up signal handling, with the SA_RESTART flag enabled.
Set up and arm the timer.
Get the window size into numrows, numcols.
Establish signal-driven I/O.
Clear the screen.
while( !finished ) {
    Handle user input and timer expirations.
}
Clear the screen and exit.
```

The body of the program's main loop is presented next. The complete program (*sigio_demo.c*) is available in the book's source code distribution.

```
while( !finished ) {
    if ( input_ready ) {        /* SIGIO received               */
        input_ready = 0;        /* Reset flag.                  */
        user_row_adjust = 0;    /* Net change in row position */
        home_cursor();
        while ( read(STDIN_FILENO, &ch, 1) > 0 && !finished ) {
            switch ( ch ) {
            case 'q':
                finished = TRUE;        /* User wants to quit.    */
                break;
```

```
            case 'd':
                user_row_adjust++;        /* Increment adjustment.    */
                break;
            case 'u':
                user_row_adjust--;        /* Decrement adjustment.    */
                break;
            case '\n':
                continue;                 /* Ignore newline.          */
            }
            moveto(TOP_ROW -1, 1);
            write(STDOUT_FILENO, CLEAR_ABOVE, clr_above_len); /* Clear line.*/
            sprintf(msg, "\rYou entered %c\r", ch); /* Format message.      */
            moveto(numrows, 1);                      /* Move to bottom row.  */
            write(STDOUT_FILENO, msg, strlen(msg)); /* Print message.        */
            home_cursor();                           /* Home cursor at (1,1).*/
        }
    }
    if ( timer_expired ) { /* Timer expiration                              */
        timer_expired = 0; /* Reset timer flag.                             */
        oldcol = col;      /* Save old position to replace with space char. */
        oldrow = row;
        row += user_row_adjust;     /* Adjust row by user's input.          */
            if ( row < TOP_ROW )    /* If above top row, move to top row.    */
                row = TOP_ROW;
            if ( row > numrows - 1 )    /* Boundary conditions to check      */
                row = TOP_ROW;
            if ( col < numcols )        /* Is it at rightmost column?        */
                col++;
            else {                      /* Yes - go to next row down.        */
                if ( row < numrows - 1 ) /* OK to go down                    */
                    row++;
                else                    /* Not OK to go down. Start at top. */
                    row = TOP_ROW;
                col = 1;
        }
        moveto(oldrow, oldcol);         /* Get set to erase old sprite.      */
        write(STDOUT_FILENO, &blank, 1);  /* Erase it.                       */
        moveto(row, col);               /* Move to new position to draw it.  */
        write(STDOUT_FILENO, &sprite, 1); /* Draw it.                        */
        user_row_adjust = 0;            /* Reset row adjustment to zero.     */
        home_cursor();                  /* Home the cursor.                  */
    }
    pause();
}
```

The program separates what the input handler does and what the timer expiration's handler does to prevent potential race conditions and unexpected behavior. The code that's executed when user input is detected doesn't update the sprite's position. Instead, the changes are recorded so that the handler for the timer interrupt can incorporate the changes before it refreshes the sprite's position. It does write a message at the bottom of the screen showing what the user entered.

This program uses ANSI escape sequences to animate the moving sprite and move the cursor. In Chapter 19, we'll see how to manage the screen using the *ncurses* library API instead. Here, we do what we can with the elementary tools at our disposal. If you build and run the program, you'll see that it meets all of the requirements we established earlier.

I chose a refresh rate of 0.1 seconds. If you increase it and enter characters at a fast enough rate, you may discover an unanticipated behavior, which I won't describe here; try to determine it yourself. I've mitigated this problem by homing the cursor at every opportunity.

Recapping, the method of input used in this program relies on a mechanism available in Linux and in BSD but which isn't part of the POSIX standard. It's partly asynchronous I/O because, although the I/O operation proceeds as the process continues its execution, the user process is informed only when input is available to be read. The input hasn't been transferred to the process when the signal's been delivered; the process has to get it by calling an input function. The next method of I/O that we'll examine is completely asynchronous and part of the POSIX.1-2024 standard.

POSIX Asynchronous I/O

The method of asynchronous I/O described in the preceding section wasn't incorporated into POSIX.1-2001 because the POSIX Working Group decided that its specification was inadequate [20]. Instead, that standard defined a new method of asynchronous I/O known as *POSIX Asynchronous I/O*, or *POSIX AIO*. This interface was implemented in *glibc* 2.1 in 1999 and has been a part of Linux distributions since then. Unlike the signal-driven I/O available by enabling the O_ASYNC flag on the file descriptor, POSIX AIO is fully asynchronous. In addition, it can be applied to I/O with any type of file descriptor, including disk files.

We'll begin with an overview of how it works and then look at the specific parts of the API that a program needs to use. It's easy to find the man pages in Linux that describe the POSIX AIO API. A search using apropos aio turns up all relevant pages. Our starting point is the aio(7) man page, which presents an overview of POSIX AIO.

Overview

The POSIX AIO interface allows programs to initiate one or more I/O operations to be performed asynchronously. When a process initiates such an operation, it runs independently. The man page says that it runs *in the background*, but it just means that it runs concurrently with the process. A program can request to be notified when the I/O operation is complete in two different ways, either by delivery of a signal or by invocation of a new thread within the process. It can also request not to be notified at all.

Many of the functions in the API are analogues to ordinary synchronous I/O system calls and have similar names. For example, the call to initiate an asynchronous read operation is aio_read(). Whereas a synchronous read() system call does not return until the data is available in the specified buffer, a call to aio_read() sets up the operation and returns immediately.

Writing is even more interesting. The write() system call does not return to the calling process until the data to be written has been completely transferred to a kernel buffer. We usually don't notice the delay because most of the time we're not sending large enough amounts of data to cause a perceptible delay. The analogue to write() is, as you might expect, aio_write(). When a process calls this function, it sets up the transfer and returns immediately, not waiting for the data to be in the kernel buffers. This is the sense in which AIO is very different from the other models of output that we've explored.

Figure 17-3 represents when the signal is generated in the process of data movement from the device to the process.

Figure 17-3: The sequence of steps in a POSIX AIO input operation showing when the notification is generated

The general sequence of events is that a process initiates an I/O operation by filling in the fields of an AIO request structure and passing that structure to a function for reading or writing. Among the fields of this structure is a member that contains the address of the data, namely a buffer in which to store input data or that contains the data to be output. That request is queued. Eventually, if the I/O operation is successful, a notification is sent to the process. The API provides several other functions, such as functions to monitor the progress of the operation and functions to suspend or cancel it.

The man page points out that the current implementation of AIO in Linux is provided by *glibc*, completely in user space. It is not implemented within the kernel. To clarify, when a process initiates a new I/O operation, the library creates a new thread to implement the operation. Each such operation is run within a separate thread. Threads within *glibc* are user-level threads, not kernel threads. As the number of operations increases, the overhead of thread management increases significantly. This is why the man page states that the current implementation scales poorly.

The AIO API

Let's turn to the details of the API, starting with the AIO object for requesting I/O, called an *asynchronous I/O control block*. This is a structure of type struct aiocb. The aio(7) man page shows its members. It also shows, incorrectly, that the required header file is *aiocb.h*; it is not. It should be *aio.h*:

```
#include <aio.h>    /* Not aiocb.h! */

struct aiocb {
    int             aio_fildes;    /* File descriptor    */
    off_t           aio_offset;    /* File offset        */
    volatile void  *aio_buf;       /* Location of buffer */
    size_t          aio_nbytes;    /* Length of transfer */
    int             aio_reqprio;   /* Request priority   */
    struct sigevent aio_sigevent;  /* Notification method */
    int             aio_lio_opcode; /* Operation to be performed;
                                       lio_listio() only   */
    // OMITTED: Various implementation-internal fields
}
```

This structure is passed to every function in the API. A program doesn't have to assign a value to the aio_reqprio, and it needs to assign a value to aio_lio_opcode only if the lio_listio() function is called. All others must be asigned a value.

Following are brief descriptions of each member:

aio_fildes   The file descriptor on which the I/O operation is to be performed.

aio_offset   The file offset at which the I/O operation is to be performed.

aio_buf   The buffer used to transfer data for a read or write operation.

aio_nbytes   The size of the buffer pointed to by aio_buf. For read operations, it's the maximum number of bytes to read.

aio_reqprio   This is a value to be subtracted from the calling thread's real-time priority. We can ignore this field for now.

aio_sigevent   The structure that specifies how the caller should be notified when the asynchronous I/O operation completes. The only possible values for the aio_sigevent.sigev_notify member of the structure are SIGEV_NONE, SIGEV_SIGNAL, and SIGEV_THREAD.

aio_lio_opcode   The type of operation to be performed. This is used only for the lio_listio() function.

AIO Functions

The POSIX AIO interface consists of the following functions. To use any of them, the program must include the *aio.h* header file, and it must be linked with the -lrt linker option, since they all use the real-time library.

aio_read()   Enqueues a read request. The asynchronous analogue of read().

aio_write()   Enqueues a write request. The asynchronous analogue of write().

aio_fsync() Enqueues a sync request for the I/O operations on a file descriptor. The asynchronous analogue of both fsync() and fdatasync(). These are the system calls that flush system buffers to disk.

aio_error() Can obtain the error status of an enqueued I/O request.

aio_return() Can obtain the return status of a completed I/O request.

aio_suspend() Suspends the caller until one or more of a specified set of I/O requests completes.

aio_cancel() Attempts to cancel outstanding I/O requests on a specified file descriptor.

lio_listio() A way to enqueue multiple I/O requests with a single function call.

Now we'll examine how to perform reads and writes. We won't explore the use of lio_listio() or the calls to suspend or cancel an operation. Afterward, we'll put together a small program that demonstrates the basics of asynchronous I/O. The aio(7) man page has a more complex example program.

The aio_read() Function

The steps to perform an asynchronous read using POSIX AIO are:

1. Fill in the fields of an asynchronous I/O control block, say aio_block. In particular, specify the file descriptor, the buffer into which data should be stored, the number of bytes to read, an initial offset in the file from which to start reading (usually 0), and how the process is to be notified. Let's assume that notification is by delivery of a SIGIO signal on I/O completion.

2. Create and establish a signal handler for SIGIO. The handler can set a flag to true when the signal is received, and the main program can check that flag, or the handler can use async-signal-safe functions to process the received input.

3. Call aio_read(), passing &aio_block, the address of the initialized block.

4. Go about executing the rest of the code.

5. On receipt of the SIGIO signal, the handler will run and the data will be available in the address pointed to by aio_block.aio_buf.

Figure 17-4 depicts the sequence of events that take place when a process initiates an AIO read operation. Compare this to Figure 17-2.

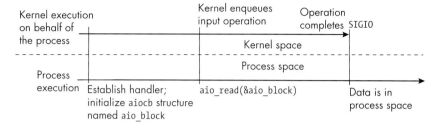

Figure 17-4: A timeline depicting the relative points in time at which events take place for an AIO input request

The aio_read() function's prototype is:

```
int aio_read(struct aiocb *aiocbp);
```

If the *aiocb control block is initialized with

```
aiocbp->aio_fildes = fd;
aiocbp->aio_buf    = buf;
aiocbp->aio_nbytes = count;
aiocbp->aio_offset = 0;
```

then calling aio_read(&aiocbp) requests an asynchronous read that's equivalent to calling the synchronous read:

```
n = read(fd, buf, count);
```

A process can retrieve the return status n of the equivalent synchronous read by calling aio_return() after the notification of completion is delivered to it. The value returned by aio_return() is the one that would have been returned by read(), which is the number of bytes actually read or -1 if it failed.

A key point to remember about reading is that when a program calls aio_read(), it doesn't continue reading where the previous call left off in the file. Each call to aio_read() starts at the absolute file offset given by aiocbp-> aio_offset. The actual file offset cannot be used by the program. This means that seeking will have no effect on asynchronous reads.

Let's consider an example. Suppose a file is 10,000 bytes long and we're reading 1,000 bytes at a time. The first time we call read, we need to assign 0 to aiocbp->aio_offset. The second time, we need to set it to 1000, the third time to 2000, and so on. This implies that, in general, if repeated reading is required, the program needs to update the aio_offset member of the control block when it receives the signal that reading is complete, and before the next call to aio_read():

```
num_bytes_read = aio_return(aiocbp);
aiocbp->aio_offset += num_bytes_read;
```

The aio_write() Function

Setting up a write operation is essentially the same as setting up a read. The control block is initialized in the same way, and the signal handler is established for the chosen signal. The aio_write() function's prototype is:

```
int aio_write(struct aiocb *aiocbp);
```

If the *aiocb control block is initialized with

```
aiocbp->aio_fildes = fd;
aiocbp->aio_buf    = buf;
aiocbp->aio_nbytes = count;
aiocbp->aio_offset = 0;
```

then calling aio_write(&aiocbp) requests an asynchronous write that's equivalent to calling the synchronous write:

```
n = write(fd, buf, count);
```

Like the read operation, each call to aio_write() starts writing at the absolute offset specified by aio_offset, unless the O_APPEND flag is enabled on the file descriptor. The call returns immediately; unlike write(), it doesn't wait for the data to be copied to system buffers.

The POSIX standard states that the write operation generates the requested notification when the write operation is completed, but it leaves the meaning of *completion* unspecified. It doesn't state whether completion means that the data has been written to the device or just to the kernel's buffer cache for the device. The *glibc* implementation of POSIX AIO generates the notification when a synchronous write of the same data to the same file descriptor would complete. In effect, whether or not the disk driver has already written the data to disk when the notification is received by the process doesn't matter, because a subsequent read of the data or the file's metadata could be satisfied from the in-memory buffers.

The aio_error() Function

Sometimes a program might need to monitor the progress of an ongoing asynchronous operation, whether it's a read or a write. The aio_error() function serves this purpose. Its prototype is:

```
int aio_error(const struct aiocb *aiocbp);
```

The return value is one of the following:

EINPROGRESS   The operation is still in progress.

ECANCELED   The operation was canceled.

0   The operation completed successfully.

e > 0   The operation failed; *e* is the value that would be put into errno by the call to read(), write(), or fsync().

In progress means that there is still an outstanding request. If a process requests a notification when the I/O operation completes and `aio_error()` is called after the notification is delivered, a return value of 0 indicates success, and a positive value is the value of `errno` that would be set by a synchronous read or write operation. The program *aio_write_demo.c* in the book's source code distribution shows how calls to `aio_write()` can be monitored with `aio_error()`.

Performance Benefits of Asynchronous I/O with Disk Files

Unlike signal-driven I/O, POSIX AIO functions can perform I/O with disk files. Doing so has the potential to make certain types of applications run faster. I'll illustrate with an example.

One of the first programs that we developed in the book was a simplified version of the `cp` command. That program consists of a loop in which it reads a fixed number of bytes from the source file into a buffer and then writes the buffer contents to a target file. Its loop is of the form:

```
while ( (nread = read(sourcefd, buffer, nrequested)) > 0 )
    write(targetfd, buffer, nread);
```

Because the write operation doesn't start until the buffer has been filled by the read operation and the read operation cannot modify the buffer while the write is copying data out of it, the reads and writes are serialized, as depicted in Figure 17-5.

read()   write()   read()   write()   read()   write()   ...

Figure 17-5: Serialized, synchronous reads and writes to copy a source file to a target file

Asynchronous I/O has the potential to make copying a file faster because the reads and writes can be partially overlapped. It is *potential* only because it may have no effect whatsoever. Some of the factors that impact the total running time are:

- The amount of system activity, which affects how long it takes for the kernel to allocate time for servicing the I/O operations

- Whether the files are on the same device (if they're on different devices managed by different drivers, the disk operations can be run in parallel)

- To what extent read operations can be satisfied from kernel buffers because the source file might have been opened recently

Although there may not be a decrease in running time, in principle, replacing the synchronous read with an asynchronous read can speed up copying. It isn't necessary to replace the synchronous write as long as the read is asynchronous.

The idea is to start the first asynchronous read of the first chunk of the file and, when the signal is delivered, start an asynchronous read of the next chunk, followed immediately by a synchronous write of the chunk just received. This sequence is repeated; each time that a read completes, the next read and write operations are started together. There's a problem, though. The process can't start the next read if it uses the buffer just filled by the previous read because whatever it reads will overwrite the buffer contents while the write is in progress, as illustrated in Figure 17-6.

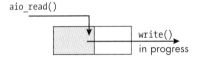

Figure 17-6: A read operation overwriting the contents of a buffer as a write operation is in progress

The solution is to employ *double buffering*.

DOUBLE BUFFERING

Double buffering is a technique used in graphics applications and window managers to speed up the rendering of images. The application maintains two buffers. At any instant of time, one buffer is what's on the screen, and the other is a *hidden* copy of the screen buffer being modified behind the scenes by the application. When the copy is ready to appear on the screen, the buffers are swapped—the copy is displayed on the screen and the previous screen buffer becomes the copy to be updated.

The program can use an array of two buffers:

```
char *buffer[2];
```

At any given time, one of these buffers is being filled by an asynchronous read, and the other, which contains the data from the preceding read, is being written to a file by a synchronous write operation. The loop, with some pseudocode, is roughly as follows:

```
// OMITTED: Set up aio_block for the first read operation.
aio_block.aio_buf = buffer[0]; /* Begin with buffer[0].        */
aio_read(&aio_block);          /* Initiate the read operation. */
i = 0;
while ( more_data_to_read ) {               /* While source file has more data  */
    // if ( aio_read() completed ) {
    num_read = aio_return(&aio_block); /* Get num bytes read.               */
    writebuf = aio_block.aio_buf;      /* write() from buffer just filled   */
    i = i^1;                           /* Same as i = (i == 0) ? 1 : 0      */
    aio_block.aio_buf = buffer[i];     /* Use other buffer for next read.   */
    aio_block.aio_offset += num_bytes_read;  /* Adjust offset for read. */
```

```
    aio_read(&aiocb));                              /* Request next read.    */
    write(target_fd, writebuf, num_bytes_read); /* Start write().        */
    }
}
```

The code omits a few details and assumes that when a read completes, the signal handler sets a global flag that indicates that aio_read() completed another read operation. The sequence of reads and writes is thus:

```
read into buffer[0];
read into buffer[1] while writing from buffer[0];
read into buffer[0] while writing from buffer[1];
read into buffer[1] while writing from buffer[0];
read into buffer[0] while writing from buffer[1];
--snip--
```

Because writing is synchronous, the next read doesn't start until the buffer can be reused.

The total running time if this idea is employed depends on whether reads and writes take roughly the same amount of time. If each read takes much longer than a write of the same data, the time to read determines the total running time, and if writing takes longer, then the writes dominate the running time. Figure 17-7 illustrates the difference.

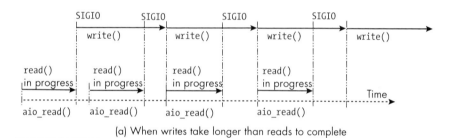

(a) When writes take longer than reads to complete

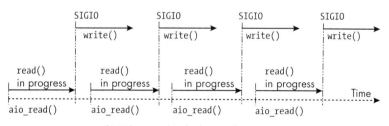

(b) When reads take longer than writes to complete

Figure 17-7: Overlapped, asynchronous reads using aio_read() and synchronous writes using write() to copy a source file to a target file

In Figure 17-7(a), writing takes longer—the read requests complete but the process can't start the next read until the write completes. In Figure 17-7(b), reading takes longer and each write completes before the next read is completed.

An AIO-Based Implementation of spl_cp1.c

Here I'll show an implementation of an asynchronous version of the simplified cp command that we developed in Chapter 4. We'll use the double-buffering technique just described.

The program sets the notification method for aio_read() completion to send the SIGIO signal to the process. The signal handler and the function that establishes it are:

```
volatile sig_atomic_t  input_ready = 0;

/* The signal handler for SIGIO */
void on_input(int sig, siginfo_t *si, void *ucontext)
{
    input_ready = 1;
}

void setup_handler()
{
    struct  sigaction sigact;

    sigact.sa_sigaction = on_input;
    sigact.sa_flags = SA_RESTART | SA_SIGINFO;
    sigemptyset(&sigact.sa_mask);
    if ( sigaction(SIGIO, &sigact, NULL) == -1 )
        fatal_error(errno, "sigaction");
}
```

The handler sets the global input_ready flag that the main program polls in its main loop. When the main program sees that the flag is set to 1, it sets up the next read and write operations.

The program uses almost all of the variables from *spl_cp1.c*, together with a few needed for the AIO version of it. The code is in two listings. The first, Listing 17-3, contains the program variables and initial configuration and setup code prior to the main loop. To save space, only the new variables are shown in this listing, and some code is omitted as well. The complete program is available in the book's source code distribution.

```
aio_cp.c   int main(int argc, char *argv[])
  Part 1   {
               // OMITTED: Declarations from spl_cp.c
               int          i = 0;      /* For choosing next buffer        */
               char        *buf[2];     /* Buffers for reads and writes    */
               char        *writebuf;   /* Pointer to buffer used by write() */
               struct aiocb  aio_block; /* AIO control block               */

               // OMITTED: Checks for correct usage
               setup_handler();         /* Set up signal handling.         */
```

```
/* Open source and target files for reading. */
if ( ((source_fd = open(argv[1], O_RDONLY)) == -1)
   || ((target_fd = open(argv[2], O_WRONLY | O_CREAT | O_TRUNC,
                      permissions)) == -1) )
    fatal_error(errno, message);

/* Allocate fixed size buffers. */
if ( (NULL == (buf[0] = calloc(BUFFER_SIZE, 1)))
   || (NULL == (buf[1] = calloc(BUFFER_SIZE, 1))) )
    fatal_error(errno, "calloc");

/* Initialize the AIO control block; zero memory first. */
memset(&aio_block, 0, sizeof(aio_block));
aio_block.aio_buf      = buf[0];
aio_block.aio_fildes   = source_fd;
aio_block.aio_nbytes   = BUFFER_SIZE;
aio_block.aio_reqprio  = 0;
aio_block.aio_offset   = 0;
aio_block.aio_sigevent.sigev_notify = SIGEV_SIGNAL;
aio_block.aio_sigevent.sigev_signo  = SIGIO;
if ( -1 == aio_read(&aio_block) )  /* Issue first read request. */
    fatal_error(errno, "aio_read");
BOOL done = FALSE;
--snip--
```

Listing 17-3: Variable declarations and setup for aio_cp.c

Listing 17-4 contains the main loop and the cleanup code that follows
it. The main loop begins by setting up the next read and then calls write().
You can't reverse the order; if it calls write() before setting up the next read,
the call to aio_read() will not start until the write completes, removing all
advantage of the asynchronous reading, since the read and write will not
overlap in time.

aio_cp.c
Part 2
```
--snip--
while ( !done ) {
    if ( input_ready ) {                  /* SIGIO received           */
        input_ready = 0;                  /* Reset flag before anything else! */
        num_bytes_read = aio_return(&aio_block);
        if ( num_bytes_read > 0 ) { /* Set up next read and write.    */
            writebuf = (char*) aio_block.aio_buf;
            i = i^1;                       /* Flip i from 0 to 1 or 1 to 0.  */
            aio_block.aio_buf      = buf[i];        /* Use other buffer. */
            aio_block.aio_offset += num_bytes_read; /* Advance offset.  */
            if ( -1 == aio_read(&aio_block) )     /* Request next read. */
                fatal_error(errno, "aio_read");
            /* Now start synchronous write(). */
            num_bytes_written = write(target_fd, writebuf,
                              num_bytes_read);
```

```
            if ( errno == EINTR )  /* Handle various errors.        */
                printf("write() was interrupted by read completion\n");
            else if ( errno != 0 ) /* Some other error              */
                fatal_error(errno, "write()");
            else /* Successful write; check if all bytes were written.  */
                if ( num_bytes_written != num_bytes_read) {
                    sprintf(message, "write error to %s\n", argv[2]);
                    fatal_error(-1, message);
                }
        }
        else  /* We're done! */
            done = TRUE;
    }
}
/* Cleanup time: Close files, free memory. */
// OMITTED: Closing files
free(buf[0]);
free(buf[1]);
return 0;
}
```

Listing 17-4: The loop in aio_cp.c

In order to test whether there's any performance gain achieved by using asynchronous I/O over the synchronous reading and writing of *spl_cp.c*, we need to follow the same procedure that we used in "Timing Programs" in Chapter 4. There, we wrote a bash script that unmounted and remounted the filesystem between successive runs of the program to clear the kernel buffers. That isn't enough to do a good comparison, because if the source and target files are on the same filesystem, the same driver will be called and the reads and writes will most likely be serialized. Therefore, it's better to copy a file in one filesystem to a directory in another. If you can create two small partitions on a disk, you can copy a file from one to the other under the time command. You can also alter the buffer size to see what effect that has on the overall running time.

Here's an example to demonstrate:

```
$ umount /temp /data
$ mount /temp /data
$ time ./aio_cp /data/ubuntu-22.04.2-src-1.iso /temp/cpy
real  0m48.565s
user  0m40.236s
sys   0m10.687s
$ umount /temp /data
$ mount /temp /data
$ time ./spl_cp /data/ubuntu-22.04.2-src-1.iso /temp/cpy2
real  1m5.005s
user  0m1.547s
sys   0m10.638s
```

These numbers shouldn't be used to draw any conclusions about the performance. We'd need to use a much larger sample. Nonetheless, we can make a few observations. First is that the system time is essentially the same. The same amount of time was spent reading and writing. Second, the AIO version spent much more time in user mode because the *glibc* implementation uses user-level threads (actually *Pthreads*) to implement the AIO API. The elapsed time in this case was much shorter for the AIO version, which is what we hope to see.

Multiplexed I/O

Let's think about the situation in which a program has to read from multiple sources of infrequent, intermittent input, such as a set of pipes or FIFOs, as well as its control terminal. Suppose that the program must respond to all of its inputs without delay.

If the program opens these file descriptors in blocking mode and then it repeatedly checks whether input is available on each descriptor one after the other, it could block on one descriptor even though data is available on others. It could, instead, open all descriptors in nonblocking mode and poll them periodically in sequence. In this case, it would waste CPU cycles polling each descriptor, especially if the input is infrequent. If it polled only infrequently, then when input did arrive, the program would take too long to receive and respond to it, leading to unacceptable response times.

Yet another alternative would be to use asynchronous reads on each descriptor. This is possible but quite messy to code, and it has the drawback that it relies on signals, which means having to write signal handlers that use only async-signal-safe functions as well as synchronization facilities to eliminate race conditions.

What we really need is a way to monitor all descriptors with a single function call. In other words, we'd like a function that can give the kernel a set of file descriptors and ask it to tell us whether any of the file descriptors in the set are ready for I/O and, if so, which ones. This capability is called I/O multiplexing. *I/O multiplexing* is a service provided by the kernel that allows a process to monitor multiple file descriptors for possible I/O activity. Unix systems support I/O multiplexing with several different functions. To find them, we can search for the term *multiplex* in the man pages. This search will yield a few different functions and system calls that are used for I/O multiplexing:

```
$ apropos multiplex
--snip--
poll (3posix)        - input/output multiplexing
pselect (2)          - synchronous I/O multiplexing
select (2)           - synchronous I/O multiplexing
select (3posix)      - synchronous I/O multiplexing
select_tut (2)       - synchronous I/O multiplexing
```

The search won't discover all such functions, but when we read any of the preceding man pages, we'll see references to a set of functions that didn't come up in this search, namely those that are part of the Linux-specific epoll() API, which is referred to as an *I/O event notification facility*.

The select() call is the oldest of these functions, first appearing in 4.2BSD. The select(), pselect(), and poll() system calls have all been part of the POSIX standard since POSIX.1-2001. In contrast, epoll() is not part of POSIX, and programs that use it will not necessarily run on other Unix distributions.

Overview

The select() and pselect() calls are nearly identical; the major difference between them is that select() waits only until a file descriptor is ready for I/O, whereas pselect() waits until either a file descriptor is ready or until a signal is caught. These two calls share a single man page, which explains how to use both and provides an example.

The poll() system call performs a similar service as select(). The primary difference between them is how the set of monitored file descriptors is specified. In addition, poll() can monitor more types of events than select() can and overcomes several limitations of select(), which will be explained shortly. The most importance difference between poll() and select() is their relative performance. If the set of file descriptors contains very large-valued descriptors, such as 900 or 1000, poll() will perform much faster than both select() and pselect().

In general, select() and poll() do not scale to large numbers of descriptors well. The time spent in the kernel is at least proportional to the number of monitored descriptors. The epoll() API is a relatively new API, first appearing in Linux 2.6, and it provides similar functionality to poll(). Unlike select() and poll(), which are level triggered, epoll() can be used as either an edge-triggered or a level-triggered interface. It has superior performance to all of the other functions. However, learning how to use its interface takes a bit more work and it is not portable.

Although the select() system call is not as efficient as the others, its performance is acceptable for small numbers of watched file descriptors, none of which is a large number. Since it's fairly easy to learn, I chose to make select() the only call I'll explain in depth.

The select() System Call

Basically, the select() call is a mechanism that allows a process to monitor multiple descriptors in a single system call. It is given three sets of file descriptors, representing I/O devices or files that the process wants to monitor, and an optional timeout value. One set contains the descriptors to monitor for input, one for output, and one for *exceptional events*, which apply only to sockets and pseudoterminals. It's a synchronous mechanism because it blocks until one of the descriptors is ready for I/O or the optional timeout interval expired.

The Form and Use of select()

The select() call has five arguments:

```
#include <sys/select.h>

int select(int nfds, fd_set *readfds, fd_set *writefds, fd_set *exceptfds,
           struct timeval *timeout);

void FD_CLR(int fd, fd_set *set);
int  FD_ISSET(int fd, fd_set *set);
void FD_SET(int fd, fd_set *set);
void FD_ZERO(fd_set *set);
```

The second through fourth arguments are addresses of objects of type fd_set, whose definition is exposed in the *sys/select.h* header file. The four functions FD_* are used for manipulating these fd_set objects. I'll explain their use shortly.

The three major arguments (readfds, writefds, and exceptfds) are the addresses of sets of file descriptors to be monitored for three corresponding classes of events— reading, writing, and exceptional events—on the specified set of file descriptors. Each of these fd_set* arguments may be passed NULL to indicate that no file descriptor in that category should be watched for the corresponding class of events.

Specifically, the arguments of the call are:

readfds The address of a set of file descriptors to be watched to see if they're ready for reading. A file descriptor is *ready for reading* if a read operation will not block. It is also ready on the end-of-file condition. When select() returns, readfds will be cleared of all file descriptors except for those that are ready for reading.

writefds The address of a set of file descriptors to be watched to see if they're ready for writing. A file descriptor is *ready for writing* if a *small* write operation will not block. A write of a large amount of data can still block if it's so large that a pipe or message queue, for example, reaches capacity. When select() returns, writefds will be cleared of all file descriptors except for those that are ready for writing.

exceptfds The address of a set of file descriptors to be watched for exceptional conditions. The select(2) man page refers us to the poll(2) man page for examples of these conditions, but as mentioned earlier, these are conditions relevant only to sockets or to pseudoterminals; most programs set this parameter to NULL. When select() returns, exceptfds will be cleared of all file descriptors except for those for which an exceptional condition was detected.

ndfs Must be set to the maximum value of all monitored file descriptors plus 1. For example, if the largest descriptor in readfds is 12 and the largest in writefds is 8 and *exceptfds is set to NULL, then ndfs must be set to 13, 1 more than 12.

timeout   The address of a `timeval` structure that specifies the amount of time that `select()` should block while waiting for a file descriptor to become ready. The call blocks until one of three events takes place:

- At least one file descriptor becomes ready.
- The call is interrupted by a signal handler.
- The timeout expires.

If `timeout` is `NULL`, there is no timeout and the call blocks until at least one descriptor is ready or it was interrupted by a signal. If both members of the `timeout` structure are 0, the call to `select()` returns immediately, updating all sets of descriptors, as if it were in nonblocking mode. If it is nonzero and the call isn't interrupted, it will wait until either the timeout interval elapses or one of the specified descriptors is ready, whichever happens first.

The return value of the `select()` call is either the number of descriptors that are ready or `-1` if there was an error. In particular, if `select()` was interrupted by a signal, `errno` will be set to `EINTR`.

NOTE   *When select() returns, each of the file descriptor sets has been modified in place to indicate which file descriptors are currently ready. Therefore, before calling select() again, as a program would do if it were in a loop, the sets must be reinitialized.*

The four macro functions for manipulating the file descriptor sets are:

void FD_ZERO(fd_set *set)   Removes all file descriptors from *set. It's the first step in initializing a file descriptor set.

void FD_SET(int fd, fd_set *set)   Adds the file descriptor fd to *set if it isn't in it already. It has no effect if it's already in the set.

void FD_CLR(int fd, fd_set *set)   Removes the file descriptor fd from *set if it's in the set. It has no effect if it's not in the set.

int FD_ISSET(int fd, fd_set *set)   Tests whether the file descriptor fd is in *set, returning nonzero if it's present and 0 if it isn't.

The fd_set data type is not necessarily a scalar. It's often an array of integers, typically 32 of them. The maximum number of descriptors in any one set is a system constant, `FD_SETSIZE`, whose value is typically 1024 (32×32 bits in the array).

The ndfs Value

The value of the first parameter (`ndfs`) must be set to the value of the largest file descriptor plus 1 because file descriptors are zero based. This parameter is used by the kernel to improve the performance of `select()`. The kernel checks every file descriptor from 0 up to ndfs − 1. Without it, the kernel would have to check all possible file descriptor values. Even so, the implementation is still not very efficient because the kernel is checking file descriptor values that don't even correspond to open file descriptors passed to `select()`. For example, if a program has four file descriptors, numbered 0, 1, 2, and 500, the kernel will check every file descriptor value from 0 through 500 (a total of 501 descriptors) when `select()` is called, even though only four need checking.

A Small Example

Following is a short code snippet that shows how to monitor just two file descriptors in a loop:

```
int     fd1, fd2, maxfd;
fd_set readset, tempset;
// OMITTED: Open 2 pipes or files and let fd1 and fd2 be their descriptors.
maxfd = fd1 > fd2 ? fd1+1 : fd2+1;

FD_ZERO(&readset);          /* Clear the bits in the mask. */
FD_SET(fd1, &readset);      /* Add fd1 to readset.         */
FD_SET(fd2, &readset);      /* Add fd2 to readset.         */
tempset = readset;          /* Copy readset to tempset.    */

while ( select(maxfd, &tempset, NULL, NULL, NULL) > 0 ) {
    if ( FD_ISSET(fd1, &tempset) ) {
        /* Read from descriptor fd1. */
    }
    if ( FD_ISSET(fd2, &tempset) ) {
        /* Read from descriptor fd2. */
    }
    tempset = readset; /* Since select() modified tempset */
}
```

Let's make a few observations about this code:

- Because the return value of select() is positive, as long as there's data to be read on either of fd1 or fd2, the loop will continue until it gets end-of-file on both file descriptors or an error occurs.

- Since select() changes the file descriptor set readset, the program makes a copy of it and passes the copy to the call. In this loop, after the call, it makes a fresh copy before calling it again.

- The sets are not modified if select() returns with an error.

- Inside the loop, it uses FD_ISSET() to test each descriptor in which the program is interested.

Select Law

One of the pages returned by our man page search at the start of this section is that of select_tut(2). After you've read the select(2) man page, you should take a look at this one. It isn't exactly a tutorial, as its name suggests, but it does provide an overview, a comparison of pselect() and select(), some guidance, and an example program. The example program is a TCP forwarding program. Because this book doesn't cover sockets, this example isn't one we can examine here.

I'd like to highlight some of what that page calls *select law*. This is advice for the safe and efficient use of select(). Some of the points that I haven't mentioned previously are as follows:

- Try to use select() without a timeout. Programs using timeouts are difficult to debug.

- Don't put a file descriptor into a set unless you plan to check its result after the call. It wastes time.

- After the call returns, always check every file descriptor to see if it's ready.

I recommend reading the other points on that page as well.

An Example Program

We'll develop a simple example here that models a server-like program and demonstrates the principles for programming with select(). The program, which I'll name *select_demo.c*, should have multiple sources of infrequent and unpredictable input as well as at least one file descriptor open for writing, on which writing may not always be possible. The terminal should be among the input sources, so that a user can enter a q to terminate the program. The terminal is a good source of infrequent, intermittent input, but the program needs more of them.

We can't use files as input sources because they'll always have input available, but we can use pipes. The program can create multiple pipes and a child process for each pipe. Each child process can open its own private pipe for writing, and the parent process can open each child's pipe for reading. If each child process writes a few bytes sporadically into its pipe at somewhat random intervals, then this will simulate an application that spawns multiple worker processes that occasionally send small messages back to the managing parent process.

Setting up a file descriptor for writing such that writes may not always be possible on it is a bit trickier. We can solve this problem with a pipe also. The program can fork a receiver process that reads from a pipe created by the parent process. The parent process will attempt to write into this pipe, but if the pipe is full, it won't be able to. Therefore, after the pipe is created but before monitoring with select(), the parent process will fill the pipe to capacity. After that, we can choreograph a dance between the child process and the parent in which the child reads enough bytes out of the pipe at a suitable rate, so that the parent will only occasionally be able to write into the pipe.

On Linux, the select() call deems the write end of a pipe to be ready for writing only if at least PIPE_BUF bytes are available in the pipe. Not all Unix systems have this behavior; on some, select() may mark a descriptor as writeable if there's room for a single byte in the pipe. Note that the behavior of select() on Linux doesn't contradict the pipe write semantics I described in Table 13-2 in Chapter 13—a process can write $n < $ PIPE_BUF bytes into a pipe that has fewer than PIPE_BUF free bytes of space, provided that n is less than the available space in the pipe. It's just that select() won't deem the file descriptor writeable in this case.

Therefore, the parent process should write PIPE_BUF bytes at a time whenever the descriptor is ready for writing, and the receiver child process should read smaller chunks at a rate so that every few seconds, the pipe has at least PIPE_BUF bytes available for a write into it.

Figure 17-8 depicts the organization of the processes in the program in terms of communication patterns.

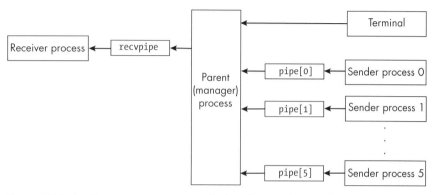

Figure 17-8: A schematic representation of select_demo.c *showing the sources of input and output monitored by the parent process using* select()

The main program will create six child processes that send small messages to it, each at a different rate. It will also read from the terminal in case the user enters a q. Finally, it will create a receiver process that will slowly drain the pipe that they share. Whenever the pipe has enough space, the parent (manager) will write a large chunk into that pipe.

The program uses the following macro constants:

```
#define  READ_END    0
#define  WRITE_END   1
#define  RECV_DELAY  4
#define  NSENDERS    6
```

The main program will be short. It offloads most of its work to a function named manager(). It needs to set up the pipes and create all processes. Its code is in Listing 17-5.

select_demo.c
main()
```
int main(int argc, char *argv[])
{
    int pipefd[NSENDERS][2];   /* Array of pipes for senders  */
    int senderpid[NSENDERS];   /* Sender process PIDs         */
    int recvpid;               /* Receiver process PID        */
    int recvpipefd[2];         /* Receiver process pipe       */

    /* Create a pipe for each child process before fork(). */
    for ( int i = 0; i < NSENDERS; i++ ) {
        if ( pipe(pipefd[i]) == -1 )  /* Create pipe[pipefd[i]. */
```

```
            fatal_error(errno, "pipe");
        switch( senderpid[i] = fork() ) {
        case -1:
            fatal_error(errno, "fork");
        case 0:                           /* Child code - the sender */
            sender(pipefd[i], (i + 1) * (1 + (rand() % 10)));
        }
    }
    if ( pipe(recvpipefd) == -1 )      /* Create receiver's pipe. */
        fatal_error(errno, "pipe");
    switch ( recvpid = fork() ) {      /* Fork the receiver.       */
    case -1:
        fatal_error(errno, "fork");
    case 0:
        receiver(recvpipefd, RECV_DELAY);
    }
    /* Parent continues here. It calls the manager() function. */
    manager(pipefd, senderpid, recvpipefd, recvpid);
    exit(EXIT_SUCCESS);
}
```

Listing 17-5: The main() function of select_demo.c

The loop creates a pipe and forks a new child that executes the sender() function, which is passed the pipe's file descriptors and a randomized number
that it uses as the number of seconds between successive writes into its pipe.
You can play around with the amount of delay and randomization. The values here make the display easy to read while it scrolls and don't delay the
program excessively.

To make the program more enlightening as it runs, the messages written
by each sender process will be timestamped with the time they were written into their pipes. When the select() call executed by the manager sees
that the read end of that sender's pipe is ready for input, it gets the current
time, reads the message with its timestamp, and computes the latency, the
amount of time the message was in transit. It prints a message to standard
output with the sender's message and the transit time. Short transit times
correspond to good response time; longer ones indicate poor response time.

To enable this feature, the program defines a message structure:

```
typedef struct _msg {
    struct timespec gen_time;    /* Time at which message was generated */
    char            content[32]; /* Text string sent by sender process  */
} message;
```

The sender() function that each child executes is fairly simple:

sender()
```
int sender(int *pipefd, int delay)
{
    message msg;                         /* Message written by sender into pipe */
```

```
        close(pipefd[READ_END]);         /* Close read end of pipe.        */
        memset(&(msg.content), 0, 32); /* Clear message content.         */
        sprintf(msg.content, "Hello from process %d.", getpid());
        while ( TRUE ) {
            sleep(delay);                /* Delay a few seconds.           */
            /* Get the current time, accurate to nanosecond. */
            if ( -1 == clock_gettime(CLOCK_REALTIME, &(msg.gen_time)) )
                fatal_error(errno, "clock_gettime()");
            write(pipefd[WRITE_END], &msg, sizeof(msg));    /* Write to pipe. */
        }
        exit(EXIT_SUCCESS);
    }
```

The receiver is somewhat symmetric to the sender processes. It sleeps a randomized amount of time, shorter than the sender's, and reads chunks of size 512 bytes. After every eight reads, the pipe is reduced by PIPE_BUF bytes, and the manager should find the write end ready for output:

receiver()
```
int receiver(int *pipefd, int delay)
{
    const int bufsize = PIPE_BUF/8;    /* Read chunks of size 512 bytes.  */
    const int usecs = 250000;          /* Used to compute delay           */
    char      buf[bufsize];            /* Buffer to store reads from pipe */

    close(pipefd[WRITE_END]);          /* Close write end of pipe.        */
    while ( TRUE ) {
        usleep(usecdelay + (rand() % usecs));        /* Delay a bit.      */
        if ( -1 == read(pipefd[READ_END], buf, bufsize) )  /* Read pipe. */
            error_mssge(errno, "read");
    }
    exit(EXIT_SUCCESS);
}
```

The manager() function is where the interesting code is. It begins by closing the ends of pipes it isn't going to use, setting up the file descriptor sets for the select() call, and filling the pipe to its capacity. The function is shown in Listing 17-6 in its entirety.

manager()
```
void manager(int sndpipe[NSENDERS][2], int *senders, int *recvpipe,
             int recvpid)
{
    char    line[512];       /* For formatted output                   */
    char    gentimestr[64];  /* For formatted time of generated message */
    char    str[64];         /* For output                             */
    char    write_msg[128];  /* For output                             */
    fd_set  readfds, writefds, readcopy, wrcopy; /* File descriptor sets */
    int     i;
    int     nbytes = 0;
    int     maxfd = 0;
```

```
char    ch = '1';
message child_msg;
int     msgsize = sizeof(message);
struct  timespec ts, diff;
char    fill[PIPE_BUF];

memset(fill, '0', PIPE_BUF);
for ( i = 0; i < NSENDERS; i++ )
    close(sndpipe[i][WRITE_END]);
close(recvpipe[READ_END]);

/* Create descriptor mask for sending children. */
FD_ZERO(&readfds);
FD_SET(STDIN_FILENO, &readfds);     /* Watch standard input.            */
FD_ZERO(&writefds);                 /* Watch write end of receiver pipe. */
FD_SET(recvpipe[WRITE_END], &writefds);
maxfd = recvpipe[WRITE_END];        /* Make this maxfd for now.         */

for ( i = 0; i < NSENDERS; i++ ) {/* Watch read end of each sender pipe.*/
    FD_SET(sndpipe[i][READ_END], &readfds);
    if ( sndpipe[i][READ_END] > maxfd )
        maxfd = sndpipe[i][READ_END];  /* Find max descriptor value.    */
}
readcopy = readfds;                     /* Make copies of descriptor sets. */
wrcopy = writefds;
fillpipe(recvpipe[WRITE_END]);          /* Fill pipe to capacity.          */
while ( select(maxfd + 1, &readcopy, &wrcopy, NULL, NULL) > 0 ) {
    /* First check pipe to receiving child. */
    if ( FD_ISSET(recvpipe[WRITE_END], &wrcopy) ) {
        if ( -1 == (nbytes = write(recvpipe[WRITE_END], fill, PIPE_BUF)) )
            error_mssge(-1, "Could not write to receiver pipe\n");
        sprintf(write_msg,"Wrote %d bytes to receiver pipe.\n\n", nbytes);
        write(STDOUT_FILENO, write_msg, strlen(write_msg));
    }
    /* Next check standard input. */
    if ( FD_ISSET(STDIN_FILENO, &readcopy) )
        if ( read(STDIN_FILENO, &ch, 1) > 0 && (ch == 'q') )
            break;  /* User wants to quit, so break loop. */
    /* Now check the pipe from each sending child. */
    for ( i = 0; i < NSENDERS; i++ ) {
        if (FD_ISSET(sndpipe[i][READ_END],&readcopy)){ /* Ready to read */
            memset(&child_msg, 0, msgsize);
            if ( read(sndpipe[i][READ_END], &child_msg, msgsize) > 0 ) {
                if ( -1 == clock_gettime(CLOCK_REALTIME, &ts) )
                    fatal_error(errno, "clock_gettime()");
                memset(&diff, 0, sizeof(diff));
                timespec_diff(ts, child_msg.gen_time, &diff);
```

```
                print_time(diff, 1, str);
                print_time(child_msg.gen_time, 0, gentimestr);
                sprintf(line, "Message from sender %d
                            (transit-time = %s):\n"
                            "    Content = \"%s\" Sent at time %s\n\n",
                            i, str, child_msg.content, gentimestr);
                write(1, line, strlen(line));
            }
        }
    }
    readcopy = readfds;                     /* Restore descriptor sets. */
    wrcopy = writefds;
}
for ( i = 0; i < NSENDERS; i++ ) /* End of loop. Terminate all children.*/
    kill(senders[i], SIGINT);
kill(recvpid, SIGINT);
while (waitpid(-1, NULL, WNOHANG) > 0 ) {}  /* Reap their status.      */
exit(EXIT_SUCCESS);
}
```

Listing 17-6: The manager process for select_demo.c

The main loop of the function repeatedly calls select(). If any file descriptors are ready for I/O, it stays in the loop; otherwise, it exits the loop. It checks the write descriptor first, the terminal input, and then each remaining read descriptor. It uses two functions not shown here. The print_time() function formats time for output, using the format *HH:MM:SS.NNNNNNNNN*, so that we have nanosecond accuracy. The fillpipe() function fills the pipe to capacity by writing into it in nonblocking mode until it gets an error. Many of the instructions in the manager() function are there to output information that could be directed instead into a log file for further analysis.

The complete program is in the book's source code distribution. Following is a small snippet showing the output of a sample run. I removed the blank lines that the program writes:

```
$ ./select_demo
Message from sender 0 (transit-time = 00:00:00.000105276):
    Content = "Hello from process 14224." Sent at time 15:53:10.944189626
Message from sender 0 (transit-time = 00:00:00.000076314):
    Content = "Hello from process 14224." Sent at time 15:53:14.944309109
Message from sender 1 (transit-time = 00:00:00.000108114):
    Content = "Hello from process 14225." Sent at time 15:53:14.944324258
Successful write of 4096 bytes to receiver pipe.
Message from sender 2 (transit-time = 00:00:00.000122340):
    Content = "Hello from process 14226." Sent at time 15:53:18.944388131
Message from sender 3 (transit-time = 00:00:00.000090107):
    Content = "Hello from process 14227." Sent at time 15:53:22.944488371
q
$
```

The transit times in this output are on the order of 0.0001 seconds because the select() function runs often enough so that available input is read quickly. If the main body of the loop spent more time in other computations, those transit times would increase.

Summary

The simple model of I/O in which read and write operations are performed in blocking mode isn't a good fit for the design of interactive programs and programs with multiple input and output connections. These types of programs typically have intermittent input that arrives at unpredictable times. Waiting for input on a single file descriptor prevents them from performing other tasks and checking other file descriptors until input is available to read.

In this chapter, we explored a few alternative methods of I/O that circumvent this problem. One is to use nonblocking I/O instead of blocking I/O. When a file descriptor is open in nonblocking mode, reads return immediately when no data is available, and writes to descriptors that aren't ready for writing also return immediately. This leads to an I/O paradigm called *polling* in which the descriptors are repeatedly checked to see if they're ready. Polling descriptors that are rarely ready is wasteful of CPU and kernel resources and can also result in increased response times.

We also considered signal-driven I/O, a form of semi-asynchronous I/O. In this paradigm, the program informs the kernel that it wants to receive a signal, SIGIO by default, whenever I/O is possible on a file descriptor by setting the O_ASYNC flag on that descriptor and establishing a SIGIO signal handler. With signal-driven input, the kernel sends the signal once the data is in kernel buffers; the program still needs to call read() or some other input function to retrieve it. This is the sense in which it is not fully asynchronous. Signal-driven I/O is available only in BSD and Linux.

POSIX asynchronous I/O, known as POSIX AIO, is an API for completely asynchronous input and output. It's more portable than signal-driven I/O because most Unix systems provide it. With POSIX AIO, a program fills in an AIO control block with information that defines an I/O request. The key members of this control block are the file descriptor, the address of a buffer, the size of the buffer in bytes, the offset in the file at which to perform the I/O operation, and the method of notification when the operation is complete. The program calls functions similar to read() and write(), but with names of the form aio_read() and aio_write().

The last model we examined can be categorized as multiplexed I/O, a form of I/O in which the readiness of multiple input and output descriptors is checked within a single system call. Servers often need this capability since they usually have connections to multiple pipes, FIFOs, and/or internet sockets. Although there are several different methods of monitoring multiple descriptors, in this chapter we explored only the select() system call. We give the call three sets of file descriptors to be monitored: those for reading, for writing, and for exceptional conditions. It returns as soon as at least one descriptor is ready for I/O. The other methods we didn't consider include the poll() call and the epoll() API, which is Linux specific. The latter is the fastest of all choices.

Exercises

1. Modify *sigio_counter.c* to use the SIGRTMIN real-time signal instead of SIGIO. Convert the signal handler to a SA_SIGINFO handler with a siginfo_t argument, and make the program output, in addition to its current output, the values of the si_fd and si_code fields of the siginfo_t structure for each arriving signal.

2. The program *mqrecv_demo.c* in Chapter 12 is one of a pair of programs that communicate through a POSIX message queue. That program currently has to be terminated by killing it with a signal. For this exercise, modify the program so that the user can enter q to terminate it. The program will use select() to monitor two input sources: the terminal and the message queue. The problem is that message queues do not have ordinary file descriptors and therefore can't be watched by select().

    To overcome this, the program will fork a child process that synchronously receives messages inside a while loop like the one in the main() function of *mqrecv_demo.c*, and each time it receives a message, it copies the message and its priority into a pipe shared by the parent process and itself. The main() function will then use select() to watch the terminal and the read end of this pipe. When the user enters q, it should terminate. When it reads the pipe, it should retrieve both the message and priority and print the same message on the terminal as it currently does.

3. Rewrite *sigio_demo.c* so that it uses the POSIX AIO API instead of signal-driven I/O. Your program should not alter the behavior of the program in any other way.

4. The select() man page describes a technique for emulating the pselect() function, which can monitor both file descriptors and signals. Because pselect() is not specified by POSIX, this is a way to create a portable version of it. It's known as the *self-pipe trick*. Write a program that uses select() to watch the standard input for possible input and that handles CTRL-C by printing CTRL-C received when a user enters CTRL-C. The signal handler for SIGINT should use the self-pipe trick, and the main program should continue to run when the signal is delivered, quitting only when the user enters q.

5. The select() system call existed well before Unix had a usleep() function. Programmers who wanted their processes to sleep for finer granularity than a second emulated usleep() with select() because it has a timeout parameter. Write a function like usleep() that is given a number of microseconds and suspends the calling process for that time, unless it's interrupted by a signal, by calling select() with suitable arguments.

18

TERMINALS AND TERMINAL I/O

This chapter sets the stage for the development of advanced interactive programs. It deals with terminals and their attributes. The programs in previous chapters haven't manipulated the terminal except perhaps by clearing the screen or controlling the cursor position. However, some programs, including system programs, do change the terminal's behavior to suit their needs. For example, they might disable the echoing of characters or prevent signals from being generated by the keyboard. Here, we'll learn how programs can take charge of the terminal, precisely so that they can make it behave in accordance with their requirements.

We'll begin by clarifying what interactive programs are and what special requirements they have. We'll then examine terminals and terminal attributes and how they can be retrieved and modified, both at the level of the shell and within programs.

About Interactive Programs

An *interactive program* is a program that expects user input while it's running. Although any program that prompts a user for input during its execution is technically an interactive program, here, we're going to consider only the subset of them that run in a terminal window, are started up from the command line, get their input from the terminal's associated keyboard device, and configure the terminal for their specific needs.

These types of interactive programs are always inextricably connected to the terminal, configuring it for their own particular needs. Programs such as text editors (vi, nano, and emacs), pagers (more and less), and administrative tools (parted and top) are tightly coupled to the terminal and control its settings and attributes. They usually don't use the standard library's input and output streams for I/O because these streams interpose a layer of buffering that interferes with their ability to control precisely how the terminal behaves. Interactive programs usually control most of the following I/O properties:

- Whether characters are echoed

- Whether characters are buffered and, if so, how many at a time

- Where the cursor is positioned on the screen

- Whether certain keypresses should have their default meaning or an application-defined meaning

- Whether timeouts should occur while waiting for input

- Whether keyboard-generated signals such as CTRL-C should be ignored, blocked, or handled immediately

In short, the issues related to terminals and their configuration for I/O in Unix are a complex topic. To better understand what attributes and aspects of their behavior a program can control, we'll begin with an overview of the software that underlies them and how it's organized.

An Overview of Terminals

People rarely use actual terminal devices anymore; instead, they use software-emulated terminals on bitmapped graphical displays. Most Unix systems run an X Window System window manager, which allows applications to run the xterm emulator, maintained by the X Consortium. An *xterm emulator* can emulate a number of physical terminals, such as the DEC VT102 or the DEC VT220. Therefore, when I use the term *terminal* here, I mean either a hardware terminal or a terminal window emulated by software.

Terminal I/O is one of the messiest and most disorganized parts of any operating system. This is partly due to the fact that I/O interfaces have developed in an ad hoc fashion over the years, responding to changes in hardware and user demands. It's also partly due to the wide variety of I/O devices that have to be accommodated under the aegis of a single I/O system and partly due to the general lack of standards that governed how terminal I/O was handled. In Unix, this was exacerbated by the rift between the BSD versions and System V versions of the operating system, which had very different sets of terminal I/O routines. The POSIX standard provided a unification of the two sets of interfaces, and modern systems provide POSIX-compliant routines. However, there are still many parts of the I/O interface that are platform specific.

If you understand how terminals work, then you'll have a better understanding of how to program terminal I/O. For example, these are the kinds of questions that you'll be able to answer:

- Why is it that we have to press ENTER in order for the typed characters to be received by a program, and is there a way to avoid this?

- How can a program suppress the echoing of characters as they're typed?

- How can a program time out while waiting for user input?

- Some programs, such as vi and emacs, override the meanings of various control sequences such as CTRL-D and CTRL-C. How can ours do that?

- If a user changes the shape of a terminal window, how can a program get the new dimensions?

- Why is it that sometimes the BACKSPACE key erases characters, sometimes the DELETE key does, and sometimes neither does? How does the terminal erase?

An Experiment

Let's begin by studying and running the following program:

upcopychars.c
```
#include "common_hdrs.h"   /* For stdlib.h, unistd.h */
#include <ctype.h>

int main(int argc, char *argv[])
{
    char inbuf;
    char prompt[] = "Type any characters followed by ENTER, Ctrl-D to exit.\n";
    if ( -1 == write(1, prompt, strlen(prompt)) )
        fatal_error(errno, "write");
    while ( read(STDIN_FILENO, &inbuf, 1) > 0 ) {
        inbuf = toupper(inbuf);
        if ( -1 == write(1, &inbuf, 1) )
            fatal_error(errno, "write");
    }
    return 0;
}
```

Before compiling and running the program, let's try to predict its behavior. By default, both standard input and standard output are connected to the process's control terminal. In its `while` loop, each time that it reads a character, it immediately writes that character in uppercase to the terminal. Converting to uppercase makes it easier to distinguish between the input and the output. It repeatedly does this until read() returns 0, which it will do if we enter CTRL-D. It follows that, if I enter the sequence abcde, when it gets the a it will write A to the screen before I enter the b, and the same for the remaining characters. In other words, we should expect that with this input, the run would look like

```
$ ./upcopychars
Type any characters followed by ENTER, Ctrl-D to exit.
aAbBcCdDeE^D
$
```

because each character is output immediately after I enter it. The ^D indicates that I entered CTRL-D to terminate the program.

Let me run it now. I enter the five characters abcde first

```
$ ./upcopychars
Type any characters followed by ENTER, Ctrl-D to exit.
abcde
```

but nothing happens. There's no output. When I press ENTER

```
$ ./upcopychars
Type any characters followed by ENTER, Ctrl-D to exit.
abcde<ENTER>
ABCDE
^D
$
```

the entered characters in uppercase appear on the next line. Even though the main loop reads a single character and immediately writes it in uppercase, nothing appears on the screen until I press ENTER. We can't attribute this behavior to the C Library's buffering since we're not using the library I/O functions. The terminal is responsible for this. Somehow, the characters that we type are stored until we press ENTER. We don't know where or why or whether that can be changed.

An Explanation

Before the advent of graphical user interfaces, the terminal was the only means for users to interact with programs. Terminal software was designed to make this interaction as convenient as possible.

For instance, we often want to edit a line before submitting it to a program. We use the BACKSPACE or DELETE keys to do so, and when we're satisfied, we press ENTER. If I run the upcopychars program and enter the five letters abcde after which I enter BACKSPACE twice followed by xyz, and then ENTER, the output would be ABCXYZ. This wouldn't be possible if every character was transmitted immediately. The line is the fundamental unit of input. This is why the terminal driver waits until a whole line is ready before it sends it off to the program. Figure 18-1 depicts the internal buffer of the terminal and the system buffer into which the read() system call stores its input before sending it to the program as I enter these characters. <BS> is the backspace code and <CR> is the code generated by ENTER. It shows that all characters are stored in this terminal buffer, but editing actions take place before it is transmitted.

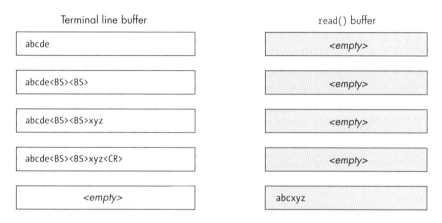

Terminal line buffer / read() buffer

abcde	<empty>
abcde<BS><BS>	<empty>
abcde<BS><BS>xyz	<empty>
abcde<BS><BS>xyz<CR>	<empty>
<empty>	abcxyz

Figure 18-1: A schematic representation of the processing of an edited input line

Imagine what it would be like if, when you entered text to a program such as upcopychars, you couldn't see the characters that you entered. Sometimes we want this, as when we enter a password, but most of the time, this would be very disconcerting; we'd have no way to know whether we entered what we intended. Normally, as we enter printable characters, they appear on the screen immediately; this is called character *echoing*, and it's what we expect. Have you ever had the experience of working on a Unix system remotely through an SSH connection and not seeing what you entered until a second or more later? That suggests that the echoing of the character is not being done only by your local machine but in part by the remote machine, and that the transmission rate happens to be slow at the time. In Unix, terminal devices do not normally echo characters; the kernel software is responsible for that.

Also consider that when we enter a control character such as CTRL-C, instead of anything being displayed on the screen, a signal is sent to our process (and all processes for which this is their control terminal).

All of these behaviors are part of a mode of operation that users expect for normal interactive use, so much so, that this collective set of properties of the terminal is called *canonical mode*.

Terminal Drivers

The preceding experiment shows that the default input mode of a terminal, called canonical mode, includes assembling the input into lines, processing various special characters such as backspace, and delivering the input lines to the process after they've been processed. Terminals can be operated in various noncanonical input modes as well. In a noncanonical mode, some part of this processing of input is disabled. Programs like emacs, vi, and less put the terminal into a noncanonical mode called *raw* mode, in which the terminal passes all input to the process with no processing.

Terminal Driver Structure

The behavior of a terminal is controlled entirely by a software component called a *terminal driver*. A terminal driver is not the same thing as a *terminal device driver*. A terminal driver consists of two subcomponents:

- A terminal device driver

- A line discipline

The terminal device driver's main function is to transfer characters to and from the terminal device; it's the software that talks directly with the physical terminal or the terminal emulator, such as xterm, at one end, and the line discipline at the other. For this purpose, the line discipline and the terminal device driver share access to a few data structures. In Linux, struct tty_struct is the major shared data structure.

NOTE *A line discipline is a software module that defines the behavior of asynchronous interfaces such as terminals, RS232 mouse drivers, Bluetooth drivers, some network protocols such as Point-to-Point (PPP), and many other drivers. In Linux, the line discipline for a terminal is of type struct tty_ldisc.*

For a terminal, the line discipline is the software that does the processing of input and output. It manages several queues, including an input queue and an output queue for the terminal driver. The relationship between these queues, the process using the terminal, and the terminal itself is illustrated in Figure 18-2. The terminal driver is the sum of the parts in this figure; it is the combination of line discipline and device driver. The queues are drawn inside the line discipline only to emphasize that it's the line discipline that manages them. The line discipline itself has no storage; it is a collection of functions and links to other structures. This is yet another example of a producer-consumer relationship within the kernel, because the device driver itself is a producer with respect to the input queue and the line discipline is a consumer. The opposite relationships are true of the output queue.

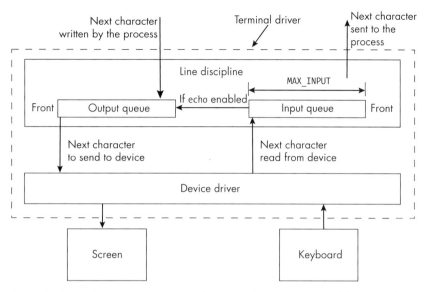

Figure 18-2: The Unix implementation of a terminal showing some of the internal queues of the terminal driver

The figure illustrates only the key components of the terminal driver. It shows that characters received from the device driver are pushed into the input queue and those to be sent to the driver are pushed into the output queue. When echoing of characters is enabled, the line discipline copies a character to its output queue when its input queue receives it, possibly after any special processing it might need to do, causing the character to be displayed on the screen.

The figure depicts that the size of the input queue is the system constant MAX_INPUT. If characters are typed faster than they are removed for processing and the queue fills up, Unix systems discard any extra characters. MAX_INPUT is specified by POSIX to be the minimum size of this buffer, but any Unix system might make the buffer larger. We've got a few different methods of finding its value. First, the getconf command can tell us:

```
$ getconf MAX_INPUT /dev/tty    # Need to give it path to terminal
255
```

A program can call pathconf() to get this same value:

max_input.c
```
#include "common_hdrs.h"
int main()
{
    printf("%ld\n", pathconf(ttyname(0), _PC_MAX_INPUT));
    return 0;
}
```

The function is given the pathname of the terminal device and the constant `_PC_MAX_INPUT` and returns the value of that parameter for the given device. When I run it on Linux 5.15, it reports that it's 255 bytes also. However, the actual maximum could be larger.

We can get its actual size from the kernel source code, or we can conduct a small experiment. To start, I'll modify the upcopychars program by deleting the code that outputs the prompt string, renaming it upcopychars2. When we enter characters from the keyboard while upcopychars2 is running without entering a newline character in between, they're all pushed into its input queue (and echoed back to us). When we press ENTER, the contents of the input queue are written to standard output. If we pipe the output of upcopychars2 to wc -c, it will output how many bytes upcopychars2 output.

If we can fill the buffer to its maximum, the output of wc -c will be the buffer size. If we try to write more characters into the buffer, they'll be discarded. But we have to enter these characters from the keyboard, not by redirecting them from a pipe or file. One way to do this is to create files containing successively larger strings without trailing newlines, and copy and paste them into the terminal window while upcopychars2 is running. If the output number is equal to the size of the file, we'll double the file size and repeat the test. If it's less, then the output number is the buffer size. If I start with a file containing a really large number of characters, I may not have to create a second file. I'll try 16,384 characters as an initial guess. If it reports less than 16,384, I found the maximum, and if not, I'll double the file size and repeat.

I'll create a file named *a.16384* containing 16,384 consecutive a characters without a trailing newline with the command:

```
% $ ( for i in `seq 1 16384` ; do echo -n 'a' ; done ) > a.16384
```

Then I'll open it, copy it into the clipboard, and paste it into the terminal window after entering upcopychars2 | wc -c. For example, here's a run in which I enter one character to the modified program:

```
$ ./upcopychars2 | wc -c
a<ENTER>^D
      2
```

The a and the newline are the two characters reported. Now I'll give it 16,384 characters:

```
$ ./upcopychars2 | wc -c
aaaaaaaaaaaaaaaa...aaaa<ENTER>^D
    4096
```

The output suggests that on this version of Linux (5.15), the buffer is 4096 bytes. The kernel source code corroborates this; the system header file *include/linux/tty.h* contains a macro definition #define N_TTY_BUF_SIZE 4096 that the kernel uses as the size of the terminal's input buffer.

The terminal driver maintains other queues besides the input and output queues. It has queues of processes waiting to read from and write to the terminal, for instance. It also has a second input queue called the *canonical input queue*. This is the queue in which input characters are processed when the terminal is in canonical mode. Canonical processing is handled by the line discipline. The terminal driver's behavior is determined by various attributes and configuration settings. Having a mental picture of the terminal driver, including its basic operations and how terminal settings affect these operations, makes it easier to understand how to program them and where to start when we need to diagnose problems related to terminal I/O.

The Terminal Driver as Seen from the Shell

Let's search for a command that can display and possibly modify the terminal settings. A man page search with apropos -s1 terminal produces too long a list, but we can filter it through grep -E (because we want to use the alternation character, |):

```
$ apropos -s1 terminal | grep -E 'setting|propert|attribute'
resize (1)          - set environment and terminal settings to current xte...
setterm (1)         - set terminal attributes
stty (1)            - change and print terminal line settings
```

The setterm command doesn't display settings; it changes them. The command we want is stty.

The stty Command

The stty command can both display and alter terminal characteristics. Without options or arguments, it displays a small subset of the current settings of the terminal connected to the shell in which the command is invoked. Different systems may display different pieces of information by default. The man page for stty provides answers to all of the questions I posed earlier. It states that the -a option displays all settings in human-readable form; following is the output of stty -a:

```
$ stty -a
speed 38400 baud; rows 24; columns 79; line = 0;
intr = ^C; quit = ^\; erase = ^?; kill = ^U; eof = ^D; eol = <undef>;
eol2 = <undef>; swtch = <undef>; start = ^Q; stop = ^S; susp = ^Z; rprnt = ^R;
werase = ^W; lnext = ^V; discard = ^O; min = 1; time = 0;
-parenb -parodd -cmspar cs8 -hupcl -cstopb cread -clocal -crtscts
-ignbrk -brkint -ignpar -parmrk -inpck -istrip -inlcr -igncr icrnl ixon -ixoff
-iuclc -ixany -imaxbel iutf8
opost -olcuc -ocrnl onlcr -onocr -onlret -ofill -ofdel nl0 cr0 tab0 bs0 vt0
ff0 isig icanon iexten echo echoe echok -echonl -noflsh -xcase -tostop
-echoprt echoctl echoke -flusho -extproc
```

Human-readable form is not the same thing as human-understandable form! Fortunately, the man page explains what each output symbol means and how to interpret the output. I'll explain more about the output and terminal settings next.

Understanding stty Output

There are three kinds of settings listed in the output of stty -a. They're displayed in one of the following three forms:

- *symbolic-value*

- *variable* or *-variable*

- *variable = value* or *variable value*

The first form is a symbolic name for the value of a fixed variable. For example, in the preceding output, the symbol tab0 indicates that the tab delay of the terminal is set to TAB0. Other possible values for the tab delay are TAB1, TAB2, and TAB3. The author of stty chose this concise form instead of the lengthier tabdly = tab0. Tab delay is one of several delay-bit attributes of a terminal. In general, delay bits specify how long a transmission stops to allow for mechanical or other movement when certain characters are sent to a terminal. The actual delays depend on line speed and system load. For software-emulated terminals, these delay bits are usually not meaningful. In fact, as of version 6, the Linux documentation states that "Linux currently ignores TABDLY, CRDLY, VTDLY, FFDLY and NLDLY. They simply aren't relevant in the world today." All symbolic values represent delays with one exception: cs8 is the character size in bits (8 bits). This cannot be changed.

The second form gives the state of Boolean variables. The Booleans are called *switches* or *flags*. I prefer the term *switch* because they act like switches—a switch prefixed with a hyphen (-) is off, and a switch that is not prefixed with a hyphen is on. Examples of switches are echo, inlcr, icanon, and icrnl.

To change the value of a switch you enter

```
$ stty [-]switch
```

where *switch* is replaced by the name of the switch, and the hyphen is present to turn it off and absent to turn it on. Thus

```
$ stty -echo
```

will turn off echo on the screen. We'll try a few changes soon, but first, before changing any settings, we need to know how to restore the terminal.

NOTE   *When all else is not working and the terminal has become a big mess, enter **reset**. If echo is disabled, you won't see what you're typing, so type slowly and carefully! You might have to enter **<LF>reset<LF>**, where <LF> is the linefeed character, which you can do by entering CTRL-J. If you'd like to restore the terminal to a sane state, enter **stty sane**. This restores most variables and values to their default settings.*

If you now enter

```
$ stty -echo
```

you won't see anything you type. Enter

```
$ stty echo
```

to restore echoing.

The last form displays the values of non-Boolean variables in one of two forms:

- *variable* = *value*

- *variable* *value*

For example, this output

```
rows 24; columns 80; line = 0; intr = ^C; quit = ^\;
```

indicates that the number of rows in the terminal is 24 and the number of columns is 80. In the expression line = 0, *line* refers to the line discipline. Line disciplines have unique small integer identifiers. For example, the *TTY* line discipline has the number 0 and the *PPP* line discipline's number is 2. The next two show that CTRL-C is the interrupt character and CTRL-\ generates SIGQUIT.

The man page explains that erase is the character that erases the last character typed. In other words, it's the character we call *backspace*. Let's look at the erase key setting:

```
$ stty -a | grep -E -o '\<erase = ...'
erase = ^?;
```

This output doesn't mean that entering CTRL-? erases a character; it does not. It means that the code generated by the BACKSPACE key is the ASCII character whose code is 127 in decimal, denoted by ^? on output, called DEL. However, entering CTRL-? doesn't erase; it sends the character whose ASCII code is 31, which is called the *unit separator* character. (Note that some systems use CTRL-H to backspace by default rather than BACKSPACE.)

Do a little experiment now. Change the erase key to X and type some text followed by BACKSPACE:

```
$ stty erase X
$ hello^?
```

The terminal displays the BACKSPACE key as ^?. Try entering text followed by X and you'll see you changed the erase key. Remember to restore it before proceeding with **stty erase ^?**.

Categories of Terminal Attributes

The terminal attributes can be categorized by how they're used and what they control.

Special characters   Characters that are used by the driver to cause specific actions to take place, such as sending signals to the process or erasing characters or words or lines. Special characters include the erase, `werase`, and `kill` characters, to name a few. Characters used to send signals include CTRL-C, which sends the SIGINT signal.

Special settings   Variables that control the terminal in general, such as its input and output speeds and dimensions. These include the `rows`, `cols`, `min`, and `time` values. The two variables `min` and `time` are used when the terminal is in noncanonical mode to control how characters are returned by read() calls; we'll explore their use later.

Input settings   Operations that process characters coming from the terminal. This includes changing their case, converting carriage returns to newlines, and ignoring various characters like breaks and carriage returns.

Output settings   Operations that process characters sent to the terminal. Output operations include replacing tab characters with the appropriate number of spaces, converting newlines to carriage returns, carriage returns to newlines, and changing case.

Control settings   Operations that control character representation such as parity, stop bits, and hardware flow control. Several of these do not apply to pseudoterminals.

Local settings   Operations that control how the driver stores and processes characters internally. For example, echo is a local operation, as is processing erase and line-kill characters.

Combination settings   Combinations of various settings that define modes such as `cooked` mode, `raw` mode, and `sane` mode.

Input switch names always begin with `i` and output switch names begin with `o`. I'll display the output of `stty -a` again, rearranged and annotated to show the categories of the variables and switches:

```
special characters:     intr = ^C; quit = ^\; erase = ^?; kill = ^U; eof = ^D;
                        eol = <undef>; eol2 = <undef>; swtch = <undef>;
                        start = ^Q; stop = ^S; susp = ^Z; rprnt = ^R;
                        werase = ^W; lnext = ^V; discard = ^O; min = 1;
                        time = 0;
control flags:          -parenb -parodd -hupcl -cstopb cread -clocal -crtscts
multibit control flags: cs8
input flags:            -ignbrk -brkint -ignpar -parmrk -inpck -istrip
                        -inlcr -igncr icrnl ixon -ixoff -iuclc ixany imaxbel
output flags:           opost -olcuc -ocrnl onlcr -onocr -onlret -ofill -ofdel
multibit delay flags:   nl0 cr0 tab0 bs0 vt0 ff0
```

```
local flags:            isig icanon iexten echo echoe echok -echonl -noflsh
                        -xcase -tostop -echoprt echoctl echoke
```

I put the character size (cs8) and the output delay constants (nl0 and so on) on separate lines because they aren't flags.

Some special characters are for editing or input purposes:

werase   Erases the rightmost occurring word to the left of the cursor. By default, it's CTRL-W.

kill   Erases an entire line. By default, it's CTRL-U.

lnext   Called the *literal next* character. Entering it before entering a special character causes the special character to be treated literally, not interpreted. By default, it is CTRL-V. To pass a CTRL-C to a process as a literal character, enter ^V^C.

Some are for job control:

susp   Generates a job control signal, SIGTSTP, that suspends the foreground process group and puts it in the background. By default, it's CTRL-Z.

And some are used for input operations:

stop   Suspends output to the terminal. By default, it's CTRL-S.

start   Resumes output to the terminal. By default, it's CTRL-Q.

In the next section, we'll examine a few terminal switches in more detail.

Experimenting with Terminal Switches

The terminal switches generally play an important role in how the terminal functions. We'll explore what two particular switches do before we dive into how to control the behavior of the terminal in our programs.

We'll start with the icrnl switch, which, when set, causes input carriage returns to be converted to newline characters. Read it as i for input, cr for carriage return, and nl for newline. The carriage return character (ASCII code 13, \r) moves the cursor to the left margin; we used it in our implementation of a progress bar in Chapter 9. The newline (ASCII code 10, \n) moves the cursor down one line without changing its column position, so that the next character starts on the line below.

We're going to conduct an experiment with this switch. I'll use the od command (od -a) to assist. This displays its file argument byte by byte, naming the characters with recognizable short names if they're not printable. First I'll run upcopychars2, redirecting its output to a file:

```
$ ./upcopychars2 > out1
abcde
fgh
ij^J
z
^D
```

In this listing, the ^J appears where I entered CTRL-J, which sends a new-line character to the terminal driver. I terminated all other lines by pressing ENTER, which sends the carriage return to the terminal driver.

Let's look at *out1*:

```
$ od -a out1
0000000   A   B   C   D   E  nl   F   G   H  nl   I   J  nl   Z  nl
0000017
```

Notice that even though the driver received a carriage return character after the e, h, and z, od shows that it was replaced by a newline, indicated by nl in the output. Here's the output of cat out1:

```
ABCDE
FGH
IJ
Z
```

It looks like what I entered, converted to uppercase, when I ran upcopychars2. I'll have more to say about this shortly.

Now I'll turn off the icrnl switch and run it again, redirecting its output to *out2*. With the switch disabled, input carriage returns will not be replaced by newlines. When we press ENTER:

- We'll see ^M appear at the cursor position.

- The cursor will not advance to the next line. It will move to the right, as if I entered a printable character such as x.

Pressing ENTER generates CTRL-M, which terminals display as ^M. Since the terminal is in canonical mode, the terminal will not deliver the input until a newline is entered, but with this switch disabled, pressing ENTER does not generate a newline; I have to enter CTRL-J to send the newline character code (10) to the driver:

```
$ stty -icrnl
$ ./upcopychars2 > out2
abcde^Mfgh^Mij^J
z^M^D
```

What we see when we enter this input is what the terminal echoes back to us. These are the characters that were put into the terminal's input queue and copied from there into its output queue. In the listing, each ^M is where I pressed ENTER. The listing displays ^J where I entered it, but in fact nothing is echoed to the terminal when I enter it. I put it into the listing so that you can see where I entered them.

Let's look at the contents of *out2*:

```
$ od -a out2
0000000   A   B   C   D   E  cr   F   G   H  cr   I   J  nl   Z  cr
0000020
```

Compare this to *out1*. The carriage returns were not converted to newlines. What follows next may surprise you. I will cat this file:

```
$ cat out2
IJHDE
$
```

Try to explain this to yourself before reading on, remembering that an input carriage return character moves the cursor to the first position in the current line, without erasing any characters.

The first carriage return causes FGH to overwrite ABC, leaving FGHDE. The next causes IJ to overwrite FG, leaving IJHDE. The newline moves the cursor to the next line and a Z is printed, but the next carriage return moves the cursor to the start of that line, and the bash prompt overwrites it.

We take the magic of the onlcr switch for granted. When our program prints a string such as "Hello world\n" to standard output, we see the *Hello world* on the screen with the cursor at the start of the line below. The newline character caused two cursor movements: It moved the cursor to the start of the row and moved it down one row. In other words, it caused the sequence \r \n to be output to the terminal's device driver.

The onlcr switch causes output newline characters to be replaced by a carriage return–newline pair. Read the name as o for output, nl for newline and cr for carriage return. What happens when we disable this switch?

Those carriage returns don't get sent to the terminal. The output is unmanageable. I'll demonstrate as follows.

```
$ stty -onlcr
cat out1
ABCDE
     FGH
        IJ
          Z
            $
```

The lack of carriage returns means that the cursor keeps moving to the right; there's no stopping it! It doesn't take long before it starts wrapping on the screen. See what happens when you enter a command such as ls with the switch turned off.

We haven't explored what happens when we disable the icanon switch. We'll cover canonical and noncanonical mode processing in greater depth in Chapter 19. The POSIX.1-2024 requirements document, Section 11.1.6, *Canonical Mode Input Processing*, summarizes what canonical mode is in conforming systems.

The Terminal Driver API

The stty command lets us see and modify terminal settings from the shell; now we'll explore how to retrieve and modify terminal settings from within programs. Searching Sections 2 and 3 in the man pages for a combination of *terminal* and *settings* fails, but if I search for *attributes* instead of settings, I find a dozen or so library functions for working with the device driver and line discipline:

```
$ apropos -s2,3 -a terminal attributes
cfgetispeed (3)        - get and set terminal attributes, line control, get a...
cfgetospeed (3)        - get and set terminal attributes, line control, get a...
cfmakeraw (3)          - get and set terminal attributes, line control, get a...
cfsetispeed (3)        - get and set terminal attributes, line control, get a...
cfsetospeed (3)        - get and set terminal attributes, line control, get a...
--snip--
tcgetattr (3)          - get and set terminal attributes, line control, get a...
tcsetattr (3)          - get and set terminal attributes, line control, get a...
termios (3)            - get and set terminal attributes, line control, get a...
```

It turns out that all of these functions share the single termios(3) man page, the beginning of which follows:

```
NAME
     termios, tcgetattr, tcsetattr, tcsendbreak, tcdrain, tcflush, tcflow,
     cfmakeraw, cfgetospeed, cfgetispeed, cfsetispeed, cfsetospeed, cfsetspeed
     - get and set terminal attributes, line control, get and set baud rate
SYNOPSIS
     #include <termios.h>
     #include <unistd.h>
     int tcgetattr(int fd, struct termios *termios_p);
     int tcsetattr(int fd, int optional_actions,
                   const struct termios *termios_p);
     --snip--
  The termios structure
     Many of the functions described here have a termios_p argument that is
     a pointer to a termios structure. This structure contains at least the
     following members:
          tcflag_t c_iflag;      /* Input modes        */
          tcflag_t c_oflag;      /* Output modes       */
          tcflag_t c_cflag;      /* Control modes      */
          tcflag_t c_lflag;      /* Local modes        */
          cc_t     c_cc[NCCS];   /* Special characters */
--snip--
```

I'll begin by examining the termios data structure, whose definition is exposed by including *termios.h*. The actual definition on any specific Unix system may include other members and therefore is contained in a file included in *termios.h*. For instance, on my Linux system, the definition is in the header file */usr/include/x86_64-linux-gnu/bits/termios-struct.h*:

```
#define NCCS 32
struct termios {
    tcflag_t c_iflag;     /* Input mode flags                */
    tcflag_t c_oflag;     /* Output mode flags               */
```

```
    tcflag_t c_cflag;    /* Control mode flags          */
    tcflag_t c_lflag;    /* Local mode flags            */
    cc_t     c_line;     /* Line discipline   NOT POSIX */
    cc_t     c_cc[NCCS]; /* Control characters          */
    speed_t  c_ispeed;   /* Input speed       NOT POSIX */
    speed_t  c_ospeed;   /* Output speed      NOT POSIX */
    // OMITTED: Two macro definitions
};
```

The structure maps closely to the different categories of terminal settings that we learned about from the stty command. Its first four members are of type tcflag_t, which is a typedef for unsigned int found in *bits/termios.h*. I will refer to these members as *flagsets*. The c_line, c_ispeed, and c_ospeed members aren't part of the POSIX standard, but they're supported in Linux. The type cc_t is a typedef for unsigned char; the c_cc member is an array of characters; these are the special characters we described earlier.

Terminal Switches

The four flagsets contain one or more bits for every distinct setting within the corresponding category. Some settings require more than one bit. The *bits/termios.h* header defines a mask for each setting; for multibit settings, the masks are also multibit. Each of bitmasks and a description of what it controls is described in the termios(3) man page. Table 18-1 describes the masks and descriptions for the c_iflag member.

Table 18-1: Bitmasks and Descriptions of the c_iflag Member

Mask name	Description
IGNBRK	Ignore BREAK condition on input.
BRKINT	Signal SIGINT on BREAK.
IGNPAR	Ignore framing errors and parity errors.
PARMRK	Mark parity errors with prefix bytes 0377,0.
INPCK	Enable input parity checking.
ISTRIP	Strip off eighth bit.
INLCR	Translate NL to CR on input.
IGNCR	Ignore CR on input.
ICRNL	Translate CR to NL on input (unless IGNCR is set).
IUCLC	Map uppercase characters to lowercase on input (not in POSIX).
IXON	Enable XON/XOFF flow control on output.
IXANY	Typing any character will restart stopped output.
IXOFF	Enable XON/XOFF flow control on input.
IMAXBEL	Ring bell when input queue is full (not in POSIX).
IUTF8	Input is UTF-8 (since Linux 2.6.4) (not in POSIX).

The c_oflag flagset masks follow in Table 18-2.

Table 18-2: Bitmasks and Descriptions of the c_oflag Member

Mask name	Description
OPOST	Perform output processing.
ONLCR	Map NL to CR-NL on output.
OCRNL	Map CR to NL on output.
ONOCR	Don't output CR if already in column 0.
ONLRET	NL performs CR function.
OFILL	Use fill characters for delay.
OFDEL	Use DEL (0177) as fill character; otherwise, NULL (0).
NLDLY	Select newline delays: NL0 or NL1.
CRDLY	Select carriage return delays: CR0, CR1, CR2, CR3.
TABDLY	Select horizontal tab delays: TAB0, TAB1, TAB2, TAB3.
BSDLY	Select backspace delays: BS0, BS1.
VTDLY	Select vertical tab delays: VT0, VT1.
FFDLY	Select form-feed delays: FF0, FF1.

Mask names ending in DLY may be more than one bit. For these, the description lists the possible symbolic values that it masks. For example, if myterm is a termios structure, then

```
myterm.c_oflag & CRDLY
```

is exactly one of CR0, CR1, CR2, or CR3; CRDLY is a two-bit mask.

Since the c_cflag member controls hardware devices, I won't display it here; it's available in both the man pages and the POSIX specifications. The c_lflag member has fewer flags and is more relevant to this material. Its mask set follows in Table 18-3.

Table 18-3: Bitmasks and Descriptions of the c_lflag Member

Mask name	Description
ISIG	Enable signal-generating characters INTR, QUIT, SUSP.
ICANON	Enable canonical mode.
ECHO	Echo input characters.
ECHOE	If ICANON is set, the ERASE character erases the preceding input character and WERASE erases the preceding word.
ECHOK	If ICANON is also set, the KILL character erases the current line.
ECHONL	If ICANON is also set, echo the NL character even if ECHO is not set.
ECHOCTL	If ECHO is also set, control characters other than TAB, NL, START, and STOP are echoed visually (not in POSIX).
ECHOPRT	Echo deleted characters back to the terminal (not in POSIX).
ECHOKE	If ICANON is set, don't output a newline after echoed KILL (not in POSIX).
NOFLSH	Disable flushing the input and output queues when generating signals for the INT, QUIT, and SUSP characters.
TOSTOP	Send the SIGTTOU signal to the process group of a background process that tries to write to its controlling terminal.
IEXTEN	Enable implementation-defined input processing.

These are the flags that enable or disable echoing in various ways, canonical mode processing, signal delivery, and so on.

Finally, you should be aware that many modern shells set the values of these flags themselves. If we want to see the true effect of changing the value of a flag with the stty command, we need to disable the shell's control of the flags. To do this in bash, for example, we need to run an instance of bash with line editing disabled:

```
$ bash --no-editing
```

Terminal Special Characters

The terminal driver's special characters are stored in the c_cc array. Array elements are accessed using symbolic constants whose names suggest their function. All of these constants begin with the letter V. For example, the symbolic constant for the array index containing the end-of-file special character is VEOF. If myterm is declared as a struct termios, then the instruction myterm.c_cc[VEOF] = 'X' sets the terminal's end-of-file character to X. The behavior of some special characters depends on what flags are enabled. For example, characters used for line editing, such as ERASE, are passed directly to the calling process when canonical mode is disabled, without causing any erasing.

Table 18-4 lists most of the special characters. Those that are neither defined by POSIX nor implemented in Linux are omitted. The table shows the symbolic name of the index (for instance, VEOF), the name by which people refer to the character (EOF), a brief description of it, its initial value on most systems, and which flags, if any, modify what the terminal driver does when the character is input.

Table 18-4: The Special Characters in the c_cc Array with Initial Values and Descriptions

Subscript	Name	Initial value	Description	Flags
VEOF	EOF	CTRL-D	End-of-file character	ICANON
VEOL	EOL	NULL	Additional end-of-line character	ICANON
VEOL2	EOL2	NULL	Another end-of-line character (not in POSIX)	ICANON
VERASE	ERASE	CTRL-?	Erase character	ICANON
VINTR	INTR	CTRL-C	Interrupt character (sends SIGINT)	ISIG
VKILL	KILL	CTRL-U	Kill line	ICANON
VLNEXT	LNEXT	CTRL-V	Literal next; quotes next input character	IEXTEN
VMIN	MIN	❶	Minimum number of characters for read	ICANON
VQUIT	QUIT	CTRL-\	Quit character (sends SIGQUIT)	ISIG
VREPRINT	REPRINT	CTRL-R	Reprint unread characters	ICANON, IEXTEN
VSTART	START	CTRL-Q	Start character; restarts output	IXON
VSTOP	STOP	CTRL-S	Stop character; stops output	IXON
VSUSP	SUSP	CTRL-Z	Sends SIGTSTP signal	ISIG
VTIME	TIME	❶	Timeout in deciseconds for read	ICANON
VWERASE	WERASE	CTRL-W	Word erase	ICANON

The subscript values are unique with one exception. The subscripts VMIN and VTIME may be the same as VEOF and VEOL subscripts, respectively. This is because the VMIN and VTIME values ❶ are used only in noncanonical mode, whereas VEOF and VEOL are used only in canonical mode. I'll explain the use of these two special characters in the discussion about noncanonical mode input processing that follows.

Terminal Attribute Modification

The tcgetattr() function gets the attributes of the terminal associated with the file descriptor fd, storing them in the termios structure pointed to by termios_p. Its prototype is:

```
int tcgetattr(int fd, struct termios *termios_p);
```

The tcsetattr() function sets attributes, but it has an additional parameter:

```
int tcsetattr(int fd, int optional_actions, const struct termios *termios_p);
```

Both tcgetattr() and tcsetattr() require that their first argument is a file descriptor for a terminal; otherwise, they'll fail, setting errno to ENOTTY.

The second parameter of tcsetattr(), optional_actions, is used to specify when the changes are supposed to be applied. Its possible values are as follows:

TCSANOW   The change occurs immediately.

TCSADRAIN   The change occurs after all output written to fd has been transmitted. This option is usually used when changing parameters that affect output, since we usually want pending output to be processed with the previous attributes.

TCSAFLUSH   The change occurs after all output written to the object referred to by fd has been transmitted. In addition, before the change is applied, all input data that hasn't been read is discarded.

TCSANOW forces changes to be applied immediately; this can cause problems if the terminal driver is writing to the terminal and the changes modify the output flags. TCSADRAIN forces the changes, but only after the output queue has been emptied by the driver. This is the action that should be chosen whenever the changes affect output to the terminal. TCSAFLUSH forces the changes only after the output queues are emptied and after it causes the input data sitting in the queue to be discarded. When restoring the terminal to its previous state, it is the safest choice to use TCSAFLUSH.

Steps for Changing Attributes of a termios Structure

Changing the attributes of the terminal that are accessible through a termios structure is a three-step procedure:

1.   Retrieve the current termios structure with tcgetattr() into a local termios structure.

2.   Make the changes to the local object.

3. Replace the existing `termios` structure by calling `tcsetattr()`, passing the modified, local `termios` structure.

Furthermore, because both of these functions fail if the file descriptor is not associated with a terminal, programs should always ensure that the file descriptor is that of a terminal. One way to do this is by calling `isatty()` on the file descriptor before making the calls.

Step 2 depends upon the type of setting to be modified. Following are the different ways to change a single attribute:

- To enable a single-bit switch whose mask constant is `MASK` in a flagset `flag`, use:

```
flag |= MASK;
```

- To disable a single-bit switch whose mask constant is `MASK` in a flagset `flag`, use:

```
flag &= ~MASK;
```

- To change the value of a multibit mask such as a delay value requires two steps. Let `MDELAY` denote the multibit mask that selects the bits in the flagset `flag` to be changed, and let `NEWVAL` be the new value that is supposed to be applied. Then the modification is:

```
flag = flag & ~MDELAY;
flag = flag | NEWVAL;
```

The first assignment zeroes out the bits of this mask, and the second replaces them with new bit values.

- To change the value of a member of the `c_cc[]` array, an ordinary assignment instruction suffices, provided that the value assigned is of type `unsigned char`, the equivalent of `cc_t`. For example, the following changes the erase character to x and changes the `MIN` variable to 4:

```
c_cc[VERASE] = 'x';
c_cc[VMIN] = 4;
```

When an array member's value is numeric, such as that of `c_cc[VMIN]` and `c_cc[VTIME]`, it has to be assignment compatible with `unsigned char`. This means, if it's an integer, it must be in the interval [0,255].

- Some settings are changed through another system call, such as `cfsetispeed()` or `cfsetospeed()`. I'll discuss those shortly.

A Program that Changes the echo Attribute

I'll demonstrate making a small change with the program in Listing 18-1 that toggles the terminal's echo state (Listing 18-1). Specifically, if echo is enabled, it disables it, and if it's disabled, it enables it.

```c
#include "common_hdrs.h"
#include <termios.h>                /* Needed for all functions in termios API */

int main(int argc, char *argv[])
{
    struct termios tty_attributes;             /* Local termios structure  */

    if ( !isatty(STDIN_FILENO) )
        usage_error("Do not redirect standard input to this program.");
    if ( tcgetattr(0, &tty_attributes) == -1 )  /* Retrieve termios struct. */
        fatal_error(errno, "tcgettattr");
    if ( tty_attributes.c_lflag & ECHO )             /* If enabled... */
        tty_attributes.c_lflag &= ~ECHO;                 /* Disable. */
    else                                             /* Else...      */
        tty_attributes.c_lflag |=  ECHO;                 /*  Enable.  */

    /* Replace termios with changed copy; use TCSANOW for immediate change. */
    if ( tcsetattr(0, TCSANOW, &tty_attributes) == -1 )
        fatal_error(errno, "tcsettattr");
    return 0;
}
```

Listing 18-1: A program that toggles the echo state of the control terminal

If the executable is named *toggle_echo*, you can enter ./toggle_echo and then type anything in the terminal to see that echo is disabled. Enter it again to turn echo on again.

A Program that Changes and Restores Terminal Attributes

A second, perhaps more interesting, application of this pair of functions changes the terminal settings only for a brief part of the program's execution and then restores the original settings. This is exactly what the login process does when it prompts us to enter a password. The prompt is visible, but when we enter the password, echo is disabled. I'll call this program *fakelogin.c*. I'll use a different strategy for ensuring that the file descriptor passed to tcgetattr() and tcsetattr() refers to a terminal—the program will call open() on the file */dev/tty*, which is essentially a link to the real device file for the terminal. This way, even if input or output is redirected, the program will not fail, because it isn't passing file descriptors 0 or 1 to these functions.

The program has to undertake the following steps:

1. Open */dev/tty* for reading and writing and assign the returned file descriptor to ttyfd. If the call fails, exit with an appropriate message.

2. Write the prompt login: to the terminal.

3. Read the user's response into a buffer, to be printed at the end of the program.

4. Call tcgetattr() to get a copy of the current terminal settings. Call this copy tt.

5. Clear the echo bit in tt and call tcsetattr() to make the change in the terminal driver.

6. Write the password prompt.

7. Read the user's response, which is hidden.

8. Set the echo bit in tt and call tcsetattr() to restore the driver to its original state.

9. Since it's not a real login program anyway, display the entered username and password as proof that it worked correctly.

Usernames are generally limited in their length. For this program, I chose a limit of 32 characters arbitrarily for both usernames and passwords. If a user enters a string that's longer than 32 characters for either variable, the program has to handle it correctly.

HANDLING EXCESS INPUT IN THE TERMINAL

When read() reads from a terminal, it doesn't receive characters until a newline is entered. Assuming that ttyfd refers to a terminal, if a program calls read(ttyfd, &buffer, 32) but the user enters 40 characters and then a newline, read() will receive the first 32 characters and store them into buffer, but there will be 8 characters and a newline remaining in the input queue. A second call to read(ttyfd, &buffer, 32) will be satisfied immediately because there's a newline in the input queue. The remaining 8 characters and the newline will be stored into buffer. If a program doesn't want these characters to be read into buffer, it can call tcflush(ttyfd, TCIFLUSH) to remove them from the input queue before reading again.

The program has code to deal with the possibility of a buffer overflow attack such as this. The program, without any error handling, is in Listing 18-2. The complete program is in the book's source code distribution.

fakelogin.c
```c
#include "common_hdrs.h"
#include <termios.h>

const char loginstr[] = "login: ";      /* Prompt for login    */
const char passwdstr[] = "password: "; /* Prompt for password */

int main(int argc, char *argv[])
{
    struct termios tt;         /* Terminal attribute structure */
    char    username[33];      /* 32 characters plus NULL byte */
    char    passwd[33];        /* 32 characters plus NULL byte */
    int     ttyfd, n;          /* File descriptor for terminal */

    if ( -1 == (ttyfd = open("/dev/tty", O_RDWR)) )
        fatal_error(errno, "open");
    memset(username, 0, 33);                    /* Zero fill username.    */
```

```
    memset(passwd,    0, 33);                   /* Zero fill passwd.       */
    write(ttyfd, loginstr, strlen(loginstr)); /* Display the first prompt. */
    n = read(ttyfd, username, 32);             /* Get user's username.    */
    if ( username[n-1] == '\n' )
        username[n-1] = '\0';                  /* Get rid of \n at end.   */
    tcflush(ttyfd, TCIFLUSH);                  /* Flush extra characters. */
    /* The next three lines turn off echo. */
    tcgetattr(ttyfd, &tt);                     /* Get current terminal state. */
    tt.c_lflag &= ~ECHO;                       /* Turn off echo bit.      */
    tcsetattr(ttyfd, TCSANOW, &tt);            /* Use this new structure. */
    write(ttyfd, passwdstr, strlen(passwdstr));  /* Display prompt.       */
    n = read(ttyfd, passwd, 32);               /* Get user's hidden typing. */
    if ( passwd[n-1] == '\n' )
        passwd[n-1] = '\0';                    /* Get rid of \n at end.   */
    tcflush(ttyfd, TCIFLUSH);
    tt.c_lflag |= ECHO;                        /* Turn echo on.           */
    tcsetattr(ttyfd, TCSAFLUSH, &tt);          /* Restore settings.       */
    printf("\nUser %s entered %s as a password.\n", username, passwd);
    return 0;
}
```

Listing 18-2: A simulated login program that shows how to temporarily disable echoing in the terminal

This program demonstrates the basic principle of making a temporary change to the terminal state. Build and run it and you'll see that it behaves just like an actual login program. If you redirect input or output, it will ignore the redirection. If you enter strings that exceed the size of the buffers, it will safely ignore the extra characters.

We used the tcgetattr() and tcsetattr() functions in *fakelogin.c*. An alternative method of terminal control is based on the ioctl() system call. Sometimes, the ioctl() system call is the easiest way to solve a programming problem. We used it, for example, in Chapter 12 in the *ulogger.c* program to retrieve terminal window dimensions. We'll explore this system call later in this chapter. In the next section, we'll undertake a larger project that primarily uses the termios(3) functions but also employs ioctl() system call.

Writing an spl_stty Command

As a more substantive exercise in working with the termios structure, we'll implement a simplified version of the stty command. Like stty, our program will be capable of displaying terminal attributes as well as modifying them, using the same syntax as the actual command. Unlike it, our program will not support any option other than -a, will let a user change only one setting at a time, and will not support setting combination modes such as sane or raw. Allowing these would require storing default values for all possible variables and switches, increasing program size and complexity. The program will allow the user to enter either of the single arguments size or speed, which the actual stty command allows. They report the terminal window size and line speed, respectively.

Another limitation is that the program will allow the user to enter control characters in only one of two ways: either by typing the actual key combination, such as CTRL-C, by preceding it with the lnext special character, CTRL-V by default, or by entering the two-character sequence ^C, but not by entering \003, for example.

Thus, to change the erase character to CTRL-H, the user can either enter the CTRL-H key combination; enter a CTRL-V followed by a CTRL-H, in case CTRL-H can't be entered because it already has special meaning; or enter the literal ^H. These limitations simplify parsing of the command line. Therefore, the different ways in which it can be invoked are:

`spl_stty`	Print a brief summary
`spl_stty size	speed`	Print size or speed
`spl_stty -a`	Print all settings
`spl_stty [-]switch`	Change the value of *switch*
`spl_stty delay-const`	Set *delay-const* in the driver
`spl_stty var value`	Assign *value* to *var*

Without any arguments or options, it prints the short list of attributes that stty displays. With -a, it prints all terminal settings. Otherwise, it is given either a single terminal switch, such as icrnl, with or without a preceding hyphen; a constant, such as cr2 or tab3; one of the words size or speed; or a variable-value pair, such as erase X. I leave various enhancements to it as exercises.

To save space, I don't present all of the code. The complete program is available in the book's source code distribution as *spl_stty.c*.

Program Data Structures

A good choice of data structures makes writing the program much easier and pretty much determines its algorithms. The program has to associate words entered on the command line, such as switch names and variable names, for instance, erase and icrnl, with corresponding symbolic mask names that select the bits of the corresponding flagset, such as VERASE and ICRNL, respectively. For example, if a user enters the command

```
$ ./spl_stty olcuc
```

to enable the lower-to-uppercase capability of the terminal driver, the program has to find the corresponding bitmask (OLCUC) and use it to enable this switch in the c_oflag member of a termios structure, say tt

```
tt.c_oflag = tt.c_oflag |= OLCUC;
```

after which it can call tcsetattr() with the modified structure to change the terminal driver settings:

```
tcsetattr(ttyfd, TCSANOW, &tt);
```

To provide a uniform and systematic way for associating the lowercase name used on the command line with the symbolic constants used as mask values, I'll define a data structure that pairs them together

```
typedef struct _maskmap
{
    int  mask;  /* Bitmap to access bits of flagset or variable array */
    char *name;  /* String name of setting entered on command line     */
} maskmap;
```

and create five separate arrays of these structures: one for each flagset and one for the c_cc[] array. The arrays are declared in file scope so that all functions have easy access to them. Here are snippets of some of them:

```
/* The map of c_iflag flag constants and command line names: */
const maskmap input_flags[] = {
    {IGNBRK , "ignbrk"},
    {BRKINT , "brkint"},
    --snip--
    {IMAXBEL, "imaxbel"},
    {IUTF8  , "iutf8"},
    {-1     ,  NULL}
};
/* The map of c_oflag flag constants and command line names: */
const maskmap output_flags[] = {
    {OPOST, "opost"},
    {OLCUC, "olcuc"},
    --snip--
    {OFILL, "ofill"},
    {OFDEL, "ofdel"},
    {-1   ,  NULL}
};
/* The map of c_cc[] index constants and command line names: */
const maskmap cc_vars[] = {
    {VINTR   , "intr"},
    {VQUIT   , "quit"},
    {VERASE  , "erase"},
    --snip--
    {VLNEXT  , "lnext"},
    {VDISCARD, "discard"},
    {-1      ,  NULL }
};
```

The last entry of each array provides a convenient stopping condition for iterating through the array, stopping when the mask member is negative. These arrays of the exact same underlying structure facilitate writing a single function that can print each flagset's current settings or a single function that can modify the value of any switch or variable.

I'll follow the same principle for working with terminal speeds; I define this data structure to associate symbolic constant baud rates such as B9600 with strings such as "9600".

```
typedef struct _baudmap
{
    speed_t baudval;  /* Macro constant that defines a speed setting      */
    char    *name;    /* String representing the numeric value of the speed */
} baudmap;
```

The program uses an array named baudrates for mapping speed settings to their numeric values entered on the command line or printed in output. Because the underlying type, speed_t, is unsigned, the sentinel is an impossible positive baud rate:

```
const speed_t NO_SUCH_BAUD = 9999;
const baudmap baudrates[] = {
    {B50 , "50"},
    {B75 , "75"},
    {B110, "110"},
    --snip--
    {NOSUCHBAUD, "unknown"}
};
```

Lastly, I define another data structure to make it easy to deal with multi-bit mask values for the output delay bits and a corresponding array:

```
typedef struct _dlymask_map
{
    int    value;  /* Bitmap to access bits of flagset or variable array */
    int    mask;   /* Multibit mask for zeroing bits to be updated        */
    char *name;    /* String name of setting entered on command line      */
} dlymask_map;

const dlymask_map output_dlymasks[] = {
    {BS0, BSDLY, "bs0"},
    {BS1, BSDLY, "bs1"},
    {CR0, CRDLY, "cr0"},
    {CR1, CRDLY, "cr1"},
--snip--
};
```

With these data structures in mind, we turn to the algorithms. I'll present the program from the top down, starting with the main() function, so that we can have a big picture of how it works.

The main() Function of spl_stty

The primary task of main() is to parse the command line and call the functions needed, based on what the user enters. For the most part, it breaks down to checking how many words are on the command line, determining what they are, and calling the appropriate function, as shown in Listing 18-3.

spl_stty.c
main()

```
int main(int argc, char *argv[])
{
    struct termios ttyinfo;   /* termios structure to store settings      */
    int    ttyfd;             /* File descriptor for control terminal     */
    int    rows, cols;        /* Window dimensions                        */
    char   speedstr[16];      /* String to store displayed or entered speed */

    /* Get file descriptor for terminal; if redirected it still gets it. */
    if ( -1 == (ttyfd = open("/dev/tty", O_RDWR)) )
        fatal_error(errno, "open");

    /* Fill termios structure ttyinfo with current settings. */
    if ( -1 == tcgetattr(ttyfd, &ttyinfo) )
        fatal_error(errno,"tcgetattr");

    if ( argc == 1 )      /* No options or arguments - show brief summary. */
        show_brief( ttyinfo );
    else if ( argc == 2 ) {   /* Several possibilities for this one word */
        if ( !strcmp(argv[1], "-a") )        /* User entered spl_stty -a.   */
            show_all( ttyfd, ttyinfo);
        else if ( strcmp(argv[1], "speed") == 0 ) {
            /* User entered spl_stty speed. */
            get_speed(ttyinfo, speedstr);   /* get_speed() gets speed.    */
            printf("%s\n", speedstr);
        }
        else if ( strcmp(argv[1], "size") == 0 ) {
            /* User entered spl_stty size. */
            if ( get_window_size(ttyfd, &rows, &cols) )
                printf("%d %d\n", rows, cols);
            else
                printf("Unable to retrieve window size\n");
        }
        else { /* User entered either a switch name or a delay constant.   */
            if ( set_switch(&ttyinfo, argv[1]) )
                /* Successfully changed requested setting */
                tcsetattr(ttyfd, TCSANOW, &ttyinfo);
            else
                /* The entered name didn't match any setting. */
                printf("spl_stty: Invalid argument %s\n", argv[1]);
        }
    }
}
```

```
        else { /* User entered two or more words after spl_stty.         */
            /* Expecting argv[1] to be a variable and argv[2] to be its value: */
            if ( set_var(&ttyinfo, argv[1], argv[2]) )
                /* Successfully changed value of variable */
                tcsetattr(ttyfd, TCSANOW, &ttyinfo);
            else { /* Was unable to make the change                       */
                printf("spl_stty: Unable to modify %s\n", argv[1]);
                exit(EXIT_FAILURE);
            }
        }
    }
    exit(EXIT_SUCCESS);
}
```

Listing 18-3: The main() function for spl_stty.c

This main program calls the following program-defined functions:

show_brief()   Displays the same information as stty does with no arguments, which is implementation dependent; this function tries to match
the output on Linux 5.15.

show_all()   Displays the same information as stty -a, not necessarily in
the same order or in the exact same format, but close to it.

get_speed()   Retrieves the terminal's input and output speeds and picks
the smaller if they differ and stores the value as a string in its second
argument.

get_window_size()   Retrieves the terminal's window size using a call
to ioctl().

set_switch()   Sets the value of any flag, whether single-bit or multiple-
bit, returning TRUE if successful and FALSE if not.

set_var()   Sets the value of any variable, whether it's one in the c_cc[]
array or one stored outside of it, such as the line, speed, and so on. It
returns TRUE if successful and FALSE if not.

The first four of these are retrieval functions; they don't change any settings.
The last two are the only ones that change the terminal settings. We'll look
at the display functions first.

Functions That Display Attributes

In order to save space in the book, I won't include listings of some lesser
functions. For example, show_brief() is a simple function that displays a small
subset of settings, which I exclude.

I'll start with the function that prints the values of the switches in the
flagset that's passed to it. Its prototype is:

```
void show_flagset(tcflag_t flags, const maskmap *map);
```

Given a flagset from a termios structure and one of the preceding map arrays, it prints the current values of the switches by visiting every entry in the

map array. For each entry, it checks whether the bit for it is set in the flagset flags. If so, it prints the lowercase name for it. If not, it prepends a hyphen to it before printing it. The loop terminates when the value member of the structure is negative:

```
void show_flagset(tcflag_t flags, const maskmap *map)
{
    int i = 0;
    while ( map[i].mask >= 0 ) {
        if ( flags & map[i].mask )  /* Flag is set.    */
            printf("%s ", map[i].name);
        else                        /* Flag isn't set. */
            printf("-%s ", map[i].name);
        i++;
        if ( i == 9 )
            printf("\n");
    }
}
```

To print all of the switch values, I'll call this function for each flagset.

We can't use this logic to print the c_cc[] array, since that output has to be of the form intr ^C; erase ^?; .... The underlying type of the c_cc[] array is unsigned char. For example, the value c_cc[VKILL] is the ASCII code for the current kill character. The values in this array are usually control characters such as CTRL-U and CTRL-C, represented on the terminal by ^U and ^C. Control characters are characters whose ASCII codes are less than 32, or the DEL character, whose ASCII code is 127. We have to display these symbols, not their ASCII codes. The character after ^ for a given control character c is the character whose ASCII code is:

```
(c + 'A' -1) & 0x7F;
```

The ASCII code for A is 65. In effect, we add 64 to the character code. If the result sets the most significant bit, as it would for the DEL character (127), we zero that bit by masking it with 0x7F. Alternatively, we could get this same character by taking the bitwise exclusive-OR of the code with 64:

```
c ^ 64
```

The function to print these variables and their values follows:

```
void show_ccvars(struct termios tt)
{
    int     i = 0;
    unsigned char ch;
    while ( cc_vars[i].mask >= 0 ) {
        if ( 0 < (ch = (tt.c_cc[cc_vars[i].mask])) )
            printf("%s = ^%c; ", cc_vars[i].name, (ch -1 + 'A') & 0x7F);
        else
            printf("%s = <undef>; ", cc_vars[i].name);
```

```
        i++;
        if ( i % 6 == 0 )
            printf("\n");
    }
}
```

The else clause is executed when the given switch is undefined in this terminal implementation.

Printing the assorted delay variables is a bit trickier. The values of these variables are in the part of the flagset masked by macros such as BSDLY and TABDLY. To understand how to do this, it's best if we take a look at their definitions, which are in the file *bits/termios-c_oflag.h*. Here is the fragment of it defining the TABDLY mask and the tab delay constants:

```
# define TABDLY 0014000   /* Select horizontal-tab delays: */
# define TAB0   0000000   /* Horizontal-tab delay type 0   */
# define TAB1   0004000   /* Horizontal-tab delay type 1   */
# define TAB2   0010000   /* Horizontal-tab delay type 2   */
# define TAB3   0014000   /* Expand tabs to spaces.        */
```

These are octal values. An expression such as tt.c_oflag & TABDLY zeroes out every bit except the bits in TABDLY that are 1s. If we shift this to the right by the number of zeros to the right of the rightmost 1 in TABDLY, we'll get the numeric value of that selector. Figure 18-3 illustrates these bitwise operations.

```
                                          rshift(TABDLY) = 11
                                          |←──────────────→|

                      TABDLY  00 000 000 000 000 000 001 100 000 000 000
                     c_oflag  01 011 100 111 110 000 001 000 010 001 110

            TABDLY & c_oflag  00 000 000 000 000 000 001 000 000 000 000
TABDLY & c_oflag >> rshift(TABDLY)  00 000 000 000 000 000 000 000 000 000 010
```

Figure 18-3: The bitwise operations to extract the value of the tab delay from the c_oflag flagset of a termios structure

In the figure, c_oflag is an arbitrary value. TABDLY has 11 zeros to the right of its least significant 1-bit. The bitwise-AND of TABDLY and c_oflag is the third row in the figure. After the shift to the right, the value is 2. Hence the tab delay in the c_oflag flagset is TAB2. The following function, which the program uses, returns the number of zero-bits to the right of the least significant 1-bit of an integer:

rshift()
```
int rshift(unsigned int value)
{
    int zero_count = 0;
    while ( (~value) & 1 ) {  /* Rightmost bit of value is 0.      */
        value = value >> 1;   /* Shift to the right and test again. */
        zero_count++;
    }
```

```
            return zero_count;
        }
```

All of the delay bits are part of the c_oflag member of the termios structure.

The following function, based on the preceding idea, prints the symbolic values of each of those delays:

show_odelays()
```
void show_odelays(struct termios tt)
{
    printf("bs%d " , (tt.c_oflag & BSDLY)  >> rshift(BSDLY)) ;
    printf("ff%d " , (tt.c_oflag & FFDLY)  >> rshift(FFDLY)) ;
    printf("cr%d " , (tt.c_oflag & CRDLY)  >> rshift(CRDLY)) ;
    printf("tab%d ", (tt.c_oflag & TABDLY) >> rshift(TABDLY));
    printf("nl%d " , (tt.c_oflag & NLDLY)  >> rshift(NLDLY)) ;
    printf("vt%d " , (tt.c_oflag & VTDLY)  >> rshift(VTDLY)) ;
}
```

The one remaining bitmask to be deciphered is CSIZE, applied to the c_cflag member of the structure. The documentation states that it specifies the character size, in bits, for both transmit and receive operations. Its possible values are defined in *bits/termios-c_cflag.h*:

```
#define CSIZE 0000060
#define    CS5 0000000
#define    CS6 0000020
#define    CS7 0000040
#define    CS8 0000060
```

We can use almost the same strategy to print the correct value as I just described for the delay bits. The difference is that we need to add a constant to get the correct number. If we don't add the required constant, we'll print out strings such as cs0, cs1, and so on, instead of cs5, . . . , cs8.

A tiny function that encapsulates this logic follows:

show_csize()
```
void show_csize(struct termios tt)
{
    int cs_shift = rshift(CSIZE);
    printf("cs%d ", 1 + cs_shift + ((tt.c_cflag & CSIZE) >> cs_shift));
}
```

The remaining functions for printing terminal settings are:

- A function to print the terminal window's rows and columns, which I'll name show_window_size()

- A function to print the values of min and time, which are stored in the c_cc[] array but not interpreted as characters, and which I'll name show_mintime()

- A function to print the line speed, which I'll name show_speed()

In Chapter 12, I wrote a program, *ulogger.c*, with a function get_winsize() that used the ioctl() system call to get the window's rows and columns, so I won't include show_window_size() here. The show_mintime() function is simple:

show_mintime()
```
void show_mintime(struct termios tt)
{
    printf("min = %d; ", tt.c_cc[VMIN]);
    printf("time = %d; ", tt.c_cc[VTIME]);
    printf("\n");
}
```

Let's deal with line speeds now. Line speeds are not meaningful in software-emulated terminals such as pseudoterminals, but they are settable and retrievable nonetheless because stty is designed to work with actual terminals and terminals connected over USB and serial lines. The termios man page lists five functions for getting and setting input and output line speeds:

```
speed_t cfgetispeed(const struct termios *termios_p);
speed_t cfgetospeed(const struct termios *termios_p);
int cfsetispeed(struct termios *termios_p, speed_t speed);
int cfsetospeed(struct termios *termios_p, speed_t speed);
int cfsetspeed(struct termios *termios_p, speed_t speed);
```

On my Linux system, input and output line speeds are the same; changing one changes the other. Nonetheless, the function to print the current speed calls both cfgetospeed() and cfgetispeed(), compares them, and if they're different, it prints the smaller of the two. Both of those functions return speed_t values, which are macro constants with names like B4800, B9600, and B19200. These are then converted to human-readable strings. This logic is encapsulated in the following function:

get_speed()
```
void get_speed(struct termios tt, char *speedstr)
{
    speed_t o_speed, i_speed, speed;
    o_speed = cfgetospeed(&tt);
    i_speed = cfgetispeed(&tt);
    speed = (o_speed > i_speed) ? i_speed : o_speed;
    /* Search for human-readable string for this speed. */
    int i = 0;
    while ( baudrates[i].baudval != NOSUCHBAUD )
        if ( baudrates[i].baudval == speed ) {
            strcpy(speedstr, baudrates[i].name);
            return;
        }
        else
            i++;
    strcpy(speedstr, "unknown");
}
```

This function is called by show_speed(), which prints the resulting string. It is omitted.

Lastly, a single function calls all of these functions in sequence so that the output matches roughly the output of stty, inserting newlines as needed (Listing 18-4).

show_all()

```
void show_all(int fd, struct termios ttyinfo)
{
    show_speed(ttyinfo);
    show_window_size(fd);
    printf("line = %d; \n", ttyinfo.c_line);
    show_ccvars(ttyinfo);
    show_mintime(ttyinfo);
    show_flagset(ttyinfo.c_cflag, control_flags);
    show_csize(ttyinfo);
    printf("\n");
    show_flagset(ttyinfo.c_iflag, input_flags);
    printf("\n");
    show_flagset(ttyinfo.c_oflag, output_flags);
    show_odelays(ttyinfo);
    printf("\n");
    show_flagset(ttyinfo.c_lflag, local_flags);
    printf("\n");
}
```

Listing 18-4: The driver function that prints all terminal attributes on the terminal

The remaining part of the program to write are the functions that change the values of terminal attributes.

Functions That Set Attributes

We need separate functions to change flags and variables. In "Steps for Changing Attributes of a termios Structure" on page 852, I described the different operations required to change flags, variables, and multibit flags, which we'll apply now.

Since the exact same steps must be taken to change a single-bit flag in any of the four flagsets, I wrote a single function that changes a single flag in a given flagset. It's given a pointer to a tcflag_t flagset, the corresponding maskmap array, and a Boolean indicating whether to enable or disable the flag:

set_switch _in_map()

```
BOOL set_switch_in_map(tcflag_t *flags, const maskmap *fmap, char *name,
                        BOOL enable) {
    int i = 0;
    while ( fmap[i].mask >= 0 ) {
        if ( strcmp(name, fmap[i].name) == 0 ) {
            if ( enable )
                *flags |= fmap[i].mask ;
            else
                *flags &= ~fmap[i].mask ;
```

```
            return TRUE;
        }
        i++;
    }
    return FALSE;
}
```

For example, to enable a switch in the c_oflags member of a struct termios
*tt, the program would call:

```
set_switch_in_map(&(tt->c_oflag), output_flags, name, TRUE)
```

When the program is given a single argument, it could be a switch in
one of these flagsets, or it could be the value of a delay constant, such as cr2.
A single function handles both cases. It's predicated on the fact that all of
these input names are unique—there is no string *s* that is used in more than
one flagset. Therefore, the function in Listing 18-5 handily sets any switch or
delay constant:

```
set_switch()  BOOL set_switch(struct termios *tt, char *name)
              {
                  BOOL state = TRUE;                 /* Assume enabling a switch.          */
                  if ( name[0] == '-' )              /* Most likely means disable switch.  */
                      if ( strcmp(name, "-tabs") != 0 ) { /* Make sure it isn't "-tabs". */
                          state = FALSE;             /* Set state to disable switch.       */
                          name = &(name[1]);         /* Search for word after leading '-'. */
                      }
                  /* Now search in each flagset, one after the other, trying to
                     find the matching entry, and if successful, change the switch
                     and return TRUE. If not, fall through to next call. */
                  if ( set_switch_in_map(&(tt->c_oflag), output_flags, name, state) )
                      return TRUE;
                  if ( set_switch_in_map(&(tt->c_iflag), input_flags, name, state) )
                      return TRUE;
                  if ( set_switch_in_map(&(tt->c_lflag), local_flags, name, state) )
                      return TRUE;
                  if ( set_switch_in_map(&(tt->c_cflag), control_flags, name, state) )
                      return TRUE;

                  /* Now handle delay bits. If we make it here, it is either
                     bad input or a delay constant such as cr0, tab0, and so on. */
                  int i = 0;
                  while ( output_dlymasks[i].value >= 0 ) {
                      if ( strcmp(name, output_dlymasks[i].name) == 0 ) {
                          tt->c_oflag &= ~output_dlymasks[i].mask;  /* Clear bits.   */
                          tt->c_oflag |= output_dlymasks[i].value;  /* Set new bits. */
                          return TRUE;
                      }
                      i++;
```

```
        }
        return FALSE;   /* Didn't find a matching name anywhere!  */
}
```

Listing 18-5: The function that modifies any switch or delay constant

The logic in this function is based on the methods described earlier.

The last piece is the code to change variables. Changing the value of a variable in the c_cc[] array is relatively straightforward:

set_ccvar()
```
BOOL set_ccvar(struct termios *tt, char *name, unsigned char value)
{
    int i = 0;
    while ( cc_vars[i].mask >= 0 )
        if ( strcmp(cc_vars[i].name, name) != 0 )
            i++; /* No match yet              */
        else {    /* Found the matching index */
            tt->c_cc[cc_vars[i].mask] = value; /* Assign new value. */
            return TRUE;
        }
    return FALSE;
}
```

The value passed to the function is of type unsigned char. The compiler will detect an attempt to pass too large a number to it. This function is called by set_var(), which is the function called by main() when it detects a command line with two arguments after the command name. It has to do a bit of tedious detective work.

First, the command line could be in any of the following forms:

- spl_stty kill @

- spl_stty erase ^C

- spl_stty min 4

- spl_stty ispeed 19200

Since argv[2] is a string, it has to be converted depending on which case it is. The first case is that argv[2] is of length 1. If so, the value is argv[2][0]. If it's of length 2, it has to detect if it's of the form ^X. For the remaining cases, it has to match argv[1] against one of the valid variable names.

It therefore begins by comparing argv[1] against the various strings, min, time, speed, and so on. If it finds a match, it either updates the corresponding variable in the c_cc[] array (as when it matches min) or calls a speed setting function if it's a speed setting. If argv[1] didn't match any of these, it checks the length of argv[2] and parses it as needed to get a value to assign to a member of c_cc[]. The function is displayed in part in Listing 18-6. The complete function is in the book's source code repository.

set_var()
```
BOOL set_var(struct termios *tt, char *name, char *val)
{
```

```
    int          i, number;
    speed_t      speed;
    unsigned char value;
    int          len;

    if ( strcmp(name, "line") == 0 || strcmp(name, "min") == 0 ||
         strcmp(name, "time") == 0 ) {
        if ( VALID_NUMBER != get_int(val, NON_NEG_ONLY, &number, NULL) )
            return FALSE;

        if ( strcmp(name, "line") == 0 ) {
            tt->c_line = number;
            return TRUE;
        }
        if ( strcmp(name, "min") == 0 ) {
            if ( number >= 256 )
                return FALSE;
            tt->c_cc[VMIN] = number;
            return TRUE;
        }
        if ( strcmp(name, "time") == 0 ) {
            if ( number >= 256 )
                return FALSE;
            tt->c_cc[VTIME] = number;
            return TRUE;
        }
    }
    else if ( strcmp(name, "ispeed") == 0 || strcmp(name, "ospeed") == 0 ||
              strcmp(name, "speed") == 0 ) {
    // OMITTED: Set speed, ispeed, and ospeed
    }
    else {
        int len = strlen(val);
        if ( len <= 2 ) {
            if ( 1 == len )
                value = val[0];
            else if ( (val[0] == '^') && (isupper(val[1])) )
                value = val[1] - 'A' + 1;
            else
                return FALSE;
            if ( set_ccvar(tt, name, value) )
                return TRUE;
        }
    }
    return FALSE;
}
```

Listing 18-6: The top-level function that determines which setting needs to be changed and calls other functions as needed

The entire program is in the book's source code distribution. Here are a few sample runs of it to demonstrate its output.

```
$ ./spl_stty
speed 38400 baud; line = 0;
brkint imaxbel iutf8
$ ./spl_stty size
24  78
$ ./spl_stty erase ^F
$ spl_stty -a | grep erase
ntr = ^C; quit = ^\; erase = ^F; kill = ^U; eof = ^D; eol = <undef>;
werase = ^W; lnext = ^V; discard = ^O; min = 1; time = 0;
```

I leave several modifications and enhancements of this program as exercises at the end of the chapter. In Chapter 19, we'll examine the various terminal driver modes and how they can be used to make interactive programs behave the way we expect them to. The last topic of this chapter is another API for controlling the attributes of not only terminals but also many other types of devices.

The ioctl() System Call

In this and previous chapters, we used the ioctl() system call for obtaining the window size but not for any other purpose. Here we'll explore this call in greater depth. The name itself is short for "input/output control."

The ioctl() system call first appeared in System 7 Unix in 1979. It was mostly used for terminal and serial line control operations. As time passed, more and more devices were handled through ioctl() calls. The POSIX Working Group developed the functions listed on the termios(3) man page as a replacement for ioctl() because they thought it was difficult to use [26]. They separated out the terminal control functions into the termios interface and left the control of all other devices to the ioctl() system call without including it in the standard. However, on Linux, *glibc* always includes ioctl(), and it's part of many other Unix distributions as well.

The ioctl() system call is a much more general-purpose tool than any of the termios functions. We can use it to access and control any I/O device for which the manufacturer provides a device driver. Although many operations on devices can be achieved by other means, most devices also have some device-specific operations that don't fit into the universal I/O model, such as:

- Changing the character font used on a terminal

- Requesting a magnetic tape system to rewind or fast-forward

- Ejecting a disk from a drive

- Playing a video file

- Maintaining routing tables for a network interface

The `ioctl()` call provides a way for user-level programs to access device drivers normally accessed only by the kernel. In fact, most `termios` functions ultimately make a call to `ioctl()`. For some programming problems, the `ioctl()` system call is the easiest tool to use. For example, in Chapter 12 we used it in the *ulogger.c* program to retrieve terminal window dimensions. To learn more about `ioctl()`, we'll start with its man page in Section 2.

The Form of an ioctl() Call

The `ioctl()` system call is a *variadic* function, which means that it can take an indefinite number of arguments, like the `printf()` function. The man page synopsis for it is:

```
#include <sys/ioctl.h>
int ioctl(int fd, unsigned long request, ...);
```

The first argument is always an open file descriptor. The second is a device-specific *request code*, also called a *command code*. Request codes are long integers, but they have symbolic names such as `TIOCGWINSZ` and `TIOCGETS`. The request codes represent different operations to perform, and they're usually called *ioctl operations* or *ioctl requests*. For example, we would say that we used the *ioctl* `TIOCGWINSZ` operation to get the window size.

The man page states that the *ioctl* request code names are located in the *sys/ioctl.h* header file. This isn't accurate. Although that header file exposes macros and definitions, they're actually defined in header files that are included in *sys/ioctl.h*. In general, request code names are defined in various header files throughout the */usr/include* directory hierarchy, depending on the category of device to which they apply. For example, on Linux, the terminal-related *ioctls* are defined in *asm/ioctls.h* or *asm-generic/ioctls.h*.

There are hundreds of different *ioctl* request codes, with unique mnemonic names. Some are defined by specific device drivers and some are defined by the kernel, which provides generic *ioctl* commands for a small set of device types. Generally speaking, the commands for the different device types have a prefix that identifies that device type. For example, terminal request codes have names in the form `TIO*` or `TC*`, and magnetic tape driver request codes are of the form `MTIO*` and are usually defined in the header file *sys/mtio.h*.

We're interested in *ioctl* operations for terminal devices. The `ioctl()` man page has a list of some other man pages related to `ioctl()` calls. Among them is the page for terminal *ioctl* operations, namely, the `ioctl_tty(2)` man page. This page documents all of the terminal and serial line–related *ioctl* request codes. We'll take a look at a few of them.

Most *ioctls* require at least one more argument, although a few don't. Table 18-5 presents a sample of the commonly used *ioctl* request codes that can be applied to terminals. For each it shows its name, its required additional argument(s), and a brief description.

Table 18-5: Some Commonly Used *ioctl* Operation Codes for Terminals

ioctl	Argument	Description
TCGETS	struct termios *argp	Equivalent to tcgetattr(fd, argp)
TCSETS	const struct termios *argp	Equivalent to tcsetattr(fd, TCSANOW, argp)
TIOCSTI	const char *argp	Insert the given byte in the input queue
TIOCGWINSZ	struct winsize *argp	Get window size
TIOCSWINSZ	const struct winsize *argp	Set window size
TIOCINQ	int *argp	Get the number of bytes in the input buffer
TIOCOUTQ	int *argp	Get the number of bytes in the output buffer
TCFLSH	int arg	Equivalent to tcflush(fd, arg)
TIOCSCTTY	int arg	Make the given terminal the controlling terminal of the calling process
TIOCGPGRP	pid_t *argp	Get the process group ID of the foreground process group on this terminal
TIOCGETD	int *argp	Get the line discipline of the terminal
TIOCSETD	const int *argp	Set the line discipline of the terminal

The first two of these are equivalent to tcgetattr() and tcsetattr(). In *fakelogin.c*, to change the echoing of the terminal, we could have used ioctl(ttyfd, TCGETS, &tt) and ioctl(ttyfd, TCSETS, &tt) instead of the calls to tcgetattr() and tcsetattr().

The third request code, TIOCSTI, is a dangerous operation because it can be used to put bytes into the terminal driver's input queue. The man page describes it as *faking input*. Many systems disable it by default because it poses a security risk. If it's enabled, you can use it only to put bytes into the input queue of the control terminal of the running process, and it must be running in the foreground. The next program shows how it's used and why it's dangerous. The error handling of system calls is omitted to save space.

fakeinput_demo.c

```
#include "common_hdrs.h"
#include <sys/ioctl.h>
#include <sys/termios.h>

int main(int argc, char *argv[])
{
    char    command[] = "/usr/bin/echo 'This is a dangerous thing to do!'";
    char    newline = '\n';
    struct termios tt;

    tcgetattr(0, &tt);          /* Turn off echoing. */
    tt.c_lflag &= ~ECHO;
    tcsetattr(0, TCSANOW, &tt);
```

```
    /* Now add the characters of command one at a time. */
    for ( int i = 0; i < strlen(command); i++ )
        ioctl(STDIN_FILENO, TIOCSTI, &command[i]);

    sleep(2);                   /* Delay a bit.      */
    ioctl(STDIN_FILENO, TIOCSTI, &newline);
    tt.c_lflag |= ECHO;         /* Turn echo back on. */
    tcsetattr(0, TCSANOW, &tt);
    return 0;
}
```

The program writes the characters of the command variable into the terminal's input queue. The command is not terminated by a newline intentionally. Echo is disabled. If it were enabled, as each character was entered, it would appear on the screen immediately. As it's written, nothing will appear for about two seconds. When the program terminates and bash runs, it displays the prompt and then it reads from the standard input of the terminal, writing that input to the screen, as if you entered it yourself. The result is that command appears after the shell prompt. Because the program sends a newline character to the input queue after writing the command into it, the command is executed by bash! This is a run of the program:

```
$ ./fakeinput_demo
$ /usr/bin/echo 'This is a dangerous thing to do!'
This is a dangerous thing to do!
$
```

The point of this program is that this *ioctl* operation can surreptitiously put a command into the input queue, which can be executed later.

One of the more useful of the operations in Table 18-5 is TIOCINQ. It gets the number of bytes in the terminal's input queue. This snippet

```
int count;
if ( ioctl(ttyfd, TIOCINQ, &count) == -1 )
    fatal_error(errno, "ioctl TIOCINQ");
printf("There are %d chars in the input queue of the terminal\n", count);
```

shows how it's used. A process can inspect the input queue of any terminal opened by the owner of the process.

Listing 18-7 monitors the size of the input queue of the terminal device given as its command line argument. It writes a line to standard output every 0.1 seconds with the current queue size.

watchtty.c
```
#include "common_hdrs.h"
#include <sys/ioctl.h>

int main(int argc, char *argv[])
{
    int count;
```

```
    int fd;

    /* Try to open given terminal device file. */
    if ( (fd = open(argv[1], O_RDONLY)) == -1 )
        usage_error("ttywatch  <device-file>");
    while ( TRUE ) {
        if ( ioctl(fd, TIOCINQ, &count) == -1 )
            fatal_error(errno, "ioctl TIOCINQ");
        printf("%d chars in queue\n", count);
        usleep(100000);  /* Delay to see changes. */
    }
    return 0;
}
```

Listing 18-7: A program that monitors a terminal's input queue size

It doesn't terminate itself; you'll have to kill it when you've seen enough.

By starting up a second process in the monitored terminal that reads from the terminal, you can see the queue being emptied. The best way to do this is to put the monitored terminal into noncanonical mode so that reads can read one character at a time without needing terminating newline characters. Listing 18-8 is a good program to run in the monitored terminal. It fills the input queue using the TIOCSTI operation and then reads one character at a time, pausing a bit so that the watchtty program can see the changes. The error-handling code is omitted.

fillqeueue.c
```
#include "common_hdrs.h"
#include <sys/ioctl.h>

int main(int argc, char *argv[])
{
    char ch = 'x', stop = 'z';
    for ( int i = 0; i < 100; i++ ) {
        ioctl(0, TIOCSTI, &ch);
        usleep(50000);
    }
    ioctl(0, TIOCSTI, &stop);
    while ( read(0, &ch, 1) > 0 && ch != stop )
        usleep(50000);
    return 0;
}
```

Listing 18-8: A companion program to run with watchtty.c, which fills its terminal's input queue and then empties it

To do this little experiment, suppose the monitored terminal is *dev/pts/1*. Start watchtty in another terminal. It will start producing lines showing an empty queue:

```
$ ./watchtty /dev/pts/1
0 chars in queue
0 chars in queue
0 chars in queue
...
```

In the second terminal, turn off canonical mode and run fillqueue:

```
$ stty -icanon ; ./fillqueue
xxxxx....
```

It will start to echo the characters filling the queue. Eventually the echoing stops and the program terminates when it receives the stop character, z. But now the output of watchtty is the queue getting larger and then smaller:

```
1 chars in queue
3 chars in queue
5 chars in queue
--snip--
99 chars in queue
100 chars in queue
98 chars in queue
--snip--
0 chars in queue
--snip--
```

When it shows 0 characters in the queue again, enter CTRL-C to terminate it.

This has been a brief introduction to the ioctl() system call's uses. It's a powerful tool, but it isn't a portable one. Whenever it's possible to use the termios API, you should. The ioctl() system call is there when there isn't a way to use termios functions to solve your problem at hand.

Summary

This chapter is an introduction to terminals and their attributes. Terminals and their configuration are complex topics that cannot be thoroughly covered in a single chapter. One objective of the chapter is to present the fundamental concepts of terminals as well as some details about their settings. Another is to show you how to learn more about them on your own. For example, the chapter discusses the attributes of the terminal driver interface, as defined by the termios structure. It presents a way to view and change these attributes from the command line using stty and with programs using functions from the termios interface such as tcsetattr(), as well as by using ioctl() operations. It doesn't describe what each and every attribute is or what effect its values have on terminal operations. It scratches the surface of the set of ioctl() operations, which are very extensive. But it does give you guidance on how to learn more, either from the relevant man pages or the POSIX standard, or for the more ambitious, by cloning the Linux source code repository and reading its system documentation. The chapter introduces the idea of terminal driver modes but does not discuss their details. Chapter 19 explores the details of canonical and noncanonical mode processing.

Exercises

1. Write a function `int istty(int fd)` that returns 1 if the file descriptor is that of a terminal and 0 if it isn't. Your function can call any function, including `termios` functions, but not `isatty()`. Write a small program that tests your function.

2. Implement the *fakelogin.c* program using `ioctl` rather than the `termios` interface.

3. Write a program that replaces the character that generates `SIGINT` with some other keyboard character and enters a loop in which it lets the user try to kill it by guessing that character. The program should keep score—each incorrect guess is counted. When the user finds the correct key, the program should print a message that it took so many guesses to find it.

4. The `ttyname()` library function, when given a file descriptor `fd`, returns the absolute pathname of the device file corresponding to `fd`. Implement a simple version of this function. Hint: First try searching the */proc* pseudofilesystem for the pathname, and if that fails, get a stat structure for `fd`, try to find an entry in the */dev* directory with the same inode and device number as in that stat structure, and if that succeeds, return the absolute pathname of that entry.

5. This one is fairly easy. Modify *spl_stty.c* to use `ioctl` commands instead of `tcgetattr()` and `tcsetattr()`.

6. Modify *spl_stty.c* so that a user can enter characters by typing their code values in the form `\0xx`, as in:

```
spl_stty intr '\003'
```

7. Modify *spl_stty.c* so that a user can enter multiple settings to be changed. Its synopsis would be

```
spl_tty [-a ]
spl_tty setting setting ...
```

where a *setting* is either a single flag possibly preceded by a hyphen (-), or it is a pair, as in *variable value*. For each setting on the command line, the program should modify the referenced attribute accordingly. The program should check that the values are within the proper range for the given variable. It should catch any invalid flag names or variable names.

19

INTERACTIVE PROGRAMMING AND THE NCURSES LIBRARY

The primary purpose of a terminal is to allow a user to provide input to and receive output from a program. A terminal's settings determine and limit the ways in which these user interactions can take place. The default terminal setting is canonical mode, which is designed to make the most common interactions convenient, but highly interactive programs such as vi, emacs, and top cannot run in canonical mode. These types of programs disable it and assign values to individual switches and variables in the terminal so that it behaves exactly as they require. They also divide the screen into distinct areas that serve different purposes, such as reserving the bottom row for messages or the top of the screen for summary information.

Previous programs in the book have used ANSI escape sequences to control the screen to a very limited extent, performing tasks such as clearing all or part of the screen and changing the cursor position. Although most modern terminal emulators support ANSI escape sequences, programs that use them are not portable to all systems.

In this chapter, we'll learn how to design and implement interactive programs that take complete control of the terminal and that also configure how different parts of the screen are used. We'll start by defining exactly what canonical mode is. We'll explore from the command line how the terminal functions when canonical mode is disabled. We'll then consider what it means for a terminal to be in noncanonical mode and explore a few different types of noncanonical modes. We'll develop a few programs that demonstrate these ideas. Finally, we'll study the *ncurses* library, which presents an API that in effect allows a program to treat a character-based terminal as a primitive drawing canvas, and we'll develop a simplified version of the top command using *ncurses*.

Canonical and Noncanonical Modes

Canonical mode is the default mode of the terminal. We're accustomed to working in a terminal configured in canonical mode. Now that we know more about the terminal driver, we can make the definition of canonical mode more precise.

Canonical Mode

Canonical mode is characterized by the following conditions:

- An input line is made available to the reading process only when one of the line delimiters \n, EOL, or EOL2 is entered, or EOF is entered at the start of line. Except in the case of EOF, the line delimiter is included in the buffer returned by read().

- Line editing is enabled. In particular, ERASE and KILL are enabled, and if the IEXTEN flag is set, then each of WERASE, REPRINT, and LNEXT is enabled as well. A read() returns at most one line of input; if read() requested fewer bytes than are available in the current line of input, then only the number of bytes requested are read, and the remaining characters will be available for a future read().

- The maximum line length is 4,096 characters, including the terminating newline character; lines longer than 4,096 chars are truncated. After 4,095 characters, input processing by ISIG and any ECHO* processing continues, but any input data after 4,095 characters, up to but not including any terminating newline, is discarded. This ensures that the terminal can always receive more input until at least one line can be read.

Let's do a little experiment to determine what it's like to work when canonical mode is disabled. We'll turn off canonical mode and run the upcopychars2 program from Chapter 18:

```
$ stty -icanon
$ ./upcopychars2
aAbBcCdDeE^D
# Prompt does not return.
```

The program behaves differently than it did in canonical mode. Each character is processed immediately, implying that the driver sends the character to read() without waiting for a newline. Notice, though, that the CTRL-D did not get translated to an end-of-file and that the program is still running. I have to terminate it with CTRL-C.

Now I'll run it again without restoring the terminal to canonical mode, but this time, I'll try to edit the line:

```
$ ./upcopychars2
aAbBcC^?^?^?xXyYzZ^C
$
```

When I entered BACKSPACE three times, it was echoed as ^? each time but did not backspace, verifying that line editing is also disabled. We take these features of canonical mode for granted.

Overview of Noncanonical Modes

The preceding experiments verified that when canonical mode is disabled, input buffering and line editing are both disabled. When canonical mode is disabled, the terminal driver is said to be in *noncanonical* mode, but noncanonical mode is not one distinct set of settings. There are thousands of possible combinations of the flags and variables when it's in noncanonical mode, each producing different terminal behaviors. Some people use the term *raw mode* to refer to any mode in which canonical processing is disabled, but this isn't accurate. Typically, raw mode also disables echoing, signal processing, most of the character conversions I described in Chapter 18, and much more. The term derives from Seventh Edition UNIX (commonly called Version 7), which defined three particular terminal modes called *raw*, *cbreak*, and *cooked*. Cooked mode was essentially today's canonical mode. Cbreak mode was a noncanonical mode with signal processing, echoing, and some character conversions enabled.

The cfmakeraw() system call puts the terminal into a raw mode almost the same as Version 7 UNIX's raw mode. The termios() man page details exactly which attributes are enabled by this function. Interactive programs often put the terminal into raw mode so that they can control exactly how user input is handled. Some put it into a mode more like cbreak mode because they want to allow keyboard signals to be generated, but they also disable echoing. For example, when we run more and press the spacebar, it isn't echoed and we don't need to press ENTER. When we're running vi, in command mode, keys like J and X aren't echoed but instead cause actions, whereas in last-line mode, characters we type are echoed. In raw mode, a program has to take charge of all editing and character handling, and as a result, it is more complex. The terminal driver interface gives us the means to fine-tune exactly how our programs will handle all possible inputs and outputs.

The MIN and TIME Parameters

One of the most important controls we can exert over how the terminal behaves is when characters entered in the terminal are delivered to our programs. Let's start by exploring the purpose of the MIN and TIME attributes of the terminal driver. In canonical mode they're ignored, but when canonical mode is disabled, they take on special roles.

Within the termios structure, the MIN value is stored in c_cc[VMIN] and the TIME value is stored in c_cc[VTIME]. Both must be in the range from 0 to 255. Taken together, they determine when a call to read() completes. Roughly, MIN determines in part how many bytes are needed in the input buffer for a call to read() to complete, and TIME is a timeout value, measured in tenths of a second, which also plays a part in when read() completes.

Their combined effect is based on which of them are zero or nonzero, leading to four possible combinations of values. The POSIX standard specifies the behavior of read operations for each of the four possible combinations. In the following descriptions, assume that the call to read() is:

```
nread = read(STDIN_FILENO, buf, numrequested);
```

You should also bear in mind that when read() is called, the driver's input buffer may already have unread data in it, and the call to read() could be satisfied by that data without the user entering more.

MIN == 0 and TIME == 0 (Polling Read)

When both attributes are 0, read() returns immediately without blocking, whether or not data is available. If no data is available, read() returns a value of 0, having read no data. Otherwise, the read buffer (buf) is filled with the smaller of the number of bytes requested (numrequested) and the number of bytes currently available. For example, if there are 6 bytes available but numrequested is 4, it reads 4 bytes, setting nread to 4. If 2 bytes are available, it reads 2 bytes and sets nread to 2.

Unlike nonblocking reads, which we've seen in previous chapters and will explore in greater depth shortly, no data does not result in a return value of -1. This is called a *polling read* because it can be called repeatedly, polling the driver without blocking the process, as if it were endlessly asking the driver, "Is there data? Is there data? . . ."

MIN > 0 and TIME == 0 (Blocking Read)

In this case, what the POSIX standard currently states is inconsistent with the implementation in all recent Linux kernels. First I'll describe the POSIX requirement, consistent with the man page description. In this case, since TIME is 0, it has no role in the behavior. In effect, the read() has infinite time and may block indefinitely, waiting for input. This is why it's called a blocking read.

The call to read() is supposed to block until MIN bytes are available in the driver or a signal is received. When it does return, it shall have read at most the number of bytes requested (numrequested). There are two cases to consider:

Case 1: MIN <= numrequested The documentation states that as soon as MIN bytes are available, MIN bytes are read into buf. The call does not have to wait for the remaining data for read() to return. This is how it behaves in Linux.

Case 2: numrequested < MIN The documentation states that as soon as MIN bytes are available, numrequested bytes are read into buf, but otherwise, read() is blocked. *This is not how recent Linux kernels implement this case.* Currently in Linux, the call to read() returns if the number of available bytes equals numrequested, even if it's less than MIN.

It's rare to set MIN to be greater than the number of bytes in a read request, and so this discrepancy normally poses no problem, but you need to bear it in mind.

The typical settings in this case are MIN == 1 and TIME == 0. Then MIN is at most the number requested. Programs use these settings in noncanonical mode so that as soon as a user presses a key, the read() returns. Soon we'll see examples that use this mode.

MIN == 0 and TIME > 0 (Timed Read)

This has two subcases:

Case 1: Driver input queue is empty at the time of the call
In this case, a timer is started as soon as read() is called. The TIME value is the number of tenths of a second after which the timer expires. The call to read() returns either because a single byte is available or the timer expired before any data became available. If the timer expired, it implies that no bytes were returned, and nread is set to 0. If read() returned before the timer expired, it implies that a single byte was transferred to the buffer, and nread is set to 1.

Case 2: Driver input queue has avail bytes at the time of the call
In this case, the smaller of avail and numrequested bytes is delivered to read() immediately and read() returns, setting nread to the number it received. Only when the queue has been emptied will the timer start.

It is called a *timed read* because it provides a way to block for a bounded number of tenths of a second controlled by a timer.

MIN > 0 and TIME > 0 (Read with Interbyte Timer)

Neither the POSIX specification nor the Linux man page describes what actually happens in Linux in this case. I will describe the way it works in Linux.

This case has several subcases because it works one way when there's data available in the queue when read() is called, and another way when there isn't. Furthermore, it has the same issues as when MIN > 0 and TIME == 0, in that what is returned to read() is not what the man page describes if MIN is greater than numrequested. Before diving into the details, let me explain why it matters. After all, when would you ever want to set an interbyte timer when reading from the terminal, as well as putting a minimum on the number of bytes to be available for read() to return?

Some applications need to distinguish between, say three characters entered slowly and three characters that are part of a single command or escape sequence. For example, the arrow keys on the keyboard generate 3-byte sequences. If you press the left arrow key, it sends the escape sequence ESC [B. If you enter these same characters slower than the timeout allows, they'll be read as three separate characters and won't cause a cursor movement. Programs such as vi that put the terminal into raw mode depend on being able to make this distinction.

Note also that the timer in this case is an interbyte timer. It's not started when read() is called but instead after the first byte becomes available, and it's restarted after another byte is received (by the driver).

Case 1: Driver input queue is empty at the time of the call

As soon as the first byte is received, the interbyte timer is started. It's restarted after each new byte is received. Suppose first that MIN <= numrequested:

- If no bytes are delivered to the driver, the timer does not start and the call to read() remains in the blocked state, possibly indefinitely.

- If at least 1 but fewer than MIN bytes have been received when the interbyte timer expires, the read() returns with that many bytes in its buffer.

- If MIN bytes are received before the interbyte timer expires, the read is satisfied and MIN bytes are delivered to read().

- If more than MIN bytes are delivered by the driver within the timeout interval, the read() returns with MIN bytes, leaving the rest in the queue for subsequent reads, even if the read request could have been satisfied with these remaining bytes.

Next assume that numrequested < MIN. In this case, the behavior is what the Linux man page describes. MIN plays no role. The read() will block until at least 1 byte is received. If numrequested bytes become available before the timer expires, read() returns with that many bytes, even though they're fewer than MIN and the timer has not expired. If more than numrequested bytes become available, the unread bytes remain in the queue for subsequent reads.

Case 2: Driver input queue has avail bytes at the time of the call

In this case, the smaller of avail and numrequested bytes are delivered to read() immediately and read() returns, setting nread to the number it received. Only when the queue has been emptied will the driver behave as described in Case 1.

The program in Listing 19-1 is designed to experiment with these values. It accepts two command line options: -m *MIN value* and -t *TIME value*. It puts the terminal into noncanonical mode and sets these variables based on the options supplied or the default of MIN == 1 and TIME == 0. It then enters a loop in which it repeatedly calls read() with a request of 6 bytes. By choosing values of MIN larger or smaller than 6, you can see how it behaves. It has a sleep in the loop to give you a chance to prefill the driver's input queue to see the effect that it has.

mintime_test_demo.c

```c
void set_non_canonical(struct termios *ttystate, int minval, int timeval)
{
    tcgetattr(0, ttystate);               /* Read current setting. */
    ttystate->c_lflag    &= ~ICANON;      /* No buffering          */
    ttystate->c_cc[VMIN]  =  minval;      /* Set MIN to minval.    */
    ttystate->c_cc[VTIME] =  timeval;     /* Set TIME to timeval.  */
    if ( -1 == tcsetattr(0, TCSANOW, ttystate) )
        fatal_error(errno, "tcsetattr");
}


void do_read()
{
    int  nread;
    char input[128];

    printf("Enter some characters or wait to see what happens.\n");
    while ( 1 ) {
        sleep(2);
        if ( (nread = read(0, input, 6)) >= 0 ) {
            input[nread] = '\0';
            if ( nread > 0 ) {
                printf("read() returned: %d; chars read: %s\n", nread, input);
                if ( input[0] == 'q' )
                    break;
            }
            else
                printf("Return value of read(): %d; no chars read\n", nread);
        }
    }
}

int main(int argc, char *argv[])
{
    int  min = 1;  /* Default is one char.                          */
    int  time = 0; /* Default is to force reads to wait for min chars. */
    int  ch;
    char optstring[] = ":hm:t:";

    struct termios current, original;

    if ( !isatty(STDIN_FILENO) )
```

```
        usage_error("No input redirection allowed.");
    if ( tcgetattr(0, &current) == -1 )     /* Retrieve termios struct.     */
        fatal_error(errno, "tcgettattr");
    original = current;                      /* Save original termios state. */

    // OMITTED: Option handling
    set_non_canonical(&current, min, time); /* Put into noncanonical mode.  */
    printf("MIN set to %d, TIME set to %d\n ", min, time);
    do_read();                               /* Call read() in a loop.       */
    if ( -1 == tcsetattr( 0 , TCSANOW, &original) )   /* Restore settings.   */
        fatal_error(errno, "tcsetattr");
    return 0;
}
```

Listing 19-1: A program designed for testing the values of MIN and TIME in noncanonical mode

By running this program with all possible configurations of MIN and TIME, you can check whether your system's implementation conforms to the behavior specified by POSIX. Assume that the number of bytes requested (nr) in the call to read() is 6:

```
$ ./mintime_test_demo -m 0 -t 0      # Polling
$ ./mintime_test_demo -m 3 -t 0      # Blocking, with MIN < nr
$ ./mintime_test_demo -m 12 -t 0     # Blocking, with MIN > nr
$ ./mintime_test_demo -m 0 -t 10     # Timed read
$ ./mintime_test_demo -m 3 -t 10     # Read with inter-byte timer, MIN < nr
$ ./mintime_test_demo -m 20 -t 10    # Read with inter-byte timer, MIN > nr
```

If on your system the semantics differ, the program will reveal this.

An Interactive Program in Noncanonical Mode

We'll develop a game-like program in order to illustrate the use of noncanonical mode. The fact that it's like a game doesn't diminish its relevance to interactive system programming. Once you see how it works and how we solve the programming problems in it, hopefully you'll see how to apply them to more serious programs like the top command. But this one is entertaining as well.

The program is derived from the snake terminal-based game of Unix antiquity. When computer terminals weren't bitmapped display devices, people invented games based on character terminals. The basic idea is that when the program starts, a snakelike object moves at a constant velocity in a single direction across the screen. Unlike a snake, the object leaves a trail of the path it's taken. In this version, it always starts in the leftmost column of the window, midway between the top and bottom rows, and moves to the right. Although it's reminiscent of snake, I call the moving object a *sprite*, the term commonly used to refer to moving objects on a computer screen.

Program Features and Issues

The user can alter the movement of the sprite in several ways. To keep the program small, since it's just an example, the allowed inputs are:

q   Quit the program.

p   Pause motion of the sprite.

c   Continue or resume the motion of the sprite.

u   Make the sprite move upward.

r   Make the sprite move to the right.

d   Make the sprite move downward.

l   Make the sprite move to the left.

The user should be able to enter these characters at any time without seeing them echoed or having to enter a newline and should see their effect immediately. Since the program has to keep the sprite moving at all times unless it's been paused, we know of two ways to approach this:

- The animation of the sprite can be implemented within a signal handler that runs at timer expirations, and the main program can use blocking waits for input from the user.

- The animation of the sprite can be implemented within the main program itself, in a loop construct, and within the loop, the program can check whether the user entered any input and respond to it if they did.

The first approach is more complex and introduces those complex problems of signal handlers involving async-signal safety and critical sections to prevent race conditions between the handler and the main program. The second approach leads to a simpler solution that is solved by changing the mode of the terminal, so that's what we'll follow. In effect, the program's main loop, in pseudocode, should be of the form:

```
while ( true ) {
    Advance the sprite in the current direction by one screen position.
    Check whether the user entered a character without blocking.
    If the user entered any input,
        Respond to the input by updating variables accordingly.
}
```

There are two ways to check for user input without performing a blocking read. One is to set the O_NONBLOCK flag on the process's connection to standard input. We haven't attempted that in any programs so far, and we won't do it here because we'd still have to set up the terminal in noncanonical mode anyway, and for reasons I'll explain later, it's not a good idea. Instead, we can do what we just learned about, namely, set the terminal driver's settings for MIN and TIME to 0 so that read() doesn't wait for input and returns 0 if there isn't any; this is called a *polling read*.

NOTE
Enabling O_NONBLOCK in the open file descriptor's flag alters only the behavior of the connection for the process reading from the terminal. Other processes are unaffected by this change. On the other hand, changing the terminal attributes affects all processes reading from the terminal. We need to bear this in mind when deciding which method to use.

In previous chapters, we used ANSI escape sequences for screen-related tasks such as clearing the screen and repositioning the cursor. Almost all terminal emulators support these sequences, making it reasonable to use them; this program will use them as well. The alternative is to use the *ncurses* library, which we'll explore in "Curses and the *ncurses* Library" on page 894.

The visual appearance of the sprite will depend on its direction of movement. When it moves to the right, it will be a > character; to the left, <; going upward, it will be ^; and going downward, v. Therefore, it will leave a trail that might look something like the following:

```
        ^>>>>>>>>>>>
        ^           v
    <<<<<<<<<<^      v
    v    ^    ^      v
    v    ^    ^      v
    v    ^    ^      v
    v    ^    ^      v
>>>>v>>>>>      <<<<<<v
    v
```

The program will also display a menu in the bottom row so that the user knows what commands they can enter, and to the right of the menu, it will display a count of how many moves the sprite has made so far:

```
quit:q; pause:p; continue:c; up:u; right:r; down:d; left:l    moves:    63
```

If the initial window size is too narrow to display the menu, or if the window is resized while the program is running and is then too small, only the count of moves will be displayed. However, to make the implementation simpler, if the user resizes the window, the screen is reinitialized, the count is reset to 0, and the sprite starts all over again. Other design decisions and features are:

- The cursor will be invisible at all times.

- If the sprite reaches a boundary, meaning the edge of the terminal window, it will always make a right-hand turn. For example, if it's moving down, it starts moving along the floor toward the wall to the left, which is a right turn when you're facing downward.

- The sprite will move at a constant speed. The program can call a sleep function in each loop iteration to define its speed. By changing the parameter of the sleep, we can make the animation faster or slower.

- If the program is sent a terminating signal by another process, it will tidy up by clearing the screen and resetting everything back to the way it was before it ran.

These design decisions lead to a useful and interesting but not overly complex program to create.

Terminal Control Functions

We'll start with terminal-related functions since that's the new material from this chapter. We'll begin with the function to put the terminal into noncanonical mode, with echoing and keyboard signals disabled, and with polling reads. I've named it init_terminal():

init_terminal()

```
int init_terminal(int ttyfd)
{
    struct termios cur_tty;
    if ( -1 == tcgetattr(ttyfd, &cur_tty) )
        return (-1);
    cur_tty.c_lflag &= ~ICANON;
    cur_tty.c_lflag &= ~ECHO;
    cur_tty.c_lflag &= ~ISIG;
    cur_tty.c_cc[VMIN]  = 0;
    cur_tty.c_cc[VTIME] = 0;
    return (tcsetattr(ttyfd, TCSANOW, &cur_tty));
}
```

The function retrieves the current settings, modifies them, and then calls tcsetattr() to modify the driver. Notice that the return value from tcsetattr() is passed back to the caller. Rather than exiting from within this function, it lets the calling function decide what to do if it failed to change the driver's state.

The program will save the current terminal settings into a global termios structure named savedtty before making these changes. If the program receives a terminating signal or if it exits normally, it will restore the terminal to the saved state. This is important because if we fail to do this, when the shell resumes, the terminal will be in noncanonical mode. Therefore, the program will have two functions for saving and restoring the terminal settings:

save_tty()

```
void save_tty()
{
    if ( -1 == tcgetattr(STDIN_FILENO, &savedtty) )
        fatal_error(errno, "tcgetattr");
}
```

restore_tty()

```
void restore_tty()
{
    if ( -1 == tcsetattr(STDIN_FILENO, TCSANOW, &savedtty) )
        fatal_error(errno, "tcsetattr");
}
```

Global Constants, Types, and Variables

Choosing good data structures and types simplifies the algorithms. The
sprite.c program uses the following types of objects:

```c
/* Directions of movement */
#define UP      1
#define RIGHT   2
#define DOWN    3
#define LEFT    4

#define USECS   400000   /* Default amount of time to sleep between updates */

const char MENU[]       = "quit:q; pause:p; continue:c; up:u; "
                          "right:r; down:d; left:l ";
const int  menu_length = strlen(MENU);

/* ANSI escape sequences for controlling the screen and cursor */
const char CURSOR_HOME[]   = "\033[1;1H";
const char CLEAR_SCREEN[]  = "\033[2J";
const char CLEAR_LINE[]    =  "\033[1A\033[2K\033[G";
const char HIDE_CURSOR[]    = "\033[?25l";
const char SHOW_CURSOR[]    = "\033[?25h";
const char USE_ALTSCREEN[] = "\e[?1049h";
const char USE_OLDSCREEN[] = "\e[?1049l";

/* Screen coordinate position */
typedef struct {
    int r;    /* Row    */
    int c;    /* Column */
} screenpos;

/* A sprite representation, consisting of a position and a glyph to draw */
typedef struct {
    screenpos pos;
    char      symbol;
} sprite;

/* The four possible unit directions of motion. By adding these to a
   position, it advances in that direction. */
const screenpos Right = {0,1};
const screenpos Left  = {0,-1};
const screenpos Up    = {-1,0};
const screenpos Down  = {1.0};

/* Global variables */
/* The sprite_state array simplifies updating the sprite when it changes
   direction. */
```

```
sprite sprite_state[] =
{ { {0,0}, ' ' }, { Up, '^' }, { Right, '>' }, { Down, 'v' }, { Left, '<'} };
struct termios savedtty;   /* Initial state of terminal; restored on exit */
int           numrows;     /* Current number of rows in terminal screen   */
int           numcols;     /* Current number of columns in terminal screen */
sprite        sprite_obj; /* The sprite object                            */
int           direction;  /* The sprite's current direction               */
int           count = 0;  /* Number of times the sprite moved             */
```

The four screenpos constants make advancing the sprite easy; we just add the appropriate constant to the sprite's position. The sprite_state[] array makes updating the sprite's direction and glyph trivial, as you'll see when we get to the main program's loop.

Support Functions

The functions used by the program fall into one (or more) of the following categories:

- Terminal control and configuration

- Screen management, using ANSI escape sequences

- Sprite control and update

- Window size and size change handling

- Signal handling

- Status and menu bar management

You've already seen the terminal control functions:

```
int  init_terminal(int ttyfd);
void save_tty();
void restore_tty();
```

Screen management functions perform tasks such as setting up and clearing the screen and moving the position of the next write to a new screen position. Their implementations aren't included here to save space. Their prototypes are:

```
void moveto(int row, int col);
void clear_screen();
void enter_alt_screen(void);
void leave_alt_screen(void);
```

The *sprite.c* program introduces the concept of the *alternate screen*. You've probably noticed that some programs, such as more and vi, seem to use a separate screen. When they're running, you can't scroll back to see your history, and when they exit, there's no trace of what was in the terminal when they ran. Terminal emulators usually support a second screen, called the alternate screen, that your program can use instead of the default screen. Two ANSI escape sequences perform this magic: one to use the alternate screen and one to leave it. They were declared in the global constants shown previously.

The functions that perform tasks related to the movement and display of sprites are:

```
void addto(screenpos *target, const screenpos adjust);
void update_sprite(sprite *sp, int dir);
int on_boundary(sprite sp, int rows, int cols, int cur_direction);
void init_sprite(sprite *sp);
```

Their implementations follow:

```
/* addto(&target, adjust) adds the screen position adjust to target. */
void addto(screenpos *target, const screenpos adjust)
{
    target->r += adjust.r;
    target->c += adjust.c;
}
```

The C language doesn't support arithmetic with structures. The addto() function is used where arithmetic is needed:

```
/* update_sprite(&sp, d) changes sp's direction and shape based on d. */
void update_sprite(sprite *sp, int dir)
{
    addto(&(sp->pos), sprite_state[dir].pos);
    sp->symbol = sprite_state[dir].symbol;
}
```

Updating a sprite requires changing its position and possibly changing its glyph. Changing its position takes advantage of the sprite_state[] array. Its indices are direction constants such as UP. For example, sprite_state[UP] contains the position to add to the sprite if the direction is upward and the character to use for its glyph when moving upward.

The on_boundary() function checks whether the next move of the sprite would go past a window boundary. This is true if and only if its current position is at the boundary and its direction of movement is toward the boundary:

```
int on_boundary(sprite sp, int rows, int cols, int cur_direction)
{
    if ( 1 == sp.pos.c && cur_direction == LEFT )
        return LEFT;
    --snip--
    else if ( rows -1 == sp.pos.r && cur_direction == DOWN )
        return DOWN;
```

```
    else
        return 0;
}
```

It returns 0 to indicate it isn't at the boundary. The init_sprite() function sets the initial position and glyph for the sprite. To save space, it isn't shown here.

There are two functions related to window size:

```
int  get_window_size(int ttyfd, int *rows, int *cols);
void on_resize(int signo);
```

We've already seen how to get the size of the window with a call to ioctl(). The second function is the signal handler for the SIGWINCH signal. If the user changes the shape of the window, this signal is sent to the program. To simplify the program's design, if the user does decide to do this while the program is running, the program will reinitialize the screen, resetting the start position of the sprite, resetting the count of moves, and redrawing the display. Anything else would require a much more complex program.

The on_resize() handler implementation follows:

```
void on_resize(int signo)
{
    struct winsize size;

    if ( ioctl(1, TIOCGWINSZ, &size) < 0 )
        fatal_error(errno, "TIOCGWINSZ error");
    numrows = size.ws_row;      /* Store new size.                   */
    numcols = size.ws_col;
    clear_screen();             /* Clear the screen.                 */
    init_sprite(&sprite_obj); /* Reset the sprite to the starting state.  */
    direction = RIGHT;          /* Set it to move to the right.      */
    count = 0;                  /* Reset the count to zero.          */
    if ( numcols >= menu_length + 16 )  /* If no room for menu, skip it.  */
        show_menubar(0);
    else {  /* Draw the menu in the new bottom row and show the move count. */
        moveto(numrows, 1);
        write(STDOUT_FILENO, CLEAR_LINE, strlen(CLEAR_LINE));
        moveto(numrows, 1);
        show_moves(0);
    }
}
```

The first step is to get the new dimensions. After that, it just does all initializations as if the program were starting up again.

I omit the signal handling function implementations. There are two signal-related functions:

```
void cleanup(int signum);
void setup_sighandlers();
```

The `cleanup()` function is the handler that's called if the program receives a terminating signal. It must ensure that the terminal is in the right state and the default screen is restored:

```
void cleanup(int signum)
{
    write(STDOUT_FILENO, SHOW_CURSOR, strlen(SHOW_CURSOR));
    clear_screen();
    restore_tty();
    leave_alt_screen();
    moveto(numrows, 1);
    raise(SIGTERM);
}
```

The function to set up signal handling isn't shown here.

The remaining functions perform tasks related to displaying the menu and move count and setting up the screen to start the program:

```
void show_moves(int count);
void show_moves_only(int count);
void show_menubar(int count);
void setup_screen(int count, sprite *sp, int *initial_dir);
```

If the window size is too small to show the menu, the program shows only the move count. One function shows the move count at the current cursor position (`show_moves()`), the next puts the cursor on the bottom row and shows the move count and nothing else, and the next shows the menu bar and move count. I omit their implementations to save space. The last function sets everything up:

```
void setup_screen(int count, sprite *sprite_obj, int *initial_dir)
{
    clear_screen();
    write(STDOUT_FILENO, HIDE_CURSOR, strlen(HIDE_CURSOR));
    if ( numcols >= menu_length + 16 )
        show_menubar(count);
    else
        show_moves_only(count);
    init_sprite(sprite_obj);
    *initial_dir = RIGHT;
}
```

Normally, the cursor is visible. We'd find it disconcerting not to see a cursor in the terminal since we wouldn't know where our typing was going. However, in this program, it's the opposite. If we don't hide the cursor, that blinking or solid shape would look like it was leading the sprite around the screen, like a horse leading a carriage. This function hides it, decides what to display in the bottom row, and initializes the sprite.

The sprite.c main() Function

The main() function is the last piece of the program. It is presented in part in Listing 19-2. To save space, some error handling is omitted.

sprite.c
main()

```
int main(int argc, char *argv[])
{
        char ch;               /* Character entered by user            */
        int  done  = 0;        /* Whether user still wants to run program */
        int  pause = 0;        /* Controls pausing of output           */
        int  delay = USECS;    /* Amount to sleep between moves         */

        setup_sighandlers();   /* Register all signal handlers.        */
        /* Check whether input or output has been redirected. */
        if ( !isatty(STDIN_FILENO) || !isatty(STDOUT_FILENO) )
            fatal_error(-1, "Not a tty");

        /* Save the original tty state and enter alternate screen. */
        save_tty();
        enter_alt_screen();

        /* Initialize the terminal, get window size, and set up initial state. */
        init_terminal(STDIN_FILENO);
        get_window_size(STDIN_FILENO, &numrows, &numcols);
        setup_screen(count, &sprite_obj, &direction);

        /* Start drawing. */
        while ( !done ) {
            if ( !pause ) {
                count++;
                switch ( on_boundary(sprite_obj, numrows, numcols, direction) ) {
                case UP    : direction = RIGHT; break;
                case RIGHT: direction = DOWN;  break;
                case DOWN : direction = LEFT;  break;
                case LEFT : direction = UP;    break;
                default    : break;  /* No change */
                }
                /* Draw sprite in next position. */
                moveto(sprite_obj.pos.r, sprite_obj.pos.c);
                write(STDOUT_FILENO, &(sprite_obj.symbol), 1);
                update_sprite(&sprite_obj, direction);
            }
            if ( numcols >= menu_length + 16 )
                show_menubar(count);
            else
                show_moves_only(count);
            usleep(delay);                        /* Delay a bit. */
            /* Do the read. If nothing was typed, do nothing. */
```

```
        if ( read(STDIN_FILENO, &ch, 1) > 0 ) {
            switch( ch ) {
            case 'q': done      = 1;     break;
            case 'p': pause     = 1;     break;
            case 'c': pause     = 0;     break;
            case 'u': direction = UP;    break;
            case 'd': direction = DOWN;  break;
            case 'l': direction = LEFT;  break;
            case 'r': direction = RIGHT; break;
            }
        }
    }
    /* Clean up - flush queue, clear the screen, and restore terminal. */
    tcflush(STDIN_FILENO, TCIFLUSH);
    cleanup(0);
    return 0;
}
```

Listing 19-2: The main() function of sprite.c

In essence, the main program sets up all variables and program state and then enters its loop. The first part of the loop updates the sprite position based on the prevailing direction and window size and draws the menu and count in the bottom row. It then adds a small delay before polling to see if the user entered a character. It's important that the delay is before the user's input, not after it. If it were after, when the user entered a command such as r, there'd be a slight delay before it took effect.

The complete program, named *sprite.c*, is available in the book's source code distribution. You can download and build it. When you run it, you'll see the value of noncanonical mode with polling reads.

Curses and the ncurses Library

It's difficult to write programs that manipulate the screen using low-level terminal driver escape sequences. Trying to make them portable is even harder. Fortunately, Unix systems include a terminal-independent, character-oriented graphics library called *ncurses* for controlling cursor movement, screen editing, and window management on ASCII display terminals. The *ncurses* library wraps the complexity of terminal management into an easy-to-use interface containing hundreds of functions. The starting point for learning about it is the ncurses(3ncurses) man page.

The *ncurses* library is vast; in this section, we examine only its basic features and functionality. Before we start our exploration, though, we need to untangle some of the confusion surrounding its name, which I'll do with a brief summary of its origin and history.

History, Standards, and Names

According to Eric Raymond, in the September 1995 issue of the Linux Journal (*https://www.linuxjournal.com/article/1124*):

> The first curses library was hacked together at the University of California, Berkeley in about 1980 to support a screen-oriented dungeon game called rogue. It leveraged an earlier facility called *termcap*, the terminal capability library, which was used in the original vi editor and elsewhere.

The original library was named *curses*, based on the phrase *cursor optimization*. Its primary developer was Ken Arnold. This is now known as the BSD version.

AT&T Bell Labs developed a different, and proprietary, version of *curses* when Mary Ann Horton, who maintained the database of terminal capabilities called *termcap* at the University of California, Berkeley, started working there. She created a new terminal capabilities library that was called the *terminfo* library and based the new version of *curses* on that library instead. This version was included in System V Release 2 (SVR2) and remained in future releases through SVR4. The SVR4 version had many attractive features, but it was proprietary and it was based on the *terminfo* format, whereas the BSD version was free and based on the *termcap* file. This made it hard to write portable *curses* programs. In 1982, Pavel Curtis solved the problem by rewriting a free version of *curses* based on the SVR1 version. Fast-forwarding, by the mid-1990s The Open Group published the X/Open Curses standard, based on the SVR4 *curses* API, and developers at UC Berkeley created a new version of *curses* compatible with SVR4 and the X/Open Curses standard, which they named *ncurses*. This standard is also referred to as *XSI Curses*.

To summarize:

- The current standard, X/Open Curses, Issue 7, defines an interface to which an implementation of the *curses* library should conform. That standard refers to the library as the *Curses* library.

- The current Linux implementation of this standard is called *ncurses*. The library file is named *libncurses*.

- Programs that link to this library are referred to in the documentation as *curses programs*, not *ncurses programs*.

- Linux has two header files, named *curses.h* and *ncurses.h*. The *ncurses.h* header is a symbolic link to *curses.h*. The man page synopsis for *ncurses* shows that programs should use the #include directive:

```
#include <curses.h>
```

Your programs should use this directive.

In the rest of this chapter, I'll use terminology consistent with the documentation, calling programs *curses* programs, calling the library the *ncurses* library, referring to the API as the Curses API, and including *curses.h* in programs. For example, the function that initializes the *ncurses* library is `initscr()`. Since `initscr()` is specified in the X/Open Curses standard, I may at times say that it's a Curses function or that it's an *ncurses* function. Everything we need to know about *ncurses* is available either on the `ncurses` man page or one of the pages that it references. The Curses library standard is available online as well at *https://pubs.opengroup.org/onlinepubs/9699909599/toc.pdf*.

Terminology

The Curses library defines a few fundamental types of objects.

Terminal

In Curses, the *terminal* is the logical I/O device within which all interactions with the user take place. The `TERMINAL` data type is an opaque data type associated with a terminal. The `TERMINAL` data structure contains information about the capabilities of the terminal, the terminal mode, and its current state of I/O operations.

Screen

A *screen* is the physical output device of a terminal. Each terminal has one screen. The `SCREEN` data type is an opaque data type that represents a screen. The `SCREEN` data structure encapsulates all of the data associated with a screen, such as the file descriptors associated with its input and output streams, buffers associated with it, screen dimensions, screen attributes, terminal driver mode, and so on.

Window

A *window* can be thought of as a two-dimensional array of characters representing all or part of a terminal screen. A window is represented by the `WINDOW` data type. The `WINDOW` data type is a C structure with many members; in addition to the internal storage for all of its screen cells, it contains the location of the window's origin on the screen (its upper-left corner), its size, the cursor position, several attributes such as its current background color and scrolling state, and its input mode.

The `WINDOW` data structure also contains a flag that indicates whether the contents of the data structure are different from its manifestation on the visible screen. When the window is changed, the flag is set. The Curses library refers to this as *touching* the window, like the Unix `touch` command that sets the modification time of a file.

A default window called `stdscr`, which is the size of the terminal screen, is created when a program calls `initscr()`.

A *subwindow* is a window created within another window, which is called its *parent window*.

Pad

The library also defines a particular type of window called a pad. A pad is a window that isn't limited to the size of the screen and whose contents aren't necessarily displayed. You can think of a pad as a canvas larger than the terminal and the terminal is then like a window that can be moved around on the canvas to make different portions of it visible. I won't cover pads in this book.

The names of several Curses functions and objects are misleading, as you'll soon discover. For example, the function newterm() creates a new screen, not a new terminal, and the objects curscr and stdscr are window objects, not screens, as their names suggest.

Compiling, Building, and Running Curses Programs

All *curses* programs must include the *curses.h* header file and the standard C I/O library header file *stdio.h*. Since the *ncurses* library file is not part of the standard library, we have to build with the -lncurses linker option, as in:

```
$ gcc -o myprog myprog.c -lncurses
```

No other libraries are needed to run a *curses* program. The behavior of *curses* programs is affected by certain environment variables. If LINES or COLUMNS are in the environment, *ncurses* will use their values instead of the information provided by terminfo. In this case, *ncurses* won't handle window resizing well. If you intend to handle window resizing events and these variables are set, then the program must remove them from its inherited environment by calling unsetenv() before calling initscr() or any other *ncurses* functions:

```
unsetenv("LINES");
unsetenv("COLUMNS");
--snip--
initscr();
```

This won't affect the environment in the shell since the process modifies only its copy of it.

Curses Basics

Here, we'll cover the key concepts and elements of the Curses library, starting with its coordinate system.

Coordinates in Curses

The coordinate system in *ncurses* is derived from matrix coordinates rather than Cartesian coordinates. The origin, (0,0), is in the upper-left corner of the screen, and the coordinate pair (y, x) represents the screen cell in row y and column x, as shown in Figure 19-1.

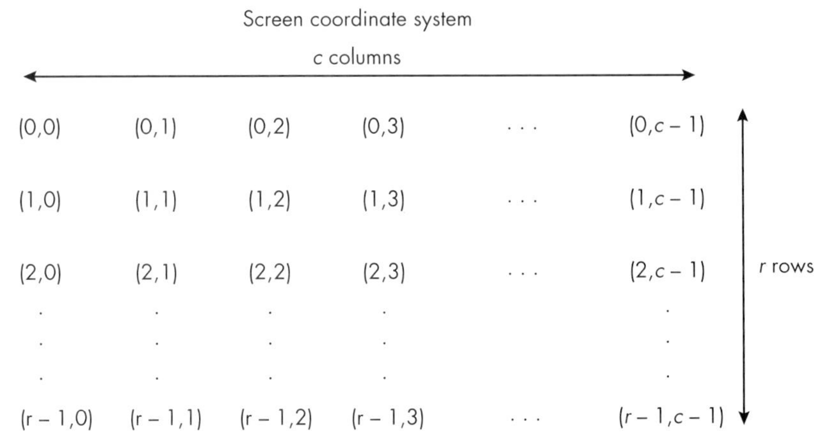

Screen coordinate system

c columns

(0,0)	(0,1)	(0,2)	(0,3)	. . .	(0,c − 1)
(1,0)	(1,1)	(1,2)	(1,3)	. . .	(1,c − 1)
(2,0)	(2,1)	(2,2)	(2,3)	. . .	(2,c − 1)
.	.	.	.		.
.	.	.	.		.
.	.	.	.		.
(r − 1,0)	(r − 1,1)	(r − 1,2)	(r − 1,3)	. . .	(r − 1,c − 1)

r rows

Figure 19-1: The Curses coordinate system

In Figure 19-1, there are r rows and c columns. Each cell is one character position on the screen.

Screen Updating in Curses

Window managing libraries, whether on Unix, macOS, or Windows, usually follow the same principle of drawing: They maintain two data structures representing the canvas on which they draw. One, the *visible canvas*, is what is currently in view on the physical display device. The other, the *hidden canvas*, is a canvas in memory on which only drawing operations take place. This terminology is not standardized and goes by various names depending on the particular system one uses. In Curses, each terminal has two such canvases. The visible canvas is called the *physical screen*, and the hidden one is called the *virtual screen*.

In Curses, when a program calls any function that modifies the screen contents, those changes are first applied to the virtual screen in memory. When the program is ready to make those changes visible on the screen, the virtual screen is used to update the physical screen. Figure 19-2 illustrates the principle.

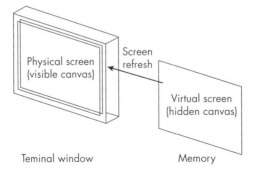

Figure 19-2: Screen refreshing in which the contents of a hidden canvas are applied to the visible canvas on the screen

The figure schematically represents the virtual screen's contents being written onto the physical screen. In fact, the *ncurses* library performs this update efficiently, comparing the two screens and modifying only the parts of the physical screen that are different from the virtual screen. In the *ncurses* documentation, the operation that updates the visible screen is called *screen refreshing*.

The actual refresh operation is actually two stages. I'll explain by way of an example. A program can write a character string to its window with the `addstr()` function. Suppose that the window's cursor is at position (5,0) on the screen. When the program calls `addstr("Hello")`, the string `"Hello"` is written to the `stdscr` window data structure. This records that line 5 now contains the string `"Hello"` in columns 0 through 4. These changes do not appear on the screen until a refresh operation takes place.

When `refresh()` is called, the first step is to map the contents of the `stdscr` window data structure into a hidden window named `newscr`, used internally by *ncurses*. Each screen has this hidden window. The `newscr` window is what the documentation calls the virtual screen. Now the string `"Hello"` is part of `newscr`. The next step is to update the physical screen, which is represented by the window `curscr`. This window's contents are the visible screen. Once our string is in it, it appears on the screen.

Every time that a program makes changes to a window, those changes only become visible when the program refreshes the screen. Two functions perform refreshing: `refresh()` and `wrefresh()`. Programs that draw on the standard screen (`stdscr`) simply call `refresh()`, whose prototype is:

```
int refresh(void);
```

A program that draws on another window, `WINDOW *win`, has to call `wrefresh(win)`. Its prototype is:

```
int wrefresh(WINDOW *win);
```

If a program has created multiple windows in the same screen and they overlap, a portion of the screen's real estate may be within more than one window. If two windows, `win1` and `win2`, overlap and `wrefresh(win2)` is called, the library determines how to redraw the screen efficiently, replacing those portions of the screen within the intersection of `win1` and `win2`. It redraws a window only if that window's content has changed in some way. A program can also call `touchwin(win)`, whose prototype is

```
int touchwin(WINDOW *win);
```

to tell *ncurses* that an entire window `win` has changed without making any actual changes to force a redraw when it calls `wrefresh(win)`.

Curses Data Types, Constants, and Variables

The *curses.h* header file defines a few data types in addition to the ones described in "Terminology" on page 896. These include:

attr_t   An integer type that is used to store the attributes of various objects in Curses

bool   A Boolean type, the same as in the C header file, *stdbool.h*

chtype   An integer type that stores a character and character attributes such as color

Curses also defines the following global constants:

```
int TRUE     /* The value 1                          */
int FALSE    /* The value 0                          */
int ERR      /* The return value indicating failure */
int OK       /* The return value indicating success */
```

When a program initializes the *ncurses* library by calling `initscr()`, the library initializes the terminal that the program will use for the Curses session. Curses creates several variables for the program, including the predefined windows stdscr, curscr, and newscr belonging to that terminal. The stdscr window is called the *standard screen*. Its size is that of the terminal screen.

The library also provides several variables associated with the terminal screen. A few basic ones are:

```
int LINES    /* The number of lines in the terminal screen             */
int COLS     /* The number of columns in the terminal screen           */
TABSIZE      /* The number of spaces used to represent a tab character */
```

I'll discuss later how *ncurses* handles changes to these variables when a user decides to resize the terminal while a *curses* program is running.

Internationalization in Curses

The *ncurses* library is locale-aware; it uses the locale of the calling process. If you want a *curses* program to use the locale, before starting up *ncurses*, it should call `setlocale(LC_ALL, "")`. If the locale isn't initialized, the library assumes that characters are encoded in the ISO-8859-1 codeset, a 1-byte code set whose lower 7 bits are the ASCII codes. Programs should always initialize the locale to avoid problems related to character codes.

Initializing and Wrapping Up

The *ncurses* library must be initialized for each program that links to it. Initialization performs many tasks, including allocating memory for stdscr and curscr and other data structures. It also changes the settings of the terminal driver. A program that uses only a single terminal window can initialize the library by calling `initscr()` before it calls any functions that work with windows or screens. Its prototype is:

```
WINDOW *initscr(void);
```

If `initscr()` fails, it returns `NULL`; otherwise, it returns a pointer to `stdscr`. That pointer can then be used as the argument to a few *ncurses* functions. Programs that set up multiple terminal windows by calling `newterm()` don't have to call `initscr()` because `newterm()` performs the required initializations of *ncurses*. Its prototype is:

```
SCREEN *newterm(const char *type, FILE *outfd, FILE *infd);
```

This returns `NULL` if it fails, and if it succeeds, it returns a pointer to the newly created screen. Later, you'll see an example that shows how to use multiple terminals.

When a program is ready to terminate, it must always call `endwin()` for each terminal that it opened to restore the terminal driver settings and release *ncurses* library resources. The prototype is:

```
int endwin(void);
```

If this function fails, it returns `ERR`; otherwise, it returns `OK`.

Programs should always have signal handlers that clean up in case they receive a terminating signal, and within the handlers, they should call `endwin()`. Not calling `endwin()` before terminating will leave the terminal in an unusable state for the shell. If this happens, at the shell prompt, enter **reset** to reset the terminal.

The Curses API

The Curses API includes several hundred different functions, some of which are much more commonly used than others. The `curses` man page lists them all, as well as some that may not be part of the XSI Curses standard. The *ncurses* library can be configured in one of two ways:

- The *normal* library handles only 8-bit characters and stores each character in a window in an object of type `chtype`.

- The *wide* library, named *ncursesw*, supports multibyte characters as well as 8-bit characters. The character representation is more complex than in the normal library.

The man page lists both normal and wide library functions. The wide library functions are usually easy to spot because their names contain a `_w` substring, such as `add_wch()`. I won't discuss the wide library here.

Many functions fall neatly into one of a few different categories, but others are harder to classify. Following is a set of categories containing many of the commonly used functions:

Initialization and configuration   Includes functions that set up and reconfigure the Curses library for the program, including setting the terminal driver input and output modes, the keyboard and mouse, and so on.

Screen, window, and pad manipulation   Includes functions that act on these objects as entities, such as creating them, deleting them, and accessing and modifying their attributes.

Input Includes all input from a keyboard as well as mouse events. The library has an extensive set of mouse-related functions, whose names usually contain the substring mouse.

Output (screen overwriting) Includes all functions that send output to windows. Because writing a character into a screen cell replaces whatever character was there before, these functions are also thought of as screen overwriting functions. This set has functions that operate on single characters and strings and includes functions that erase, delete, and modify what appears on the screen.

Cursor manipulation Includes functions that move the cursor, get its position, change its attributes, and so on.

Screen attribute management Includes functions that return information about the current state of the screen and everything in it, such as the coordinates of the window relative to its parent, the character at the current cursor position, and much more. Some contain the substring attr in their names, and some contain get. This is a large category.

We'll explore several Curses functions in this chapter, but before we do, we'll start with an example that shows the use of the most basic *ncurses* functions: initscr(), move(), addstr(), refresh(), getch(), and endwin().

A First Curses Program

The program in Listing 19-3 performs the basic operations of a *curses* program. It initializes the library, moves the cursor, prints some text, moves the cursor again, prints more text, waits for user input, and terminates when the user responds.

curses_demo1.c
```c
#include "common_hdrs.h"
#include <curses.h>

int main(int argc, char *argv[])
{
    char epoch[] = "January 1, 1970, the start of the UNIX Epoch";

    initscr();                              /* Initialize ncurses.      */
    move(LINES/2, (COLS - strlen(epoch))/2); /* Move to position so string is
                                                centered on screen.     */
    addstr(epoch);                          /* Write the string.        */
    move(LINES - 1, 0);  /* Park the cursor at bottom and display a prompt. */
    addstr("Type any char to quit:");       /* Add prompt string.       */
    refresh();
    getch();                                /* Wait for user to type a character. */
    endwin();                               /* End curses session.      */
    return 0;
}
```

Listing 19-3: A program to demonstrate basic Curses functions

Let's break down the steps in this program:

- The first call is to `initscr()`, which initializes all *ncurses* data structures after determining the terminal type and then calls `refresh()` to clear the screen.

- The program calls `move()` to move the cursor to the center row at a column position calculated so that the string in `epoch` is centered on the row. The `move()` function expects a (*row*, *column*) pair of arguments:

```
int move(int y, int x);
```

- It then calls `addstr()`, a workhorse function of Curses. Its prototype is:

```
int addstr(const char *str);
```

This outputs its string argument at the current cursor position and, by default, advances the cursor to either the next position in the line or the first position in the line below, if wrapping has not been disabled.

- The program then parks the cursor in the bottom row. *Parking* the cursor means moving it to a fixed position out of the way of any drawing routines. In this case, the program writes a message, again with `addstr()`.

- Before continuing, since all drawing has been done, the program calls `refresh()` to update the display. This step actually isn't required in this program because `addstr()` always performs a refresh operation before it returns, but it's a good habit to refresh after screen updates.

- The next function is an input function. Many interactive programs are designed so that the user enters a single character rather than a string. The Curses function `getch()` reads a single character from the current window. Its prototype is:

```
int getch(void);
```

In blocking mode, it doesn't return until the user enters a character. This program doesn't store the returned character because it doesn't use it. Any character causes the call to return.

- The last Curses function in the program is `endwin()`. When this function returns, the screen display returns to the state it was in before the program started. If we didn't have the blocking call to `getch()` before it, we'd never see our Curses screen because it would vanish too quickly.

The last point deserves a bit more discussion. Curses is designed to use the terminal driver's alternate screen. As a result, when the program exits, none of the *curses* program's outputs are in the terminal's scroll-back buffer.

Earlier in the chapter, in *sprite_demo.c*, we had to use an ANSI escape sequence to get this effect (in enter_alt_screen() and leave_alt_screen()), but Curses takes care of it for us. Compile, build, and run the program and verify that it behaves the way I just described. You won't see anything in the scroll-back buffer when it terminates.

Curses Naming Convention

The designers of the Curses API established a naming convention to make it easy to guess the name of a function based on what it does or guess what a function does based on its name. The man page specifies this naming convention. For example:

- Functions with names prefixed with w require a window argument.

- Functions with names prefixed with p require a pad argument.

- Those without a prefix generally use stdscr. I'll call these *base functions*.

- Functions with names prefixed with mv imply a call to move() prior to executing the function. They require y- and x-coordinates preceding the other arguments.

- Functions prefixed with mvw take both a window argument and x- and y-coordinates. They imply a move before executing the function in the specified window argument. The window argument precedes the coordinates, which precede the base function's arguments.

- Functions with an n preceding the base function name expect an integer argument N in the last position and process at most N characters.

This implies that each base function can have as many as eight variants including itself. For example, consider the base function addstr(s). The addstr() man page documents all possible variants:

```
int addstr(const char *str);
int addnstr(const char *str, int n);
int waddstr(WINDOW *win, const char *str);
int waddnstr(WINDOW *win, const char *str, int n);

int mvaddstr(int y, int x, const char *str);
int mvaddnstr(int y, int x, const char *str, int n);
int mvwaddstr(WINDOW *win, int y, int x, const char *str);
int mvwaddnstr(WINDOW *win, int y, int x, const char *str, int n);
```

The first four don't require a cursor movement first; the latter four do. The ones with a w work in the given WINDOW argument. The ones with an n limit output to at most n characters.

There are too many functions in Curses to cover in a single chapter. We won't explore any pad functions here or functions that manipulate color or other character and screen attributes. We won't examine any of the *ncurses* functions that access and modify the terminal information database. In general, we'll examine only base functions and not their variants. As you start to write more advanced programs, you might need to explore the ones not described here. You may also discover the *panel* and *menu* libraries that extend *ncurses* in many Unix systems but that aren't part of the XSI Curses standard.

Curses Configuration Functions

This category includes functions that set up the terminal, keyboard, and screen for your program's use. For each, I give its prototype and a brief description. You'll most likely be using all of these functions in your first few programs. You've seen a few already in the example program.

`WINDOW *initscr(void)`

Initializes the library data structures, returning a pointer to `stdscr`.

`int endwin(void)`

Releases library resources and resets the terminal.

`int clear(void)`

Clears the standard screen. It has variants to clear other windows or portions of a screen.

`int cbreak(void)`

Puts the terminal in cbreak mode. In cbreak mode, line buffering and erase/kill character processing are disabled, but interrupt and flow control characters are not disabled. It's essentially the same as turning off `icanon` in the terminal, setting `MIN = 1` and `TIME = 0`, and not modifying `isig` or `ixon` in the `termios` settings. Characters typed by the user are immediately available to the program.

`int noecho(void)/int echo(void)`

Disable or enable echoing characters when `getch()` is called in the terminal. We usually want to disable echoing. The man page has further details.

`int intrflush(WINDOW *win, bool bf)`

If `bf = TRUE`, pressing an interrupt key on the keyboard flushes all output in the terminal driver's output queue. This makes response time faster but causes Curses to have the wrong idea of what is on the screen. Disabling the option prevents the flush.

`int keypad(WINDOW *win, bool bf)`

If `bf = TRUE`, this enables keypad function key processing, and if `bf = FALSE`, it disables it. The arrow keys on the keyboard are some of the keys that become enabled by this function. When the keypad is enabled, calls to `getch()` and variants return special symbolic 8-bit character values representing arrow keys and other nonprintable character keys. They have names such as `KEY_LEFT`, `KEY_UP`, `KEY_HOME`, and `KEY_ENTER`. The *curses.h* header file defines these constants.

`int nodelay(WINDOW *win, bool bf)`

Puts the terminal into nonblocking mode when `bf = TRUE`; `getch()` and variants return `ERR` if no input is available.

There are other functions that alter the input mode, such as `halfdelay()`, `raw()`, `timeout()`, and several others. They're all described in the `inopts(3NCURSES)` man page.

A typical interactive program will include this sequence of calls

```
initscr();                /* Initialize ncurses.                     */
cbreak();                 /* Put into cbreak mode.                   */
noecho();                 /* Turn off echo.                          */
intrflush(stdscr, FALSE); /* Don't flush output on keyboard signals. */
keypad(stdscr, TRUE);     /* Turn on the keypad.                     */
```

at the start of the program. Programs that intend to poll the keyboard for input rather than waiting for it would also call `nodelay(stdscr, TRUE)`.

Curses Input Functions

We've seen getch() already; Curses has two other input functions that are worth remembering:

int getstr(char *str)
> Equivalent to a series of calls to getch() until either a newline or carriage return is entered. The terminating character isn't included in the string, which is NULL-terminated and stored at address str.

int scanw(const char *fmt, ...)
> Essentially like the C scanf() function. It is equivalent to calling getstr(s) and then calling sscanf(s, fmt, ...).

The getstr() function requires the user to enter a newline or carriage return, even in cbreak mode; otherwise, it wouldn't know when input was terminated. The following program, *getstr_demo.c*, demonstrates the use of getstr().

getstr_demo.c
```
int main(int argc, char *argv[])
{
    char str[32];
    initscr();
    cbreak();
    mvaddstr(0, 0, "Type up to 31 characters and press ENTER:");
    getstr(str);
    mvaddstr(1, 0, "You entered: ");
    addstr(str);
    mvaddstr(2, 0, "Type any character to quit.");
    getch();
    endwin();
    return 0;
}
```

The program also shows the use of the `mv` variant of `addstr()` to reduce the number of function calls. When you run it, its output will be indistinguishable from a non-*curses* program, except that the screen contents will disappear when you enter the character to terminate it:

```
$ ./getstr_demo
Type up to 31 characters and press ENTER:hello
You entered: hello
Type any character to quit.
```

After the user enters a character, the program terminates, the `bash` prompt returns, and none of the program's output is in the scroll-back buffer.

Curses Output Functions

There are a few families of functions that write to the screen. We've seen `addstr()` already, but others include:

`int addch(const chtype ch)`

Adds a single character `ch` at the current cursor position, which is then advanced. At the right margin, the cursor wraps, but see the man page for details such as how it handles backspaces, tabs, and so on.

`int addchstr(const chtype *chstr)`

Whereas `addstr()` has an argument of type `const char*`, this has an argument of type `const chtype*`. This is called a *character array* in Curses. The `chtype` data type isn't a plain character; it stores attributes such as color. Unlike `addstr()`, this doesn't advance the cursor; doesn't perform any kind of checking, such as for the newline or backspace; doesn't expand control characters to ^-escapes; and truncates the string if it crosses the right margin, rather than wrapping it.

`int insch(chtype ch)`

Inserts the character `ch` before the character under the cursor. All characters to the right of the cursor are moved one space to the right, with the possibility of the rightmost character on the line being lost. This operation does not change the cursor position.

`int insstr(const char *str)`

Similar to `insch()` except that it inserts the string `str` before the cursor, shifting all characters to the right.

`int printw(const char *fmt, ...)`

The Curses equivalent of the C `printf()` function.

In addition to functions that add characters to the screen, there are functions that remove them. These are also output functions because they alter the contents of the screen. I won't detail them all. They include `delch()`, which deletes the character at the cursor position, and `deleteln()`, which deletes all characters in the line containing the cursor.

Window Functions

A program can create and delete windows, create and delete subwindows, and more, within a single terminal screen. The window(3NCURSES) man page lists many of the window-related functions available in *ncurses*, and the util(3NCURSES) man page lists a few more. I'll describe a few from both man pages:

WINDOW *newwin(int nlines, int ncols, int o_y, int o_x)

> The call newwin(nl, nc, y, x) creates and returns a pointer to a new window with nl lines and nc columns, with the upper-left corner at screen position (y, x). The window is initialized with all default values. The man page describes what *ncurses* does when one or more of the arguments are 0.

int delwin(WINDOW *win)

> The call delwin(winptr) deletes the window pointed to by winptr, freeing all memory associated with it. It doesn't erase the window's screen image, though. We can call either werase(winptr) or wclear(winptr) to erase its screen image before deleting it.

int mvwin(WINDOW *win, int y, int x)

> The call mvwin(winptr, y, x) moves the window so that the upper-left corner is at screen position (y, x). It's an error if these coordinates would cause any part of the window to be off the screen, in which case the window would not be moved. The program has to call refresh() after the move. This function doesn't erase the old window from the screen; the program must do that.

int putwin(WINDOW *win, FILE *filep)

> The call putwin(winptr, fp) writes the contents of window winptr to the file stream pointed to by fp. This function provides a way to save a curses program's current state into a file.

WINDOW *getwin(FILE *filep)

> The call savedwin = getwin(fp) creates a window from the contents of the file stream pointed to by fp, assuming that a window was previously written into it. It returns a pointer to the new window.

Being able to create multiple windows in a screen is useful. It's a way to tile the screen into separate rectangular areas with different attributes and restrict drawing to selected regions of the screen.

Miscellaneous Useful Functions

The Curses library has a few functions that don't fit into any one category but are worth remembering. For instance, there's a function that returns the character at a given screen position and a function that returns the cursor's current position. Here's a handful of a few interesting ones:

```
void getyx(WINDOW *win, int y, int x);
/* getyx(win,y,x) gets the current cursor position in the given window and
   stores its coordinates in y and x. Notice that y and x are not pointers;
   this is a macro. */
```

```
void getmaxyx(WINDOW *win, int y, int x);
/* getmaxyx(win,y,x) puts the coordinates of the lower right-hand corner of a
   window into y and x. This is a way to get the window's size. */
chtype inch(void);
/* inch() returns the character at the cursor, as well as its attributes. */
```

We now have a repertoire of functions that will let us write many different types of *curses* programs. We'll start with a small example that shows how to use multiple tiled windows.

A Program with Tiled Windows

The program in Listing 19-4 demonstrates how to tile a terminal with a pair of Curses windows. It's designed to model programs that have a fixed information or status bar at the top of the screen and a content area below it. Usually the content changes dynamically but the information bar doesn't. We'll learn a few important rules about programs with multiple windows from this example.

tiled_windows.c
```
#include "common_hdrs.h"
#include <curses.h>

const char info_bar[] = "A menu and status information could be here.\n"
                        "Type 's' to save the content area, or 'q' to quit:";

int main(int argc, char *argv[])
{
    WINDOW *content_win;      /* The content area                          */
    WINDOW *info_win;         /* The information area                      */
    FILE   *fp;               /* File pointer for saving content window     */
    char   ch;                /* To store user input                       */
    int    infobar_length = strlen(info_bar); /* Length of fixed message   */

    if ( NULL == (fp = fopen("./saved_content.crs", "w")) )
        fatal_error(errno, "fopen");

    initscr();   /* Initialize curses.    */
    cbreak();    /* Put into cbreak mode. */
    noecho();    /* Turn off echo.        */

    /* Create a content window in the lower LINES-3 rows of the screen. */
❶ if ( NULL == (content_win = newwin(LINES-3, COLS, 3, 0)) ) {
        endwin();
        fatal_error(-1, "Could not create first window.");
    }
    mvwaddstr(content_win, 1, 0, "This is a content area.");
❷ wrefresh(content_win);                        /* Refresh this window.      */
```

```
      /* Create an information window in the top 3 rows of the screen. */
❸ if ( NULL == (info_win = newwin(3, COLS, 0, 0)) ) {
      endwin();
      fatal_error(-1, "Could not create second window.");
  }
  /* Fill the third row with a horizontal line. */
  mvwhline(info_win, 2, 0, ACS_HLINE, COLS);
  mvwaddstr(info_win, 0, 0, info_bar);     /* Add info to top window.   */
  wmove(info_win,1, infobar_length);       /* Move cursor to top window. */
  wrefresh(info_win);                      /* Refresh this window.      */

  /* Wait for input before terminating. */
  while ( (ch = wgetch(info_win)) != 'q' ) {
      if ( ch == 's' )               /* Then save the window into a file. */
          putwin(content_win, fp);
  }
  endwin();
  return 0;
}
```

Listing 19-4: A Curses program with tiled windows

The program names the two windows info_win and content_win. It opens a file with a fixed name for saving the content window and then sets up the Curses terminal, putting it into cbreak mode with echoing disabled.

It's natural to wonder why we need two windows. Couldn't we just create one window to store the information and use stdscr, which would be behind it, as the content area? You can try this, but it won't work. The ncurses man page warned us about this:

> Note that curses does not handle overlapping windows, that's done by the panel (3CURSES) library. This means that you can either use stdscr or divide the screen into tiled windows and not using stdscr at all. Mixing the two will result in unpredictable, and undesired, effects.

That's why we have two windows. The content window is created first ❶. Its height is the height of the screen minus 3, it's the full width of the screen, and its upper-left corner is at position (3,0). The program then adds a sentence to that window using the mvwaddstr() function and then refreshes that window ❷ to force the update.

The upper window (info_win) is similarly created, but it's specified so that it fits into the space at the top not occupied by the content window ❸. The program uses the mvwhline() function, which I didn't mention before. This is a line-drawing function

```
mvwhline(info_win, 2, 0, ACS_HLINE, COLS);
```

that draws a horizontal line in the info_win window, starting in position (2,0), its bottom row, using the *ncurses* ACS_HLINE character, an 8-bit character that forms a continuous line, with length equal to the screen width. Observe that the line occupies a row of the window; it isn't between two windows. The program writes a string into the window above the line, moves the cursor into this window to the left of the string, and refreshes this window.

The order of events here is significant. If the program wants the cursor to be in that screen position, it cannot refresh the content window *after* moving the cursor into position in the information window because the refresh operation on a window will move the cursor back into it.

NOTE *A screen has a single cursor no matter how many windows it has. If a program creates multiple windows in a terminal, it has to manage the position of the cursor so that it's in the window at which the next operation should take place.*

The last step is to wait for input. In cbreak mode, the user simply types a single character that's delivered immediately to the program. The program checks whether it's a q and quits if it is, and if it's not, the program checks whether it's an s, in which case it saves the window to the file using `putwin()`. If it's anything else, it iterates. When you run the program, you'll see that the screen looks roughly like the following, except with a solid line instead of the dashes:

```
A menu and status information could be here.
Type 's' to save the content area, or 'q' to quit:
--------------------------------------------------------------------------

This is a content area.
```

The primary advantage of using tiled windows rather than a single window is that a program can assign different attributes to each window. This simple program doesn't do that. There are some relatively easy extensions to this program, such as changing the backgrounds of the different windows.

A Curses Version of sprite.c

The *sprite.c* program that we developed earlier in this chapter relied on ANSI escape sequences and termios handling to manage the terminal and the screen. It's not that hard to convert it into a curses program. The program will become smaller as well, because several functions won't be needed. Some of the ways in which it becomes simpler are:

- The earlier program used a function named `moveto()` to move the cursor. In the *curses* program, we don't need that function; instead, the program calls `move()`.

- All of the terminal-related functions, such as saving and restoring the terminal state, can be deleted, since *ncurses* handles the terminal configuration.

- The program doesn't need to keep track of the size of the screen in its own private variables. It uses LINES and COLS instead. In programs in general, it's more portable coding to call getmaxyx() to get the current window size when multiple windows are open in a terminal. In this program, it isn't necessary.

- Handling window resizing events will become much simpler.

Here, I'll show all of the changed functions, beginning with the main() function. The following listing shows the changes. Code that stays the same is snipped out. All of the code in main() in *sprite.c* up to the start of its while loop is greatly simplified. The other changes are minor:

sprite_curses.c
main()

```
int main(int argc, char *argv[])
{
    char ch;                /* Character entered by user            */
    int  done  = 0;         /* Whether user still wants to run program */
    int  pause = 0;         /* Controls pausing of output           */
    int  delay = USECS;     /* Amount to sleep between moves         */

    unsetenv("LINES");      /* Unset the environment's LINES variable. */
    unsetenv("COLUMNS");    /* Same with COLUMNS; needed for resizing  */
    setup_sighandlers();    /* This doesn't change.                 */
    initscr();              /* Now Curses does the rest of the dirty
    clear();                    work of configuring the terminal, etc.  */

    cbreak();
    noecho();
    nodelay(stdscr, TRUE);
    setup_screen(count, &sprite_obj, &direction); /* No change here   */

    while ( !done ) {
        --snip--
            switch ( on_boundary(sprite_obj, LINES, COLS, direction) ) {
                // OMITTED: The same switch body as in sprite.c
            }
            /* Draw sprite in next position. */
            move(sprite_obj.pos.r, sprite_obj.pos.c); /* Curses change. */
            addch(sprite_obj.symbol);                 /* Curses change. */
            update_sprite(&sprite_obj, direction);
        }
        if ( COLS >= menu_length + 16 )               /* Curses change. */
            --snip--
        if ( ERR != (ch = getch()) ) {                /* Curses change. */
            switch( ch ) {
                --snip--
    endwin();
    return 0;
}
```

The handler for the window resizing signal is much simpler. The man page for ncurses doesn't give much guidance on how to handle these events. The problem is that the library can be configured in one of two ways, either having its own handler or not. The documentation refers us to a couple of functions for handling resizing events, resizeterm() and resize_term(). These are extensions to the standard. Using them correctly is a bit tricky and requires more advanced knowledge of *ncurses*.

The easier approach to handling SIGWINCH signals is one that only works in *xterm* windows; since most Linux window managers and many other Unix window managers use *xterm* terminal emulators, this is fairly portable. I'll use this method here. The authors of *ncurses* suggest that the easiest way to handle this signal is to call endwin(), followed by refresh(), followed by redrawing as if starting up the program for the first time (see *https://invisible -island.net/ncurses/ncurses-intro.html*). The refresh is needed to capture the new screen size. The function based on this idea follows:

```
void on_resize(int signo)
{
    int lines, cols;
    endwin();                        /* End this window and restart.        */
    refresh();                       /* Need to refresh to clean up.        */
    initscr();                       /* Reinitialize curses.                */
    clear();                         /* Clear the screen.                   */
    init_sprite(&sprite_obj);        /* Reset the sprite to the starting state. */
    direction = RIGHT;               /* Set it to move to the right.        */
    count = 0;                       /* Reset the count to zero.            */
    getmaxyx(stdscr, lines, cols);   /* Safer than using LINES, COLS        */
    if ( cols >= menu_length + 16 )  /* If no room for menu, skip it.       */
        show_menubar(0);
    else {  /* Draw the menu in the new bottom row and show the move count. */
        move(lines - 1, 0);
        show_moves(0);
    }
    refresh();
}
```

The rest of the changes are presented next. Cleaning up is handled entirely by the library. There's no need for the program to restore terminal state:

```
void cleanup(int signum)
{
    endwin();
    raise(SIGTERM);
}
```

Because Curses starts its coordinate system at (0,0) instead of (1,1), there are changes in a few other functions:

```c
int on_boundary(sprite sp, int rows, int cols, int cur_direction)
{
    if ( 0 == sp.pos.c && cur_direction == LEFT )
        return LEFT;
    else if ( COLS - 1 == sp.pos.c && cur_direction == RIGHT )
        return RIGHT;
    else if ( 0 == sp.pos.r && cur_direction == UP )
        return UP;
    else if ( LINES - 2 == sp.pos.r && cur_direction == DOWN )
        return DOWN;
    else
        return 0;
}

void init_sprite(sprite *sprite_obj)
{
    move(LINES/2, 0);              /+ Instead of (numrows/2, 1) */
    sprite_obj->pos.r = LINES/2;   /* Instead of numrows/2       */
    sprite_obj->pos.c = 0;         /* Instead of 1               */
    sprite_obj->symbol = '>';
}
```

In other words, the left margin is 0, not 1 and the right is COLS - 1, not numcols, and similarly for the top and bottom.

The rest of the changes are essentially replacing calls to write to the screen by addstr() and replacing references to numrows by LINES and to numcols by COLS:

```c
void show_moves(int count)
{
    char moves[16];
    sprintf(moves, "  moves:  %d", count);
    addstr(moves);                            /* Curses change. */
}

void show_moves_only(int count)
{
    move(LINES - 1, 0);                       /* Curses change. */
    show_moves(count);
}

void show_menubar(int count)
{
    mvaddstr(LINES - 1, 0, MENU);             /* Curses change. */
    show_moves(count);
}
```

The complete program, *sprite_curses.c*, is available in the book's source code distribution. Figure 19-3 is a screenshot of the running program.

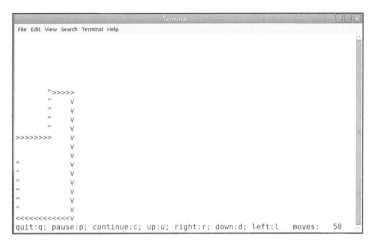

Figure 19-3: A screenshot of the running sprite_curses.c program

The screenshot captured the terminal while the sprite was moving upward along the left border of the window.

The top Program

The top command is a great example of a dynamic, highly interactive program with a complex, feature-rich user interface. It displays the real-time state of the system at regular intervals, including system summary information and a list of processes or threads currently being managed by the kernel, by default sorted by their recent CPU usage. The types of displayed system summary information and the types, order, and size of displayed process information are user configurable. The presented process information looks similar to the output of ps -ef. Whereas ps -ef presents a snapshot at an instance of time, top updates it at intervals of the user's choosing, with a default of 3 seconds. While it's running, the user can enter keystrokes that can change what's displayed, when it's displayed, and how it's displayed. The top man page, which is quite long, describes the command in great detail.

We've reached the point where we're able to implement a simplified version of top. The objective in doing so is not to replicate the command, but to integrate our new knowledge of *ncurses* with what we've learned about the kernel API and the other libraries we explored in earlier chapters in order to create an interactive system utility program. However, before I spell out the goals and limitations of this endeavor, you need to be familiar with basic use of top. If you've never run top, now is the time. Run it without any options before continuing to read by entering **top** in a terminal window at least 80 characters wide. It's better if it's even wider. Your terminal window will look like the one in Figure 19-4.

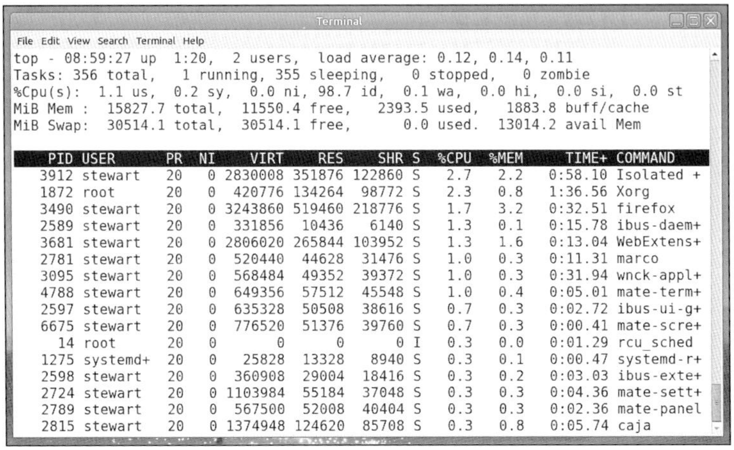

Figure 19-4: A screenshot of the running top program

The figure shows that top divides the screen into two regions: The upper region is its summary section, and the lower one is the detailed process list. The summary and process list are updated together at each refresh. The command displays only the subset of processes that can fit in the lower region, but the user can use the up and down arrow keys on the keyboard to scroll up and down the list. In Figure 19-4, processes are sorted in decreasing order of their percentage of CPU usage. The command always sorts in decreasing order unless the user reverses it by entering R. We can change the sort field with a different command sequence. If we enter f, top opens a new window containing all possible fields, and a visible cursor. We can move the cursor over a field, enter s (for select), then q (for quit), and it removes the window and sorts with the field as its sort key. There's much more to learn about top, of course; this is the tip of the iceberg.

Requirements of a Simplified top Command

The specific goals in developing this program, which I'll name *spl_top.c*, are:

- To use the *ncurses* library to implement a dynamic, multiwindow, interactive program

- To get more experience working with the */proc* pseudofilesystem

- To apply some of the advanced I/O tools we covered in the preceding chapter

These objectives guide the decision about what features and functionality our version of this command should provide. For example, whereas the actual top command has dozens of different interactive inputs, ours will offer just enough for us to learn how to implement them. Therefore, the functionality of our program is defined as follows:

1. The program will display the same summary information as the real top command, in the same order.

2. The set of fields that the program will display is the same as the default set of fields that top displays. They should be presented in the same order as well. A future enhancement will allow the user to select fields to be omitted from the display; the program should include the code and hooks to make this possible.

3. The program will update the information on the screen every three seconds. The interval should be user-adjustable by way of a command line option.

4. The screen will look the same as top's screen.

5. While the program is running, the user can enter any of the following inputs:

   c   Sort by the %CPU field.
   m   Sort by the %MEM field.
   p   Sort by the PID field.
   t   Sort by the TIME field.
   u   Sort by the USER field.
   r   Toggle the sort order.
   U   Filter the output to display only lines for a given user. This should work the same way as top's u command.
   q   Terminate the program.
   Down arrow key   Scroll downward by one line. If the bottommost line is already visible, it has no effect.
   Up arrow key   Scroll upward by one line. If the topmost line is already visible, it has no effect.

6. The program will handle all terminating signals by cleaning up the screen and exiting. If the window is resized, it will terminate after cleaning up; a future enhancement will handle window resizing by redrawing the display in the updated window.

Design Considerations

These requirements raise several questions about the overall program design. The most significant of them follow.

- How will the program handle user input mode and the cursor? In particular:
  - Should it be in cbreak mode or some other noncanonical mode?
  - Should echoing of characters be enabled or disabled?
  - Should the cursor be visible or hidden?

- How should the screen be organized? What windows do we need?

- Should the program use nonblocking I/O inside the main program's loop, implying polled input, or should it rely on blocking reads?

- Should we set up an interval timer to regulate the screen updates and handle them inside a signal handler or use a different method?

- The top command sorts the displayed lines. This is a fundamental aspect of its behavior. Our *spl_ps.c* program didn't have to sort the lines that it output; it was sufficient for it to read the contents of each */proc/[pid]* directory, construct an output line from them, and display that line on the screen. In fact, a single function, `printallprocs()`, did the job of acquiring the data and printing the lines.

  Having to sort a set of lines requires storing all of them before sorting and displaying any of them, which implies that the program needs to separate the tasks of acquiring all of the data, sorting it, and printing it. This also implies that the program needs logic to do the following:
    - Read the metadata of all processes and store it, per process, in an array.
    - Sort the array by whatever sorting criterion is in effect.
    - Print the sorted array.

- Given that the program needs to sort by different fields of the process attributes, is there a way to have a single sort function, or will it need a separate sort function for each possible field?

- What documentation do we need to read to find out which files contain the data for the summary area?

- How much of the code from the *spl_ps.c* program can we reuse for *spl_top.c*?

We'll consider each of these types of questions in turn, starting with the initial configuration of *ncurses* for user input and cursor management.

Input Mode and the Cursor

We'll put the program into cbreak mode so that input is available immediately and keyboard signals will be passed through to the program. We'll also enable the keypad so that users can enter the up and down arrow keys. The *ncurses* keypad() function does this:

```
int keypad(WINDOW *win, bool bf);
```

If the second parameter is TRUE, the keypad is enabled; otherwise, it's disabled. We'll turn off echoing of input except when it comes time for the user to enter a username when prompted by the U filtering command. The noecho() function is global; it turns off echoing of input no matter where the cursor is. To turn it on, we call echo().

We don't want the cursor to be visible, since it will be distracting. When top runs there is no cursor. The function to control cursor visibility is harder to find in a man page search, but it is listed on the curses man page:

```
int curs_set(int visibility);
```

Passing 0 to it hides the cursor; passing 1 makes it visible. It returns the previous state of the cursor. We'll put the initial configuration into the following function:

setup_curses()
```
void setup_curses()
{
    initscr();   /* Initialize curses.    */
    cbreak();    /* Put into cbreak mode. */
    noecho();    /* Turn off echo.        */
    curs_set(0); /* Hide cursor.          */
}
```

Screen Management

We'll begin by planning how we'll manage the screen and all parts of the user interface.

Program Windows

When top runs, it creates two screen regions: a summary area and an area below it, which I'll call the content area. In between is a line with the headings of the columns of the content area. The command also reserves the sixth line of the summary area for prompts and messages. If these are all created in a single Curses window, then as more lines are added to the content area than can fit on the screen, the summary area would scroll off the top of the screen. To prevent this, we can create three separate windows that are tiled horizontally, which we'll call the summary window, the heading window, and the content window. These three windows will fill the screen completely. Figure 19-5 depicts this arrangement.

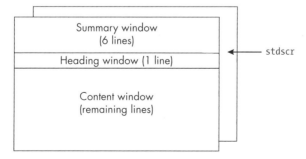

Figure 19-5: Tiled windows of spl_top.c program

If the program outputs more lines than can fit into the content window, they scroll in that window alone. In other words, scrolling downward means that the first line disappears and a new line appears at the bottom.

Figure 19-5 shows the stdscr below the tiled windows. Since every program is created with the default stdscr window, these three windows sit on top of it, essentially hiding it. However, it still exists, and we have to make sure that every *ncurses* function that the program calls operates on one of the three tiled windows, unless it's a function that configures the library globally.

The summary window has exactly six lines. We'll reserve the sixth line for prompt strings as top does. Our only use of it will be to implement filtering the lines by username. We'll mimic how top does it. If you run top and enter u, it puts the string Enter a username (blank for all): in the sixth line of the summary area and waits for the user to enter a username followed by ENTER. This is a nice little challenge that we'll revisit soon.

The heading window is in reverse video. The Curses API calls this standout mode, a term inherited from earlier hardware terminals. If you search for this term in the man pages, you find two functions: standout() and wstandout(). We can use wstandout() to put the heading window into standout mode without putting the other windows into it. That man page describes other attributes we could set if we wanted to get fancy in our programs.

The program will declare a macro constant:

```
#define SUMMARY_HEIGHT   6
```

The function that creates the three tiled windows uses the *ncurses* newwin() function:

create_windows()
```
void create_windows(WINDOW **sum_win, WINDOW **head_win, WINDOW **cnt_win)
{
    /* Create summary window in the top 6 rows of the screen. */
    if ( NULL == (*sum_win = newwin(SUMMARY_HEIGHT, COLS, 0, 0)) )
        cleanup_exit(-1, "Could not create summary window.");

    /* Create the one-line heading window below it. */
    if ( NULL == (*head_win = newwin(1, COLS, SUMMARY_HEIGHT, 0)) )
        cleanup_exit(-1, "Could not create heading window.");

    /* Create the content window in the remaining rows of the screen. */
    if ( NULL == (*cnt_win = newwin(LINES - SUMMARY_HEIGHT - 1, COLS,
                              SUMMARY_HEIGHT + 1, 0)) ) {
        cleanup_exit(-1, "Could not create first window.");
    }
}
```

Since the function allocates storage for the windows and returns a pointer to it, the parameters must be passed the addresses of WINDOW* variables, as shown in the following snippet of the main program:

```
WINDOW *content_win;        /* The content area                  */
WINDOW *heading_win;        /* The one-line heading              */
WINDOW *summary_win;        /* The summary at the top of the screen */
--snip--
setup_curses();             /* Set up curses.                    */
create_windows(&summary_win, &heading_win, &content_win);
--snip--
```

If creating any window fails, the function calls `cleanup_exit()` (in the book's code repository). Every unplanned exit from this program must call `endwin()` before exiting. Calling `endwin()` restores the terminal state, clears the screen, and releases resources used by *ncurses* in our program. This function will also be called within the signal handler that catches any terminating signals.

Window Configuration

Once the program creates the three windows, it has a bit of configuration to do. We want to disable automatic scrolling by *ncurses*. This doesn't mean we can't scroll using the mouse wheel. It means that when the bottom of a window is reached, our program decides whether to move the cursor off of the bottom line or have it stay there. We want the program to control what's visible in the content and summary windows, not *ncurses*. The `scrollok()` function enables or disables this option:

```
int scrollok(WINDOW *win, bool bf);
```

This enables or disables the scrolling feature in `win` according to whether the second parameter is `TRUE` or `FALSE`.

We also want to display the column headings in standout mode. The program can use `wstandout()` to do this. Lastly, we want to enable the keypad in the content window so that arrow and function keys can be used as inputs for controlling what's visible on the screen. The next function consolidates this logic:

configure
_windows()
```
void configure_windows(WINDOW *sum_win, WINDOW *head_win, WINDOW *cnt_win)
{
    scrollok(sum_win, FALSE);  /* Disable curses scrolling option.     */
    wstandout(head_win);       /* Put heading window into standout mode. */
    scrollok(cnt_win, FALSE);  /* Disable curses scrolling option.     */
    keypad(cnt_win, TRUE);     /* Enable arrow and function keys.      */
}
```

This is called immediately after creating the windows.

User Input and the Main Loop

Let's turn to how the program will control when and how it checks for user input. Should it block and wait, or poll? We've discussed the disadvantages of polling in this chapter and in Chapter 17, and this program gives us an opportunity to use the pselect() function introduced in Chapter 17. The pselect() function is the extension of select() that can be used to block signals while it's waiting for a file descriptor to become ready for I/O. It also provides a safe method to process caught signals in the program's main loop. In addition, it provides a simple way of implementing the refreshing of the screen at regular fixed intervals without user interval timers and signals.

Our program has just a single file descriptor to monitor, namely standard input. We don't want it to be interrupted by a signal in the middle of the code that updates the screen or internal data structures. Instead, we want the signals to be blocked in the main loop and delivered only when it's safe. That's where pselect() is useful.

The program will block all signals whose default action is to terminate it. The call to pselect() will have an empty signal mask so that when it runs, any blocked signals will be delivered to it. The call returns when it's interrupted by a signal, a file descriptor becomes available, or a timer interval expires, if it's been passed to it. Let's look at some pseudocode that shows how we'll use it:

```
Let fds be an FDSET containing STDIN_FILENO.
Let delay be a timespec storing a 3 second interval.
Block all signals that would terminate the program.

while ( 1 ) {
  ❶ Do all processing that we don't want interrupted.
  ❷ rc = pselect(1, &fds, NULL, NULL, delay, &empty_mask);
     If rc < 0 and errno is EINTR, pselect was interrupted by a signal.
        Handle it here.
     If rc < 0 but errno != EINTR, it's a bad error. Exit.
     If rc == 0, the timer interval expired, so just go back to top of loop.
     If rc > 0, input is available in STDIN_FILENO, so call getch() to get it.
}
```

The nice part of this solution is that, if there's no user input and no signals delivered to the program, the main processing code ❶ is executed every delay (3) seconds because pselect() returns ❷ when the timer expires.

The following function, iowait(), encapsulates this logic:

---

iowait()
```
int iowait (struct timespec *ts) {
        fd_set   fds;                 /* A descriptor set for pselect    */
        int      rc;                  /* Return code from pselect()      */
        sigset_t empty_mask;          /* Signal mask to pass to pselect() */
        char     mssge[32];           /* A message to be output on exit  */

        FD_ZERO(&fds);                /* Empty file descriptor set.      */
        FD_SET(STDIN_FILENO, &fds);   /* fs contains standard input only. */
        sigemptyset(&empty_mask);     /* Make empty signal mask.         */

        /* Block until either time expires, input available, or signal
           delivered. */
```

```
        rc = pselect(1, &fds, NULL, NULL, ts, &empty_mask);
        if ( rc < 0 )              /* Error from pselect()                */
            if ( errno != EINTR ) /* Not an interrupt. Clean up and exit. */
                cleanup_exit(errno, "pselect");
            else                   /* An interrupt to pselect()           */
          ❶ if ( caught_signal ) { /* Handler ran and set the flag.    */
                    sprintf(mssge, "Caught signal %d", sigcaught);
                    cleanup_exit(-1, mssge); /* Clean up and exit.      */
                }
                else
                    rc = 0;           /* Send 0 instead of -1 to caller. */
        return rc;
}
```

This function tests a global sig_atomic_t variable, caught_signal ❶, that's set
within a signal handler. If it's set, it prints a message with the number of the
signal that was delivered (sigcaught), which is also a global sig_atomic_t set by
the handler.

Let's look at how the main program can use iowait(). Listing 19-5 shows
part of it.

```
int main(int argc, char *argv[])
{
    // OMITTED: All declarations
    setup_sighandlers();
    create_sigmask(&sigmask);
    sigprocmask(SIG_BLOCK, &sigmask, NULL);
    // OMITTED: Other initializations and setting up
    /* MAIN PROCESSING LOOP */
    while ( !done ) {
        --snip--
      ❶ if ( iowait(&delay) > 0 ) /* Wait for input, timer, or signal. */
            /* Return value > 0, so a character is waiting to be read. */
            switch ( wgetch(content_win) ) {
            case 'q':
                done = TRUE;
                break;
            // OMITTED: Other input cases
            }
        }
        --snip--
    }
    endwin();
    return 0;
}
```

Listing 19-5: The role of iowait() in the spl_top.c *main function*

After all processing in the main loop is finished, `iowait()` is called ❶ to wait for input, a timer expiration, or a signal. A positive return value means a character was input. If there's input, it handles it and starts the main loop again.

The preceding functions and code snippets are the major components of the user interface of the program. Next we'll work on the harder part, namely all of the code that acquires the process metadata, sorts it as needed, filters it if the user requests it, prints it in the proper format, and so on. This is the bulk of the code.

Data Structures

Good data structures make good programs. Let's consider the program requirements with the goal of defining data structures that will simplify and clarify the program's design.

- We need a data structure that stores all of the data that is printed on a single line for each process, after suitable transformations. The `procstat` structure that we defined to implement the `spl_ps` command is a starting point. Because it doesn't contain all of the default fields that `top` displays, we'll add a few more.

- The program needs the ability to sort the lines of process data using different fields as sort keys. We don't want to write a separate sort function for every field.

- Although this version of the program may not give the user the option to remove columns, all of the code needed to do so should be in place so that we just need to modify the user interface to choose the columns to remove.

- The fields that our version of `top` will display are the ones whose column labels are

---

PID, USER, PR, NI, VIRT, RES, SHR, S, %CPU, %MEM, TIME+, COMMAND

---

in that order. Associated with each field are several pieces of information, including the format string of the column heading, the format string for the process data in that column, and the actual column heading as a string. Each field that we want to use as a sort key should have a pointer to a suitable sorting function. Every field should have a bitmask that we can use to include or exclude that column of data from the display.

Look back at the `procstat` data structure defined for the *spl_ps.c* implementation in Chapter 10 on page 527. The `top` command displays some information not in that structure and ignores some fields that are. Our program can extend that data structure to include the following new fields:

```
typedef struct {
    // OMITTED: Existing fields
    long    rss;    /* The nonswapped physical memory currently in use      */
    long    shared; /* Subset of rss that may be shared by other processes  */
    double cpu_pct;/* Percent of time since last refresh that proc used CPU */
    double mem_pct;/* Percent of total physical memory used by this process */
} procstat;
```

We'll have to do some research to find the files in */proc/[pid]* that contain this information.

Let's consider the sorting problem because that's going to play a big part in the design of our next data structure. Ideally, we want to use an existing sort function instead of writing our own. The GNU C Library (*glibc*) provides a couple of sorting functions. A man page search with apropos -s3 sort exposes qsort() and qsort_r(), which is a reentrant version of qsort(). Their prototypes are:

```
void qsort(void *base, size_t nmemb, size_t size,
           int (*compar)(const void *, const void *));
void qsort_r(void *base, size_t nmemb, size_t size,
             int (*compar)(const void *, const void *, void *), void *arg);
```

Both versions of the function have a function pointer argument. Recall that the scandir() function (see Chapter 7) has function pointer arguments as well. The qsort() function is given a pointer to an array (*base), the number of elements in the array (nmemb), the size of each array element (size), and a comparison function (*compar). A comparison function is any function that returns an integer less than, equal to, or greater than 0 if the first argument is considered to be, respectively, less than, equal to, or greater than the second. Here's an example of one:

```
int cmp_int(const void *a, const void *b)
{
    return (*((int*) a) - *((int*) b));
}
```

This compares two integers. The cast operations may look complicated, but they're necessary because a void* cannot be dereferenced. First we cast the void* argument to (int*), which can be dereferenced. Then we dereference it. The function returns a negative if a < b, positive if a > b, and 0 if equal.

If our program needs to sort by username, by PID, by percent of CPU usage, by total memory size, and so on, we need comparison functions that access the corresponding procstat fields. Since we also want to reverse the sorting direction easily, we're going to use the qsort_r() function rather than qsort(), since it lets us pass an extra variable to the comparison function. This variable can be a flag that indicates whether to sort in increasing or decreasing order.

The preceding observations lead to the following data structure for representing the information associated with a single field:

```
/* A comparison function to pass to qsort_r() */
typedef int (*compar_t)(const void *, const void *, void*);
typedef int fieldmask;
typedef struct {
    char    *name;        /* A name for future use                    */
    fieldmask mask;       /* A bitmask for this field                 */
    char    *fmt;         /* The printf format spec for this field    */
    char    *colheading;  /* The column heading for the field         */
    char    *headingfmt;  /* The printf format spec for the column heading */
    int     width;        /* The field width for calculating line size */
  ❶ compar_t sortfunc;    /* The comparison function for this field   */
} field;
```

The structure itself contains a pointer to a function ❶ that qsort_r() can call to sort by that field. We'll create an array of these structures that will supply data to several different types of functions:

```
field fieldtab[] = {
    /* NAME         MASK        FMT       COL NAME   HDNG FMT  WIDTH  SORTFUNC */
    {"pid",       F_PID,      "%7d",    "PID",     "%7s",     7,   pid_cmp},
    {"user",      F_USER,     "%-9s",   "USER",    "%-10s",  11,   user_cmp},
    {"priority",  F_PR,       "%3s",    "PR",      "%-4s",    4,   NULL},
    {"nice",      F_NI,       "%4ld",   "NI",      "%-4s",    4,   NULL},
    {"vsize",     F_VIRT,     "%8s",    "VIRT",    "%6s",     8,   vsize_cmp},
    {"rss",       F_RES,      "%7ld",   "RES",     "%7s",     8,   NULL},
    {"shared",    F_SHR,      "%7ld",   "SHR",     "%7s",     8,   NULL},
    {"state",     F_S,        "%2c",    "S",       "%2s",     2,   NULL},
    {"cpu_pct",   F_CPU,      "%6.1f",  "%CPU",    "%6s",     6,   cpu_pct_cmp},
    {"mem_pct",   F_MEM,      "%6.1f",  "%MEM",    "%6s",     6,   mem_pct_cmp},
    {"cputime",   F_TIME,     "%10s",   "TIME+",   "%10s",   10,   time_cmp},
    {"cmd",       F_COMMAND,  "%s",     "COMMAND", "%s",      8,   NULL}
};
```

The format strings and field widths are based on the formats used by top.

Now we'll create an enumerated type that can act as an index into this array:

```
enum field_t {PID, USER, PR, NI, VIRT, RES, SHR, S, CPU, MEM, TIME, COMMAND};
```

For example, fieldtab[CPU].fmt is the format to be passed to printf() to format the data in the cpu_pct field of the procstat structure.

We'll also create a set of bitmasks that the program can use for testing whether an integer mask has a bit enabled for a particular field:

```
#define F_PID       (1<<PID)
#define F_USER      (1<<USER)
#define F_PR        (1<<PR)
```

```
#define F_NI        (1<<NI)
#define F_VIRT      (1<<VIRT)
#define F_RES       (1<<RES)
#define F_SHR       (1<<SHR)
#define F_S         (1<<S)
#define F_CPU       (1<<CPU)
#define F_MEM       (1<<MEM)
#define F_TIME      (1<<TIME)
#define F_COMMAND   (1<<COMMAND)
#define F_ALL       07777
```

For example, F_VIRT is the number 1 << 4, which is decimal 16 or binary 10000. With these definitions, several tasks are simplified.

To demonstrate, the following function succinctly formats the string of column labels that is displayed in the heading window:

printtopheadings()
```
void printtopheadings(field *ftab, fieldmask fmask, char *buf)
{
    memset(buf, 0, MAX_LINE);
    for ( int i = PID; i <= COMMAND; i++ ) {
        if ( fmask & ftab[i].mask )
            sprintf(buf+strlen(buf), ftab[i].headingfmt, ftab[i].colheading);
    }
}
```

The function to print a single line of process data is not quite so simple because C doesn't have a means of writing code of the form:

```
for each member M of a structure S,
    Process S.M in some way.
```

Therefore, the function needs a switch statement. Here's its code, with repetitive parts omitted:

print_one_proc()
```
void print_one_proc(field *ftab, procstat ps, fieldmask fmask, char *buf)
{
    char  cputimestr[16];
    char *cmd;

    get_cpu_time_str(ps, cputimestr); /* Function from spl_ps.c   */
    cmd = strip_cmmd_parens(ps.comm); /* Function from spl_ps.c   */
    for ( int i = PID; i <= COMMAND; i++ ) { /* For each field... */
        if ( fmask & ftab[i].mask )    /* Is field to be printed? */
            switch ( i ) {             /* Which field?            */
            case PID:
                sprintf(buf+strlen(buf), ftab[i].fmt, ps.pid);
                break;
            case USER:
                sprintf(buf+strlen(buf), ftab[i].fmt, uid2name(ps.uid));
```

```
                break;
            // OMITTED: Other cases
            case COMMAND:
                sprintf(buf+strlen(buf), ftab[i].fmt, cmd);
                break;
        }
    }
}
```

The function is passed the fieldtab array, the process data for the given process (ps), the mask containing bits indicating which fields should be printed, and a preallocated string (buf). The loop builds a formatted string in (buf), piece by piece.

Sorting Functions

The data structures we just created make sorting by any field trivial. We can create a comparison function for each field that can serve as a sort key. Here are a few of them:

```
/* Comparison function for pid field */
int pid_cmp(const void *a, const void *b, void *dir)
{
    if ( *((BOOL*) dir) )
        return (((procstat*) a)->pid - ((procstat*) b)->pid);
    else
        return (((procstat*) b)->pid - ((procstat*) a)->pid);
}
/* Comparison function for cpu_pct field */
int cpu_pct_cmp(const void *a, const void *b, void *dir)
{
    if ( *((BOOL*) dir) )
        return (((procstat*) a)->cpu_pct > ((procstat*) b)->cpu_pct);
    else
        return (((procstat*) b)->cpu_pct > ((procstat*) a)->cpu_pct);
}
/* Comparison function for user field (which sorts by username, not uid) */
int user_cmp(const void *a, const void *b, void *dir)
{
    char name_a[11], name_b[11];
    strcpy(name_a, uid2name(((procstat*) a)->uid));
    strcpy(name_b, uid2name(((procstat*) b)->uid));
    if ( *((BOOL*) dir) )
        return strcmp(name_a, name_b);
    else
        return strcmp(name_b, name_a);
}
```

A single function named `sortprocs()` can be used to sort by any field and in either increasing or decreasing order. The first parameter is the array of procstat structures that the program would have filled by the time this is called:

sortprocs()
```
void sortprocs(procstat* procarray, int nprocs, compar_t cmpfunc,
               BOOL increasing)
{
    qsort_r(procarray,nprocs, sizeof(procstat), cmpfunc,(void*) &increasing);
}
```

The function is given a comparison function `cmpfunc` that it passes to `qsort_r()`. The main program can now sort by calling

```
sortprocs(procarray, numprocs, fieldtab[sortfield].sortfunc, sortdir);
```

where *sortfield* is a value of the enumeration previously described and *sortdir* is either TRUE or FALSE. It's now easy to sort by the sort key specified by the user.

The main program from Figure 19-5 can be filled in a little more with the call to `sortprocs()` and the code that changes the sort key and direction:

```
while ( !done ) {
    --snip--
    loadprocs(&procarray, &numprocs);  /* Not shown yet */
    sortprocs(procarray, numprocs, fieldtab[sortfield].sortfunc, sortdir);
    --snip--
if ( iowait(&delay) > 0 )
    switch ( wgetch(content_win) ) {
    case 'q': done = TRUE; break;
    case 'm': sortfield = MEM; sortdir = FALSE; startline = 0; break;
    case 'c': sortfield = CPU; sortdir = FALSE; startline = 0; break;
    case 'r': sortdir  = ~sortdir;              startline = 0; break;
    --snip--
}
```

When the user enters a character, the `switch` statement is entered, and if the character is one of the codes to pick a sort field, the `fieldtab` array index is stored in `sortfield` and the sorting direction is set to FALSE (decreasing). I'll discuss the role of `startline` soon.

Acquiring and Storing the Data

There are two types of data that the program displays: summary data and the per-process data stored in a procstat structure. We'll start by describing the steps to acquire the data displayed in the summary window and then focus on the per-process data.

Acquiring Summary Data

Summary information consists of five lines of data. We'll create four separate functions, `show_summary_line1()`, `show_summary_line2()`, `show_summary_line3()`, and `show_summary_line4_5()` that acquire and display specific lines. Because the last two lines display memory-related usage, we can use a single function to collect and print that data. A single function, `show_summary()`, will call each of these in turn. The OVERVIEW section of the top man page, specifically 2. SUMMARY Display, has detailed information about the source of the information presented in the summary window.

Summary Line 1

The first line displays the current time, the system uptime, the number of logged-in users, and the system load averages:

```
top - 11:58:50 up  3:54,  2 users,  load average: 0.09, 0.14, 0.15
```

The system uptime is the first number in the file */proc/uptime*, expressed as a fractional number of seconds. The function

---

```
void get_uptime(char *uptime);
```

---

opens that file, reads that number, and formats it as a printable string, It decides on the format based on whether the uptime is less than an hour, less than a day, and so on. To save space, that function isn't shown here.

Getting the number of users is not as simple. We can't use the user IDs stored in the `procstat` structures to count logged-in users, because it would include user IDs that aren't logged-in users, such as `root` and `systemd`. Instead we need to open the *utmpx* file to get the set of currently logged-in users. The catch is that it can have multiple entries for each user. Therefore, counting unique users requires saving user IDs already counted and checking successive entries against the saved ones. The function

---

```
int get_numusers();
```

---

uses a hash table for this purpose. The file *hash.h*, first used in Chapter 7, has a hash table interface that we can reuse in this function. The function opens the *utmpx* file, searches for USER_PROCESS records, and when it finds one, checks if the userid for that record is in the hash table. If it is, it continues to the next record. If it isn't, it inserts it and increments a counter. The function is not shown here.

The load averages come from the file */proc/loadavg*. The function to retrieve them is small enough to display:

`get_loadavges()`
```
void get_loadavges(char *loadstr)
{
    FILE  *fp;
    float avg1, avg5, avg15;
    if ( NULL == (fp = fopen("/proc/loadavg", "r")) )
        sprintf(loadstr, " load averages unknown ");
    else if ( fscanf(fp, "%f %f %f", &avg1, &avg5, &avg15) < 3 )
```

```
        sprintf(loadstr, " load averages unknown ");
    else
        sprintf(loadstr, " load average: %2.2f, %2.2f, %2.2f",
                avg1, avg5, avg15);
    fclose(fp);
}
```

The `show_summary_line1()` function gets the current local time and calls the preceding functions to collect this data and formats a string with the time, the uptime, and so on. Its prototype is:

```
void show_summary_line1(WINDOW *win);
```

After creating this string, it prints it in the window passed to it at position (0,0). That function isn't shown here to save space.

Summary Line 2

The second line has data about the number of tasks and their states:

```
Tasks: 371 total,   1 running, 370 sleeping,   0 stopped,   0 zombie
```

We can get the number of tasks by counting how many process directories we opened in the */proc* directory. When we processed those files, we collected state information and stored it in the state field of the procstat structure. We need a function that counts which processes are in which states. The top man page has details about how it counts sleeping and stopped processes. The function that displays the second line can do this work inline. It's shown in its entirety here:

show_summary
_line2()
```
void show_summary_line2(WINDOW *win, procstat *proctab, int numprocs)
{
    int count[4] = {0,0,0,0};
    enum states{RUNNING, SLEEPING, STOPPED, ZOMBIE};
    mvwaddstr(win, 1, 0, "Tasks: ");
    wprintw(win, "%d total,", numprocs);
    for ( int i = 0; i < numprocs; i++ ) {
        switch ( proctab[i].state ) {
        case 'R': count[RUNNING]++;  break;
        case 'S':
        case 'I':
        case 'D': count[SLEEPING]++; break;
        case 'T': count[STOPPED]++;  break;
        case 'Z': count[ZOMBIE]++;   break;
        }
    }
    wprintw(win, " %d running, %d sleeping, %d stopped, %d zombie ",
            count[RUNNING], count[SLEEPING], count[STOPPED], count[ZOMBIE]);
    wrefresh(win);
}
```

The number of sleeping processes might differ slightly from what top reports because it counts differently.

Summary Line 3

The third line has information about the CPUs and their statuses:

```
%Cpu(s): 0.1 us,  0.1 sy,  0.0 ni, 99.8 id,  0.0 wa,  0.0 hi,  0.0 si,  0.0 st
```

Both the top and proc man pages are enough to piece together how to compute these values. The top man page explains that a CPU can be in one of eight possible states:

- **us** Time running un-niced user processes
- **sy** Time running kernel processes
- **ni** Time running niced user processes
- **id** Time spent in the kernel idle handler
- **wa** Time waiting for I/O completion
- **hi** Time spent servicing hardware interrupts
- **si** Time spent servicing software interrupts
- **st** Time stolen from this VM by the hypervisor

The two-letter codes in top's output summarize the percentage of time that the CPU spent in each state since its last update. If there are multiple CPUs, by default, top displays the average time each CPU spent in each state. With the -1 option, it displays a line for each CPU, but in our version, we'll emulate the default behavior.

The */proc/stat* file has the data we need. A machine with multiple CPUs has a line for each CPU, but the first line of the file has the sums of the ones after it; our program needs to extract the data from the first line only. The function

```
int get_cpustates(int *states);
```

opens this file and collects the eight summary values from its first line, storing them in the states array passed to it. The tricky part is that the reported percentages are not cumulative. Instead, they're the percentages of time since the previous refresh, averaged over all CPUs, that they collectively spent in each of these possible states. This means that the program has to save the times from one refresh to another, calculate the differences between the current data and the previous data, compute percentages, and output the resulting line. The function that does all of this is partially displayed here:

show_summary_line3()

```
void show_summary_line3(WINDOW *win)
{
    int cpustate[8];  /* Sum of time each CPU spent in each of 8 states */
    static int prev_cpustate[8] = {0,0,0,0,0,0,0,0}; /* Must be static. */
    // OMITTED: Declarations of other variables
```

```
    mvwaddstr(win, 2, 0, "%Cpu(s): ");
    if ( 8 != get_cpustates(cpustate) )
        waddstr(win, "Could not get cpu state information");
    else {
        for ( i = 0; i < 8; i++ ) {
            df[i] = (cpustate[i] - prev_cpustate[i])/(1.0 * hz);
            sum += df[i];
        }
        for ( i = 0; i < 8; i++ ) {
            df[i] = 100 * df[i]/sum;        /* Compute percents.   */
            prev_cpustate[i] = cpustate[i]; /* Save current state. */
        }
        wprintw(win, " %2.1f us, %2.1f sy, %2.1f ni, %2.1f id,"
                     " %2.1f wa, %2.1f hi, %2.1f si, %2.1f st,",
                df[0], df[2], df[1], df[3], df[4], df[5], df[6], df[7]);
    }
    wrefresh(win);
}
```

The key is saving the values in the static array prev_cpustate[8] in each call. Notice that, in the wprintw() call, fields 1 and 2 are printed in reverse order. This is how top prints them.

Summary Lines 4 and 5

The last two lines of summary data report on two different types of memory: physical memory and swap space. All of that data comes from the file */proc/meminfo*. That file has the same form as the */proc/[pid]/status* files do—a sequence of lines with labels and values, such as:

```
MemTotal:       16207588 kB
MemFree:        10330164 kB
MemAvailable:   12705968 kB
Buffers:          287072 kB
Cached:          2368108 kB
--snip--
```

The function that displays the last two lines of summary data has to open this file; read one line at a time, searching for the matching labels; and extract values from the lines that match.

It calls a separate function to do this work:

```
int get_mem_summary(char *line1, char *line2);
```

To save space, I'm including only a fragment of it here:

```
--snip--
while ( count < 7 ) {
    if ( -1 == (nbytes = getline(&buf, &len, fp)) )
        if ( 0 != errno )
```

```
                cleanup_exit(errno, "getline()");
            else
                break;
        else if ( 1 == sscanf(buf, "MemTotal: %lu", &temp) ) {
            memtotal = ((double) temp)/1024;
            count++;
        }
        else if ( 1 == sscanf(buf,"MemFree: %lu", &temp) ) {
            memfree = ((double) temp)/1024;
            count++;
        }
        --snip--
        else if ( 1 == sscanf(buf,"SwapFree: %lu", &temp) ) {
            swapfree = ((double) temp)/1024;
            count++;
        }
        if ( 0 == nbytes )
            break;
}
memused = memtotal - memavail;
swapused = swaptotal - swapfree;
--snip--
```

The missing code at the end formats the lines to match top's formatting.

Acquiring Per-Process Data

The *spl_ps.c* program collected all of its per-process data in its parse_buf() function except for the user ID, which it obtained by calling stat() on the */proc/[pid]* directory and getting the user ID stored in the returned buffer. Our program has to collect a few more per-process attributes.

Acquiring Per-Process Memory Data

The top man page describes every field that it displays. It's vague about some of them, but we can compare its descriptions with the descriptions of the data in the proc man page. This detective work pays off. The vsize, rss, and shared fields come from data in the */proc/[pid]/status* file. The lines we need to parse are:

```
VmSize:       24380 kB    /* vsize: total virtual memory size    */
VmRSS:         1312 kB    /* rss: virtual memory resident set size */
RssFile:       1200 kB    /* Resident file mapping size          */
RssShmem:         0 kB    /* Shared = RssFile + RssShmem         */
```

Extracting these values uses the same logic as get_mem_summary(). We'll implement a function get_procmem_usage() to extract and store this data in the procstat structure. Its prototype is:

```
int get_procmem_usage(pid_t p, unsigned long *vmem, long *res, long *shr);
```

The function opens the *status* file in the process's */proc/[pid]/* directory and uses getline() to read successive lines, searching for the matching labels. Because the function is similar to get_mem_summary(), its code isn't shown here.

The loadprocs() Function

The loadprocs() function consolidates all of the logic for capturing the set of process data for every process represented by a directory entry in the */proc* pseudofilesystem. I'll describe its logic here and show code snippets as needed.

We've got a few problems to solve:

- The function needs to store all process data in an array, but we don't know how many processes exist unless we read the entire */proc* directory and count the numbered files in it first. This would require two passes over this directory, which is inefficient.

- It's possible that between the time we get the set of all directories and the time we start to read their *stat* files, a process terminated and its files no longer exist. We need to check for this.

- In order to compute the percentage of CPU time used by a process since the last refresh, the function needs to store the previous call's CPU time value for each process and compute the difference between the current and previous times. This implies that we need an array to store the previous times for each process. It's possible that some processes terminated since the last refresh and others were created since the last refresh. We need to handle this.

We can solve the first problem by using the scandir() function from Chapter 7. This function scans an entire directory and populates an array with those directory entries for which a filter function returns nonzero. Assume that int isprocdir(struct dirent *dp) is a filter that returns TRUE if the name of the directory in the given directory entry is only digits. Then, if namelist is an array of pointers to dirent structures, our program can call scandir() as follows:

```
struct dirent **namelist;  /* Array of proc directory entries */
--snip--
int numdirs = scandir("/proc", &namelist, isprocdir, NULL);
```

After this, it can allocate an array of procstat structures of length numdirs. I'll describe the solutions to the other problems shortly. A mix of pseudocode and actual code in loadprocs() is next, with some error handling omitted:

```
void loadprocs(procstat **proclist, int *numprocs)
{
    struct dirent **namelist;       /* Array of names of proc directories  */
    savedcpu      *prevcpu_times = NULL; /* Saved CPU times                */
    int            prevnumprocs = 0;     /* Previous number of processes    */
    long          *diff;             /* Array of CPU time differences       */
```

```
int             numdirs;        /* Current number of processes           */
// OMITTED: Other declarations

/* Call scandir() to collect the process directory entries: */
numdirs = scandir("/proc", &namelist, isprocdir, NULL);

/* If *proclist exists already, numprocs is its length. It's the previous
   proctable. We copy the CPU times in it into a second array that we
   allocate, and then free its memory. The code is roughly: */
if ( *proclist != NULL )
    // OMITTED: Check whether prevcpu_times exists, and if so, delete it.
    prevcpu_times = (savedcpu*) calloc(*numprocs, sizeof(savedcpu));
    for ( i = 0; i < *numprocs; i++ ) {
        prevcpu_times[i].pid = (*proclist)[i].pid;
        prevcpu_times[i].cputime = (*proclist)[i].utime +
                                    (*proclist)[i].stime;

    }
    prevnumprocs = *numprocs;
    free(*proclist);
}
/* We've now saved the old CPU times. */
/* Allocate memory for a new proclist and for an array to store
   differences in CPU times: */
*proclist = (procstat*) calloc(numdirs, sizeof(procstat));
diff = (long*) calloc(numdirs, sizeof(long));
// OMITTED: Allocate buffer for getline().
/* Now read the namelist[i] entries iteratively. */
j = 0;
for ( i = 0; i < numdirs; i++ ) {
    /* First get UID. */
    memset(pathname, '\0', PATH_MAX);
    sprintf(pathname, "/proc/%s/", namelist[i]->d_name);
    if ( -1 == stat(pathname, &statbuffer) ) {
        free(namelist[i]);
        continue;
    }
    (*proclist)[j].uid = statbuffer.st_uid;
    sprintf(pathname+strlen(pathname), "stat");
    /* Now set up to call getline() and then parse_buf(). */
    fp = fopen(pathname, "r");        /* Error handling not shown. */
    getline(&buf, &len, fp);          /* Error handling not shown. */
    parse_buf(buf, &((*proclist)[j])); /* Error handling not shown. */

    /* Now get memory usage. */
    get_procmem_usage((*proclist)[j].pid, &((*proclist)[j].vsize),
                & ((*proclist)[j].rss), &((*proclist)[j].shared));
    }
```

```
            memtotal += (*proclist)[j].rss;  /* Compute total memory. */
            memset(buf, 0, MAX_LINE);        /* Clean up.              */
            free(namelist[i]);
            fclose(fp);
            j++;
        }
        *numprocs = j;  /* This is the number of processes in this refresh. */
        /* Time to compute CPU time differences and compute percentages
           of CPU time used by each process. */
        if ( prevnumprocs > 0 ) {                /* Previous times exist. */
            // OMITTED: Doubly-nested loop to compute differences

        else {                          /* First time - handle differently. */
            for ( i = 0; i < *numprocs; i++ )
                diff[i] = ((*proclist)[i].utime + (*proclist)[i].stime);
        }
        /* Percent of CPU time since last refresh for process i is the time
           it spent in CPU since last refresh divided by the length of
           the refresh interval. Times are in ticks, so we have to adjust. */
        for ( i = 0; i < *numprocs; i++ ) {
            (*proclist)[i].cpu_pct = 100.0 * diff[i] / (delaysecs * ticks);
        }
        /* Percent memory use is the rss size divided by total memory. */
        for ( i = 0; i < *numprocs; i++ ) {
            (*proclist)[i].mem_pct = 100.0 * ((double) (*proclist)[i].rss)
                                        / memtotal;
        }
        // OMITTED: Clean up.
    }
```

The complete function is part of *spl_top.c* in the book's source code repository. The function that prints the data to the content window is next. This function is designed so that a user can filter out lines that don't match a given username and so that it can start printing lines starting at indices other than 0.

print_procs()
```
void print_procs(WINDOW *win, procstat *proclist, int numprocs,
                 int win_lines, int start, uid_t filter, fieldmask fmask)
{
    char psline[MAX_LINE];
    int  i = start;
    int  numprintlines = MIN(win_lines, numprocs);

    int  count = 0;
    while ( (i < numprocs) && (count < numprintlines + start) ) {
        if ( (filter == -1) || (proclist[i].uid == filter) ) {
            memset(psline, 0, MAX_LINE);
            print_one_proc(fieldtab, proclist[i], fmask, psline);
```

```
            mvwaddnstr(win, count - start, 0, psline, COLS);
            count++;
        }
        i++;
    }
}
```

If the `filter` parameter is -1, it does not filter. If it is a user ID, it only prints lines whose `uid` field match it. The `start` parameter is the index in the `proclist` array of the first process to print. It stops printing lines if either it reaches the end of the `proclist` array or the total number of lines it printed is equal to the number of lines in the content window. The index `i` iterates through the array, but the variable `count` keeps track of the number of lines printed. The instruction

```
mvwaddnstr(win, count - start, 0, psline, COLS);
```

writes at most `COLS` characters of the string `psline` in content window line `count - start`, starting in column 0.

The main() Function

We've now seen all of the major components of the program. I haven't shown several small functions, but all of the code is available in the source code repository for the book. Listing 19-6 contains fragments of the main() function.

spl_top.c
main()
```
int main(int argc, char *argv[])
{
    // OMITTED: All declarations and setup of signal handling and blocking
    setup_curses();
    create_windows(&summary_win, &heading_win, &content_win);
    configure_windows(summary_win, heading_win, content_win);
    printtopheadings(fieldtab, printfields, heading);
    mvwaddstr(heading_win, 0, 0, heading);
    wrefresh(heading_win);
    loadprocs(&procarray, &numprocs);  /* Load initial proc list. */
    ticks = get_hertz();
    delaysecs = 3;                /* Set default delay to 3 seconds. */
    delay.tv_sec = delaysecs;
    delay.tv_nsec = 0;
    --snip--
    while ( !done ) {
        show_summary(summary_win, procarray, numprocs);
        wclear(content_win);
        loadprocs(&procarray, &numprocs);
        sortprocs(procarray, numprocs, fieldtab[sortfield].sortfunc, sortdir);
        contentlines = getmaxy(content_win);
```

```
        print_procs(content_win, procarray, numprocs, contentlines, startline,
                filter_uid, printfields);
        wrefresh(content_win);
        if ( iowait(&delay) > 0 )
            switch ( wgetch(content_win) ) {
            case 'q': done = TRUE; break;
            case 'm': sortfield = MEM;  sortdir = FALSE; startline = 0; break;
            case 'c': sortfield = CPU;  sortdir = FALSE; startline = 0; break;
            case 't': sortfield = TIME; sortdir = FALSE; startline = 0; break;
            case 'p': sortfield = PID;  sortdir = FALSE; startline = 0; break;
            case 'u': sortfield = USER; sortdir = FALSE; startline = 0; break;
            case 'r': sortdir    = ~sortdir;             startline = 0; break;
            case 'U':
                filter_uid = pick_user(summary_win, username);
                startline = 0;
                break;
            case KEY_DOWN:
                if ( startline < numprocs - contentlines)
                    startline++;
                break;
            case KEY_UP:
                if ( startline > 0 )
                    startline--;
                break;
            }
        wrefresh(heading_win);
    }
    endwin();
    return 0;
}
```

Listing 19-6: The main program for spl_top.c

The program lets you sort by several different fields. It also lets you
filter the output by username; if you enter U, it prompts for a username
in the summary window's bottom line to use for filtering. In this case, it
shows only the processes of that user. If you just press ENTER in response, it
shows all users' processes. If you enter an invalid name, it displays a message,
Invalid User, that disappears in the next refresh. Otherwise, it filters by
the entered username. If you press the down arrow key, it will scroll down
one line. Similarly, if you press the up arrow key, it scrolls upward if it can.
Figure 19-6 is a screenshot of it while it's running, sorted in decreasing order
of the total time each process has run.

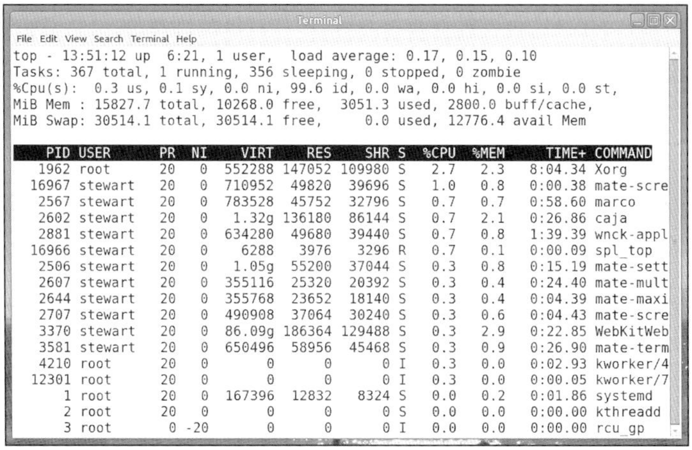

Figure 19-6: A screenshot of the running spl_top program

You can see that the appearance of the screen is almost the same as the actual top program, though you'd have to run both in different terminal windows to check whether the output values are consistent.

Concluding Thoughts

This was the most complex and largest of the programs we've developed in this book. I saved it for last because developing it combined many of the ideas from previous chapters. As complex as it might seem, the actual top program makes this one look simple.

No matter how hard a project might seem initially, by breaking it down step by step with perseverance and documentation in hand, you can master it. This is the lesson I hope you learned from this project.

Summary

The canonical mode of a terminal is the mode in which we're accustomed to working. It lets us edit lines before transmitting them to the process waiting for input. It requires us to press ENTER or another end-of-line delimiter to transmit these lines. It lets us enter thousands of characters, if we want, before sending the line. Programs that interact with their users through the terminal often need to configure the terminal in a noncanonical mode. Noncanonical modes are those that disable these features.

In this chapter we explored how programs can disable canonical mode. We studied the effects of changing the MIN and TIME terminal driver settings, as well as other settings that control the behavior of the terminal driver. We developed a program reminiscent of the snake game from the early days of Unix.

The Curses library provides a terminal-independent method of updating character screens. It includes several hundred different functions that allow a program to control exactly how its terminal screen should behave. In effect, it allows a program to treat a character-based terminal as a primitive drawing canvas. The Curses API is standardized by The Open Group. The current standard is known as XSI Curses. The *ncurses* library is a free version of Curses that is available for almost all Unix versions.

In the chapter, we explored the Curses API and developed a few programs that demonstrated some of its capabilities. We concluded by developing an implementation of the interactive top system utility, which displays process and memory statistics dynamically.

Exercises

1. Write a program that outputs either `canonical` if the terminal attached to standard input is in canonical mode or `noncanonical` if it isn't, in which case it also outputs the values of the `MIN` and `TIME` parameters.

2. Modify *sprite.c* so that when the user enters a +, the speed of the sprite increases by 1 move per second to a maximum of 20 moves per second, and when the user presses -, it decreases the speed by 1 move per second, to a minimum of 1 move per 2 seconds. In other words, pressing + has no effect at the maximum speed, and pressing - has no effect at the minimum speed. You'll notice poor responsiveness to user inputs when the speed is at the minimum. The next exercise addresses this issue.

3. The *sprite.c* and *sprite_curses.c* programs used synchronous I/O with polled, nonblocking reads. First, redesign *sprite.c* to use signal-driven I/O instead. Keep the same user interface and the same responses to user inputs. Use *sigio_demo.c* from Chapter 17 as a model for solving this problem. Then add the speed adjustments described in Exercise 2.

4. Turn *sprite_curses.c* into a game by introducing scoring. The goal is to prevent the sprite from hitting a boundary. Each time the sprite hits a boundary, the score decreases. The score increases by 1 point for every second the user runs the game. Report the score in the bottom row.

5. Modify the *spl_top.c* program to allow horizontal scrolling. Specifically, when the user presses the right arrow key, the heading and all process information lines move one column to the right, filling the left column with a space character, and when the user presses the left arrow key, the heading and all lines of process information move to the left, removing the leftmost character of the heading and each line, and space-filling the right column of the display. The right arrow should have no effect if the displayed lines start in the leftmost column of the window. It's used only to reverse what the left arrow does.

6. Modify *spl_top.c* by adding the ability to delete columns. When the user enters C, a new window containing a numbered list of all heading columns should open up on top of the screen. For example, the list could be:

```
(1)  PID
(2)  USER
--snip--
(11) TIME+
(12) COMMAND
CHOICE:
```

If the user enters a number from 1 to 12 at the cursor position after the word CHOICE, then that column is marked for removal from the display. If the user enters 0, no column is marked for removal. The window disappears after the user enters a number and, if the marked column was visible before, it is no longer visible. If it wasn't visible before, nothing is changed in the display.

7. Turn *sprite_curses.c* into a game by putting targets on the screen in random positions. A target is a single character, such as o. The objective is to move the sprite on top of the target in the fewest moves without hitting a boundary. Decide on a scoring system. For example, reaching a target could be 100 points, and the number of moves is subtracted from it.

8. Write an *ncurses* program that simulates the Game of Life. Specifically, it puts several x characters on the screen in an initial configuration. Call a cell *filled* if it contains an x and *empty* if it doesn't. Cells interact with their eight neighbors, which are the cells that are directly horizontally, vertically, or diagonally adjacent. At regular intervals, the screen is updated according to the following rules:

   - Any filled cell with fewer than two filled neighbors becomes empty.
   - Any filled cell with more than three filled neighbors becomes empty.
   - Any filled cell with two or three filled neighbors remains filled.
   - Any empty cell with exactly three filled neighbors is filled.

   The program should run until the user enters a q to quit. Some initial states will result in cycles, some will just end because of a lack of interactions, and some may run for a long time without any obvious cycles. As an extra feature, give the program a command line argument that is the name of a file containing screen coordinates, one per line, at which the initial cells will be filled.

A

CREATING LIBRARIES

Here, I'll show you how to create and use static and shared libraries in a Unix environment. This summary is tutorial and elementary. I begin by explaining a bit about software libraries in general, then proceed to describe the differences between static and shared libraries. I then describe the how-tos of creating and using both types of libraries using the tools available in a GNU-based Unix system such as Linux. The discussion here is limited to executables and libraries in the *Executable and Link Format (ELF)*, which is the format used by Linux and most Unix systems at the time of this writing. If you don't know what this means or why it might be important, that's fine; you may safely ignore this.

If you think you don't need the conceptual discussions, you can just cut to the chase and jump directly to the appropriate section, either "Creating a Static Library" (page 946) and "Using (Linking to) a Static Library" (page 947) for static libraries, or "Creating a Shared Library" (page 949) and "Using a Shared Library" (page 951) for shared libraries. For a more advanced explanation about creating and using library files, I recommend that you read David Wheeler's Program Library HOWTO at *http://tldp.org/HOWTO/ Program-Library-HOWTO/index.html*.

About Libraries

A *software library*, also called a *program library*, is a file containing compiled code and possibly data that can be used by other programs. Libraries are not stand-alone executables—you cannot "run" a library. They contain things like functions, type definitions, and useful constants that other programs can use. You have been using software libraries since your very first "Hello, world" program, whether you knew it or not. Whatever function that you used to print those words on the screen was contained in a library, most likely either the C Standard I/O Library (if you used `printf`, for instance) or the C++ *iostreams* library (if you used the insertion operator of the `cout` `ostream` object).

Perhaps you might have reached the point where you realize that you are writing useful code, code that you might want to use in more than one project, and that while you could continue to copy those functions into each new project, perhaps you would like to reuse that code in a more efficient way by creating a library file that contains it. If so, read on.

Static vs. Shared Libraries in Unix

In Unix, there are two kinds of library files, static and shared. The term *static library* is short for "statically linked library"; it is a library that can be linked to the program statically, after the program is compiled, as part of the program executable file. In other words, it is incorporated into the program executable file as part of the build of that executable. A *shared library* is a library that is linked dynamically, either at loadtime or at runtime, depending on the particular system. Loadtime is when the program is loaded into memory in order for it to execute. Runtime is the interval of time during which it is actually running. If linking is delayed until runtime, then a symbol such as a function in the library is linked to the program only when the program calls that function or otherwise references that symbol. The fact that a shared library is a dynamically linked library is not to be confused with the use of that term by Microsoft in what they call a DLL. While *DLL* is short for "dynamically linked library," DLLs are different from but serve a similar purpose to Unix shared libraries. In these notes, I use the term in the more general sense of a library that is linked to a program either at loadtime or at runtime.

Static linking, which was the original form of linking, resolves references to externally defined symbols such as functions by copying the library code directly into the executable file when the executable (file) is built. The *linkage editor*, also called the *link editor*, or just the *linker*, performs static linking. The term linker is a bit ambiguous, so I will avoid using it. The primary advantage of static linking is that the executable is self-contained and can run on multiple platforms. For example, a program might use a graphical toolkit such as GTK that may not be present on all systems. With the toolkit's libraries statically linked into the executable, the executable can run on other systems (with the same machine architecture) without requiring the users on those systems to install those library files. Another advantage is that it shields a program from changes in the library that are incompatible with how the program uses it, since the version that works is part of the executable. Once upon a time, static linking resulted in faster code as well, but the gain is negligible today.

Dynamic linking can be done either when the program is loaded into memory or while it is running and references an unresolved symbol. In the former case, the startup time of the program is slightly longer than if it had been statically linked, since the libraries have to be located in memory (and possibly loaded into memory if they were not already there) and then linked to the program before it can actually begin execution. In the latter case, the program will experience slightly longer running time, because whenever an unresolved symbol is found and must be resolved, there is a bit of overhead in locating the library and linking to it. This latter approach is the more common approach because it links only symbols that are actually used. For example, if a function from a shared library is not called during execution, it will not be linked to the library at all, saving time.

There are several advantages of linking dynamically over linking statically. One is that because the executable program file does not contain the code of the libraries that must be linked to it, the executable file is smaller. This means that it loads into memory faster and that it uses less space on disk. Another advantage is that it makes possible the sharing of memory resources. Instead of multiple copies of a library being physically incorporated into multiple programs, a single memory-resident copy of the library can be linked to each program, provided that it is a shared library. Shared libraries are dynamically linked libraries that are designed so that they are not modified when a process uses them. This is why they have the *.so* extension; it's short for "shared object."

Another advantage of linking to shared libraries is that it makes it possible to update the libraries without recompiling the programs that use them, provided the interfaces to the libraries do not change. If bugs are discovered and fixed in these libraries, all that is necessary is to obtain the modified libraries. If they were statically linked, then all programs that use them would have to be recompiled.

Still other advantages are related to security issues. Hackers often try to attack applications through knowledge of specific addresses in the executable code. Methods of deterring such types of attacks involve randomizing the locations of various relocatable segments in the code. With statically linked executables, only the stack and heap address can be randomized; all instructions have a fixed address in all invocations. With dynamically linked executables, the kernel has the ability to load the libraries at arbitrary addresses, independent of each other. This makes such attacks much harder. As noted in Chapter 10, ASLR also mitigates this problem, even in statically linked libraries.

Identifying Libraries

Static libraries can be recognized by their ending: They end in *.a*. Shared libraries have a *.so* extension, possibly with a version number following, such as *librt.so.1*. Both types of libraries start with the prefix *lib* and then have a unique name that identifies that library. So, for example, the standard C++ static library is *libstdc++.a*, and the shared real-time library is *librt.so.1*. The *rt* in the name is short for "real-time."

Creating a Static Library

The steps to create a static library are fairly simple. Suppose that you have one or more source code files containing useful functions. For the sake of precision, suppose that *timestuff.c* and *errors.c* are two such files.

1. Create a header file that contains the prototypes of the functions defined in *timestuff.c* and *errors.c*. Suppose that file is called *utils.h*.

2. Compile the C source files into object files using the command:

   ```
   $ gcc -c timestuff.c errors.c
   ```

   This will create the two files, *timestuff.o* and *errors.o*.

3. Run the GNU archiver, ar, to create a new archive and insert the two object files into it:

   ```
   $ ar rcs libutils.a timestuff.o errors.o
   ```

   The rcs following the command name consists of a one-letter operation code followed by two modifiers. The r is the operation code that tells ar to insert the object files into the archive. The c and s are modifiers; c means "create the archive if it did not exist," and s means "create an index," like a table of contents, in the archive file. The name of the archive is given after the options but before the list of files to insert in the archive. In this case, our library will be named *libutils.a*.

   This same command can be used to add new object files to the library, so if you later decide to add the file *datestuff.o* to your library, you would use this command:

   ```
   $ ar rcs libutils.a datestuff.o
   ```

4. Install the library into some appropriate directory, and put the header file into an appropriate directory as well. I use the principle of "most closely enclosing ancestral directory" for installing my custom libraries. For example, a library that will be used only for programs that I write for my Unix System Programming class will be

in a directory under the directory containing all of those programs, such as

```
~/unix_demos/lib/libutils.a
```

and its header will be:

```
~/unix_demos/include/utils.h
```

If I have a library, say *libgoodstuff.a*, that is generally useful to me for any programming task, I will put it in my *~/lib* directory

```
~/lib/libgoodstuff.a
```

with its header in my *~/include* directory:

```
~/include/goodstuff.h
```

5. Make sure that your LIBRARY_PATH environment variable contains paths to all of the directories in which you might put your *static* library files. Your *.bashrc* file should have lines of the form

```
LIBRARY_PATH=$LIBRARY_PATH:~/lib:
export LIBRARY_PATH
```

so that gcc will know where to look for your custom static libraries. If you want your libraries to be searched before the standard ones, then reverse the order:

```
LIBRARY_PATH=~/lib:$LIBRARY_PATH
export LIBRARY_PATH
```

6. Make sure that your CPATH or C_INCLUDE_PATH (or, if using C++, your CPLUS_INCLUDE_PATH) contains the path to the directory in which you put the header file. My *.bashrc* file has these lines:

```
CPATH=~/include
export CPATH
```

 Do not put your static libraries into the same directories as your shared libraries. Keep them separate.

Using (Linking to) a Static Library

To use the library in a program, you first have to tell the compiler to include its interface, that is, its header file, and then you have to tell the linkage editor to link to the library itself. The first task is accomplished by putting an

`#include` directive in the program. The second task is achieved by using the -l option to gcc to specify the name of the library. Remember that the *name* is everything between lib and the dot (.). The -l option must follow the list of files that refer to that library. For example, to link to the *libutils.a* library, you would do two things:

1. In the program, you would include the header file for the library:

```
#include "utils.h"
```

---

2. To build the executable, you would issue the command

```
gcc -o myprogram myprogram.c -lutils
```

---

or, if you did not modify your CPATH

```
gcc -o myprogram myprogram.c -lutils -I~/unix_demos/include
```

---

but in either case, do this only if you are certain that there is not a shared library with the same name in a directory that will be searched ahead of the one in which *libutils.a* is located or in the same directory as *libutils.a*. This is because gcc, by default, will always choose to link to a shared library of the same name rather than a static library of that name. This is one reason why you should not put static libraries in the same directory as shared libraries.

If you get the error message

```
/usr/bin/ld: cannot find -lutils
collect2: ld returned 1 exit status
```

---

it means that you did not set up the LIBRARY_PATH properly. (Did you export it? Did you type it correctly?)

If you want to be safe, you can use the -L*dir* option to the compiler. This option adds *dir* to the list of directories that will be searched when looking for libraries specified with the -l option, as in:

```
gcc -o myprogram myprogram.c -L~/unix_demos/lib -lutils
```

Directories specified with -L will be searched before those contained in the LIBRARY_PATH environment variable.

If you do a web search on this topic, you may see instructions for building your program of the form:

```
gcc -static myprogram.c -o myprogram -lutils
```

This will probably fail with the error message

```
/usr/bin/ld: cannot find -lc

collect2: ld returned 1 exit status
```

---

because the -static option tells gcc to statically link *myprogram.c* to all libraries, not just *libutils.a*. Since a static version of the C Standard Library is no longer included with most operating systems, the link editor, ld, will not find *libc.a* anywhere. Do not try to use the -static option. Follow my instructions instead.

Creating a Shared Library

The ar command does not build shared libraries. You need to use gcc for that purpose. Before diving into the details though, you need to understand a few things about shared libraries in Unix to make sense out of the options to be passed to gcc to create the library.

Shared Library Names

Every shared library has a special name called its *soname*. The soname is constructed from the prefix *lib*, followed by the name of the library, then the string *.so*, and finally, a period and a version number that is incremented whenever the interface changes. So, for example, the soname of the math library, *m*, might be *libm.so.1*.

Every shared library also has a *real name*, which is the name of the actual file in which the library resides. The real name is longer than the soname; it must be formed by appending to the soname a period, a minor number, and, optionally, another period and a release number. The minor number and release number are used for configuration control.

Lastly, the library has a name that is used by the compiler, which is the soname without the version number.

Example 1

The *utils* library will have three names:

libutils.so.1 Its soname

libutils.so.1.0.1 The name of the file; I will use a minor number of 0 and a release number of 1

libutils.so The name the compiler will use, which we will call the *linker name*

Example 2

If you look in the */lib* directory, you will see that links are created in a specific way; for each shared library there are often at least three entries, such as:

```
lrwxrwxrwx 1 root root    11 Aug 12 18:52 libacl.so -> libacl.so.1
lrwxrwxrwx 1 root root    15 Aug 12 18:51 libacl.so.1 -> libacl.so.1.1.0
-rwxr-xr-x 1 root root 31380 Aug  3 18:42 libacl.so.1.1.0
```

Notice that the linker's name (without the version number) is a soft link to the soname, which is a soft link to the actual library file. When we set up our *libutils* library, we need to do the same thing. Every library will have three files in the directory where it is placed: The soname will be a soft link to the actual library file, and the linker name will be a soft link to the soname.

Steps to Create the Library

1. For each source code file that you intend to put into a shared library, say *stuff.c*, compile it with position-independent code using the following command:

   ```
   gcc -fPIC -g -Wall -c stuff.c
   ```

   This will produce an object file, *stuff.o*, with debugging information included (the -g option) and with all warnings enabled (the -Wall option), which is always a safe thing to do. The -fPIC option is what generates the position-independent code (hence PIC). *Position-independent code* is code that can be executed regardless of where it is placed in memory. This is not the same thing as relocatable code. *Relocatable code* is code that can be placed anywhere into memory but that requires the linkage editor or loader to adjust its addresses before it can be executed. Instructions such as those that specify addresses relative to the program counter are position independent.

2. Suppose that *stuff.o* and *tools.o* are two object files generated in accordance with the first step. To create a shared library containing just those files with soname *libgoodstuff.so.1* and real filename *libgood stuff.so.1.0.1*, use the following command:

   ```
   gcc -shared -Wl,-soname,libgoodstuff.so.1 -o libgoodstuff.so.1.0.1  \
       stuff.o tools.o
   ```

   This will create the file *libgoodstuff.so.1.0.1* with the soname *libgood stuff.so.1* stored internally. Note that there cannot be any whitespace before or after the commas. The -Wl option tells gcc to pass the remaining comma-separated list to the link editor as options. You might be advised by someone else to use -fpic instead of -fPIC because it generates faster code. Do not do so. It is not guaranteed to work in all cases. The -fPIC option generates larger code, but it never fails to work.

3. It is time to install the library in the appropriate place. Unless you have superuser privileges, you will not be able to install your nifty library in a standard location such as */usr/local/lib*. Instead, you will most likely put it in your own *lib* directory, such as *~/lib*. Just copy the file into the directory.

4. After you copy the file into the directory, you should run ldconfig on that directory with a -n option. For example:

   ```
   ldconfig -n ~/lib
   ```

With the `-n` option, `ldconfig` creates the necessary links and cache to the most recent shared libraries found in the given directory. In particular, it will create a symbolic link from a file named with the soname to the actual library file. If there are multiple minor versions or releases, `ldconfig` will link the soname file to the highest-numbered minor version and release combination. The `-n` option tells `ldconfig` not to make any changes to the standard set of library directories. After `ldconfig` runs in our example, we would have this link:

```
libgoodstuff.so.1 -> libgoodstuff.so.1.0.1
```

After running `ldconfig`, you should manually create a link from a file with the linker name to the highest-numbered soname link. In our example, we would type

```
ln -s libgoodstuff.so.1 libgoodstuff.so
```

to create this link:

```
libgoodstuff.so -> libgoodstuff.so.1
```

5. If at some future time you revise the *goodstuff* library, you would increment either the minor version number or the release number, or perhaps even the major version number if the interface to the library changed. If you just change an algorithm internally or fix a few bugs, you would not change the major number, only the minor one or the release number. Suppose that you create a new release, *libgoodstuff.so.1.0.2*, with soname *libgoodstuff.1*. You would copy the file into the same directory as the older release and run `ldconfig` again, and `ldconfig` would change the link from the soname to the later release. A listing of that directory would then look like:

```
libutils.so -> libutils.so.1
libutils.so.1 -> libutils.so.0.2
libutils.so.1.0.1
libutils.so.1.0.2
```

Using a Shared Library

What you need to understand about how to use shared libraries is that it is a two-step linking process. In the first step, the linkage editor will create some static information in your executable file that will be used later by the dynamic linker at runtime. So both the linkage editor and a dynamic linker participate in creating a working executable.

You link your program to a shared library in the same way that you link it to a static library, using the `-l` option to gcc to name the library to which you want your program linked and using the -L*dir* option to tell it which directory it is in if it is not in a standard location. For example

```
gcc -o myprogram myprogram.c -L~/lib -lgoodstuff
```

will create the executable myprogram to be linked dynamically to the library *~/lib/libgoodstuff.so*. We can also write

```
gcc -o myprogram myprogram.c ~/lib/libgoodstuff.so
```

skipping the options -l and -L. The two methods are equivalent. If *~/lib* is in the LIBRARY_PATH environment variable, then you can also write

```
gcc -o myprogram myprogram.c -lgoodstuff
```

and this will be equivalent as well. All of this assumes that the directory containing the header file is in your CPATH or is in a standard location. Otherwise, remember to add the option -I *includedir* to this command.

This is just the first step. Your executable will not run correctly unless the dynamic linker can find your shared library file. One way to tell whether it will run correctly is with the ldd command. The ldd command prints shared dependencies in a file, meaning it displays a list of shared libraries upon which your program depends. If ldd does not display the path to *~/lib/libgoodstuff.so*, then myprogram will fail to find the file and will not run. If the dynamic linker can find my library, the output of ldd would look something like this:

```
linux-gate.so.1 =>  (0x00a31000)
libgoodstuff.so.1 => ~/lib/libgoodstuff.so.1 (0x00caa000)
libc.so.6 => /lib/libc.so.6 (0x00110000)
/lib/ld-linux.so.2 (0x00bd5000)
```

If it isn't able to find it, I will see:

```
linux-gate.so.1 =>  (0x00a31000)
libgoodstuff.so.1 => not found
libc.so.6 => /lib/libc.so.6 (0x00110000)
/lib/ld-linux.so.2 (0x00bd5000)
```

If you had the means to put your shared library file in a standard directory, this problem would be solved easily. Unfortunately, with just user privileges and not superuser privileges, you cannot do this. The easiest solution to this problem is one that is not recommended for various reasons: You can modify the environment variable LD_LIBRARY_PATH, which the dynamic linker uses at loadtime and runtime to locate shared libraries. To be precise, the dynamic linker searches the directories in this variable before any in the standard locations. Therefore, you can put the line

```
LD_LIBRARY_PATH=~/lib
export LD_LIBRARY_PATH
```

in your *.bashrc* file to have the dynamic linker search that directory at runtime. The alternative is to modify the variable every time you run the program, which is a nuisance I think, or to hardcode the path to the libraries into the executable using the -rpath option to the linkage editor, which is described in the ld man page.

There is one other option. You can define the LD_RUN_PATH variable to contain the directory in which you put your libraries in your *.bashrc* file:

```
LD_RUN_PATH=~/lib
export LD_RUN_PATH
```

If this variable is defined when you compile the executable, then the run path will be hardcoded into the executable and the dynamic linker will find your libraries at runtime.

B

UNICODE AND UTF-8

Computers store all data as sequences of bits that are essentially numbers. Numbers are used to represent all of the visual symbols that we think of as characters, such as the letters of our alphabets, the digits in our numerals, the various punctuation symbols, and the control codes that affect how and where other symbols are printed. Informally, *characters* are the smallest representable symbols used in a written language, such as the letters of the Roman alphabet, and a *character encoding* is an assignment of numbers to a set of characters.

The ASCII character encoding was the most prevalent encoding for more than 40 years. *ASCII* is the acronym for *American Standard Code for Information Interchange*. The ASCII encoding maps characters to 7-bit integers, using the range from 0 to 127 to represent 94 printing characters, 33 control characters, and the space. Since a byte is usually used to store a character, the eighth bit of the byte is filled with a 0. Well before the ASCII encoding was defined, IBM defined a different encoding named *EBCDIC*, which stands for *Extended Binary Coded Decimal Interchange*. That encoding assigned an entirely different set of 8-bit numbers to the same characters assigned by the

ASCII encoding. The existence of two different encodings of the same set of characters required programs to be aware of which encoding was used and to convert from one to the other.

One problem with both the ASCII and EBCDIC codes is that they do not provide a way to encode characters from other scripts, such as Cyrillic or Greek. They don't even have encodings of Roman characters with diacritical marks, such as é, ä, ñ, or ô. Over time, as computer usage extended worldwide, other encodings for different alphabets and scripts were developed, usually with overlapping codes. These encoding systems conflicted with one another. That is, two encodings could use the same number for two different characters or use different numbers for the same character. A program transferring text from one computer to another would run the risk that the text would be corrupted in the transfer.

Background

In 1989, to overcome these problems, the International Standards Organization (ISO) started work on a universal, all-encompassing character code standard, and in 1990 they published a draft standard (ISO 10646) called the *Universal Character Set (UCS)*. UCS was designed as a superset of all other character set standards, providing round-trip compatibility to other character sets. *Round-trip compatibility* asserts that no information is lost if a text string is converted to UCS and then back to its original encoding.

Simultaneously, the Unicode Project, which was a consortium of private industrial partners, was working on its own independent universal character encoding. In 1991, the Unicode Project and ISO decided to work cooperatively to avoid creating two different character encodings. The result was that the code table created by the Unicode Consortium, as they are now called, satisfied the original ISO 10646 standard. Over time, the two groups continued to modify the respective standards, but they always remain compatible. Unicode adds new characters over time, but it always contains the character set defined by ISO 10646-*x*.

Terminology

The Unicode Consortium defines a *character* as an abstract representation of the smallest element of a written language that has semantic value. The actual appearance or form of a character is called a *glyph*. The letter *a*, for example, is drawn using one of many possible fonts, and so its actual form can vary, but it's still an *a*. Each different way to render the letter *a* is a different glyph. Glyphs are the shapes that characters take. Character encodings assign numbers to characters, not to glyphs.

The set of all characters used together in a written natural language is called a *script*, not to be confused with the use of the same term as a type of program. For example, the characters in the Greek language constitute the Greek script, and the characters used in most of Western Europe are part of the Latin script.

The set of numbers that are assigned to all of the characters in a script is called its *codespace*. The codespace for Greek, for example, is the set of integers from decimal 880 through 1023, or hexadecimal 0370 through 03FF. An individual number in a codespace is called a *code point*.

In Unicode, a code point is denoted by "U+" followed by a hexadecimal number from four to eight digits long. For example, the code point assigned to the Greek character ψ is U+03C8, and the one assigned to ϕ is U+03C6. Most of the code points in use are four digits long. When a character has been assigned a code point, it's called an *encoded character*.

Unicode

Unicode contains the alphabets of almost all known languages, including Japanese, Chinese, Greek, Cyrillic, Canadian Aboriginal, and Arabic. It was originally a 16-bit character set, but in 1995, with Unicode 2.0, it became 32 bits. The Unicode Standard encodes characters in the range U+0000 to U+10FFFF, which is roughly a 21-bit code space. The code reserves the remaining values for future use (Figure B-1).

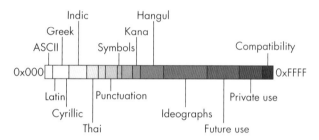

Figure B-1: Unicode layout

UTF-8

Unicode code points are just numeric values assigned to characters. They are not representations of characters as sequences of bytes. For example, the code point U+03C6 is not a sequence of two bytes containing 0x03 and 0xC6. If we were to use the number's ordinary byte representation to encode the character, there would be no way to distinguish the sequence of two characters with codes 0x03 and 0xC6 from the Greek character ϕ.

The mapping of code points to sequences of bytes is called a *character encoding form*. Because the ordering of bytes in a particular computer system can vary, such as whether it is big-endian or little-endian, the Unicode Consortium defines a *character encoding scheme* as a character encoding form together with a specification of the way in which the bytes are sequenced.

There are several Unicode character encoding schemes, including UCS-2, UCS-4, UTF-2, UTF-4, UTF-8, UTF-16, and UTF-32. UCS-2 and UCS-4 encode Unicode text as sequences of either 2 or 4 bytes, but these cannot work in a Unix system because strings with these encodings can contain bytes that match ASCII characters and, in particular, \0 and /, which have a special meaning in filenames and other C library function parameters. Unix file systems and tools expect ASCII characters and would fail if they were given 2-byte encodings.

The most prevalent encoding of Unicode as sequences of bytes is UTF-8, invented by Ken Thompson in 1992. In UTF-8, characters are encoded with anywhere from 1 to 6 bytes. In other words, the number of bytes varies with the character. In UTF-8, all ASCII characters are encoded within the 7 least significant bits of a byte whose most significant bit is 0.

UTF-8 uses the following scheme for encoding Unicode code points:

- Characters U+0000 to U+007F (that is, the ASCII characters) are encoded simply as bytes 0x00 to 0x7F. This implies that files and strings that contain only 7-bit ASCII characters have the same encoding under both ASCII and UTF-8.

- All characters larger than U+007F are encoded as a sequence of 2 or more bytes, each of which has the most significant bit set. This means that no ASCII byte can appear as part of any other character, because ASCII characters are the only characters whose leading bit is 0.

- The first byte of a multibyte sequence that represents a non-ASCII character is always in the range 0xC0 to 0xFD and it indicates how many bytes follow for this character. Specifically, it is one of 110xxxxx, 1110xxx, 11110xxx, 111110xx, and 1111110x, where the x's may be 0s or 1s. The number of 1-bits following the first 1-bit up until the next 0-bit is the number of bytes in the rest of the sequence. Thus, 1110xxxx indicates that 2 bytes follow.

  All further bytes in a multibyte sequence start with the two bits 10 and are in the range 0x80 to 0xBF. This implies that UTF-8 sequences must be of the following forms in binary, where the x's represent the bits from the code point, with the leftmost x-bit being its most significant bit:

0xxxxxxx					
110xxxxx	10xxxxxx				
1110xxxx	10xxxxxx	10xxxxxx			
11110xxx	10xxxxxx	10xxxxxx	10xxxxxx		
111110xx	10xxxxxx	10xxxxxx	10xxxxxx	10xxxxxx	
1111110x	10xxxxxx	10xxxxxx	10xxxxxx	10xxxxxx	10xxxxxx

- The bytes 0xFE and 0xFF are never used in the UTF-8 encoding.

A few things can be concluded from these rules. First, the number of x's in a sequence is the maximum number of bits that a code point can have to be representable in that many bytes. For example, there are 11 x-bits in a 2-byte UTF-8 sequence, so all code points whose 16-bit binary value is at least 0000000010000000 but at most 0000011111111111 can be encoded using 2 bytes. (Remember that code points are not bytes, but integer values that represent characters.) In hexadecimal, these lie between 0080 and 07FF. Table B-1 shows the ranges of Unicode code points that map to the different UTF-8 sequence lengths.

Table B-1: Code Point Ranges in Unicode 16.0.0

Number of bytes	Number of bits in code point	Range
1	7	00000000–0000007F
2	11	00000080–000007FF
3	16	00000800–0000FFFF
4	21	00001000–001FFFFF
5	26	00200000–03FFFFFF
6	31	04000000–FFFFFFFF

You can see that although UTF-8 encoded characters may be up to 6 bytes long in theory, code points up to U+FFFF, having at most 16 bits, can be encoded in sequences of at most 3 bytes.

Converting a Unicode code point to UTF-8 by hand is straightforward using Table B-1:

1. From the range, determine how many bytes are needed.

2. Starting with the least significant bit, copy bits from the code point from right to left into the least significant byte.

3. When the current byte has reached 8 bits including any leading required bits, continue filling the next most significant byte with successively more significant bits from the code point.

4. Repeat until all bits have been copied into the byte sequence, filling with leading 0s as required.

Conversion Example 1

To convert U+05E7 to UTF-8, we first observe that it is in the interval 0080 to 07FF, which requires 2 bytes. We write it in binary as:

```
0000 0101 1110 0111
```

The rightmost 6 bits 100111 are placed into the rightmost byte after a leading 2-bit sequence 10

```
10 100111
```

and the next least significant 5 bits 10111 are placed into the next byte after a leading 3-bit sequence 110:

```
110 10111
```

Therefore, the 2-byte sequence is

```
11010111 10100111 = 0xD7 0xA7
```

which is the decimal 215 in the upper byte and 167 in the lower byte.

Conversion Example 2

To convert U+0ABC to UTF-8, we observe that it is greater than U+07FF and therefore it requires a 3-byte code. In binary, its value is:

```
0000 1010 1011 1100
```

Following the procedure, the rightmost 6 bits are placed into the rightmost byte after a leading 10. The next 6 bits are placed into the middle byte after a leading 10. The remaining 4 bits are all 0s, so the leftmost byte is filled with four 0s after a leading 1110. The resulting bytes are, from most significant to least:

```
11100000
10101010
10111100
```

The sequence 11100000 10101010 10111100 in hexadecimal is 0xE0 0xAA 0xBC, which in decimal is 224 170 188, the Gujarati sign *nuqta*.

C

DATE AND TIME FORMAT SPECIFIERS

 The examples listed in Table C-1 are based on the date of January 19, 2038, at 03:14:07 UTC, the time at which the 32-bit Unix time representation overflows.

Table C-1: Format Specifiers for Date and Time Formatting in the EST Time Zone with Current Locale en_US.UTF-8

Format	Example	Meaning
%a	Mon	Locale's abbreviated weekday name
%A	Monday	Locale's full weekday name
%b	Jan	Locale's abbreviated month name
%B	January	Locale's full month name
%c	Mon 18 Jan 2038 10:14:07 PM EST	Locale's date and time
%C	20	Century; like %Y, except omit last two digits
%d	18	Day of month
%D	01/18/38	Date; same as %m/%d/%y

(continued)

Table C-1: Format Specifiers for Date and Time Formatting in the EST Time Zone with Current Locale en_US.UTF-8 *(continued)*

Format	Example	Meaning
%e	18	Day of month, space padded; same as %_d
%F	2038-01-18	Full date, like %Y-%m-%d
%g	38	Last two digits of year of ISO week number (see %G)
%G	2038	Year of ISO week number (see %V); normally useful only with %V
%h	Jan	Same as %b
%H	22	Hour (00–23)
%I	10	Hour (01–12)
%j	18	Day of year (001–366)
%k	22	Hour, space padded (0–23); same as %_H
%l	10	Hour, space padded (1–12); same as %_I
%m	1	Month (01–12)
%M	14	Minute (00–59)
%n		A newline
%N	0	Nanosecond (000000000–999999999)
%p	PM	Locale's equivalent of either AM or PM; blank if not known
%P	pm	Like %p, but lowercase
%q	1	Quarter of year (1–4)
%r	10:14:07 PM	Locale's 12-hour clock time
%R	22:14	24-hour hour and minute; same as %H:%M
%s	2147483647	Seconds since 1970-01-01 00:00:00 UTC
%S	7	Second (00–60)
%T	22:14:07	Time; same as %H:%M:%S
%u	1	Day of week (1–7); 1 is Monday
%U	3	Week number of year, with Sunday as first day of week (00–53)
%V	3	ISO week number, with Monday as first day of week (01–53)
%w	1	Day of week (0–6); 0 is Sunday
%W	3	Week number of year, with Monday as first day of week (00–53)
%x	01/18/2038	Locale's date representation
%X	10:14:07 PM	Locale's time representation
%y	38	Last two digits of year (00–99)

Table C-1: Format Specifiers for Date and Time Formatting in the EST Time Zone with Current Locale en_US.UTF-8 *(continued)*

Format	Example	Meaning
%Y	2038	Year
%z	-500	+*hhmm* numeric time zone
%Z	EST	Alphabetic time zone abbreviation

BIBLIOGRAPHY

[1] Alpern, Bowen, and Fred B. Schneider. "Defining Liveness." *Information Processing Letters* 21 (1984): 181–85. *https://doi.org/10.1016/0020-0190 (85)90056-0.*

[2] Alpern, Bowen, and Fred B. Schneider. "Recognizing Safety and Liveness." *Distributed Computing* 2 (1987): 117–26. *https://doi.org/ 10.1007/BF01782772.*

[3] Bourne, Stephen R. "The UNIX Shell." *The Bell System Technical Journal* 57, no. 6, part 2 (1978): 1971–90.

[4] Bovet, Daniel P., and Marco Cesati. *Understanding the Linux Kernel.* O'Reilly Media, 2005.

[5] Card, Rémy, Theodore Ts'o, and Stephen Tweedie. "Design and Implementation of the Second Extended Filesystem." In *Proceedings of the First Dutch International Symposium on Linux*, University of Groningen, Netherlands, 1995.

[6] The C Standards Committee. *Information Technology – Programming Languages – C.* ISO/IEC 9899:2024. *https://iso-9899.info/wiki/The _Standard.*

[7] DiBona, Chris, Sam Ockman, and Mark Stone. *Open Sources: Voices from the Open Source Revolution.* O'Reilly Media, 1999.

[8] Dijkstra, Edsger W. "Co-operating Sequential Processes." In *Programming Languages: NATO Advanced Study Institute: Lectures Given at a Three Weeks Summer School Held in Villard-le-Lans, 1966*, edited by F. Genuys, 43–112. Academic Press, 1968. *https://pure.tue.nl/ws/files/4279816/ 344354178746665.pdf.*

[9] Dijkstra, Edsger W. *EWD74.* 1963. *https://www.cs.utexas.edu/~EWD/ ewd07xx/EWD749.PDF.*

[10] Gray, John Shapley. *Interprocess Communications in UNIX: The Nooks and Crannies.* 2nd ed. Prentice Hall, 1998.

[11] Grudin, Robert. *Time and the Art of Living.* Harper & Row, 1982.

[12] Haff, Gordon. *How Open Source Ate Software: Understand the Open Source Movement and So Much More.* Apress, 2018.

[13] Haviland, Keith, Dina Gray, and Ben Salama. *Unix System Programming.* 2nd ed. Addison-Wesley Longman, 1998.

[14] IEEE and The Open Group. *The Open Group Base Specifications Issue 7.* IEEE Std 1003.1™-2017 (Revision of IEEE Std 1003.1-2008). 2018. *https://pubs.opengroup.org/onlinepubs/9699919799/mindex.html.*

[15] Irlam, Gordon. "Unix File Size Survey – 1993." Technical report, 1994. *https://web.archive.org/web/20071013120153/https://www.gordoni.com/ufs93.html.*

[16] Johnson, S.C., and Dennis M. Ritchie. "UNIX Time-Sharing System: Portability of C Programs and the UNIX System." *The Bell System Technical Journal* 57, no. 6, part 2 (1978): 2021–48. *https://doi.org/10.1002/j.1538-7305.1978.tb02141.x.*

[17] Kernighan, Brian W. *Unix: A History and a Memoir.* Independently published, 2019.

[18] Kernighan, Brian W., and Dennis M. Ritchie. *The C Programming Language.* Prentice-Hall, 1978.

[19] Kernighan, Brian W., and Rob Pike. *The UNIX Programming Environment.* Prentice-Hall Software Series. Prentice-Hall, 1984.

[20] Kerrisk, Michael. *The Linux Programming Interface.* No Starch Press, 2010.

[21] Killian, T.J. "Processes as Files." In *Proceedings of the USENIX 1984 Summer Conference*, 203–7. USENIX Association, 1984.

[22] Lamport, Leslie. "Proving the Correctness of Multiprocess Programs." *IEEE Transactions on Software Engineering* SE-3, no. 2 (1977): 125–43. *https://doi.org/10.1109/TSE.1977.229904.*

[23] Mahoney, Michael S. *An Oral History of UNIX.* The Unix Heritage Society. *https://www.tuhs.org/Archive/Documentation/OralHistory/.*

[24] Mauro, Jim, and Richard McDougall. *Solaris Internals.* Sun Microsystems Press, 2001.

[25] McIlroy, M. Douglas. *A Research UNIX Reader: Annotated Excerpts from the Programmer's Manual, 1971–1986.* Computing Science Technical Report No. 139. AT&T Bell Laboratories, 1987. *https://archive.org/details/a_research_unix_reader.*

[26] McKusick, Marshall Kirk, Keith Bostic, Michael J. Karels, and John S. Quartermain. *The Design and Implementation of the 4.4BSD Operating System.* Addison-Wesley Longman, 1996.

[27] Molay, Bruce. *Understanding UNIX/LINUX Programming: A Guide to Theory and Practice.* Prentice Hall, 2002.

[28] Pate, Steve D. *UNIX Internals: A Practical Approach.* Addison-Wesley Longman, 1996. *https://archive.org/details/unixinternalspra0000pate.*

[29] Ramey, Chet, and Brian Fox. *The GNU Bash Reference Manual.* Free Software Foundation, 2022. *https://www.gnu.org/software/bash/manual/.*

[30] Ritchie, Dennis M. "The Development of the C Language." In *History of Programming Languages II*, edited by Thomas J. Bergin and Richard G. Gibson, 201–8. ACM Press/Addison-Wesley, 1996.

[31] Ritchie, Dennis M. "The Evolution of the Unix Time-Sharing System." In *Language Design and Programming Methodology*, edited by Jeffrey M. Tobias, 25–36. Lecture Notes in Computer Science, vol. 79. Springer-Verlag, 1980. *https://doi.org/10.1007/3-540-09745-7_2*.

[32] Ritchie, Dennis M. "Unix Time-Sharing System: A Retrospective." *The Bell System Technical Journal* 57, no. 6, part 2 (1978): 1947–69. Also presented at the 10th Hawaii International Conference on System Sciences, Honolulu, January 1977.

[33] Ritchie, Dennis M., and Ken Thompson. "The UNIX Time-Sharing System." *Communications of the ACM* 17, no. 7 (1974): 365–75. *https://doi.org/10.1145/361011.361061*.

[34] Ritchie, Dennis M., S.C. Johnson, M.E. Lesk, and B.W. Kernighan. "Unix Time-Sharing System: The C Programming Language." *The Bell System Technical Journal* 57, no. 6, part 2 (1978): 1991–2019. *https://doi.org/10.1002/j.1538-7305.1978.tb02140.x*.

[35] Salus, Peter H. *A Quarter Century of UNIX*. Addison-Wesley, 1994.

[36] Salus, Peter H., and Jeremy C. Reed. *The Daemon, the Gnu, and the Penguin*. Reed Media Services, 2008.

[37] Silberschatz, Abraham, Peter B. Galvin, and Greg Gagne. *Operating System Concepts*. 10th ed. John Wiley & Sons, 2018.

[38] Spinellis, Diomidis. *Unix History Repository*. GitHub. *https://github.com/dspinellis/unix-history-repo*.

[39] Stallings, William. *Operating Systems: Internals and Design Principles*, 9th ed. Pearson, 2018.

[40] Stallman, Richard M. "Linux and the GNU System." *GNU Operating System*. Last modified November 2, 2021. *https://www.gnu.org/gnu/linux-and-gnu.html*.

[41] Tanenbaum, Andrew S., and Albert S. Woodhull. *Operating Systems: Design and Implementation*. 3rd ed. Pearson Prentice Hall, 2006.

[42] Tanenbaum, Andrew S., and Herbert Bos. *Modern Operating Systems*. 4th ed. Pearson, 2014.

[43] Thompson, Ken. "UNIX Implementation." *The Bell System Technical Journal* 57, no. 6, part 2 (1978): 1931–46. *https://www.tuhs.org/Archive/Documentation/Papers/BSTJ/bstj57-6-1931.pdf*.

[44] Thompson, Ken, and Dennis M. Ritchie. *The UNIX Programmer's Manual*. 2nd ed. Bell Telephone Laboratories, 1972. *https://archive.org/details/bitsavers_attunix2ndersManual2edJun72_7765885*.

[45] Tool Interface Standards Committee. *Executable and Linking Format (ELF) Specification*. Version 1.2. 1995. *https://refspecs.linuxfoundation.org/ elf/elf.pdf.*

[46] Torvalds, Linus, and David Diamond. *Just for Fun: The Story of an Accidental Revolutionary*. HarperCollins, 2001.

[47] Wheeler, David A. *Secure Programming for Linux and Unix HOWTO*. Version 3.50. August 22, 2004. *https://dwheeler.com/secure-programs/ Secure-Programs-HOWTO.pdf.*

INDEX

Conventions Used in This Index

- *System calls and library functions are indexed by their names followed by empty parentheses, as in* abort().

- *Significant functions developed in the book, such as those used by more than one program or those with their own complete listing, are indexed by their names followed by the listing or prototype label, depending on whether the implementation is given or just its prototype.*

- *Demo, or example, programs with their own complete or partial listings are indexed with the program label.*

- *Commands are indexed with the command label.*

- *Italicized page numbers refer to figures.*

Numbers and Symbols

A

RESOURCES

Visit *https://nostarch.com/introduction-system-programming-linux* for errata and more information.

More no-nonsense books from **NO STARCH PRESS**

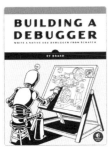

BUILDING A DEBUGGER

Write a Native x64 Debugger from Scratch

BY SY BRAND

744 PP., $69.99

ISBN 978-1-7185-0408-0

THE LINUX PROGRAMMING INTERFACE

A Linux and UNIX System Programming Handbook

BY MICHAEL KERRISK

1,552 PP., $99.99

ISBN 978-1-59327-220-3

hardcover

EFFECTIVE C, 2ND EDITION

An Introduction to Professional C Programming

BY ROBERT C. SEACORD

312 PP., $59.99

ISBN 978-1-7185-0412-7

HOW LINUX WORKS, 3RD EDITION

What Every Superuser Should Know

BY BRIAN WARD

464 PP., $49.99

ISBN 978-1-7185-0040-2

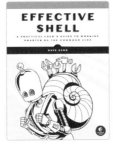

EFFECTIVE SHELL

A Practical User's Guide to Working Smarter on the Command Line

BY DAVE KERR

472 PP., $49.99

ISBN 978-1-7185-0414-1

DATA STRUCTURES THE FUN WAY

An Amusing Adventure with Coffee-Filled Examples

BY JEREMY KUBICA

304 PP., $39.99

ISBN 978-1-7185-0260-4

PHONE:
800.420.7240 OR
415.863.9900

EMAIL:
SALES@NOSTARCH.COM

WEB:
WWW.NOSTARCH.COM

Never before has the world relied so heavily on the Internet to stay connected and informed. That makes the Electronic Frontier Foundation's mission—to ensure that technology supports freedom, justice, and innovation for all people—more urgent than ever.

For over 30 years, EFF has fought for tech users through activism, in the courts, and by developing software to overcome obstacles to your privacy, security, and free expression. This dedication empowers all of us through darkness. With your help we can navigate toward a brighter digital future.